OXFORD READER'S COMPANION TO HARDY

OXFORD READER'S COMPANION TO

Hardy

Edited by Norman Page

OXFORD
UNIVERSITY PRESS

Great Clarendon Street, Oxford OX2 6DP

Oxford University Press is a department of the University of Oxford.
It furthers the University's objective of excellence in research, scholarship,
and education by publishing worldwide in

Oxford New York

Athens Auckland Bangkok Bogotá Buenos Aires Cape Town
Chennai Dar es Salaam Delhi Florence Hong Kong Istanbul Karachi
Kolkata Kuala Lumpur Madrid Melbourne Mexico City Mumbai Nairobi
Paris São Paulo Shanghai Singapore Taipei Tokyo Toronto Warsaw

and associated companies in Berlin Ibadan

Oxford is a registered trade mark of Oxford University Press
in the UK and in certain other countries

Published in the United States
by Oxford University Press Inc., New York

First published 2000

First issued without illustrations as an
Oxford University Press paperback 2001

British Library Cataloguing in Publication Data
Data available

Library of Congress Cataloging in Publication Data
Data available

ISBN 0-19-860419-X

1 3 5 7 9 10 8 6 4 2

Typeset in 8/8.75pt Minion
by Kolam Information Services Pvt. Ltd, Pondicherry, India
Printed in Great Britain
by Mackays of Chatham plc, Chatham, Kent

CONTENTS

Preface vii

Contributors x

List of Abbreviations xi

Chronology xii

Subject Index xvii

THE OXFORD READER'S COMPANION TO HARDY 1

Appendices:

A: Index of Hardy's poems 493

B: Characters in Hardy's novels 505

C: Place-names in Hardy's writings 508

D: Glossary of dialect words and expressions 510

E: Hardy in the cinema and on radio and television 515

Bibliography 517

PREFACE

THE constituency of those interested in the life and work of Thomas Hardy is, and has long been, a very broad one. It extends world-wide, and includes not only students and teachers but many who have a keen unprofessional interest in the man, his writings, and the world he lived in and wrote about. For length and continuity, Hardy's career is hard to match among English writers—he was writing poetry in his teens, and dictated his last verses on the day of his death some 70 years later—and he has some claim to uniqueness, too, in being both a major poet and a major novelist. He is, moreover, a writer whose work touches the life and ideas of his times at many points, so that, apart from its interest and value as 'literature', it has much to offer students of history and sociology, philosophy and religion, language and folklore, art, architecture, and aesthetics.

This *Companion* has been designed to provide, in an easily accessible form, a guide to Hardy's life and work and to the rich and multifarious contexts in which they can best be understood. Its entries, written by a team of more than forty scholars, range from substantial essays to short notes. A glance at the section 'Subject Index' below (pp. xvii–xx) will show its range. Major articles cover Hardy's fourteen published novels, his eight collections of verse, his autobiography, letters, notebooks, and the like, as well as such general themes as 'poetry' and 'short story', while a large number of shorter entries deal with individual stories, essays, etc. (It has not proved feasible to include individual entries for the thousand or so poems that Hardy wrote, but a very large number of them receive close attention, sometimes in a number of different articles, and Appendix A provides a guide to these references.) These largely work-specific items are supplemented by a number of entries that consider more general aspects of his writings, from humour and irony to love and tragedy.

As might be expected, the longest article in this volume is on Hardy, Thomas. The 'biographical fallacy' has itself been shown to be fallacious; the author, authoritatively pronounced dead, refuses to lie down; and it remains impossible to deny (despite his own frequent protestations to the contrary) that almost everything Hardy wrote is deeply interfused with his personal life and experiences. 'Home is where one starts from', and Hardy's family and ancestors were always of great importance to him. And though he is often depicted—in, for example, Max Beerbohm's deservedly celebrated caricature—as a lonely, introspective figure, he was a man of many friendships. There are, therefore, about 100 articles in this *Companion* that assess the significance in Hardy's life of particular individuals, ranging from his parents, siblings, and wives to fellow-artists important in their own right.

Hardy, whose contribution to the tourist industry is substantial, is often described as a regional writer; while such generalizations smooth out complexities, it remains true that, in his fiction and his verse alike, the spirit of place is potent. A further group of entries therefore reflects the places he lived in (or at least visited) and wrote about: not only in Dorset, where he began and ended, but in London, Cornwall, Scotland, Ireland, and the Continent.

To read Hardy carefully is to become aware that his work is a kind of echo-chamber of world culture, from the civilizations of the ancient world to the writers, artists, scientists, and thinkers of his own time. Some of these 'texts'—Greek tragedy, for instance, or the Book of Common Prayer, or 17th-century Dutch paintings, or the writings of 19th-century geologists and naturalists—are more than echoes, exerting a profound shaping influence upon his mind and art. A considerable amount of space in this *Companion* has been devoted to the historical, social, intellectual, and artistic contexts of Hardy's work, and to particular individuals (like Shelley or George Eliot) who exerted an important influence on him, as well as those (like Proust and Larkin) who were influenced by him.

A different kind of context is that in which Hardy functioned, struggled, and eventually prospered as a professional author. It is hardly possible to understand his work, especially his fiction, without taking into account the publishing scene of the day and the power exerted by publishers, editors, and readers. Here, too, there are both general articles on such topics as serialization and censorship, and entries on the individuals and publishing firms with whom he had dealings during a period that extended from the mid-Victorian age to the 1920s. A final major section is devoted to criticism and scholarship; in particular, the long entry on critical approaches surveys the crowded (and sometimes embattled) field of modern Hardy criticism.

The system of cross-referencing is intended to lead the user of this volume painlessly and profitably in the direction of other entries that contain additional material on the subject under investigation. Thus, for instance, information in the article on the critic and editor Leslie Stephen is supplemented by further references to Stephen in the entries on Hardy's friend Horace Moule, his publisher William Tinsley, and Stephen's daughter Virginia Woolf (herself an acquaintance as well as an admirer of Hardy), as well as in the general articles on religion, serialization, and censorship.

In addition to the entries categorized and described above, the *Companion* will reward the browser with such less predictable items as alcohol; executions, public; names; pets; and railways.

The first 'Thomas Hardy Dictionary' appeared nearly a century ago, in 1911, while Hardy's career was still in full spate. It has had a number of successors, but none as substantial and wide-ranging as the present volume, and none that so extensively exploits the collective knowledge and insights of the international community of Hardy scholars. The editor's thanks are due to all those who have assisted, through their contributions on more or less specialized areas, in bringing the volume to its final form. The contributors, drawn from five continents, also represent different generations and traditions of scholarship and criticism, and I believe that the diversity of approach gives added interest and value to this multivocal account of a writer who himself possesses the knack of constantly appearing, on each rereading, in a new and unexpected light.

A special tribute should be paid to F. B. Pinion, doyen of British Hardy scholars and author of (among much else) three admirable reference works on Hardy. Frank Pinion died suddenly when his substantial contributions to the present volume were in their final stages, and I am grateful to his daughter, Catherine Pinion, for preparing his articles for publication. His *A Hardy Companion* (1968) appeared at the very beginning of the massive surge of academic and pedagogical interest in Hardy that the past generation has witnessed; both this and his *A Commentary on the Poems of Thomas Hardy* (1976) and *A Thomas Hardy Dictionary* (1989) have been an invaluable resource in the preparation of this new *Companion*, as have R. L. Purdy's remarkable pioneering work *Thomas Hardy: A Bibliographical Study* (1954), R. G. Cox's *Thomas Hardy: The Critical Heritage* (1970), and Timothy Hands's *A Hardy Chronology* (1992).

The deaths of two other contributors whilst this book was in production must also be recorded. Desmond Hawkins died on 6 May 1999, aged 90; his writings on Hardy cover half a century, and his important contributions to the present volume show no diminution of his remarkable powers. Kristin Brady, an authority on Hardy's short stories, was killed in a road accident on 20 December 1998.

For support and advice, from the conception of this volume onwards, I am greatly indebted to Michael Cox, Pam Coote, Alison Jones, and Wendy Tuckey of Oxford University Press.

My most heartfelt thanks must go to Professor Michael Millgate, to whom my debts are both academic and personal. Without his exemplary contributions to Hardy scholarship and criticism—most notably his authoritative biography, his edition (with R. L. Purdy) of the letters, and his recension of the autobiography—we should all be less well equipped for the serious study of Hardy. He has also, with unstinted generosity, offered wise counsel and practical help, on matters of broad policy and specific detail, at every stage in the preparation of this work.

NORMAN PAGE

1999

Note to Paperback Edition

The appearance of a paperback edition of this *Companion* has given the opportunity to correct a few errors and misprints that crept into the original edition. I am very grateful to those readers and contributors who drew my attention to them, and to Rebecca Collins at Oxford University Press for her assistance in seeing this edition through the press.

NORMAN PAGE

2001

CONTRIBUTORS

General Editor

Norman Page is Emeritus Professor at the University of Nottingham. A Vice-President of the Thomas Hardy Society and former editor of the *Thomas Hardy Journal* and the *Thomas Hardy Annual*, he has published many works on literature in general, and Victorian fiction in particular, and has lectured on Hardy in many parts of the world.

Contributors

ABT	Ann Thwaite, biographer
AE	Alma Evers, King Edward VI Handsworth School, Birmingham
AT	Anthony Thwaite, poet, critic, and editor
BG	Brian Green, University of Stellenbosch
DH	Desmond Hawkins, writer and broadcaster
DJW	Donald J. Winslow, University of Boston
DT	Dennis Taylor, Boston College, Massachusetts
FBP	F. B. Pinion, University of Sheffield
HO	Harold Orel, University of Kanas
JA	James Acheson, Christchurch University, New Zealand
JB	John Bayley, St Catherine's College, Oxford
JCG	James Gibson, biographer, critic, and editor
JHS	J. H. Stape, Japan Women's University, Tokyo
JJ	Jan Jedrzejewski, University of Ulster
JVS	Jeremy Steele, Primary English Teaching Association, New Town, Australia
KB	Kristin Brady, University of Western Ontario
KW	Keith Wilson, University of Ottawa
LAB	Lennart Björk, University of Gothenburg
LO	Leonée Ormond, King's College, University of London
LStJB	Lance St John Butler, University of Stirling
MI	Michael Irwin, University of Kent
MM	Michael Millgate, University of Toronto
MPR	Mary Rimmer, University of New Brunswick
MR	Martin Ray, University of Aberdeen
MT	Michael Thorpe, Mount Allison University, Canada
MW	Merryn Williams, Open University
NMcE	Neil McEwan, Nara University, Japan
PC	Peter Casagrande, University of Kansas
PD	Pamela Dalziel, University of British Columbia
PVM	Phillip Mallett, University of St Andrews
RE	Ralph W. V. Elliott, Australian National University
RL	Robert Langbaum, University of Virginia
RM	Rosemarie Morgan, Yale University
RPD	Ronald P. Draper, University of Aberdeen
RR	Roger Robinson, Victoria University of Wellington
SD	Shanta Dutta, Jadavpur University, Calcutta
SF	Suguro Fukasawa, President, Thomas Hardy Society of Japan
SJG	Simon Gatrell, University of Georgia
TA	Tim Armstrong, Royal Holloway College, University of London
TRH	Timothy Hands, Portsmouth Grammar School
TS	Toru Sasaki, Kyoto University
YT	Yoshiko Takakuwa, Tsuda College, Tokyo

Unsigned articles are by the editor.

ABBREVIATIONS

The following abbreviations are used to refer to Hardy's works

AL	*A Laodicean*
CM	*A Changed Man*
D	*The Dynasts*
DR	*Desperate Remedies*
FFMC	*Far from the Madding Crowd*
GND	*A Group of Noble Dames*
HE	*The Hand of Ethelberta*
HS	*Human Shows*
JO	*Jude the Obscure*
L	*Letters* (see note below)
LLE	*Late Lyrics and Earlier*
LLI	*Life's Little Ironies*
LN	*Literary Notebooks* (see note below)
LW	*Life and Work* (autobiography) (see note below)
MC	*The Mayor of Casterbridge*
MV	*Moments of Vision*
PBE	*A Pair of Blue Eyes*
PN	*Personal Notebooks* (see note below)
PPP	*Poems of the Past and the Present*
RN	*The Return of the Native*
SC	*Satires of Circumstance*
TDU	*Tess of the d'Urbervilles*
TL	*Time's Laughingstocks*
TM	*The Trumpet-Major*
TT	*Two on a Tower*
UGT	*Under the Greenwood Tree*
W	*The Woodlanders*
WB	*The Well-Beloved*
WP	*Wessex Poems*
WT	*Wessex Tales*
WW	*Winter Words*

Where appropriate, references to Hardy's novels are followed by chapter numbers: thus '(*MC* 23)' signifies *The Mayor of Casterbridge*, Chapter 23. (Where the context makes it obvious which work is referred to, no abbreviation is given.) For novels divided into books as well as chapters, two figures are given: thus '(*JO* 2.3)' refers to *Jude the Obscure*, Part 2, Chapter 3.

Autobiography: references to Hardy's autobiography are to *The Life and Work of Thomas Hardy by Thomas Hardy*, ed. Michael Millgate (1984), abbreviated as *LW*, immediately followed by a page number, thus: (*LW* 123).

Letters: references to Hardy's letters are to the edition by Richard Little Purdy and Michael Millgate, 7 vols. (1978–88), abbreviated as *L* and followed by volume number and page number: thus (*L* ii 99) indicates *Letters*, Volume II, p. 99.

Notebooks: *The Literary Notebooks of Thomas Hardy*, ed. Lennart Björk, 2 vols. (1985), is referred to as *LN*, followed by volume number and page number, thus: (*LN* i 234).

The Personal Notebooks of Thomas Hardy, ed. Richard H. Taylor (1979), is referred to as *PN*, followed by the page number.

Biographies: Michael Millgate's *Thomas Hardy: A Biography* (1982) is cited as Millgate, immediately followed by a page number, thus: (Millgate 456). Robert Gittings's two-volume biography (1975, 1978) is referred to as Gittings, followed by the volume title and page number, thus: (Gittings, *Young Thomas Hardy* 77); (Gittings, *The Older Hardy* 77).

Other abbreviations:

CH	*Thomas Hardy: The Critical Heritage*, ed. R. G. Cox (1970)
DCM	Dorset County Museum
Purdy	Richard Little Purdy, *Thomas Hardy: A Bibliographical Study* (1954)
THA	*Thomas Hardy Annual*
THJ	*Thomas Hardy Journal*
THYB	*Thomas Hardy Year Book*

CHRONOLOGY

1840	2 June	Born at Higher Bockhampton, in the parish of Stinsford, near Dorchester, the first of four children of Thomas Hardy, builder and stonemason, and his wife Jemima (née Hand), who had married on 22 December 1839. Three other children (Mary, Kate, and Henry) follow in the next eleven years.
1848		Attends the newly established National School in his parish; he has by this time begun to enjoy the patronage of Mrs Julia Augusta Martin, lady of the manor and one of the founders of the school.
1849		Sees London for the first time, while travelling with his mother to pay a lengthy visit to an aunt in Hertfordshire.
1850		Is moved on his mother's initiative to a Nonconformist school in Dorchester, where he is taught by Isaac Last.
1852		Begins to learn Latin under Last.
1853		When Last starts an independent academy in Dorchester, Hardy moves with him.
1856	11 July	Enters the Dorchester office of John Hicks, architect, as an apprentice. Forms a friendship with his fellow-apprentice, Henry Bastow. Continues his studies at home, and begins to learn Greek. His earliest published work, in the shape of contributions to the *Dorset County Chronicle*, probably appears at this time.
1857	January	Death of Hardy's grandmother, Mary Hardy, who has lived in the family home since his birth. By this time, he has formed a close friendship with Horace Moule and is on friendly terms with other members of the Moule family.
1858		At about this time, writes poems, including the surviving 'Domicilium'.
1860		Having completed his apprenticeship, is kept on by Hicks as a paid assistant.
1862	April	Moves to London, and the following month begins employment with Arthur Blomfield, a distinguished architect.
	17 August	His earliest surviving letter, addressed to his sister Mary, reports that he is attending services at St Mary's, Kilburn.
	October	Is proposed by Blomfield for membership of the Architectural Association.
1863		At about this time becomes 'more or less formally engaged' (Millgate 84) to Eliza Nicholls. Wins prizes from the Architectural Association and the Royal Institute of British Architects. Makes regular visits to the National Gallery, and begins to keep the 'Schools of Painting' notebook.
1865		Begins to keep the 'Studies, Specimens, &c.' notebook. Writes some of his earliest surviving poems.
	18 March	The humorous sketch 'How I Built Myself a House' is published in *Chambers's Journal*.
1866		The relationship with Eliza Nicholls comes to an end.
1867	Summer	Leaves London and resumes work for Hicks in Dorchester. Begins his first novel, *The Poor Man and the Lady*.
1868	December	Submits the manuscript of *The Poor Man and the Lady* to Chapman & Hall.

1869	February	Chapman & Hall Hardy's reject Hardy's novel; in the following month he meets George Meredith at their London office and receives advice on a literary career.
	April	Is invited to join the architectural practice of G. R. Crickmay in Weymouth, and moves there soon afterwards, settling in lodgings in Weymouth. Submits *The Poor Man and the Lady* to Smith, Elder, who reject it; Hardy thereupon submits it to Tinsley Brothers, who later in the year also reject it. By this time he has begun work on *Desperate Remedies.*
1870	February	Moves back to his parents' home while continuing to work for Crickmay.
	7 March	Sets off for St Juliot, Cornwall, on architectural business, and meets Emma Lavinia Gifford, with whom he soon falls in love.
	April	Moves back to Weymouth. *Desperate Remedies* is rejected by Macmillan and submitted to Tinsley Brothers, who (May) offer to publish it at Hardy's expense.
	16 May	Leaves for London, having quitted his job with Crickmay.
	August	Visits Cornwall for a three-week holiday, and spends much of his time with Emma Gifford, with whom he has been corresponding.
1871	25 March	*Desperate Remedies* is published. A few days later, Hardy returns to Weymouth to resume work for Crickmay. Is now working on *Under the Greenwood Tree,* completed by the early summer.
	May	Visits Cornwall again.
	October	*Under the Greenwood Tree* is rejected by Macmillan. Is working on *A Pair of Blue Eyes* by this time.
1872		In the spring, moves back to London, working for T. Roger Smith on plans for schools.
	April	Sells the copyright of *Under the Greenwood Tree* outright to Tinsley, who publishes the novel in June, with modest success.
	August	Visits Cornwall. Emma's father rejects Hardy's request to marry her.
	September	Serialization of *A Pair of Blue Eyes* begins.
	November	Is invited by Leslie Stephen to contribute a serial to the *Cornhill Magazine.*
1873	May	*A Pair of Blue Eyes* is published in volume form.
	September	Horace Moule, Hardy's close friend and mentor, commits suicide.
	December	Visits London and Cornwall.
1874	January	Serialization of *Far from the Madding Crowd* begins.
	17 September	Marries Emma Gifford at St Peter's, Paddington, London; the honeymoon is spent in France, and the couple settle first in a London suburb, and soon afterwards in the Paddington district.
	23 November	*Far from the Madding Crowd* appears in volume form and is Hardy's first considerable success.
	December	Is invited by Stephen to contribute another serial to the *Cornhill.*
1875	July	Moves to Swanage, Dorset, where he continues work on *The Hand of Ethelberta,* serialization of which begins in the same month.
1876	March	Moves to Yeovil, Somerset.
	April	*The Hand of Ethelberta* is published in volume form.
	May	The Hardys visit Holland and Germany.
	July	The move into Riverside Villa, Sturminster Newton, Dorset.

1877	April	Submits the early portion of *The Return of the Native* to John Blackwood, who rejects it, as Leslie Stephen also does in June.
1878	January	Serialization of *The Return of the Native* begins.
	March	The Hardys move to London, settling in the neighbourhood of Wandsworth Common.
	April	Begins research in the British Museum on the background for *The Trumpet-Major.*
	June	Is elected a member of the Savile Club.
	4 November	*The Return of the Native* is published in volume form.
1879		Works on *The Trumpet-Major.*
	October	Hardy's review of William Barnes's *Poems of Rural Life* is published.
1880	January	Serialization of *The Trumpet-Major* begins.
	26 October	*The Trumpet-Major* is published in volume form. In October, after a visit to Cambridge, Hardy becomes seriously ill from an internal complaint, and work on *A Laodicean*, in progress at this time, has to be continued by dictation to his wife.
	December	Serialization of *A Laodicean* begins.
1881	April	Is able to leave the house for the first time since October.
	June	The Hardys leave London, and settle in Wimborne, Dorset. In the late summer, they take a holiday in Scotland.
	25 November	*A Laodicean* is published in volume form. Hardy is now researching the background to *Two on a Tower.*
1882	May	Serialization of *Two on a Tower* begins, the novel appearing in volume form in October. In the latter month, the Hardys take a holiday in Paris.
1883		The Hardys move to Dorchester, where the construction of Max Gate begins in November.
1884		Works on *The Mayor of Casterbridge* during this year.
1885	17 April	Finishes *The Mayor of Casterbridge.*
	June	The Hardys move into Max Gate. In the closing months of the year, is at work on *The Woodlanders.*
1886	January	Serialization of *The Mayor of Casterbridge* begins, the volume edition appearing on 10 May.
1887	4 February	Finishes *The Woodlanders*, the volume edition of which appears on 15 March.
	March	The Hardys take a holiday in Italy.
1888	4 May	*Wessex Tales* is published.
	May-June	The Hardys take a holiday in Paris.
1889		Works on *Tess of the d'Urbervilles* during this year; the half-finsihed novel is rejected by Tillotson's in September, and by *Murray's Magazine* and *Macmillan's Magazine* in November.
1890		In the early part of the year, is at work on *A Group of Noble Dames*, serialized from December (published in volume form on 30 May 1891).
1891	April	Is elected a member of the Athenaeum Club.
	4 July	Serialization of *Tess* begins.
	September	Visits Scotland.
	December	*Tess* appears in volume form.
1892	20 July	Death of Hardy's father.

	1 October	Serialization of *The Pursuit of the Well-Beloved* begins.
1893	May	The Hardys visit Dublin, where Hardy meets Florence Henniker for the first time.
	August	Begins *Jude the Obscure* at about this time.
1894	22 February	*Life's Little Ironies* is published.
	December	Serialization of *Jude* begins.
1895	March	Finishes *Jude*, which appears in volume form on 1 November. During this year the first collected edition of Hardy's work begins to appear.
1896	August–September	The Hardys take an extended holiday in England and on the Continent, their travels in Belgium including a visit to the site of the Battle of Waterloo.
1897	16 March	Revised version of *The Well-Beloved* is published in volume form.
	June	The Hardys take a holiday in Switzerland. During this year Hardy takes up bicycling with enthusiasm.
1898	December	*Wessex Poems*, Hardy's first collection of verse, is published.
1899	12 October	Outbreak of Boer War, Hardy's response to which includes a number of poems.
1901	November	*Poems of the Past and the Present* is published.
1902		During this year the firm of Macmillan become Hardy's publishers.
1904	13 January	Part First of *The Dynasts* is published.
	3 April	Death of Hardy's mother.
	May	Researches the background of *The Dynasts* in the British Museum.
1905	April	Visits Aberdeen, where he receives an honorary degree from the University.
	September	Visits Aldeburgh, Suffolk, to attend celebrations of the 150th anniversary of the birth of George Crabbe. First meeting with Florence Dugdale probably occurs during this year.
1906	9 February	Part Second of *The Dynasts* is published.
1907	September	Finishes *The Dynasts.*
1908	11 February	Part Third of *The Dynasts* is published.
1909		During this year, confides in Edward Clodd concerning his marital problems and his growing friendship with Florence Dugdale.
	3 December	*Time's Laughingstocks* is published.
1910	July	Is awarded the Order of Merit by King George V.
	November	Receives the Freedom of the Borough of Dorchester.
1911		Early in the year, Emma Hardy completes her *Some Recollections.* Later in the year, Hardy is persuaded by Sydney Cockerell to present a number of his manuscripts to various libraries and museums.
1912	April	Wessex Edition begins to appear.
	May	With Florence Dugdale, stays at Edward Clodd's house in Aldeburgh.
	2 June	Receives Gold Medal of the Royal Society of Literature.
	27 November	Death of Emma Hardy, an event that precipitates the sequence 'Poems of 1912–13', composed during the next few months.
1913	4 March	Sets off for Cornwall to revisit sites associated with Emma. During the spring Florence Dugdale moves into Max Gate.
	June	Visits Cambridge to receive an honorary degree.
	July	Accepts an honorary fellowship of Magdalene College, Cambridge.

	24 October	*A Changed Man* is published.
1914	10 February	Marries Florence Emily Dugdale at St Andrew's, Enfield, Middlesex.
	4 August	Outbreak of the Great War, to which Hardy responds creatively and in other ways.
	17 November	*Satires of Circumstance* is published.
1915	24 November	Death of Hardy's sister Mary.
1916	3 October	Publication of *Selected Poems of Thomas Hardy.*
1917		During this year, is sorting out a lifetime's papers and destroying many. Work is begun on the posthumously published autobiography.
	30 November	*Moments of Vision* is published.
1919	10 October	*Collected Poems* is published.
	December	Publication of the Mellstock Edition begins.
1920	April	Last visit to London.
	2 June	Hardy's 80th birthday elicits many messages of congratulation—from, among others, George V and the Prime Minister—as well as a deputation to Max Gate from the Incorporated Society of Authors.
1922	March	Is given an honorary degree by the University of St Andrews.
	23 May	*Late Lyrics and Earlier* is published.
	November	Accepts an honorary fellowship from Queen's College, Oxford.
1923	June	Visits Oxford.
	20 July	The Prince of Wales (later Edward VIII) visits Hardy at Max Gate.
	15 November	*The Famous Tragedy of the Queen of Cornwall* is published; it is performed for the first time by the Hardy Players on 28 December.
1924	26 November	First performance, in Dorchester, of a stage adaptation of *Tess of the d'Urbervilles*, with Gertrude Bugler, for whom Hardy by now feels a strong attraction, in the title role.
1925	20 November	*Human Shows* is published.
1927	4 November	Pays the last of his regular visits to the family graves at Stinsford and his brother's house at Talbothays.
	11 December	Onset of Hardy's final illness.
1928	11 January	Dictates his final verses, and dies following a heart attack in the evening. On the 16th, his ashes are interred in Westminster Abbey and his heart buried at Stinsford.
	2 October	Publication of *Winter Words.*
		His brother Henry dies later in 1928, his sister Kate in 1940.
		Hardy's autobiography is published, with revisions and additions, under the name of his widow in two volumes in 1928 and 1930.

SUBJECT INDEX

Works of Thomas Hardy

Prose

Novels
- *Desperate Remedies*
- *Far from the Madding Crowd*
- *Hand of Ethelberta, The*
- *Jude the Obscure*
- *Laodicean, A*
- *Mayor of Casterbridge, The*
- *Pair of Blue Eyes, A*
- *Poor Man and the Lady, The*
- *Return of the Native, The*
- *Tess of the d'Urbervilles*
- *Trumpet-Major, The*
- *Two on a Tower*
- *Under the Greenwood Tree*
- *Well-Beloved, The*
- *Woodlanders, The*

Stories
- 'Alicia's Diary'
- 'Changed Man, A'
- *Changed Man, A*
- 'Committee Man of "The Terror", A'
- 'Distracted Preacher, The'
- 'Duke's Reappearance, The'
- 'Enter a Dragoon'
- 'Fellow-Townsmen'
- 'Few Crusted Characters, A'
- 'Fiddler of the Reels, The'
- 'For Conscience' Sake'
- 'Grave by the Handpost, The'
- *Group of Noble Dames, A*
- 'Imaginative Woman, An'
- 'Interlopers at the Knap'
- *Life's Little Ironies*
- 'Master John Horseleigh, Knight'
- 'Melancholy Hussar of the German Legion, The'
- 'Mere Interlude, A'
- 'On the Western Circuit'
- 'Romantic Adventures of a Milkmaid, The'
- 'Son's Veto, The'
- 'Three Strangers, The'
- 'To Please his Wife'
- 'Tradition of Eighteen Hundred and Four, A'
- 'Tragedy of Two Ambitions, A'
- 'Tryst at an Ancient Earthwork, A'
- uncollected stories
- 'Waiting Supper, The'
- *Wessex Tales*
- 'What the Shepherd Saw'
- 'Withered Arm, The'

Non-fictional prose
- autobiography
- 'Candour in English Fiction'
- 'Dorsetshire Labourer, The'
- letters
- 'Memories of Church Restoration'
- notebooks
- prefaces
- 'Profitable Reading of Fiction, The'
- 'Science of Fiction, The'
- speeches

Drama
- *Dynasts, The*
- *Famous Tragedy of the Queen of Cornwall, The*

Poems
- ballads
- *Human Shows*
- *Late Lyrics and Earlier*
- metrics
- *Moments of Vision*
- 'Poems of 1912–13'
- *Poems of the Past and the Present*
- poetry
- *Satires of Circumstance*
- *Selected Poems*
- *Time's Laughingstocks*
- *Wessex Poems*
- *Winter Words*

Various aspects
- allusions
- characterization
- dialogue
- epigraphs
- fate
- humour
- imagery
- irony
- landscape
- language
- love
- names
- pictorialism
- plagiarism
- poetic influence, Hardy's
- sexuality

short story
style
tragedy

People

Family, friends, literary and other relationships
Allen, Grant
Allhusen, Dorothy
Antell family
Archer, William
Barnes, William
Barrie, James
Bastow, Henry
Beerbohm, Max
Benson, A. C.
Besant, Walter
Blomfield, Arthur
Blunden, Edmund
Bugler, Gertrude
Chesterton, G. K.
Child, Harold
Clodd, Edward
Cockerell, Sydney
Crickmay, G. R.
de la Mare, Walter
Douglas, Sir George
Dugdale family
Egerton, George
Elgar, Edward
Forster, E. M.
Galsworthy, John
Gifford family
Gissing, George
Gosse, Edmund
Granville-Barker, Harley
Graves, Robert
Grove, Agnes
Haggard, Henry Rider
Hand family
Hardy, Emma Lavinia
Hardy, Florence Emily
Hardy, Sir Thomas Masterman
Hardy, Thomas (d. 1599)
Hardy, Thomas (writer)
Henniker, Florence
Hicks, John
Hoare, Alda, Lady
Hobbes, John Oliver
Holst, Gustav
Hope, Laurence
Housman, A. E.
How, W. W.
James, Henry
Jeune, Mary
Kipling, Rudyard
Last, Isaac
Lawrence, T. E.
Lea, Hermann
Linton, Eliza Lynn
Malet, Lucas
Martin, Julia Augusta
Meredith, George
Moore, George
Morgan, Charles
Morris, Mowbray
Moule family
Moule, Horace
Murry, John Middleton
Newbolt, Henry
Nicholls, Eliza Bright
Oliphant, Margaret
Paterson, Helen
Patmore, Coventry
Pole, Catherine
Pound, Ezra
Powys brothers
Procter, Anne
relatives of Thomas Hardy
Sassoon, Siegfried
Shorter, Clement
Smith, Reginald Bosworth
Sparks, Tryphena
Stephen, Leslie
Stevenson, Robert Louis
Stopes, Marie
Swetman family
Symons, Arthur
Tennyson, Alfred
Thornycroft, Hamo and Agatha
Tolbort, T. W. Hooper
Tomson, Rosamund
Treves, Frederick
Ward, Mrs Humphry
Wells, H. G.
Woolf, Virginia

Sources and influences
Ainsworth, W. H.
Arnold, Matthew
Auden, W. H.
Boughton, Rutland
Britten, Benjamin
Browning, Robert
Byron, Lord
Carlyle, Thomas
Collins, Wilkie
Comte, Auguste
Dickens, Charles
Eliot, George
Faulkner, William
Fowles, John

Harrison, Frederic
Hutchins, John
Ibsen, Henrik
Keats, John
Larkin, Philip
Lawrence, D. H.
Maugham, W. Somerset
Mill, John Stuart
Milton, John
Nietzsche, Friedrich
Proust, Marcel
reading, Hardy's
Schopenhauer, Arthur
Scott, Walter
Shakespeare, William
Shelley, Percy Bysshe
Swinburne, Algernon Charles
Wordsworth, William

Places

Aldeburgh
Cambridge
clubs
Cornwall
Dorchester
Dorset
Dublin
Egdon Heath
Frome, River
Higher Bockhampton
homes
London
Max Gate
National Gallery
Oxford
Puddletown
Royal Academy
Scotland
Stinsford
Sturminster Newton
travels, Continental
Wessex
Weymouth
Wimborne

Contexts

Historical and social
agriculture
alcohol
animals, cruelty to
Boer War
calendar
class
crafts
education
emigration
executions, public
First World War
history
marriage
Napoleonic Wars
politics
railways
Titanic disaster
women
work

Science, religion, philosophy
archaeology
astronomy
Darwinism
geology
ghosts
heredity
pessimism
philosophy
Positivism
relativity
religion

Literature and language
Bible
Book of Common Prayer
classics
dialect
folklore
pastoralism
philology
realism
regionalism

Other arts
architecture
cinema
dramatizations
Hardy Players, The
hymns
music
opera
painting and sculpture
portraits and sculptures of Thomas Hardy
Tess opera
theatre

Publishing

Alden, H. M.
Aldrich, Thomas Bailey
censorship
collected editions
editors

Harper & Brothers
Heinemann, William
Holt, Henry
illustrations
Locker, Arthur
Macmillan, Frederick
Macmillan & Co.
Osgood, McIlvaine
Paul, Charles Kegan
publishers
reception
Sampson Low
serialization
Smith, Elder
Tauchnitz editions
Tillotson & Son
Tinsley, William
translations

Criticism and scholarship

biographies
critical approaches
interviews
manuscripts
societies and journals
textual studies

Miscellaneous

animals
birds
Hardy, poems about
honours
library, Hardy's
pets

A

agriculture.

> Only a man harrowing clods
>   In a slow silent walk
> With an old horse that stumbles and nods
>   Half asleep as they stalk.

'Yet this will go onward the same | Though Dynasties pass', wrote Hardy in his poem 'In Time of "The Breaking of Nations"' (1915). Yet, of course, it did not: we no longer see horse-ploughs in developed countries. Equally, of course, the basic purposes of agriculture never change. Human beings cannot do without it; the barn in *Far from the Madding Crowd* has survived better than the church or castle because it celebrates 'the defence and salvation of the body by daily bread' (22). 'The mill still worked on, food being a perennial necessity; the abbey had perished, creeds being transient', Hardy points out in *Tess of the d'Urbervilles* (35). During his lifetime he witnessed the change from a land-based to a town-based civilization, and some of the things he describes belong, like horse-ploughs, to a vanished age. These include reddlemen, labourers in long smocks, the hiring-fair where men who are probably illiterate stand around holding sheep-crooks or displaying bits of thatch or cord in their hats (*FFMC* 6). Other activities, like fruit-gathering, herding, or shearing, have scarcely changed.

His teenage poem 'Domicilium' celebrates his family's achievement in raising orchards, herbs, and flowers from what used to be a piece of heath. One of man's greatest strengths is his ability to create a garden in the wilderness, but he has to be constantly alert because nature will always fight back. People who gamble on the weather, like Henchard in *The Mayor of Casterbridge*, may lose their livelihood. *Far from the Madding Crowd*, the novel that enchanted London readers with its glimpses of a world which was quite strange to them, shows how many hazards a small farmer has to cope with. A sheepdog drives the flock over a cliff; other sheep get into the clover field and die; a storm blows up, threatening ricks which have not been covered. Or, in *Tess*, one bite of garlic by one cow can ruin the dairy's butter yield. Hardy obviously knew what he was talking about. He tells us that as a boy he had helped his father make cider—'a work whose sweet smells and oozings in the crisp autumn air can never be forgotten by those who have had a hand in it' (*LW* 96)—and while there is no reason to think that he had done other kinds of land work, he had observed them keenly. They are described with a wealth of detail, particularly in two novels, *Far from the Madding Crowd* and *Tess*.

The earlier book includes some of the high points in the agricultural year, like the shearing-supper and harvest-home celebrations. It shows farmers bringing their grain to the corn exchange for inspection, lambs being fostered, the annual sheep-shearing and bee-swarming, men harvesting oats with their scythes. Most of the action in this novel takes place on one farm, and the work is hard but satisfying; however, Tess Durbeyfield in the next generation becomes a migrant land worker, moving over a wide area and taking on work of many different kinds. As a girl at home she drives beehives to market, then works for Alec d'Urberville in a 'little fancy farm' (5) minding poultry. The artificial nature of this farm is shown by the fact that it grows strawberries out of season. At Marlott she helps with the reaping; at Talbothays she gets summer work as a dairywoman which involves a whole range of activities, all of them life-enhancing—milking cows, skimming, making butter and cheese, taking milk to the train for the benefit of Londoners 'who have never seen a cow' (30). In winter she moves 'from the pasture to the stubble' (41) and is forced to accept rough and unpleasant work—swede-grubbing, reed-drawing ('corn and swedes are all they grow' (42)), and feeding the threshing-machine.

Hardy is also interested in other kinds of agricultural work. *The Return of the Native* takes place on a heath where nothing much can be grown; the people subsist by cutting furze and related trades. The 'woodlanders' live by harvesting fruit and doing various jobs connected with timber. In Casterbridge, which is virtually an extension of the country, the chief men are grain dealers and the shops sell mainly 'scythes, reap-hooks, sheep-shears... bee-hives, butter-firkins, churns, milking stools' and so on (*MC* 4). Except for *Jude the Obscure*, where the connection between man and the land has been virtually broken, all Hardy's major novels have a rural setting.

Yet it is interesting that he does not often write directly about farmers and labourers, although he was aware that their interests often clashed and sometimes referred to the agrarian riots in the decade before he was born. Most of his farmers are unsympathetic, even brutal figures (Shiner, Groby, Troutham, Lodge in 'The Withered Arm'). In 'The Dorsetshire Labourer' (1883) he says that 'it was once common enough on inferior farms to hear a farmer, as he sat on horseback amid a field of workers, address them with a contemptuousness which could not have been greatly exceeded in the days when the thralls of Cedric wore their collars of brass'. In the same essay he praises Joseph Arch's Agricultural Workers' Union (founded 1872), which had done so much to change conditions. And he points out that town-dwellers have an utterly false impression of the labourer, whom they insist on seeing as a degraded person called Hodge. If such a reader 'were to go by rail to Dorset, where Hodge in his most unmitigated form is supposed to reside', he would find not a stereotype but a crowd of individuals: 'a number of dissimilar fellow-creatures, men of many minds, infinite in difference; some happy, many serene, a few depressed; some clever, even to genius ... each of whom walks in his own way the road to dusty death. Dick the carter, Bob the shepherd, and Sam the ploughman, are, it is true, alike in the narrowness of their means and their general open-air life, but they cannot be rolled together again into such a Hodge as he dreamt of.' Hardy felt strongly enough about this to repeat the passage almost word for word in *Tess*. Yet in most of his novels the labourers are what the Victorians called a 'rustic chorus', onlookers who merely comment on the main action. The characters with whom he sympathizes most deeply belong to an 'interesting and better-informed class, ranking distinctly above them' (*TDU* 51). They may be reduced to doing the most basic work on the land, but they are talented and aspire to better things. Henchard, who is to go a long way, has 'the walk of the skilled countryman as distinct from the desultory shamble of the general labourer' (*MC* 1). Other skilled countrymen and countrywomen include Gabriel Oak, who operates on sheep 'with a dexterity that would have graced a hospital-surgeon' (*FFMC* 21), Giles Winterborne with his 'marvellous power of making trees grow' (*W* 8), Marty, who is an expert spar-maker, Tess. These characters are at the centre of the Wessex novels.

Titles like *Under the Greenwood Tree* and *Far from the Madding Crowd* were attractive to Hardy's first readers because they promised simple stories set in a green, peaceful, undemanding place. And to some extent Hardy gave his readers what they wanted. Both these early novels end with a rural wedding and work on the land is often shown to be a positive experience. Gabriel is happy with his sheep under the stars; Clym in *The Return of the Native* finds the heath a strengthening and soothing place and enjoys furze-cutting; the orchards in *The Woodlanders*, 'lustrous with the reds of apple-crops, berries, and foliage' (28), proclaim nature's bounty. The dairymaids at Talbothays live on 'butter and eggs and milk and honey' (*TDU* 36) and Angel, when he works there, becomes 'wonderfully free from the chronic melancholy which is taking hold of the civilized races' (18) once he is used to the outdoor life. 'The Son's Veto' is about a woman who pines away in the city but revives when she meets her lover, a market-gardener bringing fresh greenstuff to Covent Garden. Hardy constantly makes the point that a healthy working relationship with nature is the basis of human life.

Yet he had always been aware that agricultural life was not, and never could be, idyllic. As a champion of animal rights in his later years he was disturbed by the killing which seems inseparable from it. Gabriel does not like to think that 'his flock ended in mutton' (*FFMC* 5), and the reaping scene in *Tess* ends with a number of small animals being driven out of the corn and 'every one put to death by the sticks and stones of the harvesters' (14). Jude presents a particularly bleak picture of farming; the only work on offer to the hero is scaring birds or raising a pig, as cottage-dwellers had done for generations, to be killed. Both actions repel him and we are invited to wonder why 'what was good for God's birds was bad for God's gardener', 'why should Nature's law be mutual butchery' (*JO* 1.2, 5.6).

Hardy was also aware that land work could be desperately hard for the labourers. An early poem, 'The Ruined Maid', describes a young woman 'without shoes or socks | Tired of digging potatoes, and spudding up docks'; her face is 'blue and bleak' with cold. People can die from prolonged soakings in the rain; labourers need to be massively built 'considering what they would have to bear at the hands of wind and weather before they returned to that mouldy nave for the last time' (*TT* 14). Tess's arm is inevitably damaged when she goes sheaf-binding—'as the day wears on its feminine smoothness becomes scarified by the stubble, and bleeds' (*TDU* 14). This novel demonstrates that work on arable farms is much less pleasant than dairy work. The girls who have been happy in 'green, sunny, romantic' Talbothays (43) have to work cheaply for the unpleasant farmer Groby, digging up swedes which have been half-eaten by livestock and drawing reeds, which makes them faint. They are half-frozen and expected to work until they are wet through—'if they did not work they would not be paid; so they worked on' (43). Low wages, eviction, man-traps, brutality were also a traditional part of agricultural life. 'As a child I knew a sheep-keeping boy who to my horror shortly afterwards died of want—the contents of his stomach at the autopsy being raw turnip only' (*LW* 335), Hardy wrote. He did not blame the labourers for wanting a change.

For changes were undoubtedly happening during his lifetime. In *The Mayor of Casterbridge* a sensation is caused by a 'new-fashioned agricultural implement called a horse-drill', which will supersede the biblical method of scattering grain by hand—'the romance of the sower is gone for good' (24). Other machines appear in *Tess*: one for reaping, dating from about 1862, another for turnip-slicing, and another for threshing—the 'buzzing red glutton' (48) which Tess feeds on Groby's farm. 'The old men... talked of the past days when they had been accustomed to thresh with flails on the oaken barn-floor; when everything, even to winnowing, was effected by hand-labour' (47). When these machines, with their garish colours and loud noises, turn up in a traditional English field, something momentous has happened. They do not necessarily improve things for the labourers—Tess and her friends hate standing on the threshing-machine, which makes them dizzy—but they do herald the beginning of a new age. Another 'machine' which profoundly interested Hardy was the railway, which had arrived at Dorchester when he was a child. When Tess and Angel take milk fresh from the cow to be picked up by the London train they are briefly in contact with 'the whirl of material progress': 'modern life stretched out its steam feeler to this point three or four times a day... and quickly withdrew its feeler again' (*TDU* 30). It is like the juxtaposition in D. H. *Lawrence's *Women in Love* of the train and the horse. Again, the machine is frightening but opens out vast possibilities.

The most striking change Hardy had observed, by the time he began to write fiction, was that people were no longer tied to their village. In his childhood few of them had ever left it: 'I can recollect the time when the places of burial even of the poor and tombless were all remembered, and the history of the parish and squire's family for 150 years back known' (*LW* 336). Ned Hipcroft in 'The Fiddler of the Reels' gets to London from Dorset by 'a six days' trudge on foot', but he is one of the last people to do so, for this is just before the Great Exhibition of 1851 when huge numbers were whirled up by train to see the marvels of modern technology. This made them realize that other ways of life were possible; compulsory education broadened the children's minds, and they and their mothers ceased working in the fields, and the Agricultural Workers' Union also helped its members to move out. Hardy and other observers, like Henry Rider *Haggard, believed that labourers would only stay if they were allowed to farm their own smallholdings. Since this did not happen, hundreds of thousands of them left the land in the second half of the 19th century (see EMIGRATION).

Gabriel Oak thinks of going to California, and Angel Clare does go to Brazil with a crowd of labourers 'dazzled by representations of easy independence' (*TDU* 49). More often, rural workers moved to the nearest town or signed on for a year at one farm and then migrated to another one. Hardy shows this happening in *Tess*: 'nearly all the labourers on Flintcomb-Ash Farm intended flight' (46). On the old-fashioned feast of Lady-Day (see CALENDAR) we witness a thoroughly modern phenomenon: 'the agricultural world was in a fever of mobility. ... When Tess's mother was a child the majority of the field-folk about Marlott had remained all their lives on one farm, which had been the home also of their fathers and grandfathers; but latterly the desire for yearly removal had risen to a high pitch. With the younger families it was a pleasant excitement which might possibly be an advantage ... and so they changed and changed' (51). The process is speeded up by the fact that 'lifeholders' who have lived in the same house for at least three generations are being expelled, so the village is losing the people who gave it stability. Hardy bitterly regretted this, comparing it to 'the tendency of water to flow uphill when forced by machinery', and noted that many village traditions, like the old dialect words, had been lost for ever. But he made a thoughtful attempt, in 'The Dorsetshire Labourer', to weigh up the gains and losses:

> Change is also a certain sort of education.... Whenever the habitually-removing man comes into contact with one of the old-fashioned stationary sort ... it is impossible not to perceive that the former is much more wide awake than his fellow-worker, astonishing him with stories of the wide world comprised in a twenty-mile radius from their homes.... It is only the old story that progress and picturesqueness do not harmonise. They are losing their individuality, but they are widening the range of their ideas, and gaining in freedom. It is too much to expect them to remain stagnant and old-fashioned for the pleasure of romantic spectators.
>
> But, picturesqueness apart, a result of this increasing nomadic habit of the labourer is naturally a less intimate and kindly relation with the land he tills than existed before enlightenment enabled him to rise above the condition of a serf who lived and died on a particular plot, like a tree.... The fields were those he had ploughed and sown from boyhood, and it was impossible for him, in such circumstances, to sink altogether the character of natural guardian in that of hireling.

The gulf between 'natural guardian' of the fields and 'hireling' can be seen when we compare the characters of Gabriel Oak and Jude Fawley, in novels published twenty years apart. The earlier works are firmly grounded in one place, which most of the characters never leave. *Tess* is a transitional novel in which labourers move about, within an area of twenty or thirty miles, walking or travelling by horse-cart and having no attachment to a particular farm. Jude thoroughly dislikes the village where he grows up—'"How ugly it is here!" he murmured' (1.2)—and the action is divided between places—'At Marygreen', 'At Christminster', and so on. Most of these places are good-sized towns and people travel between them by train, with emigration to Australia a distant possibility. Jude's links with the past have been broken and he knows little about 'the perished people of that place who were his ancestors and Sue's' (6.8).

Whereas Gabriel and Bathsheba could have a happy and satisfying life as small farmers, who have only nature to struggle with, and Talbothays dairy also offers satisfactions to those who work there, by the time of *Jude* we have moved into an age of landless, mobile workers whose problems are distinctively modern. 'The sojourning existence of the town masses is more and more the existence of the rural masses, with its corresponding benefits and disadvantages', Hardy noted in 'The Dorsetshire Labourer'. Like the old church at Marygreen, a way of life cannot be rebuilt. MW

Ainsworth, W. H. (1805–81), writer of once-popular historical romances and magazine editor. He was one of the favourite authors of Hardy's boyhood, in its account of which the autobiography contains a reference to *Windsor Castle* (1843). On Hardy's first visit to London at the age of 9 he explored with the help of a street-map the topography of Ainsworth's *Old St Paul's* (1841). It has been suggested that the description of the storm in *Far from the Madding Crowd* owes a good deal to a similar description in Ainsworth's first novel, *Rookwood* (1824), but this view has been challenged (see PLAGIARISM). More radically, Robert Gittings has argued in *Young Thomas Hardy* that the reading of Ainsworth had a profound and continuing influence on the plotting, characterization, and style of Hardy's novels.

alcohol. One of Hardy's earliest memories was of seeing his father making cider in the garden of the cottage at *Higher Bockhampton. 'Sweet cider' is the first of the great things in his poem 'Great Things', and Robert *Graves describes a visit to Hardy in August 1920 when Hardy grew 'enthusiastic in praise of cider, which he had drunk since a boy, and which, he said, was the finest medicine he knew' (Graves, *Goodbye to All That* (1929), 375). The cottage is said to have been a hiding-place for contraband goods brought from the coast by smugglers, and brandy would certainly have been available for those who wanted it. Hardy refers to the large amount of liquor drunk at the cottage by the church choir when they assembled there on Christmas Eve before going out to sing carols in the village (*LW* 16).

Asked by A. Arthur Reade to contribute to his book, *Study and Stimulants* (1883), Hardy wrote in a letter to him dated 5 December 1882: 'I have never found alcohol helpful to novel-writing in any degree. My experience goes to prove that the effect of wine, taken as a preliminary to imaginative work, is to blind the writer to the quality of what he produces rather than to raise the quality. When walking much out of doors, and particularly when on Continental rambles, I occasionally drink a glass or two of claret or mild ale. The German beers seem really beneficial at these times of exertion, which (as wine seems otherwise) may be owing to some alimentary qualities they possess, apart from their stimulating property. With these rare exceptions, I have taken no alcoholic liquor for the last two years.'

The reason for this last statement may partly have been that he had been seriously ill during that period, because there is a good deal of evidence that he did partake of alcohol. Thus in Emma Hardy's diary for 1876 she reports that while on holiday in Germany her husband was 'angry about the brandy flask', while Florence Hardy refers in her letters to his drinking champagne. Hardy wrote to Edward *Clodd on 3 December 1909: 'There should also reach you about this time the sample Burgundy I spoke of. You will of course understand that I do not send it as a fine wine in an absolute sense, but as what I think a good dinner wine, that rather takes my fancy' (*L* iv 63).

Ellen Titterington, a maid at Max Gate in the 1920s, wrote later that 'A favourite drink of Mr Hardy was Burgundy'. John Middleton *Murry, who visited the house in May 1921, describes Mrs Hardy coming into the drawing-room and saying, 'An awful thing has happened.... I've lost the keys of the wine-cellar. But there's whisky and cider' (Murry, *Katherine Mansfield and Other Literary Portraits* (1949), 224). Another visitor, Ernest Brennecke, in November 1923, had cider with lunch and then whisky and soda (*The Life of Thomas Hardy* (1925), 4–10). Leonard Woolf was offered whisky and water when he and his wife Virginia visited Hardy on 25 July 1926 (V. Woolf, *A Writer's Diary* (1953), 93).

Alcohol frequently figures in Hardy's novels. This is not surprising as it played a large part in the lives of the countryfolk who were depicted in all their variety in his writings. Hard physical work in the fields led to a thirst that needed quenching. The farmers often supplied their workers with ale and cider as part of their payment, and in the evening there was home-made cider and mead, or a visit to one or more of the many licensed houses selling their own brews. Cerne Abbas, a Dorset village of about one thousand people, had in the 1850s no fewer than thirteen public-houses. They were places of relaxation and an important part of the community, and occasional drunkenness was treated tolerantly. Hardy is tolerant, and in a short story like 'Absent-Mindedness in a Parish Choir' ('A Few Crusted Characters', *LLI*), where the village choir get themselves drunk during the sermon by imbibing a gallon of hot brandy and beer, the tone is comic, the criticism directed more at the Squire than at the choir.

Hardy was a friend of Alfred Pope, a director of the Dorchester brewers Eldridge Pope, and in *The Trumpet-Major* pays a tribute to the firm's 'Casterbridge Strong Ale': 'It was of the most beautiful colour that the eye of an artist in beer could desire; full in body, yet brisk as a volcano; piquant, yet without a twang; luminous as an autumn sunset.... The masses worshipped it, the minor gentry loved it more than wine, and by the most illustrious county families it was not despised.'

The drinking of alcohol is treated with an increasing seriousness in the novels. In *Desperate Remedies* there is an evocative description of cider-making, and in *Under the Greenwood Tree* Hardy extracts a great deal of humour out of the tapping of a cask of cider. In *Far from the Madding Crowd* the malthouse is a favourite meeting-place of the village workfolk, and they drink ale out of a large mug called the 'God-forgive-me'. After Troy has married Bathsheba, he shows his irresponsibility by forcing the workfolk at the harvest supper to drink more brandy than is good for them. Later in the same novel Joseph Poorgrass gets drunk at the Buck's Head inn with a result that has an important effect on the later development of the plot.

The plot of *The Mayor of Casterbridge* is triggered off by the rum with which Henchard's furmity is laced. His drunkenness causes the tragic error, the selling of his wife and child. Similarly, in *Tess of the d'Urbervilles* it is because Tess's parents get drunk that their exhausted daughter has to take the cart to market early next morning, falls asleep, and has the accident that kills their horse. Feeling herself a 'murderess' who has robbed her family of its main source of income, she agrees to go to Trantridge and the result is that fatal meeting with Alec. The people of Trantridge 'drank hard', Hardy tells us, and this leads to the orgiastic dancing at the inn at Chaseborough and to Tess's being rescued and then betrayed by Alec. Jude, like Henchard, has a weakness for alcohol which helps to bring about his downfall and is a sombre element in *Jude the Obscure*. What emerges from all this is that Hardy liked a drink himself, recognized drinking as a companionable activity, but was aware of its dangers if taken to excess. JCG

Aldeburgh, an ancient fishing-port on the Suffolk coast, has associations with George Crabbe, a poet much admired by Hardy, who in September 1905 attended celebrations held there to mark the 150th anniversary of Crabbe's birth. From 1891 Hardy was a frequent visitor to the house there of his rich, energetic, and sociable friend Edward *Clodd and met many distinguished fellow-guests. From the summer of 1909, at Hardy's request, Florence Emily Dugdale, later Florence *Hardy, also received invitations to Clodd's house at times when Hardy was a visitor, and Clodd was tactfully privy to the early stages of Hardy's relationship with the young Florence.

Alden, H. M. (1836–1919), American author and editor. He was for half a century (1869–1919) the editor of the American publication *Harper's Magazine*, and in this capacity published *Jude the Obscure* as a serial (December 1894–November 1895). Although Hardy had originally assured Alden that the novel would be entirely suitable for a family magazine, he asked on 7 April 1894 to be allowed to withdraw from his contract in view of the directions the story was taking in the course of composition. Alden refused, and his subsequent complaints led Hardy to bowdlerize the novel extensively. An interesting letter by Alden (29 August 1894), quoted at length by Purdy (90), states that his objections were 'based on a purism (not mine, but our readers'), which is undoubtedly more rigid here than in England. Our rule is that the Magazine must contain nothing which could not be read aloud in any family circle. To this we are pledged...'. In 1910 Alden invited Hardy to write his memoirs, for publication in his magazine, an offer that Hardy declined (*LW* 377). On 3 January 1921 Hardy sent an appreciation of Alden to his widow, who was at work on a biography.

Aldrich, Thomas Bailey (1836–1907), American author and editor. As editor of the Boston magazine *Atlantic Monthly*, he wrote to Hardy on 28 September 1881, inviting him to contribute a novel for serialization. Hardy quickly threw himself into this project, and *Two on a Tower* appeared in eight instalments from May 1882.

'Alicia's Diary', short story sold to the *Tillotson syndicate and published in the *Manchester Weekly Times* (15, 22 October

1887) and other provincial newspapers; collected in *A Changed Man and Other Tales*. The Italian scenes, which include some vivid descriptions of Venice, are based on Hardy's visit to Italy in March–April 1887 (see TRAVELS, CONTINENTAL). Alicia's younger sister Caroline becomes engaged to a handsome Frenchman while on holiday in France, but when he meets Alicia the two fall in love. The ensuing complications, which include a mock-marriage, lead to all the major characters meeting in Venice, and culminate in a suicide. Written soon after *The Woodlanders* and shortly before the 'marriage novels' of the 1890s, the story touches on many aspects of matrimony, including the legal ban on marriage to a deceased wife's sister (a subject of contemporary debate). Though Millgate finds the story 'cumbersome' (288), and though the diary form involves a measure of artificiality, the first-person narrative holds the reader's interest and at times possesses considerable dramatic power.

Allen, Grant (1848–99), novelist and journalist. Born in Canada, he settled in England and began his literary career as a popularizer of scientific subjects, contributing to the *Cornhill* and other magazines and becoming well known with his *Physiological Aesthetics* (1877). He subsequently became a prolific novelist; his first novel was published in 1884, and *The Woman Who Did* (1895) won him notoriety. This story of a liberated woman's contempt for the institution of marriage pleased neither prudes nor feminists and was disapprovingly linked by several reviewers with *Jude the Obscure*, which had just begun to appear in serial form when Allen's novel was published. The best-known of these attacks was that by Margaret *Oliphant in a review titled 'The Anti-Marriage League' (repr. in *CH*). Hardy had met Allen at the house of Edward *Clodd in 1894, and sent him a letter of congratulation (16 February 1895) after the publication of *The Woman Who Did*.

Allhusen, Dorothy, née Stanley (1877–1965). The younger daughter of Lady *Jeune by her first husband, she married in 1896 Augustus Henry Eden Allhusen (1867–1925) of Stoke Court, Stoke Poges, the Hardys being among the guests at their wedding at St George's, Hanover Square. Through his close friendship with her mother, Hardy knew Dorothy as a child and was known to her as 'Uncle Tom'. In the summer of 1905 he visited the Allhusens at Stoke Poges and stood with them beside the graveyard of Thomas Gray while the Duchess of Manchester recited from memory the whole of the 'Elegy Written in a Country Churchyard'.

Hardy wrote numerous letters to Dorothy, and when her husband died told her that he had been recalling her childhood and still possessed a picture of her at that time (see letter of 5 May 1925: *L* vi 324). When her younger daughter Dorothea died in 1926 at the age of 23, Hardy sent Mrs Allhusen a list of possible epitaphs chosen from various sources, including his own writings (see letter of 7 May 1926: *L* vii 22); not long before her death, Dorothea and her mother had visited Hardy at Max Gate.

Allingham, Helen. See PATERSON, HELEN.

allusion. Hardy's extensive use of a variety of forms of allusion demonstrates his intense awareness of the broad literary, historical, and cultural tradition in which he wrote; it also shows the significance of this tradition as source-material for the transmission, sharing, modification, and reinvention (both within and across the boundaries of historical period, area of origin, type of medium, genre, language, etc.) of a multiplicity of concepts, ideas, motifs, images, and forms of expression that were to become an essential element of the texture of his own writing. Through his use of allusions to historical events as well as popular legends, to classical mythology as well as the Bible, to science, literature, music, architecture, and painting, Hardy creates complex networks of implied associations, symbolic comments, and ironic asides, together forming an important level of the metaphorical structures of his works.

The sources of his allusions reflect his cultural, educational, and professional background and experience as much as his individual interests and tastes. Not surprisingly, given the predominantly literary character of 19th-century British culture, the majority of his allusions are either straightforwardly literary (direct quotations from or references to other texts, indirect echoes of themes, motifs, characters, phrasings, patterns of versification, etc.) or literature-related (e.g. non-text-specific references to classical, Christian, and Norse mythology). The most important of these literary influences is that of the *Bible, which Hardy knew intimately from his early years and which remained for him a major source of inspiration throughout his life, in spite of his loss of conventional Christian faith. Hardy alludes to a great variety of biblical passages from both the Old and the New Testaments, most frequently to the Psalms (quoted or alluded to in the versions given in the Book of Common Prayer or the Authorized Version of the Bible, or in the 18th-century metrical paraphrase by Nahum Tate and Nicholas Brady), the Book of Ecclesiastes, and the Book of Job. Biblical allusions are to be found throughout Hardy's writings but they are most prominent in the two novels most directly concerned with the theme of the place of institutional Christianity in the modern world, *Tess of the d'Urbervilles* and *Jude the Obscure*. The title-page of the latter includes what is perhaps the best-known of Hardy's biblical allusions, the memorable words from 2 Corinthians 3: 6 encapsulating the central message of the novel: 'The letter killeth'.

Another important source of Hardy's literary allusions was his extensive reading of the classics of English literature, particularly poetry. The central place in this respect belongs certainly to *Shakespeare, with some of the most prominent allusions coming from *A Midsummer Night's Dream, As You Like It* (the source of the title of *Under the Greenwood Tree*), and *Hamlet*. Among other poets, Hardy's literary tastes tended to favour modern authors, the Romantics and his Victorian contemporaries or near-contemporaries: those whose works are alluded to most regularly include in the first place *Shelley and *Browning, and secondly *Wordsworth, *Scott, *Keats, *Tennyson, and *Swinburne. With the possible exception of *Milton, earlier poets, well known as they were to Hardy, do not seem to have influenced his literary imagination as profoundly: quotations from and allusions to Chaucer and Spenser, Herbert and Dryden, Thomson and Gray, and numerous others are by comparison much less frequent, even if at times Hardy used them very effectively indeed, as in the allusion to Gray's 'Elegy Written in a Country Churchyard' in the title of *Far from the Madding Crowd*.

Relatively rare, too, are Hardy's allusions to works of prose fiction; while he occasionally mentions Bunyan and Defoe, one might wonder at the absence of references to Victorian novelists such as *Dickens and—most notably, given the widely recognized parallels between their works—to George *Eliot. Victorian philosophers and thinkers are represented by *Carlyle, John Stuart *Mill, and Matthew *Arnold.

Hardy's knowledge of literature in other languages may have been less thorough than his reading of English classics, but it was by no means limited, even if acquired to a considerable extent through translations. The most frequently echoed among foreign writers are classical authors such as Homer, Sophocles, Virgil, and Horace, though Hardy tends to refer to concepts and ideas derived from their works rather than to particular phrasings: he compares Clym Yeobright carrying his dying mother to Aeneas (*RN* 4.7), and describes the lives of his Wessex folk as 'dramas of a grandeur and unity truly Sophoclean' (*W* 1). (See also CLASSICS.) References to modern foreign authors are much less frequent, though, for example, among *Poems of the Past and the Present* there are short translations from Schiller, Heine, and Victor Hugo.

No less varied than Hardy's sources, literary or otherwise, are the functions his allusive techniques serve in the overall structures of his works, and the artistic effectiveness of his use of allusion as a literary device. At his best—for example, in *Far from the Madding Crowd, The Trumpet-Major, The Woodlanders*, and *Tess of the d'Urbervilles*—he integrates his allusions into the texture of his works almost imperceptibly, maintaining the consistency of his presentation of his characters and of the tone of the narratorial voice; at his weakest, as in some of his 'minor' novels, he appears to indulge in erudite allusiveness for its own sake, parading learned references, such as that to 'the well or little known bust [of William Pitt] by Nollekens' (*PBE* 4), before the reader more as a display of his own knowledge than as an element of a coherent artistic vision. This tendency can be observed even in some of the best of Hardy's works, where patterns of imagery based on extensive use of allusion can sometimes appear, for all their thematic appropriateness and consistency, either over-elaborate and thus forced (the 'Queen of Night' chapter (1.7) in *The Return of the Native*, for instance) or almost obsessively insistent (for example, the complex patterns of Christian and classical imagery in *Jude the Obscure*). JJ

Joan Grundy, *Hardy and the Sister Arts* (1979).
Marlene Springer, *Hardy's Use of Allusion* (1983).
Michael Wheeler, *The Art of Allusion in Victorian Fiction* (1979).

animals. Hardy's love of, concern for, and affinity with animals permeate his fiction. While his poetry contains much bird imagery, farm animals, in particular, abound in the novels. They are invariably treated sympathetically and frequently anthropomorphically. Despite the wealth of comment on the importance of the natural world in Hardy's work, however, there has been little close analysis of his treatment of animals.

While each species is treated with respect for its intrinsic value, horses are used with remarkable consistency throughout the whole *œuvre*. They are equated with, or form a reference point for, the toiling worker and the common soldier: plodding, burdened, unconsulted, controlled by others, and frequently uncomprehending. The short story 'The Son's Veto' and the poems 'No Buyers' and 'In a London Flat' exemplify Hardy's undiscriminating sympathy with all those enduring drudgery. Mrs Dollery's pitiful beast's lameness in the opening chapter of *The Woodlanders* prefigures that risked by Marty's wearing of clogs (*W* 5), while Jude's demoralized state can be identified with the kicked cab-horse he pities but does not defend (*JO* 6.1). The near equation of the plight of requisitioned horses and new recruits is found in Hardy's poems of the Boer War; the bewilderment of the peasant-soldier in 'Drummer Hodge' is similar to that of the doomed creatures in 'Horses Aboard', all being uprooted to die far from home. In *The Dynasts*, over a hundred references to horses indicate an analogy between these animals and the ranks in their common helplessness, most harrowingly depicted in their shared agonies during the Retreat from Moscow (*D* 3.1.7–11).

Unlike the ubiquitous working horses, sheep figure significantly only in *Far from the Madding Crowd*. Care of the flock, presented with apparent verisimilitude though actually idealized, forms a major part of the unceasing annual cycle of life-sustaining rural production which must continue, regardless of emotional crises. Primarily, however, sheep point to Gabriel Oak's twofold role. Literally, he is a caring, nurturing, healing shepherd. Metaphorically, he is Weatherbury's spiritual and moral pastor, an exemplary lay Christian, reminiscent of Piers Plowman, in a work permeated by the pastoral imagery of the Bible and Anglican liturgy.

Later, *The Mayor of Casterbridge* and *Jude the Obscure* take a bull and pigs respectively as single dominating images. The poor old bull, of vast potential strength, whom Henchard subdues (*MC* 29), parallels the muscular, blustering, bovine man, who is himself outwitted by Farfrae's superior intellect and detachment. We are, moreover, repeatedly reminded that Casterbridge is a place where bulls were once baited and are still tormented by the rabble at cattle auctions. The porcine imagery associated with Arabella in *Jude* has often been interpreted as symbolizing the 'grosser' side of the hero's nature. However, the novel can be read as charting his decline towards an inevitable, premature death, and the pig references remind the reader that, of all domesticated animals, these alone have no practical function save as carcasses. In this, as in so many respects, *Tess of the d'Urbervilles* seems a summation of authorial attitudes. Tess echoes Hardy's Monist, compassionate regard for all her sentient fellow-creatures, such as the horse Prince and the Talbothays cows, as individuals, and demonstrates the way in which Hardy wished to encourage the treatment of all animals with sensitive and undifferentiated loving-kindness. (See also next entry.) AE

animals, cruelty to. Commitment to animal welfare is clear from Hardy's *Who's Who* entry, the only personal opinions expressed therein being: 'Member of the Council of Justice to Animals; is against blood-sports, dog-chaining and the caging of birds.' He bequeathed £100 for research into transportation to abattoirs and for anti-caging education. Eventually, he became the first Honorary Member of the Wessex Saddleback Pig Society, hoping to encourage humane slaughter. Only on anti-vivisection was he sometimes equivocal, withholding absolute condemnation, but avoiding his wife Emma's Max Gate meetings and their literature as too distressing. He resisted attempts, even by as close a friend as Florence *Henniker, to persuade him to undertake public work on committees, insisting he could achieve most through his writings—even though, in the poem 'Afterwards', he reproaches himself for failure. A shared concern for animal welfare formed one of the closest bonds between Hardy and both his wives, surviving the severest marital strains, and was a major factor in many friendships, including those with Hermann *Lea, Clive Holland, and Edmund *Gosse. His highest praise for Emma Hardy after her death was that her courage on behalf of abused animals surpassed that of any woman he had ever known.

Acquaintances testify to Hardy's having avoided, as far as possible, the occasions of witnessing cruelty. Fatstock and working horses had to be faced, however. His autobiography is framed by accounts of intense distress, as a small child, at the 'pandemonium' of Smithfield market (*LW* 22) and cattle-trucks near Max Gate leaving for 'scenes of horror in a far-off city' (*LW* 468). He grieved for war-horses in South Africa; recorded, in his Notebook for July 1881, the reminiscences of an old postilion on the brutality involved in staging; and, especially, felt profound guilt at passively endorsing the ill-treatment of transport-animals, whose 'eyes ... haunted' him, seeming as they did to ask '"Where is your justice, O man and ruler?"' (*LW* 220). His press correspondence included opposition to circuses and, above all, hunting (both in Britain and of big game), an activity he regarded as being in a class of its own for depravity. (The fact that the aristocratic big-game hunter Sir Blount Constantine makes no direct appearance in *Two on a Tower* does not prevent his portrait from being a deeply unsympathetic one.)

The League for the Prohibition of Cruel Sports printed a full-page obituary of Hardy, celebrating his support, and its successor, the League Against Cruel Sports, still cites him as a champion. In *Darwinism, Hardy found confirmation of his instinctive Monism in 'the law of evolution, which ... shifted the centre of altruism from humanity to the whole conscious world' (*LW* 373). Conversely, sentience being, for him, the measure of all things, divinely ordained mutual predation was an obstacle to faith. As he remarked to the publisher Sir Newman Flower, he 'did not know why animals were here ... the suffering flung to the innocent was beyond his comprehension' (Newman Flower, *Just as it Happened* (1950), 93). This major aspect of Hardy's life and outlook has been largely underestimated, although some current assessment is beginning to acknowledge its significance. It is expressed more positively in his definition of Evolutionary Meliorism as 'the best consummation possible', before which conclusion, 'pain to all ... tongued or dumb, shall be kept to a minimum by loving-kindness' ('Apology' to *Late Lyrics and Earlier*). AE

Antell family. Hardy's mother Jemima (1813–1904) was one of several children born to Elizabeth and George Hand (see RELATIVES OF THOMAS HARDY). Her sister Mary Hand (1815–91) married John Antell (1816–78) in 1847, and during Hardy's youth at *Higher Bockhampton the Antells with their four children were living at Puddletown, only three miles across the heathland from the Hardy cottage. As Jemima had yet another sister, Maria (1805–68), who had married a James Sparks and also lived at Puddletown with her six children, there were frequent visits by the Hardys to their Puddletown relatives.

There were many Antells living in the Blackmoor Vale in the 18th and 19th centuries, some farmers but mostly labourers. A John Antell who died in Puddletown in 1849 is thought to have been a model for the Maltster in *Far from the Madding Crowd*, where Puddletown became Hardy's 'Weatherbury'. It was this John Antell's son, also John, who married Mary Hand and thus became Hardy's uncle. A shoemaker by trade, he was, like Hardy, a remarkable autodidact; he taught himself Latin, Greek, and Hebrew, took a keen interest in local affairs, was radical in outlook, and knew enough about trees and shrubs for Hardy to consult him when he moved into Max Gate in 1885. He was bitterly frustrated by his inability to use his knowledge and intelligence, took to alcohol, and was at times violent. Florence Hardy said that Hardy's Jude was partly based upon him. Of his four children, Mary (known as Polly) was best known to Hardy. She looked after Max Gate when the Hardys were away, lived with the widowed Jemima, and became the lifelong friend and companion of Hardy's brother and sisters. JCG

Arch, Joseph. See AGRICULTURE; 'DORSETSHIRE LABOURER, THE'.

archaeology. Hardy's well-known fascination with the past is perhaps most famously inscribed in the 11th chapter of *The Mayor of Casterbridge.* There, Hardy wrote, Casterbridge looks Roman, bespeaks 'the art of Rome', and conceals 'dead men of Rome': 'It [is] impossible to dig more than a foot or two deep about the town fields and gardens without coming upon some tall soldier or other of the Empire, who had lain there in his silent unobtrusive rest for a space of fifteen hundred years ...'.

The writing of this particular passage was stimulated by the Roman graves unearthed during the excavations for *Max Gate, an event which also led to Hardy's preparing an address, to be delivered before the members of the Dorset Natural History and Antiquarian Field Club (founded in 1875). Hardy had joined the Club in the early 1880s, a few years before the Dorset County Museum moved to the site it now occupies. He described, in fairly technical language, the 'relics of antiquity' unearthed in Fordington Field; these would soon become the property of the Museum. He could not resist, toward the end of his paper, a brief speculation on 'the living Durnovaria of fourteen or fifteen hundred years ago—as it actually appeared to the eyes of the then Dorchester men and women, under the rays of the same morning and evening sun which rises and sets over it now'.

A poet's sensibility was at work when Hardy listed several rhetorical questions: 'where stood the large buildings, were they small, how did the roofs group themselves, what were the gardens like, if any, what social character had the streets, what were the customary noises, what sort of exterior was exhibited by these hybrid Romano-British people, apart from the soldiery? were the passengers up and down the ways few in number, or did they ever form a busy throng such as we now see on a market day?' ('Some Romano-British Relics Found at Max Gate, Dorchester', 1884).

Hardy admitted that these vague questions occurred to him as an outsider, and might not be raised by 'initiated students'. He recommended that 'this fascinating investigation' be continued; the possibility that such questions might be answered as a consequence of the work of contemporary and future archaeologists intrigued him all his professional life.

Two decades later, the Club sponsored excavations at Maumbury Ring. Hardy, like his fellow-members, was thrilled to learn that 'the earthworks were of the palaeolithic age, and not Roman at all!' The fact that an amphitheatre had existed there in Roman times, and earthworks before that, invited Hardy's meditation on days long gone by; he did not feel restricted to the early centuries of the Christian era. For the major part of the essay that he sent to *The Times* (published on 9 October 1908) Hardy reviewed Sir Christopher Wren's interest in the sight of Dorchester's mounds; the execution of Mrs Mary Channing (who had been found guilty of murdering her husband, a grocer) shortly after her delivery of an infant son (see EXECUTIONS, PUBLIC); and the 'No Popery' procession of 'mock priests, monks, and nuns' that he had witnessed as a child.

On this occasion Hardy was responding to the invitation of Moberly Bell, manager of *The Times*, to describe for a larger audience the important work being conducted at Maumbury Ring; but there is no question that Hardy's interest in the study of antiquities—or archaeology, as the science became known in Victorian times—was deep and abiding. We have as evidence of this fascination the tale called 'Ancient Earthworks and What Two Enthusiastic Scientists Found Therein' (published in the *Detroit Post* in March 1885; subsequently retitled 'A Tryst at an Ancient Earthwork' and collected in *A Changed Man*). Here Hardy took issue with the rapacious relic-gathering habits of Edward Cunnington, whom he called (ironically, and not in any friendly way) 'our local Schliemann'.

Because barrows, or burial places of earth or stone, are scattered throughout the British Isles, and round barrows have been used by scientists and non-scientists alike as evidence of where the Celts settled, Hardy's penchant for imagining modes of thought and conduct in earlier ages was stimulated by (among other relics of the prehistoric past) the Bronze Age tumuli of Rainbarrows, Egdon Heath, and, closer still, Conquer Barrow, which was visible from the front door of Max Gate. Barrows form a rich pattern of allusions in *The Return of the Native*, *The Mayor of Casterbridge*, *The Dynasts*, and several poems, including 'The Revisitation', 'Evening Shadows', 'By the Barrows', and perhaps the most striking poem of all in this category, 'The Clasped Skeletons'. Hardy drew illustrations in which barrows were conspicuously present, and used them to accompany 'The Alarm' and 'Her Death and After' in *Wessex Poems*. As in 'My Cicely', they were meant to remind readers of how 'sleek herds trample daily the remains of flint-tipt arrows | Mid the thyme and chamomiles'.

For Hardy, then, the past lived on, and vivified the present. But more often than any popular creative writer of his time Hardy also spoke of how recklessly earlier generations had dug into barrows and destroyed the archaeological evidence, discarded anything that could not be converted to pounds and pence, and triumphantly claimed that their wanton and sometimes piratical behaviour advanced (rather than betrayed) the cause of knowledge. Some investigators took great pride in opening as many barrows as possible. One boasted of cutting into 106 in eleven days, or 777 over a lifetime; others recorded comparably staggering totals, piled up with reckless disregard of the need for precise contour-plans, the keeping of notes, the distinguishing between primary and secondary interments, and the sharing of information with those who might come later to the scene.

Before the pioneers of the science of anthropology developed methods of studying objects associated with burial-places and the skeletons of human beings found therein, the 18th century and indeed much of the 19th thought of archaeology as a minor branch of classical studies, and ignored the significance of new findings that confirmed the value of conjoining the two disciplines. Antiquarians like William Camden, John Leland, John Aubrey, Edward Llwyd, William Stukeley, and (for Hardy, the greatest of them all) John *Hutchins of Dorsetshire were gradually superseded by more methodical investigators such as William Greenwell and William Pengelly (who put paid to the once-fashionable dogma of Catastrophism), and by a growing awareness that a theoretical framework had to be developed to accommodate all the new information that was being unearthed.

We are so comfortable today with the notion of a three-age system (Stone Age, Bronze Age, and Iron Age) that we tend to forget that the sequence, developed first during the 1820s at the Danish National Museum in Copenhagen, did not receive much publicity in England for almost half a century. Not until the early 1870s were the Exhibition Rooms of the British Museum reorganized according to the three-age system. Decades were also required before Charles Lyell's *Principles of Geology*, which appeared in the early 1830s, won acceptance for its principles of organizing data. Further time was needed for them to be acted upon. One of Hardy's most dramatic scenes in *A Pair of Blue Eyes*, the one in which Henry Knight hangs from an escarpment and sees, at unnervingly close range, not only the slaty layers of the Cliff without a Name but the 'imbedded' eyes of a fossil, takes for granted a geological sophistication on the part of both Knight and Hardy's readers. In Lyell's lifetime such sophistication was possessed by very few.

Hardy's interest in archaeology was further deepened by his relationships to several individuals who were interested, in varying degrees, in research that might further elucidate their understanding of past eras. These men were always aware of possible theological objections to their enquiries, but Hardy liked their company because they were thinking along the same lines that had led him to a conviction that something like the Immanent Will controlled human destinies. They deserve to be named: Henry Joseph Moule, eldest of the seven sons of the Reverend Henry Moule (see MOULE FAMILY), who helped organize the Dorset County Museum and who on one occasion somewhat drily suggested that Hardy's Druid Stone—excavated after 2,000 years at Max Gate, along with ashes and partially charred bones—might have been a menhir rather than an irresistible magnet for ghosts, as Hardy wished to believe; Horace *Moule, who was equally knowledgeable as a student of the history of Christian oratory (the subject of his Cambridge dissertation), the Roman Republic (he prepared a guide for the use of examination candidates), and geology (he gave Hardy the two volumes of Gideon Algernon Mantell's 'condemned' work, *The Wonders of Geology*); and all the members of the Club, whose antiquarian interests are treated quietly, respectfully, and affectionately in the connecting links of *A Group of Noble Dames*.

The most important relationship, however, was that of Hardy to General Augustus Henry Lane-Fox Pitt-Rivers. The eccentric, dynamic researcher, educator, and collector of firearms (and much else—his artefacts were to become the basis of the Pitt-Rivers Museum in Oxford) did more than anyone else to make archaeology a respectable science in the second half of the 19th century. Charles Darwin, among others, sponsored his election to the Royal Society. The General was the first inspector of ancient monuments, and served as president of the Anthropological Institute. Using as a base his estate at Rushmore in Wiltshire, he excavated numerous sites in Cranborne Chase (his four-volume *Excavations in Cranborne Chase* is one of the best records of a meticulously conducted series of digs ever printed in Great Britain). He also made significant contributions to taxonomy, typology, ethnography, and prehistoric datings, and set up Larmer Grounds, an entertainment park with scientific emphases that attracted some 10,000 visitors a year. Hardy enjoyed frequent conversations with the General, visited his estate several times, and wrote frequently to Agnes *Grove, the General's daughter, in what can best be described as an idealized romance.

But, of all the dramatic scenes in Hardy's novels, the penultimate chapter of *Tess of the d'Urbervilles*, which describes Tess's coming to rest on the Great Plain of Salisbury, beneath the architraves of Stonehenge, forms perhaps the most poignant link between Hardy's creative art and his fascination with the unknowable past. Here Hardy renders full justice to the venerable age of the monoliths that 'made the black sky blacker', the hum of the wind playing its 'booming tune' upon the edifice, the insignificance of human beings in this isolated landscape.

Shortly before Pitt-Rivers's death, Hardy was interviewed by James Milne for the *Daily Chronicle*, the occasion being the announced intention of the owner of the land on which Stonehenge had been constructed to sell his property. Hardy, like many others, foresaw the possibility that Stonehenge might be disassembled and shipped to the United States. (He mentioned a 'rich American who is rumoured to have made an offer for it'.) He prepared a rough draft for Milne to use as the basis of his interview (published on 24 August 1899), and in it he spoke lovingly of 'the wonder of Salisbury Plain, and of England ... a sacred possession'. He was recording not merely his resentment of American money being able to do what the nation had thus far been unable or unwilling to do—to preserve Stonehenge in its present location—but his dismay at the stripping-away of 'associations' and 'sentiments' if Stonehenge were to be set up anywhere else, and (even if that kidnapping did not take place) the failure of the present owner to put an end to 'the dilapidation in progress', caused in large part by 'wet weather and frost'.

These twin concerns of Hardy, namely the rôle of memory in the national imagination and the need to preserve, possibly through the agency of an encircling wood, 'the solemnity and fascination of Stonehenge', show up elsewhere in his writings. Yet few passages (the memorable scene in *Tess of the d'Urbervilles* may be accounted one of them) are as eloquent as Hardy's description, in this interview, of the fascination that Stonehenge exerted for him: 'On a day of heavy cloud the sky seems almost to form a natural roof touching the pillars, and colours are revealed on the surfaces of the stones whose presence would not be suspected on a fine day. And if a gale of wind is blowing the strange musical hum emitted by Stonehenge can never be forgotten.'

Hardy's desire to understand better the artefacts of earlier ages was, of course, consistent with his views on church restoration, his love of the ancient cottages of England (possessing 'warmth and dryness', and, equally important, 'great beauty and charm'), and his habit of conjecturing, in numerous contexts, what Dorchester might have been like some 1,500 years earlier. He believed in the utility of scientific methods, and he applauded the systematic research of scientists like Pitt-Rivers. Nevertheless, his writings, both fictional and factual, are coloured by awe at the links of continuity he was continually discovering existed between his own age and any number of yesteryears. HO

Harold Orel, 'Hardy and the Developing Science of Archaeology', *THA* 4 (1986).

Archer, William (1856–1924), journalist and dramatic critic, and one of the earliest translators of Ibsen. He was a friend and correspondent of Hardy's from 1892. His translation of Ibsen's *Pillars of Society* was the first Ibsen play to be produced in London (1880); see IBSEN, HENRIK for Hardy's attendance at later productions. Their correspondence was initiated by Hardy, who sent him a presentation copy of *Tess of the d'Urbervilles* and expressed his sympathy with Archer's published views (*L* i 287). In his letters to Archer, Hardy speaks on literary matters with notable openness: a revealing letter of 24 November 1898 (*L* ii 206), for instance, explains his disinclination to write more novels. In September 1895 Archer and Edmund *Gosse were weekend visitors at Max Gate. An interview with Hardy, the text of which Hardy approved, was published in the *Pall Mall Gazette* in April 1901 and is reprinted in Archer's *Real Conversations* (1904) (see also INTERVIEWS).

An energetic campaigner against literary censorship, Archer joined the debate in 1894 concerning George *Moore's novel *Esther Waters* after W. H. Smith's circulating library had banned it for alleged indecency. His article in the *Daily Chronicle* (4 May) argues that Moore's book is less indecent than Hardy's *Life's Little Ironies*, which 'introduced into English fiction a note of sensuality from which *Esther Waters*... is entirely free'; two months earlier he had reviewed *Life's Little Ironies* favourably in the *Westminster Gazette*, and Hardy seems to have taken the comparison well. Archer nominated *Jude the Obscure* 'the book of the year' (*Daily Chronicle*, 1 January 1896); later he spoke highly of *Wessex Poems* (*Study and Stage*, 1899) but in more mixed terms of Part First of *The Dynasts* (*Daily Paper*, 3 February 1904). On his highly perceptive comments on Hardy's diction in his review of *Wessex Poems*, see LANGUAGE.

Sven Bäckman, *THJ* 3 (1987).

architecture.

Background

The expansion of the population in Victorian times led to a development in the status of the architect and his emergence as a recognized and discrete professional. The Institute of British Architects was founded in 1834, and the Architectural Association was founded thirteen years later. Stylistically, Victorian architecture was governed by historicism, especially Gothic. Thomas Rickman's *Attempt to Discriminate the Styles in English Architecture* (1819), the seminal text which Somerset recommends to Paula in *A Laodicean*, had established the accepted periods and terms of Gothic and had promulgated the idea that Gothic was not only a pre-eminent but also a national style. This ideology of Gothic was developed with liberal mixtures of scholarship, persuasiveness, and fervour by A. W. N. Pugin (1812–52), most famously in his *Contrasts* (1836), and by John Ruskin (1819–1900), whose chapter 'The Nature of Gothic' in *The Stones of Venice* (1851–3) imaginatively analyses the characteristics of the style. In the early 1860s, a reaction against High Gothic began to set in. '"Gothic is barbaric art, after all,"' Sue Bridehead declares: '"Pugin was wrong, and Wren was right"' (*JO* 5.6). The 'Modern Gothic' or 'Rogue Gothic' school centred round William Butterfield (1840–1900), E. B. Lamb (1806–69), S. S. Teulon (1812–73), F. T. Pilkington (1832–98), E. Bassett Keeling (1837–86), and W. W. White (1825–1900). These architects attempted to combine medievalism and modernity, traditional forms and new materials: their style was highly idiosyncratic and self-expressive, with particular emphasis on ornament, and they delighted in the use of new materials. Hardy studied with particular care Bassett Keeling's much-criticized Strand Music Hall, and visited one of White's early designs, All Saints, Notting Hill. More radically, other architects, especially Norman Shaw (1831–1912) and W. E. Nesfield (1835–

88), advocated a wider range of historical styles, such as Queen Anne: in the words of *A Laodicean*, 'a lull has come over the study of English Gothic architecture, through a reawakening to the art-forms of times that more nearly neighbour our own' (1.1). Hardy was to choose books by Shaw and Nesfield when in 1863 he won an Architectural Association prize.

As the century progressed, attitudes towards the issue of Gothic restoration also altered. The mid-Victorian architect, such as Sir George Gilbert Scott, with whom Hardy had tangential contact, might expect to spend at least as much of his time restoring old buildings as designing new ones, such restoration then being understood to include projects as considerable as rebuilding, redesigning, or even total destruction. Hardy's poem 'Inscription for a Peal of Eight Bells', subtitled 'After a Restoration', humorously comments on the frequently resultant lack of respect for original structures and artefacts. The formation of the *Society for the Protection of Ancient Buildings by William Morris in 1877 marked a change of mind and heart; the Ancient Monuments Protection Act (1882, amended 1900) provided supporting legislation.

Career

Hardy's sound technical education and family knowledge of building eminently qualified him for an architectural training: there is no reason to suppose that, had he wished to, he could not have pursued a career leading to prosperity and perhaps even distinction in what the *Life* terms 'the course all practical wisdom dictated—that of architecture' (*LW* 61). He was proposed as a member of the Architectural Association by Arthur *Blomfield in 1862. The next year he won first prize in the Association's competition for the design of a country mansion, as well as a silver medal awarded by the Institute of British Architects for his prize essay 'On the Application of Coloured Bricks and Terra Cotta to Modern Architecture'. Hardy's principal employment was with three architects: John *Hicks, Arthur Blomfield, and G. R. *Crickmay. In 1870 Hardy worked intermittently for Raphael Brandon, a distinguished architectural writer and practitioner, with whose writings he was well acquainted, and on whose chambers those of Knight in *A Pair of Blue Eyes* are based. In 1872 Hardy worked for T. Roger Smith (1830–1903), a Professor at the Royal Institute of British Architects, for whom he prepared designs for a competition for London Board Schools. Hardy found Smith 'able and amiable' (*LW* 94), and the success of one design led to the offer of further employment from Smith: 'This architectural success, for which he would have given much had it come sooner, was now merely provoking' (*LW* 94). Hardy declined Smith's offer, though giving his surname to the hero of the novel he was currently writing, *A Pair of Blue Eyes*, and sending that hero on an architectural assignment to Bombay, where Smith himself had undertaken commissions in the 1860s.

This decision marked the formal conclusion of Hardy's architectural career, and his returns to architecture in later life were generally limited and were motivated by personal or sentimental reasons: the restoration of Stinsford church, for example, or the design of Max Gate. Hardy did, however, become an early and regular correspondent for the Society for the Protection of Ancient Buildings, which he joined in 1881. His involvement with the Society between 1882 and 1926 on a total of sixteen projects, mostly ecclesiastical and mostly in Dorset, is fully documented in Claudius J. P. Beatty's *Thomas Hardy: Conservation Architect* (1995), where Hardy's address to the Society's Annual General Meeting in June 1906, entitled 'Memories of Church Restoration', is also reproduced. Hardy's RIBA prize essay has been lost. His early skit, 'How I Built Myself a House', is reprinted in *Thomas Hardy's Personal Writings*, ed. Harold Orel (1966). Hardy's *Architectural Notebook* survives, and has been edited by Beatty, whilst an unexecuted design for a church is reproduced in Timothy O'Sullivan's *Thomas Hardy: An Illustrated Biography* (1975), 31.

Influence on Hardy's Writings

An obituary entitled 'The Master Craftsman' in the architectural journal *The Builder* implied that Hardy wrote throughout his career with an architect's eye and pen. 'Those who have entered a church in Mr Hardy's company', Edmund *Blunden recalled, 'may remember the immediate sense of his mastery of all its various material detail.... The training he had undergone meant an additional quickness and rightness in his observation as a general habit, which was so valuable a resource in his novels and his other writings' (*Thomas Hardy* (1967 reprint), 35). Though only one novel (*A Laodicean*) is dominated by architectural discussion, three others (*The Poor Man and the Lady, Desperate Remedies, A Pair of Blue Eyes*) also have or had architects as their hero. Architectural conceptions and terms recur: Eustacia's lips and Lucetta's back are alike in their correspondence to 'the cima-recta' (*RN* 1.7; *MC* 22); and the prospect of Wintoncester in the final chapter of *Tess of the d'Urbervilles* has 'its more prominent buildings showing as in an isometric drawing', just as the lines in the buildings in Chief Street, Christminster, in *Jude the Obscure* are 'as distinct in the morning air as in an architectural drawing' (3.9).

The literature of the architectural Gothic had raised consciousness of the architectural merits of the parish church: the two copiously illustrated volumes of the Brandon brothers' *Parish Churches*, which Hardy had studied, prescribed personal inspection of the old churches of England as the only means by which the genius of medieval architects could be properly appreciated, and *A Laodicean*, in perhaps over-carefully considered detail, opens with Somerset reverently practising the art. Hardy the writer often returns for his settings to the habits and interests of Hardy the architectural pupil. In the novels, scenes set in churches or churchyards are not only prominent but also frequently portentous (as in *Desperate Remedies, A Pair of Blue Eyes, Far from the Madding Crowd*, and *Jude*). In the poems, the Brandons' advice is turned almost into a recurrent genre piece ('Drawing Details in an Old Church', 'Copying Architecture in an Old Minster', and 'While Drawing in a Churchyard'). In the first edition of *Wessex Poems* 'The Impercipient' is illustrated with a detailed pencil sketch of the interior of Salisbury Cathedral. Many poems have ecclesiastical settings (for example, 'At the Wicket-Gate', 'A Church Romance', 'A Cathedral Façade at Midnight', 'The Clock-Winder', 'A Poor Man and a Lady', 'Her Dilemma', 'In a Whispering Gallery', 'In Church', 'In St Paul's a While Ago', and 'In Sherborne Abbey').

Church restoration (*Under the Greenwood Tree, A Pair of Blue Eyes, A Laodicean, Jude*) is a recurrent motif. Writing in 1906 and looking back over the previous three-quarters of a century, Hardy concluded that 'if all the mediaeval buildings of England had been left as they stood at that date, to incur whatever dilapidations might have befallen them at the hands of time, weather and general neglect, this country would be richer in specimens to-day than it finds itself to be after the expenditure of millions in a nominal preservation during that period'. Though few knew better than Hardy, as he acknowledged, that it was easy to criticize with the benefit of hindsight, he did at a considerably earlier stage express his reservations about restoration in his imaginative writings.

Most particularly it was the restoration of his native church of Stinsford that involved Hardy personally and affected him emotionally. Hardy's family had been concerned with the upkeep of Stinsford church for many years. Though he was too young to remember the sweeping restoration of the early 1840s, its imaginative re-creation forms a central part of the narrative of *Under the Greenwood Tree*; and he was probably deputed by Hicks to undertake the restoration work of 1868, involving a new roof, window alterations, and the addition of a vestry. In April 1909 Hardy joined the Stinsford church restoration committee, advising that all works should be in accordance with 'the only legitimate principle for guidance', namely 'to limit all renewals to *repairs for preservation*, and never to indulge in alterations' (*L* iv 18). (In *A Laodicean* (1.13) Paula, after Somerset's intervention, had reached something of the same conclusion, and abandoned her plans for the construction of a new Greek court in the otherwise Gothic Stancy Castle.) In the subsequent decade, returning to the architectural notebook which he had used in the 1860s, he advised on the refurbishment of the font, and again in the next decade, two years before his death, advised the vicar on the restoration of the church bells.

The vicar of Stinsford, Arthur Shirley, who supervised both the 19th-century restorations of the church, sought to introduce to Stinsford the newest High Church practice—in fabric no less than in music or schooling. The changes are reflected in 'Afternoon

Service at Mellstock (Circa 1850)'. The poem, seemingly thrown-off, is precise in its frame of reference. The musical point is a clear one: 'Cambridge New', the tune mentioned, was used at Stinsford for the Tate and Brady version of Psalm 78, which discusses a man's responsibility for passing his faith on to the next generation. The poem deals with a fabric and a set of customs (as much as with a viewpoint) now outmoded. Everywhere there is unwelcome alteration: Tate and Brady were replaced by the Victorians with plainchant; stained glass the Victorian restorers preferred to the clear glass which once made the natural vistas of this poem possible; and, in conformity with the best High Church practice, Shirley removed the Stinsford box pews, replacing them with benches. The poem builds up a powerful feeling of vulnerable loneliness and erosion partly by an accumulation of precisely observed contemporary architectural detail.

What Hardy seems to have resented most in restoration work, as his fictional presentations of Mellstock church make clear, is a concern with buildings at the expense of people. In his poems about new or restored churches, such as 'The Church and the Wedding', 'The Children and Sir Nameless', and 'Whispered at the Church-Opening', new building work is associated with a dearth of historical and personal sentiment or understanding. The *locus classicus* is the barbed indictment of the architect of the new Marygreen church in *Jude*, an 'obliterator of historic records who had run down from London and back in a day' (1.1).

Hardy's own views on the relative merits of aesthetic elegance and memorial appeal are clear—indeed they may partly explain how he came to desert architecture for a calling he felt had more human interest. The argument that 'The human interest in an edifice ranks before its architectural interest, however great the latter may be' is developed at some length in 'Memories of Church Restoration': 'The protection of an edifice against renewal in fresh materials is, in fact, even more of a social—I may say a humane—duty than an aesthetic one. It is the preservation of memories, history, fellowship, fraternities.' The report of this lecture in the *Life* records the particular satisfaction of the audience 'that Hardy had laid special emphasis on the value of the human associations of ancient buildings... since they were generally slighted in paying regard to artistic and architectural points only' (*LW* 356).

Hardy is predictably sensitive to suiting the style of his buildings to their occupants. The poem 'Architectural Masks' implies that different styles of building can provide indications of the moral nature of their occupants. Such a hypothesis was central to Gothic theorists, for whom Gothic was not just an aesthetic preference but a statement of ideological belief: 'it was always a principle that anything later than Henry the Eighth was anathema', Hardy recalled of his early grounding in taste. Pugin's influential *Contrasts* set out to prove, by comparing medieval Gothic buildings with their later counterparts, the 'wonderful superiority' of the Gothic; Ruskin's essay on the nature of Gothic defined its 'moral elements'. Hardy's descriptions conform to these early prejudices far more frequently than might be expected: for him, as *A Laodicean* shows most plainly, architecture and morality remain deeply interfused. '"The winter rains will soon wash the unsightly smoke from the walls, and Stancy Castle will be beautiful in its decay"', Somerset tells Paula in the novel's ironic and ambivalent conclusion. '"You, Paula, will be yourself again, and recover, if you have not already, from the warp given to your mind (according to Woodwell) by the mediaevalism of that place"' (*AL* 6.5).

In general in the novels, those whose moral disposition is more likely to gain the reader's sympathy inhabit abodes which are either fully natural (Winterborne's hut, or, in still purer form, the shelter of his apple tree) or which have that architectural style (Gothic) which, according to Ruskin, had 'naturalism', a fidelity to the patterns and shapes of nature (cf. the argument of 'The Abbey Mason' and the comments on Gothic in the 1895 Preface to *A Pair of Blue Eyes*). Hardy's morally vacillating or morally dubious characters, by contrast, frequently inhabit classical buildings. In *Far from the Madding Crowd*, Bathsheba's manor is classical. Lucetta's house is Palladian and, 'like most architecture erected since the Gothic age', 'a compilation rather than a design' (*MC* 21). Fitzpiers's modishness shows in the Dutchness of his cottage and its garden: very much an adaptation of

Nesfield and Shaw. The code is at its crudest—and also perhaps most powerful—in *Tess of the d'Urbervilles.* Modern materials and an unnatural style characterize Alec's house at the Slopes (5) and the housing estates of Sandbourne (55), where he finally entertains Tess. The novel's concluding chapter is an entirely Puginesque Contrast: a medieval town, with medieval systems of charity, compared, with an acute implicit disfavour, to the altered contemporary perspective over a red-brick prison which is preparing to fulfil an unnatural law.

Stylistic Influence

A stress on the importance of function, and a resultant emphasis on originality rather than uniformity or imitation, lay at the centre of the views of the Gothic theorists. Pugin's *Contrasts* contended on its opening page that 'the great test of Architectural beauty is the fitness of the design to the purpose of the building': H. H. Statham's 'Modern English Architecture', an article which Hardy studied carefully when it appeared in the *Fortnightly Review* for 1 October 1876, urged the architect to 'commence first from the basis of practical consideration'. The principle is apparent in the poem 'Heiress and Architect' and burlesqued in the prose skit 'How I Built Myself a House'; in the design of Max Gate, a house built from the inside out, it was, as Millgate has noted (259), particularly respected.

The resultant Gothic emphasis on originality sprang also from an ideological basis. Ruskin's view that the individual workman should express his unique personality, unhindered by any self-consciousness about that personality's shortcomings, was developed in his *The Stones of Venice* into a 'universal law, that neither architecture nor any other noble work of man can be good unless it be imperfect'. Ornament was viewed as one of the principal means by which the self-expression of such imperfection could be achieved. It was central to the profession of Gothic, as also to Hardy's involvement with it: the details of design were generally the responsibility of the architectural assistant, and Hardy's prize-winning essay had been on a means of ornament (polychromatic brick) recently introduced into the architect's repertoire.

Such theories are the background to Hardy's concept of the 'cunning irregularity' which, in a considered examination of his architectural training which is opaque but which repays careful study, he saw as the chief influence of his architectural past on his literary style (*LW* 323). Elsewhere, Hardy admitted that 'being, in fact, a little careless, or rather, seeming to be, here and there' was the considered method by which he sought to bring 'wonderful life' into his writing (*LW* 108). For critics, especially early critics of the poetry, such originality was problematic: in the reception of *Wessex Poems*, for example, the oddness of including illustrations (not to mention their varying quality), the dense stresses, inverted syntax, archaisms, and strange coinages. When defending himself against such critical misunderstanding (for example, in the stinging exchange of views with Robert Lynd), Hardy argued on Gothic lines in favour of originality employed for the production of effect, and based his defence on architectural analogy (*LW* 323–4). The moral implications of the aesthetic concept of imperfection also left a considerable mark, expressed, for example, in Hardy's admiration for, and choice of quotation from, Robert *Browning, as in the allusions to 'The Statue and the Bust' in *Jude* and the choice of 'Rabbi Ben Ezra' as the last complete poem to be read to Hardy on his deathbed (*LW* 480).

The concern with idiosyncrasy and with ornament was perhaps at the expense of an overall sense of proportion. Certainly, such criticism has consistently been directed at the architectural Rogue Goths, from contemporary times to the present. Hardy, defending medieval Gothic, spoke of how 'the curved leafage of some capital or spandrel in the best period of Gothic art strayed freakishly out of its bounds over the moulding, where by rule it had no business to be' (*LW* 323). By comparison with a traditional Victorian practitioner such as Blomfield, however, Hardy (for example at Turnworth) exacerbated such a principle. He defined his art as a disproportioning of realities (*LW* 239), and a Rogue Gothic influence may well be detectable here. Architecturally as well as perhaps in his writing, there is some question as to how successfully Hardy is able to create a synthesis of the profusion of created ornament. The work of the Rogue Gothic architects possessed an emphasis on self-expression which in the view of many of its critics bordered on self-indulgence. A hostile assessment of Hardy, such as that of T. S. Eliot in *After Strange Gods* (1934), starts from a similar premiss.

Hardy's architectural training affected his respect for function and his penchant for self-expression, often achieved via eclectic or metaphorically polychromatic means. Much research on the topic remains to be done: it is notable, for example, that W. H. *Auden's brief provocative footnote in his much-admired essay in the influential centenary issue of the *Southern Review* (1940), 85, 'Hardy's fondness for complicated verse structure is perhaps not unconnected with his training as an architect', has remained an undeveloped aside. Shifting responses in public evaluation of Victorian Gothic, as well as increased attention to its academic study, may well bring particular enlightenment in future decades. Hitherto, conventional and received critical wisdom about Hardy's architectural understanding has been principally that it accounts for his overall sense of form, his sense of how to control the relationship of the parts to the whole. Future research may well reach an opposite conclusion. Hardy the architect was not in many senses best suited to becoming Hardy the literary planner. For, if the best of Hardy's career as an architect was carried over into this second career, so too were some of its quirkier characteristics.

TRH

Arnold, Matthew (1822–88), poet and literary and social critic. In a letter dated 16 May 1876 (partly quoted in *LW* 112), Leslie *Stephen advised Hardy that Sainte-Beuve and ('in a smaller way') Arnold were 'the only modern critics who seem to me worth reading', and, as the numerous entries in the *Literary Notebooks* indicate, Hardy read Arnold's critical writings with close attention. A significant passage later in the *Life* (*LW* 151) expresses disagreement with the views on 'provincialism' put forward in Arnold's *Culture and Anarchy* (1869). Hardy met Arnold in February 1880: for an interesting account of this meeting, see *LW* 137–8. Meetings in 1884 and 1887 are also on record. Hardy's novels contain a number of allusions to Arnold and his work: he is, for instance, one of the 'spectres' seen by Jude on arriving in Christminster (*JO* 2.1); the same passage cites Arnold's famous description of Oxford (Christminster), in his *Essays in Criticism: First Series* (1865), as the 'home of lost causes'. See also REGIONALISM.

astronomy appealed to Hardy's meditative temperament and consciousness of things beyond. He was 'one who had an eye for such mysteries' ('Afterwards'). The 'full-starred heavens' and the revelations of recent astronomical science enter many poems, from the early 'In Vision I Roamed', with its 'traverse through ghast heights of sky', to some of his last, such as 'Drinking Song', wryly celebrating the diminution of humanity brought by each discovery about the nature of the universe.

This reductive vision recurs. To set human vanities and aspirations in perspective, Hardy often turned to the stars, as in 'At a Lunar Eclipse', 'Shut Out That Moon', or 'And There Was a Great Calm', which summarizes the First World War with the line 'Sirius they watched above when armies fell'. This effect of contrast in scale also directs passages such as the extended star-map of the skies above Norcombe Hill in *Far from the Madding Crowd* (2), or the vision of deep space that opens the After Scene of *The Dynasts*: 'where the roars and plashings of the flames | Of earth-invisible suns swell noisily...'. The vastness of the skies, and their indifference to human concerns, are dominant, as when Tess and Abraham look up at 'stars whose cold pulses were beating amid the black hollows above, in serene dissociation from these two wisps of life' (*TDU* 4). This is when Tess calls this world a blighted apple among the stars, a superstitious element which lingered beneath Hardy's astronomical vision.

By 1880, when he started thinking about his 'Astronomical Romance', *Two on a Tower*, astronomy had become a matter of public interest. Improved telescopes; mathematical evidence (such as proving Saturn's rings to be particles in 1857); significant discoveries by amateur astronomers (such as Schwaber, Carrington, and Spörer); proof of the existence of the two moons of Mars (by Asaph Hall with the US Naval Observatory's new 26-inch telescope in 1877); Giovanni Schiaparelli's observation of the lines on Mars which he called 'canali'; his publication in 1879–81 of his maps of Mars; increased interest in those years in the work of Stanley Williams in England, H. C. Wilson in the USA, and Perrotin and Thollon in France; and the imminence of the Transit of Venus due in December 1882—all contributed to make 'the stupendous background of the stellar universe' (*TT*, Preface) one of Hardy's most topical subjects. Only sixteen years later H. G. *Wells would use it in another romance on human insignificance, *The War of the Worlds* (1898). Hardy was well-informed, capable of discussing 'the origin of things, the constitution of matter, the unreality of time, and . . . the new theory of vortex rings' with Leslie *Stephen in 1875 (*LW* 109), and of drawing William Dare's ideas on chance in *A Laodicean* partly from recent books by Richard Proctor and John Venn, which had linked astronomy, mathematics, and games of chance (see, for example, Venn's *The Logic of Chance* (1866)). In 1880 he acquired scientific information from George Greenhill, mathematics teacher at the Royal Artillery College, Woolwich, sought advice on lenses and telescopes, and in 1881 arranged to visit the Royal Observatory at Greenwich (Millgate 208, 226).

So Swithin and Viviette 'peep into a maelstrom of fire', move among 'monsters of magnitude . . . the voids and waste places of the sky', and 'more and more felt the contrast between their own tiny magnitudes and those among which they had recklessly plunged' (*TT* 1, 4, 8). Hardy provides technical and astronomical specifics, such as Jupiter riding in the elliptic opposite, 'double stars in the Lion and in the Virgin', Castor and Pollux, variable stars and diffraction rings, without distracting from the essentially metaphoric purpose. As well as immensity, the skies may represent subjectivity—'No person can see exactly what and where another's horizon is' (*TT* 6)—and even the role of human culture in representing or inscribing the universe. The Southern Hemisphere, when Swithin arrives there, is 'a heaven, fixed and ancient as the northern', but where 'Space . . . being less the historic haunt of human thought than overhead at home, seemed to be pervaded with a more lonely loneliness' (*TT* 41). This strikingly evokes a night sky Hardy never saw.

The stars also often indicate remoteness or alienation, as when Elfride and Knight in *A Pair of Blue Eyes* discuss how a star might be seen by Smith in India 'in our zenith, as it hangs low upon his horizon (*PBE* 19), or when the migrating wild mallard in *The Return of the Native* is said to have seen 'Polaris in the zenith', or when the poet imagines the bewilderment of the 'strange-eyed constellations' of South Africa in the lament for 'Drummer Hodge'.

Astronomical observers are scattered through Hardy's work. Stephen Smith sees Jupiter and Sirius, prophetically 'shedding his rays in rivalry', as he first approaches the house of Elfride (*PBE* 2), and later lies 'watching the Great Bear' (11). Clym Yeobright's watching the moon's eclipse is the pretext for a resonant catalogue of lunar locations (*RN* 3.4). Gabriel Oak regards the night sky as both a 'useful instrument' and 'a work of art superlatively beautiful' (*FFMC* 2). Tess, too, is a star-gazer, and the stars enter her world in reflection in the 'minute pools' in the cow and horse tracks, 'the vastest things of the universe imaged in objects so mean' (*TDU* 35)—another vivid image of contrast.

The Dynasts is Hardy's greatest work of galactic imagination, its whole strategy astronomical, or more accurately astronautical, with its many high-altitude perspectives of 'the peoples . . . seen writhing, crawling, heaving, and vibrating' (Fore Scene). The Spirits in their privileged overview work much like stars, or the moon in 'At a Lunar Eclipse' as the 'stellar gauge of earthly show'. Whether penetrating the 'ghastly gulfs' of space, or looking back as the Spirits do from that immense height on the diminished earth, Hardy makes full imaginative use of his age's new scientific understanding. Tess's jewels on her wedding night may turn her face and neck into 'an Aldebaran or a Sirius—a constellation of white, red, and green flashes' (*TDU* 34), but Hardy's use of the stars is never merely decorative. RR

Auden, W. H. (1907–73), poet and critic. In her introduction to Auden's *Juvenilia: Poems 1922–28* (1994), Katherine Bucknell comments: 'although he later recalled immersing himself in Hardy starting in the summer of 1923, Hardy's influence is most evident in poems Auden wrote during 1924'. In his 1940 essay 'A Literary Transference' (*Southern Review*), Auden said that it was in that summer (1923) that Hardy struck for him 'the authentic poetic note', and added that 'for more than a year I read no one else'. Though Bucknell comments that Auden exaggerated in saying this, she acknowledges that Hardy 'awakened in him an intense and long-lasting "passion of imitation", which, for the first time, established the pattern of obsession and assimilation that was to prove characteristic not only in his early development but throughout his career'. Bucknell goes on to say: 'By early 1924, he was writing poems that sounded like Hardy himself. As Auden explained, Hardy was not such a good craftsman as to make Auden feel he could never equal his achievements; on the contrary, Auden could easily see his faults: "his rhythmical clumsiness, his outlandish vocabulary were obvious even to a schoolboy".' Yet Hardy showed Auden the use of 'direct colloquial diction'.

In the same 1940 essay, Auden called Hardy 'my poetical father', saying that Hardy 'looked like my father... that broad unpampered moustache, bald forehead, and deeply lined sympathetic face belonged to the other world of feeling and sensation.... Here was a writer whose emotions, if sometimes monotonous and sentimental in expression, would be deeper and more faithful than my own, and whose attachment to the earth would be more secure and observant.' Much later, at the close of his 1956 inaugural lecture as Professor of Poetry at Oxford, 'Making, Knowing, and Judging', he referred to Hardy as his 'first Master' and read aloud the poem 'Afterwards', calling it 'a rite of homage to sacred objects which are neither gods nor objects of desire'. This was a poem that Auden had included in an anthology as long ago as 1935 (*The Poet's Tongue*, edited jointly with John Garrett); it was also the last of the thirteen Hardy poems he included in his five-volume *Poets of the English Language* (coedited with Norman Holmes Pearson) in 1952. Later still, Auden recalled that he had 'developed a passion' for the poetry of Hardy and Robert Frost 'while I was still at school' ('Letter of Introduction' to *C. Day Lewis: The Poet Laureate: A Bibliography* (1968), ed. G. Handley-Taylor and T. d'Arch Smith).

Though perhaps few direct traces of Hardy can be found in Auden's mature poems, Bucknell acutely comments that his 'Musée des Beaux Arts', written in 1938, shows something learned from Hardy: 'to feel passion for his subject, to notice its every feature, and yet to view it from a distance, with detachment'.

AT

autobiography. Shortly after Hardy's death his widow brought out, over her own name, a two-volume biography comprising *The Early Life of Thomas Hardy 1840–1891* and *The Later Years of Thomas Hardy 1892–1928*, published by Macmillan in November 1928 and April 1930 respectively. The two volumes were reissued together as *The Life of Thomas Hardy* in 1933, and it is by that title—also used for the one-volume paperback issue of 1962—that the work has generally become known. That Hardy himself had contributed much to the project was clear from the first: the title-page of *The Early Life* specifically claimed, as earnest of the work's authenticity, that it had been 'largely' based on Hardy's own diaries and memoranda and on 'oral information in conversations extending over many years'. But it was Richard Little Purdy who first revealed—briefly in a speech reported in the *New York Times Book Review* of 12 May 1940, and more substantially in his *Thomas Hardy: A Bibliographical Study* of 1954—that Hardy had in fact ghost-written almost the entire work, and that the contributions of its ostensible author, though certainly important, had remained for the most part secretarial, editorial, and supplemental.

The composition of the *Life* was for both Hardy and his wife a matter of great secrecy, but because many of the original working documents were left undestroyed by Florence *Hardy at the time of her death in 1937 (and are now in the Dorset County Museum) it is possible to reconstruct the sequence of events with a fair degree of confidence. Hardy had always been resistant to the intrusions of journalists and would-be biographers attracted by his ever-growing fame, and he had more than once declared that he would never write an autobiography. Encouraged, however, by his second wife and his friend Sydney *Cockerell, he seems in or about 1916 to have become seized with the idea that by actively collaborating during his lifetime in a prefabricated 'official' biography of himself for posthumous publication he might succeed in forestalling the dreaded proliferation of inaccurate and potentially hostile biographies by other hands.

Florence Hardy brought to the project not only her very considerable typing skills but also her experience as a writer of children's stories and her lingering ambition to be recognized as an author in her own right. No less germane was the availability of the long series of small notebooks, filled with diary entries, pencil sketches, meditations, descriptions, and ideas for plots and images, that Hardy himself had kept since at least the 1860s and extensively drawn upon as sources of material for both his fiction and his verse. When work actually began in the summer of 1917 Hardy seems first to have gone systematically through those notebooks, revisiting his past, identifying entries appropriate for quotation, and occasionally transferring unused items into his 'Poetical Matter' notebook for possible use in future poems. At the same time Florence Hardy began making what she called 'the notes', evidently based at least in part on her husband's conversation and responses to specific questions. By early 1918, however, Hardy himself was doing all of the actual writing, producing day by day, in the privacy of his study, pages of manuscript that were then handed to Florence to be typed up in three copies: the ribbon ('top') copy and two carbon copies. The second carbon became the 'rough' or working copy on which Hardy made his many subsequent revisions and additions, while the first carbon served as a copy of record to which Florence—and, increasingly, Hardy himself—transferred the 'rough' copy changes.

Once Hardy had finally approved those changes it was his wife, again, who incorporated them into the ribbon copy that was intended in due course to go to the printer. In his zeal to keep his authorship of the work a secret Hardy burned his original manuscript and sought to disguise his inscriptions on the typescripts by using the calligraphic hand he had learned as an architect. The scheme was neat enough in itself, but it tended to break down somewhat over the succeeding years as Hardy returned to the typescripts again and again and made far more extensive corrections and additions than had ever been envisaged. The copy finally submitted to the publisher has not survived but must have been largely retyped.

Once the narrative of his life had progressed into the stage of early manhood Hardy drew increasingly on the diary-notebooks as sources both of information and of the actual quotations that early reviewers of *Early Life* and *Later Years* recognized as being of particular interest and importance. It is now clear, however, that dates and other details in the *Life* are occasionally inaccurate, if for the most part unintentionally so, and that Hardy, in incorporating passages from his notebooks, did not hesitate to adjust their wording in accordance with the stylistic and, to a lesser extent, the intellectual preferences of his old age. Almost all such divergences, unfortunately, were rendered for ever undetectable by the comprehensive destruction of the diary-notebooks, most by Hardy himself, the remainder (as he had apparently requested) immediately following his death.

Somewhat more visible are Hardy's revisions to the letters incorporated into the *Life*: because the need for secrecy ruled out the possibility of asking the recipients of his letters to return or lend the original documents, Hardy drew—and with some freedom—on drafts of those letters still in his files. It is possible, for example, to detect the differences between Hardy's letter to Caleb Saleeby as included, from Saleeby's transcription, in an Appendix to *Later Years* and Hardy's revision of his own draft of the same letter that appears earlier in the volume.

The appendix containing the letters to Saleeby was inserted after Hardy's death, Florence Hardy having failed to register the element of repetition. Many of her other interventions, however, were of greater significance. Hardy, in a memorandum of 'Information for Mrs Hardy in the preparation of a biography', had specifically empowered her to introduce whatever changes she believed to be necessary, especially in order to exclude whatever seemed 'indiscreet, belittling, monotonous, trivial, provocative, or in other ways unadvisable' (*LW* xix). In practice, the additions, deletions, and alterations she made after Hardy's death are not always readily distinguishable from those she had made on his instructions during his lifetime, but it is clear that she took her responsibilities seriously and discharged them conscientiously.

Completion of the project was one of the principal tasks that Florence Hardy took in hand immediately following her husband's funeral. She consulted the two men on whom she most depended, Sydney Cockerell and Sir James *Barrie, and on their advice, supplemented by that of Daniel Macmillan and the Macmillan reader, Charles Whibley, it was decided to publish the work in two volumes rather than one, and to make cuts in Hardy's attacks on hostile critics and in the diary entries devoted to long lists of people encountered on London social occasions. Some additions were also made, among them a long passage descriptive of Max Gate and of Hardy himself as they had been in the late 1880s, and in late March 1928, just as Florence Hardy was preparing to send Macmillan the revised text for *Early Life*, she received from Barrie a long letter listing more than a dozen Hardyan anecdotes that seemed worth preserving. They included the stories of Hardy's youthful but unspoken admiration for Louisa Harding, his accepting pennies for his fiddling in order to be able to buy *The Boy's Own Book*, and his despair at the *Spectator*'s dismissive review of *Desperate Remedies*. In addition to including almost all the anecdotes Barrie had sent, Florence Hardy acted upon Barrie's further suggestion that she should seek out (from Hardy's sister Katharine) and print the texts of surviving letters written by Hardy to his sister Mary during the years 1862–7, when he was away from home for the first time and working in London.

The reviews of *Early Life* were respectful rather than enthusiastic but sufficiently favourable to justify both Daniel Macmillan and Florence Hardy in proceeding with the publication of its sequel. Florence Hardy made a far larger contribution to *Later Years* than she had done to *Early Life*. The text as Hardy had left it was in publishable form only up to the end of 1918, and in revising those first fifteen chapters she added several letters, made (or allowed others to make) quite extensive cuts to the resentful responses to critics and the exhaustive chronicling of London social events, and omitted, as she had done in *Early Life*, some of the numerous references to the first Mrs Hardy.

Beyond 1918 the working papers for the *Life*—what Hardy had called the 'Materials'—consisted chiefly of a narrative outline for 1919 and 1920 and numerous notes and drafted items, including the 'Memoranda II' notebook (see NOTEBOOKS) for the years 1921–7. It was on this basis, supplemented by diary notes of her own and solicited contributions from Charles *Morgan and Godfrey Elton, that Florence Hardy, evidently with some difficulty, put together the work's four final chapters, the first two very close to Hardy's outline for 1919–20, the last two essentially her own work. She incorporated reports on Hardy's 1920 and 1923 visits to Oxford supplied by Morgan and Elton and, in the first of three appendices, a short account of Hardy's three funeral services (Westminster Abbey, Stinsford, Dorchester) written by Harold *Child, a critic of whose work Hardy had approved. Into the second appendix she inserted the letters from Hardy to Saleeby already mentioned, and into the third three letters from Hardy to his friend Edward *Clodd.

Florence Hardy's additions to and intrusions into Hardy's text were clearly extensive and significant, to the point that it is possible to question whether the term 'autobiography' can properly be used, without qualification, of the two-volume work she published in 1928–30. Although the narrative remains essentially Hardy's, it omits a good deal of what he originally wrote, and includes, especially in its later stages, much that he neither wrote nor saw. In 1985 a more exclusively Hardyan text, based on the surviving typescripts, was published, over Hardy's own name, as *The Life and Work of Thomas Hardy*—the title the work had borne in typescript and, indeed, until after Hardy's death. Though not a substitute for *Early Life* and *Later Years*, which retain their own shared history and integrity, it does provide a clearer and fuller sense of what Hardy wished to say from beyond the grave: the self-image that he sought to project to posterity.

Though it is understandable that Florence Hardy and her advisers should have chosen to reduce or actually omit the attacks on hostile critics and the long lists of London notables, Hardy himself had presumably been voicing long-suppressed resentments and boasting a little about his genial familiarity with London and its literary, artistic, and social worlds. These aspects of the work, along with its mild glamorization of the socio-economic circumstances of his childhood, its silence about relatives outside his immediate family circle, its contrastive references to members of the aristocracy, have sometimes led to Hardy's being accused of snobbishness and social climbing. But they probably have more to do with his determination to protect his privacy after death as he had sought to do in life, the steady chronicling of external events serving to mask the lack of confrontation with contemporary experiences too private and too painful to reveal. It is true that the *Life* does offer, usually in the form of extracts from the notebooks, some intensely intimate glimpses into Hardy's feelings and thoughts, especially during the periods of his childhood and youth. In the chapters relating to the entire span of his first marriage, however, virtually nothing is said of the difficulties of that marriage, of his rejection by Florence *Henniker, or of his interest in other women.

The *Life* thus remains curiously difficult to categorize and to evaluate. As originally completed by Florence Hardy it is perhaps best considered as an official biography largely authored by its subject. As re-edited from the typescripts as an exclusively Hardyan text it has stronger claims to be considered a third-person autobiography, although such claims are diminished, even so, by the concentration upon external events—Hardy's life in his times—rather than upon personal introspection and reflection.

The *Life* is similarly compromised as a source of biographical information. Because the notebooks and other documents used in its compilation were subsequently destroyed, it remains, and will always remain, a uniquely valuable repository of biographical information, especially for the first thirty-five years or so of Hardy's life, and above all for his experiences as a child. The reliability of that information, however, is put seriously into doubt by Hardy's known readiness to adapt his sources for incorporation into the *Life*, and by the impossibility, given the absence of the original documents, of checking the accuracy of his transcriptions and datings or the validity of his generalizations. While, therefore, the work is an indispensable biographical resource, peculiarly precious as originating so largely with Hardy himself and affording some access, however limited, to the vanished notebooks, it nevertheless constitutes a virtually impassable barrier, trapping the biographer within patterns of silence, distraction, and perhaps even outright deception deliberately contrived by Hardy himself. MM

Ian Gregor and Michael Irwin, 'Your Story or Your Life: Reflections on Thomas Hardy's Autobiography', *THA* 2 (1984).

Michael Millgate, Introduction to Thomas Hardy, *The Life and Work of Thomas Hardy* (1985).

B

ballads. The traditional ballad was the literary form that most influenced Hardy as a young poet in the 1860s, when the revival of popular ballads, represented by Francis Child's edition of *English and Scottish Ballads* (1857–9) and the republication of Bishop Percy's *Reliques of Ancient English Poetry* (1765), of which Hardy owned the 1857 edition, informed his artistic apprenticeship. Hardy's experimentation with the ballad form gave expression to his serious study of avant-garde theories of metre, while satisfying his antiquarian bent. Although Hardy wrote only a dozen or so poems in the ballad stanza (an iambic tetrameter-trimeter quatrain, rhyming *abcb*), most of his over 150 narrative poems tap into the balladic lifeblood of English poetry—orally transmitted songs and stories of legendary and historical events, which he retold to keep them bright in the popular mind. As literature, his ballads are both link and foil, continuous with traditions of folk memory, and inventively involved with contemporary poetic theories and styles.

Yet by poetically inscribing Wessex customs and myths, Hardy was forced to fly in the face of his own idea of authentic balladry as an oral phenomenon, a paradox implicit in the lyric 'The Ballad-Singer', which asks the balladeer for a consoling song from either the 'country' or his 'little book'. Moreover, although his ballads catch the impersonal, objective tone of a traditional ballad, they often express the narrator's, or even the poet's, self. This shift in fictional level or aesthetic distance is considered by some a violation of ballad reserve, by others a merit, deepening Hardy's humane responsiveness as lyric poet.

The chief spin-off from these tensions in his ballads is the creative interplay Hardy achieved between lyric and narrative modes in his short poems. With his increasing absorption into, and domestication of, the ballad form (see *LW* 491) comes a historical attitude towards his personal past. Hence the balladic pervades his lyric poetry, a sense of fact informs the feeling, and the central impulses of his narrative poems—the inscrutability of Nature and the ironies of human passion—often give a primitive edge to the elegies on the death of his wife Emma, and such short poems as 'Bereft', 'One We Knew', and two that are (in his own judgement) 'possibly among the best' he wrote, 'During Wind and Rain' and 'Near Lanivet, 1872' (*L* vi 96).

By contrast, Hardy paid a price for writing ballads 'with ease' (*L* iv 117). Some may repel with their trivial anecdotage ('The Mock Wife'), melodrama ('The Workbox'), or moral and psychological prosaicness ('The Peasant's Confession', the weakest among his Napoleonic poems). Poems that are perfectly balladic in effect, adroit in versification, and evoke that 'dreamlike & confused' quality of the genre (*LN* ii 95) include 'The Harvest-Supper' (echoing the traditional ballad 'The Unquiet Grave'), 'A Sunday Morning Tragedy' (with an ominous refrain), and 'The Sacrilege' (with multiple focalization), 'A Trampwoman's Tragedy', exploiting local settings and hidden motives, Hardy included in *Chosen Poems* and may have considered 'upon the whole, his most successful poem' (*LW* 517). BG

Norman Arkans, 'Hardy's Narrative Muse and the Ballad Connection', *THA* 2 (1984).

Thom Gunn, 'Hardy and the Ballads', *Agenda*, 10 (1972).

Barnes, William (1801–86), Dorset dialect poet and philologist. He started a school in Mere, Wiltshire, in 1823 and in 1835 moved it to *Dorchester, where his pupils later included Hardy's friend Hooper *Tolbort. Ordained in 1858, Barnes was from 1862 until his death Rector of Came, Dorset. He published verses in local newspapers from 1820, and his first dialect poems appeared in the *Dorset County Chronicle* in 1833. Later publications include *Poems of Rural Life in the Dorset Dialect* (1844) and *Hwomely Rhymes* (1859).

Barnes became a remarkable linguist, teaching himself a great variety of tongues from Anglo-Saxon to Persian. He held strong and sometimes eccentric views on the need to purify the English language by purging it of classical and Romance importations and returning to its Saxon roots: he deplored, for instance, such coinages as 'photograph' and 'perambulator', suggesting 'sun-print' and 'push-wainling' as alternatives. His *An Outline of English Speech-Craft* (1878) attempts to present an English grammar while eschewing Latinate terminology: hence 'intransitive' is replaced by 'unoutreaching', 'genitive' is 'offspring case', and 'index' is 'clue to matters handled'. While such idealistic enterprises are now mere curiosities, Barnes's poetry, which was admired by Tennyson, G. M. Hopkins, and others as well as by Hardy (whose copies of Barnes's poems are heavily annotated), has an assured place in the canon.

Hardy formed an acquaintance with Barnes at about the age of 16, while working for John *Hicks, whose office in South Street, Dorchester, was next to Barnes's school, and the schoolmaster was on occasion asked to settle disputes on points of grammar between Hardy and Henry *Bastow. In later years Hardy often visited Barnes: in July 1883, for instance, he took Edmund *Gosse to hear him preach and they afterwards visited the rectory. He attended Barnes's funeral on 11 October 1886, and his poem 'The Last Signal' finely commemorates the occasion and a friendship of some thirty years. (For a later visit to Barnes's grave, see DOUGLAS, SIR GEORGE.) His obituary of Barnes appeared in the *Athenaeum* on 16 October 1886. It may be significant that the first notions of *Jude the Obscure* seem to have been conceived soon after Barnes's death: like the hero of the novel, Barnes came from humble origins (he was the son of a tenant farmer), was largely self-taught, and had a genuine passion for learning. In 1900 Hardy gave assistance with the entry on Barnes for the *Dictionary of National Biography*, and in 1907 he offered to make a selection of Barnes's poems for the Clarendon Press; published in November 1908 as *Select Poems of William Barnes*, it includes a preface and glossarial notes. In 1916 he agreed to undertake the section on Barnes in the fifth volume of T. H. Ward's anthology *The English Poets* (published November 1918). The only review he ever published was of Barnes's *Poems of Rural Life* (*New Quarterly Magazine*, October 1879).

Hardy shared Barnes's regret at the disappearance of dialect as a result of the spread of education—without, however, either committing himself so single-mindedly to a campaign for its preservation, or assuming the unfashionable mantle of dialect poet. In his preface to the *Select Poems*, he wrote: 'Since [Barnes's] death, education in the west of England as elsewhere has gone on with its silent and inevitable effacements, reducing the speech of this country to uniformity, and obliterating every year many a fine old local word.'

It has been persuasively argued that Barnes's poems exerted a significant influence on Hardy's own poetry—not only on the dialect poems (which are in any case relatively few), but on the diction and metre of other poems. This influence is most obviously detected in such locutions as 'outbreathing', 'gaingivings', 'mindsight', 'earth-track', and 'lovecraft', which have a strongly Barnesian flavour. On Barnes's influence, and on allusions to Barnes in Hardy's novels, see also PHILOLOGY.

Barnes's daughter Lucy Baxter (1837–1902) published books on art and literature under the pseudonym of 'Leader Scott'. Her biography of her father appeared in 1887. From their early years she was well known to Hardy, whose obituary of her appeared in *The Times* and the *Dorset County Chronicle* on 27 November 1902.

Samuel Hynes, 'Hardy and Barnes: Notes on Literary Influence', *South Atlantic Quarterly*, 58 (1959).

James W. Parins, *William Barnes* (1984).

C. H. Sisson, 'Hardy and Barnes', *Agenda*, 10 (1972).

Barrie, James (1860–1937), novelist and dramatist. Of humble Scots origins, he became one of the most popular writers of his day and was created a baronet (1913) and appointed to the Order of Merit (1922). While still in his twenties he published a substantial and not uncritical account of Hardy's fiction to date, 'Thomas Hardy: The Historian of Wessex', in the *Contemporary Review* (1889; repr. in *CH*). Hardy was acquainted with Barrie and his wife from the 1890s and the two men later became close friends, corresponding and meeting often in London. In 1893 Hardy took up Barrie's suggestion that he should turn his short story 'The Three Strangers' into a one-act play. In May 1919 Hardy and his second wife stayed with Barrie at his flat in the Adelphi while on a brief visit to London; they stayed there again in April 1920 (Hardy's last visit to London) and attended a rehearsal of Barrie's play *Mary Rose*, an occasion commemorated in his humorous poem 'At a Rehearsal of One of J.M.B.'s Plays'. After Hardy ceased going to London, Barrie visited him in Dorchester; on one visit, in May 1921, they went together to Hardy's birthplace.

On the day before Hardy died, Barrie, 'the friend of many years' (*LW* 480), called at Max Gate to offer assistance. Immediately after Hardy's death, and now back in London, he was active in conjunction with Sydney *Cockerell in obtaining permission for Hardy to be buried in Westminster Abbey; subsequently Barrie travelled with Hardy's body to the crematorium at Woking and conveyed the ashes to the Abbey. At the funeral he was one of the pall-bearers. In 2 September 1931 it was Barrie who unveiled the sculpture of Hardy by Eric Kennington that stands on a prominent site at Top o' Town, Dorchester. On Barrie's important role in assisting Florence Hardy in the preparation for publication of Hardy's autobiography, and on the marriage between Barrie and Florence that was contemplated in 1928, see *LW* xxi–xxii; AUTOBIOGRAPHY; HARDY, FLORENCE EMILY.

Bastow, Henry (1839–1920), a close friend of Hardy while they were both articled to the Dorchester architect John *Hicks. Brought up in Bridport and educated at 'a good school' in the London area (*LW* 32), Bastow was, like Hardy, a keen student of classics who found himself committed to the architectural profession. He was also a devout Baptist and was baptized in 1858, three years after joining Hicks's firm. After Hardy arrived there in 1856, an intimate friendship based on shared intellectual tastes developed between them. Bastow's discussions with Hardy, in and out of the office, soon moved from secular to religious studies, the sons of the Dorchester Baptist minister, Alfred and William Perkins, who were students at Aberdeen University, sometimes joining in their debates. Like the hero of *Jude the Obscure*, who also turned from the pagan classics to biblical and theological studies, Hardy was led to make a close study of the Greek Testament, acquiring, like Jude, a copy of Griesbach's edition (*JO* 1.5). A favourite topic of heated discussion was the legitimacy of infant baptism, touched on in *A Laodicean* (1.6–7), where the character of Mr Woodwell is based on the Reverend Frederick Perkins; despite his Anglican upbringing, Hardy came close to being persuaded that he should undergo adult baptism, and went so far as to seek advice from two local clergymen (*LW* 33).

After completing his four-year apprenticeship with Hicks, Bastow worked for a short time as an architect in London, then in 1860 emigrated to Hobart, Tasmania. His letters from Australia, which Hardy kept for the rest of his life, urged Hardy to remain true to the Christian faith; the correspondence, however, seems to have lapsed, and the two friends lost touch with each other. Within a few weeks of his death, Hardy, unaware that Bastow had died some years earlier, spoke to his wife about Bastow's piety and his own devotion to him (*LW* 478). (See also CLASSICS.)

Beerbohm, Max (1872–1956), author, critic, satirist, caricaturist, and dandy; knighted 1939. He became acquainted with Hardy in London; their first meeting may have been as fellow-guests at the home of Edmund *Gosse on 8 May 1904. Beerbohm visited Hardy at Max Gate in June 1923. He produced an excellent cartoon, 'Mr Thomas Hardy composing a lyric' (1913), reproduced in *Beerbohm's Literary Caricatures*, ed. J. G. Riewald (1977). Beerbohm also reviewed performances of one of the dramatized versions of *Tess of the d'Urbervilles* and of *The Dynasts* (repr. in his *Around Theatres* (1924)) and published two very effective Hardy parodies, 'A Sequelula to *The Dynasts*' (in *A Christmas Garland* (1912)) and 'A Luncheon', as well as 'Thomas Hardy and A. E. Housman' (last two items repr. in *Max in Verse*, ed. J. G. Riewald (1954)). (See also HARDY, POEMS ABOUT.)

Benson, A. C. (1862–1925), Cambridge don, prolific and successful man of letters, and compulsive diarist. He was a master at Eton and subsequently Fellow and then (1915–25) Master of Magdalene College. He came of a distinguished family: his father became Archbishop of Canterbury and one of his brothers was E. F. Benson, the novelist and autobiographer. Benson himself achieved considerable popular success with a stream of essays, biographies, poems, and novels, now mostly forgotten. With Edmund *Gosse, he visited the Hardys at Max Gate on 5 September 1912 and recorded in his (largely unpublished) diary, now at Magdalene College, Cambridge, his sharp and detailed but somewhat sour observations on Hardy, his wife, and his house (see Millgate 481–2). Hardy saw Benson during a visit to Cambridge in June 1913 and again, later in the same year, when he was back in Cambridge in order to be admitted as an honorary fellow of Magdalene (21 November). With his new wife, Florence, Hardy was once again in Cambridge in April 1914 and visited Benson among other friends.

Besant, Walter (1836–1901), novelist, philanthropist, and historian of London. He was a member of Hardy's circle of literary friends during the last decades of the 19th century. An energetic and clubbable member of the literary profession, Besant was one of the founders of the Society of Authors and was knighted in 1895. In 1879 he invited Hardy to become one of the founding members of the Rabelais Club, designed to promote 'virility' (that is, outspokenness on sexual matters) in literature; his letter of invitation (7 March 1879, DCM) pays flattering tribute to the recently published *The Return of the Native* as 'the most original, most virile and most humorous of all modern novels'. Hardy's autobiography contains a lively account of the inaugural meeting of the Club (December 1879) that includes a thumbnail sketch of its founder: 'genial Walter Besant, with his West-of-England sailor face and silent pantomimic laughter' (*LW* 135).

Besant was one of the numerous friends of Edward *Clodd and was a fellow-guest on the occasion of Hardy's first visit to Clodd's house at *Aldeburgh in June 1891. Soon afterwards he gave Hardy encouragement in the face of the hostile reception of *Tess of the d'Urbervilles.* Hardy attended Besant's funeral in Hampstead on 12 June 1901.

Bible. Hardy's relationship with the Bible was ambivalent. On the one hand, few mainstream contemporary authors were more dubious about its literal truth; on the other hand, Hardy alluded to no book more frequently or extensively.

Biblical knowledge amongst the Victorian rural working classes was remarkably high. One of Hardy's ancestors had read the Bible through seven times; and the dairymaid on whom he claimed to have based Marian in *Tess of the d'Urbervilles* had a 'marvellous power of memorizing whole chapters in the Bible', which she would repeat to Hardy in the class which he supervised at the Stinsford Sunday school (*LW* 263, 30). The Bible inevitably was central to Hardy's schooling (in both its Established and Nonconformist phases) as well as to the regular church attendance in which family tradition encouraged him.

Hardy's own enthusiasm for biblical study may be traced in bibles preserved in the Thomas Hardy Memorial Collection (DCM). These make apparent a particularly earnest period of Bible study beginning in 1861 and probably linked with a popular Evangelical Revival which affected Dorchester acutely around this time. Evangelical emphasis on Bible study was usually pronounced, and the publications of the clergy prominent in the Dorset Evangelical movement suggest no local exception. The bible which Hardy bought in 1861 was for a time a form of *vade mecum* and has become a primary source for biographers. In it Hardy often recorded his whereabouts, marked texts which reflected his thoughts and feelings, and (in some cases where shorthand and erasure have been used) entered private details which still escape biographical explication.

With Hardy's drift away from orthodox church attendance in the mid-1860s, such markings ceased almost completely, and probably with them any devotional pattern of Bible reading. However, a maintained or more probably increasing stylistic interest in the Bible is apparent in the *Life.* At around this time Hardy began turning the Book of Ecclesiastes into Spenserian stanzas, 'but finding the original unmatchable abandoned the task' (*LW* 49). A more extensive appreciation of the skill of the biblical narrators is apparent in a lengthy entry for Easter Sunday 1885, when Hardy was at work on *The Mayor of Casterbridge.* Hardy analyses 'simplicity of the highest cunning' and a 'spherical completeness of perfect art' unreached by modern narratives (LW 177).

Biblical allusions are widespread in Hardy's writings. Certain passages and books are more favoured than others: Job, 1 and 2 Kings, Psalms, the Sermon on the Mount, and (despite Hardy's fluctuating level of respect for their author) the Pauline Epistles. The poems, like the novels, frequently employ biblical allusion, but sometimes (as in 'The Face at the Casement' or 'The To-Be-Forgotten') with a particular dominance. The Bible provides Hardy with titles ('In Time of "The Breaking of Nations"', 'And There Was a Great Calm'); with epigraphs (e.g. 'The Collector Cleans His Picture', 'In Tenebris I–III', and 'In the Seventies'); with situations that can be versified ('In the Servants' Quarters'), or, more characteristically, developed with an inflammatory unorthodox purpose ('An Evening in Galilee', 'Panthera', and 'The Wood Fire'). A personal, distinctive, and finely crafted genre is the meditative poem using a biblical passage as the grounds for personal reflection: examples are 'Quid Hic Agis' and the two final poems of *Late Lyrics and Earlier*: 'After Reading Psalms XXXIX, XL, etc.' and 'Surview'.

In the novels, the number of biblical allusions is difficult to quantify precisely: 600 is the highest estimate. It is noticeable that in novels where Hardy seems to be particularly stretching his creative ambition to new levels of achievement, the number of biblical allusions is particularly high: over 60 echoes or references have been detected in each of *Far from the Madding Crowd*, *The Return of the Native*, and *Jude the Obscure*, and the highest number (87) in *Tess*. The purposes are as diverse as in the poetry—indeed necessarily more so. The biblical reference which gives *A Laodicean* its title is central to its plot and argument; the prominently positioned metrical psalms of *A Pair of Blue Eyes* (27), *Two on a Tower* (2), and *The Mayor of Casterbridge* (33) bear a particular and considered narrative and thematic weight. Julian Moynahan, furthermore, has convincingly argued in '*The Mayor of Casterbridge* and the Old Testament's First Book of Samuel' (*PMLA* 1956) that the narrative of the novel has striking resemblances to the story of David and Jonathan. The Eden imagery of *Tess* and the Jerusalem imagery of *Jude* show such structural and thematic devices developed with an even more prominent sense of purpose and cohesion.

Various thematic uses of biblical reference are consistent to the novels as a whole. Old Testament references, especially to the Pentateuch, establish the continuity of the traditions of pre-industrial Wessex. Cain Ball justifiably remarks in *Far from the Madding Crowd* that the Weatherbury parishioners 'feel all over like the children of Israel', since the novel contains 21 allusions to Genesis and Exodus alone and is liberally sprinkled with biblical parallels. The cultivation of the land and its produce is associated throughout the novels with biblical practice. In *The Mayor* (29) breeding is carried on with Abrahamic success. In *The Trumpet-Major* (17) Miller Loveday vocalizes a formula 'uttered by the proprietors of live stock ever since Abraham's day'. Farfrae will be like Jacob (*MC* 17) and Angel become 'an American or Australian Abraham' (*TDU* 19). Modern scientific or technological departures from tradition are similarly marked, perhaps most notably in the dense biblical allusions which surround the engineman and his threshing machine in *Tess* (47–8).

Hardy's legacy from contemporary intellectual agnostics shows itself in the characteristic use of biblical language to express secular love. Lady Constantine asks Swithin, '"Without the Church to cling to, what have we?"' and gets the Leslie-Stephen-style reply of '"Each other"' (*TT* 21). Hardy finds suitable language for developing this cast of idea, which is already well articulated as early as *Desperate Remedies*: the tenderness of Ambrose Graye for the young Miss Aldclyffe is expressed in an allusion to the Samson story (1), and Manston articulates his grief at the prospect of losing Cytherea in a quotation from Job (14). The motif is further developed in *Far from the Madding Crowd*, and reaches its apotheosis in *Jude*, where Sue expounds the authentic significance of the Song of Solomon, and Jude expresses his love in an adaptation of words from St Paul (3.4, 4.5).

In this latter novel, as in *Tess*, Hardy's use of biblical reference for moral and anti-orthodox purpose is at its height. A performance of an anthem based on Psalm 73 ('Truly God is Loving unto Israel') coincides with the suicide and infanticide of Jude and Sue's family (6.2); at the end of the first phase of *Tess* a reference to Elijah's goading suggestion to the prophets of Baal that their god might be sleeping prepares for the novel's closing concept of an uncaring President of the Immortals. Such biblically expressed irony, sometimes tending towards the over-blunt, contrasts with the reverence for a Pauline concept of Charity (see RELIGION) developed in both novels and poems, as well as elsewhere in Hardy's writings, and frequently expressed by reference to or adaptation of Hardy's favourite Bible passage in 1 Corinthians 13.

Hardy's close acquaintance with the Bible has an acute conceptual and stylistic influence on his writing: the language of the Bible permeated his own, and he frequently expressed his own thoughts, especially where these deviated from orthodox views, through biblical allusion. What can be less easily stated is the extent to which Hardy's more ornamental biblical references adorn or disfigure his style. R. H. Hutton's seminal *Spectator* review of *Far from the Madding Crowd* (repr. in *CH*) fastened on this as the novel's most representative feature, and developed at length a critical approach to the novel's dialogue, with its 'peculiar style, deeply infiltrated with the suggestions of a kind of moral irony mostly borrowed, no doubt, from the study of the Bible'. The ambivalence of Hardy's relationship with the Bible extends to its effect on the quality of his writing. Biblical influences are often sharply conceived, perceived, and expressed; as often, however, they can appear abstruse or belittling, or even sometimes bewildering. Hardy's use of the Bible, in short, often reflects the Bible itself, with much cross-fertilization and cross-reference as old and new strive, to the subsequent accompaniment of much critical scrutiny, for reconciliation and harmony.

TRH

biographies. Biographers naturally absorb the discoveries and correct the mistakes of their predecessors. In that sense, at least, their efforts are progressively refined. It seemed reasonable, therefore, to bypass earlier attempts and concentrate this survey on the work produced since 1975, the year in which Robert Gittings's *Young Thomas Hardy* was published. Readers exploring the life of an author they admire are probably looking for three things: a full, well-documented account of the known biographical facts; a sense of the personality of the writer concerned; and an enhanced understanding of the distinctive intelligence and imagination which produced the creative work. A biographer needs to be lucky as well as talented to excel in all three areas. The available information may be too scanty, too patchy, or too difficult to interpret.

Hardy poses the additional problem of being an elusive, even recalcitrant, biographee. He was a reticent man who claimed, pretty convincingly, 'that he took no interest in himself as a personage' (*LW* 408). His private life was undramatic. His professional career could reasonably be described as a sober, unhurried success story. There are few crises or dramas or psychological turning-points to disclose.

The recalcitrance lies in Hardy's notorious production of a pre-emptive 'official' biography, apparently written by Florence, his second wife, but effectively the product of his own pen (see AUTOBIOGRAPHY). Having created this record he destroyed most of the documents on which it was based. Genuine biographers therefore find themselves deprived of source material and compelled to depend on Hardy's own highly selective record—the very interpretation they might wish to question.

Gittings takes the *Life* as his starting-point for *Young Thomas Hardy*. Roundly denouncing the work as 'a most deliberate deception... a fake', he finds it a suspicious circumstance that 'whole areas of Hardy's life and experience are clearly omitted'. The inference he draws is that Hardy had a lot to hide, though he does concede that the omissions may not all have concerned 'sexual or deeply personal secrets'. In effect Gittings writes to a programme, setting out to discover whatever it was that Hardy wished to conceal. He falls back on the idea that 'Probably the most powerful motive was some sort of snobbery'. His thesis is that Hardy was desperate to escape from his humble background, to cut himself off from his family origins, 'to deny the rural past that had nurtured him'. It is not an argument that stands up to examination, as subsequent biographers have shown, but it slants the discussion throughout. Gittings's insistence on this reductive view seriously impairs a work which includes useful investigative elements and some interesting incidental comment—for example, on the influence on Hardy of the *Saturday Review.* He is radically out of sympathy with his subject.

Young Thomas Hardy was clearly designed to be complete in itself—as evidenced by a short final chapter briefly sketching the poet's last 50 years. *The Older Hardy* (1978) being a discrete sequel, Gittings feels compelled to find a whole new line of argument. Once again it is pejorative. He focuses on the author's alleged coldness and cruelty to his first wife, especially at the time of her death: 'His full guilt was too horrible to face. He had seen her suffer for months the utmost physical agony, had deliberately turned his eyes away and pretended not to notice...'. The hyperbolic claim has attracted much criticism. It seems to derive from Gittings's general distaste for Hardy the man. He accuses him not merely of snobbery and callousness, but of secretiveness, stinginess, voyeurism, 'perverse morbidity', deviousness, egocentricity, 'peasant rudeness', and lack of virility. The bias is present in the very grain of the prose. For example, Gittings remarks: 'there was in Hardy, for all his basic timidity, a strong strain of obstinacy'. Why not 'diffidence' rather than 'timidity'? Why not 'tenacity' rather than 'obstinacy'? Since he everywhere seems to write with these negative findings in view, Gittings is left unable to respond even to Hardy's manifest virtues. He sketches a personality remote from the writings, devoid of humour, warmth, or moral generosity. Although he has some shrewd things to say about some of the novels and many of the poems, his dislike for the man does seem seriously to encroach upon his appreciation of the artist.

By general consent Michael Millgate's *Thomas Hardy* (1982) is the definitive biography, the work of a seasoned scholar and a lucid writer, steeped in knowledge of the fiction, the poetry, and the letters. It is full and scrupulously researched, yet well-proportioned, clear, and tightly knit. As a reliable factual record it could hardly be bettered. Millgate is endlessly and usefully informative on a whole range of topics, from renovations to the Hardys' cottage to the evolution of the 'Wessex' idea. He goes into great detail about the circumstances in which various works were written, and about Hardy's relations with editors, publishers, and critics. He shows a decent sympathy in telling of Hardy's domestic life and of his various relationships with women—particularly that with Florence *Henniker. At many points he offers a useful antidote to Gittings: in particular his account of the poet's first marriage is far more persuasive than that provided by *The Older Hardy.*

One would certainly turn to Millgate concerning any matter of pure record. But the work is not without its limitations. The scrupulosity engenders longueurs. The uneventfulness of his subject's life obliges Millgate to chronicle a good deal of small beer: 'The Hardys were also on friendly terms with their solicitor, Arthur Henry Lock, whose son later recalled going to a party given by the Hardys at Shire-Hall Place for Emma's young nephew and niece, Gordon and Lilian Gifford, the children of her brother Walter, who were staying with them at the time.' More fundamentally, Hardy the man isn't brought to life by these pages any more than he is by Gittings. One doesn't hear a voice or infer a social personality. No doubt Hardy's own reticence and elusiveness are largely to blame for this absence, but Millgate, for all his knowledge of Hardy and his work, and for all his tolerant understanding, does often seem to be at odds with his subject both artistically and personally—if to a far lesser extent than Gittings. The less well-known novels tend to be patronizingly dismissed. Like Gittings, Millgate criticizes Hardy's 'ponderous displays of literary and artistic information' and his 'somewhat laborious autodidacticism'. Of *The Hand of Ethelberta* he remarks that 'Hardy's handling of upper-class characters and episodes is less disastrous than might have been anticipated'. There is a Gittings-like reference to Hardy's 'blind, sullen, unforgiving, peasant anger'. Even when Millgate is being conspicuously more judicious than Gittings about Hardy's social uncertainties or romantic attachments, it can be with the air of a potentially hostile commentator trying at all costs to be fair.

Martin Seymour-Smith's *Hardy* (1994) defines itself against the views of these two predecessors, whom he repeatedly attacks. Having little to offer in the way of fresh factual material, he is awkwardly dependent on his chosen opponents. But his concern is with matters of emphasis and interpretation. Above all he is eager to speak out on behalf of an author he takes to have been misrepresented and abused. There is a good deal of truth in his claim that Gittings depicts Hardy as 'a vain, mean and selfish egoist', and at least an element of truth in his caricature of Millgate's portrayal: 'an untutored genius—ignorant of homosexuality, over-sensitive to criticism, sexually impotent, perpetually adolescent, lacking in self-confidence, and possessed of an ageing wife and a propensity for young girls!' Always a combative, not to say truculent, critic, Seymour-Smith proclaims that Hardy is a greater artist and a nicer man than these previous biographers have allowed.

Although this reactive aggression can at times be tiresome and hyperbolic, it is refreshing to read a biographer who thinks Hardy a truly great author and actually likes him as a person. In this work Hardy's 'personal kindliness', general good humour, and sly wit all get their due. Seymour-Smith portrays no naïve autodidact, but a writer artistically sophisticated and intellectually self-confident. This Hardy is a prophetic author, ahead of his time. So far from blundering into accidental conflict with the Mrs Grundys of his day, he deliberately sets out to provoke and outwit them. The Hardy who emerges from these pages is notably more personable, more likeable, and more vigorous than Millgate's Hardy.

Undeniably, however, *Hardy* is a flawed work. At well over 800 pages it is far too long for what it sets out to do. There is a good deal of repetition, and the rambling plot-summaries are surely otiose. Much of it seems hastily and casually written. Given its academic and polemical pretensions it seems extraordinary that no footnotes are included. The guesswork concerning Hardy's sexual life is more lavishly imaginative, if more optimistic, than that of either Gittings or Millgate. Although there are some brilliant comments on Hardy's poetry, nothing very illuminating is said about the fiction or *The Dynasts*. Altogether this is patchwork—but some of the patches are top-quality material.

Two much shorter biographies have appeared in the past few years. F. B. Pinion's *Thomas Hardy: His Life and Friends* (1992) is the careful, detailed compilation one would expect from the author of the invaluable *A Hardy Companion*. The limitation here is Pinion's unwillingness to go beyond his sources. If he makes no presumptuous guesses neither does he offer significant new insights, whether psychological or critical. The speciality of the book would seem to be located in the emphasis on 'friends'. Certainly there is some useful contextual information about the likes of Leslie *Stephen, George *Douglas, and Edmund *Gosse. This element is too slight, however, to give the work a distinctive character. It offers a decently brief record of Hardy's life rather than an exploration of it.

James Gibson's *Thomas Hardy* (1996) has been shaped by the requirements of the series in which it appears, Macmillan's 'Literary Lives'. Here is a biography less than a quarter of the length of Seymour-Smith's which fulfils the aims of the series in tracing 'the professional, publishing and social contexts' which helped to shape Hardy's writing. The constraints in terms of scale and focus have been skilfully turned to positive account. Accepting Millgate's biography as definitive, Gibson is freed from the burden of exhaustive documentation and can concentrate on the intersection of the life with the literature. He is especially good at showing how Hardy's hobbies and interests—for example, music, painting, and architecture—find expression in both the form and the content of his writings. He conveys a strong sense of Hardy's warmer side, pointing out that 'very many of the visitors to Max Gate described him as friendly, kind, hospitable, modest and with a sense of humour'. Repeatedly he makes apparently simple observations that clarify a difficulty or start a train of speculation. After the disagreements of earlier biographers concerning Hardy's marriages it is helpful to be reminded that 'he said not a word in open criticism of them, whereas both Emma and Florence voiced their criticisms of him'. When Gibson remarks that nearly all Hardy's novels contain a secret, or that more than 150 of his poems begin with 'I', the comment immediately becomes part of one's received wisdom, as though one had known it all along. He remarks in his Preface that he has not tried to hide his affection or enthusiasm for Hardy. Indeed he hasn't: the book reflects his characteristic zest. For these reasons and others this, of all the biographies, is the one to recommend to students. MI

Peter J. Casagrande, '"Old Tom and New Tom": Hardy and His Biographers', *THA* 1 (1982).

birds. Songbirds seem to have been of special significance to Hardy. When in town, his personal writings suggest that what he missed most was birdsong. This sense of deprivation is enhanced by his placing comments on songbirds, in both his published and private writings, next to those on apparently unrelated and more significant matters. Juxtaposition in Hardy often provides a prime key to interpretation, a more obvious example being, in *The Mayor of Casterbridge*, Henchard's passive suicide by wilful self-neglect and the caged songbird's death through being overlooked (*MC* 45). Although not stated explicitly in his extant writings, it seems probable that Hardy connected birds with spirituality, possibly as emblems of the soul.

His heroines are also repeatedly associated with birds. In *Tess of the d'Urbervilles*, her compassionate killing of the wounded game-birds (41) emphasizes Tess's essential kindness and also the novel's dominant hunting imagery. In *The Hand of Ethelberta*, in contrast, the adaptable, tough Darwinian survivor is fascinated by a scene of potentially mortal struggle between a duck and a hawk (1). Most commonly, however, heroines are implicitly or explicitly compared to birds by specific description—for example, of Thomasin in *The Return of the Native* (3.6)—or association, as with Bathsheba in *Far from the Madding Crowd*, who progresses from early vanity and wilfulness (kingfisher, hawk: 3) to, in her more subdued condition, a beruffled, storm-beaten bird (48).

The frequent anthologizing of Hardy's poem 'The Darkling Thrush' seems partly due to attempts to impose a consistent 'philosophy' on Hardy, one which some regard as encapsulated in this poem. Birds feature in scores of his poems—far more than all other creatures—and are almost invariably treated anthropomorphically. Some poems 'spoken' by them are relatively realistic: 'Birds at Winter Nightfall' and 'Winter in Durnover Field' are direct commentaries on the apparently arbitrarily changed environment. 'The Puzzled Game-Birds' extends this reaction, while also offering a metaphor for the whole incomprehensible concept of Nature's rearing only to destroy. In 'The Caged Goldfinch', a poem related to the episode in *The Mayor of Casterbridge* cited above, the human spectator expresses the bird's bewilderment at being first confined then abandoned. Many poems present a Darwinian world of mutual, futile struggles for survival between predator and victim. In 'The Bullfinches', a bird counsels a *carpe diem* attitude to his fellows, while 'The Sleep-Worker' and 'The Mother Mourns', in dealing with animal suffering, are typical of many variations on Hardy's recurring concept of the 'Unfulfilled Intention', offering a partial explanation, partial excuse, for meaningless pain and waste.

Birds are frequently used as observers of and commentators on moments of crisis and heightened consciousness in intense human relationships, often emphasizing lovers' solipsism, sometimes with a sense of the pathetic fallacy ('Postponement', 'The Seasons of Her Year', 'The King's Experiment'). Although sometimes seen as part of the unheeding, uncaring external natural world, they are often used conversely, as the only non-human creature mentioned as present, regarded by lovers as sympathetic to their plight. White birds of passage seem to have a peculiar function as ill omens, the terrible polar visitors in *Tess* (43) being partly echoed in a number of poems, including 'The Wind's Prophecy', 'The Change', and 'Epeisodia'. AE

Blomfield, Arthur (1829–99), architect, knighted 1889. A son of C. J. Blomfield, Bishop of London, he followed an architectural career of distinction, specializing in ecclesiastical work in the Gothic style. He was elected fellow of the Royal Institute of British Architects (1867) and was awarded its gold medal (1891), but declined nomination as its president. Hardy owed his introduction to Blomfield to John Norton, an architect friend of John *Hicks, to whom Hicks had sent a letter recommending Hardy. Norton knew of Blomfield's need for a Gothic draughtsman specializing in ecclesiastical work: Hardy began work in Blomfield's office at

8 St Martin's Place, just off Trafalgar Square, on 5 May 1862, at an annual salary of £110.

Blomfield was then at the height of his considerable powers and as yet unaffected by the over-commitment to commissions which restricted the quality of his output later in life. He was currently employing two or three architectural assistants and six articled pupils: the expansion of the practice necessitated a move to 8 Adelphi Terrace early in Hardy's employment. This new office was 'a capital place', Hardy told his sister Mary in a letter of 19 February 1863, affording an exhilarating view of the Thames from premises designed by the Adam brothers, as well as the chance, with Blomfield's other employees, to torment members of the left-wing Reform League, who occupied the ground floor below them. Colleagues found the new assistant quiet, gentle, and very regular in his attendance, but rather dreamy in manner, and much given to discoursing on literature.

Blomfield, educated at Rugby and Trinity College, Cambridge (where he had rowed in the College Eight), was the son of one bishop and the brother of another. His social background and milieu, as well as the upper-class nature of his clientèle, must have struck Hardy forcefully. His company, however, was not offputting. Good-looking, witty, and highly artistic, Blomfield had a vivacious personality and his office a lively atmosphere. Glees and catches were sung at intervals during office hours by a choir into which Hardy was swiftly recruited, and Hardy's first published piece, 'How I Built Myself a House', was written for the amusement of colleagues in the office.

Blomfield used his influence on Hardy's account. He obtained for Hardy his ticket for Palmerston's funeral in Westminster Abbey on 27 October 1865, and proposed him at a noticeably early stage (October 1862) as a member of the Architectural Association (of which Blomfield had become President in 1861). Blomfield was too busy to give his assistants much attention or his pupils much instruction, and the *Life* notes that 'architectural drawing in which the actual designing had no great part was monotonous and mechanical' (*LW* 49). Afflicted by ill-health, Hardy left Blomfield's practice in 1867 to return to Dorset, but worked for the architect again briefly in 1870 and 1872.

Jobs with Blomfield particularly recalled by Hardy include the opening of the organ at St Matthias Church, Richmond; the supervision of the exhumation of corpses from Old St Pancras Churchyard, recalled in the poem 'The Two Men'; and the laying of the foundation stone at All Saints, New Windsor, by the Crown Princess of Germany, which suggested a detail in *The Poor Man and the Lady*; annotations in Hardy's hand survive on the plans of the latter church. The poem 'Heiress and Architect', dated from Adelphi Terrace in 1867, is dedicated to Blomfield, and the church of St Silas's in *Jude the Obscure* is based on one of Blomfield's designs, St Barnabas's, Oxford.

Hardy remained on friendly terms with Blomfield, who visited Max Gate in 1892 and complimented Hardy on its design. Three years later, Hardy inspected Blomfield's most significant restoration project, St Saviour's, Southwark (now Southwark Cathedral). A visit to Blomfield's home at Broadway in 1899 was prevented by Blomfield's sudden death. TRH.

'Blue Jimmy: The Horse Stealer.' See SHORT STORY.

Blunden, Edmund (1896–1974), poet, scholar, biographer, and autobiographer. He was a member of the group of young writers who were among Hardy's wide circle of friends during his later years. Blunden visited Max Gate on a number of occasions, the *Life*, for instance, recording a visit in July 1922 in the company of Siegfried *Sassoon (*LW* 450). Hardy is said to have remarked that Blunden resembled Keats in appearance. He had served in the trenches and published his best-known book, *Undertones of War*, in the year of Hardy's death. As a poet he wrote about both war and country life, and as a scholar he was influential in the revival of interest in the poetry of John Clare. His biographical and critical study of Hardy, *Thomas Hardy*, appeared in 1941.

Bockhampton. See HIGHER BOCKHAMPTON.

Boer War. The Anglo-Boer War (South African War) broke out on 12 October 1899 and was concluded on 31 May 1902 by the Peace of

Vereeniging, by which the Boers accepted British sovereignty and in turn were promised representative government and financial assistance. During hostilities, 5,774 British soldiers were killed in action and some 16,000 died of disease; Boer losses were somewhat lighter. As Michael Millgate has pointed out, Hardy 'followed the war news avidly', but his feelings about the war were 'compounded of fascination and revulsion' (Millgate 403): while his lifelong enthusiasm for military history was stimulated, not least by his first-hand witnessing of the departure of troops for the distant battle-zone, he was distressed by the sufferings of both men and horses (see ANIMALS, CRUELTY TO). On a more philosophical level, he was depressed by a so-called Christian civilization attempting to settle a dispute by resorting to methods more appropriate to distant ages of barbarism. Though the war prompted him to write a number of poems, he boasted to Florence *Henniker on Christmas Eve 1900 that 'not a single one is Jingo or Imperial' (*L* ii 277).

His creative response was prompt: as he records in his autobiography (again not without a touch of pride), the earliest of these poems appeared in the very month in which war broke out (*LW* 328). 'Embarcation', originally titled 'The Departure', was published in the *Daily Chronicle* on 25 October and stands first in the group of 'War Poems' which he later placed very near the beginning of his second collection of verse, *Poems of the Past and the Present*, a volume published while the war was still in progress. Subtitled 'Southampton Docks: October 1899', 'Embarcation' is based on a visit paid by Hardy to Southampton, where his friend Major Henniker of the Coldstream Guards (the husband of Florence Henniker) was about to set off for South Africa. In form a Shakespearian sonnet, it begins on what seems to be a note of nationalistic fervour by invoking armies of the past (the Romans, the Saxons, and Henry the Fifth setting off for France), but quickly changes key: the historical allusions turn out to be no more than a context for reproachful comments on the present, and there is sorrow and disillusion in the reflection that wars are still fought 'in the selfsame bloody mode', and warning of a 'tragical To-be'.

At about the same time Hardy wrote another sonnet, 'Departure', with the same subtitle; this questions, more radically and explicitly, current notions of 'patriotism', urging a more international sense of community and commitment. 'The Colonel's Soliloquy', with once again the same subtitle, also belongs to the opening days of the war. Another dramatic monologue, from the contrasting point of view of those left behind, is 'The Going of the Battery', subtitled 'Wives' Lament' and dated 2 November 1899; the original printing, in the *Graphic* on 11 November 1899 (in a shortened form), carried a note indicating that the departure, 'in rain and in darkness', was from Dorchester Barracks—an occasion that, once again, Hardy observed at first hand.

A slightly later stage in the conflict—not long in weeks, but representing a bitter contrast with the pageantry of the departure—is reflected in 'At the War Office, London', subtitled 'Affixing the Lists of Killed and Wounded: December 1899', first published in the *Sphere* on 27 January 1900 with the title 'At the War Office After a Bloody Battle'. But the best-known poem of this group is 'Drummer Hodge', originally titled 'The Dead Drummer' for its appearance on 25 November 1899 in *Literature*, where it also carried the note that 'One of the Drummers killed was a native of a village near Casterbridge'. Critical discussion of this fine poem has included comparisons with A. E. *Housman's 'The night is freezing fast' and Rupert Brooke's 'The Soldier'.

'A Christmas Ghost-Story' (later revised and extended) appeared in the *Westminster Gazette* on 23 December 1899: curiously, Hardy affixed the date 'Christmas-eve 1899' to this poem, a clear example ('The Darkling Thrush' is another) of a symbolical rather than a historical dating. The poem was attacked in a leader in the *Daily Chronicle* on Christmas Day, and Hardy immediately responded in a letter printed in the same newspaper on 28 December. The leader-writer's complaint that the ghost of the 'mouldering soldier' slain in South Africa was unheroic demonstrates how far Hardy was out of line with public and official attitudes to the war. With what is perhaps deliberate irony, the poem uses the (for Hardy) unfamiliar medium of the heroic couplet, and does so very effectively. 'The Souls of the Slain', though not published (in the *Cornhill*) until

April 1900, was also written in December; an interesting note included in the original printing is quoted by Purdy (109). The main thrust of this longer-than-average poem is the placing in contrast of conventional notions of military glory and the realities of personal bereavement and private grief. 'A Wife in London' is yet another poem of December 1899, while 'Song of the Soldiers' Wives and Sweethearts' came nearly a year later, in November 1900, after the return from action of the Household Cavalry. Finally, 'The Sick Battle-God' (originally 'The Sick God') returns to the idea that war cannot occupy the same place, or inspire the same feelings, in the modern world as in the historical past.

Before the Boer War had even broken out, its prospect had moved Hardy to reflect in a letter to Florence Henniker (17 September 1899) that 'It seems a justification of the extremest pessimism that at the end of the 19th Cent[ur]y we settle an argument by the Sword, just as they w[oul]d have done in the 19th Cent[ur]y B.C.' (*L* ii 229). That pessimism, and the sense that as the century expired Victorian notions of progress were being proved no more than a delusion, were not to be alleviated by what shortly followed, and were to be further deepened by the outbreak of the Great War a few years later (see FIRST WORLD WAR).

Book of Common Prayer, The (commonly known as the Prayer Book). Largely the work of Thomas Cranmer (1489–1556), it reached its final form in 1662 and constituted the official service book of the Church of England. It principally contains the daily offices of Morning and Evening Prayer (otherwise known respectively as Matins and Evensong), the forms for the administration of sacraments, and the Psalter; and it specifies the readings, collects, and other forms of prayer to be used throughout the Church's year. Hardy's copy of the Prayer Book, a Cambridge University Press edition of 1858, also contains the metrical psalms of Tate and Brady. It was purchased in 1861, and remained with Hardy throughout his life as an occasionally annotated *vade mecum*. This copy is now preserved in the Thomas Hardy Memorial Collection (DCM) and its annotations, which are most copious in the psalms and metrical psalms, have been used as a significant quarry by Hardy's biographers.

His knowledge of the Prayer Book was extensive and its influence on him is difficult to overestimate. The *Life* claims that Hardy knew the Morning and Evening services by heart (*LW* 23) and humorously recounts his childhood imitations of church services (20). The speech patterns of the Prayer Book infect his style, and its contents are often used for the effective punctuation of pointed moments of his prose and verse. Although a full-length scholarly survey of the topic has yet to appear, it is probably no exaggeration to say that Hardy gained from this book a sense of the rhythms and cadences of the Church's year, as well as acquiring the habit of Christian expressions of response to the patterns, rituals, and vicissitudes of human existence. In *The Trumpet-Major*, as the last topmast of the *Victory* fades from sight (34), Anne Loveday quotes a passage from Psalm 107 which Hardy had marked in his edition, and turns round to find John Loveday behind her; in *Jude the Obscure* Jude spots Sue at Evening Prayer at Christminster Cathedral (2.3), when another marked passage, from Psalm 119, is sung; in *Far from the Madding Crowd* Bathsheba, after her night in the brake of fern which signifies the end of her relationship with Troy, awakes to hear a schoolboy, at an earlier point in life's cycle of challenges, attempting to memorize the collect for Advent Sunday, the beginning of the Church's year (44), the humour masking the way in which the allusion prepares the reader for the religiose overtones which are to surround Bathsheba's developing relationship with Oak, and which invite or encourage the reader's approbation.

Similar practice is discernible in the poetry. For example, '"According to the Mighty Working"' takes its title from a passage in the Burial Service which Hardy had marked, whilst his reflections on his life during the troubled days of the First World War in 'Quid Hic Agis' use a Prayer Book service form and a Prayer Book reading to memorable and highly integrated effect, with the narrator gauging his own development, characteristically and significantly, against these Prayer Book-derived benchmarks.

The Prayer Book underwent textual revision for a new edition of 1928. The *Life*, linking the subject with Hardy's views on religion expressed in the Preface to *Late Lyrics and Earlier*, and remarking on his hopes during the period 1920–5 for a rationalization of the Church of England, explains Hardy's interest in the controversy thus created: 'There had been rumours for some years of a revised Liturgy, and his hopes were accordingly raised by the thought of making the Established Church comprehensive enough to include the majority of thinkers of the previous hundred years who had lost all belief in the supernatural.' However, the lack of a rationalistic revision was a considerable disappointment to Hardy, 'and from that time he lost all expectation of seeing the Church representative of modern thinking minds' (*LW* 448–9). Hardy's other 'very casual thoughts on the matter' may be found later in the *Life* (465–6). TRH

Boughton, Rutland (1878–1960), English composer. Though little remembered today, he achieved a considerable success with his opera on Celtic themes, *The Immortal Hour* (1914). Boughton paid a two-day visit to Max Gate on 4 February 1924; Hardy took a great liking to him, and they discussed Boughton's plan to write an opera based on *The Famous Tragedy of the Queen of Cornwall*. The autobiography contains an account of this meeting (*LW* 458) and notes that Hardy was 'interested in [Boughton's] political views, though he could not share them' (Boughton was a Communist). Hardy was enthusiastic about the musical project, and when the work was produced refused to take a fee. *The Queen of Cornwall* was quickly completed, and Hardy and his wife attended a performance given at the Glastonbury Festival on 24 August 1924.

Rutland Boughton, 'A Musical Association with Thomas Hardy', *Musical News and Herald* (15 February 1928).

Britten, Benjamin (1913–76), English composer. He had a long-standing interest in the musical potentialities of Hardy's work, especially his verse. In 1940, while living in America, Britten wrote the incidental music for a radio production of *The Dynasts*; 27 years later he set 'The Oxen' for voices and piano. His most substantial Hardy-inspired work is *Winter Words* (Op. 52), first performed on 8 October 1953. This is a setting for voice and piano of eight Hardy poems: 'At Day-Close in November', 'Midnight on the Great Western', 'Wagtail and Baby', 'The Little Old Table', 'The Choirmaster's Burial', 'Proud Songsters', 'At the Railway Station, Upway', and 'Before Life and After'. Although Britten's title is borrowed from Hardy's final volume of verse, only one poem actually comes from *Winter Words*, the rest being selected from several different volumes, and the choice of these particular examples—by no means the most familiar even to lovers of Hardy's poetry—is evidence of Britten's close familiarity with this large body of work. Britten's sensitive and subtle settings, though often dramatic, show great respect for the words and allow them to be heard. At about the same time he produced settings of two other poems, 'If It's Ever Spring Again' and 'The Children and Sir Nameless', but these were not included in the cycle. At some stage Britten seems also to have considered writing an opera based on *The Trumpet-Major*, but the idea was not pursued. His last orchestral work, *Suite on English Folk Tunes*, is subtitled 'A time there was', a phrase taken from the last of the poems set in *Winter Words*.

Humphrey Carpenter, *Benjamin Britten: A Biography* (1992).

Browning, Robert (1812–89), poet. Apart from two quotations from 'The Statue and the Bust' in Hardy's first published novel, *Desperate Remedies*, almost all his references to Browning come from much later in his life, and the same poem, evidently a favourite, is again referred to in *Jude the Obscure*. For a time in the 1860s Browning and Hardy had almost been London neighbours, but they did not meet. It was in the 1880s, at the home of Mrs *Procter, that they came together from time to time. Browning seems to have been to Hardy a puzzle and a contrast, rather than a model. After reading an article by Edmund *Gosse on 'Form in Poetry', for which Gosse had taken *Wessex Poems* as his text, Hardy wrote in a letter to Gosse on 6 March 1899: 'The longer I live, the more does B[rowning]'s character seem *the* literary puzzle of the 19th century. How could smug Christian optimism worthy of a dissenting grocer find a place inside a man who was so vast a seer & feeler when on neutral ground?' (*L* ii 216–17). Michael Millgate comments that 'In a much later note, prepared for inclusion in his own official "Life" but not in fact used there, he drew a specific contrast between Browning's outlook and his own: "Imagine you have to walk a chalk line drawn across an open down. Browning walked it, knowing no more. But a yard to the left of the same line the down is cut by a vertical cliff five hundred feet deep. I know it is there, but walk the line just the same' (Millgate 409).

Nevertheless, it seems likely that some of Browning's strategies in his poems suggested possible strategies to Hardy in his own. Signs of this tend to appear in Hardy's later rather than earlier poems, such as 'The Going of the Battery' (1899):

—Yet, voices haunting us, daunting us,
taunting us,
Hint in the night-time when life beats are low
Other and graver things.... Hold we to
braver things,
Wait we, in trust, what Time's fulness shall
show.

In the last few days of his life, Hardy asked his wife to read aloud to him Browning's 'Rabbi Ben Ezra'. AT

Bugler, Gertrude (1897–1992), a leading member of the *Hardy Players and Hardy's own choice for the title role in his dramatization of *Tess of the d'Urbervilles.* The daughter of a Dorset farmer, she first attracted Hardy's attention in 1913, on her début appearance with the group as Marty South in *The Woodlanders.* This immediate success was rewarded with further leading roles, including Fancy Day in *The Mellstock Quire* (1918) and Eustacia Vye in *The Return of the Native* (1920). But the Hardy Players' production of *Tess* (1924) brought Bugler her most widespread and laudatory attention. Negotiations were then entered into with the theatrical manager Frederick Harrison for a series of professional matinée performances at London's Haymarket Theatre. Terms were agreed upon, and on 12 January 1925 Bugler lunched with Hardy and Harrison at Max Gate.

Unpredictably, this was to be her last meeting with Hardy, whose parting words were 'If anyone asks you if you knew Thomas Hardy, say "Yes, he was my friend"'. In early February, Florence Hardy visited Bugler at her home in Beaminster and begged her to withdraw from the project, advancing an array of reasons, from concern about Hardy's health should he insist on attending a London performance to the possible scandal consequent upon his visiting Bugler's dressing-room and the need to dispel rumours already circulating about his infatuation with Bugler. In the face of Florence Hardy's near-hysteria, Bugler withdrew, and later that year the professional actress Gwen Ffrangçon-Davies brought Tess to the London stage. Bugler did play the role professionally soon after Hardy's death, when Philip Ridgeway revived *Tess* at the Duke of York's Theatre (1929). After this brief professional career of some 60 performances, she returned to Beaminster, where she lived for the rest of her long life. The poem 'An Expostulation' is assumed to have been inspired by Bugler. KW

Gertrude Bugler, *Personal Recollections of Thomas Hardy* (1964).
Keith Wilson, *Thomas Hardy on Stage* (1995).

Byron, Lord (1788–1824), poet. He was 'admired' by Hardy's mother (see Millgate 39 n.) and appears in records of Hardy's own early reading. In 1865 his reading-list included *Childe Harold* (*LW* 51), and in his copy of Byron on 14 May 1866 he wrote the date beside a passage from the same poem which, as Purdy speculates (297), 'seems to have had personal associations for him': the lines in question (III.85–7) refer to the hero's 'invulnerable mind'. *Childe Harold* was in his thoughts again in 1888, when he reflected on the reasons for its popularity (*LW* 216), and Byron is once more on his reading-list in 1890 (*LW* 240). On his travels Hardy showed an interest in sites with Byronic associations: in Venice, during his Italian tour of 1887, he had Byron in mind and later regretted that he had not taken the opportunity to seek out old people who might have remembered the poet (*LW* 200, 202); in Switzerland in 1897 he was conscious of 'overlooking the scene of *Manfred*' (*LW* 311); and a visit to Aberdeen in 1905 (*LW* 348) prompted thoughts of Byron's childhood in that city. Byron's treatment by the guardians of public morality produced a fellow-feeling in Hardy: in particular, the reception of *Jude the Obscure* brought to mind Macaulay's famous sentence in his review of Moore's life of Byron, 'We know of no spectacle so ridiculous as the British public in one of its periodical fits of morality' (quoted *LW* 288). In 1924, the centenary of Byron's death, Hardy was one of the signatories to a letter published in *The Times* (14 July) urging that a memorial to Byron should be placed in Poets' Corner, Westminster Abbey; the Dean of Westminster's refusal to give his consent prompted the satirical poem 'A Refusal', which also contains references to two other persecuted poets, Shelley and Swinburne.

C

calendar. Hardy's writings contain many references to festivals, saints' days, and other landmarks in the year that are now mostly forgotten but in former times were regularly observed as notable dates in the calendar. The calendar itself had been reformed (replacing the Julian with the Gregorian calendar) in 1752, nearly a century before Hardy's birth, but a relic of the Old Style calendar, in which the year began not on 1 January but on Lady Day or the Feast of the Annunciation (now 25 March), is referred to in *The Mayor of Casterbridge* (22): workers were hired at the annual fair held in Dorchester on Old Candlemas Day (2 February) to begin work the following Lady Day, though for this purpose tradition continued to reckon by the old calendar, whereby Lady Day (Old Style) fell on 6 April. The practice is glossed in a reference in *Tess of the d'Urbervilles* to 'the Candlemas Fair', which adds that 'It was at this fair that the new engagements were entered into for the twelvemonths following the ensuing Lady-Day...' (46). The same novel includes (51) an account of the migrations that took place on Old Lady Day, a topic also touched on in Hardy's essay 'The Dorsetshire Labourer'. Also in *Tess*, the 'white gowns' of the girls engaged in the traditional club-walking are described as 'a gay survival from Old Style days' (2). In *The Return of the Native* (6.4) Grandfer Cantle states his age as '"seventy-one last Candlemas-day"'. Candlemas was also known as the Feast of the Purification, and is thus referred to by a rustic speaker in *Far from the Madding Crowd* (8)—'"'twas only last Purification Day..."'.

Lady Day was also of legal and financial significance as one of the quarter days when rents and other obligations fell due (in the same second passage from *Tess* cited above, the heroine 'meant to leave' her uncongenial work at Flintcomb-Ash 'at the quarter-day'). A vaguer reference to the same fair occurs in *Far from the Madding Crowd* (6)—'a day in February, on which was held the yearly statute or hiring fair in the county-town of Casterbridge'—while the maltster reckons his period of residence from the same date, '"one-and-thirty year come Candlemas"' (8). A later chapter (15) of the same novel has Oak referring to the long lambing season ('"We shan't have done by Lady Day"'), to which one of the rustics, Joseph Poorgrass, replies that '"last year 'twere all over by Sexajessamine Sunday"', garbling the Prayer Book's Sexagesima, the second Sunday before Lent.

Of other saints' days, one of the most widely observed, though in a secular rather than a pious mood, was (and is) St Valentine's (14 February). In *Far from the Madding Crowd* (13) this is the occasion for Bathsheba's light-hearted practical joke directed at Boldwood that has serious and ultimately tragic consequences. St Swithin's Day (15 July) had and has a popular meteorological significance, the belief long being current that if it rained on that day it would rain for the next forty days. In the poem 'We Sat at the Window', subtitled 'Bournemouth, 1875' and referring to the early days of the Hardys' marriage, the speaker and a companion sit and watch on that day as 'the rain came down like silken strings'. Swithin, who was a 9th-century Bishop of Winchester and hence a Wessex figure, gives his name to the young hero of *Two on a Tower.*

St Michael's Day (29 September), better known as Michaelmas and another quarter day, is a significant date in *Under the Greenwood Tree* (2.4); there is also a reference in *The Return of the Native* to 'Michaelmas rains' (1.6). *The Mayor of Casterbridge* contains two references to St Martin's Day (11 November): Elizabeth-Jane's wedding takes place on that day (44), and there is an earlier allusion to 'Martinmas summer' (14), the modern equivalent of which is 'Indian summer'. The poem 'Last Look Round St Martin's Fair' refers to the same festival. Another saint's day is 'St Thomas's, the shortest day in the year' (*FFMC* 2), namely 21 December.

A favourite early-summer holiday time, within living memory but now largely disregarded, was Whitsuntide. Whit Sunday, the seventh after Easter, marked the beginning of Pentecost and was a favourite time for baptisms. The next day was traditionally a holiday, and *Far from the Madding Crowd* contains a reference to 'White Monday' (8), white being worn by the newly baptized. The tradition of 'club-walking', whereby members of a club or local friendly society joined in the Whitsuntide processions, is referred to in several novels, including *Far from the Madding Crowd* (33), *The Return of the Native* (1.5), and *Tess* (2). The Tuesday could also be a holiday, and Dick Dewy's father recalls an incident in the past: '"'Twas on White Tuesday—Mellstock Club walked the same day, every man two and two..."' (*UGT* 2.8). A little later in the year, on 1 August, came Lammas or Lammas-tide, a harvest celebration dating from the early history of the Church of England. The poem 'The Voice of Things' evokes a period 'Forty Augusts' earlier when the speaker 'heard the waves huzza at Lammas-tide'.

In addition to Lady Day and Michaelmas, the other two quarter days in England were Midsummer (24 June) and Christmas (25 December). Ancient superstitions and rituals associated with Midsummer Eve related especially to love and marriage. Mrs Penny in *Under the Greenwood Tree* (1.8) recalls the time before her marriage when she '"used to sit up on old Midsummer Eves to see who my husband was going to be"', old Midsummer Eve falling on 5 July rather than 23 June. A similar superstition forms the basis of an episode in *The Woodlanders* (20). A briefer reference to 'Old Midsummer eves' occurs in *Jude the Obscure* (3.8), while a personal adaptation of traditional beliefs may be found in the poem 'On a Midsummer Eve'.

The poem 'I Rose Up as My Custom Is' refers to All Souls' Day (2 November), more significant in the Roman Catholic than in the Anglican Church but (as F. B. Pinion has noted) 'merged in Hardy with old pagan beliefs of Celtic origin which are traditionally associated with Hallowe'en (31 October)' (*A Commentary on the Poems of Thomas Hardy*, 112). The poem alludes to the belief that 'souls in purgatory returned to their homes on the evening before this day'.

Christmas festivities, especially the activities of the mummers, play an important part in *The Return of the Native* (2.4–5). The custom of the waits (carol-singers) visiting the great house of the neighbourhood is the subject of the poem 'Seen by the Waits'. The tradition of carol-singing receives grimmer treatment in the short story 'The Grave by the Handpost'. Three other poems, however, display a more bitterly ironic attitude to what is conventionally viewed as the season of goodwill: 'A Christmas Ghost-Story' (dated 'Christmas-eve 1899'), 'Christmas: 1924', and 'Christmastide'. See also FOLKLORE.

Cambridge. Commenting on the diary entry that apparently contained the germ of *Jude the Obscure*—'A short story of a young man—"who could not go to Oxford"...'—Hardy made the claim that he himself 'was not altogether hindered going, at least to Cambridge, and could have gone up easily at five-and-twenty' (*LW* 216). The *Moule family, an important influence in his early years, had strong connections with Cambridge, and Charles Walter Moule became Fellow of Corpus Christi College in 1865, when Hardy was 25. During the 1860s, however, Hardy seems not even to have visited Cambridge: 'For a young assistant in Gothic architecture to avoid [both Oxford and Cambridge] suggests some feeling of social or intellectual inadequacy in Hardy' (Gittings, *Young Thomas Hardy*, 71–2). His first visit to Cambridge was on 20–1 June 1873, when he stayed as Horace Moule's guest at Queens' College and saw King's College Chapel and other sights; for Hardy this visit (briefly but poignantly described in *LW* 96) became doubly memorable as his last meeting with his friend (see also MOULE, HORACE). Another ill-starred visit followed seven years later, for it was in the course of a week's holiday in Cambridge with his wife Emma in October 1880 that he experienced the first symptoms of a serious illness.

In his later years Hardy's visits to Cambridge included one in July 1908, when he attended the Milton tercentenary celebrations and saw a performance of *Comus* at which the cast included the young Rupert Brooke; another in June 1913, when he received an honorary doctorate from Cambridge University; another in November of the same year, when he went to be installed as an Honorary Fellow of Magdalene College; and yet another in April 1914, when he attended a feast at St John's College. Hardy's friend (and later executor) Sydney *Cockerell was Director of the Fitzwilliam Museum, Cambridge, which now owns important Hardy manuscripts; other Cambridge friends included A. C. *Benson, E. M. *Forster, and A. E. *Housman.

'Candour in English Fiction' was originally printed as a contribution to a symposium in the *New Review* (January 1890) to which the other two contributors were Hardy's friend Walter *Besant and Eliza Lynn *Linton. It was written at a time when Hardy had had recent first-hand experience of the unofficial *censorship exerted by the editors and publishers of magazines intended for family consumption. In 1886 Mowbray *Morris's qualms about sexual elements in *The Woodlanders* had led to a degree of bowdlerization. Much closer to the date of the essay, in the closing months of 1889, both Morris (as editor of *Macmillan's Magazine*) and the firm of *Tillotson's had declined to publish *Tess of the d'Urbervilles*.

The essay argues that the dominance in the literary market-place of 'the magazine and the circulating library', with their emphasis upon what is deemed suitable for 'household reading', is harmful to serious contemporary fiction: such institutions 'do not foster the growth of the novel that reflects and reveals life'. In a witty passage, Hardy insists that 'the crash of broken commandments', unavoidable in any serious or tragic depiction of life, is forbidden by the 'prudery' of those controlling magazines and libraries. The reflections that follow, on the problems of the writer who begins a story in good faith but finds, after serial publication is under way, that it is leading him in unexpected and unacceptable directions, bear the stamp of Hardy's personal experience. A final section addresses the practical problem of how existing or new forms of publication might accommodate greater frankness.

Carlyle, Thomas (1795–1881), essayist and historian. Aesthetically, Hardy was much attracted to Carlyle. In 1887, in his contribution to a *Fortnightly Review* symposium on 'Fine Passages in Verse and Prose', he wrote: 'I think that the passages in Carlyle's *French Revolution* on the silent growth of the oak have never been surpassed by anything I have read, except perhaps by his sentences on night in a city, as specimens of contemplative prose . . .'. The genuineness of this public testimony is supported by Hardy's extensive copying from Carlyle into his notebooks (*LN* i 254–6); in particular the '1867 Notebook', which is aesthetically oriented (*LN* ii 455), has many quotations from Carlyle, with individual words and phrases occasionally underlined (*LN* ii 458–60, 464, 472). Hardy seems to have found his favourite criterion, an 'idiosyncratic mode of regard' (*LW* 235; see also 239, 354), both theoretically supported and practically realized by Carlyle: thus, Hardy closed his essay 'The Profitable Reading of Fiction' (1888) by quoting Carlyle's '"the eye sees that which it brings with it the means of seeing"' (see also *LN* i 179), and in 1906 he wrote that 'Carlyle . . . we take up to read as Carlyle, & not to learn about Frederick the Great or old clothes' (*L* iii 238).

Hardy did not, however, have the same high regard for Carlyle as a thinker. Although he once listed Carlyle's 'Jean Paul Richter' as a cure for despair (*LW* 59), the healing capacity Hardy attributed to it may well have been of an aesthetic nature, for other evidence suggests that he was highly sceptical of Carlyle's thought. In his well-known criticism of both Newman and Carlyle, Hardy wrote that 'Carlyle was a poet with the reputation of a philosopher. Neither was truly a thinker' (*LW* 244). LAB

J. B. Bullen, *The Expressive Eye* (1986).

censorship. In January 1890 Hardy contributed an essay on *'Candour in English Fiction' to a symposium published in the *New Review*. He was at the time having trouble in finding a publisher who would accept his new novel, *Too Late Beloved*, later to become *Tess of the d'Urbervilles*. It had been rejected by the Lancashire publisher *Tillotson, and was then offered to *Murray's Magazine*, who declined it (in Hardy's later phrase) 'virtually on the score of its improper explicitness. It was at once sent on to the . . . editor of *Macmillan's Magazine*, and . . . was declined by him for practically the same reason' (*LW* 232).

In the same passage of his autobiography, Hardy then describes how, 'with cynical amusement', he bowdlerized the book for the serial version by cutting out 'some chapters or parts of chapters', while 'in addition several passages were modified'. The bowdlerized version omits the 'seduction' and the illegitimate child, also the orgasmic scene in the outhouse at Chaseborough, which remained unpublished until 1912. Hardy's annoyance at the need to engage in this procedure and so weaken his book led him to resolve 'to get away from the supply of fiction to family magazines as soon as he conveniently could do so'. The bowdlerized version was accepted by the *Graphic*, but *Tess*, as Hardy had originally intended it, was not seen in its entirety for another 20 years.

Hardy must have welcomed the opportunity provided by 'Candour in English Fiction' of attacking the attitudes of that symbol of Victorian conventional propriety, Mrs Grundy, with which he had been forced to contend throughout his years as a novelist. He writes there that 'the great bulk of English fiction of the present day is characterised by its lack of sincerity', and this leads not only to 'imaginative deterioration' but to an inability to portray the passions as they exist in the world itself. 'Life being a physiological fact, its honest portrayal must be largely concerned with, for one thing, the relations of the sexes, and the substitution for such catastrophes as favour the false colouring best expressed by the regulation finish that "they married and were happy ever after", of catastrophes based upon sexual relations as it is [*sic*].'

Blame for this 'lack of sincerity' is put by Hardy on the magazines and the circulating libraries, whose object is not 'upward advance but lateral advance', and who want stories which can be read by the whole household without bringing a blush to the cheeks of any of them. 'What this practically amounts to', he adds, 'is that the patrons of literature... acting under the censorship of prudery, rigorously exclude from the pages they regulate subjects that have been made ... the bases of the finest imaginative compositions since literature rose to the dignity of an art. The crash of broken commandments is as necessary an accompaniment to the catastrophe of a tragedy as the noise of drums and cymbals to a triumphal march.' The result of this kind of censorship is that the writer is driven into falsifications that 'belie his literary conscience'. The essay ends with a look at possible solutions of the problem that might result in a situation where 'things that everybody is thinking but nobody is saying... might be taken and treated frankly'.

Hardy's contribution to this symposium was far more outspoken and hard-hitting than those of the other contributors, but he had suffered from Mrs Grundy more than most. Like other great writers he was ahead of his time, and found himself fighting a battle against censorship which was to last for most of his life. It began with the first novel he wrote, *The *Poor Man and the Lady.* Submitted to the firm of Macmillan in 1868, it was rejected as being too unfairly satirical about the upper classes, and he was accused of 'meaning mischief'. George *Meredith, who read the manuscript for another publisher, Chapman & Hall, advised Hardy not to be so outspoken in a first book, because 'he would be attacked on all sides by the conventional reviewers, and his future injured' (*LW* 62). The account of this episode in Hardy's autobiography continues: 'The story was, in fact, a sweeping dramatic satire of the squirearchy and nobility, London society, the vulgarity of the middle class, modern Christianity, church restoration, and political and domestic morals in general, the author's views, in fact, being obviously those of a young man with "a passion for reforming the world"... the tendency of the writing being socialistic, not to say revolutionary.'

Hardy had had his first skirmish in a fight with the Establishment that was to continue for the rest of his life. *The Poor Man and the Lady* was followed by *Desperate Remedies*, which, after being turned down by Macmillan because 'The violation of a young lady at an evening party, and the subsequent birth of a child, is too abominable to be tolerated', was published by *Tinsley in 1871. The reviews were not good, and Hardy was accused of being 'unpleasant', yet no one seems to have commented on the lesbian nature of a scene in which Cytherea Graye undresses Mrs Aldclyffe and prepares her for bed. Maybe the references were too cryptic for Mrs Grundy. That the book was a commercial failure may to some extent have been the result of the bad notices it received, which would have meant that the two big lending libraries (Smith's and Mudie's), who were relied upon by publishers to take hundreds of copies of a first edition, did not do so. Here we have an instance of the censorship of the circulating libraries to which Hardy later referred in his essay.

There was little to worry the narrow-minded in either *Under the Greenwood Tree* (1872) or *A Pair of Blue Eyes* (1873), but Hardy had problems with *Far from the Madding Crowd* (1874), which was first published as a serial in the *Cornhill Magazine*. The story is one of passion and murder, and Hardy wanted to deal with sexual relationships in an adult way, while Leslie *Stephen, the editor of the magazine, was so frightened about offending his readers that he wrote to Hardy on 11 March 1874 that he had 'ventured to leave out a line or two in the last batch of proofs from an excessive prudery of which I am ashamed; but one is forced to be absurdly particular. May I suggest that Troy's seduction of the young woman will require to be treated in a gingerly fashion, when, as I suppose must be the case, he comes to be exposed to his wife? I mean that the thing must be stated but that the words must be careful—excuse this wretched shred of concession to public stupidity; but I am a slave' (quoted in Purdy 338–9). In April Stephen complained to Hardy because he thought that 'the cause of Fanny's death is unnecessarily emphasised', and he wondered 'whether the baby is necessary at all'. On another occasion Stephen informed Hardy that 'three respectable ladies' had complained about the passage in which the fickle Mr Everdene found it difficult to be both married and happy, until he hit upon the idea of making his wife take off her wedding ring when they made love. When Hardy pointed out that *The Times* had commended this passage, Stephen replied that he 'spoke as an editor, not as a man', and added, 'You have no more consciousness of these things than a child' (F. W. Maitland, *Life and Letters of Leslie Stephen* (1906), 275).

Hardy was, in fact, cleverer than Stephen realized. It is part of the greatness of *Far from the Madding Crowd* that he conveys the sexuality and passion underlying the story by the use of highly suggestive description and imagery. As examples of this technique, which Hardy was to use repeatedly in his novels to get the better of the censor, it is worth studying the first meeting of Troy and Bathsheba, when his hard spur catches in her soft skirt (24), and the highly suggestive scene in 'the hollow amid the ferns' where Troy shows off his sword-skills (28). As so often in Shakespeare's plays, the sword is obviously a phallic symbol, and Hardy emphasizes this by describing Troy's sword as being like a living thing. This technique was a subtle and artistic way of conveying nature's sexual power, and Hardy used it repeatedly, particularly in *The Return of the Native, The Woodlanders, Tess,* and *Jude*. It is even present in such stories as 'An Imaginative Woman', where erotic imagery is used to suggest a symbolic mating.

This was one way of getting round Mrs Grundy. Hardy also used a second method: the provision of alternative versions of each novel. Twelve of his fourteen published novels appeared as serials, immediately followed by first editions in volume form, various cheaper editions, the Osgood, McIlvaine 'Wessex Novels' edition of 1895–6, and the Macmillan 'Wessex Edition' of 1912–13 (in America, the Autograph Edition of 1915), designated by Hardy the 'definitive' edition. Sometimes, as in *Tess* and *Jude*, the differences between the serial and later editions is substantial, much of the difference being the result of changes forced upon Hardy in the serials. Thus, Tess in the 1891 *Graphic* serial did not have a baby, but she did have one in the first edition, published as the serial finished. What one might call 'Grundy revisions' are to be found not just in major and minor changes to the plot but also in changes made to a few words or a sentence or two. Thus, 'loose songs' in the serial of *Far from the Madding Crowd* later became 'ba'dy [bawdy] songs', and Bathsheba's 'alarming exploits of sex', which we read today, was 'alarming potentialities of exploit' in the serial.

Textual revisions of a more serious kind were necessary in *The Return of the Native* (1878). Hardy's difficulty here was that he wanted to write a story about a passionate and sensual woman, but women in magazines were not supposed to be passionate and sensual. Leslie Stephen, perhaps aware that Hardy had got the better of him in *Far from the Madding Crowd*, refused to accept the novel until he could see the complete manuscript, because he feared that relations between Eustacia and Wildeve might develop into something too 'dangerous' for a family magazine. William Blackwood had worries too, but eventually Hardy managed, after making substantial changes, to have it accepted by *Belgravia* magazine. In the serial version the hot-blooded Eustacia suffers most, but Hardy again uses evocative imagery. From her first appearance Eustacia is associated with fire and heat. She stands by a bonfire which lights the darkness of Egdon Heath; the fire is a signal to her lover, who describes himself as suffering from 'the curse of inflammability', and refers to her 'hot little bosom' (1.6). Indignation spreads through her like 'subterranean heat', and 'scalding tears' trickle down from her eyes. Hardy is exploring dangerous moral territory, and this is revealed by the number of verbal changes that occur in later editions. Thus, Eustacia's '"but I won't encourage you any more"' of the serial and the first edition becomes '"but I won't give myself to you any more"' in the 1895 edition.

And so it went on. *The Trumpet-Major* (1880) appeared in *Good Words*, edited by one of Her Majesty's Chaplains for Scotland, who requested that a lovers' meeting fixed for a Sunday afternoon should take place on a Saturday, and that swear-words should be avoided. And as a happy ending was *de rigueur* in such a magazine, Hardy kept his unhappy ending for a later edition. With the publication of *The Mayor of Casterbridge* in 1886 Hardy found himself wanting to write about ever more serious and adult areas of human experience, and to write about them more critically. This meant that, as a little later in *Tess*, he had to make substantial changes in his plots in the different versions. In the serial of *The Mayor* Henchard marries Lucetta in the belief that his first wife is dead, and when Susan returns he has to hide this second marriage from her. However, in the volume version Lucetta is not his wife but his mistress, an arrangement that Hardy knew would not be acceptable to the editor of the *Graphic*, in which the story was being first published. This change, made more complex because in the serial the wedding had taken place only two weeks before the first wife, Susan, returned, and because the bigamous wife was just about to appear in Casterbridge, involved Hardy in far more rewriting between serial and volume version than had been required in previous novels. A typical example of the many smaller changes is found in Chapter 18, where what was '"the fact of there being a certain risk in marrying you"' in the serial became '"the fact of there being a certain risk in loving you"' in 1895.

In his next novel, *The Woodlanders* (1887), one of Hardy's themes is the unfairness of the divorce laws, which at that time allowed a husband to divorce his wife for adultery but gave no right to a wife to divorce her husband for the same reason. This required the depiction of a lecherous husband, Dr Edred Fitzpiers, whose sexual activity is not just restricted to his middle-class wife but is enjoyed with the working-class Suke Damson and the upper-class Mrs Charmond. Mowbray *Morris, the editor of *Macmillan's Magazine*, in which the serial was published, saw the dangers inherent in Suke as soon as she appeared on the scene, and wrote to Hardy: 'You will, I am sure, not mind my giving you a gentle hint on one small matter—the affair between Miss Damson and the Doctor. I am not afraid (as you may imagine) for my own morals; but we have, I fancy, rather a queer public: pious Scottish souls who take offence wondrously easily. ... If you can contrive not to bring the fair Miss Suke to too open shame, it would be as well. Let the human frailty be construed mild' (letter of 19 September 1886, in DCM). Hardy was by now used to this kind of advice, and knew how to deal with it. In the serial Fitzpiers and Suke behave on Midsummer's night in a reasonably decorous manner, but in the first edition we are told that 'It was daybreak before Fitzpiers and Suke Damson re-entered Little Hintock' (20). Again, when Mrs Charmond tells Grace of her relationship with Fitzpiers, the early editions have '"O, my great heaven!" she exclaimed, thunderstruck.... "Can it be—can it be!"', but by 1896 this has become, '"O, my great God!" she exclaimed, thunderstruck.... "He's had you! Can it be—can it be!"' (33). Even the change from 'heaven' to 'God' reveals how sensitive some of the public must have been to exclamations.

Hardy's bowdlerizations, however, did not prevent R. H. Hutton, in his review of the first edition of *The Woodlanders* in the *Spectator* (26 March 1887; repr. in *CH*), from commenting that 'Mr Hardy's story is written with an indifference to the moral effect it conveys of which we have found distinct traces before in his books'. There was a good deal of this kind of attack on Hardy, and it is a measure of his courage and his determination to drag the English novel into the adult world that his final two great novels, *Tess* and *Jude*, were more of a challenge to Grundyism and the Establishment's attempt to censor what the public were allowed to read than anything he had written before.

Something has already been said about Hardy's difficulties in finding a publisher for the serial version of *Tess*, and about the way in which he was forced to bowdlerize the book in order to overcome the moral objections of a magazine editor so sensitive that he would not allow Angel Clare to carry the milkmaids over the flooded road in his arms. Most of the cuts were restored in the first edition, and, as might have been expected, this provoked a storm of protest from the guardians of the public morals, who were particularly upset by Hardy's description of Tess on the title-page as 'a pure woman', and by what appeared to be an attack on God in the person of 'the President of the Immortals' in the novel's concluding paragraph. Hardy noted how the Duchess of Abercorn divided her friends into two groups: '"They have been almost fighting across her dinner-table over Tess's character. What she now says to them is 'Do you support her or not?' If they say 'No indeed. She deserved hanging: a little harlot!' she puts them in one group. If they say 'Poor wronged innocent!' and pity her, she puts them in the other group where she is herself"' (*LW* 258). Hardy could take comfort from the fact that there were at least as many good reviews as bad. Mowbray Morris in the *Quarterly* (April 1892; repr. in *CH*) might finish his review with 'Mr Hardy has told an extremely disagreeable story in an extremely disagreeable way', but Margaret *Oliphant in *Blackwood's Magazine* (March 1892; repr. in *CH*) thought the book 'far finer... than anything Mr Hardy has ever done before'.

Hardy claimed to be hurt by the clamour against him, and wrote that 'If this sort of thing continues no more novel-writing for me' (*LW* 259). Whether he was as upset as he made out is questionable, and an interview with Frederick Dolman in *The Young Man* in March 1894 is interesting on this point. He is quoted there as saying, 'There have been very few objectors really: as a matter of fact, my tone has been the same in regard to moral questions for the twenty years or more I have been writing. From the very beginning I resolved to speak out. I remember that in the first edition of *Desperate Remedies* there were many passages exhibiting a similar plainness to *Tess*.' And it must have been consoling that the publicity the book received made it a best-seller, made him a rich man, and led to his being taken up by London society, something he enjoyed more than he was always ready to admit. What is more, he was already planning his next book, which really would flutter the dovecotes and anger the grumbling Grundyites.

In his preface to the first edition of *Jude the Obscure*, dated August 1895, Hardy tells his readers that in this novel he 'attempts to deal unaffectedly with the fret and fever, derision and disaster, that preys in the wake of the strongest passion known to humanity; to tell, without mincing of words, of a deadly war waged between flesh and spirit'. He does this by subjecting his hero to experiences which question the whole of Victorian morality. Carried away with sexual passion, Jude has intercourse with Arabella and is forced by his own acceptance of the demands of Victorian morality into a marriage to a girl with whom he has nothing in common except sexual attraction. The inevitable separation follows, but the unhappy episode has removed his chance of marrying a woman who might be able to share life fully with him, and it plays a part in driving Sue into a loveless marriage with Phillotson. The living together of Jude and Sue was adulterous and unacceptable to the morality of the time, and yet they do find happiness together. Can this be immoral, while Jude's degrading night with his wife in the Aldbrickham hotel is moral? And are we really expected to see Sue's relationship with Phillotson as moral because it has been sanctified by a priest? Of course not, Hardy is saying, and we realize how astutely he has made adultery moral and matrimony immoral, turning received values upside-down in order to challenge the accepted views of the time.

It was Hardy's last, most aggressive, and most calculated attack on the Victorian 'censorship of prudery'. Although the serial version was bowdlerized as usual in plot and language, the editor of *Harper's Magazine* still had objections, which, he insisted, 'are based on a purism (not mine, but our readers')....Our rule is that the magazine must contain nothing which could not be read aloud in any family circle' (Purdy 90). There was an outcry when the first edition was published, and even some of Hardy's friends were shocked. Edmund *Gosse, in his review in *Cosmopolis* (January 1896; repr. in *CH*), asked, 'What has Providence done to Mr Hardy that he should rise up in the arable land of Wessex and shake his fist at his Creator?' Mrs Oliphant accused Hardy of trying to establish an 'anti-marriage league' (*Blackwood's Magazine*, January 1896; repr. in *CH*), and comments by other reviewers included 'a novel of lubricity'; 'one of the most objectionable books...ever read'; 'I thought that *Tess* was bad enough, but that is milk for babes compared to this'; 'Aside from its immorality there is a coarseness which is beyond belief'; and 'a titanically bad book'. The firm of W. H. Smith's withdrew it from its circulating library and the shelves of its bookshops, and the Bishop of Wakefield burnt a copy of it on his fire. Hardy himself, with a typical whimsical humour, claimed not to know what all the shouting was about, but so great was the financial success of both *Tess* and *Jude* that he could now afford to give up novel-writing and return to his first love, poetry.

An 1896 notebook entry quoted in Hardy's autobiography reads, 'Poetry. Perhaps I can express more fully in verse ideas and emotions which run counter to the inert crystallised opinion—hard as a rock—which the vast body of men have vested interests in supporting....If Galileo had said in verse that the world moved, the Inquisition might have let him alone' (*LW* 302). Hardy was to a large extent right. Even a cursory look at his poetry will show that it contains the strong sensual notes found in his novels, and there is his customary frankness about sexual, religious, and social matters. Yet there was very little adverse criticism. In 'At a Bridal', published in 1898, he is concerned with the difference between the stolid offspring of a conventional marriage and the 'rare forms' that might have graced a marriage based on natural love. In *Poems of the Past and the Present*, published only half-a-dozen years after *Jude the Obscure*, he was able to print three successive poems, 'The Levelled Churchyard', 'The Ruined Maid', and 'The Respectable Burgher', which satirize and make fun of sacred Victorian beliefs. These produced hardly an angry word from his reviewers, nor did 'Panthera', which questioned Christ's paternity and was published in *Time's Laughingstocks* in 1909.

However, some censorship by the journal editors still continued, and we find Hardy writing to Edward Garnett on 15 October 1907, 'In respect of the Censor, I am not sure that English literature is so disencumbered of him as you assume. The Editor is the Censor there. Last week a poem of mine ('A Sunday Morning Tragedy'), which I thought almost too obtrusive in its moral, was declined by one of our chief editors on the sole ground that his periodical was "read in families"' (*L* iii 278). (The poem was eventually published, in December 1908, in the *English Review*, whose editor, Ford Madox Hueffer (later Ford Madox Ford) later said that he had founded the magazine in order to publish it.) On 3 December 1909 Hardy wrote to Gosse agreeing with him about the threat to 'literary liberty' in a proposal by librarians to set up a committee empowered to judge the suitability for circulation of books suspected of being 'personally scandalous, libellous, immoral, or otherwise disagreeable' (*L* iv 63).

Perhaps it was because of his distinction as a novelist that Hardy the poet was very little troubled by censorship. It was a sign that he had got the better of Mrs Grundy. Another poem published in *Time's Laughingstocks* was 'One Ralph Blossom Soliloquizes', in which the seven women who have been brought on the rates by the fornication of that virile gentleman are described as thinking of the past, and by a score of five to two they decide that it was worth it. What would Leslie Stephen's 'three respectable ladies' have said about that? It is hardly surprising that Hardy never became Poet Laureate, and was never awarded the Nobel Prize for Literature.

JCG

'Changed Man, A', short story. It was completed in January 1900, published under the editorship of Clement *Shorter in the *Sphere* (21, 28 April 1900), and collected in *A Changed Man and Other Tales.* With 'Enter a Dragoon', written at the same time, it represents Hardy's farewell to prose fiction. Set in 'Casterbridge' (Dorchester), it begins as a light-hearted tale of flirtation and courtship in a provincial garrison town, but the tone unexpectedly deepens and the ending is uncompromisingly melancholy.

Attracted by the glamour of military life, Laura succeeds in catching the handsome Captain Maumbry but is dismayed when, under the influence of a local curate, he leaves the army to enter the Church and accepts a curacy in a slum area of the town, Mixen Lane (used earlier in *The Mayor of Casterbridge* and based on Fordington). During an outbreak of cholera he works heroically among his parishioners, while Laura, sent to Budmouth (Weymouth) to avoid infection, forms a liaison with a young officer. In the process of running away together to Bristol, they encounter her husband toiling at relief work and are moved to assist him. He dies of cholera, but now that Laura is free to marry the lieutenant his passion cools, their relationship fades away, and she 'died a widow'. The story re-creates in considerable detail the Dorchester of Hardy's youth, and the cholera outbreak recalls that of 1854 in which the Reverend Henry Moule (see MOULE FAMILY) took a prominent and impressive part. Hardy's letter to one of Moule's sons dated 29 June 1919 and printed in *LW* (423) states that 'I well remember the cholera-years in Fordington', and includes several graphic details earlier used in the story, including the burning and boiling of infected clothing and bedding.

Changed Man and Other Tales, A. The last of Hardy's four collections of short stories, it was published by Macmillan on 24 October 1913, priced 6*s*., and simultaneously in America by *Harper & Brothers. The size of this edition—10,000 copies, compared (for instance) with 750 copies of the first edition of *Wessex Tales* a quarter of a century earlier—is striking evidence of the growth of Hardy's fame and popular success by this date. Hardy had sent the material to Frederick *Macmillan on 19 August 1913, and the final version of the preface had followed on 12 September. The full title of this first edition was *A Changed Man, The Waiting Supper and Other Tales, Concluding with The Romantic Adventures of a Milkmaid.*

The contents are: 'A Changed Man', 'The Waiting Supper', 'Alicia's Diary', 'The Grave by the Handpost', 'Enter a Dragoon', 'A Tryst at an Ancient Earthwork', 'What the Shepherd Saw', 'A Committee Man of "The Terror"', 'Master John Horseleigh, Knight', 'The Duke's Reappearance', 'A Mere Interlude', 'The Romantic Adventures of a Milkmaid'. All twelve stories had been previously published, many of them some twenty or even thirty years earlier (see separate entries for details). The earliest, 'What the Shepherd Saw', had been written in 1881, the most recent, 'A Changed Man' and 'Enter a Dragoon', in 1899, at the end of Hardy's career as a writer of prose fiction. Most are set in the historical past.

Channing, Mary. See EXECUTIONS, PUBLIC.

characterization. Like that of most of us, Hardy's own character was compounded of the good and the bad, in a mixture whose richness and complexity was suited to the genius whom a friend candidly described as 'a great writer, but not a great man'. Readers who revered and idealized his novels often saw them, in a comfortable and comforting way, as embodying the timeless wisdom of rural England, the folk, the country routines, and their ancient values. Their author, it was felt, must himself be such a man. This impression was misleading, and most of Hardy's readers today are more aware of the dark side of his imagination: its deviousness, its fantasies and evasions, even its sadism. *Tess of the d'Urbervilles*, for instance, may seem not so much to demonstrate Hardy's impassioned plea on behalf of 'a pure woman', and her sufferings at the hands both of men and of the malign forces in the universe, as to show us Hardy's own equivocal desires and daydreams, the vision of an ideal woman, both grand and humble in her outlook and origins; a woman who obsesses his imagination by reason of the very helplessness which enabled him to summon her up and to put her there, even to possess and to persecute; a woman who can simultaneously be owned and desired as an idealized being and yet one who would have been avoided had she been a creature of flesh and blood.

Clearly Hardy was not a simple character at all, and the men and women in his novels reflect this. At the same time it is even more misleading if we see Tess solely as a creature conceived only in the shadow of Hardy's own complex secretiveness, a secretiveness that could amount to downright dishonesty. For Tess does in spite of this possess a life of her own, the same life that Hardy seemed to put so effortlessly and unconsciously into his earlier heroines—Fancy Day of *Under the Greenwood Tree*, Elfride Swancourt of *A Pair of Blue Eyes*, Bathsheba Everdene of *Far from the Madding Crowd*. The real clue to Hardy's nature, and that of his characters, seems to lie in the fact that minute and apparently involuntary powers of observation ('He was a man who used to notice such things') coexist in his creative mind with an equal capacity for dreaming and fantasizing, particularly about women. (He remarks drily of Pierston, the ageing hero of *The Well-Beloved*, that 'he was subject to gigantic fantasies still'.)

To a friend he wrote of Jude Fawley as 'my poor puppet', but this dismissive objectivity was not of course the true story, nor the real reflection of Hardy's feelings. Young Jude is alive with Hardy's own gloomy fantasy (and yet what creative fantasy by a great artist is ever really gloomy?) of what might have happened to himself, had life gone differently. The young Jude who covers his face with his straw hat to blot out reality, and watches the sunlight glinting through it, is the same younger self whom Hardy so vividly remembered, lying in the dense ferns near his father's cottage and wishing that the grown-up life in store for him would never happen.

This child's-eye view of their creator touches and transforms all Hardy's characters, giving them an inner life which balances and contrasts with the outer one they are fated to lead. They are not complex by intention, like the characters of more obviously intellectual novelists, but they become so inevitably, by reason of the divisions and separations which are a part of their provenance. To Hardy himself all this seemed perfectly obvious, or at least he professed to find it perfectly obvious; and he also professed—perhaps with an equal degree of disingenuousness—that he must have failed lamentably in the writing of a novel if his readers could not see it, if 'it requires explanation and is not self-evident'. *Jude the Obscure*, he wrote on 20 November 1895 to Edmund *Gosse, 'is all contrasts' (*L* ii 99), and he had observed to the same friend a little earlier that 'The "grimy" features of the story go to show the contrast between the ideal life a man wished to lead, and the squalid real life he was fated to lead' (*L* ii 93). This seems commonplace enough, because it leaves out the real contrast between Jude as a kind of personal fantasy, and also an objective study of what might indeed have happened to a young man of that time, and of that background, who had scholarly and intellectual aspirations.

Tess is similarly divided between her place in Hardy's own mind and heart and her objective status as a country maiden betrayed and in trouble, who goes to the bad and meets her final doom on the scaffold. That kind of story was not only traditional in the annals of country lore and mythology but had been used by writers, and later by novelists, all over the world, writing about heroines from all walks of life, from Chaucer's and Henryson's Criseyde to Richardson's Clarissa. Hardy was, in one sense, adding to a character archetype already venerable in the annals of fiction, even though his own imagination made of Tess a unique being fitted to his own fantasy's requirements, in which she could lie soft and safe without knowing it, as Keats observed of his own similar daydreams. All his life Hardy saw 'Tesses', as it were, in all kinds of contexts, rural and urban: he celebrates them in several of his poems, and recalled them in many fictions. He remarked once that the figure of Tess herself had been suggested to him by the look of a waitress seen in a Weymouth teashop, and in old age he was still falling for such chance-seen figures, as he was to do when the young and beautiful Gertrude *Bugler took the leading role in a version of Tess put on at Dorchester.

Always both introspective and sardonic in his own fashion, Hardy was well aware of these workings of his own inner consciousness. After *Tess* he could be said to have been more preoccupied in his fictions with dissimulation itself: for example, with Jude's and Sue's vagaries and self-deceptions. The contrasts there become inner contradictions of character, dramatized into event and eventual fatality: 'Sue and her heathen ends set against Jude's reading the Greek testament', and Sue's eventual and wilful transformation of herself into a Christian believer. The trouble is that there is something decidedly arbitrary in these transformations, which amount to a parody of the famous comment by the German Romantic writer Novalis that 'Character is Destiny'. This dictum had evidently struck Hardy very strongly during his earlier philosophical reading. But if character is destiny, then arbitrary and improbable accidents befalling a character can make destiny itself look as if too artificially contrived.

In the early 1890s Hardy went to see *Ibsen's plays, then a revolutionary and daring arrival on the London stage, and many critics and readers of his novels written at that time guessed, probably correctly, that he had been influenced by the dramatist's vision, or at least found his own view of things corroborated by much of what he had seen in Ibsen's personae. Irony, always a quality of his own representation of life, becomes heavier and more marked: indeed, in his final novel, *The Well-Beloved*, it has virtually become an end and method in itself. The hero Pierston, who pursues the same ideal of feminine beauty and allure from youth to old age, bears a no doubt deliberate resemblance, in however ironically stylized and simplified a guise, to Hardy's own mature awareness of himself. The much earlier quality of romantic lyricism and joyfulness which permeated all his characters when he was younger, no matter how stark their ultimate fates may become, has turned into a style of irony which seems increasingly 'unHardyan'. There had always been a kind of naïve amusement and relish—the birthright of many country people—in his earlier self. The older Hardy, and his characters, suffer in a sense from a sophistication that can strike the reader as naïve in the wrong way.

In an article for the *Westminster Review* in 1883 (repr. in *CH*)—one of the most searching and sensitive pieces ever written on the people in Hardy's novels—Havelock Ellis drew attention to Hardy's characteristic preoccupation with human weakness, his profound sympathy with it, and the way in which he separates (division and separation for Hardy are as normal as breathing) one kind of weakness from another, and particularly the male from the female. Hardy's men, like Gabriel Oak and Diggory Venn, can be strong, reliable, and supportive under all circumstances, but none of his women can be. Of course the conventions of the time, both social and moral, play their part in this, but Hardy's own inner needs are far more important to the delicacy and understanding of his creative process. As Havelock Ellis points out, to be deeply attractive to their maker all women in his novels must be weak, even when weakness is an aspect of their strength, as with Bathsheba Everdene, Sue Bridehead, or Tess herself.

The most attractive quality of Elfride, Hardy's early heroine in *A Pair of Blue Eyes*, is her 'irresolution', which fuels the plot, although in fact it has nothing to do with the final accident which brings about her death. In marked contrast to George *Eliot's women, Hardy's are in the last analysis incapable of moral firmness or ascendancy, for if they possessed it they would not attract their creator, or be seen by him and identified with as they are. Hardy's own inner nature required women to be as unlike men as possible, a point largely ignored by D. H. *Lawrence in his 1914 study of his fellow-novelist—a study, admittedly, that tells us more about Lawrence's outlook and methods than about those of Hardy. It is one of Lawrence's strengths to unify: to see the sexes, for example, in the same moral and physical context, even though he may also hold that they should retain their separate spheres of being and activity. But men and women in Hardy are, as it were, genuinely and absolutely separate beings. In this respect, if in few others, he is like that other great 19th-century novelist Tolstoy, who has just the same instinct as Hardy for keeping the things and people in his novels apart, giving them not only complete individual distinction (which Hardy too does in his own way) but a special separateness as men and women. (Consider the contrast of Anna Karenina and Vronsky, which is as total as that between Jude and Sue or between Tess and Angel Clare.)

Both Henry *James and George *Moore held that Hardy's art was fraudulent, and that a character such as Tess, whom the reading public had greeted with rapture and taken to its bosom, represented an apparent realism which was essentially false. George Moore, who had carefully studied the methods of the French realist school of novelists (see REALISM), was particularly outraged by what he considered Hardy's crude and sensational popularization. In return Hardy nursed a bitter hostility towards Moore which found expression in what is probably the last thing he ever composed, a scrap of doggerel dictated on his deathbed and for some reason preserved by his widow: 'Heap dustbins on him: | They'll not meet | The apex of his self-conceit.' This imagined epitaph on Moore reveals the bitterness which Hardy had nurtured over the years, and which perhaps explains more than any other factor his decision to quit novel-writing. He had been wounded, deeply wounded, and the grand old man of letters, for most of his admirers a figure of legendary serenity and gentleness, showed it at the end with the childish venom of a schoolboy. His admirers were also quite rightly indifferent to the criticism of Hardy's two fellow-novelists, which might justifiably have been attributed to their jealousy at Hardy's sales figures and their own comparative lack of popular acclaim.

James was particularly critical of what he considered to be Hardy's attempt to portray a fully sexual female being in Tess. Hardy might well have retorted that the British public would let him do no such thing. He professed, like many authors of the time, to despair of the hypocrisy of Mrs Grundy. But in fact the intense reality of his characters, and especially of his portraits of women, does not in the least depend upon sexual or any other kind of explicitness. The genius of his imaginative fantasy was able to impose itself with complete conviction on the mere actuality of things, producing effects like Sergeant Troy demonstrating the sword-exercise to Bathsheba in the hollow among the ferns; Elfride rescuing Knight from the cliff with a rope made of her underwear: Eustacia rocking to and fro in her misery on the great tumulus of Rainbarrow, crouching under her umbrella (a characteristically homely Hardy touch) as if some elemental force under the earth were drawing her down within it. In all these and many other instances the vivid selfhood of the characters—men and women—is achieved by the manner in which Hardy imagines and brings them to life in the strangeness, even absurdity, of their situations.

James may have felt that Hardy's characters like Tess only pretended to a sexual existence. Such was not, however, the opinion of the bishop who burnt a copy of *Jude the Obscure.* Sue Bridehead is never more terrifyingly alive than at the moment when, under the eyes of her old neighbour Mrs Edlin, she tears up the pretty nightdress she had once bought to please Jude—'the tears resounding through the house like a screech-owl' (*JO* 6.5). The imagined sound, a summation of the tension and contradictoriness within Sue, is almost physically painful to the reader, conveying as it does all Hardy's peculiar mixture of fantasy and literalness—here impressed not on the larger emotions of grief or jealousy or rage, which animate the great spaces of Hardy's earlier fiction, but on the very nerve of sexual misery and distraction. No wonder the bishop himself was distracted.

Hardy's characters live most at their moments of suddenness: he is far less effective at the extended build-up of a character, or the representation of a complete life. It is hard not to feel that his knowledge of the classics, and of what passed at the time for literary theory, had an adverse effect on his ambitious project in planning *The Mayor of Casterbridge.* The life and fate of Michael Henchard are not in fact fully or deeply considered, but move as it were in a series of jerks, animated by the build-up of coincidence and by ingenuities of plot. Suspense and the use of coincidence are perfectly acceptable when Hardy uses them in a narrative based on sudden glimpses of personality and scenes of dramatized tableaux. Henchard is conceived at his most vivid at moments like that in which he sells his wife, or in his fight in the loft with Farfrae, late on in the novel. But betweenwhiles he has hardly any imagined or documented existence; nor is his transformation at the end into a figure that is intended to recall Lear or Oedipus, setting out solitary into the heath or into a blinded exile, perhaps quite so powerful in retrospect as Hardy's earlier readers were apt to take for granted. In forsaking his twin weapons of personal fantasy and homely literalness,

Hardy sacrificed unconsciously, and in the interests of a wholly admirable ambition, his sovereign method for making his characters live.

That is true of even his most minor characters, in novels that are usually considered of slight importance. Lady Constantine and the youthful astronomer Swithin St Cleeve in *Two on a Tower* are as effectively realized as personalities as any of Hardy's more major characters. And it is they and the tower itself, as the quaint and unique determinant of their idyll and separation, that remain in the reader's mind, rather than anything of Hardy's touchingly grandiose concept of tiny lives set out and made visible like stars in an immense and indifferent universe. In terms of character, Hardy's presented moments are always more successful, more completely realized and brought off, than are his wider visions or abstractly planned perspectives.

Egdon Heath itself exists much more as a vividly realized place than as a portentously symbolic landscape. And the same is true of the persons who inhabit it, and whose lives supply the plot that is centred on the Native's return. As usual with Hardy, we can feel the presence of his own daydreams behind the topographical exactitude of setting and landscape. In an important sense he had himself returned in life to Egdon, as he also no doubt imagined himself as Clym Yeobright, falling in love with Eustacia Vye; as he imagined himself too as the poor but brilliant astronomer, fallen in love with by the grand lady who lived on an estate with a tower; or as the poor schoolmaster of 'An Indiscretion in the Life of an Heiress', who is loved by the daughter of the big house, and who unexpectedly finds himself freed, so to speak, for other fantasies of a like kind by her sudden and painless death. Hardy and his dramatic personae are seldom far away from that childhood time when he had been befriended and taught by Mrs Julia Augusta *Martin, the kind lady in the big house near his home.

The helplessness of human beings, and the elaborate artifice of coincidence, together form a contrast which Hardy's genius can make almost wholly acceptable. To dismiss his fiction, as F. R. Leavis did, as laborious and provincial is to miss its whole point. These homely characteristics are assets to Hardy's strange knack of universality, not liabilities. So even is the sheer improbability of many of his rustic scenes. It can hardly be that Diggory Venn the reddleman is, in sober fact, a mysterious red apparition, who comes and goes on the wastes of the Heath; or that Sergeant Troy should always wear the brilliant scarlet jacket that distinguished him so notably from the rustic cast of *Far from the Madding Crowd.* It is simply that these things are what make them such notable characters, rather than the twists of the tale which require Venn to revert to a homely Gabriel Oak persona (against Hardy's better judgement, as he later informed us), and Troy to end up merely as villain *ex machina.* Their character is not their destiny, but is realized in the sudden glimpses we have, say, of Troy in the dark fir coppice at night, when the opening of a dark lantern reveals him to Bathsheba.

One could say, too, in summing up, that Hardy's characters are so successful because they embody in various ways a universal human daydream. They are charged with fantasy, and at the same time filled with a day-to-day literalness of living, enjoying, suffering. It is probably time, now, that we saw Hardy—and to see him through the great moments of encounter in his novels and poems is the only way to do it—as the writer that he really is: not as one of the classic 19th-century novelists but as a new and radical breed of imaginative writer, a novelist who looks forward to the way things are going to be done in the 20th century, and to the authors who have more obviously shaped that outlook—Proust, Joyce, Woolf—the writers whose 'human shows' and 'moments of vision' have given the personal view and the inner fantasy life a universal human authority. JB

Chesterton, G. K. (1874–1936), Roman Catholic novelist and short story writer, essayist, poet, and critic. He dealt severely with Hardy in his popular study *The Victorian Age in Literature* (1913), comparing him unfavourably with George *Meredith: 'Hardy went down to botanize in the swamp, while Meredith climbed towards the sun.' The same passage contains the famous characterization of Hardy as 'a sort of village atheist brooding and blaspheming over the village idiot'. Hardy never forgot or forgave this treatment and seems to respond to it in a passage excised from earlier editions of his autobiography but restored in *LW* 381, where Chesterton (unnamed) is in turn characterized as 'a phrasemongering literary contortionist'. A few hours before he died Hardy dictated satirical verses directed at Chesterton ('Epitaph for G. K. Chesterton') and George *Moore that remained unpublished until 1970; they are included in *The Complete Poems of Thomas Hardy*, ed. James Gibson (1976).

Child, Harold (1869–1945), author and critic. He began his career as an actor but soon turned to journalism, becoming drama critic of *The Times*. For some forty years he wrote for *The Times Literary Supplement*, and he contributed extensively to *The Cambridge History of English Literature*. His *Thomas Hardy* (1916) was one of the earliest critical studies and, exceptionally, won Hardy's approval. On a number of later occasions Hardy gave Child assistance with his writings by supplying biographical and other information. Child's account of Hardy's funeral services was included by Florence Emily Hardy as an appendix to the second volume of her so-called biography, *The Later Years of Thomas Hardy* (see AUTOBIOGRAPHY).

Chosen Poems. See *SELECTED POEMS*.

cinema. The fact that his novels are all strongly plotted love stories with an abundance of dramatic action, combined with the picturesque and 'period' interest of their settings, has made Hardy a favourite source for cinematic treatment. There is even a sense in which his narrative and descriptive technique, with its varying use of 'close-up' and 'long shot', its fondness for unexpected 'camera-angles' and its propensity to 'frame' scenes and figures in, for instance, a window or an open door, may be described as 'cinematic', though all of his novels were written before the moving pictures became a popular medium. The most striking examples in all his writings, however, are to be found in his 'epic-drama' on the Napoleonic period, avowedly written for 'mental performance': for an illustrative quotation, see *DYNASTS, THE*.

Hardy's first experience of the new medium may well have been in October 1913, when he attended in London a press showing of an American version of *Tess of the d'Urbervilles*. At this stage he seems to have regarded the cinema as no more than an interesting toy, but a few years later, after witnessing in Dorchester the shooting of scenes for a film of *The Mayor of Casterbridge*, he was prepared to take a longer view—at least if we can accept the testimony of Vere Collins (*Talks with Thomas Hardy* (1928)), who reports him as remarking that 'perhaps the cinematograph will take the place of fiction, and novels will die out, leaving only poetry'. See also PICTORIALISM. For further information on film adaptations during and after Hardy's lifetime, see Appendix E.

Ellen Baskin and Mandy Hicken, *Enser's Filmed Books and Plays 1928–1991* (1993).
Tom Costello, *International Guide to Literature on Film* (1994).
David Lodge, 'Thomas Hardy and Cinematographic Form', *Novel*, 7 (1973–4).
Neil Sinyard, *Filming Literature* (1986) (contains material on Hardy, especially on John Schlesinger's *Far from the Madding Crowd* and Roman Polanski's *Tess*).

class. '"I am not red by birth, you know,"' says the reddleman in *The Return of the Native* (1.11). During the course of this novel Diggory Venn is transformed from a bizarre figure on the fringes of society into a respectable dairy-farmer, and several other characters in the Wessex novels reinvent themselves too. Class is not caste; people are constantly moving upwards and downwards through marriage, a stroke of good or bad luck, or a foolhardy or sensible personal choice. It is one of Hardy's central themes.

Twice, in his essay 'The Dorsetshire Labourer' and later in *Tess of the d'Urbervilles* (51), Hardy wrote sympathetically about an 'interesting and better-informed class' of village people, neither farmers nor workfolk. 'The metamorphic classes of society' (*HE* 39) were the ones which really interested him. This was the class to which he himself belonged; as the child of a small master-mason and a woman who had been brought up on parish relief, he had missed going to university but become a professional man, married 'a lady', and ended up as the most eminent writer of his generation. In the villages, he wrote, this class was being squeezed out as its homes were repossessed, and he made it quite clear that in his opinion this was tragic.

When Robert Gittings researched Hardy's background in the 1970s, he found that Hardy had relatives who were 'labourers, cobblers, bricklayers, carpenters, farm servants, journeyman joiners, butlers ... cooks, house-servants, ladies' maids [and] certificated teachers, regarded in the 19th century as little better than servants' (*Young Thomas Hardy*, 18). Gittings accused him of suppressing an important part of his family history because, like many other people, he wished to be considered more genteel than he really was.

Britain has been called the most class-conscious country on earth, and the Victorians did not boast about their working-class roots as their present-day descendants do; they were far more likely to be impressed by titles or 'old musty-mansioned lineages' (*TT* 36). Names like Fitzpiers, de Stancy, d'Urberville have a mysterious resonance, even if their owners are in no way remarkable. 'Blood' was considered most important and the classes were believed to be intrinsically unlike; Swithin St Cleeve as the product of a mixed marriage is suspect—'what with having two stations of life in his blood he's good for nothing' (*TT* 1).

Hardy looks on all this with the cold eye of one who is not over-impressed by human pretensions. His attitude is very similar to that of the medieval moralists, who continually pointed out that death comes to great and small alike. In his poem about the sinking of the *Titanic*, 'The Convergence of the Twain', he writes: 'Over the mirrors meant | To glass the opulent | The sea-worm crawls—grotesque, slimed, dumb, indifferent'. It is the same in *The Trumpet-Major*, where the King and his grand entourage will be reduced to dust—'a few small handfuls in royal vaults' (12). Tess's d'Urberville ancestors cannot help her, and the author has no great respect for titled families, suggesting that the Lords Luxellian in *A Pair of Blue Eyes* are 'hedgers and ditchers by rights' (2). The stories in *A Group of Noble Dames*, while not exactly attacking the aristocracy, are unlikely to make us feel there is much difference between their blue blood and the red blood of other people. Hardy certainly agreed with Angel Clare that 'the only pedigrees we ought to respect are those spiritual ones of the wise and virtuous' (*TDU* 30). He was conscious, too, that social position varied according to where one was—'Social definitions are all made relatively: an absolute datum is only imagined' (*DR* 7). He never fell into the late 20th-century error of believing class does not exist.

Yet Hardy may, as Gittings argues, have been reluctant to talk freely about his family background. Two of his early novels show a talented young person, 'delicately poised upon the social globe' (*HE* 24), who is compelled in self-defence to keep many things hidden. The architect Stephen Smith is rejected by his fiancée's father when he turns out to be 'the son of one of my village peasants' (*PBE* 9). Ethelberta, who moves among the upper classes as one of themselves, secretly belongs to a family of servants, people who 'are considered to be of different blood and bone from their employers' (*HE* 29) and are treated as if they were uniquely ridiculous. It has been pointed out that the young Hardy was also an architect from a fairly humble background, and that many women in his family, including his mother, had been servants. He may also have had affinities with Barnet in the short story 'Fellow-Townsmen', who married a woman from higher up the social scale, and was 'probably the first of his line who had ever passed a day without toil' (7). Without going too deeply into biography, it is obvious that his fiction, from *The Poor Man and the Lady, by the Poor Man* to *Jude the Obscure*, is intensely preoccupied with class and the conflicts it brings.

Hardy's novels are all about marriage, and marriage can be a way of rising out of the class one was born into. It can also be a source of extreme tension when people fall in love across the divide. When not blinded by passion, characters assess each other quite matter-of-factly: Thomasin tells Diggory Venn that her aunt 'will want me to look a little higher than a small dairy-farmer, and marry a professional man' (*RN* 1.9). *The Poor Man and the Lady*, Hardy's lost novel of the late 1860s, apparently dealt with the love between an heiress and the son of 'peasants' working on her father's estate. According to the publisher Alexander Macmillan, it was a wholesale attack on the upper classes; according to Hardy himself, it was socialistic, even revolutionary.

Some of it survives under the title *An Indiscretion in the Life of an Heiress* (see UNCOLLECTED STORIES). This has no great literary value, but it does show Hardy's concern for the poor, particularly their children, and introduces the theme of tenants being turned out of their homes, which he would take up again. When the gifted young hero falls in love with the heiress he is conscious of the cultural difference between them, and depressed 'that the habits of men should be so subversive of the law of nature as to indicate that he was not worthy to marry a woman whose own instincts said that he was worthy' (8). Evidently Hardy believed there was little chance of a happy outcome, because she dies. His later novels are full of couples who find it difficult to marry because of their class difference; Dick and Fancy, Elfride and Stephen, Swithin and Viviette, Giles and Grace, Angel and Tess. Some of these relationships survive but, more often, they do not.

Yet he was aware that women, in particular, could quite easily glide upwards through marriage: 'A woman takes her colour from the man she's walking with' (*W* 12). Much of the impression we make on other people is caused by superficial things like dress, accent, and manner. Elizabeth-Jane is reproved by her stepfather Henchard because she uses dialect words, 'those terrible marks of the beast to the truly genteel' (*MC* 20). Hardy had noted that the women he met at smart London parties would look less glamorous if they were dressed as agricultural labourers, and he shows how Tess's status sinks when she changes her clothes—'as soon as she was compelled to don the wrapper of a fieldwoman, rude words were addressed to her more than once' (*TDU* 41). A late, mordant poem, 'The Lady in the Furs', has a woman who passes as a great beauty although he believes she is no more than a scarecrow who has been decorated by 'the hands of midnight workers' in animals' skins.

So more than one of Hardy's women is suspended 'in mid-air between two storeys of society' (*W* 30) because she has had an expensive education which has distanced her from her parents. Fancy Day's father has sent her away from home to be polished in the hope that she will catch a gentleman, and she is very tempted by the vicar before she settles for Dick, who is nearer her own level. '"It is my nature—perhaps all women's—to love refinement of mind and manners ... to be ever fascinated with the idea of surroundings more elegant and pleasing than those which have been customary,"' she admits (*UGT* 4.7). Ethelberta no longer appears to have anything in common with her family after an intensive finishing course abroad. Grace Melbury has been to school with girls 'whose parents Giles would have addressed with a deferential Sir or Madam' (*W* 6); when her father sees how her education is bringing her into touch with a higher class of people, he is reluctant to let her slip back. In the scene where she and her husband Fitzpiers are watching the cider workers through their hotel window, he admits that he is proud of his ancient family and feels that he belongs 'to a different species' from them: '"And from me, too, then,"' Grace says, '"For my blood is no better than theirs ..."'—to which Fitzpiers replies, '"Ah, you—you are refined and educated into something quite different"' (*W* 25).

Angel Clare is reluctant to present Tess to his family until she has been 'familiarised with worldly ways by a few months travel and reading with him' (*TDU* 33). Even when she is again working in the fields she no longer considers the men who work with her as possible marriage partners:

> 'Is that man your husband?' he asked mechanically, denoting by a sign the labourer who turned the machine.
>
> 'That man!' she said proudly. 'I should think not!' (*TDU* 46)

Hardy clearly feels that genuine lovers should not allow class to keep them apart, but he is also aware that different backgrounds lead to different tastes and that this can cause real difficulties. Like Dickens in *Great Expectations*, he sometimes wondered whether it was worth educating bright young working-class people, if this was going to alienate them from their own kind. Grace has moments when she rejects her acquired culture and wishes that she worked in the woods, but, in the end, Hardy feels that education is precious. He seems to have a special sympathy with those of his characters (Gabriel, Elizabeth-Jane, Jude) who, like himself in his youth, spend a great deal of their spare time reading and struggling to enlarge their minds.

While women can leapfrog social barriers by marriage, men must make their own way in the world and cannot shed their previous identities quite so easily. 'Doing well', 'getting on', climbing the social ladder, are major themes in *Far from the Madding Crowd*, *The Mayor of Casterbridge*, and *Jude the Obscure*. Hardy's feelings are ambiguous; to some extent he agrees with Jude that a man '"should be as cold-blooded as a fish and as selfish as a pig to have a really good chance of being one of his country's worthies"' (*JO* 6.1), but he has considerable respect for those who work to make the best of limited opportunities, and some contempt for those who do not. *Far from the Madding Crowd*, his most optimistic novel, illustrates this very clearly. Gabriel Oak is first a shepherd and then a bailiff who is able, 'by sustained efforts of industry and chronic good spirits' (2), to become a small farmer; after losing his flock through his one act of carelessness, he starts again from the bottom and eventually achieves a worthy position. While Gabriel is admirable, Sergeant Troy, who 'wasted his gifted lot, and listed a soldier' (24), is not. '"His being higher in learning and birth than the ruck of soldiers is anything but a proof of his worth"', Gabriel points out: '"It shows his course to be downward"' (29). Damon Wildeve in *The Return of the Native* is another man who 'was brought up to better things... but he threw away his chance' (1.3), and Hardy does not admire him either, any more than the feckless Durbeyfields. Hardy himself had worked long and hard to improve his own situation, and certainly believed with one part of his mind that this was the right thing to do.

Yet he had also, like Clym in the same novel, refused to continue in a safe career because it seemed irrelevant to his deepest needs. Clym is a diamond merchant who thinks his job is useless and wants to be a poorly paid teacher; even manual work for short periods does not frighten him. This opens up an interesting debate about what 'doing well' really is. Clym's mother is concerned solely with pushing him on, and cannot understand why he should wish to '"go backward in the world by your own free choice"'. Clym justifies this on the grounds that he has duties to others: 'He wished to raise the class at the expense of individuals rather than individuals at the expense of the class' (3.2). This sounds Marxist, and Hardy did not often go deeply into politics, but it is evident that Clym belongs to the small band of men who see themselves as missionaries (perhaps without a formal religious creed), reformers, and educators. Jude is another man who feels that his only real talent is to 'accumulate ideas, and impart them to others' (*JO* 6.10). Such people are, as far as anyone can be, outside the class structure.

This tension between the urge to get on and the urge to opt out continues in later novels. It is particularly clear-cut in *The Mayor of Casterbridge*, where the labourer Michael Henchard knows himself to be capable of making a fortune. Having ruthlessly extricated himself from his family, he rises to the top of his little world. His rival Farfrae has also had to break some ties, in his case with his homeland, because that is the only way to gain 'the prizes of life' (8). Farfrae is the model self-made individual, becoming 'Mayor and man of money' (37) without deliberately wronging anyone. Yet, paradoxically, Hardy and the reader feel much more affection for Henchard, who loses his high position largely through his own fault, becomes a labourer again, and does not attempt to make a fresh start because 'he had no wish to make an arena a second time of a world that had become a mere painted scene to him' (44).

Hardy asks some searching questions about class in this novel. Farfrae and Elizabeth, who achieve a modest happiness by 'making limited opportunities endurable', are obviously to be admired, perhaps more than Henchard. There is no difference between 'being respected in the nether parts of Casterbridge and glorified at the uppermost end of the social world' (45). But this little community, which seems so harmonious, has its dark side, with bitter power struggles between the leading men and an underclass which enjoys getting small revenges on its betters. Farfrae loses some of his popularity after he becomes successful, and his wife is also resented. '"I do like to see the trimming pulled off such Christmas candles"' (37), one woman spitefully says. On the skimmity-ride, which, though not precisely violent, results in a death, Hardy comments that 'the tempting prospect of putting to the blush people who stand at the head of affairs' is the 'supreme and piquant enjoyment of those who writhe under the heel of the same' (42).

'Writhing under the heel' sounds extreme, yet in his last three major novels Hardy does show various ways in which the rich exploit the poor. *The Woodlanders* has a very definite social ladder, with Mrs Charmond at the top; she owns the woods (but takes no interest in them) and turns Giles out of his home in a fit of temper. Hardy had strong feelings about the practice of evicting families who had lived in one place for generations, and would use the same situation in *Tess*. Fitzpiers has no property but has the assurance and prestige of an upper-class man; Giles (after he has been evicted) and Marty are landless labourers. Somewhere in the middle is Grace, who has money but no background, and her social position will be determined by the man she marries. Robert Creedle brutally sums up her value in conversation with Giles: '"Ye've lost a hundred load o' timber well seasoned; ye've lost five hundred pound in good money; ye've lost the stone-windered house that's big enough to hold a dozen families; ye've lost your share of half-a-dozen good waggons and their horses—all lost!—through your letting slip she that was once yer own!"' (25) It is as cold-blooded as the marriage market in Jane Austen.

What is clear is that Hardy's sympathies are with Giles, Marty, and to some extent Grace, and against the aristocrats Fitzpiers and Mrs Charmond who casually take away everything they value (even Marty's hair). The balance of sympathies is the same in his next novel. Tess is descended from an ancient family, and the author makes the general point that 'many of the present tillers of the soil were once owners of it' (*TDU* 30), but for all practical purposes she and her fellow field-workers are the exploited, while Farmer Groby and Alec (whose family, it seems, has also evicted copyholders) are exploiters. Alec takes advantage of Tess just as her own ancestors probably did of peasant girls generations earlier. Angel's class background also makes him insensitive to her problems because he cannot understand the pressures she has to face.

It is in *Tess* that Hardy makes one of his few statements about what a harmonious society might be like. He says that Talbothays dairy offers 'perhaps the happiest of all positions in the social scale, being above the line at which neediness ends, and below the line at which the *convenances* begin to cramp natural feeling' (*TDU* 20). Talbothays has a primitive class structure, and does not offer Tess a permanent home, but it does represent something of real value.

A group of short stories written in the 1880s show the class war at its starkest. 'The Three Strangers' deals with the escape of a man condemned to death for sheep-stealing; the point is made that he is a skilled man (a member of the 'interesting and better-informed class') who could not get work and was unable to feed his family. We know that Hardy had been devastated by his father's account of a half-starved boy who was hanged merely for being present at a rick-burning, and in 'The Withered Arm' he returns to the hanging of the innocent. Rhoda is a milkmaid who has been seduced by a farmer before he goes on to make a conventional marriage; their son is executed 'to make an example of him, there having been so much destruction of property' (8), and the farmer's wife tries to take advantage of his death. The women in 'Barbara of the House of Grebe' (in *A Group of Noble Dames*) and 'The Son's Veto' are both cruelly sacrificed to class feeling; Barbara's husband punishes her viciously for having preferred a non-aristocratic man to himself, and Sophy's son, educated in his father's values, refuses to let her marry the man from her own background who could have made her happy. In each case the woman dies.

'A Tragedy of Two Ambitions' shows two brothers who, in effect, murder their father because he is about to destroy their respectable image. Their sister is able to rise in the traditional way, by getting married, but the best they can achieve is a low rank in the Anglican Church, which seems hopelessly worldly: 'The Church is a poor forlorn hope for people without influence. . . . A social regenerator has a better chance outside' (5). This story foreshadows *Jude the Obscure*, which is perhaps Hardy's most devastating attack on established religion and the class system of his day.

Readers are often depressed by this novel because it offers few chinks of hope that hard-working people can do anything to improve their situation. The boy Jude has no close family or nurturing community, like Talbothays; his relationship with the farmer, Troutham, is one of master and servant, and his adult life is spent maintaining the fabric of colleges in which he will never study. Hardy believes that the Church and the ancient universities have lost sight of their original purposes; Christminster was founded for poor students with a 'passion for learning', but they were 'elbowed off the pavement by the millionaires' sons' (3.4).

This point is underlined on the very last page, where Jude lies dead with his battered books around him while various 'illustrious gents' are being given honorary degrees. It is noticeable that no member of the university shows any sympathy with his wish to study; the heads of colleges snub him, and even the more thoughtful undergraduates, with whom he knows himself to have much in common, ignore him: 'he was as far from them as if he had been at the antipodes. Of course he was. He was a young workman in a white blouse, and with stone-dust in the creases of his clothes; and in passing him they did not even see him, or hear him, rather saw through him as through a pane of glass at their familiars beyond' (2.2). In the end he is forced to realize that he belongs with 'the manual toilers... unrecognised as part of the city at all by its visitors and panegyrists, yet without whose denizens the hard readers could not read nor the high thinkers live' (2.6).

This reminds us that Hardy's thought is deeply practical, indeed materialist—'What was most required by citizens? Food, clothing, and shelter' (1.5)—and it is a terrible indictment of the university that it should ignore those who keep it going. The only optimistic notes are struck when we hear that working-class students may one day get a chance (Ruskin College was founded in 1899), and when Jude maintains that it was right to try to achieve his dream, even though he was born too early. There is, perhaps, hope for the future, but Hardy feels keenly how much has been lost: '"Too late for me... and for how many worthier ones before me!"' (6.10)

In the Wessex novels, class is as inescapable as it is unnatural. Jude's hands, like Marty South's, are subdued to what they work in: 'As with so many right hands born to manual labour, there was nothing in its fundamental shape to bear out the physiological conventionalism that gradations of birth show themselves primarily in the form of this member. Nothing but a cast of the die of destiny had decided that the girl should handle the tool; and the fingers which clasped the heavy ash haft might have skilfully guided the pencil or swept the string, had they only been set to do it in good time' (*W* 2). In *The Poor Man and the Lady* there appears to have been a scene where the squire's daughter is watching the labourers' children walk home in the rain, and says patronizingly, '"Poor little wretches!"', to which the schoolmaster-hero retorts, '"Say poor little children, madam"' (*An Indiscretion in the Life of an Heiress*, 4), and, in a sense, all Hardy's novels make this point. MW

classics. Hardy's first recorded encounter with classical literature came *c.*1848 when his mother gave him a pocket edition of Dryden's translation of Virgil—a book 'for which she had a great liking', as he noted shortly after her death (*Daily Chronicle*, 9 April 1904). In 1850 she sent him to the British School in Dorchester, partly because the headmaster, Isaac *Last, was known as a good teacher of Latin. Within two years, at the age of 12, he was launched into Latin for an extra fee.

Latin at School

The Latin grammar and texts of Eutropius and Caesar that Hardy remembered starting with (*LW* 27) were still in his library at Max Gate at the time of his death, as were many other classical books (see LIBRARY, HARDY'S). His second-hand Eton grammar (1846), in which he wrote his name in 1852, had its origins in the early 16th century. Studded with doggerel Latin hexameters to be learned and chanted by rote, its tone was inescapably grim. A second-hand *King Edward VI Latin Grammar* (*c.*1844), which he probably acquired at school, followed much the same discouraging pattern at greater length. It was here that he coloured the genders in watercolour (*LW* 27), using red for masculine, blue for neuter, and leaving feminine white. The effect, suitably varied over five pages, remains alluring. Eutropius' compact survey of Roman history down to AD 364 has the merit of simplicity, but it is dull and now largely forgotten. Hardy's signature in his 1846 text, again second-hand, is dated 1854. However, his copy of Caesar's *De Bello Gallico* (1854) was new, and its condition indicates that he studied part of Book 1 and all of Book 4, doubtless chosen because it included Caesar's first expedition to Britain. This early reading was to flower in a gloriously unhistorical reference to Caesar escaping the glooms of Egdon Heath before the autumnal equinox (*RN* 1.6).

Hardy also had a copy of the newly published Cassell's *Lessons in Latin* (1853), a rigorous teach-yourself primer, which he signed on 6 December that year. (His mother rather than Last is the likely source.) The author, the Reverend J. R. Beard, confessed that he was partly self-taught himself, and he provided much more help than the traditional classroom grammar. Even so, learning Latin from Beard's lessons and exercises alone would have been arduous. At one point he warned his students against Ainsworth's Latin dictionary, 'common at old book-stalls'; nevertheless in 1854 Hardy acquired a ninth edition (1813), which he covered in brown paper with elaborately decorative titling. Although abridged for schools it was quite substantial, with illustrative quotations in the Latin–English section, and he seems never to have replaced it.

A year before leaving school he was given a Latin Testament inscribed 'T. Hardy. A reward for diligence in studies from Mr. Last. Mids[ummer] 1855.' The only passage he marked in the text was John 9: 4, from which he borrowed 'the night cometh' at the end of his 'General Preface to the Novels and Poems' (1912). On the front endpaper (after 1870, to judge by the hand) he wrote the Latin of one of St Paul's more radical statements, Hebrews 12: 27. Angel Clare quotes it in argument with his father (*TDU* 18), and Hardy used it again in the 1922 'Apology' prefaced to *Late Lyrics and Earlier.*

The four years of Latin under Last gave Hardy a useful grounding and may have extended to some reading of verse—Virgil, Horace, or Ovid. Yet he knew no Greek, and set against the curriculum of schools with the traditional classical bias, even his achievement in Latin looks relatively small.

Study at Home

Hardy was not to let his classics lapse, however. Almost immediately he was encouraged to continue by a fellow architectural pupil he met in John *Hicks's Dorchester office in July 1856. Henry *Bastow had done Greek as well as Latin at school, and he readily agreed to begin reading with Hardy. Hicks, who had some classics himself, regarded their arrangement indulgently, and William *Barnes, a fine linguist, could be consulted at his school next door. Hardy began to get up early to study at home—as early as four in the summer. It was a habit he later transferred to the brothers Halborough in the short story 'A Tragedy of Two Ambitions', where Joshua remarks that the mechanical element in translation meant he could do it even when he felt '"too dreary to read a novel"': an illuminating qualification of the cheerful tone of the autobiography at this point. Hardy recalled that early rising got him through some Horace, Ovid, and several books of Virgil's *Aeneid* (*LW* 32). It is likely that during this period he turned to an unusual edition of *Aeneid* 1 (1827), in which the text is preceded by a section that rearranges the Latin to match the word order of an interlineated translation. Hardy's copy of this 'crib' is also of interest because it contains a pencil draft of his own version of the poem's opening in three hexameter lines. (The probable date of the draft is the mid-1860s, though the choice of 'Willers' to render Virgil's 'gods' may be a later revision.) He also made use of a small edition (1838) by J. C. Jahn, where he noted finishing *Aeneid* 2 in 1859. It is the only complete text of Virgil recorded from his library.

No record of a text of Ovid survives, and which one he studied at Bockhampton remains unknown. Indeed, although he had an 1876 prose translation of the *Fasti, Tristia,* and *Pontic Epistles,* Ovid seems never to have engaged him deeply. Horace, however, he would return to; now he began on the *Odes* in an 1855 school edition uniform with his Caesar. His markings, mostly glosses, indicate that he concentrated on Book 1, and the most interesting is one associating his father with the essential innocence evoked in Ode 22, 'Integer vitae'. Later, with some irony, he was to use his own verse translation of the first two lines in the prelude to Angel Clare's wedding-night confession (*TDU* 34; *L* i 282).

Taking up Greek

Within a year or so Hardy began Greek, which meant learning a different script as well as a new language: no easy undertaking, despite Bastow's companionship. He seems to have started with a well-used copy of a progressive series of sentences, Valpy's *Delectus Sententiarum Graecarum* (1832), an old-fashioned classroom text which exhales rather the same cheerless atmosphere as his Eton Latin grammar. He also got Moody's *New Eton Greek Grammar* (1852). It made no concessions to solitary students either, but optimistically Hardy wrote the Greek for 'I shall teach you everything' on the fly-leaf. For a dictionary he seems to have relied on a battered 1832 copy of Donnegan's lexicon, where he dated his bookplate 1858. (His equally battered 1823 copy of *Lemprière's Classical Dictionary* was also bought now, if not earlier.) Donnegan is commemorated not only in the Halboroughs' early study of the Greek Testament, but in one of Hardy's wittiest poems, 'Liddell and Scott', which celebrates the immense labour of the compilers of the lexicon that replaced Donnegan's.

Hardy tackled his first text, Homer's *Iliad*, in a two-volume edition with Latin commentary by Samuel Clarke. First published in 1729, it included a Latin translation at the rear of each volume. His 1818 copy, which he signed in 1858, was already well used, and the markings are not a reliable guide to the extent of his reading. Nevertheless the pencilled note of his two places of study, 'Bockhampton, Dorchester', at the beginning of Book 1, and 'Thomas H.' at the end, indicate he got through that much at least. Book 4 is the most heavily marked in the first volume, but no reader seems to have made much use of the second.

Hardy's assault on Homer was in any case interrupted after little more than a year by an energetic dispute with Bastow about infant baptism. Bastow was reinforced by two sons of the local Baptist minister, both undergraduates who enjoyed an easy command of the Greek original of the New Testament. For a time Hardy abandoned his other classical reading to concentrate on this crucial text, even though it meant learning another dialect—one, moreover, that he had not even mentioned in an early handwritten note pasted into his *Iliad*. He continued to find the Greek dialects frustrating, and his worry that Greek literature had been 'at [their] mercy' (*LW* 96) looks like a case of anxiety transferred.

The baptism dispute, later reflected in *A Laodicean* (1.6–7), seems to have peaked in the summer of 1859. Subsequently the two pupils continued to study the Greek Testament more companionably, and Hardy got a new text, Griesbach's in the 1859 Bohn edition, which he signed in February 1860. Only one marked passage (1 Corinthians 7: 14) bears on the baptism issue; however, 'Bockhampton' pencilled at the beginning of Hebrews suggests early reading. Hebrews frames 'A Tragedy of Two Ambitions', and the Greek quoted at the end of that story ('endured the cross, despising the shame': 12: 2) is underlined in the Griesbach text. Other markings include 'Dynasts—"the mighty"', noted against Luke 1: 52, and the lining of Acts 17: 23, which supplied the unknown god of the last title in *Poems of the Past and the Present*.

With Bastow's departure from Dorchester by the middle of 1860, Hardy had to take his profession more seriously. Nevertheless, now lodging in the town, he read more of his pagan authors: Homer, Horace, and probably Virgil. He acquired a complete text of Horace, a worn copy (*c.*1826) of the 1691 Delphin edition with a Latin paraphrase and commentary. (His library also contained a Delphin Martial of 1701 and a Lucretius of 1680.) One of his signatures, dated 1860, is placed in the first of Horace's *Satires*, just above the source for the title of Chapter 53 in *Far from the Madding Crowd*, 'Concurritur—Horae Momento'.

A list of five passages pencilled inside the cover of the first volume of his *Iliad* may well also date from this period. He marked them off in the text, signing two. An erased cross-reference in the second volume makes it clear that the list came from someone else—quite possibly Horace *Moule, a gifted classical scholar whom he had known for at least three years. Moule was a tutor and mentor he could respect more than Bastow, and it was Moule's advice he followed in terminating a tentative exploration of Greek drama (probably in Paley's 1855 edition of Aeschylus) towards the end of his term with Hicks.

The expiry of Hardy's pupillage also marked the close of his serious study of Greek, which would remain weaker than his Latin. He knew enough to work out a passage that particularly interested him, but henceforth he would rely mainly on translations for fluent reading. The idea floated in the autobiography (*LW* 38) that he might have gone to university and become a classical don seems to be an indulgence of his old age. More realistically, in 1866 (*L* i 7), he had dismissed a similar notion of going to Cambridge to prepare for the Church as impractical and far-fetched.

Homer and Virgil

Three translations of Homer are recorded from Hardy's library: Chapman's *Iliad* (an 1884 copy, scarcely marked); Pope's *Iliad* and *Odyssey*; and an *Iliad* in literal prose. No text of the *Odyssey* is recorded, though he may well have had one. Occasionally he noted translations of Homer amongst his reading (for example, in 1887: *LW* 212), but there is no doubt that he felt a greater affinity with Virgil as well as being more at home in Latin. Allusions to Virgil throughout his work easily outnumber those to Homer, and range from *Desperate Remedies* (1871), where the *Aeneid* is used ingeniously as a hidden key to the mother-son bond between Cytherea Aldclyffe and Aeneas Manston, to an evocation of the Virgilian underworld in the poem 'To My Father's Violin' (1916).

The *Aeneid* was the mainspring of Virgil's attraction for Hardy; he showed much less interest in the rural *Eclogues* and *Georgics*. All his life he relished a good story, and Virgil's epic provided several, tinged with a distinctive pathos. He preferred the first half (Aeneas' wanderings) to the second (the fighting in Italy): Books 1, 4, and 6 were his favourites, centred respectively on Aeneas' arrival in Carthage, his affair with Dido, and his visit to the underworld. These preferences are evident both in his allusions and in the pattern of markings in his translations. The pocket Dryden given him by his mother is by far the most heavily marked, and furnishes a record of his early reading. He also had a larger edition of Dryden's version (1819), where the few notes include parallels with English poets, and a prose version by Lonsdale and Lee (1894), which clearly disappointed him. The only line he marked in all three versions, adding the Latin in two, was 'Fate, and the dooming gods, are deaf to tears' (Dryden's free rendering of *Aeneid* 6.376). One of his earliest poems, 'Hap' (1866), presents 'crass Casualty' and 'dicing Time' as 'purblind Doomsters'; much later Virgil's line became an emblem of the profound disillusion induced in him by the Great War (*LW* 398), and he added it as a second epigraph to *The Dynasts*, apparently for the limited edition of 1927.

Classics and Social Class

In the autobiography Hardy wanted to show that his schooling had been quite respectable, yet not of a quality that detracted from his own efforts afterwards. This delicate balance (which he managed skilfully) was an important part of the process of blurring his social origins, for education, particularly a classical education, could be a class marker. His sensitivity on this subject was expressed as early as *A Pair of Blue Eyes* (1872), partly in the friendship between Smith and Knight, where the element of patronage reflects his experience with Horace Moule. But it is more sharply focused in the satirical portrait of Parson Swancourt, who has a propensity for dropping isolated Latin tags as a sign of his social status. Initially he welcomes Smith as an equal, delighted to find someone who 'is gentleman and scholar enough to continue a quotation' (from the last of Horace's *Epodes: PBE* 7). However, as Smith's eccentric pronunciation reveals, his classics are based on four years' postal tutoring from Knight at Oxford, and when Swancourt discovers that he is no 'gentleman' after all, he dismisses the young man's ability to play the quotation game as spurious, simultaneously declaring that he himself hasn't looked at a classical text for eighteen years (9).

Hardy was not entirely free from a similar tendency to flourish his learning. Particularly when he was trying to establish himself as a writer of fiction, he was quite capable of introducing classical allusions casually or awkwardly, as if to display his social and cultural credentials. He was ready to make use of short cuts, too: for instance, in 1864 he bought C. T. Ramage's *Beautiful Thoughts from Latin Authors*, published that year, which he marked quite heavily and used as a quarry.

The classical grind is a prerequisite for the Halboroughs' social rise through the Church—a small but vital component in the story of their soured ambitions, written in 1888. In the same year Hardy noted, rather fiercely, an idea for another story about a young man's unsuccessful struggles to go to Oxford (*LW* 216), which ultimately found shape in *Jude the Obscure*. The novel develops a distinctive vein of social protest, and a good deal of its power derives from the resonances of Jude's solitary efforts to master the classics, Hardy's surviving texts reinforce a belief that here more than anywhere else he drew on aspects of his own experience: the Latin grammar that blasts Jude's expectation of an easy system for changing one language into another might have been the Eton grammar; his early reading is selected from Caesar, Virgil, and Horace (though he relies entirely on old Delphin editions, covering up the Latin paraphrases); he uses Clarke's *Iliad*, and has read the five passages listed in Hardy's copy; he restricts himself for a while to the Greek Testament in Griesbach's text and gets a better edition; like the youthful Hardy (*LW* 32) he talks to himself in Latin on lonely walks; he is troubled by the Greek dialects, feels inadequate with the Greek of the dramatists, and is generally more secure in Latin.

Jude's progress, wholly dependent on 'unanticipative, clumsy books' (2.6), is harder won than Hardy's was. But Hardy had done quite enough isolated study to know the self-discipline required to keep going through the inevitable confusions and drudgery (an experience that prepared him well for the demands of writing as a profession). Equally he knew the peculiar rewards of 'digging out the thoughts of these minds so remote yet so near' (*JO* 1.5) from times innocent of Christian tradition.

Reading in London, 1862–7

The five years spent working as an architectural assistant in London brought Hardy's first serious immersion in English poetry and the beginnings of his own work as a poet. However, he also read more Latin poetry: he had returned to Horace by 1865 (*LW* 51, 53), and a few notes he took from Lucretius' *De Rerum Natura* can be dated to 1866.

Whether or not he had acquired his Delphin text of Lucretius, he relied mainly on a Bohn prose translation (1851). Lucretius, concerned to free people from their fear of death and the supernatural, expounded a materialist view of the world based on atomic theory. Hardy was struck by the parallels with contemporary science, noting 'Survival of the Fittest' against the hypothesis (in Book 5) that many creatures must have perished because they were ill-adapted to life. Overall he was impressed by the extraordinary physicality of Lucretius' imagination, and he was later to describe him as 'that glorious Double-man—poet & scientist' (*L* ii 143). The teasing epigraph on the title-page of *The Hand of Ethelberta*, 'Vitae post-scenia celant', is a rare borrowing, though it may have been taken from Ramage's anthology, where it is heavily marked. 'Men conceal the back-scenes of their life' was Ramage's translation.

Unlike Lucretius, Horace presented himself and his experience as distinctly individual. Hardy was clearly drawn to his balance, resilience, and distaste for city life, and the way that his acceptance of transience and death was moderated by a belief in the survival of his poetry. Returning to him now in London, Hardy relied on the Delphin text and Christopher Smart's 1756 prose translation, revised and reissued in the Bohn series. His markings are most frequent in the *Odes* and *Ars Poetica*, and sometimes he added the Latin or his own version to the translation. The didactic *Ars Poetica* was to have some influence on his practice, and he quoted from it in 'The Profitable Reading of Fiction' and the autobiography (*LW* 51). Yet his familiarity with Horace is evident in echoes scattered right through his published writings, notes, and letters, down to 'A Private Man on Public Men' in *Winter Words*. The earliest borrowing, a verse translation of three lines from *Odes* 4.13 in *Desperate Remedies* (12), he tentatively attributed to Congreve when he pencilled it in his Delphin text. A phrase from *Epistles* 1.12 that particularly arrested him, 'rerum concordia discors', was to emerge in the After Scene of *The Dynasts*, first as 'the droning tune of Things' and then, after 1920, as 'the chordless chime of Things'.

In the mid-1860s Hardy also read *The Thoughts of the Emperor Marcus Aurelius Antoninus* in George Long's 1862 translation—a New Year gift from Horace Moule in 1865. The number of his markings indicates that he was impressed, particularly by Aurelius' self-questioning and disciplined concentration on moral action in the present. Moule's inscription included a quotation from Book 8: 'This is the chief thing: Be not perturbed: for all things are according to the nature of the universal.' Although that may seem close to fatalism, Aurelius was a Stoic and believed in a universe governed by reason; everything that happened conduced to the good of the whole, even if individual components seemed to suffer in the process. It was a faith that Hardy found increasingly difficult to share, and there is a poignant irony in his choosing this book to contain Moule's funeral card after his suicide in 1873. His later references to Moule's quotation, in *A Laodicean* (4.1), *Tess* (39), and a note from New Year's Eve 1885 (*LW* 183), have their share of irony too, as has the epigraph to Part Fifth of *Jude*, taken from Book 11.

A flirtation with verse drama may have led Hardy to look at Aristotle's *Poetics* shortly before he left London. His Bohn translation (1850) shows him interested in broad principles rather than illustrative examples: for instance, he picked out Aristotle's preference for the universal truths of poetry over the particular truths of history, and his emphasis on the central importance of plot in tragedy. Ideas like these helped to shape Hardy's own practice as a writer, and the presence of Aristotle can particularly be felt in his essay 'The Profitable Reading of Fiction', not only in the direct invocation of Greek drama to praise the 'constructive art' of Richardson, but in phrases like 'the well-knit interdependence of parts' or 'less the transcript than the similitude of material fact'. Much the same point ('no question of bare "imitation"/p.122') is noted inside his presentation copy of S. H. Butcher's edition of the *Poetics* (1902). There, though he left the text and translation clean, he marked a few passages in the accompanying essays, including two bearing on Aristotle's preference for 'the true tragic ending'. It was a requirement he had fulfilled more than once, and his 1912 Preface to *Jude* directly invokes the Aristotelian concept of catharsis in its defence.

Greek Tragedy

The years following Hardy's return to Dorchester in July 1867 were divided between architectural work and building his career as a writer. The *Aeneid*, 'of which he never wearied' (*LW* 61), is the only classical reading he recorded (and that was in 1868). By January 1876, however, he had completed six novels and could afford some leisure. One result was the opening of a new literary notebook, where, between April and June 1876, he made four entries about Prometheus from the Bohn translation of Aeschylus (*LN* i, 280, 281, 297). These brief notes mark the revival of his interest in Greek tragedy, dormant since 1861–2, and foreshadow its penetration of his fiction. Prometheus was to be a potent figure in his next novel, *The Return of the Native*, both in terms of 'Promethean rebelliousness' and the fire imagery which characterizes Eustacia Vye and her unsatisfied passions.

Hardy had new copies of the Bohn Aeschylus and Sophocles. Both now lack title-pages, but bound-in advertisements date their issue between 1873 and 1878. His two-volume Bohn Euripides (1850; 1867) and a complete text of Greek drama, Dindorf's *Poetici Scenici Graeci* (1841), were second-hand, and so acquisition dates are less certain. Yet, besides showing that he marked translations much more than texts, these books can be seen to endorse what his own writing suggests: his sustained reading of Greek tragedy began in 1876. For Aeschylus' text he relied mainly on Paley's edition, mentioned earlier, and the plays most heavily marked there and in the Bohn translation are *Agamemnon* and *Prometheus Vinctus*. The Bohn version of the latter supplied his most notorious Aeschylean borrowing, 'the President of the Immortals' at the end of *Tess*, and the phrase is noted in both his texts (in Dindorf as 'best translation'). In the play it refers to Zeus, characterized as a brutal oppressor, and it is clear that Prometheus' outrage, defiance, and loyalty to humankind powerfully engaged Hardy's sympathies.

The first chorus in *Agamemnon* is the source of the words that haunt Jude after the death of his children ('Things are as they are, and will be brought to their destined issue': *JO* 6.2), and Hardy quoted the refrain ('Chant Aelinon, Aelinon! but may the good prevail') in both 'Candour in English Fiction' and a late poem, 'Compassion'. A suggestion in the next chorus that the beacon which signals the fall of Troy might be 'some delusion of the gods' drew an unusual cluster of markings from Hardy, and he expanded its meaning in the After Scene of *The Dynasts*. The character and motivation of Clytaemnestra (who kills her husband towards the end of the play) particularly fascinated him, and her presence colours a note of August 1889, when he was working on *Tess* (*LW* 231), as well as another late poem, 'On the Portrait of a Woman about to be Hanged'.

The bold simplicity of Aeschylus' imagery was very much to Hardy's taste, as was the grand scale of his imagination, which has an analogue in the design of *The Dynasts*. Aeschylus was persistently concerned with the interpenetration of divine and human and their moral relationship, and his sense of forces beyond human control was deeply congenial. So too was his attempt to understand them and give some account of the human condition that recognized its painful incongruities but avoided despair.

Like his Aeschylus, Hardy's Bohn Sophocles indicates that he read all seven of the surviving plays. However, he was most interested by the three 'Theban' plays and *Trachiniae*. For the latter he used a school text (1877), edited and presented by his friend Alfred Pretor. Although he was held by the whole action, it was Hyllus' final speech condemning the injustice and callousness of the gods that really bit into his mind. Uniquely, he copied the Greek onto a slip of paper and inserted it beside the Bohn version, which he altered to universalize the protest. His intention to transform it into a 'lyric', noted in 1897 (*LW* 303), seems to have been satisfied by attributing its essence to the Spirit of the Pities after Nelson's death (*D* 1.5).

Hardy was looking at Jebb's edition of *Oedipus Tyrannus* in the British Museum in July 1889 (*LW* 230), and later got his own copy (1893). It is the only example of a full-dress scholarly edition of a single Greek play recorded from his library, and it testifies to a deeper engagement than is suggested by the markings in his Bohn translation, which were probably made earlier. In the first part of the action he was exercised by the problem of knowledge: the terrible discrepancy between Oedipus, ignorant of his past, and the seer Teiresias, who knows that *his* knowledge of that past is too terrible to share. 'Alas, how dreadful to have wisdom where it profits not the wise!', Teiresias exclaims. This is Jebb's version of lines 316–17; Hardy double-lined it, adding a cross-reference to Gray's 'Ode on a Distant Prospect of Eton College'. It was a particularly sharp expression of his belief that human consciousness had evolved in severe disproportion to human suffering, and is to be associated with his marking of the Chorus' reaction later on to the appalling disclosures about their king: 'For where, where is the man that achieves more of happiness, than barely so much as to fancy he has it, and so fancying to fall away from it?' (Bohn version of lines 1189–92).

For *Oedipus Coloneus* Hardy had no separate edition, and the fairly sparse markings in his Bohn version suggest that he was less interested in the action than in Oedipus' view of himself and the reflections he utters or generates. The most pregnant passage occurs when the Chorus of old men reflect on the pains inseparable from life. Hardy put a marginal line against most of it and underscored their pivotal judgement—'Not to have been born at all is superior to every view of the question'. Probably in 1895, he drafted a sonnet version which he left unpublished ('Thoughts from Sophocles'), and Oedipus seems to have become an icon of the despair and alienation which afflicted him in the 1890s (see Jeremy Steele, 'Thoughts from Sophocles', in *The Poetry of Thomas Hardy*, ed. Pat Clements and Juliet Grindle (1980)).

Antigone moves towards the tragedy of Creon rather than Antigone herself, and Hardy's numerous markings, scattered through the Bohn version, reflect this. Yet it was Antigone who took root in his imagination. One of two passages he distinguished from her death lament—'O, woe is me! who am neither a dweller among men nor shades, the living nor the dead'—is remembered by Jude as he drifts through Christminster with Arabella, mortally chilled by his last journey to see Sue (*JO* 6.9). The other passage—'What ally can I invoke, since at least by observing piety, I have obtained the reward of impiety?'—appears transposed to a different key in the final paragraph of the story 'For Conscience' Sake', first published in 1891. However, the analogy drawn there between the fates of Antigone and Millborne was not part of Hardy's original conception, nor was anything like it. A quotation from Euripides' *Hippolytus* was introduced, rather clumsily, by a marginal insertion in the manuscript, only to be replaced in the magazine proofs by the *Antigone* reference, which follows the curve of the story more faithfully.

Describing Little Hintock in *The Woodlanders*, Hardy contended that such isolated communities produce 'dramas of a grandeur and unity truly Sophoclean' because of 'the concentrated passions and closely-knit interdependence of the lives therein' (*W* 1). In the 'General Preface' of 1912 he unashamedly returned to the comparison, pointing to 'our magnificent heritage' of Greek drama to justify the self-imposed constraints of his Wessex. Earlier, while working on *The Return of the Native*, he had made a note of tragedy arising 'from the gradual closing in of a situation' (*LW* 123)—a manœuvre Sophocles could execute with unsurpassed remorselessness. The rigour of Sophoclean design also gave a keener edge to his more pessimistic preoccupations. For, unlike Aeschylus, Sophocles did not attempt to explain suffering in terms of a governing order, but presented it as a condition of life to be endured. In this sense the outlook of Elizabeth-Jane expressed in the closing lines of *The Mayor of Casterbridge* remains peculiarly Sophoclean.

Although Hardy read most of Euripides (only three of the nineteen plays in his two Bohn volumes are unmarked), there are very few traces of that reading in his work. In dramas that tend to be loosely structured anyway, a rhetorical talent frequently tempted Euripides to elaborate a speech or scene at the expense of the whole. Consequently many of the passages Hardy marked are detachable thoughts or commonplaces: 'But the tearless dead forgets troubles' is a typical example from *Troades*, and where it is echoed on the next page Hardy added a parallel from *Hamlet*. The two plays he most admired are both exceptionally taut designs. Above Dindorf's text of *Bacchae* he initialled his opinion that this was 'The *best* of Euripides'; a similar note praises the second chorus, and here he evidently turned to the Greek unusually often. The second play, *Hippolytus*, which is the most heavily marked in translation, sets the acceptance of sexuality (Aphrodite) against its rejection or sublimation (Artemis)—an opposition which runs right through Hardy's own work. It is neatly caught in the description of Grace Melbury as having 'more of Artemis than of Aphrodite in her constitution' (*W* 42), and is perhaps most keenly felt in *The Well-Beloved*. A third play, *Andromache*, which is energized by the jealousy between two 'wives', prompted Hardy to pencil a marginal running summary of the action. Unique in his set of Bohn translations, it may be associated with his 1902 note of an idea for a bigamous plot (*PN* 29), which ends with a reference to the play.

In the first Bohn volume Hardy recorded his dissent from *Swinburne's opinion that Euripides ran a poor third to Aeschylus and Sophocles. Essentially, however, Euripides provided a supplement to what Hardy found in the two older tragedians, and affected him less distinctly.

Later Reading

Hardy's later reading certainly included an 1887 Bohn Catullus, probably linked to his Italian journey that spring, which produced one imitation ('Catullus: XXXI'). But neither this nor Myers' translation of Pindar (1895) had the impact of Wharton's elegant edition of the slender remains of Sappho, which he bought in 1895. 'How I love her', he wrote to Florence *Henniker soon afterwards (*L* ii 84), and shortly he was introducing quotations from Sappho into the texts of *Jude the Obscure* (epigraph to Part Third) and *The Well-Beloved* (1.2, 2.6). He opened his first collection of verse with Sapphic stanzas ('The Temporary the All'), and included 'Sapphic Fragment' in his next.

He also seems to have come late to the Greek Anthology. Five selections of translations into English verse, presented or acquired between 1889 and 1925, are of much less importance than Mackail's *Select Epigrams*... (1911), a scholarly edition with Greek text and prose translations, inscribed for him in 1917. Here he marked twenty poems, including the sources for his 'Epitaph on a Pessimist' (Anon.) and 'The Bad Example' (Meleager). A fragment of Mackail's translation, 'O my heart, leave the rest alone', underlined in Agathias' Greek, supplied the opening line of his valedictory poem 'He Resolves to Say No More', where at first he only changed 'alone' to 'unknown'.

Throughout his life Hardy's study of Greek and Latin literature was supplemented by classical elements in his wider reading (partly recorded in his surviving notebooks). And though the sum of evidence is necessarily incomplete, it is clear that the imagined worlds of Greece and Rome claimed an abiding place in his mind. On the half-title of his early Griesbach New Testament he had pencilled the Greek for 'and the truth shall make you free' (John 8: 32). It is a promise he was to echo ironically in the bleak close to his final volume, *Winter Words*. By then the pagan ancient world had shown him other versions of the truth.

Sources

The above account is based on an examination of the most significant classical texts and translations Hardy is known to have possessed. The majority of these are now held by Frederick B. Adams, Colby College, DCM, and Yale University (Purdy Collection). W. R. Rutland was able to survey the Max Gate library before its dispersal, and Chapter 2 in his *Thomas Hardy: A Study of His Writings and Their Background* (1938) gives a selective account of Hardy's classical reading informed by the books therein. While unreliable in detail, it provides a record of an irrecoverable opportunity. JVS

Clodd, Edward (1840–1930), banker, rationalist, and writer on popular science and anthropology. Originally intended for the Baptist ministry, he went into business and was for more than forty years Secretary of the London Joint Stock Bank (1872–1915). He was President (1895–6) of the Folk-Lore Society and co-founder of the Omar Khayyám Club, of which Hardy became a member. In 1881 he was elected to the Savile Club, of which Hardy had been a member since 1878. In 1906 Clodd became Chairman of the Rationalist Press Association, and is portrayed (as 'Edwin Dodd') in H. G. *Wells's novel *Boon* (1915).

Like Hardy, his exact contemporary, Clodd was largely self-educated and became an agnostic with wide-ranging intellectual interests. The two met in about 1891, and a close friendship, based on congeniality of outlook, soon developed. Thereafter they were often in each other's company and exchanged many letters, Hardy's correspondence with Clodd being notable for its relative candour and openness. As well as personal and literary matters, their letters touch on folklore, anthropology, comparative religion, spiritualism, and other topics. According to Millgate, Hardy gradually became 'more intimate with [Clodd]... than with any other of his male companions, always excepting his brother Henry' (462).

A sociable man and a generous host, Clodd welcomed a stream of friends to his house on the Suffolk coast (Strafford House, *Aldeburgh, enlarged from the cottage that had been his parents' home), and on visits there (the first in June 1891) Hardy encountered among his fellow-guests Grant *Allen, William *Archer, James *Barrie, James Frazer (author of *The Golden Bough*), Edward Whymper the mountaineer (who described to Hardy his ascent of the Matterhorn), and many others. In turn, Clodd was a visitor to Max Gate, and there were other meetings in London. In September 1905 Hardy visited Aldeburgh to take part in celebrations to mark the 150th anniversary of the birth of George Crabbe, whose realism he greatly admired.

Clodd was a confidant of both Hardy and Florence Dugdale (later Florence Hardy) in the early stages of their relationship. During a visit to Aldeburgh in early July 1909, Hardy seems to have told him both of his marital problems and of his interest in the young Florence; later in the same month, at Hardy's request, Clodd accompanied Florence to a performance of the opera *Tess* in London at which Hardy was also present. Soon afterwards, in mid-August, Clodd invited them both to Aldeburgh. During this visit Clodd, Hardy, and Florence were out boating on the River Alde, found themselves stuck on a mudbank, and had to be rescued; the incident was reported by the local press, and Hardy showed some anxiety lest it get into the national newspapers. Other, less eventful—or at least less well-publicized—visits followed in 1911 and 1912.

Clodd's autobiographical volume *Memories* (1916) contains discreet references to Hardy.

clubs. Hardy was a member of two leading London clubs. He was elected to the Savile Club in June 1878 and to the Athenaeum in April 1891 (he had asked Lord Carnarvon to propose him for the latter in July 1888), and made frequent use of both during periods spent in London. Of the Savile, where Hardy often met his close friend Edmund *Gosse, 'it was at one time said that to become a member you had either to be an atheist or to have written a book' (Tom Girtin, *The Abominable Clubman* (1964), 152), while the membership of the Athenaeum has traditionally been literary, academic, and ecclesiastical. For Hardy's association with the Rabelais Club, a dining-club founded in 1879, see Walter *Besant. Hardy was also a founder-member of the Omar Khayyám Club, a dining-club co-founded in 1892 by his friend Edward *Clodd: for Hardy's attendance at a notable dinner given by the club, see George *Meredith. Nearer home, he belonged from about 1880 to the Dorset Natural History and Antiquarian Field Club, to which he delivered in 1884 a paper on 'Some Romano-British Relics Found at Max Gate, Dorchester' (see ARCHAEOLOGY).

Cockerell, Sydney (1867–1962), museum director and bibliophile. He became a confidant of Hardy's in the writer's later years, and afterwards one of his literary executors. He had worked as secretary to the Kelmscott Press (1891–6), and became Director of the Fitzwilliam Museum, Cambridge (1908–37). In the latter capacity he wrote to Hardy in 1911 requesting the gift of manuscripts for the Museum; on 29 September he visited Max Gate and was successful in persuading Hardy to allow him to distribute such of his literary *manuscripts as were then in his possession among various institutions, largely according to Cockerell's own judgement (*LW* 384). Letters from Cockerell to Hardy written in September and October 1911 (now in DCM) indicate that he submitted for Hardy's approval a scheme for the allocation.

Cockerell became an intimate friend of both Thomas and Florence Hardy, was frequently at Max Gate during Hardy's later years, gained a considerable degree of control over Hardy's literary affairs, and exchanged many letters with Hardy and Florence. On 11 February 1914, for instance, Hardy wrote to Cockerell justifying his decision to remarry (*L* v 9). He was privy to the composition of the *autobiography that was later passed off as Florence's biography of her husband, and which she reported to Cockerell in August 1922 as 'finished, so far as is possible'. He also assisted in seeing *Late Lyrics and Earlier* and *Human Shows* through the press.

In 1916 Hardy appointed Cockerell his literary executor, with Florence Hardy as co-executor. Cockerell was later reported as saying that immediately after Hardy's death he 'spent a whole morning' destroying Hardy's notebooks. With Sir James *Barrie he was instrumental in arranging Hardy's funeral in Westminster Abbey and supervised arrangements for the cremation. Before long he and Florence Hardy had quarrelled violently over their duties as executors. Cockerell's attempts to gain control of Hardy's manuscripts and literary estate, and his insistence on burial in the Abbey despite Hardy's own wishes and those of his family, have laid him open to criticism: Robert Gittings, for example, refers to him as 'tireless and shameless' and to his 'powerful and insinuating personality' (*The Older Hardy*, 143). He was knighted in 1934. Cockerell's unpublished diaries (British Library), covering a great span of years, contain references to Hardy. For Cockerell's role in the dispersal of the Max Gate library, see LIBRARY, HARDY'S.

Michael Millgate, *Testamentary Acts: Browning, Tennyson, James, Hardy* (1992).

collected editions. When in 1890 Hardy began negotiating with Clarence McIlvaine of the publishers *Osgood, McIlvaine for the publication of a collected edition of his work, it marked an epoch for him. The dignity of a collected edition—'Thomas Hardy's Works'—would mean that there could no longer be any question of whether he had arrived as a novelist. Hardy's current publishers, *Sampson Low, had been for a while issuing such novels as they controlled in uniform bindings, but the prospect of a deliberately constructed and complete edition fired

Hardy's imagination afresh. Though he was dealing at the same time with the serialization and publication of *Jude the Obscure*, between 1894 and 1896 he reread each of his novels and his three collections of short stories, and made substantial revisions to all of them, as well as adding to each a preface, sometimes of considerable importance. Of particular significance to him was the opportunity to re-envisage his early novels as part of the fully matured conception of *Wessex that had emerged only towards the end of writing *Tess of the d'Urbervilles*. Wessex was in this collected edition for the first time explicitly defined by the author, since Hardy appended to each volume a map of the district, the outlines those of south-western England, the names mostly those of the fictional Wessex.

Hardy more or less substantially revised the environment of each novel in order to bring it into the Wessex scheme of things, an act which sometimes obliterated significant details, as in *The Return of the Native* or *The Trumpet-Major*; and to put, as it were, his final copyright-mark on the region, the series was identified on the half-title page of each volume as 'The Wessex Novels'. It would be misleading, though, to imply that topographical revision was Hardy's only concern in this edition; the changed social climate, for instance, allowed him to use more candour in describing the sexual relations of his characters; he took the opportunity to rethink the dialect of rural speakers; and he made many local adjustments to the imagery and rhythm of his prose. It is a matter for debate whether he altered any of his works of fiction in sufficiently fundamental ways that one might be justified in thinking of them as new works, but it is certainly true that, say, *Under the Greenwood Tree* of 1896 was a substantially different novel from that which Hardy had published in 1872.

The Osgood, McIlvaine edition was handsomely produced, in dark-green cloth with gold blocking and an elegant 'TH' monogram on the front cover, surrounded with swirling water-lilies. The type was quite small, but the paper of excellent quality and a pleasant colour. The publishers commissioned H. Macbeth Raeburn to produce drawings of places prominently featured in each volume, and splendid engravings accompany each novel, with the authenticating note 'drawn on the spot'—tying Wessex still more closely to observable reality.

The first editions of *Jude the Obscure*, *The Well-Beloved*, *Wessex Poems*, and *Poems of the Past and the Present* were issued in the same format (though *Harper & Brothers had taken over Osgood, McIlvaine in 1898), and when Hardy's final collection of short stories, *A Changed Man*, was published in 1913 it was also, for the sake of completeness, brought out in this livery by *Macmillan, who had become exclusively Hardy's publisher in 1902.

In that year Macmillan began to reissue the 'Wessex Novels' in a different binding, without engravings, as the Uniform Edition; Hardy made a few revisions for this re-impression, including some of significance in *Tess* and *Far from the Madding Crowd*. In 1906 the same plates were used for another publishing enterprise, Macmillan's thin-paper Pocket Edition. However, in 1912 there began appearing the first volumes of a quite new collected edition. Originally it had been intended to be a limited *édition de luxe*, but those plans were shelved. Again Hardy reread all of his work, and revised it, though not as extensively as he had in the 1890s: Hardy's care for his texts and his stamina into his seventies are remarkable. The revisions for the Wessex Edition (as it was called) follow for the most part the same pattern as those for the Osgood, McIlvaine edition, though his self-image as recorder of vanished or vanishing Wessex evidently weighed even more heavily upon him. Instead of engravings, there were photographs taken by Hardy's friend Hermann *Lea, and there was an improved map of Wessex. The major innovation was the division of his fiction into three categories: novels of character and environment, romances and fantasies, and novels of ingenuity.

The edition was a somewhat less satisfactory production than Osgood, McIlvaine's; though the page and the type were larger, the paper, except at the heaviest weights, had considerable show-through, the photographs were on the whole dull, and the smooth maroon binding was prone to discoloration. Nevertheless, Hardy considered it the authoritative edition, and from time to time during the remainder of his life attempted (unsuccessfully) to ensure that all forms in which his work was sold embodied these texts. In this respect he was particularly unsuccessful with his poetic texts, because there occurred a decisive textual split between the separate collected edition of his poems, first published in 1919 and expanded (and revised) thereafter as Hardy published new collections, and the Wessex Edition volumes containing verse (also revised). He was never able to reconcile the two textual traditions, and an inspection of Samuel Hynes's critical edition of Hardy's poetry reveals the extent of the variations.

The planned de luxe edition appeared in two instalments, both of 500 copies. The first, in America, was Harper's Autograph Edition of 1915, essentially using the plates of the English Wessex Edition (save for the works copyright in America); each copy of *Tess of the d'Urbervilles* had a leaf signed by Hardy (five years later this edition was published in unlimited form as the Anniversary Edition). The second, in 1919–20, was Macmillan's Mellstock Edition, entirely reset, printed on watermarked paper, bound in blue, but only very slightly revised by Hardy; the first volume of *Tess* was also signed by the author.

Hardy's stories were published in one collected volume in 1928, two months after his death. There were no revisions. With the exception of this last, all the unlimited English editions were kept in print by Macmillan until the 1970s, when (in anticipation of the expiry of their copyright in 1978) they issued the New Wessex Edition, with its essentially flawed texts. See also TEXTUAL STUDIES.

SJG

Collins, Wilkie (1824–89), novelist. A leading exponent of 'sensation' fiction, his intricately constructed novels of melodrama, mystery, and suspense are widely assumed to have influenced Hardy's early fiction. In 1869, George *Meredith, having read Hardy's first novel, *The Poor Man and the Lady*, in manuscript, advised him to write a novel 'with a more complicated plot', whereupon Hardy 'set about constructing the eminently "sensational" plot of *Desperate Remedies*' (*LW* 64). The latter shares with *The Woman in White* (1860), Collins's most famous work, a villain of illegitimate birth, a woman with a mysterious past, and a woman masquerading as another. Also, as F. B. Pinion has pointed out (*Thomas Hardy: Art and Thought* (1977), 1–9), resemblances may be found between *Desperate Remedies* and Collins's earlier *Basil* (1852), in which the very phrase, a 'desperate remedy', occurs more than once: the villains in these two novels have similar names (Manston and Mannion) and physical appearances, and are alike accorded Satanic powers.

Although the extent of Collins's influence is hard to assess, the sensation genre doubtless intrigued Hardy, and as late as 1888 he was still exploring the possibility of a novel 'in which the sensationalism is ... not physical but psychical' (*LW* 213). Indeed, from this perspective, one can claim, as Richard H. Taylor has done, that 'every one of [Hardy's] novels is a sensation novel' (*The Neglected Hardy: Thomas Hardy's Lesser Novels* (1982), 13).

Upon Collins's death, Harry Quilter, the editor of the *Universal Review*, started a campaign for a memorial in Westminster Abbey or St Paul's. Hardy was on the committee, and when the plan did not materialize, he expressed surprise in a letter to Quilter (13 March 1890), and agreed to his proposal, which was later acted upon, to use the money that had been raised in order to 'purchase a library of fiction for the People's Palace' in the East End of London (*L* i 210).

TS

'Committee-Man of "the Terror", A.' This short story was first published in the 1896 Christmas Number of *the Illustrated London News* and collected in *A Changed Man and Other Tales*. Though dated 1895 by Hardy, it seems not to have been completed until the following year (*L* ii 101, 126, 129). His source was *The Journal of Mary Frampton* (1885), where the original incident takes place in London rather than Wessex (F. B. Pinion, *A Hardy Dictionary* (1989), 63). Purdy (155) gives details of the working notes included in Hardy's manuscript.

A historical tale set 'at the time of our brief peace with France in 1802–3', it concerns two French exiles who meet by chance in *Weymouth, then enjoying its heyday as a fashionable resort favoured by George III. A young governess, herself living in exile, is horrified to recognize a man who, as a member of the 'Committee of Public Safety' (active from

1792), has condemned members of her family to the guillotine. Despite this inauspicious beginning, a relationship develops between them, he proposes marriage and emigration together to Quebec, and at last she agrees. As in 'The Fiddler of the Reels', the situation is one in which a mysterious and almost morbid sexual attraction, apparently based on masculine domination, overrides all other considerations: 'Contrary to all reason and sense of family honour she was, by some abnormal craving, inclining to a tenderness for him that was founded on its opposite.' At the last moment she runs away, then returns only to find that he too has had second thoughts and left her. The story is introduced by a description of the narrative situation in which 'The writer, quite a youth' has heard the tale from an old woman of 80 who has in turn learned it from her mother, an acquaintance of the Frenchwoman. Though the story also apparently exists in written form, this narrative setting qualifies it as oral history and is typical of Hardy's fondness for establishing links with the historical past through individual human experience.

Comte, Auguste (1798–1857), French philosopher known as the founder of *Positivism. Hardy read Comte's *Positive Philosophy* in 1870 (*LW* 79), and studied both Comte and other Positivists so widely before the writing of *Far from the Madding Crowd* that his vocabulary had acquired Positivist overtones to an extent that made reviewers attribute the novel to George *Eliot (*LW* 100). Hardy also owned a copy of Comte's *A General View of Positivism* (1865), a gift from Horace *Moule. In 1876 he entered into his *Literary Notebooks* numerous excerpts from Comte's *Social Dynamics, or the General Theory of Human Progress* (*LN* i 64–80), and in 1880 excerpts from *Theory of the Future of Man* (*LN* i 133).

Hardy seems to have read Comte to find secular moral and ethical alternatives to Christianity: if, he speculated, Comte had introduced Christ into his system of thought, Positivism would have become 'tolerable to thousands who... now decry what in their heart of hearts they hold to contain the germs of a true system' (*LW* 150–1).

In addition to Positivism's 'Religion of Humanity', Hardy was also attracted by Comte's anti-rationalist view of human nature, which was similar to the affective psychology he had earlier been drawn to in the Utopian Socialist Charles Fourier (*LN* i 239–41). Late in his novel-writing career Hardy also found Comte's 'dynamic' historical perspective on human psychology useful, especially Comte's analysis of the 'Theological stage', with its three subdivisions, fetichistic, polytheistic, monotheistic (*LN* i 69–74), a terminology Hardy applied in describing Tess's singing—'And probably the half-unconscious rhapsody was a Fetichistic utterance in a Monotheistic setting' (*TDU* 16)—and in defining the milkmaids' lives as 'essentially polytheistic' (in the *Graphic* serial version; see *LN* i 316). LAB

Lennart A. Björk, *Psychological Vision and Social Criticism in the Novels of Thomas Hardy* (1987).

Cornwall. In 1869 Hardy was still having to earn his living as an architect, although his ambition was to become a writer. His previous employer, John *Hicks of Dorchester, had died, and he was working for the Weymouth architect G. R. *Crickmay, who had taken over some of Hicks's work. A job that Hicks had agreed to do was the rebuilding of the church of St Juliot, near Boscastle in Cornwall, and in February 1870 Crickmay asked Hardy to travel to Cornwall to draw up plans. Hardy was finishing off *Desperate Remedies* at the time, but, after first refusing, he agreed to go.

Early on the morning of 7 March he set out on what he later described as a 'journey of seeming unimportance... yet it turned out to have life-long consequences for him' (*LW* 67). The major consequence was that he met at St Juliot the woman he was to marry, Emma Lavinia Gifford (see HARDY, EMMA LAVINIA). Emma was the daughter of a solicitor, and had been born and brought up in Plymouth. The Giffords were a snobbish middle-class family with an alcoholic father, and their way of life depended upon the money of the grandmother. On her death in 1860 they were forced to leave Plymouth and settle in Kirland in Cornwall, not far from St Austell. It was a lonely place, and Emma missed the social life of Plymouth. In 1867 her sister Helen married the Reverend Caddell Holder, Rector of St Juliot, a small, even lonelier parish a mile or so outside Boscastle, and Emma went with her to keep her company and help in any way she could.

On Emma's death in 1912 Hardy found that two years previously she had written down her memories of her early life in Plymouth and of her meeting with him. Her little book was written on ordinary exercise-paper and then bound up in brown paper. Emma gave it the title *Some Recollections*, and it was found by Hardy among her possessions shortly after her death on 27 November 1912. On reading it he was so moved that he prepared it for publication, but it was not until 1961 that it was published under the editorship of Evelyn Hardy and Robert Gittings (Evelyn Hardy's transcription includes a number of errors, corrected in the second edition of 1979, from which the quotations in the present entry are taken).

In spite of Emma's uncertain English and her obvious vanity, snobbery, and pretentiousness, it is a book that charms by its genuineness and the vividness with which she writes of her life in Plymouth and then in Cornwall. She describes St Juliot as a romantic spot some sixteen miles from a railway station, where the local people still believed in witchcraft. It was a poor parish, and the church had been so neglected that the tower was cracked, the carved bench-ends were rotten, and the bells had been removed to the north transept, where they stood 'with their mouths open upward' (30). She and her future husband could not, she says, have had a 'much more romantic meeting with its unusual circumstances, in bringing them together... at this very remote spot, with beautiful sea-coast, and the wild Atlantic ocean rolling in with its magnificent waves and spray, its white gulls and black choughs and grey puffins, its cliffs and rocks and gorgeous sunsettings sparkling redness in a track widening from the horizon to the shore' (p. 31).

Hardy had started his journey to Cornwall on that never-to-be-forgotten day, 7 March, by rising at four in the morning, and he arrived at the Rectory in the early evening after what Emma called 'a sort of cross jump-journey, like a chess-knight's move' (p. 33). The Rector had gout and was in bed, and it fell to Emma to receive the visitor. 'I was', she said, 'immediately arrested by his familiar appearance, as if I had seen him in a dream—his slightly different accent, his soft voice; also I noticed a blue paper sticking out of his pocket' (p. 33). Later she was to learn that the blue paper was not a plan of the church but the manuscript of a poem.

Hardy's own description of the four days he spent at the Rectory on this first visit is to be found in his autobiography (*LW* 75–8). It seems to have been almost 'love at first sight', and the poem 'At the Word "Farewell"' may refer to their first parting at the end of his visit. During those four days he worked on his plans for the church, visited Tintagel, and went on to Penpethy slate-quarries with a view to the church roofing. In the evenings there was music, and Hardy was never to forget the songs that Emma sang to him. As she rode her horse along Beeny Cliff he walked beside her, and his 'Cornish Romance' began.

A poem he almost certainly wrote at about this time, but which was not published until 1914 and after Emma's death—it is an irony that she may never have known of its existence—is 'When I Set Out for Lyonnesse'. As he explained, it 'refers certainly to this first visit, it having been his custom to apply the name "Lyonnesse" to the whole of Cornwall' (*LW* 78). Here is love's 'first fine careless rapture', and the poem conveys something of the sense of magic which many visitors to Cornwall have experienced. On his return to Dorset he presented Crickmay with his expense account for £6. 10*s*. 9*d*., and on 16 May recorded in his notebook the fact that he had left his heart in Cornwall (*LW* 79).

He was back in Cornwall in August and, shortly after, the builders started work on the rebuilding of the church. Hardy was sad to see the old tower and north aisle and transept destroyed, but wondered what else could have been done. He found Emma transformed from the 'young lady in brown ... thickly muffled from the wind' into 'a young lady in summer blue', and he was driven 'to various picturesque points on the wild and rugged coast... among others to King Arthur's Castle, Tintagel' (*LW* 81). Their shared interests in music and literature brought them closer together, and a sketch by Hardy, dated 22 August 1870 and showing Emma sitting in the rain on Beeny Cliff, still survives (DCM). There has been speculation that Emma, who was about the same age as Hardy when they met (that is, almost 30), saw him as an attractive way of escaping from the dullness of life in St Juliot, and that there was a family conspiracy to marry her off to him. Possibly so. However, what seems certain is that she had no real idea of Hardy's humble background, and that Hardy himself, paying only short visits at long intervals to Cornwall, had little opportunity of really knowing his wife-to-be.

There were further visits to Cornwall in 1871 and 1872, but he was not present when the restored church was opened on 11 April 1872. It seems likely that it was in that year that he and Emma became engaged—in spite of some opposition from Emma's father, who is said to have described Hardy as 'a base churl' not good enough for his daughter. When Hardy in later years referred to Emma's 'loyalty', he may have been thinking of her support of him against her father's wishes, and of her insistence on his persisting in his attempt to make a career as a writer even after the failure of his first published novel, *Desperate Remedies* (1871), and the difficulty of finding a publisher for his second, *Under the Greenwood Tree* (1872). William *Tinsley, who did publish this short novel, was impressed by it and accepted Hardy's proposal of a full-length novel. With the promise of serial publication in *Tinsleys' Magazine*, to be followed by an edition in three volumes, it at last looked as if Hardy might be able to earn his living as a writer, and so be able to support a wife who had no money of her own.

The new book was to be called *A Pair of Blue Eyes*, and serial publication was from September 1872 to July 1873. Hardy was under pressure from the publishers, and it is understandable that, working so rapidly, he should have drawn heavily on his own recent experiences and the places that were uppermost in his life at the time. Although he repeatedly denied that the novel could be in any way regarded as autobiographical, it is inescapable that it is: not only does his life tell us something about the novel, but the novel tells us something about his life. Most of the action takes place (just as some of the novel was written) in Cornwall, and the heroine, Elfride Swancourt, is the daughter of the Rector and has a character and physical qualities like those of Emma. She lives in Endelstow Rectory, which is very similar to St Juliot Rectory, while Endelstow House in the novel has features of Lanhydrock House, and Hardy identified the 'Cliff Without a Name' as Beeny Cliff. (For other identifications, see Denys Kay-Robinson, *The Landscape of Thomas Hardy* (1984).) One of the characters in the story is Stephen Smith, a young architect of humble background who arrives to plan the rebuilding of the church and falls in love with Elfride. Her snobbish father rejects Stephen when he discovers his background, and Stephen's father and mother have something in common with Hardy's own parents.

With Emma's death in 1912 there was no longer any need for equivocation (had she never recognized herself in Elfride?), and when Macmillan published the Mellstock Edition of Hardy's works in 1919–20 almost the only changes in the texts that Hardy requested were to *A Pair of Blue Eyes*. Significantly, these involved changing 'vicarage' to 'rectory' throughout the book; locating more exactly the church and rectory so that they are more easily identifiable as those of St Juliot; and giving the title of a song that Elfride sings in Chapter 3 as 'Should He Upbraid', one of Emma's favourites. After Emma's death, Hardy visited the then Rector of St Juliot, who wrote to a friend in 1936: 'Mr Hardy on both his visits talked freely about his first wife and his novel *A Pair of Blue Eyes*, and told us that the heroine of that book was indeed Miss Emma Gifford. He said that nearly all the incidents in the story were true, as inventing fiction was too much trouble.' When the concept of 'Hardy the *Wessex* novelist' came to Hardy a year or two after the first publication of *A Pair of Blue Eyes*, he got over this little local difficulty by describing 'Castle Boterel' (his name for Boscastle) as lying 'near to, or no great way beyond, the vague border of the Wessex kingdom' (1895 Preface to the Osgood, McIlvaine edition).

Hardy and Emma were not to have children, but *A Pair of Blue Eyes* may be regarded as the first literary fruit of the 1870–4 Cornish visits. The magic in his eyes which he brought back from Lyonnesse was to last a lifetime, and something of that magic is found in *A Pair of Blue Eyes*. Its isolated setting in what at that time was a remote part of a distant county, with the descriptions of the wild, lonely hills, the bare black edifice which is St Juliot church, and the haggard cliffs of the coast—all these contribute to a poetic background that seems to have some mysterious power over the imagination. It is not surprising that it was a favourite novel of at least two poets, *Tennyson and Coventry *Patmore. Hardy's increasing confidence in himself as a novelist is shown by the fact that *A Pair of Blue Eyes* was the first of his novels to bear his name on the title-page.

Hardy and Emma met twice more in Cornwall and once in Somerset in 1873, and he probably spent Christmas of that year at St Juliot. His poem 'The Seven Times' seems to be a not altogether accurate account of his visits to Emma in those years. It was the success of his next novel, *Far from the Madding Crowd* (1874), that seems eventually to have given Hardy the financial confidence to marry, and on 17 September 1874 he at last married Emma at St Peter's, Paddington. The wedding ceremony was performed by Emma's uncle, who was later to become Archdeacon of London (something of which Emma was inordinately proud). None of the four parents was present at the wedding, and no one came up from Cornwall to what was a low-key affair attended only by the officiating clergyman, Emma and Hardy, a young brother of Emma's, and the daughter of Hardy's landlady, who acted as one of the witnesses. For Emma in *Some Recollections* it was 'a perfect September day...not a brilliant sunshine, but wearing a soft, sunny luminousness, just as it should be' (37).

The courtship in Cornwall had lasted four years, the marriage lasted 38, until Emma's death in 1912, and it was a matter of sadness for Hardy after her death that not once during their years of marriage had they returned to Cornwall together. For all the charm that Cornwall had for him, Hardy seems never to have revisited it during Emma's lifetime, and her last visit was probably to her sister at St Juliot when the latter's husband died in November 1882. The reason for this may well be that during the early years of the marriage they were too busy, and that as they grew apart in the later years it would have been too painful to visit again 'those olden haunts'.

But with Emma's death all was changed. The shock of her death and the reading of *Some Recollections* filled Hardy with a sadness, remorse, and nostalgia which led over the next year to the writing of some of the most beautiful elegiac love-poems in the language. In his collection of verse published in 1914, *Satires of Circumstance*, where they appeared for the first time, Hardy grouped these poems together under the title *'Poems of 1912–13', with a Virgilian epigraph, *Veteris Vestigia Flammae* ('relics of an old love'). The opening poem, 'The Going', is dated 'December 1912', and the first eleven are all located in or near Max Gate. Then the poem 'A Dream or No' asks the question 'Why go to Saint-Juliot?', and the next few poems, including three of the very greatest—'After a Journey', 'Beeny Cliff', and 'At Castle Boterel'—are located in the Cornwall he had known and loved 40 years earlier.

On 6 March 1913, almost exactly 43 years to the day after that first visit to Lyonnesse, Hardy had arrived in Boscastle again and visited the places that they 'once had visited'. He saw once again the Valency Valley, Beeny Cliff, Boscastle harbour, St Juliot church and the Rectory, and his remarkably retentive memory brought back the past as if it had been yesterday. In Plymouth on the journey home he arranged for a tablet to be placed in St Juliot church in Emma's memory.

The renewed call of Cornwall took him again to Boscastle and St Juliot in September 1916, and this time he brought a somewhat jaundiced second wife, Florence, with him. They had tea at the Rectory, where the Cornish Romance had all begun in 1870, and a visit to Tintagel may have provided the idea for what was later to become *The Famous Tragedy of the Queen of Cornwall*. Published in November 1923, this was the last work to result from his emotional involvement with Emma and Cornwall. It is a poetic drama based upon the story of Tristram and Iseult, and, once again, there are autobiographical references. Hardy described Emma as an Iseult of his own. His attempt to write it as a 'play for mummers' and to observe the three unities is brave, but it is not a work that has found favour, and it is for *A Pair of Blue Eyes* and the love poems about Emma that we must be grateful to Crickmay for sending Hardy to Cornwall. JCG

crafts. Nowhere do we feel more strongly that Hardy is chronicling a vanished culture than when he refers to the traditional crafts of his region. Even at the time of writing, many of them seemed archaic. Willowes in 'Barbara of the House of Grebe' (in *A Group of Noble Dames*) has a grandfather who was 'the last of the old glass-painters', which suggests a way of life that is intrinsically worthy, but doomed. The same note is struck in the 1912 Preface to *The Woodlanders*: technological advances have 'almost extinguished the handicrafts classed formerly as "copsework", and the type of men who engaged in them'.

Hardy is writing not about a throwaway age, like our own, but one in which common household objects were rare and precious. People who had any stability in their lives were surrounded by things 'that date from the days of their mothers' mothers' ('Old Furniture'). Giles's pack of cards has been stained by 'the touch of generations of damp and excited thumbs, now fleshless in the grave' (*W* 10), and the family mug—there is only one—in 'The Three Strangers' has been drunk from by many people now dead. In the same story, several sheep-crooks of various types hang on the wall as ornaments. They have been bought at the fair; there are few shops in the Wessex novels, and certainly no factories.

Instead, people make the few things they need, or get them from the local specialist. *Under the Greenwood Tree*, one of the most old-fashioned of the novels, has the singing boys dressed in 'snow-white smock-frocks, embroidered . . . in ornamental forms of hearts, diamonds and zigzags' (1.4), no doubt by their wives and mothers. One man is an expert boot- and shoe-maker, another constructs hoops. They carry lanterns made from cow-horn, and most households brew their own mead or wine.

The brewing of drink (see also ALCOHOL) is often described in almost lyrical terms, and it takes skill to get the flavour just right. Hardy notes the old-fashioned mead made from 'the purest first-year or maiden honey' by the shepherds in 'The Three Strangers'; non-alcoholic furmity in *The Mayor of Casterbridge*; the celebrated local 'strong beer' in *The Trumpet-Major*; and, in *The Woodlanders*, the cider-making 'natural to the locality at this time of the year'. 'Down in the heart of the apple-country nearly every farmer kept a cider-making apparatus and wring-house for his own use' (*W* 25), but there are also men who travel round with their own equipment, like Giles. 'Behind him on wheels, in readiness | His mill, and tubs, and vat, and press': in these lines Hardy evokes one such cider-maker from his youth in the poem 'Shortening Days at the Homestead'. Other specialists could be seen on the roads, like the reddleman with his 'bright pigment', but 'since the introduction of railways' (*RN* 1.9) they have disappeared.

Women do needlework at home, useful or ornamental. Bathsheba has a sampler which she describes as 'out of date—horribly countrified' (*FFMC* 44); Anne Garland and her mother work sporadically on a rug (*TM* 1). Basket-makers cut 'osiers' ('The Lady Penelope', in *A Group of Noble Dames*). In *The Return of the Native*, Olly Dowden gets a living by making heath brooms. Elizabeth-Jane has 'a wonderful skill in netting of all sorts-acquired in childhood by making seines [i.e. fishing-nets] in Newson's home' (*MC* 30). In *The Woodlanders*, an entire community subsists on the crafts related to trees. Marty is first seen splintering hazel wood to make 'spars, such as are used by thatchers' (*W* 2). According to Giles it is a 'trade' (3), and she is good enough to go far. Melbury's business includes the making of hurdles and 'sawing, crib-framing and copseware manufacture in general' (4). Others work in the 'hollow-turnery trade' and produce 'wooden bowls, dishes, spigots [pegs], spoons, cheese-vats, funnels and so on' (29). In one scene (19), Melbury's workers are removing bark from oaks, to be sold for tanning. All these crafts require care and skill; as Marty says in her lament over the grave of Giles, '"whenever I split a gad, and whenever I turn the cider wring, I'll say none could do it like you"' (48). They have died out, Hardy tells us in the Preface to the same novel, because of 'the adoption of iron utensils and implements in agriculture, and the discontinuance of thatched roofs for cottages'.

He is also interested in those who work with stone. As a boy Pierston in *The Well-Beloved* carves chessmen 'out of bits of stone from the soft-bed of his father's quarries' (1.3). Jude begins by 'copying the heads and capitals in his parish church' (*JO* 1.5) and goes on to 'monumental stonecutting, gothic free-stone work for the restoration of churches, and carving of a general kind' (2.1). Later he does cheap headstones for his neighbours, 'a lower class of handicraft than ... his former performances as a cathedral mason' (5.1). 'He was a handy man at his trade, an all-round man,' Hardy says with approval, 'as artisans in country towns are apt to be' (2.4). Jude's frustrated creativity also comes out in making edible models of colleges, or 'Christminster cakes'.

Whether or not these activities are well-paid, or considered worthwhile, Hardy sees them as intrinsically valuable. Like Ruskin, he believed that people should not be employed in one monotonous task all their lives, but needed work which gave scope for their talents. Traditional crafts, extinct or not, are always described with respect. MW

Craigie, Pearl. See HOBBES, JOHN OLIVER.

Crickmay, G. R. (1830–1907), architect. The Weymouth-based Crickmay, having taken over the practice of John *Hicks on the death of the latter in 1869, requested Hardy's assistance with a number of unfinished ecclesiastical commissions. The most significant of these was the rebuilding of Turnworth church, a design on which Hardy exerted a far greater than usual influence. Crickmay subsequently offered Hardy three months' further employment. Hardy's resultant residence in Weymouth influenced the locale of *Desperate Remedies*; Edward Springrove in that novel was, Hardy claimed, based on a new assistant at Crickmay's (possibly Hardy himself).

Hardy also worked for Crickmay subsequently, on terms which by their flexibility were advantageous to Hardy at the start of his novel-writing career. These ecclesiastical projects, all acquired from Hicks, included the churches at West Lulworth and Hinton Martel, and the momentous commission at St Juliot in *Cornwall, which Hardy first visited on 7 March 1870. As well as these ecclesiastical projects, Hardy was probably involved for Crickmay with work during 1871 on Weymouth hospitals, the restoration of Stoke Wake church, schools in and near Weymouth, and alterations to Slape House, Netherbury. TRH

critical approaches.

Introductory Survey

Hardy criticism had a rather mixed start in his lifetime; respectful and less than respectful reviews of the earlier work gave way to the violent debates that followed the publication of *Tess* and, even more, of *Jude*. Then a dozen books were published in the early years of the 20th century, along with a handful of chapters and articles, devoted largely to his 'thought'. A polemical tone pervades these early studies by Lascelles Abercrombie, Lina Berle, Ernest Brennecke, Samuel Chew, H. C. Duffin, F. A. Hedgcock, Arthur *Symons and, unsurprisingly, those by E. M. *Forster and G. K. *Chesterton. One needed, then, to be For or Against Hardy.

After Hardy's death the polemics continued: F. R. Leavis's dismissal of most of the poetry in his *New Bearings in English Poetry* (1932) and T. S. Eliot's sneerings at the novels in *After Strange Gods* (1934) were matched by the insightful oddity of D. H. *Lawrence's opinions (for instance, in the long essay included in his *Phoenix*, published posthumously in 1936).

Less engaged, more objective approaches to Hardy began in the 1940s. The New Criticism, along with its British version in the shape of Leavis again, made a serious attempt on Hardy in the now famous issue of the *Southern Review* of Summer 1940, issued to commemorate the centenary of Hardy's birth. Henry Nevinson wrote the first of a whole series of books that were to bear the same simple title, *Thomas Hardy*, in 1941, and Lord David Cecil published his solidly appreciative *Hardy the Novelist* in 1943. James Southworth (*The Poetry of Thomas Hardy*, 1947), Harvey Curtis Webster (*On a Darkling Plain: The Art and Thought of Thomas Hardy*, 1947), Albert J. Guerard (*Thomas Hardy: The Novels and Stories*, 1949), Desmond Hawkins (*Thomas Hardy*, 1950), Ezra *Pound (*ABC of Reading*, 1951), R. A. Scott-James (*Thomas Hardy*, 1951), Edmund *Blunden (*Thomas Hardy*, 1954), Douglas Brown (*Thomas Hardy*, 1954), C. Day Lewis (*The Lyrical Poetry of Thomas Hardy*, 1957; originally delivered as a lecture in 1951), and some others published books and (though this was less common) articles during the 1940s and 1950s. By 1960 this generally more balanced attention (though one would never accuse Pound of balance) had been paid to most of Hardy's work, with the possible exception of the 'minor' fiction and *The Dynasts.*

The 1960s saw the beginning of the professionalization of Hardy studies in that the majority of writers concerning themselves with his work were now university academics. He has always attracted the amateur enthusiast, for better or worse, but, equally for better or worse, his reputation since 1960 has been largely in the hands of Academia. Typically of this tendency, the 1960s witnessed a multiplication of journal articles devoted to single novels (the staple of a certain kind of academic gesture), and a dozen or more essays were written on each of the 'major' (and fashionable) texts during the decade: *Tess of the d'Urbervilles, The Mayor of Casterbridge, The Return of the Native,* and *Jude the Obscure.* Lectures and essays by John Holloway (in *The Charted Mirror,* 1960), J. I. M. Stewart (in *Eight Modern Authors,* 1963), Raymond Williams ('Thomas Hardy', *Critical Quarterly,* 6 (1964)), Arnold Kettle (*Hardy the Novelist: A Reconsideration,* 1966), and David Daiches (in *Some Late Victorian Attitudes,* 1967) established a consensual academic respectability for Hardy. The volumes published, however, were far fewer in number, and, although they included Albert Guerard's academic, even pedagogic anthology *Hardy: A Collection of Critical Essays* of 1963 and Roy Morrell's *Thomas Hardy: The Will and the Way* of 1965, they also included George Wing's brief *Hardy* of 1963, Richard Carpenter's *Thomas Hardy* of 1964, and Trevor Johnson's short 1968 book of the same name; these last show fewer signs of being written with an academic audience in mind.

Recognizable modernity in criticism can be discerned in the late 1960s. Alan Friedman's fascinating *The Turn of the Novel* (1966) situated Hardy himself at the critical entry-point into modernity. In that same year the poet Philip *Larkin wrote an impassioned plea entitled 'Wanted: A Good Hardy Critic' (*Critical Quarterly,* 8) which lambasted recent work and asked for a simpler recognition of Hardy's own simplicities. Four years later a good critic, one of the best there has been, Joseph Hillis Miller, published *Thomas Hardy: Distance and Desire,* and the period of modern criticism had begun. Not all subsequent critics have had the sophistication or the critical armoury (or acumen) of Miller. He himself, moreover, has taken Hardy criticism in different directions since 1970, but here was the first voice speaking in at least some of the new language that has had so profound an impact on our approach to all writers, not just Hardy, in the last 30 years. In 1972, manifesting the unease that was then being felt at the state of Hardy studies, F. R. Southerington wrote a short essay entitled 'Lives, Letters, and the Failure of Criticism, 1928–1972' (*Agenda,* 10), in which the shortcomings of current thinking about Hardy are pointed out.

The 1970s, then, mark a transition from an older style of criticism to the newer style informed by structuralist and poststructuralist thinking, although there were studies that clearly wanted no part of the new approach and which formed (and still form) an alternative, as it were, to the 'Alternative' rereadings that have become fashionable; a paradigm example would be Margaret Drabble's anthology of essays significantly entitled *The Genius of Thomas Hardy* (no contestation of canonical status here) of 1976. This contains interesting essays by John Betjeman (no poststructuralist he), Geoffrey Grigson and, 33 years on, Lord David Cecil again, but it is not a leading-edge-intellectuals' volume. It might well be contrasted with Dale Kramer's *Critical Approaches to the Fiction of Thomas Hardy* (1979). Here we find names from the poststructuralist era: David Lodge (perhaps still a Structuralist), Elaine Showalter and Mary Jacobus, known for their feminist readings, Michael Ryan, author of a book on deconstruction and Marxism, and several others. Typically this second volume is written almost entirely by practising academics and seems to belong to a world with few points of contact with the Drabble collection.

Another example of the two tendencies in Hardy studies that emerged in the 1970s was the Macmillan New Wessex Edition of Hardy's works, published in London and New York between 1974 and 1979. Some of the volumes have introductions by the pre-Theory species of critic (Barbara Hardy introduced *The Trumpet-Major* and *A Laodicean,* F. B. Pinion *Two on a Tower*), while others have the young (and not-so-young) Turks to present them to a new public (Terry Eagleton introduced *Jude the Obscure*, David Lodge *The Woodlanders*, J. Hillis Miller *The Well-Beloved*). One might make some sort of correlation here between the texts chosen and their editors: theorized critics have tended to be attracted to the major fiction at the expense of the minor, although some re-canonization has gone on, with *The Well-Beloved* rising in the charts at the hands of such as Hillis Miller and Patricia Ingham. A final point concerning the 1970s would be that Hardy criticism, like the criticism of many other writers, expanded enormously during the decade. The Gerber and Davies bibliographies make the point: Volume 1 (1973), with its supplement, lists over 4,200 items for the near-century 1871–1969, while Volume 2 (1983) lists 1,400 items for the nine years 1970–8. This was not altogether welcome to certain practitioners in the field: William E. Buckler, surveying Hardy criticism in 1981, suggested not altogether fairly that in the 1970s Hardy studies were rather 'busy' than 'inspired'. Donald Davie, writing in 1982, called Hardy studies an 'academic growth-industry' for 'second-class minds'.

By the 1980s nobody in the academic or literary world could be ignorant that major changes were taking place in the way we read. It was now a question of being either For or Against the *nouvelle critique*, and Hardy seemed happy hunting-ground for the newer critics, though by no means for everyone. I well remember one distinguished Hardy critic saying to me, at a Thomas Hardy Society conference in Dorchester in 1986, that as far as the poststructuralist enterprise was concerned, he was 'keeping his head down and hoping it would go away'. A history of 'modern Hardy criticism' written in the closing years of the present century must recognize that there are two streams flowing: on the one hand theorized criticism, more 'modern', more in tune with the new thinking, and on the other hand a continuation of the different strands of 'traditional' criticism of a largely untheorized kind.

In what follows, then, I shall be concerned with Hardy criticism as it has developed in the 1970s and, particularly, the 1980s and 1990s. Apart from the two main streams into which it can be divided (which I would call theorized and non-theorized), there are further subdivisions. Thus one non-poststructuralist school of critics has worked on Hardy's language, while others have worked on Wessex regionalist matters, on his religion and philosophy, or on psychological readings of the fiction in pre-Lacanian terms. The theorized critics have concentrated on the usual areas of their style of reading: feminism is notably to the fore, along with Marxism and deconstruction, and there is a kind of essay that shows its allegiance to the new thought without specifically adhering to any 'ism'.

Non-Theorized Criticism

1. *Language*

Before 1970 but of founding importance in paying close attention to Hardy's language was David Lodge's essay 'Tess, Nature and the Voices of Hardy', a chapter in his *Language of Fiction: Essays in Criticism and Verbal Analysis of the English Novel* (1966). This is a superb example of Lodge's efforts to get readers to consider prose in the same detailed stylistic light as verse, and, of course, Hardy provides Lodge with examples of a prose that is every bit as dense as some poetry—notably the scene between Angel Clare and Tess in the garden at Talbothays. Later Lodge would regret that he had confined his analyses in this book to passages of narration and diegesis; the possibility of a stylistics that would also include characters' represented speech only came to him once he had digested the work of Mikhail Bakhtin, a theorist highly apt for the Hardy critic.

A more sociological and less 'prestructuralist' approach was taken by Patricia Ingham in her essay on 'Dialect in the Novels of Hardy and George Eliot' in the volume *Literary English since Shakespeare* (1970), edited by George Watson. Here Hardy's characters are seen as using dialect for the expression of deep feeling and, alternatively, to mark social inferiority. These Bakhtinian notions were supported, at least by implication, in Norman Page's essay 'Hardy and the English Language' in his own collection *Thomas Hardy: The Writer and his Background* (1980). Page stresses the variety of Hardy's languages in a useful way; more sophisticated, more technical, and in the end more promising as a model for future analysts is

Peter Grundy's essay 'Linguistics and Literary Criticism' (*English*, 1981). Here we see, following the Lodge example and that of stylistics in general, a linguistic analysis of the end of 'The Maiden' from *Tess*. The results are fascinating and, as usual, reveal a subtler, more deliberate and thoughtful image of Hardy than the one we normally have in our heads as we read. Ingham's class-analysis of dialect is taken further by J. B. Smith's 'Dialect in Hardy's Short Stories' (*THA* 1985).

Ralph Elliott's *Thomas Hardy's English* (1984) considers the sources of Hardy's 'Englishes' and includes detailed consideration of his prosody, grammar, and pronunciation. A more introductory study, less exciting, less detailed and scholarly, but none the less of use to students of this question, is Raymond Chapman's *The Language of Thomas Hardy* (1990). But the most substantial and scholarly of recent studies in the field of Hardy's language must be Dennis Taylor's *Hardy's Literary Language and Victorian Philology* (1993). Taylor takes on the hoary topic of Hardy's awkwardnesses but situates this problem in terms of Victorian thinking about language and the information revealed by the *Oxford English Dictionary*. This impressive monograph underlines yet again that Hardy knew what he was doing and, so far from writing in some 'natural' or spontaneous (read rustic? ignorant?) way, was responding very precisely to the new philology of the 1860s and working on his language consciously. Again and again Taylor reveals that Hardy's reviewers were wrong in attributing rank neologism to him: odd words he uses can be shown to have entered the language recently or not yet fully to have died out from it. Hardy is 'on the cutting edge of a style that provokes ... contrary responses', not merely floundering about in search of a stunning word.

2. *Philosophy and Religion*

Although more or less all Hardy criticism, from the very beginning and with the exception only of the driest and most scholarly bibliographical and textual research, involves some sort of assessment of his views on the universe and the largely intractable question of his 'beliefs', there have been periods when philosophy and religion have bulked larger in the criticism than at other times. The 1970s, for example, seemed to be less interested in 'Hardy's philosophy' than earlier and later decades. F. R. Southerington's *Hardy's Vision of Man* of 1971 is a mild exception, concerned as it is with Hardy's 'thinking' and therefore his personal temperament. T. B. Tomlinson in 1973 published a study of *Tess* in the *Critical Review* in which he considered Hardy's 'positive agnosticism' in this novel, and in 1975 Valentine Cunningham produced a full-length study of dissenters in Victorian fiction (*Everywhere Spoken Against*) that includes a chapter on Baptists in *A Laodicean* and Alec-as-preacher in *Tess*.

Later critics have from time to time tried to put Hardy into one or other philosophical or religious framework. As with any great writer this has tended to yield remarkably coherent results—although, of course, one has to accommodate one's agreement with one critic's viewpoint to one's subsequent agreement with another critic's quite different viewpoint. Thus, for instance, in 1982 Mary Ann Kelly made the not-unexpected comparison between Hardy and Schopenhauer ('Hardy's Reading in Schopenhauer', *Colby Library Quarterly*). In 1983 Bruce Johnson produced a full-length Husserlean study of the fiction, *True Correspondence: A Phenomenology of Thomas Hardy's Novels*. There is much of interest in this book and, although it has to be admitted that Phenomenology is more than usually flexible in its accommodation of disparate ideas, and that, therefore, some of this study involves close reading of a more general and less Phenomenological kind than one might fear, in the end a case is made out for reading Hardy alongside Husserl. As he is not the best-understood philosopher of modern times it might have been better if Johnson had explained a little more of Husserlean theory before plunging into his readings, but the attempt is revealing none the less.

More typical of the 1980s in this area, however, might be two essays that appeared in 1984, tracing quasi-Christian themes: Sandy Cohen's 'Blind Clym, Unchristian Christian and the Redness of the Reddleman' (*THY*), an essay about *The Return of the Native* offering Diggory Venn as a sort of attenuated Christ figure; and Myrddin Jones's 'Hardy and Biblical Narrative' in the *Thomas Hardy*

Society Newsletter, where Henchard in *The Mayor of Casterbridge* is compared with Cain.

The religion or philosophy deployed does not necessarily have to be Christian or even Western. In 1985 the Indian scholar Jagdish Dave made a highly plausible connection between Hardy and Buddhist (and Hindu) ideas in *The Human Predicament in Hardy's Novels*. This astonishing *tour de force* involves a constant crossing and recrossing of the East–West divide as Camus, Sartre, and Marcus Aurelius are deployed as a preparation for the main comparison between Hardy's aims and those of the Buddha. The value of this sort of approach lies in its liberation of new areas of thinking and the creation of a new Hardy *pour nos jours*.

A more conventional study of Hardy's thinking appeared in 1990: Deborah Collins's *Thomas Hardy and His God*. This calm and penetrating survey, though apparently written without benefit of Jagdish Dave's insights, revisits the familiar topoi of Positivism, Darwin, Schopenhauer, *et al.*, to present us with a complex but not inconsistent Hardy who is both pessimistic and *in search*, trying to make some compassionate sense of a universe of only provisional meanings. A quasi-Christian commitment to 'lovingkindness' puts Hardy more or less where the Buddhist interpretation puts him. Is this the latest consensus about his views?

One of the most promising approaches to the question of Hardy's 'beliefs' might be a style of reading that emerges from the general area of Discourse Analysis. Here the question of language and the question of thought are less easily separable than elsewhere. We cannot say, at the level of discourse, that *Jude the Obscure*, for instance, has a Judaeo-Christian surface and an atheist or agnostic 'content'. Intertextuality cannot rest content with this distinction: there is no such thing as mere surface in intertextual relations, and where there is Christian discourse, for instance, there is, precisely, *Christian* discourse. Jude as a Jesus figure is not merely decorative metaphor: the triple, simultaneous hanging-up-to-die of the children is not merely analogically related to the Crucifixion. In this context I would recommend the typological readings of Victorian writers pioneered by George Landow among others, taken up in Barry Qualls's *Secular Pilgrims of Victorian Fiction* (1982), and exemplified, however poorly, in the present writer's chapter on Hardy in his *Victorian Doubt* (1990).

3. *Psychology*

In 1972 Perry Meisel's book *Thomas Hardy: The Return of the Repressed* broke new ground in the increasing sophistication of Hardy criticism. Although this is not a post-structuralist study of the sort associated with the names of Lacan and Kristeva, it includes a substantial orientation towards Freudian theory, as its title suggests, and should be read alongside *biographies of Hardy for a broader picture of the psycho-intellectual sources of his *angst*. There has been, none the less, some reluctance to follow this promising path very much further.

Also in 1972 Elliott Gose used some of the psychoanalytical arsenal to approach, in a chapter of his *Imagination Indulged*, the text that has proved the most fertile hunting-ground for this sort of criticism, *The Return of the Native*. The archetypal, folkloric elements of that novel provoke us to read Eustacia, and the other characters, as psychological embodiments of mythical elements. This approach engendered its own sub-genre of *Return of the Native* criticism, from Frank Giordano's 'Eustacia Vye's Suicide' (*Texas Studies in Literature and Language*, 1980) through Katherine Hanley's 'Death as Option' essay of 1981 (about female suicide in 19th-century fiction, and focusing on Eustacia), to M. E. Jordan's 'Clym Yeobright and Melancholia' (*American Imago*, 1982).

Frank Giordano had earlier examined *Far from the Madding Crowd* from a psychological perspective in his 'Farmer Boldwood: Hardy's Portrait of a Suicide' (*English Literature in Transition*, 1978). He also took a look at *The Woodlanders*, contributing to *THA* (1984) a fascinating study of 'The Martyrdom of Giles Winterborne' which is an almost classic Freudian account of Giles's self-repressions, displacements, and unconscious drives. These ideas of Giordano's were developed in 1984 in a full-length study entitled 'I'd Have My Life Unbe': Thomas Hardy's Self-Destructive Characters. Some of the sharp Freudian thrust is lost in the wider concerns of this book, which is more about suicide than about psychology (if such a difference has any meaning).

A more generally psychological study had appeared in 1981: Rosemary Sumner's *Thomas Hardy: Psychological Novelist.* Sumner develops the obvious but insufficiently examined proposition that Hardy was a psychologist before Freud and the founding fathers of psychoanalysis had marked out the territory. Sensibly, she tries to associate particular psychic traits and disturbances with particular characters: Sue Bridehead as neurotic, Michael Henchard as suicidal, the 'Well-Beloved' spirit that haunts Jocelyn Pierston as the Jungian Anima, and so on. From a later perspective this study now looks a little thin on the actual psychology, although it is none the less a very good study of Hardy; there is a tendency on Sumner's part to drift off into philosophical and social considerations that detract from the sharpness of her analytical focus.

Something of the same comment might be made about Leon Waldoff's essay on *Tess* that appears in Dale Kramer's *Critical Approaches* volume of 1979. Despite the title ('Psychological Determinism in *Tess*'), there is more interesting material here about determinism and moral responsibility than about the work of Sigmund Freud. One must not be too negative about such processes: Freud himself would have been the first to argue that where desire is involved, displacement is inevitable, and one of the constant unspoken themes of all Hardy criticism is that there is, precisely, a surplus of desire in his texts, an unexploded charge that one might not have to deal with, for instance, in the work of Henry *James. Distortion and concealment seem inevitable.

This is very apparent if one reads the fascinating essay by John Fowles, 'Hardy and the Hag' (see FOWLES, JOHN), which appeared in the present writer's collection *Thomas Hardy After Fifty Years* (1977). I take no credit for the essay, but the circumstances are revealing: who would have expected a novelist at the height of his fame to take time off to contribute an original article to an academic collection? But Fowles did, and surely the reason for his generosity is connected with the surplus of desire that one can so readily identify both in the work of Hardy and in the work of John Fowles. The essay associates the very springs of artistic creativity with the profoundest of all psychological events, the separation from the mother, and speculates most fruitfully about Hardy's endless search for reparation. The topic is taken up most instructively by Ann Benway in *THY* (1986), in an article entitled 'Oedipus Abroad: Hardy's Clym Yeobright and Lawrence's Paul Morel'.

4. *Wessex and Sociology*

A safe topic for Hardy critics, even in recent decades, has been the regionalist and gently sociological tendency towards 'Wessex Studies'. Obviously the biographers have been particularly interested in this area, and Michael Millgate has made a comparison between Hardy's Wessex and William *Faulkner's Yoknatapatawpha. The normal line for other traditional critics to take has been that under Hardy's pen Wessex concerns expand into universal concerns. Thus a representative example would be R. P. Draper in *THJ* (1985), where the universalist claim is clearly and effectively made, as it had been in different ways by Michael Irwin and Ian Gregor in 1977 (*Thomas Hardy after Fifty Years*), by W. J. Keith (in Dale Kramer's *Critical Approaches* volume of 1979), and by Maire Quinn ('Wessex and the World', *THY* 1976). This last is particularly interesting because it focuses on Hardy's anxiety about appearing provincial, thus forming a sort of mirror-image of the anxiety of the critic for whom Hardy must not be allowed to be provincial lest the critic him- or herself be, *ipso facto*, relegated to the margins.

Another related topic in modern criticism is that of Hardy's own views of the regional, as expressed in the novels in particular. There is a constant harping in the fiction on the impact of change, and that change, as exemplified for instance by the last paragraph of the first chapter of *Jude the Obscure*, is an invasion from the centre, the urban, the modern, a threat to the old, rural, regional. This is the theme, for instance, of George Wing's essay 'Hardy and Regionalism' in Norman Page's *Thomas Hardy: The Writer and His Background* (1980). For a contrast, see my comments on Peter Widdowson's 'Hardy, "Wessex" and the Making of a National Culture' in the 'Theorized' section of this entry below.

The principal names that spring to mind, however, when we are considering the Regional must be those of Raymond Williams and Merryn Williams. The former, from very early days, was a champion of the margins—a protester against the London—Oxbridge assumption of centrality—as any reader of his novel *Border Country* or his panoramic *The Country and the City* will know. Specifically referring to Hardy in *The English Novel From Dickens to Lawrence* (1970), he objects to the patronizing of provincial novelists as 'autodidacts', wondering whether many Oxbridge-educated critics could compete with George *Eliot, say, or by implication with Hardy himself, in a contest of erudition. The constant reiteration by Williams of versions of his basic ideas on this topic between 1964 ('Thomas Hardy' in *Critical Quarterly*) and 1980 (with Merryn Williams, 'Hardy and Social Class', in Norman Page's *Thomas Hardy: The Writer and His Background*) signals the enduring interest readers have in his approach. In a sense Williams is trying to eliminate the terms of the original question: it is not a problem that Hardy was not a Londoner or a university man or a public-schoolboy; the problem lies with those who think this to be a problem. It is not surprising that we should hear so commanding a voice as his from the margins when we remember that the margins are only marginal from a certain centralist perspective.

Merryn Williams followed the path blazed by her father, Raymond Williams, in her first book, *Thomas Hardy and Rural England* (1972). Here she establishes a tradition of ruralist writing in earlier 19th-century English fiction, and goes on to praise the breadth and depth of Hardy's handling and treatment of his rustics. Not surprisingly, the theme recurs in her next book, *A Preface to Hardy* (1976). Objections to the Williamses' approach are to be found in Arthur Pollard's 'Hardy and Rural England' (*THA* 1982), but in the same year a sort of 'serious-regionalist' study by Noorul Hasan (*Thomas Hardy: The Sociological Imagination*) redressed the balance by again stressing Hardy as the novelist of painful change. Another view had been heard in Andrew Enstice's *Thomas Hardy: Landscapes of the Mind* (1979); here Hardy's locations and landscapes are seen not so much as Wessex places but as something like objective correlatives of states of being experienced by the characters in the novels.

Alongside Wessex matters, mostly to do with the fiction, has gone an interest in Hardy as rural or regional poet, inevitably associated with the name and work of William *Barnes. Two representative examples of this sort of study are C. H. Sisson's 'Hardy and Barnes' (*Agenda*, 1972) and W. J. Keith's *The Poetry of Nature: Rural Perspectives in Poetry from Wordsworth to the Present* (1980).

5. *Other Topics*

One could subdivide the themes of Hardy criticism endlessly; what is important here is to signal the breadth and energy of the many non-theorized Hardy critics of the last three decades. Academics, and occasionally non-academics, have been interested in the following topics among others:

Hardy and Painting. Critics such as J. B. Bullen (*The Expressive Eye: Fiction and Perception in the Work of Thomas Hardy*, 1986) and Annie Escuret ('Thomas Hardy and J. M. W. Turner', in Lance St John Butler (ed.), *Alternative Hardy*, 1989) have considered Hardy's relationship to Turner, Ruskin, and later 19th-century art in general. Joan Grundy's *Hardy and the Sister Arts* (1979) also compares Hardy to Impressionism. There is a sub-genre of articles covering this ground, too, such as Rosemary Sumner's 'Some Surrealist Elements in Hardy's Prose and Verse' (*THA* 1985).

Hardy and Other Writers. Marlene Springer's *Hardy's Use of Allusion* (1983), without being fully cognizant of intertextual theory, is only one of a number of studies to appear that work on the relationship between Hardy's texts and those of others. Ray Martin has considered Eustacia Vye as Lady Macbeth *rediviva* (*THYB* 14 (1987)); Patrick Diskin has compared Joyce's 'The Dead' with the ending of *The Woodlanders* (*Notes and Queries*, NS 30/4 (1983)); Lesley Higgins has found 'Shelleyan Echoes' also in *The Woodlanders* (*THA* 5 (1987)); Diana Basham has written on '*Jude the Obscure* and *Idylls of the King*' (*Thomas Hardy Society Review*, 1/10 (1984)). Other writers set alongside Hardy in the last 30 years have included Yeats, Milton, Faulkner, Lawrence, Henry James, Sherwood Anderson, Kipling, and Rider Haggard.

Hardy's Poetry. This may seem an odd category to relegate to a list of 'other topics', but there have been many articles (usually on one or two poems only) devoted to the poetry as poetry rather than as a contribution to an overall assessment of what Hardy was and meant. The most readily available example of this sort of approach is the Macmillan *Casebook* on the poetry edited by James Gibson and Trevor Johnson in 1979, but R. P. Draper and Martin Ray's invaluable *Annotated Critical Bibliography of Thomas Hardy* (1989) lists fifteen other volumes, either collections of essays or monographs, dedicated to the poetry, and no fewer than 30 pages of articles on the same topic.

A myriad other topics find their place in modern Hardy criticism. Articles have appeared on Hardy's *Darwinism, his relationship to science, his sociology, his handling of *tragedy; along with these there is a steady stream of pieces considering the now conventional topics of his *pessimism, his view of *fate, the role of chance or of mythological thinking in his work. Even 'traditional' 'close criticism' has not dried up, in spite of the poststructuralist tidal wave, and there is many an honest respectable article that discusses (to give some examples concerned with *Tess* as a representative and popular case) 'Time' or 'Nature and Paganism' or 'Mastery and Abandon [*sic*]' or 'Hardy's Universe' in connection with that novel, and in pretty conventional terms. Without doubt, there are many more Thomas Hardys to come, and many more ploughs will rework the furrows I have listed here.

Theorized Criticism

If it is a little surprising to find so many critics still approaching Hardy in some of the old ways as late as the 1990s, it is also surprising to find that the *nouvelle critique* has been somewhat slow in turning its mind to what must be one of the most promising writers for its purposes. Not an enormous number of deconstructionists or New Historicists have written at any length on Hardy; not much Marxist or Bakhtinian or Reader-Response work has been done on him. The major exception to this is feminist critique, which has been practised extensively against Hardy; 'against' here is partly figurative but partly meant literally in that some feminist critics have accused Hardy of a sort of complicity with the male perspective on the females in his fiction. A *locus classicus* of this sort of thinking is to be found in Rosemarie Morgan's admittedly brilliant *Women and Sexuality in the Novels of Thomas Hardy* 1(988): see, for instance, her analysis of the role of the male gaze in *Far from the Madding Crowd*.

'Theory' and its Limits

As already noted, in 1979 Dale Kramer edited a volume entitled *Critical Approaches to the Fiction of Thomas Hardy*, a collection which Kramer himself starts off with an essay ('Making Approaches to Hardy') that assesses and locates the different strategies, structuralist, deconstructive, feminist, and so on, that his contributors have adopted. His explicit suggestion is that Hardy responds particularly well to these methods, and that the grounding insight they have in common lies in the polysemy of his texts: Hardy's meanings are multiple, overlapping, and interconnected in a way that is highly congenial to the poststructuralist approach. This suggestion, although its optimism was perhaps not justified by the event of subsequent writing on Hardy, would not have been possible a decade earlier. The new approaches Kramer had assembled were a product of the 1970s, and he presumed, not unreasonably, that they would sweep all before them in the coming decade. In fact, much criticism proceeded just as before.

A clue to the relative failure of Hardy to become, paradoxically, a central figure in the new, poststructuralist canon of much-deconstructed authors is perhaps offered in Peter Widdowson's article 'Hardy in History: A Case Study in the Sociology of Literature' (*Literature and History*, 1983). This article looks at the phenomenon of 'Hardy', a figure constructed by criticism and by those who set the typical examination syllabus. This Hardy has had plenty of fairly 'traditional' criticism devoted to him, as we have seen above, and has been seen as a tame target at which those with the tender sensibilities of youth can be invited to shoot. His work is neither too religious nor excessively anti-religious (not 'deep down'), nor too obviously political, nor apparently too erotic, and it can be made to conform readily enough to the unspoken liberal-humanist agenda that is suitable to the education of the young. In other words, we have created a 'Hardy' (as we create every other writer we name, read, think about), and he happens to be one that we can live with without the dangers and difficulties of poststructuralist analysis.

This is an odd situation, since it is, presumably, those writers most obviously inserted whole into the traditionally acceptable patterns who offer the most tempting challenge to deconstructive practice. A writer such as Samuel Beckett, for instance, at the rebarbative opposite end of the scale from Hardy, remains largely unexplored, by Derrida at least, for the very reason that he is too obviously in the process of deconstructing himself as he writes. Hardy, or 'Hardy', is not. None the less it simply is the fact that, in contrast, say, with the poetry of the Romantic period or with Renaissance theatre in English, there does seem to be a surprising lack of modern criticism of Hardy in all areas except the feminist. But the surprise is relative; I only mean that there is not the plethora of such criticism that we might well expect. Sometimes, of course, it is a little difficult to tell whether a particular critic is approaching Hardy with his or her poststructuralist hat on or off. A collection such as Annie Escuret's Special Issue of *Cahiers Victoriens et Edouardiens* (1980) signals the split by including such venerable pieces of thinking as F. B. Pinion's 'Hardy's Literary Imagination' (admirable but quite untroubled by the likes of Roland Barthes) alongside such postmodern special-effects pieces as J. Senechal-Teissedou's 'Focalisation, regard et désir dans *Far from the Madding Crowd*' or Escuret's own '"Tess des d'Urbervilles": le corps et le signe'. These French essays lead us naturally to such pieces as Haig Stirling's '"By the Rivers of Babylon": Water and Exile in *The Mayor of Casterbridge*' (*THY* 1984) (reading for flow or some other semi-concrete, semi-abstract conception is quite typical of the more recent style of criticism). But there are essays elsewhere which, within their own compass, seem to be uncomfortably situated both within and outside the new vocabulary.

Thus even a good modern critic such as Patricia Ingham shows signs of not being prepared to go the whole textualist hog in an essay such as her 'Hardy and "The Cell of Time"' of 1980 (in Patricia Clements and Juliet Grindle (eds.), *The Poetry of Thomas Hardy*). The conception of time that she deploys is sophisticated enough, but the assumptions on which the article is written are not quite those of a paid-up poststructuralist. Similarly, Juliet Grindle in her 'Compulsion and Choice in *The Mayor of Casterbridge*' of 1979 (in Anne Smith (ed.), *The Novels of Thomas Hardy*) discusses power most interestingly without reaching for her Foucault in what would nowadays be considered a compulsory gesture.

The split between theorized and non-theorized work on Hardy is rather clearly marked if we consider the Penguin Critical Studies series of small monographs on some of the individual novels. The volume of *Tess* by Graham Handley (1991) is almost entirely innocent of the new thinking, while Cedric Watts's volume on *Jude* (1992) discusses Marxist, feminist, and other approaches at some length without, however, adopting them too strenuously.

Structuralism, Poststructuralism, Deconstruction

Apart from David Lodge and some French critics, notably the Greimasians Henri Quere and Janie Senechal in their 1989 essay 'Hardy's Alternatives in *The Woodlanders*, Chapter 39' (in *Alternative Hardy*, ed. Lance St John Butler), it is not easy to find many obviously structuralist accounts of Hardy. But structuralism only lasted a very short time before it gave way to what is recognizably poststructuralist, and what I have just said about Hardy could be said of almost any writer currently being studied.

The term 'poststructuralist' is best reserved as a blanket expression to cover the whole vast range of 'modern criticism' in so far as it has taken account of and learnt the vocabulary of the Barthes–Derrida–Lacan–Foucault school. It would thus include feminist and other such approaches—approaches that it has informed, reinvigorated, and placed on a more usefully insecure basis than before (although to hear some modern critics speak you would think that they had received the Tables of the Law from Paris). But sometimes the term 'poststructuralist' is used more narrowly to delimit an area of thought more or less coterminous with 'deconstruction'. I prefer to use the latter term for this area, and to keep 'poststructuralist' for the broader matter. (After all, it is what has come in 'structuralism's wake' that has upset so many of our applecarts, so the 'post-' is pretty clear in its meaning.)

Under 'deconstruction', then, pride of place must be given to the work of Joseph Hillis Miller. In 1968, before becoming as deconstructive as he later became, his *Forms of Victorian Fiction* included a close analysis of a chapter of *A Pair of Blue Eyes* in which, without donning a fully Derridean cap (Derrida was virtually unknown when Miller was writing this book), he stresses the multiplicities of Hardy's text: there are, for instance, different time-scales in the novel, notably those of the reader and the author as well as those of the narrator and the characters, which multiply possibilities of interpretation. We have already mentioned Miller's *Thomas Hardy: Distance and Desire* of 1970 (thus 'early' in these terms), which looks now like a first step towards the advanced position he is now in. His essay 'Fiction and Repetition: *Tess of the d'Urbervilles*', included in Alan Friedman's *Forms of Modern British Fiction* (1975), sets a deconstructive standard which others might have emulated to advantage. Miller focuses on the considerable number of recurrences of all sorts in the novel, and denies that any of them, particularly those with an apparent explanatory power, can really be taken as some sort of final explanation or 'Hardy's own view'. Hardy is thus liberated at a stroke from a monologic 'position', from the tyranny of 'authorial intention', and from having to tie all his moral ends neatly together. And in fact it is truly hard to see, in *Tess*, an overarching meaning; indeed, is it not, if the paradox is permitted in this deconstructive terrain, the point of the novel that it has no final point? That fiction, and suffering, move without necessarily arriving? That the heroine's fate is not any sort of resolution or the bringer of catharsis?

Also in 1975, Miller edited *The Well-Beloved* (New Wessex Edition), a novel whose rehabilitation from the ranks of 'lesser' Hardy novels he is largely responsible for. His introduction is a model of the new thinking, reading Jocelyn and his predicament not as psychological oddities, items in a personal development, but as ambiguous signs, themselves groping, as novelist and reader are alike doing, towards an elusive meaning.

Miller's essays on *Tess* and *The Well-Beloved* were revised for his volume *Fiction and Repetition: Seven English Novels* (1982). Anyone wanting to see a brilliant deconstructionist at work on Hardy would be well advised to read this book; it is not easy, but then it does not seek to simplify a highly complex topic, or, if you prefer, to simplify the complexities of a great writer. He approached Hardy's poetry, too, not only in the early (1968) essay on 'Wessex Heights' (*Critical Quarterly*, 10), but also, well into his post-structuralist stride, in his essay on 'The Torn Letter' in *Taking Chances: Derrida, Psychoanalysis and Literature* (1984), and in his essay 'Prosopopoeia in Hardy and Stevens', which deals with 'The Pedigree', in the 1970 symposium *Alternative Hardy*. These essays find, in poems not always of an apparently promising nature, things undreamt of by less acute critics. In Miller's hands they become exercises in the impossible elucidation of meaning, including their own meaning as poems; they become multiplied, infinitely available for re-inscription by 'us', by criticism, by readers.

In the wake of Miller's work there have been one or two articles that concentrate on the play in Hardy's polysemic texts. During the mid-1980s Alexander Fischler worked on Hardy's punning (*Studies in the Novel*, 13/3 (1981)), J. M. Rignall on uncertainty of interpretation in *The Trumpet-Major* (*Essays in Criticism*, 34/1 (1984)), and Romey Keys on 'shifting levels of reality' in 'The Withered Arm' (*Texas Studies in Literature and Language*, 27/1 (1985)). The undermining of apparent authorial intention by the text is the thesis of Laura Claridge's 'Tess: A Less than Pure Woman Ambivalently Presented' (*Texas Studies in Literature and Language*, 28/3 (1986)). Vincent Newey gives a textualist version of *Jude* (*Proceedings of the English Association North*, 1 (1985)).

Roger Ebbatson, in his *Hardy: The Margin of the Unexpressed* (1993), mentions Miller by name repeatedly in the first half of his book, which is the deconstructive half, entitled 'Reading Desire'. Rather typically of the deconstructive tendency towards 'marginal' thinking, this first part of Ebbatson's book is devoted to examples of the 'minor' fiction:

Desperate Remedies, The Trumpet-Major, Our Exploits at West Poley, and three of the short stories. He speaks of the 'surplus of undecidability' in Hardy and the novelist's (and reader's) willingness 'to rest in uncertainty' in moves clearly indebted to Derrida (he also cites Barthes), and is interested in the repetition, punning, unconscious forces, historical misconceptions, and other elements that he identifies in his material.

There are deconstructive elements in other recent studies, too, but these are perhaps best discussed under other headings below. The point to be made here is simply that 'modern criticism', here modern theory, is a garment cut out of one large piece of cloth, and it is hard to separate its different parts. Marxist and feminist critics, for instance, certainly use deconstructive techniques to assist with their analyses.

Marxism

Perhaps the 'sociological' approach to Hardy taken by the Williamses in the 1960s and 1970s (see above) seemed adequate to critics of a Marxist inclination, and led them to leave his work alone. Whatever the reason for it, however, there is no doubt that until recently only a handful of those working on Hardy have taken the leftish line that one would have thought to be an obvious strategy—after all, class structure and social change are essential elements, in the fiction at least, and *Jude*, to go no further, a Pandora's Box of subversive elements. None the less, there are some substantial exceptions to this neglect.

Arnold Kettle, a Marxist of the old school, has an essay on *Tess* in his *Introduction to the English Novel* (1953) which covers the ground one might expect. In his account Tess becomes a figure representative of the English peasantry (Kettle assumes that there was such a class, an assumption that has been challenged more than once), and her destruction at the hands of Alec and the law symbolizes the destruction of her class by the forces both of reaction and of the new capitalist, bourgeois class that did so well out of the *laissez-faire* arrangements of the 19th century. The argument is interesting but hardly fully convincing. To accept it means reducing one's perspective on the novel to a very narrow focus indeed.

In 1971 F. R. Southerington, in his *Hardy's Vision of Man*, divided the fiction into the two categories 'personal' and 'ideological', but no Marxist would rest content with the definition offered of the latter category. In 1976 G. W. Sherman published his *magnum opus, The Pessimism of Thomas Hardy*, in which the motivation behind the novels and poems is claimed to be a frustrated radicalism of the *Poor Man and the Lady* sort. Hardy is presented as consistently sympathetic to the working-class characters, and consistently hostile to the upper classes. All this is set in a matrix of ideas about the 19th century of an avowedly Marxist kind, and, there being no doubt that if Marx's analyses work anywhere they work for the century he was analysing, there are some useful points made about Hardy's 'background'. But the sense of strain is quickly apparent and the book often hard to follow into its remoter corners.

A more modern Marxism is apparent in the often inspiring introduction written by Terry Eagleton for the New Wessex edition of *Jude the Obscure* in 1974. Eagleton manages, with his usual brio, to de-sentimentalize Jude and his life (though one might think such a proceeding unnecessary) and to locate the story at the critical points of weakness in late-Victorian ideology. Vulgar Marxism gives place here to an emphasis on such topics as education and gender roles. Moving on from this sort of approach to the even more modern style of late Marxism known as 'cultural materialism', George Wotton published *Thomas Hardy: Towards A Materialist Criticism* in 1985. This text, typical of its decade, explicitly argues for a taking of sides; its purpose is to rescue Hardy from the liberal-humanist ideology in which most critics have trapped him, and to establish a Hardy who is, consciously or unconsciously, in revolt against the economic and class arrangements of his day. With a study such as this, highly theoretical and at times difficult to follow, we can see the immense distance we have come, not all of it over hospitable terrain, since Lord David Cecil 50 years earlier.

Also typical of the 1980s, and also interested in the 'construction' of a Hardy to suit political purposes, is Peter Widdowson's 1986 essay 'Hardy, "Wessex", and the Making of a National Culture' (*THA* 4). This swashbuckling piece takes some pretty effective swipes at the figure of Hardy the poet of the English countryside and the creator of a Wessex about which we can be nostalgic. It makes the undoubtedly salutary point that Hardy himself, though afflicted by nostalgia, was never dewy-eyed about the rural past he evoked, and that perhaps we should not be too sentimental either.

Perhaps the most striking recent publications on Hardy that are in a Marxist vein are those by John Goode (*Thomas Hardy: The Offensive Truth*, 1988; two years later, Goode produced an essay explicitly entitled 'Hardy and Marxism') and Roger Ebbatson (*Hardy: The Margin of the Unexpressed*, 1993). In both of these the Marxism is not of a pure and unadulterated kind. Both authors rely heavily on a wider battery of critical weapons than those provided by Marxist thinking, and make it clear that the poststructuralist endeavour is not easily to be divided up into neat parcels. Ebbatson's book, for instance, is in two halves: the first, as we have seen, is a series of generally poststructuralist pieces entitled 'Reading Desire'; only the second takes us noticeably leftwards, called as it is 'Speaking Class'. Goode moves freely between Marxist and other ideas, including Lacan, Barthes, and Bakhtin, as well as Marx, Macherey, Lukács, and others.

Goode's debt to Frederic Jameson's *The Political Unconscious* of 1981 is explicit; he refers to 'the pervasive assistance I have received from Jameson's important text in thinking about the theoretical implications of my approach to Hardy'. And indeed, with a little help from Gramsci and Marx, Goode sets up a Hardy marked by radical alienation who works along the ideological fault-lines of late 19th-century capitalism. Some of this is convincing: Hardy's earlier novels do indeed show him rather unsuccessfully trying to maintain 'a continuity between human relationships and a larger wisdom' (we may think of Clym Yeobright at the end of *The Return of the Native*), and the later novels could perhaps be seen as moving 'nearer to the possibility of a new ideological project which does not seek wisdom, but seeks to represent instead the opposition of structure and agency, the project of the ideological break itself'.

Such clauses, taken out of context, may unfairly seem more opaque than they are, but Goode descends at times into what, in or out of context, must count as the incomprehensible; Hardy himself might have found the following definition of the 'break' of alienation worrying: 'Hardy's ideological formation is to be located at an exact point before the radical disenfranchisement of the empirical calculus capitulates to the symbolic order in the name of the Other.' This sort of thing is not universal in Goode or in Marxist criticism in general, but it lies in wait for those who take the leftward path. What is best about Goode is the radical, deconstructive nature of his more comprehensible passages; on the end of *Tess*, for example, he is illuminating, confining his Marxist tendencies to a mere peroration to the interesting effect that 'Justice' (as in the dreadful sentence that comments on the hanging of the Pure Woman, 'Justice was done') was the title of the newspaper of William Morris's Social Democratic Federation, and that Hardy sent Morris a copy of the novel.

Ebbatson, relying on Lukács, Macherey, Benjamin, and others, discusses, in his 'Speaking Class' section, two highly relevant texts, *An Indiscretion in the Life of an Heiress* and 'The Dorsetshire Labourer'. Neither is treated very sympathetically by this sort of Marxism. Egbert Mayne in the former is seen as a sort of attenuated and weedy revolutionary, caught up in the dilemma of being without the courage to rebel properly, and thus ultimately complicit with the destructive nature of capitalism. Hardy's essay on the Dorset workfolk may be his 'most overtly sociological' piece, but it does not in the end, for Ebbatson, live up to the promise of its references to agricultural disturbances and the abortive attempts to set up trade unions in the county. The critic feels able to berate Hardy in terms such as these: 'Hardy fails to delineate or imagine ... the emergence of any specifically working-class movement with its own life and culture.' The 'fails' here is not neutral. The overall impression given, in connection with both texts, is that there is only one way of creating useful literary meaning, and that is by adherence to a sociological view based on the historical 'realities' of the period in question. This, of course, is by no means the only possible opinion in these matters.

Present behind the arguments of Goode and Ebbatson is the Foucauldian notion of

Power that has sustained the cultural-materialist version of Marxism, and this leads them at times to consider closely some of the physical and economic detail available in Hardy. George Wotton makes an explicit bid in this direction in his 1993 study *Thomas Hardy: Towards a Materialist Criticism*. This approach can be fruitful; equally, the fairly frequent reference to Mikhail Bakhtin in these left-leaning critics can yield good results. If there is one theorist whose work is more promising for the reading of Hardy than another, it must be this Russian stylistician; and indeed, Dennis Taylor laments, in his volume on *Hardy and Nineteenth-Century Philology* mentioned above, that nothing truly Bakhtinian has yet been done on him. Goode and Ebbatson seem to contradict this assertion and, when talking of the languages in which Hardy writes, are able to make some excellently Bakhtinian points. Who better than Hardy to demonstrate the importance and significance of voices in 19th-century England?

Feminism, Gender, and Sexuality

John Goode refers to Penny Boumelha's *Thomas Hardy and Women: Sexual Ideology and Narrative Form* (1982) as 'the first sustained poststructuralist analysis of Hardy' (*Thomas Hardy: The Offensive Truth*, 173). This may help to demonstrate the interconnectedness of all elements of the emerging modern paradigm; it is, indeed, 'ideology' which sustains sexism (as it also sustains feminism) in the way that Goode points out in another of his essays, 'Sue Bridehead and the New Woman' (in Mary Jacobus (ed.), *Women Writing and Writing about Women*, 1979).

Before the new thinking took hold, there was, as any reader of Hardy knows, much to be said about his women. D. H. Lawrence, writing in 1914–15, famously analyses Sue, Tess, and others in what has become a *locus classicus* of engaged criticism (*Phoenix*, 1936). No later critic is quite without an opinion on at least some aspect of the female in Hardy, but perhaps serious feminist analyses started in the wake of Mary Jacobus's essays on 'Sue the Obscure' (*Essays in Criticism*, 25 (1975)) and 'Tess's Purity' (ibid. 26 (1976)). Debate raged through the later 1970s and early 1980s as to the nature of Hardy's meanings, especially in relation to Sue. Is she meant to be neurotic or revolutionary? Is she weak and a tease, or the first emancipated woman in fiction?

At least a dozen essays can be identified that canvass these and related topics, and they are complemented by Elaine Showalter's 'The Unmanning of the Mayor of Casterbridge' (in *Critical Approaches to the Fiction of Thomas Hardy*, 1979); by essays on Eustacia and her suicide by Frank Giordano (*Texas Studies in Literature and Language*, 30 (1980)) and Katherine Hanley (*College Language Association Journal*, 25/2 (1981)); and by regular chapters on the topic of women, mostly from an identifiably feminist perspective, in general studies of Hardy or of aspects of the novel, such as John Lucas's 'Hardy's Women' (in his *The Literature of Change*, 1977), Gail Cunningham's 'Thomas Hardy: New Women for Old' (in her *The New Woman and the Victorian Novel*, 1978), and Patricia Stubbs's *Women and Fiction* of 1979. Such work then leads us through Boumelha's book of 1982 to Pamela Jekel's *Thomas Hardy's Heroines* (1986), and on to Patricia Ingham's *Thomas Hardy* (1989) in the Feminist Readings series. Ingham is particularly useful as a feminist reader: for her, the lesson of deconstruction having been learnt, there are far fewer dividing lines between the sexes in Hardy than one might suppose; especially in the later fiction, women become more and more complex at Hardy's hands, and lose much of their allotted Victorian status, in spite of their often terrible fates.

All this is but the tip of an iceberg of feminist reading of Hardy. It is an iceberg that has come to have some very familiar contours indeed: it consists of a million undergraduate essays, written in English departments often, though not exclusively, by female undergraduates, hundreds of MA and Ph.D. theses, and dozens of published articles. The familiar contours include a list of the crimes that Victorian sexism perpetrated against women, a close analysis of Hardy's language, and the presentation of his characters, notably the female characters, in the light of this history of oppression. Ideology looms fairly large, but sexuality even larger. Here are some representative titles from the 1980s and 1990s, all concerned in one way or another with the 'treatment of women' question: 'Thomas Hardy, the Man Who "Liked" Women' (article, 1981); 'The Habit of Misogyny (dissertation, 1981); 'Pure Tess: Hardy on Knowing a Woman' (article, 1982); 'An Affinity for Birds: Kindness in *Jude*' (article, 1981); 'Fictional Consensus and Female Casualties' (chapter in book, 1983); 'History, Figuration and Female Subjectivity in *Tess*' (article, 1983); 'Angles of Vision and Questions of Gender in *Far from the Madding Crowd* (article, 1986); 'Tess of the d'Urbervilles: Misfortune is a Woman' (article, 1989); 'Fictions of Feminine Voice: Antiphony and Silence in *Tess*' (chapter, 1990); 'Gender and Silence in Thomas Hardy's Texts' (chapter, 1992); all the articles in *The Sense of Sex: Feminist Perspectives on Hardy*, ed. Margaret Higonnet (1993); 'Hardy's Sue Bridehead and the "New Woman"' (article, 1993); 'Towards a Feminist Theory of Description' (dissertation, 1993); 'The Feminine Voice in the Poetry of Thomas Hardy' (article, 1992); 'Inner Landscape in Three of Hardy's Characters' (dissertation, 1994); 'The Male Bias of Language and Gender Hierarchy: Hardy's Bathsheba Everdene...' (article, 1995); 'Female Characterisation in Thomas Hardy's Early Fiction' (dissertation, 1995); 'The Quiet Women of Egdon Heath' (article, 1996); and, to bring this very selective listing full circle, 'Thomas Hardy: A Man Who "Liked" Women' (dissertation, 1996).

Closely connected to these essays—there are full-length books, too, including *The Decline of the Goddess: Nature, Culture and Women in Thomas Hardy's Fiction*—and obviously to the whole question of 'Gender', is 'Sexuality', another growth industry in Hardy studies since the mid-1980s. The major publication in this area is undoubtedly Rosemarie Morgan's *Women and Sexuality in the Novels of Thomas Hardy* (1988). Morgan sees Hardy's heroines not so much as passive victims but as active and, particularly, sexually active. Using and enjoying their sexuality, these women emerge as far stronger than traditional criticism has supposed; not least they pose a threat that is virtually political in its power.

Here are some titles of theses and articles that have contributed to the sense that this has been, alongside feminism, the central area of modern thinking about Hardy. The titles themselves reveal much: '"Swinburne Planteth, Hardy Watereth": Victorian Views of Pain and Pleasure in Human Sexuality' (article, 1984); 'Bathsheba's Lovers: Male Sexuality in *Far from the Madding Crowd*' (article, 1984); 'The Late Nineteenth Century Novel and the Change towards the Sexual: Gissing, Hardy and Lawrence' (article, 1985); 'Tess: A Less Than Pure Woman Ambivalently Presented' (article, 1986); 'Androgyny, Survival and Fulfilment in ... *Far from the Madding Crowd*' (article, 1988); '"You Did Not Come": Absence, Death and Eroticism in *Tess*' (chapter, 1990); 'Sexual Ideology and Narrative Form in *Jude*' (article, 1989); '"A Little More than Persuading": Tess and the Subject of Sexual Violence' (chapter, 1991); 'Male Relations in Thomas Hardy's *Jude*' (article, 1991); 'Hardy's Sexual Evasions...' (article, 1993); 'Ruinous Bodies: Women and Sexuality in Hardy's Late Fiction' (article, 1993); 'The Signification of Arabella's Missile: Feminine Sexuality...' (article, 1996). To this list may be added a couple of books: *Sexual Tyranny in Wessex: Hardy's Witches and Demons of Folklore* (1993) and *The Stone and the Scorpion: The Female Subject of Desire in the Novels of Charlotte Brontë, George Eliot and Thomas Hardy* (1994). These listings could be greatly extended, in a way they could not for any other topic in the world of Hardy criticism.

Other Topics

There are many lesser topics that have engaged the poststructuralist attentions of recent critics, but none to compare with this one. Thus Reader-Response critics have made something of certain texts, from Dale Kramer's 'How to Read *A Few Crusted Characters*' of 1975, through Wayne Anderson's 'The Rhetoric of Silence in Hardy's Fiction' of 1985, to Judith Mitchell's 'Hardy's Female Reader' of 1993 (which brings together two aspects of the poststructuralist project rather neatly).

Psychological studies of a modern kind have not been wanting, from Carol and Duane Edwards's article '*Jude the Obscure*: A Psychoanalytic Study' of 1981, through Romey Keys's 'Reading of "The Withered Arm"' of 1985, to Jeff Nunokawa's 'Tess, Tourism and the Spectacle of the Woman' of 1992, which combines historical and materialist elements with gender and psychoanalytic approaches.

Besides these, Hardy has provoked a whole host of less common poststructuralist work, ranging from postcolonial topics (Simon Gatrell, 'England, Europe and Empire: Hardy, Meredith and Gissing', 1992) to philosophical questions relating to such mainstream deconstructionist topics as Subjectivity, History, Mythography, and so on.

The current state of Hardy criticism seems to me to be very healthy. In the battle between the Ancients (here represented by New Criticism and 'traditional' ways of thinking) and the Moderns (here read 'poststructuralists'), there is good work on both sides. My prediction must be for eventual victory for the Moderns, but this would be without more traditional views and techniques having to abandon the field altogether. The continuing interest in the 19th century and in Hardy's biography almost guarantee the survival of a minority view. Perhaps the two will merge in a new consensus in the 21st century.

A final note: a neat summary of all Hardy criticism from the beginning until 1990 is available in Charles Lock's *Thomas Hardy*, Criticism in Focus (1992). LStJB

D

dance. See MUSIC.

Darwinism. Hardy was 'among the earliest acclaimers' of *The Origin of Species* (*LW* 158), and remained committed to the dire truthfulness of Darwin's ideas. His last lines of verse, dictated on his deathbed, mock G. K. *Chesterton for claiming to refute Darwin ('Epitaph for G. K. Chesterton'). Hardy was unusual in the post-Darwin era in eschewing popular meliorist compromises such as 'moral evolution', 'creative evolution', or social Darwinism. He was unique in making great tragic literature from the belief that 'the surviving organism is not necessarily the better... though it must be that which is most in harmony with surrounding conditions' (*L* i 40).

The *Origin* probably confirmed rather than caused his disbelief in a beneficent personal deity, and he found no difficulty in reconciling the ideas of Charles Darwin and T. H. Huxley with the peasant fatalism of his upbringing (Millgate 91, 132). The notebooks show, however, that serious and well-informed thinking on Darwinism remained a habit, with entries on creative evolution, archebiosis, beetles, butterflies, crabs, compound eyes, Herbert Spencer on Political Integration, Samuel Butler on evolution by mechanization, the evolution of 'the woman of the future', and many more.

His literary work forms a rich response to the implications of Darwinian science. The gravest of these was the loss for humanity of any divinely given superiority or purpose. 'Does Mr Huxley claim apes on his grandmother's or his grandfather's side?' thundered Bishop Wilberforce, but Hardy made Darwin's revelation that 'We all are one with creeping things; | And apes and men | Blood-brethren' one of science's crucial discoveries, in his ironic 'Drinking Song'. Man 'is not the central point of the universe... He is no more than a zoological species...' (*LN* ii 98–9). The sense of loss is poignant: 'So here we are, in piteous case | Like butterflies | Of many dyes | Upon an Alpine glacier's face' ('Drinking Song'). This consciousness of diminished importance makes vivid many of the novels' images: Henry Knight confronting the vastness of geologic history as he clings for life to the cliff (*PBE* 22); Viviette and Swithin as 'two infinitesimal lives against the stupendous background of the stellar universe' (*TT*, Preface); the various rendezvous in *The Mayor of Casterbridge* at the age-old venues of Maumbury Ring or Mai-Dun Castle; or Tess and Marian 'moving like flies' over the wintry brown surface above Flintcomb-Ash. Chronologically, geographically, and biologically, humanity is now infinitesimal. *The Dynasts*, too, pulls back its lens until the great men and affairs of the *Napoleonic Wars appear 'Like meanest insects on obscurest leaves'.

For Jude and Sue, their 'horrible sensitivity', their 'development of emotional perceptiveness' (*JO* 6.3), was to Hardy evolution's 'blunder of overdoing': 'The emotions have no place in a world of defect' (*LW* 153). Another note, in 1889, affirms the 'woeful fact—that the human race is too extremely developed for its corporeal conditions, the nerves being evolved to an activity abnormal in such an environment...' (*LW* 227). This is what cripples or kills Boldwood, Viviette, Clym, Giles, Henchard, Tess, Jude, and Sue, who all embody Hardy's questioning 'if what we call Nature... so far back as when she crossed the line from invertebrates to vertebrates, did not exceed her mission' (*LW* 227). The poem 'Before Life and After' locates the tragedy of the human condition at 'the birth of consciousness' and 'the disease of feeling'. Other poems dealing with this evolution of suffering through sensitivity include 'A Plaint to Man', 'The Mother Mourns', 'I Travel as a Phantom Now', and 'New Year's Eve'. Hardy followed Darwin, too, in the belief that natural selection does not always produce perfection; adaptation is often imperfect, and misery and defeat ensue, as for Henchard, a superseded species fighting for lost territory with the wrong weapons.

Hardy is always prone to present attraction between the sexes in biological terms, from showing women as 'fishers of men' who 'set out their fascinations', and the 'animal' quality of Manston's loving in *Desperate Remedies* (4.2, 12.4) to the 'conjunctive orders from headquarters, unconsciously received by unfortunate men when the last intention of their lives is to be occupied with the feminine' in *Jude the Obscure* (1.6). His observation of the natural world, too, always fine and meticulous (like Darwin's), takes on the Darwinian awareness of conditioning by environment. This includes the seasonal shaping of *Under the Greenwood Tree* and *Far from the Madding Crowd*, the colouring of Miller Loveday and Diggory Venn by their trades, the dress of many characters, and the participation of the heath-dwellers, woodlanders, and labourers in the 'great battle for life'. The Darwinian allusion is unmistakable in the description of trees 'wrestling for existence' among 'Dead boughs scattered about like ichthyosauri in a museum' (*W* 42).

Characters such as Gabriel Oak and Marty South are, like the fieldwomen in *Tess*, 'merged' with their terrain. Others fail to adapt as the environment changes. Tess's story, like Henchard's, is charted consciously in these terms, her every state conditioned by the terrain she moves across. And however near extinction, she embodies that other Darwinian tenet, the striving for felicity, to fulfil the intention of evolutionary perfection.

While writing *Tess*, Hardy became increasingly conscious of another constraint on individual action, *heredity. His treatment of this and other forces is never wholly deterministic, however. Tess and her fellow dairymaids may be 'each... but a portion of one organism called sex', forced to writhe 'feverishly under the oppressiveness of an emotion thrust on them by cruel Nature's law' (*TDU* 23), but for each also the 'consciousness upon which [Clare] had intruded was the single opportunity of existence ever vouchsafed... her every and only chance' (25). So Tess insists '"Call me Tess"', and refuses to be classed as 'one of a long row only' (19), and Henchard ends the note in which he demands oblivion with a thumping assertion of individuality: 'To this I put my name. MICHAEL HENCHARD.' Hardy is probably the most powerful artist of the Darwinian crisis because he so honestly confronted the implications of the message Darwin brought, yet also defiantly affirmed the inviolate significance of each individual's 'precious life'.

RR

Gillian Beer, *Darwin's Plots: Evolutionary Narrative in Darwin, George Eliot, and Nineteenth-Century Fiction* (1983).
—— *Open Fields: Science in Cultural Encounter* (1996).
John Holloway, 'Hardy's Major Fiction', in *The Charted Mirror* (1960).
Peter Morton, *The Vital Science: Biology and the Literary Imagination 1860–1900* (1984).
Roger Robinson, 'Hardy and Darwin', in Norman Page (ed.), *Thomas Hardy: The Writer and His Background* (1980).

de la Mare, Walter (1873–1956), poet and novelist. He stayed with the Hardys at Max Gate in June 1921 and was taken by Hardy to inspect the Stinsford graveyard. It was on this occasion (17 June) that Hardy gave his visitor the recently written poem 'Voices from Things Growing in a Churchyard' to read and told him that the 'Fanny Hurd' of the opening stanza was Fanny Hurden, a schoolfellow who had died at the age of 20 and whose grave, with headstone, can be seen at Stinsford; Hardy had been romantically attracted to her, and it was a matter of permanent regret to him that, as a result of a childish accident, he had caused her hands to suffer burns from the schoolroom stove. Another visit to Max Gate, by de la Mare and his wife, took place in May 1923. On his deathbed Hardy asked for de la Mare's poem 'The Listeners' to be read to him.

Walter de la Mare, 'Meeting Thomas Hardy', *Listener* (28 April 1955).

Desperate Remedies. The earliest of Hardy's fourteen published novels.

Composition

Hardy began the novel in 1869, after trying for some months to find a publisher for his first novel, *The Poor Man and the Lady*. The novelist George *Meredith had read *The Poor Man* for Chapman & Hall; in an encounter widely (though not quite accurately) seen as the genesis of *Desperate Remedies*, he advised Hardy to withdraw *The Poor Man* and write a novel with more of a plot. In the spring of 1870 Hardy submitted the nearly complete manuscript of *Desperate Remedies* to Macmillan, who rejected it, and then to Tinsley

Brothers, who had offered to publish *The Poor Man* if Hardy put up money against potential losses. William *Tinsley was willing to publish, subject to revisions based on the reader's report, and an advance from Hardy of £75. Oddly, Hardy did not try Chapman & Hall, who despite Meredith's misgivings had offered to publish *The Poor Man* for only £20. Perhaps, as he suggests in the *Life* (*LW* 79), Hardy did not want *Desperate Remedies* to be read as the outcome of Meredith's advice.

Although no manuscript of *Desperate Remedies* survives, one change made at this point is identifiable. In his reader's report for Macmillan, John Morley complains about making 'the violation of a young lady at an evening party' the key to the novel's action (quoted in Charles Morgan, *The House of Macmillan* (1943), 93–4), but in the 1871 text only the vague statement that Miss Aldclyffe is 'cruelly betrayed' (21) by her cousin remains. Tinsley also asked that Anne Seaway be made less obviously Manston's mistress; in the event the simple excision of the word 'mistress' seems to have sufficed.

Publication

Like its immediate successor, *Under the Greenwood Tree, Desperate Remedies* is exceptional among Hardy's novels in not having originally appeared as a serial. Tinsley published the work in three volumes, at the traditional price of one-and-a-half guineas (31*s.* 6*d.*), on 25 March 1871. In 1874 the novel appeared in the United States as part of Henry *Holt's Leisure Hour series, and at Holt's request Hardy readjusted Miss Aldclyffe's sexual history, this time changing her shameful secret into clandestine marriage to a criminal (an alteration he never transferred to later editions). For the 1889 Ward and Downey edition Hardy made extensive revisions to style and to passages criticized by reviewers; perhaps at the request of the publishers, he also toned down some risqué and sensuous expressions. The apparent censorship was oddly inconsistent, leaving largely intact scenes such as Miss Aldclyffe's visit to Cytherea's bed and Manston's first meeting with Cytherea. Hardy also nudged the Springroves' social status up slightly and decreased the amount of dialect in the elder Edward Springrove's speech. Finally, he changed some fictional place-names, probably in order to distance *Desperate Remedies* from 'Wessex', his developing fictional world. The county town, for instance, became 'Troominster'; the original, 'Froominster', might have suggested Dorchester in the Frome valley and by extension 'Casterbridge', Dorchester's Wessex counterpart.

Hardy never revised *Desperate Remedies* as thoroughly again, although he changed place-names and distances, this time in order to bring the novel into 'Wessex', for the 1895–6 Osgood, McIlvaine collected edition: 'Froominster'/'Troominster' became 'Casterbridge', for instance, and 'Creston' became 'Budmouth'. There were also some verbal and dialect changes in 1896, as there were again in 1912 for the Macmillan Wessex Edition.

Reception

As a novel by a new and anonymous author, *Desperate Remedies* attracted predictably little attention on its first appearance. Each of the five reviews it received made some positive remarks, especially about scenes involving the rustic characters, but the plot came under fire, especially in the *Spectator* (22 April 1871; repr. *CH*), which suggested that the novel, though demonstrating considerable talent, was probably itself a desperate remedy for 'ennui or an emaciated purse'. A long and favourable commentary by Hardy's friend Horace *Moule appeared in the *Saturday Review* (30 September 1871; repr. in *CH*), but too late to have a material effect on the poor sales of the novel, already being offered at reduced prices.

Plot

Ambrose Graye's death impoverishes his children, Cytherea and Owen. They move to Budmouth, where Owen has found work, and Cytherea falls in love with Edward Springrove. Pledging his love but hinting at impediments, Edward leaves Budmouth for London. Cytherea becomes maid and then companion to Miss Aldclyffe of Knapwater House. Miss Aldclyffe, having discovered that Cytherea is her namesake and the daughter of her lost love Ambrose, alternately bullies and pets her. Cytherea learns of Edward's longstanding engagement to Adelaide Hinton, and shortly afterwards meets the new Knapwater steward Aeneas Manston, who fascinates and terrifies her. She breaks off her engagement to Edward, but continues to love him. Though deeply attracted to Cytherea, Manston turns out to be already married. Miss Aldclyffe forces him to bring his estranged wife to live with him at Knapwater, but the inn Eunice Manston goes to upon her arrival burns down, and she is presumed dead.

Edward's father, the innkeeper, loses everything, and Miss Aldclyffe can legally force him to rebuild several cottages destroyed in the fire. Using Mr Springrove's vulnerable position and misleading 'evidence' of Cytherea's feelings, Manston and Miss Aldclyffe coerce Edward into renewing his engagement to Adelaide. Manston begins courting Cytherea, though without success until Owen develops a mysterious lameness. Medical bills and Owen's inability to work put the Grayes under severe financial pressure, and Manston exploits this to make Cytherea marry him. Before the marriage can be consummated, it is called into question by the revelation that Eunice, having left the inn before the fire, may still be alive. Manston advertises for her with apparent reluctance, and in due course a woman assumed to be Eunice joins him at Knapwater. Cytherea is now free, though in a dubious social position, and Adelaide has jilted Edward to marry a richer man. Edward persuades the now-recovered Owen to help him prove Manston a wilful bigamist, but they discover instead that the woman living with Manston is an impostor, and that Manston has killed Eunice. Now a fugitive, Manston tries to claim Cytherea as his wife, but is caught on the point of raping and/or abducting her. He writes a confession, and hangs himself in his prison cell. Miss Aldclyffe falls ill at the news and dies, after telling Cytherea that Manston was her illegitimate son, that her past compelled her to give up Ambrose Graye, and that she had hoped to retrieve Ambrose vicariously through Manston's marriage to Cytherea. Edward and Cytherea marry and live at Knapwater; Edward manages the estate, and their children will inherit it.

Critical Approaches

Until recently, *Desperate Remedies* has not fared well critically. Its deployment of such popular sub-generic modes as sensation fiction, the Gothic romance, and the detective story appears to isolate it from 'Wessex' and the matrix of concerns that came to be seen as genuinely Hardyan, especially after the publication of *Far from the Madding Crowd*. As early as Havelock Ellis's 'Thomas Hardy's Novels' (*Westminster Review*, April 1883; repr. in *CH*), *Desperate Remedies* seems out of place; for Ellis it is in the more emphatically rural world of *Under the Greenwood Tree*, 'far away from the murky atmosphere of *Desperate Remedies*', that Hardy finds his vocation. The cultural status of sensation, like that of Gothic and the detective story, has always been low; the focus on crime and various kinds of deviance in their heavily plotted stories has made sensation novelists such as Mary Elizabeth Braddon (1837–1915) and Wilkie *Collins critically suspect, despite their popularity, and *Desperate Remedies* has undoubtedly suffered from its association with the genre. Until quite recently, even sympathetic and detailed discussions, such as that in Richard H. Taylor's *The Neglected Hardy: Thomas Hardy's Lesser Novels* (1982), have not challenged received opinion about the book's 'minor' status.

Hardy himself apparently encouraged readers to set *Desperate Remedies* aside. In his 1889 preface he notes that it was his first novel, written 'at a time when he was feeling his way to a method', and excessively dependent on 'mystery, entanglement, surprise and moral obliquity'. He reinforced these deprecatory remarks by placing it among the 'Novels of Ingenuity' when he classified his work for the 1912 Macmillan Wessex Edition, and again in the *Life*, where he contrasts the rejected, radical *Poor Man and the Lady* with *Desperate Remedies*, supposedly a novel written almost to order, simply to get published (*LW* 64). Often invoked as proof that *Desperate Remedies* was an accident, the unfortunate mistake of a young novelist who 'took Meredith's advice too literally' (*LW* 64), this contrast cannot be wholly verified or disputed, since *The Poor Man* survives only as fragments borrowed for other works. As Pamela Dalziel has argued, however, the many passages which appear in both *Desperate Remedies* and *An Indiscretion in the Life of an Heiress* (the novella Hardy constructed from the remains of *The Poor Man* in 1878: see UNCOLLECTED STORIES) make the opposition between his first two books questionable ('Exploiting the *Poor Man*'). Hardy certainly cannibalized a good deal from his first novel in writing *Desperate Remedies*, just as he took poetry he had written during the 1860s and, 'after dissolving it into prose' (1912 Preface to *DR*), used it for *Desperate Remedies* (and likely for *The Poor Man* before that). Moreover, the judgements he applied to his works years after their first appearance do not necessarily define his sense of their merit, especially those judgements made once he began to establish himself as a poet and wanted to deflect critical interest away from his fiction. Catherine Neale argues that Hardy's public comments on his novels are not only slippery but also strategic, and mediated by reviewers' and critics' responses.

For many years most commentators who discussed *Desperate Remedies* at all tried to separate it from its genre, as it were, hiving off passages or characters which seem to anticipate later novels, and ignoring the 'sensational' elements as far as possible; these efforts may even take their cue from Hardy's 1889 preface, which raises (only to dismiss) the possibility of reissuing the novel as an anthology of the few parts worth saving. Yet there is a remarkable disagreement as to what any such division of the novel should save, suggesting a similar lack of consensus as to what defines 'genuine' Hardy: for some it is the cider-making scene, for others the imagery, or Cytherea's poignant cry to Owen in Chapter 13 that '"Nobody can enter into another's nature truly"', and for still others the scene in which Anne Seaway, a detective, and Miss Aldclyffe observe each other and all three spy on Manston as he moves and buries Eunice's body.

One episode often singled out (though not always for praise) is the bedroom scene between Miss Aldclyffe and Cytherea. Defining the extent of Hardy's awareness of lesbian desire—or indeed anyone's awareness of it in the England of the 1870s—is difficult. Some readers speculate that Hardy did not know what he was writing, and Robert Gittings suggests that he merely transcribed an anecdote recounted by one of his servant cousins (*Young Thomas Hardy*, 143). However one accounts for them, though, conflicting currents of desire and social domination make the episode disturbing: whether Miss Aldclyffe's offer of love is sexual or passionately platonic, Cytherea's subordinate status certainly makes it coercive. Others have noted cross-gender parallels with Hardy's own childhood experience as the favourite of Julia Augusta *Martin, the lady of the Kingston Maurward manor (the 'original' of Knapwater House); this may provide what Roger Ebbatson calls the 'nexus of sexuality and class condescension [which] fuels the lesbian scenes of *Desperate Remedies*' (*Hardy: The Margin of the Unexpressed*, 21).

Separating the 'real' from the sensational Hardy sometimes takes the form of searching out Hardy's 'sources', as if to shift the blame for the plot onto Wilkie Collins, for instance, first mentioned as a likely model by the reviewer in the *Morning Post* (13 April 1871). Parallels with Collins's *The Woman in White* (1860) and *Basil* (1852) are emphasized by several critics and are explored in detail by W. R. Rutland (*Thomas Hardy: A Study of His Writings and Their Background* (1938; repr. 1962), 141–6) and by F. B. Pinion (*Thomas Hardy: Art and Thought* (1977), 2–9). Gittings notes the influence of Harrison *Ainsworth, whose Gothic novel *Old St Paul's* (1841) Hardy was fond of as a child (*Young Thomas Hardy* 139–40). Most assume that the influence of Collins and/or Ainsworth was unfortunate, part of the 'mistake' Hardy made in turning to sensation fiction in the first place, but Roy Morrell's *Thomas Hardy: The Will and the Way* (1965) argues that *Desperate Remedies* systematically undermines the notion of Providence that Collins's (and Ainsworth's) novels generally invoke.

In *Thomas Hardy: His Career as a Novelist* (1971), Michael Millgate also sees Hardy's appropriation of the sensation form as having a point, despite an element of opportunism; Millgate suggests that the novel attempts to reach beyond generic boundaries towards a new kind of sensation novel (pp. 34–5). Support for this reading comes from an 1888 note of Hardy's, recorded in the *Life*, about the possibility of 'psychical' sensation fiction, where 'the casualty or adventure is held to be of no intrinsic interest, but the effect upon the faculties is the important matter to be depicted' (*LW* 213); this may indicate that even in 1871 sensation meant more to Hardy than simply a way of getting published.

The critical desire to rescue the 'good' from the 'bad' in this novel seems to reflect critics' sense that the book is better than it ought to be, given its 'unHardyan' genre: Irving Howe, for instance, sees in it the 'raw evidence of art' and a 'coarse and indefensible power' (*Thomas Hardy* (1966), 35). This idea that the novel is an uneasy combination of 'power' and 'rawness' finds an echo in several other commentators, and may explain why *Desperate Remedies* has continued to attract attention even from critics who cannot quite bring themselves to take it seriously. At times the feeling that it is more than a sensation novel turns into the complaint that it has too many divergent impulses in it to succeed, either as sensation fiction or as the 'real' Hardy novel that struggles against the limitations of the genre.

The numerous *allusions in this novel are a significant part of its unruly and diverse energies, and to many they have seemed excessive. Not only the narrator, but also the characters, protagonists and antagonists alike, produce telling quotations from Virgil, Keats, Milton, Shakespeare, Shelley, the Bible, and several other sources—even on one occasion the letters of Laurence Sterne. Hardy's ability to handle allusion in general has been widely debated, but his use of it in *Desperate Remedies* has attracted especially pejorative attention. Even Marlene Springer's positive discussion registers dissatisfaction with several 'intrusive' allusions in the novel (*Hardy's Use of Allusion* (1983), 30), and others complain more insistently, often reading the allusions as the unfortunate effect of self-education or of the insecure writer's need to show off his knowledge. Hardy's allusions to Virgil's *Aeneid* are especially vulnerable here, since they can often seem outrageously inappropriate, as when the chaste warrior Camilla from the *Aeneid* is invoked to describe the attitudes of Anne Seaway, Manston's mistress and (the narrator hints) a former prostitute.

Some more recent critical comments, by contrast, suggest that these apparent solecisms form part of a wider strategy. Joe Fisher, for instance, in *The Hidden Hardy* (1992), sees the 'processes of naming and allusion' (p. 29) as crucial elements of the book's subversive subtext; to Fisher the novel's plot, with its overt reinforcement of gender and class ideologies, is continuously disrupted by subtextual critiques of those ideologies, to the point where the entire book can be read as a sustained joke. Fisher's argument tends to overreach itself, but it does suggest new approaches to allusions such as the Camilla one, and to the 'indefensible power' of the book as a whole.

Other recent discussions of this novel also tend to focus on subversive subtexts which undo the apparently conventional plot, and to give the book a more central place within Hardy's fictional *œuvre* than it has usually been assigned in the past. An especially significant reading of this kind is Ebbatson's, which uses a variety of theoretical perspectives to address the novel's disjunctive form and 'textual polyphony' (*Hardy: The Margin of the Unexpressed*, 15), and mobilizes the concept of the 'flaneur', derived from (among others) the Marxist theorist Walter Benjamin, in a suggestive commentary on the novel's urban scenes, and the connection between detection and narration.

Several feminist critics have addressed *Desperate Remedies*, often seeing Cytherea (and sometimes Miss Aldclyffe as well) as the victim of a variety of patriarchal plots and of a barrage of aphoristic generalizations about women. Patricia Ingham, however, argues that in this novel, as elsewhere in Hardy, the plots are subtly undermined, and the aphorisms tend to destabilize the very 'truths' about women which they appear to inscribe (*Thomas Hardy* (1989), 14–22). Corresponding to Ebbatson's and Fisher's, Ingham's reading sees a value in the very disruptive qualities of *Desperate Remedies* which earlier critics tended to read as flaws.

Thanks to an increasing tolerance for and even interest in novels which breach generic decorum, and in popular art forms such as sensation fiction, there has recently been an upsurge of critical interest in *Desperate Remedies.* The greater range and liveliness of the debate, together with the appearance of new paperback editions, may restore this book to a wider readership, and encourage readers to broaden their notion of the 'real' Hardy to include his first published novel. MPR

Pamela Dalziel, 'Exploiting the *Poor Man*: The Genesis of Hardy's *Desperate Remedies*', *Journal of English and Germanic Philology*, 94 (1995).

Roger Ebbatson, *Hardy: The Margin of the Unexpressed* (1993).

Catherine Neale, '*Desperate Remedies*: The Merits and Demerits of Popular Fiction', *Critical Survey*, 5 (1993).

'Destiny and a Blue Cloak.' See UNCOLLECTED STORIES.

dialect. Hardy's attitude to and understanding of the Dorset dialect was formed, like so much else in his creative life, by his parents. Both spoke with a marked local accent, but his mother, very ambitious for her children, consciously eliminated from her speech many non-standard lexical and grammatical formations, and urged her son to do the same. His father, on the other hand, was unashamed in his use of the full range of the dialect. Hardy wrote of Tess Durbeyfield that she 'spoke two languages; the dialect at home, more or less; ordinary English abroad and to persons of quality' (*TDU* 3), and Hardy as a young man had a similar bilingualism—though probably he used the dialect at home less rather than more. In fact, in early versions of *Tess of the d'Urbervilles*, this account of Tess's speech read differently: she spoke in dialect 'only when excited by joy, surprise or grief'—and this may well have been Hardy's own youthful experience.

As Hardy matured he learned other dialects, amongst them that of the literary élite, as is ironically shown in the language of an account he wrote quite early in his career of his practice in representing dialect in his fiction: 'if a writer attempts to exhibit on paper the precise accents of a rustic speaker he disturbs the proper balance of true representation by unduly insisting upon the grotesque element; thus directing attention to a point of inferior interest, and diverting it from the speaker's meaning' (*Athenaeum*, 30 November 1878). In this Hardy pandered to his middle-class university-educated critics. A casual reading of *Under the Greenwood Tree* (1872)—or even of *The Hand of Ethelberta* (1876), which is not usually thought of as a novel enriched by dialect—shows that though Hardy did not follow his countryman and friend William *Barnes in writing *in* the Dorset dialect, he was committed not just to representing a Dorset speaker's meaning, but also to showing his urban, middle-class audience the richness, the vitality, and indeed the occasional satisfying grotesqueness of Dorset speech. In *Ethelberta*, a lad transplanted from Wessex to London says: 'if I talk the Wessex way 'tisn't for want of knowing better; 'tis because my staunch nater makes me bide faithful to our old ancient institutions' (18). It is worth noting in passing that for Hardy until around 1890, Dorset and Wessex were coterminous.

By 1881 his publicly expressed attitude, if not his practice, was changing; in a less defensive piece of self-analysis he wrote: 'The rule of scrupulously preserving the local idiom, together with the words which have no synonym among those in general use, while printing in the ordinary way most of those local expressions which are but a modified articulation of words in use elsewhere, is the rule I usually follow'; and he added: 'It must, of course, be always a matter for regret that, in order to be understood, writers should be obliged thus slightingly to treat varieties of English which are intrinsically as genuine, grammatical, and worthy of the royal title as is the all-prevailing competitor which bears it [i.e. the Queen's English]' (*Spectator*, 15 October 1881).

In October 1881 he was preparing to write *Two on a Tower*, which has, in the few chapters devoted to Dorset speakers, a high concentration of unique dialect words. In the first of these scenes the vicar and the village choir are rehearsing hymns, and there is an exchange significant for this discussion:

> the bass contingent at last got under way with a time of its own:
>
> 'Honwerd, Christen sojers!'
>
> 'Ah, that's where we are so defective—the pronunciation,' interrupted the parson. 'Now repeat after me:
>
> "On-ward, Christ-ian, sol-diers."'
>
> The choir repeated like an exaggerative echo:
>
> 'On-wed, Chris-ting, sol-jaws!'
>
> 'Better!' said the parson... (3)

This is the first-edition version. The interchange is followed by the refusal of the choir-members to respond to the vicar's attempt to make them use the new-fangled tonic sol-fa as 'out of the order of nater', and then by their singing the hymn in accord with an old tuning-fork 'wrought before pianoforte builders had sent up the pitch to make their instruments brilliant'. All these details are directly or metaphorically emblematic of resistance to the supersession of the Dorset dialect by the Queen's English.

In 1883 Hardy made the decision to build a house in Dorchester, and one of the youthful acquaintances he renewed then was with William Barnes, poet, teacher, clergyman, and advocate of the Dorset dialect. Barnes died only three years later, and in an obituary notice in the *Athenaeum* (16 October 1886), Hardy acknowledged Barnes's role in establishing the significance of the dialect: 'he has shown the world that far from being, as popularly supposed, a corruption of correct English, it is a distinct branch of Teutonic speech, regular in declension and conjugation, and richer in many classes of words than any other tongue known to him'.

In the same year *The Mayor of Casterbridge* was published, and an exchange between Michael Henchard and Elizabeth-Jane shows effectively why dialect speech was rapidly being replaced by standard English:

> One grievous failing of Elizabeth's was her occasional pretty and picturesque use of dialect words—those terrible marks of the beast to the truly genteel.
>
> ...'If you'll bide where you be a minute, father, I'll get it.'
>
> '"Bide where you be!"' he echoed sharply. 'Good God, are you only fit to carry wash to a pig-trough, that ye use such words as those?'
>
> ...in time it came to pass that for 'fay' she said 'succeed'; that she no longer spoke of 'dumbledores' but of 'humble bees'; no longer said of young men and women that they 'walked together', but that they were 'engaged'; that she grew to talk of 'greggles' as 'wild hyacinths'; that when she had not slept she did not quaintly tell the servants that she had been 'hag-rid', but that she had 'suffered from indigestion'. (*MC* 20)

The narrator's pleasure in the dialect words as 'pretty and picturesque' does not reflect Barnes's scholarly seriousness about Dorset dialect as a separate language, nor even Hardy's less dedicated acknowledgement of its abiding value, but rather the still less committed interest of a cultivated middle-class gentleman confronted with charming rural irregularities—Hardy, as often, inventing a narrative voice that will appeal to the experience of the majority of his readers.

When Hardy revised all of his fiction for the first collected edition of his work in 1895–6, his concern for the representation of dialect, as one of the distinguishing marks of Wessex, was at its height. In every novel the dialectal content of the speech of those characters who occasionally or habitually used dialect vocabulary or constructions was increased. It is particularly interesting that, when the standard-English-speaking schoolteacher-friends Phillotson and Gillingham meet in *Jude the Obscure* (4.4) (written just before the Osgood, McIlvaine edition was published), Hardy has them occasionally revert to dialect forms in their conversation—a powerful marker of intimacy, in an instinctive acknowledgement of their shared childhood, before standardization had taken them over.

In 1908 Hardy edited a selection of Barnes's Dorset poems, and he felt constrained to add glosses and paraphrases for the information of the standard English speaker, but he regretted the necessity: 'it may be assumed they are but a sorry substitute for the full significance the original words bear to those who read them without translation, and know their delicate ability to express the doings, joys and jests, troubles, sorrows, needs and sickness of life in the rural world as elsewhere'.

In the light of this further evidence of Hardy's high valuation of the dialect, it comes as something of a surprise to find that the universal tendency of the revision Hardy made in 1912 for the Wessex Edition of his works was to diminish the presence of the local language. Some changes, like that from 'naibours' to 'neighbours', might be thought of as cosmetic, the original spelling indicating no particular spoken distinction from standard English; others, such as that from 'nate' to 'neat', do represent a change in pronunciation from local to standard, if not in dialect (these alterations are in the majority); but there are some—the change from 'I mid so well go' to 'I may as well go' is one example—that are removals of dialect vocabulary or grammar (all these examples are from *Under the Greenwood Tree*). The extent of such changes is not great, and the overall effect more substantial in some novels than others, but the cause for the trend is unclear, especially since in other ways Hardy's revisions at this time added significantly to the record of Wessex.

As a practical example to illustrate this brief analysis, the poem 'The Bride-Night

Fire', the only one Hardy wrote completely in the Dorset dialect, is useful. Like many of Hardy's poems it was first written in 1866 or 1867 when he was working in London as an architect. But we cannot know how it then read, for, though it was the earliest poem that Hardy ever managed to get published—in the *Gentleman's Magazine* in November 1875—it appeared there in a bowdlerized form, and most probably with fewer dialect words or phrases than when initially inscribed. In 1894 the poem was reprinted unbowdlerized in the poet Lionel Johnson's pioneering critical study *The Art of Thomas Hardy*, for which version Hardy read proof. When compared with the *Gentleman's Magazine* version it contained a few new representations of Dorset pronunciations modelled on Barnes's usage—'peäir' for 'pair' (12), 'woone' for 'one' (13), 'zeed' for 'seen' (27)—and some new, lexically non-standard readings like 'He roamed... ath'art field' for 'He roamed... across field' (21), or 'caddle' for 'stoor' (82). However, it was when the poem was included in *Wessex Poems* in 1898 that there were the most radical alterations to the dialect. Hardy's sensitivity to dialect issues had been enhanced by the experience of making the revisions for Osgood, McIlvaine's collected edition, and thus, for example, 'crabbed' became 'thirtover' (3), 'frightened' became 'gallied' (45), 'at length' became 'bylong' (73), 'in a terrible way' became 'in a mortal bad way' (91), while the word 'vlankers' (33) was added.

In 1912, however, the process, to a small degree, was reversed for the Wessex Edition, so that for 'clinking off wi' her' there was 'vanishing wi' her' (10), for 'bylong' there was 'erelong' (73), and 'halter-path', added in 1898, reverted to 'bridle-path' (73).

It is a small example of the complex situation surrounding Hardy's poetic texts that the first and last of these remained unchanged in the 1919 and subsequent editions of Hardy's *Collected Poems*, while the second was altered to 'ere long'. Further along the same line, the title of the poem in *Wessex Poems* was 'The Fire at Tranter Sweatley's'; in the 1912 printing of the Wessex Edition it became 'The Bride-Night Fire | (Wessex Dialect)'; for *Collected Poems* it became 'The Bride-Night Fire | (A Wessex Tradition)'; but a year later, when the Wessex Edition was reprinted, the title appeared as 'The Bride-Night Fire | Or, The Fire at Tranter Sweatley's | (Wessex Dialect)'. For both the Wessex Edition and *Collected Poems* Hardy gave thirty translations of dialect words as footnotes (not reproduced in the standard *Complete Poetical Works*). It seems ironic that at the time Hardy added the subtitle 'Wessex Dialect' he should actually remove examples of what he claimed to be exhibiting.

SJG

Ralph W. V. Elliott, *Thomas Hardy's English* (1984).

dialogue is a conversation between two or more people, ranging from informal exchange of ideas and opinions on everyday subjects to serious discussion of important topics like religion, marriage, and death. For Hardy dialogue proved an essential ingredient in his art, in verse as well as in his prose fiction. It enabled him to create individual traits by letting his characters speak for themselves, by using different levels of language to indicate a speaker's background, social position, sex, and age. In Chapter 6 of *The Hand of Ethelberta*, for example, the two sisters are talking about love, the elder, Ethelberta, wiser and more experienced, the younger, Picotee, innocent and 'an absurd child' in her sister's view. The chapter hints at feminine interests in clothes and jewels and how to attract men, as Ethelberta advises: '"Ah, Picotee! to continue harmless as a dove you must be wise as a serpent."' The entire chapter is in dialogue telling the reader much about the two young women.

In a drama like *The Dynasts* or *The Famous Tragedy of the Queen of Cornwall* Hardy relied largely on dialogue, apart from brief explanatory comments and stage directions. Similarly, a poem like 'At Wynyard's Gap' is really a short one-act play, the speakers identified simply as 'She' and 'He' with a brief one-line appearance of a 'Carrier'. Other poems employ dialogue to varying extent, the speakers being the poet himself talking with the Lord Most High in 'God-Forgotten' or with the moon in 'To the Moon'. In 'The Two Houses' a smart new house converses with an old, cracked, wormy one to learn a salutary lesson. In 'A Sound in the Night' a dialogue between two newly-weds in an eerie castle leads to a tragic dénouement. In such cases Hardy uses dialogue in verse to describe an episode, to give voice to an emotion, to probe a belief, or to record what in the 'Apology' prefaced to *Late Lyrics and Earlier* he called 'a series of fugitive impressions'. In his verse, dialogue proved an important means for Hardy to express his own views and sentiments, whether speaking in his own person or through the mouth of a fictional character.

Yet it is especially in his fiction that dialogue assumes the important role it performs in Hardy's art as a writer: his characters become recognizable personalities by being endowed with distinctive voices. Individuals reveal themselves in dialogue, as when Michael Henchard angrily berates Elizabeth-Jane in *The Mayor of Casterbridge* (20) for slipping into dialect. By contrast, Donald Farfrae's speech in the same novel is courteous and straightforward, made distinctive by his Scottish accent. In *A Pair of Blue Eyes* Henry Knight is portrayed as a man of academic temperament by filling his speech with abstractions and recondite allusions, inviting parody (17). Among Hardy's villains, Aeneas Manston in *Desperate Remedies* lards his dialogue with biblical references—' "Ah—true. I read Deuteronomy myself" ' (11.3). The disagreeable William Dare in *A Laodicean* reveals his twisted character from his first pronouncements; there is 'a wiry unreasonableness in his voice' when he talks with Somerset at Monte Carlo (4.4). But it is Alec d'Urberville whose voice betrays 'a ghastly bizarrerie' as he utters words of Scripture after his conversion. Yet it is as the flattering, ingratiating libertine that his speech marks him throughout his relationship with Tess, until 'sharper words' are uttered in response to her final tragic denunciation (*TDU* 56).

Hardy's women are similarly endowed with distinctive voices. The difference between Arabella and Sue in *Jude the Obscure* is as much in how they speak as how they look and act. The earthy, colloquial vulgarity of Arabella's talk, its 'humorous impudence' (3.8), is effectively contrasted with Sue's fastidious nature as revealed when she speaks of marriage and sex and Christianity (e.g. 5.1). Other women's voices in Hardy's fiction are likewise distinguished: Tess, Bathsheba Everdene, Eustacia Vye, and not least Marty South in her memorable, almost wholly monosyllabic farewell over Giles's grave at the very end of *The Woodlanders*. Like Marty's role, Mother Cuxsom's in *The Mayor of Casterbridge* is not a central one, yet hers too is a distinctive voice, whether speaking of her late husband—' "Ah, yes, Cuxsom's gone, and so shall leather breeches!" ' (13)—or delivering her homely threnody on the death of Susan Henchard (18).

Dialogue is used by Hardy to indicate social distinctions, as in the contrasting modes of speech between the Chickerel brothers Sol and Dan and the aristocratic members of their sister's circle in *The Hand of Ethelberta*. Social distinctions are articulated in the dialogue of Angel Clare's elder brothers in *Tess of the d'Urbervilles*, where snobbish self-importance takes precedence over Christian charity towards their rustic brother (25). The mysterious stranger in the summer shelter in 'The Romantic Adventures of a Milkmaid' (*CM*) immediately reveals himself to be a foreigner whose superior rank Margery regularly acknowledges by addressing him as 'sir'.

Strong emotions find their outlet in dialogue. The distracted mother in *The Return of the Native* (4.6) unburdens her heart to little prattling Johnny Nunsuch; Jude's final outpouring to Mrs Edlin at the end of *Jude the Obscure* is a tragic 'rambling' to which the old woman 'could hearken all day' (6.10); and more monologue than dialogue, although it elicits a couple of brief responses, is Fitzpiers's impassioned confession in *The Woodlanders* (35), while sitting in a befuddled state in front of his father-in-law on the latter's horse.

The confessional function of dialogue is akin to its revelatory role, and both can have comic overtones, like butler Chickerel's revelation of his daughter's parentage to his astonished employers in *The Hand of Ethelberta* (42), or Elfride Swancourt's sobbing confession to Knight in *A Pair of Blue Eyes* (32) that she had loved two other men before him. In *Two on a Tower*, the Bishop of Melchester ascribes Viviette's acceptance of his hand in marriage to 'the persuasive force of trained logical reasoning' (39) rather than to her 'condition', whose nature she did not reveal to him. Fitzpiers's horseback confession of his adultery (already referred to) has a comic flavour, but its earlier revelation from

Felice Charmond's own lips to Fitzpiers's wife, while both are lost in the woodlands, is devastatingly poignant, 'a revelation transcending her utmost suspicion'—' "He's had you! Can it be—can it be!" ' (*W* 33). It is from Lucetta that Elizabeth-Jane learns of her former liaison and her present infatuation in *The Mayor of Casterbridge*, a novel filled with painful revelations. And can one forget how, after Tess's revelation of her past to her just-wedded husband, Hardy uses dialogue effectively to expose both their characters as well as to pinpoint a crucial moment in the unfolding of the plot (*TDU* 35)?

It was a happy inspiration that persuaded Hardy to introduce into his first published novel, *Desperate Remedies* (1871), characters who in their dialogue used the speech of local country folk. One reviewer, although scathing in his overall judgement of the novel, remarked on the author's 'happy facility' in reproducing the manners, the language, and 'the tone of thought' of the 'gaping village rustics', a facility which Hardy had already displayed in two early dialect poems written in 1866, although not published until later: 'The Bride-Night Fire' (originally entitled 'The Fire at Tranter Sweatley's') and 'The Ruined Maid', the latter consisting entirely of dialogue.

Hardy persevered with 'Wessex' dialogue in his next novel, *Under the Greenwood Tree*: a wise decision, for rustic dialogue was to become one of the hallmarks of his fiction. Already in the latter novel the speakers are differentiated to some extent by their speech, and thereafter Hardy relied increasingly on dialogue and different voices, not only among the 'work-folk'. These latter, however, frequently perform an almost choric function, commenting on happenings in the story, relating anecdotes and traditions of the countryside, or offering sage pronouncements on any topic from the weather to too much liquor. In Chapter 10 of *Far from the Madding Crowd* the assembled rustics are presented individually by their appearance and their speech, the dialogue alternating appropriately between the Dorset speech of the men and women, sometimes in unison, and the Standard English of the presiding Bathsheba Everdene. One 'poor gawkhammer mortal' is reduced to little more than ' "Heh-heh-heh" ', while another, being 'a stammering man', collapses into a comic stutter, although ' "'A can cuss, mem, as well as you or I, but 'a can't speak a common speech to save his life" ', as Henery Fray helpfully explains 'in an undertone'. Some of the appeal of the Wessex novels is undoubtedly due to Hardy's 'happy facility' in rendering dialogue, not least in local speech. It is there, skilfully handled, from *Desperate Remedies* to *Jude the Obscure*, where Phillotson and his friend Gillingham 'occasionally used a dialect word of their boyhood' (4.4), and where even the young Australian Father Time 'had learned to use the Wessex tongue quite naturally by now' (5.7). (See also DIALECT.)

RE

Raymond Chapman, *Forms of Speech in Victorian Fiction* (1994).

—— ' "Good Faith, You do Talk": Some Features of Hardy's Dialogue', in Charles P. C. Pettit (ed.), *New Perspectives on Thomas Hardy* (1994).

Dickens, Charles (1812–70), novelist. Referring in his autobiography to his move to London in the spring of 1862, Hardy observes that 'It was the London of Dickens and Thackeray' (*LW* 43); about twelve months later he heard Dickens give one of his celebrated public readings, and the experience was repeated in 1865. In turning to the composition of fiction later in the same decade, he may well have been partly influenced by the example of Dickens and others who had emerged from obscurity and achieved great fame and financial success as novelists; as the popularizer of serialized fiction, Dickens was soon to influence him indirectly in another way. Their fictional territories were, however, to prove quite distinct, Dickens being a great comic and satirical novelist and primarily a depicter of the urban scene. A letter of 31 October 1903 makes an interesting comparison between Dickens and Victor Hugo: describing himself to Sir George *Douglas as 'a Victor-Hugo-ite still', Hardy adds that Hugo's 'misérables are not so real as Dickens's, but they show, to my mind, one great superiority, that of universality' (*L* iii 81). Hardy contributed to a centenary symposium on Dickens published in the *Bookman* ('Charles Dickens: Some Personal Recollections and Opinions', February 1912), stating that his own works did not owe much to the influence of Dickens but adding that 'No doubt they owed something unconsciously, since everybody else's did in those days'. He also expressed the view that Dickens's best novel is *David Copperfield*.

Michael Slater's essay 'Hardy and the City', in *New Perspectives on Thomas Hardy*, ed. Charles Pettit (1994), contains an interesting comparison between Dickens and Hardy.

'Distracted Preacher, The', short story. It was originally published as 'The Distracted Young Preacher' in *New Quarterly Magazine* (April 1879) and, in five instalments, in the American *Harper's Weekly*, and was later collected in *Wessex Tales*. A note added when the story was reprinted in the Wessex Edition of 1912 refers to 'the true incidents of which the tale is a vague and flickering shadow', and the origins of the story lie in the anecdotes of smuggling on the Dorset coast, especially the Lulworth area, that Hardy had heard in his youth (see Millgate 207). It is set in the 1830s, the decade before Hardy's birth.

Richard Stockdale, a naïve young Methodist minister, lodges with a young widow, Lizzy Newberry, in the village of Nether-Moynton (based on Owermoigne, Dorset), and soon falls in love with her. He discovers, however, that, along with most of the other inhabitants of the village, she is regularly involved in smuggling spirits brought over from France. For Lizzy the smuggling is a family tradition ('"My father did it, and so did my grandfather..."') and provides not only her source of livelihood but a welcome excitement. Stockdale's strict principles, however, do not permit him to accept her views, which prove an obstacle to their marriage. A coda to the story, set two years after his departure from the village, transforms this impasse into a happy ending, but Hardy's 1912 note makes it clear that this ('almost *de rigueur* in an English magazine at the time of writing') was not the ending he originally intended. It can be argued, though, that the ironic realism of the ending printed, which has the vivacious Lizzy removed from her rural home into a Midlands town and transformed into a biddable minister's wife and the author of an anonymous tract on the evils of smuggling, has its own bittersweet effectiveness. Lizzy herself is a spiritual sister of Bathsheba Everdene in *Far from the Madding Crowd* earlier in the same decade: an independent-minded, and economically independent, woman, whose 'experienced manner and bold indifference' contrast with her lover's inexperience and conventionality at the same time as being for him part of her attractions. She responds to his moral objections to smuggling by telling him: '"You dissent from Church, and I dissent from State.... And I don't see why we are not well matched."' A natural 'dissenter' or rebel, enjoying a freedom that would have been unthinkable for a young woman in the bourgeois urban society of her day, she also has much in common with Sally Hall, the heroine of *'Interlopers at the Knap', a slightly later short story also included in *Wessex Tales*.

'Doctor's Legend, The.' See UNCOLLECTED STORIES.

Dorchester. Hardy's deeply retrospective nature endowed him with an abiding interest in history, and the Dorset into which he was born was rich in memories of the past, with Dorchester, now its county town, at the centre of it all. The town is surrounded by the remains of ancient Celtic settlements, the most important of these being Maiden Castle, an enormous Neolithic camp conquered by the Romans *c.* AD 44. They established a settlement by the river *Frome, and over the next three and a half centuries of their occupation Durnovaria became a thriving town. One visible relic of that period in modern Dorchester is Maumbury Rings, prominently featured by Hardy in *The Mayor of Casterbridge*. This began its life as a Neolithic henge, and was used by the Romans as an amphitheatre. It was large enough, it was said, to hold up to 10,000 people for the games so loved by the Romans, an indication of the importance and size of the town. (See also ARCHAEOLOGY.)

The Roman occupation had a special fascination for Hardy, but he was also very conscious of Dorchester's later history: the attacks on the town by the Vikings, the visits to it of King Alfred, the arrival of the Norman invaders, its part in the Civil War, the cruel punishments meted out by the 'Hanging Judge', Judge Jeffreys, after the Battle of Sedgemoor (1685), and the impact of the *Napoleonic Wars with the threat of invasion.

Hardy's birthplace at *Higher Bockhampton, some two to three miles to the east of Dorchester, was built in 1801 close to a Roman road which he mentions in his poem 'The Roman Road'. In this poem he describes his mother 'Guiding my infant steps' when they 'walked that ancient thoroughfare, | The Roman Road'. At the age of 9 he was sent to school in Dorchester, and one of the strongest memories of his youth must have been of walking into the town along the road from *Puddletown which crossed Grey's Bridge, on which there was, and still is, a plaque, dated 1827–8, warning that 'Any person wilfully injuring any part of this County Bridge will be guilty of felony, and upon conviction liable to be Transported for Life'. Hardy attended school in Dorchester for seven years, and was then apprenticed to an architect in the town and walked that road for another six years until 1862, when he was 22.

In *The Mayor of Casterbridge* Elizabeth-Jane and her mother approach Casterbridge on this road, and the town lying before them is described by Hardy just as he must have seen it almost every day for so many years: 'Its squareness was, indeed the characteristic which most struck the eye in this antiquated borough... at that time, recent as it was [the late 1840s], untouched by the faintest sprinkle of modernism. It was compact as a box of dominoes. It had no suburbs.... Country and town met at a mathematical line' (4). There follows a vivid and detailed description of the town based upon his own memories of the past, and it is clear that Casterbridge is Dorchester, even if the scrupulous Hardy feels that the changes in it required by his fictional purposes called for a change of name. So exact are his descriptions of places that there is no difficulty in recognizing them, and where there is no need to change the name he sometimes uses it. Thus, Ten Hatches Hole, in which Henchard nearly commits suicide, is the actual name of the place Hardy describes, and it is there, near Grey's Bridge and somewhat reduced in size, at the present day.

Hardy the architect must have found something satisfying in the basic structure of Dorchester, with its three main roads forming a letter T, the horizontal being High Street (the two parts of which are generally known as High East Street and High West Street) and the vertical South Street. After crossing Grey's Bridge one meets High East Street, and it was not only Henchard in *The Mayor* who came this way so often trodden by Hardy himself. In *Under the Greenwood Tree*, Parson Maybold, having just learnt of Fancy Day's engagement to Dick Dewy, leans over the parapet of Grey's Bridge and 'saw without heeding... how the water came rapidly from beneath the arches, glided down a little steep, then spread itself over a pool in which dace, trout and minnows sported at ease among the long green locks of weed that lay heaving and sinking with their roots towards the current'.

It is to the Swan Bridge 'of weather-stained brick... immediately at the end of High Street', some 300 yards further into the town than Grey's Bridge, that Sergeant Troy in *Far from the Madding Crowd* comes to wait for Fanny Robin, unaware that she has passed over this bridge already and is now lying dead in the Dorchester workhouse. Later in the same novel, Farmer Boldwood, having murdered Troy, walks this road on his way to surrender himself at the County Gaol. In Chapter 32 of *The Mayor of Casterbridge*, Swan Bridge (sometimes called Town Bridge) is described as being, of the two eastern bridges, that to which 'those of lowest character' gravitated, for they 'did not mind the glare of the public eye'.

The large brick building seen so prominently from Grey's Bridge is the new prison built in 1884–5 on the site of the former gaol, of which only the old stone archway entrance survives. It was on top of this latter building that in August 1856 Martha Browne was publicly executed, and Hardy stood in the crowd watching her hanged, a sight he was never to forget (see EXECUTIONS, PUBLIC). Not far from this old entrance to the gaol is Hangman's Cottage, which is mentioned by Hardy in two short stories, 'The Withered Arm' and 'The Three Strangers'. In his *Thomas Hardy* (1941) H. W. Nevinson mentions being shown Hangman's Cottage by Hardy in 1906: 'he showed me the railings he used to climb up as a boy to watch the hangman having his tea at a cottage in a hollow below on the evening before an execution, and wonder how the man could eat anything so soon before his terrible task' (p. 18). The

Frome runs round this northern side of the town, and, because of the darkness of that side, Hardy in *The Mayor* calls it the 'Schwarzwasser [black water] of Casterbridge' (19).

Also visible from Grey's Bridge, on a small hill to the south-west, is the church of St George, Fordington. The vicar of St George's for more than 50 years, from 1829 until his death in 1880, was the Reverend Henry Moule (see MOULE FAMILY). A man of many interests and talents who showed great courage during a cholera epidemic in 1854 (see Hardy's short story 'A Changed Man'), Moule begat seven remarkably gifted sons, of whom one, Horace *Moule, became a friend and mentor of Hardy. Horace was a brilliant scholar and teacher, a lover of music, a writer and reviewer, and his influence on Hardy in the 1850s and 1860s was considerable. However, he suffered from personality weaknesses which meant that at Cambridge he never achieved the high academic success that he merited, and he committed suicide in 1873. Hardy was deeply shocked by the loss of such a close Dorchester friend. The funeral, attended by Hardy, took place in a portion of the graveyard of St George's church which can be seen from the road below. His poem, 'Before My Friend Arrived', with its mention of 'the towered church on the rise', is about Moule and his funeral.

The Dorset volume (1972) in the Penguin *Buildings of England* series comments that 'The one essential is to walk the length of the High Street, which has a truly urban feeling from one end to the other, an appearance really very little changed since the late nineteenth century'. There have been a number of changes since those words were written, but, above shop level, the houses are still very much as they would have been in Hardy's time. As he began his daily walk up High East Street, he would have seen the carts parked in the road and in the forecourt of the White Hart Inn, waiting to carry people to their rural destinations. It was the bus-station of that time. It was from here, in the group of short stories called 'A Few Crusted Characters', that 'Burthen, Carrier to Longpuddle' set out. Further up on the right-hand side was the Three Mariners' Inn, which makes an appearance in *The Mayor of Casterbridge*, but it was pulled down at the end of the 19th century. Sadly, little is left, either, of the Phoenix Inn, scene of the poem 'The Dance at the Phoenix'.

However, on the right-hand side of the road, the King's Arms, which also plays a part in *The Mayor* as well as in *Far from the Madding Crowd*, is still functioning as a hotel. It is easily recognizable by its great bay window on the first floor; looking west, one can now see more clearly the three churches in the High Street which Hardy would have known well. The first on the left-hand side, identifiable by its spire, is All Saints' (see the poem 'The Casterbridge Captains'). It was the choir of this church that Michael Henchard made sing the 109th Psalm in the Three Mariners (*MC* 33). The second church, on the right-hand side, just where High West Street begins, is St Peter's. As an architectural pupil, Hardy drew a plan of St Peter's, and he features this building, the oldest by far of the three churches, in *The Trumpet-Major* as well as in *The Mayor of Casterbridge*, where he refers to its 'massive square tower'. The bells whose ringing is referred to in his poem 'The Chimes' are those of St Peter's. They rang out the curfew until the 1940s and would often have been heard by Hardy, who in his autobiography describes how he went to St Peter's belfry at the end of 1884 'to the New-Year's-Eve ringing. The night-wind whiffed in through the louvres as the men prepared the mufflers with tar-twine and pieces of horse-cloth ...' (*LW* 176).

The third church, Holy Trinity, a little higher up High West Street, was rebuilt in the mid-1880s, but the original church of that name dated from medieval times, and one of its rectors in the 17th century was the Reverend John White, a Puritan who played a large part in the foundation of Massachusetts by raising money for the emigrants and by procuring a charter for them. This was one of the few pieces of Dorchester's history that receives no mention anywhere in Hardy's writings. Hardy likewise wrote nothing in his books about the Tolpuddle Martyrs, who, not long before his birth, had been tried in the courtroom of Shire Hall, further up High West Street on the right.

The heart of the town in Hardy's time, called by him 'the cross', was where the three roads—High East Street, High West Street, and South Street (the northern end of which is called Cornhill)—meet. The three churches, the King's Arms hotel, the Corn Exchange and Town Hall, the Dorset County Museum, the Antelope hotel (renamed 'The Stag' in *The Mayor of Casterbridge*), Judge Jeffrey's lodgings and court-room, are all to be found within a hundred yards, and at their centre, in the middle of Cornhill, is an obelisk marking the location of the old Town Pump.

Here the townspeople would gather to chat, and the bi-weekly markets (mentioned by Hardy on several occasions) took place. Lucetta's house in *The Mayor* is the grey stone building in Glyde Path Road, now used as a Dorset Council Club, but Hardy moves it to a site in the High Street overlooking the market and the centre of the town, where Lucetta and Elizabeth-Jane can observe events important to the plot. In one scene (24) they look out and see the 'new fashioned agricultural implement called a horse-drill' which Donald Farfrae has bought, and later in the same chapter Hardy describes something he must often have witnessed, the thinning away of the market at the end of the day, and the arrival on the scene of the field-labourers and their wives and children, coming from the villages for their weekly shopping. In *Time's Laughingstocks* the group of poems titled 'At Casterbridge Fair' are located in this busy centre of the town.

Two important buildings in that centre call for further comment: the Town Hall and Corn Exchange, and the Dorset County Museum. The present Town Hall was erected in 1848, the last major building on the north side of High East Street. The Corn Exchange was added to it in 1867, and they may be regarded as one building. There was an earlier Corn Exchange on the site, and it is this to which Bathsheba goes in *Far from the Madding Crowd.* Of this earlier building, Hermann *Lea says in his *Thomas Hardy's Wessex* (1913)—the only guide-book to Hardy places of which Hardy himself approved—that 'The Corn Exchange was a "low though extensive hall, supported by beams and pillars". If we enter the present building on a market day we shall be struck with the similitude of its human scenes now to what they are described as being then. Here are the farmers with their sample bags of corn, pouring out the contents into their hands—just as we read of Bathsheba doing' (p. 38). The Corn Exchange today is no longer used for its original purpose. It has become a hall that can be hired for many different functions, one of which is as the location of the Thomas Hardy Society's biennial international conference.

The Dorset County Museum is at the beginning of High West Street, right next to St Peter's Church and at the heart of Dorchester. The growing interest in science, and particularly in geology and archaeology, in the early Victorian period led to the founding of Dorchester's first museum in 1845. It was located at first in two rooms in Judge Jeffrey's lodgings in High West Street, opposite the present museum. In 1857 it moved to larger premises in Trinity Street, and in 1884 the present museum, which had been specially built for this purpose, was opened by the Earl of Shaftesbury. To Hardy, who was then living just round the corner, it was a great boon, since it had an excellent library and reading-room in which copies of journals and the London newspapers were available.

About 1880 Hardy had become a member of the Dorset Natural History and Antiquarian Field Club, which met in the Museum; he was a zealous supporter of its work, and in 1884 read a paper to its members about the Roman remains discovered in digging the foundations of *Max Gate. He used the Museum as the setting for the meeting of the imaginary 'Wessex Field and Antiquarian Club' in his book of short stories, *A Group of Noble Dames.* The Museum meant a great deal to him: as early as 1911 he presented it with his holograph of *The Mayor of Casterbridge,* and as late as the autumn of 1927 he attended a meeting there about the preservation of a recently discovered mosaic pavement. On the death of his widow, Florence Hardy, in 1937, a great collection of manuscripts, books, letters, and articles was bequeathed to the Museum on condition that they were 'placed on exhibition in a separate room'. Today the Dorset County Museum houses an unsurpassed collection of Hardy material, including his reconstructed study.

One of the newspapers that Hardy would have read in the Museum reading-room was the *Dorset County Chronicle.* It had begun publication in 1821, and became the county's leading weekly newspaper. It may be that an anonymous letter, signed 'The Wareham

Town Pump', that appeared in the *Chronicle* as early as 6 March 1856 (when Hardy was only 15) was written by him (Purdy 291). This was followed in 1883 by an obituary of a friend and, almost certainly, obituaries of several of his relations were written by him.

More important was the methodical reading by Hardy in the 1880s of back numbers of the *Chronicle*, which provided him with material for his novels. This dredging up of the local past was invaluable. Thus, he would have read in the *Chronicle* of 4 November 1886 a graphic account of how a horse took fright near Cornhill, rushed through a shop window, and was so badly injured that his throat had to be cut. The article ends, 'The street after the horse had been killed presented a sickening spectacle, the road, pavement and gutter being literally deluged with blood.' Not long after, Hardy was describing the killing of Prince the horse in *Tess of the d'Urbervilles*. The *Chronicle* expired in 1957.

Cornhill and South Street stretch out to the south from the junction of High East and High West Streets, and are closely associated with Hardy's years of training as an architect. The office of John *Hicks, his architectural tutor, was near the bottom of the road on the right-hand side, and now bears a plaque commemorating Hardy's time there. Among the shops in Cornhill was that of a furniture dealer named Treves from whom Hardy 'as a boy purchased his first writing-desk' (*LW* 457). The shopkeeper's son, later Sir Frederick *Treves, became a famous surgeon whose patients included the Elephant Man and Edward VII, and Hardy and he were lifelong friends. The Antelope hotel (a hotel no longer) was close to the Town Pump. The King's Arms and the Antelope were the two chief coaching inns until the arrival of the railway in 1847.

On the opposite side of the road to the Antelope is the house, also marked with a plaque, that Hardy imagined as Henchard's house in *The Mayor of Casterbridge*. Not far from the bottom of South Street was Dorchester South Station, which Hardy would have used on hundreds of occasions when travelling to London. The poem 'In a Waiting-Room' may well have been conceived here, and he wrote several other poems about trains and stations (see RAILWAYS). To provide more room for Eldridge Pope's brewery (built in 1881), the South Station was moved further south and rebuilt in the 1990s. The firm of Eldridge Pope had been founded in 1837 by Charles and Sarah Eldridge, and was bought by the Popes in the 1870s. Hardy was a close friend of Alfred Pope, with whom he shared a great love of Dorset and an interest in the past, and he described Pope's Dorchester ale in *The Trumpet-Major* (see ALCOHOL).

Many other Hardy 'places' in Dorchester cry out to be mentioned, but space will not allow. However, Hardy's interest in war and soldiers requires mention. At the top of High West Street is an important crossroads called 'Top o' Town'. There today can be seen the memorial statue of Hardy that was unveiled by Sir James *Barrie on 2 September 1931 (see PORTRAITS AND SCULPTURES OF THOMAS HARDY). It stands, ironically, where the roar of traffic is never-ending. A little further west, at the beginning of the road to Bridport, will be found a stone keep which is today a military museum but was in Hardy's time the entrance to the military barracks originally established here in 1795. Hardy's war poems include 'The Going of the Battery', which describes what is almost certainly a piece of personal observation: soldiers leaving the barracks on their way to the *Boer War.

What had been Hardy's contact with Dorchester since the age of 22? For the next five years he was working as an architect in London, but because of health problems he returned to the Higher Bockhampton cottage of his family at the end of the summer of 1867. In his autobiography he tells us that 'A few weeks in the country—where he returned to his former custom of walking to the Dorchester architect's office from his mother's house every day—completely restored him' (*LW* 57). Most of the next seven years, until his marriage in 1874, were spent in Bockhampton, and his first four novels were written during this period. For the first nine years of his marriage he and Emma moved somewhat restlessly from place to place, but the native returned to his origins in June 1883. Maybe by then he had realized that he wrote best when he was most fully the Wessex Novelist writing about the places in which he and his family had grown up and had their roots. Michael Millgate puts the matter very well: 'Hardy had returned to Dorchester precisely in order to be in closer touch with all the traditions and customs and values of his family and his region'; he had fallen back 'upon his oldest, deepest, and surest creative resources' (Millgate 247). It was a sensible move, its first fruit being the novel that immortalized the town and made so much use of it, *The Mayor of Casterbridge*.

Work on this novel began early in 1884, when the Hardys were living in lodgings in Shire Hall Place, very close to Colliton House and the centre of Dorchester, where so much of the action of the novel takes place. Hardy had for some time been giving consideration to making Dorchester his permanent home, and in June 1885 he moved into Max Gate, a new property about a mile from the centre of the town, designed by Hardy himself and built by his father and brother. This was to remain his home until his death in 1928. In it he wrote three of his greatest novels, *The Woodlanders*, *Tess*, and *Jude*, as well as *The Dynasts* and most of his poetry. Until about 1910 Hardy and Emma went to London every year for the two or three months of the 'season', but from then until his death Hardy very seldom left home, and the famous and not-so-famous who wished to meet him had to make their pilgrimage to Dorchester. Here, at Max Gate, they were sure of a warm welcome (usually an invitation to tea), and were often taken by Hardy on visits to places of interest in Dorchester.

In spite of the demands of his professional life, he found time to take part in some of the abundant life of the town. He became a local magistrate in 1884 and a county magistrate ten years later, and during the 1914–18 war he was a member of the bench trying food-profiteering cases. Another Dorchester activity that very much involved him was the dramatic productions of what began as the Dorchester Debating, Literary and Dramatic Society and later became the *Hardy Players. The first of a series of plays based upon Hardy's fiction and *The Dynasts* was a production of *The Trumpet-Major* in 1908, and a period which linked Hardy to an interesting collection of Dorchester people ended with a production of his own dramatization of *Tess* in 1924.

It was in the Corn Exchange on 16 November 1910 that Hardy received the Freedom of the Borough of Dorchester, an honour that, because of his lifelong association with the town, moved him greatly. He made a speech on that occasion emphasizing how much Dorchester had meant to him. 'Mr Mayor,' he began:

> In simply expressing my sincere thanks for the high compliment paid me by having my name enrolled with those of the Honorary Freemen of this historic town, I may be allowed to confess that the Freedom of the Borough of Dorchester did seem to me at first something that I had possessed a long while, had helped myself to (to speak plainly), for when I consider the liberties I have taken with its ancient walls, streets and precincts through the medium of the printing-press, I feel that I have treated its external features with the hand of freedom indeed. True it might be urged that my Casterbridge (if I may mention seriously a name coined off-hand in a moment with no thought of its becoming established and localized) is not Dorchester—not even the Dorchester as it existed 60 years ago, but a dream-place that never was outside an irresponsible book. Nevertheless, when somebody said to me that 'Casterbridge' is a sort of essence of the town as it used to be, 'a place more Dorchester than Dorchester itself', I could not absolutely contradict him, though I could not quite perceive it.

Hardy goes on to express his regret at the destruction of so much of the past in the town, but appreciates that change has to occur:

> The power to preserve is largely an illusion.... Here in Dorchester, as elsewhere, I see the streets and the turnings not far different from those of my schoolboy times; but the faces that used to be seen at the doors, the inhabitants, where are they? I turn up the Weymouth Road, cross the railway-bridge, enter an iron gate to 'a slope of green access', and there they are. There is the Dorchester that I knew best; there are names on white stones one after the other, names that recall the voices, cheerful and sad, anxious and indifferent, that are missing from the dwellings and pavements. Those who are old enough to have had that experience may feel that, after all, the permanence or otherwise of inanimate Dorchester concerns but the permanence of what is minor and accessory. (*LW* 378–80)

JCG

Dorset is one of the smaller English counties, equivalent in size to the island of Madeira. Its historic character has been much changed by two recent alterations of the county's administrative boundaries and by the progressive imbalance of the modern coastal development that now extends almost unbroken from Poole Harbour to Christchurch. During his lifetime Hardy saw the phenomenal rise of Bournemouth from a population of 1,330 in 1851 to 91,761 in 1921. When the first house was built there in 1811 the town was in Hampshire; transferred to Dorset in 1974, it is now a major conference centre with an internationally acclaimed symphony orchestra, a newly founded university, and a population of 154,677. For comparison, Dorchester's population in 1851 was 3,513 and 15,100 in 1991. The rural communities engaged in agriculture, which contributed so much vivacity and colour to Hardy's novels, are now greatly diluted by commuters and retired incomers.

Nevertheless, Dorset does obstinately retain much of its quintessential character. Its special icons are there to be seen: the Chesil Bank, the Cerne Giant, the Abbotsbury Swannery, Sherborne Abbey, 18th-century Blandford, the turf sculpture of King George III riding his white horse on the downs at Weymouth, and Gold Hill in Shaftesbury, 'that mountain town', as Hardy described it. Here, too, are the celebrated memorials of ancient people, the Iron Age hill-forts overlooking the course of the river Stour, the long barrows and the Bronze Age cursus of Cranborne Chase, historic individual sites such as Maiden Castle, Badbury Rings, and Knowlton Circles.

Geologically, Dorset has unusual variety in a small space, so that the passing of only a few miles brings completely fresh scenes. Sandy heath, clay vale, chalk downland ring the changes with marble, sandstone, and shale to create the landscapes that feature so strongly in Hardy's writings. He liked to prepare his novelistic descriptions from the real scene, as a painter would do, and in this he was helped by the fact that he had also lived at various times, if only briefly, in Weymouth, Swanage, Sturminster Newton, and Wimborne. Throughout his lifetime of nearly 88 years, his home during 77 of them was in Dorset. In a conversation with William *Archer published in *The Critic* (New York) in 1901, Hardy is reported as saying, 'I suppose it is an advantage to be thoroughly at home in one region, however narrow.' Wessex was to become his special province but, within that province, his native county had pride of place because of its deeper intimacy with his formative years and the imaginative power he drew from it. The most memorable characters in his novels—Tess, Henchard, Bathsheba, Giles Winterborne, Gabriel Oak, Marty South, to pick some at random—are Dorset folk, and it is in the towns and fields of Dorset that we find them (call it 'South Wessex' though we may). Jude, in this as in other ways, is an exception, but he too is cryptically a child of Egdon Heath. When he lies down on the pig-sty litter (*JO* 1.2), pulls his straw hat over his eyes, and wishes to prevent himself from growing up, he is renewing a profound experience of Hardy's own boyhood, expressed in the poem 'Childhood among the Ferns' and also narrated in Hardy's autobiography (*LW* 20).

Dorset gave Hardy five centres of rich resource: the coast; the contrasting towns of Dorchester (Roman and homely) and Weymouth (Georgian and glamorous); the dairying river valleys; Egdon Heath; and the downlands and the woodlands with their village communities. The coast at once suggests the subject of smuggling, to which the story 'The Distracted Preacher' is the response. Poole and Purbeck (including Corfe) occur incidentally, but it is Portland that seized Hardy's imagination. 'That Gibraltar of Wessex' was his description of the gaunt, forbidding rock that, in the poem 'The Souls of the Slain', serves as a landmark to the souls of the men killed in the Boer War; and it was into the dreaded Race off Portland Bill that those with bitter memories of home plunge headlong in the poem's dramatic climax. The savage nature of the Race and the long tally of ships battered to destruction on a lee shore in Deadman's Bay was a continuing interest of Hardy's. In a very different mood Portland provided the setting for *The Well-Beloved*, based on John Smeaton's account of Portland's premarital custom.

Weymouth and Dorchester run through Hardy's writings in many contexts—primarily in *The Trumpet-Major* and *The Mayor of Casterbridge*, but as important elements also in his verse. The dairying valleys were an integral part of Hardy's immediate experience. The milkmaids of the Froomside farms were his familiars in Sunday school and barn-dance. Blackmore Vale was the prize of the two years he spent at Sturminster Newton; so too were the woodlands and cider orchards of the Hintocks.

The two last to be mentioned here are perhaps the most intimately personal of all. The great heath behind Hardy's birthplace was the first landscape of childhood and the most deeply imprinted, 'the unrecognized original of those wild regions of obscurity which are vaguely felt to be compassing us about in midnight dreams of flight and disaster, and are never thought of after the dream till revived by scenes like this' (*RN* 1.1). Belonging to a later stage in his life is the celebration of those 'Wessex Heights' to which he withdrew in spirit for his refreshment. Their names run like a litany through his writings, and of their nature they respond to a temperament that valued solitude. In the poem of that name they have been extended to embrace Wessex. In terms of Dorset they are the downland scarp that extends westwards from Bulbarrow to Nettlecombe Tout, High Stoy, Bubb Down, and Toller Down, a sort of bastion that gives a finish to the gradual upward incline of the county. DH

Desmond Hawkins, *Hardy at Home* (1989).
Llewelyn Powys, *Dorset Essays* (1935).
Frederick Treves, *Highways and Byways in Dorset* (1906).

Dorset County Chronicle. See DORCHESTER.

Dorset County Museum. See DORCHESTER.

'Dorsetshire Labourer, The.' One of Hardy's most substantial and important essays, it was first published in *Longman's Magazine* (July 1883) under the title 'The Dorsetshire Farm Labourer', its appearance coinciding very closely with the Hardys' final move to Dorchester. As Purdy notes (50), it was used 'a few years later as a quarry for several passages in *Tess of the d'Urbervilles*', notably the description of house-moving on Old Lady Day.

The essay begins by questioning, and eventually demolishing, the popular stereotype of 'Hodge', which dates back to the Middle Ages but had recently been given fresh currency by Richard Jefferies's *Hodge and His Masters* (1880). (Curiously enough, Hardy himself was to revert to the term nearly twenty years later in his poem 'Drummer Hodge'.) As generally conceived, Hodge is 'a degraded being of uncouth manner and aspect, stolid understanding, and snail-like movement', with barbarous speech habits and a hangdog manner, and dwelling amid 'fever and misery'. Anyone familiar with the reality rather than the stereotype, Hardy insists, will be aware of the human individuality of the agricultural labourer class.

The ensuing account of the life of this class, with a number of case-histories evidently drawn from personal experience, includes a detailed description of the old Candlemas hiring fairs, which Hardy had evoked in *Far from the Madding Crowd* (6) and was to depict again in *Tess of the d'Urbervilles* (23); the 'day of removal' consequent upon the taking up of new employment is also described from personal observation. Hardy even-handedly notes the substantial improvement in the lives of these workers, compared with the gross exploitation to which they had been subjected in earlier times; but he also feels acutely the losses—in terms of sensibility and outlook rather than economics—that have proceeded from the changes in their lives. Increased mobility has generated 'a less intimate and kindly relation with the land he tills'; gains in economic power and personal freedom are offset by a breakdown in the relationship that formerly existed between rural workers and their surroundings ('they have lost touch with their environment, and that sense of long local participancy which is one of the pleasures of age'). Rural communities, too, are breaking down: 'The occupants who formed the backbone of the village life have to seek refuge in the boroughs.'

The essay includes a laudatory reference to the work of Joseph Arch (1826–1919), and a personal reminiscence of his speeches in Dorset. Arch, who had himself been an agricultural worker and later became a Liberal MP, played an outstanding role in the betterment of conditions for this class of worker. He formed the Agricultural Labourers' Union in his native Warwickshire in 1872, and in the same year the National Agricultural Workers' Union, with the object of improving the conditions of farm-labourers. (See also AGRICULTURE.)

Michael Millgate, *Thomas Hardy: His Career as a Novelist* (1971), 206–20.

Douglas, Sir George (1856–1935), 5th Baronet, Scottish landowner and author. He met Hardy in 1881 while on a visit to his younger brother, who lived near the Hardys in *Wimborne. The acquaintance was presumably sought by Douglas, who in the previous year had published an admiring sonnet, 'To the Author of "Far from the Madding Crowd"'. They became close friends, visited each other's homes, met in London, and exchanged many letters. At Easter 1890, for instance, Douglas stayed at Max Gate and he and Hardy went together to the grave of William *Barnes; in September 1891 the Hardys stayed at Douglas's Scottish estate, Springwood Park. Hardy's correspondence with Douglas is frank and friendly, showing shared literary interests and a respect for Douglas's literary judgement. Among much else, Hardy commented to Douglas on Tennyson (19 December 1897: *L* ii 183), on Victor Hugo (21 October 1903: *L* iii 81), and on a meeting with *Swinburne (1 July 1905: *L* iii 175). Hardy told Douglas of his dismay at the hostile reception of *Jude the Obscure*, and in January 1896 Douglas published in the *Bookman* an article defending Hardy ('On Some Critics of *Jude the Obscure*'). There is a humorous reference to Douglas (though he is not named) in the preface to *The Mayor of Casterbridge*, as having provided assistance with the dialogue given to the Scots character Donald Farfrae. See also SCOTLAND.

dramatizations of Hardy's works divide into three broad categories: those prepared by Hardy himself, those prepared by other adapters during his lifetime, and those made since his death. Inevitably it is the first two groups that are of the greatest importance here, although they were not necessarily the most successful in actual performance.

Hardy's interest in adapting his own work for the stage was more substantial and enduring than the sparseness of the end results might indicate. He sketched out numerous outlines for possible dramatizations, most of which never bore fruit in actual playscripts. Surviving schemes range in preparation dates from the 1890s to close to the end of Hardy's life, and in originating text range from short stories—'Enter a Dragoon', 'The History of the Hardcombes', and 'The Duchess of Hamptonshire'—to major novels. *A Pair of Blue Eyes, The Return of the Native, The Trumpet-Major, Two on a Tower, The Mayor of Casterbridge*, and *Jude the Obscure* all generated scenarios, some in multiple versions. None was developed by Hardy into actual plays, however.

Hardy's apparent diffidence in seeing dramatic projects through to fulfilment may have owed something to his unfortunate earliest experience in adaptation, the 1879–80 collaboration with J. Comyns Carr on a dramatization of *Far from the Madding Crowd*. While a stageable play, entitled *The Mistress of the Farm*, was eventually prepared, it soon became the centre of controversy. Initially accepted by Hare and Kendal, the managers of the St James's Theatre, it was subsequently rejected, although at some point Kendal's wife conveyed the play's outline to Arthur Wing Pinero. When the St James's subsequently staged Pinero's *The Squire*, whose plot bore striking similarities to that of the rejected collaboration, Hardy's indignation took very public form. His letters (2 January 1882) to *The Times* and the *Daily News* provoked a brief *plagiarism furore.

This was further enlivened by the ability of the theatre-going public to make its own judgement when a revised version of the collaboration, now under the title *Far from the Madding Crowd*, opened at the Prince of Wales Theatre in Liverpool on 27 February 1882, with Marion Terry appearing as Bathsheba. Hardy himself attended the last Liverpool performance on 11 March, and after a brief provincial tour the play opened at London's Globe Theatre (29 April 1882), with Mrs Bernard Beere playing Bathsheba and Charles Kelly, the husband of Ellen Terry, as Gabriel Oak. Its most striking feature was the excision of Boldwood from the novel plot and his replacement by an entirely new character, Fanny Robin's brother Will, a saturnine gipsy whose main function is 'to cower behind hedges, and come in and out of doors and windows for three acts, in order to shoot Sergeant Troy before the curtain falls' (*The Theatre*, 1 April 1882, 246). The Pinero play was praised for its pastoralism, the Hardy-Comyns Carr adaptation condescended to for its melodrama, better suited to the provinces and 'a miscellaneous rather than a select audience'.

For more than ten years Hardy made no further attempts at dramatization himself, although he was flattered by Robert Louis *Stevenson's unfulfilled ambition to adapt *The Mayor of Casterbridge* (*L* i 146), and suggested minor modifications to the unperformed script for *The Woodlanders* prepared by Jack Grein and Charles Jarvis (1889). But it was not until 1893 that, at James *Barrie's suggestion, he transformed his short story 'The Three Strangers' (*WT*) into a one-act play, *The Three Wayfarers*. This was originally performed with other short pieces at Terry's Theatre on 3 June 1893, and occasionally revived, Hardy famously declaring, in response to 'requests from music-halls', that 'I am willing to let anybody play it for a guinea a night' (*L* iv 193). The story's innately melodramatic situation—the chance encounter of an escaped condemned convict and his brother with the hangman who has been sent to perform the execution—translated well to a circumscribed stage format.

The same cannot be said of Hardy's much more ambitious (initially five-act) adaptation of *Tess of the d'Urbervilles*, first prepared in 1895. Negotiations with potential managements, most extensively with J. Forbes-Robertson, came to nothing in the 1890s, despite the interest in playing Tess shown over the years by actresses as various and eminent as Mrs Patrick Campbell, Elizabeth Robins, Eleonora Duse, Olga Nethersole, Sarah Bernhardt, Lillah McCarthy, and Sybil Thorndike. The difficulty of distilling a complicated novel plot into coherent dramatic form continued to plague, throughout the many years of its sporadic evolution, this sole completed attempt by Hardy to dramatize a major novel. It was eventually performed in 1924 by the *Hardy Players, with Gertrude *Bugler as Tess. Further adjustments were made by A. E. Filmer, and, with Philip Ridgeway directing and Gwen Ffrangçon-Davies in the title role, *Tess* finally reached the professional stage at the suburban Barnes Theatre, opening on 7 September 1925. It subsequently transferred (2 November) to the West End's Garrick Theatre, where it ran until 12 December before going on tour, with Christine Silver as Tess, in the new year.

The reviews were very mixed, identifying as the central problem an episodic and intransigently untheatrical script rather than the acting. E. A. Baughan of the *Daily News* (8 September) gave the most forthright condemnation: 'At every moment... one saw how scene after scene was failing to make its proper effect, because the author of the play had not thought out his subject either in terms of drama or even in terms of the theatre.' In 1929, after Hardy's death, Ridgeway brought Gertrude Bugler to the Duke of York's Theatre in a revival of the play.

Hardy's other involvements with actual performance of his own dramatizations centred on poetic dramas rather than prose fiction. Shortly after the outbreak of the First World War, Harley *Granville-Barker wrote to Hardy with a proposal to stage some scenes from *The Dynasts*. A close collaboration developed between the two, with Granville-Barker selecting the scenes and Hardy helping to reshape and connect them. The play opened at the Kingsway Theatre, London, on 25 November 1914. While its episodic nature and the original's expansive scene-setting stage directions created presentational problems, these were partially solved by foregrounding as a central character a 'Reader', played by Henry Ainley. The adaptation was well received as a significant contribution to the national war effort, and it was staged again by the Oxford University Dramatic Society in 1920. The success of the collaboration with Granville-Barker may have encouraged Hardy to make his own much briefer adaptation entitled *Wessex Scenes from 'The Dynasts'*, for performance in Weymouth and Dorchester by the Hardy Players in 1916.

In 1923 the Hardy Players were also allowed to premire (on St George as aforetime acted by Dorset Mummers' and of the Dorset folk-piece 'O Jan! O Jan! O Jan!') the only work by Hardy written from the outset with actual stage presentation in mind, *The Famous Tragedy of the Queen of Cornwall*. He incorporated into this rendering of the end of the Tristan and Iseult story many of his ideas ahout dramatic unity, most particularly his belief 'that the rule for staging nowadays should be to have no scene which would not be physically possible in the time of acting' (*LW* 245). New scenes were signalled by change of characters rather than scenery, and a chorus of Chanters commented on unfolding events with what in performance by an amateur group became somewhat opaque incantatory intensity. But the play was well received, not least by T. E. *Lawrence, who in a letter to Florence Hardy (2 December 1923) conveyed how moving he had found it ('one of the best hours I've had in my life').

Of the adaptations made in Hardy's lifetime by other people, the most successful was the one over which geographical circumstance gave Hardy least influence. While negotiations in the 1890s for a stage *Tess* came to nothing in England, in America the adaptation (1897) made by Lorimer Stoddard, with Minnie Maddern Fiske in the title role, was a considerable success and helped to establish Fiske's career. Tess's complex psychology, particularly her motivation for returning to live with Alec at Sandbourne, always proved difficult to convey in Hardy's own telescoped stage plotting. Stoddard emphasized the conflict between Tess's own moral nature and her family's plight by enlarging the characterization of her manipulative and feckless parents. This made Tess's responses all too plausible in their desperation. She does not surrender to Alec's renewed importunities until her starving brother and sister have tried to consume horse fodder, her mother has unsuccessfully appealed to the sheriff's men as her worldly goods are carted off, her brother has collapsed into unconsciousness, the horse has died, and Alec has provided apparent proof of Angel's death. Only then does Tess wearily exclaim, 'I don't care what happens. Take me.'

Extremities such as these may help account for the farces *Tess of the Vaudevilles* and *Tess of Darbyville* staged in New York and Philadelphia in the wake of the Stoddard/Fiske success (see Marguerite Roberts, *Tess in the Theatre*, 211–12). Like *Far from the Madding Crowd* before it, the American play also generated controversy in London when an unauthorized and poorly received adaptation by Hugh Arthur Kennedy opened at Notting Hill's Coronet Theatre on 19 February 1900, with Mrs Lewis Waller (Florence West) playing Tess. It immediately provoked a letter from Hardy to *The Times* (21 February) disavowing all connection with the production. Subsequently transferred to the Comedy Theatre, this version was eventually closed by an injunction from Fiske, who claimed that Kennedy had based his script on Stoddard's.

The difficulty of reconciling the conflicting demands of stage comprehensibility and fidelity to a novel-length plot plagued all the adaptations made, with varying degrees of assistance from Hardy, by A. H. Evans and T. H. Tilley for the series of Dorchester-based Hardy Players productions. These did little more than sew lumps of Hardy's own novel dialogue into patchworks of the best-known elements of the story-line. While this worked quite well for scenes of rustic humour, it proved inadequate to the tragic intensities of novels like *The Return of the Native* (staged in 1920) or even the melodrama of *A Desperate Remedy* (1922). Although Gertrude Bugler's renderings of three of Hardy's greatest tragic heroines—Marty South (*The Woodlanders*), Eustacia Vye (*The Return of the Native*), and Tess—received substantial praise, on occasion even from sophisticated London critics, these plays were little more than local amateur theatricals that attracted national attention because of Hardy's eminence and partial involvement.

The interest provoked in 1924–5 by the staging of *Tess* led to the last Hardy-sanctioned adaptation, John Drinkwater's version of *The Mayor of Casterbridge*. The play was not a success and closed little more than two weeks after opening, again under Philip Ridgeway's direction, at the Barnes Theatre (8 September 1926). It was taken down to Weymouth for a 'flying matinée' on 20 September, attended by the Hardys, where it elicited one of Hardy's tarter comments: 'Beautiful afternoon, scene outside the theatre finer than within' (*LW* 467). The occasion was Hardy's last visit to a theatre.

Since his death, Hardy's work has continued to attract theatrical attention, particularly on the provincial fringe circuits, where minor adaptations of the major novels are frequently produced. There have been two prominent incursions into the West End. Ronald Gow's version of *Tess* (1946), a vehicle for Gow's wife, Wendy Hiller, moved with moderate success from Bristol to London, first to the New Theatre and subsequently to the Piccadilly. Frank Harvey's *The Day after the Fair*, a dramatization of the short story 'On the Western Circuit', enjoyed a very successful run at the Lyric Theatre (1972), in considerable part because of the casting of Deborah Kerr as Edith Harnham. But, as in Hardy's lifetime, the two most ambitious and original stage adaptations have been versions of *The Dynasts*. The Hugh Durrant adaptation (1980), performed in Exeter Cathedral, was the first major professional attempt to translate at least some of the vast work into stageable form since Granville-Barker's 1914 production. Patrick Garland attempted something similar at the Chichester Festival Theatre in 1989, declaring his emphasis on national myth in his adaptation's assertive title *Victory!* These versions made considerable demands of energy on both actors and peripatetic audiences.

That a work 'intended simply for mental performance, and not for the stage' (Preface to *The Dynasts*) should have provoked such ingenuity in adapters determined to stage it, while what would seem quite theatrically encompassable fictions often had such troubled transformations into dramatic form, casts appropriate ironic light on Hardy's own theatrical experiments. For all his career-long toying with drama, contemporary plays always remained for him 'a lower form of art: what is called a good play...being distinctly in point of artistic feeling & exhibition of human nature no higher than a third rate novel' (*L* ii 43). KW

Desmond Hawkins, *Hardy: Novelist and Poet* (1976), 'Appendix 2: Dramatizations'.

Marguerite Roberts, *Tess in the Theatre* (1950).

Keith Wilson, *Thomas Hardy on Stage* (1995).

Dublin. On 18 May 1893 Hardy and his wife Emma left London for Dublin, travelling via Holyhead and Kingstown. There they were (until 29 May) the guests of the Viceroy, Lord Houghton (1858– 1945), later Marquess of Crewe. (Hardy had known his father, the first Lord Houghton (1809–85), formerly Richard Monckton Milnes, politician and man of letters, and the first biographer of Keats.) On arrival they were received by his host's sister, Mrs Arthur Henniker (see HENNIKER, FLORENCE)—Hardy's first meeting with a woman who was to become one of the closest of his female friends.

During their stay at the Viceregal Lodge on the edge of Phoenix Park, Hardy visited Dublin Castle, Guinness's Brewery, and other sights in the city and neighbourhood, including the Killarney lakes. His diary of the tour (reproduced in *LW* 270–2) faithfully records his meetings with various notabilities; but—to quote a passage included in the typescript but deleted from the published version of the *Life*—'The chief significance of Hardy's visit to Dublin was his meeting there with Mrs Arthur Henniker...'.

Dugdale, Florence. See HARDY, FLORENCE EMILY.

Dugdale family. Florence *Hardy's father Edward Dugdale was for many years the stern headmaster of the St Andrew's National (Church of England) School for Boys in the London suburb of Enfield, his forceful character having taken him from a working-class background to a position of some local prominence (for example, as a founder of the Enfield Independent Building Society). His wife, born Emma Taylor, was a former governess whose somewhat more affluent family claimed a connection to John Taylor, the publisher of Keats. Their five children, all daughters, were given educations designed to keep them securely within the middle class: Ethel (later Richardson, 1877–1956), Florence (1879–1937), and Constance (1884–1959) were trained as teachers, Eva (1887–1971) became a nurse, and Margaret, known as 'Marjorie' (later Soundy, 1893–1979), studied domestic science.

Hardy seems to have met all of the Dugdale sisters before he married Florence in 1914—most of them, indeed, while Emma Hardy was still alive—and they all spent time at Max Gate during the ensuing years, often substituting for Florence at times when she needed hospital treatment or was summoned back to Enfield by parental illnesses. Hardy seems to have preferred the company of Ethel and Constance, both interested in books and music, but Eva's nursing skills were in demand at times of emergency, including Hardy's final illness and death, and Margaret, Florence's favourite sister, not only spent her honeymoon at Max Gate in February 1917 after marrying an officer in the Royal Flying Corps, but stayed there again with her new baby throughout the spring of 1918.

Conscious of being in a better position, financially, than any of her sisters, Florence tried to help them—especially the two youngest—during her lifetime and left a will that chiefly benefited Eva and the children of Ethel and Margaret. MM

Letters of Emma and Florence Hardy, ed. Michael Millgate (1996).

Robert Gittings and Jo Manton, *The Second Mrs Hardy* (1979).

'Duke's Reappearance, The', short story. First published in the 1896 Christmas Supplement of the *Saturday Review*, it was collected in *A Changed Man and Other Tales*. In the latter version 'several slight touches were added to identify it as a family tradition' (Purdy 153). When he gave the manuscript to Edward *Clodd, Hardy added a footnote to the first line: 'Christopher Swetman was one of the author's ancestors on the maternal side' (Purdy 155). In the *Life* Hardy states that the *Swetman family 'seem to have been involved in the Monmouth rising', and that one 'indubitably true' family tradition held that 'after the Battle of Sedgemoor [1685] two of the Swetman daughters—Grace and Leonarde—were beset in their house by some of the victorious soldiery' and narrowly escaped being raped (*LW* 10–11).

Though the names are used in the story, the events are modified into a romantic anecdote of the defeated Duke of Monmouth, an unsuccessful claimant to the throne, taking refuge, incognito, in the home of Hardy's ancestor Christopher Swetman at Melbury Osmond, Dorset ('King's Hintock' in the story).

Dynasts, The. This work is so massive and ambitious an undertaking that its position within the Hardy canon was problematic from the dates of first publication (Part First, January 1904; Part Second, February 1906; Part Third, February 1908). Early reviewers hardly knew what to make of Part First, and most made disparaging remarks that dismayed Hardy; Part Second was also received coolly; but his determination to complete the work was not seriously crippled by the negative elements in early reviews. Some of Hardy's closest friends regretted that its composition had diverted the author's energy from the writing of more novels. The oddity of its genre (Hardy called it, after considerable thought, an 'epic-drama') meant that its literary form—whatever Hardy chose to call it—defied assimilation to the venerable epic tradition of English poetry. Many devoted readers of Hardy are unfamiliar, to this day, with either the intentions or the achievement of a work to which Hardy devoted a major part of his life: perhaps understandably so, since a large number of books dealing with Hardy, whether biography or criticism, barely mention its existence.

Yet *The Dynasts*, roughly equivalent in length to all of Hardy's more than 900 shorter poems, was the key event of his seventh decade; on it he lavished so much of his energy that he could honestly say that he had become, while writing it, a contemporary of Nelson and Wellington. It, more than his novels, was responsible for the new King's conferral of the Order of Merit upon him in June 1910. It was singled out for praise at the time he received his honorary degree of Doctor of Letters at Oxford (1920). His lifelong dedication to the craft of poetry earned him the glowing commendation of more than 100 younger poets; St John Ervine, in 1921, thanked him for all his work, but 'most of all, perhaps', for *The Dynasts*. Ellen Glasgow recalled, years later, that Hardy had spoken to her about it as either his 'greatest' or his 'best' work (the precise adjective escaped her). At any rate, *The Dynasts*, in Hardy's mind, was his bid for poetic immortality, his masterwork.

Tracing its genesis takes us back to the ghost of an idea recorded in a note dated 13 March 1874: 'Let Europe be the stage & have scenes continually shifting.' In fact, Hardy's fascination with the Napoleonic era had germinated decades before that, when he read issues of the periodical *A History of the Wars* and C. H. Gifford's *History of the Wars Occasioned by the French Revolution, from the Commencement of Hostilities in 1792 to the End of the Year 1816* (2 vols., 1817), a work that Hardy was to use for several scenes in *The Dynasts*. At an early age he knew well the historical writings of Thomas *Carlyle, J. B. H. R. Capefigue, Sir W. F. P. Napier, and Edward Pelham Brenton. He borrowed most heavily from Louis Adolphe Thiers's *Histoire du Consulat et de l'Empire*, which was available to him in the edition of 1847–62, as well as D. F. Campbell's translation of 1845–62 (he owned both editions, each set consisting of 20 volumes). In the 1870s he visited Chelsea Hospital to interview veterans of Waterloo, and conducted extensive research at the British Museum for *The Trumpet-Major*, a novel set in 1804–5; he would use his notes on both primary and secondary sources a second time when he came to the writing of *The Dynasts.* No creative artist in Great Britain had read more widely on the Napoleonic era, or to better effect, than Hardy.

Hardy's concept expanded from a series of interlinked ballads dealing with Napoleon's early campaigns, Moscow, and the Hundred Days, to a historical drama that swept the European stage from 1805, when Napoleon placed the crown of Lombardy on his head at Milan Cathedral, to 1815, Waterloo, and Napoleon's belated recognition that his lot was not 'to shoulder Christ from out the topmost niche'. His Nemesis was too great and powerful, too indifferent to his aspirations, for him to succeed; as he mused in the wood of Bossu, while his generals and their soldiers sought avenues of retreat, 'Great men are meteors that consume themselves | To light the earth. This is my burnt-out hour.'

A poem of such length and scope required, as Hardy saw it, a philosophical substructure. *The Dynasts* contains Hardy's fullest working-out of his concept of the Immanent Will. Hardy, on his own, had come to much the same conclusions about the bitter relationship between human beings and the gods who rule the universe as Eduard von Hartmann, in his *Philosophy of the Unconscious* (translated into English in 1884), and Arthur *Schopenhauer, in *The World as Will and Idea* (familiar to Hardy in the translation of 1890).

Since Hardy readily admitted that the simple faith of his childhood had been destroyed by developments in Victorian science, a brief summary of the case argued by Hardy is in order. (Despite protestations to the contrary, he was not a neutral observer of the decade he was reviewing.) The Immanent Will, as a non-human force operating behind the scenes, is poorly understood, and perhaps can never be apprehended in all its awesome dimensions; it is the sum of all wills, weaving Its 'eternal artistries in Circumstance'. A poet's difficulty in trying to speak about 'it' in language that is intelligible to his audience derives partly from Its obscurity, but more importantly from the fact that an anthropomorphic vulgarization of the 'Great Necessitator' (also called the 'Eternal Urger' and any number of similar names) is almost impossible to avoid. Hardy rejected the 'Divine personages' of mythology as principles of Causation; he believed that his contemporaries had done the same as soon as they began to think in terms of a 'First or Fundamental Energy'.

Thus, men and women are deluded if they think they have free will: they are mannikins moving with little self-knowledge through a terrestrial tragedy. A would-be 'dynast' like Napoleon may believe that he is hurling other dynasts from their thrones and establishing a new world-order; but his empire, built upon shaky foundations, cannot last. Hardy entertained no illusion that those who succeeded Napoleon had a higher concept of 'loving-kindness' (Hardy's coinage) than the Emperor. It is all the more striking, therefore, that *The Dynasts* concludes on a muted note of hope, and that this bleak limning of history ends with the Chorus chanting 'But—a stirring thrills the air | Like to sounds of joyance there, | That the rages | Of the ages | Shall be cancelled, and deliverance offered from the darts that were, | Consciousness the Will informing, till It fashion all things fair!' (Part Third, 'After Scene'). These, the very last words of Hardy's work, reinforce his doctrine: the Immanent Will cares not for the misery It inflicts on the human race; compassion as a concept is alien to Its being; but after aeons of time (Hardy is not specific as to how long the process will take) the Will *may* develop some awareness of Itself, and work to alleviate the unhappiness of mankind.

The Dynasts was expansive enough to develop and incorporate a formidable cast of Spirits (Hardy's version of the 'celestial machinery' that had served Homer, Virgil, and Milton): the Spirit of the Years, the Spirit of the Pities, the Spirit Ironic, and the Spirit Sinister. Though not as sharply differentiated one from the other as their names indicate, they speak some of the drama's most beautiful and poetic lines, and much of the time they verbalize Hardy's own views.

Nevertheless, they constitute only a small fraction of the 297 characters who are given lines. These, in turn, range from military and naval figures, members of royal households, and politicians (all of whom are historically based), to ordinary soldiers, peasants, and Dorset folk operating at different social levels. The range of diction on display compares favourably with that exhibited in any Wessex novel.

Moreover, to accommodate his appetite for variety, Hardy employed more than 30 rhyme-schemes. As Ruth A. Firor pointed out in her *Folkways in Thomas Hardy* (1931), his use of folk-rhythms, ballads, jigs, reels, 'favourite quicksteps', and even a morris-dance tune, is astonishingly sophisticated. A more recent study, Dennis Taylor's *Hardy's Metres and Victorian Prosody* (1988), gives Hardy's versatility an equally respectful treatment.

The action unfolds in localities that change from London's House of Commons to bloody battlefields in western Spain, to Borodino and (eventually) Moscow, while numerous scenes are vividly and ingeniously described as from a great height. The chosen perspective frequently anticipates later cinematic techniques. One example may be cited: 'The nether sky opens, and Europe is disclosed as a prone and emaciated figure, the Alps shaping like a backbone, and the branching mountain-chains like ribs, the peninsular plateau of Spain forming a head. Broad and lengthy lowlands stretch from the north of France across Russia like a grey-green garment hemmed by the Ural mountains and the glistening Arctic Ocean. The point of view then sinks downwards through space...' (Fore Scene, 'The Overworld'). As the camera's eye moves effortlessly, and incredibly swiftly, toward the necessary close-up before the main action can commence, it begins to examine, in a manner almost brutal in its objectivity, the peoples of Europe 'distressed by events which they did not cause ...writhing, crawling, heaving, and vibrating in their various cities and nationalities'.

Some of this emphasis on grandiose perspectives is due to Hardy's interest in the concept of sublimity given wide currency by Edmund Burke in his famous *A Philosophical Enquiry into the Origin of our Ideas of the Sublime and Beautiful* (1756). Hardy's knowledge of German metaphysics may have included some familiarity with Gotthold Lessing's annotations (attached to a translation Lessing had made himself); but even closer at hand, in addition to Burke's English text, were John Morley's study of Burke (1867) and Leslie *Stephen's *History of English Thought in the Eighteenth Century* (1876), with their fair-minded assessments of Burke's aesthetics. The numerous panoramic vistas of *The Dynasts* are consistent with Burke's conviction that 'we are more struck at looking down from a precipice, than at looking up at an object of equal height', and with the equally provocative notion that disorder in nature can create 'an idea of grandeur'. Burke cited 'the starry heaven', with individual stars lying in 'apparent confusion', as a prime example of sublimity; unable to count the stars, we comfort ourselves by believing that our recognition of failure brings us closer to an understanding of infinity.

Hardy knew, even as he undertook his massive project of making sense of a turbulent decade, that he would be unable to unify his wildly diverse materials: for example, naval strategies were important only in Part First, and Napoleon was personally not present in the lengthy passages dealing with the Peninsular Campaign. The rise and fall of the French Emperor, requiring as it did the slaughter of hundreds of thousands of armed combatants, the misery of millions of civilians, and the spatial dimensions of an entire continent, provided a crowded cavalcade of impressions. Each impression is individually etched with fine-grained detail.

Nobody understands why events happen as they do. Hardy never underestimates Napoleon's intelligence, but even Napoleon fails to make clear sense of the overarching Reality that governs his life. The Emperor blames a force within himself that baffles his intent and harries him onward. At Tilsit, when, hand held over his heart, he gives Queen Louisa of Prussia a rose, she throws herself on his mercy; Napoleon, though momentarily moved by her emotion, tells her that he cannot give her Magdeburg because his star is to blame: 'It is unswervable!' (2.1.8). He is one of the few in Europe, according to the Spirit of the Years, who discerns, however faintly, the working of the Will. And yet his premonitions amount to only a clouded awareness that he, too, is unable to exercise free will. At Charleroi, a few hours before Waterloo, he falls into a troubled sleep, and a vision passes before him: 'corpses in divers stages of decay...the flesh dropping from them...[including] his intimate officers who have been slain...'. He cannot wake from the nightmare in which he finds himself entangled, and mutters, 'Why hold me my own master, if I be | Ruled by the pitiless Planet of Destiny?' (3.6.3).

At first Hardy did not want *The Dynasts* to be staged. His work was intended 'simply for mental performance', and perhaps, he mused, his kind of verse-drama might at some future time take the shape 'of a monotonic delivery of speeches, with dreamy conventional gestures, something in the manner traditionally maintained by the old Christmas mummers ...'. Nevertheless, he was unprepared for the half-serious suggestion of the theatre critic A. B. Walkley, printed in the *Times Literary Supplement* (29 January 1904), that the dramatic portions might be put on-stage as a puppet-show, or a series of shadow pictures. A spirited correspondence between Hardy and Walkley, arguing the case for and against the theatrical viability of *The Dynasts*, followed on 5, 12, and 19 February.

Perhaps Hardy overstated his case for the work's unsuitability for the stage. In 1914–15, in the opening half-year of the Great War, Harley *Granville-Barker put on a successful three-hour production, adapting some 30 scenes of *The Dynasts*, at the Kingsway Theatre, London. In numerous productions of selected moments staged over the next 70 years in Dorchester, Oxford, London, and (perhaps most spectacularly) Exeter Cathedral, as well as four BBC radio programmes, *The Dynasts* proved its dramatic potential (see also DRAMATIZATIONS).

The issue of literary form, much debated in Hardy criticism, may obscure the more significant connection between Hardy's patriotic intention and the public's receptivity to his theme, particularly during the crises of both World Wars. Hardy was correct in pointing to the failure of his fellow-artists to treat the British contribution to the defeat of Napoleon. In his Preface, he wrote that the role played by the British in the 'vast international tragedy' had received 'only slight regard' from Continental writers. Minor efforts by English writers included what Thackeray had written in a few scenes in *Vanity Fair* (1848), George *Meredith in some 1,000 lines, and Robert Buchanan in *The Drama of Kings* (1871), an epic that devoted two of its three parts to the war of 1870–1. Hardy correctly saw that there was room for 'a new handling of the theme which should re-embody the features of this influence in their true proportion...'.

What Hardy did, in brief, was to present to his readers English heroes: Nelson, his fellow-captains, and their crews; Sir Arthur Wellesley (afterwards Duke of Wellington), Sir John Moore, and those who fought in Spain and Belgium; and the common folk who fought against the French threat to their existence. They rose to the challenge posed by Pitt in the House of Commons, a challenge to save England by her exertions and Europe by her example (1.5.5). The emphasis on courage, ethical and moral responsibility, and the determination of countless Englishmen and Englishwomen to do the right thing, seriously undercuts Hardy's dour view of human strivings (stated, for example, by the Spirit of the Years in the Fore Scene) that Napoleon's actions make human beings 'gyrate like animalcula | In tepid pools'. Moreover, there are other heroes—Marshal Ney on the French side, General Kutuzov on the Russian, and indeed all those who refused to think of themselves as (in Hardy's phrase) mean insects crawling on the obscurest leaves.

Hardy believed, with some justification, that the objections to *The Dynasts*, however they were phrased, were largely aimed against his bluntly stated doctrine of Predestination. England's educated élite objected to his characterization of Christianity as 'a local cult', and could not accept his championing of the concept of the Immanent Will as a useful way to understand man's place in a brutal, and largely uncaring, universe. But he did not intend, during the fifteen years that he concentrated on writing the work, that the 'hard Pyrrhonism' of the Spirits would remain hard for ever; it could not remain so if indeed the Immanent Will were developing, however slowly, a consciousness of Itself. He insisted, with some justification, that those who accused him of unremitting pessimism misread his text. (In the 1920s, because of the savagery of the Great War and the ineptitude of those who drew up the Treaty of Versailles, Hardy declared that he foresaw a new Dark Age; that men's minds appeared to be 'moving backwards rather than on'.)

In recent years *The Dynasts* has more than once been described in language that would meet E. M. W. Tillyard's desiderata for a true epic as enumerated in *The English Epic and Its Background* (1954): high seriousness in approach, a correspondingly high quotient of talent, amplitude of subject-matter and variety of technique, sophistication of execution, and choric appropriateness.

In addition to the unusual aspects of *The Dynasts* already cited, the epic-drama also provides, in its numerous scenes dominated by Napoleon, a remarkably complex portrait. This Napoleon is not only peremptory, fitfully cruel and arbitrary, and emotionally unmoved by the carnage of one battlefield after another, but a leader who earns the obedience and devotion of his staff as he destroys one outmoded royal house after another.

If, after Borodino, Hardy increasingly stressed Napoleon's physical deterioration, he did so not merely because the data for such a change were recorded in his sources, but because he wanted to show that the Emperor's increasing decrepitude symbolized a tragic decline from a condition that once approximated godhead. The price that Napoleon exacted from the peoples of Europe was excessive. In its dramatizations of the killing fields of Austerlitz, Albuera, the bridge of the Beresina, and the roads leading from Smolensko to Lithuania, *The Dynasts* is surely one of the most eloquent and moving anti-war jeremiads of world literature.

Hardy's empathy with pain and suffering permeates its 131 scenes, and perhaps never with greater poetical insight than in the speech given to the Chorus of the Years, when the fate of helpless coneys, moles, larks, snails, butterflies, and hedgehogs at Waterloo looms fully as large as that of entire armies: 'Trodden and bruised to a miry tomb | Are ears that have greened but will never be gold, | And flowers in the bud that will never bloom' (3.6.8). It is an extraordinary moment of quiet before the storm, one in which Hardy succeeds in creating a poetic moment that combines beauty of language with a powerful insight. *The Dynasts* contains a surprisingly high number of such moments. Those who love Hardy cannot afford to pass it by. (See also NAPOLEONIC WARS.) HO

Susan Dean, *Hardy's Poetic Vision in 'The Dynasts'* (1977).

Harold Orel, *Thomas Hardy's Epic-Drama: A Study of 'The Dynasts'* (1963).

Walter F. Wright, *The Shaping of 'The Dynasts': A Study in Thomas Hardy* (1967).

E

editors. All of Hardy's published novels except the first two, *Desperate Remedies* and *Under the Greenwood Tree*, appeared originally as serials, a process that involved him in relationships, sometimes strained, with a variety of editors. William *Tinsley, who had rejected *The Poor Man and the Lady* but subsequently issued the two novels named above, published Hardy's first serial, *A Pair of Blue Eyes*, in *Tinsleys' Magazine*. Its two immediate successors, *Far from the Madding Crowd* and *The Hand of Ethelberta*, appeared in the prestigious *Cornhill Magazine* under the distinguished editorship of Leslie *Stephen. Before its eventual publication in *Belgravia*, owned by the publishing firm of Chatto and Windus, *The Return of the Native* had been considered but not taken up by Leslie Stephen, John Blackwood (*Blackwood's Magazine*, which later published 'The Withered Arm'), and George Bentley (*Temple Bar*). (Stephen, who had had anxious moments about the treatment of Fanny Robin and her baby in *Far from the Madding Crowd*, smelt danger in the opening portion of the new novel.) *The Trumpet-Major* made its first appearance in *Good Words*, whose Scots editor, Donald Macleod, asked Hardy (as he later recalled) 'to make a lover's meeting, which I had fixed for a Sunday afternoon, take place on a Saturday, and that swear-words should be avoided' (Purdy 32–3). *A Laodicean* appeared in the European Edition of the American *Harper's New Monthly Magazine*, as did the later *Jude the Obscure*; the editor was H. M. *Alden, but Hardy's negotiations were partly conducted through the owner, J. Henry Harper of *Harper & Brothers. *Two on a Tower* appeared in another American magazine, the *Atlantic Monthly*, edited by T. B. *Aldrich.

As editor of the *Graphic*, Arthur *Locker published the original versions of *The Mayor of Casterbridge*, *A Group of Noble Dames*, and *Tess of the d'Urbervilles*, the second and third of these enterprises being fraught with difficulties. *Tess* had earlier been rejected by the *Tillotson newspaper syndicate, by *Murray's Magazine* (which, under Edward Arnold's editorship, had already published one of Hardy's short stories, 'The Waiting Supper'), and by *Macmillan's Magazine* (edited by Mowbray *Morris). Serialization of *The Woodlanders* in *Macmillan's Magazine* had been beset by milder difficulties as authorial outspokenness came into collision with editorial caution, Morris showing an amiable nervousness about the handling of Fitzpiers's affair with Suke Damson. The original version of *The Well-Beloved* was contracted for by the Tillotson syndicate, under whose auspices it appeared in the *Illustrated London News*. Further information is given under entries for individual novels and editors.

Apart from those mentioned above, Hardy was involved with a number of other editors in connection with the publication of his short stories and poems. For an example of a short story that achieved magazine publication only after significant editorial interference, see 'On the Western Circuit'. Among the poems, a notable case is 'A Sunday Morning Tragedy', an uncompromising ballad concerning an abortion attempt that ends disastrously. On 3 October 1907 this was refused by W. L. Courtney of the *Fortnightly Review* on the grounds that its subject was unsuitable for younger readers of the magazine; it was eventually published by Ford Madox Hueffer in the *English Review* (December 1908). (See also CENSORSHIP; SERIALIZATION.)

education. Hardy's own formal education was limited to about eight years, between the ages of 8 and 16, and the traditional description of him as an autodidact, though not one he relished, is not unfair. In September 1848 he was the first pupil to enter the newly built National School at Lower Bockhampton, established largely under the patronage of the lady of the manor, Mrs Julia Augusta *Martin; it is recalled in his poem 'He Revisits His First School' and in his autobiography (*LW* 21). There, by his own account, he 'excelled' in arithmetic and geography. In

September 1850 he was moved on his mother's initiative from this Anglican establishment to the British School in Dorchester, which was run on Nonconformist lines. Jemima Hardy's motivation, however, was not doctrinal but related to the reputation of the master, Isaac *Last (though a difference of opinion between mother and patroness was evidently also involved). Under Last's care Hardy was enabled, from 1852, to study Latin. When, in 1853, Last started a 'commercial academy' or private school in Dorchester, Hardy moved with him, remaining there until he left school in 1856 to become an architectural apprentice.

The autobiography speculates that, if he had received different advice from his friend and mentor Horace *Moule, he might at a later stage have abandoned architecture 'for a University career' (*LW* 38); in another passage, referring to the origins of *Jude the Obscure* as 'the story of a young man—"who could not go to Oxford"', Hardy states that he himself 'was not altogether hindered going, at least to Cambridge, and could have gone up easily at five-and-twenty' (*LW* 216). Cambridge was Moule's own university, but that 'easily' may well be questioned.

In any case, the plan of a university education was not pursued; instead he studied with great dedication and perseverance, for the most part outside working hours and in the solitude of his bedroom in his parents' cottage. It was a subject on which he remained sensitive and defensive to the end: his copy of F. A. Hedgcock's 1912 study of his life and work (in DCM) has a wounded and indignant annotation against the description of him as self-educated, to the effect that he was 'taught Latin & French at School and College'. The statement, without being mendacious, is misleading (or perhaps self-deluding), his experience of 'College' being limited to a short period of attendance at evening classes in French held at King's College, London. See CLASSICS for a detailed account of his study of Latin and of Ancient and New Testament Greek—efforts that may fairly be described as heroic, and that in some instances bear a close resemblance to those attributed to his last tragic hero, Jude Fawley.

In Hardy's fiction, education plays a prominent role, working both positively and negatively to determine human happiness or (more often than not) frustration and even misery: it can be, as it had been for Hardy himself, a potent instrument of liberating opportunity and social mobility, but it can also produce divisiveness and estrangement between an individual and his background, and can generate conflict in relationships, especially in love and marriage and between parents and children. '"I am better educated than you,"' Bathsheba, who had originally thought of becoming a governess, tells Gabriel Oak (*FFMC* 4), and she clearly regards it as an obstacle to his candidature for her hand; for his part Gabriel has to admit to her, '"You speak like a lady—all the parish notice it."' Grace Melbury, disqualified by her genteel schooling from feeling contented in her old home, reaches the point of telling her father '"I wish you had never, never thought of educating me"' (*W* 30). Hardy's first, lost, and heavily autobiographical novel *The Poor Man and the Lady* evidently presented a hero who was the clever child of humble parents, did well at school, became an architect, and aspired to the hand of the squire's daughter—a paradigmatic Victorian success story that was partly wish-fulfilment but in the event was to be largely enacted by Hardy himself.

In the very early *Under the Greenwood Tree* the heroine, Fancy Day, is a trained schoolteacher, as were Hardy's sisters and his cousin Tryphena *Sparks. The first products of the newly established training colleges had emerged in 1853 and had been memorably depicted by Dickens in *Hard Times* (1854) and *Our Mutual Friend* (1865). Though the elementary-school teacher carried little social weight in that period—the schoolmaster-hero of *An Indiscretion in the Life of an Heiress*, painfully aware of this fact, is impelled to seek less socially disadvantageous employment—Fancy's salaried status grants her financial independence and a home of her own, and hence makes her different from most women of her time in fact and fiction. Like such later heroines as Bathsheba and Ethelberta, Fancy's role in the community is not exclusively domestic and subordinate. As with a much later heroine, Grace Melbury in *The Woodlanders*, her education has been part of a life-plan drawn up for her by an uneducated but socially ambitious father. That parents of this kind are a recurring character-type in Hardy's fiction—a striking example occurs in the short story 'To Please His Wife'—is a phenomenon for which his own mother must perhaps bear some of the responsibility.

Two of the rivals for Fancy's hand, the tranter's son Dick Dewy and Parson Maybold, represent, respectively, the uneducated class out of which she has moved and the educated and socially esteemed class to which she aspires. Grace Melbury faces a similar choice, between the countryman Giles Winterborne and the gentleman-doctor Edred Fitzpiers. In these cases, as elsewhere, questions of education are intimately bound up with those of class, status, social mobility, and economic power. In the context of contemporary attitudes and prejudices, it counts for nothing (except for Hardy) that Fitzpiers is morally unprincipled and his scientific research mere dabbling, whereas Giles is not only his moral superior but possesses genuine and communally valuable skills of a practical order. Fitzpiers's upper-class education, as much as his Norman-French name, is a guarantee of blood and breeding, and confers an automatic (and richly undeserved) prestige.

Rivalry in love between two men who are also representatives of different kinds of knowledge is a theme that had been explored in the novel immediately preceding *The Woodlanders*. In *The Mayor of Casterbridge*, the insider-outsider pattern (already used in, for instance, *Far from the Madding Crowd*) had been placed within a historical and even Darwinian framework: while Henchard represents traditional (and now outmoded) ways of doing business, Farfrae brings scientific method to the corn trade and prospers accordingly. The antithesis is between instinct and training, the self-taught and the educated man: professionalism has invaded an area of life in which unschooled experience has hitherto been paramount. Like earlier heroes such as Giles, Henchard is the possessor of distinctive skills, and the very first page of the novel depicts him as no common labourer but one with a marketable expertise. His misfortune, or misjudgement, is to enter into rivalry with a man who is not merely skilled but educated, for in 19th-century England education is power.

Education plays a different role in another relationship in the same novel, for Henchard is another parent whose social ambitions are partly displaced on to his child (in this instance an adoptive daughter). Brought up in poverty, and with very little in the way of formal education, Elizabeth-Jane is expected to qualify herself for a more affluent existence by acquiring manners to match her new status. For Henchard, such manners are most readily identified with the more polished forms of speech associated with his social superiors: specifically, they demand the avoidance by Elizabeth-Jane of traditional and local words and expressions that are by definition lower-class. Hardy's ironic comment makes it clear that this misguided quest for the bourgeois gentility of Standard English involved a loss of expressiveness and picturesqueness: doing her best to avoid causing linguistic offence, 'when she had not slept she did not quaintly tell the servants next morning that she had been "hag-rid", but that she had "suffered from indigestion"' (20).

The English novel has a long tradition of exploiting speech as a social badge, more often than not for comic or grotesque purposes; but Hardy shows a profounder interest in the ways in which self-consciousness concerning speech-behaviour and attempts to modify it could have disruptive and divisive effects on individuals and their relationships. Some of his characters are well aware that speech-differences can constitute a barrier. In *Far from the Madding Crowd*, as already noted, Gabriel is a man of knowledge, skill, and wisdom—but not of education in the formal and institutionalized sense. In *Tess of the d'Urbervilles*, one of the first things Tess notices about Angel Clare is his accent: she has no interest in other dancing-partners who 'did not speak so nicely as the strange young man had done' (3).

In Hardy's own early years, his contacts with middle-class patrons like Mrs Martin and the Moule family cannot have failed to make him sharply aware of such non-standard elements as his own speech and that of his family possessed. As a sensitive child he must, too, have perceived, if only half-consciously, the difference between his father's broad dialect and the language and accent of his mother, who had taken pains to purge her speech of local elements, and who no doubt impressed on her children the importance of talking 'properly' if they wished to succeed in the world.

It is not surprising, therefore, that the ambitious and upwardly mobile individual embarrassed by his own lack of social polish, or by an uneducated or at least socially inferior parent, is another recurring character-type. In the story 'The Son's Veto', Henchard's situation is reversed, with an obnoxious Etonian son feeling ashamed of the dialect speech of his Dorset-born mother; for her part, though marriage to a clergyman has removed her from the social sphere in which she grew up, she has retained both the speech-behaviour of her provincial youth and a deep attachment to the rural past of which it was a part. In another short story, 'A Tragedy of Two Ambitions', Joshua, a clergyman of humble origins, feels a deep shame on account of the rough-mannered father who threatens to haunt his newly acquired middle-class existence until death obligingly snatches him away.

In that story Joshua has been a schoolteacher before entering the Church, having shrewdly identified the teaching profession as an accessible rung on the social ladder. Since the Church of England exerted such extensive control over education, from elementary schools to training colleges and universities, it is not surprising to find the Church frequently associated with educational ambitions or shortcomings. (The association had played a part in Hardy's own early life, when he had contemplated a career in the Church.) Jude Fawley, in a novel whose opening chapter begins with the word 'schoolmaster' and ends with the image of a rebuilt church, at one stage sees a bishopric as the desiderated goal of his educational aspirations.

Both Tess and Jude have, arguably, had their contentment marred by their schooling. Tess has 'passed the Sixth Standard in the National School under a London-trained mistress' (3); later in the same chapter the narrator returns to the point, commenting sardonically on 'her trained National teachings and Standard knowledge under an infinitely Revised Code'. (The Revised Code of 1862, further amended in 1867, made standardized examinations important by instituting a system of payment by results.) However, it is clear that this schooling has not taken her very far: she has heard the word 'centurion' in the classroom, but uses it with wild (and touching) inappropriateness, and her flounderings in the deep waters of an educated vocabulary expose her to the mild teasing of both Angel and Hardy (30).

To Hardy, such half-a-loaf knowledge seems worse, not better, than none. He, like Tess, had attended a National School—though only briefly, before being removed to a superior establishment offering Latin as an 'extra'. Established early in the 19th century by the National Society for Promoting the Education of the Poor in the Principles of the Established Church, the National Schools did valuable work in promoting the spread of education in the generations immediately preceding the 1870 Act, which made the provision of schools the responsibility of the state. But her schooling, it seems, has done little more than to unsettle Tess, creating rifts and divisions in her life. In Chapter 3 her minimal education, it is implied, is a poor exchange for the traditional culture represented by her mother—'superstitions, folk-lore, dialect, and orally transmitted ballads'—even though this is unsentimentally characterized as 'lumber'.

Tess's uneasy relationship to two different worlds is symbolized in her speech, for she 'spoke two languages: the dialect at home, more or less; ordinary English abroad and to persons of quality' (3). That unobtrusive 'more or less' speaks volumes concerning Hardy's sense of the loss inflicted by an 'education' that has put so little in the place of what it has taken away. That 'London-trained mistress' has, by precept and example inhibited Tess from speaking with the homely vigour of her father without turning her into the conversational equal of Angel or his family.

Much earlier, in *The Return of the Native*, Hardy had touched more lightly on the spread of education and the minimal nature of some of its recipients' attainments. In this novel published in the same decade as the passing of the Education Act (1870) that had established the Board schools and the principle of universal literacy, a minor character comments unconsciously on the limited progress that has been taken towards this goal: '"The class of folk that couldn't use to make a round O to save their bones from the pit can write their names now without a sputter of the pen, oftentimes without a single blot..."' (1.3). This speech by Olly the besom-maker has begun with the observation that people '"strive after"' education. Yet others who have had access to it without striving value it less highly: Damon Wildeve, who has occasioned these remarks, is a qualified engineer who has taken to keeping an inn, so that '"His learning was no use to him at all"'.

In the same novel, Clym Yeobright's case is both similar and different. He is another educated man who has followed a gentlemanly profession as a diamond merchant, but abandons his glamorous career. His motivation, however, is more idealistic, for he dreams of taking up the ill-esteemed job of village schoolmaster. Subsequently, under the pressure of necessity, he is not ashamed to become a furze-cutter. Inherent in the presentation of Clym may be a questioning of the value of education, or at least of its worldly rewards in the shape of social advancement and economic success—a questioning that becomes more persistent in Hardy's later fiction. Throughout his work, most of the characters who seem intended to engage the reader's sympathy and admiration most deeply (Dick Dewy, Gabriel Oak, Giles Winterborne, Tess Durbeyfield) have received little education, while the well-educated (Damon Wildeve, Edred Fitzpiers, Alec d'Urberville) are frequently flawed. Even in the problematic case of *The Mayor of Casterbridge* it is, for all his shortcomings of nature and temper, Henchard rather than the shallow Farfrae who emerges as tragic hero.

In *The Return of the Native*, Clym's rejected ambition later reasserts itself under his mother's influence, but now redefined in terms of a multi-tiered and socially conscious educational profession: his quixotic and missionary zeal to give 'rudimentary education to the lowest class' yields to the less unworldly notion of establishing 'a good private school for farmers' sons' and ultimately qualifying himself for a public school headship (3.3). As so often the links between education and worldly success, for teacher and taught, are strong.

Clym's earlier sense of vocation, however, had been genuinely philanthropic and intended for the Jude Fawleys of the world. The novel of which Jude is the hero seems to have had its starting-point, or one of its starting-points, in an idea for a story, noted in Hardy's diary, on the theme of a young man's frustrated quest for a university education. Largely self-taught, Jude battles even more heroically than Hardy himself had done with the almost insuperable obstacles in the path of a poor boy aspiring after an élitist education: even laying his hands on a textbook is a heavy task, and the account of his despair at discovering that learning Latin and Greek involves no simple formula for changing one language into another, but prolonged drudgery, is deeply touching.

Behind the piercingly dramatized detail of Jude's frustrated quest for an education lies a problem of anachronism. In the later 19th century Jude's ambitions—to study the classics, Church history, and the like, go to Oxford, and enter the Church—are already outmoded. Earlier figures such as Wildeve and Farfrae had represented the science and technology of the age (though it is true that neither is sympathetically presented), and the hero of *Two on a Tower* is an astronomer (though admittedly, or perhaps redeemingly, Swithin St Cleeve seems to have been largely self-taught). Jude, however, reverts to a pre-Victorian model for his longed-for but unfulfilled educational career. Partly, of course, this is because he has no one to turn to for counsel; partly because Oxford itself had shown little inclination to adapt to the new age; and partly because in this novel of the *fin de siècle* the middle-aged Hardy was to some extent drawing on his own hopes and dreams of three or four decades earlier. Significantly, as noted above, Jude follows the educational programme that Hardy himself had followed: even their reading-lists are virtually identical.

Of the other three major characters in the novel, two are also associated with education, and specifically with the teaching profession. Phillotson, the 'schoolmaster' of the book's opening sentence, has his own ambitions but enjoys little more success than Jude in realizing them. Sue Bridehead attends a training college whose description is closely based on that in Salisbury, the Anglican establishment at which Hardy's sisters had trained. For Sue, as for Fancy Day much earlier, the teaching profession has offered one of the few opportunities for independence available to a woman of her background. Hardy's last novel thus depicts diverse levels of the educational system of the country, from village school to ancient university. At the same time the hero is even more of an autodidact than Hardy himself had been.

The advice Jude receives from the Master of Biblioll College (probably Hardy had in mind the famous Benjamin Jowett, classical scholar and Master of Balliol from 1870 to 1893) seems heartless but is practical in its recognition of the contemporary realities: Jude's life would have been less tormented, and might have been longer, if he had not pursued a dream whose chances of fulfilment had always been remote. (This is not to minimize the fact that educational disappointment is only one of the sources of his un-happiness.) In Hardy's later novels there is a pervading sense of education as a disturber of the peace. Grace Melbury's expensive schooling disqualifies her for a happy marriage with Giles; Tess's cheaper and more limited schooling creates a barrier between herself and her family without equipping her to deal with the problems with which life presents her; Jude, who might have been a contented craftsman, is destroyed, as Hardy's uncle John Antell seems to have been (see ANTELL FAMILY), by the itch for knowledge. One of the most poignant moments in all Hardy's fiction occurs on the last page of *Jude the Obscure*, where his few shabby books—a 'dog-eared' Greek Testament and 'superseded' editions of the classics—stand close to his corpse as silent commentators on the futile and misguided efforts that are now at an end. The implication that it would have been better for these efforts never to have been made is strong.

This radical questioning of the value—or at least the practical effects—of education seems to subvert the Victorian applauding of self-help, and may seem odd coming from Hardy. For his own career had been—and, as his fame and affluence increased and the honours accumulated in his later years, was to continue ever more resoundingly to be—a testimony to the efficacy of education, including self-education, as an agent of liberation and self-fulfilment. Yet he seems to have wondered, at any rate intermittently, whether it had all been worth while, and there is a quiet eloquence in the remark made within a few weeks of his death that '"if he had his life over again he would prefer to be a small architect in a country town"' (*LW* 478). It is a remark that, at least momentarily, seems to wish all the books unwritten and unread, all the notebooks unfilled.

Philip Collins, 'Hardy and Education', in Norman Page (ed.), *Thomas Hardy: The Writer and His Background* (1980).

Egdon Heath was Hardy's collective name for the many individual heaths which extend east of Dorchester to the Avon valley. Historically this was unproductive waste land, with thin acid sandy soil overlying a so-called 'iron pan' that defied traditional forms of plough. Its vegetation of gorse and heather was gathered for firing and grazed by ponies known as heath-croppers. To Hardy it was the familiar scene of his boyhood, and it retained a powerful atmosphere of hostility to civilization, as a refuge for the outcast and the rejected. Its incarnation as the setting of *The Return of the Native* is considered a supreme example of Hardy's command of the interplay between a landscape and the characters who inhabit it. His emphasis on Egdon's unchanging character was modified in the story 'The Withered Arm'.

The introduction in the mid-18th century of the rhododendron to ornamental grounds and game coverts produced an early alteration in the vegetation which has become a problem. The misplaced zeal of the agricultural improvers of the time, who saw the heath as almost a challenge to their virility, began the whittling away of the majestic size of Egdon, from about 40,000 hectares in 1750 to 23,000 by 1900. Twentieth-century policy has followed two conflicting courses. One holds that the advanced technology for land-reclamation for farming and forestry can bring heathland, like a converted heathen, into the general harmony of a rural economy. The other sees Egdon as irredeemable but capable of a new destiny as so many parcels of characterless acres on which a variety of modern installations may be sited. Meanwhile the area of heather, gorse, and bracken has shrunk to about 5,000 hectares, mostly scattered in small lots. DH

Ralph Wightman, *The Wessex Heathland* (1953).

Egerton, George (1859–1945), pseudonym of the Irish short story writer, novelist, and dramatist Mary Chavelita Dunne. She created a sensation by her frank treatment of female sexuality in her remarkable volume of short stories *Keynotes* (1893). A copy (now in the Beinecke Library, Yale University) was lent to Hardy by Florence *Henniker, and he read it very attentively, marking passages with marginal comments and emphases. He was so impressed by *Keynotes* that he copied five extracts—mostly from the first story, 'A Cross Line'—into his notebook (*LN* ii 60–1). His marginal comments and queries, intended for the eyes of Mrs Henniker, on the essential nature of woman, the institution of marriage, and the relation of the sexes are particularly interesting, since at this time he was working on the final version of *Jude the Obscure.* The characterization of Arabella in that novel as a 'female animal' probably shows the influence of Egerton's repeated use of this phrase and her emphasis on the physicality of her female protagonists; Sue Bridehead, too, possibly owes something to the 'nervous' and 'quivering' Egerton heroines. Michael Millgate suggests, however, that 'while Hardy's marginal annotations have to be read as contributions to the half-humorous debate being carried on with Mrs Henniker, they nevertheless indicate some hostility towards women in general or, at the least, a tendency to fall back upon the standard male attitudes of his time' (Millgate 356).

Literary admiration seems to have been mutual, since after reading *Jude* Egerton wrote to Hardy (letter of 22 November 1895, DCM) thanking him for presenting a 'true psychological study' in the character of Sue Bridehead. In his reply (22 December 1895) Hardy returned the compliment by praising the 'verisimilitude' of Egerton's stories. On a more personal note, congratulating her on the birth of a son, he confessed his regret at his own childlessness. In 1901 Egerton divorced her husband, George Egerton Clairmonte, and married Reginald Golding Bright, a theatre agent and critic. Although Hardy and Bright corresponded concerning possible dramatizations of some of Hardy's works, there seems to be no evidence that Hardy either met or corresponded again with George Egerton. SD

Elgar, Edward (1857–1934), English composer; knighted 1904, appointed to the Order of Merit 1911, and created baronet 1931. In 1913 he explored the possibility of writing an opera based upon one of Hardy's works. An interesting letter to Elgar from the author and critic Sidney Colvin, dated 20 July 1913 and written from Hardy's home at Max Gate, indicates that—evidently at Elgar's request—Colvin had floated this idea with Hardy, and that it had been enthusiastically received: 'I find the old man not only willing but *keen* to co-operate in an opera with you.' He adds that Hardy had made three specific suggestions: *The Trumpet-Major* ('pleasant and picturesque materials'), *The Return of the Native* ('a strong country tragedy'), and part of *The Dynasts*, 'particularly the 100 Days section'. Hardy had also expressed his willingness to meet Elgar for discussions, but the project came to nothing. (Colvin's letter is quoted by Jerrold Northrop Moore in his *Edward Elgar: A Creative Life* (1984), 649.)

Eliot, George (1819–80), novelist. Her influence is evident in several of Hardy's early novels. Both her *Felix Holt* (1866) and Hardy's *Desperate Remedies* five years later present ladies with illegitimate sons, and a scene of substitute affection in Eliot's novel is repeated in one that shows the transference of Miss Aldclyffe's thwarted love to her maid (*DR* 6.1). The possibilities of the instrumental choir in *Under the Greenwood Tree* were certainly suggested by the opening of Eliot's story 'Amos Barton', included in her *Scenes of Clerical Life* (1858), and the Christmas party in Hardy's novel has parallels with the New Year's dance in *Silas Marner* (1861), one detail closely followed being that of Miss Crumpler moving so smoothly in the figure 'that one might think she rolled on castors'. The scene at the Rainbow in *Silas Marner*, in which local worthies discuss the leading events of the story and function like the Greek chorus, exemplifies a technique that Hardy used more humorously in *Far from the Madding Crowd* and *The Return of the Native.*

When reviewers of *Far from the Madding Crowd* were reminded of George Eliot, Hardy thought it expedient to try a new tack in *The Hand of Ethelberta.* The reference in the 'Author's Introduction' to *Felix Holt* to 'churchyards, with their grassy mounds and venerable headstones' may have suggested the reference to Gray's 'Elegy' in the title of

Far from the Madding Crowd, while the opening of the barn shearing-scene in the same Hardy novel echoes less resoundingly 'For the great barn-doors are thrown wide open...' in Eliot's *Adam Bede* (1859), the description of the hero of which probably suggested Gabriel Oak's name and character—men like Adam are said to resemble strong oaks with no 'bending languor'. The image also recalls 'Mr Gilfil's Love Story', another of the *Scenes of Clerical Life*, where the hero is compared to an oak of the finest grain, the main trunk of his nature remaining 'loyal to a first and only love' like Gabriel's. *Adam Bede*, in which Hetty Sorrel is seduced by Arthur Donnithorne, may furthermore have suggested the story of Fanny Robin's seduction in *Far from the Madding Crowd*.

The Mayor of Casterbridge contains echoes of *The Mill on the Floss* (1860). Both novels quote Novalis's epigram 'Character is fate', and the maxim applies as much to Henchard as to Tulliver. Like the Mayor, the latter belongs to the old rule-of-thumb world of provincial business, and is the victim of circumstance. Tulliver's curse on Wakem and his sadistic revenge (resisted by Henchard when he has Farfrae at his mercy) may have suggested scenes in Hardy's novel.

A chapter in Eliot's *Romola* (1863) provided the image of the heroine in *Desperate Remedies* (12.6) and *Tess of the d'Urbervilles* (45) 'as one in a boat without oars', drifting helplessly and without hope. Maggie Tulliver's remark on astronomers and women in high towers in *The Mill on the Floss* could well have suggested the theme of *Two on a Tower*. In *Silas Marner* (10) a comment on the advantage of church-going in securing a place in heaven may have prompted the discussion between Joseph Poorgrass and Coggan on the soul-saving advantage held by chapel-folk over churchgoers (*FFMC* 42). The image of the snow extinguishing both the landscape and Dorothea's illusions in Chapter 28 of Eliot's *Middlemarch* (1872) is intensified to symbolize the extinction of Fanny Robin's hopes (*FFMC* 11). In the same Eliot novel, the 'crystalline feather-touch' which shook Lydgate's flirtation with Rosamond Vincy into love (31) is perhaps echoed in Hardy's poem 'At the Word "Farewell"', though both writers could have derived the idea from Sir Walter *Scott. A reflection in Chapter 17 of Eliot's *Daniel Deronda* (1876) on girl-tragedies and the dying of wounded birds after being shot for sport seems a likely source of a scene in *Tess* (41). Alec d'Urberville's first appearance at Flintcomb-Ash, a black speck in the distance (*TDU* 46), may have been suggested by the menacing appearance of Raffles as seen by Bulstrode in *Middlemarch* ('an ugly black spot on the landscape'). Another passage in *Daniel Deronda*, on 'the sort of lovers' vows at which Jove laughs' (45), perhaps finds an echo in the reference, on the last page of *Tess*, to the President of the Immortals and his 'sport' with that novel's heroine. Eliot's comment on *caritas*, in a letter of 29 December 1862, that it represents 'the highest love... which I am happy to believe that no philosophy can expel from the world' is paralleled in Jude's vaunt that the verses on charity in 1 Corinthians 13 will 'stand fast' when all that Sue calls religion has passed away.

The conviction expressed in *Daniel Deronda* that romance and poetry exist in science and railways was shared by Hardy in *A Laodicean*, which introduces telephony (1.2) and the engineering triumph of a railway tunnel (1.12) as well as in poems such as 'The Change', 'After a Romantic Day', and 'Nobody Comes'. Both authors put their faith in *Positivism; each had a scientific outlook, assuming that our life on earth is the only one of which we can be certain, and that everything possible therefore should be done for the general good. Eliot's writings strengthened Hardy's belief in altruism, but he was less optimistic than she, concluding in his later years that man was too much swayed by 'unreason'. Eliot believed that the 'impulses of love and justice' could be raised by 'the aesthetic teaching of great literature', 'the slow stupendous teaching of the world's events', and even the 'unhistoric acts' of everyday life. Hardy recognized 'her genius as a philosopher', but thought that 'her powers as a story-teller, an exhibitor of life' were overestimated, as he told William Blackwood (*L* ii 299), who had hoped (in vain) that Hardy might write a book on her. FBP

Lina Wright Berle, *George Eliot and Thomas Hardy: A Contrast* (1917).

Michael Squires, *The Pastoral Novel: Studies in George Eliot, Thomas Hardy, and D. H. Lawrence* (1974).

emigration recurs throughout Hardy's fiction, but almost always as a cause of disruption and loss rather than fulfilled happiness. Typical is the pointedly named Lackland in 'A Few Crusted Characters' (*LLI*), who returns after 35 years only to find that he must 're-establish himself from the beginning', since even in his native place no 'roots and tendrils' have survived.

Emigration was a conspicuous fact of British society throughout Hardy's lifetime, a solution to economic problems at home which also solidified the global Empire. Several novelists attempted extended treatments of emigrant life: Dickens in *Martin Chuzzlewit* (America), Thackeray in *Vanity Fair* (India) and *The Virginians* (America in an earlier period), Trollope in *John Caldigate* (Australia), Butler in *Erewhon* (New Zealand), Schreiner in *The Story of an African Farm*, and many more. Hardy's many emigrants depart and return, but the narrative remains unremittingly local. The four paragraphs that sketch Angel Clare's sufferings in Brazil (*TDU* 41, 49) are his fullest account. They are highly stylized, with the vignette of 'mothers from English farms' burying their babes with bare hands, and geographically suspect, misplacing Curitiba and misrepresenting its climate. Otherwise he provides only glimpses, usually retrospective: of Newson and Susan in their cottage in Canada (*MC* 4), Sergeant Troy making 'a precarious living' in America (*FFMC* 50), Sir Blount Constantine 'marrying' his African princess (*TT* 32), old Halborough banished to 'that cursed country' Canada in 'A Tragedy of Two Ambitions' (*LLI*), the Reverend Alwyn Hill pining in his Boston college for his lost Duchess of Hamptonshire (*GND*), or Arabella Donn serving in her Australian husband's Sydney hotel (*JO* 3.9).

More vivid than these are the scenes that show the feelings of those left behind, like Mrs Martin preserving her grandson Swithin's 'jim-cracks and tangleys as he left 'em' and sadly waiting six months for a letter (*TT* 38); of those about to leave, like the fretful Timothy Tangs, 'not happy' that emigration to New Zealand 'was dividing him from his father' (*W* 46); and of those who return, at best deracinated and at worst destitute, like Lackland, Arabella, even Stephen Smith in *A Pair of Blue Eyes*, one of the few prosperous migrants in his Bombay bank, but still faded from Elfride's affections, or like the failed and exhausted Philip Hall, whose sudden return from Australia precipitates the action of 'Interlopers at the Knap' (*WT*). The more natural course seems to be to stay home. Gabriel Oak and Michael Henchard both seriously think of emigrating, to California (*FFMC* 56) and, in Farfrae's intended footsteps, to America (*MC* 32) respectively, yet both are unthinkable out of their Wessex context.

It may be that Hardy's dislike of emigration went back to resentment (perhaps his mother Jemima's resentment) at the loss to the family of Martha Hand, her sister, to Canada in 1851, and of two of the Sparks sisters, her nieces, to Queensland in 1870. That recent departure appears in *The Hand of Ethelberta*, where the butler Chickerel's daughters emigrate to Queensland with their farmer husbands (*HE*, sequel). Queensland is also the intended destination of Agatha Pollins's uncle, and thus the cause of her problems, in the uncollected story 'Destiny and a Blue Cloak'. Family loss goes deeper than just the personal pining of Mrs Martin or Timothy Tangs. When Barnet in 'Fellow-Townsmen' leaves to wander America, Australia, India, and the Cape, the narrator sounds like a biologist mourning the end of a species: 'the name became extinct in the borough of Port Bredy, after having been a living force therein for more than two hundred years' (*WT*).

The Darwinian note is characteristic. A notebook entry shows Hardy's belief that the migrant must not only age, but change, by inevitable adaptation to the new environment. On the California frontier, 'Every man jack . . . was changed' (*LN* ii 89). Another entry foresees future Australians adapting into a people 'energetic', 'caring much for easy society', 'growing and drinking wine', and reshaped by their new concept of distance (*LN* i 228). Those that cannot adapt must suffer, like the English farm-workers in Brazil, whose frames 'had resisted all the weathers to whose moods they had been born', but not 'the weathers by which they were surprised on Brazilian plains' (*TDU* 41). To be alien, for Hardy, is to be tragically displaced, like 'Drummer Hodge' in South Africa, bewildered by 'Strange stars amid the gloam'.

So Hardy's native can never truly return. Alien experience enforces change, even if the journey has been only to Paris, as for Clym Yeobright, or to school, as for Grace Melbury. Introduced species, too, can wreak havoc. The products of the new world are rootless and dangerous interlopers. It is an 'Italianized American, a South Carolinian by birth' who murders Felice Charmond in *The Woodlanders*; an actress from Philadelphia who precipitates Aeneas Manston's tragedy in *Desperate Remedies*; a Dutch Guianan with a worthless wife in Quebec who deprives Lady Icenway of her happiness in *A Group of Noble Dames*; a fortune from Canada that lets Wildeve lure Eustacia to her death in *The Return of the Native*; and a young Australian who hangs his siblings and himself in *Jude the Obscure*—'one of those preternaturally old boys ... from new countries'. Little Father Time, whose face 'took a back view over the great Atlantic of Time', acquires extra meanings as a native of that age-old continent which was also a new country (*JO* 5.4, 5.3). Mrs Doncaster in *The Hand of Ethelberta* is not alone in taking as her measure of undesirability the offspring of an 'Antipodean miscreant'. A citizen of the world like William Dare in *A Laodicean*, who has 'lived mostly in India, Malta, Gibraltar, the Ionian Islands, and Canada', is as careless of 'social rules and troublesome observances' in England as his father hoped they might be in 'America or New Zealand' (*AL* 2.5).

Hardy's emigrants are the despairing and lovelorn (Alwyn Hill), the ambitious (Suke Damson), the malcontent (Arabella), the fugitives (Troy, or Mopp Ollamoor in 'The Fiddler of the Reels'), or the fantasists, like Sergeant John Clark, whose patter about New Zealand is his seduction technique ('Enter a Dragoon', *CM*). Those who go in honest hopes of self-improvement, like Newson and Susan in *The Mayor of Casterbridge*, usually fail. RR

'Enter a Dragoon', short story. Published in the New York magazine *Harper's Monthly* (December 1900), it was collected in *A Changed Man and Other Tales*. Though dated December 1899, it had been begun in November 1899 and was completed in January 1900, and with 'A Changed Man', written at about the same time, represents Hardy's farewell to prose fiction. Written and published during the *Boer War, its historical background is the Crimean War of nearly half a century earlier. The situation of marriage preparations interrupted by the appearance of a man believed dead had been used a dozen years earlier, with variations, in 'The Waiting Supper'.

Three years before the story opens, Selina Paddock of Mellstock has been on the point of marrying James Clark, a soldier, when he has been called away to fight in the Crimea. He is believed to have been killed in action, and Selina, who has borne Clark's child, is now about to marry Miller, a wheelwright, when Clark turns up. She decides to keep her original promise to marry him, and agrees to his plan to emigrate to New Zealand. However, he has a fatal heart attack on the evening of his arrival (he has been 'in the hospital at Scutari', and is exhausted by a long journey and a vigorous dance). After these three abortive attempts to marry, Selina remains single, though passing herself off as Clark's widow. On a visit to his grave she meets a woman whom Clark has married in Yorkshire before his return to Selina, and who has also borne him a child. The final ironic tableau of the two women confronting each other over the grave anticipates Hardy's series of poems 'Satires of Circumstance' in the volume thus titled.

epigraphs. Hardy followed the example of Sir Walter *Scott, George *Eliot, and others in affixing epigraphs to many of his works and parts of works. As the examples that follow will suggest, they exhibit the range of his reading and also point to certain notable favourites among classic and modern authors. Their effect is often, as in *The Woodlanders* and *Tess of the d'Urbervilles*, to draw the reader's attention at the outset, more or less provocatively, to some significant aspect of the story that follows; at the same time, like the numerous other quotations and allusions embedded within the text, they link the particular work, and the limited world it portrays, with traditions of ancient and modern writing and the much broader depiction therein of human life, thought, and feeling.

Though his first published novel, *Desperate Remedies*, bears on its title-page a prose quotation from Scott, Hardy's preferred sources of epigraphs lay overwhelmingly in the direction of poetry, including poetic drama. *Tess of the d'Urbervilles* has at its beginning a quotation from *Shakespeare's *Two Gentlemen of Verona*; *The Return of the Native* some lines from *Keats's *Endymion*; *Two on a Tower* an apt extract about love and the 'new astrology' from the 17th-century Roman Catholic poet Richard Crashaw; *The Hand of Ethelberta* a brief phrase in the original Latin from the Roman poet Lucretius. Crashaw turns up again as the provider of the epigraph for Part First of *The Well-Beloved*, the other two parts of this novel being prefaced by quotations from, respectively, Sir Thomas Wyatt and Shakespeare, whilst the title-page carries a brief but entirely apposite phrase from *Shelley's *Revolt of Islam*. Hardy's last novel, *Jude the Obscure*, is generously supplied with epigraphs: St Paul's stern admonition 'The letter killeth' (2 Corinthians 3: 6) stands at the beginning, and each of the six parts of the novel has one or two epigraphs—from the Apocryphal Book of Esdras; *Swinburne and Ovid; Sappho; *Milton; Marcus Aurelius; another book of the Apocrypha, Esther; and *Browning.

But of all Hardy's works, the two most lavishly furnished in this respect are *A Pair of Blue Eyes*, each chapter of which bears a brief unattributed quotation at its head, and the story *An Indiscretion in the Life of an Heiress*, which also has an epigraph for every one of its short chapters—from Shakespeare (four times), Browning (four times), Shelley (twice), Tennyson, Byron, Dryden's translation of Virgil's *Aeneid*, Waller, and the Old Testament. Another story, 'Enter a Dragoon', carried epigraphs (from O'Shaughnessy, Donne, Barnes, Jonson, and Shakespeare) at the head of each of its five sections for its original magazine publication, but Hardy may have reached the conclusion that this was a little overdone since he deleted all of them when he collected the story in *A Changed Man*. Three important examples of epigraphs in his poetical works remain to be noted: *The Dynasts* is headed by brief quotations in Latin and English; a Latin phrase from Virgil's *Aeneid* stands strikingly at the beginning of the sequence of elegies for his dead wife, 'Poems of 1912–13'; and the three poems grouped under the title 'In Tenebris' each carry an epigraph from the Book of Psalms. On a Sophoclean epigraph given in the manuscript of one of Hardy's short stories but later dropped, see 'THE GRAVE BY THE HANDPOST'.

executions, public. These were not abolished in England until 1868, and in his youth Hardy witnessed two that left a permanent impression upon him. On 9 August 1856, aged 16, he was well to the front of a crowd of three or four thousand people outside Dorchester jail who watched the hanging of Martha Browne. Nearly seventy years later he retained a vivid memory of the scene: an account written on 20 January 1926 (*L* vii 5) has an unmistakably erotic component in its description of the woman's body, in its 'tight black silk gown' soaked by the rain, turning as it dangled from the rope. Two years after Martha Browne's execution Hardy watched, in different circumstances, the hanging of James Seale on 19 August 1858: this, too, was vividly recalled in his old age, the autobiography describing how, standing on high ground not far from his home and training a telescope on the jail three miles away, he saw the condemned man drop (*LW* 32–3).

Another local execution, but in a distant generation, also took a powerful and permanent hold on Hardy's imagination: that of Mary Channing, who was burned to death at Maumbury Ring in 1705 after being found guilty, like Martha Browne, of murdering her husband. This is briefly referred to in *The Mayor of Casterbridge* (11) and described at fuller length, with a wealth of harrowing detail, in an article Hardy published in *The Times* on 9 October 1908; a version of the story is also the basis of his poem 'The Mock Wife'. A further reference dated 1919 is evidence of Hardy's horrified fascination over a long period with this ghastly episode (see *PN* 38). In the same year he is on record as having insisted on recounting details of the grisly circumstances of the woman's death to guests at a Max Gate tea party, the group including the 15-year-old daughter of Lady Ilchester, and it is not going too far to say that he was obsessed by this appalling example of institutionalized injustice and barbarity.

Throughout his life, it seems, Hardy was fascinated by executions, especially of women, even after they ceased to be held in public. He took a strong interest in the case of Mary Wheeler, executed on 23 December 1890 for the brutal murder of the wife and child of a man with whom she had a relationship that seems to have been comradely rather than sexual. Michael Millgate has suggested (347) that this aspect of the case—the subject of specific comment in a *Times* leader—may have influenced the presentation of Sue Bridehead in *Jude the Obscure*, who desires a similar relationship with the Christminster undergraduate and later with Jude himself.

At the end of *Tess of the d'Urbervilles*—a novel whose composition is close in date to Mary Wheeler's execution—the heroine's hanging takes place inside the jail at 'Wintoncester' (Winchester), and is announced by the hoisting of 'a black flag'. Two stories in *Wessex Tales*, however, refer to a much earlier period. 'The Three Strangers', set in the 1820s when penal savagery could condemn a poor man to death for stealing to feed his starving family, has a hangman (on his way to 'Casterbridge' jail) and his unrecognized victim as two of the principal characters. 'The Withered Arm', set in the same period, offers much circumstantial detail concerning a hanging, also at 'Casterbridge'. The story is set 'in those days, when men were executed for horse-stealing, arson, and burglary'; rural folk will walk up to twenty miles each way 'in one day, solely to witness the spectacle'. The hanging takes place at midday, after the arrival of the mail-coach from London, in case of a last-minute reprieve; after the hanging, the crowd 'still waited to see the body taken down'; and portions of the rope are sold afterwards 'by the inch' as souvenirs. The whole occasion is regarded as a 'hang-fair'. Several details in this story correspond to those given in Hardy's account of the hanging of James Seale (see above): the 'white flat façade' of the gaol, with the gallows erected on the roof, seems to be based on Hardy's memory of 'the white stone façade of the gaol, the gallows upon it' (*LW* 33). In another short story, 'The Melancholy Hussar of the German Legion', set at the beginning of the 19th century, two deserters are executed by firing-squad; the witnessing of this event from a distance by the lover of one of them again recalls Hardy's experience of the hanging of James Seale.

In the preface added to *Wessex Tales* in 1896, Hardy offers (perhaps only half-seriously) an apology for including 'two stories of hangmen', and notes that 'in the neighbourhood of county-towns hanging matters used to form a large proportion of the local tradition'. He adds that as a boy he had had 'the privilege of being on speaking terms with a man who applied for the office, and who sank into an incurable melancholy because he failed to get it', and the grim joke is kept up at considerable length. (For another relevant quotation from the same preface, see 'WITHERED ARM, THE'.)

Hardy's enduring fascination with the subject began even earlier than the youthful instances cited above: at the end of his life, he could still 'recall what his mother had said about the Rush murder when he was about the age of six: "The governess hanged him." He was puzzled, and wondered how a governess could hang a man' (*LW* 475). (He was actually a little older than 6, since James Rush was hanged for a double murder, largely on the evidence of his mistress, in 1849.) This lifelong fascination is evident not only from his autobiography and his fiction but from a number of poems, including the one he thought his most successful, 'A Trampwoman's Tragedy', which is set in the 1820s and describes the hanging of the speaker's lover 'at Ivel-chester jail'. Another poem, 'On the Portrait of a Woman about to be Hanged', is dated 6 January 1923 and was prompted by a widely publicized murder case. Three days after the latter poem was written, Mrs Edith Thompson and her lover were hanged for the murder of her husband. Nearer our own time, Hardy would surely have been gratified by the comment on Mike Newell's film *Dance with a Stranger* (1985), the subject of which is Ruth Ellis, the last woman to be hanged in Britain, that it 'has an unexpected but authentic Hardyesque quality. Ruth is a Tess of the 1950s . . .' (Neil Sinyard, *Filming Literature* (1986), 50).

F

Famous Tragedy of the Queen of Cornwall, The, poetic drama and one of Hardy's last works. It shows him near the end of his long life imaginatively revisiting scenes associated with that life's most important emotional landmark: the meeting with, and subsequent courtship of, Emma Lavinia Gifford in Cornwall. In the summer of 1870, soon after their first meeting, he and Emma had visited Tintagel, with its romantic setting and strong Arthurian associations, and three years later, in the preface to *A Pair of Blue Eyes*, he had described the area as 'the region of dream and mystery'.

But the poetic drama based on the spot and the legends attaching to it, however early meditated, was not to be begun until 1916. In the September of that year he revisited Tintagel, now in the company of his second wife, Florence, and began to plan the work. Soon laid aside, however, it was not to be finished until 1923. The first performance was given by the *Hardy Players in Dorchester on 28 November 1923; the printed version had appeared some two weeks earlier. The full title, as given on the title-page, is *The Famous Tragedy of the Queen of Cornwall at Tintagel in Lyonnesse: A New Version of an Old Story, Arranged as a Play for Mummers in One Act, Requiring no Theatre or Scenery.* The manuscript is in DCM, which also has the originals of the two illustrations drawn by Hardy himself. See also DRAMATIZATIONS. On the opera based on Hardy's play, see BOUGHTON, RUTLAND.

Far from the Madding Crowd. The fourth of Hardy's fourteen published novels.

Composition

Keenly interested in the anonymously published *Under the Greenwood Tree*, Leslie *Stephen, the editor of the *Cornhill Magazine*, took measures to discover its author's identity. He was informed by Hardy's friend Horace *Moule of the authorship, and invited Hardy in November 1872 to provide a serial story for the *Cornhill*. For the relatively unknown writer that Hardy then was, this excellent offer from a leading periodical provided a signally important occasion to advance his career. Still busy writing *A Pair of Blue Eyes*, he could not immediately comply with Stephen's request and instead he sent a brief outline of a pastoral tale in which the chief characters would be a woman-farmer, a shepherd, and a sergeant of cavalry.

Stephen was willing to wait. In March 1873, Hardy finished *A Pair of Blue Eyes*, and in April the editor renewed his enquiry. Hardy submitted some specimen chapters at the end of September, and on the strength of these Stephen accepted the novel for serial publication. Hardy wrote to Stephen of the advantage of being actually among the people described at the time he was depicting them. In September 1873, he walked over to Woodbury Hill Fair, on which his Greenhill Fair (*FFMC* 50) was to be based. In October, at Stephen's request, Hardy agreed to an earlier publication date than had originally been contemplated. He finished the writing, all of which was done at *Higher Bockhampton, in July 1874. Owing to his impending marriage, the last few chapters were done, Hardy confessed, 'at a gallop' (*LW* 103).

The manuscript, which Hardy later thought lost, was discovered in the offices of *Smith, Elder & Co. in 1918, and is now at the Beinecke Manuscript and Rare Book Library, Yale University. Two fragments of the first draft also survive: one (7 leaves) contains material that is in the present Chapter 23; the other (11 leaves), which—judging from references to Troy, who has a fist-fight with Oak—may have been intended for the August instalment (Chapters 34–8), bears little relation to the final version. These leaves, bound together, are housed in DCM.

Serialization

The novel appeared anonymously in the *Cornhill* from January to December 1874, in 12 monthly instalments, as follows: January, Chapters 1–5; February, 6–8; March, 9–14; April, 15–20; May, 21–4; June, 25–9; July, 30–3; August, 34–8; September, 39–42; October, 43–7; November, 48–51; December, 52–7. In America it was serialized in *Every Saturday* from January to October 1874 (when the magazine was absorbed by *Littell's Living Age*); in *Littell's Living Age* from January 1874 to January 1875; in the *Eclectic Magazine* from March 1874 to February 1875; and in the *New York Semi-Weekly Tribune* from June to December 1874.

Chronological and seasonal references in the fictional world of this novel closely correspond to the times at which readers of the serial encountered the relevant portions (though the action covers more than one year). The first instalment deals with occurrences in December; the next one starts with a fire in Bathsheba's farm which takes place in February; the sheep-shearing scene appeared in the May number; a summer storm in the August number; and the last instalment opens on Christmas Eve.

A few passages in the manuscript were not printed: the farm labourers' idle chat at the malthouse in Chapter 15 (about 450 words); the table conversation at the shearing-supper in Chapter 23, which contains Pennyways's suggestion to Bathsheba that Fanny Robin is now a 'ruined' woman (1,100 words); a dialogue between Bathsheba and Liddy in Chapter 43 concerning Fanny and her baby in the coffin (500 words); and Troy's abortive search for his clothes on the shore after he is saved by the boat in Chapter 47 (500 words). Some of these excisions and various other small emendations were caused by Stephen's editorial acumen, from which Hardy profited, and others by Stephen's keen awareness of the prudery of Victorian readers. In addition, five drawings Hardy included in the manuscript of the hoof-marks that Oak and Coggan follow in Chapter 32 were not published. The deleted passages and the drawings are restored in Suzanne B. Falck-Yi's edition in the Oxford World's Classics series (1993). Chapter 16 is not in the manuscript, and appears to have been an afterthought added at the proof stage.

Illustrations

Every instalment in the *Cornhill* was accompanied by a full-page illustration and a vignette initial by Helen *Paterson. There were no illustrations in American serializations.

Volume Publication

The novel was published by Smith, Elder & Co. in two volumes at a price of one guinea (21*s*.), in an edition of 1,000 copies (twice the size of that of any of Hardy's previous novels) on 23 November 1874. The last five chapters of the first American edition, published in the same month by Henry *Holt, differ slightly, because they were set from a handwritten draft of earlier date than the manuscript used for the *Cornhill*.

Over the years Hardy made a number of revisions. (Since he thought the manuscript had been lost, he was not able to use it for this purpose.) There appears to be a general tendency to gentrify Troy and to amplify the description of Boldwood's psychology, but these later alterations do not effect a substantial change in the content. Hardy revised the text most extensively for the first complete collection of his works, the Osgood, McIlvaine Wessex Novels (1895), when he co-ordinated the topographical details of *Wessex—a term first employed by Hardy in the manuscript of Chapter 50 of this novel. (The term, however, did not appear elsewhere in the serial or the first edition, other occurrences being later additions.) He partially reinstated the coffin scene, making a direct reference to Fanny's baby; he spelled out Troy's illegitimate birth; and it is now Bathsheba and Oak, not Bathsheba and Troy, who suspect Boldwood's madness (55). The Preface was also added on this occasion. After the 1901 Sixpenny Edition, Hardy made alterations to show that Bathsheba suspects that Troy is still alive, rather than that she thinks he was drowned.

Rosemarie Morgan's *Cancelled Words: Rediscovering Thomas Hardy* (1992) is a detailed study of Hardy's revision of this novel.

Reception

On 15 January 1875, less than two months after the novel's publication in volume form, George Smith, its publisher, wrote to Hardy that 'nearly the whole' of the first edition had been sold, and that a 'second edition' (actually a second impression) of 500 copies was being prepared (Purdy 18–19). Although nothing remarkable by the standards of Victorian best-sellers, this was a marked improvement as far as Hardy was concerned, and the novel is usually considered his first commercial success. No doubt partly responsible for this was the fact that it was very widely reviewed, drawing more attention than any of Hardy's previous work.

On the whole critics received the novel favourably. That here was a new talent was broadly recognized, and Hardy's vivid depiction of rural surroundings was unanimously praised. The *Guardian*, *The Times*, and the *Saturday Review* seized on the novel's 'idyllic' or 'pastoral' quality with enthusiasm, and, not surprisingly, reviewers often evoked the name of George *Eliot. (Hardy himself was both pleased and irritated by this: he admired Eliot as a thinker, but in his view she was 'not a born story-teller by any means', and she 'had never touched the life of the fields' (*LW* 100).) The *Spectator*, after the appearance of the first instalment, went so far as to suggest that the novel was written by Eliot (they corrected their misattribution in February 1874, and this is where the author's identity was first made public). The *Westminster Review* made the laudatory remark that the novel stood to all contemporary fiction precisely as Eliot's *Adam Bede* (1859) had done to other novels of its period.

Negative opinions, however, were also expressed. The last reviewer, for example, found the novel marred by sensationalism. Similarly, the *Athenaeum* complained that the extravagance of some of the scenes was worthier of Charles Reade than of Eliot. R. H. Hutton, in the *Spectator*, also observed that, unlike Eliot, Hardy confused his own ideas with those of the dramatic figures, and put the author's thoughts and words into the rustics' mouths, thereby rendering these characters unbelievable. Other critics, including Andrew Lang writing for the *Academy*, pointed out this fault.

Of all the reviewers the most critical was the young Henry *James. In the *Nation* (New York), he observed that the novel was diffuse, and severely criticized its inartistic execution. He found Bathsheba 'inconsequential, wilful, mettlesome'. He was not alone in this: the heroine generally provoked hostile reactions (notably from the *Observer*), and was deemed a failure, whilst Troy and Boldwood were considered better drawn. But James went further than most critics in asserting that 'Everything human in the book strikes us as factitious and insubstantial; the only things we believe in are the sheep and the dogs'.

Plot

A chance encounter between Gabriel Oak, a farmer of gentle nature and temperament, and Bathsheba Everdene, a high-spirited, self-assured beauty, leads to his offer of marriage, which she rejects. Bathsheba becomes the mistress of a farm inherited from her uncle. Oak, after accidentally losing the greater part of his flock of sheep, starts working for her as a shepherd. Bathsheba frivolously sends a Valentine card to a prosperous neighbouring farmer, Boldwood. The joke misfires, when the latter falls violently in love with her. He begins to pursue her, and passionately asks her to marry him. Fanny Robin, a servant girl at Bathsheba's farm, is in love with the handsome Sergeant Troy, and their marriage is about to take place, when the ceremony is frustrated by her late arrival at the church, owing to a misunderstanding. Troy is infuriated, and they separate. He then chances upon Bathsheba, overwhelming her with flattery and his dazzling sword-practice. To Boldwood's despair, Bathsheba marries Troy, but Troy soon tires of her. Fanny dies in the Union workhouse, and when her body is brought back to the farm, Bathsheba discovers the corpse of a baby beside her in the coffin and learns that the father is Troy. The sergeant, who brutally declares that Fanny was the only girl he ever loved, disappears after her burial. His clothes are found on a beach, and he has been seen drifting out to sea, so he is presumed drowned. Boldwood again starts to court Bathsheba, and out of remorse she cannot refuse him. Boldwood's fantasy, however, is shattered by the returned Troy, whom he shoots dead in a burst of anger. Bathsheba is finally ready to see the worthiness of Oak, and accepts his hand.

The various cross-references (some anticipatory) to other novels from his own pen suggest that Hardy seems to have imagined the action as taking place in the early 1860s. Keeper Day of *Under the Greenwood Tree* is mentioned in Chapter 8; the Casterbridge lawyer Long, mentioned by Troy, later appears as a member of the Town Council in *The Mayor of Casterbridge* (37); and Everdene and Boldwood are among the creditors of Henchard elsewhere in that novel (33).

Critical Approaches

The title of the novel is taken from Thomas Gray's 'Elegy Written in a Country Churchyard' (1751), where the poet refers to the quiet way of life of the villagers:

> Far from the madding crowd's ignoble strife
> Their sober wishes never learned to stray;
> Along the cool sequestered vale of life
> They kept the noiseless tenor of their way.

Although the 'noiseless tenor' of Gray's poem may hardly seem appropriate to the novel's melodramatic character, it does resonate with the latter's ground note sounded by the rustic chorus, the labourers who gather at Warren's Malthouse. The harmony is disturbed, but is re-established at the end; the novel's world is essentially that of comedy. As in the poem, the contrast between rural (unifying, enduring Nature) and urban (modern, self-centred) values is present, but the latter's destructiveness is by no means as insistent as in the later tragic novels. Hardy's method here is not typical, either; as Roy Morrell points out, he presents his theme through a central character who is successful, rather than through a failed hero.

Indeed, *Far from the Madding Crowd* significantly differs from Hardy's later novels in some respects. The novelist himself was aware of this: more than twenty years after its publication he wrote to Frederic *Harrison that the novel seemed to him like 'the work of a youngish hand, though perhaps there is something in it which I could not have put there if I had been older' (29 July 1901: *L* ii 294). The point is that *Far from the Madding Crowd* brims with the kind of energy and charm not habitually associated with a major Hardy novel. It is unassumingly free from a burden of significance that tends to weigh down the world, great as it is, inhabited by Tess or Jude. This may, on the other hand, be equated with lack of substance. The burgeoning novelist wrote to Leslie Stephen in February 1874 that he was satisfied with being considered 'a good hand at a serial', and showed his willingness to accommodate himself to the demands of serial literature. This does not, however, mean that he wrote against the grain of his imagination. In fact Hardy managed, in this novel, to combine the melodramatic profusion of incidents of *Desperate Remedies* and *A Pair of Blue Eyes* with the closely observed rural realism of *Under the Greenwood Tree.* The result is a marked advance on his previous work.

One of the salient features of this vigorous narrative is that it is punctuated by striking tableaux: Troy's cruel gulling of Boldwood, withholding the fact that Bathsheba is already married to him, or Bathsheba's opening Fanny's coffin to discover the baby. Although some almost seem to be detachable set pieces, the best are not only visually compelling but also thematically highly charged. Virginia Woolf calls them 'moments of vision', taking the phrase from the title of a Hardy poem (or perhaps his 1917 collection), and they are precisely where Hardy's gift as a poet most happily combines with his novelistic talent.

A case in point is the scene where Oak fights the storm (36–7). It is often said that Hardy lifted this from Harrison *Ainsworth's *Rookwood*, a romance recounting the adventures of Dick Turpin, to which he had been attached as a boy. (The inclusion of Troy's performance as the highwayman might be a further indication of this influence.) This may be so, but the sensory details, and the thematic richness packed into this scene, are uniquely Hardy's own: Oak's stepping on a large toad, the hot breeze fanning him, the flash leaping out with the 'shout of a fiend', and the silver-coloured lightning gleaming 'like a mailed army'. Together with all this, there is a sense of cosmological magnitude against futile mortal activities; everything human 'seemed small and trifling in such close juxtaposition with an infuriated universe'. The humans, however, are not entirely helpless. As Morrell suggests, 'Nature is one of Gabriel's resources; but he is never controlled by her, nor, in any Wordsworthian sense, does he ever trust her' (p. 63). The able shepherd studies the workings of Nature, and lives in accordance with them. Oak sees a female form in the flash of the thunder, and realizes that it is Bathsheba. The silhouette, made by the lightning, of the two atop the haystack is visually striking. Emphasizing the virtue of work, this tableau, more than anything else, prepares the reader for the union of the couple at the end.

Another particularly rich 'moment of vision' is the scene where at night Bathsheba meets Troy for the first time, her lantern showing up his brilliant figure: his 'sudden appearance was to darkness what the sound of a trumpet is to silence' (24). Here Troy's spur biting into Bathsheba's skirt is pregnant with sexual implications. (It possibly looks forward to the scene in *The Woodlanders* (47) where Grace's skirt is bitten off by a mantrap.) The sexual violence implied in this meeting comes to the fore in the famous scene of Troy's sword-practice (28); the very landscape, 'the hollow amid the ferns', is strongly suggestive of female genitalia. Indeed, the chief male characters, the three suitors of the heroine, are all equipped with phallic instruments—Troy's sword, Boldwood's gun (with which he kills Troy at the end), and Oak's trocar (surgical instrument). This nocturnal encounter is thus a node of expressive metaphors in the novel.

Far from the Madding Crowd shows, moreover, a distinctive development in characterization. The main characters are more interesting and memorable than those in Hardy's previous work. He achieves this not by delineating psychology as such in any depth, but by externalizing it in significant action.

Boldwood is admittedly a crude creation, but an important one. He is the only character who rises towards anything like tragic stature, and he foreshadows the emotionally disturbed characters that Hardy is increasingly to deal with in his later novels. Hardy's intuitive insights into this character, Rosemary Sumner argues, anticipate Freud's theory of repression. Boldwood's repressed sexual desire is powerfully realized in the scene where he looks at the Valentine which was capriciously sent to him by Bathsheba: his continuous gaze is so intense that the large red seal becomes 'a blot of blood on the retina of his eye'. He is an obsessive dreamer, and his fierceness is also captured later, in the scene where gifts he has bought for her are found in packets labelled 'Bathsheba Boldwood' (55). His clothes fetishism, however, is not the only point here. This is in keeping with a thematically vital thread, the motif of possession, which combines materiality and sexuality: the branding of the flock with Bathsheba's initial (the red seal pressing upon Boldwood's retina is immediately followed by Oak's pressing brands upon the lambs), and Bathsheba's words, '"I *hate* to be thought men's property"' (4).

One remembers Oak as the character who embodies the virtue of work and is distinguished by his skill: he twice saves Bathsheba's farm, from fire and storm, and only he can save the lambs that have eaten poisonous young clover. He is, however, presented somewhat differently in the early chapters. There he is introduced as a man who yawns during the Sunday service (later he becomes a diligent member of the church choir), and he is even careless enough to be almost suffocated in his hut. An important early episode that sets off Oak's moral journey is the one in which his young dog wildly drives all his ewes over the edge of the cliff, thereby crushing his hopes of becoming an independent farmer. (The sheep are not insured—again, possibly, through his carelessness.) This incident has a symbolic significance in that the dog's behaviour might be read as an externalized picture of Oak's aroused sexual desire for Bathsheba. The motif of desire endangering work recurs when Oak injures a sheep with the trocar, when his attention is distracted by Boldwood courting Bathsheba. (Boldwood's neglect of his farm is another variation of this motif.) In the course of the novel Oak learns to discipline his desire.

Troy disturbs not only Bathsheba's fortune, but also that of the whole rural community. The sergeant, committed only to the present, lacks a sense of time, and his readily offering his watch to Bathsheba is a telling gesture. He has no sense of continuity with the past, and when, as Bathsheba's husband, he becomes 'a farmer of a spirited and very modern school', he is placed in marked opposition to the timeless, eternal 'great barn' that is celebrated as the moral centre of the labourers in Chapter 22. Troy is the villain of the piece, but he is not entirely negatively conceived. On the occasion of the sword-practice, he says that it *is* not magic but mere dexterity. But it is magic, for he has the sexual attraction that *is* truly magical. As D. H. Lawrence notes, Troy 'is the only man in the book who knows anything' about Bathsheba, and he can, like Alec d'Urberville, 'reach some of the real sources of the female in a woman, and draw from them'. This power is something absolutely denied to Oak. When the rain spoils all his efforts at Fanny's grave, one feels that Hardy is laughing at Troy with the gargoyle. But given that Hardy takes pains to grant Troy noble blood, and his own fondness for such a lineage, one cannot help suspecting that he secretly admires this charmer.

True to her biblical name, which recalls the story of King David secretly observing the woman bathing, Bathsheba is very much visually conceived. When Oak sees her for the first time, she is looking at a mirror on a waggon. In this doubly visual moment, one of her key features, vanity, is brought forward. Oak also observes her executing a tricky ride on horseback, and is captivated by her, just as de Stancy is by Paula Power when he spies upon her at her gymnastic exercises in *A Laodicean* (2.7). Bathsheba is undeniably the novel's main creative focus, and what is most interesting about her is that, as in the case of Troy, one suspects that Hardy entertains an ambiguous attitude towards her: he is intrigued by, and at the same time somewhat afraid of, this character.

Considering that the novel was being written shortly before Hardy's marriage, it is perhaps curious to find a series of misogynistic remarks made by the narrator: for example, 'The facility with which even the most timid women sometimes acquire a relish for the dreadful when that is amalgamated with a little triumph, is marvellous.' J. I. M. Stewart notes that generalizations of this kind 'all take origin in some specific aspect of Bathsheba's behaviour'. Towards the end of the novel Boldwood asks Oak, '"Does a woman keep her promise, Gabriel?"', and the shepherd answers, '"If it is not inconvenient to her she may."' It is with 'faint bitterness' that he speaks here. Stewart observes: 'We certainly end by feeling that this bitterness haunts Oak's creator too' (p. 90).

Thus, although the novel apparently depicts Bathsheba's growth from a vain, irresponsible girl into a morally mature woman who can understand Oak's true worth, there are critics who see this 'growth' as problematical. While Peter J. Casagrande argues that in view of Hardy's idea of the tragic unalterability of things Bathsheba is not completely curable, feminist critics tend to read the story of her education as a taming process, a gradual breaking of her spirit. Rosemarie Morgan, for example, asserts that Oak encloses her by his male ideology: 'as surely as Bathsheba attempts to maintain her independence and prove her talents, so Oak attempts to subdue and reduce her'. Oak's spying is nothing but his policing activity, and, in her view, the novel expresses this 'more insidious form of subjugation' (p. 44), with the author in sympathy with his heroine. Linda M. Shires is perhaps more subtle. According to her, the novel certainly destabilizes the conventional view of masculinity and femininity, but in 'allowing Oak the positions of both phallic male and castrated male while awarding Bathsheba the contradictory position of powerful and dependent female, Hardy is not denying power and sexuality to either sex'. The redefinitions proposed in this novel serve no agenda in particular, 'except growing uncertainty at the end of the nineteenth century about: what is woman?' (p. 64).

On Hardy's collaborative adaptation of this novel for the stage, see DRAMATIZATIONS.

TS

Peter J. Casagrande, 'A New View of Bathsheba Everdene', in Dale Kramer (ed.), *Critical Approaches to the Fiction of Thomas Hardy* (1979).

D. H. Lawrence, 'A Study of Thomas Hardy', *Phoenix* (1936).

Rosemarie Morgan, *Women and Sexuality in the Novels of Thomas Hardy* (1988).

Roy Morrell, *Thomas Hardy: The Will and the Way* (1965).

Linda M. Shires, 'Narrative, Gender, and Power in *Far from the Madding Crowd*', in Margaret R. Higonnet (ed.), *The Sense of Sex: Feminist Perspectives on Hardy* (1993).

J. I. M. Stewart, *Thomas Hardy: A Critical Biography* (1971).

Rosemary Sumner, *Thomas Hardy: Psychological Novelist* (1981).

Virginia Woolf, 'Thomas Hardy's Novels' (1928), in *The Essays of Virginia Woolf*, ed. Andrew McNeillie, Vol. 4 (1994).

fate. Hardy, like those other great 19th-century artists Beethoven and Brahms, was deeply aware of the power of fate in human lives, and, like them, made the operation of fate a central element in his work. At the same time, Hardy was appalled by the misery and agony he observed everywhere about him. This perception was the most powerful in his life, and the attempt to understand it and come to terms with it drove through the sequence of his novels. He accepted that a part of human suffering was self-inflicted, and showed how damaging such failures in self-preservation could be; but, like very many before him, he grew steadily more oppressed by the question, why are we made to experience so much pain? (not 'why *do* we?').

In his youth Hardy accepted the Christian explanation—or explanations—but through his twenties he gradually lost the faith that could sustain them, as many others did in the 1860s. By the time he came to write *The Return of the Native* in 1878 he could offer a disengaged criticism of the position generally accepted in his culture. He describes and analyses the thoughts of Clym Yeobright, whose wife, mother, and brother-in-law have all unnecessarily died:

> He did sometimes think he had been ill-used by fortune so far as to say that to be born is a palpable dilemma, and that instead of men aiming to advance in life with glory they should calculate how to retreat out of it without shame. But that he and his had been sarcastically and pitilessly handled in having such irons thrust into their souls he did not maintain long. It is usually so, except with the sternest of men. Human beings, in their generous endeavour to construct a hypothesis that shall not degrade a first cause, have always hesitated to conceive a dominant power of lower moral quality than their own; and, even while they sit down and weep by the waters of Babylon, invent excuses for the oppression which prompts their tears. (6.1)

However, Hardy never lost belief in an agency of causation in the world, and in his later novels we are accustomed to read, in the narrative voice, of this agency as fate, or destiny, or chance, or circumstance, or fortune, or providence (though not, on the whole, Providence, which, as an abbreviation and personification of divine providence, belongs to Christianity and to some of the characters in the novels)—an impersonal random force for good or evil as occasion and human action allows, the force that allows one crucial letter to arrive just too late to prevent a death (*The Return of the Native*), another to be read at the precise moment when it can do most psychological damage to the reader (*The Mayor of Casterbridge*), and yet another, pushed under a door, to slip under the carpet rather than on top of it, so that it is never read (*Tess of the d'Urbervilles*). It is Hardy's hypersensitivity to the pain in the world that dictates that most of the random actions of fate cause sorrow or disaster.

At the same time, in Hardy's work as elsewhere, fate and destiny and fortune are also used to refer to what happens to an individual, as in this exchange from *Desperate Remedies*:

> 'I used to think 'twas your wife's fate not to have a liven husband when I sid 'em die off so,' said Gad.
>
> 'Fate? Bless thy simplicity, so 'twas her fate; but she struggled to have one, and would, and did. Fate's nothen beside a woman's schemen!'
>
> 'I suppose, then, that Fate is a He, like us, and the Lord, and the rest o' em up above there,' said Gad, lifting his eyes to the sky... (8)

This fragment also introduces in a lighthearted way a further aspect of Hardy's understanding of our relationship with fate-as-cosmic-force: the idea that how we deal with it is of intense significance in our lives.

Though Hardy quite often appears to use fate or destiny with the implication that the pattern of the lives of his characters, and by extension of his readers, is already laid out ahead of them, that they have no control over their future, that implication is more apparent than real. In this respect the central text is *The Mayor of Casterbridge*, in which Hardy quotes Novalis's precept that 'character is fate', that what sort of person we are influences to a very great degree what will happen to us. That is not to say that Michael Henchard's character is not tested by the actions of fate; wherever possible the timing of events in the novel is designed by the novelist to give him the most pain, to such an extent that a reader might be inclined to exclaim that it is more appropriate to see the novelist as fate. Hardy would not have been perturbed by such a response; the novel is a crucible for testing the man; if cosmic fate is perpetually harsh to Henchard, the more vividly his essential nature will be revealed through his responses. And the idea that 'character is fate' is not thereby rendered valueless—indeed it becomes of the greater significance. How we respond to these senseless acts of cruelty is the ultimate measure of the quality of our humanity.

In this respect *The Return of the Native* also offers instruction: the reactions of Clym

Yeobright and his wife Eustacia are fundamentally opposed. Clym adapts himself to disastrous fate to live a low-key version of his idealistic ambitions; Eustacia fights disastrous fate with her whole nature, and cannot survive. Most readers have felt that hers is the greater or nobler character, but that perhaps is because we have been weaned on Aeschylus and Shakespeare. Hardy, if we return at the end of the novel to reread its first chapter, is not so sure; Clym's maimed resilience is the modern virtue embodied by Egdon Heath. He finds a purpose in endurance which Michael Henchard cannot. Though neither, it has to be said, can Tess Durbeyfield or Jude Fawley. All three embrace death willingly, two because the love which, by the end, alone gave purpose to their lives has been withdrawn from them, the other because, though that love is now at its height, she knows it will later be withdrawn.

All three have been harried by that desire of the novelist to show the reading world how powerful adverse circumstance can be; but if they are in part victims of fate, they are also victims of society, victims of the self-gratifying urges of other humans, and victims of their own natures. It is in *Jude the Obscure*, Hardy's last novel, that this nexus of forces operating on individual destiny, thickening as Hardy grew more experienced as a man and a writer, becomes most dense—to the degree that the multiplicity of agency becomes too complex and sometimes too contradictory for readers to accept with any gratitude, and we long for the relative simplicities of *The Return of the Native.* At the same time the pain experienced has become more vivid and more intense, the need for an explanation more urgent. After Tess Durbeyfield's fate had been violently altered by Alec d'Urberville under the trees in the Chase, the narrator comments with anguished bitterness:

> Why it was that upon this beautiful feminine tissue, sensitive as gossamer, and practically blank as snow as yet, there should have been traced such a coarse pattern as it was doomed to receive; why so often the coarse appropriates the finer thus, the wrong man the woman, the wrong woman the man, many thousand years of analytical philosophy have failed to explain to our sense of order. One may, indeed, admit the possibility of a retribution lurking in the present catastrophe. Doubtless some of Tess d'Urberville's mailed ancestors rollicking home from a fray had dealt the same measure even more ruthlessly towards peasant girls of their time. But though to visit the sins of the fathers upon the children may be a morality good enough for divinities, it is scorned by average human nature; and it therefore does not mend the matter. (11)

By the time of *Jude the Obscure* the fate in Jude's consciousness has become more a recognition of the fact that some desired future has been rendered impossible by a complex of causes—personal, social, circumstantial—which might be thought of collectively as constituting the driving force behind one's personal fate. In a moment of insight, Jude gazes over the Christminster colleges:

> He saw that his destiny lay not with these, but among the manual toilers in the shabby purlieu which he himself occupied, unrecognized as part of the city at all by its visitors and panegyrists; yet without whose denizens the hard readers could not read, nor the high thinkers live. (2.3)

He was unable to sustain this insight, or to find it sustaining, because of aspects of his nature, because of his upbringing, because of his marriage, because of Victorian social and cultural attitudes, as well as because certain incidents in his life occurred when they did, where they did. This complexity driving life had always existed, but Hardy only understood it fully as he matured. Later, when Sue Bridehead is about to be married to Phillotson, and has asked Jude to give her away, they are walking in Melchester:

> By the irony of fate, and the curious trick in Sue's nature of tempting Providence at critical times, she took his arm as they walked through the muddy street—a thing she had never done before in her life—and on turning the corner they found themselves close to a grey Perpendicular church with a low-pitched roof—the church of St Thomas.
>
> 'That's the church,' said Jude.
>
> 'Where I am going to be married?'
>
> 'Yes.'

It is the combination here of 'the irony of fate' and 'the curious trick in Sue's nature of tempting Providence at critical times' that marks the dominant note of this novel in this respect, the sense that though fate is almost always only noticed by humans when it seems 'ironic' or even malicious, there is most often an accompanying human trait or characteristic or failing that permits fate to have an effect, or a more powerful effect, upon the lives of those affected.

Indeed, by the end of the novel this becomes one of the central ideas. Sue and Jude's children have been murdered by Jude and Arabella's child. The shock turns Sue's mind inside-out; at first she sees the deaths as an act of revenge by fate for the natural joy she and Jude had taken in their (sexual, socially unsanctioned) life together: '"now Fate has given us this stab in the back for being such fools as to take Nature at her word!"' (6.2). A little later the idea of vengeance has worked further in her mind, and fate becomes socially sanctioned Jehovah: '"All the ancient wrath of the Power above us has been vented upon us, His poor creatures, and we must submit.... It is no use fighting against God!"' But Jude remains clearer-eyed: '"It is only against man and senseless circumstances"'—that is, against society and random, neutral fate. He does not add, 'and against our own errors', for that would not have helped his immediate case, but he is well enough aware that this is the triad his life has been spent struggling with—not fate alone.

It is a measure of the deepening dissatisfaction that Hardy felt with the world—society, culture, individual human development— that the character in *Jude the Obscure* who shows, through adaptation to the actions of men and senseless circumstance, that she is fittest to survive is Arabella Donn. When she finds the marriage she has contracted is not doing what she hoped it would for her, she goes to Australia, where she marries someone else. When having her son with her is inconvenient she abandons him; when conformity to social convention is profitable she conforms. She acts as fate to Jude, from the moment she flings the pig's pizzle at him to the moment she abandons him to his death in order to find another slender staff to bend to her will for a while. She treats social conventions as it suits her, ostentatiously conforming when it is advantageous to do so, setting them aside when her interest demands. To reflect upon the progression of those who survive the operation of fate, from Gabriel Oak, through Clym Yeobright, to Arabella Donn, is to understand much about Hardy's changing view of humanity and of agency in the world.

To turn to Hardy's poetry is at once, in this context as in so many others, to return to simplicity. The whole question of fate is at the heart of *The Dynasts*, refined and codified in the concept of the Immanent Will, an unconscious first cause working 'Eternal artistries in Circumstance' (*D* 1.1.1). By the end of the drama, Napoleon confesses to himself, 'I have ever known I That such a Will I passively obeyed!' In the final scene the Spirit of the Years outlines the universal scope of the Immanent Will, and summarizes it as a 'vast and singular confection' with no apparent meaning, while the Spirit of the Pities speculates that since man evolved 'cognition with the flux of time' why should not 'the Force informing them'. Hardy told a correspondent that though his view that the first cause is unconscious was not new, he believed his idea that 'consciousness is creeping back towards the origin of force' was original (*L* v 70).

These notions underlie much of his poetry, but amongst those that explicitly confront them might be mentioned 'Doom and She' from *Poems of the Past and the Present*; the brief sequence in *Time's Laughingstocks*, 'Before Life and After', 'New Year's Eve', and 'God's Education'; while in *Moments of Vision* there are 'The Blow' and 'Fragment', both of which anticipate the 'Immanent Doer' awakening to consciousness and regretting what it has caused. But perhaps the most celebrated poem detailing acts of the Immanent Will is 'The Convergence of the Twain', Hardy's contribution to the continuing fascination with the **Titanic* disaster.

SJG

Faulkner, William (1897–1962), American novelist, author of *The Sound and the Fury*, *Absalom, Absalom!*, and many other novels and short stories. Although he never acknowledged any indebtedness to Hardy, Faulkner owned the 1917 Modern Library edition of *The Mayor of Casterbridge* and was certainly aware of Hardy's example as a regionalist and creator of a fictional world. A distinctively Southern writer, he set most of his works in the 'little postage stamp of native soil' he called Yoknapatawpha County, conceived and created as a predominantly rural area closely corresponding in outline and topography to the actual Lafayette County, Mississippi. Jefferson, the imaginary county's administrative centre, was based mainly on the university town of Oxford, Mississippi, where Faulkner lived for most of his life, but partly on Ripley, Mississippi, where he spent much of his childhood.

The structural similarities between Yoknapatawpha and Wessex coexist with significant functional differences. The recurrence of characters (e.g. Quentin Compson, Gavin Stevens) and settings (e.g. the Old Frenchman place, the Jefferson courthouse) is much more intensive and substantial in Faulkner's fiction than in Hardy's, and Faulkner's emphasis, unlike Hardy's, is always on the interplay—what he often called 'counterpoint'—within and between texts and on the overall integration of his fictional world, ideally conceptualized as 'one compact thing which could be picked up and held in the hands at one time'. Both writers, however, identified themselves closely with the areas in which they were born and continued, for the most part, to live; both drew and published maps of their imaginary territories as part of the process of claiming 'authority' over them; and both were, implicitly, pastoralists, requiring their mainly urban readers to measure their own sophisticated assumptions against the customs and values of simpler places and times. MM

Michael Millgate, 'Unreal Estate: Reflections on Wessex and Yoknapatawpha', in *Faulkner's Place* (1997).

J. R. Rabbetts, *From Hardy to Faulkner: Wessex to Yoknapatawpha* (1989).

'Fellow-Townsmen', short story. Presumably written at Upper Tooting, it was published in the *New Quarterly Magazine* (April 1880) and the American *Harper's Weekly* (five instalments, April–May 1880), and later collected, in an extensively revised version, in *Wessex Tales*. Set in and near 'Port-Bredy' (Bridport), it is a bleak narrative of marital discord and successive failures in the attempt to redeem a past error—a favourite Hardyan theme that he returned to in the later story 'For Conscience' Sake'.

George Barnet has inherited wealth and makes a disastrous marriage to a woman who is his social superior: a relationship that contrasts painfully with the happy union of his friend Downe, a much less prosperous solicitor from the same town. Both women are involved in a boating accident: Downe's wife dies, but Barnet's, thanks to his own efforts after a struggle of conscience, survives. Lucy, a woman he has loved and forsaken before his marriage, reappears in his life but refuses to renew her association with him, even after his wife has first abandoned him and then died. Instead she marries Downe, but even after the latter's death many years later she persists in rejecting Barnet. In a final ironic turn of events, she changes her mind, only to discover that he has left the town, and she is unable to trace him.

Somewhat overweighted with a plot that is at times clumsily contrived, and almost unrelievedly gloomy in tone, the story opens 'five-and-thirty years ago', but 21 years pass after Lucy's marriage to Downe and Barnet's disappearance from the town to wander the globe; it is, therefore, a story of the 1840s and the 1860s. In this respect it differs from most of its companions in *Wessex Tales*, which are set in earlier periods, and in its treatment of domestic life, marital disharmony, and failed aspirations it looks forward to such stories of the 1890s as 'An Imaginative Woman' and 'On the Western Circuit'.

'Few Crusted Characters, A', the second linked short-story sequence that Hardy wrote in the early 1890s. When it was published as a serial in *Harper's New Monthly Magazine* (March–June 1891), it was entitled *Wessex Folk* (thus a second deliberate piece of assertion, after *Wessex Tales* of 1888, of his interest as author in the regional name). Instead of giving the sequence a separate volume publication, he included it (with the changed title) as the last element in the collection *Life's Little Ironies* in 1894.

The surviving manuscript of *Wessex Folk* (Berg Collection, New York Public Library) is of the greatest interest, for parts of it are the only substantial pieces of first draft we have, giving the student of Hardy's creative process most valuable information. There are lists of trial character- and place-names, and notes from Hardy to himself proposing different plot-lines; some of the material is in the barest note form with many alternative ideas, other parts consist of the simplest narrative, while 'Old Andrey's Experience as a Musician' is missing altogether. One leaf of a subsequent fair-copy manuscript, presumably the one used by the serial's printers, was reproduced in a magazine in the 1920s, but its present whereabouts are not known.

There is in the sequence an evident contrast with its predecessor, *A Group of Noble Dames*: having presented a mostly middle-class group indulging in mildly scandalous gossip about the dead gentry of Wessex, Hardy decided to turn to a collection of villagers retelling tales about (mostly) dead inhabitants of their village. His storytellers are folk from Longpuddle, returning thence from Casterbridge by carrier's waggon; they all belong to the class of Hardy's own family, the people who provided the village with essential services—the postmistress, the groceress, the schoolmaster, the master-thatcher, and the like. This was the class that for Hardy provided village life with its continuity and essential character, but which was being, as he wrote in 'The Dorsetshire Labourer', driven away by changes in the economics of farming. They are joined in their journey by John Lackland, a child when his family emigrated 35 years ago, who has now returned with the idea of settling in the village he had left as an 11-year-old. Lackland asks for information about people he had once known, and his fellow-travellers oblige, though not really to his satisfaction. Each of their narratives has something remarkable about it, something that in conventional terms justifies the telling, something that makes for 'a good story'; but they disappoint Lackland, who is 'less interested in the questionable characters of Longpuddle and their strange adventures than in the ordinary inhabitants and ordinary events'. Lackland is in the end a sad figure. He does not return with his fortune made: 'even in the new countries, you know, there are failures,' he says, and once he reaches Longpuddle he wanders ghostlike about the village for a few days, finds he has no connection with the place anymore, and disappears. The melancholy tone he supplies to the frame-narrative contrasts vividly with the vitality of the stories he hears.

The nine tales and anecdotes that he is told are less closely linked in theme than those of *A Group of Noble Dames*, but Hardy works hard to contrive that the close of one shall suggest the next. For instance, it is at the wedding-party of 'Tony Kytes, the Arch-Deceiver' (the account of a young man who manages to propose to three girls in an afternoon, and does marry one of them), that 'The History of the Hardcomes' begins to unfold its ironies, while a little later there are three wryly amusing stories—'Andrey Satchel and the Parson and the Clerk', 'Old Andrey's Experience as a Musician', and 'Absent-Mindedness in a Parish Choir'—that follow naturally one from the other, the last two being incidents that have a harmony with *Under the Greenwood Tree* and the poems Hardy wrote about the band of Mellstock singers and players.

The best of the stories, though very different from each other in tone, are 'The History of the Hardcomes' and 'Absent-Mindedness in a Parish Choir'. The first tells how the cousins Steve and James Hardcome, both engaged to thoroughly compatible young women, were seduced by the intoxicating sensuousness of rhythm and proximity, as each danced with the other's fiancée, into agreeing to exchange brides. This powerful effect of music and dance as a sexual stimulation suppressing all reason is experienced by many other of Hardy's characters. After a few years, all four regretted their decision, and the climax comes when Steve and James's wife are drowned while rowing on Weymouth Bay. Their bodies are found in a loving embrace. James then marries Steve's widow as originally intended. The strength of the slight story is in the calm acceptance of the rightness of the love-death of one couple, and the certainty of the narrator that the other two by marrying fulfilled 'their destiny according to Nature's plan'. 'Absent-Mindedness in a Parish Choir' parallels in brief *Under the Greenwood Tree*, in that it accounts for the ejection of another band of church musicians from its west gallery: weary and primed with hot brandy and beer on the Sunday after Christmas, they accidentally play the dance-tune 'The Devil Among the Tailors' in the middle of the service. The squire has them replaced by a barrel-organ, with 'a really respectable man to turn the winch'. See also MANUSCRIPTS.

SJG

Simon Gatrell, *Hardy the Creator: A Textual Biography* (1988).
Martin Ray, *Thomas Hardy: A Textual Study of the Short Stories* (1997).

'Fiddler of the Reels, The', short story. It was published in *Scribner's Magazine* (New York) in May 1893, and collected in *Life's Little Ironies.* Hardy had completed it towards the end of 1892, and had sent it to Scribner's on 12 January 1893. One of Hardy's most powerful short stories, it draws on his early passion for music and dancing (see MUSIC). Its opening reference to 'Exhibitions, World's Fairs, and what not' alludes to its original appearance in a special 'Exhibition Number' of *Scribner's* intended to commemorate the Chicago World Fair, and its subsequent references to the Great Exhibition of 1851 locate it in the period of Hardy's childhood.

It is, however, a story with supernatural or paranormal as well as realistic aspects: the erotic effects of Mop Ollamoor's fiddle-playing may, in combination with his magnetic personality, constitute a form of musical hypnotism but seem to go beyond rational causes. There are implications of black magic and diabolism: he is described as 'weird and wizardly', 'impish' and 'elfin', has never entered a church, and plays only 'the devil's tunes' (that is, secular rather than sacred music). His ostensible trade as horse-doctor allies him to a traditional rural world, whereas his rival Ned moves to London and becomes a mechanic, thus placing in antithesis the world of ancient lore and superstition and that of modern science and rationalism. Mop's uncanny appearance at the Great Exhibition in Hyde Park— itself a celebration of Britain's technological pre-eminence in the modern world—sets these two worlds in dramatic conflict. At the same time, for all the precision of its early-Victorian chronology, the story has overtones of the ballad or folk-tale, and the grotesque and unearthly elements in the character of Mop enable Hardy to present his irresistible sexuality with greater frankness, and less risk, than would be possible in a wholly realistic tale.

First World War. Hardy's feelings concerning war, nationalism, and patriotism had been exercised and articulated by the *Boer War, and the outbreak of the Great War a dozen years later confirmed his deep antipathy to war and his distrust of patriotism as commonly conceived. A summarizing comment in the *Life* declares that 'so mad and brutal a war destroyed all Hardy's belief in the gradual ennoblement of man, a belief he had held for many years'. The further comment that 'he would probably not have ended *The Dynasts* as he did end it if he could have foreseen what was going to happen within a few years' (*LW* 398) reinforces the sense that the events of 1914–18 effected a radical change in his philosophical outlook, and rendered meliorism no longer a tenable position.

His diary for 4 August 1914 recorded the outbreak of war at 11 p.m., and another entry a few days later refers to 'War excitement' (*LW* 394), a popular sentiment from which he seems to have been exempt. Within less than a month, though, he was making a contribution to the war effort appropriate to an elderly author: on 2 September he travelled to London to co-operate with other 'well-known men of letters', including his friends and acquaintances Sir James *Barrie, Arthur *Benson, John *Galsworthy, Sir Henry *Newbolt, and others, in producing 'public statements on the strength of the British case and principles in the war' (*LW* 395). His private and poetic statements were, however, to prove less wholeheartedly morale-boosting. The relevant poems were to be collected in a section titled 'Poems of War and Patriotism' in *Moments of Vision* (1917), but many of them had been previously published much closer to the date of composition.

It is true that the *alla marcia* rhythms of 'Men Who March Away', apparently composed on 5 September 1914 (presumably in the afterglow of enthusiasm generated by the London meeting), appear to celebrate and endorse the 'faith and fire' of the departing soldiery; but even there a significant note of questioning ('Is it a purblind prank, O think you...?') is expressed by a 'Friend with a musing eye' who has at least something in common with Hardy himself. This poem had appeared in *The Times* on 9 September, with a note indicating that copyright was not reserved: in other words Hardy (and *The Times*) made a present of it to anyone who wished to use it for patriotic purposes.

Subsequent poems, however, express deeper doubts—indeed, a sense of tragic waste and futility that is sometimes not far from that expressed by a combatant-poet such as Wilfred Owen. The very title of 'The Pity of It', dated April 1915 but actually written in February and published in the *Fortnightly Review* in April, anticipates Owen's emphasis (in the posthumously published preface to his poems) on 'the pity of War'. Apparently prompted by reading an article on eugenics, Hardy's sonnet opens reflectively, but quickly moves into a mood of anger and fulmination. Strolling 'in loamy Wessex', he observes the similarity between the local dialect and the German language, comments that English and Germans are after all 'kin folk kin tongued', and expresses outrage at the wickedness of those whose leadership has set two such closely related peoples in conflict.

On the day before the outbreak of hostilities between Britain and Germany, the latter had invaded Belgium, and the ensuing flood of refugees to Britain prompted three poems. The sonnet 'On the Belgian Expatriation' was written on 18 October and published in a volume intended to aid a fund for the refugees; 'An Appeal to America on behalf of the Belgian Destitute' was written in December and published soon afterwards in various American newspapers; and 'Cry of the Homeless' was written in August 1915 at the instigation of Henry *James and Edith Wharton, and appeared in another fund-raising volume. Poetry-to-order was not Hardy's forte, and the literary quality of these productions is slight. They do, however, indicate his wish to do what he could for the sufferings of the innocent victims of war, and in the second of the three there is an appeal to the 'lovingkindness'—that quintessentially Hardyan concept—of the American people.

In an entirely different class, and universal rather than 'occasional', is the best-known of these poems, 'In Time of "The Breaking of Nations"'. Its twelve short lines present three separate but intimately related (and significantly ordered) vignettes of timeless rural existence, symbols of continuity that have no place in 'history' as conventionally conceived, but that will outlive 'War's annals'. The implicit contrast between officially sanctioned 'history' and the unwritten but valid histories of the obscure links the poem with the Wessex novels, whose narrator or 'chronicler' is often presented in the role of a historian of the 'unhistoric'.

The note of affirmation in this poem is all the more striking when one remembers that the date is 1915, when the slaughter on the Western Front was at its height. Of the vast number who died on active service during that year, one was very close to Hardy. Frank George, killed, aged 35, in the Gallipoli campaign in August, was a distant relative (the son of a second cousin) of whom Hardy had become very fond and whom he even regarded as a potential heir. In April 1915 Frank had paid a last visit to Max Gate, an occasion recalled in the poem 'Before Marching and After', which Hardy cared enough for to include in his *Selected Poems*. Another poem of 1915, 'Then and Now', contrasts the time 'When battles were fought | With a chivalrous sense of Should and Ought...' with the callous mass-destruction of modern warfare, and strikingly embodies the ambivalence that often lies just beneath Hardy's musings on war. It might be objected that his notions of 'knighthood', with its 'honourable rules' and 'heroic schools', represent no more than an idealized, even childish fantasy, and that war, at least in the ranks, was never very different in kind, though it may have been different in scale. But as *The Trumpet-Major* as well as some of the Boer War poems remind us, Hardy (like A. E. *Housman) was fascinated by the glamour of redcoats and cavalry, military campaigns and drum-and-trumpet glory: even as a child, physically weak and under-developed, he had found the life of action, seen from a convenient distance, irresistible. At the same time, emotionally, morally, and philosophically, he was repelled by the idea of men seeing it as their 'duty' to kill perfect strangers, and the horrors of 20th-century warfare confirmed and authenticated these convictions.

folklore. The omnipresence in Hardy's fiction and poetry, from the early novels through to *Winter Words*, of references to popular folk customs, beliefs, and traditions is a direct reflection of his deep interest in and intimate knowledge of the folklore of the South-West of England. Presented with a consistently meticulous attention to the accuracy of ethnographical detail, descriptions of the traditional mores of the people of

Wessex combine to produce a realistic image of the disappearing world of rural England—'a fairly true record of a vanishing life' ('General Preface' to the Wessex Edition).

Hardy's fascination with Wessex folklore stemmed from the experience of being brought up in the rural environment of mid-19th-century Dorset. Both the Hardy household and the broader communities *Higher Bockhampton, *Stinsford, and *Dorchester were still, in the 1840s and 1850s, in many ways immersed in traditional ways of life, vividly remembered if not always actively practised. Many of the traditional stories, beliefs, and customs Hardy knew and used in his works came to him through his grandmother, Mary Hardy (see RELATIVES OF THOMAS HARDY), while his father (ibid.) introduced him to the heritage of traditional Dorset *music, both religious and secular. In course of time, with the gradual erosion of the role of ancient customs and beliefs in the community at large on the one hand, and with Hardy's own adoption of a middle-class lifestyle on the other, his experience of Dorset folklore became less direct; however, although he may never have 'studied it systematically' (*L* v 111), his autobiography, notebooks, and correspondence offer ample evidence of a continued interest in matters as diverse as local family legends, the subtleties of the Dorset dialect, and the details of the construction and operation of traditional agricultural tools. All these memories Hardy preserved with the zeal of a committed antiquarian, stressing that 'every superstition, custom, etc., described in [his] novels may be depended on as true records of the same (whatever merit in folklorists' eyes they may have as such)—and not inventions of [his own]' (*L* ii 54).

These records of folklore constituted for him not only documentary evidence of local social and economic history, but also a tangible link with the communal past, rapidly disintegrating as a result of the processes of modernization and industrialization that, in the course of Hardy's lifetime, utterly transformed the character of the English countryside. It is perhaps an appropriate testimony to the consistency and intensity of Hardy's interest in folklore that one of the last semi-public controversies in which he engaged should have concerned the origins and development of popular and folk dances in 19th-century England.

The range of Hardy's references to folklore is extremely broad: he mentions local beliefs and superstitions as well as details of agricultural technology, and he describes ancient rural festivals and celebrations (see CALENDAR) as well as traditional patterns of the socio-economic life of the rural community of Dorset. This diversity of motifs and images derived from folklore contributes, particularly in the 'Novels of Character and Environment' and in some of the poems, to the sense of organic unity that characterizes Hardy's Wessex: Gabriel Oak's ability to understand and interpret natural phenomena, and Giles Winterborne's skills in cider-making, are as much part of the cultural heritage of Wessex folklore as they are distinctive features defining the two characters as individuals.

In much the same way, folklore-related motifs often play an integral role in the development of Hardy's plots: the action of *The Mayor of Casterbridge* grows from an incident of wife-selling, a traditional folk form of divorce; the dénouement of 'The Withered Arm' (*WT*) is triggered by the characters' belief in the curative powers of touching the neck of a man who has just been hanged; and the Durnover church bells are unexpectedly silenced on New Year's Day after the singers have sacrilegiously 'swilled the Sacrament-wine' ('No Bell-Ringing', *WW*). On the contrary, when, as in *Jude the Obscure*, Hardy's characters move from country to town, their sense of uprootedness and of social and cultural isolation is underlined by the relative sparseness of references to the traditional lore of the rural communities in which they grew up.

Perhaps the most immediately prominent aspect of Hardy's presentation of folklore is his use of popular beliefs in a variety of forms of the supernatural—*ghosts, witches, spells, omens, premonitions, and so on. Hardy's characters believe in ghosts appearing in old houses (*TDU* 34), on moors (*RN* 1.3), on the sites of crimes ('What the Shepherd Saw', *CM*), at crossroads ('Where Three Roads Joined', *LLE*), in graveyards ('Friends Beyond', *WP*), in their old homes ('To Please His Wife', *LLI*), and in places they knew in life ('The Superstitious Man's Story' in 'A Few Crusted Characters', *LLI*). Ghosts can be seen and/or heard at Christmas ('The Dead Quire', *TL*), on Midsummer Eve (*JO* 3.8), and on All Souls' Eve ('I Rose Up as My Custom Is', *SC*). Eustacia Vye is widely believed to be a witch, and indeed encourages such notions: she compares herself to the biblical Witch of Endor (*RN* 1.6), and she offers Johnny Nunsuch a crooked sixpence, believed to be a charm against witchcraft (1.7). As a result, she is thought capable of casting spells (2.8), the effects of which Johnny's mother Susan tries in turn to prevent by magic of her own. This consists first in pricking Eustacia with a stocking-needle (3.2), and then in making a wax figure of her, inserting in it numerous pins, and melting it over the fire while reciting the Lord's Prayer backwards (5.7). Also suspected of witchcraft are Elizabeth Endorfield (*UGT* 4.3)—whose surname seems indeed to confirm the superstition—and Rhoda Brook ('The Withered Arm'), and the common explanation of why horses are sometimes found sweating in the morning is that they have been, literally, hag-ridden (*W* 28).

In moments of crisis, Hardy's characters sometimes resort to consulting 'conjurors', local people believed to have the power to mediate between supernatural powers and ordinary mortals. Michael Henchard sees Conjuror Fall about the weather at the time of the forthcoming harvest (*MC* 26); Gertrude Lodge seeks advice from Conjuror Trendle in an attempt to find a cure for her arm ('The Withered Arm'); and Dairyman Crick expects to have to ask Trendle's son for help when the milk in his churn will not produce butter—even though the son may not prove as reliable as his father or as other conjurors of olden days, such as Conjurer Mynterne (*TDU* 21).

Widely held in Hardy's Wessex are beliefs in omens and premonitions, of both good and bad luck. The swarming of the bees on the day of their wedding is a good sign for the future happiness of Dick Dewy and Fancy Day (*UGT* 5.1); being born with a caul (as Dickens's David Copperfield also was) is supposed to bring good luck to Christian Cantle (*RN* 3.7); and Miller Loveday believes the arrival of a letter from his son Robert has been foreshadowed by the appearance of a letter in the flame of a candle (*TM* 12). Even more numerous are bad omens: bad weather on the wedding-day spells trouble for the couple (*DR* 13.1; 'The Country Wedding', *LLE*); Elfride Swancourt believes that a gift of hair brings bad luck to lovers (*PBE* 30); the breaking of a key portends misfortune for Bathsheba Everdene (*FFMC* 33); and being born at a time when there is no moon bodes ill for the child (*RN* 1.3). Omens of sickness and/or death are legion: a cock's crowing in the afternoon (*TDU* 33), an owl screeching ('Premonitions', *HS*), the sighting of a raven (also in 'Premonitions') or of a single magpie (*FFMC* 8), an old clock striking unexpectedly ('Premonitions' yet again) or falling ('The Waiting Supper', *CM*), a corpse with its eyes open (*MC* 18) or still limp when put into the coffin ('Signs and Tokens', *MV*), the shadow of a sundial pointing at people ('In the Garden', *MV*), the dull sound of a church bell ('The Superstitious Man's Story', 'Premonitions'), and many others.

Some of Hardy's characters demonstrate powers of premonition, often associated with dreams: on the night after her brief encounter with Clym Yeobright, Eustacia sees herself dancing with a knight in shining armour (*RN* 2.3); in the same novel, Christian Cantle's dream foreshadows Mrs Yeobright's important conversation with Diggory Venn (5.2); Grace Melbury experiences feelings of anxiety before her planned wedding to Edred Fitzpiers (*W* 24); and Tess Durbeyfield has a vague sense of uncertainty about the prospect of working at The Slopes (*TDU* 6). Linked to the belief in premonitions are attempts at divination, most frequently in relation to one's marriage prospects: Mrs Penny remembers waiting for her future husband on a Midsummer Eve at a table laid out with bread, cheese, and beer (*UGT* 1.8); Bathsheba uses the method of the Bible and key (*FFMC* 13); and the young women of Little Hintock try sowing hempseed (*W* 20).

Hardy's interest in folklore is also evident in his presentation of traditional methods of farming, weather-lore, popular medicine, and so on. The skills of Hardy's ideal farmer, Gabriel Oak, include animal surgery (*FFMC* 2); later, in a singular feat of inventiveness, he puts together a makeshift lightning conductor while struggling to save, during a storm, Bathsheba's ricks of barley (37). The people of the Hintocks understand the woodland and the complexities of the timber trade (*W* 7) as much as Dairyman Crick knows about cows (*TDU* 17) and the Donns about the practicalities, cruel as they might be, of pig-farming (*JO* 1.8–10).

Weather can be predicted not only on the basis of the observation of the sky and the clouds (*FFMC* 36), but also from the behaviour of animals (*D* 1.2.5). The Wessex folk—at least some of them—have their ways of curing warts and scrofula (*MC* 26) and of finding an antidote for an adder bite (*RN* 4.7); they use love potions (*JO* 5.5) and abortion-procuring herbs ('A Sunday Morning Tragedy').

On the borderline between folklore and local and social history lies another major area of Hardy's antiquarian interests: that of traditional occupations, celebrations, and pastimes reflecting the various patterns of the life of the rural community, from personal and family occasions through religious festivals to customs reflecting the rhythm of nature and of the agricultural year. The reader is offered accounts of christenings ('The Three Strangers', *WT*), weddings (*UGT* 5.1; 'The Country Wedding'), and funerals ('The Grave by the Handpost', *CM*), as well as of traditional community activities such as club-walking (*TDU* 2) and the burning of bonfires on Egdon Heath (*RN* 1.3). The influence of religion on Wessex folklore is to be seen primarily in the accounts of various aspects of Christmas celebrations: Christmas parties are held at the Dewys' (*UGT* 1.7–8), at Farmer Boldwood's (*FFMC* 52–3), and at Mrs Yeobright's (*RN* 2.5–6); musicians go carolling (*UGT* 1.4–5; 'The Rash Bride', *TL*; 'The Dead Quire', 'Seen by the Waits', *SC*); and animals are believed to kneel in homage to the new-born Christ ('The Oxen', *MV*).

Parallel to the rhythm of the Christian year is that of the seasons and of agricultural work; this is reflected in the presentation of scenes of sheep-shearing (*FFMC* 22), harvesting (*MC* 27), and wheat-threshing (*TDU* 47) as well as of shearing-suppers (*FFMC* 23) and harvest feasts (*FFMC* 36; 'The Harvest-Supper', *HS*). The more practical aspects of the socio-economic reality of the traditional life of rural Dorset include agricultural fairs (*FFMC* 12; *MC* 3; 'At Casterbridge Fair', *TL*), hiring-fairs (*FFMC* 6), and Old-Lady-Day migrations (*TDU* 51–2). An essayistic rather than fictional treatment of these subjects, demonstrating Hardy's profound awareness of and sympathy for the plight of simple Dorset workfolk, is to be found in 'The Dorsetshire Labourer'.

Directly related to Hardy's interest in folklore is his treatment of numerous other dimensions of Wessex life, such as the tradition of folk music, song and dance, or the idiosyncrasies of local dialects (see DIALECT).

JJ

Joanna Cullen Brown, *Figures in a Wessex Landscape* (1987).

Ruth A. Firor, *Folkways in Thomas Hardy* (1931).

'For Conscience' Sake', short story. It was published in the *Fortnightly Review* (March 1891) and collected in *Life's Little Ironies.* The manuscript is in Manchester University Library. Written during the same period as *Tess of the d'Urbervilles*, it takes one of the key situations of that novel—a girl seduced and then abandoned by her lover—and explores a different outcome, ironic rather than tragic.

The germ of the story is probably to be found in an anecdote related to Hardy in December 1882 by 'a very old countrywoman'; the account of their conversation in his autobiography is followed by the comment that 'The eminently modern idea embodied in this example—of a woman's not becoming necessarily the chattel and slave of her seducer—impressed Hardy as being one of the first glimmers of woman's enfranchisement; and he made use of it in succeeding years in more than one case in his fiction and verse' (*LW* 162–3).

Twenty years after he has seduced and then abandoned her, a bachelor of independent means, living in London, seeks out the woman in question, who has passed herself off as a widow, has brought up their daughter single-handed, and has achieved a position of respectability in the cathedral city of Exonbury (Exeter). The long-delayed marriage to which he persuades her is not a success, demonstrating the contention that it is wrong to marry in order to satisfy the demands of society. A subplot concerns the courtship of the daughter by a curate who takes fright when he learns of her illegitimacy—another example of the anticlericalism widespread in this collection of stories. The story includes a scene, simultaneously comic and illustrative of Hardy's interest in *heredity (compare in this respect 'An Imaginative Woman' in the same volume), in which, under the effects of seasickness, the girl's face betrays her relationship to her unacknowledged father. Like much else, the title is ironic in its questioning of 'conscience' as a moral guide, since the seducer's motivation is fundamentally if unconsciously egotistical. The theme of redeeming a past error had been treated somewhat differently in the earlier story 'Fellow-Townsmen', and is taken up again in Angel's return to Tess.

Forster, E. M. (1879–1970), novelist, short-story writer, essayist, and biographer. He made the acquaintance of Hardy and his second wife Florence in March 1919 through the poet Siegfried *Sassoon. A friendly connection appears to have been rapidly established, but this relationship remained more formal than intimate, with Forster intermittently visiting Max Gate for tea or lunch.

Forster was privately disappointed with Hardy's personality. In July 1922, he reported entertainingly on a 'Simple, almost dull tea at the Hardys' which had been followed by a visit to the pets' cemetery in the garden at Max Gate (*Selected Letters of E. M. Forster*, ed. Mary Lago and P. N. Furbank (1985), ii. 31), and a visit in late September of the same year, recounted to Virginia Woolf, yielded the characterization of Hardy as (in Woolf's words) 'a very vain, quiet, conventional, uninteresting old gentleman' (*The Letters of Virginia Woolf*, ed. Nigel Nicolson (1976), ii. 559). In late September 1923, Hardy showed Forster proofs of his play The **Famous Tragedy of the Queen of Cornwall* and regaled him with an account of the recent visit of the Prince of Wales. Forster's essay 'Clouds Hill' (1938), collected in his *Two Cheers for Democracy*, recalls an occasion when the Hardys arrived at T. E. *Lawrence's home while Forster was staying with him. While Forster regarded Hardy more highly as a poet than as a novelist, Hardy for his part praised Forster's novel *A Passage to India* (1924).

Forster touches on Hardy's fiction in his Clark Lectures, delivered at Cambridge and published as *Aspects of the Novel* (1927). In his account of plot he specifically mentions or alludes to *The Return of the Native, The Trumpet-Major, The Woodlanders, Tess of the d'Urbervilles,* and *Jude the Obscure,* and places Hardy as a much greater writer than *Meredith, whose once very large reputation had already waned, yet a less successful novelist. He particularly objects to Hardy's sacrifice of character to causality, and discerns this as a fundamental 'flaw' at odds with the generic conventions of the form itself. JHS

Fowles, John (b. 1926), novelist. In 'Notes on an Unfinished Novel' (1977), Fowles reveals that Hardy is one of his favourite Victorian novelists. Why this is so is clear from Fowles's preface to Jo Draper's *Thomas Hardy's England* (1984), and also from his essay, 'Hardy and the Hag', included in *Thomas Hardy After Fifty Years*, ed. Lance St John Butler (1977). In the former, Fowles speaks of sharing Hardy's interest in the 19th-century transformation of England from a rural into an urban economy, a subject Hardy treated not only in his novels but in his important essay 'The Dorsetshire Labourer' (1883).

Another preoccupation—or, as Fowles puts it in 'Hardy and the Hag', 'obsession'—he shares with Hardy has to do with the irrecoverable past. In his own novels, and particularly in *The Collector* (1963) and *The French Lieutenant's Woman* (1969), Fowles says in his essay, he is aware of having sought to recover, at an unconscious level, the lost young mother of his infancy. Similarly, he sees in *The Well-Beloved* Hardy's effort to recapture his love for Tryphena *Sparks, and also Hardy's attempt to assuage his guilt over his failure to love his first wife. Pierston, the main character of *The Well-Beloved*, is, Fowles says, a surrogate for Hardy, and Pierston's successive love affairs with the three Avices is an oblique description of the love for Tryphena that might have been. If *The Well-Beloved* is not one of Hardy's greatest novels, Fowles adds, it is because it reveals too much of the author's own life: he argues in 'Hardy and the Hag' that Hardy's decision to limit himself to poetry after 1896 was taken because 'verse is, in this context, a less "naked" medium than prose; not an exposed field, but a shady copse'. JA

Frome, River. Often mentioned by Hardy, and usually spelt 'Froom' by him, it rises in the Dorset village of Evershot (one of the locales of *Tess of the d'Urbervilles*), flows past Maiden Newton, *Dorchester (where it skirts the northern edge of the town and is joined by the River Cerne near Fordington), and Lower Bockhampton, through the 'Valley of the Great Dairies' (another scene of the action of *Tess*), to Wareham, entering the English Channel at Poole. There are many allusions to the Froom in *Tess*, and there is a description of it in *The Mayor of Casterbridge* (19). It is also often mentioned in Hardy's poems—for example, in 'Wessex Heights' ('There's a ghost in Froom-side Vale...') and 'She Hears the Storm' ('The Froom in flood upon the moor...').

G

Galsworthy, John (1867–1933), novelist and dramatist. In April 1906 he sent Hardy a presentation copy of his novel *A Man of Property*, which Hardy began but did not finish. Another presentation copy, of *The Freelands*, may have fared somewhat better, Hardy reporting to the author in August 1916 that his wife Florence was reading it aloud to him. Other presentation copies followed, and the two writers corresponded on literary matters: Hardy expressed admiration (February 1921) for Galsworthy's *In Chancery* and regret (October 1921) that the 'Forsyte Saga' series was concluded.

In the previous year, on Hardy's 80th birthday, Galsworthy had been a member of a small deputation from the Society of Authors that visited Max Gate. Galsworthy and his wife Ada visited Max Gate very near the end of Hardy's life, on 6 September 1927, *LW* recording (474–5) a striking conversation that took place during this visit concerning Hardy's memories of his early childhood. Four months later Galsworthy was one of the pall-bearers at Hardy's funeral in Westminster Abbey. H. V. Marrot's *Life and Letters of John Galsworthy* (1935) contains numerous references to Hardy.

geology, and the related science of paleontology (fossil remains), made rapid advances in the 19th century. Revelations about the scale of terrestrial history by Charles Lyell, Richard Owen, and others, together with Darwin's work in biology and Weismann's in *heredity, entered deeply into Hardy's thought. As an architect, he had more than ordinary knowledge of the qualities of stone (see the account of the Casterbridge bridges in *The Mayor of Casterbridge* (32)), and acquired a well-informed amateur's interest in such matters as rock strata and soil content. In his writings these enhance rather than replace his acute countryman's recognition of terrain. Thus as Fitzpiers 'skirted a high plateau of the chalk formation . . . the calcareous upland appeared but as a deposit of a few years' antiquity upon the level vale', and Phillotson moves 'downwards till the soil changed from its white dryness to a tough brown clay. He was now on the low alluvial beds . . .' (*W* 28, *JO* 4.4). Such movements over changing soils are common and important, most vividly in Tess's journeyings between the differing vales of Blackmoor and Froom, and across the 'calcareous downs' with their outcrops of flint, 'siliceous veins in the chalk formation' (*TDU* 2, 43). In *Jude the Obscure*, Hardy writes of 'the solid barrier of cold cretaceous upland', again the geological word validating the metaphorical effect.

The main message of geology for Hardy was the earth's immense antiquity, usually in contrast with transitory human affairs. The relativities of time occupied his imagination, for instance the way skeletons from 1800 BC can become relics merely of 'yesteryear' in the presence of 'the fossils near you' ('The Clasped Skeletons'); or as d'Urberville history is diminished by stones 'older than the centuries' at Stonehenge; or as Egdon Heath, 'having defied the cataclysmic onsets of centuries, reduced to insignificance by its seamed and antique features the wildest turmoil of a single man' (*TDU* 58, *RN* 5.3). His most striking single use of geology is in *A Pair of Blue Eyes*, when Henry Knight, clinging to a cliff, finds himself confronting 'an imbedded fossil . . . one of the early crustaceans called Trilobites'. In a vision receding 'across millions of years' through early geologic eras, 'Time closed up like a fan before him' and Knight arrives back, like H. G. Wells's time traveller twenty years later, among 'the lifetime scenes of the fossil confronting him' (*PBE* 22). The scene anticipates the more sustained presence of the 'Titanic form' of Egdon Heath in *The Return of the Native*, 'obsolete', 'superseded', 'untameable', 'antique', 'prehistoric', 'unaltered', with its 'ancient permanence' and continuance of 'the ancient world of the carboniferous period' (*RN* 1.1, 3.5).

Hardy's other most geological texts are *Our Exploits at West Poley* and *The Well-Beloved.*

The children's story depends on the ancient Mendips cave where the boys divert an underground spring. The rock formations are evocatively described, with 'skeletons of great extinct beasts' and 'beautiful natural ornaments [in] the form of pills, lace, coats of mail'. The story is an ecological fable, which appeals through the boys' ability to change a form of nature that dates 'from geological times', yet warns against the environmental and social consequences of doing so. In *The Well-Beloved* the Isle of Slingers (Portland) is a constant presence. The setting is a 'peninsula carved by Time out of a single stone', 'a rocky coign of England' with 'houses built of solid stone', a 'towering rock ... a solid and single block of limestone four miles long' (*WB* 1). The words 'rock' and 'stone' recur, often specified as 'oolite'. Pierston's name is doubly stony, and even in London, as he seeks to define love's impermanence through sculpture, the blocks from his father's quarries, 'tons of freestone' in 'white cubes and oblongs', are unloaded across the Thames (*WB* 1.9). The only permanence of his loving is its 'instability', yet it compulsively returns to its original form, as the trees at Sylvania Castle are merely the current surface of 'the underlying stone-beds, where a whole forest of conifers lay as petrifactions ... blown down by the gale in the Secondary geologic epoch' (3.1). Even Rome reminds Pierston only 'of the quarries of maiden rock at home' (3.1). The 'lump of rock' that is the Isle of Slingers is essential to the novel's exploration of instability, permanence, and recurrence in human feelings, with 'hereditary persistence' closely associated with the 'unreckonable geologic years' of the layers of oolite.

The poem 'Green Slates' is a similar meditation, and several of the 'Poems of 1912–13' take 'those red-veined rocks far west' to epitomize timelessness. Here, however, this antiquity does not diminish human love, but rather reinforces its permanence to those immersed in its experience. So in 'At Castle Boterel', the 'Primeval rocks' show up 'the transitory in earth's long order', yet also 'what they record in colour and cast | Is—that we two passed'. Subjectivity overcomes geology.

Behind petrous permanence lies also the new awareness of entropy (probably most readily available in the work of Max Müller), most explicitly in 'By the Earth's Corpse', with its vision of a future 'when flesh | And herb but fossils be'. Hardy could turn entropy into a sardonic metaphor for the cooling of amorous passion, 'a lover's heart after possession being comparable to the earth in its geologic stages ... first a hot coal, then a warm one, then a cooling cinder, then chilly' ('Barbara of the House of Grebe', *GND*).

Such geologic metaphors are quite frequent. The year 1851 is 'a precipice in Time ... a geological fault' ('The Fiddler of the Reels', *LLI*); Bob Loveday's scar is 'like the geological remains of a lobster'; Miller Loveday's wardrobe is layered with 'the hard stratification of old jackets, waistcoats, and knee-breeches'; dried mud in a gateway may be a 'geological record' of footprints (*TM* 39, 16, 6); the mummers' play is 'a fossilized survival' (*RN* 2.4); and Giles and Grace stare into a cloudy sky of 'fancied cairns, logan-stones, stalactites and stalagmites of topaz' (*W* 28). Thus Hardy made colourful and often powerful use of the discoveries of a period in which geological 'science was ... ardent ... the pursuit of the unknown' (*Our Exploits at West Poley*). RR

ghosts offer a useful distinguishing mark of difference between Hardy's fiction and his verse. The characteristic 'ghost' in Hardy's novels is Johnny Nunsuch's vision of the reddleman in *The Return of the Native*, or Michael Henchard's of his *doppelgänger* in *The Mayor of Casterbridge*—rationally explained as the consequence of the misperception of reality by one of heightened sensitivity and apprehension. There are one or two possibly genuine ghosts in his stories, in which he did not feel the demands of narrative realism so strongly; but once Hardy was no longer so constrained, he could explore his personal understanding of the matter. Very soon after he had ceased to contemplate novels, he wrote one of his great ghost-poems, 'Wessex Heights', and thereafter never ceased to embody fresh hauntings.

'Wessex Heights' and the 'Poems of 1912–13' that he wrote after his wife's death show most vividly what was at the back of Hardy's thorough acceptance of ghosts. The spirits that haunted him existed for himself alone, and though, as in 'The Voice', he may wonder whether their existence is solely in his imagination, ultimately he insists on their effective reality—though his marginal doubt is one source of the sharp poignancy of these poems. For the most part, too, the ghosts are associated with particular places; 'At Castle Boterel' offers a brilliant intense example of this, but the associations did not have to be his own: wherever Hardy went—in old houses, near often-handled implements, to places where incidents of high passions had occurred—he was at once aware of the presence of the past lives that had left behind their invisible but palpable mark. Three lines from a seldom-read poem called 'The Re-Enactment' put the matter succinctly: 'here some mighty passion | Once had burned, | Which still the walls enghosted'. Or one might turn to 'Old Furniture': 'I see the hands of the generations | That owned each shiny familiar thing | In play on its knobs and indentations . . .'.

These are Hardy's essential ghosts, the ones he would vouch for, but in fact there is a considerable variety of less personal ghosts in Hardy's poetry. Music released spirits for him, as in 'The Choirmaster's Burial' (an almost straightforward ghost-story), 'Jubilate', or 'The Paphian Ball'. So, naturally enough, did war: there is 'The Souls of the Slain', or 'A Christmas Ghost-Story', or the wryly ironical 'Channel Firing', in which the dead wake up, thinking the noise of heavy naval guns is that of the Judgement Day. There are also other poems voiced for spirits, like 'I Rose Up as My Custom Is', or 'Ah, Are You Digging on My Grave?'; and, to take a step further, there is 'Voices from Things Growing in a Churchyard', in which the plants in a graveyard speak of the lives of those buried beneath. The tone of these ghost poems ranges from the bitter to the comic, from pathos to satire: in fact they reflect the variety available in Hardy's work as a whole. See also FOLKLORE and, for Hardy's sighting of a 'real' ghost, PHILOSOPHY. SJG

Gifford, Emma Lavinia. See HARDY, EMMA LAVINIA.

Gifford family. Hardy's first wife was born Emma Lavinia Gifford, the younger daughter of John Attersoll Gifford (1808–90) and his wife Emma (née Farman), who died in 1891. John Gifford had been a solicitor in Plymouth, but well before the time at which Hardy became involved with the Giffords he had given up his practice in slightly mysterious circumstances and settled at Kirland Manor near Bodmin in Cornwall. He was distinctly hostile towards Hardy as a suitor, treating him patronizingly and even insultingly, and was in other ways a difficult man, given to bouts of heavy drinking.

Emma's elder sister Helen (d. 1900) married an elderly widower, the Reverend Caddell Holder, who was Rector of St Juliot, Cornwall, and Hardy's momentous meeting with his future wife took place at the Rectory, where Emma was then living as a no doubt welcome escape from the parental home. Emma's parents were not present at their marriage in 1874, but her brother Walter (1847–1904), an official in the Post Office, was one of the witnesses; his daughter Lilian was later on friendly terms with both her aunt Emma and with Hardy. The marriage was performed by Emma's uncle, Canon Edwin Gifford (1820–1905), who had been a Cambridge don and a headmaster, was then an Honorary Canon of Worcester and later became Archdeacon of London and Canon of St Paul's—a family connection of which Emma was to be inordinately proud, and one to which Hardy himself drew attention both in the newspaper announcement of his marriage and, much later, in his *Who's Who* entry.

After Emma's death, Hardy made an attempt to identify the graves of her parents and grandparents in Plymouth, which, as the scene of Emma's childhood and youth, features in 'The Marble-Streeted Town' and other poems. The death in 1920 of Archdeacon Gifford's daughter Evelyn, a cousin of Emma Hardy, prompted the poem 'Evelyn G. of Christminster'. 'Rou'tor Town' in the poem 'I Rose and Went to Rou'tor Town' is based on Bodmin, near where Emma's father lived, and his treatment of Hardy as a prospective son-in-law may be reflected in the behaviour of Elfride's father in *A Pair of Blue Eyes* (9).

Gissing, George (1857–1903), novelist. His realistic stories of poverty and failure to some extent invite comparison with Hardy's later work, especially his final novel, *Jude the Obscure*, and such short stories as 'The Son's

Veto'. In June 1886 Gissing approached Hardy with the request to visit him in London in order to seek advice on the writing of novels. Gissing had at that time published two novels, *Workers in the Dawn* (1880) and *The Unclassed* (1884). The visit duly took place, and Gissing afterwards sent Hardy a copy of *The Unclassed* with a letter (partly quoted in *LW* 189) expressing high admiration for Hardy's work; Hardy's reply (1 July 1886: *L* i 149) refers to the difficulties he was experiencing with the writing of *The Woodlanders*, then in process of serialization. The acquaintance did not flourish, however: 'Always warily appreciative of each other's work, Hardy and Gissing were distinctly uncomfortable in each other's company...' (Millgate 366). There seem to have been no further meetings until July 1895, when they were fellow-guests and fellow-speakers at a dinner given by the Omar Khayyám Club in honour of George *Meredith. On that occasion Hardy encouraged Gissing to keep in touch, and soon afterwards invited him to Max Gate for a weekend: on this visit, in September of the same year, Gissing (unlike some other visitors) judged his host's residence 'a very nice house', but found his hostess 'an extremely silly & discontented woman'. (For some revealing comments on Hardy's behaviour in his wife's presence, see *The Letters of George Gissing to Edouard Bertz 1887–1903*, ed. A. C. Young (1961), 206.) When, in 1899, Gissing published an article in the *Review of the Week* attacking the jingoistic and warmongering sentiments of a sonnet by *Swinburne, prompted by the Boer War and published in *The Times*, Hardy sent him a warm letter of congratulation.

Adrian Poole, *Gissing in Context* (1975).

Gosse, Edmund (1849–1928), prolific critic, biographer, and poet. He became one of Hardy's closest friends and most frequent correspondents. He and his wife Nellie celebrated their golden wedding in 1925, at which time Hardy sent a telegram: 'CONTINUED HAPPINESS FOR BOTH FROM ONE WHO THINKS HE HAS KNOWN YOU THE WHOLE TIME.' This was indeed the case. Hardy and Gosse first met as guests at the Savile Club in the winter of 1874, nine months or so before the Gosses' marriage. At this time the 25-year-old Gosse was already at the heart of the London literary scene, and was meeting *Swinburne almost daily when released from his work at the British Museum. Gosse later became a leading figure in the literary establishment (H. G. Wells called him the 'official British man of letters'), and numbered among his many friends Henry *James and R. L. *Stevenson as well as Hardy. He was knighted in 1925.

In many ways and for long periods Gosse was Hardy's most intimate friend. Nearly 300 letters from Hardy to Gosse survive, and Hardy preserved more of Gosse's letters than of anyone else's. Some of Hardy's are mere notes, acknowledging invitations, books, birthday greetings, and so on, but others are among his most interesting letters, full of humour, modest pleasure in their mutual admiration, and gratitude for Gosse's perceptive championing of his work. Gosse was not merely a hero-worshipper, however. He needed his heroes to care about him, and Hardy certainly did.

Hardy saw Gosse as someone who would always 'perceive, if nobody else does, what I have aimed at' (*L* i 110). In November 1895, after the publication of *Jude the Obscure*, he wrote to Gosse: 'Your review is the most discriminating that has yet appeared. It required an artist to see that the plot is almost geometrically constructed...' (*L* ii 93). 'A review from a practising poet', as he once told Henry *Newbolt, 'is worth hundreds of pages from a mere critic' (*L* iv 5). Hardy admired Gosse's poetry. 'Lying in the Grass' Gosse dedicated 'To Thomas Hardy', and there was also a more substantial dedication in one of his collections of essays, *Critical Kit-Kats* (1896).

Gosse thought that Hardy was the 'living glory' of English literature, 'our greatest novelist'. He described him as 'the man whom of all my living contemporaries I admire and delight in the most'. Even so, Gosse did, on one occasion, make Hardy 'angry' with his casual use of the word 'indecent' in relation to *Jude*. The context was a lunch-table discussion. Our knowledge of it comes from a totally friendly reference in a letter ten years later to 'the only time you ever made me really angry' (*L* iv 33). It is a measure of friendship to feel able to say what one really thinks.

Gosse endeared himself to Hardy by visiting him when he was seriously ill in

Arundel Terrace, Tooting, in the winter of 1880–1. By that time they were both members of the Savile Club, where they saw each other regularly over the years. After he moved back to Dorchester, Hardy would nearly always call on the Gosses, at Delamere Terrace and later Hanover Terrace, during his London visits. Edward Marsh would report that Hardy did not talk much, 'content to bask in Gosse's beams'. Gosse paid his first visit to Dorchester in July 1883. When Max Gate was built, Gosse was Hardy's first 'sleeping visitor', 'when all was in the roughest state' (*L* iv 239). Hardy was eager that the Gosses should themselves buy a cottage in Dorset: 'I shall pester you with advice. Look at the enclosed—& jump at it.' This was in 1890, at the height of their close friendship. He humorously called Max Gate 'Porta Maxima' in the address on one letter to Gosse, as he did to no one else. A series of snapshots taken with Gosse's new Kodak on a holiday that year included one of a beloved dog who died soon after. Even so, Hardy wrote, 'The most interesting to me is where we are standing together—you and I' (*L* i 218).

One of the foundations of their friendship was their shared background. With Gosse, Hardy did not have to conceal anything. Gosse's grandmother had been a domestic servant, as Hardy's mother had been. Gosse's father had been born in lodgings over a shoemaker's shop, in circumstances no grander than those of Hardy's stonemason father. If these things were not much discussed, they were known, and the young writers certainly compared notes on their West Country roots. They fantasized that as children (Hardy nine years older than Gosse) they might have brushed against each other in the streets of *Weymouth. Gosse took a photograph of Hardy and their two wives on the pier to commemorate the connection.

It seems that Hardy and Gosse were easy with each other when they were together, but their relationship had its share of fluctuations and misunderstandings. Hardy had commiserated with Gosse at the time of his worst hour, when Churton Collins denounced his 'Shakespeare to Pope' lectures as full of error. He wrote perceptively and comfortingly, and from Rome the following year he sent Gosse two pressed violets from Keats's grave.

In 1924 Hardy felt let down when Gosse failed to criticize George *Moore for his attack on Hardy in his *Conversations in Ebury Street*. Gosse had his opportunity, Florence Hardy said, and did not take it. She thought it 'appalling' that there was a chance of Gosse being Hardy's literary executor: 'I cannot imagine what he was doing when he arranged that' (*Letters of Emily and Florence Hardy*, 187). Florence was deeply suspicious of Gosse, of his love of gossip and the way he was always 'dancing attendance on the famous'. There is little evidence that Hardy himself felt neglected in the last years when he rarely went to London. He continued to admire Gosse's 'genial and responsive insight into life and its humours', his articles 'teeming with ideas', his 'lightning power of reading a book and writing a penetrative valuation of it . . . in such a flash of time', and above all his *Father and Son* (1907).

It was certainly true that 'we have not met often of late', as Hardy wrote, welcoming Gosse's proposed visit with Arthur *Benson in 1912. Gosse's last visit was in June 1927, when the famous photograph was taken of the two old men on the garden-seat at Max Gate. 'He is a wonder,' Gosse wrote, 'full of spirit and a gaiety not quite consistent in the most pessimistic of poets.'

Gosse admired Hardy's poetry as much as his prose. Hardy wrote some interesting letters when Gosse was working on his article 'Mr Hardy's Lyrical Poems' for the *Edinburgh Review* (April 1918). In a broadcast made in 1928, in the short period between Hardy's death and his own, Gosse suggested that it was 'the fashion to over-estimate his poetry' and 'to underrate his novels'. He thought that the future would realize that 'this remarkable man was equally distinguished in the two arts of prose and verse'. So it has turned out. It is appropriate that Hardy's last letter was written to Gosse, and that he was a pall-bearer at Hardy's funeral. ABT

Ann Thwaite, *Edmund Gosse: A Literary Landscape* (1984).

Granville-Barker, Harley (1877–1946), actor, producer, dramatist, and critic. He was involved in a theatrical adaptation of *The Dynasts*, and subsequently, with his wife Helen (herself an author), became a friend of Hardy and his second wife.

In the autumn of 1914 Hardy was engaged in correspondence with Granville-Barker concerning the latter's adaptation and production of *The Dynasts*, a venture that Hardy viewed with mixed feelings. The production, for which Hardy wrote a new Prologue, opened on 25 November at the Kingsway Theatre, London; Hardy had attended a rehearsal, and later went to one of the performances.

Subsequently they corresponded concerning the dramatization of *Tess of the d'Urbervilles* staged in Barnes, Surrey, in the autumn of 1926; earlier (3 December 1924) Hardy had asked Granville-Barker to go to see another production of the same work in Weymouth. The Granville-Barkers paid visits to the Hardys' home (for example, in May 1923, with Max *Beerbohm and his wife) and also received visits from them at their Devon home, Netherton Hall. The last of these visits by the Granville-Barkers was on Hardy's 87th birthday: for Helen Granville-Barker's account of this occasion, see *LW* 471. A few weeks before his death Hardy read Granville-Barker's recently published preface to *King Lear*, one of a well-known series of Shakespearian essays written originally for *The Players' Shakespeare* series.

'Grave by the Handpost, The', short story. Originally published in the 1897 Christmas number of *St James's Budget* and (on 4 December 1897) in the American *Harper's Weekly*, it was collected in *A Changed Man and Other Tales*. Though it revives, with touches of affectionate humour, the church choir described a generation earlier in *Under the Greenwood Tree*, the tale, offered as an episode from 'village history', is predominantly grim and even macabre.

Making their traditional carol-singing round just after midnight on Christmas morning, the band and singers encounter the burial of a suicide at a crossroads, and charitably sing a carol over his grave. Soon his soldier-son arrives, believing himself to be the cause of his father's death and full of remorse, and arranges with the villagers for the surreptitious transfer of the body to consecrated ground and the erection of a gravestone. After his departure, however, it is learned that the corpse has had a 'six-foot' stake driven through it, and it is decided that it would be inconvenient to proceed with the exhumation. Years later, the son returns, discovers that his father still lies at the crossroads, and eventually kills himself.

Though the dominant tone is of black humour, there is an element of clerical satire in the opposing views of clergymen in neighbouring parishes as to the rights of a suicide to Christian burial. A final ironic twist reveals that the son's wish to be buried with his father at the crossroads has been disregarded, and he has been buried 'in the ordinary way in the churchyard'.

'Chalk-Newton' in the story is based on the village of Maiden Newton, eight miles from Dorchester and mentioned in Hardy's recollections of his family's music-making as having formerly possessed a strong church band (*LW* 14). The action is set during the Napoleonic Wars, with the son serving in the Peninsular Campaign and retiring to his native region after Waterloo. For a description of the manuscript (in private hands), see Purdy 154. Purdy notes that the manuscript version carries an epigraph from Sophocles' *Antigone*, a drama turning upon the question of giving decent burial to a loved one: 'Consider if thou wilt help me in the work.'

Graves, Robert (1895–1986), poet, novelist, autobiographer, and critic. He was introduced to Hardy by Siegfried *Sassoon. In August 1920 Graves and his wife (Nancy Nicholson) stayed with the Hardys, and Graves's autobiographical *Good-bye to All That* (1929) contains (Chapter 28) brief descriptions of Hardy and his home, and a vivid (though probably not entirely reliable) account of their conversation, which ranged over such topics as the Russian Revolution, poetic composition, Hardy's novels (about which he spoke 'disparagingly'), and Nancy's short hair. (On the inaccuracy of Graves's account, see Gittings, *The Older Hardy*, 204.) Graves was also one of the young writers who in 1921 presented Hardy with a first edition of Keats to mark his 81st birthday.

Great War. See FIRST WORLD WAR.

Group of Noble Dames, A. The volume contains the following stories, divided into two groups as shown (where they are different, the titles for serial issue are noted in parentheses):

Part First: Before Dinner
'The First Countess of Wessex'
'Barbara of the House of Grebe' ('Barbara, Daughter of Sir John Grebe')
'The Marchioness of Stonehenge' ('The Lady Caroline (Afterwards Marchioness of Stonehenge)')
'Lady Mottisfont'

Part Second: After Dinner
'The Lady Icenway'
'Squire Petrick's Lady'
'Anna, Lady Baxby'
'The Lady Penelope'
'The Duchess of Hamptonshire' ('The Impulsive Lady of Croome Castle')
'The Honourable Laura' ('Benighted Travellers')

The early history of the nucleus of the stories that make up the collection titled *A Group of Noble Dames* (1891) is intimately bound up with that of *Tess of the d'Urbervilles*—indeed, the stories were composed in the gap between the writing of the first and second halves of that novel, in the early part of 1890. The manuscript of the stories (now in the Library of Congress) was sent to the *Graphic* on 9 May, but produced no reaction from the editor until six weeks later, when Hardy was bluntly told that the stories would have to be radically bowdlerized if they were to appear in the magazine. Hardy complied in two or three stages; particularly noteworthy are the blue-pencil alterations (which here appear for the first time in one of Hardy's manuscripts) of material to be excised from the serial version but retained for the book-issue. Examination of the effects of such censorship on one of these stories will give some idea of the scale to which Hardy was prepared to go rather than write a replacement.

At the heart of 'Lady Mottisfont', as of several others in the sequence, is an illegitimate child (something the directors of the *Graphic* could not tolerate), the daughter of Sir Ashley Mottisfont and an unnamed Contessa. Sir Ashley is widowed, and when he marries again he manages to interest his wife in Dorothea, whom he 'found one day in a patch of wild thyme'—the more easily since it seems the couple can have no child of their own (a central theme of the collection). The Contessa, however, decides that she wants the child, and as Lady Mottisfont works out slowly the parentage of Dorothea, she reluctantly agrees; in a while the Contessa wishes to marry, and tries to return Dorothea to the Mottisfonts. Lady Mottisfont, however, is pregnant at last, and no longer has room in her affections for her husband's illegitimate child. So Dorothea is farmed out to the peasant-woman who had cared for her as a baby, is unhappy for a while, but eventually marries an engineer, a man who does something useful in the world.

The most convincingly created character in the story is Sir Ashley, whose low-key affection is well-established in a series of speeches and actions. But the *Graphic* would not accept the result of his loving encounter with the Contessa, and so, quite cynically, Hardy substituted for the slightly sketched but genuine dilemmas and ironies at the centre of the original story a two-paragraph tale of secrecy, suicide, crime, and poltroonery. In the space of this special serial account Sir Ashley's character is reversed. Dorothy is now the child of an early secret marriage, ended when this wife (sister of the Contessa) was driven by him to suicide because, as a result of her father's conviction for forgery, he refused to acknowledge her. Sir Ashley also refuses to acknowledge the (perfectly legitimate) baby, who is 'handed over to the tender care of a villager as though she were a child of shame'. The serial-reader must have been puzzled indeed to reconcile this account of a heartless husband and father with the many details still remaining in the story that showed his quiet good-nature. The English serial-reader, that is, for readers of *Harper's Weekly* in America got more or less the whole story, and one or two extra details as well that Hardy added on the emended *Graphic* proofs he sent across the Atlantic.

The same pattern is observable to a greater or lesser degree in all the stories the *Graphic* commissioned—'Barbara of the House of Grebe', 'The Lady Caroline', 'Lady Baxby', 'The Lady Icenway', 'Squire Petrick's Lady', and 'Lady Mottisfont'—but when *A Group of Noble Dames* appeared in volume form early in 1891 the narratives were substantially restored to their original form, some titles changed, and their order altered. To these six Hardy added four tales published elsewhere, 'The First Countess of Wessex', 'The Lady Penelope', 'The Duchess of Hamptonshire', and 'The Honourable Laura', the first at the beginning of the book, the others at the end. These stories do not have the same cynical edge to them.

For the *Graphic* Hardy had followed a pattern made popular by Dickens in his Christmas numbers, and presented the stories as if they were told to pass the time by members of the Mid-Wessex Field and Antiquarian Club, unexpectedly snowed in at the end of a meeting. This frame-narrative was altered and expanded for the first edition, and Hardy made some superficial changes to the stories, intended to render them more appropriate to their tellers; but he did not go far enough. This happened in 'The Lady Icenway', told by the churchwarden, where on a few occasions 'of' was changed to 'o'' and a phrase like 'families of note' became 'folk o' note'—but the narrative voice remains essentially that of the *Graphic* group as a whole. For all that Hardy stresses that this particular Field club was remarkably 'inclusive and intersocial' in character, and points out that the members who had swapped tales in such a cosy fashion would, the evening over, split into social groupings that would scarcely acknowledge each other's existence, neither the content nor the telling of the stories supports this pretension to social diversity.

Hardy acknowledges as much in introducing the churchwarden, who, 'now thoroughly primed, proceeded to relate in his own terms what was in substance as follows, while many of his listeners smoked' ('Lady Mottisfont'). And yet 'The frost of class-division and social prejudices' ('The Marchioness of Stonehenge') is one of the primary themes of these anecdotes; and Hardy may well have been making an ironic allusion to the *Graphic* editor's notion that these were 'smoking-room' stories, fit only for male consumption—and of course the Club's membership is exclusively male.

Another pervasive theme of the book is the idea of marriage and consequent legitimate childbirth as a purely dynastic contract; sometimes it is the failure to marry, sometimes it is the failure to conceive, particularly to conceive a son, which is the issue.

Though one of the stories ('Squire Petrick's Lady') is described by an auditor as a 'subtle and instructive psychological study', the reader is left to wonder at the mind that could think it so. Indeed the Club-members are as much criticized by the narrator as any of the boorish gentry in the stories who so thoroughly mistreat their women; some of the members, for instance, believe that an early death is an appropriate punishment for a woman who marries three times ('The Lady Penelope').

In fact Hardy fairly often wrote about aristocrats, though not in his most popular novels: *The Hand of Ethelberta, A Laodicean,* and *Two on a Tower* have centrally important characters from the upper classes, and all of them are viewed critically, even to some degree Lady Constantine, the heroine of *Two on a Tower.* Their social and personal assumptions are held up for scrutiny, and found without value to compensate for their ugliness. There is, however, in novels and stories, a tendency to distinguish between the male and female of the species: the males are mostly concerned about issues of inheritance and property, while women are their instruments and victims; women for their part are most often concerned with maintaining a social façade of propriety over their sexual indiscretions.

This typology is more nakedly effective in *A Group of Noble Dames,* and ultimately the stories may be seen purely in terms of a critique of an archetypal patriarchal society. However, the thematic content of the narratives is often so threadbare, and the treatment so perfunctory, that one might wonder why Hardy wanted to write them at all, unless the very casualness of the dismissal of Lord Uplandtowers, or the off-hand relegation of Dorothy Mottisfont to a farm-cottage, are part of the attack on a class that can show so many examples of such behaviour. See also SHORT STORY. SJG

Kristin Brady, *The Short Stories of Thomas Hardy* (1982).

Martin Ray, *Thomas Hardy: A Textual Study of the Short Stories* (1997).

Grove, Agnes (Lady) (1863–1926). The subject of Hardy's elegiac poem 'Concerning Agnes', she was the daughter of General Augustus Pitt-Rivers (1827–1900) and Alice (1828–1910), daughter of the 2nd Baron Stanley of Alderley. In the Stanley tradition she was very much a child of the Whig aristocracy, and Bertrand Russell was one of her cousins. In 1882 she married Walter Grove

(1852–1932), 2nd Baronet (1897), by whom she had three sons and two daughters. The Grove estate, Ferne, adjoined the Pitt-Rivers estate, Rushmore, Tollard Royal, Wiltshire.

She first met Hardy when he visited Rushmore in 1895 to attend the annual festivities in the Larmer Tree Gardens, ornamental grounds created by her father. Dancing together in the grounds lit romantically by many hundreds of Vauxhall lamps, she and Hardy found a quick rapport—he troubled by hostility to *Jude the Obscure*, she wrestling with the problem of what a young mother should tell her children about religion and sex. Her emancipated, feminist approach epitomized the new generation he wished to reach, and was the basis of their lifelong friendship. He encouraged her to write and to send him her first efforts, which he corrected and proof-read. To some extent she replaced Florence *Henniker in his desire for a sympathetic pupil among the society beauties whose company gave him so much pleasure.

Agnes Grove published four books: *Seventy-One Days Camping in Morocco* (1902); *The Social Fetich* (1907), which was dedicated to Hardy; *The Human Woman* (1908); and *On Fads* (1910). She was polemically and politically active in the campaigning causes of the Edwardian years, including women's suffrage, anti-vivisection, and the Women's Liberal Association: Gladstone had been her hero and the Asquiths were her friends. But the Great War destroyed her world. She lived on in ill-health and near-poverty, to be given, in her death, the enduring memorial of Hardy's poem. DH

The Grove Diaries, ed. Desmond Hawkins (1995).

Desmond Hawkins, *Concerning Agnes* (1982).

Nancy Mitford (ed.), *The Ladies of Alderley* (1938).

—— *The Stanleys of Alderley* (1939).

H

Haggard, Henry Rider (1856–1925), novelist. He is now remembered chiefly for such popular romances as *King Solomon's Mines* (1885), but he also had a strong interest in agriculture, and sought assistance from Hardy when working on his *Rural England* (1902). A letter of March 1902 quoted in Hardy's autobiography (*LW* 335–7) responds to Haggard's request for information concerning the history of the Dorset agricultural labourer. (Hardy had written earlier on the same subject in his essay 'The *Dorsetshire Labourer'.) Quoting Hardy's letter in *Rural England*, Haggard describes him as one 'who, as all the world knows, has made lifelong observation of this and kindred matters connected with the land'. A letter of condolence sent by Hardy after the death of Haggard's young son contains one of the most striking remarks in all his correspondence: that the death of a child is 'never really to be regretted, when one reflects on what he has escaped' (?May 1891, *L* i 235). Haggard was knighted in 1912.

Hand family. Hardy's mother (see RELATIVES OF THOMAS HARDY) was born Jemima Hand, the daughter of George Hand (1773–1822), who in 1804 had married Elizabeth (Betty) Swetman (1778–1847) (see SWETMAN FAMILY). George was the eldest of a family of nine children. His father, William Hand (1752–1828) of *Puddletown, had married Betty Symonds (1752–1828) of Melbury Osmond, Dorset, in 1773. Betty Swetman, the daughter of a yeoman farmer, married beneath her: though George Hand is often described as having been a servant, Millgate notes that he 'seems to have worked, when he worked at all, as a gardener or as a shepherd'; he was, moreover, a heavy drinker who could be violent when drunk, and Millgate also suggests that Jemima's recollections of her father, transmitted to her son, 'contributed major strands in the creation of such characters as Michael Henchard and Jude Fawley' (Millgate 12).

George's death from consumption in his late forties, when the youngest of his seven children was only 6 years old, plunged the family into poverty, even destitution, and his widow became dependent on poor relief from the parish of Melbury Osmond. According to Hardy, she had been left nothing in the will of her father (who died in the same year as her husband), though he had been 'in comfortable circumstances'; consequently she was 'at her wit's end to maintain herself and her family, if ever widow was' (*LW* 12). Hardy adds that his mother experienced 'poverty' and 'stressful experiences' in her youth, and a surviving letter written by her own widowed mother and quoted by Millgate (13) painfully bears this out.

Jemima's elder sister Maria (1805–68) was brought up by her paternal grandparents after her father's death, and later married (1828) James Sparks, a Puddletown cabinetmaker of good family (see SPARKS, TRYPHENA). Of Jemima's two younger sisters, Mary (1815–91) married (1847) John Antell, a Puddletown shoemaker (see ANTELL FAMILY), and Martha (1816–59) married (1841) John Sharpe, with whom she moved away from Dorset and later emigrated to Canada. Jemima also had three brothers: Henry, sometimes known as Henery (1807–83), William (1810–80), and Christopher (1811–86). All became builders, William in Melbury Osmond while the others settled in Puddletown. Christopher later became (like Hardy's father) a mason, but like his brothers and his own father before him was a heavy drinker. All the brothers, like all their sisters, married and had issue, and since the Hands went in for large families Thomas Hardy was well provided with cousins as well as with uncles and aunts.

Hand of Ethelberta, The. The fifth of Hardy's fourteen published novels.

Composition

In December 1874, impressed by the success of *Far from the Madding Crowd*, Leslie *Stephen, the editor of the *Cornhill Magazine*, in which it had been appearing, asked Hardy for another serial, to begin in April 1875. He submitted a rough draft of the new story in January, and its first chapters in March. Hardy started the novel in Surbiton and London, wrote its greater part in Swanage, where he moved in July, and finished it in January 1876. The manuscript does not survive; according to Purdy (22), some portion of it was returned to Hardy by the publisher, *Smith, Elder, in 1918, along with the manuscript of *Far from the Madding Crowd*, but he subsequently destroyed it.

Serialization

The novel appeared monthly in the *Cornhill* from July 1875 to May 1876, divided thus: July, Chapters 1–4; August, 5–9; September, 10–15; October, 16–21; November, 22–6; December, 27–30; January, 31–4; February, 35–8; March, 39–42; April, 43–6; May, 47–50. Serialization in the United States was in the Sunday issues of the *New York Times* from 20 June 1875 to 9 April 1876.

As with *Far from the Madding Crowd*, Stephen showed his sharp awareness of the prudery of his Victorian readership. In May 1875 he suggested that Ethelberta's writing be described as 'sentimental' instead of 'amorous', and in August he objected to 'the very close embrace in the London churchyard'. Hardy made alterations accordingly (see Simon Gatrell, *Hardy the Creator: A Textual Biography* (1988), 19–20). The *Cornhill* proof-sheets, extensively revised in Hardy's hand, survive, except for the three instalments of February–April. They are now housed in the Beinecke Manuscript and Rare Book Library, Yale University. Every instalment in the *Cornhill* featured a full-page illustration and a vignette initial by George du Maurier.

Volume Publication

The novel was published on 3 April 1876 by Smith, Elder in two volumes, priced at one guinea (21*s*.), in an edition of 1,000 copies. Fearing that some readers might understand 'comedy' to mean farce, Stephen had asked Hardy to drop the subtitle ('A Comedy in Chapters') for the work's serial appearance, and this now appeared for the first time. The American edition was published by Henry *Holt & Co. in May. In 1895, Hardy wrote the Preface for *Osgood, McIlvaine's edition of the Wessex Novels, revised the novel, and reduced it from its original 50 to 48 chapters.

Robert Gittings has pointed out that some autobiographical details were lost in this revision (*Young Thomas Hardy*, 206, 210). Christopher Julian's pallid sister Faith was originally named Mary, like Hardy's unobtrusive younger sister. The description in Chapter 5 of candles as 'clammy and cadaverous as the fingers of a corpse' originally read 'as the fingers of a woman who does nothing' (Hardy had recently married a middle-class woman who had never worked). Neigh's character as 'a terrible hater of women... particularly of the lower class' (25) was stated as being caused by his father's 'goings-on', which included marrying his cook (Hardy's own mother had actually been a cook in a Dorset vicarage). Hardy excised portions of Chapters 9 and 12, and included the remaining material in the present Chapters 8 and 11. The omitted passages contained details pertaining, respectively, to Christopher's recognition of Ladywell as his rival, and Faith's realization of Picotee's love for Christopher. For *Macmillan's Wessex Edition of 1912 Hardy made some minor revisions and added a Postscript.

Reception

The Hand of Ethelberta was not commercially or critically as successful as *Far from the Madding Crowd*. Although the first edition sold relatively well, and only 61 copies were left in 1878, more than half of the single-volume edition of 1,000 copies published in 1877 was remaindered in 1882. Owing to the success of its immediate predecessor, the novel was extensively reviewed; it received mixed reactions. R. H. Hutton, in a representative review in the *Spectator*, declared: 'A more entertaining book than the *Hand of Ethelberta* has not been published for many a year'; he added that no one would read the novel 'without being aware from beginning to end that a very original and a very skilful hand is wielding the pen'. However, Hutton found the characterization weak on the whole: Ethelberta is 'so much of a riddle to us, and so little of a living figure', and other characters are 'vivacious shadows, who amuse us without impressing us'. But there are a few points where we find opposed judgements. While some criticized Hardy's style, George Saintsbury in the *Academy* noted a 'stylistic improvement' (that is, less laboured eccentricity) in this novel, a view echoed by the *Atlantic Monthly.*

Hardy's attempt at a new direction was, one suspects, strongly motivated by his wish not to be categorized as a follower of George *Eliot, but comparisons with her *Daniel Deronda*, then running as a serial, were mooted by *The Times* and the *Westminster Review*—the former negatively, and the latter positively. Another interesting area of mixed reactions concerns the question of genre in relation to the novel's 'improbability'. The *Athenaeum* found it improbable and of the second order, but the *Examiner* reviewer, most enthusiastic and perhaps most perceptive of all, took a directly opposite view. Hardy, it was observed, is here deliberately working outside a rigid standard of probability, and the novel, actually 'what may be called ideal comedy, in which fancy is permitted to range beyond the limits of real life', was in this reviewer's opinion an admirable success; for from 'whatever point of view we regard the work, we find deliberate artistic aims and unflinching fidelity of execution'. The review concludes: 'We doubt whether *Ethelberta* possesses the popular interest of some of Mr Hardy's previous novels... but it is more masterly as a work of art—it reveals a progress in technical excellence which makes us look forward with curiosity to his next publication.'

Plot

Ethelberta Petherwin, a young and attractive widow, arrives at Anglebury, South Wessex, near her old home. A servant's daughter, she had been married to an upper-class youth who died shortly after their honeymoon. She chances upon the impoverished music teacher Christopher Julian, her former suitor, who lives with an unmarried sister, Faith. He again comes to be interested in Ethelberta, while Picotee, her younger sister, falls in love with him. Ethelberta's anonymously published book of poetry is the talk of fashionable society. After quarrelling with her rich mother-in-law, who does not allow her to recognize her own family, she becomes a professional story-teller in London, counting upon her literary talent to earn her a living.

She is so successful that she is able to establish a London residence with most of her family masquerading as servants. Eustace Ladywell and Alfred Neigh, two gentlemen who move in society, are fascinated by Ethelberta, while Julian faithfully courts her, but is too sexually and economically powerless to attract the strong-minded, ambitious girl. Feeling that her performance is losing its fresh appeal with the public, Ethelberta begins to entertain the idea of an advantageous marriage, in order to support her large family. Neigh proposes, but she does not accept his offer. In the meantime, Lord Mountclere, an old lecher, becomes besotted by her, and when she goes across the Channel to Rouen to visit her aunt, he eagerly follows her, as do Neigh and Ladywell. She asks her three suitors to wait for a month.

Back in England, invited to Lord Mountclere's country seat, Ethelberta gives a story-telling performance, in which she recounts the story of her own life. When she realizes that Lord Mountclere has been aware of her background, she accepts his offer of marriage. Lord Mountclere's brother Edgar, Mr Chickerel (Ethelberta's father, and butler in the service of the Doncastles, a middle-class family living in west London), her carpenter brother Sol, and Christopher, each discover that she is going to marry Lord Mountclere, and try to prevent the marriage. They arrive at the church simultaneously, but too late. After the formalities have taken place, Ethelberta is horrified to learn that Lord Mountclere has a mistress. She sends for help, and Christopher comes to rescue her, but his attempt is foiled by Lord Mountclere. Ethelberta is reconciled to her husband, and comes to dominate him. Christopher marries Picotee.

Critical Approaches

Hardy knew his public wanted him to write another *Far from the Madding Crowd.* He did not, however, capitalize on the success of that novel, but made 'a plunge in a new and untried direction', for he 'had not the slightest intention of writing for ever about sheepfarming' (*LW* 105). Consequently, *The Hand of Ethelberta*, although stressing the contrast between the country and the city, is essentially an urban social comedy rather than a pastoral novel. Hardy modelled it after the Restoration and 18th-century comedy of manners. The chapter-headings indicate the scenes of action, and the subtitle, 'A Comedy in Chapters', is a variation on that of a play, such as 'A Comedy in Three Acts'. In addition, there are accidental meetings and other similar contrivances, the playful naming of some characters, and some farcical elements. But Hardy was not merely imitating the genre. Ethelberta is by no means a stage heroine, and Hardy deliberately upsets conventional generic expectations. This is not a story in which a proud heroine finally learns her lesson and marries the patient humble hero, on the pattern of *Far from the Madding Crowd.*

Hardy does, however, continue his study of a woman of striking independence, here giving a different kind of complexity to the characterization of the heroine. '"Experimentally, I care to succeed in society; but at the bottom of my heart, I don't care,"' Ethelberta declares, and this 'experimental' attitude is the most significant feature of her psychological make-up. She can cope with the loss of Christopher, not so much because she knows that this man without ambition does not suit her, as because she is at bottom detached from her own emotions. The novel hinges upon the question, 'Whom will Ethelberta marry?', and when she has to make that decision, she considers first her family, then her social ambition, and, lastly, her romantic feelings.

Hardy does not want us to regard her action as selfishly motivated, for he presents her as concerned about the survival of her family more than anything else. Nevertheless, possibly because she herself is detached from her emotions, one does not feel involved with Ethelberta, as one does, for instance, with Tess. Different from Hardy's other heroines in important respects, Ethelberta invites a unique response from us. *Fate has little to do with her: she is largely in control of herself. Crucially, she is not caught in the mesh of sexual love, which she replaces with reason and will-power. (Ethelberta's first marriage is practically non-existent, and she is compared to the biblical virgin Abishag in Chapter 45. It is interesting to note Hardy's continued use of female figures associated with King David, following Bathsheba in his previous novel.) No suitor affects her seriously in sexual terms: there is no Alec d'Urberville. All this was deliberate on Hardy's part, for, referring to the novel's subtitle, he remarks in a letter to Stephen that 'My meaning was simply, as you know, that the story would concern the follies of life rather than the passions, & be told in something of a comedy form, all the people having weaknesses at which the superior lookers-on smile, instead of being ideal characters' (21 May 1875: *L* i 37).

The reader, then, is meant to maintain a sense of distance from the characters, even from Ethelberta. The novelist, another detached 'looker-on', is here being 'experimental' himself, placing the strong heroine in a comedy that has no sexually dangerous men. The prevailing detachment is paradoxically related to the fact that this is a deeply personal novel, in which Hardy projects much of himself, particularly his class anxiety, onto the protagonist. Ethelberta's secret marriage ceremony is not unlike Hardy's own, with his wife's uncle and brother the only guests, since the two families, belonging to different classes, were hostile to one another.

The novelist and the heroine share the same background, their family members and relatives consisting of servants, carpenters, and schoolmistresses. On Hardy's mother's side there were people in service. Given that his mother's maiden name was Hand, Hardy may have been wryly amused by a private resonance in the novel's title. Ethelberta's encounter with London society reflects Hardy's own experience at the time of the novel's composition, when he was just beginning to socialize with the metropolitan literati. The novelist, like the heroine, made his way into this new territory through writing, and had anxieties about his social background. Their artistic careers follow a similar path: Ethelberta first publishes a book of poetry, then becomes a story-teller in order to earn a living, while Hardy himself wanted to be a poet, but turned to novel-writing to 'keep base life afoot' (*LW* 105). Ethelberta's composing an epic poem corresponds to Hardy's own project, *The Dynasts,* conceived at the time of his writing the novel.

When the heroine says to her brother Sol, '"Whether you like the peerage or no, they appeal to our historical sense and love of old associations"', the novelist himself in a way shares this sentiment seriously, for here is a clear symptom of what might be called Hardy's 'D'Urberville Complex', a conflict between the dignified solidarity with country labourers and the irrepressible yearning for ancient aristocratic lineage. Given all this, one is led to speculate that, in addition to Hardy's 'experimental' attitude towards the novel, a careful distancing through which the novelist objectifies himself has much to do with the sense of detachment in the portrayal of Ethelberta.

Class awareness, a major preoccupation of Hardy throughout his career, had up to this point never been so pronounced except for his very first work of fiction, *The Poor Man and the Lady*, which had possibly some close links with *The Hand of Ethelberta*. Hardy's statement that in the latter he made 'a plunge in a new and untried direction' may need qualification, for in a sense he went back to his first, unpublished novel, finished in 1868. The manuscript of this work being lost, we have no way of knowing its exact content, but it was, Hardy records, 'a striking socialistic novel', the targets of its 'sweeping dramatic satire' including 'the squirearchy and nobility, London society, the vulgarity of the middle class', and its 'most important scenes were laid in London' (*LW* 58, 62–3). *The Hand of Ethelberta* is by no means a 'socialistic' novel, but it does deal with a serious issue which is of central importance to Hardy's artistic career. We should not be so blinded by the novel's oddity (the urban setting, comedy, and so on) as to overlook its continuity with his other fiction.

When preparing the Wessex Edition of 1912, Hardy divided his fiction into three groups, and put this novel in the slighter category of 'Novels of Ingenuity', or 'Experiments', which 'show a not infrequent disregard of the probable in the chain of events'. The truth, however, is that he does not much respect probability even in the 'Novels of Character and Environment', usually thought of as his major works. These 'Novels of Ingenuity' simply display this attitude to a more marked degree. By the same token, Hardy boldly 'experimented' with the class issue in *The Hand of Ethelberta*, presenting an extreme case of a marriage between a viscount and a servant's daughter without involving the heroine in sexual complications. When he wrote the novel, Hardy was perhaps not yet ready to confront the issue in a more realistic mode. 'Comedy', then, was to some extent a safeguard, whereby he could say, as he does in the 1895 Preface, that 'there was expected of the reader a certain lightness of mood' in dealing with this 'somewhat frivolous narrative'.

Indeed, the novel's 'comedy' has presented difficulties to critics since its publication, but it is by no means simply 'frivolous'. In Michael Millgate's view, most of the comedy 'can be related, in one way or another, to the question of appearance and reality which provides one of the novel's continuing themes'; Ethelberta 'plays so many superimposed parts' that 'her "true" personality proves finally elusive—perhaps even to Hardy himself' (*Thomas Hardy: His Career as a Novelist*, 112).

A key to the problem is provided in a letter, particularly revealing in the present context, that Hardy wrote to J. B. Priestley (8 August 1926: *L* vii 38), who had just published a book on George *Meredith. Stressing Meredith's role as a successor to the writers of artificial comedy of the Restoration period, Hardy says that he did not 'let himself discover the tragedy that always underlies Comedy if you only scratch it deeply enough'. Richard H. Taylor argues that in *The Hand of Ethelberta* 'we do not have to scratch very deeply to discover the potential tragedy', and that 'in a real moral sense Ethelberta's success is a tragedy' (*The Neglected Hardy*, 68).

Millgate and Taylor are exceptions to the general tendency of modern critics to treat the novel summarily. Recently, however, it has become a focus of much serious attention from materialist and feminist critics. Representative of the former school, Peter Widdowson examines the way in which this novel self-consciously foregrounds issues of social class, gender relations, and the artifice of realist fiction writing. What the novel really does, in Widdowson's view, is to expose the very artificiality of these conceptions by its own artificiality and improbability, its use of coincidence, unreal characters, farcical absurdities, and other uncompromisingly fictive contrivances. Even the novel's awkward style is an effective weapon that contributes to the whole defamiliarizing effect.

Feminist critics mainly concentrate on the issue of gender, emphasizing various elements that confound patriarchal values, such as Ethelberta's active part in giving her hand in marriage, and the reversed gender-roles (the masculine Ethelberta and the feminine Christopher) that undermine essentialist accounts of women. In their view, Ethelberta is not an inscription by the male pen on a blank page, but a creative writer who can manipulate the 'male gaze'. The novel demonstrates, Sarah Davies argues, that 'the feminine figure of the realist novel is a social and therefore male construct, a myth rather than a reality or truth'. TS

John Bayley, *An Essay on Hardy* (1978).
Sarah Davies, '*The Hand of Ethelberta*: De-Mythologising "Woman"', *Critical Survey*, 5 (1993).
Michael Millgate, *Thomas Hardy: His Career as a Novelist* (1971).
Richard H. Taylor, *The Neglected Hardy: Thomas Hardy's Lesser Novels* (1982).
Peter Widdowson, *Hardy in History: A Study in Literary Sociology* (1989).

Hardy, Emma Lavinia (1840–1912). Hardy met Emma, who became his first wife, on 7 March 1870 in the tiny Cornish hamlet of St Juliot, inland from Boscastle. He had been asked by his then employer, the Weymouth architect George *Crickmay, to make a survey of the dilapidated church preparatory to its restoration. Upon arriving at the rectory after a day-long journey (memorialized in the poem 'When I Set Out for Lyonnesse'), he was greeted by a 'young lady in brown' (*LW* 77), Emma Gifford, whose elder sister, Helen, had recently become the second wife of the rector, the Reverend Caddell Holder.

Emma and Helen were the children, along with three brothers, of John Attersoll Gifford, a Plymouth solicitor, and his wife Emma, née Farman (see GIFFORD FAMILY), and Emma's artlessly charming *Some Recollections*, written late in life, gives an impression of an essentially happy childhood that was none the less shadowed by several removals within Plymouth and by her father's drinking, to which she freely refers. Perhaps for financial reasons, perhaps because of some professional embarrassment, Gifford in or about 1860 abandoned his practice and took his family to live at Kirland, a remote manor-house near Bodmin. Isolation and financial necessity drove Helen Gifford to take employment as a governess and companion, and eventually to marry Holder, her senior by 35 years. Emma herself, though lacking any formal education, also worked briefly as a governess, and was evidently glad enough—perhaps because of her father's continued drinking—to join her sister at St Juliot in 1868.

She had little occupation in that lonely spot, however, apart from playing the harmonium in the church on Sundays, and few prospects of marriage. When Hardy appeared in her 30th year she seems not only to have set aside her reservations about his appearance and economic prospects but to have represented herself as younger than she actually was, and more actively courted by local suitors. Hardy, for his part, was immediately fascinated by Emma's spectacular and as yet unfaded corn-coloured hair as well as by her middle-class accomplishments, literary enthusiasms, and provocative unpredictability.

The wild Cornish landscapes and seascapes provided a seductively romantic setting, and by the end of Hardy's second visit to St Juliot, in August 1870, the couple were effectively and perhaps formally engaged. Their actual marriage, however, was still four years off, a period largely of separation during which they conducted an active correspondence that Hardy claimed to have been comparable to the famous courtship letters of the Brownings, but that Emma comprehensively destroyed towards the end of her life.

Emma was strongly supportive of Hardy's risky career shift from architecture to literature in the early 1870s, and directly assisted him by preparing a fair-copy manuscript of *Desperate Remedies* and co-operating in the composition of *A Pair of Blue Eyes*, a novel containing numerous elements drawn from their courtship and a heroine based in many respects on Emma herself. Hardy, meanwhile, had begun to doubt the wisdom of his choice, not least because of his exposure to John Attersoll Gifford's class-based contempt for the social pretensions of the Hardys, and the corresponding resentment towards the Giffords evinced by his own parents and siblings. When the wedding finally took place, at St Peter's Church, Paddington, on 17 September 1874, it was opposed by both families,

Emma being supported only by her brother Walter, and Hardy only by the daughter of his London landlady.

Emma's honeymoon diary, though far from intimate, contains no hint of marital tensions, and indeed the early years of the marriage, spent in Surbiton, Swanage, Yeovil, and Sturminster Newton (see HOMES), seem to have been happy enough, though clouded by the non-appearance of children. Emma's confidence in Hardy's future was amply vindicated by the success of *Far from the Madding Crowd*, and she eagerly sought opportunities—some real, others artificially created—to associate herself with her husband's writing.

She often exaggerated her role in the composition of the novels, however, and her desire to figure in the metropolitan literary scene as the wife and helpmate of a successful author was clearly a factor in prompting their ill-fated move of March 1878 to the London suburb of Tooting—where, as Hardy later noted, 'their troubles began' (*LW* 128). When Hardy fell seriously ill in Tooting during the serialization of *A Laodicean*, it was Emma who nursed him and acted as his indispensable amanuensis, but the subsequent retreat from London to Dorset, first to *Wimborne and then to *Dorchester itself, brought her into direct conflict with Hardy's family, all of whom—but especially Jemima, his mother, and Mary, the older of his sisters—remained permanently unreconciled to the marriage.

Because so few of Emma's letters have been preserved, and because Hardy maintained so high a level of personal privacy, it is difficult to trace at all precisely the stages by which the marriage deteriorated. The daily routines of domestic life at Max Gate seem always to have been kept up in a reasonably stable fashion; the Hardys took a number of Continental holidays together, the last in 1897 (see TRAVELS, CONTINENTAL); for many years they rented a London house or flat for several weeks of the spring 'season'; and when Hardy was in London by himself, his letters home were largely devoted to practical details and expressive neither of hostility nor of particular affection.

Emma's surviving letters, on the other hand, give voice to complex marital resentments dating back at least to the beginning of the 1890s. She felt eclipsed by her husband's fame, denied participation in his work, and largely excluded from his lionization in 'society' circles following the publication of *Tess*. Her own intensifying religious beliefs made her hate what she saw as the irreligiousness of *Jude*, and she took personally its attack upon the institution of marriage. She also knew that Hardy enjoyed in London the flattering attentions of women such as Rosamund *Tomson and Florence *Henniker with whose education, beauty, and style she could not hope to compete.

Above all, perhaps, she remained bitterly at odds with Hardy's unforgiving mother and with Mary Hardy—accusing the latter, in a remarkable letter of 22 February 1896, of being 'a witch-like creature' who had done her 'irreparable mischief' by calling her 'mad' and conspiring to turn her husband against her: 'Your brother has been outrageously unkind to me—which is *entirely your* fault' (*Letters of Emma and Florence Hardy*, 7–8).

There can be no doubt that Hardy increasingly sided with his family against Emma, and sought to minimize her participation in both his intellectual and his social life. But sympathy for her predicament has to be balanced by recognition of the degree to which Hardy found his wife's eccentricities a source of public embarrassment, a burden on his emotional resources, and a disruption of his everyday routines as a professional writer. Emma, as her letters show, could be abrasively quarrelsome; she was a strenuous advocate, in and out of season, of aggressively Protestant religious views; friends and acquaintances often commented on her oddities of dress and behaviour; and she readily shared with outsiders her increasingly paranoid criticisms of her husband's writings, opinions, and marital conduct.

To what extent her condition amounted to serious mental instability it is difficult to judge, although Hardy certainly added the epigraph 'And I saw the figure and visage of Madness seeking for a home' to his early reminiscence of Emma in the poem 'The Interloper', evidently in the belief that some inherited strain of insanity had lurked in her since birth. A partial amelioration of their difficulties was eventually found in what seems to have been a mutual agreement to live more separate lives, and Emma began taking holidays on her own, or in company with her niece, Lilian Gifford, and spending most of her time at Max Gate in an attic that was later enlarged to allow for the accommodation of a personal maid.

Emma seems quite early in the marriage to have attempted some writing of her own, notably a romantic and partly autobiographical short story entitled 'The Maid on the Shore' (typescript in DCM). Around the turn of the century—prompted in part by a desire to compete with her husband—she managed to place a few poems and articles in newspapers and magazines. Rather more interest now attaches to the deeply engaged letters she wrote to newspapers on such topics as religion, female suffrage, and cruelty to animals—this last a cause she shared with her husband, who always praised her passionate readiness to intervene whenever she personally encountered instances of mistreatment. Following another burst of writing in 1910–11, when Florence Dugdale acted as her typist, Emma gathered fifteen poems into the privately printed *Alleys* of 1911 and some brief prose meditations into the companion volume, *Spaces*, of 1912.

It was also in 1912 that she seems to have completed the manuscript of *Some Recollections*, hiding it away with the secret diaries in which, over a period of some twenty years, she had vigorously recorded her grievances against her husband. It was apparently Hardy himself who discovered these documents following Emma's death, and while he soon destroyed the diaries, he spared *Some Recollections*, thus making available for subsequent publication what seems to have been by far the liveliest and most attractive of his first wife's compositions.

Emma's sudden death, aged 71, on 27 November 1912 seems to have been entirely unexpected. She had indeed been something of an invalid in her last years—often needing to be towed to church in a bathchair—and her death was attributed by the attending physician to a combination of heart failure with the normally painful condition of impacted gallstones. Even so, it is by no means clear that Hardy was guilty (as has sometimes been alleged) of callously ignoring his wife's suffering over an extended period. She had kept up her social life as well as her secret writing, and although she was certainly taking sedatives from time to time, she seems neither to have consulted a doctor nor to have complained openly of any serious pain.

Hardy was shocked by Emma's death and by his subsequent discovery of her bitter diaries, and his inscription on her funeral wreath ('From her lonely husband, with the old affection') provided an early hint of the direction his response was taking. From cold indifference he span into a dark vortex of self-pitying regret and self-flagellating remorse. His guilt at the neglect and unhealed divisions of recent years mingled with idealized re-imaginations of their earliest times together, and in March 1913—precisely 43 years after his first encounter with Emma—he made what was virtually a pilgrimage to St Juliot in the company of his brother Henry.

Essentially coterminous with this profoundly emotional if perhaps partly willed process was the period of intense creativity that resulted in the *'Poems of 1912–13'. First published in the *Satires of Circumstance* volume of 1914, these poems of celebration and regret constituted for Emma herself a kind of posthumous triumph—for Florence Hardy a burden to be borne. Indeed, while the initial intensity of Hardy's expiatory mood dissipated over time, it became one of his second wife's perennial complaints that he persisted in his revisionist estimate of his first wife—and kept his desk calendar permanently set at that 7 March date of their first meeting. MM

Emma Hardy Diaries, ed. Richard H. Taylor (1985).

Emma Lavinia Hardy, *Poems and Religious Effusions*, Monographs on the Life, Times and Works of Thomas Hardy, no. 29 (1966).

Letters of Emma and Florence Hardy, ed. Michael Millgate (1996).

Denys Kay-Robinson, *The First Mrs Thomas Hardy* (1979).

Millgate 121–5, 127–30, and *passim*.

Hardy, Florence Emily (1879–1937), Hardy's second wife. She was the second of the five daughters of Edward Dugdale, headmaster of the St Andrew's (Church of England) boys' school in Enfield, Middlesex, and his wife Emma (née Taylor). The Dugdales owned and occupied 5 River Front, a substantial semi-detached villa in the centre of Enfield, and lived there in solid lower middle-class comfort and respectability. Her father had at school the reputation of a disciplinarian, quick to resort to corporal punishment, but he seems at home to have maintained a more genial regime that none the less demanded strict observance of the standard moral, religious, and domestic proprieties. Little is known of Florence's childhood, her relatives having respected her privacy both before and after her death and destroyed almost all of her family letters, but the household seems to have been generally happy and united, and Florence always remained devoted to her parents. Her self-confidence, however, was already shadowed by the melancholia and delicate health that increasingly dogged her later years.

Florence attended the St Andrew's girls' school until she was 12 and then went on to the local Upper Grade School, where she came top of her class in 'Composition' in July 1892. At the age of 15 she became a pupil-teacher—one of the few employment options then available to a young woman of her class—and returned in that role to the St Andrew's girls' school, where the stressfulness of her daily tasks was intensified by poor working conditions and by the recurrent laryngitis and pharyngitis that would eventually force her out of teaching altogether. Denied on medical grounds the place at a training college for which she had qualified by her good marks in the Queen's Scholarship Examination in 1897, it took her until 1906 to obtain an Acting Teacher's Certificate based on a combination of teaching experience (in her father's school) with part-time attendance at a non-residential training college in central London. Depression, however, and frequent illness—she sometimes lost her voice for months at a time—eventually convinced her that she was both temperamentally and physically ill-suited to teaching, and she began to seek for other means of earning a livelihood.

During the winter of 1906–7, before her final abandonment of teaching, she seems to have spent several months in Dublin as companion to the wife of Sir Thornley Stoker, a distinguished and wealthy surgeon who knew and entertained many of the leading Irish writers of the day. But her ambition was to support herself by writing—a profession she had long viewed in romantic terms. She presented a paper on Tennyson to the Enfield Literary Union as early as 1901, taught herself to type, wrote articles for the local newspaper, and developed warm friendships with the Irish novelist Katharine Tynan Hinkson, then living in Enfield (and probably the originator of the arrangement with the Stokers), and especially with Alfred H. Hyatt, a struggling Enfield writer whose early death from tuberculosis she greatly mourned. She was employed as a journalist for a time—probably by the *Sphere*, an illustrated weekly edited by Clement *Shorter, certainly by the London daily newspaper the *Standard*—but found the work no more congenial than schoolteaching. She also became, from about 1905 onwards, a prolific, if poorly paid, author of short stories for children. Among her published volumes were *Jennie, Who Did Not Like Christmas* and other moral tales for the Society for Promoting Christian Knowledge, *Country Life*, *Eminent Women*, and *Old Time Tales* for Collins, *In Lucy's Garden* for Hodder and Stoughton, and, most notably, three titles—*The Book of Baby Beasts*, *The Book of Baby Birds*, and *The Book of Baby Pets*—illustrated by the well-known artist E. J. Detmold.

Though Florence in later years gave varying accounts of her first meeting with Hardy, it had certainly occurred by the end of 1905, and had apparently taken the form of her seeking and obtaining permission, as an ardent admirer of his work, to call upon him at Max Gate. By the spring of 1907 Florence was making occasional visits to the British Museum to check historical details Hardy wanted to include in *The Dynasts*, while Hardy, for his part, was attempting to forward her literary career: it was largely at his instigation, for example, that the *Cornhill Magazine* published her story 'The Apotheosis of the Minx' in May 1908.

Over the next few years they spent much time in each other's company in London and elsewhere—they went together, for example, to some of Edward *Clodd's intellectual house-parties in *Aldeburgh—and Hardy became increasingly dependent on Florence's quiet devotion as well as on her skills as a typist. The possibility that their relationship became actively sexual cannot, of course, be ruled out, but there was a 38-year difference in their ages and evidence other than inferential is in any case entirely lacking. Florence, with her deeply conventional upbringing and romantic view of literature, seems to have been motivated primarily by literary hero-worship and a desire to be of use. That she had some reservations about Hardy even so is suggested by her private remark (recorded in Clodd's diary for 23 June 1910) that he was a great writer but not a great man.

An apparently accidental meeting between Florence Dugdale and Emma Hardy in the early summer of 1910 led to Florence's being invited to Max Gate later that same year to assist in the typing and prospective publication of Emma's writings. A friendship between the two women briefly flourished, only to fade as Florence became increasingly distressed by Emma's eccentricity and by the prevailing Max Gate climate of domestic dissension. Though the letters she wrote to Emma at this period can seem distinctly disingenuous when read in the light of later events, there is no clear indication of Florence's having cherished thoughts of an eventual marriage with Hardy. When, however, Emma suddenly died in late November of 1912, Florence Dugdale was summoned, along with Mary and Kate Hardy, to Hardy's assistance, and over the next fourteen months she spent much of her time at Max Gate, effectively taking over responsibility for its management. As she frankly reported in her letters to Clodd, her situation was made difficult and often painful by local gossip, by Hardy's descent into what she could only regard as excessive depths of grief and guilt, and by the hostile presence of Emma's niece Lilian Gifford, indulged by Hardy precisely because of her resemblance to his dead wife.

But as the time passed Florence became ever more inextricably involved in Hardy's life, and by the late spring or early summer of 1913 she had consented to a marriage that she doubtless already saw partly as a life-solution, partly as a life-sentence. As late as the beginning of January 1914 she was still insisting on the departure of Lilian Gifford as a precondition of that marriage, but the concession was made and the wedding itself took place in Enfield Parish Church early in the morning of 10 February 1914, in circumstances of extreme privacy dictated by Hardy's fame and his determination to frustrate the attentions of reporters and photographers. No one was present other than the minister, Hardy's brother, and Florence's father and youngest sister, and the couple returned immediately to Max Gate, successfully avoiding the especially dreaded risk of a civic reception at Dorchester station.

Although it was much easier to live in Dorchester as Mrs Hardy than as Miss Dugdale, some of Florence's basic difficulties persisted into, and even throughout, her marriage. Max Gate itself was redecorated, and various improvements and modernizations gradually introduced, but Florence found the house cold and the tree-surrounded garden gloomy, worried over the costs and complications of housekeeping, and was never entirely at ease in dealing with the servants. Her secretarial duties became steadily more demanding as Hardy's increasing fame stimulated an ever-greater volume of correspondence, and in addition to typing her husband's letters—together with his poems and, in due course, his ghost-written biography—she found herself conducting active correspondences with such friends as Rebekah Owen and Lady *Hoare essentially on his behalf. Hardy's habit, too, of spending much of each day closeted in his study meant that she was often left on her own for long periods with only the dog Wessex for company, while the after-dinner routine each evening was that she read aloud to her husband for an hour or more, sometimes straining her voice in the process. Her health, indeed, remained always delicate, and she underwent operations on her nose in 1915 and on her neck (for the removal of a potentially cancerous tumour) in 1924.

Her position had, of course, its compensations. She was socially established and financially secure, and she had the satisfaction of knowing that she was daily enhancing the health, comfort, and creative vitality of one of the world's greatest writers. Being the mistress of Max Gate might bring with it the awkward responsibility of protecting her husband from unwanted intrusions, but it also placed her in the centre of his wide circle of famous and interesting friends, among whom she became most attached to Sir James *Barrie and T. E. *Lawrence. But Florence's disposition was as melancholic as Hardy's, and at times of distress—for example, when she read the 'Poems of 1912–13' in *Satires of Circumstance* (1914) as Hardy's declaration that Emma was irreplaceable and his second marriage a failure—her misery was all too likely to flow over into whatever letters she happened to be writing. In her intimate and intensive correspondence with Hardy's friend and adviser Sydney *Cockerell, for example, she typically mingled concern for her husband's welfare and health with complaints about his behaviour or conditions at Max Gate.

Particularly difficult, though for very different reasons, were the stressful years of the *First World War, which broke out within six months of the marriage, and the period, in the mid-1920s, of Hardy's infatuation with Gertrude *Bugler, whom Florence, in her genuine if exaggerated fear and jealousy, treated with a bullying hostility that she later regretted, and that has certainly damaged her posthumous reputation. Some marital tension was also created by Florence's persistence in keeping up her journalistic work. For her this was essentially a small but significant gesture of personal and financial independence, but Hardy had little patience with the unsigned reviews of new novels she supplied to Clement *Shorter's *Sphere* magazine, and was distinctly embarrassed by the appearance in popular newspapers of such articles as 'The Dress Bills of Wives', attributed in the *Weekly Dispatch* of 8 April 1923 to 'Mrs. Thomas Hardy, wife of the great author'.

The marriage remained amicable and affectionate, however, and Hardy continued to be remarkably healthy, if increasingly frail, as he moved into his middle and late eighties. The onset, late in 1927, of what proved to be his final illness thus took Florence and his doctors by surprise. She did most of the nursing herself, assisted by the professional skills of her sister Eva Dugdale, and after the death her exhaustion and distress enabled Barrie and Cockerell, summoned to Max Gate only at the last minute, to get her consent to funeral arrangements she subsequently deplored. She soon quarrelled with the overbearing Cockerell, with whom she shared the literary executorship under the terms of Hardy's will, and became further embittered by the falling away of many who had cultivated her friendship during her husband's lifetime. She seems at one point to have anticipated that Barrie would marry her, and the evaporation of that possibility only exacerbated her sense of a loss of direction and purpose.

Max Gate, especially in winter, now seemed gloomier and more isolated than ever, and since she was now relatively wealthy she bought a car, hired a chauffeur, and pursued the hope of a more stimulating social and intellectual life in London. Among the apartments she rented there at various times was one in Adelphi Terrace, a building in which Hardy had once worked and Barrie now lived. But the promise of London proved in the end illusory, and Max Gate with its contents (including Hardy's study), associations, and responsibilities could not in any case be altogether abandoned.

The immediate task of completing, revising, and publishing Hardy's ghosted biography (see AUTOBIOGRAPHY), published over her own name as *The Early Life of Thomas Hardy* (1928) and *The Later Years of Thomas Hardy* (1931), had been accomplished early on, but Hardy's literary estate required some degree of management, and requests for access to his books and papers had also to be dealt with. As time passed, Florence spent more time in Dorchester and found satisfaction and purpose in taking an increasingly active role in its civic life as a magistrate, a leading member of the Dorchester Hospital Management Committee, and the chairman of the Mill Street Housing Society, an effective provider of cheap but good quality housing in the town's poorer areas. She also held her melancholia partly at bay by keeping up with old friends such as Barrie, Dorothy *Allhusen, T. E. Lawrence, and Max *Beerbohm and his wife Florence (whom she once visited at their home in Rapallo), forming important new friendships with, among others, Stephen Tennant, Sir Arthur Pinero, Adelaide Phillpotts, and the American Hardy scholars Frederick Adams and Richard Purdy, and keeping a watchful eye on the needs of her own family, especially those of her youngest sister, Margaret Soundy, and her two children, Thomas and Barbara, in whom she had always taken a particular interest.

It was Margaret Soundy who came to Max Gate to assist Florence when she was diagnosed with inoperable cancer of the bowel in the late spring of 1937. Always ill and in pain, cared for by professional nurses, and wheeled outside from time to time to enjoy the summer pleasures of the Max Gate garden, she managed to survive until 15 October of that same year, a good deal longer than her doctors had predicted. She was only 58, and the life she had chosen and worked at had always been lived too largely at second-hand. But the courageousness and serenity of her dying perhaps reflected a final justified recognition of her indispensable contribution to the astonishing creativity of Hardy's last years. MM

Letters of Emma and Florence Hardy, ed. Michael Millgate (1996).

Thomas Hardy, *The Excluded and Collaborative Stories*, ed. Pamela Dalziel (1992), 332–47.

Robert Gittings and Jo Manton, *The Second Mrs Hardy* (1979).

Millgate 444–7 and *passim*.

Michael Millgate, *Testamentary Acts: Browning, Tennyson, James, Hardy* (1992), 139–74.

Hardy, poems about. Poems addressed to Hardy repeatedly honour his compassion. Siegfried *Sassoon's 'At Max Gate' (1950; *Collected Poems* (1961)) concentrates the dual vision of Hardy first described in *Siegfried's Journey* (1945) in two faces: one of an amiable, inoffensive old man, the other of 'the Wessex wizard' or 'seer' thought-rapt over a flickering fire. Edmund *Blunden's 'Thoughts of Thomas Hardy' (1940; *Poems of Many Years* (1957)) similarly images Hardy (as in some photographs) 'with forehead bent downward', attentive to the fall of a single leaf that symbolizes 'a vaster threne of decline'. Walter *de la Mare's 'Thomas Hardy' (1938; *Complete Poems* (1969)), partly imitating one of Hardy's own poems, the long-lined 'Afterwards', plays upon the motif of noticing from that poem, concluding: '"O Master," I cried in my heart, "lorn thy tidings, grievous thy song; | Yet thine, too, this solacing music, as we earthfolk stumble along"'. Charles Tomlinson's 'In Memoriam Thomas Hardy' turns upon the universal emotional impact of 'His besetting word... "Afterwards"' (*Written on Water* (1972)).

More fancifully, John Betjeman's 'The Heart of Thomas Hardy' (1937; *Collected Poems* (1958)) apotheosizes Hardy's resurrected heart 'in golden nimbus', about which reverently radiate the risen corpses of Wessex characters he created. Betjeman handles the hexameter line with Hardyesque skill (but see Donald Davie, *Thomas Hardy and British Poetry* (1973), 109–10, for justified reservations about this poem). Clive Sansom also conjures, in 'Thomas Hardy' (*'The Witnesses' and Other Poems* (1956)), a transcendent vision of Hardy's 'loving wraith' revisiting Stinsford, 'quietly brooding upon his rhymes', still asking the 'eternal Why?'. The refrain 'Times, ay Times' of the church sexton who has seen the ghost is Hardyesque. C. Day Lewis's 'Birthday Poem for Thomas Hardy' (*Poems 1943–1947* (1948)) addresses Hardy's spirit in five fluently rhymed sestets, celebrating the poet's abiding life 'in us warmer-hearted and brisker-eyed | Since you have been'.

Writing in 1968, Philip *Larkin considered that 'there are no successful imitators of Hardy' (*Required Writing* (1983), 176). John Powell Ward plausibly suggests why: 'I couldn't copy Hardy's style, except by chance. He does his imperfection so perfectly that it leaves nothing to do but gasp' (*THJ*, February 1995, 31). An exception is C. Day Lewis, in several poems of regret, crossed love, and mourning. While not imitating Hardy's forms precisely, Lewis's are technically similar, with Hardyesque compounds, neologisms, lyrical refrains, and incantations. See the following, all included in *Poems of C. Day Lewis*, edited by Ian Parsons (1977): 'The Album', 'Cornet Solo', 'Hornpipe', 'The Fault', 'The Rebuke', 'On the Sea-Wall', 'Ewig'; also, in *Poems 1943–1947*, 'The House-Warming'. Lewis's *Italian Visit* (1953) contains an acknowledged pastiche, 'Singing Schoolchildren: Lucca della Robbia', which closes 'Would I had sung my last ere joy-throbs dwindled | Or wan faith froze!', with which may be compared Hardy's own 'The Dead Quire' and 'A Cathedral Façade at Midnight'.

Hardy's arch-parodist is Max *Beerbohm. His 'A Luncheon', composed in Hardy's voice, is in one version subtitled 'Th*m*s H*rdy M*x Gate, July 20th 1923', when the Prince of Wales paid the Hardys a notoriously awkward visit. The middle stanza plays upon the Prince's remark, related by Hardy to Sassoon, that 'My mother tells me that you have written a book called [... er... er] *Tess of the d'Urbervilles*. I must try to read it some time':

Beautiful weather? Sir, that's true,
Though the farmers are casting rueful looks
At tilth's and pasture's dearth of spryness—
Yes, Sir, I've written several books—
A little more chicken, Your Royal Highness?
(*Max in Verse*, ed. J. G. Riewald (1963), 118)

Beerbohm's 'A Sequelula to *The Dynasts*', first published in his volume *A Christmas Garland* (1912), reassembles the Spirits and Choruses of Hardy's epic-drama to hear the Recording Angel recite the 'parasite' Thomas Hardy's account 'of our (for so we deemed it) private visit' to Earth. After the reading, and the expulsion of the mischievously partisan Spirit of Clement *Shorter, Hardy's devotee and Bonapartist, the Spirits unanimously condemn Hardy's presumptuous 'vision' as, according to the Spirit of the Pities, 'Striving to belittle things that are | Little enough already'. The Spirits revisit Earth on Christmas Day, only to be guided by Hardy's spirit to the County Gaol, Casterbridge: 'This well-kept castle whose great walls connote | A home of the pre-eminently blest'. Ironically, the harsh regimentation witnessed within compels the Spirit of the Years to acknowledge

... the soundness of the central thought
In Mr Hardy's drama. He was right.
Automata these animalcula
Are—puppets, pitiable jackaclocks.

John Betjeman's pastiche 'Dorset', included in his *Collected Poems*, successfully imitates Hardy's 'Friends Beyond': such as T. S. Eliot and Brian Howard rub shoulders in the refrain with Tranter Reuben (see Davie, *Thomas Hardy and British Poetry*, 108–9). 'Thomas Hardy in the Cowshed', a delightfully humorous encounter with Hardy's spirit, by his biographer Robert Gittings, echoes Hardy's diction, movement, and metaphysic; it concludes,

'Who *are* you?' I lipped; but his visage of elderly grizzle
Rebuked by misprision, 'Who *was* I were meeter for them
Who view thus my ghost! Go, visit my tomb where they chisel
"Thomas Hardy, O.M." '
(*People, Places, Personal*, 1985)

Many poems about Hardy are largely topographical—celebratory explorations of Hardy country and its associations with his life and work. The following can be found in *THJ*: Andrew Deane, 'The Last Tryst' (February 1992); David Holbrook, 'Hardy Country' (May 1992); Ronald Tomkins, 'Emma' (May 1994); Christine O'Connor, 'Play On', and David Burnett, 'Hardy' (October 1994); Gavin Ewart, 'T.R.O.T.N.' and 'The Thomas Hardy Blues' (May 1995); Jack Clemo, 'Tryphena', and Gavin Ewart, 'The Allotment of Sex in *The Woodlanders*' (February 1996). Michael Thorpe's 'Eight Poems for Thomas Hardy' appeared in various issues of *THJ* and are collected in his *Loves and Other Poems* (1997). MT

Hardy, Sir Thomas Masterman (1769–1839), of Portisham, Dorset. He is best remembered as captain of Nelson's flagship, the *Victory*, at Trafalgar (and the recipient of his famously disputed dying words). He was created baronet in 1806, and concluded a distinguished career as a vice-admiral. According to Hardy he 'belonged to a branch of the Dorset Hardys, of whom the subject of this memoir belonged to another' (*LW* 350). A letter of 24 January 1920 quoted later in the *Life* puts the matter rather more tentatively: 'All that I can state with certainty is that both Admiral Sir Thomas Hardy's family and my own have been Dorset for centuries, dwelling within a few miles of each other, and that they are reputed to come from the same ancestry, as is antecedently probable for several reasons. But they branched apart before the Admiral's time' (431). Admiral Hardy is commemorated in his native county by the Hardy Monument, erected in 1846; this notable landmark, visible from Max Gate, is also mentioned in the *Life* (472).

In the late 1870s Hardy corresponded with Emily Chatteris (born 1809), a daughter of Admiral Hardy, concerning her father. However tenuous his own family connection, it must have helped to nourish Hardy's lifelong interest in the Napoleonic period, and his namesake, who appears briefly in *The Trumpet-Major*, and also in *The Dynasts*, seems often to have been in Hardy's thoughts. After a visit to Max Gate, Cynthia Asquith noted that 'The only thing he takes the least pride in is his descent from the Trafalgar Hardy...' (quoted in Millgate 537 n.).

Hardy (or Hardye), Thomas (d. 1599), of Melcombe Regis, Dorset. This Elizabethan namesake 'endowed the Dorchester Grammar School' (*LW* 9) and is also claimed as one of Hardy's ancestors in the *Life*, which reproduces the memorial to him in St Peter's, Dorchester. The connection (whatever its precise degree of closeness may have been) led Hardy to feel pleasure in his own appointment as a Representative Governor of the school, an office he held from 1909 to 1925. The 'Elizabethan philanthropist... whose namesake I have the honour to be' is referred to at some length in the speech (printed in *LW* 472–3) that Hardy made on 21 July 1927, when he laid the foundation stone of a new building for the school; there he is also described as 'this first recorded Thomas Hardy of the Frome Valley'.

Hardy, Thomas (1840–1928), novelist and poet. He was born on 2 June 1840 in the Dorset hamlet of *Higher Bockhampton, located in the parish of *Stinsford just to the north-east of *Dorchester, the county town. He was his parents' first child, arriving rather more than six months after their marriage on 22 December 1839. His father, Thomas Hardy senior (1811–92), was a stonemason and jobbing builder whose own father, yet another Thomas Hardy, had at the turn of the century built the family cottage (now one of the National Trust's most famously picturesque properties) in an isolated situation at the very end of the hamlet's single street, among trees and on the very edge of open heath (see HOMES). His mother, born Jemima Hand (1813–1904), had known much hardship as a child in the north Dorset village of Melbury Osmund, and had worked for a time as a cook for relatives of the Earl of Ilchester. (On Hardy's parents and other family members, see RELATIVES OF THOMAS HARDY.) Money was short during the early years of the marriage, Thomas Hardy senior's sanguine temperament rendering him an unaggressive tradesman, but Jemima Hardy's resourcefulness and somewhat grim tenacity brought the family through its difficulties to increasingly better times. There would be three more children: Mary (1841–1915), much the closest to Hardy in age and sympathies, Henry (1851–1928), and Katharine, usually known as Kate (1856–1940). Mary and Kate became schoolteachers; Henry assisted and then succeeded his father in the family building business; all remained unmarried.

Early Years

Hardy himself said that he was almost given up for dead at the time of his birth, and he certainly remained small and delicate throughout his childhood. Kept protectively at home in his earliest years, he spent much time with his mother and his sister Mary and became intensely familiar with his immediate surroundings of heath and woodland. He absorbed—from his parents, both of whom had lively narrative gifts, from other relatives, and from neighbours—a great deal of local *folklore and traditional *music as well as the oral history of Stinsford parish stretching back over several generations. As he later acknowledged, much of his work in prose and verse derived directly from his childhood experience, as did his lifelong fascination with the world his parents and grandparents had known. In the novel *Under the Greenwood Tree*, for example, he memorialized the disbandment, around the time of his own birth, of the Stinsford church 'quire', in which his father and grandfather had been leading instrumentalists. Hardy himself began to play the violin at an early age and, when he was a little older, he occasionally went with his father to provide the music at local dances and parties. Music remained emotionally important to him throughout his life—he once said that he found the history of the concert hall of far more interest than the history of the theatre—and his particular attachment to the music and rituals of the Church of England remained undiminished by his eventual agnosticism.

Hardy may have gone to a village dame-school at some point, but he had no regular schooling until September 1848, when—as recalled in the poem 'He Revisits His First School'—he presented himself early on the opening day of the new National (i.e. Church of England) school in Lower Bockhampton. He had already attracted, and would always fondly remember, the affectionate attentions of the school's principal founder, Julia Augusta *Martin, wife of the owner of Kingston Maurward House and effectively (though not technically) lady of the manor. Jemima Hardy, however, strongly disapproved of the relationship and sought to break it up, some element of class-antagonism doubtless reinforcing her natural possessiveness. She took her son out of the school in the autumn of 1849 in order that he could accompany her to Hatfield on an extended visit to her younger sister Martha Sharpe (Hardy's model, years later, for Bathsheba in *Far from the Madding Crowd*), and in September 1850 she sent him to the Dorchester British School, an elementary school run on Nonconformist principles. Mrs Martin, taking offence on both religious and personal grounds, is said to have ensured that Hardy's father did no further work for the Kingston Maurward estate.

Because Hardy was still not strong, he was sometimes exhausted by his daily walk of three miles in each direction between Higher Bockhampton and Dorchester. But the school itself was well suited to his needs, and he remained with its able headmaster, Isaac Glandfield *Last, when the latter set up his own 'commercial academy' in Dorchester in 1853. Last's standard curriculum emphasized mathematics and mechanics, but Hardy was reading widely by this time and even acquiring a few books of his own—some of them preserved in the Dorset County Museum—and his parents paid for him to take Latin as an extra (see CLASSICS). At some point he began—perhaps with the help of Horace *Moule, classicist son of the evangelical Vicar of Fordington—to work at Greek on his own, apparently with the long-term ambition of going to university, taking orders, obtaining a curacy in a country parish, and devoting himself largely to the writing of verse. It was an ambition rendered remote by his lack of money and, indeed, of an adequate classical education, but he did not entirely abandon it until many years later.

Hardy's parents had more immediate and more obviously practical plans for their eldest child. They had long recognized that he was insufficiently robust to succeed his father as a stonemason and builder, but his cleverness at school now evidently suggested that he might draw upon his background and education, and find a route into the middle class, by pursuing an architectural career. In 1856, therefore, Hardy was apprenticed to John *Hicks, an architect whose office in South Street, Dorchester, was next door to the school kept at that time by the Reverend William *Barnes, the Dorset dialect poet.

Hicks's office proved a congenial workplace, and Hardy became especially close to a fellow-pupil, the evangelically minded Henry *Bastow, who emigrated to Australia shortly afterwards. He also deepened his friendships with the brilliant but deeply troubled Horace Moule and his much stabler brother Charles. Hicks seems to have provided his apprentices with an excellent technical grounding, and because the practice specialized in ecclesiastical work Hardy was able to develop his skills as a draughtsman even as he significantly broadened his knowledge of the churches and landscape of west Dorset (see also ARCHITECTURE). Dorchester itself, as the county town, had a busy and various life of its own, and Hardy saw there, along with much else, some of the circuses he so loved (despite his later concern for the welfare of animals) and the never-forgotten public hanging of Martha Browne for murder in the summer of 1856 (see EXECUTIONS, PUBLIC). He kept up meanwhile his private study of Latin and Greek, mainly in the early morning hours before setting off for work, taught Sunday school at Stinsford church from time to time, and seems to have found his way, at least indirectly, into print: he later claimed not only to have supplied technical information to the *Dorset County Chronicle* reporter assigned to cover the rededication ceremonies of churches Hicks had repaired but also to have tricked the same newspaper into printing a humorous squib of his own.

The earliest surviving photograph of Hardy dates from the beginning of his time with Hicks. Taken by a Dorchester photographer, it shows a tight-lipped, slightly built young man with dark hair, incipient moustache, and modest aspirations towards sartorial elegance, evidently somewhat unsure of himself and of the photographer. Hardy would always be somewhat below the average in height; he grew a beard in the 1880s, but reverted to a moustache in the early 1890s; and while concern for his appearance certainly did not survive into his old age, it was sustained at least through the 1890s, the many studio photographs of that period tending to show him smartly turned out and with his moustache almost militarily waxed.

In London

Hardy stayed on with Hicks for a time after the completion of his apprenticeship, but in April 1862, shortly before his 22nd birthday, he set off for London: a move primarily economic in its motivations but perhaps influenced in its timing by an emotional or religious crisis of some kind. His first lodgings were in Kilburn, then on the outskirts of the city, but from the spring of 1863 onwards he rented a room at 17 Westbourne Park Villas, close to Paddington Station, the main terminus for the Dorchester trains. 'Dickensian' London was in the 1860s fast vanishing in the face of extensive expansion and rebuilding, and Hardy quickly found employment with one of its busiest architects, Arthur *Blomfield, an exponent of French Gothic, who moved his office, shortly after Hardy's arrival, from Trafalgar Square to Adelphi Terrace, overlooking the as yet uncompleted Thames Embankment. Hardy worked diligently at his profession and was soon on friendly terms with his colleagues and with Blomfield himself. He was elected to the recently established Architectural Association, and in 1863 won both an Association prize for the design of a country mansion and the Silver Medal of the Royal Institute of British Architects for an essay, later destroyed, on the use of coloured bricks and terracotta in architecture. The letters Hardy wrote from London to his sister Mary in the early 1860s vividly testify, as do the pages devoted to this period in his autobiographical *Life*, to his sense of enjoyment and excitement as he watched and shared in the processes of urban growth and change, went to plays and operas, visited galleries and museums, and attended different churches (including, on at least one occasion, the Jesuit chapel in Farm Street, in the company of Horace Moule).

Hardy in fact lost his religious faith during the 1860s—in part, perhaps, because of his reading of Darwin's *On the Origin of Species* (1859)—and he eventually abandoned his dreams of university and eventual ordination. Journalism seemed for a time an alternative means of subsidizing a devotion to literature, and his preparations for such a career included evening classes in French, the study of shorthand and art history, and the writing of compositional exercises suggested by Horace Moule. A humorous prose sketch entitled 'How I Built Myself a House' was published, and paid for, by *Chambers's Edinburgh Journal* in March 1865, but instead of following up this success with other lightly written pieces Hardy seems to have turned almost immediately to the cultivation of his more serious literary ambitions and set deliberately about the task of turning himself into a poet. The Dorset County Museum holds several dictionaries and volumes of poetry purchased in 1865 (see LIBRARY, HARDY'S), and the same date appears at the front of a rare surviving notebook, headed 'Studies, Specimens &c.' (published 1994: see NOTEBOOKS), that gives some indication of the technical and vocabulary-building exercises by which he sought to acquire the basics of the poet's trade. No poems by him appeared in print in the 1860s, but many of those he drafted or outlined at that time would be effectively reworked for publication 30, 40, 50, and even 60 years later.

Return to Dorset

The dirt and smoke of London were meanwhile damaging Hardy's health, and in the summer of 1867 he returned to Higher Bockhampton and resumed his work as a country architect, first for Hicks and then for G. R. *Crickmay, the Weymouth architect who took over the practice when Hicks died. Over the next few years Hardy worked on a number of decaying village churches, and at Turnworth, in north-east Dorset, and perhaps at one or two other locations, both the design and the on-site supervision seem to have been almost exclusively in his hands. He clearly took satisfaction in his work, especially at Turnworth, but later accepted the view, most notably pioneered by William Morris, that church 'restoration' had all too often been radically destructive both of the fabric of buildings and of their centuries-old associations: in an address, indeed, that he wrote in 1906 for delivery to the Society for the Protection of Ancient Buildings he apologized publicly for the damage he had himself unwittingly caused. In the late 1860s his cherished literary ambitions were already drawing him away from architecture, although sheer economic realism—the necessity for making an alternative living—had by now caused him to put poetry at least temporarily aside and seek a career as a professional novelist.

His first novel, *The *Poor Man and the Lady*, written in the first person, was begun in the autumn of 1867, finished in first draft by the following January, and submitted in a revised fair copy to Alexander Macmillan, the publisher, in late July of 1868. Macmillan and his reader, John Morley, were both impressed by the energy of Hardy's writing, but while Macmillan wrote sympathetically to Hardy about his manuscript he finally declined to publish a book so openly hostile towards the upper classes. George *Meredith, reading the manuscript for another publisher, Chapman & Hall, was also deterred by what Hardy himself later called the 'socialistic' (*LW* 63) aspects of the book and recommended the young author to begin his career with a novel written along more conventional lines. Hardy's response, strongly influenced by the example of Wilkie *Collins, took the form of a 'sensation' novel called *Desperate Remedies* that was published—anonymously and on a shared-cost basis—by Tinsley Brothers in 1871. The book was praised in the *Athenaeum* and the *Morning Post*, but its fate was chiefly determined by the contemptuous condemnation it received in the *Spectator*, and Hardy in fact forfeited a significant portion of the £75 he had contributed towards its publication. Tinsley Brothers nevertheless brought out another book of his in 1872, again anonymously but without a publication subsidy. This was *Under the Greenwood Tree*, the brief, brilliant, and richly humorous idyll, subtitled 'A Rural Painting of the Dutch School', that Hardy had in part quarried (as he would later quarry portions of other novels and stories) from the otherwise abandoned manuscript of *The Poor Man and the Lady*.

Love, Courtship, and Marriage

Hardy returned to London early in 1872 in response to an invitation from T. Roger Smith, a prominent architect of the day, but was under increasing pressure to decide whether his writing should remain a part-time occupation alongside architecture or replace architecture as a full-time career. Two factors determined the choice he finally made in the summer of 1872. One was the professional status and commitment implied in an invitation from Tinsley Brothers to write a full-length serial for *Tinsleys' Magazine*. The other was the enthusiastic support of Emma Lavinia Gifford, the woman to whom he was now engaged to be married. This was not, of course, Hardy's first affair of the heart. His responsiveness to female beauty and sexuality is richly evident from his novels and stories, and his poems and reminiscences are full of direct and indirect allusions to the real or fancied love-affairs of his youth and young manhood.

He speaks, for example, of the erotic suggestiveness of Mrs Martin's silk flounces, of his fascination with the reigning village beauties of his boyhood, and of his silent adoration of Louisa Harding, the daughter of a local farmer. During his London years of the 1860s he formed an attachment, possibly amounting to a form of engagement, with a serious-minded young Dorset woman named Eliza Bright *Nicholls, who was working as a lady's maid and can with some confidence be identified with the 'She' of the 'She, to Him' sonnets. Hardy seems to have broken with Eliza before he left London in 1867—perhaps because the erosion of his religious faith had become too starkly incompatible with Eliza's evangelicalism—and to have transferred his affections shortly thereafter to his cousin Tryphena *Sparks, then in her mid-teens and pupil-teaching at the Puddletown village school.

Hardy's fond remembrance of Tryphena in the poem 'Thoughts of Phena: At News of Her Death' certainly indicates that he had come to think of her, in retrospect, as a 'lost prize', as someone whom he might have married. But there is only meagre and doubtful evidence to support past speculations as to the importance, intimacy, and consequences of the actual relationship, let alone to show why the lively and attractive Tryphena should have developed any long-term interest in a not especially prepossessing cousin eleven years her senior. Before the end of the decade Hardy had in any case become more interested in Catherine ('Cassie') *Pole, the pretty if apparently somewhat insipid daughter of the butler at West Stafford House.

All previous emotional involvements, however, were eclipsed by a romantic encounter in a tiny Cornish hamlet on 7 March 1870: the date to which Hardy's desk calendar was in his last years permanently set. He had been asked by Crickmay to inspect the badly decayed church of St Juliot, and, when he finally reached the Rectory after his long and tedious journey from Dorset, he was greeted at the door by the vividly attractive Emma Lavinia Gifford, whose older sister had recently married the elderly Rector, Caddell Holder, as his second wife. The daughter of a Plymouth solicitor (see GIFFORD FAMILY), Emma Gifford had been brought up with middle-class assumptions and expectations, only to find herself, at the age of 29, living in rural isolation, unmarried, and with few resources or prospects. Hardy, for his part, was flattered by Emma's class superiority and captivated by her social graces, flowing ringlets, and teasing flirtatiousness, especially as encountered amid the romantic wildness of the Cornish setting, and his second visit to St Juliot in the summer of 1870 was probably the occasion of their becoming engaged.

They were rarely together during the four years that intervened before their actual marriage, Emma remaining for the most part in Cornwall and Hardy in London, but Emma's genuine literary interests made a significant contribution to her side of an active correspondence and to her warm endorsement of Hardy's decision, in the summer of 1872, to undertake the *Tinsleys' Magazine* serial, and so embark upon a new career as a professional novelist. She also co-operated in the writing of the serial as it took shape as *A Pair of Blue Eyes* and evidently made no objection to Hardy's incorporation of episodes from their courtship, or to his creation of a heroine whose appearance and personality sometimes bore striking similarities to her own.

For Hardy the period was one of unexpected successes and equally unexpected disasters. Among the successes were the generally positive reviews of *A Pair of Blue Eyes* and the arrival of an invitation to write a serial for the *Cornhill Magazine*, a journal distinctly more prestigious and better-paying than *Tinsleys'*. The immediate disaster was the suicide in Cambridge in September 1873 of Horace Moule, his literary lodestar and dearest male friend, but recognizable at least in retrospect were the foreboding shadows cast over his forthcoming marriage by the unconcealed hostility of Emma's intensely class-conscious father, by his own family's opposition to the idea of his marrying 'up', or perhaps even marrying at all, and by the extent to which he felt attracted, early in 1874, to Helen *Paterson (later Helen Allingham), his *Cornhill* illustrator. The wedding itself, at the newly built (and now closed) church of St Peter's, Paddington, on 17 September 1874, was conducted by Emma's uncle, Dr Edwin Hamilton Gifford, later Archdeacon of London, but the Giffords were otherwise only minimally represented, the Hardys not at all.

Professional Novelist

The other major event of 1874 was the unexpected popularity of *Far from the Madding Crowd*, the serial Hardy had written for the *Cornhill*, then under the editorship of Leslie *Stephen. The interest aroused by its monthly serial appearances from January to December 1874 was confirmed and reinforced by the numerous and generally positive reviews that greeted its publication in volumes in November 1874. *Far from the Madding Crowd*, in short, made Hardy famous for the first time and placed him immediately in the front rank of contemporary novelists. It also served to identify him—more securely, perhaps, than would always prove convenient in later years—with rural and indeed agricultural characters and settings and with the specific fictional region that he called *Wessex and based very closely on the actual topography of his native Dorset and the counties adjacent to it. Wessex was introduced for the first time during the serialization of *Far from the Madding Crowd*, and while Hardy obviously perceived from the first the potential advantages of writing a series of linked fictions, as *Scott and Trollope had done, he can scarcely have envisaged the importance that Wessex would eventually assume in his own work, let alone the mapped permanence and visitable solidity it would attain in the popular imagination. Wessex is an ancient name, but its current acceptance as a regional designation is entirely attributable to its deployment in Hardy's novels, stories, and poems.

The Hardys' two-week honeymoon in Brighton, Rouen, and Paris was for both of them a first trip abroad (see TRAVELS, CONTINENTAL), but while Emma's lively diary of the trip (published in the volume of her *Diaries* in 1985) is full of incidental details, it unfortunately provides little insight into the relations between the couple at this early point. Upon their return to England they took rooms in a house called St David's Villa in the London suburb of Surbiton, but the location proved less convenient than anticipated, and in March 1875 they moved closer in to London, to 18 Newton Road in the Paddington area, where Hardy had lived alone during the 1860s and again in the years immediately preceding his marriage. Hardy was now writing *The Hand of Ethelberta* as a second serial for the *Cornhill*, and was profiting from Leslie Stephen's intellectual companionship even more than from his shrewd but not always sympathetic editorial advice. The shift to settings and characters predominantly urban probably reflected Hardy's desire to display his virtuosity as a professional novelist, and Stephen's disappointment in the directions the novel was taking may have influenced Hardy's decision to finish writing it in Dorset, he and Emma renting West End Cottage in the seaside resort of Swanage from July 1875 until the following spring.

Similar factors may have affected Hardy's decision to delay the start of his next book, apparently—so Lennart Björk has suggested (*LN* xx–xxi)—in order to take stock of his situation, do some reading and thinking, and reach some decisions as to the kinds of novel he wanted to write. He certainly purchased several books on philosophy and sociology in the mid-1870s and began to compile the notebooks, headed 'Literary Notes', in which (occasionally with Emma's assistance) he recorded quotations from, and notes upon, his current reading in such areas as philosophy, history, aesthetics, and literary criticism. These notebooks, kept up in some form almost to the end of his life, are movingly reflective of the continuing autodidactic strain in his intellectual background, and of his sensitivity to his lack of a university education. Though only fragments remain of the diary-pocketbooks he kept from early in his career, a few other *notebooks do survive to testify to the serious practicality with which he sought to accumulate material that might prove useful in his work.

The Hardys' departure from Swanage was followed by a brief house-hunting stay in Yeovil and a holiday (of which Emma again kept a diary) in Holland, Germany, and Belgium, Hardy's already well-developed fascination with the Napoleonic period inevitably mandating a visit to the Waterloo battlefield. In June 1876 they made what was projected as a long-term move to a newly-built semi-detached house charmingly situated on a bank overlooking the River Stour in the small north Dorset market-town of Sturminster Newton. Hardy later recalled Riverside Villa as 'their first house and, though small, probably that in which they spent their happiest days' (*LW* 115). They bought furniture for the first time, and settled quickly into the life of the town, making friends and attending local events, and Hardy eagerly explored the surrounding area of the Vale of Blackmoor, previously known to him chiefly through the poetry of William Barnes.

When, however, he began work on his next novel, *The Return of the Native*, he chose as its setting the south Dorset heathlands he had known from his childhood, emphasizing the identification by the sketch-map, disoriented but still recognizable, that he supplied as a frontispiece to the first edition. The likelihood that this gesture was related to Hardy's personal situation is strengthened by his incorporation of many of his mother's characteristics into the representation of Mrs Yeobright. Jemima Hardy's continuing disapproval of her son's marriage—despite, or perhaps because of, the visit that he and Emma made to Higher Bockhampton at Christmas 1876—may even have found its reflection in the disastrous consequences of Mrs Yeobright's hostility to her daughter-in-law.

Though rebuffed by the editors of more prestigious journals, Hardy eventually placed the serialization of *The Return of the Native* with *Belgravia*, a magazine specializing in 'sensation' fiction. By the time the first instalment appeared in January 1878 he and Emma had decided to move back to London, his sense of the professional advantages of living in the metropolis chiming, for the time being, with her desire for a wider social world. They again chose a suburban rather than a central location, and on 22 March 1878 spent their first night at 1 Arundel Terrace, Upper Tooting, not far from Tooting and Wandsworth Commons and the Wandsworth Common railway station.

It was not to prove a happy move. Hardy certainly took advantage of his nearness to London by joining the Savile Club and developing friendships with writers, editors, publishers, and artists that would be important to him in subsequent years. It is also clear from a notebook he kept at the time (published in *PN*) that the accessibility of the Reading Room of the British Museum greatly facilitated the researches into newspapers and magazines of the Napoleonic period that he was undertaking in preparation for the composition of *The Trumpet-Major*, the relatively lightweight historical novel that was serialized in *Good Words* (with occasional revisions to accommodate the religious scruples of the editor) from January to December 1880, and published in volumes in late October 1880. But difficulties were developing in the Hardys' marriage, some no doubt sexual and related to its continuing childlessness, and Tooting always remained in Hardy's memory as the place where 'their troubles began' (*LW* 128).

It was also at Arundel Terrace that Hardy suffered the serious illness, apparently originating in complications from a bladder infection, which kept him in bed, his feet raised higher than his head, for much of the autumn and winter of 1880–1. The illness struck shortly after the beginning of the serialization of *A Laodicean* in *Harper's Monthly*, and it was only Emma's assistance as nurse and amanuensis that enabled him to turn in instalments and return proofs on schedule, and so maintain his reputation for professional reliability.

The entire episode, painful and debilitating in itself (as indicated by the poem 'A Wasted Illness'), contributed significantly to the weakness of *A Laodicean* and to Hardy's association of London with ill-health and 'mechanical and ordinary productions from his pen' (*LW* 154). He and Emma therefore decided to give up the Tooting house and return once more to Dorset, and in June 1881 they rented 'Lanherne', a small detached villa in The Avenue, *Wimborne—an ancient east Dorset town that was still (like Sturminster Newton) well away from the vicinity of Bockhampton and Hardy's family. They made new friends in Wimborne, joined a Shakespeare reading group, and participated in other local activities.

There was an exciting but frustrating episode that winter when Arthur Wing Pinero's play *The Squire* was widely accused of being partly plagiarized from *Far from the Madding Crowd*, which Hardy had himself dramatized a short while before. Hardy's adaptation (see DRAMATIZATIONS), revised and rendered more melodramatic by J. Comyns Carr, was itself staged in Liverpool early in 1882 (Hardy and Emma travelling north to see the production), and later in London, but without quite matching the success of *The Squire*.

Much of the summer of 1882 was devoted to the composition of the novel *Two on a Tower* for serialization in the American-based *Atlantic Monthly*, but once the final instalment was sent off the Hardys took an extended holiday in Paris that Hardy later blamed for his failure to revise and strengthen the novel prior to its publication in volumes that October.

The Hardys made a number of visits to London in May and June of 1883, and over many subsequent years they developed a regular pattern of renting a house or apartment during the London 'season' and taking the opportunity to see friends, attend theatres, concerts, and galleries, and keep abreast of the latest metropolitan gossip, fashions, and literary trends. Hardy was a regular visitor to the Savile Club at these times, even after his election to the more prestigious but distinctly staider Athenaeum in 1891, and an occasional presence at dinners organized by ostensibly literary though primarily convivial associations such as the Rabelais Club (see CLUBS).

The Return to Dorchester

No more than Sturminster Newton did Wimborne prove a permanent solution, however, and in the summer of 1883 the Hardys moved finally to Dorchester itself, taking a rented house in Shire-Hall Lane while on the town's south-eastern outskirts Hardy's father and brother and their workmen built, slowly but solidly, the red-brick villa that Hardy had himself designed, that he lived in from the summer of 1895 until the day of his death, and that is now the property of the National Trust. The site was a one-and-a-quarter-acre plot of open downland, bare of trees, that Hardy first leased and then purchased from the Duchy of Cornwall—at some point changing its existing name, Loud's Gate, to *Max Gate, in humorous deference to the Henry Mack who had for many years operated a nearby toll-gate on the Wareham Road.

For Hardy the move had obvious creative advantages in that it returned him to the centre of the world he had known in childhood and youth and spoke directly to his already developed fascination with its history. No less importantly, his mature recognition of the centrality of Dorchester to Dorset's predominantly agricultural economy stimulated a reconception of Wessex both as a linking device for a series of distinct novels and as a means of writing authentically about the regional past. Shortly after arriving in Shire-Hall Lane he began reading his way through local newspapers of the 1820s and 1830s in preparation for the writing of *The Mayor of Casterbridge*, in which Casterbridge itself would be transparently modelled upon early 19th-century Dorchester.

The move back to Dorchester was also purposive in social terms. Hardy promptly became an active member of the Dorset County Museum (of which his old friend Henry J. Moule, one of Horace's brothers, had recently become curator), involved himself in local politics as a supporter of the Liberal party, and (perhaps as a political reward) was soon appointed a Justice of the Peace for Dorchester—a position he continued to hold and value long after he had ceased to be active politically. And Max Gate itself, though not a large house as originally built, clearly proclaimed its owner's aspirations to middle-class status by the way in which it sat securely and (until the trees that Hardy had planted grew up around it) very visibly in its own grounds. Such aspirations, however, were slow to be recognized in a place where his humbler background was well known and where many of his relatives were still living working-class lives, and Emma in particular always felt insufficiently 'accepted' by the arbiters of local and 'county' society.

Despite his constant involvement in the building of his new house, Hardy managed to complete *The Mayor of Casterbridge* well before its first serial instalment appeared in the *Graphic* in January 1886. In order to meet the perceived demands of weekly (rather than monthly) serialization in a popular magazine, he understated sexual issues and introduced excessive narrative complications, and was obliged to engage in extensive revision ahead of publication of the two-volume first edition in May of that year. The publisher's reader is said to have complained of a 'lack of gentry among the characters' (*LW* 186), and the novel, now regarded as one of Hardy's major achievements, did for some reason sell poorly at its first appearance and for a considerable time thereafter. Its successor, *The Woodlanders*, proved particularly hard to complete, perhaps because the plot-line would not admit of any ending readers were likely to find pleasing, perhaps because its central character, Giles Winterborne, shared many characteristics with Hardy's father and its setting was based on a part of Dorset intimately associated with Hardy's mother.

By mid-March of 1887, however, just as *The Woodlanders* was being published, Hardy felt free to set off with Emma on an extended visit to Italy (see TRAVELS, CONTINENTAL), most of their time being spent in Florence (where William Barnes's daughter, Lucy Baxter, was their frequent guide), Rome (where Hardy picked and sent back to his friend Edmund *Gosse some violets from Keats's grave), and Venice (where they were entertained by Browning's friend Mrs Bronson). The trip was obviously important to Hardy, and later received particularly full coverage in the autobiographical *Life*, Emma's travel diary (published in *Diaries*) providing a valuable supplement on which Hardy may himself have sometimes drawn.

Hardy had since the 1870s been publishing short stories in British and American magazines, and in 1888 he brought out *Wessex Tales*, a first collection of such stories. Another collection, *A Group of Noble Dames*, appeared in 1891, to be followed in 1894 by *Life's Little Ironies*, in 1914 by *A Changed Man and Other Tales*, and in 1992 by a final posthumous gathering of *The Excluded and Collaborative Stories*—among them the important *An Indiscretion in the Life of an Heiress*, first published in 1878, and drawn directly from *The Poor Man and the Lady*. The production and publication of such stories remained to the end of the 19th century an important element in Hardy's life and career, both as a significant source of income and as an impressive aspect of his professionalism, and although the stories themselves are of variable quality, several clearly deserve to be reckoned among his best work.

His final decade, however, as a writer of prose fiction was distinguished above all by the production of two deeply compassionate and unmistakably major novels, *Tess of the d'Urbervilles* and *Jude the Obscure*, published in 1891 and 1895 respectively. Both aroused opposition by the directness of their treatment of social issues and especially sexual relationships—portions of *Tess* were omitted prior to its serialization, while the serial version of *Jude* was extensively bowdlerized (see also CENSORSHIP)—and together they served to bring Hardy to levels both of fame and of notoriety that he had not previously known. Lionization as 'the author of *Tess*' gave him access to London social circles still more rarefied than those he had previously frequented and brought him into contact with glamorous and intelligent women who eagerly sought his company. In the late 1880s he had first pursued and then, apparently, fled from the beautiful, provocative, but socially transgressive poet Rosamund *Tomson. In the early 1890s, he fell seriously—and frustratingly—in love with the handsome but rigidly conventional Florence *Henniker, daughter of Richard Monckton Milnes (Lord Houghton), wife of a senior army officer, and author of a number of novels and short story collections. In the mid-1890s he was attracted to another beautiful woman with literary interests and ambitions, (Lady) Agnes *Grove, the daughter of General Augustus Pitt-Rivers, the archaeologist and anthropologist.

Different though these attachments were in kind and degree (his feeling for Agnes Grove was evidently no more than what he liked to call 'romantical'), there can be no doubt that his long-cherished devotion to Florence Henniker constituted a profound emotional defection from his marriage. Emma's unpredictability of temper, eccentricities of manner and dress, and growing religiosity had become an irritant to Hardy at home and an embarrassment in public, while Emma, for her part, continued to feel isolated in Dorchester, openly returned the sustained hostility of Hardy's family, and deeply resented the persistence with which Hardy himself took sides against her, walking regularly to the Higher Bockhampton cottage on Sundays even when other communication between Max Gate and the cottage had effectively been broken off. Hardy was much moved by the death of his father in 1892, but since Thomas Hardy senior had always been the member of the family least antagonistic towards Emma the feud continued unabated—as it did even after Jemima Hardy died, aged 90, in 1904, for there was still Mary Hardy, whom Emma seems to have regarded as the worst of her enemies, and the like-minded but less passionate Kate.

The situation worsened meanwhile with Emma's perception of both *Jude* and *The Well-Beloved* (the latter serialized in 1891, and revised for book publication in 1897) as attacks upon marriage and, by implication, upon herself; and although a veneer of domestic routine was maintained at Max Gate right up until the time of Emma's death, husband and wife in fact lived increasingly separate lives, Hardy secluding himself in his study for the better part of every day and Emma taking refuge in two attic rooms at the top of the house. They were as one, however, in their hatred of cruelty to animals and their particular devotion to the animals later buried in the pets' cemetery at Max Gate (see also ANIMALS, CRUELTY TO; PETS).

Farewell to Prose

In 1895–7 the London-based but American-owned firm of *Osgood, McIlvaine brought out the first collected edition of Hardy's novels and stories, and thus provided him with a welcome opportunity to revise his texts, consolidate his matured conception of his fictional region of Wessex, and write a series of retrospective prefaces (see also COLLECTED EDITIONS). It was in certain respects a farewell performance, since he effected shortly afterwards his long-contemplated return from fiction to poetry.

The hostility some critics had displayed towards his last three novels, especially *Jude the Obscure*, doubtless helped to precipitate his decision, but the principal determinants seem to have been the imminence of his 60th birthday and the enhanced sense of economic security created by the success of *Tess*, the availability of American copyright protection, and the assurance of continuing royalties from the works he had already published.

The contents of his first verse collection, *Wessex Poems*, published in 1898, showed that Hardy had not only gone back to revise some of the verses he had drafted in the 1860s, but had continued to be active as a poet during the decades publicly devoted to fiction. The result, as in several of his subsequent volumes of verse, was uneven and somewhat miscellaneous—an impression only intensified in this instance by the inclusion of a series of interesting if distinctly idiosyncratic drawings by the poet himself. Most reviewers were respectful but puzzled, and there was a good deal of criticism of what was seen as the clumsiness of Hardy's technique and the provinciality of his language.

There were no drawings in *Poems of the Past and the Present* (1901) or *Time's Laughingstocks* (1909)—nor, indeed, in any of the later verse collections—but Hardy's persistence in ranging so widely and inventively in his verse-forms and lexical choices continued to bemuse contemporary criticism and to slow his emergence as a major poet and powerful influence upon younger poets. His sensitivity to this situation was reflected in his frequent insistence, in both public and private utterances, upon the superiority of his verse to his prose.

By the time *Wessex Poems* appeared, the firm of Osgood, McIlvaine had been absorbed into the New York house of Harper & Brothers, leaving Hardy with an American publisher for his British as well as his American publications. He felt dissatisfied with this situation and in 1902 transferred all British editions of his books, both prose and verse, to the house of *Macmillan. It was a comfortable and mutually profitable relationship that lasted to the end of his life, and beyond. Macmillan published in 1912–13 (with subsequent additions) the textually significant 'Wessex Edition' of the novels and poems, followed by the de luxe 'Mellstock Edition' of 1919–20 (see COLLECTED EDITIONS).

Earlier, the firm had brought out *Time's Laughingstocks* and, in 1904, 1906, and 1908, the three distinct 'parts' of *The Dynasts*, the ambitious verse-drama that was the end-product of Hardy's long-standing fascination with the *Napoleonic Wars. *The Dynasts* met with a mixed critical reception, but its completion consolidated Hardy's reputation as the greatest British author of his day (it was in 1909 that he received the exceptional honour of appointment to the Order of Merit), and its national theme, reinforced by Harley *Granville-Barker's stage production of 1914, gained it additional respect and relevance during the First World War and for a considerable period thereafter. It has not been widely read or discussed during the last generation or two, however, and has figured only marginally in the rise in Hardy's reputation as a poet during those years.

Bereavement and Remarriage

The Hardys' marriage continued its undramatic deterioration during the Edwardian years, and as Emma became more of an invalid and recluse they kept up only intermittently the pattern of renting London accommodation every spring. Hardy himself still spent a good deal of time in London, however, and was increasingly in the company of Florence Emily Dugdale (see HARDY, FLORENCE EMILY), a young teacher and aspiring writer (chiefly of children's stories) who had first approached him as an admirer in 1905. She did typing for him, checked historical references for *The Dynasts* in the British Museum, and occasionally accompanied him to the lively intellectual gatherings hosted by Edward *Clodd, the rationalist, at his house in *Aldeburgh, on the Suffolk coast.

Whether they became lovers it is impossible to know. For a period in 1910–11 Florence Dugdale was on very friendly terms with Emma Hardy, staying at Max Gate while typing Emma's manuscripts and encouraging her literary ambitions, and going on at least one seaside holiday with her. Although (or perhaps because) Emma had been in poor health for so long, her sudden death, in November 1912, seems to have been quite unexpected. Florence Dugdale came at once to assist Hardy's sisters in running Max Gate, created some local scandal by staying on in the house for extended periods, and eventually overcame her numerous hesitations, expressed particularly in her letters to Edward Clodd, and agreed to become the second Mrs

Hardy. The marriage itself took place, in conditions of great secrecy, in the parish church of her home town of Enfield, Middlesex, on 10 February 1914. There was no honeymoon—Hardy's main concern was to rush straight back to Max Gate before the newspaper reporters got on the trail or the townsfolk of Dorchester had time to organize a civic welcome—but they did make a short trip to the Devon coast later in the month.

Hardy, meanwhile, had responded to Emma's death and the discovery of her private diaries—full of vituperative comments upon himself—by plunging into a period of profound remorse at having failed to halt the long erosion of what had begun so romantically at St Juliot that March evening more than forty years before. His rediscovered love for Emma would have its magnificent creative result in the *'Poems of 1912–13', first published in *Satires of Circumstance* in 1914. To Florence, however, it registered as a wilful act of self-laceration and as another burden to add to those she necessarily bore as the second wife of a world-famous author 38 years her senior who had long become rigidly settled into his daily domestic and working routines. Though she recognized the excellence of the 'Poems of 1912–13'—Hardy, indeed, always valued her criticisms of his work—she could not help regretting what she saw as the public exposure of her insufficiency as a substitute for her predecessor.

The early years of the marriage were saddened by the death of Hardy's much-loved sister Mary (see RELATIVES OF THOMAS HARDY) in November 1915; by the outbreak and disastrous course of the *First World War; and by the news, in August 1915, that a favourite Hardy cousin, Frank George, had been killed at Gallipoli. Hardy, so Florence reported, had imagined and confronted the war's worst possible consequences right from the start, and could therefore respond with some resilience to wartime pressures and privations; but he was already 74 years old when the war began, and as he moved through his late seventies and into his early eighties he became increasingly set in his ways: hypochondriac, though rarely ill; frugal, though financially secure; obsessively industrious, though now in his ninth decade; acutely sensitive to criticism and public opinion, though so universally admired; and deeply pessimistic, though plainly fortunate in so many aspects of his life.

Florence Hardy was in some respects well suited to cope with the special demands made upon her. She was an excellent typist, a devoted nurse, and a determined protector of her husband's privacy. But she was also depressive, insecure, quick to despair and complain, and too cruelly self-deprecating to respond well to the kind of crisis represented—for her at least—by Hardy's yearning and at times openly besotted response, extending over a period of years, to the appealing beauty of Gertrude *Bugler, the young local actress who played Eustacia Vye, Marty South, and, above all, Tess Durbeyfield in dramatizations of Hardy's novels produced by the group within the Dorchester Debating and Dramatic Society that came to be known as the *Hardy Players.

As time passed, Florence's specifically secretarial responsibilities became increasingly onerous, even though she had the assistance for a time of a young poet named May O'Rourke. Hardy's fame brought him a very large correspondence, and while he answered some letters in his own hand, replies to the others would be typed up by Florence from draft outlines her husband had supplied. She also typed up the drafts and fair copies of the many poems he was still producing, and played a crucial role, as typist and revising editor, in the secret composition of the third-person but essentially autobiographical 'Life and Work of Thomas Hardy', written by Hardy himself but always intended for posthumous publication as an official biography authored by his widow (see AUTOBIOGRAPHY). After Hardy's death the scheme was faithfully carried through. Florence, as Hardy had envisaged, made revisions, deletions, and additions to the existing text—even Hardy could not, in the nature of things, have narrated his own death—and then brought it out over her own name in two volumes: *The Early Life of Thomas Hardy* (1928) and *The Later Years of Thomas Hardy* (1930), now better known by their conflated single-volume title, *The Life of Thomas Hardy.* Because the work emanated from Max Gate, offered extensive quotations from Hardy's notebooks, and was clearly authoritative, it amply served its immediate purpose of deterring alternative biographies. Because Hardy ensured the destruction of almost all the notebooks and other materials drawn upon during its composition, it has remained important as a unique source for many aspects of Hardy's life.

Last Years

Hardy made his last visit to London in May 1920, shortly before his 80th birthday, in order to attend the wedding of Harold Macmillan and Lady Dorothy Cavendish. He remained modestly active in local Dorchester affairs thereafter, but rarely left Max Gate for more than a few hours. A large portion of each day was typically spent secluded in his study, dealing with correspondence, writing new poems, revising old drafts, and from time to time checking copy and proofs for the successive verse collections he continued to produce with a regularity altogether remarkable in a man of his years: *Moments of Vision* (1917), *Late Lyrics and Earlier* (1922), *Human Shows* (1925), and the posthumous *Winter Words* (1928), together with a carefully considered *Selected Poems* (1916), and the verse-drama called *The Famous Tragedy of the Queen of Cornwall* (1923).

At about four o'clock he customarily descended to the drawing-room to chat lightly over tea with the day's quota of visitors. Some of these were or became famous, among them Virginia *Woolf and her husband Leonard Woolf, H. G. *Wells and Rebecca West, Siegfried *Sassoon, Edmund *Blunden, Harley *Granville-Barker, Walter *de la Mare, E. M. *Forster, T. E. *Lawrence, and Sydney *Cockerell—these two last being perhaps the most frequent and most welcome. The Prince of Wales made a formal and highly publicized visit in 1924. Many callers, however, some of them Hardy or Hand cousins, came from Dorchester itself and the surrounding area, while still others were simply literary pilgrims, often from overseas, who had made their way to Max Gate in the hope of catching a glimpse of the great man and had been lucky enough to find themselves introduced into his house and his company. In the early evening he and Florence might take the dog Wessex for a short walk, and after dinner Florence would read aloud for an hour or so, generally from a recent novel, biography, or collection of essays.

Although Hardy worried a good deal about his health, he seems in his last years to have suffered little beyond colds and minor bladder problems that were perhaps related to his illness of 1881–2. He kept walking and cycling well into his eighties, performed with considerable vigour in August 1927 the laying of the foundation stone for the new Dorchester Grammar School buildings, and was welcoming visitors—including Edmund *Gosse, one of his very oldest friends—right through the autumn and early winter of that year. He seems also to have been enjoying a fresh burst of creative energy that impelled the writing of a number of new poems and the assembling of the further collective volume that became *Winter Words*. In mid-December, however, he experienced a sudden loss of energy, and by Christmas he was seriously ill. Florence's sister, Eva Dugdale, a professional nurse, soon arrived, doctors and specialists were consulted, and there seemed some hope of a recovery. On 11 January 1928 Hardy had energy enough to joke with his doctor and dictate to his wife unforgiving epitaphs on two people, George *Moore and G. K. *Chesterton, with whom he felt he had scores to settle. At nine o'clock that evening, however, he suffered a massive heart attack and died almost immediately, crying to his sister-in-law, 'Eva, what is this?'

Hardy's family had always taken it for granted that he would be buried in Stinsford churchyard, alongside his parents, his sister, and his first wife, and that seems also to have been Hardy's own wish. It was, however, the strong opinion of such influential friends as Sir James *Barrie and Sydney Cockerell (chosen by Hardy as one of his literary executors) that Hardy, despite his reputation as an agnostic, was too famous and important a figure to be allowed to rest anywhere other than in Westminster Abbey. The consent of the Dean of Westminster was quickly obtained, but protests from Dorset led to a somewhat macabre compromise by which Hardy's heart was removed, for separate interment at Stinsford, prior to the cremation of the rest of his body and Abbey burial of the ashes. The two funerals, one national, the other local, both took place on 16 January 1928. MM

Thomas Hardy, *The Life and Work of Thomas Hardy*, ed. Michael Millgate (1985).

The Collected Letters of Thomas Hardy, ed. R. L. Purdy and Michael Millgate (7 vols., 1978–88).
The Personal Notebooks of Thomas Hardy, ed. Richard. H. Taylor (1978).
The Literary Notebooks of Thomas Hardy, ed. Lennart Björk (2 vols., 1985).
The Architectural Notebook of Thomas Hardy, ed. C. J. P. Beatty (1966).
Emma Hardy Diaries, ed. Richard H. Taylor (1985).
Letters of Emma and Florence Hardy, ed. Michael Millgate (1996).
Robert Gittings, *Young Thomas Hardy* (1975).
Robert Gittings, *The Older Hardy* (1978).
Michael Millgate, *Thomas Hardy: A Biography* (1982).
Richard Little Purdy, *Thomas Hardy: A Bibliographical Study* (1954; rev. edn. 1968).

Hardy Players. Originally an offshoot of the Dorchester Debating, Literary and Dramatic Society, the amateur acting group who became popularly, and ambiguously, known as the Hardy Players staged adaptations of Hardy's fiction between 1908 and 1924. The earlier adaptations—*The Trumpet-Major* (1908 and 1912), *Far from the Madding Crowd* (1909), *The Mellstock Quire* (1910), *The Three Wayfarers* and *The Distracted Preacher* (1911), and *The Woodlanders* (1913)—were, with the exception of *The Three Wayfarers* (Hardy's own dramatic version of his short story 'The Three Strangers'), made by A. H. Evans, a Dorchester chemist, who also directed. After Evans's removal to London, responsibility for direction fell to T. H. Tilley, a monumental mason and sometime Mayor of Dorchester. During the First World War, only Hardy's patriotic compilation *Wessex Scenes from 'The Dynasts'* (1916) and a revival of *The Mellstock Quire* (1918) were staged. Fuller productions resumed with two adaptations by T. H. Tilley, *The Return of the Native* (1920) and *A Desperate Remedy* (1922). The Players' final and most ambitious productions were of plays written by Hardy himself: *The Famous Tragedy of the Queen of Cornwall* (1923) and *Tess* (1924).

Hardy's direct involvement with the Players varied, increasing as Tilley took over more responsibility and as the staging of Hardy's own plays made greater demands on the amateur actors. But his interest and willingness to advise were always far greater than he acknowledged publicly. Because of the Hardy connection, the performances received critical attention in the national press and a degree of fashionable patronage out of all proportion to the quality of the plays or expertise of the players.

The initial strength of the group resided in the dialect humour of some of the older players, such as Walter Bawler and T. H. Tilley himself. It also depended on the familiarity of local audiences with both Hardy's fiction and the actors, many of whom were quite prominent in the cultural and professional life of the community. For anyone unfamiliar with the original works, the contraction of substantial novels into stage cameos often generated somewhat opaque plot-lines. As the novels chosen moved increasingly towards high tragedy and made greater demands on the actors, reviewers became more guarded in their praise, especially after the plays began to be staged not only in Dorchester and Weymouth but also before the Society of Dorset Men in London. Particularly after the emergence into prominence of Gertrude *Bugler, playing such tragic roles as Marty South, Eustacia Vye, and Tess Durbeyfield, newspaper hyperbole often led audiences to expect more than mere amateur dramatics. But amateur they unequivocally were.

Tess was the Players' greatest triumph and inevitable swansong. Many of the original actors were no longer suited to juvenile leads, divisions had begun to appear in the group, and, in the wake of the final Hardy-authored plays, T. H. Tilley was no longer sufficiently confident to attempt further adaptations himself. Florence *Hardy was also concerned at the toll the productions were taking on Hardy's energy, as well as being alarmed by his apparent infatuation with Gertrude Bugler. But while they lasted the Hardy Players provoked considerable national attention and provided a valuable outlet for Hardy's stage interests. KW

Norman J. Atkins, *Thomas Hardy and the Hardy Players* (1980).
Gertrude Bugler, *Personal Recollections of Thomas Hardy* (1962).
Keith Wilson, *Thomas Hardy on Stage* (1995).

Harper & Brothers, American publishers, became Hardy's publishers after absorbing the firm of *Osgood, McIlvaine. Much earlier, in 1881, they had published the first American edition of *A Laodicean*, and at that time Hardy had conducted his negotiations partly through their London agent, R. R. Bowker (1848–1933). Subsequently Harper's had published American editions of *Jude the Obscure* and *The Well-Beloved*. After taking over from Osgood, McIlvaine, they published the first English and American editions of *Wessex Poems*, in connection with which they declined Hardy's offer to bear any financial loss that the volume might incur. They also published his next volume of verse, *Poems of the Past and the Present*.

Harper's themselves had gone into receivership in December 1899, but resumed business under new management in February 1900. Later in that year they brought out a sixpenny edition of *Tess of the d'Urbervilles*: Hardy reported this as 'a great commercial success' (20 July 1900: *L* ii 265), and the 100,000 copies printed were quickly sold. It was followed in 1901 by a sixpenny edition of *Far from the Madding Crowd*. Also in 1901 Hardy gave Harper's the right for three years to publish in America a cheap uniform edition of his novels and poems 'at 50 cents a volume' (*L* ii 295).

During this time much of Hardy's literary business with Harper's was conducted through their London representative, Clarence McIlvaine, though he also corresponded with J. Henry Harper (1850–1938), head of the firm and grandson of one of its founders. So far as the publication of Hardy's work in England was concerned, most of his contracts expired in April 1902; he had been feeling for some time the unsatisfactoriness of having as his sole publisher a firm based in New York, and he then—to Harper's considerable dismay—decided not to renew the contract but to transfer his affairs to the London firm of *Macmillan, who remained his publishers for the rest of his life.

Harper's did, however, issue the first American edition of the volume of short stories *A Changed Man* in 1913. They also published various magazines in which major works by Hardy had made early appearances: *The Woodlanders* and *Tess of the d'Urbervilles* had their American serialization in *Harper's Bazar*, *The Return of the Native* and *A Laodicean* likewise made their American début in *Harper's Monthly Magazine*, while *Jude the Obscure* appeared simultaneously on both sides of the Atlantic in *Harper's New Monthly Magazine*; and *Harper's Weekly* published the serial version of *The Mayor of Casterbridge* in America. Many of the stories included in *A Group of Noble Dames* also made early appearances in the firm's publications, as did several other stories and the poem 'The Abbey Mason', first printed in *Harper's Monthly Magazine* in December 1912.

Eugene Exman, *The House of Harper* (1967).
E. McC. Fleming, *R. R. Bowker: Militant Liberal* (1952).
J. Henry Harper, *The House of Harper* (1912).

Harrison, Frederic (1831–1923), author. The leading English Positivist, he was also Hardy's most important friend among the English advocates of *Positivism. Their friendship came to an end, however, in 1919, when Harrison criticized the pessimism of Hardy's *Moments of Vision* (Millgate 529), for which Hardy took him to task in the 'Apology' prefaced to *Late Lyrics and Earlier* in 1922 (see also *L* iii 230–1). Before that Hardy and Harrison had carried on a relatively regular correspondence for over twenty years (*L* ii–vi), the letters suggesting a harmony of attitudes and taste in various areas: on *Carlyle (*LN* i 255–6), political and social events (*L* iii 46), the 'Positive view of the Universe' (*L* iii 98), and, as Hardy generously wrote after reading Harrison's *Memories & Thoughts* (1906), on 'Sport, Tobacco, Church-restoration, & endless other things' (*L* iii 230).

Hardy's familiarity with Harrison's ideas was thus far from limited to the relatively few entries in the *Literary Notebooks* from between 1880 and 1882 (*LN* i 135, 146), for, as he wrote to Harrison in 1888, 'I am always glad to see anything of yours in the Reviews or elsewhere' (*L* i 176). In addition to his attendance at Newton Hall, the Positivist Society's centre from 1881 onwards, where Harrison lectured for many years, Hardy also owned and read other of Harrison's publications: for instance, his copy of *The Choice of Books and Other Literary Pieces* (1887) has several passages marked (*LN* i 255–6, 371), and he commented on *The Positive Evolution of Religion* (1913) to Harrison (*L* iv 319). Harrison's appreciation of Hardy's novels is well documented (*LN* i 312), and he complimented Hardy for being 'saturated with human and anti-theological morality'.

LAB

Harrison, Mary St Leger. See MALET, LUCAS.

Heinemann, William (1863–1920), publisher. He obtained Hardy's permission—granted after an initial refusal—to bring out a 'Popular Edition' of *Desperate Remedies* in 1892. Two years later Heinemann's control of the book was withdrawn as a result of the wish on the part of Hardy and his publishers, *Osgood, McIlvaine, for a uniform edition of his novels to be produced.

Henniker, the Hon. Florence Ellen Hungerford (1855–1923). She was the daughter of Richard Monckton Milnes, 1st Lord Houghton, who was a friend of Tennyson, Thackeray, Swinburne, and many other writers and was himself a poet and the first biographer of Keats. She married in 1882 the Hon. Arthur Henniker-Major (1855–1912), youngest son of the 4th Lord Henniker and a professional soldier who was at that time a Lieutenant in the Coldstream Guards, and who eventually rose to the rank of Major-General. With her father's encouragement she had composed poems as a young child; later she published six novels, beginning with *Sir George* in 1891, as well as short stories.

Hardy, who had known Lord Houghton in the early 1880s and was already acquainted with her brother, the 2nd Lord Houghton, met Mrs Henniker on 10 May 1892 at the Vice-Regal Lodge, Phoenix Park, Dublin. Hardy and his wife Emma had been invited there as Lord Houghton's guests, and Mrs Henniker, already an admirer of Hardy's work, was present as hostess for her brother, the then Lord-Lieutenant of Ireland. Hardy's diary of the visit is reproduced in his autobiography (*LW* 270–2), where his first impression of Mrs Henniker is of a 'charming, *intuitive* woman, apparently'. The close friendship that quickly developed is played down in the *Life*, where, as R. L. Purdy has said, Mrs Henniker is given a 'carefully inconspicuous' place (see Purdy's valuable essay printed as Appendix IV in his *Thomas Hardy: A Bibliographical Study*). They met frequently in London and elsewhere; at one time the Hennikers had a house in Southsea, and she and Hardy would meet in Winchester or Salisbury. A large number of letters were exchanged over a period of nearly thirty years. Like Hardy, she campaigned against cruelty to animals.

In 1894 she dedicated her volume of short stories *Outlines* to Hardy, who gave her a considerable amount of help and encouragement with her writing, and urged editors to accept her work. He wrote a short account of her, published anonymously in the *Illustrated London News* (18 August 1894), which refers to her 'note of individuality' and 'emotional imaginativeness' as well as, not uncritically, to her work. For their collaboration, in the year in which they first met, on the short story 'The Spectre of the Real', see UNCOLLECTED STORIES.

On Hardy's side at least, the relationship was one of profound importance, especially during the three years or so after their first meeting: indeed there is little doubt that during the first few months of their friendship he was infatuated with her and took every opportunity to contrive a meeting. Both were married, but Mrs Henniker, unlike Hardy at this period, was happily married, and his feelings were not reciprocated.

The extent of the influence exerted upon his work by these emotions and aspirations, though difficult to assess, is certainly considerable. When they first met he had just begun work on *Jude the Obscure*, and the character of Sue Bridehead, whose second name is 'Florence', is said to have been based to some extent on Mrs Henniker. She seems likely also to have been the model for the central character in the short story 'An *Imaginative Woman'. Though none of his poems specifically refers to her by name, there is good reason to believe that a significant number (including 'A Broken Appointment', 'At an Inn', 'The Division', and 'In Death Divided') refer to their relationship. While 'A Thunderstorm in Town', subtitled '(A Reminiscence: 1893)', suggests no more than a flirtation, such poems as 'A Broken Appointment' and 'In Death Divided' indicate much deeper feelings. 'At an Inn' starts by playing with the dangerous idea of their being mistaken for a couple engaged in an affair, and seems to conclude by wishing that this were indeed so; 'He Wonders About Himself', dated November 1893, expresses perplexity, and perhaps dismay, at the havoc created in his emotional life by his infatuation; 'Come Not; Yet Come!' expresses a conflict of feelings; 'The Month's Calendar' acknowledges that he can hope for no happy ending to his feelings for her, and hints that she has told him as much; and 'Last Love-Word', dated '189–' but not published until after Mrs Henniker's death, confesses that he has let his feelings get out of control and 'did not mean that this should come'. She has also been speculatively identified as the 'rare, fair woman' referred to in 'Wessex Heights', which candidly declares that 'my love for her in its fulness she herself even did not know'.

'A.H., 1855–1912' was written, evidently at the suggestion of Florence Dugdale, on the occasion of the death of Mrs Henniker's husband. Earlier, when Major Henniker was leaving for active service in South Africa, Hardy had gone to Southampton to see him off, a visit with creative results (see BOER WAR). Florence Dugdale, who subsequently became Hardy's second wife, had been brought to Max Gate by Mrs Henniker to meet him in 1904. Mrs Henniker and Hardy continued to meet until near the end of her life, and a visit that included 'a delightful drive' is recorded as late as July 1922 (*LW* 450). Less than twelve months later she was dead, Hardy copying in his diary the *Times* announcement of her death on 4 April 1923 with the comment '"After a friendship of 30 years!"' (*LW* 452).

One Rare Fair Woman: Thomas Hardy's Letters to Florence Henniker 1893–1922, ed. Evelyn Hardy and F. B. Pinion (1972).

heredity, that 'wonderful subtlety of the threads which bind flesh and flesh together' ('Lady Mottisfont', *GND*), was for Hardy a source of complex and creative feeling. Through most of his novel-writing career this focused on the privilege of pedigree. Several novels and half his short fictions take their problems and plots from socially unequal love and mixed heredity. The opening image of *An Indiscretion in the Life of an Heiress* is of Geraldine unattainably reclined under 'a vast marble monument, erected to the memory of her ancestors'. Most of the *Group of Noble Dames* stories, written to give human colour to the 'pedigrees of our county families', are of love across the boundaries of birth and its consequences for the next generation, as are 'The Waiting Supper' (*CM*), 'The Romantic Adventures of a Milkmaid' (*CM*), 'The Son's Veto' (*LLI*), and others.

Clearly Hardy was fascinated by inherited privilege, especially in well-dressed and educated women. Equally clearly he disapproved of it, a common ambivalence in England. He declared himself politically 'opposed to aristocratic privilege' (*LW* 213), and habitually mocked those who claimed it, though reserving his strongest mockery for those who invented their claims, like Mrs Troyton's 'raked up pedigree as long as my walking-stick' (*PBE* 12), or Simon Stoke 'constructing his family tree' as a 'work of imagination' (*TDU* 5). The glamour of pedigree is destructive to those it attracts: to Melbury and his daughter, seduced by Fitzpiers's 'poor old ramshackle family' (*W* 25); to John Durbeyfield and his daughter, deluded by a spoon and a vault; and to Timothy Petrick and his son, whom he ceases to love on discovering that he is not, after all, the natural son of an aristocrat imbued with 'hereditary force and brilliancy' ('Squire Petrick's Lady', *GND*). Hardy purported to prefer Miller Loveday's plain pedigree, which 'ascertained that Mr Loveday's great-grandparents had been eight in number'; though even there, in *The Trumpet-Major*, he could not resist a role for his own illustrious naval ancestor (see HARDY, SIR THOMAS MASTERMAN).

The most sustained attacks on aristocratic presumptions are *The Hand of Ethelberta*, which satirizes the belief that personal worth and grace can be found 'only in those whose vestibules are lined with ancestral mail', Ethelberta mockingly vowing to 'get a Herald to invent an escutcheon of my family, and throw a genealogical tree into the bargain' (*HE* 1, 24); and *A Laodicean*, where Paula must choose between Somerset's 'nobility of talent and enterprise', with his 'intellectual line of descent' as an architect, and her predilection for 'hoary medieval families with ancestors in alabaster and primogenitive renown' and the allure of de Stancy's 'tentacle from their genealogical tree' (*AL* 1.24, 3.5, 5.7, 3.2).

The Dynasts, too, takes its ironic title from Napoleon's betrayal of his egalitarian principles, and some of its most dramatic scenes from his pathetic hereditary hopes for his sickly son. Josephine expresses the meritocratic George Somerset argument: 'value best | That high heredity from brain to brain | Which supersedes mere sequences of blood' (*D* 2.2.6).

In late 1890 Hardy's preoccupation with pedigree became a more scientifically informed interest in heredity, when he read *Essays on Heredity* by the German neo-Darwinian August Weismann (*LW* 240). Anticipating modern genetics, Weismann postulated the 'germ plasm' as the immutable conveyor of inherited traits and impulses across the generations. This entered Hardy's revisions of the manuscript of *Tess of the d'Urbervilles* in the drastically heightened emphasis on the heroine's ancestry. Additions included the title, the opening on Parson Tringham's revelation, the spurious kinship between heroine and villain, the visit to the family's vault as the nadir of their fortune, the arrogant d'Urberville portraits at Wellbridge, and the ironic obituary comment that 'the d'Urberville knights and dames slept on in their tombs unknowing'.

Jude the Obscure and *The Well-Beloved*, too, are deeply concerned with heredity, the latter almost emblematically. So are the poems 'Heredity', 'The Pedigree', 'Family Portraits', 'Old Furniture', and 'Sine Prole'. These all set the value of individual feeling in dynamic tension against its negation by genetic conditioning. Thus Tess's defiance of Alec with the gauntlet may be merely a 'recrudescence' from 'her armed progenitors', Jude's misery is ordained by a family 'not made for wedlock' and a son impelled by a 'ground swell from ancient years of night', Pierston is entrapped by 'hereditary persistence', and the poet in 'The Pedigree' is abased to discover that 'I am the merest mimicker and counterfeit!— | Though thinking, "I am I, | And what I do I do myself alone"' (*TDU* 47; *JO* 1.3, 5.3; *WB* 2.6). One variant of this conditioning is the decay of family energies, which afflicts Tess, Jude, and de Stancy. The 'ancestor-worship' of Hardy's later years mixed pride that he 'derived from the Jersey le Hardy's' with the belief that he suffered from their 'spent social energies' (Millgate 566, 519).

Heredity's irrepressible power is dramatized in scenes where inherited features assert themselves: in sleep, when Henchard recognizes Newson's face in Elizabeth-Jane's; in seasickness, 'revealing a strange pantomime of the past' in the face of Millborne's daughter ('For Conscience' Sake'); and on first encounter, as when Sue meets Little Father Time and cries, '"I see you in him!"' (*JO* 5.3). Hardy's macabre language implies that the living are being controlled by the dead: 'buried genealogical facts, ancestral curves, dead men's traits' (*MC* 19); 'the spectral presence of entombed and forgotten ancestors' ('For Conscience' Sake', *LLI*); 'the family face; | Flesh perishes, I live on...' ('Heredity'); 'the spectral past' ('Sine Prole'). It is a ghoulish subtext to a scientific idea.

Hardy adopted the science of heredity in part as a new kind of tragic determinism, replacing the 'deus ex machina' or Wheel of Fortune. But genetic predisposition is never his whole story. 'An Imaginative Woman' (which may also derive from Weismann) affirms the shaping power of individual desire (*LLI*). In *Tess* and *Jude* he makes effectively an existentialist cry of defiance on behalf of the individual. Tess is Tess, with 'her precious life' (*TDU* 25), as well as 'of the d'Urbervilles'. Hardy never resolved this conflict, but some of his best fiction and poetry emerged from confronting it. RR

J. O. Bailey, 'Ancestral Voices in *Jude the Obscure*', in Howard M. Harper and Charles Edge (eds.), *The Classic British Novel* (1972).

Peter Morton, *The Vital Science: Biology and the Literary Imagination* (1984).

Roger Robinson, 'Hardy and Darwin', in Norman Page (ed.), *Thomas Hardy: The Writer and His Background* (1980).

August Weismann, *Essays on Heredity*, 2 vols. (English translation 1889, 1892).

Hicks, John (1815–69), Dorchester architect. On 11 July 1856, soon after his sixteenth birthday, Hardy was articled to Hicks for three years. The *Life* (*LW* 31) represents Hicks as a business associate of Hardy's father, and suggests that Hicks became interested in Hardy after observing him assist on a survey. Hicks's practice, on the ground floor of 39 South Street, Dorchester, was congenially sited (next door to William *Barnes's school) and sympathetically staffed: Hicks was genial, well-educated, informal, and indulgent, whilst Hardy soon struck up with a fellow-pupil, Henry *Bastow, one of his earliest and closest friendships. Hicks, the son of a clergyman, specialized in ecclesiastical architecture, more specifically construction and restoration in the Gothic style. Hardy's own specialism was thus (not necessarily unwillingly) determined. Commissions on which Hicks worked during Hardy's time with him included churches at Athelhampton, Bridport (St Mary's), Coombe Keynes, Dorchester (St Peter's), Powerstock, Rampisham, and Shipton Gorge: some of the reports on these projects that appeared in the *Dorset County Chronicle* are thought to have been written by Hardy. Hardy's responsibilities as an articled pupil would have included making measurements and surveys: Hicks particularly valued Hardy's gifts as a draughtsman, and Hardy copied or traced existing plans as well as 'improving'—that is, adding detail to—Hicks's initial sketches.

Hardy's articles with Hicks were extended for a further year on account of Hardy being considered young for his years; Hardy entered Hicks's employment as a paid assistant in the summer of 1860 and remained with the practice until departure for London in April 1862. Hicks supplied letters of introduction which brought Hardy to the attention of Arthur *Blomfield, and when Hardy decided to leave Blomfield's London practice in July 1867, Hicks offered him employment as an assistant with church restoration projects, the terms being favourably arranged to allow Hardy opportunity for time in which to write. On Hicks's death the work of his practice was taken over by G. R. *Crickmay. The poem 'The Abbey Mason' is dedicated to Hicks. In 1927, Florence Hardy noted Hardy's comment that 'if he had his life over again he would prefer to be a small architect in a country town, like Mr Hicks at Dorchester' (*LW* 478). TRH

Higher Bockhampton is the name of the hamlet, hardly more than a handful of houses along a side-lane leading nowhere, in which Hardy was born. It is a part of the parish of *Stinsford, only three or four miles or so from the county town of *Dorchester, but remote enough in the 1840s. On the earliest Ordnance Survey map of 1811 it is called New Bockhampton, and there were then only three houses along the lane, of which the Hardys' was the first to be built, at the beginning of the century. Lines from Hardy's youthful poem 'Domicilium' give some sense of how isolated it was:

That road a narrow path shut in by ferns,
Which, almost trees, obscured the passer-by.
Our house stood quite alone....
Snakes and efts
Swarmed in the summer days, and nightly bats
Would fly about our bedrooms.

However, the place was ripe for expansion, and by the time Hardy was growing up there were eight dwellings in what was known as Cherry Alley. Hardy describes the lane on the first page of his autobiography: 'The domiciles were quaint, brass-knockered, and green-shuttered then, some with green garden doors and white balls on the post, and mainly occupied by lifeholders of substantial footing like the Hardys themselves.' This page also has a description of Hardy's birthplace itself; the Dewys' house in *Under the Greenwood Tree* is a version of the same building, and the parish of Mellstock in that novel closely resembles Stinsford.

Nowadays the hamlet is much visited, since Hardy's birthplace is owned by the National Trust and is open to the public. The house remains much as it was in the 1840s, and is still the last in the lane, which still peters out into fragments of heathland, though much of the land is now under Forestry Commission plantation. SJG

history. Although not a historical writer in the vein of Sir Walter *Scott, Hardy was nevertheless deeply interested in history, both as a record of the individual, communal, national, global, and indeed cosmic past, and as a continuous process of adaptation and change operating throughout time according to unchanging principles that define and shape the present and the future in the same way as they defined and shaped the past. In consequence, some of his works, such as *The Mayor of Casterbridge* and *Tess of the d'Urbervilles*, are in many ways historical works in the sense that they offer, in their descriptions of the agricultural communities of *Wessex, a paradocumentary analysis of the socio-historical reality of 19th-century rural England in transition from its traditional pre-industrial ways, symbolically represented by Michael Henchard and Tess Durbeyfield, to the world of modernity epitomized by Donald Farfrae and Alec (Stoke) d'Urberville.

On the other hand, in some of the works of an ostensibly 'historical' nature, such as the stories of 'The Lady Icenway', 'Squire Petrick's Lady' (both in *GND*), and 'Master John Horseleigh, Knight' (*CM*), the historical setting plays a comparatively minor role, functioning as an attempt to remain formally faithful to the context of the anecdotes Hardy used as his source material rather than offering insights into patterns of living and thinking distinctively different from those characteristic of more modern times.

Hardy's interest in history dates back to the years of his childhood, in particular to his family traditions and to the memories of the past, going back to the late 18th century, told to him by his grandmother, Mary Hardy (see RELATIVES OF THOMAS HARDY). Throughout his life, Hardy maintained that he was descended from the Jersey le Hardy family, whose members had settled in Dorset in the 15th century; whether or not that had been the case, the supposed connection provided him with an important sense of personal link with local and indeed national history, which manifested itself in his literary work as well as in his private and public life. That earlier Sir Thomas *Hardy who was captain of the *Victory* appears as a character in both *The Trumpet-Major* and *The Dynasts*, while an even earlier Thomas *Hardy, the 16th-century founder and benefactor of the Dorchester Grammar School, was the subject of an address Hardy gave a few months before his death at the ceremony of the laying of the foundation stone of the school's new buildings (see SPEECHES). It was also the importance for Hardy of that sense of a personal link with the past that accounted for the antiquarian zeal with which he noted anecdotes, stories, and recollections of countless anonymous informants remembering, in their old age, times as distant as the late 18th century and the period of the Napoleonic Wars—among them, local people from around Dorset, and retired soldiers, including Chelsea pensioners.

Hardy's appreciation of the direct, tangible presence of the past in the modern world is evident also in his attitude to the documents of history, whether material—fossils, prehistoric artefacts, sites of historical interest, ancient buildings—or non-material, such as legends, customs, beliefs, and traditions, many of them rooted in local Dorset folklore but others, such as changing forms of linguistic usage or patterns of Christian liturgy, deriving from a variety of other spheres of historical experience. In Hardy's opinion, the duty of the modern age is to protect, record, and preserve those relics of history, not only out of a sense of reverence for their antiquity but because of the baggage of associations they carry with them. He expresses the view in the context of his favourite subject of architecture: 'The protection of an ancient edifice against renewal in fresh materials is, in fact, even more of a social—I may say a humane—duty than an aesthetic one. It is the preservation of memories, history, fellowship, fraternities' ('Memories of Church Restoration'). Hardy's co-operation with the Society for the Protection of Ancient Buildings was but one of the forms in which his antiquarian zeal expressed itself.

For all the importance for Hardy of the local, personal, immediate aspects of history, his detailed factual knowledge of the past derived predominantly from his reading, both of the classics of British historiography such as Gibbon and Macaulay and of books more directly pertinent to his specific interests, such as John *Hutchins's *The History and Antiquities of the County of Dorset* (1773) and histories of the Napoleonic era, including C. H. Gifford's *History of the Wars of the French Revolution* (1817) and Adolphe Thiers's *Histoire du Consulat et de l'Empire* (1845–62). Those works in which the historical background is re-created in most detail, *The Trumpet-Major* and *The Dynasts*, required further research: the evidence of Hardy's literary and personal notebooks, specifically of the 1878–9 notebook he used while working on the background to *The Trumpet-Major* (see NOTEBOOKS), demonstrates the comprehensiveness of his study of the period around 1804–5, in which the action of the novel is set. Gathering his evidence from the national and local press as well as from historical and biographical sources, Hardy notes details of matters as diverse as George III's visits to Weymouth, the internal structure and regulations of army regiments stationed in Dorchester, and details of women's fashions current at the time. The preparations for the writing of *The Dynasts* involved further work, which included, apart from extensive library research, careful on-site study of the field of the Battle of Waterloo.

Largely as a result of the extensive knowledge of the past that Hardy had acquired over the years, the range of historical reference in his writings is remarkably broad, extending from the prehistoric, indeed cosmic, past to a comprehensive presentation of Wessex at a number of points throughout the 19th century. Hardy is aware of the relative insignificance of the timescale of human history when perceived against the context of what could be labelled cosmic time and geological time—the temporal perspectives of, respectively, scenes involving the Spirits in *The Dynasts* and the cliff-hanging scene in *A Pair of Blue Eyes* (22).

In a rather similar way, Hardy is aware of the insignificance of personal histories when perceived against the context of the history of the human race, expressed in terms of what could in turn be described as archaeological time and ethnological time. The former perspective, conveyed primarily through references to the history of Roman Britain, is particularly evident in *The Mayor of Casterbridge* and, in a less solemn way, in 'A Tryst at an Ancient Earthwork' (*CM*) and poems such as 'Aquae Sulis' (*SC*). As for the perspective of ethnological time, contrasting the transitoriness of the individual human existence with the continuity of the life of the community, it finds its best expression in the Egdon Heath chapter of *The Return of the Native* (1.1), though echoes of it can be heard elsewhere—for example, in the history of Tess Durbeyfield (especially the scene of her seduction/rape, *TDU* 11), or in the presentation of the patterns of life in the Isle of Slingers in *The Well-Beloved*.

The variety of historical timescales adopted by Hardy stands in direct contrast to the comparative narrowness of his range of locations: Hardy's history remains first and foremost local history, not only when it concerns the family histories of the Wessex nobility (*A Group of Noble Dames*) or the archaeological past of local historical landmarks ('A Tryst at an Ancient Earthwork'), but also when it becomes a reflection of national or global history. Whatever happens beyond the borders of Wessex only becomes part of Hardy's world when it begins to materialize in Casterbridge or on Egdon Heath, whether by directly affecting the lives of local people or, if those are no longer available for Hardy's scrutiny, by leaving marks on the landscape. Roman Britain exists for Hardy in so far as it produced roads still used by the people of Egdon (*RN* 1.1) and the ancient amphitheatre of Dorchester/Casterbridge ('Maumbury Ring'; *MC* 11); the Arthurian legend is for him not so much an intercultural medieval myth as a local story of Lyonnesse (*The Famous Tragedy of the Queen of Cornwall*); even Hardy's admiration for the splendours of medieval architecture is mediated through the story of the architect who, in designing the church that was later to become Gloucester Cathedral, invented Perpendicular Gothic ('The Abbey Mason', *SC*). Echoes of the Civil War are heard in the story of 'Anna, Lady Baxby' (*GND*) and echoes of the Monmouth Rebellion in 'The Duke's Reappearance' (*CM*). In Hardy's own time, the drama of the *Boer War comes alive as the reader is presented with the images of South Africa-bound ships departing from Southampton ('Embarcation', 'Departure', 'The Colonel's Soliloquy', all *PPP*) and of Wessex people dying and buried far from their homes ('Drummer Hodge', *PPP*), while some of the most tragic ironies of the First World War are brought to the fore as Hardy points out the similarities between ancient linguistic forms typical of the Wessex dialect on the one hand and modern German on the other ('The Pity of It', *MV*).

A similar pattern characterizes much of Hardy's presentation of the Napoleonic era (see NAPOLEONIC WARS). *The Trumpet-Major* is indeed a Wessex novel first and a historical novel second; its meticulous re-creation of period detail serves the purpose of enhancing the qualities of the story as a costume drama, with the events of the war offering some extra background colour as well as a useful mechanism ensuring that characters can enter and exit as the novel's romantic plot requires. However, the perspective of the novel remains curiously provincial. Much the same approach is adopted in the short stories and poems set in or alluding to the same period: 'A Tradition of Eighteen Hundred and Four', 'The Melancholy Hussar of the German Legion' (both *WT*), 'The Grave by the Handpost', 'A Committee-Man of "the Terror"' (both *CM*), 'San Sebastian', 'Leipzig', 'The Peasant's Confession', 'The Alarm' (all *WP*), etc. In all of them the context of one of the most dramatic periods in European history provides little more than a background for an evocation of personal memories, a colourful anecdote, or an account of curious emotional experiences or of a bizarre coincidence—in the majority of cases more or less firmly embedded in the local context of Wessex.

To a certain extent, the same method is applied in *The Dynasts*: the most colourful and in many ways the most appealing scenes of Hardy's 'epic-drama' are set among ordinary people, civilians and soldiers, in Wessex, London, and on the Continent. Here, however, Hardy's objective goes far beyond attempting to create a period piece or to tell a picturesque tale. The scenes set among the peasants of Wessex, together with those involving the monarchs, politicians, and generals from all sides of the conflict, from George III to Napoleon and Alexander of Russia, from Pitt to Talleyrand and Metternich, and from Nelson and Wellington to Murat, Blücher and Kutúzof, make up a composite picture not just of modern Europe at a critical moment of its political and military history but of all humanity, presented as one living organism, in the context of all time.

The cosmic overview of the events presented, afforded to the reader by the Phantom Intelligences, reduces the royals and the usurpers, the heroes and the cowards, the powerful and the powerless alike to mere ignorant puppets acting out the designs of the Immanent Will, which 'works unconsciously, as heretofore | Eternal artistries in Circumstance' (*D* 1, Fore Scene). History, then, is not the creation of humans—'shapes that bleed, mere mannikins or no, | [of whom] each has parcel in the total Will' (ibid.): it is ruled by some form of fate, over the direction of which neither individuals nor masses have power or influence—until, that is, a conscious effort of all humanity to achieve 'loving-kindness' leads to universal peace, with 'consciousness the Will informing, till It fashion all things fair' (*D* iii After Scene). JJ

Samuel Hynes, 'Hardy's Historians', *THA* 5 (1987).

R. J. White, *Thomas Hardy and History* (1974).

Hoare, Alda, Lady (1861–1947). One of the high-born ladies (the group also including Florence *Henniker and Mary *Jeune) whom Hardy numbered among his close friends in his later years, she was the wife of Sir Henry Hoare (1865–1947), 6th Baronet, of Stourhead, the magnificent house and estate in Wiltshire, where Hardy and his new wife Florence spent a weekend in the summer of 1914. The Hoares' only son was killed in action in 1917. Lady Hoare shared Hardy's concern for the suffering of animals, and campaigned for the reform of slaughterhouses. She became a confidante of Florence *Hardy: see, for example, a revealing letter from Florence concerning her relationship to Hardy (Millgate 499–500), and another letter throwing light on Hardy's important but mystifying poem 'Wessex Heights' (excerpted in Gittings, *The Older Hardy*, 87).

Hobbes, John Oliver, pseudonym of Pearl Craigie (1867–1906), née Richards. She was active during the 1890s as a novelist, dramatist, critic, and journalist. Born in Massachusetts of American parents who later settled in London, she married in 1887 but left her husband in 1890, securing a divorce in 1895; unhappy marriage is a recurring theme in her fiction. In 1895 she wrote to Hardy, praising his handling of the 'marriage question' in *Jude the Obscure*; a few weeks later, however, she told Florence *Henniker that she had found the 'bedroom scenes' in that novel 'profoundly unpleasant'. She had met Hardy in 1893, two years after the successful appearance of her own first novel, *Some Emotions and a Moral*: recalling their first meeting, Hardy later described her as 'that brilliant woman' (*LW* 272). Subsequently they met on various social occasions, and were fellow-guests at the homes of Mrs Henniker and Lady *Jeune; on the latter occasion they took a long walk together in the course of which she told Hardy of her conversion to Roman Catholicism. In June 1895 she visited the Hardys at their London flat. After her death, Hardy praised her 'intellectual brilliancy' and remembered her as 'entertaining and ebullient' (*L* iii 221, 239). He was present at the unveiling of a memorial to her at University College London in July 1908. Earlier (6 December 1906) he had sent to her father the letters he had received from her.

J. M. Richards, *The Life of John Oliver Hobbes, Told in Her Correspondence with Numerous Friends* (1911).

Holst, Gustav (1874–1924), English composer of Swedish extraction, closely involved in the English folksong revival. His early *Six Baritone Songs*, Op. 15 (1902–3), includes settings of three poems by Hardy; when one of them, 'The Sergeant's Song' (based on lines in Chapter 5 of *The Trumpet-Major*), was published, Holst sent a copy to Hardy, who later sent the composer a presentation copy of *Time's Laughingstocks*, evidently in the hope that he might find material therein for further musical settings.

Holst visited Hardy at Max Gate in April 1922, and again on 9 August 1927. The invitation for the second visit was prompted by Holst's request to dedicate to Hardy his tone-poem *Egdon Heath*, Op. 47, inspired by the opening chapter of *The Return of the Native* as well as by a walking tour in the Egdon Heath area at Easter 1926. Hardy gave permission, but never heard the piece, which was first performed a few weeks after his death. Holst paid tribute to Hardy's personal qualities in a lecture delivered at Harvard University in 1932.

Holt, Henry (1840–1926), American publisher. He met Hardy in July 1879 at a garden party at the home of the publisher Alexander Macmillan, on which occasion they had a conversation about British and American spelling and idiom (*LW* 131). Well before this date, however, they had had a quite extensive business relationship. Five years earlier Holt had published the first American edition of Hardy's first novel, *Desperate Remedies*, some bowdlerization of the text of which had been undertaken by Hardy at Holt's request. Even earlier, Holt's New York firm had produced in its 'Leisure Hour' series editions of *Under the Greenwood Tree* (June 1873)—which thus became the first of Hardy's novels to appear in America—and *A Pair of Blue Eyes* (July 1873); other novels later appeared in the same series. In November 1875 Holt had arranged for the publication in America of Hardy's first poem to appear in print, 'The Fire at Tranter Sweatley's', later retitled 'The Bride-Night Fire' (in *Appletons' Journal*, simultaneously with British publication), and in May 1876 his firm had brought out the American edition of *The Hand of Ethelberta*. Later, in May 1886, Holt & Co. was to publish the American edition of *The Mayor of Casterbridge* very shortly after the novel's first appearance in volume form in England.

Holt thus played an important role in establishing Hardy's American readership and reputation, and the royalty of 10 per cent on the retail price of these editions (Millgate 197) must have been a useful addition to his income in his early years as a professional author. Hardy enjoyed a good working relationship with Holt, and his published correspondence includes letters to him.

homes. Hardy was born, and spent the first 21 years of his life, at the cottage in *Higher Bockhampton, in the parish of *Stinsford, Dorset, and some three miles from *Dorchester, that now belongs to the National Trust (open to visitors). It had been built about 1801 by his great-grandfather John Hardy for his son Thomas, who had married Mary Head (see RELATIVES OF THOMAS HARDY), and it had been occupied by the Hardy family ever since. The cottage stood on the Kingston Maurward estate, which in 1835 granted a new lease on the lives of Thomas Hardy, the writer's grandfather, and his two sons (one of the latter being the writer's father)—an arrangement that must have fuelled Hardy's interest in the system of 'lifehold' occupancy, used as a plot-device in *The Woodlanders* and elsewhere.

Its position was isolated and on the very edge of the heathland that, as *Egdon Heath, plays an important role in *The Return of the Native* and other novels. The original structure was smaller than the cottage we see today, with an interior somewhat differently arranged, extensions having been made shortly before Hardy's birth and other structural alterations taking place during his childhood. The cottage continued to be occupied by members of the Hardy family until 1913, completing an unbroken period of well over a century.

Hardy moved to London in April 1862, and lived at first in lodgings in a house (now demolished) in Clarence Place, Kilburn, sharing rooms with a fellow-architect employed in the offices of Arthur *Blomfield.

Kilburn, now a North London suburb, then still retained a semi-rural character. In the following year Hardy moved to 16 Westbourne Park Villas, Bayswater, a more convenient location for central London, and also very close to the house in which Eliza *Nicholls was working. This quite handsome house still stands, marked by a commemorative plaque, and the address is a familiar one to readers of Hardy's early poems, several of which carry an appended note referring to it (sometimes abbreviated to 'W.P.V.'). It evidently suited him well, since he remained there until his return in July 1867 to Dorset.

For the next couple of years he lived in his old home, until moving in the spring of 1869 to 3 Wooperton Street, *Weymouth, after joining the firm of G. R. *Crickmay in that seaside town. There much of *Desperate Remedies* was written as well as a number of poems marked 'Weymouth'. The next twelve months were mostly spent in Weymouth, though he was back at his parents' home for a time in February 1870, and in the following month made his momentous visit to St Juliot, Cornwall. On 16 May 1870 he returned to London, lodging now at 23 Montpelier Street, off the Brompton Road. On 30 March 1871 he resumed work for Crickmay in Weymouth, returning to his former lodgings in Wooperton Street but later apparently moving to 1 West Parade nearby. By the early spring of 1872, however, he was back in London, now at 4 Celbridge Place (now part of the Porchester Road and numbered 50), not far from his former lodgings in Westbourne Park Villas. There he lived on and off until September 1874, with periods spent in Bockhampton and Cornwall during this time.

His marriage to Emma Gifford at St Peter's Church, Paddington, on the 17th of that month inaugurated a new phase of his life, but did not put an end to his somewhat unsettled existence. Indeed, it seems curious that Hardy, to whom place, habit, tradition, and association meant so much, should have waited until he was in his forties before acquiring a home of his own. For some years, the couple do not seem even to have possessed any furniture. Economic factors were partly involved, but Hardy seems also to have been unsure about the most desirable location for a professional author. As Fran Chalfont has pointed out, it is also significant that the various temporary homes they occupied in Dorset during their early married life were all at some distance from the homes of Hardy's relatives, with some of whom his wife was not on good terms.

After returning from their honeymoon in France, they lived first (from October 1874) in furnished rooms at a house called St David's Villa in Hook Road, Surbiton, Surrey, then an outlying suburb of London. After nearly six months there they moved, in March 1875, to rooms in 18 Newton Road, Westbourne Grove—much closer to central London, and familiar ground for Hardy, since it was close to his old lodgings in Westbourne Park Villas. Within a few months, however, they decided to leave London, and after some fruitless house-hunting in other Dorset towns settled, in July 1875, in the coastal resort of Swanage. Their rented home there, West End Cottage (still standing), is the scene of the poem 'The Lodging-House Fuchsias', and is also depicted in *The Hand of Ethelberta*, which was completed during their residence. Delightful as this spot sounds, the Hardys were there no more than eight or nine months, moving in March 1876 to lodgings at 7 St Peter's Street, Yeovil, a terraced house now demolished. Then, understandably tired after nearly two years of marriage of living among other people's possessions, and perhaps also prompted by 'hints from relatives' that they 'appeared to be wandering about like two tramps' (*LW* 114), they made a further move within Dorset, to Sturminster Newton, where they took a 'pretty cottage overlooking the Dorset Stour' (ibid., and see also the poem 'Overlooking the River Stour'). This was the semi-detached Riverside Villa (still standing), which remained their home for nearly two years from 3 July 1876, and it was there that *The Return of the Native* was written.

The Hardys seem to have been happy in Sturminster Newton, perhaps happier than anywhere else, but Hardy clearly was in two minds about the wisdom of a successful novelist burying himself in the country, and very early in 1878 he was contemplating a move back to London. In February he signed a three-year lease on 1 Arundel Terrace (now 172 Trinity Road, and marked with a plaque) in the South London suburb of Upper Tooting, and very close to Wandsworth Common. They moved in at the beginning of

April and remained there until their final return to Dorset in 1881. *The Trumpet-Major* was written at Upper Tooting, and poems such as 'Snow in the Suburbs' and 'Beyond the Last Lamp' (the latter subtitled 'Near Tooting Common') reflect this period of suburban residence.

When the lease ran out, they once again returned to Dorset, at first to *Wimborne, where from June 1881 they rented 'Lanherne', 16 Avenue Road, a detached red-brick house still standing. Though still not home-owners, the Hardys had definitely moved up in the scale of dwellings, from furnished rooms to small houses, and now to a dignified middle-class residence. But before the end of 1882 Hardy was expressing concern that their proximity to the River Stour was unhealthy (to Edmund Gosse, *L* i 110), and declaring his intention of leaving Wimborne. In any case he was now a well-established writer who could afford to own his own home; for deeper reasons, too, he at last felt ready to return to the neighbourhood in which he had grown up; and he took the decision, natural in one who had practised the architect's profession for some fourteen years, to design a house for himself. The result was *Max Gate, where he was to live for the rest of his life.

On 30 November 1882, after considering other sites on the edge of the county town, he applied to the Duchy of Cornwall for a 99-year lease in order to erect, on land on the Wareham Road, on the outskirts of Dorchester, 'a villa Residence and Offices, Stabling, etc.... to cost £1000 at least'. On June 1883 the Hardys moved from Wimborne to Dorchester in order the more conveniently to supervise the work, renting a temporary home in Shire-Hall Lane, near the centre of Dorchester; and it was there that Hardy's Dorchester novel, *The Mayor of Casterbridge*, was written. But it was nearly twelve months from the date of application before the lease went into effect, and building work did not begin until the end of November 1883. It was 29 June 1885 before the Hardys slept there for the first time.

Opinions have differed concerning the architectural merits and general atmosphere of Max Gate (the name was originally Mack's Gate, after a Dorchester toll-keeper), but by the standards of its period it seems to have been a reasonably handsome, dignified, and comfortable house set in a large garden (later somewhat darkened by the two or three thousand trees that Hardy planted). There were subsequent alterations and extensions to the interior. The house is now in the hands of the National Trust (open to the public). During the Max Gate years Hardy regularly spent part of the year in London, roughly corresponding to the social 'season', until he was too old to do so: his numerous rented homes there, beyond the scope of this entry, are described in the third of a series of well-illustrated articles by Fran Chalfont (*THJ* 8–9, 1992–3), which provide fuller information on virtually all of Hardy's homes and temporary residences.

honours. Hardy, who left school at 16, and whose last novel bitterly attacks the inequality of educational opportunity, was the recipient of many academic honours in his later years. He accepted an honorary degree (LL.D.) from Aberdeen University in 1905; another (Litt.D.) from Cambridge in 1913, becoming an honorary fellow of Magdalene College, Cambridge, in the same year; and a D.Litt. from Oxford in 1920, becoming an honorary fellow of Queen's College in that university two years later. In March 1922 he accepted an LL.D. degree from St Andrews, and in July 1925 a Litt.D. from Bristol; his age made it impossible for these awards to be conferred in person, but on the latter occasion a deputation from the University performed the ceremony in private at Max Gate. The outstanding national recognition of his pre-eminence, however, was the award of the Order of Merit in 1910. Announced in the Birthday Honours List of 9 July (the Prime Minister's letter conveying the news to Hardy is dated one week earlier), this came only a few weeks after Hardy's 70th birthday and only two months after the accession of George V. (Unlike most national honours, the Order of Merit is bestowed as the personal gift of the sovereign.) It has been suggested that this honour was prompted by the vast and widely acclaimed achievement of *The Dynasts*, publication of which had been completed in 1908. When Hardy attended the investiture on 19 July, his wife Emma did not accompany him, but instructed Florence Dugdale (later Florence Hardy) to ensure that he was correctly attired for the occasion. Earlier, in November 1908, he had declined the offer of a knighthood from the then Prime Minister, H. H. Asquith (though his initial response to Asquith's letter of 2 November had been to ask for time to consider the matter). Later in 1910, he was given (16 November) the freedom of the Borough of Dorchester (see SPEECHES): this 'meant more to him, precisely because it was local, than any national or international recognition could do' (Millgate 471).

For speculations on Hardy's failure to receive the Nobel Prize for Literature, or to be appointed Poet Laureate after the death of Alfred Austin in 1913, see the conclusion of the article on *TIME'S LAUGHINGSTOCKS*.

Hope, Laurence, pseudonym of Adela (also known as Violet) Nicolson (1865–1904), poet. She came from an army family, and spent much of her short life in India, having married in 1889 Malcolm Nicolson (1843–1904), a professional soldier who entered the Indian army and rose to the rank of major-general. Hardy met her only once, in London, but was much struck by her beauty. The news of her suicide in Madras, which followed the death of her husband two months earlier, seems to have affected him deeply, and he wrote a short obituary of her for the *Athenaeum*. Published anonymously on 29 October 1904, it suggests that 'the tragic circumstances of her death seem but the impassioned closing notes of her impassioned effusions'. At about the same time he suggested to Arthur *Symons that an appreciation of her should be written. He later described her as 'the gifted and impassioned poetess' (*LW* 346).

She is chiefly remembered for her collection (allegedly of translations) *The Garden of Kama and Other Love Lyrics from India* (1901), which attracted a good deal of attention on its appearance (many taking it for the work of a man), and was reprinted several times. One poem, 'Pale hands I love', became immensely popular through a musical setting. Two other collections followed, one posthumously.

Housman, A. E. (1869–1936), poet and classical scholar whose verse has certain elements in common with Hardy's. He made his poetical début with *A Shropshire Lad* (1896) at about the same time as Hardy (*Wessex Poems* appearing in 1898). They met in London in June 1899, possibly at the home of Edmund *Gosse, and the following summer Housman was a guest at Max Gate. When Housman, in November 1912, wrote a letter of condolence to Hardy on the death of his wife Emma, he recalled meeting her 'several times' at the Gosses', and it seems likely that Hardy too had been present on some or all of these occasions. He and Housman certainly met twice in Cambridge in 1913 (Housman had become Professor of Latin there in 1911): on 10 June, when Hardy received an honorary degree and they dined together at Jesus College, and on 15 November, when Hardy went to be installed as an Honorary Fellow of Magdalene College. In 1919 Housman contributed a poem to a presentation volume organized by Siegfried *Sassoon and given to Hardy on his 79th birthday. He was one of the pall-bearers at Hardy's funeral in Westminster Abbey in 1928.

Housman's Oxford contemporary Alfred Pollard, recalling their undergraduate days, tells us that 'among novelists his favourite was Thomas Hardy, and I think Hardy's influence went far deeper than [Matthew] Arnold's'. (This would have been the earlier Hardy: *The Return of the Native* had appeared near the beginning of Housman's second year at St John's College.) After Hardy's death Housman told a correspondent that 'For Hardy I felt affection, and high admiration for some of his novels and a few of his poems' (*Letters*, 329). In 1922, the year of his own *Last Poems*, he seems to have agreed to produce for publication a selection from Hardy's verse, and actually chose the contents, though for some reason the project was abandoned. Hardy for his part is on record as an admirer of Housman's poetry, his favourite being 'Is my team ploughing?' (*A Shropshire Lad* XXVII). When Florence *Henniker gave Hardy a copy of *A Shropshire Lad* as a Christmas present in 1902, he wrote assuring her that he was carrying it in his pocket, though the implied tribute may be to the donor rather than the poet.

The Letters of A. E. Housman, ed. Henry Maas (1971).

How, W. W. (1823–97), Bishop of Wakefield 1888–97. Celebrated in his day as the author of 'For all the saints' and other well-known hymns, as well as many popular devotional works, he is remembered by students of Hardy for his vigorous, even dramatic condemnation of *Jude the Obscure*. The official biography by his son, F. D. How (1898), describes him as 'fond of a good novel' but concerned at 'the danger of the "realistic" school'. On 9 June 1896 the *Yorkshire Post* published a letter from How stating that, having bought a copy of *Jude*, he was 'so disgusted with its insolence and indecency that I threw it on the fire'. Hardy did not learn until the publication of F. D. How's biography that the bishop had also used his influence to have the book withdrawn from W. H. Smith's circulating library, and to secure 'an assurance that any other books by the same author would be carefully examined before they were allowed to be circulated'. For Hardy's account (simultaneously regretful, indignant, and ironic) of this episode, see *LW* 294–5, 315.

Simon Curtis, *THJ* 11 (1995).

'How I Built Myself a House.' See UNCOLLECTED STORIES.

Human Shows. Subtitled 'Far Phantasies, Songs, and Trifles', this was Hardy's seventh volume of verse. It appeared on 20 November 1925, having been expeditiously proof-read by him throughout September, and expediently released in time for Christmas. That it would be the last volume he saw published, he could not know. If its purpose was to bring out 'in book form' the 25 magazine poems 'accumulated' since *Late Lyrics and Earlier* (*L* vi 338), there was no preface declaring that some of them originated in existing material stored in papers and notebooks, a few from the 1860s. Since nineteen of the early poems are marked as such, the bulk of the 152 poems were presumably composed after the war. While reviewers considered the volume 'gloomy and pessimistic', Hardy characterized the content of only about sixty poems as 'tragedy, sorrow or grimness' and the remainder as poems of 'Reflection, love, or comedy', some even 'flippant, not to say farcical'.

If the provisional title, 'Poems Imaginative & Incidental: with Songs and Trifles', suggested a vague ephemerality, the published form accurately projects the considered music of the compilation. For the main title has evolved into an adjective-noun doublet: 'HUMAN SHOWS' and 'FAR PHANTASIES', printed on consecutive lines in large capitals, with a slow, trochaic—spondaic flow that causes a concentration of thought which is then relaxed in 'Songs, and Trifles'. Moreover, the linear parallelism and graphic equivalence of the main title set up an antithesis suggestive of Hardy's preoccupation with, on the one hand, visualization and, on the other, the recognizably human and the remote nonhuman, the conflict between body and soul, consciousness and the unconscious. His lifelong concern with picturing and feeling once again committed him to the Johnsonian criterion of exhibiting or showing human nature (see *L* ii 43).

In embodying his deepest creative themes, *Human Shows, Far Phantasies* fulfils Hardy's poetic undertaking in a poem not published until long after his death to 'set in view | Life and its secrets | Old and new' ('A Jingle on the Times')—to disturb habits of mind, open eyes, and reveal new meaning and value, by making his readers aware of the perpetual interaction between the wasting and quickening processes of time, Nature, society, and mind. In its explorations and exhibitions of reality, the volume contains, if not Hardy's best poems, certainly some of his least negligible and most representative and assured. Of those reprinted in *Chosen Poems* (see SELECTED POEMS), three have frequently been anthologized: 'Waiting Both', 'A Sheep Fair', and 'Snow in the Suburbs', the latter, together with 'When Oats were Reaped' and 'This Summer and Last', esteemed by Philip *Larkin. Other popular poems are 'The Best She Could', 'No Buyers', 'Nobody Comes', and 'Shortening Days at the Homestead'.

As for design, the volume seems like a discordant, jumbled medley. But miscellaneity is typical of Hardy's two previous volumes, and essential to the distinctive Hardyan tone and tenor. On the one hand, defects of style derive from his refusal to adjust the metrical ideal to fit the experiential actual. On the other hand, the loose arrangement is attributable to his readiness to accommodate a fluid sequence of poems and avoid a narrowly controlled design. True to his exalting of emotion above expression (*LW*

334), and to his aesthetic idea of a calculated carelessness, 'the art of concealing art' in 'cunning irregularity' (*LW* 323; see also 108), Hardy forgoes conformity between the design and execution of this volume. What *Human Shows* does artistically 'conceal' is that its arrangement is not merely accumulative, but supported by a broadly thematic substructure. What seems at first casual and clumsy relies on an inclusive, imaginative format. Fundamental to the structure of the entire volume is the tension generated by the opposition between method and randomness, pattern and disproportion, skeletal symmetry and fluid experience. The antithetical title initiates the tension, which is reinforced intermittently by contrastive imagery (for example, light and dark, sun and moon). Metrically, too, contrariety is a shaping spirit in a book that is remarkable for its innovative, often visual, stanzaic forms, using several different types of verse line in the same poem.

While rhyming couplets, for instance, coordinate the middle lines in 'Snow in the Suburbs', the number of beats in each line varies from three to five, pulling against prosodic cohesion and making the lines seem independent of one another. Even when attention focuses on those lines that begin with 'And', one hears behind this word the stylistic influence of biblical usage, where instead of any real (causal) continuity, there is an abrupt juxtaposition, evoking images that are, if not at odds, quite distinct. An initial 'And', used as a phantom marker of linkage, is a dominant conjunction in Hardy's poetry and usually features at the end of a stanza or poem, as in the poem in question: 'A black cat comes wide-eyed and thin; | And we take him in', a couplet that completes the interplay between setting and actors. Here the reader becomes involved as conscious observer ('we') in the entire process of the poem, imaginatively making connections in terms of the obvious dissonances, until out of the disconnectedness comes reconciliation. For there is, in fact, a measure of continuity imaged in the falling snow, but this is counterpointed by the interruptive, deadening effect of its coming to rest.

The dynamic process of this poem, in which texture enhances theme, functions as a *discordia concors* (the Renaissance doctrine that beauty and harmony are the offspring of contraries) to organize Hardy's entire volume, setting poem against poem. Abrupt juxtaposition, ungainly dislocation, freakish digression—all are held in a harmonious tension. In a poem placed at the centre of the volume, 'Genitrix Laesa' (meaning 'The Injured Earth-Mother'), Hardy unchivalrously uses the standard classical formula of beauty and harmony to pour salt into Nature's wounds: 'Life that rhythmic chime is holding: | (Yes; so deem it you, Ladye— | This "concordia discors"!)...'. The sting is in that Latin oxymoron, and Hardy goes on to imply that the traditional synonymous inversion, *discordia concors*, would be a truer, more realistic, description of the disappointing achievement ('world-work') of a damaged Nature: 'Good in dream, in deed below it: | (Lady, yes: so sight it we!) | Thus, then, go on fondly thinking...'. Paradoxically, Hardy's sarcasm deconstructs the imperfect arrangement of his own book even while it justifies his quest as an artistic explorer and exhibitor of reality.

When, in writing this poem, Hardy assimilated the metres of 12th-century Latin hymns in the Sarum Missal, he was doing much more than technically enriching his native verse (*LW* 329): he was also fulfilling his mission as a poet. The essential paradox of the theory of *discordia concors* is found in statements like 'Art is a disproportioning...of realities, to show more clearly the features that matter in those realities' (*LW* 239), or formulations such as 'The business of the poet...is to show the sorriness underlying the grandest things, and the grandeur underlying the sorriest things', and 'To find beauty in ugliness is the province of the poet' (*LW* 178, 222). To Hardy, a true poet would see the union in the variance of natural things, and use Nature's very deformities, defects, and contradictions to create a compensatory beauty, even if the volumes of such verse were unwieldy, jarring, and uneven. At least they would have a harmonious diversity or, in Millgate's phrase, 'a homogeneous miscellaneity' (560), and a structure that was at times dynamic.

Some such principle of arrangement would seem to govern a miscellany like this volume, parts of which are more continuous and coherent than others. Three 'groupings' of poems stand out on account of their date of composition, genre, or theme. Five poems dated 1912 or 1913 are about Emma's death, four contiguous with 'far', philosophical, fantasies. Five poems of uneven quality composed in the 1890s are scattered throughout the book. Of the two poems dated in the 1860s, one ('Retty's Phases') survives in a draft that provides the earliest specimen of a poem in Hardy's handwriting; the other ('Discouragement') serves an important transitional function at the end of the volume. The ballad form (see BALLADS) features more than any other genre, most times singly, but twice clustered, first near the middle of the book and again towards the end. Songs occur only slightly less frequently, and never in a series.

The most interesting grouping, whether serial or sporadic, is by theme, and Hardy uses several techniques to develop and embody a dominant thematic line. The volume begins on a philosophical note with 'Waiting Both', a naïve conversation dramatizing the shared doom of all creation, in which a biblical allusion ('Till my change come': Job 14: 14) suggests the utter hopelessness of man's unique condition ('degree'). In a universe of temporal process, for the speaker to call his death a 'change' is an absurdly wishful euphemism, a grim irony enforced by the echoic response of the star which itself must ultimately die.

In the rest of the opening section, further images of human limitation ('the hammering clock'), emaciation ('a rag drawn over a skeleton'), and obsolescence ('making meaningless | The coded creeds of old-time godliness') reinforce the withering passage of time. Faced with the evidence of the utter loss of life's meaning and purpose, Hardy searches his mind for joys and values ('once full-defined') of the past. With mortality and powerlessness established as thematic points of reference, these philosophical concerns about the meaning of human existence are then offset by ballads and songs about familiar social events, personages, and places. When Hardy resumes the initial thematic line, it quickly gains a new emphasis. By depicting the destructive potential of the sexual instinct in poems on the personal torments and social consequences of erotic love (with some of guilt about Emma), he is able to widen the scope of his philosophical topic to include the processes of society and Nature.

These new dimensions of interest are registered in images of travelling and seasonal change, more specifically in images of the sun (connoting the virtues of wisdom, generosity, and kindness) and moon (characterized by cold, sinister, ominous realism). The seasonal image of falling leaves occurs so frequently that it comes to symbolize the sad loss resulting from all three thematic processes of time, Nature, and society, and also to be associated with snowflakes, feathers, and anything small, delicate, and light in air. Then the kinetic image of a living creature on a journey is highly significant in these poems, whether conjuring up places, presenting life as a journey through time, space, and social environment, or projecting the mind in memory or fantasy.

All of these key images are set up in the first third of the volume and come together in a memorable series of descriptive poems, six poems on winter. This grouping of poems illustrates another embodying technique of Hardy's, in which he first depicts a minutely detailed setting, then infuses emotion and significance into the scene by bringing on an agent or stationing an observer. They also celebrate, or treat ironically, the imperceptible processes of time, Nature, and society, as they interrelate with the mind seeking to make sense of human existence. The scene in 'Life and Death at Sunrise' works as an objective equivalent for intuitions about life and death. As the observer's perceptions gradually connect with the routines and rhythms of rural life, so the poem embodies the mind's capacity to discover coherence and worth amid the discordance of the amoral, objective world in motion between two states of being. Even when natural processes are disrupted, as in the contraposed poem 'Night-Time in Mid-Fall' (where 'Leaves totter down still green'), and the breakdown extends to social processes, the flippant, melodramatic enumeration of events blurs these starkly grotesque omens of disaster.

The theme of mortality recurs in 'A Sheep Fair', where the mass of vivid, pictorial minutiae conveys the experiential immediacy of all creatures entangled in the community of existence and extinction. When the black cat in the playful centre-piece, 'Snow in the Suburbs', finds a temporary refuge inside a suburban home, it escapes to a Victorian dwelling designed to blend rural and urban impulses, for personal solitude and for social interdependence. Here is a place that represents detachment and identification perfectly intermingled, when an act of loving-kindness creates a moral-emotional space where all anguished, lonely souls can feel safe awhile, a liminal world between the dream of utopia and the doom of the grave. A characteristic inflection of this poem is the next, 'A Light Snow-Fall after Frost', in which the interrelatedness of three human figures (including the closely observing poet), and their affinity with their wintry surroundings, prevent them from discerning the microscopic effects of the snow. Instead, the subtle changes are embodied as a fusion of the processes of Nature and the mental faculties of perception and imagination. Quiet wonder is the effect of this poem, implying as it does that the precise instant of transformation is not for a man to know. He is alone even in the ignorance of his own change.

After three variations on the theme of homespun unwittingness and communal solidarity, Hardy re-enacts the fusion of mental and natural processes in a courtship elegy on Emma, 'The Frozen Greenhouse'. The limiting relativity of human consciousness, the lack of self-apprehension, is again used, here as a source of irony. Short lines, simple rhymes, and plain diction create a childlike innocence all the more touching for Emma's intense alarm and pity at the negligent death of the plants, little thinking that, like Hopkins's Margaret, she grieves for herself. As the poet's inward focus shifts, he realizes his loss afresh, just as the 'frost' of the present brings out into visibility the 'cobwebs' of the past.

At the spatial midpoint of the volume stands a small cluster of philosophical poems (including 'Genitrix Laesa', already discussed), a grouping made complex and significant by its varied subject-matter (time, death, mind, Nature, and life), no less than by its layout. For, after exposing both time and death as sham monarchs, Hardy inserts a string of dramatic narratives. Passionate love, on which this balladic interlude centres, exists in contrast with inevitable disaster or death, a process imaged by the 'hot' sun yielding to the 'cold' moon ('Last Look Round St Martin's Fair'). The idea of doom and diminishment acts as a thread linking these poems to the more abstract, philosophical ones, but it also prepares us for the problem of consciousness ('this disease | Called sense') and its solution: 'Limit its registerings to good, | And hide from it all anguishment.' In 'The Prospect', for instance, a comparison superimposed on a reminiscence provides a vignette showing the 'good' which can come from a dynamic intermingling of mental and natural processes. Here the restorative double exposure, which blends life and death in the aged poet's mind, surfaces in the activity of skaters and boys who enliven a sluggish winter scene. The 'health and vigour' of Emma 'last July' and that of the youth 'th[is] December' together reanimate his consciousness of her and energize the desire to be in her vital presence (see *LW* 386–7). Then, after the scathing parody of a hymn to Mother Nature, Hardy reverts to the healing effect that the processes of his poet's mind have on him, administered through the wit, honesty, and tenderness of four elegies celebrating Emma. This deployment of elegies expresses the sense of philosophical, local, and personal continuity and interdependence in which his mind is rooted. Finally, in '"What's There to Tell?"', a narrow account of life as short, impersonal, and wretched is couched in a song of benign resignation, which invests the concept with a sense of inevitability and finality, adding a pathos to the melancholic protesting of the philosophical poems.

After this curious mix of passionate nostalgia and intellectual enquiry, the elegiac and the anti-elegiac, come poems that arguably form the most trivial and fancifully managed section of the volume. The idea of man's mortality in an impersonal universe (presented in a succession of poems on death) reasserts itself and leads us into the closing part. Here, in order to effect a forceful transition, Hardy inserts one of his earliest poems, a satiric sonnet, 'Discouragement', which demarcates an apt conclusion with four poems that span the last 60 years of his poetic career. This 'coda' refocuses the opening theme of mortality and mankind's lot. But as the volume begins ironically with a tone of hopeful sufferance, so it ends on a solemn note of disillusioned assertiveness. No longer small, starry-eyed, and submissive, like the aged speaker in 'Waiting Both', the poet now validates his attitude towards living in a place dominated by chance ('hap') and will ('whim').

Knowing that death and the passage of time often carry away what is precious, and feeling the futility of what they leave behind, Hardy justifies his going through the dehumanizing motions ('mechanic repetitions') of daily life, in the book's final poem, 'Why Do I?' (included in *Chosen Poems*). His personal apologia for living in a world of pain, failure, and imperfection, where the natural order of things works so uncompromisingly against the fulfilment and dignity of mankind, he grounds in an attachment of great devotion and tenderness. And when the image of 'wondrous wings' superseding a 'dusty cloak' unites the processes of the poet's mind and the natural order in a metaphor for death, the transformation acts as a heartening variation on the pervasive 'falling leaf' imagery. It also works as a linking device, nicely revising the question-and-answer mode of the book's keynote poem, 'Waiting Both'. What the image points us towards is the stupendous 'change' that occurs in the poet's mind, where the thought of the physical death of the beloved transforms itself into an inward reality of strength, freedom, and beauty. We are left with a double evocation of boredom set against refreshment, pitiful decay against regeneration. The liberating revelation affirms, too, that Hardy's lonely, long-awaited 'change' was now of no consequence to him. All that mattered was a personal relationship and a mind still capable of opening with wonder. BG

humour. Like most other things about him, Hardy's humour can be decidedly equivocal. Its most obvious and least rewarding feature, conscientiously exercised in the early novels, is also its most derivative. From Chaucer and Shakespeare to Scott and Dickens, rustic humours had been a reliable tradition of English writing, guaranteed to raise a laugh; and Hardy sets himself to explore this narrative vein, drawing on his own rich and first-hand knowledge: recollections of how the country people of his childhood had actually spoken and thought. He has to be careful, for although genteel Victorian readers had been conditioned to approve picturesque speech and idiom, they still had no stomach for coarse jokes and genuine earthiness of expression, matters with which Hardy had become quite familiar as he accompanied his father to play the fiddle at local gatherings, and of which he gives us a good glimpse in the first, unexpurgated version of his ballad poem 'The Fire at Tranter Sweatley's' (later retitled 'The Bride-Night Fire').

He can do this rollicking style of humour, and it is evident that he can enjoy it, but his own personal sense of humour (and nothing is more personal than what each of us separately finds funny) is very different. A kind of deadpan fantasy, peculiar to himself and easily missed or misunderstood by the reader, frequently seems his most characteristic way of almost secretly enjoying his own play of thought and word as he composes. A good instance comes from his first published novel, *Desperate Remedies*. The young heroine, Cytherea Graye, is as lively a feminine portrait as Hardy was ever to draw, her peculiar charm, like that of such young girls in all ages, being her own private mixture of vivacity and indifference, a combination which clearly both amuses and entrances her creator. She is extremely bored as she watches a presentation of Shakespeare in the town hall of Hocbridge, Hardy's name for what may well be Banbury in Oxfordshire: 'The town was intentionally bent upon being attractive by exhibiting to an influx of visitors the local talent for dramatic recitation, and provincial towns trying to be lively are the dullest of dull things' (1.3). The humour is implicit, as his own style of humour always is in Hardy. Rustics, as Hardy well knew (and as he shows us in the mumming scene in *The Return of the Native*), take their own pleasures happily if mechanically, but nothing equals the tedium engendered by more refined folk, who are required to rise to a cultural occasion. Hardy's odd and undercover sense of humour finds such boringness droll in itself.

In the words of the comic song, 'There was nothing to laugh at at all' for the young heroine, but her boredom is soon to be alleviated. There follows one of the most striking tableaux that Hardy ever created, and its suggestiveness is both dreadful and dreadfully comic. The young girl's 'idling eye' has a view of the church spire under repair nearby, and of the group of builders who are at work upon the scaffolding—a group that includes her own father, an architect: 'The height of the spire was about one hundred and twenty feet, and the five men engaged thereon seemed entirely removed from the sphere and experiences of ordinary human beings. They appeared little larger than pigeons, and made their tiny movements with a soft, spirit-like silentness.' Hardy proceeds to a private joke, of the kind which his critics tend to pass over with a shrug of pained exasperation. The amateur theatricals in the town hall are meaningless and pretentious: the real show on the scaffolding has the silent oblivious concentration of true work, taking place here as if in another world. The 'idling eye' passes over both, and the young lady is 'as listless and careless as one of the ancient Tarentines, who, on such an afternoon as this, watched from the Theatre the entry into their Harbour of a power that overturned the State' (1.3).

Why on earth drag in the ancient Tarentines, except as an out-of-place demonstration of the youthful author's reading and learning? But the point lies precisely in its apparent unsuitability: it takes its allotted place in the unfolding of what seems to become for Hardy a complex and doleful joke. For the heroine's life is about to be changed, totally and for ever, by what now takes place. Her father slips and falls from the scaffolding, 'immediately disappearing downwards'. Had he disappeared *upwards*, we infer, all would have been well, and the story would never have been written. But gravity, like historical destiny, can only play its prescribed role. The scene concludes with a typical piece of Hardyan 'noticing', whose incongruity summates the whole sinister but strangely languid tragi-comedy of what has gone before. As Cytherea is helped home she sees 'white sunlight shining in shaft-like lines from a rift in a slaty cloud'; and 'Ever after that time any mental agony brought less vividly to Cytherea's mind the scene from the Town Hall windows than sunlight streaming in shaft-like lines'. It seems all part of the joke that we have to read that sentence two or three times before grasping which way it works.

The scenes in the servants' hall in the same novel are alive with a humour both rich and subtle, in some ways even more effective (Hardy's mother had begun her working life as a London housemaid) than are the comfortable rustic humours of the late novels. Hardy returned to a scene with indoor servants in *The Hand of Ethelberta*, in which they gather upstairs for a silent and hilarious dance of their own, imitating their betters in the ballroom below.

It used to be rather patronizingly assumed by some readers and critics that all such 'humour' in Hardy, in so far as it existed at all, was as involuntary and unintentional as its results often seemed laborious. Nothing surely could be further from the truth. As the craftsmanship of his poems shows, Hardy was very well aware of every subtle effect he wished to obtain, and his humour is an integral part of his own personal style of working a subject. As he said more than once, and with his usual smouldering annoyance at the stupidity of his critics, they mistook the verbal and metrical ingenuities in his poems for clumsiness, and his sly humour for naïvety. The *Lyrical Ballads* that are largely the work of *Wordsworth, one of Hardy's youthful influences, are often unintentionally comic through earnestness and over-emphasis. That does not happen with Hardy's poems, where effects of the incongruous, even of absurdity and banality, have been carefully timed for his own purposes.

An instance would be 'The New Boots' in Hardy's last and posthumous collection, *Winter Words*. It is a poem that might have been written in old age, or alternatively put aside much earlier and then reworked. It takes the form of a dialogue, or rather a series of exchanges mixed with monologue, the exchanges being the sort that Hardy might have had with some neighbour—at least when he was young, for when old he did not go in for such casual social visiting. The poem has asked a woman about the boots that hang on the wall, and she says her husband bought them: '"He bought them for the wet weather, | And they are of waterproof leather"'. The poet then asks 'a neighbour of hers I knew' why the husband never wears them, and his reply is enigmatic, having the unfathomable quality of rustic exchange: '"Ah, those boots. Aye. | He bought them to wear whenever | It rained. But there they hang ever". There is no hurry. Extreme leisureliness is the point of the cheerless little comedy ('"Ah, those boots. Aye"'). And the poet still does not know what has happened to the husband, whose cheerfulness about the new boots is reported in the next stanza. In the last one the neighbour finally comes to the point:

> '... Anyhow,
> As you see them hanging now
> They have hung ever since he died
> The day after gaily declaring:
> "Ha-ha, now for wet wayfaring.
> They're just the chaps for my wearing!"'

Hardy was accustomed to dwell on 'life's little ironies' and its 'satires of circumstance', and often with a good deal of heavy-handedness, not to say crudity. But the impact of these two characteristic samples—one from his first published novel, the other from one of his last written, or rewritten, poems—shows the same kind and degree of richness and subtlety in the deployment of his own personal kind of humour, a humour often decidedly unobvious but rewarding to explore. It is a notable feature of 'The New Boots' that the joke itself is far more evident than is the sly demure skill with which it is enjoyed and brought out by the poet. Hardy clearly preferred his private relish in such 'ironies' to any more expansive social reception.

A distinction can in fact be drawn between Hardy's open and obvious comedy and irony, and the more private, even secret, sort. The former is great fun, the latter more pleasurable to reflect on and return to. Joseph Poorgrass meekly responding with his own name to the owl's repeated 'Who—who' in the silent wood, and adding 'Sir' as a mark of deference, is wholly and engagingly in the Shakespearian vein; but there is more of Hardy himself, and his own secretive brand of amusement, in the story, also in *Far from the Madding Crowd*, which is told about Bathsheba Everdene's father, a masterful man given to acts of piety such as belabouring errant choirboys, but also one who finds the state of marriage so incompatible with love and desire that he persuades his wife to remove her wedding-ring when he wishes to embrace her (and, by presumption, make love to her). Hardy was clearly fascinated by this state of mind (a good foundation, one might say, for grim jokes of the style he loved), and in the context of the narrative there is about it a wholly unexpected and startling intimacy, the scrap of revelation about her parent even shedding light of its own ambiguous sort on Bathsheba's subsequent conduct. She too dislikes the thought of the humdrum and quotidian nature of marriage, and she herself makes a disastrous marriage in consequence, the kind of marriage that should, and indeed in a sense does, end like a tragic love affair. She only comes to value the steady and unromantic affection of Gabriel Oak when she has found out (as probably Hardy himself never did) that love of the kind she really loves cannot last.

A tale whose grim humour emphasizes this in its own rather odious, because coldly facetious and detached, way is 'Barbara of the House of Grebe' (*GND*). It was singled out by shocked reviewers, and later on by influential critics like T. S. Eliot, as an example of Hardy's 'morbidity', a morbidity concealed under the mask of the author's countryman's relish for a bizarre or quaintly gruesome narrative. Hardy defended himself against his critics, not very convincingly, by protesting that his tale was a robustly humorous one, written in the vein of comic-gruesome melodrama that he had enjoyed as a boy, and which possessed, after all, a long and venerable literary history.

However that may be, 'Barbara of the House of Grebe' is certainly a nasty story, nor is it much of an excuse that it is told in a dramatized and impersonal setting, in the manner of *Browning's monologues or Chaucer's *Pardoner's Tale*. For it repeats in its own macabre way a favourite, not to say obsessive, theme of its author and his wryly humorous view of life. We learn that a lover's heart is 'comparable to the earth in its geologic stages... first a hot coal, then a warm one, then a cooling cinder, then chilly—the simile shall be pursued no further'. Hardy frequently pursued this theme, and its merry equivalent, but he did so in his great fictions, where perception, sadness, sympathy, and above all humanity mingle with humour in a way they do not begin to do in a story like this one. Humour in his novels and in most of his poems is always a more or a less subtle adjunct to Hardy's vision of human life and how it was to be lived: never a substitute for it. JB

Hutchins, John (1698–1773), topographer and antiquary. Born in Bradford Peverell, Dorset, he was educated at Dorchester Grammar School and Balliol College, Oxford. He spent the rest of his life as a clergyman in his native county and is buried in St Mary's, Wareham. His life's work, the *History and Antiquities of Dorset*, was published posthumously in 1774. Hardy owned a copy (now in DCM) of the third edition, in four volumes, and drew on it as a source for the stories in *A Group of Noble Dames*, the preface to which includes a reference to the genealogical tables to be found on 'the pages of county histories', as well as in the short story 'Master John Horseleigh, Knight'.

hymns and metrical psalms. Though metrical psalms (nowadays generally subsumed in hymns) were a legacy of the Reformation, hymn writing and hymn singing are mainly an invention of the 18th century. They gained impetus from the rise of the Nonconformist and Evangelical movements, with authors and divines such as Isaac Watts and the Wesley brothers making notable contributions, and were also fostered by the High Church or Oxford Movement, two of whose leaders, John Keble and John Henry Newman—both studied by Hardy—were prominent hymnodists. By the middle of the 19th century hymn singing was firmly established, and hymnals such as *Hymns Ancient and Modern* (1861) consolidated their appreciation and use.

Hardy had from childhood an acute interest in and sensitivity to hymns: an early page of his autobiography vividly depicts him, as a very small child, reciting to himself at sunset a line from one of Watts's hymns, 'And now another day is gone', 'with great fervency' (*LW* 20)—though his motivation, as he scrupulously points out, was aesthetic rather than religious. This interest was maintained for the rest of his life. The staple (and old-fashioned) fare of Stinsford is described in detail in his autobiography (*LW* 16), and included in particular the metrical psalms of Tate and Brady. Musical memories implanted so early were not forgotten, and in 1910 he contributed to the yearbook of the Society of Dorset Men in London a short article, 'Some Old-fashioned Psalm-Tunes Associated with the County of Dorset', that included an introductory note and facsimile reproductions of ten tunes.

Later Hardy certainly came in contact with more modern Evangelical attitudes to the hymn: a copy of one of the most famous Evangelical compositions, 'Just as I am without one plea', is retained inside one of his early copies of the Bible. After his move to London, he also experienced modern High Church practice: on 17 August 1862 he wrote to his sister Mary, mentioning approvingly the hymns used at St Mary's, Kilburn, where *Hymns Ancient and Modern* was already in use (*L* i 1). He also worshipped at All Saints, Notting Hill, where the musical tradition had benefited from the appointment of the distinguished hymn composer H. J. Gauntlett as organist. Hardy comments on the development of the hymn during his lifetime in the poem 'Apostrophe to an Old Psalm Tune'. W. H. Monk, the editor of *Hymns Ancient and Modern*, who is referred to in this poem, was organist at King's College, London; there is, however, no evidence that Hardy encountered him when he received tuition there.

In 1895 Hardy felt unable to respond to a newspaper enquiry about 'Hymns that have helped me' (*LW* 290–1), but submitted the names of three hymns which 'have always been familiar and favourite hymns of mine as poetry'. These were 'Thou turnest man, O Lord, to dust' (Tate and Brady's version of Psalm 90), 'Awake, my soul, and with the sun' (Bishop Ken's so-called 'Morning Hymn'), and Newman's 'Lead, kindly light'.

Many of the hymn tunes best loved by the Stinsford choir, as itemized by Hardy (*LW* 16), make an appearance in his writings. These include the following tunes used for metrical psalms: 'Old Hundredth' ('The Chapel-Organist'); 'New Sabbath' (*AL* 1.1); 'Devizes' (*TT* 2); 'Lydia' (*RN* 1.5); and 'Cambridge New' ('Afternoon Service at Mellstock'). Two of his particular Stinsford favourites also appear in his work: Ken's 'Evening Hymn', sung at Stinsford to 'Tallis', is recalled by Jude (*JO* 2.1) and the composer of the tune for Ken's 'Morning Hymn' is the subject of 'Barthélémon at Vauxhall'. Another poem, 'On the Tune Called the

Old-Hundred-and-Fourth', contains a reference ('Ravenscroft's terse old tune') to another of Hardy's favourite hymn tunes, Thomas Ravenscroft's setting of Psalm 104 in his *Whole Book of Psalms* (1521).

Hymns feature prominently in several of the novels. 'Lead, kindly light' plays a significant part in the conclusion of *Far from the Madding Crowd*, just as 'New Sabbath' seizes Somerset's attention at the start of *A Laodicean*. In both instances the words of the hymns have a close relevance to the events taking place. In *The Mayor of Casterbridge* (33) a metrical version of Psalm 109, sung '"to the tune of Wiltshire"' (a melody by George Smart), is put to startling dramatic use, and is quoted at length.

But Hardy's familiarity with hymns extended more deeply than casual or even expanded reference. Many of the stanza forms of his verse are influenced by hymn forms, or are in some cases a deliberate parody of them, or at least an ironic allusion to them: it is scarcely an accident, for instance, that 'The Impercipient', a partly regretful, partly embittered lament for his loss of faith set in the context of a cathedral service, should employ such a form. More particularly, his sentimental and musical attachment to hymns encouraged, and perhaps to a certain extent fed, the air of wistful sentimentality frequently characteristic of his attitude to religion and the Church, and exemplified in a poem such as 'The Oxen'. TRH

I

Ibsen, Henrik (1828–1906), Norwegian dramatist, and one of the founding fathers of modern European drama. Hardy's admiration for Ibsen is discussed in the various biographies of the two writers, especially Michael Meyer's *Ibsen: A Biography* (3 vols., 1967–71; abridged one-volume edn., 1974). In 1891 Hardy joined George *Meredith, A. W. Pinero, and others in supporting the establishment of the Independent Theatre Society, which was devoted to the performance of plays by Ibsen and other 'serious' dramatists. In 1891, he attended with Edmund *Gosse the first performance in an English translation of *Hedda Gabler*; he saw another production of the same play in 1893, as well as *The Master Builder* and *Rosmersholm*, and three years later urged Florence *Henniker to go to see *Little Eyolf*. (For a possible influence on one of Hardy's short stories written during this period, see 'IMAGINATIVE WOMAN, AN'.) Hardy was completely out of sympathy with the 'blinkered insular taste' of critics who condemned Ibsen for his lack of idealism and branded his plays 'Ibscene'. In 1898, together with Henry *James, Bernard Shaw, J. M. *Barrie, A. C. Bradley, and others, he contributed to a 70th birthday present for Ibsen. Yet Hardy was not entirely uncritical of the Norwegian dramatist's work, commenting in 1890 that 'Ibsen's edifying is too obvious'. It was not Ibsen's didacticism that appealed to Hardy, but his concentration on some of the harsher issues of everyday life, which the plays present bluntly and without apology, just as some of Hardy's novels do. JA

illustrations. The first of Hardy's works to be illustrated was *A Pair of Blue Eyes*, serialized in *Tinsleys' Magazine* in eleven monthly instalments (September 1872–July 1873), each accompanied by a full-page woodblock drawing by James Abbott Pasquier. Hardy sent Tinsley preliminary sketches for the first two illustrations, and thus began his lifelong involvement in the visual representation of his work. That Pasquier made use of these sketches is suggested by the resemblance between his Elfride and Emma Gifford, Hardy's 'original', and perhaps also by the particularly effective composition of the first two illustrations, which dramatically depict Elfride's observation of Stephen embracing a woman at Endelstow House and Stephen's alarm at Elfride's precarious position on the cliffs.

There is no evidence that Hardy contributed to any of the later *Pair of Blue Eyes* illustrations, most of which are weak in terms of both design and execution. Faced for the first time with the pressures of writing for serial publication, he found it difficult to meet his deadlines and perhaps had insufficient time to produce additional sketches. That Pasquier may in any case have objected to such explicit authorial direction is indirectly suggested by Hardy's concern for the sensitivities of his next illustrator. Writing to the publishing firm of *Smith, Elder about the *Cornhill* illustrations to *Far from the Madding Crowd* (January–December 1874), Hardy offered to supply the as yet unnamed artist with sketches of various 'out-of-the-way things that might have to be shown', and then concluded: 'but if he is a sensitive man and you think he would rather not be interfered with, I would not do so' (*L* i 25).

The new illustrator was in fact a woman, Helen *Paterson, who married the poet William Allingham shortly afterwards and became, as Helen Allingham, a successful artist best known for her watercolours of country cottages and gardens. Whether she in fact received the proffered 'outlines of smock-frocks, gaiters, sheep-crooks, rick-"staddles", a sheep-washing pool, one of the old-fashioned malt-houses', etc., is not known, though probable enough. Hardy evidently 'gave her a few points' when they first met in May 1874, during the course of the novel's serialization (*LW* 103); on 7 May he sent her 'a few particulars of the story', and promised to forward 'any other information, or any sketch', she might require (*L* i 30); and there survive pencil sketches of a milking-bucket and shepherd's crook, signed with his address as if for posting.

Hardy's later references to Helen Allingham as the best of his illustrators are somewhat surprising, given that her interpretation of *Far from the Madding Crowd* as pastoral idyll was distortingly idealized and ignored almost entirely the novel's more passionate and disturbing elements. The illustrations are quite attractive, however, and for the most part well drawn, and Hardy was no doubt willing to countenance a one-sided representation that was likely to enhance the novel's commercial success; indeed, he may even have recognized that the visual idealization served to disguise the more subversive aspects of a text that continually threatened to transgress the limits of conventionality. His retrospective praise of Allingham's artistry may in any case have been influenced by his 'romantical' feelings about her person (*L* iii 218), especially since her own recollections suggest that he was initially less impressed with her work than he later claimed to be: although 'fairly complimentary' on the occasion of their first meeting, he 'said it was difficult for two minds to imagine scenes in the same light' (quoted in Marcus B. Huish, *Happy England, as Painted by Helen Allingham, R.W.S.* (1903), 39).

This difficulty was of course intrinsic to the entire illustration process, and although Hardy had at least tried with both Pasquier and Allingham to assist them in imagining the scenes of his fiction, he seems for whatever reason to have had little or no contact with his next illustrator, George du Maurier, during the serialization of *The Hand of Ethelberta* (July 1875–May 1876), again in the prestigious *Cornhill*. Hardy may well have been preoccupied with the completion of his own text, and in any case it perhaps seemed both inappropriate and unnecessary to offer advice to such a celebrated artist, especially given that the novel was a social comedy and du Maurier was best known (then as now) for his *Punch* satires of contemporary manners and mores. It would appear that du Maurier would in fact have preferred to work in close collaboration, though in telling Hardy so, in response to the latter's praise of the completed drawings, he sounded more than a little apologetic: 'If we were neighbours and I could have consulted you easily I should have been better able to realize your conceptions, and in many cases I should have asked you by some trifling alteration in the text to help me to a better picture or to a different choice of subject' (DCM). Hardy's admiration of the *Hand of Ethelberta* illustrations was not shared by the reviewers, who were disappointed by the resemblance between Ethelberta and du Maurier's familiar 'pretty lady' in *Punch* and, for the most part, found the drawings unremarkable in composition, style, or execution—a judgement echoed by subsequent generations of art and literary critics.

Hardy took an active, if not always approving, interest in the work of Arthur Hopkins, the illustrator of *The Return of the Native for Belgravia* (January–December 1878). Hardy claimed to have 'liked... much' the opening illustration of the heathfolk gathered around the bonfire (*L* i 52), but he so disliked the drawing of Eustacia on Rainbarrow (February 1878) that he sent Hopkins a 'corrective' sketch, followed by specific suggestions designed to ensure that his heroine, even if morally flawed, would henceforward be portrayed as conventionally attractive in both face and figure. While Hopkins did eventually succeed in representing Eustacia to Hardy's satisfaction, he was clearly more comfortable with the unambiguously 'good' characters like Thomasin, whom he acknowledged to be his favourite. Hardy declined to offer detailed advice on the representation of Clym—'A thoughtful young man of 25 is all that can be shown' (*L* i 55)—but he was eager, as always, to provide sketches of unusual items, twice sending drawings of mummers' costumes. He also expressed his hope that the mummers would figure in one of the drawings, and Hopkins obligingly included them in his illustration to the May 1878 instalment.

Accuracy of detail continued to be a major concern of Hardy's as he sought an illustrator for his next novel, *The Trumpet-Major*, to be serialized in *Good Words* (January–December 1880). His first choice was Charles Keene, well-known for his *Punch* illustrations and 'considered by army men to draw soldiers remarkably well' (*L* i 66), but Keene, pleading pressure of work, declined his invitation. Hardy subsequently approached John Collier, who accepted the commission and promised to 'spare no pains to insure correctness in the costume and accessories' (29 August 1879, DCM). Aided by numerous sketches by Hardy, including a drawing of the miller's kitchen used for the February 1880 illustration, Collier achieved what he had promised, but the accuracy of his architectural and sartorial details is rarely complemented by effective execution of facial features or expressions, and the illustrations as a whole demonstrate an almost complete inability to capture either emotion or drama.

In April 1880, during the course of the *Trumpet-Major* serialization, Hardy agreed to provide a new novel (*A Laodicean*) for the inaugural issues of the European Edition of *Harper's New Monthly Magazine*, offering, should the story be illustrated, to 'furnish the artist with hints, rough sketches &c. precisely as I should do for an English magazine' (*L* i 72). Harper's asked Hardy to find a first-class artist, and in early June he made unsuccessful approaches to Helen Allingham, Frank Dicksee, and William Small, before du Maurier, having been invited to recommend other illustrators, expressed an interest in doing the work himself. Harper's promptly accepted du Maurier's terms for a full-page illustration monthly over a 13-month period (December 1880–December 1881), and Hardy embarked on his closest collaboration with any of his illustrators: du Maurier's frequent lunch invitations—perhaps somewhat too frequent from the point of view of a busy author—seem expressive in themselves of his eagerness to consult Hardy about all aspects of the illustrations. By 22 June Hardy was offering to read du Maurier the newly completed opening chapters of the novel and to find 'a photograph or two for the chief characters' (*L* i 76). It is not clear what specific input Hardy had into the opening illustration of Paula's refusal to be baptized (December 1880), but he certainly suggested the arrangement of the figures in the next illustration (Paula's luncheon party) and provided a sketch of furniture; at du Maurier's insistence he also approved these first two illustrations in both draft and final form. Du Maurier requested a photo or drawing of the chapel of Stancy Castle for the third illustration, but by the time one was sent on 24 October—the day after Hardy realized he was seriously ill—he had already drawn a different scene. Hardy's prolonged indisposition abruptly ended their active collaboration: bedridden and often reduced to dictation, Hardy was forced to direct all his energies towards meeting the serial deadlines.

Even the collaborative early illustrations to *A Laodicean* are not particularly successful, however, and du Maurier seems, as with the *Hand of Ethelberta* illustrations, to have been conscious of having fallen below his own standards: when, in December 1880, Harper's London agent expressed disappointment on the publisher's part, du Maurier replied that 'he was better at working his own will in social satire than under the limitations of other people's stories' (quoted in E. McClung Fleming, *R. R. Bowker* (1952), 156). Several of his later *Laodicean* drawings are in fact effective examples of social satire—Hardy himself wrote to praise the final illustration of Paula and Somerset on the beach at Etretât—and the illustrations as a whole have been criticized precisely because they emphasize the *Punch*-like social situations at the expense of the novel's more dramatic events: a criticism directed more towards du Maurier's interpretation of the text than his artistic abilities.

The Mayor of Casterbridge (serialized weekly in the *Graphic*, 2 January-15 May 1886) was the next of Hardy's novels to be illustrated, the task being assigned to Robert Barnes, one of the magazine's staff illustrators. In the spring of 1885 Hardy sent to the *Graphic* a list identifying the 'originals' of his fictional places, which was duly forwarded to Barnes with the suggestion that he contact Hardy directly. Although no further documentary evidence exists, author and artist must almost certainly have communicated in some way—perhaps orally—and Barnes's own professionalism is in any case evinced both in his desire to visit the scenes of the story before illustrating them and in the high quality of the drawings themselves, which are striking and attractive, if at times idealized, attempts to represent sympathetically the narrative's drama of relationships.

What Hardy thought of Barnes's work—arguably the finest of all the illustrations to his fiction—is not known. Nor is it known what he thought of the illustrations to *Tess of the d'Urbervilles*, also serialized in the *Graphic* (4 July–26 December 1891), though a sufficient endorsement can doubtless be found in his hanging at Max Gate not only Hubert von Herkomer's splendid opening illustration of Tess returning from the dance but also his more conventional illustration (29 August 1891) of searching for garlic in the meads. Herkomer, however, drew only six of the 25 illustrations, his students Daniel Albert Wehrschmidt, Ernest Borough Johnson, and Joseph Syddall undertaking the remainder. This diversity of hands and levels of competence (the illustrators failing even in self-consistency) unfortunately rendered the principal characters virtually unrecognizable from one instalment to another. Tess, the most frequently depicted character, undergoes particularly noticeable fluctuations in her facial features, her figure, and even her apparent age. The illustrations are also uneven in quality, although several do effectively render the dramatic tensions of the novel and a few—notably Herkomer's opening illustration and Wehrschmidt's treatment (15 August 1891) of Tess discussing the transmigration of souls—even succeed in capturing something of Tess's undefinable essence.

Hardy knew Herkomer and probably collaborated with him to some extent; it is not at all clear, however, that he knew either Walter Paget, the illustrator of *The Pursuit of the Well-Beloved*, serialized in the *Illustrated London News* (1 October–17 December 1892) and later published in heavily revised form as *The Well-Beloved*, or William Hatherell, the illustrator of *The Simpletons/Hearts Insurgent*, the serial version of *Jude the Obscure*, as it appeared in *Harper's New Monthly Magazine* (December 1894–November 1895). Nor is his reaction to Paget's drawings recorded, even though the visual representation of the novel's central character bears in some of the illustrations a rather striking resemblance to the novel's author. What is known is that Hardy greatly admired Hatherell's sympathetic response to *Jude* and wrote to him to express 'sincere admiration' of the final illustration, 'Jude at the Milestone': 'The picture is a tragedy in itself: & I do not remember ever before having an artist who grasped a situation so thoroughly' (*L* ii 94). Hatherell's illustrations are consistently successful in their evocation of mood and emotion, and Hardy later had a set of them hung in his study at Max Gate.

Both Paget and Hatherell had already illustrated Hardy short stories. Paget's drawings for 'On the Western Circuit' (*English Illustrated Magazine*, December 1891) are undistinguished, but Hatherell's full-page illustration to 'The Fiddler of the Reels' (*Scribner's Magazine*, May 1893) is an attractive and emotionally evocative, if conventionally idealized, delineation of a rural scene. Hatherell's assignment to *Jude*, however, was presumably the result not of any intervention on Hardy's part but rather of the artist's existing connection with American magazines, and in 1900 it was again for *Harper's Monthly* that he illustrated 'Enter a Dragoon', the last of Hardy's short stories to be published during his lifetime.

Although Hardy seems, with one or two exceptions, to have had little or no contact with the numerous artists who illustrated his short stories for the magazines of the day, he was by no means indifferent to the visual representation of these works. In discussing 'The First Countess of Wessex' (*GND*) a year before its December 1889 publication in *Harper's New Monthly Magazine*, he specified that the story's illustrator should have special skill in 'the delineation of old English manor-house architecture, & woodland scenery, with large gnarled oaks &c., beside, of course, figures, in the costume of George the Second's reign' (*L* i 181). He also suggested possible illustrators: Helen Allingham ('The best illustrator I ever had'), Alfred Parsons ('knows that part of the country thoroughly'), Charles Green ('fairly good at architecture—possibly he is good at winter foliage'), and William Small ('has done some good illustrating'). The letter, though tentatively phrased, was not unproductive: while the well-known American artist Charles Stanley Reinhart supplied the four 'First Countess of Wessex' illustrations depicting the interactions between characters, Parsons drew the headpiece and three illustrations of architectural and geographical locations (having visited in Hardy's company at least one of the scenes of the story during his stay at Max Gate in January 1889). Two years later Parsons was again commissioned by Harper's to draw the Dorchester High Street headpiece for 'Wessex Folk' (*Harper's New Monthly Magazine*, March–June 1891), the seven (non-architectural) illustrations being supplied by Green.

Hardy's closest and most sustained involvement in the selection of locations for illustration occurred during the preparation of two collected editions, the Osgood, McIlvaine Wessex Novels edition of 1895–6, and the Macmillan Wessex Edition of 1912–13 (with subsequent supplementary volumes). Each of the Osgood, McIlvaine volumes included an engraving by Henry Macbeth-Raeburn of a scene from the story 'Drawn on the spot', and there is ample evidence of his extensively consulting Hardy, both by letter and in person. Hermann *Lea, who photographed the scenes used as frontispieces to the Wessex Edition volumes, was already a friend of Hardy's at the time the edition was initiated, and their close co-operation went beyond the frontispieces themselves to the publication, in matching format, of Lea's extensively illustrated *Thomas Hardy's Wessex* (1913).

For each of the two collected editions Hardy also drafted a map of 'Wessex' to be included in every volume. Years earlier, in 1878, he had drawn the sketch-map prefaced to the first edition of *The Return of the Native*, the first of several instances of his choosing to be both author and illustrator: in 1880 he drew for the cover of *The Trumpet-Major* the vignettes of camp and mill connected by a winding path; in 1898, still more remarkably, he supplied his own famously idiosyncratic drawings to *Wessex Poems*; and in 1923 he included in his verse-drama *The Famous Tragedy of the Queen of Cornwall* precisely detailed sketches of the exterior and interior of Tintagel Castle 'at the Time of the Tragedy'.

Hardy's verse was also illustrated by professional artists, especially during the 1920s, when his reputation as a poet had become well established. It seems unlikely that Hardy actively collaborated with any of these illustrators, but the illustrations themselves possess an independent interest as examples of the extraordinary range of visual responses to his work—from Edward Blampied's quaintly sentimental drawing of an aged father waiting for his daughter ('The Forsaking of the Nest', *Nash's Magazine*, February 1912; an early version of 'The Third Kissing-Gate') to Rockwell Kent's powerful Blakeian woodcut of a giant male figure lying across a stark landscape ('An Ancient to Ancients', *Century Magazine*, May 1922), or from Arthur Wragg's elegant Klimtian border ('The Last Leaf', *Nash's and Pall Mall Magazine*, November 1924) to Harry Clarke's Beardsleyesque rendering of nightmare ('The Portraits', *Nash's and Pall Mall Magazine*, December 1924; an early version of 'Family Portraits'). One poem, 'The Turnip-Hoer' (*Cassell's Magazine*, August 1925), simultaneously attracted quite contradictory representations: the poem itself is accompanied by conventionally idealized drawings of the turnip-hoer as first contented and then discontented labourer, while on the cover of the magazine he is sensationally depicted as carrying a distinctly vampiric Duchess.

In August 1927 the poem 'Yuletide in a Younger World' was published, together with two drawings by Albert Rutherston, as the first of the Faber & Gwyer Ariel Poems booklets. It was the last of Hardy's works to be illustrated during his lifetime. During the five and a half decades that had passed since the appearance of the first instalment of *A Pair of Blue Eyes*, Hardy's response to the illustration of his work had varied considerably, ranging from non-participatory interest to an active involvement that included supplying his illustrators with preliminary sketches, suggesting scenes for possible illustration, and providing detailed descriptions (sometimes accompanied by drawings or photographs) of characters, settings, and unusual items. The intensity of Hardy's engagement chiefly reflected his active interest, at once professional and financial, in the critical acceptance and commercial success of his published works, but something must also be attributed to his educated interest in the visual arts. He was, after all, trained as an architect, during his early years he seriously considered becoming an art critic, and, as his illustration of *The Famous Tragedy of the Queen of Cornwall* demonstrates, he continued even into old age to take pleasure in the exercise of his own modest graphic skills. PD

Pamela Dalziel, 'Anxieties of Representation: The Serial Illustrations to Hardy's *The Return of the Native*', *Nineteenth-Century Literature*, 51 (1996).

—— '"She matched his violence with her own wild passion": Illustrating *Far from the Madding Crowd*', in Charles P. C. Pettit (ed.), *Reading Thomas Hardy* (1998).

Arlene Jackson, *Illustration and the Novels of Thomas Hardy* (1981).

imagery. While Hardy's imagery has not been studied as systematically as (for example) his diction and his metres, the evidence suggests that from the beginning of his career he collected images for possible future use in the same way as he noted down ideas for stories, or details from paintings. The notebook 'Memoranda, I' (see NOTEBOOKS) has such entries as these: 'August [1870]. In Cornwall. The smoke from a chimney droops over the roof like a feather in a girl's hat.' 'Apl. 1871. In Church. The sibilants in the responses of the congregation who bend their heads like pine-trees in a wind.' 'Nov. 13 [1872]. The first frost of autumn... open-air cucumbers have collapsed like green umbrellas with all the stays broken' (*PN* 5, 9, 12). These seem to have been gathered with no particular work in mind, to be used as occasion offered: the bent pine trees could as readily be compared to a congregation at prayer, or the feather to the smoke, as the congregation to the trees and the smoke to the feather. This is not to say that such images may not have some more general significance, since collectively they imply that links may be drawn between the human and the natural worlds, making each part of what Hardy was later to call the 'great web' of existence (*W* 3). But if this is their effect, it seems unlikely that it was their intention.

It was Hardy's fate to be regarded as a poetic novelist, and then, when he emerged as a poet, to be told that he had left his best poetry in the novels. It is clearly true that some of the novels are structured, in part at least, around patterns of associated images. Hardy was not of course alone in this; the fires in *Wuthering Heights* and the fogs in *Bleak House* were seen and noted by contemporary readers long before they became the subject of academic study, and Victorian criticism of Shakespeare in particular had shown how imagery could be used to suggest theme or argument, rather than as simply a means of decorating a text. But Hardy went further than his contemporaries in treating scenes, episodes, and even characters as images. In doing so he was making a conscious departure from Victorian realism.

The use of scenes rendered so distinctly and powerfully that they come to have a significance over and above that given by their function in the plot can be illustrated from *Far from the Madding Crowd*. Bathsheba's night by the swamp after Troy's departure both recalls and contradicts the display of Troy's swordsmanship in the hollow amid the ferns. Then Bathsheba was 'enclosed in a firmament of light', dazed by an '*aurora militaris*' (28); now she is exposed to 'the essences of evil things in the earth and in the waters under the earth', as the reality of Troy's betrayal of her sinks in (44). In a note made in 1887, Hardy wrote that his interest was in 'the deeper reality underlying the scenic', when the mind is awakened to the 'tragical mysteries of life' and brings to what it perceives a mood or feeling which 'coalesces with and translates the qualities that are already there' (*LW* 192). This is what happens here, where the natural world is seen in a manner which echoes and intensifies the human feeling.

In most of the novels there are some episodes which operate rather as the scene does in *Far from the Madding Crowd*. Knight's experiences on the Cliff without a Name in *A Pair of Blue Eyes* are on one level the occasion for a meditation on the transience of human experience, but at another the passage images or sums what it feels like for a middle-aged bachelor to find himself suddenly in love: it feels as if he is clinging for dear life above a sea of passion, at any moment to fall. There is a similar instance in *The Well-Beloved*. In the 1892 serial version Pearston is tempted to end his life and pushes himself out to sea in a boat without an oar; as the boat is caught up by the current, the lightship, the only object to give him his bearings, appears sometimes on his right, sometimes on his left. The episode images Pearston's lack of will, and his inability to make passion and desire submit to the dictates of his reason. It is characteristic of Hardy's economy that the missing oars and the lightship reappear in the 1897 revised version, when Avice the Third and Henri Leverre elope together. What the image now suggests is the inexperience and impulsiveness of the young lovers, as against the rigidity with which Pierston (as Hardy now calls him) follows his chosen course in trying to wed the third Avice.

In such instances, the physical scene, and actions within the physical world, are described in ways that turn them into images, or what T. S. Eliot was soon to call objective correlatives, that is, external facts or events correlated to and evocative of human moods and feelings. The extremest example of this technique is in *Jude the Obscure*, in the presentation of Little Father Time. Where we expect to see a boy, albeit an unhappy one, we are given 'Age masquerading as Juvenility' (5.3). He is less a character than an image or summation of the condition of the life open to Jude and Sue; as Hardy puts it, he becomes 'their nodal point their focus, their expression in a single term' (6.2). Hardy's 1887 note refers to late paintings by Turner, but the example of Little Father Time suggests a closer parallel with the work of Expressionist painters at the turn of the century—Munch, perhaps, or Emil Nolde. Part of the reason Hardy abandoned novel-writing must have been that he had taken his own experiments as far as he could; it was the task of a new generation of novelists to carry them further.

In both *The Return of the Native* and *The Woodlanders*, and to an extent in *The Well-Beloved*, the constant use of the same scene allows Hardy to make significant use of recurring or associated images to illustrate or rather to work out the moral theme of a novel. Throughout *The Woodlanders*, Hardy reminds the reader that the battle for survival in this pastoral world is as intense as it is in the harshest city slums. The struggle of the trees for light and water figures the battle between Fitzpiers and Giles for Grace. Giles, the gentler and perhaps the nobler spirit, is not equipped for such battles; if he is morally in advance of the blind evolutionary struggle around him, he fails in the struggle for survival, and the Winterborne family line dies with him. But the imagery tells us that in a world where the lichen eats the stalk, the ivy destroys the 'promising sapling', and the trees are 'disfigured with wounds' received in the wrestle for existence, we should not expect events to harmonize with our sense of moral fitness (7, 42).

The contradiction between the desired and the inevitable is reflected here, as also in *Tess of the d'Urbervilles*, in some of Hardy's most striking, even shocking, single images. On the day when Melbury sends Giles to fetch Grace home—an event which ought to be the start of their life together—the dawn sky appears as 'the bleared white visage of a sunless winter day... like a dead-born child' (4). When Tess is disturbed by Dairyman Crick's story of another deceived maiden, the evening sun is suddenly 'ugly to her, like a great inflamed wound in the sky' (21). In one case the perception of the external world is informed by the foreknowledge of the narrator, in the other by the sadness of the character: in both, the narrative reaches beyond the mere truth of material fact.

The most restricted setting in Hardy's novels is that of *The Return of the Native*, and many of the images which shape this novel are implicit in its opening pages, in the deeply equivocal account of Egdon Heath. On the one hand Egdon has 'a lonely face, suggesting tragical possibilities'; it is the original of our 'midnight dreams of flight and disaster'—precisely what it offers at the close of Book 5—and it thus serves as a stage or arena which focuses and intensifies the hopes and fears which make up the tragic sense of life.

But it is also, more prosaically, a tract of land known to antiquarians through their studies, and to furze-cutters through their daily work, and its dark uniformity suggests a 'satire' on the vanity which leads men and women to seek to be original, or to demand personal fulfilment. The question of what Egdon images, of the nature of the deeper reality behind the scenic, is in one sense the issue of the novel. Is life to be seen as a Promethean struggle for fulfilment, a struggle which makes men and women godlike; or is the assumption of our individual importance a mere conceit, and life properly to be understood as a matter of keeping the community intact? Is the ground of our being imaged by Egdon's 'nightly roll into darkness', or by the white road traced out by those who have in their different ways cautiously occupied the heath, and accommodated themselves to it (1.1)? The moral world of the novel seems (especially with the added sixth book) to endorse the values of the community, as it reconstitutes itself around the maypole, yet the imagery associated with Eustacia seems to support the individual who tries to stand against it, and in place of the routines of the Heath demands 'what is called life' (4.6). It was the imagery, not the plotting or the moral commentary, that D. H. *Lawrence had in mind when he said that Hardy put the great morality of life itself into his novels, behind the foreground of human drama.

There is a similar use of linked images in *Tess of the d'Urbervilles*. Here again the idea of red, the colour of blood and of fire, echoes throughout the book. Tess's red ribbon and white dress, the splashes of Prince's blood on her skirt, the strawberries Alec presses on her, the red letters warning against adultery, the red buzzard of the threshing machine which begins to exhaust her energy and weaken her till she surrenders again to Alec, the red-brick building where her life ends—all these, as the novel progresses, suggest that Tess has been marked out. Understandably, some accounts of the novel have been as fatalistic as Tess's own family: 'It was to be' (11). Other readers, less excited by the imagery, have emphasized the moments of choice and decision which Hardy is eager to insist on. Both elements have to be acknowledged in our reading of the novel. As in *The Return of the Native*, the imagery sets up a different kind of reading from the one which focuses on the critical moments of moral decision; it reminds us that in Hardy (as later in D. H. Lawrence) the most significant parts of human life may not be those which take place in the consciously choosing mind.

Used in these ways, Hardy's images are more than decorative. They can be so when used in other ways too. Two examples must suffice. There is a key sentence in *Tess*: 'A piece of blood-stained paper, caught up from some meat-buyer's dust-heap, beat up and down the road without the gate, too flimsy to rest, too heavy to fly away; and a few straws kept it company' (44). Like an ideogram or an Imagist prose poem, the sentence focuses what we may take away emotionally from this novel, as if the novel were an exploration into the elemental qualities of blood and straw and wind. It is in this sense that we might most rewardingly see Hardy as a poetic novelist, rather than by referring simply to his powers of description. A second example suggests that images can be used heuristically, as if they held in suspension a range of possible meanings, which might be released by different ways of using them. In both the 1892 and the 1897 versions of *The Well-Beloved* Hardy used the image of a fireworks display and the framework on which it is set up. In 1892, when Pearston loses the third Avice, he sees the 'black framework' where once there had been illuminations which 'dazzled' his eyes; the image suggests the moment when illusion is replaced by clarity and disappointment. In 1897, however, it is used differently: here the blemishes of ordinary human life, so unromantic that the second Avice is a washerwoman, are lost sight of against the 'shining out' of the 'more real' person within, just as the framework of a fireworks display is irrelevant while the fireworks blaze. The same image suggests both the creative seeing made possible by love, and the colder undeceived light of love lost: the inner shining of the beloved, and the self-deception by the lover.

This is perhaps the closest one comes to finding an organizing image in Hardy's writing, one which links poetry and prose. Imagery of vision (and of its absence—sight as opposed to vision) features throughout both novels and poems. So, for example, the poem 'At Waking' picks up the ideas and much of the vocabulary of *The Well-Beloved*: the light of love goes out, to reveal the 'bare | Hard lines' of a 'blank' reality. So persistent is the imagery that Hardy's men seem to fall in love as much with a trick of the light as with the woman herself. Fancy Day is lit 'nebulously' by a candle when Dick Dewy first sees her, and at once falls in love with her (*UGT* 5); Stephen Smith sees Elfride within 'a nebulous haze of light', again from a candle (*PBE* 3); Angel Clare is most drawn to Tess when her face has 'a sort of phosphorescence on it' in the dawn mist (*TDU* 20). In contrast, Bathsheba is wounded when she realizes that Gabriel Oak sees her 'in the cool morning light of open-shuttered disillusion' (*FFMC* 20). Both the charm of this misseeing, and its terrible dangers, are among Hardy's central concerns as a poet and novelist dealing with human love: the 'aureate nimb' that may or may not have lit Tryphena's last days in 'Thoughts of Phena'; the 'hint of rose' that comes and goes in 'Wives in the Sere'; the 'radiance rare and fathomless' which comes with love in 'When I Set Out for Lyonnesse', but which cannot illumine the 'darkening dankness' of Emma's death in 'The Going'.

The imagery suggested by such words as *radiant, radiance, irradiate*—with, as a rule, a corresponding notion of radiance lost, or refused—extends beyond the love poems to those sometimes described as philosophical. So, the speaker in 'A Sign-Seeker' cannot, as others can, 'Read radiant hints of times to be', and 'A Meeting with Despair' ends as darkness overcomes 'Heaven's radiant show'. Such images fit themselves easily to Hardy's preoccupation with the passing of time. Frequently the pattern of the poetry is to reveal a present or future bareness which discloses that a past brightness was a deception: the lady's sunshade, once 'silked in its white or pink', is reduced to a 'skeleton' ('The Sunshade'); 'market-dames, mid-aged' were once 'muslined pink young things', but now neither love nor memory can 'transfigure' them ('Former Beauties'); the 'brightest things' a family owned are exposed to the same weather which with the passage of time will erode even the names on their tombstones ('During Wind and Rain').

In this context 'Shut Out That Moon' may be seen as the quintessential Hardy poem. It is a meditation both on the attractions of the moon, starlight, and the fragrance of boughs at midnight, and on the need to refuse them, to avoid later disappointment by attending to the 'dingy details' of daily life rather than the bright vision conjured up by 'immense Orion's glittering form'. But if Hardy's poetry is often dark, the gloom is rarely unrelieved, and the image of starlight to suggest the mystery of things appears throughout the poems: 'strange-eyed constellations' reign over the dead soldier in 'Drummer Hodge'; in 'Afterwards' the 'full-starred heavens' help to suggest that death will not be the end; and in one of Hardy's greatest moments, at the close of 'Channel Firing', the last verse reminds us not only of 20th-century England and the great guns firing out at sea, but of 'Camelot, and starlit Stonehenge'.

The *'Poems of 1912–13' also share a pattern of images, associated with the ghost-girl-rider, the woman on a horse by the sea, who is at once Emma Lavinia Gifford and an archetype of the haunted imagination. This is a figure which can be summoned but not made to stay; who can haunt, but remains unseen; who plays on the shore of our experience, and on the shore of life and death, on the boundary between the world we know and the world of which we dream. These poems include separate images of great beauty—the lonely dreamscape where 'the shy hares print long paces' ('The Haunter'); the 'pale mews' which haunt over the surface of a jewelled sea ('Beeny Cliff'); the stars closing their shutters as 'the dawn whitens lazily' ('After a Journey'). But just as often the power of these poems comes from the directness of Hardy's speech, where he seems to eschew imagery which might draw attention to itself. There is a fine example in the last stanza of 'At Castle Boterel', where the images—love's domain, the sands of time—are so familiar as to be barely noticed, and what remains with the reader is the nakedness of 'I look back at it amid the rain | For the very last time'.

This is finally one of Hardy's characteristics. Striking as the diction is, his words often seem to invite the reader to pass through them, not to notice them. The obvious contrast among his contemporaries would be with Hopkins at one end of Hardy's poetry-writing career, and the later Yeats at the other. Hardy is more suspicious than they are of the visionary, and more mindful of what he does not know or cannot say: tentative, reserved, loyal to the familiar, he rarely provides the linguistic excitement of, say, 'The Windhover' or 'Byzantium'. But this is perhaps what we should expect, and value, in a poet who was content with 'the homeliest | Of heart-stirrings' ('Any Little Old Song'), who celebrated 'deeds of home' rather than 'glory and war-mightiness' ('The Souls of the Slain'), and was ready to learn 'Earth-secrets' from 'God's humblest' ('An August Midnight'). PVM

'Imaginative Woman, An', short story. It was written in 1893, and first published in the *Pall Mall Magazine* (April 1894). Hardy had offered it (at that stage unwritten) to a literary agent, W. M. Colles, on 14 April 1893, and had sent him the story exactly five months later. Originally collected in the American edition of *Wessex Tales* (1896) published by Osgood, McIlvaine, it was moved to *Life's Little Ironies* for Macmillan's Wessex Edition (1912). In both collections it stands first. The manuscript, which shows numerous revisions and is titled 'A Woman of Imagination', is now in the library of the University of Aberdeen.

The sources of the story seem to be both intellectual and personal: Hardy's reading in 1890 of August Weismann's *Essays on Heredity* supplied some of its ideas, but a more immediate impetus came from his meeting in May 1893 with Florence *Henniker, whose 'emotional imaginativeness' he later referred to. Some of the details in the story may well allude to Mrs Henniker: she had, for example, lived at Southsea, the 'Solentsea' of the story; like the heroine, Ella Marchmill, she had literary aspirations; her second name, Ellen, is not far from Ella; and her husband's military profession was not far removed from that of Marchmill, the gun-manufacturer who is married to the heroine. In the manuscript the poet's name is Crewe, that of Mrs Henniker's mother, though Hardy tactfully changed it to Trewe. In many details the figure and career of Trewe are based on those of Dante Gabriel Rossetti, whose portrait by Holman Hunt seems to have been the basis of Hardy's description (see F. B. Pinion, *A Hardy Dictionary*, 277). The theme of loveless marriage connects the story with *Jude the Obscure*, while its treatment of the frustrations of philistine bourgeois life in a provincial town may owe something to *Ibsen, some of whose plays Hardy saw in London in June 1893. The story, which moves towards an effective ironic conclusion, is one of the finest studies of contemporary life in Hardy's shorter fiction.

Martin Ray, '"An Imaginative Woman" from Manuscript to Wessex Edition: A Textual Study', *THJ* 9 (1993).

Indiscretion in the Life of an Heiress, An. See UNCOLLECTED STORIES.

'Interlopers at the Knap', short story. First published in the *English Illustrated Magazine* (May 1884), it was collected in *Wessex Tales*. Farmer Darton visits The Knap, the King's-Hintock home of Sally Hall and her mother, with the intention of proposing to Sally, but complications arise when Sally's brother turns up unexpectedly, having returned with a wife and two children from Australia after a five-year absence. Darton has formerly been the lover of Philip Hall's wife Helena, and, sensing this, Sally turns him down. Philip promptly dies and Darton marries Helena. (A comparable situation, with the death of a spouse offering the opportunity to make good a wrong committed in the past, had been used a little earlier in the story 'Fellow-Townsmen'.) After her death he vainly renews his attentions to Sally, who declares her intention of never marrying.

Compared with other stories in the same volume, such as 'The Three Strangers' and 'The Withered Arm', 'Interlopers at the Knap' is low-keyed and lacking in drama. The atmosphere of rural life is convincingly rendered, but there is perhaps too much plotting for a story of this length: much of the action is narrated summarily rather than dramatically, and the two deaths are undeniably convenient. Its main interest is in the figure of Sally, whose lively and independent spirit recalls Fancy Day in *Under the Greenwood Tree*: a liberated woman within the constraints of traditional rural society, Sally rejects an advantageous marriage, and exercises her right to choose her own way of life (the story's quiet but striking final words are 'steadily adhered to her purpose of leading a single life').

Darton's journey to visit Sally at the beginning of the story is said to have been based on a family tradition concerning Hardy's father's journey to Melbury Osmond on the eve of his wedding (see Millgate 15). Darton's attempt to atone for past errors by marrying the woman he has wronged looks forward to the theme of a later short story, 'For Conscience' Sake', while the return of the failed Australian emigrants is an idea that was taken up again in *Jude the Obscure*.

interviews. Hardy's attitude towards interviews changed radically during his professional life as a writer. During the 1870s and early 1880s his income as a novelist was never large, and he needed all the publicity he could get, even though he was by nature a quiet and reticent person. And there was another problem. England was a class-conscious society, he was writing for middle-class readers, and his own origins were distinctly working-class. Publicity, then, had to be obtained to help the sales of his books and provide an income sufficient for a married man, and the interviews with him had to be falsified in certain biographical areas. Hardy the professional writer did not regard himself as being on oath to tell the truth about his private life, and he worked hard during those early years to establish the right kind of public persona. Thus, he made journal editors aware that he was willing to give interviews, and, if necessary, was prepared to write the interview himself for a journalist to publish as his own work, just as he would later pretend that his wife had written his *autobiography.

A very few recollections of Hardy survive from the first 30 years of his life (1840–70), and there were not many interviews with him during the novel-writing years of the 1870s and 1880s. One example of an interview almost certainly written by Hardy himself is to be found in the *Literary World* (Boston) for August 1878. Who else would have written the sentence, 'His attention, however, during this period was not wholly devoted to architecture, literature receiving his attention to a considerable extent, and his higher education being looked after by an able classical scholar and Fellow of Queens' College, Cambridge'? (The reference is, of course, to Horace *Moule.) Other articles that have Hardy written all over them include Richard Bowker's 'Thomas Hardy: The Dorset Novelist' in *Harper's New Monthly Magazine* (June 1888), and an anonymous article, 'Celebrities at Home', in the *World* (February 1886). Useful interviews from this period are those of Dr Frederick B. Fisher, the Hardy family doctor (*Christ Church College (Cawnpore) Magazine*, March 1930); Sir George Douglas, *Gleanings in Prose and Verse* (Galashiels, n.d.); Lady St Helier, *Memories of Fifty Years* (1909); and Edith Wharton, *A Backward Glance* (1934).

Just as there is a dearth of interviews before 1890, there is a glut after that date. Hardy the well-known novelist became Hardy the famous novelist after the publication of *Tess* in 1891 and the even more sensational *Jude* five years later. He was now the subject of countless newspaper and journal articles, and there is a substantial change in Hardy's attitude towards those who wished to interview him. In 1894 we find him, in a letter to Florence Henniker (*L* ii 44), complaining that 'I find that these men, out of one visit, will make 4 or 5 interviews, for various papers', and he refers to 'the cloven hoof of the interviewer'. With fame and fortune, the problem was not too few requests for interviews, but too many.

There had to be some kind of protection of his private life and his early years, about which he was still very sensitive, and, with the coming of the 20th century, interviews were not so welcome as they had previously been, although he was remarkably generous to young writers and genuine scholars. Those whom Hardy agreed to meet were warned that on no account were they to talk about his personal life, interpret his novels in an autobiographical way, or ask him to sign copies of his books, and they were usually forbidden to take down any notes. Even so, one visitor, Vere H. Collins, was treated very generously by Hardy and interviewed him on a number of occasions in 1920–2. Then, as soon as Hardy died in 1928, Collins published a book, *Talks with Thomas Hardy at Max Gate*, which has 84 pages of dramatized duologue with Hardy. Was Collins allowed to take notes, and how otherwise could he claim to report Hardy's words exactly? Florence, Hardy's widow, was very annoyed by this publication.

Because of Florence's moodiness and her regret that Hardy, by the time she married him, was unwilling to leave home for more than a day or two at a time, and because of her grumbles about how lonely she felt at Max Gate, the impression has been given that in his later years Hardy lived the life of a recluse. This is not true, and there was a never-ending stream of visitors until almost the moment of his death. The Max Gate visitors' book was signed by more than 70 visitors in 1927, the last complete year of Hardy's life, and not everyone who visited signed the book. Many of his friends wrote down their memories of him, and published them after his death. There are several hundred recorded interviews, and probably as many more that have not been traced. Because of this it is possible to mention briefly only a few.

Among the most worthwhile interviews of the 1890s are those of Raymond Blathwayt, who published interviews in *Pall Mall Gazette*, 2 January 1892, and *Black and White*, 27 August 1892 (see also *Cassell's Saturday Journal*, 25 June 1892, and *The Young Man*, March 1894); G. K. Chesterton, in his *Autobiography* (1936); George Gissing (*Letters* (1961)); John Cowper Powys (*Autobiography* (1967)) and Llewelyn Powys (*Virginia Quarterly Review*,

Winter 1939); and Christine Wood Homer and Hermann *Lea. The reminiscences of these last two will be found in the series *Monographs on the Life, Times and Works of Thomas Hardy* (Toucan Press, Guernsey), which contain much useful information as well as occasional trivialities.

From about 1900, American professors and others began to arrive in search of an article on Hardy, or a chapter in a book. One of the best of these productions is by William Lyon Phelps (*Autobiography with Letters* (1939)), and one of the most amusing in its obtuseness that of Hamlin Garland (*Afternoon Neighbours* (1934)), whom Hardy found so boring that he began asking silly questions such as 'Is Harvard a girls' school?' An important interview that took place in 1901 was with William *Archer (*Real Conversations* (1904)). It is in duologue form but, unlike that of Vere Collins, clearly had Hardy's approval. Although Frank Hedgcock aroused Hardy's ire by daring to write a book that made use of biographical material gathered during a visit to Max Gate in 1919, his reminiscences of Hardy in the *National and English Review* (October–November 1951) are full of interest.

Of the flood of interviews that was to follow in the remaining years of Hardy's life, the ones that most deserve mention are those of his fellow-writers. The contrasting accounts of a visit to Max Gate in 1912 by A. C. *Benson and Edmund *Gosse, described in Ann Thwaite's *Portraits from Life* (1991), reveal how important it is in interpreting any interview to take into account the attitude of the interviewer. Siegfried *Sassoon first visited Hardy in 1918, and there are many references to Hardy in his letters and diaries: see especially *Siegfried's Journey 1916–20* (1945).

Sassoon seems to have introduced Robert *Graves, who visited Max Gate in 1920, and this meeting is described in the *Sphere* (28 January 1928). It was Graves who in turn introduced T. E. *Lawrence, who, in *his* turn, introduced E. M. *Forster to Hardy. Lawrence and Forster both wrote about Hardy in several of their letters. Other interviews of value will be found in John Middleton *Murry's *Katherine Mansfield and Other Literary Portraits* (1949), Lady Cynthia Asquith's *Portrait of Barrie* (1954), Walter *de la Mare's article in *The Listener* (28 April 1956), the monographs in the Toucan Press series by Norman Atkins, May O'Rourke, and Harold L. Voss, Eden Phillpotts's *From the Angle of 88* (1951), Rutland *Boughton's article in the *Musical News and Herald* (15 February 1928), Gertrude *Bugler's article in the *Listener* (29 June 1939), and Virginia *Woolf's *A Writer's Diary* (1954). JCG

Thomas Hardy: Interviews and Recollections (1999), ed. James Gibson.

irony. So pervasive is ironic thought, statement, and situation in Hardy's fiction and poetry, as well as in his personal writings, that it is less useful to consider irony in Hardy by invoking conventional notions such as rhetorical irony, Romantic Irony, etc. than to think of irony in Hardy as an expression of basic outlook and temperament. That things are not what they appear to be, might be, or should be, is for Hardy less a matter of intellectual strategy than a response to the authority of his consciousness and experience.

In Hardy's vision of things the ironies inherent to existence stem from what in *The Dynasts* (1.5) the Spirit of the Pities describes as 'the intolerable antilogy of making figments feel'. To this the Spirit Ironic replies: 'Logic's in that. It does not, I must own, quite play the game.' The Spirit Ironic's 'It' is the Unconscious Will, which is, as that Spirit acknowledges, as coldly unaware 'as glacial snow' of humanity, its joys and sorrows.

The very language of Hardy's titles registers the depth of his ironic sense. The phrase 'Tess of the d'Urbervilles' signals a nominal aristocracy concealing an actual poverty concealing in turn the indomitable, ineradicable aristocracy of Tess Durbeyfield's character. The phrases 'Under the Greenwood Tree' and 'Far from the Madding Crowd' bespeak pastoral idyllicism, while the novels they name exhibit on nearly every page the intolerable anguish of that feeling called love. If 'The Woodlanders' calls attention to the human denizens of a wood, the language of *The Wood-landers* exposes their kinships with the tormented non-human lives (vegetal, insect, animal) whose struggle for existence surrounds Giles, Marty, and others and replays in uncanny ways their suffering through love and marriage. The words of the title *The Mayor of Casterbridge* invite attention to a man of character and status who is in truth a venal, if forgivable, man of temper capable of selling wife and daughter for a few guineas.

The Dynasts targets what was for Hardy the great tragic irony of 19th-century European history, the perversion of humanitarian idealism by military and political power, the example of Napoleon the liberator become Bonaparte the tyrant. *Time's Laughingstocks, Satires of Circumstance, Human Shows*—these titles of three of Hardy's eight volumes of poetry convey what hundreds of the poems in these and other volumes exhibit: that time, circumstance, and experience will, because they must, undo expectation, idealism, and hope. The title of another collection, *Moments of Vision*, illustrates, in some 70% of its 160 poems, that Hardy's moments of vision were moments of insight into the irony at the heart of things: that education and experience do not bring understanding ('Afternoon Service at Mellstock'), that a man can admire a lover's youthful photograph more than the ageing lover herself ('The Rival'). Hardy was simply capable of inventing, repeating, and playing the changes on hundreds of ironic situations.

Hardy's use of ironic titles, as well as multitudes of ironic circumstances and comments, confirms that his is an irony of outlook, a philosophic irony intimately tied to his fundamental sense of things. That he resists classification as a Romantic Ironist illustrates his refusal to embrace nihilism, or even a radical philosophic scepticism. What sets Hardy's irony off from Byron's, Thackeray's, or Meredith's is his use of it to expose the cosmic disorder behind the human struggle, rather than to expose a social disarray rooted in human infirmity.

So Hardy's ironic vision is also his metaphysic; it serves the ends not of satire, absurdist discourse, or pessimism, but rather the purposes of a sad celebration for the beauty of the inherent sadness, the tears, in things. In sum, Hardy's irony is less Byronic than it is Sophoclean, less a sneer or a whine than a stern or smiling pronouncement on the insight contained in the phrase from *The Dynasts* recalled above. This remarkable phrase exposes the controlling paradox of Hardy's ironic vision. 'Antilogy', literally 'against knowing', is his archaic word for paradox. The 'figments' are those living, breathing beings—vegetal, animal, human—victimized by the 'making' of an unconscious force that can neither know nor care about the consequences of its insentient doings. That living things should be made capable of feeling is an unbearable absurdity, an 'intolerable antilogy', because to live is to know pain. For Hardy, irony can be neither a rhetorical devising nor an existential posturing, but rather a (perhaps the) central fact of sentient existence. PC

Wayne C. Booth, *A Rhetoric of Irony* (1974).

Anne K. Mellor, *English Romantic Irony* (1980).

Douglas Colin Muecke, *Irony and the Ironic* (1982).

J

James, Henry (1843–1916), novelist. Born an American, he settled in England and became a British citizen near the end of his life. He reviewed *Far from the Madding Crowd* for the New York *Nation* (24 December 1874, repr. in *CH*), where his comments on the novel's verbosity and 'padding' and his patronizing remarks that the author was 'evidently very much at home among rural phenomena', and that 'the only things we believe in are the sheep and the dogs', would not much have endeared him to Hardy. The two were acquaintances in London from at least the early 1880s, but never became close friends: Hardy, indeed, though admiring James's artistry and sense of vocation, seems not to have cared for him as a man, while James found it difficult to admire fiction so different in purpose and method from his own, and perhaps also found Hardy's lack of sophistication and a cosmopolitan outlook unappealing. They met frequently, however, at the homes of mutual friends such as Edmund *Gosse and became fellow-members of the Athenaeum (see CLUBS).

Hardy read some of James's work with admiration: at an early stage of both their careers, he read *Roderick Hudson* (1876), as well as James's biography of Hawthorne (1879), and his essay on Balzac in *French Poets and Novelists* (1878); in 1888, reading *The Reverberator* soon after its publication, he reflected that novelists could hardly continue to be preoccupied by 'the minutiae of manners', but *The Wings of the Dove* (1902) moved him to describe James, in an unwonted and striking burst of enthusiasm, as almost the only novelist he could read (*L* iii 56). A later letter (5 November 1915: *L* v 130) contains the equally striking statement that, though not now much interested in novelists, he could 'always . . . read' James. Less than two months before James's death, Hardy wrote to him on behalf of the Society of Authors, offering congratulations on his naturalization and on the award of the Order of Merit.

A generation earlier, in letters to R. L. *Stevenson not published until after James's death, James disparaged the recently published *Tess of the d'Urbervilles*, describing it as 'chock-full of faults and falsity', though at the same time possessing 'a singular beauty and charm'. The same letter (19 March 1892) refers condescendingly to 'The good little Thomas Hardy'. On 17 February 1893, evidently responding to Stevenson's defence of Hardy, James attacked both the sexuality and the style of the same novel, conceding only that it contained 'some pretty smells and sights and sounds'—a reversion to his much earlier attitude of condescension towards *Far from the Madding Crowd*. Hardy, evidently deeply wounded by the explosion of this time-bomb, quotes part of this second letter, with sardonic comments, in *LW* (259–60). (See also CHARACTERIZATION.) For an instance of Hardy's posthumous malice towards James, see PROCTER, ANNE.

J. T. Laird, 'Approaches to Fiction: Hardy and Henry James', *THA* 2 (1984).

Jeune, Mary (1845–1931), society hostess, philanthropist, and journalist. She married (1) Colonel the Hon. John Constantine Stanley (1827–78), second son of the 2nd Lord Stanley of Alderley; her younger daughter by this marriage also became a valued friend of Hardy's (see ALLHUSEN, DOROTHY); (2) Francis Jeune (1843–1905), lawyer and later judge, knighted in 1891, created Baron St Helier in 1905. She served as an alderman of the London County Council, and was created a Dame of the British Empire in 1925. She became a close friend and frequent correspondent of Hardy's, and from about 1890 was 'the closest of his London friends' (Millgate 304); they met frequently at social gatherings, he was a regular visitor to her house in Harley Street, and the *Life* contains many references to her and her second husband.

At her request Hardy wrote an epilogue for a special performance of Shakespeare's *The Taming of the Shrew* given at the Lyceum Theatre on 23 July 1890 in aid of a children's charity; spoken on that occasion by the actress Ada Rehan, these lines had been written at the Savile Club the previous evening, and were eventually printed (as 'Lines') in *Wessex Poems.* At Hardy's urging, Lady Jeune wrote a letter to the *Daily Chronicle* (published 8 May 1894), defending *Life's Little Ironies* against the charge of immorality brought by William *Archer in a letter four days earlier.

Hardy's first wife Emma was distantly connected with the Jeune family, since her uncle, Canon Edwin Gifford, had married a daughter of Francis Jeune (1806–68), late Bishop of Peterborough and father of the Francis Jeune who in 1881 became Mary Stanley's second husband. Robert Gittings has suggested (*The Older Hardy,* 29) that both the name and something of the character of the husband of Lady Constantine, heroine of *Two on a Tower,* were based on those of Lady Jeune's first husband.

Jude the Obscure. This is in *effect* Hardy's last novel, even though *The Well-Beloved* appeared in volume form for the first time in 1897. An earlier version of the latter had been serialized in the closing months of 1892, while the serial version of *Jude* appeared from December 1894 to November 1895. The virulent attacks on *Jude* (which were in fact, however, not so universal as Hardy felt) cured him, as he wrote in the 1912 Postscript to the preface, 'of further interest in novel-writing'. It is because *Jude's* reception was one of the factors that caused Hardy to abandon novel-writing and return to poetry that it is *effectively* Hardy's last novel.

Composition

Hardy's Preface to the First Edition, dated August 1895, summarizes various stages in the novel's development: 'The scheme was jotted down in 1890, from notes made in 1887 and onwards, some of the circumstances being suggested by the death of a woman in the former year. The scenes were revisited in October 1892; the narrative was written in outline in 1892 and the spring of 1893, and at full length, as it now appears, from August 1893 onwards into the next year; the whole, with the exception of a few chapters, being in the hands of the publisher by the end of 1894.' The distinction between 'scheme' and 'outline' is not altogether clear, but a diary entry for 28 April 1888, quoted in the *Life,* shows that the educational theme that looms so large in the completed novel was already in Hardy's mind at this time: 'A short story of a young man—"who could not go to Oxford"—His struggles and ultimate failure ...' (*LW* 216). The 'woman' referred to in the preface was Tryphena *Sparks, who had died in March 1890. The 'scenes ... revisited' in October 1892 were in Oxfordshire, not far from 'Christminster' itself: Hardy's grandmother Mary Head (see RELATIVES OF THOMAS HARDY) had spent her early years very unhappily in the village of Great Fawley, which both gives Jude his surname and is the model for 'Marygreen', in which the novel opens. From this evidence it seems likely that *Jude* occupied Hardy, from start to finish, for longer than any of its predecessors. The date given at the end of the manuscript (now in the Fitzwilliam Museum, Cambridge) is March 1895.

Serialization

Hardy was under contract to provide a serial for *Harper & Brothers, who at an early stage expressed concern that the story should be 'in every way suitable for a family magazine'—to which he had offered the assurance that it would be one that 'could not offend the most fastidious maiden'. By April 1894, however, he admitted to them that it was developing along unforeseen lines, and he asked to be released from the agreement. This request was not granted, and in response to pressure from the magazine editor, H. M. *Alden, Hardy set about the highly uncongenial task of bowdlerizing his novel—an unwelcome repeat of what he had done in respect of *Tess of the d'Urbervilles.* These changes ranged from minor stylistic adjustments (such as changing 'kissing' to 'shaking hands', 'sex' to 'affection', and 'bed' to 'couch') to extensive omissions, especially in those parts of the action dealing with the hero's relationships with Arabella and Sue.

In this mangled and emasculated form the novel appeared in *Harper's New Monthly Magazine* in twelve monthly instalments from December 1894 to November 1895, appearing simultaneously in New York and London. In the first instalment the title was given as *The Simpletons;* in the second, and for the rest of the run, it was changed to *Hearts Insurgent,* apparently because it had been realized that there might be confusion with Charles Reade's *A Simpleton,* which

Harper's had published more than twenty years earlier.

The division of the novel into monthly portions was as follows: December 1894, 1.1–6; January 1895, 1.7–11; February, 2.1–5; March, 2.6–3.3; April, 3.4–7; May, 3.8–4.2; June, 4.3–5; July, 4.6–5.3; August, 5.4–7; September, 5.8–6.3; October, 6.4–7; November, 6.7 (contd.)–11.

Illustrations

Each monthly instalment was accompanied by an illustration by W. Hatherell. These are in a vein of harsh realism befitting the tone and texture of the novel, and were much admired by Hardy.

Volume Publication

The novel appeared in volume form, now as *Jude the Obscure*, in London, priced at 6s., on 1 November 1895, as Volume VIII in *Osgood, McIlvaine's collected edition of Hardy's novels ('Wessex Novels'), which was then in progress (see COLLECTED EDITIONS). Later in the same month an American edition was issued by Harper & Brothers. In accordance with a common custom applying to books published near the end of a year, both editions were dated 1896. For these editions, which reproduced Hatherell's illustrations, Hardy added a short but interesting preface and very largely restored the cuts and revisions made for the serial version. There were further revisions when Macmillan reissued the novel in 1902, and a substantial 'Postscript' to the preface was added when it appeared in the Wessex Edition of 1912.

Reception

Jude the Obscure aroused more controversy than any of Hardy's other novels, a fact that no doubt helped to make it the terminus of his novel-writing career. Disapproval of the novel by contemporary reviewers in England and America, though not unanimous, was often vehement and sometimes scurrilous. As R. G. Cox has noted, reactions 'went to ridiculous extremes among ordinary readers as well as critics' (*CH* xxxvi): the most notorious of such reactions was that of W. W. *How, Bishop of Wakefield, who not only claimed to have burned the book but ensured its banning by W. H. Smith's, a leading circulating library.

Of published criticisms, R. Y. Tyrrell in the *Fortnightly Review* (June 1896; repr. in *CH*) judged the work 'a deplorable falling-off' and characterized it as 'a treatise on sexual pathology', while the *Athenaeum* (23 November 1895; repr. in *CH*) judged it 'a titanically bad book' and the *Pall Mall Gazette* (12 November 1895; repr. in *CH*) dubbed it 'Jude the Obscene'. In more moderate tones, J. B. Allen asked in the *Academy* (15 February 1896), 'why should a novelist introduce subjects normally avoided in conversation?' The novel was, however, taken more seriously by a number of critics. An anonymous writer in the *Saturday Review* (8 February 1896) made the memorable comment that Jude's is 'the voice of the educated proletarian, speaking more distinctly than it has ever spoken before in English literature', and the *Illustrated London News* (11 January 1896; repr. in *CH*) declared that 'most of our fiction is to *Jude the Obscure* as a hamlet to a hemisphere'. Havelock Ellis, in a long article in the *Savoy Magazine* (October 1896; repr. in *CH*), responded to Hardy's attackers, and uncompromisingly concluded that 'if the Young Person should care to read *Jude* we ought for her own sake, at all events, to be thankful'. Another of Hardy's defenders was his friend Sir George *Douglas, who responded to some of the attacks in an article in the *Bookman* (January 1896).

References are made later in this article to other reviews, including the important ones by Margaret *Oliphant and by Hardy's friend Edmund *Gosse.

Plot

The depiction of Jude Fawley's orphaned childhood in the village of Marygreen shows his extreme, indeed excessive, idealism, in his idealization of his schoolmaster Phillotson and the place Phillotson moves to, Christminster (Oxford), in order to be near the university. We see Jude's hesitation to walk in a pasture for fear of crushing earthworms, and his protection of the birds he has been hired to scare away. He loses the job, disappointing the great-aunt who has adopted him. Feeling more unwanted than ever, the boy lies down near a pig-sty, glimpsing the world through the interstices of a straw hat he has pulled over his face: the thought 'that mercy towards one set of creatures was cruelty towards another sickened his sense of harmony' (1.2). For the first time Jude faces the ironic disparity between the ideal and the real.

By the age of 19, Jude has been intensively studying the Latin and Greek classics and the Greek Testament with a view to preparing himself for admission to the university at Christminster. He is walking home one evening, thinking of all he has read and all he has still to read, when he is struck in the face by a piece of pig's flesh (a penis) that has been thrown by the laughing Arabella, a pig-breeder's daughter and 'a complete and substantial female animal' (1.6). Jude, who has never noticed women before, is now awakened to sex, another aspect of reality—the pig theme locates this reality both inside and outside Jude. In a short time he has been lured into Arabella's bedroom, and tricked into marrying her when she claims to be pregnant. He is quickly disillusioned when he discovers that Arabella's hair and dimple are as false as her pregnancy. She turns against him when he makes a mess of killing their pig because of his tenderheartedness. Jude begins drinking, and she leaves for Australia with her family: 'Their lives were ruined', says Hardy, attacking marriage, because they 'based a permanent contract on a temporary feeling' (1.11).

Jude is now free to resume his purpose by moving to Christminster, where he meets his cousin Sue. Jude, who works as a stonemason, finds Sue selling Christian statuettes and other religious objects in a church shop. But we note the division in her character when we see her in her own time buying pagan statuettes and reading *Swinburne's anti-Christian poetry (2.3). Jude falls in love with Sue. On their first meeting he suggests a visit to Phillotson, whom he finds, to his disillusionment, still a village schoolmaster, his ambitions unfulfilled. Jude sees that Phillotson, though twenty years older than Sue, is falling in love with her, but can do nothing to advance his own cause since he is still married to Arabella.

Jude is frustrated again when, after applying to various colleges for admission, he receives a reply from one of them advising him, since he describes himself '"as a workingman"', to remain in his '"own sphere"' and stick to his '"trade"' (2.6). The effect is to drive him back to drink, and he is dismissed by his employer. In despair he returns to Marygreen, where a local curate gives him a new hope—to enter the Church in a humble capacity as a licentiate (licensed preacher rather than ordained priest).

Having received a letter from Sue informing him that she has entered a teachers' training college at Melchester (Salisbury), Jude decides to go there to continue his studies. He finds work that suits him, repairing the Cathedral, though Sue insists that it is the railway station rather than the Cathedral that is now the real centre of the town. The college discipline does not agree with her, and Jude takes her out for a meal to relieve her tension; there she announces 'with the perverseness that was part of her' (3.1) that she has promised to marry Phillotson after she has finished her course of training, when they will work together in the boys' and girls' departments of a school. The college reprimands Sue and confines her to her room for going out with Jude, but she appears one evening at his lodgings soaking wet, having escaped through her window and crossed the river. Jude lends her his Sunday suit and, in a striking scene, finds 'a slim and fragile being masquerading as himself on a Sunday' (3.3). Sue describes her '"peculiarity"' that she has no fear of men's books and has '"mixed with [men] ... almost as one of their own sex"'; she tells how she and a Christminster undergraduate planned to live together '"like two men almost"', but the young man could not bear the sexual frustration involved and, she fears, died of it. '"I have never yielded myself to any lover,"' she continues: '"People say I must be cold-natured—sexless—on account of it. But I won't have it!"' Jude is left depressed by 'her strange ways and curious unconsciousness of gender' (3.4).

On a trip to Christminster, Jude is amazed to recognize Arabella serving as barmaid in a pub he has entered. They spend the night together discreetly in a neighbouring town (for, unlike Jude and Sue, Arabella manages to stay within the conventions), where she reveals her secret—that she has 'married' again in Australia. Soon afterward the Australian 'husband' turns up and she joins him. By way of contrast to Arabella, Sue reveals her repugnance towards a sexual relationship with her new husband, Phillotson: '"What tortures me so much is the necessity of being responsive to this man whenever he wishes"' (4.1). '"One ought to be allowed,"' she continues (and here Hardy shows *Jude* to be, among other things, a novel of ideas), '"to undo what one has done so ignorantly!"' (4.1). She kisses Jude, and the kiss makes him realize that he can no longer aspire to be a preacher. Each of his aspirations, he reflects, has been checked by a woman. Sue's aversion to Phillotson takes such extreme forms—she finally throws herself out of the window to avoid his attentions—that he agrees to let her go to her cousin Jude, and later grants her a divorce, an act of generosity that ruins his own career.

Arabella for her part grants Jude a divorce, so he is now free to marry Sue; but she shrinks from marriage. Twice they try to get married, but retreat; finally they slip away to London, letting it be known on their return that they are married. However, they are not believed, which ruins Jude's stone-cutting business, forcing them to leave Aldbrickham (Reading). Jude's life with Sue is a mixture of happiness and frustration. They produce two children and a third is on the way, but their sexual life together is evidently insufficient to satisfy Jude. Before the conception of these children, Arabella has sent them a strange sad little boy who, she insists, is Jude's son: 'He was Age,' we are told, 'masquerading as Juvenility' (5.3), and is nicknamed 'Little Father Time' (5.4). He stands out in the realistic context as an almost allegorical figure, disturbing to some critics. The book's tragic dénouement is brought about by the dangerous mixture of this preternaturally old little boy with Sue's peculiarities. Both are presented as distinctively modern phenomena.

Sue's fear of sex shapes the conversation with the boy that leads to his suicide and his murder of the other two children. Jude has taken the family back to Christminster in order to witness the academic ceremonies on 'Commemoration Day'; lodgings are difficult to find, and Father Time watches as they are turned away by unfriendly landladies on account of the children. After they have at last found lodgings with space for Sue and the children but not for Jude, Sue unnecessarily confesses to the landlady that she and Jude are not married, which causes the family's eviction. This eviction, and further refusals at other lodgings, make a terrible impression on the boy, who concludes that '"It would be better to be out o' the world than in it, wouldn't it?"' Instead of comforting him, Sue agrees with this grim sentiment. Sue's failure to conceal the truth about the expected baby, and to reassure the boy by telling him she loves him, betrays a lack of instinct.

After the children's deaths she comes to the 'awful conviction that her discourse with the boy had been the main cause of the tragedy' (6.2); she has '"wanted to be truthful"' but now feels guilty because she failed to tell him '"the facts of life"'. Sue's fear of sex is always the deeper motive beneath her apparent ones. Yet she subscribes—illustrating Hardy's analysis here and elsewhere of self-deceiving idealism—to ideals of free sex and freedom from Christian dogma. When, after the tragedy, Sue returns as a penance to her 'lawful' husband (though Phillotson is no longer that except in a quixotic sense), the penance begins as a way of putting an end to her sexual life.

The parting with Sue kills Jude, who tells her that '"Perhaps the world is not illuminated enough for such experiments as ours!"' and accuses her of never having loved him as he has loved her ('"Yours is not a passionate heart.... You are... a sort of fay, or sprite—not a woman!"' (6.3)). Apprised of what has happened, Arabella begins her campaign to recapture Jude: she appears on his doorstep begging for shelter, since her father (she tells him untruthfully) has turned her out. Jude reluctantly lets her stay in his attic, and later, finding him in a tavern, she gets him drunk and, in a replay of her first seduction of him, takes him home to her bedroom. Her father tells him that he must make an honest woman of her; she has the licence and the parson ready; and Jude remarries her. Thus Hardy renews his attack on marriage and religion.

Soon after their marriage, Jude falls ill and Arabella regrets her bargain. He resolves to go and see Sue again, and, still a sick man, walks the five miles from the station to Marygreen in a driving rain. Their meeting, in which Jude tells Sue that she is '"not worth a man's love!"', is the novel's most passionate scene. They kiss, but Sue tells him to leave and later, in self-punishment for her 'sin', asks Phillotson to let her into his bed. When Jude, after another long walk in the rain, returns to Christminster, he finds Arabella waiting for him at the station; when she tells him he has '"done for"' himself, he tells her that this is what he meant to do, and she expresses incredulity that he should wish to '"kill yourself for a woman"'—summing up the extreme realism she has represented throughout (6.9). Hardy, a Darwinian, credits her with a strong instinct for survival lacking in Jude and Sue.

Hardy presents Jude's death with great skill, counterpointing it ironically against the Commemoration festival outside, which Arabella has gone off to enjoy. He dies repeating the words of Job, and cursing the day he was born.

Critical Approaches

Hardy complains in the 1912 Postscript to his preface that the attacks on *Jude* dwelt mainly on 'some twenty or thirty pages of sorry detail [on sexuality]', whereas the main point for him was 'the shattered ideals of the two chief characters'. He delineates the book's ideas: that 'a marriage should be dissolvable as soon as it becomes a cruelty to either of the parties—being then essentially and morally no marriage'; that it was difficult to acquire 'knowledge in letters without pecuniary means'; that 'artistic effort always pays heavily for finding its tragedies in the forced adaptation of human instincts to rusty and irksome moulds that do not fit them'. Hardy quotes a German reviewer who associated Sue Bridehead with 'the woman of the feminist movement... the intellectualized, emancipated bundle of nerves that modern conditions were producing'—as, in other words, a New Woman. All these ideas were subjects of discussion among advanced intellectuals in the 1890s.

Irving Howe, in his *Thomas Hardy* (1967), opens his chapter on *Jude* by calling it 'Hardy's most distinctly "modern" work, for it rests upon a cluster of assumptions central to modernist literature: that in our time men wishing to be more than dumb clods must live in permanent doubt and intellectual crisis; that for such men... life has become inherently problematic' (pp. 134–5). *Jude* is also 'modern', I would add, in its location in towns (rather than the country, the locale of Hardy's other major novels), through which Jude and Sue wander, indicating their modern rootlessness.

In his favourable review of *Jude* in *Cosmopolis* (January 1896), Edmund Gosse perceives its geometrical structure, a perception confirmed by Hardy in his letter to Gosse of 10 November 1895 (*L* ii 93), in response to Gosse's first review of the novel in the *St James's Gazette* on 8 November. H. M. Daleski, in his *Thomas Hardy and the Paradoxes of Love* (1997), analyses the structure, pointing out that this story of two couples is like a quadrille in which each couple begin together—Jude with Arabella, Sue with Phillotson—then move apart, only to return to each other, in Jude's remarriage to Arabella and Sue's to Phillotson. Daleski also discerns a principle of repetition: 'the ultimate effect of Jude's wanderings is to bring him back to where he started: to Christminster, the city to which he first moves, and to Marygreen, the site of his last despairing and suicidal journey to see Sue and the place from which he originally set out'. Each episode moves to a defeat of Jude's hope, but ends with renewed hope as he changes direction, until, in the final episodes, the death of the children, the separation of Jude and Sue, and Jude's death conclude 'the systematic frustration of all aspirations' (pp. 181–3).

It is in the characterization of Sue that Hardy makes a definitive break with the Victorian novel, in which the problem is to arrive at the point of sexuality by finding the right mate while observing the laws of God and society. With Sue, sexuality itself becomes the problem, whether a problem in pathology or the relation between the sexes. With Sue, Hardy makes a first attack on the cult of virginity, showing how virginity can become a pathological state of mind. Sue remains psychologically a virgin even after she has slept with Jude and given birth to his children.

Sue's sexuality has been recognized as a problem since the first reviews of *Jude*. Margaret Oliphant, herself a prolific novelist, considered Sue's way of holding Jude 'on the tiptoe of expectation, with a pretended reserve' as 'almost more indecent' than Arabella's frank and open fulfilment of his desires (*Blackwood's Magazine*, January 1896; repr. in *CH*). Another female reviewer in the same month considered Sue 'not well fitted for married life'. Edmund Gosse wrote of Sue, again in the same month: 'She is a poor, maimed "degenerate", ignorant of herself and of the perversion of her instincts...

ready to . . . play at loving though she cannot love' (*Cosmopolis*; repr. in *CH*).

It is, however, D. H. *Lawrence, in his *Study of Thomas Hardy* (1914), who created the most vivid and influential characterization of Sue as sexually deficient. Sue's 'was no marriage', he says, because she 'is scarcely a woman at all, though she is feminine enough'. He remarks of the sublimated quality of Sue's intellectual idealism that she wanted 'to contain the body within the mind. One of the supremest products of our civilisation is Sue, and a product that frightens us.' It was wrong of Jude to have forced sex upon her, and wrong of her to have borne children in order to make a false show of being a woman. Lawrence sees in Sue's return to Phillotson a sign that she loathed her body: 'That, too,' he continues, 'should be scourged out of existence. . . . All that remained of her was the will by which she annihilated herself' (*Phoenix* (1936), 496–7).

Hardy himself, in a letter to Gosse responding to his review, accounts for Sue's behaviour in a more moderate way: 'There is nothing perverted or depraved in Sue's nature. The abnormalism consists in disproportion, not in inversion, her sexual instinct being healthy as far as it goes, but unusually weak and fastidious. . . . Her intimacies with Jude have never been more than occasional.' She fears the marriage ceremony, Hardy adds, because she wants to feel 'at liberty to yield herself as seldom as she chooses. This has tended to keep his passion as hot at the end as at the beginning, and helps to break his heart.'

Recent feminist critics, on the other hand, defend Sue against the charge of sexlessness and frigidity. In *Thomas Hardy and Women* (1985), Penny Boumelha, while admitting that Hardy's revisions increase Sue's sexual reserve, argues against equating 'such changes with a total absence of sexual feeling, or with frigidity'. The reserve is connected with the intellectual 'woman's sense of selfhood': 'it is a necessary stand against being reduced to the "womanly"' (p. 143).

Whereas previous critics blamed Sue for the failure of the relationship, the feminists blame Jude. Sue's consciousness, says Boumelha, is mainly filtered 'through the interpretations of Jude, with all their attendant incomprehensions and distortions' (p. 148). Rosemarie Morgan argues that Sue is sexually disarmed by Jude's idealization of her. Jude makes love to Sue by saying, '"All that's best and noblest in me loves you, and your freedom from everything that's gross has elevated me."' 'How can Sue yield now', Morgan comments, 'out of any other feelings than guilt and responsibility, and a frightening sense that at all costs she must not appear "gross" (sexually passionate)?' (*Women and Sexuality in the Novels of Thomas Hardy* (1991), 140). We can learn from the feminist critics to respect Sue's intelligence and autonomy. Nevertheless we cannot deny Sue's fear of sex, and the reader's impression that she does not derive much pleasure from sex.

It is, in the end, Arabella and not Sue who discovers Jude's death and fetches two women to 'lay out' the corpse. And it is she and Widow Edlin who attend his funeral. It must be said in Arabella's favour that she did Jude less harm than did Sue. The contrast between Sue and Arabella is the contrast between attractive idealism and unattractive reality, and reality in Hardy is always respected.

Jude the Obscure is Hardy's gloomiest and most tragic novel. The early reviewers complained that it lacked the humour to be found in his earlier novels. But here Hardy was concentrating all his forces toward a single accumulating tragic effect. Besides, the issues here are too serious and too wide-ranging to admit of humour. For the novel is a bitter protest against everything: against the injustice of nature, society, and God. See also EDUCATION; RAILWAYS; TRAGEDY. RL

Gail Cunningham, *The New Woman in the Victorian Novel* (1978).

David J. De Laura, '"The Ache of Modernism" in Hardy's Later Novels', *Journal of English Literary History*, 34 (1967).

John Goode, 'Sue Bridehead and the New Woman', in Mary Jacobus (ed.), *Women Writing and Writing about Women* (1979).

Patricia Ingham, 'The Evolution of *Jude the Obscure*', *Review of English Studies*, 27 (1976).

Elizabeth Langland, 'Becoming a Man in *Jude the Obscure*', in Margaret R. Higonnet (ed.), *The Sense of Sex: Feminist Perspectives on Hardy* (1993).

Anne B. Simpson, 'Sue Bridehead Revisited', *Victorian Literature and Culture*, 19 (1991).

Michael Steig, 'Sue Bridehead', *Novel*, 1 (1968).

K

Keats, John (1795–1821), poet. His poetry, encountered early in Palgrave's *Golden Treasury*, made a great impression on Hardy, who frequently quotes his felicitous phrases and memorable images in the novels. Among other instances, 'leaden-eyed despair' and 'spectre-thin'—both from Keats's 'Ode to a Nightingale'—appear in his first published novel (*DR* 3.2, 3.3); the same poem is quoted again in *Desperate Remedies* (10.4) and in *A Laodicean* (2.7), as well as supplying the title of one of Hardy's poems, 'The Selfsame Song'; the casement in 'The Eve of St Agnes' appears in *Far from the Madding Crowd* (57), and may have suggested a scene in *A Pair of Blue Eyes* (32); Sue's remark to Jude about the garland and heifers of sacrifice (*JO* 5.4) alludes to the 'Ode on a Grecian Urn'; the sonnet 'On First Looking into Chapman's Homer' is referred to in two novels (*PBE* 23, *TT* 14); 'La Belle Dame Sans Merci' is also quoted in *A Pair of Blue Eyes* (7); in *The Woodlanders* (27) the striking phrase 'glued up with frozen thawings' is appropriated from Keats's lyric 'In drear-nighted December', which has the line 'Nor frozen thawings glue them'; and the title-page of *The Return of the Native* bears an epigraph from *Endymion*.

Of all Keats's poems the 'Nightingale' ode seems to have been Hardy's favourite, if one can judge by the number of times he refers to it (in addition to the examples already cited, see *FFMC* 23); the phrase 'the fever and the fret' in that poem was one that haunted Hardy's memory with particular persistence (see *PBE* 2, *HE* 34, *AL* 1.2, *W* 33, the 1895 preface to *JO*). Even in his non-fictional prose Hardy remembers Keats, as when he uses the phrase 'high-piled granary' (freely adapted from the sonnet 'When I have fears that I may cease to be') in 'The Profitable Reading of Fiction'. The poem 'At Lulworth Cove a Century Back' was written in the mistaken belief that Keats (as his friend Joseph Severn wrongly supposed) wrote his 'Bright star' sonnet soon after landing on the Dorset coast on his final journey to Rome.

In 1887 Hardy visited Keats's grave in Rome, and sent to his friend Edmund *Gosse two violets he had picked there; he also visited the house in which Keats had died (see the poem 'Rome: At the Pyramid of Cestius'). In 1906 he signed an appeal published in *The Times* for the acquisition and maintenance of the latter, and in 1920 he joined the National Committee formed to negotiate the purchase of Wentworth Place, another property with Keatsian associations (see his poem 'At a House in Hampstead', first published in 1921 in a memorial volume marking the centenary of Keats's death). Fittingly, on Hardy's 81st birthday in that year a group of younger writers that included Robert *Graves, James Joyce, Siegfried *Sassoon, and Virginia *Woolf presented him with a first edition of Keats's 1820 poems.

FBP

Kipling, Rudyard (1865–1936), precocious, prolific, and very popular writer of fiction and verse. He met Hardy in the summer of 1890; Kipling had come to London from India a few months earlier, and was enjoying a remarkable success (*The Times* had published a leading article on his work on 25 March). The conversation at their first meeting is briefly recalled in Hardy's autobiography: '"He talked about the East.... He told curious details about Indian life"' (*LW* 236). At about the same time Hardy met, at the home of Edmund *Gosse, Caroline Balestier, an American who married Kipling in 1892.

Soon after his first meeting with Hardy, Kipling had been involved in a controversy with the American publishing firm of *Harper & Brothers, whom he accused of pirating his work. On 8 November 1890 Hardy told James Osgood that he wished to express his support for the firm of Harper, and on 22 November he was a co-signatory (with Walter *Besant and William Black) of a letter to this effect published in the *Athenaeum*. Kipling responded with the satirical ballad 'The Rhyme of the Three Captains', which appeared in the *Athenaeum* on 6 December and refers to Hardy as 'Lord of the Wessex coast, and all the lands thereby'.

Their friendship recovered from this difference of opinion, however, and in the following year Hardy was one of those who proposed Kipling for membership of the Savile Club. Kipling settled permanently in England in 1896, and in September 1897 the Kiplings, who were considering the purchase of a house in Dorset, visited the Hardys, and the two writers spent several days bicycling together. Kipling was one of the pall-bearers at Hardy's funeral.

Kipling's short story 'A Conference of the Powers', first published in May 1890 and collected in *Many Inventions* (1893), includes a character (Eustace Cheever, a successful middle-aged novelist) who bears some similarity to Hardy, and it has been suggested that Kipling may have been expressing his attitude towards some of the distinguished writers he encountered soon after his arrival in London. Another story, 'My Sunday at Home', first published in April 1895 and collected in *The Day's Work* (1898), includes a reference to *Tess of the d'Urbervilles*, and has been interpreted as a 'counter-statement' to Hardy's tragic view of life.

L

landscape is an element of greater importance in Hardy's writings than in the work of almost any other comparable novelist. Partly this may be due to his training as an architectural draughtsman: he had a discriminating visual sense, which was enhanced by a keen interest and pleasure in the landscape paintings by great artists displayed in the galleries he visited frequently in his formative years. To match them in words was sometimes a deliberate act. In *A Pair of Blue Eyes* (29) the description of the rising of the sun on the south Devon coast as seen from the steamer *Juliet* approaching Plymouth is a bravura piece in which Hardy revels in the effect of light on a marine landscape. Such elaborate detail is more than the immediate action the story demands, and a writer in a different style might have been content with little more than a curt stage direction. For Hardy, however, the human figures he portrays move in well-defined landscapes. Increasingly, as he mastered his craft, he found correlations of emotion and mood between his characters and the surrounding scenes in which they are revealed. Landscape thus became an additional and potent factor in the human drama, adding a bass chord to the individual theme.

The types of landscape available to Hardy were well contrasted. The chalk of the downs, the limestone of Portland and Mendip, the clay vales, the fenny marshland of the Somerset Levels, red sandstone, greensand, and the acid sandy tracts of heathland were the dominant factors, with the granite and slate of north Cornwall adding their more dramatic qualities. During the 19th century much of Wessex would have been green round the year, a sward of meadow for hay and pasture for grazing livestock, well watered by its climate.

The rivers were more impressive by their numbers than their size, many being little more than winterbornes. The watershed hills seldom approach 1,000 feet (305 metres), but their downland contours and steep-sided coombes have a dynamic quality that Hardy relished. The technique of using rivers to irrigate grassland by 'drowning' was at its height in his lifetime and added a distinctive landscape feature in *Tess of the d'Urbervilles* (31). Another man-made modification of the Wessex landscape is the work of the turf-sculptor carving representations of white horses and other large images on the broad sloping sides of the downs. Chalk, contrasting its whiteness with the surrounding turf, is the ideal medium for such images. In England's tally of these hill-figures all but four are in the chalk areas of southern England; of the seventeen horses, eleven are in Wessex. Their preservation requires scouring at intervals to preserve them from being lost under a fresh growth of vegetation, and some have undoubtedly disappeared in this way.

In addition to the well-known white horses, the subjects displayed in Wessex include the regimental badges at Fovant Down, between Shaftesbury and Wilton, and the slogan 'Drink more Milk' burnt into the same down with weedkiller during a period of distress among dairy farmers between the Wars; but the most notable is the Giant of Cerne, 180 feet (55 metres) tall and 44 feet (13 metres) across the shoulders. Other dimensions are best studied on site, at Trundle Hill, Cerne Abbas. Hardy made a careful record in his notebook, dated 12 September 1890, of the local legend of the Giant who terrorized the villagers until they killed him and cut his figure on the hill. In a scene at Flintcomb-Ash (*TDU* 48) Hardy mentions 'Giant's Hill by Abbot's Cernel' as a landmark, and in *The Dynasts* (1.2.5) he uses the Giant legend effectively to parody the sort of atrocity story that circulates in wartime, when an unnamed woman hints at Napoleon's ultimate iniquity: 'They say that He lives upon human flesh, and has rashers o' baby every morning for breakfast—for all the world like the Cernel Giant in old ancient times.'

In Hardy's larger treatment of downland landscapes two outstanding examples are the poem 'Wessex Heights' and the night scene on Norcombe Hill in *Far from the Madding*

Crowd (2). While the poem belongs to a later stage in Hardy's development of landscape writing, the first major example of what became his characteristic technique is the manner of his introduction of Gabriel Oak in the two opening chapters of the novel. After a slight, seemingly trivial encounter with Bathsheba Everdene he appears next as no more than the sound of a flute that he is playing in the solitude of a winter's night on one of the uplands in the Toller Down area. The atmospheric description of this lonely scene is meticulous in its detail, particularly in its sounds (always an important feature of Hardy landscapes). Norcombe Hill itself is described as 'a shape approaching the indestructible as nearly as any to be found on earth. It was a featureless convexity of chalk and soil—an ordinary specimen of those smoothly-outlined protuberances of the globe which may remain undisturbed on some great day of confusion, when far grander heights and dizzy granite precipices topple down.'

Norcombe Hill, in short, was a survivor. It is a paradigm of Oak himself, in contrast with the 'far grander heights and dizzy granite precipices' which represent his later rivals, Troy and Boldwood, and will 'topple down on some great day of confusion'. Hardy emphasizes this middle-of-the-road, unobtrusive, unchallenging nature in Oak, describing him in the previous chapter as 'one who felt himself to occupy morally that vast middle space of Laodicean neutrality' and to be 'a man whose moral colour was a kind of pepper-and-salt mixture'. Implicitly the landscape is reinforcing our first apprehension of the kind of man Oak will turn out to be. 'Laodicean' was a favourite colour on Hardy's palette.

Tess of the d'Urbervilles is particularly rich in landscapes, partly because of the various moves that punctuate Tess's life. The two dairying areas were both within the compass of Hardy's most intimate knowledge, and he shows them in their changing interplay with Tess's moods and circumstances. The Vale of the Little Dairies is the Blackmore Vale, the Valley of the Great Dairies the valley flanking the River Froom (Hardy's preferred spelling: see FROME, RIVER) below Dorchester. In his portrayal of Blackmore Vale he makes the point that it is 'for the most part untrodden as yet by tourist or landscape-painter' and then proceeds to describe it as a landscape-painter might see it: a fertile and sheltered tract of country 'in which the fields are never brown and the springs never dry'. The atmosphere 'is so tinged with azure that what artists call the middle distance partakes also of that hue, while the horizon beyond is of the deepest ultramarine' (2). Hardy's friend Frederick *Treves described it in his *Highways and Byways in Dorset* (1906) as 'that valley of the Blue Mist in whose soft shadows will be found the very heart of England', adding that 'Everywhere are there cows, for the smell of cows is the incense of North Dorset'. A further attribute that Hardy adds is the persistence of superstitions on heavy soils such as that of Blackmore Vale. When Tess returns from Flintcomb-Ash to her family home at Marlott (*TDU* 50), she descends at night from Bulbarrow into the Vale and at once recognizes the contrast from the chalk downland in the tread and smell of the soil. Her consciousness becomes alert to half-remembered folk-memories that generate a potent atmosphere of nameless fears, the same fears that made her mother insist that the magical properties of her battered copy of *The Compleat Fortune-Teller* were such that the book must not remain in the cottage overnight, but must be hidden in the thatch of the outhouse (*TDU* 3).

The Valley of the Great Dairies is first presented in terms of the contrasts its landscape offers to the Blackmore Vale. Everything appears to be on a larger, more opulent scale, with bigger fields, more numerous herds of cattle and the beasts themselves of a superior grade. The rivers likewise could hardly differ more strongly: the Stour, turbid and silent, flowed over beds of mud in Blackmore Vale, while the Froom was clear and rapid as it prattled over pebbly shallows. To emphasize the difference between the two rivers Hardy chooses as symbols the characteristic flower of each: the water-lily of the Stour that he had known so well when he lived beside the river at Sturminster Newton, and on the Froom the white flowers of water-crowsfoot, with their butter-golden centres making a carpet of colour on the water.

Here, at the beginning of Phase the Third, the scene is set for Tess's start of a new life, with all Nature in accord with the lyrical mood of her new hopes. The air has the scent of thyme, birds are hatching, and she starts impulsively to sing the Benedicite, rejoicing with 'ye Green Things upon the Earth'. Now, as she settles into her place among the green pastures of the Froom valley, and her relationship with Angel Clare develops, the landscape finds a consonance of its own with her personal drama. In the first stage of their mutual awareness they are in a landscape of arborescence, the leafy time of strengthening bud and rising sap (20). The burden of Tess's guilty secret of her dead child finds an outward expression in the crouching, searching figures looking in the meadow grass for the unsuspected agent which has tainted the day's milk, the foul root of wild garlic which must sooner or later be found and extirpated (22).

For all its tensions, the Froom valley never loses its genial quality as the scene of Angel's courtship. The landscape of Flintcomb-Ash in winter was the epitome of bleak despair (43). After her rejection by Angel, Tess joined Marian, one of the dairymaids from Talbothays, on this lofty downland farm where no tree grew and the large fields were devoted to corn and swedes. Where the swedes had been eaten off by the livestock, it was the task of the girls to grub up the remainder. In a landscape completely devoid of shelter, exposure to the driving icy rains of winter was cruel and incessant. With its spectral birds arriving on a direct flyway from the Arctic this must be the most inhospitable Wessex landscape that Hardy created.

Hardy's care in the choice of a landscape for the final moments of a leading character is strongly marked in *Tess*. The choice of Bournemouth (alias Sandbourne) for Alec d'Urberville's dying moments serves to emphasize the lack of the ballast of reality in him. His different roles as descendant of an ancient family or as lay-preacher are a sort of fancy dress worn in a masquerade. Bournemouth, described by Hardy as 'a Mediterranean lounging-place on the English Channel', had not grown up from the grass roots of trading or strategic dynamics but had burst into existence in 1811 'like a fairy place suddenly created by the stroke of a wand'. Its soil was the heathy soil of Egdon, still—within a mile of the town—unbroken since the days of the Caesars. Like Alec it was an affluent interloper flaunting the lofty roofs, chimneys, gazebos, and towers of the 'numerous fanciful residences of which the place was composed'.

At the other extreme of age, Stonehenge emphasizes the long chain of generations that crystallize in Tess as she shares her farewell moments with Angel at the dawning of the day on Salisbury Plain: 'The band of silver paleness along the east horizon made even the distant parts of the Great Plain appear dark and near; and the whole enormous landscape bore that impress of reserve, taciturnity, and hesitation which is usual just before day. The eastward pillars and their architraves stood up blackly against the light, and the great flame-shaped Sun-stone beyond them; and the Stone of Sacrifice midway. Presently the night wind died out, and the quivering little pools in the cup-like hollows of the stones lay still' (58). Tess's expression of pleasure in the place because it is 'so solemn and lonely... with nothing but the sky above my face' recalls Hardy's own pleasure in 'Wessex Heights' 'when one's next neighbour is the sky'.

It is seemingly by chance that Tess comes to Stonehenge, but with Michael Henchard the case is very different (*MC* 45). After his final rejection he walks out of Casterbridge instinctively to the true unyielding Egdon as the setting for the bitterness of his death as an outcast. In his preparation for the scene Hardy reanimates his vision of 'that ancient country whose surface never had been stirred to a finger's depth, save by the scratching of rabbits, since brushed by the feet of the earliest tribes'. As with Tess the ultimate retreat is to this pristine landscape of prehistory, in which the visionary moments of Hardy's own childhood were spent. This is the occasion to recall that Hardy created his Wessex in equal parts of reality and dream. The Egdon Heath that he portrayed most fully in the opening chapter of *The Return of the Native* is shot through with the imaginative, poetic qualities of that dream: 'The untameable, Ishmaelitish thing that Egdon now was it always had been. Civilisation was its enemy.'

From the heath Hardy drew a new aesthetic of landscape, based on what today would be called 'wilderness values'. Where Dorset's historian John *Hutchins had considered the heathland to be the one deplorable blot on an otherwise beautiful county, Hardy rejected this orthodox idea of beauty in favour of a more sombre and austere preference for the 'chastened sublimity of a moor, a sea or a mountain' as more in keeping with the moods of the more thinking among mankind; and he forecast that 'to the commonest tourist, spots like Iceland or the sand-dunes of Scheveningen may become what the vineyards and myrtle-gardens of South Europe are to him now'. DH

J. H. Bettey, *The Landscape of Wessex* (1980).
H. J. Massingham, *English Downland* (1936).
Morris Marples, *White Horses and Other Hill Figures* (1981).

language. Writing about Hardy's poetic language, Edmund *Blunden, one of his most perceptive critics, noted that it is 'sometimes a peculiar compound of the high-flown and the dull. If he means "I asked" he is liable to say "I queried" or rather "Queried I"; he is liable to "opine" instead of think.... He goes his road in the matter of expression, unworried about grinning faces, and in this spirit he arrives at numberless decisive ways of putting things.' The idiosyncrasies to which Blunden draws attention are not confined to Hardy's verse, although they are more concentrated there than in his prose. The reader is more likely to be baffled by a couplet like 'These umbered cliffs and gnarls of masonry | Outskeleton Time's central city, Rome' in the poem 'Rome: Building a New Street in the Ancient Quarter', than by prose sentences containing words like 'the langterloo jingle', or 'his fugleman', or 'the ceorl, Giles Winterborne', all in *The Woodlanders*, which was written at the same time. Hardy's esoteric diction was not intended to puzzle his readers, nor to impress them, even if perhaps he did assume 'from the start', as one critic has suggested, 'that a writer was expected to be cultured'. His language exhibits, from his earliest fiction and verse, a constant quest for the right word, and in his search he turned to whatever source was available, ancient or modern, obsolete or contemporary. It was his friend William *Archer who summed up Hardy's attitude to language in a memorable comment in his review of *Wessex Poems* in December 1898: 'There are times when Mr Hardy seems to lose all sense of local and historical perspective in language, seeing all the words in the dictionary on one plane, so to speak, and regarding them all as equally available and appropriate for any and every literary purpose.' Hardy thought that 'seeing all the words of [*sic*] the dictionary on one plane' was a 'happy phrase'—a fair assessment of his linguistic practice, rather than a stricture.

But language is more than just choosing the right words. It embraces grammar, syntax, social distinctions, received standards and local dialects, sounds and cadences. For a writer of fiction there is also *dialogue, the language of spoken conversation, and for the poet, certainly for Hardy, there are also considerations of form and metre and rhyme. Syntax, 'the traffic rules of language', is the arrangement of words in sentences. Although in most respects Hardy's syntax conforms to the accepted norms of Victorian English, he readily departs from these in order to achieve a particular effect, as in the last four words of this sentence: 'She was at last driven to desperation: her natural common sense and shrewdness had seen all through the piece how imaginary her emotions were—she felt herself to be weak and foolish in permitting them to rise; but even then she could not control them: be agonized she must' (*DR* 6.1). The cadence of these four words is vintage Hardy, even at this early stage of his writing. The effect of unconventional word-order, such as placing a predicate before the subject and verb, may be disturbing, as in this sentence: 'Unpleasant to Stephen such remarks as these could not sound' (*PBE* 5), or when Hardy is pondering Knight's predicament later in *A Pair of Blue Eyes* (20): 'Throw up his cards and go away he fain would have done, but could not'; but to rearrange the sentence in more conventional mode—'He fain would have thrown up his cards and gone away, but could not'—would have lost the collocation of the emphatic 'would' and 'could' and might have given more prominence to the archaic 'fain' than Hardy perhaps intended.

What in 'A Mere Interlude' (*CM*) Hardy calls 'the inconveniences of syntax' clearly did not greatly trouble him. He followed his own bent, for example, to create the impression of informal dialogue, as when Mrs Smith in *A Pair of Blue Eyes* (36) says to her husband: '"You always will go poking into town in your working clothes. Beg you to change how I will, 'tis no use."' Here the final clause suggests an appropriate shaking of the head or other gesture of frustration. And in much the same way the reader can hear, as no doubt Hardy meant us to hear, Sue saying to Jude, '"I don't think of you like that means!"' (*JO* 3.5). To emphasize a pronoun Hardy often inverts normal word-order. Here Wildeve is speaking to Eustacia: '"I think I drew out you before you drew out me"' (*RN* 1.6); and here is Felice Charmond speaking to Grace: '"I cannot give him up until he chooses to give up me!"' (*W* 33). In both sentences the order is deliberately inverted to emphasize the word 'me'. A similar effect is achieved in straight narrative: 'The more briskly they walked the more briskly walked she' (*TDU* 44).

Similarly in verse: 'Midnight on Beechen, 187-' opens with the line 'On Beechen Cliff self-commune I', and the first stanza of 'The Memorial Brass: 186-' concludes: 'Well, all pay the debt that paid he!' Not only pronouns are placed in unexpected positions. For the sake of rhyme or rhythm a verb or preposition may be similarly moved. The reader may 'grin', but the result is often striking. The penultimate stanza of 'In Tenebris I' reads: 'Tempests may scath; | But love can not make smart | Again this year his heart | Who no heart hath.' In 'I Have Lived with Shades' Hardy writes 'Since forth from cot and croft | I went mankind among', where the preposition 'among' is made to rhyme with 'long'. In the poem 'Faintheart in a Railway Train', first printed when Hardy was 80, occurs the superbly hesitant question 'Get out to her do I dare?' The variable positioning of adverbs is another common feature of Hardy's language, both in narrative and in dialogue: 'Much he deplored trifling with her feelings for the sake of a passing desire' ('On the Western Circuit', *LLI*); 'He could not love long a kimberlin' (*WB* 2.3); '"Ah, pore widow-woman! she cried her heart out about it almost"' (*FFMC* 10); 'His spirits were oozing out of him quite' (*FFMC* 42).

What appear to be grammatical oddities in Hardy's language may be reflections of uncertainties of usage in Victorian English, in which tradition, purism, and contemporary colloquial speech are at odds. The pronoun *whom*, for example, which is practically extinct in late 20th-century English, is often replaced by *who* in Hardy, as in '"You know, I suppose, who I married?"' (*JO* 5.8), or '"Who have we lost on board here?"' (*D* 1.5.4). In *Desperate Remedies* (2.2) Hardy originally wrote: 'Young women have a habit, not noticeable in men, of putting on at a moment's notice the drama of whomsoever's life they choose.' When a reviewer described 'whomsoever's' as 'an odd formation', Hardy changed it in 1889 into the clumsier 'whosesoever's', but eventually decided on 'whosoever's' in the edition of 1896.

Hardy mirrors popular usage, including *dialect, in blurring the distinction between different cases of pronouns. '"No, faith. 'Tis nothing to I,"' says Uncle Benjy in his inimitable, colloquial way (*TM* 6); and '"Then it was he I saw far away on the road,"' says Ethelberta (*HE* 31), where *he* seems to convey stronger emphasis than the objective *him* would have done. And here is Marty South in a truly characteristic utterance: '"Then things don't fay with she any more than with we!"' (*W* 5). The retention of reflexive pronouns where they are now generally omitted is an archaic feature surviving in dialect, thus contributing to the 'Wessex' character of Hardy's language: 'Poor Abel, as he was called, had an inveterate habit of over-sleeping himself' (*MC* 15). In verse Hardy's retention of a reflexive pronoun may often be prosodic: 'That one I loved vainly in nonage | Had ceased her to be' ('My Cicely'); 'Let me sit me down amid them' ('The Bridge of Lodi'). The need to aid the rhythm may also account for the insertion of a superfluous pronoun in a line like 'Soon, soon that lover he came' ('Julie-Jane').

Among grammatical features pounced upon by critics of Hardy's language are such alleged misdemeanours as split infinitives, absolute constructions which are a form of syntactic compression in place of longer subordinate clauses, and so-called dangling or hanging participles—that is, sentences in which the subject of the main clause is not the same as that implied in the participial phrase. All these features are present in Hardy's writings from the start, as in his early story *An Indiscretion in the Life of an Heiress* (1.7): 'He determined at all events to put the case clearly before her, to heroically set forth at their next meeting the true bearings of their position, which she plainly did not realize to the full as yet.' Here the emphatic placing of 'heroically', splitting the infinitive, is as deliberate as the strategically positioned 'as yet' at the very end of the sentence. In the same novel Hardy begins a sentence with an absolute construction which defines both the moment reached and the mental activity leading up to it: 'The decision come to, his impatience could scarcely preserve him from rushing to Tollamore House that very daybreak' (1.4). Such constructions occur in all Hardy's later fiction: split infinitives like 'to precisely describe a human being' and 'to unambitiously devote her life', both in *The Woodlanders* (5, 12); absolute constructions like 'There being no knocker, she knocked by means of a short stick which was laid against the post for that purpose; but nobody attending, she entered the passage, and tried an inner door' (*TM* 6); and dangling participles like 'While leaning thus upon the parapet, his listless attention was awakened by sounds of an unaccustomed kind from the town quarter' (*MC* 38).

Hardy's language invites comparison with his early profession of *architecture in the subsuming of individual parts in the total design, the absorption of single incongruities in the entire edifice. What the eye accommodates in a building, the ear as readily accepts in Hardy's prose and poems. This is not to overlook or deny the grammatical quirks to be found in Hardy's writings; as Blunden pointed out, they are as much as his other idiosyncrasies the stamp of his individuality. His frequent use of passive constructions is yet another instance. Perhaps this was a way of stressing anonymity or of suggesting unnamed forces acting on persons or events: 'The superstratum of timidity which often overlies those who are daring and defiant at heart had been passed through, and the mettlesome substance of the woman was reached' (*RN* 5.3). The passive phrase 'was reached' occurs elsewhere: 'The shed was reached' (*W* 3); 'Trendle's house was reached at last' ('The Withered Arm', *WT*); and in that poignant passage where superhuman will power and a stray dog combine to drag Fanny Robin finally to Casterbridge Unionhouse: 'Thus the town was passed, and the goal was reached' (*FFMC* 40). In *The Dynasts* the general anonymity of war is expressed in such passive phrases as 'The battle is begun', 'a dust is raised', 'moans of men and shrieks of horses are heard', 'the see-saw is continued' (*D* 2.2.7).

A verbal form which has been called the expanded tense in a passive sense, and which was common in 18th- and early 19th-century writers but has long been obsolete in modern English, is still occasionally used by Hardy. Thus he describes a flower-garden 'in process of clearing from weeds and rubbish' (*L* 1.3), and, in *The Woodlanders* (6), 'in the kitchen dinner was preparing'. Such instances are part of a recurrent archaizing tendency in Hardy's language, both in prose and verse, as are obsolete forms of verbs like the past tenses 'clave', 'glode', 'trode', and 'upclomb', as well as colloquial forms used by local speakers: '"Really, sir, 'tis thoughted by many"' (*UGT* 2.4), and '"Another case I knowed was when the man was catched in a man-trap"' (*UGT* 5.1). The colloquial 'ain't' is used variously for 'am not', 'is not', and 'are not' among local folk from *Desperate Remedies* to *The Well-Beloved* and *The Dynasts*, along with other dialect forms like 'mid' for 'may' or 'might', 'getten' for 'getting', 'hae' for 'have', 'doos' for 'does', and others.

The use of the subjunctive in 19th-century English to express supposition, doubt, or wish was often a matter of personal preference, or sometimes of social class. Thus Hardy wrote to his friend Edmund *Gosse in January 1900: 'Time will show if this be true or not' (*L* ii 244); and in the following month to Florence *Henniker: 'I take a keen pleasure in war strategy & tactics, following it as if it were a game of chess' (*L* ii 248). Similarly, Hardy uses the subjunctive in conditional clauses in his fiction: '"If he wish me to"', says Anne in *The Trumpet-Major* (39); and in 'A Changed Man' (2) Hardy writes: 'The acting was for the benefit of such and such an excellent charity—nobody cared what, provided the play were played.' On the other hand, Tess uses the indicative when among her family: 'And if I was quite sure how it would be living there, I would go any-when' (*TDU* 6).

A noteworthy characteristic of Hardy's language is his treatment of adjectives and adverbs unhampered by conventional rules of grammar. He freely turns adjectives into adverbs (*anciently, exteriorly, whitely*); he creates unusual comparatives like *forwarder* and *tearfuller*, and superlatives like *ancientest, ownest, purplest*, and *yellowest*, comically in Mrs Day's '"The parishioners about here... be the laziest, gossipest, poachest, jailest set of any I ever come among"' (*UGT* 2.6). Already in his early poem 'Hap' Hardy had written of one 'Powerfuller than I', and towards the end of his life he made Tristram in *The Famous Tragedy of the Queen of Cornwall* (14) say: 'Your father dealt me illest turn in this.'

Hardy's scouring of the English language, his seeing all the words in the dictionary on one plane, entailed a deliberate restoration of good old English words, whether in dialect or in received literary usage, all testifying to his tireless quest for the right word. That this applies even more to his poetry than to his prose is easily explained by the requirements of metre and rhyme, for Hardy was a careful, if not fastidious, craftsman in verse, as his frequent revisions testify. But in prose, too, he was anxious not merely to display his word-hoard, as in the early novels, but to explore the resources of a millennium of English history to get his meaning across in the manner which best suited his aim and his ear. All parts of speech play their part in this. Hardy was as ready as Shakespeare was to play with grammatical categories, to turn the adjective dismal into 'the deepest fit of the dismals' in *The Hand of Ethelberta* (10), or to have horses called for 'by the brisk' in *A Pair of Blue Eyes* (14). He turns nouns into verbal adjectives as in 'that abundantly daughtered woman' (*PBE* 14), and prepositions into adjectives in 'such old-fashioned and far-between people' in 'The Fiddler of the Reels' (*LLI*). Shifting of grammatical categories is not uncommon in English, which is largely devoid of inflections, but even more important in Hardy's lexical explorations was the revival of good words fallen into desuetude, like the rare word *inimic* in *The Dynasts* (2.4.5), or *armipotents* in 'I Met a Man', or *brumal* in *Two on a Tower* (23), where tropical climes are contrasted with 'the brumal rigours of Britain'—a word whose very sound conveys wintry chills, as it does in the 'frosty and brumall' passage in Gavin Douglas's 15th-century version of Virgil's *Aeneid*. In his poem 'He Abjures Love' Hardy follows Miles Coverdale and the King James Bible in using the word *daysman*, and in 'Rake-Hell Muses' occurs the word *intermell* (conflict).

An instructive example of Hardy's lexical eclecticism is his monody on the death of *Swinburne, whose poems Hardy greatly admired. 'A Singer Asleep', first published in April 1910, echoes Shakespeare's 'orts of love' in *Troilus and Cressida* in Hardy's line 'Whose very orts are love incarnadine'. Although *incarnadine* is an adjective here it also carries Shakespearian echoes, while *orts* (fragments, scraps) dates from the 15th century, and *brabble* (carping, quarrel), also in this poem, dates from the 16th. In the second line of the poem, sentry is used as a verb, a rare Victorian innovation; of only three instances of this usage cited in the *Oxford English Dictionary* one is Hardy's. In referring to Swinburne's 'fulth of numbers freaked with musical closes', Hardy's *fulth* is a medieval English word which survives in dialect, along with such words as *greenth*, in 'The Tree and the Lady', and *blooth* (bloom, blossoming) in several novels as well as in the compound *apple-blooth* in 'The Dance at the Phoenix'.

Hardy's fondness for compound adjectives finds expression in the Swinburne monody in *fresh-fluted, love-anguished, unslumbering*, and *world-encircling*, while the final line of the same poem, 'Upon the capes and chines', harks back to the English of King Alfred the Great of Wessex in the late 9th century: a *chine* is a 'fissure or ravine' in Old English, and is used by Hardy in the poem 'A Woman Driving' and with reference to England's 'chalky chines' in *The Dynasts* (2.1.8).

That the dialect of Wessex should play a prominent part in Hardy's language is to be expected, although he took care not to puzzle his readers unduly, nor to turn his country folk into the uncouth 'Hodge' image berated in his essay 'The *Dorsetshire Labourer'. For Hardy dialect words were yet another enrichment of his language, with their special meanings, sounds, and cadences—like the word *griff*, which is a dialect word denoting a small valley or cleft, but has the poetic sense of a grip or claw in Hardy's 'The Clock of the Years'. Dialect words largely confined to Dorset include many picturesque expressions, like *borus-snorus* (*UGT* 2.2), *hontish* (*MC* 37, *TDU* 12), *mollyhorning* (*RN* 3.1), and *teuny* (*W* 4).

Not content with adopting words from dialect and from earlier periods of the language, Hardy proved himself a deft coiner of words. Indeed, his verbal inventiveness is without doubt one of the most distinctive features of his language. The creation of compound words was a rich source of metaphorical language for Hardy, as it had been in Old English poetry, and many of Hardy's 'decisive ways of putting things', in Blunden's phrase, ensued, as in 'A Singer Asleep'. We also recall the verb *outskeleton*, mentioned earlier, one of several *out*-words Hardy coined, like *outheave* (*D* 3.3.3) and the memorable 'The Century's corpse outleant' in 'The Darkling Thrush', a poem further enriched by the sombre words *spectre-gray*, *fervourless*, and *blast-beruffled*. Among fruitful prefixes Hardy found *in*-, as in 'Where such inbe' in 'The Two Houses' and *inscroll* in 'A Sign-Seeker', which also includes the verb *subtrude* (to thrust or steal in stealthily), Hardy's being the only citation in the *OED*. Another prefix is *dis*-, as in *discompose* (*HE* 47) and in 'a long line of disillusive centuries' (*RN* 3.1); both these usages are also cited in the *OED*, the latter as the only instance. Other coinages using common prefixes include *remutinied* (*JO* 1.3), *ensphered* (*HE* 34), *upclosing* ('Panthera'), and the noun *under-whistle* in the opening chapter of *Under the Greenwood Tree*. The most commonly used prefix for Hardy was *un*-, not uncharacteristic of his vision of things, as in *unhale*, *unhope*, *unworth*, and in the memorable line in 'Tess's Lament' 'I'd have my life unbe'.

Many of Hardy's compounds, especially nouns and adjectives, add a strongly visual or aural element to his language. One recognizes the pictorial quality in words like *frizzle-headed* in the description of that 'frizzle-headed brawny damsel' driving Durbeyfield's chaise in the second chapter of *Tess of the d'Urbervilles*, or in Tess's own 'lash-shadowed eyes' (46), or in that telling epithet *mouldy-minded* in the reference by the Spirit of the Years to 'Europe's mouldy-minded oligarchs' in *The Dynasts* (2.6.7). One of Hardy's poems notably rich in such pictorial compounds is 'Afterwards', with words like *delicate-filmed*, 'the dewfall-hawk', 'the wind-warped upland thorn', 'the full-starred heavens'. Hardy's tendency to coin words admittedly had its pitfalls. Even a young man as eager for classical learning as Jude is hardly likely ever to have said '"After all ... it is not altogether an *erotolepsy* that is the matter with me, as at that first time"' (*JO* 2.4), using a word which even Hardy found it necessary to italicize, having taken it straight from a Greek word meaning 'smitten with love'. On the other hand, he did not italicize his neologism *dolorifuge*, which occurs early in *Tess* (6), where it fits in well: 'The children, who had made use of this idea of Tess being taken up by their wealthy kinsfolk ... as a species of dolorifuge after the death of the horse, began to cry at Tess's reluctance.' Unlike Jude's *erotolepsy*, *dolorifuge* possesses an English cadence despite its Latin elements, because the Latin *dolor* (pain) and the Latin *fugere* (to flee) have been active roots in the formation of good English words like 'condolence' and 'refugee'. Not surprisingly, Hardy's *dolorifuge* has found its place in major English dictionaries among other Hardy coinages.

As most of Hardy's central characters are women, his portrayal of attractive women demanded appropriate language, one word in particular recurring several times—flexuous. A Renaissance word, *flexuous* has the basic meaning 'being full of bends and curves, undulating', in which sense Hardy uses it in the poem 'The Sheep-Boy', where 'Flexuous and solid, clammy vapour-curls | Are rolling over Pokeswell Hills'. The word is used of water in 'A Mere Interlude' (*CM*), and of massed humanity in the dumb show in *The Dynasts* (3.4.1) where armies are twice seen as 'flexuous and riband-shaped', marching 'in flexuous courses of varying direction'. But already in *Far from the Madding Crowd* the word is applied to women, the haymakers consisting of 'gnarled and flexuous forms, the former being the men, the latter the women' (25). Later in the novel the word describes Fanny Robin, whose 'general contours were flexuous and child-like' (40), and subsequently it is applied to Lucetta in *The Mayor of Casterbridge*, to Charlotte in *A Laodicean*, to Tess Durbeyfield, and to Sophy the parlourmaid in 'The Son's Veto' (*LLI*). The word had served Hardy well.

Hardy's language, albeit firmly rooted in his native Wessex, transcends the boundaries of both space and time. In his letters he happily uses modern words like *flattites* (dwellers in flats), *sex-mania, romantical*, and even occasional Americanisms (although he deplores their growing infiltration into Standard English), and his dialect speakers use many words and expressions found also in other regions well beyond Wessex. But even within Wessex there were two distinct languages: 'the dialect at home, more or less; ordinary English abroad and to persons of quality' (*TDU* 3). Whereas Tess had passed 'the Sixth Standard in the National School', like Stephen Smith in *A Pair of Blue Eyes*, Mrs Durbeyfield habitually spoke the dialect. The difference between mother and daughter is, as Hardy was well aware from his own family background, between Tess's mother's 'fast-perishing lumber of superstitions, folk-lore, dialect, and orally transmitted ballads', and the daughter 'with her trained National teachings and Standard knowledge under an infinitely Revised Code'—'a gap of two hundred years as ordinarily understood' (*TDU* 3). 'Persons of quality', the 'high compa-ny' of the comic poem 'The Ruined Maid', who speak ordinary English appear in all Hardy's fiction, even if 'modern developments have shaken up the classes like peas in a hopper', as Lord Mountclere rustically puts it (*HE* 38), and as Hardy himself was poignantly aware when as a budding writer he describes 'a wondrous man of the world talking of vast Schemes, radical Errors, and saying such words as the "Backbone of Society", the "Tendency of Modern Thought", and other things like that' (*An Indiscretion in the Life of an Heiress*, 1.8).

In *The Hand of Ethelberta* Hardy deliberately set out to write a story contrasting the folk in the servants' hall with their masters in the drawing-room. Downstairs young Joey talks 'the Wessex way' (18); upstairs, as Lady Petherwin avers, '"as regards some words, as well as some persons, the less you are acquainted with them the more it is to your credit"' (10). Both as novelist and as poet, Hardy created a distinctive language which combined the old and the new, colourful local speech and Standard English, idiosyncratic grammar and syntax with accepted Victorian usage, into a unique blend, which may indeed cause an occasional grin, but which did enable him to arrive at numberless decisive ways of putting things. RE

Raymond Chapman, *The Language of Thomas Hardy* (1990).
Ralph W. V. Elliott, *Thomas Hardy's English* (1984).
Norman Page, 'Hardy and the English Language', in Norman Page (ed.), *Thomas Hardy: The Writer and His Background* (1980).
Dennis Taylor, *Hardy's Literary Language and Victorian Philology* (1993).

Laodicean, A. The eighth of Hardy's fourteen published novels.

Composition

On completing *The Trumpet-Major* in April 1880, Hardy proposed another serial to the publishing firm of *Harper & Brothers, finalizing negotiations by late May. Writing, at his home in Upper Tooting, apparently began in June or July, and before falling seriously ill in late October Hardy had completed the equivalent of some three serial instalments. Confined to bed until April 1881, he dictated most of the novel to his wife Emma as composition and serial publication proceeded hand-in-hand. He completed the work on 1 May 1881. Hardy later destroyed the manuscript. An incomplete and mixed set (galley and page proofs) of marked serial proofs of the European edition are preserved in the Library of Congress.

Serialization

The novel was serialized in *Harper's New Monthly Magazine* (European edition) in thirteen monthly instalments from December 1880 to December 1881, with an illustration by George du Maurier in each. (For details of the division of the text for serial publication, which bears a somewhat complex relationship to the chapter-divisions in the volume-version, see Purdy 37.) In America it was serialized in *Harper's* from January 1881 to January 1882. The American serial retitled du Maurier's illustrations, and omitted that of Sir William de Stancy's funeral procession.

Volume Publication

Harper & Brothers of New York published the novel in one volume, at 20 cents, on 25 November 1881. The English edition, in three-volume format, was published by *Sampson Low of London during the first week of December at the price of one-and-a-half guineas (31*s.* 6*d.*). The final serial instalment appeared simultaneously with the book edition. Sampson Low, which remaindered its edition to Mudie's circulating library in February 1882, published a cheap one-volume edition later in the year. *Tauchnitz offered the novel for sale on the Continent in its 'British Authors' series in 1882. *Osgood, McIlvaine of London published the novel in 1896 in its uniform edition (see COLLECTED EDITIONS), for which Hardy revised the text and supplied a preface. In 1912 the novel appeared in the Wessex Edition published by Macmillan. On this occasion Hardy again made a few revisions, and added a brief postscript to the 1896 preface.

Reception

A Laodicean received mainly approving and respectful notices, but reviewers regretted Hardy's abandonment of the detailed depiction of rustic mores and personalities; the principal characters were found to be insufficiently engaging and lacking in credibility; and plot and treatment were criticized. The *Spectator* objected to the lack of 'thrilling incidents, or situations, or violent emotions of any kind' (4 March 1882), and, presaging the controversy that would surround the reception of later novels, reviewers questioned the moral tone. The *Athenaeum* was disturbed by the undercurrent of eroticism, and, in a general survey of Hardy's work in the *Contemporary Review* (1889), J. M. *Barrie opined that the novel was not only 'dull' but 'here and there nasty'. A few reviewers saw beyond obvious flaws to Hardy's essential interests and experimental aims. Confident that the novel presented evidence of continuing artistic growth, Havelock Ellis, in an astute general evaluation in the *Westminster Review* of April 1883, detected a deepening of vision, and praised the book highly.

Plot

The novel is a love story with a typical comic plot, the initial hindrances to the eventual happy union of the hero and heroine being gradually removed. George Somerset, a London architect interested in church architecture, first observes Paula Power when she refuses to be baptized by the well-disposed Reverend Mr Woodwell in the dissenting chapel erected by her late father, John Power, a railway magnate. Following a telegraph wire to a castle, Somerset returns to explore the building, and soon finds that the young woman who changed her mind at the baptism is the heiress to a fortune and is the owner of the castle. Friendly relations quickly develop under the eye of Paula's doting guardian, Mrs Goodman, and her companion, Charlotte de Stancy, a scion of the castle's historic owners now fallen on hard times. (Her father, Sir William, lives in a modest modern house near their ancient family seat.)

Paula plans to restore Stancy Castle with the help of Havill, a local architect; convinced of Somerset's greater skill, she none the less devises a design competition out of fairness and to avoid accusations of favouritism. Somerset engages Will Dare, a troublingly ambiguous young man, to assist him. Dare, who has in fact obtained his position by purloining the letters of application submitted by the better-qualified applicants, quickly proves unsatisfactory and insolent, and is dismissed. As Paula and Somerset drift into a romantic entanglement, Havill and Dare, hostile to Somerset, steal his design and plot against the love match. On the arrival of Sir William's son, Captain William de Stancy, Dare, who is the Captain's illegitimate son, reveals his plan to see de Stancy married to Paula, who is sentimentally interested in the ancient family. Dare tricks his father into watching her at exercise, and de Stancy, breaking a vow to remain single, resolves to woo her.

At a charity performance of Shakespeare's *Love's Labour's Lost*, de Stancy angers Somerset by feigning to kiss Paula. Her Uncle Abner, who arrives from a prolonged absence abroad, encourages de Stancy's suit and permits him to join Paula's party for a Continental sojourn, while Somerset, increasingly in love but distressed by Paula's coolness, begins work on the castle, having won the competition. After frustrating communications, which eventually lapse, he sets out to see Paula on the Continent. He runs into Dare, who succeeds in thwarting Somerset's suit by tricks that blacken his name in the eyes of Paula and her companions. De Stancy now gains the upper hand, and on learning of his father's death receives Paula's consent to marry. In the meantime Somerset has resigned his commission as her architect.

Abner Power, having discovered the truth about Dare's parentage, threatens public revelation, but Dare, who has discovered Power's own criminal and anarchistic past, contrives Power's disappearance from the scene as the two face out each other at gun point.

Having returned to England to wed the new Sir William, Paula learns from Charlotte about Dare's plot to ruin Somerset's reputation. As she insists on legal retribution for Dare, de Stancy is forced to reveal himself as his father. Paula breaks off the marriage and, accompanied by Mrs Goodman, sets out in search of Somerset, who is then engaged in sketching old churches in Normandy. Ill and heartbroken, Somerset is finally found, and their love is reaffirmed. Newly married, they return to England, staying in the village as the castle's renovations are about to be completed. On the night of their arrival Dare achieves his revenge, setting fire to the castle with the de Stancy family portraits. Watching the blaze, Paula and Somerset determine to renounce the medievalism the building represents, and to build a modern house.

Critical Approaches

The novel returns to themes, character-types, and plots used in Hardy's earlier fiction. It displays his characteristic strengths, in particular the finely detailed observation of a wide range of emotions, an intense concentration on physical detail, and the tenacious exploration of a variety of controversial topical questions, as well as typical flaws, including a tendency towards unnecessarily complicated plotting, an over-reliance on coincidence, and the spinning out of incidents of little thematic importance.

The main thematic interest is the exploration of the awkward and stressful transition to modernism, and the effects of this on individuals and social relationships. Like *Tess of the d'Urbervilles*, the novel is also concerned with the decay of a once great lineage, and in symbolic terms with the waning of energies and ideas that had shaped and influenced English life and history. The loss of age-old and reassuring certainties, the emergence of new technologies, the destabilization and slow but progressive reordering of society and its long-established rituals are, however, concerns worked out within the confines of a traditional comic plot.

Much of the weight of Hardy's emphasis on change and dispossession is borne by Paula Power, the title-character. Overly self-aware and consequently hesitant, she symbolizes an emergent modernism not yet at one with itself. Incompletely formed, in being linked neither to the rural past nor to the ancient aristocracy of birth, she uneasily inhabits the medieval castle she has inherited. Her search to make an appropriate home in Stancy Castle, an effort to place herself within a ready-made identity forged out of past circumstances and customs, necessarily and appropriately ends in stalemate, while her attempt to restore her castle, as well as her seemingly aimless Continental wanderings, suggest a desire to define herself anew. This pressing modern need is a version of the medieval quest, with the hero overcoming deceit, illusion, and error to emerge aware of an identity and destiny. Identification with place does not in the end help Paula with her task, and, as a symbol of a society in the midst of widespread changes, she must finally, even if reluctantly, accept displacement and discontinuity as essential conditions of modern life.

Hardy diagnoses this in part as a problem for the 'New Woman', who from personal experience must forge a system of values and a philosophy of life. While not quite a 'New Woman', because she lacks a political consciousness about her situation, Paula none the less is directly confronted with the altered conditions of modernism, and faces the discovery of original solutions to new problems. Unable to commit herself wholeheartedly to a religious creed or a romantic relationship (traditional answers to questions of identity), she must yet contend with the urgent necessity of self-definition. Her orphanhood, great wealth, and status as an outsider in the communities that surround her castle likewise emphasize her profound separateness. While these conditions do not quite add up to a state of alienation, they situate her outside the social mainstream. And in her financial circumstances she is also distinctly and inescapably 'modern', in that the former basic condition of feudalism—the economic and social interdependence between lord and labourer—has disappeared.

Paula's 'Laodiceanism'—a word taken from Revelations to denote lukewarmness, and doubtless more readily recognizable to the Bible-reading culture of Hardy's day—is for Hardy a condition that defines the modern spirit's reluctance to fix itself firmly upon unalterable and determining positions. Her lukewarmness is also an attempted protest against enforced roles and responsibilities, and thus a delaying tactic allowing her to discover provisional solutions to the questions her problematic situation poses. It is, however, double-edged: its negative side brings her to the very brink of an inappropriate marriage, while its positive aspects will permit her to adapt when she is deprived of her castle and of the solidity, order, and continuity it symbolizes.

Her surname, Power—she is sarcastically referred to on one occasion as 'Miss Steam-Power'—is multi-layered in its ironies. As heiress to her father's fortune, she resembles in at least some respects the aristocrats of old whose authenticity and authority she longs for: like them she is constrained by a network of circumstances that she inherits rather than creates. As she becomes entangled in the web elaborately spun for her by Will Dare, she is increasingly 'power-less', is deprived of crucial information and (partly through her own temperamental lack of strong feeling) denies her instinctual knowledge of Somerset's goodness. Even her attempted restoration of Stancy Castle, a symbolic revitalization as much as an attempted appropriation of the past, is frustrated by external intervention as Dare, the last and decadent representative of an ancient lineage, wreaks his revenge for his social marginalization by destroying the ancestral home that he believes himself to have been deprived of. (In psychological terms, this act of parricide also dramatizes his desire for self-destruction.)

George Somerset, like Paula, falls victim to circumstance, and his own lukewarm response to life's chances, together with his tendency to respond passively rather than to initiate action, are symbolized by his apparently accidental entrapment in one of the castle's turrets, a version of the mythic labyrinth. This situation, which ironically reverses the situation of the knight who rescues the chatelaine from the threatening ogre, betokens much that follows as the trio of villains collude to isolate Somerset, and to deprive him of his lady-love.

While Paula and Somerset must come to understand that the devil has not entirely disappeared from the world, but has simply assumed a modern shape, their growth in knowledge lies mainly in another and traditional direction: in the gradual discovery of their authentic selves. This occurs through a double love-plot involving Paula's initial rejection of the true man for the false one. In developing this plot, Hardy plays a game of cat-and-mouse with the reader, confecting various suspense elements, and gradually propelling his tale to the inevitable scene of recognition in which the hero and heroine at last perceive their true selves and their destinies as clearly as the circumstances of their time permit them. The symbolic climax of this search in marriage—the orthodox solution to problems of social placement and personal identity—is, however, subtly undermined by the placement of the proposal and the wedding off-stage on the Continent.

Hardy's modern-dress revival of topoi and figures derived from medieval romance—in Dare, the devil and the changeling; in Paula, the innocent damsel enchanted by the evil magus; and in Somerset, the knightly champion who undergoes trial and ordeal to liberate the virtuous maiden from the monster imprisoning her—creates a mythical background that highlights both the fissures and the continuities between the medieval past and the late-Victorian present. However much these elements from the medieval imagination may have assisted Hardy in developing his thematic materials, the 'Merrie England' of collective fantasy and the sometimes sentimentalized medievalism of the mid-century's Pre-Raphaelite writers and painters is implicitly refuted by sharply drawn contrasts in plotting, incident, and character.

Hardy thus contends that, for the modern individual, medieval dress can never be more than an ill-fitting costume. By the conclusion the attempt to revive the past, with its confident belief in a single purpose for human existence and its feudal pieties rigidly governing social intercourse, has become an untenable basis for adapting to a future shaped by technology (here the railway and the telegraph) and its consequences of increased social and geographical mobility and the wide dissemination and exchange of diverse ideas and beliefs. While Hardy argues that imitating the past is futile, he also demonstrates that the past itself is inescapable, enduring as a deep substratum beneath modern experience. The discovery of the ancient foundations of Stancy Castle, which causes a modification to Somerset's plans for its restoration, convincingly symbolizes this interpenetration and interdependence. Similarly, Dare and de Stancy represent earlier, less developed types that, rather than disappearing with time, persist under the surface trappings of modernity.

The persistence of the past is also partly suggested by Hardy's heterogeneous narrative strategies. Self-consciously constructed out of various literary predecessors—the morality play, the comedy of manners, the melodrama, and the contemporary travelogue—the novel uses these to articulate philosophical observations on late-Victorian life and mores. Its highly mixed origins complement its central focus on the consequences of lukewarmness: it is itself at times indeterminate about its generic identity, sometimes veering towards the long-established conventions of romance, and sometimes towards the 'newer' modes of psychological and social realism. Appropriately, and like its heroine and hero, the novel casts a lingering and half-regretful glance backwards, while steadfastly turning towards the challenges, questions, and techniques of the future.

In turning, even if reluctantly, towards an uncertain modernism, the novel enjoins an abandonment of Victorian earnestness, and its ambivalent and nuanced rejection of optimism and of certain belief in an overarching sense of purpose is highly effective. Partly a matter of Hardy's own temperamentally passive stand, the novel's irresoluteness serves as a deliberate rejection of Victorian fictional methods, and provides the formal means of elaborating Hardy's own philosophical stance. That an acknowledgement of the workings of fate and contingency, and an acceptance of a circumscribed universe—serious concerns for Hardy and his audience—are ideas explored in a love-story with a happy ending, a highly unusual mixture of materials, suggests the large ambitions this novel essays.

Modern critics continue to be divided into two camps over how successfully *A Laodicean* meets these ambitions, some straightforwardly condemning the work as a poorly crafted and embarrassing effort, even Hardy's worst novel. Others, while admitting its defects, argue for a balanced appraisal, and discern in the novel the seeds of later, more accomplished work. The negative case centres on inadequacies noted by the early reviewers, but also takes much stronger exception to its melodramatic elements. A. J. Guerard's revisionist study of 1949 (*Thomas Hardy: The Novels and Stories*) framed the terms of modern critical debate. Singling out the opening chapters as among 'the finest and most controlled' that Hardy wrote, he judged the later sections marred by 'woolly abstract summarizing... a grotesquely theoretical psychology' and 'the dullest European journey' in fiction, while the 'charmingly modern and ambiguous' Paula dwindles into a 'paragon of Victorian smugness and evasion' (pp. 54, 25).

While fewer in number, the novel's defenders have offered more nuanced views. F. B. Pinion asserts that, in the light of the circumstances of composition, the novel is a 'considerable' achievement (*A Hardy Companion* (1968), 36), and in her introduction to the New Wessex edition of this novel (1975) Barbara Hardy has strenuously argued for appreciating Hardy's art and large, if only partially met, aims.

While assessment remains a critical preoccupation, criticism since the 1970s has focused on particular facets of the work. In his *The Metaphor of Chance: Vision and Technique in the Works of Thomas Hardy* (1971), Bert G. Hornback suggests that, despite the wooden characterization, Hardy's development of Paula's confrontation with the past served him as a preparation for Tess. George Wing observes that the flawed development and presentation of the villains is in some measure responsible for their gain in stature as outcasts from middle-class society ('Middle-Class Outcasts in Hardy's *A Laodicean*', *Humanities Association Review* (1976)). In the most suggestive discussion of *A Laodicean* to date, John Bayley argues that its hero and heroine 'remain suitably unrealized and negative figures... remarkably alive in terms of the novel's negative form' (*An Essay on Hardy* (1978), 155). See also TRAVELS, CONTINENTAL.

JHS

Valentine Cunningham, *Everywhere Spoken Against* (1975). (This study of Dissent in the Victorian novel includes a chapter on the Baptist elements in *A Laodicean*.)
Richard H. Taylor, *The Neglected Hardy: Thomas Hardy's Lesser Novels* (1982).

Larkin, Philip (1922–85), poet. In a number of articles, reviews, interviews, and broadcasts, Larkin was almost extravagantly generous in acknowledging Hardy's beneficial influence on his own poems. The earliest public statement seems to be the Introduction which Larkin wrote for the reissue of his first book of poems, *The North Ship*. This collection had originally been published in 1945, at a time when the young Larkin was, by his own later account, heavily under the influence of W. B. Yeats. But in the 1965 Faber and Faber reissue, Larkin wrote of his reaction against this influence, 'undramatic, complete and permanent'. It was, he wrote, in 'early 1946' that he had by his bedside 'the little blue *Chosen Poems of Thomas Hardy*: Hardy I knew as a novelist, but as regards his verse I shared Lytton Strachey's verdict that "the gloom is not even relieved by a little elegance of diction". This opinion did not last long; if I were asked to date its disappearance, I should guess it was the morning I first read "Thoughts of Phena at News of Her Death"'.

Over more than twenty years, Larkin often wrote and spoke about Hardy: in such reviews of biographical and critical books as his notices of Emma Hardy's *Some Recollections* (*Critical Quarterly*, 1962); of Roy Morrell's *Thomas Hardy: The Will and the Way* and Carl J. Weber's *Hardy of Wessex* (*Critical Quarterly*, 1966); his BBC Radio 4 broadcast 'A Man Who Noticed Things' (1968); and his long review-article on Robert Gittings and Jo Manton's *The Second Mrs Hardy* (*Encounter*, 1979). All these were included by Larkin in his collection of 'miscellaneous pieces 1955–82', *Required Writing* (1983). There are also a number of other pieces on Hardy by Larkin, scattered in various periodicals, which are in the process of being gathered together in a further collection of Larkin's prose—perhaps most importantly his review ('The Hidden Hardy') of *One Rare Fair Woman: Thomas Hardy's Letters to Florence Henniker, 1893–1922*, which appeared in the *New Statesman* (2 June 1972).

The key quotation, one which became almost a talismanic text for Larkin, was from Hardy's notebook, under the date 1 July 1879 (quoted in *LW* 131), and is taken from Leslie *Stephen: 'The ultimate aim of the poet should be to touch our hearts by showing his own, and not to exhibit his learning, or his fine taste, or his skill in mimicking the notes of his predecessors.' Larkin quoted this in a letter dated 22 July 1953; it appears at the beginning of one of his poetry notebooks; and he was never tired of repeating it. AT

Last, Isaac (1814–66), Dorchester schoolmaster. He was teaching at the British School in Greyhound Yard, Dorchester, when Hardy, then aged 10, was moved to this Nonconformist establishment in September 1850 after attending the National School nearer home. Last had a considerable local reputation as 'an exceptionally able man, and a good teacher of Latin' (*LW* 22), and the move was instigated by Jemima Hardy's ambitions for her son. Later Hardy began to study Latin with Last as an 'extra', and in 1853, when Last started an 'academy' or private school, Hardy moved with him, remaining there until he left school in 1856. Hardy did well under Last's tuition, and received prizes from him. Later Last's health made him unable to continue teaching, and he became a grocer.

His son William became Director of the Science Museum at South Kensington, and his grandson a classical scholar and head of an Oxford college. Referring to the former in his autobiography, Hardy states that 'The obituary notices that appeared in *The Times* and other papers gave details of a life more successful than his father's—though not of higher intellectual ability than that by which it had been Hardy's good fortune to profit' (*LW* 383). See also CLASSICS.

***Late Lyrics and Earlier*.** Hardy's sixth collection of verse was published on 23 May 1922, some four and a half years after its immediate predecessor, *Moments of Vision*, in an edition of 3,200 copies. There were two reprints before the end of the year. Hardy had sent the manuscript (now in DCM) to his publisher, Macmillan, on 23 January. Of its 151 poems, 'about half... were written quite lately', according to the long and important 'Apology' with which Hardy prefaced the volume (see PREFACES). The rest, as Purdy has pointed out (226), exhibit, chronologically speaking, 'the same surprising range' as some of the earlier collections: 'The earliest is dated 1866, the latest 1921, and every decade between (save the 80's) provides some verse. In many respects the volume is the most representative of Hardy's whole career.' Twenty-two of the poems had already appeared in print.

As usual, a number of the poems refer to individuals important in various ways in Hardy's personal life. 'I Sometimes Think' is a tender and touching tribute to the way in which his second wife, Florence, has transformed his existence: she has been (the poem claims) unique in recognizing and appreciating his exertions to make the world a better place. The short and simple poem blends the expression of his love for Florence with a sense of hurt and disappointment at what he perceived as the world's indifference to his altruistic endeavours. Most of the poems in this group, however, refer to the dead. '"Sacred to the Memory"' and 'The Sun's Last Look on the Country Girl' are further evidence of his response, already evident in *Moments of Vision*, to the death of his beloved sister Mary (see RELATIVES OF THOMAS HARDY). The latter poem is dated December 1915, very shortly after Mary's death on 24 November. The title of the undated '"Sacred to the Memory"' is taken from the inscription on Mary's tombstone, designed by Hardy himself, in Stinsford churchyard; this brief but deeply felt poem seeks to make amends for the 'bare conventionality' of the inscription by insisting that the 'full script' of his feelings for the dead woman is inscribed on the landscape she knew. The perception of both tombstone and landscape as 'texts' is characteristic.

Much less close to Hardy, and the object of a very different kind of emotion, was Helen *Paterson, the subject of 'The Opportunity', who nearly 50 years earlier had illustrated the serial version of *Far from the Madding Crowd*. (The opening reference to 'Forty springs back' suggests that the poem was written some years before publication.) That Helen Allingham, as she became, was still living makes the publication of the poem a little surprising, though it is true that her identity was partly concealed under the initials 'H.P.'. Hardy had met Helen Paterson in May 1874; on 25 July 1906 he told Edmund *Gosse that he had 'never thought of her for the last 20 years'; he added, perhaps jokingly, that 'but for a stupid blunder of God Almighty' he might easily have married her. This sense of a lost opportunity (a favourite Hardyan theme) finds somewhat more serious expression in the poem.

Another lost opportunity is the subject of 'Faintheart in a Railway Train', a more obviously light-hearted poem (which is not to say that the feeling is not genuine) about a 'radiant stranger' who is unidentified and may well have been fictitious. Two poems referring discreetly but more unequivocally to individuals are 'The Passer-By' and 'An Old Likeness'. The 'L.H.' of the former is Louisa Harding, a farmer's daughter (see *LW* 30) who was the object of the young Hardy's romantic interest for a year or so, and who, not long before Hardy's death, was to be the subject also of 'To Louisa in the Lane', included in the posthumous collection *Winter Words*. The manuscript has 'In Memoriam L—— H——. (She speaks)', which indicates the nature of the poem as a dramatic monologue in which Hardy, 'well-trimmed and brushed' and blushing with shyness, sees his younger self from the outside; it also dates the poem subsequent to Louisa's death in 1913. The 'R.T.' of 'An Old Likeness' has been plausibly identified as Rosamund *Tomson, the entry for whom comments further on this poem.

The stream of poems about Emma *Hardy that had flowed through Hardy's previous two collections had still not by any means dried up in this volume of 1922. 'The West-of-Wessex Girl', with its infectious rhythm, is noted as '*Begun in Plymouth, March 1913*'—that is to say, in the course of Hardy's painful and penitential revisiting, a few months after Emma's death, of scenes associated with her early life and the early stages of their relationship (she had been born in Plymouth, and spent the years before her marriage in Devon and Cornwall). Before he left Plymouth in March 1913, Hardy ordered a memorial tablet to Emma, to his own design, to be placed in St Juliot Church, and 'The Marble Tablet', precisely dated '*St Juliot: 8 September 1916*', refers to a visit he paid with Florence to ensure that the work had been properly carried out; another poem, 'The Monument-Maker', included in *Human Shows*, also originated in this visit. ('The Marble Tablet' invites comparison with '"Sacred to the Memory"', referred to above.) 'Her Song' and 'A Wet August' recall, respectively, his first two visits to *Cornwall more than 40 years earlier. Particularly haunting—an apt word in relation to poems in which Emma's ghost is much in evidence—is 'A Man Was Drawing Near to Me', a counterpart, from Emma's point of view, of the no less haunting 'When I Set Out for Lyonnesse' in the previous collection, and a powerful expression of Hardy's private myth of the first encounter with Emma as not only momentous but an intensely dramatic working out of destiny. 'End of the Year 1912', 'The Marble-Streeted Town' (referring again to Plymouth), 'On a Discovered Curl of Hair', 'A Woman Driving', and 'Best Times' are among other poems based on memories, early or late, of Emma, who may also be the subject of the more generalized but effective poem of unexpected loss, 'The Last Time', and of 'The Strange House', discussed below.

Love and loss, memory and regret: these themes, widespread in earlier collections, persist in *Late Lyrics and Earlier*, as do such other diverse but typically Hardyan themes as *ghosts, old age, *birds, and *animals. Emma's is by no means the only ghost that haunts the poet, and as in *Moments of Vision* the presence of the dead is often felt through some common object, unremarkable in itself but given potency by its 'associative power'. 'Quite a row' of the dead sit lightly on a disintegrating piece of garden-furniture in the song-like poem 'The Garden Seat'. In another metrically delicate poem, 'The Little Old Table', the creaking of an old wooden table is the voice through which it speaks of the person (perhaps his mother) who gave it to him long ago; it is surely a significant point that the table creaks when touched 'with elbow or knee', as if symbolical contact is being made with the dead. 'The Strange House' envisages the state of Max Gate in the year 2000, haunted by the ghosts of not only its human inhabitants but its very furniture, with a ghostly piano playing 'Just as a ghost might play'. In the well-known and (again) song-like 'Voices from Things Growing in a Churchyard', named individuals now dead are not only associated with particular specimens of plant life but have been literally metamorphosed into them in the manner already touched on in 'Transformations' (*MV*). (For further comments on this poem, see DE LA MARE, WALTER.) The anecdotal 'The Old Neighbour and the New' implies that the presence of the departed in a familiar spot can be felt at least as keenly as that of the one who has taken his place.

Old age is treated, for once, impersonally in a poem about a grim marital jest, 'At the Dinner-Table'. A young wife, catching sight of herself in a mirror, is horrified to see the 'Wrenched wrinkled features' of old age, then learns that her husband has substituted a distorting mirror for the original. The joke turns out, however, to be a prophecy; for 50 years later, after his death, she looks in the mirror again and sees, this time without distortion, the same hideous features. This slight but in some respects characteristic poem seems to represent a development of the more personal 'I Look into My Glass' (*WP*), while the woman's experience of the ravaging effects of time is also paralleled in the experience of Marcia near the end of *The Well-Beloved*.

As befits a volume in whose title the term 'lyric' is prominent, music is, in many aspects, a strong presence throughout. A number of poems are subtitled 'Song' (one, 'The Rift', has the subtitle 'Song: Minor Mode'); others bear such more precise musical indications as 'Nocturne' ('Murmurs in the Gloom') and 'Scherzando' ('A Military Appointment'). Singers and singing feature in several poems: 'On Stinsford Hill at Midnight' has 'a woman's muslined form | Singsonging airily'; another woman sings in 'To a Lady Playing and Singing in the Morning' (probably referring to Emma Hardy); a wartime poem, 'At the Entering of the New Year', recalls 'The contrabasso's measured booming' as part of the cheerful prewar welcoming of a new year. 'The Maid of Keinton Mandeville' refers to a specific song that had strong personal associations for Hardy—'Should he upbraid', set by Henry Bishop. The origin of this poem is to be found in a concert Hardy attended, and a singer he heard, at Sturminster Newton in 1878.

Emma Hardy's fondness for music is the subject of 'A Duettist to Her Pianoforte', a dramatic monologue in which she recalls music-making at St Juliot Rectory before her marriage with her sister Helen. Another poem about music-making, 'Haunting Fingers', subtitled 'A Phantasy in a Museum of Musical Instruments' (Hardy may have had in mind the Horniman Museum in London), endows a series of instruments with voices that recall in inactivity their active past. 'A little boy with a violin', as Hardy himself had once been, plays to a convict in the exquisite 'At the Railway Station, Upway', one of several poems in this collection selected by Benjamin *Britten for setting in his *Winter Words*. 'An Ancient to Ancients', discussed further below, includes both dances and popular operas in its humorous survey of bygone fashions; and dancing 'on the ball-room's smooth floor' is also alluded to in 'A Gentleman's Epitaph on Himself and a Lady, Who Were Buried Together'. Church music, to which Hardy had a strong attachment from his early years, is the point of departure for 'On the Tune Called the Old-Hundred-and-Fourth', which refers to one of Hardy's favourite *hymns, Ravenscroft's setting of Psalm 104: addressed to Emma, the poem is another of regret for missed opportunities of shared experience. 'The Chapel-Organist' owes something, metrically and otherwise, to *Browning, and can even be read as a counterweight to his 'Abt Vogler'.

Many of the poems so far referred to revive the past, and often the distant past, but a few others are more firmly topical. A literary centenary, that of *Keats's most important volume, the *Poems of 1820*, is commemorated in two poems, 'At a House in Hampstead' and 'At Lulworth Cove a Century Back', dated respectively July and September 1920. Topical in a different way are the war poems. 'Jezreel', though precisely dated 24 September 1918 and prompted by a military success very near the end of the Great War, characteristically places modern history in the context of the remote (here the biblical) past; '"And There Was a Great Calm"' marks the armistice on 11 November of the same year; and the anecdote 'After the War' is more informal and ironic.

This rich collection contains a number of other noteworthy poems that do not lend themselves readily to categorization. 'Weathers', which stands at its head, is a deservedly popular anthology-piece, song-like and exquisitely precise in its observation and diction; for an analogy we must turn to a Shakespearian song such as 'When icicles hang by the wall', similarly remarkable for its rapid succession of precisely delineated vignettes of the visible world and human activity. 'If It's Ever Spring Again' has something of the same quality, but with greater poignancy and wistfulness. 'The Children and Sir Nameless' is, in less familiar vein, a moral fable about the pride that has a long-term fall, embodied in a typically Hardyan awareness of the historical decline of once-great families, and a no less typical capacity to have his imagination quickened by church monuments and other artefacts surviving from the distant past.

In contrast, 'Last Words to a Dumb Friend', dated 2 October 1904, is addressed to one of the accident-prone Max Gate cats, identified as 'Snowdove' (see PETS). 'The Whipper-In' and 'A Military Appointment' are both dialogue poems recounting a simple but sardonic narrative. The love-poem 'After a Romantic Day' turns out to propose a very modern rejection of traditional notions of a 'poetry of place' harmonizing with human feelings: for the modern lover, 'the blank lack of any charm' in a railway cutting does not disqualify it from forming an appropriate setting for the (presumably fictitious) subject's emotions. Distinctively modern, too, is 'In a London Flat' (the term 'flat' was itself recent enough to give rise to comment in *The Well-Beloved*), where the language and verse-movement, no less than the theme of loneliness and isolation, irresistibly bring to mind the poetry of T. S. Eliot, and remind us that *Late Lyrics and Earlier* belongs to the same year as *The Waste Land*: 'Reading late on a night of gloom, | And a cab-hack's wheeze, and the clap of its feet | In its breathless pace on the smooth wet street . . .'.

'After a Romantic Day' portrays the sides of the cutting as 'a convenient sheet whereon | The visions of his mind were drawn', and the preoccupation with different forms of 'text' provided by the circumstantial world that is evident in *Moments of Vision* is no less striking in this later collection. Anything from a mirror ('At the Dinner-Table') to a memorial tablet ('The Marble Tablet'), a photograph ('An Old Likeness') to a gravestone ('"Sacred to the Memory"') or a milestone ('The Milestone by the Rabbit-Burrow'), lends itself to one or other kind of 'reading' and interpretation.

Three poems of old age and retrospect at the end of the volume are unmistakably personal. 'An Ancient to Ancients' surveys Hardy's life, tastes, and beliefs, noting that many once admired—including Etty, Mulready, and Maclise among painters, and *Tennyson among poets—are now out of fashion. There is a slightly boastful or defiant personal application in the reminder that many of the greatest thinkers and writers have done much of their best work in their old age ('Burnt brightlier towards their setting-day'). As F. B. Pinion has observed, the tone of this poem is 'genial, confident, and even sprightly, befitting an after-dinner speech' (*A Commentary on the Poems of Thomas Hardy* (1976), 199). Even the reference to Emma, who once read Tennyson aloud to him ('Even she who voiced those rhymes is dust'), is without intensity, and indeed the stanza in which that line appears looks very like a parody of the early Tennyson. 'After Reading Psalms XXXIX, XL, etc.' and 'Surview' both use biblical texts as devices for reviewing and assessing his own experiences. The former is of interest for its clear-eyed inspection of the very early stages of Hardy's career as a poet. Its audacious rhymes ('tryst, I' with the Latin '*fecisti*', for instance) have a Browningesque flavour. All three poems provide, in their vigorous rhythms and their sometimes self-mocking wit, an unexpectedly upbeat conclusion to the collection.

Lawrence, D. H. (1885–1930), novelist and poet. In his *Study of Thomas Hardy*, written in 1914 but published posthumously, Lawrence implicitly acknowledged Hardy as the main influence on his novels. Although he criticizes Hardy for allowing his metaphysic or moral judgement to outweigh his sympathy for his convention-breaking characters, Lawrence writes about Hardy's novels with such affectionate understanding that his admiration is what we remember. Hardy's 'feeling', he writes, 'his sensuous understanding is... apart from his metaphysic, very great and deep, deeper than that, perhaps, of any other English novelist' (*Phoenix: The Posthumous Papers*, ed. E. D. McDonald (1936), 480).

Lawrence took from Hardy the new subjects of sex and the unconscious. Writers, of course, have always dealt with sex: the difference in Hardy, and especially in Lawrence, is that sex has become self-justifying, not subject to other values. But Hardy, says Lawrence, too often turns the merely relative judgements of society against his sexually active characters, making Tess, Jude, and Sue, for example, internalize society's condemnation of them. Actually Hardy is no less critical than Lawrence of society and its relative judgements, as when the narrator in *Tess of the d'Urbervilles* remarks that Tess's desire for Angel 'was not to be controlled by vague lucubrations over the social rubric'. Hardy shows his understanding of the unconscious when, in the same sentence, he describes Tess's desire as 'that tremendous force which sways humanity to its purpose, as the tide sways the helpless weed' (*TDU* 30). When he says that Angel would have been nobler 'with more animalism' (36), Hardy is on his way to becoming Lawrence. Lawrence, on the other hand, in the *Study*, rewrites Hardy's novels, criticizing their deficiencies in such a way as to arrive at his own novels.

RL

Robert Langbaum, 'Hardy and Lawrence', in *Thomas Hardy in Our Time* (1995).

Lawrence, T. E. (1888–1935), popularly known as 'Lawrence of Arabia', archaeologist, soldier, and author. He met Hardy in April 1923, and soon afterwards described him in a letter to Robert *Graves (8 September 1923) as 'so pale, so quiet, so refined into an essence' (quoted in Millgate 549). Lawrence, who had in the previous year enlisted in the ranks of the Royal Air Force, was at this time living at Clouds Hill, Wool, Dorset. He made a very favourable impression on both Hardy and his wife: according to an undated letter by Florence *Hardy (quoted in Gittings, *The Older Hardy*, 204), Hardy was 'utterly captivated' by him, and he quickly became one of the circle of younger men who formed close friendships with Hardy during his final years. There were frequent meetings: for example, on 30 December 1923 (with G. B. Shaw),

Lawrence lunched at Max Gate, and on 6 September 1924 (with Siegfried *Sassoon) he had tea there, while on another occasion Hardy, his wife, and E. M. *Forster went to tea at Clouds Hill.

He was one of those who knew of the existence of Hardy's autobiography, Florence Hardy sending him a copy of the typescript early in 1926. On 21 April 1925 he had written to the publisher Jonathan Cape: 'a very distinguished person's wife once asked me if I would care to edit or "ghost" her husband's diary. . . . I haven't said either yes or no . . . The existence of the material is not known, even to Macmillan's' (*The Letters of T. E. Lawrence*, ed. David Garnett (1938), 474–5). A letter to Florence Hardy (p. 498) dated 21 June 1926 makes it clear that he has seen the manuscript of the *Life* as it then stood.

Hardy's autobiography contains a touching account (*LW* 468) of Lawrence's departure after his last visit to Hardy. A passage deleted from the autobiography states that 'Hardy was devoted to this world-famous soldier, and their not infrequent meetings during the last few years of Hardy's life were a source of great interest to both' (*PN* 279–80).

Ronald D. Knight, *T. E. Lawrence and the Max Gate Circle* (1988).

Lea, Hermann (1869–1952), author and photographer. He is best known as the author of both text and photographs of *Thomas Hardy's Wessex* (1913), a guide to the environments of Hardy's work. Lea and Hardy worked closely together on the project (Lea's photographs also formed frontispieces for the Wessex Edition: see COLLECTED EDITIONS), and it seems not too much to say that Lea and Hardy became friends, to the degree that Hardy in his sixties was open to friendship. They bicycled together in the early years of the century, and when Lea acquired a car they drove out together, and of course they walked together. When Hardy's brother and sisters left the birthplace in *Higher Bockhampton in 1913, Lea, with Hardy's blessing, assumed the lease, and their walks together then were most often on Puddletown Heath.

Lea wrote down some accounts of his relationship with Hardy, which suggest that over time there was a growth of intimacy and an interchange of confidences between the two men, confidences which Lea took with him to his grave. The image of the older Hardy that he offers in these unshaped biographical fragments, collected in *Thomas Hardy Through the Camera's Eye* (1964), is subtly different from the larger portraits of Robert Gittings or Michael Millgate. He dwells on Hardy's sense of humour, his generosity, his openness to all shades of opinion on controversial issues, his love of heights and the prospects therefrom, the pleasure he took in planning excursions, his wholehearted interest in the little things of life—ordinary delights. In fact Lea was unlike most others who came at all close to Hardy: he was not gentry, he was not a woman, he was not literary; and he seems to have experienced a side of his friend that was less public and less reserved than most people were offered. SJG

Hardy's Wessex Today: Modern Photographs and Texts by Vera Jesty; Original Photographs by Hermann Lea (1990).

letters, for Hardy, were a veritable 'gale of correspondence', as he called it. He was a constant correspondent: his personal letters in the seven volumes of the Purdy–Millgate edition, which excludes letters written for publication, cover 65 years, from August 1862 to December 1927. Hardy's letters were handwritten until, after his second marriage in 1914, his wife Florence typed many of them, assisted in the last few years of Hardy's life by the part-time secretary May O'Rourke.

Many of the letters are addressed to the firm of Macmillan, his principal publishers from 1902, and reveal a sound business sense; others deal with public affairs, literary and linguistic topics, and subjects close to his heart, like animal welfare. There are frequent references to his health, but it is those touching on what in one letter he calls 'inner things' that are of especial interest. In his letters, whatever the topic, Hardy is speaking in his own voice, in the first person, as in many of his poems. This is not the voice of the narrator of his fiction, nor that of the impersonal narrative of his 'autobiography'. This is Thomas Hardy, from 1885 onwards in his study at Max Gate, sharing his thoughts with close friends, women and men, with other writers, acquaintances, and even strangers, with Emma and Florence, dealing with domestic matters, responding to questions about his beliefs, his writings, his feelings, on topics as diverse as growing onions and the future of humanity.

A natural courtesy pervades Hardy's letters. Only rarely does he react with irritation to some accusation or misrepresentation. He disliked inveterate autograph-hunters, especially those who are 'in the habit of sending me my own books for the purpose, & (as I regret to find) selling them afterwards for double the price they paid for them' (*L* v 168). As the flood of requests continued, Hardy suggested to Sir Frederick *Macmillan, who approved, that a charge of one guinea be made for each autograph in support of the Dorset County Hospital (*L* vi 168). A letter from an Australian correspondent in 1924 received a curt, dictated response, objecting to 'the tone in which you write', and concluding: 'Were Mr Hardy to answer the mass of letters he received from strangers like yourself he would have no time whatever for any work of his own, or even for taking rest' (*L* vi 286–7).

Hardy's sensitiveness to reviews is well known: he resented being misunderstood, aware that he 'has been misrepresented so much' (*L* v 319), referring elsewhere to 'the blood-puppies of the *Daily Express*' who 'cock up the hind leg over the pages' (*L* v 20). In August 1907 Hardy wrote to the journalist and magazine editor Clement *Shorter in light-hearted tone, yet deeply felt: 'I endeavour to profit from the opinions of those wonderful youths & maidens, my reviewers, & am laying to heart a few infallible truths taught by them: e.g.,—That T.H's verse is his only claim to notice. That T.H's prose is his only real work. That T.H's early novels are best. That T.H's later novels are best. That T.H's novels are good in plot & bad in character. That T.H's novels are bad in plot, & good in charr. That T.H's philosophy is all that matters. That T.H's writings are good in spite of their bad philosophy. This is as far as I have got at present, but I struggle gallantly on' (*L* iii 266).

In 1908 Hardy thanked the poet-novelist Alfred Noyes for a very generous review of the third part of *The Dynasts* (*L* iii 296), but many years later he severely berates Noyes for asserting in a lecture that Hardy believed that 'the Power behind the Universe was an imbecile jester' (*L* vi 52). A week later, responding to Noyes's reply, Hardy argues persuasively that readers and critics should recognize 'the vast difference between the expression of fancy and the expression of belief' in his writings. It was the failure of one critic to do so, commenting on Hardy's poem 'To My Father's Violin' that 'truly this pessimism is insupportable.... One marvels that Hardy is not in a madhouse', that led to the concluding words to Noyes: 'Such is English criticism; and I repeat, why did I ever write a line! However I will go no further. And perhaps if the young ladies to whom you lectured really knew that, so far from being the wicked personage they doubtless think me at present to be, I am a harmless old character much like their own grandfathers, they would consider me far less romantic and attractive' (*L* vi 53–5). This letter, along with a number of other selected letters, is also included by Hardy in the *Life*.

Hardy himself did not hesitate to comment on other writers, living and dead, in his letters, although he confesses to being but 'a poor critic of bygone authors—I mean dead authors' (*L* v 323). There are, for example, comments on Spenser, *Shelley, Whitman, and Goethe. On Shakespeare he wrote to the influential Shakespearian theatrical director Harley *Granville-Barker that 'I always feel that Shakespeare is largely wasted in acting' (*L* vi 373), and to J. W. Mackail, who had just delivered the Annual Shakespeare Lecture of the British Academy, in 1916, that he thought Iago 'the greatest failure in S's characters... I shouldn't wonder if he (Iago) didn't "slip idly from" S. just as a matter of potboiling' (*L* v 173–4). Hardy's dislike of 'the new ugly school of poetry' (*L* iv 300) is a recurrent theme in his later years. He deplores that 'a fashion for obscurity rages among young poets, so that much good verse is lost by the simple inability of readers to rack their brains to solve conundrums' (*L* v 275). Writing to Ezra *Pound in 1921, Hardy admits: 'As I am old-fashioned, and think lucidity a virtue in poetry, as in prose, I am at a disadvantage in criticizing recent poets who apparently aim at obscurity. I do not mean that you do, but I gather that at least you do not care whether the many understand you or not' (*L* vi 77). In a letter to Robert Bridges he compliments the latter on endeavouring 'to save our young poets from the woeful fogs of free verse worship' (*L* vi 165).

There are many casual remarks and observations on matters of general interest in Hardy's letters—*politics, war, art, for example—and others of more personal concern, like *religion, *marriage, and the treatment of *animals. Such comments figure frequently in the letters to friends, among them Edmund *Gosse, Edward *Clodd, and Sydney *Cockerell, and women like Florence *Henniker and Agnes *Grove. Writing, almost prophetically, in 1903 on 'the enormous specific gravity of China amongst the nations of the earth' (*L* iii 79), Hardy realized, while working on the battle of Jena in Part Second of *The Dynasts*, that 20th-century war is very unlike earlier wars which throbbed 'with enthusiasm & romance' (*L* iii 135).

These words were written to Florence Henniker when memories of the Boer War were still fresh. A year later, Hardy writes again to Mrs Henniker that 'politics have played me a shabby trick of coming to a crisis just at the moment when I meant to bring out Dynasts II.... I feel rather gloomy about it, as indeed about most things' (*L* iii 190). War, with its inhumanity and suffering, affected Hardy deeply. Thus he writes to Cockerell in December 1915: 'It is a gloomy time, in which the world, having like a spider climbed to a certain height, seems slipping back to where it was long ago' (*L* v 135). Humanity has 'retrograded' in civilization in view of 'the cold scientific slaughter of hundreds of thousands that we see going on now'—that is, in 1918 (*L* v 270). And a year later: 'All development is of a material & scientific kind—& scarcely any addition to our knowledge is applied to objects philanthropic or ameliorative' (*L* v 309). 'So why', he asks Mrs Henniker in the same letter, 'does not Christianity throw up the sponge & say I am beaten, & let another religion take its place.'

'Theological lumber is still allowed to discredit religion', Hardy had written to Clodd in 1902 (*L* iii 5), and 24 years later he wrote, again to Clodd, that rational religion was not making much progress—'indeed the movement of thought seems to have entered a back current in the opposite direction. These however are not uncommon in human history' (*L* vii 32). His hope that the Christian Church 'could be made to modulate by degrees ... into an undogmatic, non-theological establishment for the promotion of that virtuous living on which all honest men are agreed' (*L* i 136) was patently doomed to remain an idle dream.

After the publication of *Jude the Obscure* (1895), Hardy elaborated in several letters his views on 'the marriage question', writing, for example, to the critic William *Archer, who praised the book, that the novel was 'concerned merely with the doom of hereditary temperament & unsuitable mating in marriage' (*L* ii 104). To Sir George *Douglas he wrote that 'a bad marriage is one of the direst things on earth, & one of the cruellest things, but beyond that my opinions on the subject are vague enough' (*L* ii 98). About his own two marriages Hardy wrote to Florence Henniker that 'according to my own experience a second marriage does not, or need not, obliterate an old affection' (*L* v 19). Some of Hardy's other affections also survived the passage of time: writing to Gosse in 1906, he mentioned feeling 'quite romantical' about the artist Helen *Paterson (subsequently Mrs William Allingham), who had illustrated *Far from the Madding Crowd* many years earlier, and who 'but for a stupid blunder of God Almighty' might have become his wife (*L* iii 218).

Of other topics, a cause close to Hardy's heart was the welfare of animals (see ANIMALS, CRUELTY TO). In many letters he voiced his concern about vivisection, cruel methods of slaughtering, circus performances, and conjuring tricks. In 1904 he wrote to an Anglican clergyman about the 'barbarism' of blood sports, wondering, in the manner of Swift's *Modest Proposal*, 'why the children, say, of overcrowded families should not be used for sporting purposes. There would be no difference in principle' (*L* iii 110). Hardy's interest in art and, on an even more personal level, in *architecture is reflected in many letters, from his earliest surviving letter, written in 1862 to his sister Mary and referring to a chapel by Pugin (*L* i 1), to a letter of 1924 about Portland stone (*L* vi 234–5).

That comments on English usage, including dialect, are scattered throughout Hardy's correspondence is not surprising in one so deeply involved in the art of writing. He abhorred slovenly writing and, declining an invitation to a conference of Professors of English in America in 1922, expressed the view that 'the English language is in danger of utter ruin, largely as it seems by the multiplication of half-illiterate publications' (*L* vi 147). Presumably he included in this ruin 'the rawest American' which he had mentioned in a letter to John Lane in 1910 (*L* iv 131), but not imparted to the American professors.

Hardy's often indifferent health, his recurring bouts of influenza and other afflictions, are frequently alluded to; on the other hand, he relates with obvious satisfaction his bicycle tours, even in his seventies, until just before his 80th birthday he admits to the novelist Anthony Hope to not bicycling far nowadays, adding for good measure: 'I ought to be a dignified figure sitting in a large armchair (gilded for choice) with a footstool' (*L* vi 18). When cycling became too strenuous, the motor-car offered many opportunities for comfortable travel: in 1915 alone Hardy made over 30 excursions by car with his photographer friend Hermann *Lea (see *L* v 116). Other modern inventions also proved useful: a telephone was installed at Max Gate late in 1919 (*L* vi 1–2), and in 1924 Hardy was 'inveigled into setting up Wireless', in time to listen to J. C. Squire broadcasting a talk in celebration of Hardy's 84th birthday—'our dog listened attentively' (*L* vi 252–3). Wessex, a wire-haired terrier, was usually the noisiest member of the household, and barked furiously when the telephone rang, but there were more serious problems with servants, judging by words like 'great trouble' and even 'rebellion', which suggest that life at Max Gate did not always run smooth.

In style Hardy's letters range from formal politeness to familiarity and, when writing to his lady friends, to affection. There is some vacillation in modes of address and concluding phrases. Within less than three weeks in 1916, for example, Hardy uses three different forms of address to Sir Frederick Macmillan, signing himself once 'Yours very truly' and twice 'Sincerely yours'. While his earlier letters are more concerned with Hardy's life and literary labours, the later ones tend to be more expansive and, as the editors of the *Collected Letters* point out, more directly revelatory of Hardy's attitudes and beliefs. RE

Evelyn Hardy and F. B. Pinion (eds.), *One Rare Fair Woman: Thomas Hardy's Letters to Florence Henniker 1893–1922* (1972).
Michael Millgate (ed.), *Letters of Emma and Florence Hardy* (1996).
Richard Little Purdy and Michael Millgate (eds.), *The Collected Letters of Thomas Hardy*, 7 vols. (1978–88).

library, Hardy's. By the time of his death Hardy had accumulated at Max Gate a sizeable library that overflowed from his study into many other parts of the house. Little direct evidence survives of how and when these books were acquired. A small number (including bibles, prayerbooks, language primers, and classical texts, on which see CLASSICS) dated back to his childhood and schooldays; the editions of canonical British poets seem mostly to have been purchased in the 1860s; several significant works of philosophy, social theory, and local history were added in the 1870s; and towards the end of the century came the historical and biographical studies of the Napoleonic period later drawn upon for *The Dynasts*. Hardy also purchased many miscellaneous titles during these years (such as guidebooks for his Continental travels), but for new novels and other current publications, including many of those mentioned in his *Literary Notebooks*, he seems largely to have depended on Mudie's Select Library and, later, The Times Book Club, or on the libraries of the Athenaeum and the Dorset County Museum.

As his fame increased so did the number of presentation copies he received from friends, admirers, and publishers, and such involuntary acquisitions were primarily responsible for the library's expansion during his three final decades. While, therefore, the surviving volumes from the Max Gate library are of immense interest, especially since they often contain markings and annotations in Hardy's hand, it is important to keep in mind that many of the books in the library had not been chosen by him and that his reading was by no means confined to the titles he actually owned.

Unfortunately, the dispersal of the Max Gate library following Florence Hardy's death resulted in many of Hardy's personal copies becoming difficult, even impossible, to find. Although Hardy sometimes wrote his name inside his books, he did not insert bookplates in any of them, nor was any catalogue of the library compiled during his lifetime. Early in 1928 Sydney *Cockerell, as co-literary executor with Florence Hardy of Hardy's estate, visited Max Gate and removed from the shelves an unspecified number of volumes he deemed to be ephemeral or otherwise uninteresting, although it is not clear that these were actually disposed of at the time. He also had 'Max Gate' book-labels printed in two versions, red-on-white and black-on-white, and personally pasted red labels into books that contained Hardy's signature or annotations, leaving Florence Hardy to arrange for the black labels to be inserted into the remaining volumes. Hostility, however, soon developed between the two literary executors, Florence Hardy never did insert the black labels, and when she died in 1937 her will directed that the library should be sold subject to the prior selection of the more important and 'characteristic' of Hardy's books for deposit and display in the Dorset County Museum. But because the selection (by Irene Cooper Willis, Florence Hardy's executor) was not very expertly carried out, a number of significant items were sold even while some relatively uninteresting volumes were reserved for the Museum. Even so, the Museum's collection of some 475 volumes from the library, supplemented as it is by Hardy's copies of many of his own books, remains of the first importance.

The first, and major, auction sale of books from the Max Gate library was conducted in London by Hodgson & Co. on 26 May 1938. Further items, almost all of minor importance, were included in another sale on 10 June 1938. While, however, the Hodgson catalogue for 26 May is of considerable interest as an overall reflection of the contents and character of Hardy's library, its value as a research tool is greatly lessened by its low levels of comprehensiveness and specificity, each lot typically comprising a number of volumes of which only one or two are identified by title. And in the 10 June sale 29 uncounted lots of miscellaneous books were offered simply as 'parcels'. That the catalogues also failed to discriminate between Hardy's own books and those belonging to his wife was pointed out by Cockerell in a letter to *The Times Literary Supplement* of 17 September 1938.

At both sales, however, almost all the lots were bought by booksellers, and while a few were acting wholly or partly on commission for specific customers, the majority—including Maggs Bros., W. Heffer & Sons, Frank Hollings, Bertram Rota, and Elkin Mathews—subsequently issued their own catalogues in which the Max Gate volumes were, with varying degrees of fullness, individually listed and described. Potential problems were created, as Cockerell also noted in his September 1938 letter, by the random insertion of some of the black book-labels both before and after the Hodgson sale and, worse, by the widespread post-sale insertion of imitation labels produced by the booksellers themselves. Although there is no evidence of deliberate deception, the presence of a Max Gate book-label does not in itself constitute proof of Max Gate provenance, and such labels are not in any case to be found in the books that Hardy's widow gave to Hardy's friends and relatives.

Inevitably, the Max Gate volumes became widely dispersed, and many have entirely disappeared from view. In addition, however, to those in the Dorset County Museum, such volumes are to be found in significant numbers in the Beinecke Library at Yale University, the Humanities Research Center at the University of Texas, the Colby College library, the School Library of Eton College, and the private collection of Mr Frederick B. Adams. A comprehensive reconstruction of the library, based on auctioneers' and booksellers' catalogues supplemented by inspection of currently traceable volumes, is being compiled by Michael Millgate, but useful references to the library and its contents are already available in a number of sources, including those listed below. MM

Michael Millgate, 'The Max Gate Library', in Phillip V. Mallett and Ronald P. Draper (eds.), *A Spacious Vision: Essays on Hardy* (1994).

Dennis Taylor, *Hardy's Literary Language and Victorian Philology* (1993).

Walter F. Wright, *The Shaping of 'The Dynasts': A Study in Thomas Hardy* (1967).

Life's Little Ironies, the third of Hardy's four collections of short stories, was published on 22 February 1894 by *Osgood,

McIlvaine, with the subtitle 'A Set of Tales with Some Colloquial Sketches Titled A Few Crusted Characters'. An American edition was published in the following month by *Harper & Brothers. Hardy had assembled the collection in the autumn of 1893, and it had been ready for the publisher before the end of October. Its position in the list of Hardy's published works between *Tess of the d'Urbervilles* and *Jude the Obscure* is significant in relation to the themes of several of the stories. All of the nine stories included had been previously published in magazines; for details see under separate entries for 'The Son's Veto', 'For Conscience' Sake', 'A Tragedy of Two Ambitions', 'On the Western Circuit', 'To Please His Wife', 'The Melancholy Hussar of the German Legion', 'The Fiddler of the Reels', 'A Tradition of Eighteen Hundred and Four', 'A Few Crusted Characters'. 'On the Western Circuit' had been extensively bowdlerized for magazine publication, and was then revised for its volume appearance.

Most of the stories had been written during the winter of 1890–1, though 'The Fiddler of the Reels' was not written until 1892, and 'A Tradition of Eighteen Hundred and Four' had been completed in 1882. Hardy wrote a short preface for a later edition in 1896. When he came to revise his writings for the Wessex Edition of 1912, he moved 'An Imaginative Woman' from *Wessex Tales* into this collection, and transferred two stories, 'The Melancholy Hussar of the German Legion' and 'A Tradition of Eighteen Hundred and Four', from *Life's Little Ironies* to *Wessex Tales*, thus reducing the number of items in the former collection to eight. These changes were prompted by the desire to give greater coherence to the volume. In its final form, it opens with five stories all of which deal largely with bourgeois life in a contemporary and often an urban setting, in marked contrast to the 'Wessex' settings and historical or traditional subjects of the earlier collection. In this respect, as also in its concern with the themes of marriage, education, and social mobility, *Life's Little Ironies* shares many common elements with *Jude the Obscure*. Comparing *Life's Little Ironies* with George *Moore's *Esther Waters*, which had been attacked for indecency, William *Archer commented on the 'note of sensuality' in Hardy's stories, and it remains true that in their quite different ways such stories as 'An Imaginative Woman' and 'The Fiddler of the Reels' deal perceptively and courageously with aspects of love and sexuality. Among other notable features of the collection are a recurring concern with the price that has to be paid for social advancement, a number of depictions of unhappy marriages, and several unflattering portraits of clergymen. The Oxford World's Classics edition (1996) of *Life's Little Ironies* contains much information on its textual history.

Linton, Eliza Lynn (1822–98), novelist. The first woman in England to pursue a career as a full-time journalist, she became famous for her controversial articles in the *Saturday Review* (1866–8), especially 'The Girl of the Period', and the 'Wild Women' series published in *The Nineteenth Century* (1891–2). Her *Saturday Review* articles, published anonymously, take an aggressively anti-feminist stand, and prompted many contemporaries, including Hardy, to conjecture that the writer was a man. In a letter to Linton (24 December 1888) Hardy states that he has read her articles with interest, although he 'never suspected the sex of the writer'. The same letter expresses regret that the conventionality of editors prevented him from depicting in his own work what was true to life. This is also the tenor of his contribution soon afterwards to the symposium on 'Candour in English Fiction' (*New Review*, January 1890), to which Linton and Hardy's friend Walter *Besant were also contributors. Here Linton complained that the combined tyranny of the 'British Matron' and the 'Young Person' had emasculated British fiction to a schoolgirl standard. Having faced the brunt of publishers' Grundyism in relation to *Tess of the d'Urbervilles*, Hardy probably sympathized with Linton's indictment of literary censorship.

Linton presented many contradictions. Herself an independent woman (she separated amicably from her husband, William James Linton) and a professional writer, she became increasingly reactionary in her views on women's issues. Although such early novels as *Amymone* (1848) strongly advocate women's rights, her later periodical writings are hostile to women's bid for higher education, entry into male-dominated professions, and the vote. Such inconsistencies did not appear to trouble Hardy, who sent her in 1888 a copy of his recently published short story 'A Tragedy of Two Ambitions' as a mark of his respect. In her reply Linton warmly praised Hardy's story. He visited her in January 1891—a delightful encounter recorded in a letter written by Linton to her sister (see George Somes Layard, *Mrs Lynn Linton: Her Life, Letters and Opinions* (1901), 277). Linton's unfinished reminiscences, *My Literary Life* (1899), contain, however, no reference to Hardy. SD

Locker, Arthur (1828–93), novelist and journalist. He was editor of the *Graphic* from 1870 to 1891, and *The Mayor of Casterbridge* was the first of three important works by Hardy to appear in this weekly under Locker's editorship. According to Hardy's own somewhat confusing account, late in 1889, after the early portion of *Tess of the d'Urbervilles* had been declined by two other editors, he sent Locker an expurgated version of what he had written, with the intention of publishing some of the excised material elsewhere; later Hardy described this stratagem as 'unprecedented in the annals of fiction' (*LW* 232). On 9 May 1890 he sent Locker the manuscript of *A Group of Noble Dames*, only to be faced in June with requests for bowdlerization. An interesting extract from the letter of complaint and reproof written by William Locker (Arthur's son and his assistant editor) is quoted by Millgate (305). Hardy responded by calling on Locker at his office, only to be told that it was not the editor himself who raised objections but 'the Directors'. As Purdy says, this painful experience would have been 'instructive' (73) for Hardy as he worked on *Tess* during the rest of 1890.

London. 'Mr Hardy seems to be in the way to do for rural life what Dickens did for that of the town.' This statement, in a review of *The Trumpet-Major* (*Athenaeum*, 20 November 1880; repr. in *CH*), is characteristic of a conception of Hardy's fictional forte on the part of his contemporaries, and it was one that he himself was to reinforce later in the same decade by his systematic identification of the world of his novels with 'Wessex'. The role of a chronicler of 'rural life' was not, however, one that he had eagerly embraced in the earlier stages of his career. Ever sensitive to a patronizing snub, especially if it appeared to reflect on his social origins, he must have been impelled by some of his early critics—for example, Henry *James, in his condescending review of *Far from the Madding Crowd*—to try to prove that he could write about the upper reaches of metropolitan society as well as about shepherds and dairymaids. There is a distinct note of resentment as well as sharpness in his comment that reviewers were prone to remind him 'not to write of a place he was unacquainted with, but to get back to his sheepfields' (*LW* 64)—and a perceptible defensiveness in his claim, in the same passage, that he was sometimes mistaken for 'a born Londoner'.

The fact is that he knew London well, lived there during a crucial stage of his personal development, and continued to visit the city until old age made the long journey difficult. London, moreover, makes many appearances in his prose and verse. His first attempt at fiction, *The Poor Man and the Lady*, begun in 1867, was later characterized as, among other things, a satire on 'London society', and there are London scenes in his last novel to be published in volume form, *The Well-Beloved*, exactly 30 years later.

London was important to Hardy, imaginatively and practically, from his earliest years. His first knowledge of the metropolis would have come to him, like so much else, from his mother, who before her marriage had been in service in London, and is likely to have told her firstborn tales of her life in the city. It was his mother who took him to London for the first time, when he was 'eight or nine years old': they merely passed through the city on their way to visit Jemima's sister in Hertfordshire, making a one-night stopover in Clerkenwell, but Hardy never forgot the places they glimpsed—not only the grandeur of 'Cumberland Gate into Hyde Park, which then could boast of no Marble Arch', but the deafening horrors of Smithfield market (*LW* 21–2).

Hardy's move to London in April 1862, as a young architect nursing secret ambitions to become a writer, had a certain inevitability but must also have been undertaken with not a few doubts and hesitations: when he set out, cautiously purchasing a return ticket from Dorchester, he can hardly have foreseen that he would make his home there for five years. During this period he made full use of the cultural opportunities offered by the city, including, 'for many months', daily lunch-hour visits to the *National Gallery, which was situated conveniently close to Blomfield's office, 'confining his attention to a single master on each visit' (*LW* 53)—studies that bore fruit not only in the 'Schools of Painting' notebook but in numerous *allusions in his writings. He also attended 'every one' of Samuel Phelps's Shakespeare productions at the Drury Lane Theatre, earnestly viewed from the pit with 'a good edition of the play' in his hand (*LW* 54). The British Museum and the opera were other favourite destinations, and he took evening classes in French at King's College. For Hardy's church-going during this period, see RELIGION.

Less uplifting, but perhaps equally fascinating, were his observations of the life of the streets and especially of the West End, then notorious throughout Europe as a centre for prostitution: the poem 'From Her in the Country', written in 1866, muses discreetly but with evident fascination on 'city din and sin', and 'The Ruined Maid', also dated 1866, links with humour and even cynicism the city that was his adopted home and the rural world he had left behind. The *Life* admits to his having 'once at least visited' Evans's supper-rooms . . . in an underground hall in Covent Garden' (*LW* 43)—an establishment with a somewhat louche reputation—and the later poem 'Reminiscences of a Dancing Man' recalls the celebrated dance-halls, the Argyll Rooms and the Cremorne Gardens. As the *Life* reminds us (*LW* 43), the London of Hardy's youth was still *Dickens's London: *Our Mutual Friend*, with its panoramic portrayal of London life at every social level, appeared during his time there, and he heard Dickens give his sensational public readings in 1863 and again in 1865.

There is—a little unexpectedly, given his accepted standing as a countryman and a provincial or regional writer—a touch of pride in the passage in the autobiography already referred to, in which Hardy claims sometimes to have been taken for 'a born Londoner', and speaks of 'between five and six years' constant and varied experience—as only a young man in the metropolis can get it—knowing every street and alley west of St Paul's' (*LW* 63–4). As this suggests, his base was firmly in the western part of the rapidly growing city, especially in the area near Paddington station—the arrival and departure point for those who ventured to the capital from Dorset. (On his lodgings during this period, see HOMES.) It is from the standpoint of a Londoner that he writes, in his first published novel, *Desperate Remedies*, that 'provincial towns trying to be lively are the dullest of dull things' (1.3).

Hardy left London in the summer of 1867 to return to the cleaner air and more tranquil surroundings of Higher Bockhampton, and it was not until the spring of 1872 that he returned, this time to work on designs for Board Schools for the prominent architect T. Roger Smith. He stayed in London no more than a few months, a period interrupted by a summer holiday in Cornwall, and by the autumn he was back in Dorset to work on *A Pair of Blue Eyes*. In the following summer, after visits to London and Cambridge, Dorset was once again his chosen base for working on *Far from the Madding Crowd*: a pattern was already emerging whereby London was the scene of his social and cultural activities, but Dorset the place of choice where his writing was done. This instinctive sense of where he could work best becomes conscious and explicit in a letter of 9 January 1874, when he tells Leslie Stephen that he has 'decided to finish' his novel in Bockhampton, 'within a walk of the district in which the incidents are supposed to occur. I find it a great advantage to be actually among the people described at the time of describing them' (*L* i 27). And yet, very revealingly, the standpoint of that remark is surely a Londoner's rather than a countryman's: 'to be actually among the people described' has the tone of the outsider, the observer, even the anthropologist, rather than the resident.

In July 1874 Hardy left Bockhampton, where he was never again to live for any substantial period, and two months later married Emma Gifford at St Peter's Church in Elgin Avenue, Paddington. Upon returning from the honeymoon, the still-happy couple settled at the eminently suburban address of St David's Villa, Hook Road, Surbiton—exchanged after only six months for a more central location in the Paddington area. For a number of years after his marriage and the launching of his career as a professional novelist, the Hardys' unsettled lifestyle reflects a chronic uncertainty whether London or the West Country should be his base. Now that he no longer enjoyed his bachelor freedom, and was no longer quite so young, the city held fewer attractions for him; he seems to have come to believe, moreover, that it was bad for his health. On the other hand, though he could pursue a writer's career anywhere in the land, he was conscious of the professional advantages of being 'on the spot', close to publishers, editors, and the social life of literary circles. Furthermore, as long as he entertained ambitions to write on urban as well as rural subjects, he needed to be close to his material: Hardy may have felt at times a little of the anxiety that plagued Joseph Conrad, who often complained that his life as a mariner had left him in ignorance of social and domestic life on shore, the basic raw materials of the fiction-writer's trade.

In July 1875 the Hardys left London for the West Country, living for varying periods of time, and always in rented accommodation, in Bournemouth, Swanage, Yeovil, and Sturminster Newton. In retrospect, the move to London in 1878 that terminated the 'Sturminster Newton idyll' must have seemed a serious mistake, but Hardy was at the time confident enough of the rightness of his decision to take a three-year lease on a house in Upper Tooting, close to Wandsworth Common in south London, and there they remained until 1881. The long illness during which *A Laodicean* was painfully composed settled the matter, and the move back to Dorset in 1881 was final. This did not prevent Hardy, however, from making frequent visits to 'Town' and taking advantage of his membership of leading gentlemen's *clubs, and both he and Emma for many years spent the 'season' in London, usually taking a house or flat, entertaining and being entertained by the increasingly grand social circles to which Hardy's success and fame granted him admission. His *letters and his *autobiography are scattered with mainly gratified references to dinners, evening parties, receptions, and other gatherings, and to the famous men and beautiful women encountered there. There is, though, the occasional spurt of rebellion and distaste, as when, after attending 'a crush at the Jeunes'' (see JEUNE, MARY) and being fascinated by the 'great eyes' of Agatha *Thornycroft, he writes afterwards in his diary: 'But these women! If put into rough wrappers in a turnip-field, where would their beauty be?' (*LW* 235).

This is 1890, in the London of Oscar Wilde, and Hardy is by this time himself leading a double life, moving between the crowded social life of the metropolis and his quiet existence at *Max Gate. Though it is natural to think of *Dorchester as Hardy's true setting by this time, and the base from which he and Emma made their regular forays to London, he sometimes seems to have tried to convey to his London friends the opposite impression, referring to his Dorset home in the terms a city-dweller might apply to a country cottage, and suggesting that it was merely a useful place to get on with his writing.

But these fashionable and brilliantly lit occasions had been reached by a hard and painful road. The experience of the protagonist of *The Poor Man and the Lady* was, by Hardy's own account, based partly on 'the life of an isolated student cast upon the billows of London with no protection but his brains' (*LW* 58), and it is probably not too rash to detect an autobiographical element in this statement. The reference to 'the billows of London' is echoed in the statement that his early experience included 'years of London buffeting' (*LW* 76). Such phrases suggest that the years spent in London as a young man saw not a little stress and unhappiness, and the poems that survive from the 1860s—not to mention what is now known of his relationship with Eliza *Nicholls—confirm this.

In a valuable essay (to which the present entry is greatly indebted), Michael Slater has suggested that 'London induced in Hardy an even deeper anxiety than the one relating to class and sex. In the crowded city the individual could lose his or her identity, the very sense of selfhood' (p. 47). If Hardy felt this as a young man, he was able to view it more objectively, and to give it more direct expression, in later years when he returned to London after an absence. Some diary entries for March 1888, quoted in the *Life* (*LW* 215–16), are relevant here: in the British Museum Reading Room, for instance, he is conscious of 'Souls . . . gliding about here in a sort of dream . . .', a surrealistic or nightmarish vision of the anonymous crowds that represent the opposite pole of human experience from the near-empty Wessex landscapes in which the individuality inspires curiosity and respect. Watching the Lord Mayor's Show in 1879, he is overwhelmed by the sense of the crowd as 'an organic whole, a molluscous black creature having nothing in common with humanity' (*LW* 134).

It remained true for Hardy, though, that London was the focus of literary and artistic activity, and he continued to go there to meet fellow-writers, to attend exhibitions and soirées at the *Royal Academy, to listen to the music of which, in the days before gramophone and radio, anyone living in the country could feel starved. As Slater notes, 'It is significant that the protagonists of Hardy's two London novels, *Ethelberta* and *The Well-Beloved*, are both artists' (p. 49). Both novels contain descriptions of cityscapes that find painterly beauty in the urban scene, and especially in the chromatic effects created by the smoky atmosphere: in *The Well-Beloved*, for instance, we read of 'those marvellous sunset effects which, if they were not known to be made up of kitchen coal-smoke and animal exhalations, would be rapturously applauded' (3.5).

Elsewhere in Hardy's fiction, London is more likely to be marginal, a place that people arrive from or depart for. In *Tess of the d'Urbervilles*, for instance, it has been the scene of Angel Clare's youthful sexual lapse, and it is the destination for the milk that Angel and Tess convey from the dairy to the train. Angel observes that the milk will probably have been watered by the time it reaches the Londoners' breakfast-tables, and in other respects London sometimes gets a bad press in Hardy's writings. The short story 'The Son's Veto' poignantly evokes the fate of a countrywoman exiled and heartsick in London, and the poem 'Coming Up Oxford Street: Evening' depicts, less memorably, the situation of the city-clerk 'Who sees no escape to the very verge of his days | From the rut of Oxford Street into open ways . . .'. Hardy had made his own escape into 'open ways', and as the years passed going to the city seems to have become less of a joy and more of a chore. Nevertheless, the five years spent there during his highly impressionable young manhood had a permanent influence on his sensibility, and the calculation of the days spent in London during his long career as a writer would produce a large figure. See also HOMES.

Michael Slater, 'Hardy and the City', in Charles P. C. Pettit (ed.), *New Perspectives on Thomas Hardy* (1994).

love.

She sat here in her chair,
Smiling into the fire;
He who played stood there,
Bowing it higher and higher.

Childlike, I danced in a dream;
Blessings emblazoned that day;
Everything glowed in a gleam;
Yet we were looking away!

'The Self-Unseeing' recalls Hardy's childhood in a way that is wholly characteristic of him. The three of them—mother, father, son—were supremely happy at moments like these because they loved each other; but they did not know it, or at least did not bother about it: they were 'looking away'. Only in his maturity, as the poet implies, did he come to realize, and supremely value, such old moments of love as this, between parent and child. And by then it was too late to do more than express it in a poem.

Love for Hardy is mainly a matter of enchanted retrospection. But some of his most moving poems commemorate a first love moment, in which the scale might have been turned 'by a feather' against falling in love: 'But crimson one cheek of hers burned | When we went in together.' He 'came back from Lyonnesse | With magic in my eyes' because he had met there, or at least in North *Cornwall, the woman to whom he was to be married for many years. It was on the whole a woeful marriage, with misunderstanding and increasing dislike on both sides, but with what is probably the balance of blame on Hardy's side, since early on in marriage he seems to have retreated into himself, and in a sense never emerged again as long as his wife lived. But no sooner had she died than he visited their old Cornish haunts and began at once to write love poems of astonishing tenderness and intensity.

'Hereto I come to view a voiceless ghost; | Whither, O whither will its whim now draw me?' 'After a Journey' describes Hardy's sense of his dead wife's ghost, a strangely neutral presence, haunting the cliffs and shore that she once loved. She has drawn him down here but has nothing to say to him, whereas he has much—and much of love—to say to her:

> Trust me, I mind not, though Life lours,
> The bringing me here; nay, bring me here again!
> I am just the same as when
> Our days were a joy, and our paths through flowers.

Hardy's longing to be 'just the same as when' is touching, and perhaps not so much self-deceiving as self-fulfilling: as a poet, and in his own feelings, he really can be just the same. That indeed is a great part of the function of his art as a poet: to make love last. For in lyric poetry it can last, or seem to do so, and Hardy always thought of himself as primarily, and above all, a poet. He wrote his novels for a living, and love in the novels is an entirely different matter.

Indeed, one would be hard put to it to find a case in Hardy's novels where love endures, or at least settles down into any steady state of affection, trust, or understanding. This is partly due to the old conventions of romance and melodrama, styles of popular fiction in which Hardy was mostly happy to work, at least until the planning of his last and most ambitious novel, *Jude the Obscure*. He wanted his novels to display his learning, his own approach to life, and the tragic sense that was intended to make Egdon Heath, or the Mayor of Casterbridge, or the story of Tess, alive with parallels from the ancient classics and the great literature of the past. But it is hard to escape the conclusion that he did not write about 'grown-up' love devotion, in the sense that George *Eliot or even Trollope could do so well, because he himself had no experience of it: he just did not know what it was like.

The most moving moments in *Tess* are those in which the star-crossed lovers have their brief doomed idyll together, after Tess has murdered Alec, in the solitary and shut-up country house. They are like children whose childhood cannot last and who have only a few brief adult hours in bed together before the end. In bed together, because the scene is in its own brief way explicit, as such love passages in Hardy (and he certainly knew all about sexual attraction) usually are. It would have been impossible for his imagination to consider Tess and Angel as married and settled down together, for his imagination recoiled from any such picture. He could only deal with the idea in a satirical poetic vein, imagining two lovers who have eloped, and then married, at which point their 'leapings each to each' decline into 'frigid syllables austere | Of household speech'. An unattractive comedown, certainly; and it seems not to have occurred to Hardy that mature married life might be anything more than a compound of taciturn frigidity and austerity.

Whether it could have been different if he had married a different woman is hard to say, but given his temperament, and the habit of his mind, the chances must seem against it. His mother, the most powerful submerged influence in his life, seems in her own masterful way—and perhaps from her own experience—to have taken it for granted that her four children should not marry, and apart from Hardy himself none of them did. His mother's instinct for family closeness had somehow seen to it that they did not grow up to be the marrying kind. Probably Hardy should have continued to fall endlessly in love, but somehow to escape the conventions of the time and never marry. In that case, however, whatever else he might have written, we should not have had such wonderful verse-cycles as the one he produced after his first wife's death. By then, too, a marriage of some sort had become a habit with him, even though a gloomy one.

A significant illustration of Hardy's in many ways perverse refusal to understand or imagine a happy love situation comes in a comparatively tranquil moment of *Jude the Obscure*, when Jude and Sue are enjoying themselves together at the agricultural show. '"Happy?"' Jude murmurs, and the narrator continues: 'She clasped his arm, and they went along silently as true comrades ofttimes do.' The sentence jars, and not only because of that coy word 'ofttimes'. Hardy seems to be wistfully imagining a comradely state in the relation of the sexes, when the wife (if she is a wife) makes no demands on the husband, nor he on her. Hardy might well have been thinking of his own wife's unspoken resentment at the way he excluded her from his work, his habits, and his powers, if any, of continued and overt affection. He seems—and very typically—to be envisaging a situation in which a married couple, or at least a cohabiting couple, should be able to live together but separate, without disturbing or bothering one another, rather as if they were two animals grazing peacefully together in the same field: a homelier Hardyan version of the married state which D. H. *Lawrence was to envisage, with a couple revolving round each other like twin stars.

If solitude and self-sufficiency are for Hardy the proper natural state of human beings, or at least of those who live a quiet country existence and follow its routines, an emotional disturbance in their way of life is all the more devastating. This is what Clym Yeobright in *The Return of the Native* finds, and Farmer Boldwood in *Far from the Madding Crowd*. More powerfully than almost any other novelist, Hardy can make his reader feel the violence and the ecstasy of such a primal urge, and he makes the reader feel, too, the corresponding and contrasting strength of feminine passion. Eustacia and Bathsheba are passionate women, and passion leads them astray, for in the nature of things it cannot last. 'Thus they mutually oppressed one another even while they loved', as Hardy observes in that curious and shrewdly wish-fulfilling little fantasy *An Indiscretion in the Life of an Heiress*. Living idyllically together in the solitude of Egdon Heath, Eustacia and Clym are none the less consuming their mutual passion together 'at a terrible rate', as if love was a commodity which could all too quickly be used up, as Hardy certainly came to think it was.

One of the few women to escape its oppressions, Elizabeth-Jane in *The Mayor of Casterbridge*, does so 'in discovering . . . the secret (as she had once learnt it) of making limited opportunities endurable' (45). Her own concluding marriage with Farfrae is set to be humdrum but contented, and about such a rational arrangement Hardy has no more to say. The only solution to love, in his view, seems to lie in the words of Sir Walter *Scott's poem in *The Bride of Lammermoor*: 'Vacant heart and hand and eye, | Easy live and quiet die.' And yet we are made to feel how the novelist's whole creative being rebels against such quietism. How well he could describe the swift violence and joy of love's onset, as the young Jude, a would-be cloistered scholar, finds his view of learning blotted out and himself 'lost to all conditions of things in the advent of a fresh and wild pleasure'. True, by the time he came to write *Jude*, Hardy strove, as it were, to be hard-boiled about love and its conflict of emotions, and what has turned Jude on is the shameless invitation contrived by that designing and experienced woman Arabella, who throws the pig's pizzle at him. When Hardy became, or at least tried to sound, wholly cynical, it was no doubt time for him to stop writing novels. For, as with his poems, all the most moving and memorable scenes in his novels are about the helpless vulnerability of love and lovers—but about their joys too, however ephemeral. JB

M

Macmillan, Frederick (1851–1936), publisher. The eldest son of Daniel Macmillan, co-founder of the Macmillan publishing house (see next entry), and his wife Frances (née Orridge), he went to Uppingham School but was otherwise trained up specifically in the family business, spending the years 1871–6 with the recently established Macmillan branch in New York. Returning to England with an American wife (née Georgiana Warrin), he became a partner in the firm and increasingly, as his uncle Alexander Macmillan gradually withdrew, its central figure, largely responsible for its evolution as a world-wide operation at once large, profitable, and highly respected, not least for its impressive literary list. Macmillan became a powerful, and essentially conservative, figure in the book trade, twice president of the Publishers' Association and particularly remembered for his energetic advocacy of the Net Book Agreement of 1890. In 1907 he was knighted for his work on behalf of London hospitals.

Macmillan had an early sense of Hardy's importance. When in New York he drew *Under the Greenwood Tree* to the attention of Henry *Holt, who became Hardy's first American publisher, and in the 1880s and 1890s it was he who corresponded with Hardy about *The Woodlanders* and *Wessex Tales* and the inclusion of all his fiction titles in the Macmillan Colonial Library. Hardy's responsive admiration for Macmillan's professional and personal qualities seems largely to have determined his decision to transfer all his British rights to Macmillan & Co. in 1902, and they enjoyed a productive partnership thereafter. Hardy, managing his own business affairs without the assistance of an agent or accountant, relied increasingly on Macmillan's expert and confident advice, to the point that Florence *Hardy, in November 1926, could say that Sir Frederick was the only person who had any real influence over him. MM

Macmillan & Co., Hardy's principal publishers. Daniel Macmillan (1813–57) and his brother Alexander (1818–96), the sons of a Scottish crofter, first went into business together in Cambridge as booksellers, a trade to which Daniel had been apprenticed. In 1843 they adventured into publishing and enjoyed an early success that was interrupted by the death of Daniel, the more dynamic of the two. Alexander, however, not only took his brother's widow and family into his own household but expanded the business, moved its headquarters to London, and in 1859 founded *Macmillan's Magazine.* The firm's financial strength in the late 19th and early 20th centuries owed much to its successful marketing in educational and professional fields, but it also attained a high literary reputation as the publisher of such figures as Kingsley, Dodgson (Lewis Carroll), Arnold, Tennyson, James, Kipling, Shaw, and Hardy himself.

It was to Macmillan that Hardy in July 1868 sent the 440-page manuscript of his first novel, *The Poor Man and the Lady*, accompanied by a letter of recommendation from Horace *Moule, whose Hulsean Prize dissertation had been published by Macmillan in 1859. Remarkably for an unsolicited first novel, it was read with care both by John Morley, the firm's chief adviser on literary manuscripts, and by Alexander Macmillan himself. Macmillan's long letter to Hardy, published in Charles *Morgan's centenary history, shows him to have been sympathetically responsive to Hardy's writing and yet unable to accept the bleakness of the novel's portrayal of the upper classes: it was, he finally decided, 'a class of book' the firm could not publish. Macmillan tried, unsuccessfully, to help Hardy find another publisher for his novel, but his own firm rejected *Desperate Remedies* and then hesitated so long over *Under the Greenwood Tree* that Hardy took it, too, elsewhere.

Intermittent friendly relations were maintained over the ensuing years, especially when the Hardys were living close to the Alexander Macmillans in Tooting in 1878–81, but the firm published nothing of

Hardy's until *The Woodlanders* was serialized in *Macmillan's Magazine* from May 1886 to April 1887, and issued in three volumes in March 1887. Macmillan also published the first edition of *Wessex Tales* in 1888 and included that same title, together with *The Woodlanders* and *The Mayor of Casterbridge*, in their Colonial Library. But Mowbray *Morris, the editor of *Macmillan's Magazine*, objected to what he saw as the sexual openness of *The Woodlanders*, and his refusal to serialize *Tess of the d'Urbervilles* was largely responsible for driving Hardy to the *Graphic* and then, for volume publication, to the firm of *Osgood, McIlvaine & Co. Macmillan, now increasingly in the hands of Alexander's son George and Daniel's sons Frederick and Maurice, raised difficulties over the inclusion of their Hardy titles in Osgood, McIlvaine's 'Wessex Novels' collected edition of 1895–7, but good feelings were soon restored and endorsed by Macmillan's publication of Colonial editions of all of Hardy's fiction.

Hardy's publishing agreements with Osgood, McIlvaine expired in 1902, by which time the firm had been absorbed by *Harper & Brothers of New York. While not objecting to Harper's as his American publisher, Hardy decided to transfer his British rights to a British publisher—specifically to the house of Macmillan, where he was warmly welcomed by Frederick *Macmillan. An agreement signed on 2 April 1902, and maintained with minor revisions during Hardy's lifetime, specified royalties of one-fourth on sales at six shillings, one-fifth on sales between four and five shillings, and one-sixth on cheaper books, and thus effectively ensured the relative affluence of Hardy's final decades.

By 1902 Hardy had abandoned fiction for poetry, and his early volumes of verse, including the three Parts of *The Dynasts*, did not sell especially well. On first becoming Hardy's publisher, however, Macmillan reissued the Osgood, McIlvaine prose volumes in a cheaper format (incorporating occasional revisions), and this 'Uniform' edition remained profitably in print during and after Hardy's lifetime, though outsold from 1907 onwards by the trim volumes of the cheaper 'Pocket' edition. In 1911 Hardy undertook further revisions to his prose and verse texts and prefaces for Macmillan's handsome Wessex Edition (1912–31), intending it to be textually 'definitive'. A few additional revisions were incorporated into the limited, signed Mellstock Edition of 1919–20, and all editions except the Mellstock were progressively expanded to incorporate the later poetry volumes, including the posthumous *Winter Words* of 1928.

After Hardy's death the next generation of Macmillans, Maurice's sons Daniel (1886–1965) and, to a lesser extent, Harold, later Lord Stockton (1894–1986), worked with Florence *Hardy in publishing the two volumes of the official biography, and continued to advise her until her death in 1937. During the Second World War Macmillan purchased from Florence Hardy's estate the copyrights to all of Hardy's published works, and it was ownership of those copyrights—extending originally to 31 December 1978, but reinstated for the period ending 31 December 1998—that subsequently enabled the firm to maintain its position as the leading publisher of Hardy's works and of materials related to them. The long and important relationship between Hardy and the house of Macmillan is richly documented by the correspondence, publication records, and other materials contained in the extensive Macmillan Archive in the British Library. MM

Charles Morgan, *The House of Macmillan (1843–1943)* (1943).

Malet, Lucas, pseudonym of Mary St Leger Harrison (1852–1931), author. A daughter of the novelist Charles Kingsley, she married (1876) the Reverend William Harrison and herself became a popular novelist whose books gained a reputation for outspokenness. She and Hardy were acquainted by 1892, and his diary (quoted in *LW* 258), recording a meeting during that year, refers to her striking appearance and attractive personality. In February 1892 he mentions that he has read two of her novels 'with the deepest interest', and gives special praise to *Colonel Enderby's Wife* (1885). In an interesting letter written in the following month (*L* vii 119–20), he thanks her for sending him *The Wages of Sin* (1891) and comments on the problems of women writers in dealing with issues of sexual morality. (On the evidence of a slightly later letter to another correspondent, however, he seems to have found the novel's conclusion disappointingly fainthearted.) Her recollections of Hardy are included in William *Archer's *Real Conversations*.

Mansfield, Katherine. See MURRY, JOHN MIDDLETON.

manuscripts. The surviving manuscripts of Hardy's fiction are almost all working drafts betraying one or more different stages of development; his poetry manuscripts, however, are very close to being fair copies, written out once the selection and order had been decided on for each volume, and he left remarkably few early holograph versions of individual poems.

Almost all of these manuscripts are now in public collections, and are available on microfilm to the interested reader. Some have been published in photographic facsimile. But for anyone seriously interested in analysing Hardy's working methods and the development of his texts, such publications are only a first step, for until digital images of the manuscripts are available, there is much evidence in the documents themselves that photography cannot reveal.

The study of Hardy's fiction manuscripts is a highly rewarding but also frustrating business. It is often possible to discern some of Hardy's earliest ideas about a novel from fragments of early draft material incorporated in later work. Sometimes the evidence is in cancelled passages, sometimes in leaves written on a different kind of paper from the majority of the manuscript, or in a different ink; sometimes Hardy frugally preserved discarded sheets and wrote new matter on the other side; sometimes he employed different systems of numeration at different times in a novel's development, and often he altered names of places and persons. It is possible to gather much from the study of such details, but Hardy had no idea of providing a transparent record for posterity of the successive layers of his work on a text, and the available evidence almost always leads the investigator into further speculation.

One advantage such an investigator possesses is the superb clarity of Hardy's hand, even when he was writing in a hurry with the pressure of a serial deadline in his mind; there are occasional possible ambiguities—the difference, for instance, between 'flare' and 'glare' is sometimes hard to discern, as is that between 'house' and 'home'—but such situations are very infrequently found. On occasion his first wife Emma helped him by copying passages from one draft to another, a practice which has led to some fruitless speculation about her possible original contribution to the narratives. Hardy was sensitive about this matter, and it is certain that when he presented the manuscript of *The Mayor of Casterbridge* to the Dorset County Museum he removed from it a substantial number of leaves she had inscribed. It is possible that other manuscripts, like that of *Tess of the d'Urbervilles*, are now defective for the same reason.

Perhaps the most consistently remarkable feature of Hardy's manuscripts, when compared with the printed versions of the same texts, is the highly individual nature of Hardy's punctuation, the essential feature of which is that he attempted to represent through his punctuation the cadence and rhythm of a sentence, or especially of a speech, as he heard it in his mind while writing. Here is an example from *Under the Greenwood Tree*, Fancy Day speaking: '"Now Mr Dewy—no flirtation, because it's wrong and I don't wish it"' (3.1). The compositors who set Hardy's manuscripts were trained to use punctuation according to prescriptive rules, and none was prepared to accept Hardy's expressive pointing (though some were more receptive than others). This is how Fancy's teasing speech appeared in print: '"Now, Mr. Dewy, no flirtation, because it's wrong, and I don't wish it"'—correct, but lifeless. By Victorian standards, Hardy's punctuation was light, and from first novel to last, several thousands of marks of punctuation were added or made heavier (commas changed to semicolons, for instance) when each was first put into type. This regularization makes a distinct difference to the reading experience, but is most damaging when it leads to an alteration in meaning, as it does in many places in each novel: in *Tess*, for instance, as Tess and Angel become estranged, she says that she supposes he will not live with her for long, and Angel in the manuscript answers: '"I cannot,... without despising myself, and what is worse, perhaps despising you".' In all the printed versions the passage reads: '"I cannot,... without despising myself, and what is worse, perhaps, despising you"' (36). The added comma makes Angel say something much more unpleasant: not that he might despise Tess, which would be worse than despising himself, but that he *would* despise Tess, which might perhaps be worse than despising himself.

One manuscript of particular significance is that of the short story sequence now known as 'A Few Crusted Characters', which appears in *Life's Little Ironies.* (This manuscript is now in the Berg Collection at the New York Public Library.) It is the only substantial document containing first draft material, which is almost in note form; all other surviving manuscripts are at least one generation of copy beyond that stage. Some of the manuscripts written by Hardy under time-pressure for magazines (*The Trumpet-Major* is an example) exhibit a kind of intermediate stage in which quite often the initial inscription is a bare line of narrative with minimal indications of colour, and richness of characterization and description is added in a second layer—a process not so much of revision as of fleshing-out. In the majority, however, the original is fully developed, and additions and cancellations represent second and third thoughts.

There is little to say about the manuscripts of Hardy's poetry and drama. Some of the collections have more revisions than others, and in this respect *Wessex Poems* is noteworthy. Perhaps most interesting of all is a note to the printers at the head of *Poems of the Past and the Present*, instructing them that the punctuation was to be as in the manuscript. His instruction was not followed, but it is surprising that the editor of the critical edition of the poems has chosen not to follow the instruction either.

Information on the location of individual manuscripts is given in the separate entries for the volumes in question. On the distribution of the manuscripts existing in 1911, see COCKERELL, SYDNEY. SJG

Simon Gatrell, *Hardy the Creator* (1988).

marriage. In a letter written in November 1906 in response to Millicent Garrett Fawcett on the 'Marriage Question', Hardy touches briefly upon the issue of 'woman-suffrage', observing that 'the tendency of the woman's vote will be to break up the present pernicious conventions in respect of manners, customs, religion, illegitimacy, the stereotyped household (that it must be the unit of society), the father of a woman's child (that it is anybody's business but the woman's own, except in cases of disease or insanity) (*L* iii 238). Two important tenets, both central to Hardy's thinking, inform this juxtaposition of ideas interlinking the private domain (of sexuality, home, family) with the political arsenal of institutions and ideologies (Church, law, and state).

The first tenet, transparently Hardyan, pertains to his iconoclastic interrogation of the status quo. As early as 1867 with his first (unpublished) novel, *The Poor Man and the Lady*, Hardy chose to portray himself as a writer driven by '"a passion for reforming the world"... the tendency of the writing being socialistic, not to say revolutionary' (*LW* 63). However, during the decades that followed, which involved endless, salutary, and often humiliating negotiations with the discomfited editor, the protesting reviewer, the enraged ecclesiarch, all of which productively braced Hardy, artistically speaking, to circumvent these 'Grundyan' agencies of censorship, his revolutionary passion eventually modulated to a less immoderate, more judicious caution. Or so he hoped, and so he strived. Certainly, on the marriage question, an aspect of gravity and steady forbearance tempers his private correspondence—to wit, his dispassionate words to Garrett Fawcett, which echo from a distance his equally even-tempered but no less contentious thoughts on modern marriage as 'a survival from the custom of capture and purchase, propped up by a theological superstition' (to Edward Clodd, 10 November 1895: *L* ii 92). The revolutionary tone has mellowed, yet the reformist zeal lives on.

This brings us to the second tenet, closely related to the first: Hardy's meliorism. Encapsulated by the poetic phrase, 'if way to the Better there be, it exacts a full look at the Worst' ('In Tenebris II'), the pursuit of truth, in art as in life, becomes, for Hardy, precarious, self-exposing, and in no sense a safe refuge. Correlatively, the meliorist in Hardy neither romanticizes nor sanctifies the institution of marriage—a position which, for a Victorian of repute and influence, came dangerously close to hubris. Yet his views on contemporary matrimonial codes and practices were fundamentally humanitarian. Regarding the institutionalization of love relationships as, in itself, a sure way to imperil them, Hardy felt that to govern the human heart by rigid social conventions and ineluctable ideologies was to endanger, by over-regulation, the very thing the law sought to protect. Worse still, the very same rules and conventions degraded the female half of the partnership by rendering the wife the legal property of her husband upon marriage. If he were a woman, Hardy told Florence *Henniker in the more liberated climate of 1918, he would think twice about entering matrimony 'in these days of emancipation, when everything is open to the sex' (*L* vi 283). Twenty years earlier such emancipated 'openings' had seemed remote. In reformist terms, the potentially educative effect of *Jude the Obscure* (1896) was in fact perceived by many a harsh critic to have the opposite effect: doing more harm than good. Hardy was devastated. Bitterly despondent, he himself turned hostile, or at any rate perceptibly defensive. In response to the editor of the *Daily Graphic*, who had requested an interview on the topic of the marriage problem, Hardy retorted: 'I can only say... that as I have already written so much on marriage—(in the novel *Jude the Obscure*, 9 years ago) I am not prepared at this time to write or say anything more about that sacred institution' (*L* iii 144).

Sarcasm is an act of self-defence; and if the anomalous 'sacred institution' appears thoroughly insincere, it does indicate Hardy's sense of his own vulnerability—his need to appease. He is covertly begging asylum. Critical attacks on *Jude*, reputedly burned by the Bishop of Wakefield and withdrawn from W. H. Smith's circulating library, had, at this point in his novel-writing career, left him with the conviction that, 'if he wished to retain any shadow of self-respect' (*LW* 309), he should abandon prose fiction altogether. This conviction, now engendering paranoia (he even feared walking the streets at night alone), spurred the defensive Hardy to adopt yet another self-protective posture, denial: 'I did not intend', he protests to one correspondent, 'to argue it [the marriage question] at all... my opinions on the subject are vague enough' (*L* ii 98). And to another: 'The very last charges I expected them to bring against [the book] were that it was an attack on marriage' (*L* ii 104). And yet again: 'My own opinions are nowhere given' (*L* ii 97).

Nevertheless, the truth was that *Jude* had openly held in question every important aspect of that venerated Victorian institution—from its sacramental foundations in Church dogma as a lifelong union ('let no man put asunder'), to its statutory underframing in law and its innumerable social ramifications. All of the latter ratified the absolute authority of the male head-of-household, including his conjugal right-of-access to his wife (with or without her consent), and his appropriation of her property, of which he became sole owner upon marriage, down to the very last nuance of class and sexual discrimination. In sum, *Jude* had openly routed that hallowed preserve so highly esteemed by the Victorian dominant culture as 'the unit upon which a constitutional Government has been raised which is the envy and admiration of mankind' (W. Cooke-Taylor, quoted in H. L. Beales, 'The Victorian Family', in *Ideas and Beliefs of the Victorians* (1966), 348).

At the narrower, personal level of discourse, in his letter to Garrett Fawcett, Hardy challenges, specifically, the liberal-feminist ideals of his correspondent and her compeers. These ideals were based on a firm belief in the doctrine of 'separate spheres'—a form of apartheid between the sexes. Above all else, woman should uphold, as her highest mission, the pieties of selfless wifehood and angelic motherhood, and man, the exemplar of all that was knightly and chivalrous, would serve as her protector, her provider, her sovereign lord. Exposed in his daily commerce with the world to brutalizing forces, man's moral character and spiritual sustenance would be refreshed, nourished, purified upon return to the sanctity of hearth and home. In line with these ideals, liberal feminism adopted a gradualist approach to matrimonial reform, vigorously upholding the centrality of woman's angelic role and ennobling influence in contributing to the national good by preserving her 'power behind the throne'.

Ranged against this faction a radical feminist fringe took arms, most notably against the Institution of Matrimony itself; and although Hardy rarely pledged his allegiance to specific organizations or societies, he did lend his support to individuals in this minority group. As early as the mid-century, John Stuart *Mill had railed against the doctrine of 'separate spheres'. Mill had argued that the subordination of women was as endangering to the moral health of society as any form of slavery could ever be; had claimed that, where sexual difference was made the groundwork of inequality, society could only be the loser; had stipulated that the free direction of all faculties of all citizens, including the female half of the world, would lead to a healthier, more progressive society. 'The wife', protested Mill in his *Three Essays on Religion* (1874), 'is the actual bond-servant of her husband: no less so, as far as legal obligation goes, than slaves commonly so called', but whereas the slave can refuse her master 'the last familiarity', the wife can be forced to suffer the 'lowest degradation... that of being made the instrument of an animal function contrary to her inclinations'. A solution (of a kind) would be to level the sexual differences (equality of education), to abolish the sexual double-standard (equality under the law), and to revise the marriage codes (institutional reform).

Hardy had long since been familiar with the work of Mill; and in common with those radical feminists campaigning, later in the century, for a more equitable role for women, it early became clear to him that alternative opportunities beyond marriage should feature in the life of a woman's personal expectations. Broadly speaking, the 'radical feminist fringe' held strong anti-marriage views and stood in opposition to prevailing laws and conventions favouring the notion that wifehood and motherhood formed the ultimate and most desirable fulfilment of a woman's sexuality. Mona Caird, author of many anti-marriage tracts, was openly supported by Hardy. By contrast, liberal feminists such as Millicent Garrett Fawcett remained less oppositional and more optimistically gradualist in their approach to the emancipation of women and reformation of Victorian marriage laws. Fawcett rationalized her position, in the 1880s, by claiming that woman's suffrage would come as a necessary corollary of other recent political changes—a 'corollary' still in abeyance some 30 years on.

If, among the radical feminist fringe, the 'anti-marriage' lobbyists loomed large, for Hardy they voiced more than a complaint against the condition of women. The plight of women being also that of men, the issue turned, ultimately, upon the welfare of all humanity.

The practice of drawing upon autobiography or any other extratextual documentation in order to 'explain' specific works of literary imagination remains a spurious evidentiary procedure. An exception arises when a literary canon reflects, over a period of two or three decades, a consistent point of view to which the author's life and extratextual writings bear a close correspondence. The creative mind at work unquestionably transcends the world, reshapes places, people, and events in order to forge alternative state of being and consciousness, while representing, with clarity and vision, the 'inner heart of things', as Hardy would say. Thus, when he laments to a friend that 'a bad marriage is one of the direst things on earth, and one of the cruellest' (*L* ii 98), his readers may be reasonably assured that this deprecation, in echoing down the years from a life beyond the novel, will almost certainly take dramatic shape and form when seized upon by the all-transcendental imagination.

As early as *The Return of the Native* (1878), and for the next two decades up until the publication of *Jude the Obscure* (1896), this lamentation rings loud and clear and with increasing vehemence as the novels proceed. Among those unions most to be repented are the mismatches that result from inequitable relationships—as in *Far from the Madding Crowd* (1874), *The Return of the Native* (1878), *The Woodlanders* (1887), *The Mayor of Casterbridge* (1886)—the inequity invariably being exacerbated by the sexual double standard, notably in *A Pair of Blue Eyes* (1873) and *Tess of the d'Urbervilles* (1891), and, for women, from an ignorance of their own bodies and sexual needs (*A Laodicean* (1881) and *Jude*).

Beyond the world of the novel, the Victorian cultural valorization of chastity, purity, and sexual innocence in women frequently led to what could be termed 'sexual anaesthesia'—less a sexual frigidity (as Hardy tried to explain to his critics with regard to his characterization of Sue Bridehead), than an unreadiness, a want of consciousness. Conversely, female sexual self-knowledge—culturally devalued as coarseness, moral degeneration, impurity of mind and body—endangers more love-unions in Hardy than does sexual ignorance. From Henry Knight's persistent disparagement of Elfride's bounding sexual vitality in *A Pair of Blue Eyes*, to Angel Clare's abandonment of Tess on her bridal night on the grounds of her prior relationship with Alec, the sexually active, voluptuous woman, with the exception of Arabella in *Jude*, is deemed a wholly unworthy candidate for marriage.

Many love-unions in Hardy also have to bear the weight of personal self-delusions and romantic projections of passion which fail to flow on and beyond into broader, fuller, companionate partnerships. Placed in a historical context, it would be true to say that acculturation to the 'separate spheres' ideology, which prescribed one set of rules and roles for women and another for men, would render companionate relationships very difficult indeed to attain. Certainly for Hardy's characters, for those struggling to find a common ground between the sexes, a set of shared interests or working arrangements, the social impedimenta they come against often prove be to insurmountable. And this despite the fact that most of Hardy's settings are rural, part of a village world (or world village), where, as opposed to the urban community, there should be 'common ground' enough. For example, in the ancient tradition rural labour is proportionately shared between the sexes; natural disasters such as storms and fires bring out the entire community; eating is frequently communal; the byways and highways are traversed by all, and often on foot, allowing for meetings, conversations, assignations; and the agricultural world, inevitably the interest and concern of all, provides a predestinate 'common ground' of a kind the urbanite may only dream of.

Thus, the world-village setting should furnish multiple opportunities were it not for the fact that this is not in any way Hardy's concern. If 'Wessex' functions, as it does, as something of a Homeric universe, the events and characters inhabiting it represent less an idyllic past than a universal human condition. To take one of Hardy's most independent heroines, Bathsheba, who moves into the farming community of Weatherbury with a decided competency to govern her own property, her own agricultural lands, there is no doubt that from the outset the odds are so heavily stacked against her that no 'common ground' will ever be found which will afford her an equitable love-relationship. From the sexual discrimination she has to face on all fronts and in all manner of forms, to the mismanagement of her business by her husband, Frank Troy, to his eventual appropriation of her hard-earned income—to which he is legally entitled, and which he squanders at will—there will be little left for her at the end of the day other than falling back on the traditional role prescribed for women of becoming, body, soul, and mind, dependent upon the all-providing male.

This is possibly one of Hardy's most astute 'marriage' novels, if it can be so called. In his characterization of Bathsheba, Hardy portrays, with sensitivity and concern, the numerous, complex dilemmas facing a young and inexperienced woman struggling to hold her own in the world of men—or, as Bathsheba would say, a world made by men for men. One of Hardy's most 'astute' moments in this novel lies in the dénouement and Bathsheba's eventual fall into dependency upon Oak. Whatever Victorian readers might have felt about the failure of this closure, the sense remains, for most readers, of disappointment. Of all Hardy heroines Bathsheba comes closest, with Gabriel Oak, to finding herself in a companionate marriage. Yet there is an incompletion here. The text insists upon withholding this—and for good reason, since Oak does not fully accord her an equal footing. His endeavour to shape her into a 'meek and comely woman' does not augur well for an equitable union.

This is, after all, the ultimate dilemma. For behind, beneath, and beyond all other contingencies, there is invariably the double standard, which finds its own true correspondence in the iniquitous, inequitable marriage laws. For Hardy, the matrimonial dilemma lies in its institutionalized values and legal ramifications; it denatures human love-relationships. This takes on an anomalous aspect in *Jude*, at an early point in the novel, where, by statutory requirement, Jude's marriage to Arabella obliges them to swear, on oath, 'that at every other time of their lives till death took them, they would assuredly believe, feel, and desire precisely as they had believed, felt, and desired during the few preceding weeks. What was as remarkable as the undertaking itself was the fact that nobody seemed at all surprised at what they swore' (*JO* 1.9). The anomaly is no less grave for its apparent lighthearted irony.

Hardy's thoughts on divorce, as expressed beyond the novel, would be as familiar to readers of his fiction as are his thoughts on marriage. In 1911 he tells Florence Henniker:

> You know what I have thought for many years: that marriage should not thwart nature and that when it does thwart nature, it is no real marriage, and the legal contract should therefore be as speedily cancelled as possible. Half the misery of human life would I think disappear if this were made easy: where there were no children at the wish of both or either: where there were children after an examination of the case by a court, and an order for certain provisions to be made. There would, of course, be difficulties, as you point out, but they would not be insuperable. Every kind of reform is met with the objection that it would be impossible, would have monstrous results, etc, yet the reform takes place, and the impossibility vanishes. (*L* iv 177)

The case of *The Woodlanders* (1887) is perhaps the first to come to mind in the divorce context. Melbury's conviction that he can secure a divorce for his daughter, Grace, on the grounds of her husband's adultery and subsequent desertion, is based on misinformation, is acted upon with thoughtless haste, and, worse, inflicts unwarranted pain upon the innocent Grace and Giles.

It is clear, from Hardy's characterization of Lawyer Beaucock, Melbury's misinformant (a charlatan and a drunkard), that Hardy sought to subvert the whole issue of judicial integrity, justice, and equity, to a level of malformation, scandal, and false representation. The much-lauded Matrimonial Causes Act, which had created a new secular court to exercise jurisdiction in matrimonial matters hitherto exercised by the ecclesiastical courts, and its subsequent 1878 amendment, which empowered magistrates to grant legal separation with maintenance to wives whose husbands had been convicted of assault, in actual fact did not provide equality under the law, and did not abolish the archaic principle of one law for the rich and another for the poor and women. True, the new laws did abolish the highly expensive procedure of gaining a private Act of Parliament for the granting of a divorce, which only the very rich and (invariably) male spouse could afford. But the double standard remained. Whereas a husband could now divorce his wife on the grounds of adultery or desertion, she, in similar circumstances, would have to provide evidence of the following (quoted verbatim from the 1857 Statute): 'Incestuous Adultery, or of Bigamy with Adultery, or of Rape, or of Sodomy or Bestiality, or of Adultery coupled with such cruelty as without Adultery would have entitled her to a Divorce *a Mensa et Thoro*, or Adultery coupled with Desertion, and without reasonable excuse, for Two Years or upwards.' Alternatively, according to the 1878 amendment, she would have to prove 'aggravated' assault—that is, gain a conviction—and even then would be entitled only to a legal separation.

Correlatively, Melbury's clumsy handling of the divorce procedures is as dire as the law he invokes. In apt alignment with an iniquitous justice system, first Beaucock then Melbury himself enact a form of prosecution in which patriarchal malformations of the world exact a high price in terms of human suffering. Returning home following his meeting with Beaucock, the first undertaking Melbury performs is that of renewing his promise to Giles Winterborne of the transfer of property he had originally intended to make. Upon Grace's initial return home from her expensive boarding-school, it had been his intention to offer her as a token of reparation for his own sins: she would be his 'gift' in marriage to Giles. However, upon examination of his 'investment', he feels he should aim for a better bargain, and he instructs her to make herself desirable to Dr Fitzpiers. When this marriage flounders, but before the divorce option is even embarked upon, Melbury usurps the law and repeats his offer to Giles: '"My boy, you shall have her yet—if you want her"' (*W* 37).

By presenting current divorce procedures as (in the first instance) an equitable solution to a dire marriage, '"no longer one law for the rich and another for the poor"', but then subsequently putting all out of bounds,

Hardy establishes a harsh irony: that human incompetence and the law go hand in hand. By association, the unscrupulousness of the law's advocate reflects back upon the very laws he invokes, which turn out to be no less of a sham than he. They are more misleading than remedial; they offer no solution whatsoever to this particular 'dire' marriage. In this manner Hardy ensures that the anomalies of contemporary divorce law reforms, originating in the Matrimonial Causes Act of 1857, intersect—as anomalies *per se*—with aligned narratorial structures to synchronize all aspects of aberration, whether attached to the nature of the 'legal' character, or the misguided actions of patriarchy, or the estrangement of men and women. All are purposefully anomalous, that is, all desired ends work against the interests of those involved.

The outcome of these negotiations, in which Grace herself has not at any point been consulted, simply compounds those 'pernicious conventions' Hardy speaks of to Millicent Garrett Fawcett. In this instance, the focus is upon the prevailing marriage laws, which entail women as 'chattels' (to use Grace's own word to her father) to be settled as property-transactions between men, whereby the honest poor (in this instance the humble Giles) also serve as mere pawns in a patriarchal system that thrives by divide and rule—that is, by engendering and exploiting class and sexual division.

Later, in *Jude*, Hardy elaborates on this theme, but with a shift in emphasis to the issue of the sexual double standard in law. Earlier, in *Tess*, he had treated the double standard as a personal issue between Angel Clare and Tess (the former a legatee of bourgeois cultural values), ultimately to become a public issue with Angel's desertion of his young bride and her subsequent murder of Alec and death by hanging. Broadening this base from the personal to the public arena, Hardy now moves, in *Jude*, to the legal ramifications of the sexual double standard under the prevailing divorce laws. Seeking to be released from her marriage with Phillotson, and observing that hers is not one of the natural tragedies of love, '"but a tragedy artificially manufactured for people who in a natural state would find relief in parting!"' (*JO* 4.2), Sue Bridehead levels her criticism at state and institution. At root, the body politic is the denaturing agent. Since the marriage contract enforces specific sexual and legal inequalities upon a love-based union, but at the same time disallows a means of departure in the event of divergent feelings or changed circumstances, Sue has no legal right to gain 'relief in parting'. She has no admissible grounds for divorce: not even on the basis of the mental cruelty she suffers in having to submit, against her will, to her husband's sexual pleasure. Consequently, having no recourse to law, no legal claim to freedom, she has to grovel, plead, and beg with Phillotson to allow her that 'relief'.

As a displaced but urgent indicator of her needs, of her painful sense of being emotionally and spiritually destroyed, Sue degenerates into self-mutilating behaviour. She subjects herself to physical discomforts and injuries—imprisoning herself and jumping from windows—driven by an inchoate sense of self-destruction that has, in some form or other, to be given physical expression. All this, to gain his consent: not to be granted grounds for divorce in her own right, but to be rendered, herself, the guilty party; the husband, alone, remains the sole party who can avail himself of the law.

Here the double standard is fully exposed. A wife's refusal to cohabit with her husband was sufficient grounds for divorce in itself: as Phillotson says, if she refuses to stay after he has said he has forgiven her, the legal tie can be dissolved altogether. Not so the other way round. Alternatively, whereas adultery would not have sufficed for suing the husband, it suffices well enough for suing the wife. In addition, the husband can sue for compensation: the wife, deemed the legal property of her husband, has a price on her head, and upon divorce Phillotson is entitled to claim damages for the loss of his goods.

In *Jude*, as in *The Woodlanders*, Hardy purposefully sets up a contrast between the 'pernicious conventions' of modern marriage and the more flexible, less rigorously codified forms of the past. To this end, just as it is the disreputable Lawyer Beaucock who speaks for the (discreditable) law in *The Woodlanders*, so, inversely, it is the kindly Widow Edlin, in *Jude*, who speaks on behalf of the more benign matrimonials of an earlier order. And to ensure that her voice will be heard, Hardy has this otherwise marginal character enter the scene three times over to make the point clear.

In the first instance, she introduces a noticeably lighthearted tone; this effectively contrasts with Sue's high seriousness on the marriage problem while placing the latter in a subtly different light. Shuddering with anxiety at the thought of institutionalized marriage, Sue meets with a snort of derision from Widow Edlin: '"Chok'it all.... if this is what the new notions be leading us to! Nobody thought o'being afeard o'matrimony in my time, nor of much else but a cannon-ball or empty cupboard! Why when I and my poor man were married we thought no more o't than of a game o' dibs!"' (*JO* 5.4). Later, taking issue with Phillotson on his determination to reinstate his matrimonial contract regardless of Sue's mental breakdown, the good-humoured Widow turns sharply on his heedless cruelty in this matter and emphatically refuses to attend the renewed marriage ceremony: '"No. Be hanged if I can.... I don't know what the times be coming to! Matrimony have growed to be that serious in these days that one really do feel afeard to move in it at all. In my time we took it more careless; and I don't know that we was any the worse for it! When I and my poor man were jined in it we kept up the junketing all the week, and drunk the parish dry, and had to borrow half-a-crown to begin housekeeping!"' (*JO* 6.5). But if the good Widow Edlin here succeeds in muting outrage with overtones of jaunty defiance, her later words are more ominous: '"Ah! Poor soul! Weddings be funerals 'a b'lieve nowadays. Fifty-five years ago, come Fall, since my man and I married! Times have changed since then!"' (6.9).

These schismatic undercurrents—paradigms inimical to modern marriage—are nothing new in Hardy's work. At one level they provide a kind of rear-view mirror to the world in perspective which, in turn, seeks to illuminate the 'pernicious conventions' framing the institution of modern marriage. At another level they add cultural depth and dimension to what appears (with institutionalized marriage) to be primarily a hazard of bourgeois capitalism. And at yet another level they bespeak alternative values. Not that Hardy, at any point in his artistic career, stepped out of line and tried to provide solutions: rather that he painted-in contrasting colorations in oddly unexpected places where they might add a jarring note or a measure of tonal dissonance, a way of accentuating and illuminating the underlying theme of social criticism.

Weddings, in the Wessex chronicles, are invariably undermined, to some purpose, by means of this narrative technique. Getting-married-and-living-happily-ever-after, the traditional literary mode of closure in all but works of tragedy, remained, for Hardy, an undesirable, ethically unjustifiable, narrative convention. In terms of mimesis alone he considered it a false representation of the world. Paying lip-service to this convention was, it appears, the length to which he would go, and no further. Subtextual structures of ambivalence, incertitude, and indeterminacy would ensure, for readers looking in that direction, that the 'happy ending' closure would be subtly and permanently compromised. Clearly Sue's self-annihilating act of returning to Phillotson requires no added touch of dissonance. In fact, the minor note of discord introduced by the kindly Widow as an implicitly negative commentary on modern marriage is, in one sense, ameliorative, in so far as it does serve to show that things might have been, could have been, altogether different.

The Woodlanders also concludes with schismatic 'last words' in much the same vein as in *Jude*. Grace reunites with the inconstant Fitzpiers, and does so with a naïve optimism that leaves her father bemused and the local community scratching their foreheads. Yet again, as with Widow Edlin, it is one of the rustic 'good souls' who speaks out of the historical past, at this point of closure, putting the 'matrimonial' present in a slightly different perspective. Recalling a time, before the advent of the rigidified codes and constitutional strictures of modern marriage, when there was less concern with conjugal rights and entitlements and considerably more unrepining levity in domestic relationships, the neighbourly rustic now recounts the story of a woman he once knew whose husband

> ...went away for four-and-twenty year. And one night he came home when she was sitting by the fire, and thereupon he sat down himself on the other side of the chimney-corner. 'Well,'

says she, 'have ye got any news?' 'Don't know as I have,' says he; 'have you?' 'No,' says she, 'except that my daughter by the husband that succeeded 'ee was married last month, which was a year after I was made a widow by him.' 'Oh! Anything else?' he says. 'No,' says she. And there they sat, one on each side of that chimney-corner, and were found by the neighbours sound asleep in their chairs, not having known what to talk about at all. (*W* 48)

At surface level, choric utterances of this kind seem to carry minimal thematic weight in the immediate context. But in so far as they rumble on insistently in the background of the novel, schismatic from the very first to the very last, they satisfy all the conditions of relevancy and sincerity of purpose on Hardy's part.

Far from the Madding Crowd is possibly the best of all testaments to Hardy's schismatic method. It is his most renowned 'pastoral idyll', yet, on closer inspection, it turns out to be his most subversive anti-pastoral (see PASTORALISM). Readers and critics have continued to debate, from the date of its first publication up to the present day, whether or not the dénouement fulfils the pastoral's customary promise of regeneration and renewal, traditionally symbolized, at the closure, by nuptials. Is there, in fact, an authentic 'happy ending'? Victorian readers were by no means convinced that Bathsheba's conflictful growth to womanhood, with Oak as her strictest disciplinarian, ultimately 'reforms' her unwomanly ways. Does she, convincingly, emerge the meek-and-comely woman Oak tries to fashion? Is she conventionally equipped for dutiful wifehood—the 'Angel in the House'? Evidently not. To many critics, including Henry James, she remained a 'hussy' first and foremost, and Oak should have known better than to marry her.

The purposeful ambivalence that subverts this 'happy marriage' ending is textually induced in the closing sequences by Hardy in several subtle ways. First there is the misapplication of the allusion to the Song of Solomon, which speaks, in purported relation to the union of Bathsheba and Oak, of a 'love as strong as death', but which is, in fact, a travesty of the Old Testament original, which celebrates, in the main, a woman's erotic desire for her male lover. Then there is the concluding chapter, the 'wedding' chapter, which is not only given an indeterministic title, 'A Foggy Night and Morning', but also features a shadowy configuration of two blurred forms disappearing into the mist on their way to their nuptials. And finally, in place of wedding bells and jubilation, a somewhat mawkish array of villagers arrives to pay tribute to the bride and groom, who receive, instead of grand Hosannas, an irrelevant quotation made by Poorgrass in allusion to Hosea, that 'it might have been worse'. Evidently, if the reader's expectations were of a happy-marriage celebration, Hardy's were not.

This brings us back to 'pernicious conventions' and, by way of a conclusion, to Hardy's treatment of the theme of marriage in his poetry. There are some 50 or more Hardy poems in which betrothals, weddings, and matrimonial separations feature in one way or another. Significantly, the so-called 'schismatic' element predominates. Whether the topic is a mismatch, an infidelity, a long separation, a wrongdoing, a heartfelt regret, a premonition of death or impending tragedy, the speakers tend, more often than not, to be the Mrs Edlins—in varying guises, sexes, ages—of Hardy's Wessex world.

In general, light irony is to the fore: verbal, situational, and structural. Frequently, the irony turns upon a situation that should have been catastrophic but becomes subsumed, in the telling, to absurdity. Thus, when a wife sews her drunken husband into his bedsheets to prevent his unwanted embraces, only to wake up the next morning to find he has suffocated, a situational irony seems self-evident. But as the poem's title ('Her Second Husband Hears Her Story') hints, the incongruity of the act subtly shifts from the past to the present moment in which the wife relates this tale to her second husband as he lies beside her in the selfsame bed. The tone she employs is wry, and her rhetorical form is understatement or, at any rate, flatly unexaggerated; hence her listener never raises an eyebrow, and the only indication the reader has that he should be forewarned hangs in his last line, which is simply, 'Well, it's a cool queer tale!' The incongruity of the wife's 'cool' air opens up a gap between the act of manslaughter and the imperfection or shortcomings of the account. Turmoil is absent. All appropriate emotions, from regret to horror, are absent. And in that absence there lies a dim sense of foreboding.

In historical context, those rural betrothals (so fondly recalled by the Mrs Edlins of Hardy's world), which pre-dated the Victorian institutionalization of marriage, varied considerably in custom and practice from region to region. In Wessex alone, one locality might deem a betrothal promise between two lovers sufficient ceremony in itself to constitute a sworn union, while a neighbouring locality (notably the Portland area) might not deem that promise consummate until a child was born of the union. Shades of these ancient betrothal customs infuse the 'marriage' poems more pervasively than the Wessex novels, where, one would surmise, their presence might have caused a Victorian reading public to raise more than an eyebrow. Unlike the formal rites of matrimony, they did not require that a man and a woman should swear, in the words already quoted from *Jude the Obscure*, 'that at every other time of their lives till death took them, they would assuredly believe, feel, and desire precisely as they had believed, felt, and desired during the few preceding weeks'. Betrothals were frequently no more than a loving couple's expressed desire to commit to each other, although they were no less sanctified for all that, as Hardy records in the poem 'A Poor Man and a Lady': 'We knew it was not a valid thing, | And only sanct in the sight of God. . .'. After exchanging promises, the lovers part without consummating their union; but, believing this betrothal to be a sworn union, the male speaker later confronts his beloved when he discovers that she intends to marry another, reminding her that she is already married to him. She heartlessly denies this bond, and leaves.

Clearly, one advantage to such a promissory betrothal is that it pre-empted the need for divorce. On the other hand, the registration of marriages, births, and deaths, before their bureaucratic organization under the central Westminster government, could be a hazardous affair. Maintained by the parish and kept in the local church vestry, these demographic records could fall foul of all sorts of human vagaries. For example, who, in *Far from the Madding Crowd*, would have recorded the birth and death of Fanny's infant (by Frank Troy), if Oak had had his way and permanently erased all knowledge of it as chalked on the coffin, and if the discovery of the stillborn babe had never been made by Bathsheba?

It may not come as a surprise to experienced Hardy readers that many of his 'marriage' poems are deeply forgiving. Infidelities may hurt, but they are also compassionately understood, by husbands and wives in equal measure. 'The Burghers' and 'Her Late Husband' are memorable in this context, but 'A Wife and Another' is possibly one of the most touching. In this poem, the childless wife plans to intercept her husband with his lover, but upon meeting the other woman, who, she now discovers, is with child, 'Something snapped'. In an extraordinary moment of compassion the wife sees herself 'the snarer—them the trapped':

> My hate dies, and I promise,
> Grace-beguiled,'
> I said, 'to care for you, be
> Reconciled;
> And cherish, and take interest in the child.

Later in the poem something characteristically Hardyan occurs. Leaving her husband and his lover 'alone embracing', the legal wife retreats with the gentle thought: '"He joins his wife—my sister."' It is one of those moments in Hardy when the words, feelings, and heartfelt thoughts of the living poet—who, beyond the text, speaks of 'lovingkindness' as the most important of all human gifts to humanity—gives this precious quality dramatic enactment, as, in the voice of the woman left behind, the verse concludes with 'I held I had not stirred God wrothfully'. See also WOMEN. RM

Martin, Julia Augusta (d. 1893). One of the formative influences in Hardy's early years, she was the wife of Francis Martin, who in 1845 purchased the Kingston Maurward estate, not far from Hardy's early home. As 'lady of the manor' (*LW* 23) she was a charismatic figure in Hardy's childhood, and arguably the subject of far-reaching and creatively fruitful fantasies. Wealthy but childless, she seems to have taken a fancy to little 'Tommy' early in his life, and to have been in the habit of cuddling and kissing him until his schooldays and perhaps after. He attended for a time the National School that, as a staunch Anglican, she had had a hand in establishing at Bockhampton, and she later claimed to have taught him to read (she may have taught him to write, but he seems to have been reading before her arrival in the district).

Michael Millgate comments that 'Hardy did not forget, then or ever, the woman who had overwhelmed him not only by her fond and flattering encouragement but also by a cultivation and elegance, a voluptuousness of dress and person, that were altogether new to his experience' (Millgate 47). Hardy returned her attachment and long afterwards described his precocious feeling for her as 'almost that of a lover' (*LW* 24). However, an estrangement with the Hardy family followed when Mrs Martin took offence at Jemima Hardy's decision to move her son to a Nonconformist school in Dorchester. A brief but (on the child's part at least) deeply and unforgettably emotional reunion at a harvest-supper is vividly recorded in the autobiography (*LW* 24–5).

They did not meet again for a dozen years or so, when Hardy called on her at her Bruton Street home soon after he settled in London, the Martins having left Dorset in 1853. The meeting was not a great success, Hardy being taken aback by the signs of ageing that were now unmistakable, and he did not take up her invitation to repeat the visit. A dozen years later still, she wrote to congratulate him after the success of *Far from the Madding Crowd*, but though he replied to her letter there was no personal contact and they never met again. The passage in the *Life* recording this last episode (1874) is of great interest; in his old age Hardy sharply recalled the erotic thrill caused by the '"frou-frou"' of her silk dress 'when she had used to bend over him, and when [it] brushed against the font as she entered church on Sundays'—an experience reproduced 'in exact detail', as Robert Gittings notes (*Young Thomas Hardy*, 12), in the short story 'The Withered Arm'. The same passage speculates startlingly on the direction that their relationship might have taken after her husband's death and before his own marriage (*LW* 104–5).

These memories and fantasies, articulated long after her death, are deeply revealing about the adult Hardy, and there is no doubt that Mrs Martin made an important contribution to his childhood experiences. Her compound of feminine attractiveness (Millgate's 'voluptuousness of dress and person') and social standing may have been the origin of his preoccupation with 'a constant theme in most of Hardy's early novels, sexual attraction across class barriers' (Gittings, *Young Thomas Hardy*, 11). More specifically, *Two on a Tower* seems to follow closely the lines of Hardy's partly real, partly fantasized relationship with Mrs Martin. In that novel Viviette, the lady of the manor, is pious and childless but becomes interested in the intellectual pursuits of a much younger man who is her social inferior, and falls in love with him. Hardy's discreet comment, in his autobiographical account of the harvest-supper (see above), that Mrs Martin's husband, 'the squire', was 'by no means strait-laced' may be reflected in the contrast between Viviette's delicacy and piety and the vein of coarseness evident in her husband. At the conclusion of the novel, like Hardy meeting Mrs Martin again in 1862, Swithin is shocked to see how much Viviette has aged when they meet again after a long separation. That Swithin's grandmother is named Mrs Martin may be a private or even unconscious allusion to the lady who had afforded him, very early in life, his first glimpse of a world of elegance and affluence.

'Master John Horseleigh, Knight', short story. Published in the 1893 Summer Number (12 June) of the *Illustrated London News* and in the American *McClure's Magazine* (July 1893), it was collected in *A Changed Man and Other Tales*. John *Hutchins's *History and Antiquities of Dorset* was an important source of material (see Purdy 156). The story, set in the 16th century, concerns a mysterious stranger who marries a young widow and is killed by her brother, who believes him to be already married; it turns out that he has married the girl in good faith, knowing his aristocratic marriage to be invalid as a result of events beyond his control. Despite its historical setting in a period when, as the suspicious brother observes, '"The King's new-made headship of the Church hath led men to practise these new tricks lightly"', the concern with marriage and the relationship between its legal and moral implications connects this lightweight story with the major novels of the same period.

Maugham, W. Somerset (1894–1965), novelist and playwright. Maugham's novel *Cakes and Ale* (1930) caused a literary scandal as it was perceived to be a vicious satire of Hardy and his second wife, Florence, soon after Hardy's death. A leading character in *Cakes and Ale* is an elderly novelist called Edward Driffield, who, like Hardy, has been awarded the Order of Merit and has a much younger second wife who protects him from the public. Despite the numerous differences between Hardy and Driffield, Hardy's supporters saw the novel as a direct attack on his work and his private life. Driffield is criticized for his purple prose, melodrama, and tedious scenes of peasants speaking in dialect. He is also dishonest, and his second wife exploits his reputation before and after his death to support her own pretensions.

Debate about the resemblance between Hardy and Driffield began as soon as *Cakes and Ale* was published. In a review J. B. Priestley deplored Maugham's literary ethics in presenting a character who was bound to be identified with Hardy. In another review, Evelyn Waugh defended Maugham, arguing that the public's urge to find real-life originals for a novelist's characters is an insult to literary creativity. Maugham denied that Driffield was based on Hardy, and in the 1963 preface to a reissue of *Cakes and Ale* states that he met Hardy only once, that he 'knew little of Hardy's life', and that the similarities between Hardy and Driffield are 'negligible'. However, Ted Morgan's biography of Maugham (1980) cites an unpublished letter in which Maugham admits that his novel was inspired by the pomp of Hardy's funeral in Westminster Abbey. Any suggestion that Mrs Driffield was based on Florence Hardy is dismissed in Robert Gittings and Jo Manton's biography, *The Second Mrs Hardy* (1979). JA

Max Gate. The Hardys moved from *Wimborne to a rented house in *Dorchester in the summer of 1883. Shortly afterwards, Hardy set about building on the one-and-a-half-acre plot on the town's south-eastern outskirts that he had leased from the Duchy of Cornwall, the principal landowner in the area. The property, formerly called Loud's Gate, was renamed Max Gate in humorous tribute to the Henry Mack who had once kept the nearby toll-gate on the Wareham Road. Work on preparing the exposed and unbroken downland site began in November 1883, Hardy planting with his own hands many of the hundreds of trees, mostly beech and Austrian pine, that progressively sheltered the house but eventually shut it in to an almost claustrophobic degree. At various times he also planted a small orchard and a variety of native trees, such as holly, wych elm, and spindle. Skeletal remains of the Romano-British period were discovered during the digging of the foundations and driveway, and recent excavations have revealed the underlying presence of a neolithic causewayed burial enclosure. The building work went slowly, and Hardy and Emma did not move in until June 1885; purchase of the freehold, for the then considerable sum of £450, was completed eighteen months later, in December 1886.

The new house was designed by Hardy himself (some of the drawings are in DCM) and built by the Hardy family firm, under Henry Hardy's direction, of bricks from the family brickyard at Broadmayne, the stable and carriage-house being constructed first, even though the Hardys seem never to have owned a horse or vehicle of their own. As a mid-Victorian villa standing in its own generous grounds, fronted by a brick wall almost six feet in height and a horseshoe-shaped driveway, Max Gate in its raw red newness clearly announced Hardy's attainment of solid middle-class status. Often criticized, then and since, as ugly and uncomfortable, it certainly lacked conventional architectural distinction and proportion: the front porch is offset, the windows are of different shapes and sizes, and it was several years before the curious square turret at the south-west corner of the house was balanced by the addition of a similar turret at the south-east corner (the attractive sundial it now carries was designed by Hardy but not erected until after his death). Hardy seems to have been chiefly concerned with such issues of interior convenience as adjustment of the size and shape of the windows to the position and purpose of the rooms (the south-facing living-room, for example, was given a window exceptionally large), and the house as originally built was quite compact and fully up to contemporary standards of comfort and convenience.

Such standards took for granted the availability of servants, and during Hardy's lifetime there seem always to have been at least two and sometimes as many as four live-in servants: cook, scullery maid, parlourmaid, and sometimes an assistant parlourmaid or an all-purpose 'man' or 'boy', one of whose tasks in the early 1900s was to pull Emma Hardy in her bath-chair to church. A full- or part-time gardener was also employed to tend the two formal lawns, the shrubbery (location of the pets' cemetery), the tree-lined walk that extended along two sides of the property, the several flower-beds, and the sizeable kitchen garden. In the 1920s Florence Hardy purchased an adjoining paddock, primarily as a run for her chickens.

As the Hardys' sense of economic security increased, various additions were made to the back of the house, the most extensive in 1895–6 and 1907. These alterations, again designed by Hardy and carried out by his brother, were somewhat sprawling in their overall effect, but they significantly enlarged the kitchen and scullery, increased the number of bedrooms, and provided Hardy, who had already moved his study twice, with the spacious eastward-facing final study that has recently received a full-scale reconstruction in the Dorset County Museum. Although there had been from the first an indoor flushing toilet, it was not until 1920, well into Hardy's second marriage, that an indoor bathroom was created by reducing the size of the principal bedroom. Well-water had still to be pumped to the top of the house by disgruntled servants, however, and installation of electric light had to wait until after Hardy's death.

Hardy sometimes referred to Max Gate as his country retreat or 'writing box', and he certainly found it an efficient place in which to live and write—not least because of its location in the centre of the region he had made fictionally his own. Domestically, it proved less happy. Emma Hardy never felt at home in Dorchester, where she had few friends and was constantly at odds with Hardy's family, and as their marriage deteriorated she and her husband lived increasingly separate lives, she withdrawing to her attic 'eyrie', he to his study. They entertained less and less and allowed the house itself to become somewhat dingy and run down. Emma's death and Hardy's marriage to Florence Dugdale brought many changes: rooms were redecorated and furniture re-covered; a conservatory was added to the living-room, a new double-oven range installed in the kitchen; and Max Gate became a more hospitable place, Hardy often taking tea with the literary pilgrims who constantly descended upon him.

Florence, however, found Max Gate, its massed trees now fully grown, depressingly dark and damp, and when Hardy died and left her the house she was perpetually torn between her desire for escape and her sense of responsibility towards a place so profoundly associated with her husband and his work. Though she left Hardy's study virtually untouched, she had reached no clear decision about the future of Max Gate by the time of her death in 1937, simply directing in her will that the property and its contents should be sold, Hardy's specifically literary remains only excepted. The contents, apart from furniture presented to the Dorset County Museum or retained by Florence Hardy's sisters, were duly sold by the Dorchester auctioneers Hy. Duke & Son on 16 February 1938, while Hardy's *library, apart from approximately 475 volumes deposited in the Dorset County Museum, was similarly dispersed in London three months later. But when Max Gate itself was auctioned on 6 May 1938 it was purchased by Hardy's sister Kate and subsequently left by her to the National Trust. Housing estates have reached out towards and beyond Max Gate over the years, and the Dorchester bypass now runs through a cutting immediately alongside it, but the house and, especially, its garden can still provide the visitor with a sense of the lives once led there by Thomas, Emma, and Florence Hardy, their successive servants, their many visitors, and the pets who alone still remain.

MM

Mayor of Casterbridge, The. The tenth of Hardy's fourteen published novels. (On the various forms taken by its title and subtitle, see below.)

Composition

This was to be the first of the five novels written after Hardy made his home in *Dorchester, though composition took place at his temporary residence in Shire-Hall Lane, before the move to Max Gate (see HOMES). The bulk of it was written during 1884, and it was completed on 17 April 1885, on which day Hardy noted in his diary that it had been 'begun at least a year ago, and frequently interrupted in the writing of each part' (*LW* 177). At the end of the manuscript, which survives in incomplete form and is now in the Dorset County Museum, Hardy has noted simply '(Written 1884–1885)'. The manuscript also indicates that the names of some of the characters were originally different: Michael Henchard was Giles (a name used in Hardy's next novel, *The Woodlanders*), and Donald Farfrae began as Alan Stansbie. Henchard was at first designated a 'woodman' (like the later Giles), then a stonemason (like the hero of *Jude the Obscure*), before becoming a hay-trusser; he was to have been somewhat older at the beginning of the story, married five years (rather than two) and with two daughters (rather than one), one of whom remained with him after the separation from his wife.

Serialization

The Mayor appeared first as a weekly serial in the *Graphic*, under the editorship of Arthur *Locker, from 2 January to 15 May 1886, divided as follows: 2 January, Chapters 1–2; 9 January, 3–5; 16 January, 5 (contd.)–7; 23 January, 8–9; 30 January, 10–12; 6 February, 13–15; 13 February, 13 (contd.)–17; 20 February, 18–19; 27 February, 20–1; 6 March, 22–3; 13 March, 24–5; 20 March, 26–7; 27 March, 27 (contd.)–29; 3 April, 30–2; 10 April, 33–4; 17 April, 35–6; 24 April, 37–8; 1 May, 39–41; 8 May, 41 (contd.)–43; 15 May, 44–5. It was serialized simultaneously in the American magazine *Harper's Weekly*. Hardy later came to feel that he 'had damaged [the novel] more recklessly as an artistic whole in the interest of the newspaper in which it appeared serially, than perhaps any other of his novels, his aiming to get an incident into almost every week's part causing him in his own judgment to add events to the narrative somewhat too freely'; later still, however, he reflected that the plot was 'quite coherent and organic, in spite of its complication' (*LW* 185–6). Purdy notes that the novel was 'considerably rewritten before its publication in book form, with significant alterations in plot and many deletions. Chaps. 12, 18, 34, 43, and 44 particularly show important revisions' (52). Some of these alterations had the effect of reducing the number of 'incidents': for example, a scene in the serial version involving a meeting between Susan and Lucetta that is witnessed by Henchard was dropped. On these and other textual points, the Oxford World's Classics edition of the novel by Dale Kramer (1987) may be consulted.

Illustrations

Each of the twenty weekly instalments carried an illustration by Robert Barnes, not reproduced in subsequent editions; six of them are now in DCM. Hardy thought highly of them and hung them on the wall at Max Gate. (See also ILLUSTRATIONS.)

Volume Publication

On 10 May 1886, a few days before the completion of serial publication, the novel was issued in two volumes by the London firm of *Smith, Elder & Co. at the price of one guinea (21*s.*). Before the end of the same month it had been published in America by Henry *Holt & Co. Purdy notes that it was 'widely pirated' in America (53). A one-volume edition appeared in 1887. For the Wessex Novels edition issued by *Osgood, McIlvaine in 1895, Hardy added an interesting preface; he also restored a passage that had been deleted from Chapter 44, and made minor revisions, some of which, affecting the Scots speech of Donald Farfrae, appear to have been suggested by his friend Sir George *Douglas (see Hardy's preface). When *The Mayor* was included in the 1912 Wessex Edition Hardy made minor revisions to his preface.

Reception

Contemporary reviewers were slow to recognize *The Mayor* as one of Hardy's greatest achievements, and Laurence Lerner and John Holmstrom's judgement in *Thomas Hardy and His Readers* (1968) that the early criticism is 'not very interesting' is hard to dispute. The *Guardian* found it 'not a pleasant book . . . its outlook is narrow, its tone is prosaic, and its last word is elaborately pessimistic'. The *Saturday Review* (29 May 1886) found it not only 'not equal to the author's great and most picturesque romance of rural life, *Far from the Madding Crowd*' but deemed it 'a disappointment': the same anonymous reviewer added that 'The story, which is very slight and singularly devoid of interest, is, at the same time, too improbable'. What earned praise from this reviewer was not the story's psychological interest or tragic power but the descriptions of Casterbridge and the portrayal of 'peasants', especially through their dialogue. In similar terms the *Athenaeum* (29 May 1886) praised Hardy's knowledge of 'the ways and humours of country folk' but compared *The Mayor* unfavourably with *The Trumpet-Major*, partly on account of their having, respectively, a 'self-willed' and an 'unselfish' hero. A notable exception to these variously dismissive or lukewarm verdicts was a substantial review by the leading critic R. H. Hutton in the *Spectator* (5 June 1886). This discusses at length the characterization of Henchard, which is seen as producing 'a curiously strong impression of reality'. Hutton also praises the presentation of Elizabeth-Jane, but finds Farfrae much less satisfactory. (The last three reviews cited are all reprinted in *CH*.) A much more perfunctory notice in the *Westminster Review* also gives high praise to the protagonist ('a grand study which has not, as far as we recollect, its prototype in fiction'). Among private responses, Hardy quotes in his autobiography, with evident satisfaction, a letter from R. L. *Stevenson expressing 'sincere admiration' for the book: 'Henchard is a great fellow, and Dorchester is touched in with the hand of a master' (*LW* 186).

Plot

Michael Henchard, a hay-trusser, gets drunk at a fair at Weydon-Priors and 'sells' his wife Susan to a sailor, who disappears with the woman and the couple's child. The next morning Henchard vows not to touch drink for 21 years; he later learns that his family appear to have emigrated. Settling in Casterbridge, he prospers and becomes a leading dealer in corn and hay, and eventually mayor of the town. After the sailor's presumed death many years later, Susan and her daughter Elizabeth-Jane, now about 18 years old, come to Casterbridge to seek help from Henchard. (At this stage Henchard does not realize that the girl is not in fact his own daughter, who has died, but a child subsequently born to Susan.) Eventually he goes through a form of marriage to Susan (who has in fact been his legal wife throughout), and Elizabeth-Jane, an intelligent and sensitive girl, now enters into a life of affluence.

In the meantime Henchard has persuaded a shrewd and ambitious young Scot, Donald Farfrae, who is passing through Casterbridge on his way to North America, to stay and help run his business. Henchard forms a close bond with the young man and confides to him the story of his relationship with Susan and also the secret of his affair with a young woman, Lucetta Le Sueur, in Jersey. Soon, though, Henchard's attachment turns to distrust and dislike when Farfrae becomes a popular figure in the town and, having left Henchard's employment, a business rival. Farfrae also shows a romantic interest in Elizabeth-Jane. Susan dies and, just after telling Elizabeth-Jane that she is his daughter and not merely a stepdaughter as she had supposed, Henchard discovers a letter written by Susan that makes it clear that the girl is the child of the sailor, Newson. Henchard's manner towards her becomes cold, even hostile, and she goes to live as a companion to Lucetta, whom she has met by chance and who, under her new name of Templeman (adopted after inheriting property from an aunt), has come to live at High-Place Hall in the town in the hope of marrying Henchard. Lucetta and Farfrae fall in love, so that the latter is now Henchard's rival in love as well as in business and local politics.

Thanks to impulsive speculations, Henchard's financial affairs seriously deteriorate, and the old woman who has sold him alcohol at the fair turns up and reveals the secret of his wife-selling—this marking the turning-point in the fortunes of Henchard, who is soon declared bankrupt and becomes a lodger in a cottage, while Farfrae buys his business, house, and furniture, marries his former lover, and becomes mayor of the town. For his part, Henchard becomes a journeyman hay-trusser and, the period of his oath having expired, takes to drink. Henchard's carelessness causes letters written to him by Lucetta at the time of their affair in Jersey to fall into the hands of strangers, who stage a 'skimmington ride' (designed to expose the immoral to public ridicule and disgrace) in the town; the shock of this event causes Lucetta to have a miscarriage and die. Newson, who has not after all been drowned at sea, arrives to claim his daughter, but Henchard selfishly informs him that she is dead, with the result that he himself continues to enjoy her company for a time. Soon, however, she is courted by Farfrae. Henchard leaves Casterbridge, dressed as he had been when he entered the town as a young man. Newson reappears and is reunited with his daughter, who marries Farfrae. Revisiting Casterbridge at the time of the wedding, Henchard finds his hopes of a reconciliation are dashed when he is reproached by Elizabeth-Jane for coming between her and her real father. A little later his death in a remote cottage is discovered by Elizabeth-Jane and Farfrae.

Critical Approaches

Hardy and his wife moved from Wimborne to Dorchester in June 1883, and before the end of the year the building of *Max Gate on the outskirts of that ancient town had begun. A few months later, as the building of the house slowly proceeded, Hardy was at work on *The Mayor of Casterbridge*, the novel that celebrates and commemorates his return to the neighbourhood of his youth. Though the chronology of the story is not entirely clear, the main action evidently takes place during the period of Hardy's childhood. As part of his research for the work, Hardy studied the files of the local newspaper, the *Dorset County Chronicle* (see DORCHESTER), beginning from 1826. It is thus a novel with significant connections to both personal history and local history, the former drawing on the early memories of a writer now in his mid-forties, the latter involving not only Dorchester's early-Victorian past but its history from the time of the Roman occupation and, earlier, its prehistoric settlers.

The action opens 'before the nineteenth century had reached one-third of its span', but the first two chapters turn out to constitute no more than a prologue (though a crucial one), and nearly twenty years elapse before Susan Henchard's reappearance in Chapter 3. Even so, for the late-Victorian reader this must have had very much the feel of a historical novel, re-creating a vanished past, though one within the memory of elderly or even middle-aged readers: during the period of the action, the railway, for instance, had not yet been extended to Casterbridge (it reached Dorchester in 1847), and the Prince Consort (who died in 1861) is still very much alive as the prototype of the 'Royal personage' of Chapter 37. A rough analogy might be with a novel of our own day that was set in the period immediately following the end of the Second World War.

Hardy's preface makes a large claim for the historical basis of his story as well as for the firmness and coherence of its chronology: 'The incidents narrated arise mainly out of three events, which chanced to range themselves in the order and at or about the intervals of time here given, in the real history of the town called Casterbridge and the neighbouring country.' It is not, however, a claim that need be taken too literally. For one thing, wife-selling was not a practice by any means confined to that time and place. It occurred throughout England over a long period, and in a letter written in 1906 Hardy seems to concede that he had encountered, presumably in his reading of old newspapers, more than one such case: 'There were frequent instances here [in Dorset] between 1820 and 1830, the supposed date of the sale...' (*L* iii 241). (This cheap method of 'divorce' and bizarrely pragmatic corner of social history is thoroughly explored in Samuel Pyeatt Menefee's *Wives for Sale: An Ethnographic Study of British Popular Divorce* (1981).) Nor can it really be maintained that the royal visit of 1849 furnished the novel with more than a vivid incident. (The third of the 'three events' referred to is the repeal of the Corn Laws in 1846.) As so often, Hardy's strategy in his prefatory declaration may be to conceal the more personal origins of a story that, among much else, re-creates an important chapter of his own past. It is worth remembering, for instance, that as an intelligent child of 9 Hardy could well have heard, and had his curiosity stimulated by, gossip about Prince Albert's visit to Dorchester, and it was in the following year that he began to attend a school in that town.

Hardy is prepared, too, to take liberties with historical fact when it suits his purpose, so that the 'Royal personage' is compelled to complete his journey to Casterbridge by road in the absence of a railway, even though Dorchester had been linked to the railway system two years before the historical royal visit. To this extent a precise matching of the fictional

Casterbridge with the town in which Hardy made his home is misleading. Paramount for Hardy is the necessity of depicting Casterbridge as an isolated, conservative, and thoroughly traditional community, with a social organization belonging to the pre-railway age: in both its rough-and-ready business methods and its superstitions and folk customs, it is a survival from the past, and the novel, especially in the person of Farfrae, depicts and dramatizes the intrusion of the modern world and the beginning of a process of radical and irresistible change. Repeatedly the narrative reminds the reader, from the standpoint of the 1880s, that the hand of change has fallen heavily on such places as Casterbridge. The Three Mariners Inn is 'now, unfortunately pulled down' (6); more happily, the slum of Mixen Lane is also 'in great part pulled down' (36); the curfew formerly 'rung in Casterbridge' has been 'silenced for many years' (4). A footnote reference to 'time and progress' in Chapter 9 is unmistakably ironical. While 'pulled down' is several times applied to buildings, 'extinct', with its Darwinian overtones, is applied in Chapter 36 to a form of social organization. In this way the story offers a series of receding perspectives, from the late-Victorian present to an early- and mid-19th-century past, and beyond that to the Romans who built and occupied Durnovaria, and the prehistoric settlement of Maumbury Ring ('The Ring at Casterbridge' of Chapter 11: see ARCHAEOLOGY).

As often, Hardy was slow to settle on a final title for his novel. In the manuscript it stands as simply *The Mayor of Casterbridge*, but the first edition adds the subtitle *The Life and Death of a Man of Character*, modified in the editions of 1887 and 1895 to *A Story of a Man of Character*. Finally, the 1912 title-page carried an amalgam of these various notions, *The Life and Death of the Mayor of Casterbridge: A Story of a Man of Character*. The two interesting features are the 'life and death' formula and the somewhat enigmatic phrase 'man of character'. The former perhaps echoes such Renaissance models as Shakespeare's *The Life and Death of King John*, and possibly also such moralistic works as Bunyan's *The Life and Death of Mr Badman*; it promises the whole sweep of a human life, and seems also to hint at tragedy.

At the same time the emphasis on 'character', like the epigram from Novalis, 'Character is fate', that Hardy quotes in Chapter 17, defines the story as one of events that result from human choices and actions rather than blind chance. The impulsive sale of his wife in the opening episode determines the rest of Henchard's life, and that act proceeds, as Hardy perceives the matter, from the deep and permanent core of Henchard's nature: even when, thanks to a rigorous and sustained self-discipline, he has become prosperous, respectable, and well-regarded, 'Mayor and churchwarden and what not', there is 'still the same unruly volcanic stuff beneath the rind of Michael Henchard as when he had sold his wife at Weydon Fair' (17). From that 'unruliness' almost every one of his actions in the novel proceeds. In its more benign forms it emerges as a capacity for impulsive (but also possessive) affection, as in his rapidly formed attachment to Farfrae, whom a shrewder and more dispassionate man—Farfrae himself, for instance—would have identified as a potential rival and seen off briskly for foreign parts. Too often this quality works against Henchard's own interests, so that many commentators have seen in his conduct an unconsciously self-punishing, self-destructive element—the legacy of guilt-feelings proceeding from his effective abandonment of his family. In Albert J. Guerard's phrase, he is 'a man of character obsessed by guilt and so committed to his own destruction' (*Thomas Hardy: The Novels and Stories* (1949)).

Like most of Hardy's novels, *The Mayor* is rich in allusions to a range of literature, ancient and modern, and in broader terms the outlines of its story have much in common with certain earlier texts. In this way, rather as simple Susan Henchard in her death lies with long-perished ladies of the Roman Empire (20), a tale of an obscure individual living and dying in a remote corner of England is seen to be no more, and no less, than a variation on familiar and sad stories of the death of kings that belong to world literature. Julian Moynahan has persuasively demonstrated, for instance, the striking similarities between Henchard's story and that of Saul in the First Book of Samuel in the Old Testament. Others have noted Henchard's resemblance to an earlier Wessex figure,

Shakespeare's King Lear, who also had a tormented relationship with a daughter and also died in wretchedness. Like Lear, Henchard by an act of folly gets rid of his family at the beginning of the story and, in his desperate loneliness and need for love, spends the rest of it trying to regain family ties—for it should be remembered that he has 'sold' a child as well as a wife, and the relationship with Elizabeth-Jane is perhaps the most touching element in the book. Henchard, physically powerful and authoritative in manner, and one 'who knew no moderation in his requests and impulses' (12), has the makings of a tragic hero. In some respects, too, he anticipates Solness in *Ibsen's *The Master Builder*, not produced in England until 1892. (Relevant discussions of the tragic dimensions of the novel include a 1959 essay by John Paterson in *Victorian Studies*, and Jeanette King's 1978 book *Tragedy in the Victorian Novel*.)

Henchard is, though, the victim of history as well as of his own nature, for Hardy makes it clear that the changing world has no more room for the likes of him than for a dinosaur. Farfrae, whose 'character was just the reverse of Henchard's' (17), is the man of the future, rational and scientific rather than impulsive and intuitive; the fact that he is a more superficial personality, less capable of feeling, will not prevent him from succeeding in a world that is learning to prize efficient business methods and shrewd managerial abilities. Hardy shows considerable skill in exposing Farfrae's limitations, which are evident from his first appearance and his rendering of sentimental songs about the native land he is in such a hurry to leave for ever. For Douglas Brown (*Thomas Hardy* (1954)), Hardy's tale is one of 'the struggle between the native countryman and the alien invader', and depicts, in a wider context, 'the tension between the old rural world and the new urban one'. (It is worth noting that the role of 'alien invader' is shared by Farfrae with Lucetta, whose new wealth enables her to assume a place in Casterbridge society to which she can lay no claim by virtue of birth or labour.) It can also be argued, however, that a 'sociological' reading of this kind displaces what after all seems to be Hardy's chief preoccupation: the psychology of his protagonist. Thus, to cite a notable example, Elaine Showalter's feminist reading identifies the central achievement of the novel as its offering 'the fullest nineteenth-century portrait of a man's inner life', and describes the work as 'more Shakespearean than Victorian' ('The Unmanning of the Mayor of Casterbridge', in *Critical Approaches to the Fiction of Thomas Hardy*, ed. Dale Kramer (1979)).

Though the story is from one point of view linear, moving from Henchard's youth to his middle age and death, it simultaneously possesses a well-emphasized circularity. The opening of the third chapter deliberately echoes the opening of the first, and more importantly Henchard's resumption of his former trade and former costume in Chapter 43 brings him back to the point at which the story started. Such patterns based on repetition, with the implication that progress and advancement are no more than illusions and delusions, are common in Hardy. The traditional idea of Fortune's wheel seems not far from Hardy's mind in his account of Henchard's rise and fall, and indeed it becomes almost explicit when the furmity-woman's revelations in the police-court are noted as marking 'the edge or turn in the incline of Henchard's fortunes' (31). If the drama of 'rise and fall' gives Henchard's career its basic pattern, though, the narrative attends much more closely to the fall than to the rise, which takes place in the many years that silently elapse between the end of the second and the beginning of the third chapter. Hardy's real interest, it seems, is in Henchard's decline and fall. With Susan's return, and the invasion of the prosperous present by the shameful past, his decline, though at first imperceptible, begins.

The family walking along the road on the first page of the novel; Susan and her daughter peering with shy curiosity at the public evidence of Henchard's success at the beginning of the third chapter; Henchard again trudging the road in the same dress twenty years later—these and numerous other key-passages suggest the extent to which Hardy's narrative is conducted through a series of detailed verbal pictures, often seen from a specific angle or viewpoint (as when Lucetta and Elizabeth-Jane observe the market-day activities from an upstairs window). This is a novel in which Hardy's *pictorialism, so often a striking feature of his writing, is particularly in evidence, as is his favourite motif of the watcher or voyeur. The narrator is at times one of these voyeurs, and is a sophisticated manipulator of viewpoint who is often closer to Christopher Isherwood's camera-eye than to the old-fashioned, omniscient chronicler. On that first page we do not learn the names of the characters, but we are enabled to 'observe' in great detail the visible signs in, for instance, the very precisely detailed description of the male figure, and we are aided in the interpretation of what is described and 'seen' by the interpretative comments of one with specialized knowledge: 'His measured, springless walk was the walk of the skilled countryman as distinct from the desultory shamble of the general labourer...'. Later these visual techniques are applied to buildings as well as people, so that Casterbridge, 'the pole, focus, or nerve-knot of the surrounding country life' (8), with its social, economic, and architectural variety ranging from fine residence to slum, becomes intimately known to the reader.

In the 'General Preface' written for the Wessex Edition of 1912, Hardy reminds us that his 'Wessex' is, though small in geographical terms, roughly equivalent to the region of Ancient Greece in which the dramas of the great tragic writers are set. Casterbridge is only a tiny part of Wessex, but virtually all the action of the novel takes place there or in the immediate vicinity. Susan goes to Canada and returns: Farfrae hails from Scotland and sets out for the New World (but abandons his plan); nearer home, Henchard, Lucetta, and Jopp have all spent some time in Jersey; the furmity-woman is an itinerant who disappears for a long time and then returns. This larger world, however, lies offstage. But for all the reader's sense of a confinement unusual in a novel of this length, Hardy's themes are (to employ a phrase he was to use in his next novel, *The Woodlanders*) of a 'Sophoclean grandeur' (see also TRAGEDY).

Robert Kiely, 'Vision and Viewpoint in *The Mayor of Casterbridge*', *Nineteenth-Century Fiction*, 23 (1968).

Jeannette King, '*The Mayor of Casterbridge*: Talking about Character', *THJ* 8 (1992).

Laurence Lerner, '*The Mayor of Casterbridge*': *Tragedy or Social History?* (1975).

J. C. Maxwell, 'The "Sociological" Approach to *The Mayor of Casterbridge*', in Maynard Mack and Ian Gregor (eds.), *Imagined Worlds: Essays on Some English Novels and Novelists in Honour of John Butt* (1968).

Julian Moynahan, '*The Mayor of Casterbridge* and the Old Testament's First Book of Samuel: A Study of Some Literary Relationships', *PMLA* 71 (1956).

John Paterson, '*The Mayor of Casterbridge* as Tragedy', *Victorian Studies*, 3 (1959).

'Melancholy Hussar of the German Legion, The', short story. It was delivered to the *Tillotson syndicate on 22 October 1889, published (under the title 'The Melancholy Hussar') in the *Bristol Times and Mirror* (4, 11 January 1890) and other provincial newspapers, collected in *Life's Little Ironies*, but transferred to *Wessex Tales* for the Wessex Edition (1912). A tale of 'nearly ninety years ago', it is presented as the product of oral tradition: the middle-aged narrator has heard it more than 30 years earlier, as 'a lad of fifteen', from an old woman who is also the protagonist; he has promised to keep it a secret until after her death, and has more than kept his promise. Phyllis, living as a young woman in an isolated spot with an eccentric and curmudgeonly father, falls in love with Corporal Matthäus Tina, a young German posted in Budmouth with 'the King's German Legion'. Her father plans to marry her to Humphrey Gould, a socially well-placed but shallow man whose attentions are intermittent. On the point of eloping with the German, with whom she will make her way to his home in Germany, she changes her mind when it appears that Gould has returned to claim her. It turns out, however, that he has merely come to announce his marriage to another; in the meantime Matthäus and his friend Christoph have been arrested as deserters, and Phyllis witnesses from a distance their execution by firing-squad.

The reliance of the story on local history is stressed at its conclusion by a transcription from the parish register and references to the graves of the dead, including Phyllis herself. Hardy's 1896 preface to *Life's Little Ironies* states that 'the extract from the register of burials is literal, to be read any day in the original by the curious', and refers to his own meeting with the original of Phyllis. Hardy's diary for 27 July 1877 (excerpted in *LW* 119) records material gleaned during his research for *The Trumpet-Major*: 'James Bushrod of Broadmayne saw the two German soldiers [of the York Hussars] shot [for desertion] on Bincombe Down in 1801'; a note adds that the story uses the actual names of the two soldiers. The graves in question are in Bincombe churchyard.

'Memories of Church Restoration', one of the most interesting of Hardy's essays, was originally written as a paper to be delivered to a meeting in London of the Society for the Protection of Ancient Buildings on 20 June 1906; however, in his 'enforced absence' (*LW* 356), it was read by another member on his behalf. It was printed both in the Society's *Transactions* and in the *Cornhill Magazine* (August 1906). Millgate describes it (56) as 'a kind of public confession of the part he had himself unwittingly played' as a young architect in the destruction of ancient churches, and Hardy defines his own position as that of one who 'look[s] back in a contrite spirit at my own brief experience as a church-restorer'. To a large extent, however, the tone is one of relaxed and sometimes humorous reminiscence. The paper begins seriously enough by declaring that England would be richer in ancient ecclesiastical architecture if the efforts of 19th-century 'restorers' had never been made, and there follow many instances of irreversible damage done in the name of preservation to the fabric and contents of churches. The problem is that a church is both an aesthetic object and a building for practical use, but Gothic architecture should be preserved intact at all costs, for both 'material' and 'spiritual' reasons: no modern skill can replace the original work, and the 'human associations' of the original disappear with it. The emphasis on what he elsewhere calls 'associativeness', a recurring theme in Hardy's reflections on relics from the past, is eloquently reinforced: what is at issue is 'the preservation of memories, history, fellowship, fraternities'. But there will always be conflict between 'the purely aesthetic sense and the memorial or associative', and he concludes that, on balance, 'To do nothing, where to act on little knowledge is a dangerous thing, is to do most and best'. The paper contains a number of anecdotes based on his own inspection of churches as well as references to specific churches and cathedrals in many parts of England. He regrets the damage and destruction done not only to church buildings but to pews and other woodwork, to memorials, and to gravestones: the comments on 'innumerable instances in which head-stones have been removed from their positions, the churchyard levelled, and the head-stones used for paving the churchyard walks, with the result that the inscriptions have been trodden out in a few years' are paralleled in the poem 'The Levelled Churchyard', written in 1882 at *Wimborne, where the Minster (identified in the original manuscript of the poem) had been extensively 'restored'. See also ARCHITECTURE.

'Mere Interlude, A', short story. It was sold to the *Tillotson syndicate, published in the *Bolton Weekly Journal* (17, 24 October 1885) and other provincial newspapers, and collected in *A Changed Man and Other Tales*. Set in Cornwall ('Off-Wessex') and the Scilly Isles ('the Isles of Lyonnesse'), this briskly narrated story is a black comedy or (to use a term that appears in its final paragraph) 'tragi-comedy'. In its concern with marriage and the compromises enforced by that institution, it looks forward to *The Woodlanders* and other 'marriage novels' of the next ten years.

Baptista Trewthen, daughter of a small farmer on one of the islands, has something in common with Fancy Day, the heroine of *Under the Greenwood Tree*. She has attended a teachers' training college on the mainland but dislikes the profession, and decides to return home to marry a rich and elderly tradesman. Delayed by missing a boat, she meets a young man she has known at college, impetuously marries him, and is immediately widowed when he drowns while bathing. She continues her journey and, arriving home, says nothing of what has happened, so that her second marriage takes place on the day after the first. The 'mere interlude' of the first is not, however, shaken off so easily: on the honeymoon she finds herself, to her horror, occupying a room next to that in which the corpse is lying; she attends her first husband's funeral; and on returning home she is blackmailed by one of the witnesses to her first wedding. Confession to her husband is greeted by confession on his part of a former liaison that has produced four daughters, of whom she must now take charge; Baptista thus finds herself back where she started, in the uncongenial role of teacher. A brief coda of unexpected gravity depicts her not only accepting this fate but learning in time to love her instant family.

Meredith, George (1828–1909), novelist and poet. He worked (1862–94) as a reader for the London publishing firm of Chapman & Hall, and in this capacity advised against the publication of Hardy's first novel, *The *Poor Man and the Lady.* Hardy's meeting with Meredith at Frederick Chapman's office in March 1869 is vividly described in his autobiography (*LW* 62–4), and was crucial in determining the early direction of his career as a novelist. Meredith suggested that, though the book was acceptable, its passionate social satire would damage the young novelist's career at the outset; he also advised him to write a novel with a stronger plot. Hardy took this advice seriously, the result being *Desperate Remedies*, and it was advice that may have had a decisive effect on his literary career.

A generation later, as an established novelist, Hardy visited Meredith at his home at Box Hill, Surrey, on 30 April 1894, accompanied by Edward *Clodd; other visits, in 1899 and 1905, are also on record, and the two writers often corresponded. In January 1898 Hardy was involved, with Edmund *Gosse and others, in the preparation of a 70th birthday tribute to Meredith. When Meredith died on 18 April 1909, Hardy learned of the news from a newspaper poster in Dover Street, London, when he was on his way to the Royal Academy, went instead to the Athenaeum club, and forthwith wrote the poem 'George Meredith', published (as 'G.M.') in *The Times* on 22 April, the day of Meredith's funeral. Hardy attended the memorial service held in Westminster Abbey on the same day (permission for Meredith's burial there had been refused by the Abbey authorities, and Hardy himself was later to be the first novelist since Dickens to be buried in the Abbey). In the last year of his own life Hardy wrote 'G.M.: A Reminiscence' at the request of Meredith's son, W. M. Meredith, who was editor of *The Nineteenth Century and After*; it was sent to that journal on 12 October 1927, but not published until February 1928, just after Hardy's death.

metrics. Looking back at the publication of his first volume of poetry, *Wessex Poems* (1898), Hardy spoke of the aesthetic principles of his metres:

> In the reception of this and later volumes of Hardy's poems there was, he said, as regards form, the inevitable ascription to ignorance of what was really choice after full knowledge. That the author loved the art of concealing art was undiscerned. For instance, as to rhythm. Years earlier he had decided that too regular a beat was bad art.... He knew that in architecture cunning irregularity is of enormous worth, and it is obvious that he carried on into his verse, perhaps in part unconsciously, the Gothic art-principle in which he had been trained—the principle of spontaneity, found in mouldings, tracery and such like—resulting in the 'unforeseen' (as it has been called) character of his metres.... He shaped his poetry accordingly, introducing metrical pauses, and reversed beats. (*LW* 323)

Hardy's remarks reflect an important period in the history of English metrical theory, the discovery of the true nature of accentual-syllabic rhythm. In one of his many notebook entries on the subject, he quoted Basil de Selincourt's 1911 article, 'English Prosody': 'The principle which we deduce may be expressed thus: so long as the structure of a verse shows either in itself or in its context the number of accents which it ought to have and the places where they ought to fall, so long as the mind hears the implied accents in their places, the number and position of the accents which naturally occur is of no consequence' (*LN* ii 209).

What may seem like common sense to us was in fact a hard-won insight first expressed with full understanding in the Victorian period by Coventry *Patmore in an 1857 essay, 'English Metrical Critics' (*North British Review*). The simplicity of the insight is its virtue, in that it provides both for rule and variation, the rule which determines the number of accents within a given number of syllables, the variation which allows much flexibility in the placement of these accents. (The analogy to rule and variation in Gothic architecture is also made by Patmore and John Ruskin.)

Many important poetic developments were taking place in the 1860s as Hardy began his poetic career. *Tennyson was at the height of his reputation, *Browning and the Pre-Raphaelites were coming into prominence, and *Swinburne burst on the scene with his *Poems and Ballads.* Sonnet sequences were common; *Hymns Ancient and Modern* (1861) and Francis Child's *English and Scottish Ballads* (1859–) established the canon of hymns and ballads; the decade of the 1860s witnessed a great revival of imitations of classical metre. Palgrave's *Golden Treasury* (1861) became the most popular of all anthologies and was a major source for Hardy, from which he copied some of the entries for his poetic notebook, *Studies, Specimens &c.* (see NOTEBOOKS).

When Hardy began writing poetry in the 1860s, he explored the resources of various kinds of metrical line, and was fascinated by their 'ordered liberty'. His earliest surviving poem, 'Domicilium', is in Wordsworthian blank verse, but thereafter Hardy almost invariably preferred rhyming stanzaic verse. The line that most fascinated him at first was the rhyming iambic pentameter, employed in 27 sonnets written by 1901, and in other verse forms many of which Hardy invented. In 'She, to Him II', the woman complains that her lover might become for her merely 'A Thought—as I in your life seem to be!' The momentary awkwardness of adjusting the metre to the sense produces the following intonation: 'as I in *your* life *seem* to be!'—that is, as I in *your* life ('by comparison with you in *my* life') *seem* to be ('indeed my whole motive for saying any of this is that I seem to be nothing to you').

This capacity of the accentual-syllabic line to create dramatic emphasis fascinated Hardy through the next half-century and more of his verse writing. While experimenting with the pentameter line he was also intrigued by other line types, as in song stanzas, with their two-beat lyrical punctuation:

> I marked her ruined hues,
> Her custom-straitened views,
> And asked, 'Can there indwell
>   My Amabel?'

The comic musicality of the refrain cuts across the serious theme of the stanza, and evokes a wry Wessex song tradition. Sometimes, as in 'Postponement', the dimeter line punctuating the stanza evokes a very different tradition, that of classical sapphic verse with its dactylic-trochaic refrain line:

> Snow-bound in woodland, a mournful word,
> Dropt now and then from the bill of a bird,
> Reached me on wind-wafts; and thus I heard,
>   Wearily waiting...

Hardy also explored the staple resource of the iambic tetrameter and trimeter lines in his early ballads like 'The Dance at the Phoenix', written during the novel-writing years: 'Now Jenny's life had hardly been | A life of modesty...'. 'Módestý' reminds us of the potentially wrenched accent the ballad metre imposes on the plain language. Hardy eventually wrote over 150 poems in standard ballad or hymnal forms. Ballad rhythms can be shaped into rollicking trisyllabic dance rhythms, as in the early 'The Bride-Night Fire': 'They had long met o' Zundays—her true love and she— | And at junketings, maypoles, and flings...'. The trimeter lines can be stretched into long lines that unroll the meaning in a long drum roll, as in the early 'The Dawn after the Dance':

> And there stands your father's dwelling with its
>   blind bleak windows telling
> That the vows of man and maid are frail as filmy
>   gossamer.

This metrical experimentation achieves its finest early subtlety in 'Neutral Tones', which evokes both classical sapphic structure, with its concluding short line, and the ballad structure of tetrameter and trimeter, and its anapaestic potential:

> Since then, keen lessons that love deceives
> And wrings with wrong have shaped to me
> Your face, and the God-curst sun, and a tree,
>   And a pond edged with grayish leaves.

Again, the last two lines play with the counterpoint between metre and language to achieve their expressiveness:

> Your fáce, and the Gód-*curst* sun, and a trée,
>   And a pónd *edged* with gráyish léaves.

Here, 'curst' and 'edged' are engraved with emphasis by being 'extra', strongly stressed syllables in normally unaccented positions.

Thus, early in his career, Hardy had mastered the various metrical constituents of English poetry. What is interesting then to see is how Hardy combines and recombines them for expressive purposes. For example, in a series of poems, in increasingly complex ways, Hardy creates a journey rhythm through metrical means. 'My Cicely' was probably written in the latter half of Hardy's novel-writing career, and uses a conventional though somewhat exotic 'ghazal' stanza (using a recurrent rhyme) to convey the obsessive movement of the lover to capture his past love:

> I mounted a steed in the dawning,
> With acheful remembrance,
> And made for the ancient West Highway
> To far Exonb'ry.

This rhythm continuing through the poem establishes the basic irony of Hardy's journey poems, that they dramatize a movement that advances—into the past. This ironic theme, and expressive journey rhythm, is present in the famous 'Wessex Heights' with its *aabb* stanzas composed of seven-beat lines or traditional fourteeners:

> So I am found on Ingpen Beacon, or on Wylls-
> Neck to the west,
> Or else on homely Bulbarrow, or little Pilsdon
> Crest,
> Where men have never cared to haunt, nor
> women have walked with me,
> And ghosts then keep their distance; and I know
> some liberty.

The interest of 'Valenciennes', completed in 1897, the year after 'Wessex Heights', is that it brings together three metrical line types, the tetrameter, trimeter, and pentameter, to render the remembered movement of the soldiers in an old man's memory:

> We trenched, we trumpeted and drummed,
> And from our mortars tons of iron hummed
> Ath'art the ditch, the month we bombed
> The Town o' Valencieën.

Ten or more years later, Hardy writes 'Beyond the Last Lamp', where the expressive effect is achieved by the answering back and forth of falling and rising rhythms:

> Beyond the last lone lamp I passed
> Walking slowly, whispering sadly,
> Two linked loiterers, wan, downcast;
> Some heavy thought constrained each face
> And blinded them to time and place.

Only gradually do we realize that the 'I', th narrator, is one of the 'loiterers' he is watching, and that he is enacting an ancient memory, where the spell of the vision in fallin rhythm keeps crossing the waking consciousness of the present in rising rhythm.

And so it goes with these developing journey poems, with subtle effects achieved b new metrical means in *'Poems of 1912–13 such as 'The Phantom Horsewoman', 'After Journey' (with its intriguing dipodic rhythms), and many of the others enactin Hardy's real and imagined journey to th Cornwall of his past romance. Finally, abou 1917, Hardy writes 'The Five Students', whic uses five metrical line types (tetrameter, trimeter, pentameter, hexameter, and dimeter) t render the complicated advance-regressio of these figures in Hardy's life:

> The sparrow dips in his wheel-rut bath,
> The sun grows passionate-eyed,
> And boils the dew to smoke by the paddock
> path,
> As strenuously we stride,—
> Five of us, dark He, fair He, dark She, fair She, I
> All beating by.

The human advance turns into a horrifi Düreresque stasis, as the seasons advanc more subtly like the tortoise that overtake the frantic human striving.

We can see this kind of expressive metrica development at work in many other series o poems by Hardy, poems imitating the repetitive beating of the clock, or musical rhythms or the motions of storm and rain, or the pla of light and shadow.

Another aspect of the metrical scheme tha fascinated Hardy was its sheer abstraction, it way of freezing language in an a-tempora frame, but a frame that comes to look lik the stone permanence of a tombstone. Man of his early reviewers attacked the versification: 'His verse often halts or dances in hob nails' (quoted in Taylor, *Hardy's Metres an Victorian Prosody*, 199). They did not see th expressive and dramatic principle of the versification. Hardy said he kept 'quantities o notes on rhythm and metre, with outline and experiments in innumerable origina measures.... These verse skeletons wer mostly blank...' (*LW* 324). Hardy love 'verse skeletons', and their potential to ente into the drama of the poem. Thus, when h writes 'The Monument-Maker', the stanza form itself has the engraved visual status of a monumental design:

> I chiselled her monument
>   To my mind's content,
> Took it to the church by night,
> When her planet was at its height,
> And set it where I had figured the place in the
>   day-time.
>   Having niched it there
> I stepped back, cheered, and thought its outlines
>   fair,
>   And its marbles rare.

Hardy had little use for free verse, which he saw as a 'jumble of notes' (*L* vi 186). Nevertheless, he is an interesting bridge figure between traditional metrical verse and the era of free verse. His poems are not just aurally complex, they are visually complex. While he always maintained accentual-syllabic stanza forms, he moved toward poems composed in unique and complex stanzas increasingly conscious of their own visibility in the manner of the free-verse poem. (The visually complex 'Thoughts of Phena', at the beginning of his 1890s return to poetry, looks forward to these later poems.) The late poem 'Ice on the Highway' is interesting in that it consists of one unrepeated complex stanza form, and thus could almost be a William Carlos Williams poem. The difference is that the indentation indicates the line types, pentameter, trimeter, dimeter:

> Seven buxom women abreast, and arm in arm,
>   Trudge down the hill, tip-toed,
>   And breathing warm;
> They must perforce trudge thus, to keep upright
>   On the glassy ice-bound road,
> And they must get to market whether or no,
>   Provisions running low
>   With the nearing Saturday night,
> While the lumbering van wherein they mostly
>   ride
> Can nowise go:
> Yet loud their laughter as they stagger and slide!

Also in this poem, Hardy takes the next step in his journey-rhythm poems and creates a visual equivalent of motion in the verse form.

Hardy wrote poems in more metrical forms than any other major English poet, indeed perhaps than any other poet. For about 1,093 poems, he used almost 800 different metrical forms. He invented more verse forms than any other poet in the accentual-syllabic tradition: over 620 stanza forms. His poetry is also full of imitations of other verse forms, over 170 of them. A glossary of his metrical borrowings serves as a comprehensive guide to the English metrical tradition. Thus W. H. *Auden said of Hardy that 'no English poet, not even Donne or Browning, employed so many and so complicated stanza forms. Anyone who imitates his style will learn at least one thing, how to make words fit into a complicated structure and also, if he is sensitive to such things, much about the influence of form upon content' ('A Literary Transference', *Southern Review*, 1940). DT

Dennis Taylor, *Hardy's Metres and Victorian Prosody* (1988).

Mill, John Stuart (1806–73), philosopher and economist. Hardy claimed to have known Mill's *On Liberty* 'almost by heart' in the 1860s (*LW* 355), and he listed 'Of Individuality' as one of his 'cures for despair' in 1868 (*LW* 59). Perhaps because Hardy was so familiar with Mill's ideas, he felt no need to copy much from him into his *Literary Notebooks*, where there are only two brief entries from Mill (*LN* i 172, ii 40) and one from a review of Leslie Stephen's biography of him (*LN* ii 357–8). Mill, however, inspired Hardy in several ways, particularly through his rejection of Nature as a moral guide and through his exposition and dissemination of *Positivism, although Hardy preferred Mill's more individualistically oriented psychology (*LN* i 132). Mill's criticism of Christian self-denial and promotion of pagan self-assertion is also likely to have struck a chord in Hardy: see, for instance, Hardy's copying and underlining of the observation on 'the virtue of Paganism in making a virtue of joy', quoted in a review in 1892 (*LN* ii 55). The entry is echoed in *Jude the Obscure* as Sue laments in her retrospective view of her and Jude's pagan revolt against society, a revolt she thinks ironically led to the death of their children: '"We said . . . that we would make a virtue of joy"' (*JO* 6.2). Perhaps Hardy's best-known artistic use of Mill's ideas is found in Sue's impassioned evocation of Mill in her plea to Phillotson to set her free: '"She, or he, 'who lets the world, or his own portion of it, choose his plan of life for him, has no need of any other faculty than the ape-like one of imitation'. J. S. Mill's words, those are..."' (see also a quotation from *On Liberty* in *JO* 4.3). LAB

Milton, John (1608–74), poet. Hardy had a close familiarity with Milton's verse and prose writings, and quotes from them freely in his own fiction and poetry (see list in F. B. Pinion, *A Hardy Companion* (1968), 211). His copy of Milton (now in DCM) has interesting markings and annotations. Though Miltonic allusions are to be found in his work as early as *Desperate Remedies*, they are particularly numerous in his later work, especially *Tess of the d'Urbervilles*, *Jude the Obscure*, and *The Dynasts*. The last of these was conceived as an epic-drama, and at an early stage Hardy reread Milton, the most important epic poet in English (see *LW* 212). In a letter of 20 February 1908 (quoted *LW* 492) he links Milton's name and his own: 'like *Paradise Lost*, *The Dynasts* proves nothing'. Joan Grundy, however, has argued that it is *Tess* rather than *The Dynasts* that is Hardy's *Paradise Lost*, and has noted in this novel a number of direct or indirect allusions to Milton's epic: among others, Alec d'Urberville, the heroine's tempter, is explicitly compared to Milton's Satan, and Tess herself is compared to Eve (50), while the closing words of the novel may echo those of the poem.

In *Jude the Obscure* it is Milton's prose, and specifically his pamphlet *The Doctrine and Discipline of Divorce*, that is more in evidence than his poetry: the pamphlet provides the epigraph for Part Fourth of this novel, and a sentence from it ('Milton's wormwood words') is adapted in the final two lines of Hardy's poem 'Lausanne: In Gibbon's Old Garden: 11–12 p.m.', dated 27 June 1897. Another poem, 'A Philosophical Fantasy', first published in the *Fortnightly Review* in January 1927, has an epigraph from Walter Bagehot, 'Milton . . . made God argue'.

Elsewhere, it is clear that Hardy thought of himself as a fellow-sufferer of Milton and other writers who had been persecuted or reviled for truth-telling: referring to the hostile reception of *Jude*, and specifically to its condemnation by Bishop W. W. *How, he writes that 'Shelley, Milton, and many others of the illustrious, reaching all the way back to the days of Protagoras, had undergone the same sort of indignity at the hands of bigotry and intolerance' (*LW* 294). In a speech given on 16 November 1910 (see SPEECHES), he quotes from Milton's pamphlet on the freedom of the press, *Areopagitica*. On 10 July 1908 Hardy attended the Milton tercentenary celebrations in Cambridge, and saw a performance of *Comus* in which one of the actors was the young Rupert Brooke.

Joan Grundy, 'Hardy and Milton', *THA* 1 (1985).

Mistress of the Farm, The. See DRAMATIZATIONS.

Moments of Vision. Hardy's fifth collection of verse, was published by *Macmillan in an edition of 3,000 copies on 30 November 1917, almost exactly three years after *Satires of Circumstance*, and five years to the day after the funeral of Emma *Hardy. The manuscript had been sent to the publisher on 21 August. With 159 poems, it contains more than any of his other volumes of verse. Nine poems had appeared for the first time in Hardy's **Selected Poems* in the previous year; apart from these, only six had seen earlier publication. After Hardy's death the manuscript was given, by his request, to Magdalene College, Cambridge.

As Purdy points out (207), most of the contents appear to have been written between 1913 and 1916—that is, in the period immediately following the death of Emma, memories of whom dominate the collection. These years, which saw both his second marriage and the outbreak of the *First World War, were clearly a highly creative period for Hardy. Only five poems are definitely known to belong to earlier phases of his life before the turn of the century. Apart from a group of 'Poems of War and Patriotism' near the end, *Moments of Vision* is, then, for the most part a highly personal collection. Hardy was 77 when it was published and the poems reveal him reflecting on the past—not only on Emma but on his family, his childhood, his friends, and Time itself—in a persistent endeavour to trace patterns in the experiences of a long lifetime. To this extent the volume represents a process that was to be continued in the *autobiography, work on which was begun at about this time.

Poems based on memories of his family include 'Logs on the Hearth', one of several tributes to his sister Mary, dated December 1915 (she had died on 24 November), and 'To My Father's Violin', dated 1916. (Mary Hardy is also the subject of the hauntingly rhythmical 'Molly Gone'; her initials are appended to another poem of 1915, 'In the Garden'; and her name is linked with those of Hardy's two wives in 'Conjecture'.) Both of these exemplify a recurring feature in Hardy's recreations of the past, whereby specific individuals or experiences are evoked through inanimate objects associated with them. That the objects have survived their original users is often an underlying or even explicit irony. In 'Logs on the Hearth' the fire consumes wood from an apple-tree that Hardy and his dead sister climbed as children: the logs are known almost as intimately as the faces of old friends, and are also texts on which remembered history is inscribed ('Where the bark chars is where, one year, I It was pruned and bled . . .'). In this and many other poems the effect of reliving memories with such circumstantial precision is to call up a ghost. 'The Sunshade' works similarly but more speculatively, linking the discarded object with its unknown but possibly dead owner, who, like the writer's dead sister ('her young brown hand awave'), is depicted in sharp physical detail ('Little thumb standing against its stem'). 'Old Furniture' is another poem that finely expresses deep feelings for dead forebears through apparently commonplace, even banal objects: the living hands grasping the drawer-handles of some humble item of furniture long in the family are in intimate proximity to the skeleton or ghostly hands of former users.

Some of the poems of childhood relate to the Hardy family's Christian faith and observances, and Hardy's own subsequent loss of belief. 'Afternoon Service at Mellstock' has, by anticipation, a curiously Betjemanesque flavour: beginning in a tone that blends affectionate nostalgia with wry detachment, it concludes with an entirely serious questioning of the value of a lifetime's earnest intellectual struggles. Its subtitle ('Circa 1850') places it firmly in Hardy's childhood, and its metrical form is appropriately, if also ironically, hymn-like. A better-known poem, 'The Oxen', uses a legend Hardy had heard from his mother, and had alluded to earlier in *Tess of the d'Urbervilles* (17) to point a similar contrast between early faith and subsequent scepticism; the final stanza poignantly conveys the wish to believe in the face of firm intellectual convictions to the contrary.

There is evidence, too, of a continuing preoccupation with family history and especially with the sense, explored in the late tragic novels, of inherited characteristics (see HEREDITY), and of the exhaustion or extinction of a family line. The temptation to read 'She, I, and They' as a direct autobiographical statement ought to be resisted, but it may well express Hardy's regrets (not to put it more strongly) that he and his siblings were all childless (he was in fact the only one of the four to marry). More positively, 'Heredity' presents family resemblances as constituting a kind of immortality.

Two poems about dead friends—and it might be said both that most of Hardy's poems of friendship are about the dead, and that by this date a large proportion of Hardy's friends had died—re-create scenes from the past, sometimes in precise and pictorial detail, without being specific about the individuals concerned. 'During Wind and Rain' is one of the finest of all Hardy's poems, striking in its series of contrasting images and exceptionally intense in its language. The other, 'The Five Students', names no names, but identifications of all but one of the four (Hardy himself is the fifth) can be confidently made: 'dark He' is Horace *Moule, 'dark She' Helen Holder (sister of Emma Hardy), 'fair She' is Emma herself, but 'fair He' remains a puzzle, though various candidates have been proposed. 'The Last Signal', on the other hand, is an unambiguous tribute to William *Barnes which, like so much else in this volume, embodies the spirit of its title by communicating a particular instant of experience through a sharply focused visual image. Less powerfully than these, 'The Pink Frock' and 'In Her Precincts' refer to women who played minor roles in Hardy's life (respectively, Marcia, Lady Yarborough, and a niece of Julia Augusta *Martin).

An unusually ecstatic and uncomplicated view of love is expressed in the modest but engaging 'First Sight of Her and After', which F. B. Pinion dates with proper tentativeness as 'probably' a poem of March 1870 (*Commentary on the Poems of Thomas Hardy*

(1976), 123), when Hardy returned from his first visit to *Cornwall and his first encounter with Emma. If this dating can be accepted, this poem of return forms an attractive counterpart to the equally attractive and equally enchanted poem of departure, 'When I Set Out for Lyonnesse', in Hardy's previous collection. In simple but at the same time innovative language ('moonshades on the way', 'Sky-glancing travellers'), it exquisitely catches the lover's sense of privilege in breathing a purer air than folk to whom it 'Has been a common day'. More characteristic, however, is the Swithin's Day poem, 'We Sat at the Window', subtitled '*Bournemouth, 1875*' and hence belonging to a date less than a year after his marriage to Emma. The sense of an opportunity missed is intensified by the implications of bad weather on St Swithin's Day (see CALENDAR): the omens are that the failure of understanding, like the rain, will long continue. Another poem of failure and disappointment in love, though this time the incident is probably fictitious, is 'At the Wicket-Gate'.

It is Emma Hardy who, by a very considerable margin, dominates *Moments of Vision*. The great sequence of elegies titled *'Poems of 1912–13' and published in *Satires of Circumstance*, though it includes the most familiar of the poems inspired by her death, represents only a fraction of Hardy's sustained creative response to this landmark in his emotional life. The outpouring of poems of grief, regret, and memory in the immediate aftermath of Emma's death continued for several years, and both the length of *Moments of Vision* and its rapid production attest to a preoccupation that bordered on obsession. Here again he returns in memory to the scenes of their early days together, though rarely if ever in a simple vein of comforting reminiscence: 'Near Lanivet, 1872' recalls a disturbing premonitory incident of their courtship to depict an Emma 'crucified', and there is more than a hint of guilt in the words Hardy puts into her mouth: '"If no one is bodily crucified now, | In spirit one may be!"' 'The Figure in the Scene' and 'Why Did I Sketch' both have appended to them the phrase '*From an old note*', seemingly as a guarantee of their autobiographical status; the sketch to which they refer survives and bears the date 22 August 1870—that is, in the course of the very happy three-week holiday Hardy spent in Cornwall, during which the couple reached an understanding that they would eventually marry. The former poem makes explicit the recurring association of Emma with specific places, notably in Cornwall, that possess for Hardy the potency of ingredients in a private myth: she is 'the Genius still of the spot' that, after the single unforgettable occasion, she has never revisited.

Not all of the poems referring to Emma go so far back in time, however. The spirit of place is again in evidence in 'Old Excursions', where the place-names seem to indicate the period after the couple settled at Max Gate. In 'Something Tapped' (dated August 1913, some nine months after her death) the brushing of a moth against a window-pane creates the momentary illusion of a ghostly visitation. 'An Upbraiding' grants the dead woman, self-punishingly on Hardy's part, a reproachful voice. 'Paths of Former Time' seems to embody, as F. B. Pinion suggests, recollections of 'walks with Emma Hardy in the Frome meadows between Max Gate and Stinsford' (*Commentary on the Poems of Thomas Hardy*, 154). 'Conjecture' characteristically speculates on the way in which different chances and choices would radically have altered his life and, perhaps a little unexpectedly, places Emma in the company of his second wife, Florence, and his sister Mary. Other Emma-centred poems, too numerous to list here, abound.

It is important to remember that, since their relationship had extended over more than 40 years, in contemplating the life and death of his first wife Hardy was also subjecting to review and reflection the greater part of his own existence. If love is one of his major poetic themes, time is another, as a poem that stands second in the collection makes clear. The three stanzas of 'The Voice of Things' record three visits to the same spot at intervals of twenty years; the unstated scene is Cornwall, and the first visit is evidently that of August 1870 (referred to above), the second a fictitious one at the time of his soured marriage-relationship, the third after Emma's death.

The pathetic fallacy (something of an addiction for Hardy) is evident in the contrast between the first two linguistically audacious tanzas: at first 'The waves huzza'd like a nultitude below', but later he 'heard the vaters wagging in a long ironic laughter'. 'In . Museum', on the other hand, presents a osmic rather than a personal view of time: wo distinct experiences, the sight of the fossilized remains of an extinct bird (and by mplication its long-silent song), and the ound of the 'contralto voice I heard last ight', are almost surrealistically blended n a single 'full-fugued song'. It is highly haracteristic of Hardy that what may seem n extravagant, almost Metaphysical fancy hould actually have a scientific basis, and he famous cliff-hanging scene in *A Pair of Blue Eyes*, with its image of time closing up like a fan', comes to mind as an analogue to his poem. On a more human scale, but still cientifically conceived, time in relation to he history of families is the subject of 'Herdity' (already referred to), while 'Transormations' places human life in the context f the earth's chemical cycle. (We have Hardy's word for it that the scene is Stinsford hurchyard.) Time takes on a more deeply ersonal dimension, however, in 'At Middle-'ield Gate in February', where boyhood nemories of joyful activity are contrasted vith a present in which the poet seems the nly survivor of 'a bevy now underground'.

Hardy's preoccupation in this volume, and enerally in his verse and prose, with memries of the dead and with their ghostly nanifestations is by no means confined to Emma. His poems are themselves like hurchyards in that the dead tend to outumber the living, and many of the poems lready cited touch on the sense of the dead s felt presences sometimes so powerful as to mount to a kind of haunting. 'On a Midummer Eve' describes three acts of unconcious invocation to the ghost of Emma; the upposed occasion is one traditionally assoiated with the supernatural, and there are lso references to ancient superstitions. 'A anuary Night', apparently based on an exerience of 1879, when the Hardys were living n Tooting, is less personal and less concluive, but is noteworthy for the precision and ividness of its largely monosyllabic diction 'The east wind snarls and sneezes'). In 'I Travel as a Phantom Now' Hardy has himself ecome a ghost before his death (a recurring dea in his last years): somewhat unexpectedly, this brief poem of 1915 touches on his most radical philosophical ideas (wondering whether 'Man's consciousness | Was a mistake of God's'), and then, a further surprise, undergoes a transformation of mood to something like joy in its final allusion to human life (and, possibly, a specific reference to his feelings for Florence *Henniker).

Many of the poems referred to, and many others, convey ideas about love, death, and time partly or even largely through visual images—a feature of which the title of this collection provides fair warning. With Hardy, poems that are primarily concerned to express general ideas can at the same time accommodate cinematic close-ups of the observed world: 'At Middle-Field Gate in February', already discussed, establishes in its fifteen lines the familiar and interconnected antitheses between past and present, youth and old age, summer and winter, joy and sorrow, life and death, but still finds room for a delicately detailed account of a foggy day when the mist condensing on a five-barred gate forms droplets 'Like silver buttons ranged in a row, | And as evenly spaced as if measured...'. Such details are not merely decorative, since the inclement weather is part of a pattern of season-symbolism. 'The Ageing House' presents similar antitheses through the contrasting images of a house once new and later decayed.

The concept of 'images' takes on a more precise significance in many poems in which some such representation as a drawing, painting, or photograph is the medium through which the past is preserved and becomes an ingredient of the present. The 'portraits of our fore-folk... Framed and glazed' constitute the third party in 'She, I, and They', in which the emotions of the dead seem to have, through their visual presence, equal currency with those of the living.

'The Photograph' is a more puzzling and more disturbing poem: though Hardy identified the scene as Max Gate (and thereby implicitly acknowledged a factual basis), neither the date nor the woman concerned is known. The speaker, engaged in 'a casual clearance of life's arrears', destroys the long-preserved picture of a woman with whom he has presumably once had a close relationship, but of whom he now knows nothing, not even whether she is alive or dead. But the 'casual' act suddenly acquires significance, and he utters 'a cry of hurt', as he observes the process of destruction: there is not only Hardy's habitual voyeurism but something erotic and even sadistic in the speaker's watching 'furtivewise | Till the flame had eaten her breasts, and mouth, and hair'. The simple act of burning an old photograph has become a kind of homicide. As often, Hardy seems to be able to experience a more fully liberated and fully articulated relationship with a representation or icon than with a living reality.

Other poems with a photographic motif include 'The Rival', an ironic monologue by a female speaker, and 'Looking at a Picture on an Anniversary', addressed to Emma a few months after her death. As already noted, 'The Figure in the Scene' and 'Why Did I Sketch' revive memories of the distant past through the medium of one of Hardy's own drawings, while, much more impersonally, the moral tale 'The Enemy's Portrait' concerns a painting. Other visual representations are to be found in mirrors and even waxworks ('At Madame Tussaud's in Victorian Years').

To return to our starting-point: in these poems of his old age Hardy can be constantly detected in the process, common enough among elderly folk who are not great poets, of trying to come to terms with the past, of reviving in memory and bringing together experiences separated by long tracts of time, and of seeking to discern pattern and significance in the seeming chaos of deeds, thoughts, and emotions. The patterned structure of a poem such as 'The Voice of Things' is one way of imposing pattern on the fluidity of experience, and revisiting was one of Hardy's favourite gambits both in his life and in his art—one of the reasons for the dualistic structure of so many of his poems. Like the *Wordsworth of (for example) 'A slumber did my spirit seal', Hardy habitually invites us to compare what was with what is and to draw our own conclusions. The repeated phrases 'Show me again...' and 'Love lures life on' that open and close each stanza of the 'Lines to a Movement in Mozart's E-Flat Symphony' are another kind of patterning, designed with a similar purpose. The very precisely dated 'Apostrophe to an Old Psalm Tune' ('*Sunday, 13 August 1916*') creates a sense of the changing phases of a life through a more linear structure.

Moments of Vision, a highly personal collection reflecting an intensely felt private history, contains near its end a group of seventeen 'Poems of War and Patriotism' that reflect the momentous public history of the years during which most of the contents of the volume were written. The majority bear dates ranging from the autumn of 1914 (war had broken out on 4 August of that year) to 1916, and some are highly topical, as titles like 'On the Belgian Expatriation' indicate. The best-known is 'In Time of "The Breaking of Nations"', which seems to have originated at the time of the Franco-Prussian War in 1870. (Hardy cites it in his autobiography (*LW* 408) as a striking example of his 'faculty... for burying an emotion in my heart or brain for forty years, and exhuming it at the end of that time as fresh as when interred'—an observation whose metaphors provide food for thought.) Its three economically expressed vignettes of timeless human activities insist on the primacy of private over public histories: 'Though Dynasties pass', the lives of the obscure persist over uncounted generations. Less familiar, but worth mention, is 'The Pity of It' (a title that seems to anticipate the war poems of Wilfred Owen), which in April 1915, when fighting on the Western Front was at its height, offers a quiet reminder that, ethnologically and linguistically, Germans and British are brothers, 'kin folk kin tongued' (see PHILOLOGY); also 'Then and Now', in which Hardy's lifelong infatuation with the *Napoleonic Wars leads him to reflect on modern warfare as something entirely different from the time 'When battles were fought | With a chivalrous sense of Should and Ought'. Such poems remind us that *Moments of Vision* was a wartime publication; as with his earlier poems about the *Boer War, Hardy's poetic voice speaks quietly but firmly, in very different tones from the hearty and clamorous jingoism that characterizes much of the once popular poetry concerned with the same events.

Moore, George (1852–1933), Anglo-Irish novelist whose work was influenced by French realist fiction. His *Esther Waters* (1894) was provocatively compared with Hardy's *Life's Little Ironies* by William

*Archer: on the relationship of Moore's novel to Hardy's *Tess*, see REALISM.

Hardy met Moore at the home of Edmund *Gosse, and a marked and enduring hostility, both literary and personal, developed between the two novelists. In his *Conversations in Ebury Street* (1924), Moore launched a bitter attack on Hardy's use of language as well as his status as a living classic; his strictures are especially directed against *Tess of the d'Urbervilles*. Hardy was angered as well as upset by the attack: thanking J. M. *Murry for defending him in an article in the *Adelphi*, he remarked that 'Somebody once called [Moore] a putrid literary hermaphrodite, which I thought funny, but it may have been an exaggeration' (28 March 1924: *L* vi 242–3). Unforgiving to the last, Hardy dictated on his deathbed a squib attacking Moore ('Epitaph for George Moore: On one who thought no other could write such English as himself'). (See also CHARACTERIZATION.)

Morgan, Charles (1894–1958), novelist, dramatist, and critic. He went to Oxford belatedly in 1919, and, as Manager (subsequently President) of the Oxford University Dramatic Society, was one of those who in December 1919 invited Hardy to attend a production of scenes from *The Dynasts*. With his wife, Hardy travelled to Oxford by train on 9 February 1920, the University conferring on him the honorary degree of Doctor of Letters during the same visit. For Morgan's long and interesting account of the visit, written in 1929 at the request of Florence Hardy for inclusion in the second volume of her 'biography', see *LW* 524–8. Morgan saw Hardy again when they both attended a dramatization of *Desperate Remedies* in Dorchester. As the official historian of the publishing firm of Macmillan, Morgan later described Hardy's relationship with the firm in *The House of Macmillan (1843–1943)* (1943).

Morris, Mowbray (1847–1911), editor of *Macmillan's Magazine* from 1885 to 1907. In this capacity he was responsible for the serial publication of *The Woodlanders*. Hardy's manuscript was subjected to an editorial censorship that, though it was not extensive, Hardy seems to have found irksome: on Morris's tactful but firm letter of advice (19 September 1886) 'not to bring the fair Miss Suke [Damson] to too open shame', see CENSORSHIP. With Frederick *Macmillan, Morris was responsible for choosing the title of the novel from the options submitted by Hardy: since the alternative offered was *Fitzpiers at Hintock*, their taste can only be applauded. Morris was later one of those who turned down *Tess of the d'Urbervilles* (*LW* 232). His generally unfavourable review of *Tess* in the prestigious *Quarterly* (April 1892: repr. in *CH*) wounded Hardy, and prompted the well-known response, '"if this sort of thing continues no more novel-writing for me"' (*LW* 259).

Moule, Horace (1832–73), fourth son of the Reverend Henry Moule (see next entry), was probably the most intimate of all Hardy's male friends, exerted a profound influence on Hardy's early development, and for a considerable time served as a role-model. Moule had studied at both Oxford (Trinity College, 1851–4) and Cambridge (Queens' College, to 1858) but for reasons that are not entirely clear had left both universities without a degree, graduating from Cambridge belatedly in 1867. Despite this unconventional academic record, he had in 1858 won a Cambridge prize for his dissertation on *Christian Oratory*, and had published a book on *The Roman Republic* (1860).

From 1857, despite the social and educational gulf between them as well as the eight-year age-gap, he and Hardy were close friends, and Moule took a strong interest in Hardy's reading, lending or giving him books—including, for example, in 1857, Jabez Hogg's *Elements of Experimental and Natural Philosophy*; in 1858, G. A. Mantell's *The Wonders of Geology*; and, in 1865, Comte's *General View of Positivism*. He also encouraged Hardy to read the controversial *Essays and Reviews* (1860), and introduced him to the *Saturday Review*. In Hardy's own words, Moule was 'always ready to act the tutor in any classical difficulty' (*LW* 38), and his role in relation to the young man whose formal education had ceased some time earlier seems to have been a combination of older brother, teacher, and friend. As well as being a gifted classical scholar, Moule was interested in music and poetry, wrote poems himself, and gave Hardy copies of Palgrave's

Golden Treasury and a translation of Goethe's *Faust*. He also gave him the crucial advice to abandon the study of Greek, and his hopes of a university career, and to persist with his architectural training. After Hardy's move to London, guidance continued to be sought and given through correspondence and occasional meetings. Hardy's earliest surviving letter (17 August 1862), written from Kilburn to his sister Mary, mentions Moule, recording a visit from his friend during which they attended a service at the Jesuit chapel in Farm Street.

Moule sought to make a career as a journalist and reviewer for the London periodicals while living for a time at home and supporting himself as a private tutor. But he suffered from bouts of serious depression, and by 1860, when he took a job as a tutor in Salisbury, there is evidence that he was drinking heavily and also taking opium. For a time (1865–8) he was a master at Marlborough College, and towards the end of his life he became an assistant Poor Law inspector for East Anglia (1872), living at this time in his Cambridge college. He had earlier become a contributor to the progressive and lively *Saturday Review*, founded in 1855, and later published there reviews of both *Desperate Remedies* (30 September 1871: repr. in *CH*) and *Under the Greenwood Tree* (28 September 1872: repr. in *CH*).

Moule also gave private encouragement to Hardy's early attempts at writing. At his suggestion, Hardy sent the manuscript of *The Poor Man and the Lady* to Alexander Macmillan on 25 July 1868, Moule providing a letter of introduction. The character of Henry Knight, the literary journalist in *A Pair of Blue Eyes*, seems to be partly based on Moule; Knight's patronizing attitude towards the socially inferior Stephen Smith may well reflect Hardy's awareness, and even resentment, of a similar attitude on the part of Moule.

Hardy's last meeting with Moule was when he visited him in Cambridge, and stayed as his guest at Queens' College, on 20–1 June 1873. Exactly three months after their final parting, on 21 September 1873, Moule committed suicide in his Cambridge rooms. There had been earlier indications of a suicidal disposition, and Moule's bouts of heavy drinking may have led him to fear he would lose his job. It seems, too, that the governess to whom he was engaged had recently broken off their relationship. Hardy heard the news of his friend's suicide on the 24th, and attended his funeral at Fordington two days later. The poem 'Before My Friend Arrived' describes a visit to the freshly dug grave on the eve of the funeral.

Outside his poetry, Hardy's published references to Moule are brief and restrained, but he always kept by his bedside the copy of *The Thoughts of the Emperor Aurelius Antonius* that Moule had given him on New Year's Day, 1865. In October 1922 the *London Mercury* published a note by Hardy written to accompany the reprinting of one of Moule's poems, 'Ave Caesar', originally published 60 years earlier, in 1862; in this note Hardy suggests that Moule possessed the potentiality to become 'a distinguished English poet'.

Other poems referring to Moule include 'An Experience', in which he is referred to as 'my friend' (a title not lightly bestowed by Hardy), and the early sonnet 'A Confession to a Friend in Trouble', dated 1866, which poignantly expresses Hardy's concern over Moule's problems, and his sense of guilt over wishing to avoid further knowledge of them. Moule is also the 'dark He' of 'The Five Students'. Most enigmatically, and perhaps most hauntingly, of all, 'Standing by the Mantelpiece' appears to refer to Moule's prediction of his own death in the course of Hardy's last visit; it has been suggested that this poem also implies Moule's confession of homosexual feelings towards Hardy, and the latter's rejection of them, though such an interpretation remains purely speculative.

A long-delayed addition to Moule's tragic history was provided by a story told by Hardy's widow, according to which Moule had had an affair with a girl of the Dorchester slums who was well-known for her promiscuity; she had become pregnant, had emigrated to Australia, and had borne a son who was eventually hanged. The story presumably came from Hardy himself, and may well have suggested elements in the plot of *Jude the Obscure*. The early poem 'She at His Funeral' may also be associated with this story.

Moule family. The Reverend Henry Moule (1801–80) was Vicar of Fordington, on the outskirts of *Dorchester, for more than 50 years, from 1829 until his death. In a letter (11 February 1880: *L* i 70) written to Moule's youngest son shortly after his father's death, Hardy expresses his great admiration for the late vicar, and states that he always regarded himself as one of his parishioners. In a later letter, to Florence Henniker (25 February 1900: *L* ii 248), he indicates that Moule was to some extent the model for Angel Clare's father in *Tess of the d'Urbervilles.* It seems likely, too, that Clare's clerical brothers owe something to Moule's clergymen-sons.

A man of strong convictions and great energy, Moule threw himself into a variety of causes ranging from the immorality of his rural parish to the low standard of church music, and was widely unpopular until his courage and practical assistance during a cholera epidemic in 1854 turned him, as Robert Gittings has said, into a kind of folk-hero (*Young Thomas Hardy,* 36). The protagonist of Hardy's story 'A Changed Man' is based on Moule, and the story closely follows the historical circumstances of the epidemic. Moule's interest in sanitary reform led him to invent and patent the 'dry earth system' of sewage disposal, which was widely adopted. Among his many publications on a variety of topics, the most notable is a series of eight letters prompted by the cholera epidemic, and originally sent to the Prince Consort.

By his wife Mary, Moule had seven sons, as follows:

(1) Henry (1825–1904) was an antiquary who became curator of the Dorset County Museum. When he died, Hardy reflected that their friendship reached 'much further back than that of any person now alive'; the same letter includes a description of the funeral, which Hardy attended (to Arthur Moule, 20 February 1904: *L* iii 114–16). To Edward *Clodd, Hardy wrote that Moule's death terminated a friendship extending over 47 years, and described him as 'a man whose opinions differed almost entirely from my own on most subjects: & yet he was a good and sincere friend' (22 March 1904: *L* iii 117).

(2) George (1828–1912) became the first Anglican Bishop of Mid-China. Hardy was prevented by illness from attending his consecration in St Paul's Cathedral in 1880.

(3) Frederick (1830–1900) also became a clergyman.

(4) Horatio (Horace): see previous entry.

(5) Charles (1834–1921) became a tutor and later President of Corpus Christi College, Cambridge.

(6) Arthur (1836–1918), like George, became a missionary in China. Hardy declined an invitation to review his book *New China and Old* (1891).

(7) Handley (1841–1920) became Bishop of Durham. When his *Dorchester Poems* appeared in 1878, he sent a copy to Hardy; later Hardy read with pleasure his account of his Fordington childhood in *Memories of a Vicarage* (1913). Handley is probably the 'religious man' referred to in an interesting letter to Florence Henniker on the subject of the Boer War (25 February 1900: *L* ii 248).

Murry, John Middleton (1889–1957), critic and editor, and one of Hardy's circle of younger friends during his final years. On 7 November 1919 he published in the *Athenaeum,* of which he was the influential editor (1919–21), a highly eulogistic review of the first volume of Hardy's *Collected Poems* ('Mr Hardy stands high above all other modern poets...'), singling out for special praise the *'Poems of 1912–13'. On 9 December 1920 Hardy sent him his poem 'At the Entering of the New Year' for publication in the *Athenaeum.* On 28 March 1924 (*L* vi 243) he expressed his gratitude to Murry for attacking George *Moore's criticisms of Hardy in his *Conversations in Ebury Street.* (Murry's comments are contained in a review published in the April number of the *Adelphi,* and reprinted later in the year in a limited edition of 500 copies as *Wrap Me Up in My Aubusson Carpet.*) In the last weeks of Hardy's life, he was instrumental, through Edmund *Gosse, in obtaining a grant from the Prime Minister for Murry, who was in financial difficulties.

In 1918 Murry married Kathleen Mansfield Beauchamp (1888–1923), the New Zealand short-story writer better known under the pseudonym Katherine Mansfield. She shared her husband's enthusiasm for Hardy's poetry, and her *Journal* (1927) contains references to her reading of it. After Murry had visited Hardy in May 1921, he reported to her that Hardy had read her volume *Bliss, and Other Stories* (1920), and particularly wished her to know of his admiration for 'The Daughters of the Late Colonel'.

music. Hardy's lifelong interest in music was inherited. In introducing the reader to himself and his family in his autobiography (*LW* 17–21), he dwells extensively on his father's musical accomplishments and the family's musical traditions. He also mentions his mother's interest in folksong and in watching her children practise on a piano that she herself felt frustrated at being unable to play. In the poem 'A Church Romance', his parents' relationship is reported—somewhat idealistically, as the title seems to acknowledge—as arising out of a musical attraction.

In introducing himself, Hardy mentions his precocious interest in reading, but music comes a close second. He explains that he was 'able to tune a violin when of quite tender years. He was of ecstatic temperament, extraordinarily sensitive to music, and among the endless jigs, hornpipes, reels, waltzes, and country-dances that his father played of an evening in his early married years, and to which the boy danced a *pas seul* in the middle of the room, there were three or four that always moved the child to tears, though he strenuously tried to hide them' (*LW* 19). The situation evoked in his poem 'The Self-Unseeing', where the child dances to his father's accompaniment while his mother looks on, closely corresponds to that described here. (The poem 'To My Father's Violin' recalls the instrument itself and its past performances.) The same passage in the *Life* goes on to name several of the tunes in question: one of them, 'Miss Macleod of Ayr' ('an old Scotch tune to which Burns may have danced'), is the 'quaint little tune' to which Donald Farfrae dances so energetically with Elizabeth-Jane in *The Mayor of Casterbridge* (16).

The poem 'One We Knew', written in 1902 in memory of his paternal grandmother, places foremost among her remembered narratives the reminiscences of her dancing days in the late 18th century (she was born in 1772), with which she would regale the eager ears of the young Hardy:

> She told how they used to form for the
> country dances—
> 'The Triumph', 'The New-Rigged Ship'—
> To the light of the guttering wax in the
> panelled manses,
> And in cots to the blink of a dip.
>
> She spoke of the wild 'poussetting' and
> 'allemanding'
> On carpet, on oak, and on sod...

Hardy also learned to play the violin and in 1852 began to accompany his father to local festivities and to take part in the music-making: on one occasion, when he was 'thirteen or fourteen', an anxious hostess had to bring his playing to a halt through fear that his sustained performance might cause him to '"burst a bloodvessel"' (*LW* 28). Nearly 70 years later, hearing an anthem by Croft sung in Exeter Cathedral, Hardy felt that he would have liked to have been a cathedral organist more than anything else in the world (*LW* 434).

Hardy was deeply familiar with a wide range of folk music, both songs and dances. His interest in transcribing folksongs (*LW* 86) was considerably in advance of the English folksong revival, and his knowledge and enthusiasm were deeply rooted, for he had been from childhood steeped in the tradition of such music, the incidents, textures, patterns, and associations of which often play a significant and even a central role in his narratives. In *Far from the Madding Crowd* Troy leaves Fanny to the accompaniment of 'The Girl I Left Behind Me' (10); 'The Soldier's Joy' is performed appropriately at the Harvest Supper (36); and 'Jockey to the Fair' is twice associated with Gabriel Oak (6, 8), who is himself a musician accomplished enough to earn money by his flute-playing. In *The Woodlanders* Suke Damson sings a snatch of 'The Foggy Foggy Dew' to entice Fitzpiers into a nocturnal meeting (20), and Tess's seduction (*TDU* 11) is accompanied by the same meteorological conditions and folkloric associations.

Lists of dances are not uncommon in his work, as in the story 'The Romantic Adventures of a Milkmaid' and the poem 'The Dance at the Phoenix', the latter specifying 'the throbbing "Soldier's Joy"', as well as '"Fancy-Lad"' and '"Maiden Coy"'. Nor is there any doubt in this poem, and even more particularly in such stories as 'The Fiddler of the Reels' and 'The History of the Hardcomes', of his awareness that sexual passion could readily be aroused by such dances. Another story, 'Absent-Mindedness in a Parish Choir' (included, like 'The History of the Hardcomes', in the sequence 'A Few Crusted Characters'), has the befuddled musicians, with unwitting blasphemy, play the dance-tune 'The Devil Among the Tailors' in the middle of the church service.

The dances with which he became familiar during his early years in London are recalled in the 'Reminiscences of a Dancing Man'. Before he left Dorset his appetite had been whetted by an older and somewhat more sophisticated fellow-pupil in Hicks's Dorchester office, who returned from London 'whistling quadrilles and other popular airs, with accounts of his dancing experiences at the Argyle Rooms and Cremorne' (*LW* 38): the young Hardy was clearly fascinated by this glimpse at one remove of fashionable metropolitan ballrooms, and one particular quadrille—unidentified despite strenuous efforts on his part—haunted him for years. A little later, working and living in Weymouth, he himself joined a quadrille class (see the poem 'The Dawn after the Dance').

A very different aspect of Hardy's early musical experience is represented by the church choir. In a letter to Florence Henniker dated 30 December 1896, he termed the Mellstock choir 'the characters that I like best in my own novels' (*L* ii 141). A basic account of the history and membership of the original choir is given in the *Life* (*LW* 14–17). Hardy was too young to remember the discontinuation of the Stinsford string choir as an ecclesiastical body and its replacement by an organ; however, this forms the central subject of *Under the Greenwood Tree*, where his recurring theme of transition assumes a specifically musical expression. The Mellstock choir, or individual members of it, are the source of anecdotes in *The Return of the Native* (1.5) and *Tess of the d'Urbervilles* (17). They also feature in a number of poems, including 'The Rash Bride', 'The Dead Quire', 'The Paphian Ball', 'The Choirmaster's Burial', and 'Winter Night in Woodland', as well as in the short stories 'The Waiting Supper', 'The Fiddler of the Reels', and 'A Few Crusted Characters'.

Hardy's interest in music was, characteristically, powerful but also idiosyncratic. Its eclecticism is illustrated by a paragraph in his autobiography referring to the time he spent in London during the 1890 'season': beginning by remarking that he seemed at that time 'to have had a humour for going the rounds of the music-halls', it proceeds to offer some interesting reflections on the art of opera, prompted by a performance of Bizet's *Carmen*, and then describes a visit to 'a ballet at the Alhambra' (*LW* 237). If he could enjoy Bizet and Verdi, however, he could also relish Lottie Collins's rendering of 'Ta-ra-raboom de-ay' at the Gaiety—'really a very unusual performance', as he assured Sir George *Douglas, '& not altogether so silly as people say' (13 April 1892).

However, the musical knowledge and understanding of, say, George *Eliot was not in any way Hardy's. He appears to have known no Bach, little Mozart (despite the 'Lines to a Movement in Mozart's E-Flat Symphony'), less Beethoven, some Grieg, and less Wagner. Unlike Eliot he was not an informed attender of the orthodox repertoire, nor a cultivator of the company of composers (despite a sympathetic meeting with Gustav *Holst and a mooted collaborative project with Edward *Elgar), with the single exception of his close attraction to the young Rutland *Boughton. Vera J. Mardon, the young Dorchester pianist invited to Max Gate in Hardy's later years, recalled how he would lay classical pieces to one side: 'I gathered from the general conversation that his love was for the old tunes. He never discussed classical music', she recalled (*Monographs on the Life, Times and Work of Thomas Hardy* No. 15, p. 11). Though with opera the situation was somewhat different, it is generally fair to conclude that Hardy's musical taste did not expand significantly beyond the provincial music of his childhood, the country dances of the village band, and the repertoire of the parish choir. As 'Any Little Old Song' candidly puts it, 'Newest themes I want not | On subtle strings, | And for thrillings pant not | That new song brings'. He admitted to Rutland Boughton in 1924 that he was unfamiliar with modern music, including Boughton's own: '"The Blue Danube", "The Morgenblätter Waltz", and the "Overture to *William Tell*" interested him more strongly, and also church music, mainly on account of the association with his early days' (*LW* 458).

He did, however, possess an enthusiasm for romantic opera, especially Italian opera, and the extent of his familiarity with the standard repertoire—or its influence on his work—has not always received sufficient recognition. Even before he left Dorset for London he may have attended his first opera, for Verdi's *Il Trovatore* was performed by a touring company in Dorchester in February 1860. Whether he saw *Il Trovatore* for the first time then or a little later in London, it remained one of his favourite operas (see the poems 'An Ancient to Ancients' and 'The Dead Man Walking'). An interesting passage in the autobiography (*LW* 320–1) draws an analogy between his own career and Verdi's; the phrase used of Verdi and quoted by Hardy, 'amazing old man', could as well have been applied to himself. As a young man in London he had frequently attended operatic performances at Covent Garden and other theatres.

More broadly speaking, musical terms and a musical awareness impregnate Hardy's style. The pitch of a character's voice, for instance, is frequently identified in musical terms. Boldwood has a basso profundo (*FFMC* 23) and Tess a 'fluty' voice, with a 'stopt-diapason note' (*TDU* 14, 18). The sounds of nature likewise undergo musical analysis and expression. The elms in *The Woodlanders* sing 'Gregorian melodies' (13); the beeches in *Far from the Madding Crowd* 'wailed or chaunted to each other in the regular antiphonies of a cathedral choir' (2); the heath in *The Return of the Native* has a variety of 'treble, tenor and bass notes' to which the holly tree adds a 'baritone buzz' (1.6); an even more extensive set-piece (a sort of 19th-century literary tone poem) is the description of the Casterbridge waterways (*MC* 41); while the opening sentence of *Under the Greenwood Tree* declares that 'To dwellers in a wood almost every species of tree has its voice as well as its feature'.

More fundamentally, music has psychological relevance and power in Hardy's life and work. To a certain extent an overheard tune had the same effect on Hardy as a sip of tea on Proust. Music was for him a marker of significant moments and a potent trigger of remembered incident. His life, as recalled by him, has almost the feel of a Wagnerian opera about it: leitmotifs, musical moments replete with significance and inner meaning, mark many poignant instants of experience. This applies not just to his parents' first meeting but also to the vicissitudes of his relationship with Emma ('On the Tune Called the Old-Hundred-and-Fourth', 'A Duettist to her Pianoforte'), and, in his earliest surviving poem, 'Domicilium', the itemization of his grandmother's favourite dances.

Music can underpin the structure of a novel and be deliberately used to aid its characterization. *The Mayor of Casterbridge*, where musical vocabulary is especially in evidence, shows the technique used with what appears to be a particularly conscious sense of system. Henchard is 'highly strung' (44), whereas Farfrae has the charm of 'a well braced musical instrument' (23). Farfrae can express himself and attract others by his singing ability: Elizabeth-Jane had never heard 'any singing like this' (8); by contrast Henchard can only summon up the 'bass note' with which he awakens Abel Whittle (15). Yet Henchard, like Saul, is deeply moved by music (the narrative has much in common with the biblical story of Saul and David) and 'high harmonies transsubstantiated him' (41), whereas Farfrae's musical accomplishments perhaps conceal an emotional hollowness. After his second marriage Farfrae is heard 'giving strong expression to a song of his dear native country that he loved so well as never to have revisited it' (44), and we are told, in a statement that repays scrutiny, that his 'voice musically undulated between two semi-tones' (14)—hardly an expansive range. Many of the novel's major events are marked by performances by the town band of brass players; string bands appear on less formal and more personal occasions. Only on the generally harmonious occasion of Elizabeth-Jane's wedding do the two appear together. The instrumentation and anarchic individualism of the 'rude music' that accompanies the skimmington ride (39) forms a strong contrast to this harmony.

Much use is made in Hardy's fiction of 'off-stage' musical effects such as the psalm that accompanies the discovery of the children's bodies in *Jude the Obscure* (6.2) and the military and brass bands of the same novel's final chapter. Though hymns frequently supply the music involved, the technique itself may owe much to Hardy's enthusiasm for opera, in which such effects are frequent.

Folksongs and hymns undoubtedly influenced Hardy's metrical practice: at least three poems ('Timing Her', 'Meditations on a Holiday', 'O I Won't Lead a Homely Life') were composed to folk tunes. (See also HYMNS AND METRICAL PSALMS; METRICS.) In addition, Hardy claimed that his sensitiveness to melody was patently at odds with the frequent assertions of critics that his verse lacked musicality (cf. *LW* 21). A discerning resolution of this conflict is provided by Joan Grundy in her *Hardy and the Sister Arts* (1979): 'Hardy's writing acquires a musical character and texture, even without overt musical reference. His concern with mood and sensation and the expression of these, together with an acute sense of order and relationship, which also forms part of a musical sensibility, is chiefly responsible. Hardy responds to experience through its tones, rhythms and harmonies, its changing tempos, chords and keys' (p. 167).

Hardy's writings have been a source of inspiration to a number of composers: the Wessex Novels, especially *The Return of the Native*, are the basis for Gustav Holst's *Egdon Heath*, while of various settings of Hardy poems the most impressive are to be found in Benjamin *Britten's song-cycle *Winter Words*. See also OPERA.

Transcriptions or arrangements of dances and carols which the Hardy family knew have been published as *The Wessex Tunebook*, arr. Elna Sherman (1963); *The Dorchester Hornpipe*, ed. Joan Brocklebank (1977); *The Mellstock Carols*, ed. A. D. Townsend (1989); and *The Musical Heritage of Thomas Hardy*, ed. Roger Trim (1990). Roger Trim, as a member of the musical group The Yetties, has also been involved in a number of commercial recordings, some using Hardy family instruments. TRH

Simon Gatrell, 'Hardy's Dances', in his *Thomas Hardy and the Proper Study of Mankind* (1993).

Brian Maidment, 'Hardy's Fiction and English Traditional Music', *THA* 4 (1986).

N

names. Naming characters was an aspect of his art that Hardy took seriously, and his choices are often worth attention. Although many personal names in the novels are ordinary ones, sometimes drawn from places or families in Dorset, others are symbolic and influence our sense of the characters in various ways. Sometimes Hardy found a local name that would fit. 'Troy' was formerly a Dorset place-name; it has just the right note of exaggerated swagger, combined with ill-omen, in 'Sergeant Troy'. *Far from the Madding Crowd* includes several other distinctive names, notably Gabriel Oak's. Deeply rooted, he endures, as Bathsheba notices: 'What a way Oak had, she thought, of enduring things' (43). Gabriel, moreover, acts as her guardian angel. 'Pennyways', for Bathsheba's dishonest bailiff, belongs to an old, originally dramatic, tradition of whimsical and label-like names, still flourishing in Thackeray and Trollope, but sparingly deployed in Hardy. There are also poetic names such as 'Joseph Poorgrass', noted as 'excellent' for a bashful countryman in Henry *James's review (*Nation*, 24 December 1874; repr. in *CH*). Throughout the novels there are some names that affect our feelings about a major character, as with the inappropriately baptized Angel Clare in *Tess*, while others add a pleasant touch to a minor figure. Shiner is a rich, showy young farmer in *Under the Greenwood Tree*, and Owlett, the smuggler in 'The Distracted Preacher' (*WT*), is a night bird.

We are reminded in *The Return of the Native* of how Hardy's contemporaries often had Bible stories in mind when naming children, when it is said of Eustacia Vye that 'she would have christened her boys such names as Saul or Sisera in preference to Jacob or David' (1.7). The original Bathsheba, whose beauty provoked David to murder her husband, belongs in the unconventional, if not ungodly, 'Saul or Sisera' category. Perhaps Hardy chose it in the same spirit of fun that inspired 'Cain Ball', for a rustic whose parents were muddled about Cain and Abel (*FFMC* 10); if so, he was more profoundly influenced later by the dramatic, queenly, and enigmatic figure in 2 Samuel and 1 Kings.

Hardy's care in naming appears in his frequent manuscript revisions. He improved 'Stansbie' into 'Farfrae', for the Scot in Wessex in *The Mayor of Casterbridge*, 'Alfred', for Troy, into the ironic 'Frank', and 'Jack' into 'Jude'. 'Strong' was rejected in favour of the stronger name 'Oak'. These alterations often help editors by identifying stages in composition. Michael Henchard is called 'Giles' and 'James', in the manuscript of *The Mayor*, in passages belonging to an earlier version. Tess is called 'Rose-Mary' and 'Sue' in early stages of her story's evolution, where Hardy's imaginative grasp of the character was less certain; it is as though he found her name when he learnt her nature. Eustacia Vye had a prototype called 'Avice' (a name salvaged in *The Well-Beloved*); the manuscript of *The Return of the Native* shows that she was to have figured as a witch. Hardy's autobiography tells us that 'Eustacia' was taken from the name of a lady of the manor in medieval Dorset (*LW* 120). Unlike Avice, the ladylike Eustacia (to be addressed as 'Miss Vye') speaks standard English and dreams of living in Paris. Here the baptismal name denotes a higher social class as clearly as the surname 'd'Urberville', debased into 'Durbeyfield', does in Tess, and also wider cultural horizons.

Hardy exploits the potency that names can develop in intimate relationships. When Angel Clare (rather in Hardy's own manner) calls Tess 'Artemis' or 'Demeter', she demurs: '"Call me Tess," she would say askance; and he did' (*TDU* 20). 'Tess' sounds remarkably poignant here, calling to mind Shakespeare's phrase quoted on the title-page, 'Poor wounded name!' It is at such dramatic moments that the evocative 'Tess' (with echoes of 'tress', 'tears', 'tease', 'tenderness') is most effective. Gabriel Oak's 'my beautiful Bathsheba', when finally accepted, is another resonant, intimate naming, especially after she has made him say 'Miss Everdene' for so long (*FFMC* 56).

Some fictional names had a private meaning for Hardy which his earliest readers could not have guessed. 'Fawley' is one. Hardy visited the village of Fawley, near Oxford, the former home of his grandmother Mary Head, when planning *Jude the Obscure* in 1892. He renamed the village 'Marygreen' in the novel, and Jude 'Fawley' (earlier versions included 'Hopeson' and 'Head'). 'Mary' and 'Head' found their way into 'Sue [Susanna Florence Mary] Bridehead'. Hardy admits to some personal associations. His autobiography mentions that 'Clement', in *The Return of the Native*, was taken from Clement le Hardy, a possible ancestor (*LW* 120). A reference to 'Hardys' occurs in Dairyman Crick's list of old families come down in the world (*TDU* 19). Hardy was modest about 'Thomas': the only fictional one in the novels is the simpleton Thomas Leaf, who finally proves 'clever enough to tell a story' (*UGT* 5.2).

Recurring names help to date events in Wessex history. Farmer Everdene and 'a silent, reserved young man named Boldwood' make brief appearances in *The Mayor of Casterbridge* (31), implying that *Far from the Madding Crowd* (in which they had already appeared) is set about a decade later, in the 1860s. A reference to 'Keeper Day' (*FFMC* 8) implies that Bathsheba's people are acquainted with folk from *Under the Greenwood Tree.* Such playful strokes add to our sense of Wessex, which extends to the world of the poems. Parson Thirdly (*FFMC* 8) is mentioned in 'Channel Firing' (*SC*).

Hardy's rural titles, such as 'Farmer Oak', 'Miller Loveday', 'Tranter Dewy', or 'Jack Durbeyfield, the haggler', help to create a sense of life in a small locality. The reddleman Diggory Venn remarks on how children speak as though there were only one fox, one devil, and one reddleman (*RN* 1.8); Hardy himself often speaks in this way, of 'the reddleman', 'the trumpet major', 'the Native', 'the mayor of Casterbridge'. Wessex has one of each. The actual world does sometimes pay Hardy the tribute of adopting one of his names or titles. Ruskin College was not named after Jude, a possibility mentioned in the novel's 1912 Postscript; but there is today a pub near Oxford's 'purlieu of Jericho' (as Hardy referred to the counterpart of his 'Beersheba') called the Jude the Obscure.

NMcE

Napoleonic Wars. Although Hardy is not primarily a writer of historical fiction, his longest work, *The Dynasts*, begins in 1805 (35 years before the year of his own birth), and ends only a decade later; if any single historical period exercised his imagination, it was the quarter-century covering Napoleon's rise and fall. Hardy's scholarship in this era was wide-ranging. He knew and used J. Holland Rose's *The Life of Napoleon I* (1801); P. Coquelle's *Napoléon et l'Angleterre, 1803–13* (1804; read by Hardy in preparation for writing the last two sections of his epic-drama); Pierre Lanfrey's *Histoire de Napoléon I* (first volume published in 1869; Hardy used the 1876 edition); and works as lengthy as J. B. H. R. Capefigue's ten-volume *L'Europe pendant le Consulat et l'Empire de Napoléon* (1840), as well as brief but telling excerpts and clippings from the *Gentleman's Magazine* (1806), the *Morning Chronicle* (various dates), and summaries of Parliamentary debates. He seldom quoted directly or slavishly; his piquant touches, intended to dramatize otherwise sombre moments, are frequently imaginative inventions independent of his sources.

The issue of whether Hardy gave fair credit to his sources loomed large at one time. This is not the same problem as the one that plagues the readers of all historical fictions: namely, the difficulty of reviewing thoroughly the factual works on which a given story is based, in order to determine how much was borrowed and how much might be accounted as new. An authoritative judgement could not be made until the Napoleonic-era items in Hardy's library were carefully reviewed, and this kind of analysis was not undertaken until more than half a century after Hardy's death.

Hardy unfortunately transcribed some 275 words of a lengthy passage written by the American author A. B. Longstreet (who in turn was adapting a widely known work about military drilling for a chapter entitled 'The Militia Company Drill' in *Georgia Scenes*, published first in 1835). When he used this passage in *The Trumpet-Major* (1880), however, Hardy was not borrowing from Longstreet, but from C. H. Gifford's *History of the War Occasioned by the French Revolution* (1817). Perhaps more meticulous crediting of sources would have made no difference; the drilling passage caught the attention of several critics, who levied unpleasant charges of *plagiarism in the *Critic*, the *Academy*, and several other American magazines. Hardy finally recognized the justice of the accusation (and said as much in his 1895 preface to the novel). He never again laid himself open to the charge of unethical borrowing from his sources. (The issue is worth mentioning, if only because Hardy was so concerned about the legal rights surrounding his own intellectual properties.)

Several poems use the Napoleonic years as background or subject-matter. *Wessex Poems* alone contains 'The Sergeant's Song', dated '1803', deriding the threat of a French invasion; 'Valenciennes', a war-ballad with a complex background history of Hardy's research; 'San Sebastian', about a sergeant who felt marked 'with a God-set brand | Like Cain'; 'Leipzig' and 'The Peasant's Confession', both belonging to a planned ballad-sequence on the Napoleonic wars; and 'The Alarm', a very precise and fact-based treatment of an invasion scare. This last poem should be read in conjunction with the short story 'A Tradition of Eighteen Hundred and Four', which deals with a supposed visit by Napoleon to the English coast; the possibility of a French invasion seemed most ominous in that year, and Hardy, who published the story in 1882, learned much to his surprise that what he had written as fiction was a well-established tradition in the very region he had set his story.

Some of these are powerful poems; they illustrate Hardy's fascination with a past that still remained vivid to the pensioners at Chelsea Hospital, whom he interviewed on several occasions, and to many Dorset residents, whose tales he had heard while growing up. Other conflicts—the *Boer War and the *First World War in particular—take up a more prominent residence in subsequent volumes of poems. Collections of poems after *Wessex Poems* speak much less directly about the Napoleonic years (with the notable exception of 'The Bridge of Lodi' in *Poems of the Past and the Present*, a poem commemorating the victory in 1796 that persuaded Napoleon he would conquer an empire). But a significant number of poems written during the same period that he was embarked upon *The Dynasts* develop views that were shaped by Hardy's meditations upon, and slow brooding about, the meaning of Napoleon's fall from grace. Hardy never wanted to turn away from what became, relatively early in his life, an obsession, and in important ways it served his art well. HO

National Gallery. Founded in 1824, the National Gallery was housed in its present building in Trafalgar Square when Hardy came to London in 1862. While employed by Arthur *Blomfield in the early 1860s, Hardy visited the gallery for twenty minutes each day, concentrating upon a particular painter (*LW* 53). At that period, the National Gallery was also the site of the annual exhibitions of the *Royal Academy, at which Hardy was also a regular exhibition-goer.

Hardy alludes directly to several paintings in the National Gallery collection in his fiction and poetry. In the poem 'The Respectable Burgher on "The Higher Criticism"', the speaker illustrates his religious doubts by reference to the figure of Lazarus in Sebastiano del Piombo's *Raising of Lazarus*, and the same painting provides a point of comparison for Clym Yeobright's appearance when rescued from drowning in *The Return of the Native* (5.9), and for that of Aunt Drusilla in *Jude the Obscure* (3.9). Most of Hardy's references to National Gallery paintings relate to moments of tragedy. Angel Clare, returning from abroad in *Tess of the d'Urbervilles*, is compared to the Christ in Carlo Crivelli's *Pietà* (53), while the bowed heads of Clare and Liza Lu, after the hanging of Tess, are compared to those of two saints (59) in a picture then believed to be by Giotto, but now attributed to Spinello Aretino.

From its first decade, the National Gallery has had considerable holdings of Dutch 17th-century landscape works, and the structure of these considerably influenced Hardy's own method of landscape description. He particularly noted a painting of a man on a path bordered by trees, *The Avenue of Middleharnis* by Meindert Hobbema. Of equal importance in their effect on Hardy's writing were the paintings of J. M. W. Turner. As a result of the Turner Bequest to the nation of 1856, he was able to see paintings of which he later expressed admiration, including *Rain, Steam, and Speed—The Great Western Railway*, on the walls of the National Gallery.

In *The Well-Beloved* Hardy's hero, Jocelyn Pierston, returns to the National Gallery in his sixties, and finds himself unmoved by those paintings which had previously delighted him, including works by Perugino and Titian, and even the del Piombo *Raising of Lazarus* fails to interest him (3.8). LO

Newbolt, Henry (1862–1938), poet and man of letters. He achieved considerable eminence in his day, but is now chiefly remembered (not entirely respectfully) for a handful of patriotic poems. An active member of the literary profession, he was knighted in 1915. He and Hardy were fellow-members of the Omar Khayyá m Club (see also CLODD, EDWARD); a friendship developed between them, and he dedicated to Hardy his *Collected Poems 1897–1907* (1910). In 1912, on Hardy's 72nd birthday, Newbolt, accompanied by W. B. Yeats, visited Hardy on behalf of the Royal Society of Literature and presented him with the gold medal of the Society. Newbolt reviewed the first part of *The Dynasts* on its publication in 1904; Hardy sent him on 9 February 1906 a presentation copy of the second part, and on the appearance of the completed work Newbolt published a long and enthusiastic review of it in the *Quarterly Review* (January 1909; repr. *CH*) under the title 'A New Departure in English Poetry'.

Nicholls, Eliza Bright (1840–1918). The eldest daughter of George and Jane Nicholls, she was born in Sussex but spent part of her childhood at Kimmeridge Bay, on the south Dorset coast, where her father was stationed as a coastguard. By 1861, however, George Nicholls was in retirement, apparently as a result of an illness or injury, and keeping the Running Horse inn in the Sussex village of Findon, while Eliza was in service in London as the personal maid of Emma Hoare (née Mansel), of Smedmore House.

Hardy and the serious-minded Eliza were linked for some years in an 'understanding' of some kind, its course reflected in Hardy's 'She, to Him' and related sonnets. A drawing of Clavel Tower, on the cliff-top at Kimmeridge, accompanies the poem 'She, to Him. I' in *Wessex Poems*, and Hardy could have met Eliza in Dorset in the late 1850s, although the proximity of the Hoares' house to Hardy's lodgings at 16 Westbourne Park Villas makes a first encounter in London equally likely. Eliza's duties took her away from London before the end of 1863, however, and by early 1865 she seems to have been living with her parents. She and Hardy exchanged letters, and Hardy visited her in Findon—the drawing of Findon church ('Ch. near the Downs'—in his *Architectural Notebook* is dated 1866), but in 1867 the engagement (if such it was) evidently foundered on Hardy's developed preference for Mary Jane Nicholls, Eliza's younger and livelier sister. Hardy's 'Neutral Tones' captures the bitterness and perhaps the scene of that parting.

Eliza Nicholls died unmarried. She kept the photograph Hardy had given her (now in the Beinecke Library of Yale University), and what she said was his ring, and when he became a widower in 1912 she called to see him, apparently in the hope that their relationship might yet be renewed—only to be told that he planned to marry Florence Dugdale. Eliza's voice is heard, however, in some of Hardy's early sonnets, and the 'prosing' of 'She, to Him. II' at a moving moment in Chapter 13 of *Desperate Remedies* lends credence to her claim to have been the 'original' of Cytherea Graye. MM

Nietzsche, Friedrich Wilhelm (1844–1900), German philosopher. Whereas Hardy may have felt some interest in Nietzsche's criticism of Christianity and views on tragedy and aesthetics, his overall attitude to the German philosopher was negative (*LN* ii 511–12). In his first entry on Nietzsche in the *Literary Notes* (see NOTEBOOKS) from 1888 or 1899, Hardy quotes the opinion that 'N.'s sounder doctrines were put forth during his early life, & that his later utterances were tainted with insanity', and then caustically adds: 'The latter words are true enough' (*LN* ii 75). Nietzsche nevertheless held his interest, and Hardy quoted from John Addington Symonds's analysis of Nietzsche on *tragedy in 1902 (*LN* ii 127–8), and from another article in the same year (*LN* ii 166). He also seems to have tried to translate a brief passage from Nietzsche on aesthetics into his *Literary Notes* in 1908 (*LN* ii 240). Yet, in a much-publicized letter in 1902, he wrote that 'to model our conduct on Nature's apparent conduct, as Nietzsche would have taught, can only bring disaster to humanity' (*LW* 339). The tone was even more acrid in a letter on the German bombardment of Rheims Cathedral in 1914: if deliberate, Hardy wrote, this destruction 'will strongly suggest that a disastrous blight upon the glory and nobility of that great nation has been wrought by the writings of Nietzsche.... I should think there is no instance since history began of a country being so demoralized by a single writer, the irony being that he was a megalomaniac and not truly a philosopher at all' (*Manchester Guardian*, 7 October 1914; quoted *LN* ii 512; see also *L* v 50–1). LAB

M. May, *Nietzsche and the Spirit of Tragedy* (1990).

Eugene Williamson, 'Thomas Hardy and Nietzsche: The Reasons', *Comparative Literature Studies* (1978).

notebooks. Hardy was a compulsive note-taker and kept numerous notebooks, the great majority of which were destroyed after his death (see Michael Millgate, *Testamentary Acts: Browning, Tennyson, James, Hardy* (1992)). The most important extant notebooks have all been published, as described below. The unpublished material consists of a volume of notes and cuttings entitled 'Facts from Newspapers, Histories, Biographies, & other chronicles (mainly Local)' in the Memorial Collection at the Dorset County Museum, and a microfilm of the 'Poetical Matter' notebook, made by R. L. Purdy and now in the Beinecke Library at Yale University; the whereabouts of the original of this microfilm, if it still exists, are unknown (see also Millgate 89–90).

The published notebooks are as follows:

(1) *The Architectural Notebook of Thomas Hardy*, ed. C. J. P. Beatty (1966). Hardy's architectural career (see ARCHITECTURE) spans some sixteen years, from 1856 to 1872: as apprentice in Dorchester, 1856–62; as assistant in London 1862–7; and as part-time assistant to Dorset architects from 1867 to 1872. All but eleven pages of the *Notebook* contain material from the decade 1862 to 1872. As a whole the *Notebook* may be called, Beatty maintains, 'a microcosm of the Victorian age', since many pages touch on 'every aspect of Gothic church architecture and the plans of big houses', and others 'have a direct bearing on industry and commerce and the day-to-day living of ordinary people in town and country' (p. 5).

Architecture plays a part in Hardy's writings, both directly and indirectly: some of the characters in his novels are architects, and there are numerous intricate descriptions of different kinds of buildings. Most significantly, perhaps, there is the analogy between architecture and poetry that Hardy himself perceived and also emphasized in his autobiography: 'He knew that in architecture cunning irregularity is of enormous worth, and it is obvious that he carried on into his verse, perhaps unconsciously, the Gothic art-principle in which he had been trained' (*LW* 323).

(2) *The Personal Notebooks of Thomas Hardy*, ed. Richard H. Taylor (1979), includes four notebooks: 'Memoranda, I', 'Memoranda, II', the 'Schools of Painting Notebook', and the 'Trumpet-Major Notebook'; an appendix includes 'Typescript passages omitted from *The Life of Thomas Hardy*'. Being mostly excerpts from earlier notebooks from the period 1867–1920 which were subsequently destroyed, the Memoranda notebooks provide insights into various stages of Hardy's careful selection of potential material for his *autobiography. He stopped entering notes into 'Memoranda, I' in 1920, and used 'Memoranda, II' from 1922 or 1923 until September 1927. As Taylor points out in his introduction, Hardy's closing of the first notebook in 1920 coincided with the end of his own part in the composition of the autobiography (up to and including chapter 36). Significantly, there is a note in Hardy's hand on the original typescript at this point: 'The rest is in small Notebooks of Memoranda beginning 1921' (p. xiv). The entries in the Memoranda books constitute a highly idiosyncratic collection of notes, representing in Taylor's definition three general categories: literary and antiquarian, social, and personal (p. xv).

The 'Schools of Painting Notebook', consisting of factual information, reflects Hardy's autodidactic endeavours generally, as well as his ambition at one time to become an art critic.

The 'Trumpet-Major Notebook' is unique in that it is, as far as we know, the only notebook Hardy kept with a specific novel in mind. It contains diverse notes on, for instance, ladies' and gentlemen's clothing, plays, actors and actresses, items from local histories, and military matters from Napoleonic days. The notebook also seems to have been used for *The Dynasts* (see Emma Clifford, 'The "Trumpet-Major Notebook" and *The Dynasts*', *Review of English Studies*, NS 8 (1957); Walter F. Wright, *The Shaping of 'The Dynasts'* (1967)).

The 'Typescript passages omitted from *The Life of Thomas Hardy*' offer insights into the revision and editing of the original typescripts by Hardy before his death and/or by his widow. The introduction details the subterfuge engaged in by Hardy and his wife in the writing of the disguised autobiography, as well as the roles played by J. M. *Barrie and T. E. *Lawrence.

(3) *Thomas Hardy's 'Studies, Specimens &c.' Notebook*, ed. Pamela Dalziel and Michael Millgate (1994). This small notebook ($6\frac{1}{8} \times 3\frac{3}{4}$ inches; 15.6×9.6 centimetres), produced as a 'typographical "facsimile"' (reproducing the page and line-by-line divisions of the original), comprises 89 pages. Most of the entries date from the mid-1860s—that is, from Hardy's first London period (1862–7)—but with some entered as late as 1869. The notes confirm Hardy's previously known reading of, for instance, Shakespeare, the Romantic poets, Swinburne, and the Bible, but there are also excerpts from Jean Ingelow, Isa Craig, and Robert Buchanan; in addition, the notes testify to his careful reading of the 16th- and 17th-century selections in Palgrave's *Golden Treasury*. The focus of the notes is lexical, Hardy's aim being to increase his vocabulary generally and his poetic diction in particular, and not to study technical or formal aspects of poetry. In the process, Hardy engages, towards the end of the notebook, in some limited playing and experimenting with vocabulary he has quoted, which makes it possible to discern a 'progression from a self-educative to an actively creative agenda' in the notebook (p. xxi). Yet the nature of the lexical studies suggests to the editors that this stage of Hardy's development was marked by 'naiveté, educational deprivation, and painful autodidactic effort' (p. xxii).

(4) *The Literary Notebooks*, ed. Lennart A. Björk, 2 vols. (1985). Compiled over a period of more than 50 years, the 'Literary Notes', as Hardy entitled them, constitute the fullest extant record of his reading for his career as a writer, the earliest note dating from 1863 and the last from 1927. They range from the Greek dramatists to Shaw; from the radical French Utopian writer Charles Fourier to Cardinal Newman; and from *The Milliner and Dressmaker and Warehouseman's Gazette* to Einstein. The books incorporate materials from other notebooks and show traces of having been reread and annotated by Hardy.

The inception of these notebooks coincides with the time off from writing that Hardy took after the mixed reception of *The Hand of Ethelberta* in the spring of 1876 (*LN* i xx). In a letter to a publisher he indicated that he did not 'wish to attempt any more original writing of any length for a few months, until I can learn the best line to take for the future' (*L* i 43). Hardy seems to have thought that reading literary criticism would help him choose 'the best line', and he contacted Leslie *Stephen for advice (*LN* i xix–xx). Stephen advised Hardy against reading criticism—a piece of advice to which Hardy did not pay much attention, it seems—and there are many extracts from Matthew *Arnold, whom Stephen did recommend. In any case, Hardy suspended his novel-writing for about one year, and in the meantime seems to have started on a determined course of study and note-taking, reflected in *The Literary Notebooks*.

It is possible to divide the notes into two general categories that relate to Hardy's own distinction in his essay 'The Profitable Reading of Fiction' between two kinds of literary elements that readers might profit from. On the one hand, there are the 'accidents and appendages of narrative . . . trifles of useful knowledge, statistics, queer historical fact'; on the other, there is the 'true object' of fiction, 'a lesson in life, mental enlargement', which can only be derived from 'elements essential to the narratives themselves and from the reflections they engender'. *The Literary Notebooks* contain both kinds of notes: there are 'accidents and appendages' later to be used in rather obtrusive allusions, as well as more ideologically oriented notes which were to be interwoven into the very fabric of Hardy's writing (see L. A. Björk, 'Hardy and his "Literary Notes"', *THA* 1 (1982)).

It would seem as if Hardy's concept of his notes gradually changed from the first category to the second, for the first novel after the inception of these notebooks, *The Return of the Native*, is fuller of 'accidents and appendages' material than any later work. One example is Hardy's use of a 'queer historical fact' entry from Macaulay's essay on Warren Hastings: 'The Speech of Sheridan on the Oude charge—The finest delivered within the memory of man. Not reported—lost to us' (*LN* i 7). Grandfer Cantle's exaggerated description of a musical performance is put into the same class: 'As with ... Sheridan's renowned Begum Speech, the fortunate condition of its being forever lost to the world invested the deceased Mr Yeobright's tour de force on that memorable afternoon with a cumulative glory which comparative criticism, had that been possible, might considerably have shorn down' (*RN* 1.5).

The clearest examples of Hardy's use of *Literary Notebooks* material intended for 'mental enlargement' are found in his last novels. The ideological frameworks of *Tess of the d'Urbervilles* and *Jude the Obscure* especially are conspicuously underpinned by both implicit and explicit references to moral, philosophical, and religious authorities that Hardy had copied from into his *Literary Notebooks*: Arnold, classical literature, Comte, Huxley, English Positivists, Mahaffy, Morley, Gibbon, Mill, Milton, Newman, Shelley, Symonds, Voltaire, and others (*LN* i xxii–xxx). LAB

'Old Mrs Chundle.' See UNCOLLECTED STORIES.

Oliphant, Margaret (1828–97), née Wilson, prolific Scots novelist, editor, and reviewer. She wrote to Hardy on 20 July 1882 inviting him to contribute an article on 'the labouring poor in the countryside' to *Longman's Magazine*; the result was his important essay 'The Dorsetshire Labourer', published there in July 1883. As a reviewer she frequently attacked the immorality of Hardy's fiction and specifically his questioning of female chastity and the sanctity of marriage. An unsigned article in the *Spectator* (18 January 1890) refers to the 'grotesque indecency' of the heroine's action in *Two on a Tower* in marrying in order to secure a father for the child she is expecting by another man; the same criticism was reiterated in *Blackwood's Magazine*, March 1892. In *The Victorian Age of English Literature* (1892), written jointly with her son, F. R. Oliphant, she has praise for some of Hardy's earlier novels, but attacks 'the sacrifice of . . . female virtue' in *Tess of the d'Urbervilles*; her review of *Tess* in *Blackwood's* (March 1892; repr. in *CH*), however, while expressing strong reservations, recognizes the novel as Hardy's finest achievement to date.

Her most notable attack on Hardy was in 'The Anti-Marriage League' (*Blackwood's Magazine*, January 1896; repr. *CH*), where *Jude the Obscure* is reviewed in tandem with Grant *Allen's *The Woman Who Did*. R. G. Cox has described this as 'perhaps the most thorough-going condemnation that *Jude* received'. Hardy refers to this attack in his 1912 postscript to the preface to *Jude* ('the screaming of a poor lady in *Blackwood* that there was an unholy anti-marriage league afoot'). She also wrote to Bishop W. W. *How, commending his well-publicized burning of a copy of *Jude*; for Hardy's embittered reaction to this, see *LW* 295. After meeting her in May 1895, he described Mrs Oliphant as 'propriety and primness incarnate'.

J. S. Clarke, *THJ* 5 (1989).
Norman Page, *Victorian Newsletter*, 46 (1974).

'On the Western Circuit', short story. It was first published in the *English Illustrated Magazine* (December 1891) and the American *Harper's Weekly* (28 November 1891), and collected in *Life's Little Ironies*. The manuscript was given by Hardy to the Manchester Central Public Library in 1911. Earlier titles were 'The Amanuensis' and 'The Writer of the Letters'.

The story was completed early in 1891, at about the time Hardy was dealing with the proofs of *Tess of the d'Urbervilles*, and concerns the courting and seduction of a servant girl by a young London barrister, Raye, while the latter is on a professional visit to the provinces. Since she is illiterate, his subsequent correspondence with her is conducted by her mistress, a lonely woman trapped in a loveless marriage who gradually becomes infatuated with the young man. Though he marries the girl under the pressure of social conventions and moral obligations, both he and the older woman come to recognize that their marriages are doomed, and that, in different circumstances, they might have been happier together.

The story thus forms part of Hardy's extensive fictional examination of the institution of marriage at this stage of his career. In the seduction of a simple girl by a man who is her social superior, it echoes the treatment of Tess by Alec; and in the social and educational inequality of the lovers and the fascination of an educated man with an unsophisticated 'child of nature', it reworks the relationship of Tess and Angel Clare. (Compare in this latter respect, *'The Son's Veto' in the same volume.) The situation of the married woman, Edith Harnham, has much in common with that of Ella Marchmill in another story of this period, 'An Imaginative Woman'. In having the girl's love letters written by another, Hardy may have been recalling his own early experiences of writing letters to absent sweethearts on behalf of village girls.

The frank treatment of sexuality, both in the seduction and pregnancy of the village girl and in the married woman's intense feelings for another man, created difficulties for Hardy, who was forced to make substantial changes before the story was accepted for magazine publication. In the bowdlerized version, for instance, the married woman is a widow. The original version was restored for volume publication. For discussion of these various versions, see Alan Manford's 'Note on the Text' in the Oxford World's Classics edition of *Life's Little Ironies* (1996). On the dramatic version of the story staged in 1972, see DRAMATIZATIONS.

opera. On the opera based on *Tess of the d'Urbervilles*, see TESS OPERA. An opera by Stephen Paulus based on *The Woodlanders* (libretto by Colin Graham) was produced in St Louis in 1985. On the opera based on *The Famous Tragedy of the Queen of Cornwall*, see BOUGHTON, RUTLAND. On unfulfilled plans to turn works by Hardy into operas, see BRITTEN, BENJAMIN; ELGAR, EDWARD.

Osgood, McIlvaine was one of the most important of the publishing firms with which Hardy had dealings. James Ripley Osgood (1836–92) was an American publisher whose firm, James R. Osgood & Co., acquired the rights to serialize *Far from the Madding Crowd* in the USA. In 1888, in his capacity as London representative of the American firm of *Harper & Brothers, he corresponded with Hardy concerning the publication of 'The First Countess of Wessex' (later collected in *A Group of Noble Dames*) in *Harper's New Monthly Magazine*, and they subsequently met in London. With Clarence W. McIlvaine (1865–1912), Osgood formed in 1890 Osgood, McIlvaine & Co., which became Hardy's publishers in 1891 and remained so during an important phase of his career, issuing *A Group of Noble Dames*, *Tess of the d'Urbervilles*, and *The Well-Beloved* as well as a significant collected edition, 'The Wessex Novels', in 1895–6 (see COLLECTED EDITIONS).

Osgood had died suddenly in 1892 and Hardy attended his funeral in Kensal Green Cemetery (the letter describing this occasion to his wife (*L* i 269) contains some unexpected touches). Subsequently the firm was absorbed by Harper & Brothers, which took over as Hardy's publishers, McIlvaine becoming their London representative.

'Our Exploits at West Poley.' See UNCOLLECTED STORIES.

Oxford. Among those attending Hardy's funeral service in Westminster Abbey on 16 January 1928 was the Provost of Queen's College, Oxford, which had elected Hardy to an honorary fellowship in November 1922. Nearly three years earlier, in February 1920, the University had conferred on him the honorary degree of Doctor of Letters, which Hardy received during his stay in Oxford to attend a performance of *The Dynasts* by the Oxford University Dramatic Society. He could hardly have expected any of this when he paid a visit to Oxford in May 1875 to watch the college boat races and, at the invitation of an undergraduate club, spoke at the Second Annual Shotover Dinner.

In striking contrast to Hardy's acceptance by the academic community of Oxford is the rejection of Jude, the hero of Hardy's deeply personal novel, by 'Christminster', his fictional Oxford. Jude dies alone on Remembrance Day, again a fictional version of Oxford's Commemoration (Encaenia), his ambition to be admitted to the University having been denied by the Master of Biblioll (Balliol) College and others long before. Hardy, who made a special point of being in Oxford for Commemoration in June 1893, draws in this novel a very accurate picture of the city and its moods. Beginning with Jude's arrival in the working-class district of 'Beersheba' (Jericho), he goes on to describe Jude's wanderings through the city, not forgetting to bring in the 101-stroke curfew rung on Great Tom at five minutes past nine. The figures that crowd Jude's mind at that time, ranging over more than two hundred years, are also easily identified: Ben Jonson, Edward Gibbon, the Tractarians, A. C. Swinburne, and others.

The last time Hardy slept away from Max Gate was his first and only visit to Oxford as a Fellow of Queen's College, in June 1923. On this visit he particularly wished to see the curve of the High Street ('Chief Street' in *Jude the Obscure*), the Martyrs' Memorial, and the Shelley Memorial. YT

P

painting and sculpture, both classical and modern, played an important part in the formation of Hardy's personal aesthetic and, specifically, in his own mode of writing. As a boy and young man he made numerous pencil drawings, and his gifts as a draughtsman helped to promote his choice of *architecture as a profession. Hardy's early knowledge of the fine arts came from works like Cassell's *Illustrated Magazine of Art* and the *Art Journal* and through occasional glimpses of country house collections. It was only on his arrival in London in 1862 that he could enjoy the experience of studying original works. During his period as assistant to Arthur *Blomfield, Hardy paid daily visits to the *National Gallery. He was also a regular attender at the 1862 International Exhibition, with its extensive art sections featuring displays of Old Masters and modern British paintings. The chance to see this exhibition was apparently a factor in Hardy's decision to work in London. Another regular haunt was the South Kensington Museum (now the Victoria and Albert Museum), where Hardy studied the collections bequeathed by John Sheepshanks and Robert Vernon, both featuring important modern works. In later years, Hardy often went to the winter exhibitions of Old Masters held at the *Royal Academy, as well as exhibitions of more modern art at the French Gallery and the Grosvenor Gallery.

As he became more prosperous, Hardy was able to visit a number of European museums and galleries (see TRAVELS, CONTINENTAL), including the Louvre, which he first saw on his honeymoon in 1874, and to which he returned throughout the next two decades. In 1876 he was in Holland, Belgium, and Germany, taking in the Hague, Antwerp, and Brussels. His visit to the Wiertz Museum in Brussels, which houses the macabre paintings of the early 19th-century artist Antoine Wiertz, eventually bore fruit in the passage in *Tess of the d'Urbervilles* where, after Tess's confession, Angel Clare's vision of life is described as like 'the staring and ghastly attitudes of a Wiertz Museum' (39). A journey to Italy in 1887 gave Hardy the chance to see many of the best-known galleries and churches, including the Uffizi and Pitti galleries in Florence, the Vatican and Capitoline Museums in Rome, and the Accademia in Venice. In 1896 he was again in Belgium, looking closely at works by three Flemish artists, the 15th-century Hans Memling, and two early 17th-century painters, Frans Pourbus and Peter Paul Rubens.

The majority of Hardy's comments on the paintings and sculptures that he saw and admired refer to the Old Masters. In 1863, when he was still learning the names of artists and schools, he wrote out a list of painters (the 'Schools of Painting Notebook'), sometimes appending brief notes and apparently working from a work of reference (repr. in R. H. Taylor, *The Personal Notebooks of Thomas Hardy* (1979), 103–14; see also NOTEBOOKS). In 1887 Hardy's admiration for the directness of approach which he found in the work of the early Renaissance painters led to a declaration that 'My art is to intensify the expression of things, as is done by Crivelli, Bellini, etc., so that the heart and inner meaning is made vividly visible' (*LW* 183). Such a reaction was entirely in tune with the aestheticism of the 1880s, which had firmly established a public taste for early Italian art.

Hardy's novels show the effect of his study of the Old Masters, and are marked by frequent allusions to works of the Italian Renaissance, to Dutch 17th-century painters, and, occasionally, to classical sculptures. Many of these allusions suggest particular facial characteristics for Hardy's women characters. In the opening chapter of *A Pair of Blue Eyes*, for example, the novelist compares the appearance of the heroine to those of women seen in works by three Old Masters, Raphael, Rubens, and Correggio. Titian, Greuze, and the Dutch masters Terburg, Dou, and Cuyp are among other artists to whom Hardy compares female characters in the novels up to *The Mayor of Casterbridge.*

Predictably, Hardy developed a keen interest in landscape paintings, and his own descriptions show the influence of the traditional structures of landscape painting, particularly those of Dutch 17th-century masters like Meindert Hobbema and Jacob van Ruisdael, both well represented in the National Gallery. Hardy's practice of opening a novel with a meeting of characters travelling along a road directly parallels the style of these painters, for whom a road or path provides a characteristic means of leading the eye of the beholder into the canvas. Two of the works which Hardy most admired were Hobbema's *The Avenue at Middleharnis* (1689, National Gallery) and a modern work using the same device of a figure on a path, *The Morning Walk* by Giovanni Boldini (1873, private collection). Perhaps surprisingly, it is not to these great artists, but to two little-known late 16th- and early 17th-century Flemish painters, Denis Van Alsloot and Antoon Sallaaert, that Hardy turns when seeking to give an extra dimension to his description of the Vale of the Great Dairies in *Tess of the d'Urbervilles* (16), or of Mrs Yeobright's sense of community in *The Return of the Native* (3.3). The crowded processional paintings of these artists provided Hardy with a parallel for the mass of hedges, trees, and cattle seen from high ground. Hardy's language in such landscape descriptions is often paralleled in the technical terms of the artist with his use of expressions like 'foreground', 'middle distance', and 'background'.

In the first chapter of *The Return of the Native*, Hardy speculates that future generations will prefer dark and desolate landscapes to the bright southern scenes popular with the earlier Victorian public. Here again, Hardy was reflecting a change in public taste. The popularity of landscape paintings like *February Fill Dyke* by Benjamin Robert Leader (1881, Birmingham City Museum and Art Gallery), or the late Scottish scenes of John Everett Millais, including *Chill October* (1870–1, private collection), indicates just such a swing from bright southern scenes to melancholy mood pieces as Hardy predicted.

Of all landscapists, Hardy probably most admired J. M. W. Turner, whose preoccupation with effects of light and shade is reflected in Hardy's own. Hardy was familiar with the Turner Bequest paintings in the National Gallery, and it is known that he was reading Ruskin's *Modern Painters*, which championed Turner, in 1862. Seeing a group of watercolours by the artist in the Royal Academy in 1889, Hardy noted his admiration for Turner's treatment of light, and the devices by which the artist gave his landscapes the effect of reality, while recognizing the impossibility of representing the world as it is. Among the watercolours was one representing Stonehenge, which was to become an important point of focus in the penultimate chapter of *Tess*. Hardy admired several of the impressionistic late works by Turner, which were much derided at the time, including *Rain, Steam and Speed* (1842, Tate Gallery) and *Snowstorm and a Steamboat* (1842, Tate Gallery).

Hardy's admiration for Turner's landscapes presumably encouraged his enthusiasm for the work of Claude Monet when he saw a group of '"impression" pictures' in 1889 (*L* i 191). In the same year Hardy noted the work of John Singer Sargent, who, with his fellow American painters, Edwin Austin Abbey and Frank Millet, became a personal friend of the novelist. Among the older Academicians, Hardy had a particular admiration for the genre painter William Powell Frith, whose work he had known from his early days in London. Lawrence Alma Tadema Hardy knew as the brother-in-law of his close friend Edmund *Gosse, but it seems unlikely that he had any great feeling for Tadema's paintings of classical life. Hardy established cordial relationships with his illustrators, including George du Maurier (the illustrator of *The Hand of Ethelberta* and *A Laodicean*) and Helen *Paterson (later Allingham). Alfred Parsons, who illustrated 'The First Countess of Wessex' (*A Group of Noble Dames*), was requested by Hardy to paint scenes of the Wessex countryside, and Parsons stayed at Max Gate while he worked on these.

Hardy's feeling for sculpture is less apparent in his fiction than his response to painting, but occasional references in novels and stories, together with a number of poems, make it clear that he became increasingly fascinated by the plastic art. Antique and Renaissance statues provoked a meditative response. He describes himself, on his journey to Italy in 1887, sitting on the steps of the

Loggia dei Lanzi in Florence, looking at the works of Donatello and Michelangelo, and noticing that it was the accidental effects of the surface of the marble, the cracks and the scratches, which held his imagination, not the more ideal intention of the original sculptor (*LW* 199). In the Room of the Muses in the Vatican, where stood such famous works as the Apollo Belvedere, Hardy found the statues blurring before him. In his poem 'Rome: The Vatican: Sala Delle Muse', the speaker tells of a deep anxiety about which of the arts he should follow, or which of them should be pre-eminent; in his imagination, a single female figure representing the arts appears, assuring him that an artist must follow an inspiration from within, not from outside.

From Rome Hardy brought back memories of another celebrated sculpture, the Laocoön, which finds its way into *The Mayor of Casterbridge* (12) and *Jude the Obscure* (2.7). The many statues of Antinous, the beloved of the Emperor Hadrian, seem also to have struck him, although another example was to be found in the British Museum. Hardy compares the radiant good looks of Swithin St Cleeve, the hero of *Two on a Tower*, to those of Antinous (5), and the same ideal beauty provides a parallel for Tess's love for the face of Angel Clare (*TDU* 57). Another parallel for Antinous is found in the short story 'Barbara of the House of Grebe' (*GND*), where the arrival of a life-size sculpture of the handsome Edmund Willowes, the heroine's first husband, who has subsequently been hideously disfigured in a fire, becomes an object of worship for Barbara, and provokes the cruelty of her second husband. Ironically, she could not bear the sight of Willowes once his beauty was destroyed.

Hardy was a habitué of the British Museum Reading Room, and he may well have looked at the antique collections on his many visits to that institution. A late poem, 'Christmas in the Elgin Room', reveals a familiarity with the Elgin Marbles.

Among the sculptors of the Renaissance, Hardy, like his contemporaries and successors, most admired Michelangelo. In the 1870s, he was reading histories of art and instructing his wife to write comments on Michelangelo into notebooks.

Hardy was friendly with a number of sculptors of his own day, Thomas Woolner and Hamo *Thornycroft among them, and he no doubt drew upon his knowledge of their lifestyle and work for his late hero, the sculptor Jocelyn Pierston in *The Well-Beloved.* Pierston's father is a quarry-owner and has been a stonemason, like Jude Fawley in *Jude the Obscure*, who is employed to recut statues on the public buildings in Oxford.

One element in Hardy's understanding of art and artists came as a direct result of his growing fame. Later in his life, he was painted and sculpted by some of the most enterprising artists of his day, including Jacques-Emile Blanche, Hamo Thornycroft, William Strang, and Augustus John (see PORTRAITS AND SCULPTURES OF THOMAS HARDY). See also PICTORIALISM. LO

J. B. Bullen, *The Expressive Eye: Fiction and Perception in the Work of Thomas Hardy* (1986).
Joan Grundy, *Hardy and the Sister Arts* (1979).
Alistair Smart, 'Pictorial Imagery in the Novels of Thomas Hardy', *Review of English Studies*, 12 (1961).

Pair of Blue Eyes, A. The third of Hardy's fourteen published novels.

Composition

In *Life and Work* Hardy claimed that he had written down the plot of this novel 'long before' he met and began to court Emma Gifford in 1870 (*LW* 77), though the context of this assertion is his attempt to refute biographical readings of the work, especially the identification of himself with Stephen Smith, Elfride's architect-suitor. By 24 July 1872, when Hardy verbally agreed to sell the serial and three-volume publication rights to William *Tinsley for £200, the composition of what was then entitled 'A winning tongue had he' had apparently still not progressed beyond the rough sketching out of the opening chapters and general outline. The first instalment (to be published on 15 August 1872) was hurriedly written in London, where Hardy was currently completing a project for the architect T. Roger Smith; on 7 August Hardy travelled to Cornwall, writing the second instalment in the company of Emma Gifford and with some assistance from her. Later that month Hardy decided to give up architecture as a profession and devote his time entirely to writing; after a brief return to London in September he went on to Higher

Bockhampton, where he completed the novel, posting the conclusion on 12 March 1873.

The surviving manuscript (Berg Collection, New York Public Library) is fragmentary, consisting only of the setting copy for the September, October, and January serial instalments (Chapters 1–8 and 15–18). Its revisions were primarily stylistic, though a few were designed to distance somewhat the fictional text from Hardy's personal background and courtship experiences, as in the alteration of Stephen's father's occupation from master-mason to mason and of the Swancourt residence from a rectory to a vicarage.

Serialization

The novel was serialized in *Tinsleys' Magazine* in eleven monthly instalments, from September 1872 to July 1873, divided as follows: September, Chapters 1–5; October, 6–8; November, 9–11; December, 12–14; January, 15–18; February, 19–21; March, 22–5; April, 26–8; May, 29–31; June, 32–6; July, 37–40. Although Hardy read proof for *Tinsleys'*, he made very few revisions at this stage, presumably because most of his time was taken up with primary composition as he attempted to cope with the unfamiliar pressures of writing for serial publication.

Illustrations

Each of the eleven *Tinsleys'* instalments was preceded by a full-page woodblock illustration by the painter and illustrator James Abbott Pasquier. The drawings are highly uneven in quality; the most effective in terms of both composition and execution are the first two, depicting Elfride's sight of Stephen embracing a woman at Endelstow House, and Stephen's alarm at Elfride's precarious position on the cliffs. Hardy sent Tinsley preliminary sketches for both, and the resemblance between Pasquier's Elfride and Hardy's 'original' Emma Gifford suggests that the artist made at least some use of them.

Volume Publication

The novel was published in three volumes at 31*s*. 6*d*. (half a guinea per volume) by Tinsley Brothers in the last week of May 1873 (i.e. after the 15 May publication of the June instalment). In revising the text for volume publication Hardy omitted the opening description of Elfride's emotional response to reading a tragic romance; he also increased the financial independence of the Smiths and modified some of the more strident examples of social criticism.

Revisions for the one-volume edition published by Henry S. King in 1877 included the deletion of several passages of self-conscious narratorial commentary and the abridgement of the 'Pennie's the jewel that beautifies a" chapter, both of which had been criticized by the *Spectator* reviewer (see below). Hardy also eliminated Somerset and Dorset references in an attempt to confine all local references to Cornwall.

The 1895 Osgood, McIlvaine edition introduced standard 'Wessex' names and altered distances to conform more closely to the actual, in keeping with Hardy's general 'Wessexization' of the fiction for the Wessex Novels collected edition. Other significant revisions included the enhancement of the Smiths' social and financial status, the reduction of articulations of narratorial sympathy for Elfride, the omission of much of the social criticism in the Rotten Row scene, and the suggestion that Mrs Jethway's presence aboard the *Juliet* is a figment of Elfride's disordered imagination.

For the 1912 Macmillan Wessex Edition Hardy introduced further changes which continued the patterns of revision established in 1895 with respect to geographical authenticity, the Smiths' social position, narratorial sympathy for Elfride, and the sensationalism of the *Juliet* scenes. He also explicitly identified the cause of Elfride's death as a miscarriage, and, as with other Wessex Edition volumes, undertook a thorough general revision of the text—tightening his prose style, eliminating much of the compositorially imposed punctuation of earlier editions, and attempting to sort out inconsistencies of detail.

A Pair of Blue Eyes was the only novel Hardy substantially revised for the Macmillan Mellstock Edition. Published in 1920, eight years after the death of Emma Hardy, this final version identified the setting more precisely and explicitly with the Cornwall of the Hardys' courtship.

Reception

The tone for most of the 1873 reviews was set by the *Spectator*, source of the hostile review of *Desperate Remedies* that had so profoundly distressed Hardy two years previously. Its *Pair of Blue Eyes* review (28 June 1873) was, however, essentially laudatory: criticism of the novel's sentimental title, occasional stylistic affectation, and heavy-handed social criticism is overwhelmed by admiration of its sparkling humour, 'true moral instinct', subtle character-analysis, and exquisite evocation of natural scenery, qualities which combine to produce 'a really powerful story, well proportioned in its parts, of varied and deep interest'. Praise of the depiction of 'the humble neighbours' includes the standard reference to George *Eliot, while the 'breathless description' of the cliff-hanging scene is said to be reminiscent of Sir Walter *Scott.

The specifics of the *Spectator*'s criticism and commendation were largely echoed by the brief notice in the *Graphic* (12 July 1873) and the more substantial reviews in the *Saturday Review* (2 August 1873)—almost certainly written by Hardy's friend and mentor, Horace *Moule—and the *Pall Mall Gazette* (25 October 1873). All of these reviews were sympathetic, if essentially condescending, towards Elfride. The tone of the *Pall Mall Gazette* is typical: 'There was no wise motherly influence to warn and guide the girl; and so it may be inferred there was a good deal of moral weakness in Elfride. But she was profoundly loveable, especially to men, and she loved to be loved...'

Occasional dissenting voices were heard, however, with respect to both Elfride and the novel as a whole: the *Athenaeum* (28 June 1873), for example, was lukewarm at best, describing Elfride as self-willed and her story as farcical, while *The Times* (9 September 1873) was still less complimentary, chastising Hardy for his 'ridiculous' language and insisting on Elfride's 'extraordinary folly and extraordinary deceit'.

Almost all of the reviews were sympathetic—and *not* condescending—towards the 'strictly manly' Knight (*Spectator*), acknowledging his harshness but emphasizing his integrity. The *Saturday Review* did suggest that Knight was both unnatural and priggish, but if the author of this review was indeed Moule he was perhaps concerned primarily to challenge any resemblance between himself and the fictional reviewer (see below).

The 1877 one-volume edition was briefly but favourably noticed by a number of periodicals—'a genuinely powerful story' (*Birmingham Daily Gazette*, 21 August 1877); 'full of fresh, vigorous thought' (*Liverpool Weekly Albion*, 15 September 1877)—and evaluation of the novel in relation to other Hardy works was by no means dismissive: the *Bath Chronicle* (16 August 1877), for example, described it as not equal to *Far from the Madding Crowd* but still of 'very considerable merit', while *John Bull* (15 September 1877) insisted that if some of the other books were more artistically written, Elfride remained the most perfectly conceived of Hardy's female characters.

A Pair of Blue Eyes retained a high place in the Hardy canon throughout the 19th century. It was the declared favourite of both Coventry *Patmore and Alfred *Tennyson, and overviews of Hardy's novels, from Alexandra Sutherland Orr's in the *New Quarterly* (1879) to W. L. Phelps's in the *North American Review* (1909), almost always ranked it as one of the best. Hardy placed it early in the Osgood, McIlvaine collected edition—fourth, in fact, after *Tess of the d'Urbervilles*, *Far from the Madding Crowd*, and *The Mayor of Casterbridge*—and its eventual relegation to 'minor' status may indeed have been a consequence of his deciding (after considerable vacillation) to classify it as the first of the 'Romances and Fantasies' rather than the last of the 'Novels of Character and Environment' in the Wessex Edition. Certainly the publication history of *A Pair of Blue Eyes* bears witness to its having been one of the more lastingly popular of Hardy's novels throughout the late 19th and early 20th centuries.

Plot (1873 version)

When Stephen Smith, a young architectural assistant, makes a professional visit to Endelstow vicarage to prepare drawings for the church's restoration, he is quickly captivated by the blue eyes of the vicar's clever and high-spirited daughter. For her part, Elfride Swancourt is attracted not only to Stephen's handsome face and gentle bearing but also to the sense of mystery which surrounds him. Although disappointed to learn that the mystery consists only in the humbleness of Stephen's origins—his father is a mason employed by the neighbouring landowner, Lord Luxellian—Elfride none the less defies parental opposition and remains true to their youthful lovers' vows. A clandestine attempt to marry fails when Elfride insists on returning home at the last moment, necessitating an all-night train journey in Stephen's company. Their indiscretion is successfully concealed from everyone except a grief-crazed neighbour, Mrs Jethway, who blames Elfride for the premature death of her only son, Felix.

Stephen goes to India 'to make his fortune' while Elfride remains with her father and wealthy new stepmother (formerly their neighbour Mrs Troyton). Elfride's experience of men is broadened by the visit of Henry Knight, who is (rather conveniently) the new Mrs Swancourt's cousin, Stephen's much-admired mentor, and the hostile reviewer of Elfride's medieval romance. Scenes of the courtship with Stephen are replayed, but with the gender roles reversed: it is now Knight rather than Elfride who consistently has the upper hand. Her interest in Knight increases, in spite of (or perhaps because of) his condescension, and she struggles to remain faithful to Stephen.

A life-and-death encounter, which leaves Knight suspended on the precipice of a cliff until saved by Elfride's ingenious creation of a rope from her underclothes, concludes with the revelation of their mutual affection on the day of Stephen's arrival from India. Stephen soon learns of the new relationship, but his continued love for Elfride and regard for Knight prevent him from pressing his own claims or exposing Elfride. She feels increasingly unable to tell Knight herself about her previous engagement, especially when she learns that much of his attraction to her stems from his belief that she is as sexually inexperienced as he is. Terrified of losing the man she now passionately loves, Elfride becomes entangled in prevarications and untruths. By the time the dreaded exposure finally arrives in the form of a vengeful letter from Mrs Jethway, Elfride has so magnified the seriousness of her attempted elopement with Stephen that she is unable to defend herself against Knight's accusations. He, believing her to have had sexual relations with her former (and still unidentified) fiancé, deserts her.

Fifteen months later a world-weary Knight meets Stephen, recently returned to England after a successful architectural career in India. Stephen discovers that Knight and Elfride are not married, Knight that Stephen was Elfride's suitor and that their relationship was sexually innocent. Each believes that he is Elfride's true beloved and accordingly sets out for Endelstow to ask her to marry him. The rivals end up travelling on the same train, accompanied, as they eventually and painfully discover, by a funeral carriage bearing the body of Elfride, who has died not for love of either of them but from an unspecified illness ('miscarriage' in late editions) after a brief marriage to the handsome, wealthy, and aristocratic Luxellian.

Critical Approaches

Until the advent of revisionist readings of Hardy in the 1980s, the dominant critical approach to *A Pair of Blue Eyes* during this century has been biographical. The similarity of Stephen Smith's profession and circumstances to Hardy's was remarked upon as early as 1881 by Charles Kegan *Paul in the *British Quarterly Review*, and continued to be the focus of critical attention in spite of Hardy's attempts in *Life and Work* and elsewhere to dissociate the novel's characters from himself and his intimate circle—always excepting Elfride, whom he readily acknowledged was based upon Emma Gifford. As numerous critics (most notably Michael Millgate) have demonstrated, Hardy in fact dealt with the unfamiliar pressures of writing for serial publication by drawing heavily upon autobiographical material, not only his courtship experiences but also his family background and relationship with Moule (Knight's 'original').

Apart from its biographical interest, *A Pair of Blue Eyes* has until recently been treated as 'minor', hence either ignored or dismissed with brief comments pointing up what are perceived to be flaws in structure, style, or characterization. Although both Millgate and Richard H. Taylor do each devote an entire chapter to the novel, their concern to detail weaknesses frequently overwhelms more constructive insights, such as Millgate's reading of Knight as a Hamlet figure, or Taylor's recognition of the similarities between the review of Elfride's romance and those of Hardy's *Desperate Remedies*.

A relatively early exception to this fault-finding tendency is John Lucas's 1977 study, which not only posits that *A Pair of Blue Eyes* has been 'badly underestimated' but also offers a proto-feminist reading of Elfride as a woman 'struggling to realize her sense of herself, which means trying to keep it free from those coercive visions of her which her lovers have' (pp. 126, 137). Subsequent feminist critics have continued to analyse the representation of Elfride, frequently focusing on the disjunction between the sympathetic realization of this often unconventional heroine and the location of her within the narrator's essentialist and largely negative commentary on womankind. Rosemarie Morgan argues that Hardy was intentionally attempting 'to placate the Grundyists' by superimposing on the narrative a censorial voice (p. 12); Patricia Ingham that this voice constitutes only one among several of the text's discourses which in combination generate 'unease' with the conventional female stereotype (p. 16); and Mary Rimmer that Hardy distanced, without actually disowning, his anxieties about female power by projecting them onto an 'obviously fallible' narrator (p. 214). A similar variety of opinion can be found in recent responses to the novel's conclusion, ranging from Roger Ebbatson's disappointment with its arbitrariness and failure to embody a *Tess*-like critique of patriarchy to Ingham's celebration of it as the ultimate realization of Elfride's triumph over Stephen and Knight (see also Morgan, Jo Devereux, and Pamela Dalziel). The range of response reflects the critics' attempts to make sense of a representation which—as so often in Hardy's texts—seems contradictory, its challenge to hegemonic conceptions of gender problematized by its reinscription of the conventional punitive plot (erring heroine killed off).

Similar contradictions beset the representation of class in *A Pair of Blue Eyes*. On the one hand, the narrator explicitly criticizes social snobbishness and sympathetically portrays the Stephen–Elfride relationship, yet another incarnation of the **Poor Man and the Lady* story. And, indeed, substantial sections of that first unpublished novel, which Hardy himself defined as 'socialistic, not to say revolutionary' (*LW* 63), seem to have been incorporated into *A Pair of Blue Eyes*. On the other hand, the plot reaffirms hegemonic class structures: Elfride 'corrects' her grandmother's and mother's imprudent matches by marrying the aristocratic Luxellian—though one could perhaps revisionistically argue that her death should be read as a punishment not for her unconventionality but for her inability to resist her father's class expectations.

In any case, as the work of numerous critics makes clear, issues of gender and class are inexorably intertwined in this novel. Ingham, for example, trenchantly argues that the categories of 'lady' and 'poor man' are not entirely discrete—humiliation transcends gender boundaries—and that woman becomes a vehicle of metaphor for the marginalized male. Stephen, frequently described as 'feminine', internalizes society's disvaluation of himself, absorbing its class prejudices as Elfride uneasily accepts its standards of womanliness. Rimmer also explores the conflation of gender and class codes as inscribed within the game of chess and its 'club laws' in her astute interrogation of Hardy's use of the chess matches to define Elfride's relations with Stephen and Knight.

Other revisionist readings include Mary Jacobus's analysis of Knight's cliff-edge visions in relation to both Hardy's capacity for posthumous self-projection and his confrontation of the destructive powers of the imagination; Judith Bryant Wittenberg's discussion of the text's voyeuristic moments, from Elfride as object of the male gaze to such 'sight-engendered crises' (p. 161) as Mrs Jethway's watching Stephen's watching; and John Goode's ruminations on *A Pair of Blue Eyes* as Hardy's 'scientific game', his search for a narrative and fictional language which plays off 'public expectation against "real thoughts"' (pp. 10–11). Issues of perception, identity, and language are also explored by Ebbatson, who provides both a good introduction to recent approaches to the novel and a valuable contribution to the critical debate.

An aspect of this novel which would benefit from further examination is the representation of the rural labourers, hitherto either dismissed as comic relief or cursorily discussed in relation to Hardy's family.

PD

Pamela Dalziel, Introduction to Thomas Hardy, *A Pair of Blue Eyes*, Penguin Classics (1998).
Jo Devereux, 'Thomas Hardy's *A Pair of Blue Eyes*: The Heroine as Text', *Victorian Newsletter*, 81 (1992).
Roger Ebbatson, Introduction to Thomas Hardy, *A Pair of Blue Eyes*, Penguin Classics (1986).
John Goode, *Thomas Hardy: The Offensive Truth* (1988).
Patricia Ingham, *Thomas Hardy* (1989).
Mary Jacobus, 'Hardy's Magian Retrospect', *Essays in Criticism*, 32 (1982).
John Lucas, *The Literature of Change: Studies in the Nineteenth-Century Provincial Novel* (1977).
Michael Millgate, *Thomas Hardy: His Career as a Novelist* (1971).
Rosemarie Morgan, *Women and Sexuality in the Novels of Thomas Hardy* (1988).
Mary Rimmer, 'Club Laws: Chess and the Construction of Gender in *A Pair of Blue Eyes*', in Margaret Higonnet (ed.), *The Sense of Sex: Feminist Perspectives on Hardy* (1993).
Richard H. Taylor, *The Neglected Hardy: Thomas Hardy's Lesser Novels* (1982).
Judith Bryant Wittenberg, 'Early Hardy Novels and the Fictional Eye', *Novel*, 16 (1983).

pastoralism as commonly perceived is an escapist genre (and is so defined in the *Oxford Companion to English Literature*); but this is misleading, especially with regard to Hardy's use of it. Much pastoral literature, it is true, is situated in an Arcadian never-never land where shepherds loll about on the grass serenading their loved ones, or, more often, lamenting their frustrations in love; and in such literature the harsh realities of nature and the economic basis of sheep-farming are rarely mentioned. But there is also a long tradition of pastoralism that creates an idealized picture of life for the purpose of contrasting it with the very un-idealized quality of life in the real world. The myth of the Golden Age—so closely associated with pastoral that it is virtually impossible to separate the two—implies a contrast with the decadent conditions of subsequent Ages, in the Ovidian tradition designated Silver, Brass, and Iron, and the purpose of the myth is to emphasize the deterioration. By conflating the Golden Age with the biblical Eden, Renaissance classicism gave further emphasis to the contrast between a prelapsarian and a fallen world, and the Christian identification of the shepherds with Christ, the saviour and protector of his flock, while heightening still further the idealism of pastoralism, by the same token increased awareness of the wretched condition of 'the hungry sheep' who (as in Milton's 'Lycidas') 'look up and are not fed'.

Hardy both idealizes and records with graphic realism the country life he knew at first hand in Dorset. The very titles of *Under the Greenwood Tree* and *Far from the Madding Crowd* are redolent of pastoral literature (the first drawn from a song in *As You Like It*, the second from a line in Gray's 'Elegy'), and their living representation of old country customs constantly suggests the charm and humanity of a plainer and simpler life than that known to most of their readers. But, characteristically, the old is seen as under threat from the new, which is the contemporary, with its snobbery, greed, and selfishness. In *Far from the Madding Crowd* in particular, the dream of living 'Far from the madding crowd's ignoble strife' is shattered by the flashy intruder, Sergeant Troy, and the exposure of his alien qualities includes a vividly real demonstration of his inadequacies in the face of a violent storm which not only shows nature in one of its harshest moods but is also reckoned in terms of its damaging effects on the farming economy. Likewise, the seemingly idealized qualities of Gabriel Oak as the tender shepherd and sensitive member of the rural community are offset by the misfortunes he suffers and his reduction to a journeyman's trade. The ancient 'et ego in Arcadia' theme, the grim intrusion of death into the pastoral world, is also echoed in the tale of Fanny's seduction and its bitter consequence. If the debt here is just as much to the ballad tradition, with a generous overlay of Victorian sentimentality, its modifying effect on the supposedly sheltered world of pastoral cannot be seen as anything but conscious and deliberate.

The pastoralism in Hardy's later novels becomes increasingly anti-escapist. David Lodge makes the interesting suggestion that the form of *The Woodlanders* is that of the classical pastoral elegy, 'a formalised literary development from rituals designed to celebrate and promote the renewal of Nature's fertility', but with the emphasis (as in Marty's final threnody over Giles's grave) on remembrance rather than renewal. Nevertheless, the world of this novel is fundamentally Darwinian, opposing a competitive nature engaged in the ruthless struggle for survival to the pathetic fallacy of a nature that sympathizes with the sufferings of man. It is a matter of studied irony that Fitzpiers should be the character to uphold the literary vein of pastoralism in his self-flattering ideal of finding a calm retreat in the woodland world: he becomes the modern serpent in its Eden. And if Giles and Marty are representatives of the true old rural pattern, that pattern is seen as obsolescent and self-defeating—weakened in its resistance to the destructively modern by its own outmoded adherence to such virtues as loyalty and self-effacement.

This sense of the pastoral in decay becomes still more the note of *Tess of the d'Urbervilles* and *Jude the Obscure*, though arguably the latter makes a complete break with the pastoral tradition. Tess has great pastoral moments, including the heroine's 'bird's-eye perspective' of the Valley of the Great Dairies at the beginning of her 'rally' and the midsummer dawn scene of Chapter 20, where the 'spectral, half-compounded, aqueous light' gives Tess and Angel Clare 'a feeling of isolation, as if they were Adam and Eve'. However, these are subjectively deceptive moments.

Tess is Hardy's most sustained effort to create an image of the innocent pastoral girl who stands, like Shakespeare's Perdita, for the restorative and recuperative powers of nature, and yet is also a realistically convincing woman of the Dorset countryside. But in thus bringing together the ideal and the real, he also shows, unusually, the corrupting effect of the ideal. Angel's inability to see her, and accept her, as she is—to come to terms not with a literature-conditioned and sentimentalized icon, but with the strengths and weaknesses of a living woman—move this novel from pastoralism to tragedy. *Tess* is thus both pastoral and anti-pastoral: a comment on the deep appeal of the genre, and a criticism of the false idealism it may generate. What is left in *Jude* is more like harsh satire: the country lad whose idealism focuses on the impossibly dreaming spires of Christminster, set against the coarse country wench who brings sexual fantasy down to the level of a pig's pizzle.

There are also important elements of pastoralism in *A Pair of Blue Eyes*, *The Return of the Native*, and *The Trumpet-Major*, and there is an example of sustained pastoral romance in the long story 'The Romantic Adventures of a Milkmaid'. Fiction aside, Hardy's remaining links with the pastoral are to be found in certain of his poems. The great majority deal with country life and country people, usually, however, in a more realistic vein (as exemplified by 'A Sheep Fair') than is generally associated with the epithet 'pastoral'. But the simple lyricism of poems like 'Great Things', 'Weathers', and 'Timing Her', and the backward-looking idealism of 'Domicilium' and 'The Oxen', have something of the feeling that belongs to Golden Age pastoralism. By contrast, a poem like 'The Ruined Maid' deliberately mocks pastoral assumptions as the luxuries enjoyed by the kept woman are compared with the hard slog endured by the virtuous country maid.

More explicitly, 'In a Wood' (with its avowed connection with *The Woodlanders*) is an anti-pastoral pastoral. This poem adopts the point of view of a weary urban persona, 'Heart-halt and spirit-lame, | City-opprest', who turns to the woodlands for 'sylvan peace', only to encounter disillusionment in the face of the trees' Darwinian struggle for survival that shows them 'to men akin— | Combatants all!' 'The Pine Planters' is a derivative from the same novel: subtitled 'Marty South's Reverie', it offers a versified variant on her elegy for Giles Winterborne. Other elegies, such as 'Bereft' and 'She Hears the Storm', also have pastoral overtones; but Hardy's most interesting use of the pastoral elegy is in 'Transformations' and 'Voices from Things Growing in a Churchyard', where the traditional renewal theme is given an original, and disconcertingly witty, twist as the dead combine with the organic processes of nature to persist eerily 'as nerves and veins... in the growths of upper air'.

Other poems which owe at least some of their effect to an implicit contrast with conventional pastoralism include 'Neutral Tones' and 'The Darkling Thrush'. The pathetic fallacy in the former paints a starkly modern picture of an unsympathetic, unbenign nature; and the pastoral elegy, adapted in 'The Darkling Thrush' to the subject of New

Year's Eve, underlies the poem's structure—offering in its first two stanzas a bleak 'death-lament', counterbalanced in the second two by the unexpectedly 'full-hearted evensong' of an aged thrush. However, in typically ambivalent Hardyan fashion, the 'blessed Hope' thus suggested is something 'whereof he [the bird] knew | And I was unaware'. To find a rare example of new-minted pastoralism which Hardy does not undercut, one must turn to that extraordinary minor masterpiece 'An August Midnight'. Here the meeting of the human and natural that is characteristic of pastoralism (and is too often marked by a predictable use of the pathetic fallacy) is successfully defamiliarized. It comes across with a new, open-ended quality, and holds the imagination by a genuinely pastoral quietness and modesty of tone. RPD

John Alcorn, *The Nature Novel from Hardy to Lawrence* (1977).

R. P. Draper (ed.), *Thomas Hardy: Three Pastoral Novels* (1987).

Michael Squires, *The Pastoral Novel: Studies in George Eliot, Thomas Hardy and D. H. Lawrence* (1974).

Paterson, Helen (1848–1926), artist and illustrator. She produced the illustrations for the serial version of *Far from the Madding Crowd* in 1874. Hardy's autobiography recalls his surprise at opening the issue of the *Cornhill* in which the first instalment appeared, and discovering that it was not only given pride of place but was illustrated by a woman (*LW* 100). In May 1874 Hardy met Helen Paterson at the home of Leslie *Stephen, the *Cornhill*'s editor; the meeting served the purposes of both business and pleasure, for he not only 'gave her a few points' (*LW* 103) for her illustrations, but was evidently attracted to her. They also met on other occasions and corresponded, his letters including drawings of rustic articles to give assistance and authenticity to her own representations of rural life.

In August 1874, a month before Hardy's own marriage, Miss Paterson married William Allingham (1824–89), the Irish poet, who was almost twice her age. In June 1880 Hardy sought in vain to enlist her as the illustrator of *A Laodicean*. A generation later, on 25 July 1906, in response to an enquiry from Edmund *Gosse, he stated that she was the 'best illustrator' he had ever had, adding the curious but characteristic reflection that he might easily have married her rather than Emma. (Mrs Allingham's own views on this point are not on record.) The idea or fantasy of what might have happened 'Forty springs back' also prompted the poem 'The Opportunity (For H.P.)', which opens with that phrase but was not published until it appeared in *Late Lyrics and Earlier* in 1922.

Patmore, Coventry (1823–96), Roman Catholic poet. He wrote to Hardy on 29 March 1875, though at the time they had not met, to tell him of the 'extraordinary pleasure and admiration' with which he had read his novels, and in particular the recently published *A Pair of Blue Eyes*. Patmore's letter (DCM) suggests, however, that the novel is essentially poetic in conception, and expresses the regret that it should not have taken poetic form. Hardy cites this letter in an important passage of his autobiography in which he describes himself as 'committed to prose' at that stage of his career (*LW* 107–8). In the same work he notes with pride that *A Pair of Blue Eyes* was 'the favourite novel of two eminent poets', *Tennyson and Patmore (*LW* 93). On 11 November 1886 Hardy thanked Patmore for a flattering reference to him in an article on William *Barnes. At the invitation of Edmund *Gosse, Patmore reviewed *The Woodlanders* in *St James's Gazette* on 2 April 1887 (repr. *CH*). Most of the review is devoted to a very favourable account of Hardy's work in general, but *The Woodlanders* is subjected to harsh criticism.

Paul, Charles Kegan (1828–1902), author and publisher. He was one of Hardy's earliest literary friends, and one of those who proposed him for membership of the Savile Club. A man of unorthodox views, Paul was a vegetarian and a Positivist who had been an Anglican priest but later resigned his living, and later still became a Roman Catholic. In 1877 he took over the publishing firm of H. S. King and established Kegan Paul, Trench & Co. Hardy expressed his pleasure (*L* i 67–8) at the article 'Mr Hardy's Novels' published anonymously under Paul's editorship in the *New Quarterly Magazine* (October 1879) and written by Mrs Sutherland Orr; he was also gratified (*L* i 89) by Paul's own article with the same title, published anonymously in the

British Quarterly Review (April 1881)—more surprisingly in this case, since it contained (as his interesting letter points out) 'personal remarks', such as a reference to his descent from 'a race of labouring men', of a kind that Hardy did not customarily relish.

Paul was also one of the first to recognize Hardy's authoritative depiction of the landscape and inhabitants of *Wessex, and his anonymous article in the *Examiner* ('The Wessex Labourer', 15 July 1876) praises Hardy's skill as a regional novelist. His autobiography, *Memories* (1899), refers to Hardy's depiction of Dorset life as 'absolutely true to life'. Paul knew what he was talking about, for he had been vicar of Sturminster Marshall, Dorset (1862–74), and had been associated with Joseph Arch's work on behalf of the agricultural workers of Dorset (see AGRICULTURE; 'DORSETSHIRE LABOURER, THE'); Hardy himself 'once spoke of Kegan Paul as the only man who knew Dorsetshire better than himself' (Millgate, *Thomas Hardy: His Career as a Novelist*, 118). In a letter to Hardy (25 December 1891: DCM), Paul described *Tess of the d'Urbervilles*, then under attack, as a 'really great novel', but also pointed out that no clergyman would have behaved like the one in the novel and refused Tess's appeal for her baby to be buried in consecrated ground.

The friendship between Hardy and Paul was a close one, based on mutual esteem. It was at a dinner-party at Paul's home that Hardy met T. H. Huxley (*LW* 125). Paul's firm published one-volume editions of *A Pair of Blue Eyes* and *The Return of the Native*, and under his editorship the *New Quarterly Magazine* published Hardy's novella *An Indiscretion in the Life of an Heiress* (see UNCOLLECTED STORIES) and his short stories 'The Distracted Preacher' and 'Fellow Townsmen', as well as his review of William Barnes's *Poems of Rural Life in the Dorset Dialect*.

pessimism. The word 'pessimism' has been linked so frequently with Hardy's fiction and poetry, from Victorian times to the present, that it seems to have been forgotten that pessimism was for Hardy not an end in itself but an instrument for exposure of his highly refined sense of reality—a sense better captured by the phrase 'tragic realism' than the word 'pessimism'. Hardy consistently rejected charges of pessimism, on the grounds that what his readers saw as his making the worst of things was in reality his use of such a viewpoint to take the measure of things. Take the case of the 'In Tenebris' trilogy of poems and the oft-quoted partial-line from it, 'if way to the Better there be, it exacts a full look at the Worst'. Frequently used as a touchstone for Hardy's pessimism, the seemingly pessimistic 'full look at the Worst' actually serves for Hardy as a road to the Better, to that state of affairs in which men and women's hopes and needs are consistent with the demands of their circumstances. It is never acknowledged that Hardy does not deny the possible existence of 'the Better', but rather questions the existence of a way to it, a possibility he none the less regards as so powerful as to 'exact' our full attention.

When operative, Hardy's use of pessimism—in *Jude the Obscure*, for example—is less misanthropic than humanitarian. He looks upon his men and women with sadness rather than with contempt. They are not in his eyes 'odious little vermin, smitten with pride' (in Swiftian phrase), but, rather, almost always knowing, accepting puppets of forces greater than they, creatures sadly willing to learn the beauty of the sad truth that all things decay. The fault, in Hardy's view, is not in Jude, or in Sue, but rather in the incompatibility between their temperaments and their society's and the gods' demands on them. In holding them not ultimately responsible, he does not deprive them of choice; rather he shows the severely limited choices at their disposal. The supposed victims of his pessimism keep trying to choose; too often they cannot choose correctly, or their choices are limited. So Hardy's pessimism, though often taken as serving satiric, philosophic, or even political ends, instead serves aesthetic ones. Because he placed supreme value on the spectacle of always-futile human striving against an indifferent cosmic backdrop, the pleasure of observing the beauty of the sadness of the hopeless striving was always for him the thing of first importance. His deepest pleasure seems to have been in shaping balanced and antithetical arrangements of this spectacle, or in 'repetitive symmetries', to borrow a phrase from his younger contemporary, Marcel *Proust. *Tess of the d'Urbervilles*

(1891) and *Jude the Obscure* (1895) illustrate most dramatically his taste for statement and counterstatement: the tragic spectacle of Alec's and Angel's ruin of Tess set off against the morbidly comic spectacle of Arabella and Sue's ruin of Jude. Contemporary cries of 'Tessimism' and 'Jude the Obscene' missed the mark because the undoubtedly pessimistic treatment of things in both novels is more than overshadowed by the tragic grandeur of Tess and the pathos of Jude.

Hardy's aestheticized pessimism is best illustrated by his telling, retelling, and telling yet again the story of homecoming: a comic homecoming in Fancy Day's return to Mellstock in *Under the Greenwood Tree* (1871), a tragic version of the same in Clym Yeobright's return to Egdon Heath in *The Return of the Native* (1878), a tragi-comic rewriting of the same in Grace Melbury's return to the Hintock woodlands in *The Woodlanders* (1887). Hardy's pessimism, at work to different degrees in each of these homologous narratives, can be defined for literary purposes only by its service to the project at hand: as a foil to the playful irony of the first; as an element of the brooding melancholy of the second; as a possible interpretation for the naturalistic paralleling of human and non-human lives of the third.

To approach Hardy in the belief that he is a writer inclined to impose the worst possible interpretation on things is to ignore his restless experimentation throughout his fiction and poetry with various interpretations of things. In the 1890s, when he took up once more the project (begun in the 1870s) later to be titled *The Dynasts*, he may be seen as doing so in the service of his attempt to articulate an 'evolutionary meliorism'—that is, a view that the process of change in nature is not an arbitrary or capricious one, but one guided by an unconscious will to improve the lot of human and non-human lives. In fact, Hardy's engagement with these ideas was but one more attempt at a gloss on things as he found them in all their mystery. It has been said that the spectacle of the *First World War destroyed whatever faith he might have gained in an Immanent Beneficence. However, in the context of his entire career up to 1914–18, *The Dynasts* (1903–8) is best viewed as one more effort to exhibit a 'way to the Better' by taking a 'full look at the Worst': namely, at the spectacle of Napoleon the liberator becoming Napoleon the tyrant.

In sum, Hardy's supposed pessimism is less a set attitude or frame of reference than it is an instrument of his ongoing enquiry into the nature of things on behalf of the beauty of the always sad spectacle of their working. Because his essential outlook is an ironic one, a sense that things are not as they seem to be, should be, or might be, and because his was an age governed from various influential quarters by optimism and belief in progress, he is easily mistaken for a doctrinaire pessimist, like *Schopenhauer or Swift. In fact, Hardy's ironic outlook and tragic realism, because most widely encountered in his romantic narratives with their cosmic overtones, is easily mistaken for full-blown pessimism. If it is true that Hardy's people always end worse than they begin, it is also true that in that end they enjoy hard-won dignity, strength beyond their stations, and, most important, a beauty of situation that (however severe) is absolutely genuine. Consider Jude Fawley dying to the sound of Christminster bells, Tess Durbeyfield going to her hanging without complaint, Clym Yeobright preaching sermons no one wishes to hear, Michael Henchard resolutely imposing his will upon his survivors, and Marty South at Giles Winterborne's grave uttering anything but a pessimist's eulogy ('"...you was a good man, and did good things!"'). Tess, Jude, Clym, Henchard, Giles—as flawed and foolish as they are good—end not as fools, villains, hypocrites, or Faustian predators, but rather as pillars of human strength and dignity exposed by that 'full look' into human weaknesses. PC

G. W. Sherman, *The Pessimism of Thomas Hardy* (1976).

Jeffrey Paul Von Arx, *Progress and Pessimism: Religion, Politics, and History in Late Nineteenth-Century Britain* (1985).

pets. Hardy's affection for and sympathy with animals in general (see ANIMALS; ANIMALS, CRUELTY TO) is seen in concentrated form in his relationships with his many pets. By far the best known of these is the Edward VII terrier Wessex, who was brought to Max Gate, on her marriage, by Florence Dugdale. Wessex displayed the familiar characteristics of an animal who has long been the close companion of a neurotic owner: he was without house-training, vicious, and, except to his doting owners, highly objectionable. Lady Cynthia Asquith described him as 'the most despotic dog guests had ever suffered under... [with] the longest biting history of any domestic pet!' (BBC talk, 1956). The proposal was made to keep a record of every visitor who had been assaulted by Wessex, T. E. *Lawrence being almost the only exception. In her letters, Florence Hardy sounds somewhat of a buffer between Hardy and Wessex's victims, constantly anxious about the local wish to have the dog put down. Nevertheless, Hardy adored him and, on his death in 1926, wrote the heart-broken poem 'Dead "Wessex" the Dog to the Household'. He is buried, with predecessors, in the Max Gate garden, in a pets' cemetery of the kind made fashionable by Queen Victoria, his headstone, 'drawn up by Hardy and carved from his design', describing him as 'THE FAMOUS DOG WESSEX... Faithful, Unflinching' (*LW* 469, which also quotes relevant entries from Hardy's diary).

Hardy, however, was primarily a cat-lover. At Max Gate, many residents were joined each afternoon by guests for saucers of milk on the lawn. Like Emma, many of Hardy's closest friends, including Edmund *Gosse, shared his passion. Towards the end of her life, when relations with Emma were most strained, the two could still correspond with warmth and in detail about their cats. The subject-matter of their letters ranges from damage to a maid's hat to the gardener's being instructed to drown kittens and a maid being required to comfort their mother. Such occasional tough realism, by proxy, is similarly suggested by Hardy's refusal to allow the gardener to restrain a hare from regularly feasting on their vegetables, but his willingness also to eat this same animal, cooked after it was killed by one of the cats. Hardy's grief at the death of a favourite cat is expressed in the poem 'Last Words to a Dumb Friend', which expresses his sense of a deeply distressing void left in the household by the death of 'Snowdove', whose gravestone was carved by Hardy himself. Many portraits of Hardy show him with a cat companion; these include the drawing by Jacques-Emile Blanche, and a number of photographs, such as the very late one with 'Cobby', a grey kitten and a last birthday present.

Florence Hardy was, apparently, also a (selective) animal-lover. She used anecdotes about pets in her articles as a journalist, and, with E. J. Detmold, produced a series of baby animal books, which encouraged children to treat pets kindly. (Nevertheless, within a few months of her arrival at Max Gate, all the cats were dead.) Though frequently mentioned in correspondence with friends, pets—with the exception of the caged goldfinch in *The Mayor of Casterbridge*, and a number of poems lamenting real or imaginary bereavements—figure only marginally in Hardy's writings. AE

philology. The 19th century was the great age of English philology, the historical study of English and the comparative study of related languages, especially the Germanic languages of northern and central Europe. Several influential learned societies devoted to philological scholarship were founded in Britain, including the Philological Society (1842), the Early English Text Society (1864), which published 295 volumes during Hardy's lifetime in its Original and Extra series, and the English Dialect Society (1873). At the same time works by Continental philologists were keenly studied in Britain, among them the *German Grammar* (1819) of Jakob Grimm, which offered the first historical study of the Germanic languages and included the well-known rule governing consonantal changes in several related languages that became known as Grimm's Law. In *Jude the Obscure* (1.4) Hardy describes young Jude naïvely believing that the grammar of every language has a rule or 'secret cypher, which, once known, would enable him, by merely applying it, to change at will all words of his own speech into those of the foreign one. His childish idea was, in fact, a pushing to the extremity of mathematical precision what is everywhere known as Grimm's Law.' The name 'Grimm's Law' was given currency in Britain by the Anglo-German comparative philologist Max F. M. Müller. Hardy's 'Literary Notes' contain a quotation from Müller taken from an essay in 1876, suggesting an interest in philology on Hardy's part, as does the passing reference in *Two on a Tower* (1) to the name Haymoss as 'the encrusted form of the word Amos, to adopt the phrase of philologists'.

An important result of the flourishing of philological studies was the proliferation of dictionaries, with some of which Hardy was familiar, and some of which he owned. In Gabriel Oak's modest 'library' was 'Ash's Dictionary' (*FFMC* 8), the work of a Dorset-born Baptist minister, published in 1775, but clearly still a prized possession among Dorset folk, with its proud title *The New and Complete Dictionary of the English Language*. Hardy himself owned a copy. Other dictionaries followed in the next century, becoming more ambitious and comprehensive with advances in philological scholarship. Noah Webster's *The American Dictionary of the English Language* was published in 1828 and proved popular not only in America. A few years later, in 1836–7, Charles Richardson's *New Dictionary* was distinguished by a wealth of illustrative quotations, a lexicographical innovation introduced by Dr Samuel Johnson in his famous *A Dictionary of the English Language* of 1755. P. A. Nuttall's *The Standard Pronouncing Dictionary of the English Language* appeared in 1864. Hardy owned a copy and wrote under the title: 'Used by T.H. when writing Far from the Madding Crowd.' He marked many of the words in this dictionary as of particular interest.

A century after Johnson, in the summer of 1857, the then Dean of Westminster, Richard Trench, prompted by the philologist and literary scholar Frederick J. Furnivall, read a paper to a meeting of the Philological Society entitled 'On Some Deficiencies in our English Dictionaries', outlining the principal objectives which a major new English dictionary should achieve. The Society forthwith embarked on preparations for the new dictionary, a work that was to dominate English lexicography for generations to come: the *Oxford English Dictionary* or *OED*. The first editor was Herbert Coleridge, grandson of the poet Samuel Taylor Coleridge, who was appointed in 1859 but unfortunately died in 1861. F. J. Furnivall succeeded him, but his contribution lay rather in fostering the stream of publications of the Early English Text Society, which made possible the inclusion of numerous early English words and quotations not previously accessible. Furnivall, in turn, was succeeded as editor by the Scottish schoolmaster whose name is most commonly associated with the *OED*, James (later Sir James) Murray, who edited the work from 1879 until his death in 1915. The first volume was published in 1884, the final volume in the year of Hardy's death, 1928.

In the *Life* Hardy mentioned meeting 'Sir James ("Dictionary") Murray and others' at a gathering in Cambridge in 1908 (*LW* 369), and again in Cambridge in 1913, on the occasion of Hardy's receiving the honorary degree of Doctor of Letters (*LW* 390). In July 1903 he had written a reply to Murray (*L* iii 69–70), explaining his use of the term 'pair-royal' in the raffle scene of *The Return of the Native* (3.7) and applied there to dice rather than to cards showing three identical numbers. Apart from an occurrence in connection with 'raffle', dated 1656, Hardy's is the only citation in the *OED* for 'pair-royal', although the dialect form 'prial' was used by Thomas de Quincey in 1840, and is recorded in the *English Dialect Dictionary* with reference to cards. Hardy's affinity with the *OED* is also apparent from a letter he wrote in May 1912 (*L* iv 214) to Sydney *Cockerell, director of the Fitzwilliam Museum in Cambridge, saying that he somewhere referred to a rabbit's nest as its 'form', which normally refers to a hare. He could have used the dialect word 'stop' for a hole in the ground in which a rabbit deposits her young. 'I wish', he adds, 'I had sent "stop" to Murray for his dictionary—but perhaps he will have it all the same.' It is indeed in the *OED*, citing William Cobbett's *Rural Rides*, and in Joseph Wright's *English Dialect Dictionary*, the *EDD*, published 1898–1905, as a southern English dialect word.

Hardy's linguistic resourcefulness, nourished by the fruits of contemporary philology, knew no bounds, but he was upset by critics condemning his dialectal usages, his archaisms and coinages. When one critic complained of Hardy's expression 'his shape smalled in the distance', Hardy wondered what else he could have written. When on a few occasions he had looked a disputed word up in the dictionary, he discovered that the sole authority quoted was himself in a half-forgotten novel. Hardy was not the first to use 'small' as an intransitive verb, but the *OED* cites his poem 'Departure' as an example: 'All smalling slowly to the gray sea-line.' Altogether there are well over 2,000 citations from Hardy's works in the *OED* and *EED*, many of them first occurrences, according to the painstaking investigations of Professor Yoshinoshin Goto of Japan.

The study of dialects, which culminated in the foundation of the English Dialect Society and led to the publication of the *EDD*, formed an important part of Victorian philology, and here Hardy was singularly well placed, growing up and living for much of his life in a region of England whose local speech had its roots in the Wessex of King Alfred the Great in the 9th century. Hardy's own Wessex extended geographically and dialectally beyond his native Dorset, and in this he differed from his mentor, 'the Dorsetshire poet and philologer', William *Barnes. They became friends, and their friendship continued until Barnes's death in 1886, the year of the publication of the second, much revised, edition of the 'philologer's' *A Glossary of the Dorset Dialect with a Grammar of its Word Shapening and Wording*, which had first appeared in 1863.

Barnes's idiosyncratic technical vocabulary of 'word shapening', and 'breathpennings', and 'twysound', and similar attempts at 'purifying' the language cannot disguise his wide-ranging philological scholarship and knowledge of languages. Hardy did not embrace Barnes's often eccentric Anglo-Saxonizing of his vocabulary, but he responded with his own creative genius to the recovery of our linguistic past. In his obituary of Barnes, published in the *Athenaeum* in 1886, Hardy paid tribute to his friend's 'systematic study of his native dialect, as a result of which he has shown the world that far from being, as popularly supposed, a corruption of correct English, it is a distinct branch of Teutonic speech, regular in declension and conjugation, and richer in many classes of words than any other tongue known to him'. One of the fruits of Barnes's Anglo-Saxonizing of his language was his creation of compound words in the manner of Old English, thereby greatly enriching his dialect poems—a facility which Hardy also possessed. In Hardy's poem 'The Last Signal—A Memory of William Barnes', the compound words 'yew-boughed' and 'grave-way' are perhaps a deliberate recognition of his friend's linguistic legacy. In *Far from the Madding Crowd* (56) and in *Jude the Obscure* (4.4), Hardy quotes directly from Barnes's poems 'Woak Hill' and 'Shaftesbury Feair' respectively, and in 1908 he edited *Select Poems of William Barnes* for the Clarendon Press, complete with a Preface and Glossarial Notes.

Dennis Taylor aptly describes Hardy's literary language, especially the language of his poetry, as Hardy's 'philological laboratory'. Here he experimented with every linguistic facet known to him. He had learnt much from Barnes, but in the course of his long life Hardy's own philological interests widened, inspired by the work of many English and foreign grammarians, lexicographers, and comparative philologists like Jakob Grimm and Friedrich von Schlegel, Müller and Furnivall, Richard Trench and Alexander Ellis. Two indefatigable editors of early English texts who merit special mention are Henry Sweet, the model for George Bernard Shaw's Henry Higgins in *Pygmalion*, whose *The Oldest English Texts* appeared in 1885 and whose *Anglo-Saxon Reader* of 1876 has remained a popular textbook for more than a century, and W. W. Skeat, among whose masterpieces is the six-volume edition of the works of Chaucer, published in 1894.

Two societies specifically concerned with the English language of which Hardy became a member were the English Association, founded in 1906, 'to foster and develop the study of English as an essential element in our national education', and the Society for Pure English (SPE), founded in 1913. Hardy took the aim of 'pure' English seriously, albeit not quite in the manner of Barnes. One of the founders of the SPE was the American-born writer Logan Pearsall Smith, to whom Hardy wrote in 1913 that in *Wessex Poems* he had 'tried to popularize some good old English words, still living, down here' (*L* iv 318). And in 1919 he wrote to Robert Bridges, another of the founders of the SPE, that 'never was pure English in more need of help—owing to the influence of American journalism, I suppose. Even in our leading newspapers the headlines are appalling. It is curious that there seems to be no good English Grammar in existence. I wish one of the Society wd take that up' (*L* v 333).

A matter of philological as well as emotional interest for Hardy was the close relationship between the English and German languages. The dialect he heard 'in loamy Wessex lanes' with its 'Er war' and 'Ich woll', inspired the 1915 poem 'The Pity of It' with its recognition that 'kin folk kin tongued even as are we', English and Germans. Even the *First World War could not destroy the sentiment; on the contrary, he thought that the young German prisoners of war sent to work in the garden at Max Gate were 'amiable'. Already in *The Woodlanders*, some three decades earlier, Hardy had ascribed to Grammer Oliver such dialect usages as 'Ich woll' and 'Ich have', with its retention of the Old English personal pronoun, so close to the corresponding German word.

Hardy was able to traverse a thousand years of English linguistic history, to compare English with other languages, and to introduce into his 'philological laboratory' many ancient words, Anglo-Saxon, medieval, or Renaissance words, some extinct, others archaic, but all given new life and meaning and resonance in his own literary language. In this process he had access increasingly to dictionaries of older English and of other languages, products of the philological labours of scholars in Britain and abroad. Among the more important of these works were the monumental *Greek-English Lexicon* by H. G. Liddell and Robert Scott of 1843, which Hardy celebrated in his humorous poem 'Liddell and Scott', and Lewis and Short's *Latin Dictionary* of 1879. Anglo-Saxon dictionaries, an Icelandic–English dictionary, and etymological dictionaries of English, German, and French were all published in the course of Hardy's life. And all the while 'was fashioning' (as Hardy wrote of the *Titanic*) the *Oxford English Dictionary*, that great monument of Victorian philology. As Dennis Taylor has perceptively remarked: 'Hardy's words travel from dictionary to novels and poems and back to the dictionary.'

RE

Dennis Taylor, 'Hardy, Professor Goto, and the Oxford English Dictionary', *THJ* 4 (1988).
—— *Hardy's Literary Language and Victorian Philology* (1993).

philosophy. Hardships in her early years made Hardy's mother feel that nothing in life should be taken for granted, and this attitude was transmitted to her firstborn. After a happy summer with Emma Gifford in Cornwall, Hardy wrote (30 October 1870): 'Mother's notion, & also mine: That a figure stands in our van with arm uplifted, to knock us back from any pleasant prospect we indulge in as probable' (*PN* 6–7).

Familiar at first hand with 'nature red in tooth and claw' on 'Egdon Heath' and in the woods near his home, he was 'among the earliest acclaimers' of Darwin's *Origin of Species* (1859) (see DARWINISM), published while he was still in his teens, though he was never one to share Darwin's sense of grandeur in the evolutionary theory of the survival of the fittest: he was always on the side of the Pities, while acknowledging the truth of the Years in the dialectic of *The Dynasts*. By the age of 25 he had clearly studied much scientific and agnostic thought. He had developed an early interest in *astronomy, as is evident from the sonnet 'At a Lunar Eclipse' (apparently written in his twenties) and, more extensively, *Two on a Tower*.

It also seems most unlikely that he would have neglected such an epoch-making book as Sir Charles Lyell's *Principles of Geology* (1830–3). Geological time is seen by Henry Knight in the celebrated cliff-hanging scene in *A Pair of Blue Eyes* as he gazes at an 'imbedded' fossil trilobite and pictures 'the varied scenes ... between this creature's epoch and his own'. The poem 'At Castle Boterel', one of the elegies commemorating the death of his first wife, sees her in their first courtship days and reflects how much the 'primeval rocks' they passed on the Boscastle road had witnessed 'of the transitory in Earth's long order'. (See also GEOLOGY.)

This finds a counterpart in a notebook entry concerning 'the enthusiasm of Sir Charles Lyell, who when travelling along a cutting gazed out of the railway carriage as if the sides were hung with beautiful pictures' (*LN* ii 116). Nineteenth-century science had taught him that transitoriness is the condition of the physical world as of human existence, and characteristically the first poem in his first collection of verse begins 'Change and chancefulness in my flowering youth time' ('The Temporary the All', *WP*). In the fourth poem in the same collection ('Hap'), 'Time' conspires with 'Crass Casualty' to mete out good and ill fortune indifferently.

His major characters suffer from chance misfortune: Tess's 'single opportunity of existence ever vouchsafed... by an unsympathetic First Cause—her all, her every and only chance' (35) is blighted, like the apples in the orchard. (The uncompromising phrase 'single opportunity of existence' had been used much earlier of Cytherea, the heroine of *Desperate Remedies* (13.4).) The same chapter of *Tess* ends with a bleak reference to 'the harrowing contingencies of human experience'. Hardy accepted *Swinburne's views, expressed in his 'Hymn to Proserpine' (in *Poems and Ballads* (1866), an early enthusiasm of Hardy's): 'Nay, for a little while we live, and life has mutable wings, | A little while and we die; shall not life thrive as it may? | For no man under the sun lives twice, outliving his day, | And grief is a grievous thing...'.

In a later conversation with William *Archer, Hardy claimed that his 'practical philosophy' had been melioristic (rather than pessimistic) and said that his books had been a plea 'against "man's inhumanity to man"—to woman, and to the lower animals'. 'Whatever may be the inherent good or evil of life,' he added, 'it is certain that man makes it much worse than it need be.' Such feelings were certainly much intensified by the horrors of the *First World War.

From an early period, when under the spell of Shelley's thought, he had accepted the view that neither chance nor purpose governs the universe but 'necessity'. As he noted in his later years, such a view approximated to those of Spinoza and Einstein (*LW* 364). Necessity could be regarded as a web of circumstance linking widely separated and apparently unconnected elements: in *The Woodlanders*, the death of Mrs Charmond (at the hands of a lover from South Carolina) is related to the American Civil War. Such determinism allows the individual little choice: Hardy envisages only a 'modicum of free will', 'conjecturally possessed by organic life when the mighty necessitating forces—unconscious or other... happen to be in equilibrium, which may or may not be often' ('Apology' to *Late Lyrics and Earlier*; cf. *LW* 361).

Hardy believed, however, that there was an 'inherent will to enjoy' in organic life, from human to ephemeron, thwarted as humans know by circumstance: 'So the two forces were at work here as everywhere, the inherent will to enjoy, and the circumstantial will against enjoyment' (*TDU* 43). He believed that creatures live in their own worlds. The darkling thrush in 'blast-beruffled plume' sings joyfully without apparent reason for hope. How does the bird or the crocus know, when there is no change in temperature, that spring approaches? is the question he raises in 'The Year's Awakening'. When four of 'God's humblest' creatures are drawn to his lamp, 'so meet we five' he writes, as if he were in no way their superior, or were even their inferior: 'They know Earth-secrets that know not I' ('An August Midnight').

A special feature of Hardy's presentation of Darwinian ideas is the struggle for existence between trees, which are 'to men akin— | Combatants all!' ('In a Wood'). Their vocalized sorrows and visible wounds are vividly presented in *The Woodlanders* (especially 3, 43). Within a wood may be found (as Hardy declares in Shakespearian tones) 'Fair growths, foul cankers, right enmeshed with wrong, | Strange orchestras of victim-shriek and song, | And curious blends of ache and ecstasy' ('The Sleep-Worker'). Nature is like Shelley's Necessity, 'whose sightless strength for ever | Evil with evil, good with good, must wind | In bands of union, which no power may sever' (*The Revolt of Islam* 9.27). From Nature's sightlessness proceed 'those fearful unfulfilments' in her 'world-webs' and 'that red ravage through her zones | Whereat all creation groans' ('The Lacking Sense', a poem that also echoes Shelley's 'sightless', while St Paul's reference to all creation groaning is cited again in *JO* 6.2). In 'Doom and She' Nature is once more 'Unlit with sight' and tells God that 'Shapings that eyelessly I dare | Maybe I would undo'. Nature had not proposed a creature like man, intelligent enough to discern her defects, 'Each flaw and each stain', and one who could declare, '"Give me... but the matter | And means the gods lot her, | My brain could evolve a creation | More seemly, more sane"' ('The Mother Mourns').

A diary entry of 9 May 1881 notes that, after 'infinite trying to reconcile a scientific view of life with the emotional and spiritual, so that they may not be interdestructive', he had formulated the general principles of a theory of the 'unfulfilled intention', much of it based on ideas he had encountered in John Stuart

*Mill's *Three Essays on Religion* (1874): this held that 'Law' (i.e. Nature) 'has produced in man a child who cannot but constantly reproach its parent for doing much and yet not all, and constantly say to such parent that it would have been better never to have begun doing than to have *over*done so decisively; that is, than to have created so far beyond all apparent first intention (on the emotional side), without mending matters by a second intent and execution, to eliminate the evils of the blunder of overdoing. The emotions have no place in a world of defect, and it is a cruel injustice that they have developed in it.' The note adds that 'If Law itself had consciousness, how the aspect of its creatures would terrify it, fill it with remorse!' (*LW* 153). A little earlier, in *The Return of the Native*, Clym Yeobright 'already showed that thought is a disease of the flesh, and indirectly bore evidence that ideal physical beauty is incompatible with emotional development and a full recognition of the coil of things'. Clym's was 'the typical countenance of the future.... That old-fashioned revelling in the general situation grows less and less possible as we uncover the defects of natural laws, and see the quandary man is in by their operation' (*RN* 2.6, 3.6).

Later, regretting that the human race was too nervously developed for its 'corporeal conditions', Hardy thought that this state extended to higher animals, and questioned whether Nature 'did not exceed her mission' when she 'crossed the line from invertebrates to vertebrates' (*LW* 227). This diary entry of 7 April 1889 concludes by reflecting that 'This planet does not supply the materials for happiness to higher existences. Other planets may, though one can hardly see how.' With J. S. Mill he believed that we should co-operate with beneficent powers in Nature and 'Assist her where thy creaturely dependence can or may, | For thou art of her clay' ('The Lacking Sense'). In another poem, 'He Wonders About Himself', he asks the question, 'Part is mine of the general will, | Cannot my share in the sum of sources | Bend a digit the poise of forces, | And a fair desire fulfil?'

Such an 'intent... Of that enkindling ardency from whose maturer glows | The world's amendment flows' ('A Commonplace Day') activates the Pities until, at the end of *The Dynasts*, they hear stirrings which make them believe that the Will, blind and insentient from the beginning, is becoming conscious and will 'fashion all things fair'. These spirits, 'In fair compassions skilled', love 'the true, the excellent', and exert civilizing influences. The 1914–18 War, however, 'gave the *coup de grâce* to any conception [Hardy] may have had of a fundamental ultimate Wisdom at the back of things', and he came to regret having concluded *The Dynasts* with the expression of a belief in 'the gradual ennoblement of man' that 'he had held for many years', since recent history suggested that 'the never-ending push of the Universe was an unpurposive and irresponsible groping in the direction of the least resistance' (*LW* 398).

Three thinkers who exerted an especially important influence on Hardy were Herbert Spencer, whose *First Principles* (1862) used to act on him 'as a sort of patent expander' whenever he had been 'particularly narrowed down' by life; T. H. Huxley, the biologist; and Leslie *Stephen, his editor and friend. Spencer was an evolutionary before Darwin's conclusions were published; Stephen's philosophy (Hardy wrote) 'was to influence his own for many years, indeed, more than that of any other contemporary' (*LW* 102). Stephen owed much to J. S. Mill, and Mill to the French philosophical sociologist Auguste *Comte, a translation of one of whose works Hardy read in 1865. Further study of Comte followed at later periods, and he became friendly with some of Comte's principal adherents in England.

Comte's *Positivism was based on the argument that, having no assurance of life after death, we should concentrate our efforts on the amelioration of life on earth; his 'religion of humanity' aimed at the raising of standards through education and science and the active, zealous promotion of justice and altruism. Mill's 'new commandment' was 'to love one another'; it is, according to Clym Yeobright's preaching (*RN* 6.3), the eleventh commandment and is echoed in the 'loving-kindness' of the 'Apology' to *Late Lyrics and Earlier*, where Hardy's hope for the future lies in the minimization of pain for all on earth through loving-kindness and the use of science. 'Altruism, or The Golden Rule, or whatever "Love your Neighbour as Yourself" may be called, will ultimately be brought about... by the pain we see in others reacting on ourselves, as if we and they were a part of one body' (*LW* 235), he wrote in 1890; in 1909 he maintained that 'the law of evolution, which revealed that all organic creatures are of one family, shifted the centre of altruism from humanity to the whole conscious world collectively' (*LW* 373). In the poetic fantasy 'A Plaint to Man'—the best expression of Hardy's hope for the future—the dying God insists that since 'tomorrow the whole of me disappears | The truth should be told, and the fact be faced | That had best been faced in earlier years: | The fact of life with dependence placed | On the human heart's resource alone, | In brotherhood bonded close and graced | With loving-kindness fully blown, | And visioned help unsought, unknown'. Progress will come, he believed, when people realize that they must rely on their own resources and not on imagined help from Providence.

It is not easy to understand how Hardy, who was an evolutionary meliorist and had written *The Dynasts* from that point of view, could think that mankind would be better off if it returned to the state when it was devoid of feeling and thereby no longer suffered the pains of sickness, love, loss, regret, or 'whatever crash or cross brought wrack to things'. But the 'life of emotion' to which he surrendered as a poet made him subject to inconstant moods, and in 'Before Life and After' he prefers 'primal rightness' to civilizing advance: 'But the disease of feeling germed, | And primal rightness took the tinct of wrong; | Ere nescience shall be reaffirmed | How long, how long?' This is the regressive alternative of his Unfulfilled Intention, the opposite of his Positivist beliefs which by and large gave him strength, and of the view that concludes 'Fragment' (in *Moments of Vision*) that the Ultimate Cause will become conscious of his earthly wrongs: '"By some still close-cowled mystery | We have reached feeling faster than he, | But he will overtake us anon | If the world goes on."' Hardy's theory of the Unfulfilled Intention, memorably dramatized in a vivid passage in *The Woodlanders* (7), had included Mill's assumption that the powers of the First Cause were limited and it was unable to provide all that it originally intended to bestow on us.

Positivism had made Hardy incredulous of life after death: 'When a man falls he lies', he wrote in 'A Sign-Seeker'. Life could survive death only in the memory of those who outlived the deceased, and for most people that could not last long. As he observes in another poem, 'A Shade but in its mindful ones | Has immortality' ('Her Immortality'). The thought is developed in 'His Immortality' and 'The To-Be-Forgotten', in the latter of which the question arises: '"For which of us could hope | To show in life the world-awakening scope | Granted the few whose memory none lets die | But all men magnify?"' Yet, after the death of his first wife in 1912 and of his sister Mary three years later, the old assurance had gone. In 'He Prefers Her Earthly' he thinks of Emma, the fearless pony-rider of St Juliot, and imagines her 'Changed to a firmament-riding earthless essence' as he gazes at the 'glory-show' of an 'after-sunset'. In 'Paradox' he wonders if Mary remembers those she has left, and concludes: 'Can she, then, know how men's fatings befall? | Yea indeed, may know well; even know thereof all.' What a blessing it would be, he had written in 'A Sign-Seeker', 'In grave-yard green, where his pale dust lies pent | To glimpse a phantom parent, friend, | Wearing his smile, and "Not the end!" | Outbreathing softly: that were blest enlightenment'. On Christmas Eve 1919 he was convinced he saw a ghost after placing a sprig of holly on his grandfather's grave; when Hardy followed it into Stinsford church it had vanished. In such an episode we have moved far from the novelist who insisted of two of his heroines (Cytherea and Tess) that their lives were their sole existence.

Having been too absolute himself, Hardy was ready in his later years to admit that man's knowledge and perceptions were too limited to fathom the mysteries of life. In 'Drinking Song' he is at one with the *Tennyson who wrote in *In Memoriam* that 'Our little systems have their day: | They have their day and cease to be'; his theme is the discrediting of conclusions drawn by thinkers on life and the universe from Thales of Ancient Greece onwards. He agreed with Herbert Spencer's 'doctrine of the Unknowable' (*LW* 400) and complained that his own works were treated as if they constituted a system of philosophy, insisting that they were in fact no more than a record of 'seemings', provisional only and 'used for artistic purposes because they represent approximately the impressions of the age, and are plausible, till somebody produces better theories of the universe' (*LW* 406). At the end of 1920 he protested that he had no philosophy, 'Merely what I have often explained to be only a confused heap of impressions, like those of a bewildered child at a conjuring-show'; 'it is my misfortune that people *will* treat all my mood-dictated writing as a single scientific theory', he concluded (*LW* 441). It is open to question, however, whether this striking late pronouncement may be taken as representative of a consistent and lifelong belief.

FBP

pictorialism. To recall a Hardy novel is to recall pictures: Angel Clare sleep-walking with Tess in his arms (*TDU* 37), Michael Henchard peering down from a bridge at his effigy in the waters below (*MC* 41), Diggory Venn and Damon Wildeve gambling by the light of glow-worms (*RN* 3.8). Hardy is manifestly a pictorial novelist in the basic sense that he enables the reader to see what he describes. The generalization holds true for both characters and scenery, as in 'a short man with a nose resembling a copper knob, a damp voice, and eyes like button-holes' (*MC* 1); or 'a chappie with no chin, and a moustache like a lady's eyebrow' (*JO* 3.8); or 'On the right hand the sun, resting on the horizon-line, streamed across the ground from below copper-coloured and lilac clouds, stretched out in flats beneath a sky of pale soft green. All dark objects on the earth that lay towards the sun were overspread by a purple haze, against which a swarm of wailing gnats shone forth luminously, rising upward and floating away like sparks of fire' (*DR* 12; see also *RN* 3.5).

Although nearly all the great Victorian novelists show a concern with the visual, their work tends to be weighted towards commentary and dialogue. In Hardy less is said and explained, more is seen. In any case, few could emulate his freshness of simile or powerful command of effects of light, shade, and colour. He is a writer who both sketches and paints. Colour adjectives proliferate, fastidiously precise. He pays particular attention to the shifting brightness of sunrise and sunset, and to the dramatic potentialities of fire-light and candle-light. But more fundamentally his very mode of description is expressive of meaning: he illustrates and interrogates what he takes to be the human tendency to experience life itself in terms of pictures.

Hardy has often been called a cinematic novelist, and the anachronistic compliment is well justified. Everywhere he shows us what his characters see, or what 'an observer' might see. He deals in close-up, cross-cutting, juxtaposition, tracking. Many of his descriptive passages could be read as direct instructions to director or camera-man:

> they both contemplated the picture presented in front, and noticed how the farmer's wife sat flattened between the two men, who bulged over each end of the seat to give her room till they almost sat upon their respective wheels: and they looked too at the farmer's wife's silk mantle inflating itself between her shoulders like a balloon and sinking flat again at each jog of the horse. (*UGT* 3.1)

> The present writer... can never enter the old living-room of Overcombe Mill without beholding the genial scene through the mists of the seventy or eighty years that intervene between then and now. First and brightest to the eye are the dozen candles scattered about regardless of expense, and kept well snuffed by the miller, who walks round the room at intervals of five minutes, snuffers in hand, and nips each wick with great precision, and with something of an executioner's grim look upon his face as he closes the snuffers upon the neck of the candle. Next to the candlelights show the red and blue coats and white breeches of the soldiers—nearly twenty of them in all, besides the ponderous Derriman—the head of the latter, and, indeed, the heads of all who are standing up, being in dangerous proximity to the black beams of the ceiling. (*TM* 5)

Both passages are powerfully imagined, acutely observed, carefully placed. We see 'the picture' through the eyes of Dick and Fancy, 'the scene' through the eyes of Hardy himself. Though only the latter episode makes use of the present tense, from the reader's point of view both are happening in a continuous present: one is timed by the jog of the horse, the other by the miller's candle-snuffing. This immediacy of presentation, as of something directly experienced, does much to give Hardy's work its extraordinary vitality.

Yet he is anything but a naïve picture-painter. *Desperate Remedies*, his first published novel, shows him already explicitly testing out the limits of description. At the simplest level he is intrigued by the problem of making his characters visualizable. Having devoted almost a page to an account of his heroine, Cytherea Graye, he immediately adds a reservation: 'But to attempt to gain a view of her—or indeed of any fascinating woman—from a measured category, is as difficult as to appreciate the effect of a landscape by exploring it at night with a lantern—or of a full chord of music by piping the notes in succession' (1). In a very few pages he returns to the topic. When Cytherea asks her brother about Edward Springrove, a new acquaintance he has mentioned, Owen replies: '"I can't exactly tell you his appearance: 'tis always such a difficult thing to do"' (2). Yet in response to a deft line of questioning he is induced to venture: '"He has dark hair, almost a Grecian nose, regular teeth, and an intellectual face..."'. Cytherea cries: '"Ah, there now, Owen, you have described him!"' Nevertheless, eager to learn more, she continues her questioning. Later, when she comes to meet Springrove, quite unexpectedly, it happens that 'she acquired perceptions of the new-comer in the following order: unknown trousers; unknown waistcoat; unknown face' (2). Only when he has introduced himself and taken off his hat does she have a chance—which gives Hardy a chance—to 'examine the appearance' of her future lover. The mode swiftly moves from the literal to the impressionistic: 'his glance sometimes seeming to state, "I have already thought out the issue of such conditions as these we are experiencing."'

Even from this early sequence it is possible to infer certain of Hardy's habitual attitudes towards physical description: that it can have at least a serviceable defining force, that much may depend on the conditions in which the person or thing is seen, and that what is visible on the surface may be far less significant than what can be deduced from it. Despite his talent for sketching a face, Hardy insists that a countenance should not merely be seen, but be read—especially the countenance of a thinking, feeling man such as Clym Yeobright: 'Hence, people who began by beholding him ended by perusing him. His countenance was overlaid with legible meanings.... He already showed that thought is a disease of flesh...' (*RN* 2.6). It follows that many of the faces which Hardy pictures in visual terms he then proceeds to interpret.

Early in *Desperate Remedies* can be found linked illustrations of a further aspect of Hardy's interest in the complexities of seeing and picturing. From the Town Hall Cytherea notices her architect father and four workmen standing on the scaffolding enclosing a newly built church spire: 'The picture thus presented to a spectator in the Town Hall was curious and striking. It was an illuminated miniature, framed in by the dark margin of the window, the keen-edged shadiness of which emphasized by contrast the softness of the objects enclosed' (*DR* 1). Repeatedly in his fiction Hardy frames a 'picture' in this way, usually by means of a window. Obviously this habit of presenting a composed scene, carefully lit, reflects his keen interest in the visual arts; but there is more to it than that. Here is the earliest example of the sustained tensions in his work between narrative and description and between sensationalism and decorum. Held motionless for a moment in this 'illuminated miniature' Mr Graye is about to plunge to his death—just out of frame. The episode could have been extravagant, but the presentation distances it. 'The picture' is soundless, disciplined, stylized, and precise. Similarly the disruptive deaths of Alec d'Urberville and Michael Henchard take place off-stage, and are distilled into controlled visual images—respectively of a blood-stained ceiling and a ruined cottage. In all these cases, and many others of a less melodramatic kind, an event is translated into a single, memorable picture.

But the episode in *Desperate Remedies* is to make a further point—almost a converse point—about the relationship between seeing and feeling. Just as a painful event can be mediated through a depersonalized image, so may a neutral image come to project feelings that have been arbitrarily associated with it. Cytherea faints upon seeing her father fall. When she comes to herself, 'her eyes caught sight of the south-western sky, and, without heeding, saw white sunlight shining in shaft-like lines from a rift in a slaty cloud.

Emotions will attach themselves to scenes that are simultaneous—however foreign in essence these scenes may be—as chemical waters will crystallize on twigs and wires. Ever after that time any mental agony brought less vividly to Cytherea's mind the scene from the Town Hall windows than sunlight streaming in shaft-like lines' (*DR* 1).

In the same way Gabriel Oak's grief at the death of his sheep is to be linked in his mind with the bleak pond he sees as he reflects on his loss: 'All this Oak saw and remembered' (*FFMC* 5). The speaker in the early poem 'Neutral Tones' describes another pond, beside which he and a lover have quarrelled. The conclusion is similar in its effect: 'Since then, keen lessons that love deceives, | And wrings with wrong, have shaped to me | Your face, and the God-curst sun, and a tree, | And a pond edged with grayish leaves.'

For Hardy, in short, 'pictures' can be charged with powerful emotions. They may enable the reader to experience, or at least to infer, the feeling concerned. The most enigmatic exercise of this kind is probably 'On the Esplanade'. The poem moves from past to present tense as a scene and a particular moment are vividly evoked—but evoked solely in relation to some unspecified drama which the narrator is about to enter upon:

> Inside a window, open, with undrawn blind,
> There plays and sings
> A lady unseen a melody undefined:
> And where the moon flings
> Its shimmer a vessel crosses, whereon to the strings
> Plucked sweetly and low
> Of a harp, they dance. Yea, such did I mark. That, behind,
> My Fate's masked face crept near me I did not know!

Hardy is appealing to common experience: 'You know how a place can become retrospectively memorable when it proves to be the site of a decisive incident in one's life.' Though the ensuing story is not told, the picture that emerges from the poem remains intriguing, surrealistically suspended, charged with mysterious potentiality.

To a remarkable extent Hardy's very narrative method is founded upon seeing. Where most novelists establish relationships between their characters by means of social encounters—visits, conversations, chance meetings—Hardy typically deals in 'sightings'. Dick Dewy sees Fancy framed by her window (*UGT* 1.5), Gabriel sees Bathsheba lying flat on the back of her horse (*FFMC* 3), Captain de Stancy sees Paula Power exercising in her private gymnasium (*AL* 2.7), and effectively each of the three is immediately in love. In *A Pair of Blue Eyes* Hardy remarks: 'Every woman who makes a permanent impression on a man is usually recalled to his mind's eye as she appeared in one particular scene, which seems ordained to be her special form of manifestation throughout the pages of his memory' (3). A similar, but slightly different, point is made in *Desperate Remedies*. Hardy speaks there of an early stage of love 'when on the man's part, the mistress appears to the mind's eye in picturesque, hazy, and fresh morning lights, and soft morning shadows; when, as yet, she is known only as the wearer of one dress, which shares her own personality; as the stander in one special position, the giver of one bright particular glance...' (3). The sense here is that such an impression will come to be collated with, or overlaid by, others—and that an accumulation of such pictures is the nearest one can get to full knowledge.

In nearly all such cases the mood or disposition of the seer has an implied effect on what is seen. When Knight, in *A Pair of Blue Eyes*, peers down from the cliff-face to which he is clinging, 'The sea would have been a deep neutral blue had happier auspices attended the gazer: it was now no otherwise than distinctly black to his vision' (22). If Gabriel were not in the 'listlessly' wretched mood occasioned by the loss of his sheep the pool he contemplates might not seem to glitter 'like a dead man's eye'. The emphasis can vary as between the facts of the scene and the mood of the observer. The bleak dawn landscape which confronts Boldwood after his receipt of Bathsheba's valentine is a reflection of his own confusion and apprehension (*FFMC* 14). Disorderly feelings have been ordered into a picture.

It is only after this night of crisis that Boldwood 'for the first time really looked at' Bathsheba, and 'thought her beautiful' (17). Hardy regularly shows how romantic predisposition can colour what we see. In *The Woodlanders* Fitzpiers explains to Giles

Winterborne that love is a matter of projection: had 'any other young lady' appeared before him at the appropriate time he would have felt the same love for her as he claims to feel for Grace Melbury (16). Hardy would surely endorse his earlier, rather different, observation, that love involves 'an idea which we project against any suitable object in the line of our vision' (16). There is more to the matter than mere projection: Grace is 'suitable' for Fitzpiers in a way which Suke Damson is not. To an extent we choose the pictures that we see, and colour them according to our emotional tastes.

For Hardy what is true of our romantic responses is true of our responses to life in general. In the preface to *Jude the Obscure* he speaks of his repeated attempts 'to give shape and coherence to a series of seemings, or personal impressions'. He offers a number of these in his autobiography—for example, an observation at a First-Aid class: 'A skeleton—the one used in these lectures—is hung up inside the window. We face it as we sit. Outside the band is playing, and the children are dancing. I can see their little figures through the window past the skeleton dangling in front' (*LW* 163). Here the juxtaposition produces its own ironic 'seeming'. In the fiction, neutral images can elicit a powerfully subjective response: 'Fitzpiers had observed some of Melbury's men dragging away a large limb which had been snapped off a beech-tree. Everything was cold and colourless. "My good God!" he said as he stood in his dressing-gown. "This is life!"' (*W* 30). For that man, in that mood, the scene offers a chilling comment on the emptiness of existence.

These particular vignettes are highlighted, isolated. But Hardy's fiction can be fully appreciated only when it is understood that his 'pictorialism' in general—his prevailing habit of visual description—goes far beyond providing picturesque backgrounds. It is charged with possible meanings for his characters and for the reader. For this reason his novels, for all their cinematic qualities, are not readily translated into successful films. It is easier to replicate the visual effects than to capture their implied significance. Hardy's verbal pictures offer not only possible 'meanings' but a tacit commentary on the human tendency to seek or impose them. MI

plagiarism. Carl J. Weber has suggested (*Review of English Studies*, 17 (1941)) that the storm scene in *Far from the Madding Crowd* (37) relies heavily on a similar description in Harrison *Ainsworth's *Rookwood* (Book II, Ch. 1), a novel with which Hardy is known to have been familiar from boyhood: 'He did not copy it word for word . . .', writes Weber, 'but he came close to doing so.' This claim has been challenged: see, for example, V. T. Hopkins in *Thomas Hardy Society Review*, 1 (1978), and the vigorous dismissal by Robert Gittings (*Young Thomas Hardy*, 191), who insists that 'Being so close to his originals in real life, Hardy had no need of literary models'.

Among acknowledgements to his sources, 'oral and written', in the 1895 preface to *The Trumpet-Major*, Hardy writes: 'The drilling scene of the local militia received some additions from an account given in so grave a work as Gifford's "History of the Wars of the French Revolution" (London, 1817).' This statement seems to be a response to strictures in the *Critic*, the *Academy*, and other American periodicals, alleging that he had plagiarized a passage in a work by an American author, A. B. Longstreet's *Georgia Scenes* (1835). The situation seems to have been, however, that Longstreet had based his own account of military drill on Gifford's book. (See also NAPOLEONIC WARS.)

On Hardy's protests against the alleged plagiarism of his *The Mistress of the Farm*, a dramatization of *Far from the Madding Crowd*, in A. W. Pinero's play *The Squire*, see DRAMATIZATIONS.

'Poems of 1912–13'. Hardy paid a tribute to his own memory when he wrote that 'I believe it would be said by people who know me well that I have a faculty (possibly not uncommon) for burying an emotion in my heart or brain for forty years, and exhuming it at the end of that time as fresh as when interred' (*LW* 408). The 'Poems of 1912–13' show how true this was. Dates and anniversaries meant a great deal to him, and one that he was never to forget was the meeting on 7 March 1870 with Emma Lavinia Gifford (see HARDY, EMMA LAVINIA). He was then in his thirtieth year, an aspiring poet and novelist who had so far failed to get anything of importance published, but a successful architect, specializing in work on ancient churches. The Weymouth architect by whom he was then employed sent him to the tiny hamlet of St Juliot, near Boscastle in *Cornwall, to draw up plans for the restoration of the dilapidated church of St Julitta. He left his home very early on that morning of 7 March, and on arrival at St Juliot Rectory met the Rector, his wife, and her sister Emma. Both Hardy and Emma were in their thirtieth year, both more than ready for marriage, and love soon grew up between them. Hardy's poem 'When I Set Out for Lyonnesse' may well have been written about this time, though it was not published by Hardy until after Emma's death.

They were married in September 1876 and lived together until her death nearly forty years later, in November 1912. It was at first a happy relationship, and the two years they spent at *Sturminster Newton in 1876–8 were later described by Hardy as idyllic. By the mid-1880s, however, that first fine careless rapture had gone, and the couple were drifting apart. This is seen in Hardy's increasing concern in his later novels, and particularly in *The Woodlanders* (1887) and *Jude the Obscure* (1896), with the marriage 'problem': 'given the man and woman, how to find a basis for their sexual relation' (preface to *The Woodlanders*).

It is never easy for the outsider to know what is happening in a marriage, but we do know that Emma was a snob who looked down on Hardy's humble origins and his relatives; that she was almost fanatically religious and resented Hardy's agnosticism; that she also resented his growing success as a novelist; that she was very upset by the moral views expressed so powerfully by her husband in *Jude*; and that she could not come to terms with his relationships with upper-class society and the women who took advantage of him in order to advance their own careers as writers. He, for his part, sometimes acted towards her with an insensitivity that was completely out of keeping with his sensitivity as a writer. Children would have helped, but as Hardy put it in a note quoted in his autobiography, 'never a sign of one is there for us' (*LW* 119). However, they stayed together, as so many couples do, and at least shared memories of the past and their love of animals.

It was these memories that inspired Emma, only two years before her death, to write about her childhood in Plymouth, her three years in St Juliot with her married sister, and finally the arrival there in 1870 of the architect she was to marry four years later. Her little book, written on exercise paper and loosely bound together with brown paper, was given the title *Some Recollections*, and was not read by Hardy until after her death. It is an interesting and charming piece of writing that brings the past vividly alive, and it was an important part of the inspiration that resulted in the poems that are considered by many to be the best of Hardy. Some of these poems echo words and passages written by Emma. Hardy prepared *Some Recollections* for publication, but it was not until 1961 that it was published.

There can be no doubt that Emma's death came as a shock to Hardy. She had been in failing health for several years, and he had no reason to believe that death was imminent. He was now overcome by grief, remorse, and nostalgia for a past that had gone for ever, and the reading of *Some Recollections* made him realize that Emma had not forgotten their Cornish romance. The wreath he laid on her grave bore the inscription, 'From her lonely husband—with the old affection'. Poetry had always been for Hardy a form of catharsis, and he now began to write a whole series of poems about his loss. In his own words, 'it was quite natural; one looked back through the years and saw some pictures' (diary of A. C. *Benson).

It was ironic that Hardy and Emma had never visited Cornwall together during their married life, but that within a few months of her death, in March 1913, almost exactly 43 years after that first visit in 1870, he returned to Boscastle and St Juliot. Here he stood on the hill-road and remembered how, during their courtship, he and Emma had climbed it together. He walked along the Valency Valley and wrote a poem about a picnic during which they had lost a tumbler while Emma was trying to wash it in a little waterfall. His astonishingly retentive memory took him back to those days in the 1870s as if they had been yesterday, and poem after poem grew out of this pilgrimage, among the greatest of them being 'After a Journey', 'At Castle Boterel', 'Beeny Cliff', and 'The Voice'.

These poems were grouped together with others written before and after the visit to Cornwall and given the title 'Poems of 1912–13', with an epigraph from Virgil's *Aeneid*, 'Veteris vestigia flammae', variously translated as 'Traces of an ancient flame' and 'Relics of an old love'. It was a poetic miracle that this profoundly emotional experience happened to Hardy at a moment when he was at the height of his poetic powers, and that Emma's death should be transcended by the universality of his poignant expression of sorrow. As Irving Howe so well puts it, 'What begins as an obscure private hurt ends with the common wound of experience' (*Thomas Hardy* (1967), 183).

It is an indication of the particularly personal nature of these poems that not one of them appeared in periodicals before their first public appearance as the second group of poems in *Satires of Circumstance*, published in November 1914. The group then consisted of eighteen poems. The first, 'The Voice', is dated 'December 1912', and is a natural introduction as it begins with Emma's death. It is followed by 'Your Last Drive' (also dated December 1912), 'The Walk', 'Rain on a Grave' (31 January 1913), 'I Found Her Out There', 'Without Ceremony', 'Lament', 'The Haunter', 'His Visitor' (1913), and 'A Circular'. All these are located in or near the Hardy home at Max Gate. There is then a poem that links Dorset to Cornwall ('A Dream or No' (February 1913)) by asking the question, 'Why go to Saint-Juliot?' As we know, Hardy went to Cornwall in March, and the remaining six poems, 'After a Journey', 'A Death-Day Recalled', 'Beeny Cliff', 'At Castle Boterel', 'Places' (Plymouth, March 1913), and 'The Phantom Horsewoman', are all located there. In later editions 'The Spell of the Rose', 'St Launce's Revisited', and 'Where the Picnic Was' were taken out of the first group and put at the end of 'Poems of 1912–13'.

The greatness of these poems about Emma was recognized from the beginning. Laurence Binyon in 1915 described them as 'deeply personal' and 'intense with loss' (*Bookman*, February 1915). Harold *Child thought them 'the most musically and suggestively beautiful poems that Hardy ever wrote.... They are intimate, they are personal, they are gentle' (*Thomas Hardy* (1916), 88). In November 1919 John Middleton *Murry, writing in the *Athenaeum*, described the 'Mr Hardy of the love poems of 1912–13' as 'not a man giving way to memory in poetry; he is a great poet uttering the cry of the universe'. Arthur McDowell in 1931 thought that they were 'central among the poems.... Almost any one of them, by itself, might take its place among the others, but they cling together with the unity and veracity of a profoundly real experience' (*Thomas Hardy*, 233). In 1954 Douglas Brown commented on Hardy's 'peculiar flair for catching the timbre of the perceived "moment" and for recording a sudden profundity of sensation', and described the poems as 'the summit of Hardy's achievement' (*Thomas Hardy*, 152, 176). Even F. R. Leavis, not a great admirer of Hardy's writings, had to concede that 'After a Journey' was 'a poem that we recognize to have come directly out of life; it could... have been written only by a man who had the experience of a life to remember back through. And recognizing that, we recognize the rare quality of a man who can say with that truth "I am just the same", and the rare integrity that can so put the truth beyond question. It is a case in which we know from the art what the man was like; we can be sure, that is, what personal qualities we should have found to admire in Hardy if we could have known him' (*Scrutiny*, 19). It is a final irony that so much great poetry grew out of such a sad situation. JCG

Poems of the Past and the Present. Hardy's second volume of verse, though dated 1902, was in fact published by *Harper & Brothers in England in November 1901 and in America a month later, in an edition of 1,000 copies divided equally between the two markets. It sold well, and a second printing, this time of 250 copies for each market, was required within a few weeks. In 1902 Hardy changed publishers, moving from Harper to *Macmillan, and in 1903 *Poems of the Past and the Present* appeared with some corrections as Volume XIX of Hardy's *Works* in Macmillan's Uniform Edition; the same plates were used for Macmillan's 'Pocket Hardy' (1907), where the collection appeared together with *Wessex Poems* as Volume XVIII. There were two sets of major revisions: for the Wessex Edition of 1912, where it appeared in Volume L, again with *Wessex Poems*, and for the *Collected*

Poems of 1919. There were minor corrections for the Mellstock Edition of 1920 (Volume XXIV, once more with *Wessex Poems*), and for the 1920 and 1923 editions of *Collected Poems*. Hardy chose 28 poems from *Poems of the Past and the Present* for inclusion in his *Selected Poems* of 1917. The holograph, a corrected fair copy, is in the Bodleian Library, Oxford (MS Eng. Poet. d. 18).

Composition and Reception

The volume contained 99 poems, almost twice as many as *Wessex Poems*, but unlike that volume it had no illustrations. Fourteen of the poems had already been published. Two, 'The Ruined Maid' and 'Her Reproach', bear dates from the 1860s; nine come from Hardy's European tour of 1887, and two more from a visit to Switzerland in 1897, though the poems were for the most part written up later (*LW* 196, 313); eight poems on the Boer War are dated 1899. The opening poem, on the death of Queen Victoria, is dated 27 January 1901; 'The Darkling Thrush' is dated 31 December 1900, though it first appeared in the *Graphic* two days earlier. In other cases where dates are attached they seem to have no immediate significance, and, as usual with Hardy, internal evidence as to the date of composition of other poems is inconclusive. 'Tess's Lament' presumably postdates *Tess of the d'Urbervilles*, though in the holograph table of contents its title is given simply as 'A Lament'; a letter of 1909 makes it clear that the comet of 'The Comet at Yell'ham' was the one first noticed by Donati, at its brightest in October 1858—it features in William Dyce's well-known picture of 'Pegwell Bay'—which might argue for an early date (*L* iv 54). Several poems seem to bear the impress of strong personal experience, such as 'Her Reproach', which may derive from Hardy's relationship with Eliza *Nicholls, and 'A Broken Appointment', which R. L. Purdy associated with Florence *Henniker, but for the most part they resist attempts to fit them neatly into the biography. In the Preface to *Wessex Poems* Hardy had described his subject-matter as 'dramatic or personative'; in the Preface to *Poems of the Past and the Present* he used the more familiar and emphatic form 'impersonative', and the reader of the poetry, if not the biographer, will do best to take him at his word.

The *Life* records, unconvincingly, that Hardy 'seems to have taken no notice of the reception accorded to the book by the press' (*LW* 333). The reviews were mixed but broadly favourable. The *Saturday Review* (11 January 1902) thought Hardy had 'discredited' his reputation with *Wessex Poems*, but now found him a 'profoundly interesting' poet, albeit one without 'a singing voice'—a conclusion somewhat at odds with the sensitive account of the music of 'The Mother Mourns', which, as the reviewer notes, is held together by the single rhyme sound ('lane', 'unchain', etc.) used at the end of each of 22 four-line stanzas, so that 'the queer ingenious metre, with its one rhyme set at wide... intervals, beats on the ear like a knell'. Like other reviewers, T. Herbert Warren in the *Spectator* (5 April 1902) thought Hardy's best poetry was in his prose fiction, and worried that *Poems of the Past and the Present* was too often morbid or gruesome ('He is especially attracted to the charnel-house'). The *Athenaeum* (4 January 1902) was loftily dismissive, and for reasons which were to become familiar: Hardy's diction was clumsy, his neologisms ugly, his mood unvarying—all these, according to the reviewer, the signs of Hardy's lack of judgement and self-criticism. The *Academy* (23 November 1901) was more tolerant of the mood of the poems, and discerning enough to recognize that Hardy's mistrust of the scheme of things prompted him to urge kindness and tolerance between man and man. In an astute phrase, Hardy is described as 'an unbelieving mystic', and the review concludes justly that whatever its faults 'no other living writer could have written this book'.

'War Poems'

The first sequence in the collection, entitled 'War Poems', comprises eleven poems written in response to the outbreak of the *Boer War in October 1899, nine of them completed before Christmas. Hardy's projected title for the volume was 'Poems of Feeling, Dream and Deed', and these were perhaps to be the poems of deed. If so, the final title was no less appropriate; as 500,000 troops came from every corner of the British Empire to engage in what soon settled into a long war of attrition, Hardy's poems were very much of 'the present'. Hardy wrote to Florence Henniker that while he deplored the barbarism of war between civilized nations (he put 'civilized' in scare quotation marks) few persons liked better 'to write of war in prose or rhyme' (*L* ii 232). A year into the war he wondered how many of the 40,000 who had died would, given the choice, really wish to have their lives back again: not perhaps the most tactful of letters, since Major Henniker was serving in South Africa at the time (*L* ii 269). But if events in South Africa reinforced Hardy in the view he expressed in February 1901, that 'not to have been born is best' (William Archer, *Real Conversations* (1904), 45), it also filled him with dismay that 'this late age of thought' ('Embarcation') had found no better way to resolve disputes. The phrase was carefully chosen. The pro-war party justified the war in part by reference to contemporary Darwinian notions of the survival of the fittest; the anti-war faction saw it as evidence of an evolutionary falling-off, a reversion to the mores of an earlier age and hence an anomaly in this late age. Hardy, a meliorist as well as a pessimist, clung to the view expressed in the last poem in the sequence, 'The Sick Battle-God', which offers the comfort that a modern sense of the 'many-sidedness of things' has weakened the hold on the human imagination of the God of Battles. Years later he was to remark that the outbreak of the *First World War gave the lie to such a hope (*LW* 394–5).

Four of the poems deal with embarkations and departures, some of which Hardy had witnessed, both at Southampton Docks and from 'Casterbridge'—as if to bring the events within his own imaginative world, Hardy used the Wessex name. The best of these, 'The Going of the Battery', subtitled 'Wives' Lament', oddly couples the women and the guns, love and death: the guns, 'upmouthed to the night', gleaming despite the rain, and the women's 'pale faces outstretched for one kiss', lit by the same glimmering of the gaslamps. Hardy's sense of the irony of things is usually mediated through a human consciousness, most often that of the speaker of the poem; here, however, it is left implicit in the juxtaposition of weapons and women.

'A Wife in London' also works by ironic juxtaposition. The first section tells how the wife receives the news of her husband's death; the second recounts the arrival of a letter written before the battle, dreaming of the 'new love that they would learn'. Another poet might have reversed the two sections, and shown death as intruding on hope; Hardy makes the second letter echo and deepen the desolation brought by the first. The longest poem in the group, 'The Souls of the Slain', is full of effects that might be taken as characteristic of Hardy: the ironic rhyme of 'sweethearts' and 'fleet hearts', the rejection of 'war-mightiness' in favour of the 'homely acts' and 'old kindness' of domestic life, the poet's reverence before the mysteries of life and death, as he listens with 'breathings inheld' to the spirits of the dead. This was, rightly, one of the poems the reviewers singled out for praise.

Two of the war poems have proved controversial. In 'A Christmas Ghost-Story' the phantom of a dead soldier asks why the Christian 'Law of Peace' has been set aside. When the poem was first published in the *Westminster Gazette*, Hardy described his soldier simply as a 'fellow-mortal', and made no comment about which side he had been fighting on ('be he or be he not your countryman'). A Christmas Day leader in the *Daily Chronicle* questioned this vision of the soldier, and recalled the Dublin Fusiliers who cried out in the midst of battle 'Let us make a name for ourselves!' In reply, Hardy suggested that the ghost of a fallen soldier might well have risen to a patriotism which knew nothing of national boundaries and come to look with regret at 'the battles of life and war in general'. The letter was reprinted in W. T. Stead's anti-war paper, *War against War in South Africa* (for the text, see Harold Orel (ed.), *Thomas Hardy's Personal Writings* (1967), 201–2). Hardy meanwhile amended the poem, so that the soldier becomes 'your countryman', but if this seems to limit the duty of grief to mourning only for those who die on one's own side, it also reminds the reader in whose interests they die, and the revised version is in its own way as critical as the one first published.

The other poem which has caused some dispute is 'Drummer Hodge', which has been read in opposition to Rupert Brooke's later poem 'The Soldier'. The 'richer dust' of Brooke's soldier turns a corner of a foreign field into a spot 'which is forever England'; Hardy's Drummer Hodge is absorbed into a foreign landscape, not richer or poorer but 'unknown' and ruled over by 'strange-eyed constellations'—both strange to Hodge's eyes and eyeing him strangely. To Mrs Henniker Hardy wrote that none of his war poems was 'Jingo or Imperial' (*L* ii 277), and certainly 'Drummer Hodge' is not. Part of the power of the poem comes from the way it brings together two perspectives. Hodge lives his short life as the type of the English rustic, and he dies as the epitome of the unknown soldier, thrown without ceremony into an unmarked grave; but if his life story is unimportant when measured against events on the scale of the Boer War, in his death, as he becomes part of the landscape, he suggests the still wider scheme in which the War itself is only a minor episode.

'Poems of Pilgrimage'

The second sequence in the volume, 'Poems of Pilgrimage', is less rewarding. The Italian tour of 1887 is discussed in Chapter 15 of the *Life*, and the Swiss tour of 1897 in Chapter 24 (see also TRAVELS, CONTINENTAL). Hardy comments there that he 'grasped very little' of the history of Rome and left the city 'with some relief' (*LW* 198–9), and the sense of fatigue is apparent in several of the poems. The one clear success is 'Shelley's Skylark', again marked by the change of perspective as the bird that once inspired the poet is commemorated as a 'pinch of unseen, unguarded dust'. The best of the other poems in this group, 'Lausanne', records the evening in Switzerland in 1897 when Hardy sat in the garden where, 110 years earlier, Gibbon had finished his *Decline and Fall*; few writers were more alert than Hardy to such anniversaries, and he clearly sympathized with a writer who felt that those who wished to speak the Truth were compelled to do so indirectly, 'in phrase askance'. (Only a couple of years earlier Gibbon had been referred to in this context in *Jude the Obscure*.)

'Miscellaneous Poems'

The next 67 poems are grouped under the heading 'Miscellaneous Poems'. Placed at the beginning of this section are a number of poems of the kind usually described as 'philosophical'. In October 1896 Hardy had speculated that 'Ideas and emotions which run counter to the inert crystallized opinion' (*LW* 301), especially on matters of faith and doubt, might be heard with more patience if expressed in verse rather than prose—as it were, 'in phrase askance'—but for the most part these poems are if anything too direct and insistent. They typically take the form of dialogues with or meditations on a figure, sometimes named as God, sometimes as Nature, who whether through inattentiveness or incapacity wounds or at least fails to help or protect humankind. In a letter of May 1902 to the *Academy*, Hardy set out in plain prose the essential argument that the presence of pain proves that Nature (or God) 'is blind, and not a judge of her actions, or that she is an automaton, and unable to control them' (*LW* 338). There is more variety of mood in the poems than the reviewers allowed, but too many of them do little more than elaborate on their titles: 'The Lacking Sense', 'Doom and She', 'The Sleep-Worker', 'God-Forgotten', 'By the Earth's Corpse'. The world-view stated here (both 'world-view' and 'stated' seem justified by the explicitness of the poems) was shared, more or less, by other poets of the time. W. E. Henley, A. E. *Housman, Rudyard *Kipling, A. C. *Swinburne, all could write of a world indifferent to suffering. Unlike these writers, however, Hardy rarely strikes a stoic or defiant pose, but is more often stirred to compassion; alert to the 'undervoicings' of human loss at the end of 'A Commonplace Day', mindful of the 'creaturely dependence' which may make good what Nature cannot in 'The Lacking Sense', or hoping in despite of reason that the future will bring 'Joys seldom yet attained' in 'To an Unborn Pauper Child'.

Hardy's personal voice is more apparent in the three 'In Tenebris' poems, which seem to have been written within rather than about the same mood, though by giving to each of them an epigraph taken from the Psalms Hardy perhaps wished to suggest that the feeling expressed was not merely personal. The third, with its wish that death could have come earlier, recalls Hardy's childhood feeling that 'he did not wish to grow up' (*LW* 20); the second is both an apology and a defence for being 'one shaped awry', at odds with the more confident voices of the age. The most compelling of the three is the first, wonderfully resourceful in its use of the spondee (note especially the first line of each stanza) and in the daring of its diction;

the poem closes on the coined word 'unhope', the prefix calling briefly into existence the positive it then denies—much as 'Hap' in *Wessex Poems* asks 'why unblooms the best hope ever sown?'—which sounds the ground-note of much of the volume.

There is another small sub-group of poems dealing with plants and animals. The best-known of these is 'The Darkling Thrush', which has become one of the most anthologized of all Hardy's poems. It was first published in the *Graphic* with the subtitle 'By the Century's Deathbed', which seems to align it with the philosophical poems discussed above. Considered on its own, it has rather too much the appearance of a poem aimed at the anthologies. It ends with the word 'unaware', as Hardy or his persona scrupulously refuses either to endorse or to reject the thought that the bird's song carries within it some 'blessed Hope', but the use of the upper case for Hope invites the reader to expect that the speaker's doubts will soon be cancelled by the growth of that awareness which the poem, if only hesitantly, brings into being. That suggestion is, however, diminished in *Poems of the Past and the Present*, where the poem stands between 'The Last Chrysanthemum', in which the speaker firmly rejects the idea that the flower has sense or reason, and 'The Comet at Yell'ham', which measures human affairs against the time and space of the astronomers.

There are among the 'Miscellaneous Poems' some to which that title seems more appropriate. These include a handful of triolets and a villanelle, forms which had been made fashionable in the early 1870s by writers like Austin Dobson and Hardy's friend Edmund *Gosse. There are several narrative or ballad-like poems, including 'The Lost Pyx', which provides a more cheerful account of the origin of the Cross-in-Hand pillar on Batcombe Hill than that given in Chapter 45 of *Tess of the d'Urbervilles*, and 'The Dame of Athelhall', which turns on the kind of irony which Hardy had explored in the novels and has a family resemblance to *Browning's 'The Statue and the Bust', a poem Hardy greatly admired. Of several humorous poems, much the best is 'The Ruined Maid', which plays on the irony that for a country girl her sexual ruin might be the way, if not to make a fortune, at least to escape poverty. The volume closes with two brief sections, one of 'Imitations' from other poets, from Sappho to Victor Hugo, the other called 'Retrospect', consisting of two poems which look back into the past from an imagined future, and 'Αγνωστωι Θεωι' (*Agnosto Theoi*), addressed to an unknown and unknowing God.

Reading through *Poems of the Past and the Present* in sequence, it is easy to understand why the reviewers were unsure what to make of it; it clearly contains a number of fine poems, but it is quirky in organization and uneven in quality. Of poems already mentioned, a re-reader might turn first to 'The Souls of the Slain', 'Drummer Hodge', 'Shelley's Skylark', 'Tess's Lament', 'A Broken Appointment', 'In Tenebris I', and 'The Darkling Thrush'. Two others demand comment. In 'An August Midnight' the chance meeting of poet, longlegs, dumbledore, moth, and fly leads only to a musing question, not a statement of significance: a good example of the modesty of much of Hardy's poetry, the unwillingness to push for the really big poem which has puzzled so many of his critics. Much the same might be said of 'The Self-Unseeing', a delicate re-creation of things past, which is at once an elegy for what is lost and a celebration of what is held in the memory. Hardy has been both admired (by Philip *Larkin) and criticized (by Donald Davie) because he is not a transcendent writer, but instead renders back to us the world in which we live. On the evidence of the best poems in this collection, this should be seen as a considerable achievement.

PVM

poetic influence, Hardy's. Hardy's poetry perceptibly influenced three generations of English poets: that of the 'Georgian' period, of the Thirties, and of the Fifties and beyond (for his influence continues). In his *Thomas Hardy and British Poetry* (1973), Donald Davie initiated the study of this largely unrecognized debt, the most far-reaching 'of the last fifty years' (p. 3). If little 'acknowledged', this was perhaps because Hardy's achievement, though valued by poets as varied as Ezra *Pound, D. H. *Lawrence, W. H. *Auden, and Dylan Thomas, escaped definition. Also, in Davie it draws an ambivalent response, between his judgement that, failing in his poetry to transcend and transform reality, Hardy 'sold short... the poetic vocation' (p. 40), and his admiration for the 'monumental art' with which Hardy confronted the ineluctable ironies of existence (pp. 181–2). Certain of the poets whom Hardy influenced share Davie's ambivalence.

The first generation includes a number of First World War poets and the Georgians. The strongest acknowledged influence was upon *Siegfried Sassoon, who states that 'the influence of Hardy's *Satires of Circumstance* (1914) is fairly perceptible' (*Siegfried's Journey* (1945), p. 49) in his collection *The Old Huntsman* (1917). This volume was dedicated to Hardy, who wrote to Sassoon on 18 May 1917 a letter appreciative of 'the grim humour' and 'pathos' of certain poems (*L* v 213). Sassoon opens his 1917 *Diary* with a quotation from *The Dynasts*, which had accompanied him into the trenches. Although Sassoon's war experiences taught him to esteem Hardy's 'grim, wise fatalism' (*Diaries 1915–1917*, 171), he later praises Hardy somewhat ambiguously as a 'splendid craftsman with a commonplace mind' (*ibid.* 282). (On minor stylistic influences, see Michael Thorpe, *Siegfried Sassoon: A Critical Study* (1966).)

In his 1922 diary, Sassoon remarks of his fellow war poet Edmund *Blunden that 'He has a good deal in common with old Hardy. A simplicity and honesty beyond praise, and a quality of being one with his work to which he has such a noble devotion' (*Diaries 1920–1922* (1981), 174). Blunden would later publish his study of Hardy (1942) and already in his own practice, like Sassoon, followed Hardy in preferring closed, traditional forms, employing a wide range of intricate stanzas. The ironies of his war poetry and its pity for suffering nature are Hardyesque (see Michael Thorpe, *The Poetry of Edmund Blunden* (1971)). Hardy's 'loving-kindness' would become a shared paramount value.

More generally, in the second and third decades of the twentieth century, Hardy was, as James Reeves notes, 'father-figure' to the Georgians. Though he was not himself a Georgian, since 'his muse was rustic', Hardy's 'influence was strong' (James Reeves, *Georgian Poetry* (1962), pp. xvi, xxii). Sassoon, Blunden, and Walter *de la Mare—another traditional stylist whose forms Hardy actually imitates himself—all embraced the 'pastoral mode'. The Hardyesque influence, observes John Heath-Stubbs, lay in 'reaching back to the organic past; remembered as a concrete reality, but felt as already dead and dying', yet unlike many of the Georgians, who sought a retreat to innocence, these three poets are most akin to Hardy in feeling, with varying intensity, 'the shadow of metaphysical evil' (John Heath-Stubbs, *The Faber Book of Twentieth-Century Verse* (1953), 24–5). In de la Mare, who was not a war poet, this may be felt in melancholy lyrics of wistful loss such as 'The Ghost' and 'The Voice'.

In the predominantly modernist Thirties, Hardy's poetic influence becomes less perceptible. Blunden, Sassoon, and de la Mare are peripheral to the main currents—and all have turned toward religious affirmation. Among younger poets, C. Day Lewis stands out: 'Hardy is behind much of the very best that Day Lewis wrote' (Ian Parsons (ed.), *Poems of C. Day Lewis 1925–1972* (1977), p. xiii). Day Lewis adhered to traditional forms, within which he was, like Hardy, an innovative experimenter. A plangent, elegiac lyricism, an intense feeling for things that pass, is his Hardyesque note. (This is also felt in another Hardy admirer, John Betjeman, whose subject-matter, like Day Lewis's, links the 'rustic' with modern urban realities that the Georgians shunned.) In *The Poetic Image* (1947) Day Lewis, appraising Hardy's 'To an Unborn Pauper Child' at length, distinguishes Hardy's 'personal poetry' as standing apart from the modernist, Eliot-inspired vogue for impersonality: it 'breathes in all the best of it that singular sweetness of disposition, that simplicity, warmth and magnanimity to which all who knew him have attested' (p. 152).

Lewis's generalization that 'with Hardy's poetry it is impossible to detach technique and imagination from character' (p. 152) may be linked with F. R. Leavis's 'Hardy's great poetry is a triumph of character' (*New Bearings in English Poetry* (1932), 59). Hardy's influence is indeed in his *poetic character*—his integrity of temperament and tone—rather than in his technique, which is almost inimitable. G. S. Fraser speaks of 'the paradox of Hardy's expressive clumsiness' (*The Modern Writer and His World* (1964), 257).

Both W. H. Auden and Philip *Larkin embrace this 'paradox' in their tributes.

Auden recalled in his later years that 'My first master was Thomas Hardy.... He was a good poet, perhaps a great one, but not *too* good.... This gave me hope where a flawless poet might have made me despair. He was modern without being too modern (*Making, Knowing and Judging* (1956), 10). Larkin wrote that 'When I came to Hardy it was with a sense of relief that I didn't have to try and jack myself up to a concept of poetry that lay outside my own life.... One could simply relapse back into one's own life and write from it. Hardy taught one to feel rather than to write...' (*Required Writing* (1983), 175). Auden has indicated his manifold debts of tone and attitude to his 'poetical father' in his essay 'A Literary Transference', and these debts have been thoroughly explored in Andrew Robert Deane's '"Tiny Observer of Enormous World": Thomas Hardy and W. H. Auden' (*THJ* 10 (1994)). Larkin opened his *Oxford Book of Twentieth-Century Verse* (1973) with 28 poems by Hardy, more than by any other poet in that anthology.

If, introducing the *New Lines* anthology in 1956, Robert Conquest put down Hardy as, with *Kipling, an 'odd eccentric' who was not influential enough 'to correct a mood'—of the Forties, that is—he was presumably then unaware of Hardy's resurgent influence in Larkin, one of his chosen poets. Larkin may be connected with Day Lewis in continuing what G. S. Fraser, in the study already cited, describes as 'the tradition of ruminative and ironic Victorian poets like Clough and Hardy and Browning' (p. 299). The ironic element, so characteristically English, has been traced by Jahan Ramazani to the 'ironic irresolution' of 'The Darkling Thrush' as kin to the uncertainties of Yeats, Auden, Larkin, and Heaney (*Poetry of Mourning: The Modern Elegy from Hardy to Heaney* (1994)). However, following Sydney Bolt, Donald Davie argues that we should discriminate between Hardy's 'cosmic irony' and the 'strategic' irony of the modernist which 'relies upon the reader's tact, sense of literary tradition, or sense of values' (*Thomas Hardy and British Poetry* (1973), 131–2). Samuel Hynes makes a similar point in distinguishing the Hardy from the Eliot line ('The Hardy Tradition in Modern English Poetry', in N. Page (ed.), *Thomas Hardy: The Writer and His Background* (1980), 180).

MT

poetry. Hardy claimed that the critical furore over *Tess of the d'Urbervilles* and *Jude the Obscure* caused him 'to abandon at once a form of literary art he had long intended to abandon at some indefinite time, and resume openly that form of it which had always been more instinctive with him, and which he had just been able to keep alive from his early years, half in secrecy, under the pressure of magazine writing' (*LW* 309). He had earlier written that 'Perhaps I can express more fully in verse ideas and emotions which run counter to the inert crystallized opinion—hard as a rock—which the vast body of men have vested interests in supporting. To cry out in a passionate poem that (for instance) the Supreme Mover or Movers, the Prime Force or Forces, must be either limited in power, unknowing, or cruel...will cause them merely a shake of the head.... If Galileo had said in verse that the world moved, the Inquisition might have let him alone' (*LW* 302).

In fact Hardy had been a practising poet long before 1896, when his last novel, *Jude the Obscure*, was published. His earliest known poem, 'Domicilium', was begun in 1857. In the mid-1860s he started composing a series of poems in the hope of earning his living as a poet; but on their rejection by editors he reluctantly became a novelist. Nevertheless he continued to produce poems throughout his novel-writing years. From 1870 until 1896, when he stopped writing novels, he wrote about 50 poems which have been preserved. In the aftermath of *Jude*, he began to gather these poems into volumes. The result is that many of his volumes are combinations of current and early poems rescued from drawers, where they had 'been lying about for many many years' (*L* ii 202). His first collection, *Wessex Poems* (1898), was reviewed favourably, 'though by some critics not without umbrage at Hardy's having taken the liberty to adopt another vehicle of expression than prose-fiction without consulting them' (*LW* 319).

The prophetic Hardy, the Hardy who wanted to 'cry out', is also evident from the beginning. The vision Hardy wished to share, however, was a vision of loss. While many of his contemporaries, it seemed to him, were proclaiming the gospel of Victorian success, Hardy insisted on seeing the underside. His sense of loss was both biblical, like that of Job and the Psalms, and late-Victorian. He carried this vision into the 20th century, when he continued to write poems until 1928, in his 87th year.

Hardy's poetic vision of loss is almost exhilarating in its comprehensiveness and its ingenious imbedding in multiple poetic forms. From the despair of the country girl to the self-questioning of the philosopher, Hardy develops a grammar of loss in multiple forms, from sonnet to ballad, from personal lyric to dramatic monologue and epic drama. The coherence of poetic forms seems itself called into question, as the poetics of loss undermine the traditional claims for the transcendence of literature. Jude lived in a universe where 'Events did not rhyme' (*JO* 1.2). Thus Hardy's 'Hap' proclaims a vision of chance and universal incoherence in a sonnet form traditionally associated with design:

—Crass Casualty obstructs the sun and rain,
And dicing Time for gladness casts a moan....
These purblind Doomsters had as readily strown
Blisses about my pilgrimage as pain.

We can discern the following stages in Hardy's development as a poet:

1. Poems of 1860–74

These represent Hardy's beginnings as a poet, while he was also working as a Gothic architect and making his transition to novel-writing. Many of these early poems are grouped together at the beginning of *Wessex Poems*; another grouping seems to be gathered in a section entitled 'More Love Lyrics' in Hardy's third collection, *Time's Laughingstocks* (1909); and occasional others are (as indicated by the dates often appended to them) scattered through the various other volumes. Among the early poems from this period are many sonnets, including a series entitled 'She, to Him', in imitation of traditional sonnet sequences, 'part of a much larger number which perished' (*LW* 55); songs like 'Amabel'; comic ballads like 'The Ruined Maid', and ballad narratives like 'The Bride-Night Fire'; classical imitations like 'The Temporary the All (Sapphics)', which influenced the modified Sapphic form in 'Neutral Tones', Hardy's most important early poem. 'Neutral Tones' is Hardy's definitive early lyric of loss, the loss of love, a lesson learned too late in a universe of 'tedious riddles of years ago'. Hardy's collections of poetry will continue to show an amazing versatility of theme and variety of verse forms.

2. Poems of 1878–1901

These belong to the novel-writing years and the 'return' to poetry in the 1890s, the period reflected in the latter half of *Wessex Poems* and in Hardy's second volume, *Poems of the Past and the Present* (1901). The 1878–1901 poems include the following:

(a) A set of narrative poems or short Wessex ballads composed *c.*1875–83 is grouped in the middle of *Wessex Poems*. These were written after the success of Hardy's fourth published novel, *Far from the Madding Crowd* (1874), and his marriage to Emma, and they represent his attempt to exploit poetically the Wessex he was creating in the novels. In 1875 he makes 'first mention ... of the idea of an epic on the war with Napoleon' (*LW* 109–10), and the poems now try out the Napoleonic themes which he will later develop into *The Dynasts*. The most remarkable of these narrative ballads is 'The Dance at the Phoenix', finished about 1878 (the year in which Hardy published *The Return of the Native*), which uses a ballad stanza form to capture those dance-rhythms that he would often return to again in his poetic career:

That night the throbbing 'Soldier's Joy',
    The measured tread and sway
Of 'Fancy-Lad' and 'Maiden Coy',
    Reached Jenny as she lay
Beside her spouse; till springtide blood
Seemed scouring through her like a flood
    That whisked the years away.

(b) Hardy's return to poetry in the 1890s is represented by a group that seems to begin with 'A Sign-Seeker' in *Wessex Poems*; other poems from this period are collected in *Poems of the Past and the Present* and later volumes. We can see the beginnings of Hardy's return to poetry as early as 'Thoughts of Phena', dated 'March 1890' and written as Hardy was at work on *Tess of the d'Urbervilles* (1891). About these poems Hardy later said that 'he had found an awkwardness in getting back to an easy expression in numbers after abandoning it for so many years; but that soon wore off' (*LW* 310). This statement is misleading in two respects. First, Hardy, as we have seen, had not completely abandoned poetry during the novel-writing years. Also, while he may have become more skilful, there remains a certain deliberate awkwardness in Hardy's metres and language that challenges Tennysonian notions of musicality and gracefulness. It was Hardy's sense that his language should reflect the continuous challenge of new idioms, consistent with his belief that 'the English language was liable to undergo great alterations in the future, whereas Latin would remain unchanged' (*LW* 517).

These poems also show significant elaborations of meditative and metrical form. A most important Hardy poem, probably of the early 1890s, is 'Nature's Questioning', an example of a poem which brings together two key aspects of Hardy's art, the personal meditation and the philosophical discourse, each consistent with the other. As the poem discourses about a world of incompletion and interruption, so also it proceeds to its own interruption and incompletion at the end:

> Thus things around. No answerer I....
> Meanwhile the winds, and rains,
> And Earth's old glooms and pains
> Are still the same, and Life and Death are neighbours nigh.

Interruption is a rich theme in Hardy, as the momentary interruption of the meditative reverie portends the more fateful interruption of life by death. This interruptive lyric form is Hardy's aesthetic achievement for conveying the realizations of loss.

(c) The 'Poems of Pilgrimage' in *Poems of the Past and the Present* were inspired by Hardy's journeys to Italy in 1887 and 1889 (see TRAVELS, CONTINENTAL). These visits, in which he travelled as a literary pilgrim to spots associated with Keats, Shelley, Byron, and the Brownings, were sparks for his resumed career, resulting most spectacularly in 'Shelley's Skylark'—probably, like 'Genoa and the Mediterranean', 'written a long time after' the 1887 trip (*LW* 195). The journeys also produced a series of 'Imitations' grouped at the end of *Poems of the Past and the Present*.

(d) The cosmological poems in an opening group of 'Miscellaneous Poems' in *Poems of the Past and the Present* are the poems most relevant to Hardy's ambition in the 1890s to 'cry out in a passionate poem that (for instance) the Supreme Mover or Movers must be either limited in power, unknowing, or cruel'. Hardy must have felt his ambition realized when a letter arrived from a reader of these poems, saying that Hardy was 'like some terrible old prophet crying in the wilderness' (*LW* 328). Thus 'God's Funeral', written at this time but published later, dramatizes the growth and decay of the theological idea of God. This group was probably initiated by 'Nature's Questioning'. Several of these poems—'The Mother Mourns', 'The Lacking Sense', 'Doom and She', 'The Sleep-Worker'—echo or are echoed by Jude Fawley in Hardy's last novel, and in turn their ideas 'were further elaborated in *The Dynasts*' (*LW* 333). This interplay between poems and passages in the novels is a continuing phenomenon in the work of Hardy, who used each form as fodder for the other. As he said as he returned to poetry in the 1890s, 'He had mostly aimed... to keep his narratives... as near to poetry in their subject as the conditions would allow' (*LW* 309). 'A Commonplace Day' is the most distinguished example in this group, and achieves a beautiful interaction of mind and setting, as the expansions and contractions of the meditation are mirrored in the expansions and contractions of the flame in the grate.

(e) Hardy's love lyrics of the 1890s are grouped in 'Miscellaneous Poems' in *Poems of the Past and the Present*. 'A Broken Appointment', written in 1893 or shortly thereafter, is one of a number of 1890s poems reflecting Hardy's eroticized relationship with Florence *Henniker. Here Hardy crafted a beautiful relic of the Petrarchan sonnet sestet, within a two-beat refrain ('You did not come', 'You love not me'), a refrain that suggests the 'onomatopoeia' of the rhythm of the clock which interrupts the speaker's strained reasoning.

(f) 'War Poems' in *Poems of the Past and the Present* were written mostly in 1899, and respond to the *Boer War. These poems significantly develop the war insights only played with in the Napoleonic poems of the novel-writing years. A major achievement is 'Drummer Hodge', where the world of the Wessex worker becomes implicated in international themes:

His landmark is a kopje-crest
That breaks the veldt around;
And foreign constellations west
Each night above his mound.

In this group, 'The Souls of the Slain' is Hardy's most impressively orchestrated meditative poem of the 19th century: a great war poem in which an extended meditation about the ghosts of the dead takes place in a darkening oceanic setting. The interaction of the speaker's mind and the ocean setting is beautifully detailed:

The thick lids of Night closed upon me
Alone at the Bill
Of the Isle by the Race—
Many-caverned, bald, wrinkled of face—
And with darkness and silence the spirit was on me
To brood and be still.

The speaker's awakening at the end of the poem is beautifully accommodated to the dispersing of the ghosts into 'sea-mutterings'.

(g) Animal poems written *c.*1899–1900 are grouped together in 'Miscellaneous Poems' of *Poems of the Past and the Present.* In 'An August Midnight' the bugs smearing the ink offer a humorous allegory of the interruption experienced by the writer in the act of writing. 'The Darkling Thrush' (dated 31 December 1900) is an assessment of the end of a century in which truth seemed less and less possible: 'The land's sharp features seemed to be | The Century's corpse outleant....'.

3. Poems of 1902–12

This period is reflected in *Time's Laughingstocks* (1909) and in the section entitled 'Satires of Circumstance' in the 1914 volume of the same name. This is the era of *The Dynasts,* when the shorter poems seem somewhat secondary to the enormous energy expended on the epic, which was published in three parts in 1904, 1906, and 1908. These are also years of continuing deterioration in Hardy's marriage, and his poetic career was not to take wing until Emma's death late in 1912. Nevertheless, Hardy said in the preface to *Time's Laughingstocks*: 'As a whole they will, I hope, take the reader forward, even if not far, rather than backward.'

The 1902–12 poems include the following groupings:

(a) A large miscellany of poems constitutes the balance of *Time's Laughingstocks,* including the opening set of poems and 'Pieces Occasional and Various', a grouping at the end of the volume. Some of the most notable poems are 'A Trampwoman's Tragedy', which Hardy 'considered... upon the whole as his most successful poem' (*LW* 517); 'A Sunday Morning Tragedy' (see CENSORSHIP); 'She Hears the Storm', a perfection of the ballad form; and 'The Man He Killed', a consummate war poem that plays on clichés that have become dead weights: '"I shot him dead because—| Because he was my foe, | Just so: my foe of course he was; | That's clear enough..."'.

(b) 'A Set of Country Songs' in *Time's Laughingstocks.*

(c) 'Satires of Circumstance' is a grouping placed at the end of the volume *Satires of Circumstance,* and was composed in 1910, two years before the seismic event of Emma's death: 'The scales had not fallen from my eyes when I wrote them, & when I reprinted them they had' (*L* v 260). Their satire is nevertheless effective, as in the anecdote of the popular preacher who is seen to re-enact 'at the vestry glass | Each pulpit gesture in deft dumb-show | That had moved the congregation so' ('II. In Church').

(d) 'Miscellaneous Pieces' in *Satires of Circumstance* contains lyrics written between *The Dynasts* and 1912. There is a noticeable contrast between 'Lyrics and Reveries', which begins the volume, and these 'Miscellaneous Pieces' placed later, just before the 'Satires of Circumstance'. 'Miscellaneous Pieces' represents Hardy's full-time resumption of the lyric poem after *The Dynasts,* but before Emma's death in November 1912. The poems Hardy included here, and thus did not choose to highlight in 'Lyrics and Reveries', are generally either long narrative poems or poems that have the satiric tone he came to regret in 'Satires of Circumstance'.

The best poem in the group is 'The Abbey Mason', which reflects the powerful formative influence of the Gothic Revival on Hardy, with its ancient but now obsolete patterns 'as dead as a fern-leaf in a lump of coal' (*JO* 2.2). Thus the poem celebrates 'Petrified lacework—lightly lined | On ancient massiveness behind', and suggests the aesthetic principle behind Hardy's earlier perception: 'the seer should watch that pattern among general things which his idiosyncrasy moves him to observe, and describe that alone. This is, quite accurately, a going to Nature; yet the result is no mere photograph, but purely the product of the writer's own mind' (*LW* 158).

4. Poems of 1912–17

These represent Hardy's greatest achievement in poetry, a period reflected in 'Poems of 1912–13', and include poems published in *Satires of Circumstance* (1914) and *Moments of Vision* (1917). The following groupings may be noted:

(a) 'Lyrics and Reveries' in *Satires of Circumstance* is a transitional group introducing the volume and consisting of poems mostly written a few years before and shortly after November 1912. 'Lyrics and Reveries' is a very rich and interesting group of poems. It seems to represent Hardy's assessment of the best of his left-over and recent work (excepting 'Poems of 1912–13'), a selection made from the perspective of all he had learned since 27 November 1912, the day of Emma's death. Thus the group contains both pre- and post-1912 poems. Its love poems, poems of memory, nature poems, philosophic poems, and elegies constitute a miscellany—but, like the miscellany of *Moments of Vision*, one of deeply imagined poems. 'Channel Firing' is an anti-war poem that relies on Hardy's sense of the grotesque for its satirical vision of the end of the world:

> We thought it was the Judgment-day
>
> And sat upright. While drearisome
> Arose the howl of wakened hounds:
> The mouse let fall the altar-crumb...

'The Convergence of the Twain', about the **Titanic* disaster and the Immanent Will, eerily forecasts the *First World War. Other classics are the Proustian 'Under the Waterfall', and Hardy's wonderful tribute to Swinburne, 'A Singer Asleep'. 'The Ghost of the Past' is his consummate poem of vision become memory, and memory become pure loss:

> It looms, a far-off skeleton
> And not a comrade nigh,
> A fitful, far-off skeleton
> Dimming as days draw nigh.

(b) The well-known sequence titled *'Poems of 1912–13' is placed after the transitional 'Lyrics and Reveries' in *Satires of Circumstance*. Hardy seems to have been thinking of 'Poems of 1912–13' when he wrote that 'Many poems were written... at the end of the previous year and the early part of this—more than he had ever written before in the same space of time' (*LW* 389). What Hardy meant by the 'falling of the scales' from his eyes (quoted above) was that the myths he had satirized in others (in 'Satires of Circumstance') he now saw operating in himself, the myth of a timeless romantic life so garishly exposed in the afterlight of Emma's death. 'So much shadow domestic and public had passed over his head since he had written the Satires that he was in no mood now to publish humour or irony' (*LW* 396). Hardy had become his own satire of circumstance. In 'The Phantom Horsewoman' the speaker is spellbound by a 40-year-old image which he cannot distinguish from the present moment:

> But she still rides gaily
> In his rapt thought
> On that shagged and shaly
> Atlantic spot,
> And as when first eyed
> Draws rein and sings in the swing of the tide.

Here the various aspects of Hardy's art come together: the sense of a meditation frozen in time but soon to be interrupted; the sense of a life caught in a vision whose pastness is about to be revealed; the formality of the poetic structure that reflects a brittle vision about to break. The picture of his past life becomes most clear just as he sees it evaporating, as in 'At Castle Boterel':

> I look and see it there, shrinking, shrinking,
> I look back at it amid the rain
> For the very last time; for my sand is sinking,
> And I shall traverse old love's domain
> Never again.

'The Walk' conveys with marvellous economy the 'difference' in the familiar scene: 'Only the underlying sense | Of the look of a room on returning thence'. And 'The Voice' ends with a striking portrait of the ghost-haunted lover:

> Thus I; faltering forward,
> Leaves around me falling,

Wind oozing thin through the thorn from
norward,
And the woman calling.

(c) 'Poems of War and Patriotism' comprises Hardy's new series of war poems in *Moments of Vision.* The war poem that Hardy had developed, in response first to the *Napoleonic Wars and then to the Boer War, he now develops further for the Great War. About this war he said: 'It was seldom he had felt so heavy at heart as in seeing his old view of the gradual bettering of human nature, as expressed in these verses of 1901, completely shattered by the events of 1914 and onwards' (*LW* 395). The most distinguished of this group is 'In Time of "The Breaking of Nations"', with its apocalyptic pastoral critique of war:

Only thin smoke without flame
From the heaps of couch-grass;
Yet this will go onward the same
Though Dynasties pass.

Indeed, Hardy sees more clearly the connection between war-fever and apocalyptic fever, the lust to make time stop in one final burst of flame, as in 'A New Year's Eve in War Time':

In the dark there careers—
As if Death astride came
To numb all with his knock—
A horse at mad rate
Over rut and stone.

(d) Hardy published *Moments of Vision* in 1917. Of this collection R. L. Purdy commented that 'Where it is possible to date the poems, they seem to be almost wholly the product of the years 1913–16, and only five (with varying dates 1871–98) give any evidence of earlier work' (Purdy 207). Hardy's versatility is most evident here. 'There is absolutely no observation too minute, no flutter of reminiscence too faint, for Mr Hardy to adopt as the subject of a metaphysical lyric', Edmund Gosse observed in an essay on 'Mr Hardy's Lyrical Poems' published in the *Edinburgh Review* in 1918.

'Copying Architecture in an Old Minster' is an archetypal meditative moment in Hardy's work: the speaker sketching in a church begins to muse, and suddenly wakes to find that his sketching pad is on the floor and the late evening fog has come in. Hardy continues to make us see the process which turns fresh insights into archaic formulas, tentative expressions into rigid expressions, spontaneous rhythms into repetitive patterns. 'To my Father's Violin' dramatizes in its complex verse-form the continuing hold of an old melody, while 'The Pedigree' paints the patterns of a family tree forestalling 'every heave and coil and move I made'. 'The Figure in the Scene' and 'Logs on the Hearth' are skilful mimeses of, respectively, rain-led and fire-led meditations.

'During Wind and Rain' is Hardy's ultimate poem of interruption and loss. Each stanza portrays a stage of life harshly interrupted by the storm: 'Ah, no; the years, the years; | Down their carved names the raindrop ploughs.' Hardy said in 1921 that this 'was possibly among the best I have written' (*L* vi 96). 'A Merrymaking in Question' takes Hardy's theme of memory to its ultimate point, where memory becomes a static, obsolete vision of itself, an apocalyptic image masking permanent absence:

From the night came the oddest of answers:
A hollow wind, like a bassoon,
And headstones all ranged up as dancers,
And cypresses droning a croon,
And gurgoyles that mouthed to the tune.

And yet there is always the consummate simplicity of 'The Oxen': 'We pictured the meek mild creatures where | They dwelt in their strawy pen . . .'. Hardy's reputation as a major poet could easily rest on *Moments of Vision* alone.

5. Poems of 1918–22

This is the period of *Late Lyrics and Earlier,* published in 1922. The collection includes the great tribute to *Keats, 'At a House in Hampstead', and the great tribute to Hardy's musical ancestors, 'Haunting Fingers'. It also contains a war poem, '"And There Was a Great Calm"', where war becomes the ultimate interruption, a symptom of apocalyptic, dream-like frenzy exploding into the real world, like a return of the repressed. In the 'Apology' prefaced to *Late Lyrics and Earlier* he expressed anxiety that 'we seem threatened with a new Dark Age'. Hardy seems most ghost-haunted in these years.

Apocalypse is now the finale of memory that can no longer distinguish the changing world; such is the subject of 'Going and Staying':

> Then we looked closelier at Time,
> And saw his ghostly arms revolving
> To sweep off woeful things with prime,
> Things sinister with things sublime
> Alike dissolving.

Surreal and apocalyptic themes continue in 'The Wanderer', 'Voices from Things Growing in a Churchyard', and 'He Follows Himself', until we arrive at the wizened cosmic gaiety of 'An Ancient to Ancients'. In his 'Apology' Hardy also stated his rationale for poetry on the dark side: 'let me repeat what I... wrote much earlier, in a poem entitled "In Tenebris":

> If way to the Better there be, it exacts a full look at the Worst:

that is to say, by the exploration of reality and its frank recognition stage by stage along the survey, with an eye to the best consummation possible: briefly, evolutionary meliorism'.

Hardy also realized something about the nature of his own poetic language, with its layering of archaic and anomalous diction, when he said of the translators of the Authorized Version of the *Bible that 'They translated into the language of the age; then the years began to corrupt that language as spoken, and to add grey lichen to the translation; until the moderns who use the corrupted tongue marvel at the poetry of the old words' (*LW* 416). The language of Hardy's own 'prophetic' poetry is consistent with this insight. In 1920 he wrote: 'The value of old age depends upon the person who reaches it. To some men of early performance it is useless. To others, who are late to develop, it just enables them to complete their job' (*LW* 435).

6. Poems of 1922–8

This is the period of *Human Shows* (1925) and *Winter Words* (published posthumously in 1928). It includes an important grouping of pastoral poems, in which Hardy dramatized a fluid and almost comic interaction between mind and nature very different from the tragic collisions that were still his main focus. This is a time of final resignation and detachment. An entry like the following is typical of Hardy's eighth decade: 'Walked to top of High Stoy (probably for the last time), thence back home. A beautiful drive' (*LW* 450). Hardy's pastoral is actually the other side of the coin of his tragic nature poems; where nature gently moulds the mind in Wordsworthian fashion in pastoral comedy, in tragedy it collides tragically with the human.

Thus we can enjoy the cascading images in 'Snow in the Suburbs', because we know their tragic implications elsewhere:

> A sparrow enters the tree,
> Whereon immediately
> A snow-lump thrice his own slight size
> Descends on him and showers his head and eyes,
> And overturns him,
> And near inurns him,
> And lights on a nether twig, when its brush
> Starts off a volley of other lodging lumps with a rush.

Similarly we know much of the tragic lives of Hardy's Wessex characters behind the comic relief of 'Ice on the Highway', whose very form reflects a mimetic liveliness we might expect in a happier nature poet. In any event, Hardy's tragic sense leads to a detachment which is very close to pastoral remove: 'I am the one whom ringdoves see | Through chinks in boughs.... "Oh, it's only he."' Hardy said that 'he preferred to be "the man with the watching eye"' (*LW* 465).

But the pastoral in Hardy is always close to the tragic patterns ('discover the tragedy that always underlies Comedy if you only scratch it deeply enough': *LW* 474). These patterns enclose the human and produce eerie realizations for the living, as in the marvellous poem 'Lying Awake', which metamorphoses subjective selves into objective tombstones:

> You, Meadow, are white with your counterpane cover of dew,
> I see it as if I were there;
> You, Churchyard, are lightening faint from the shade of the yew,
> The names creeping out everywhere.

The articulations of these patterns, enclosing the mind and the life in obsolete forms stretching out from the past, is rendered in 'The Prospect', one of a series of poems where Hardy explores the patterns of pattern: here, inner patterns of vein and nerve are compared to outer patterns of tree-branch and cobweb, symbolizing the vast cosmic patterns, internal and external, in which one is caught: 'The twigs of the birch imprint the December sky | Like branching veins upon a thin old hand.'

This period includes the surreal effect of 'Nobody Comes', where the self is eerily split between inside and outside: 'And mute by the gate I stand again alone, | And nobody pulls up there.' Also there is great if obscure human drama in 'Standing by the Mantelpiece' and 'Family Portraits'; a fine rendering of dance rhythms in 'Concerning Agnes'; and continual evocations of the epigrams of the *Greek Anthology*, as in 'Two Lips'. There continues to be, in these volumes as in earlier ones, the same great miscellany of narrative and lyrical poems, of simple and complex stanzas. Finally, in 'He Resolves to Say No More', Hardy lays down the prophet's wand:

> Let Time roll backward if it will;
> (Magians who drive the midnight quill
> With brain aglow
> Can see it so,)
> What I have learnt no man shall know.

The great poet of loss was about to be silent. In 1927 Hardy was reported to say: 'His only ambition, so far as he could remember, was to have some poem or poems in a good anthology like the *Golden Treasury*' (*LW* 478). On his deathbed he listened to Browning's 'Rabbi Ben Ezra' with 'wistful intentness', then asked for a stanza from Edward FitzGerald's translation of the *Rubáiyát* (*LW* 480–2). What is perhaps Hardy's last poem, 'Epitaph for George Moore', is an indirect defence of his own poetic style against the conformist norms of the critic who would say, 'No mortal man beneath the sky | Can write such English as can I.'

Hardy composed over a thousand poems during a period of nearly 70 years. His full-time poetic career, from 1860 to 1928, lasted longer than that of any other Victorian, indeed almost any other English poet. It encompassed the mid- and late Victorian periods, the Edwardian and Georgian periods, the War and postwar period, and the twenties. Despite his demurrers, Hardy is one of the great novelists of the language. But he is also one of the great poets, whom readers continually discover to their surprise. Mark Van Doren said it well in his *Autobiography* (1958):

> The immense, rambling country house of his *Collected Poems* has so many rooms that one could live in it forever. I have heard it called too large a house, with too many low rooms in it where the furniture is old and ugly, and where there is the odour of rats in the wainscot. Too many of Hardy's poems, that is to say, are not 'good'. And I agree; but I am always changing my mind as to which ones those are; I never tire of opening old doors that resist me a little; and my conclusion is that the building as a whole should be left just as it lies, hugging the dark ground over which Hardy's eyes wandered for decades, peering at every visible shape, human or unbreathing. (pp. 167–8)

DT

Donald Davie, *Thomas Hardy and British Poetry* (1972).
Samuel Hynes, *The Pattern of Hardy's Poetry* (1961).
Tom Paulin, *Thomas Hardy: The Poetry of Perception* (1975).
Dennis Taylor, *Hardy's Poetry, 1860–1928* (2nd edn., 1989).
—— *Hardy's Literary Language and Victorian Philology* (1993).
Walter F. Wright, *The Shaping of 'The Dynasts'* (1967).

Pole, Catherine ('Cassie') (1845–91). Cassie Pole was born in the Dorset village of Chettle to James Pole and his wife Sophia (née Wilson). By the early 1860s James Pole had become the butler to John Floyer at West Stafford House, across the river from Lower Bockhampton, near Dorchester, but Hardy's attraction to his daughter presumably dated from the late 1860s, when she was the personal maid of Emily Fellowes at Kingston Maurward House. Little is known of either the nature or the duration of their relationship, but there is evidence to suggest that Hardy went so far as to purchase an engagement ring—indeed, that Cassie Pole, rather than Tryphena *Sparks, was originally to have been the recipient of the ring that Hardy later gave to Emma Gifford.

Hardy seems to have broken rather abruptly with Cassie following his first meeting with Emma in March 1870, and when Emily Fellowes went to London to be married early in 1872 her maid went with her. In early January 1874 James Pole was 'borrowed' by the rector of West Stafford, the Reverend Reginald Smith, and his wife, the parents of

Hardy's friend Reginald Bosworth *Smith, to act as butler at a dinner at which Hardy was one of the guests. Pole's distress, at once class-conscious and parental, at being required to wait upon the stonemason's son who had spurned his daughter, apparently contributed, shortly afterwards, to both the themes and the situations of *The Hand of Ethelberta*. Cassie herself, in London, married Charles Hutchin, landlord of the New Chesterfield Arms in Shepherd's Market, but in September 1894, aged only 48, she died of cancer at that address—an event that Michael Rabiger has convincingly linked to Hardy's poem 'At Mayfair Lodgings'. MM

Michael Rabiger, 'The Hoffman Papers', *THYB* 10 (1980).

politics. Born into the labouring class, conscious of his talents, and deriving from his reading of Shelley a passion for reforming the world, Hardy freely disclosed his class-prejudices in his unpublished first attempt at novel-writing, *The *Poor Man and the Lady*. It was, according to his own account, among other things 'a sweeping dramatic satire of the squirearchy and nobility, London society, the vulgarity of the middle class', 'the tendency of the writing being socialistic, not to say revolutionary'. Ironic satire of this order is inherent in *The Hand of Ethelberta*, where the contrasts of working-class merit and the limitations of fashionable society (including Mammonites and a decadent aristocrat) are to the fore: see, among much else, the tart observations on 'ancestors' in Chapter 28.

Hardy did not rate politicians highly. Meeting a number at a crush in 1885, he found that they had gathered in the hope of hearing the news of General Gordon's murder, which would precipitate the fall of Gladstone (*LW* 179). This experience prompted the reflection that 'The offhand decision of some commonplace mind high in office at a critical moment influences the course of events for a hundred years.... A row of shopkeepers in Oxford Street just as they came would conduct the affairs of the nation as ably as these' (*LW* 179). In the following year he noted in his diary, 'Plenty of form in their handling of politics, but no matter or originality' (*LW* 187), an observation echoed in *The Well-Beloved* (2.1).

Seeing 'most beautiful women' at another crush in 1890, he wondered where their beauty would be if they were set to work in a turnip-field (*LW* 235)—he no doubt had Tess in mind—and, visiting a training-college for girls in the following year, he reflected: 'How far nobler in its aspirations is the life here than the life I met at the crush two nights back!' (*LW* 246–7). He disapproved of the attitude towards the peasantry displayed by the novelist Henry Fielding, describing it as 'aristocratic, even feudal' (*L* ii 195).

A diary entry of 24 January 1888 (*LW* 213) defines his political position: he is 'neither Tory nor Radical' but 'an Intrinsicalist', opposed to 'privilege derived from accident of any kind' regardless of the class one belonged to—for 'democratic privilege' ('the arrogant assumption that the only labour is hand-labour') was even more repugnant to him than 'aristocratic privilege'. He noted that Tories often did 'by way of exception to their principles more extreme acts of democratism' than Radicals did 'by rule' (*LW* 235). His distaste for class distinctions made him demur when Asquith offered him a knighthood in 1908, and his reservations when his friend Edmund *Gosse accepted one may be inferred, partly from his delay in sending his congratulations (*L* vi 323).

After the *Boer War, Hardy thought that nations would be too sane to go to war again (see the poem 'The Sick Battle-God'), and expressed satisfaction that none of his war poems was jingoistic or imperialistic (*L* ii 277). The Great War of 1914–18 (see FIRST WORLD WAR) convinced him that 'patriotism' should be 'extended to the whole globe' (*LW* 405), and his depression at the likelihood of a sequel is evident at the end of *Winter Words*. FBP

Poor Man and the Lady, The. Hardy's first, unpublished, and now lost novel was begun in the late summer of 1867, shortly after he had left Arthur *Blomfield's London office to resume employment with the Dorchester architect John *Hicks. Written over the next several months during the intervals his architectural work afforded him, the novel was recopied (and revised) between 16 January and 9 June 1868, before being dispatched on 25 July to the publisher Alexander Macmillan (see MACMILLAN & CO.). The manuscript, entitled *The Poor Man and the Lady; By the Poor Man*, divided into two parts totalling 440 pages, and accompanied by a letter of reference from Horace *Moule, was received on 27 July and forwarded the same day to John Morley, Macmillan's principal reader of fiction.

Morley's report was mixed, his evident admiration countered by blunt criticism: 'A very curious & original performance: the opening pictures of the Christmas Eve in the tranters [*sic*] house are really of good quality, much of the writing is strong & fresh. But there crops up in parts a certain rawness of absurdity that is very displeasing, and makes it read like some clever lad's dream...' (Macmillan Archive, British Library). Macmillan was sufficiently interested to read the novel himself and to write a long, detailed letter to Hardy on 10 August, praising the 'dignity & power' of his writing while criticizing his improbable plot and unremittingly bleak—hence 'exaggerated & untrue'—depiction of the upper classes (DCM). Enclosing a copy of Morley's report, Macmillan promised to seek the advice of another reader as to whether a revised version of the story might be publishable.

What that reader thought, if in fact anyone else did read the manuscript, is not known, but it was subsequently returned, revised, and resubmitted, only to be rejected in December as not 'a class of book' the firm could publish. Macmillan did, however, suggest that another publisher might take a different view, and gave Hardy a letter of introduction to Frederick Chapman (*LW* 60).

Hardy left the manuscript at the London offices of Chapman & Hall, and on 8 February 1869 he was informed that their reader had advised against its acceptance, largely because it lacked 'an interesting story' as a basis for its 'episodic scenes' (DCM). When Hardy responded in person to this letter, however, Chapman agreed to publish the novel if £20 were put up as a guarantee against loss. Then, in late February, Chapman invited Hardy to meet with him and the novel's reader, George *Meredith, who warned the young novelist 'not to "nail his colours to the mast" so definitely in a first book', insisting that the reviewers would be 'about his ears like hornets' if he published such a radical satire of society (*LW* 62, 63).

Hardy returned to Bockhampton with the manuscript, subsequently submitting it to at least two more publishers: on 15 April to *Smith, Elder, who rejected it within a fortnight, and in early June to Tinsley Brothers (see TINSLEY, WILLIAM), who three months later offered to publish it on terms Hardy considered beyond his means. Efforts to publish the work in its entirety were then abandoned, though Hardy freely incorporated many of its scenes into his next three novels (see below), used it as the basis of his novella *An Indiscretion in the Life of an Heiress*, and in his seventies even considered reconstructing the original novel from memory and a fragment of the manuscript then still in existence. That reconstruction never materialized, however, and Hardy's subsequent destruction of the manuscript fragment allowed his extraordinary claims for the novel—'It was the most original thing (for its date) that I ever wrote' (*L* iv 130)—to remain essentially unchallenged.

According to *Life and Work*, Hardy's original intention was to write 'a striking socialistic novel' based upon materials derived from his own contrasting experiences of 'West-country life in its less explored recesses, and the life of an isolated student cast upon the billows of London with no protection but his brains' (*LW* 58). The result was unconventional both in structure (the original subtitle was *A Story with no plot; Containing some original verses*) and in content. Hardy himself described it as 'a sweeping dramatic satire of the squirearchy and nobility, London society, the vulgarity of the middle class, modern Christianity, church restoration, and political and domestic morals in general' (*LW* 62–3).

Morley's report and Macmillan's letter are the only surviving first-hand responses to the lost novel, but other (somewhat less reliable) sources of information exist, including Hardy's own remarks in *Life and Work*, Edmund *Gosse's plot synopsis based on a conversation with Hardy in 1915, and the two creative works drawn directly from *The Poor Man: An Indiscretion in the Life of an Heiress* and the poem 'A Poor Man and a Lady'. Taken in combination, they provide reasonably reliable evidence for reconstructing the basic *Poor Man* plot, which revolves around the thwarted love of Will Strong, a young man of humble origins and exceptional abilities, and Miss Allancourt, the beautiful and spirited daughter of the local landowner. When the lovers' relationship is discovered by Miss Allancourt's family, the young people are separated and Strong, trained as an architect, goes to London to establish himself. He becomes a political radical and recounts his life story in an address to working men. A chance encounter with Miss Allancourt concludes with a renewal of affection, but separation is again parentally enforced, and she becomes engaged to marry the heir of a great landowner. A subsequent meeting leads to another mutual declaration; whether or not they then marry (as in *An Indiscretion*) is not clear, but certainly Miss Allancourt (like Geraldine Allenville) dies suddenly from a haemorrhage of the lungs.

The novel's scenes of country life were clearly based upon Hardy's own Bockhampton experiences, and it is not difficult to recognize autobiographical elements in Strong's story. Nor is it difficult to identify the reuse of the poor-man-and-the-lady motif in Hardy's subsequent work (see the book by Patricia Ingham cited below), while the socio-political issues invoked in this first novel re-emerge throughout his career, most explicitly in his last novel, *Jude the Obscure*. Less obvious but more tangible is Hardy's deployment of fragments of the *Poor Man* manuscript in his early work: one considerable segment, including the Christmas Eve scenes praised by Morley, evidently made its way into *Under the Greenwood Tree*, just as the Rotten Row scenes admired by Macmillan became part of *A Pair of Blue Eyes*. Marked verbal parallels between passages in the early novels (including *Desperate Remedies*) and *An Indiscretion* further suggest that Hardy incorporated extensive material from his unpublishable 'revolutionary' (*LW* 63) novel into the natural and architectural descriptions, courtship scenes, and dialogue of his more readily publishable fiction, permanently establishing *The Poor Man* as a haunting ghostly presence. PD

Pamela Dalziel, 'Exploiting the *Poor Man*: The Genesis of Hardy's *Desperate Remedies*', *Journal of English and Germanic Philology*, 94 (1995).

—— (ed.), *Thomas Hardy: The Excluded and Collaborative Stories* (1992).

Patricia Ingham, *Thomas Hardy* (1989).

Charles Morgan, *The House of Macmillan (1843–1943)* (1943).

portraits and sculptures of Thomas Hardy. Hardy iconography includes images of the author by artists in various media: drawings, etchings, oil paintings, sculptures in marble and bronze, and photography. Although Hardy did not sit to as many artists as, say, Pope or Johnson or Carlyle, he was an interesting subject for portraiture. Of the approximately 40 artists who portrayed him, four became important in his personal life.

The chronology of Hardy portraits may be divided into three periods: the 1890s, or the final stages of his career as a novelist; around 1910, after *The Dynasts*, when he received the Order of Merit; and the last decade of his life, the 1920s, when he was the Grand Old Man of English literature. There is another general division of his portraiture, especially in cartoons and caricatures, based on the double nature of his life: the London theatre-going sophisticate of the formal portraits, and the Wessex countryman. The Wessex tone is evident in the posthumous statue by Eric Kennington (unveiled by Sir James *Barrie on 2 September 1931) at Top o' Town, Dorchester. It depicts a seated Hardy in country suit, hat in hand, surrounded by floral vegetation—his contemplation of which makes him resemble, according to Augustus John, 'a frustrated market-gardener'.

Hardy's figure was not impressive, for he was only 5 feet 6 inches tall, rather slightly built, and unprepossessing in his general appearance—'great brow, frail frame'. (This disproportion is caricatured in Max *Beerbohm's well-known drawing of 1913.) However, many of the artists who did Hardy commented on the appeal of his head. Even as a young man of 24 in London, he was made aware of the particular shape and size of his head by having a phrenological reading of his cranium done by a noted phrenologist who had examined many famous Victorians. After he became famous himself, rising young artists asked for permission to portray him; in his later years they became something of a nuisance, for he found sittings tiring and was concerned that the artist might expect him to buy the resulting portrait. He probably found sitting for a sculptor somewhat less demanding, for he was freer to move about. Earlier portraits were generally done in the artist's studio in London, sometimes taking several months to complete. In his later years, after he had given up going to London each spring for the 'season', artists had to come to *Max Gate, frequently living in the house for several days, often to Hardy's irritation. Many requests to sit were turned down with the excuse of health and age.

None of the painted portraits of Hardy shows him during the years when he wore a full beard, only photographs of the 1870s and 1880s (when beards were especially popular). In the 1890s an oil portrait was done by a little-known artist, Winifred Hope Thomson, who, through the influence of Hardy's friend Lady *Jeune, managed to obtain the novelist's consent to sit for her in London. A larger canvas than most of the later portraits, the Thomson portrait (DCM) is a three-quarter length, showing an affable, sophisticated gentleman, slightly balding and with a dapper moustache with upturned, possibly waxed, ends. Even in later years Hardy prized this early portrait over some by superior artists, and kept it at Max Gate.

One artist whose interest in Hardy as a subject extended from the 1890s to 1920 was William Strang. His portraits, some ten in all and mainly drawings and etchings, began in 1893 with an etching and an oil painting, and ended in 1920 with another oil, the latter (Glasgow Art Gallery) showing an unusually imaginative background influenced by Gauguin's Tahitian works. Hardy was pleased not only with Strang's portraits but also with his other art works, especially the grotesques and the darkly ominous ones, and he found Strang a genial companion. Representations of Hardy intended for the general public included a reproduction of one of Strang's etchings used as the frontispiece to Volume I of the Mellstock Edition (1919–20). The Strang portraits remain among the best, and his small oil (1893) on display in the National Portrait Gallery is one of the most widely familiar images of Hardy.

Less well known, and scarcely counting as a true portrait, is a large group painting done by Strang in 1913, '*Bal Suzette*' (*The Café Royalists*), now in a private collection: this shows twelve costumed theatrical figures (predominantly women), and four gentlemen in formal dress as observers of the scene. Hardy has often been considered to have been the model for one of the latter group; Strang himself is among the costumed figures in the background. Only one other group portrait depicts Hardy, a painting that reflects his social life in London and also raises unanswered questions. This is *First Night* (in private hands), a large painting by a Belgian artist, Alfred Stevens, and shows the audience at the Palace Theatre in 1893 or later, with Hardy sitting in a row with handsome women and well-dressed men (including, it has been suggested, Joseph Conrad and Richard D'Oyly Carte). Once again, as so often, Hardy appears in profile, looking down as though reading a programme, with only his head showing beyond the large feather fan held by an attractive young lady at his side.

Other artists portrayed Hardy in the early years of the 20th century. William Rothenstein did sketches; Mary Hardy did three oils of her brother; Walter William Ouless of Jersey did a portrait that has in recent years been used on a postage stamp issued in Jersey; Vernon Hill's ineffective etching was used in a later edition of Lionel Johnson's *The Art of Thomas Hardy*, replacing a fine one by Strang in the original edition of 1894. But these works are overshadowed by the productions of such artists as Blanche, Herkomer, Thornycroft, Eves, and Augustus John.

A French and a German artist, both Anglophiles and highly respected portrait-painters who conducted their own art schools, were both important portrayers of Hardy. In 1906 Jacques-Emile Blanche did two quite different portraits in oil, and Hubert von Herkomer did one in 1908. Blanche became a good friend of the Hardys and wrote entertainingly about the experience of painting Hardy. Emma Hardy had requested him not to make Hardy look 'miserable', but her plea was obviously ignored. Blanche's first, unfinished portrait (Tate Gallery) shows Hardy with a sad, even forlorn, countenance. His other portrait (Manchester City Art Galleries) is more formal and conventional. Herkomer ran the Bushey School of Art just outside London, though he had a studio in the city. Since he was a busy teacher and professional painter, there were, much to Hardy's irritation, frequent delays in the sittings. His portrait (DCM), though full front face and certainly not sad, is quite dark with a greenish cast. Hardy himself never liked it.

Among all these artists the closest friend was the well-known sculptor Hamo *Thornycroft. In 1915, having long been an admirer of Thornycroft's style, Hardy accepted his request to do a bust. There had previously been only a little terracotta bust of Hardy, no more than a few inches high, done by William Carter Unwin of the Poole Potteries, Dorset. Thornycroft made two original versions, one in bronze (National Portrait Gallery), the other in marble (DCM). These busts reveal the aspect of Hardy that appealed to many artists: the shape of his head.

At the age of 84 Hardy was persuaded by another sculptor, the Franco-Russian Serge Youriévitch, to have his head done in bronze, but the sittings tried his patience sorely. The location of the original is unknown, but two small copies exist (University of Texas; plaster cast at DCM). Maggie Richardson (Mrs George Mitchell) did a bronze head of Hardy (DCM) that is more youthful than the Thornycroft one. Considerably better than these are two medallions, one by Theodore Spicer-Simson, the other by Hardy's cousin James Sparks. In the 1930s, after Hardy's death, Madame Tussaud's in London exhibited a waxwork of Hardy among a group of assorted literary notabilities ranging from Chaucer to H. G. Wells.

Several portraits of Hardy (Tate Gallery, National Portrait Gallery, DCM) were done in his later years by Reginald Eves. These show the elderly, white-moustached author with dark blue eyes and the familiar serious, resigned expression. Of the two in DCM, one portrays Hardy in academic dress.

Probably the best of all the portraits as a work of art is that executed in 1923 by Augustus John (Fitzwilliam Museum, Cambridge). The technique is unusual in that the oil paint was lightly applied, the canvas showing through in places. Hardy is seated with bookshelves behind him, looking off to his right; the shape of his head is clearly shown, and the raised eyebrows contribute to a greater than usual animation. Both hands, holding the lapels of his coat with the thumbs elongated, are prominent. John, who was a noted Bohemian, got along well with Hardy: someone is said to have remarked that it was a case of a successful womanizer and a failed one. In any case the result is a fine portrait and, according to Helen Granville-Barker (quoted *LW* 471), Hardy expressed his appreciation of it: 'I don't know whether that is how I look or not—but that is how I *feel*.' (Another anecdote, however, has him remarking, 'Well, if I look like that the sooner I am under ground the better.') Plans for J. S. Sargent to paint Hardy later in 1923 came to nothing, as Hardy was unwilling to go to London for sittings.

Hardy's lifespan covers a period when photography was developing rapidly, and he became a frequent subject for many professional as well as amateur photographers. Certainly for his early and middle years, bearded or not, these are the only images we have. Possibly the best of all the photographs is that taken by Emil Otto Hoppé *c.*1913–14 (National Portrait Gallery); another notable photograph is by Olive Edis (1914, also National Portrait Gallery). DJW

Series of articles in *THJ* by Donald J. Winslow: on Blanche (8, 1992); Herkomer (7, 1991); Strang (7, 1991; 9, 1993); Thomson (1, 1985); Thornycroft (3, 1987).

Positivism. 'I am not a Positivist, as you know... but no person of serious thought in these days could be said to stand aloof from Positivist teaching & ideals', Hardy wrote in 1903 (*L* iii 53). In fact, by then he had immersed himself in Positivist thought for over 30 years (*LN* 618 n.), by reading *Comte and the main English exponents of Positivism: Edward Spencer Beesly (*LN* i 312), John Henry Bridges (*LN* i 50–1), George *Eliot (*LN* i 381), Frederic *Harrison (*LN* i 370–1), G. H. Lewes (*LN* i 14–15), Harriet Martineau (*LN* i 100–1), John Stuart *Mill (*LN* i 368), Cotter Morison (*LN* i 396–7), John Morley (*LN* i 292), and Leslie *Stephen (*LN* i 341–2).

Hardy's Positivist sympathies were noted at an early stage, and contemporary reviews attributed *Far from the Madding Crowd* to George Eliot (*LW* 100). In *The Return of the Native*, Clym is explicitly related to Positivism, as his social morality is pointedly associated with 'ethical systems popular at the time' in Paris (3.2). Positivist psychology, with its anti-rationalist basis and attendant social criticism, constitutes a major element in Hardy's fiction (see L. A. Björk, *Psychological Vision and Social Criticism in the*

Novels of Thomas Hardy (1987), 79–106). There is, for example, a strain of anti-rationalism in the novels—in narrative commentary, characterization, and thematic implications—that finds support in a good many of Hardy's notes (*LN* i 3–4, 68; ii 55), in his autobiography (*LW* 107, 153, 169, 332, 432), and in his literary essays (*Thomas Hardy's Personal Writings*, ed. H. Orel (1966), 127, 107, 115, 146).

It is significant that the more philosophically and morally outspoken Hardy's novels became, the more conspicuous is his use of Positivist notions. *Tess of the d'Urbervilles* is a case in point, as Frederic Harrison recognized in calling it 'a Positivist allegory or sermon' (*LN* i 312). Equally relevant in this context is the fact that, at the time Hardy was smarting from the attacks on *Tess* in the press on moral and religious grounds (*LN* i 292–3, 320), he should have marked passages in his copy of Morley's *Diderot and the Encyclopaedists* directly relevant to the moral issues in the novel. One example is Morley's explanation for the decline of faith and morals in the reign of Louis XIV: 'This [decline] must always be the natural consequence of building sound ethics on the shifting sands and rotting foundations of theology' (quoted in Björk, p. 116). This distinction between morals and theology is precisely the key point in Tess's argument with Angel: 'She tried to argue, and tell him that he had mixed in his dull brain two matters, theology and morals...' (*TDU* 47).

Hardy's acceptance of Positivism was not absolute. As his own writings consistently indicate, he shared neither Positivism's attitude to marriage, nor its evolutionary optimism, nor its Idea of Progress (*LN* i 312–13; Björk, pp. 46–50). It was in fact the general optimism of Positivism that in 1919 severed Hardy's friendship of almost 40 years with Harrison. LAB

Pound, Ezra (1885–1972), American poet and critic. He invited Hardy to contribute to the New York magazine the *Dial* in 1920; Hardy's letter of refusal (28 November: *L* vi 47) includes a graceful compliment that shows his awareness of Pound's own poetry. Thus encouraged, before the end of the same year Pound sent Hardy presentation copies of his *Quia Pauper Amavi* (1919) and *Hugh Selwyn Mauberley* (1920); Hardy's discussion of them in a letter dated 18 March 1921 (*L* vi 77) indicates that he had read them carefully and sympathetically. Pound later remarked, with more enthusiasm than accuracy, in relation to Hardy's *Collected Poems*, 'There *is* the harvest of having written 20 novels first' (*Letters of Ezra Pound, 1907–41*, ed. D. D. Paige (1950), 294).

Powys brothers. Hardy was acquainted with the novelist John Cowper Powys (1872–1963) and his brothers Theodore (1875–1953), Albert (1881–1936), and Llewelyn (1884–1939). J. C. Powys wrote widely about Dorset and other parts of 'Wessex' in such works as *A Glastonbury Romance* (1932) and *Maiden Castle* (1936). He paid several visits to Hardy at Max Gate; in a letter to his brother Llewelyn written after a visit in 1919 he refers to Hardy as conversing 'gaily and cheerfully', and describes Florence Hardy as resembling 'a grave ascetic art student or a Chelsea socialist, follower of William Morris' (Millgate 525).

Llewelyn, a journalist and essayist whose books include *Dorset Essays* (1935), also visited Max Gate, and later described Hardy as 'a very old dapper country gentleman moving about quickly, jerkily like a sparrow or Tom Tit'. Theodore, a novelist writing as T. F. Powys and best remembered for the rural allegory *Mr Weston's Good Wine* (1927), was another visitor to Max Gate: 'On his notoriously weird approach, Hardy jumped in the air in alarm, but Florence calmly carried off the situation' (Gittings, *The Older Hardy*, 204, based on an account by J. C. Powys). Hardy corresponded on architectural subjects with Albert Reginald Powys, an architect who was secretary of the Society for the Protection of Ancient Buildings.

Two Essays by Llewelyn Powys, Toucan Press Monographs No. 70 (1971).
R. P. Graves, *The Brothers Powys* (1983).

prefaces. It was Harold Orel in his edition of *Thomas Hardy's Personal Writings* (1966) who first collected together all the prefaces that Hardy wrote for his novels and collections of poems, and thus enabled us to see them as a continuous self-assessment.

The first time Hardy thought it good or necessary to introduce one of his novels was in 1889, when a revised edition of *Desperate Remedies* was published. Alone of his novels this one had not been issued in a cheap one-volume form soon after its first publication, and Hardy felt that some justification for the belated reissue was required. The tone is essentially deprecatory, stressing that in the novel 'he was feeling his way to a method'.

In 1889 Hardy was writing *Tess of the d'Urbervilles*, and perhaps the composition of this brief note convinced him of the value of direct conversation between author and reader, because the first, three-volume edition of *Tess* (1891) was prefaced with an 'Explanatory Note'. In part this note accounted in neutral terms for differences between the serial and the book versions of the novel; but it concluded with a significant sentence attempting through attack to pre-empt (or to provoke) criticism, saying that the novel offers in artistic form 'a true sequence of things', and demanding that the 'too genteel reader, who cannot endure to have said what everybody nowadays thinks and feels' should consider St Jerome's words: 'If an offence come out of the truth, better it is that the offence come than that the truth be concealed.'

This sentence shows clearly the kind of response Hardy expected; and when he got it, though in smaller proportion than he had expected, he took the earliest opportunity—that provided by the publication of a one-volume edition of *Tess* in 1892—to add a much more substantial preface to the novel. In this he thanks the majority of readers who have welcomed the book, and then reviews the hostile criticism and rebuts it, sounding pleased that there was at least an occasional 'genteel reader' with whom he could take issue. The combative nature of this introductory material is of a piece with Hardy's essay *'Candour in English Fiction' of 1890, in which he writes disgustedly of the falsity imposed upon novelists by the *de facto* censorship exercised by magazine editors and the circulating libraries.

When, in 1895, Hardy began to work through all his novels for his first collected edition, he continued the idea of introductory prefatory notes. *Tess of the d'Urbervilles* and *Far from the Madding Crowd* were the first two to be prepared. For the former, Hardy only felt it necessary to apologize for the tone of the 1892 preface (though allowing it to stand 'as something once said'); for the latter, however, Hardy wrote perhaps the most important of all the forewords to his fiction, for it introduces the idea of Wessex, which he then called a 'merely realistic dream-country'. It was, given the nature of the revisions he was going on to make to the environment of all of his novels, already a misleading description, and he changed it for the second collected edition in 1912 to the familiar, and more accurate, 'partly real, partly dream-country'. The preface is also characteristic of many of those he was to write during the following year and a half, in that, after introducing Wessex, he offers a brief primer to details in the novel that he thinks of as characterizing the past or passing culture of Wessex. In this instance he also accounts for their disappearance, as he had done in 'The *Dorsetshire Labourer', by the replacement of a permanent village population with a stream of migratory labourers.

Readers who bought each volume of the Osgood, McIlvaine collected edition as they came out will have found as they read that in these first two of the set they had already met the topics most frequently addressed in subsequent prefaces: self-justification and details of Wessex. There follow brief notes on the significant elements in each, in the order in which the novels appeared:

The Mayor of Casterbridge: The significance of the state of the harvest in England before free trade in grain was permitted in 1846; the reintroduction of a chapter deleted from the English editions; the Scottish speech of Farfrae.

A Pair of Blue Eyes: The futility of church-restoration in Cornwall; a justification for including Cornwall in Wessex; an account of the district as 'a region of dream and mystery' that has details used later in *'Poems of 1912–13'.

Two on a Tower: The theme, 'the emotional history of two infinitesimal lives against the stupendous background of the stellar universe'; the hostile reviews, and counter-arguments, some of which are self-consciously mischievous; environmental details.

The Return of the Native: Topography—Budmouth and Egdon Heath.

The Woodlanders: Marriage (decidedly mischievous); the beauty of the novel's landscape.

Jude the Obscure (the first edition of the novel): An account of the novel's composition; an attempted pre-emptive defence of its treatment of 'the strongest passion known to humanity', and of its philosophical inconsistencies.

The Trumpet-Major: An account of the oral and written sources for the historical elements of the novel.

The Hand of Ethelberta: An explanation of the 'somewhat frivolous narrative', in which Hardy is unable to say directly that he was writing social satire, but concluding with the belief that a story told from the perspective of the servants' hall would be more acceptable now than when first written.

A Laodicean: The theme of the novel as exhibiting the romance of modern scientific and cultural developments; the story should give pleasure to those who think marriage the ultimate goal in life.

Desperate Remedies: Topographical alterations, and an allusion to similarities between the novel and *Jude the Obscure.*

Wessex Tales: On hangmen in Wessex; on the relation between reality and fiction; on smuggling.

Life's Little Ironies: On the relation of a teller to his tale; other anecdotes of Parson Toogood ('Andrey Satchel and the Parson and the Clerk').

A Group of Noble Dames: On the source-material for the stories, and Hardy's acquaintance with present members of some of the noble families.

Under the Greenwood Tree: A long and loving account of the originals behind the Mellstock quire.

The Well-Beloved (the first edition of the novel): On the nature of Portland/the Isle of Slingers; that the novel has been rewritten since its serialization.

When, in 1912, a second freshly revised collected edition was issued, Hardy added to or amended most of these prefaces. The most important changes were to those in *Tess* and *Jude.* In a Postscript to the latter, Hardy reviewed with sadness the violent critical response to the first publication of the novel, and gave his response, especially on marriage, noting finally that it had also been suggested that Sue was the first 'woman of the feminist movement' in fiction. Hardy did not add much to the preface for *Tess* itself—primarily the information that the subtitle was added at the last minute to the first edition—but he did include in the volume a substantial 'General Preface to the Novels and Poems'. In it he covers the classification of the novels adopted for the edition, Wessex (again), his poetry, and the philosophy in his writing. Otherwise many of the brief notes added for 1912 refer to environmental details; with *Under the Greenwood Tree* the note was one of regret that he had not taken the quire seriously; with *A Pair of Blue Eyes* it was to point out the thematic connection with Tess; with *Desperate Remedies* to explain why the novel seemed to embody ideas found in his poems.

The preface to *The Dynasts* was perhaps the most necessary of all of Hardy's introductory pieces, for the whole conception was unfamiliar to his audience. He begins: 'The spectacle here presented to the mind's eye in the likeness of a Drama . . .', at once warning the reader that the play is not for acting. He explains why he has become interested in Napoleon, and then outlines the spirit-framework of the drama, the 'phantasmal intelligences', concluding with a discussion of the viability of a drama unintended for performance. As in many of his prefaces, he is essentially on the defensive; and the same is true of the last, and the most substantial—the 'Apology' that introduced his sixth book of verse, *Late Lyrics and Earlier*, in 1922.

It might seem that at this late date—Hardy was 81, and 'a writer whose books are fairly well received lately' (*L* vi 116)—such an introduction was unnecessary; but Hardy was still being accused of pessimism as if it were a crime against humanity, and the first few pages of the 'Apology' (a title Hardy used as being more 'piquant' than 'Preface', thus suggesting irony) are a response to such attacks. He then turns to more general considerations, suggesting that 'we seem threatened by a new Dark Age', and offering the hope that religion, 'which must be retained unless the world is to perish', might be allying itself with 'complete rationality, which must come, unless also the world is to perish, by means of the interfusing effect of poetry'.

SJG

Procter, Anne (1799–1888), née Skepper, veteran literary hostess, whose memories of the distant past were a source of fascination to Hardy. The widow of B. W. Procter (1787–1874), poet, who used the pseudonym 'Barry Cornwall', she met Hardy in March 1880 and he became a frequent visitor to her salon, often meeting Robert *Browning there. Hardy was fascinated not only by her octogenarian vivacity but by her memories of some of the Romantic poets—she would recount, for instance, how Leigh Hunt once called on her, accompanied by a young man he introduced as Mr Keats—and he described her as 'a remarkable link with the literary past' (*LW* 139). At Hardy's suggestion, she once made a list of all the celebrities she had known. On another occasion he went with her to visit *Tennyson (*LW* 140).

The extracts from her letters quoted in the autobiography are racy in style, and suggest a survival of Regency manners in the late-Victorian period. She admired Hardy's work, and wrote to him enthusiastically about *Far from the Madding Crowd* and *The Return of the Native*: on 4 September 1874, she wrote of the serialized version of the former, 'I can hardly make you understand, how one wants the next Number. It is perhaps a taste of Purgatory, to wait for the drop of cold water' (DCM). She was, on Hardy's own admission, the model for Anne Loveday in *The Trumpet-Major*. As late as 1886, in her late eighties, she visited the Hardys' temporary London home and regaled them with anecdotes of Macaulay and Sydney Smith. Henry *James, who was one of her favourite visitors, described her as 'the best talker I have met in England' and, after her death, as 'a kind of window in the past'. In his autobiography Hardy quotes from a diary entry of 24 March 1880 (*LW* 140) to the effect that, during a lunch visit to her house, she had shown him a photograph of James and stated that James (44 years her junior) had proposed to her. Hardy's quoted speculation '"Can it be so?"' is perhaps disingenuous and not untinged with malice: the truth seems to be that she and James carried on a mock-flirtation enjoyed by both but taken seriously by neither (see Leon Edel, *Henry James: The Conquest of London 1870–1881* (1967)).

'Profitable Reading of Fiction, The.' This essay appeared in the New York magazine *Forum* in March 1888 and was the first of three essays on the novel written by Hardy in 1888–91 (see also CANDOUR IN ENGLISH FICTION and SCIENCE OF FICTION, THE)—a period during which his own relationships with editors, publishers, reviewers, and the reading public were becoming more problematic. Its subject, evidently proposed by the magazine's editor, is 'novel reading considered with a view to mental profit', and the first kind of 'profit' considered is simple relaxation or escapism. Hardy stresses the importance of a 'somewhat absorbing' narrative and the value of a 'change of scene... as if the reader had taken the hind seat on a witch's broomstick'. For such purposes novels should not be read in a critical spirit.

Hardy next turns to the 'intellectual or moral profit' that can be gained from novel-reading, at first identifying such extrinsic features as 'didactic reflection', 'trifles of useful knowledge', and 'quotations from ancient and other authors'. Though he comments ironically and even patronizingly on these attractions for the serious reader of fiction, and cites examples from Johnson, Hugo, Disraeli, and Fielding, his own novels provide ample supplies of all these characteristics. More seriously, he proceeds to define good fiction as 'that kind of imaginative writing which lies nearest to the epic, dramatic, or narrative masterpieces of the past'. Modern fiction is again linked with classical prototypes in the Aristotelian declaration that 'the best fiction... is more true, so to put it, than history or nature can be'. In turning to specific examples, Hardy finds in Richardson a 'constructive art' comparable to that of Greek tragedy; he does not, however, share the conventionally high estimation of the plot of Fielding's *Tom Jones*, ranking *Scott's *The Bride of Lammermoor* above it in this respect. More generally, he stresses the importance of formal elements in a work of fiction: though not many novel-readers may pause to consider this element, 'to a masterpiece in story there appertains a beauty of shape no less than to a masterpiece in pictorial or plastic art'.

Hardy seems to come nearest to his own practice as a novelist in praising the kind of novels 'which impress the reader with the inevitableness of character and environment in working out destiny, whether that destiny be just or unjust': it is this kind, he maintains, that 'must have a sound effect, if not what is called a good effect, upon a healthy mind'. He was later to use the formula 'character and environment' to designate his own major fiction.

Proust, Marcel (1871–1922), French novelist. Hardy and Proust shared the view that man's deepest love may be for a 'nostalgic phantom' that inhabits a series of individuals and serves as a source of artistic inspiration. Proust read four of Hardy's novels in translation: *Jude the Obscure* in 1906, *A Pair of Blue Eyes* and *The Well-Beloved* in 1910, and *Far from the Madding Crowd* in 1911. After finishing *The Well-Beloved*, he remarked to Robert de Billy that he had just read 'something very beautiful' which resembled what he himself was writing; some years later, Hardy noted that as in *The Well-Beloved*, so in Proust, the lover harbours within himself an ideal image of the beloved, and projects it onto a succession of flesh-and-blood women. Yet Proust and Hardy differ in the conclusions their characters reach. Pierston, the artist-hero of *The Well-Beloved*, loses his artistic inspiration when the third of the Avices he had hoped to marry elopes with another man; instead, he marries the woman to whom he was attracted years before. He renounces art, in other words, and also the folly of youthful romance, settling for a woman who will be a good companion and nurse to him in his old age. By contrast, the narrator of Proust's *A la recherche du temps perdu* (1913–27) arrives in the end at a new sense of artistic creativity, and devotes himself to art, relinquishing forever love, marriage, and even friendship. For Hardy's own analogy between the ideas embodied in *The Well-Beloved* and those expressed 'many years later' by Proust, see *LW* 303; for his transcription of two passages from Proust in the original French, again in connection with *The Well-Beloved*, see *LW* 466–7. JA

publishers. During his long literary career Hardy had dealings, for longer or shorter periods, with a great variety of English, American, and Continental publishers. From 1902 *Macmillan & Co. were his principal publishers, but in his earlier years he frequently changed allegiances and also worked for different publishers more or less simultaneously. His fiction of the 1880s, for instance, appeared from three different firms: *Smith, Elder (*The Trumpet-Major* and, six years later, *The Mayor of Casterbridge*); *Sampson Low (*A Laodicean* and *Two on a Tower*); and Macmillan (*The Woodlanders* and *Wessex Tales*). The most important of these firms and individuals are the subject of separate entries: see, in addition to those already noted, HARPER & BROTHERS; HEINEMANN, WILLIAM; HOLT, HENRY; PAUL, CHARLES KEGAN; MACMILLAN, FREDERICK; OSGOOD, MCILVAINE; TAUCHNITZ EDITIONS; TILLOTSON & SON; TINSLEY, WILLIAM. The articles on Hardy's various volumes of fiction and poetry contain details of their publication, including, in some instances, changes of publisher in later editions. See also COLLECTED EDITIONS.

Puddletown, in earlier times Piddletown, played a large part in Hardy's early years, and is the scene of much of the action in *Far from the Madding Crowd*. It was and is a large village about five miles north-east of *Dorchester on the road to Bere Regis (Hardy's 'Kingsbere'). Many of Hardy's closest relatives were associated with the place. His paternal great-grandfather spent much of his life in Puddletown, and his maternal grandmother passed the last years of her life there. The Puddletown Hardys included Elizabeth, widow of his great-uncle John, and several of her children, who were contemporaries of Hardy and his sisters and brother. Two of Hardy's mother's sisters had settled at Puddletown: Mary, who had married John Antell, and Maria, who had married James Sparks. Both had several children, and Hardy and his mother frequently walked across the heathland from their own cottage at *Higher Bockhampton to Puddletown, a journey of about two miles, to visit their many relatives. In the late 1860s Hardy had a romantic relationship with his cousin Tryphena *Sparks.

Hardy's novels are all written about places he knew well, and this is particularly true of *Far from the Madding Crowd*. When asked by the editor of the prestigious *Cornhill Magazine* in 1873 to write a serial for him, Hardy located it in and around the Puddletown he knew so well, and called the village 'Weatherbury'. He could not resist a joke at the expense of his Puddletown relatives, and describes the Weatherbury folk as 'by no means uninteresting intrinsically. If report spoke truly they were as "hardy, merry, thriving, wicked a set as any in the whole country"'. Puddletown's fine church, which still retains its musicians' gallery, was the scene of some of the action, as were several of the local buildings.

John Antell's father had been a maltster in Puddletown at the beginning of the 19th century, and was a model for the maltster in the novel. More importantly, John Antell himself played a part in the creation of Jude Fawley in *Jude the Obscure*. As a self-educated working-class man (he was the Puddletown shoemaker), Antell was frustrated by the lack of opportunity to realize his potential, and became bitter and an alcoholic. As Hardy listened to his Puddletown uncle criticizing the class-system and the fate that kept him down, he would have been storing ideas and feelings that were to manifest themselves throughout his career as a writer. See also ANTELL FAMILY; RELATIVES OF THOMAS HARDY.

JCG

R

railways. Born in 1840, Hardy was in time to witness during his early childhood some of the last moments of the pre-railway age. When 8 or 9 years old, he accompanied his mother on a visit to his aunt in Hertfordshire; his autobiography describes this as 'his first experience of travel' (*LW* 21), and relates how, on the return journey, they travelled by coach to London, the Great Northern Railway being then 'only in process of construction'; in London they stayed at a coaching inn, the Cross-Keys in Clerkenwell, before proceeding to Waterloo and completing their journey by train, the line to Dorchester having been recently opened. Later, as a young architect in London, he was at one time assigned macabre duties in relation to the removal of coffins and bones from Old St Pancras Churchyard, the site of a cutting for the Midland Railway (*LW* 46–7).

In his fiction Hardy frequently depicts a community existing beyond, but only just beyond, the steadily extending network of the railways. In the opening chapters of *The Well-Beloved*, the 'Isle of Slingers' (Portland) remains untouched by modernity, and to travel to London the hero must first go to 'Budmouth' (Weymouth), a few miles in distance but marking the boundary of two worlds and two historical epochs. In *Tess of the d'Urbervilles* the pastoralism of the Valley of the Great Dairies belongs to the pre-railway age, but Tess and Angel do not have far to travel to 'a little railway station' (30) in order to deliver the milk for conveyance to the urban centres where it will be consumed—a reminder that the apparently self-enclosed rural world is now linked to the wider world.

Such a situation is contrived, with cavalier disregard to history, in *The Mayor of Casterbridge*: describing a royal visit to Casterbridge, the narrator states that 'The railway had stretched out an arm towards Casterbridge at this time, but had not reached it by several miles as yet; so that the intervening distance . . . was to be traversed by road in the old fashion' (37). Prince Albert's journey to Dorchester in July 1849, on which this episode is based, had, however, been conducted entirely by train, since the line to Dorchester had been opened some two years earlier. Despite his prefatory claim to historical foundations for his story, it suited Hardy to push the royal visit back into a period when Casterbridge was still untouched by the railway.

At a time when the railways had not yet penetrated the remoter corners of Wessex, a journey of any length could sometimes involve different modes of transport, combining the old-fashioned and the newfangled. In the story 'A Changed Man'—almost Hardy's last venture into fiction, but set in an earlier period—an eloping couple, wishing to travel from Casterbridge (Dorchester) to Bristol, first take a fly (light carriage let out for hire) to Ivell (Yeovil, Somerset), and then pick up the train, since 'The Bristol railway was open to Ivell'. Narratives extending over a period of years sometimes embody dramatic changes in modes of transport, and consequently in social life. In the earlier part of the short story 'Fellow-Townsmen', apparently set in the 1840s, 'Port-Bredy' (Bridport) has 'no railway within a distance of many miles', but by the closing section, set 21 years later, 'a railway had invaded the town, tying it on to a main line at a junction a dozen miles off'.

Of all Hardy's novels it is the last, *Jude the Obscure*, that most fully exploits the mobility that railways had now placed at the disposal of nearly all sections of society. Sue Bridehead, indeed, offers the aggressive generalization that it is the railway station rather than the cathedral that is '"the centre of the town life now"' (3.1): she might have added that some Victorian railway stations could easily have been mistaken for cathedrals. On a more practical level, the rootless and restless lives of the principal characters in that novel involve them in constant journeys, more often by train than by any other means: Sue travels by train from Melchester to Shaston; Jude and Arabella travel from Christminster to Aldbrickham and back; Jude goes from

Melchester to Kennetbridge 'by a series of crooked railways' and returns 'by the slow Sunday train'; Phillotson meets Sue at the station after she has travelled from Alfredston to Shaston; Sue takes '"the six-thirty train"' from Shaston when she leaves her husband; Jude meets Arabella off the seven o'clock train at Christminster; Jude, now dying, makes his painful journey to visit Sue partly by train from Christminster to Alfredston—and this list is by no means complete. The first reference to the railway occurs at the beginning of the third chapter, where we learn that the young Jude—anticipating the fate of his own son a generation later—has been 'deposited by the carrier from a railway station'. But perhaps the most memorable of all the train journeys in this novel is the one Hardy also made the subject of a fine poem (finely set by Benjamin Britten), 'Midnight on the Great Western': that of Little Father Time, the 'journeying boy' on the Great Western Railway.

Some of the cross-country journeys made by characters in the same novel involve combinations of train, other forms of transport, and walking, and Hardy shows considerable interest in the logistics of late 19th-century mobility. To cite a single instance: when Sue returns to Phillotson, she leaves Christminster by train, travels as far as Alfredston Road, and then transfers to a steam-tram, finally hiring a horse-drawn vehicle to take her to Marygreen, thus experiencing the history of transport in reverse as she travels from the city to the village.

But perhaps the most dramatic, or melodramatic, of all the numerous railway journeys in Hardy's fiction occurs near the end of *A Pair of Blue Eyes* (39). The two rivals in love, Smith and Knight, travel by 'the ten o'clock train from Paddington' and change at Plymouth 'for Camelton, the new station near Castle Boterel and Endelstow'—only to find on arrival that Elfride's coffin has accompanied them all the way from London. The discovery casts a grim retrospective irony on the comedy of the exchanges that have taken place between the two men while 'the train continued rattling on'. Earlier in the same novel, a pivotal part in the plot has been played by an overnight train journey in which Elfride and Stephen innocently but compromisingly travel together.

For Hardy there was nothing unromantic about railway travel. The point is made explicit in the description of a railway tunnel in *A Laodicean* (1.12), introduced by the observation that 'The popular commonplace that science, steam, and travel must always be unromantic and hideous was not proven at this spot'. Similarly, in the poem 'After a Romantic Day', a railway cutting is the entirely acceptable setting for a lover's emotions. Such passages echo an entry in Hardy's notebooks that refers to 'the enthusiasm of Sir Charles Lyell, who when travelling along a cutting gazed out of the railway carriage as if the sides were hung with beautiful pictures' (*LN* ii 116).

Steam was indeed intimately associated with one of the most important days in Hardy's entire emotional life, 7 March 1870, when he had travelled, largely by train, from his Dorset home to St Juliot in Cornwall, and had met Emma Gifford. The poem 'A Man Was Drawing Near to Me', written from Emma's point of view, traces that momentous journey in some detail without actually referring to the mode of travel. Two other poems, 'Faintheart in a Railway Train' and 'After a Romantic Day', associate love with railway travel more explicitly, while the banal locale of a station platform is the setting for the ironic anecdote touchingly recounted in 'At the Railway Station, Upway'.

A final real-life example: it was while changing trains at Plymouth Hoe station on the last day of 1873, on his way home from a visit to Cornwall, that Hardy bought a copy of the January issue of the *Cornhill Magazine* and found the first instalment of *Far from the Madding Crowd* placed at the beginning of the magazine—a moment of exhilaration, in its mundane and noisy setting, that heralded his first commercial success as a novelist.

reading, Hardy's. In approaching Hardy's reading it is well to keep in mind what his friend Edmund *Gosse hypothesized on the relationship between Hardy's reading and his legendary *pessimism: Hardy's pessimistic ideas were 'already present in his [Hardy's] mind and conversation' when the two men met in the 1870s, Gosse maintained, and were 'the result of temperament and observation, rather than of "influence"' (*L* iv 37 n.). Nevertheless, the records of Hardy's reading offer potentially useful insights into the complex matrix of intellectual and emotional contexts out of which his writing emerged.

The present overview is divided into two main parts: the first goes up to the mid-1870s, thus including what was Hardy's most formative period, but one from which the records are scarce and the dating somewhat uncertain. The second period starts in the mid-1870s, and covers more or less the rest of Hardy's life. This division is motivated partly by the fact that Hardy started on a focused and deliberate course of self-study, a significant part of which is documented in his *Literary Notebooks* (*LN* i xi ff.), a record of reading and notetaking that he started in 1876 and kept up until the year before his death. These notes, in addition to other extant *notebooks, his *autobiography, his *letters, and his *library, constitute the main records of Hardy's reading.

As previous studies have suggested, there is nothing very remarkable about Hardy's early reading, for the romantic tales of Bernardin de Saint-Pierre, Dumas, James Grant, G. P. R. James, W. H. *Ainsworth, Sir Walter *Scott, and others offered the young Hardy an emotionally exciting but not intellectually disturbing view of life. Similarly, there is nothing to suggest that Hardy's lifelong reading of the *Bible, so pervasively reflected in his own writings, was anything but devout at the time (*LN* ii 259).

By the mid-1860s, however, Hardy had started reading texts that would change and extend his theological, philosophical, and scientific beliefs and attitudes. These texts also seem to foreshadow major trends and preoccupations in his future reading and writing. The texts from this period may be divided into three general categories. The first comprises classical literature, and Greek drama in particular. Hardy's commitment to Aeschylus and Sophocles (see CLASSICS) seems to have been particularly strong, and he maintained in his essay 'The Profitable Reading of Fiction' that *Shakespeare (another lifelong reading commitment) and Greek drama provided the highest aesthetic and moral criteria in literary art (*LN* i 267–8).

The second significant category of Hardy's reading from this period consists of a great number of poems that he studied very carefully in order to prepare himself for a career as a poet, a course of reading at least partly reflected in a notebook headed 'Studies, Specimens &c'. Although the quotations he entered from, for instance, *The Golden Treasury*, Spenser, Shakespeare, Burns, *Byron, *Wordsworth, Scott, *Tennyson, and *Swinburne primarily seem to have been motivated by his desire to work up a literary vocabulary (Millgate 88), Hardy is not likely to have ignored the religious or philosophical content. It seems likely, for instance, that *Shelley's social radicalism helped to stimulate Hardy's own interest in that direction, an interest that was soon to find a voice in *The *Poor Man and the Lady*. He may also have been drawn towards Shelley's Hellenism, especially in combination with his almost idolatrously enthusiastic reading of Swinburne's *Poems and Ballads* and *Atalanta in Calydon*, with their pagan themes (*LN* i 379–80).

A third category of Hardy's reading from 1857 onwards, partly under the guidance of Horace *Moule, is found in articles in Victorian periodicals, especially in the *Saturday Review*, about Victorian social evils, hypocrisy, and sentimentality. Although of a conservative bent, the *Saturday Review* may well have contributed, as Robert Gittings argues, to the 'corrective scepticism' that is expressed in Hardy's early novels (*Young Thomas Hardy*, 39).

It is also possible to identify a few individual works that are likely to have left an impact on Hardy's mind before 1865, both for their ideological content and for the mode of thinking they promoted: Darwin's *The Origin of Species; Essays and Reviews*; Walter Bagehot's *Estimates of Some Englishmen and Scotchmen*; Ruskin's *Modern Painters*; and John Stuart *Mill's *On Liberty*. Hardy claimed that 'as a young man' he was 'among the earliest acclaimers' of *The Origin of Species* (*LW* 158), and to have known *On Liberty* 'almost by heart' (*LW* 355). And in Bagehot's *Estimates* he may for the first time have come across a more sustained and formal discussion of the beliefs of authors with whom he later on identified himself: for instance, Gibbon's struggle with the old problems of 'fate, free-will, fore-knowledge absolute', and Shelley's atheism, social radicalism, idealism, and revolutionary views on love and marriage (*LN* i 367). In Bagehot Hardy also found his attention drawn to certain ideas about literary matters, especially Bagehot's emphasis on the importance of what Hardy himself was later to call the 'idiosyncratic mode of regard' (*LW* 235) in writers such as Cowper, Gibbon, Macaulay, and Shelley.

Yet it is to be noticed that Hardy does not seem to have been immediately or easily influenced by the new scientific, social, religious, and philosophical ideas—or at least he did not allow the theological consequences of such ideas to prevent him from contemplating entering the Church in 1865 (*LW* 52–3). Hence, the main long-range effect of these books may well have been lodged in their various applications of the principles of inductive science and the 'historic method', considered by John Morley to be 'the most important intellectual cause of nineteenth-century thought and sentiment' (J. H. Buckley, *The Triumph of Time* (1966), 20), and thus potentially instrumental in Hardy's later assimilation of the radical thought of, for example, Herbert Spencer, Thomas Henry Huxley, Auguste *Comte, and others whom he read and from whom he started excerpting material into his 'Literary Notes' in 1876.

The very first entry in the 'Literary Notes' is from a book that Hardy read in the early 1860s but decided not to mention in his autobiography: *The Passions of the Human Soul* by Charles Fourier, the French Utopian writer. Hardy was sufficiently impressed by Fourier to draw a chart captioned 'Diagrams shewing Human Passion, Mind & Character Designed by Thos Hardy. 1863' and insert it into his *Literary Notebooks* (*LN* i 4). Hardy's reading of Fourier is important because of its apparent relevance to his own psychological vision and to his social criticism, two central areas of concern in his *Literary Notebooks* and future writings. Fourier was a Utopian extremist (which may account for his exclusion from Hardy's autobiography), but Hardy found similar psychological ideas voiced by the considerably more authoritative Auguste Comte, from whose *Social Dynamics, or The General Theory of Human Progress* he copied more into his *Literary Notebooks* than from any other single source. As in Fourier, Hardy found in Comte abundant support for an affective psychology, with its emphasis on the instinctual and emotional life, and he entered the observation that 'Feeling [is] the great motor force of human life' (*LN* i 68). Hardy's interest in affective psychology and Positivist social psychology is also reflected in his reading in a wide variety of other writers with Positivist tendencies, such as J. H. Bridges, George *Eliot, Frederic *Harrison, G. H. Lewes, J. S. Mill, John Morley, George Sand, and Leslie *Stephen.

There seems to be a strong link between Hardy's interest in the affective psychology and social criticism promoted by *Positivism, and his emerging interest in Hellenism in the mid-1870s (see Lennart A. Björk, *Psychological Vision and Social Criticism in the Novels of Thomas Hardy*, 79–140). The gradual shift in Hardy's social criticism towards a combination of Positivist and 'Hellenic' viewpoints can be traced in his novels, from the Comtean overtones of Clym Yeobright's social ethics in *The Return of the Native*, via Angel Clare's provocation of his clergyman father in *Tess of the d'Urbervilles* 'that it might have resulted far better for mankind if Greece had been the source of the religion of modern civilization and not Palestine' (*TDU* 25), to the evocation of 'Greek joyousness' in *Jude the Obscure* (5.5). This shift is also reflected in Hardy's extensive reading about Ancient Greece and in the writings of Matthew *Arnold from the mid-1870s onwards: before and during the writing of *The Return of the Native*, Hardy read and quoted from a *History of Greece*, Plato, articles on Aeschylus, on the Pagan view of suicide, J. P. Mahaffy's *Social Life in Greece from Homer to Menander* (about 80 entries altogether), and John Addington Symonds's *Studies of the Greek Poets* (Björk, pp. 130 ff.). The intertextual nature of Hardy's reading and writing is manifest in, for instance, the condemnation of Angel's behaviour towards Tess: 'His inconsistencies rushed upon him in a flood. He had persistently elevated Hellenic Paganism at the expense of Christianity; yet in that civilization an illegal surrender was not certain disesteem' (*TDU* 49). Hardy had copied the identical point from Mahaffy some fifteen years before the publication of *Tess* (*LN* i 52).

Hardy's notetaking suggests that Arnold is also likely to have played a role in his understanding of Hellenism, for example in his account of Greek culture in general (*LN* i 13), Greek joyousness, and the contrast between the Hellenic and Hebraic (*LN* i 130)—a contrast that is prominent in Hardy's later novels. Arnold, of course, was a touchstone also in other respects, especially aesthetic matters such as the idea of art as a representation, not a transcript, of life (*LN* i 256–9), and the notion that 'the most essential part of poetic greatness' is 'the noble and profound application of ideas to life' (*LN* i 118).

No account of Hardy's reading, however brief, can leave out his reading in more general philosophical and religious areas. His autobiography and *Literary Notebooks* are full of quotations from, for instance, Spencer, Huxley, *Schopenhauer, and von Hartmann, of whom the former two, in Hardy's opinion, exercised greater influence on him than Schopenhauer (*L* vi 259), although, against Maeterlinck's 'vindication of Nature', he believed more in 'the original difficulty recognized by thinkers like Schopenhauer, Hartmann, Haeckel... and by most of the persons called pessimists' (*LW* 338). Hardy read Spencer early in life, copied the title of Part I of *First Principles* ('The Unknowable') into the 1867 Notebook (*LN* i 335), and paid a glowing tribute to this work in 1893 (*L* ii 24–5). Extant records of Hardy's reading of Huxley are from the 1880s (*LN* i 377), but he had met Huxley socially earlier (*LW* 125), and thought very highly of Huxley's effort to 'shake... off' contemporary 'Theological lumber' (see also *TDU* 46). Hardy may well have been introduced to, and acquired perspectives on, some of the more professional philosophers by Leslie Stephen, 'whose philosophy', Hardy acknowledged, influenced his own 'for many years, indeed, more than that of any other contemporary' (*LW* 102; see also *LN* i 341–2).

It is quite impossible, of course, to give an adequate account of an extensive reading such as Hardy's. After all, his early reading pre-dated Darwin and his late reading extended beyond Einstein (*LN* ii 544). The overview attempted here has not, for instance, included Hardy's reading in contemporary and near-contemporary novelists and dramatists—for example, Balzac, Hugo, *Ibsen, *James, *Kipling, Thackeray, Hawthorne, and Zola, all of whom he read and referred to in his *Literary Notebooks.* LAB

Lennart A. Björk, 'Hardy's Reading', *THA* 1 (1982).

—— *Psychological Vision and Social Criticism in the Novels of Thomas Hardy* (1987).

Michael Millgate, *Thomas Hardy: His Career as a Novelist* (1971).

Walter F. Wright, *The Shaping of 'The Dynasts'* (1967).

realism. Although towards the end of his time as a novelist Hardy began to show great interest in the formal idea of 'realism', as practised by the modern French authors and by such an English disciple as George *Moore, it was a method that in an important sense remained wholly unsuited to his temperament and to his imagination as a creator. Everything great in the art of his novels depends on a kind of freshness. This puts the matter in what may seem a naïve way, but Hardy himself remained in many ways a naïve and even childlike man, however much that simplicity was tempered with a native cunning and shrewdness. He is quite simply no good at what the French call *déniaiserie*—the spoken or unspoken claim to a wholly and professionally unenchanted view of things. Zola, in his Rougon-Macquart series of novels, implies almost as a condition of a novelist's success that he must exhibit a detached and dispassionate—indeed a quasi-scientific—overview of the human condition, if his work is to make a real impact and to retain a lasting authority. It is true that Zola's practice belied his own theory, which in one way makes him the fascinating writer he is. The more he threw the lyric soarings and subjective excitements of the old romanticism out of the door, the more apt they were to return in a different shape through the window. Not for nothing did an amused but admiring French critic, Sainte-Beuve, remark of his novels that 'it is in Médan [Zola's country retreat outside Paris] that the Last Romantic is in hiding'.

There was of course no question of Hardy being 'a last romantic', just as there is no real question of his being among the first British 'realists'. He would instinctively have known how little such labels really counted for a writer immersed in 'the seemings of things', creating what from instinct and observation he had himself felt and discovered. Hardy was an organic writer, professional only in the sense that he knew the value of his work in money and had a shrewd idea of how to set about getting it, both in his dealings with publishers and in his instinct for what the public wanted, or what they would not tolerate. He was genuinely shocked by what he felt to be the rejection of *Jude*, his most ambitiously conceived novel and the one to which he must have attached the most importance. And yet for all its pseudo-modernity and its exploration of current ideas—class issues and the Woman Question—*Jude*, like its predecessor *Tess*, remains essentially a rich ragbag of narrative, daydream, and graphic or tragic effects. The tragedy itself is rather too obviously fabricated for the ideas behind it to impress themselves deeply on the reader, even though the drama of Little Father Time, and his dutiful execution of his siblings, is as moving and in its own unique way as upsetting to read as is the violent death on the dark road of the horse Prince, in *Tess*.

Hardy's implicit claim that Sue Bridehead represents modern womanhood, or woman as in the new age she may become, is also an implicit claim to the realism that, in the view of its exponents, must go with modernity. But it seems probable that in terms of realism, as he and his French masters conceived of it, George Moore would have regarded Sue with as much derision as he did Tess. His objection to Tess was precisely that she was a romantic and romanticized figure whom Hardy had striven to make realistic by giving her some accurately contemporary characteristics, such as the fact that she spoke both the 'Standard English' drilled into her at school and the broad Dorset dialect which had come to her in early childhood. (This is realism in the important sense: by contrast, Dickens's Oliver Twist inherits the romance of fairytale convention that a hero is exempt in speech or behaviour from his actual circumstances.) Tess's speech, together with the undoubted fact that (like not a few country girls) she had accidentally inherited an ancient genealogy, would for George Moore none the less have constituted the sole features in Tess of contemporary 'realism' or modernity. Zola himself, who would certainly have been interested by the emphasis on Tess's inherited class characteristics, would also have been extremely sceptical of their authenticity.

In a much more 'scientific' spirit Zola had himself portrayed the predestined influences of heredity in his Rougon-Macquart series. And yet, as the French critics had noted, Zola mingled the wish for objective and scientific reality with more colourful and personal enthusiasms. When he described the Paris meat market, or the city's vast new department stores, his imagination projected a world which was in one sense strictly and accurately observed, but in another sense as grotesque and outlandish as any marvels in the *Arabian Nights*. The grim naturalism with which he had examined the coal mines for his novel *Germinal* also turned them into a terrifying and exciting underground world, almost akin to the fantasy world of H. G. Wells's *The Time Machine*, published in the same year as *Jude*. The idea of the Time Machine was also conceived in a scientific spirit, as was the prophesied division of the human species into underground Morlocks and their prey, the decorative Eloi of the surface world. But the adventures of the scientist, the time traveller, can none the less only be conceived in terms of traditional fantastic fiction.

The first readers of *The Return of the Native* may well have been struck by the comparable separation between the heath folk living their strange and self-sufficient lives and the other classes of society around them. That separation is even more marked in *The Woodlanders*, where the trees themselves, together with the secluded folk who live among them and depend on them, are drawn by Hardy in something like the Darwinian spirit of struggle and survival. His vision of the forest, a vast overcrowded mass of individual trees struggling upwards for air and light, contrasts oddly with the pastoralism also implicit in the novel. But it is precisely the strength of Hardy as a creator to be able to combine without any appearance of self-consciousness the new outlook and new ideas with old traditions and ways of life, and old ways of writing about them. His fictions demonstrate that this placid pluralism can work to great effect, apparent incongruities seeming to strengthen the overall vision.

On the other hand, it was the mixture of old conventions and new methods which irritated some of Hardy's readers and critics, as well as writers like George Moore and Henry *James, who should, we may now feel, have been more in sympathy. Moore's novel *Esther*

Waters (1894) is in some sense a deliberate rejoinder to *Tess*, a demonstration by the author of the way the thing should be done. Esther is a young girl of the same class as Tess, but her creator is rigorously determined not to let his own consciousness enter into her, to falsify an exact and sober portrait of what such a girl was and how her life might develop. The novel is well written, Moore was thoroughly familiar with his heroine's background, and it deserved the success it obtained. It is also moving, for the reader can enter into Esther's situation, if not into her heart and mind. She is not susceptible to the kind of daydreaming process in which Hardy conceives and imagines Tess, but from a less conscientiously realistic angle this could be said to impoverish Esther unfairly. There is no question but that Tess is Hardy's creation, and also that she seems to exist in her own right.

Moore's portrait reveals the inherent fallacy in realism: the writer not being able to do anything but present his own view of the subject, however much he may try to observe the convention that it is an 'objective' one. This difficulty is clearly shown by Flaubert's memorable portrait of Madame Bovary, Flaubert himself being the master most revered by disciples like Moore. In so far as Emma Bovary is seen objectively, she seems a devitalized and patronized figure, however incisively the predicament brought about by her romantic illusions is presented. His or her own illusions about life are just as real to the individual as are the facts of his or her case; and this is something that Hardy's art can take for granted. Flaubert's own penetrating intelligence made him realize all too well that to the extent that Emma 'existed' it could only be in his own mind, which was the reason for his famous and rueful reported comment, 'Madame Bovary, c'est moi.'

It did not prevent Henry James making the equally penetrating comment that Emma has too 'mean' a consciousness to be the heroine of so ambitious a work. James no doubt perceived that Flaubert was in a sense fatally divided by his refusal to let Emma learn, understand, be mentally alive in her own selfhood, because this would falsify the bleak image of the provincial girl he wished to create. His intelligence is at work upon her, but is never, so to speak, inside her. The severe exponents of the new realism, as well as writers who had pondered the matter, like Moore and James, were fully entitled to object that Hardy's country girl (like, in a different sphere of technique, Dickens's Oliver Twist or Pip) was simply endowed with the author's consciousness, irrespective of upbringing and background.

But in all these cases success—whether or not the author pulls it off—might be held to be the true and only criterion, and there is no denying the success that Hardy's heroes and heroines achieved with the public, and in terms of his own highly individualized kind of art. In practice Hardy uses 'realism' to great effect, although at the time of his early novels (the settings of *Desperate Remedies*, for instance, are highly realistic) he would not have thought of it that way; but he possessed (also perhaps unknowingly) the secret of mixing his own sort of realism so effectively with other literary modes—all seeming to become a part of his own vision—that its use is never insistent, or in the least doctrinaire. In his first published novel the heroine's situation is every bit as sober and realistic, in terms of the authority with which it is done, as is that of Esther Waters herself; and the Gothic melodrama Hardy uses and obviously enjoys makes neither Cytherea Graye nor Tess in the least unreal, but all the more lively and convincing. In *Jude the Obscure*, on the other hand, what is lively and realistic as well as soundly documented has begun to suffer from realism as a method, as opposed to the simply *realistic*, although even in *Jude* Hardy's unique separations and combinations of mode are still sound, and seldom fail him.

Indeed, by any possible criterion, the most realistic scenes in Hardy's novels are those most heavily charged with the author's own imaginative powers. Such scenes are never fanciful or fantastic: they are never touched by the various modes of 'magic realism', and they appear to exist for no other reason than that Hardy himself has imagined them, and imparted to them his own sort of homely and factual sobriety. When Elfride in *A Pair of Blue Eyes* rescues Knight from the cliff edge by means of a rope made of her underwear; or Sergeant Troy, who has reassured Bathsheba by telling her his parade sword is blunt and harmless, cuts a scarf of skin from his hand to show her afterwards how sharp it is; or Diggory Venn and Damon Wildeve in *The Return of the Native* stir up the glow-worms on the heath to give light by which to read the dice—it is then that the reader sees ('To make you *see*' was Conrad's ambition as a novelist) and believes absolutely. Perils, rescues, melodramas, grotesque accidents, and ludicrous mishaps, such as occur in *Tess* as well as in *Two on a Tower* or *A Laodicean*, are all authenticated by Hardy's brilliantly workmanlike imagination. And that is the secret of his own peculiar style of realism. JB

reception. There would appear to be three main phases in the critical reception of Hardy's novels. In the first phase, from 1871 to the mid-1880s, reviewers frequently complained about Hardy's style, especially the allegedly implausible conversations of the rustics. Reviewers also occasionally noted improbable twists of plot and unconvincing characterization, while there was some mild disquiet about matters of sexual propriety. The novels attracting the most favourable reviews during this period were *Far from the Madding Crowd*, which established Hardy's reputation, and *The Trumpet-Major*. The middle phase is marked by the publication of *The Mayor of Casterbridge* and *The Woodlanders* in the 1880s, when Hardy's pessimism began to be discussed (the term 'Tessimism' was later coined). The third and final phase of the evolution of Hardy's reputation as a novelist is the storm of controversy that was provoked by *Tess of the d'Urbervilles* and, even more so, by *Jude the Obscure*, reviewers of both of which were often obsessed with issues of philosophy and morality.

Hardy's first published novel, *Desperate Remedies*, received some very positive reviews, except for the savage notice published anonymously in the *Spectator* (22 April 1871; repr. in *CH*), which began by observing that at least the novel was published anonymously and so would not disgrace the family name. When he first read this, sitting on a stile, Hardy wished himself dead, showing that extreme sensitivity to hostile criticism which remained with him throughout his career. The reviews, he said, taught him not to dabble in plot, while the praise of his rustic characters and scenery led him to write next a pastoral novel, *Under the Greenwood Tree*. This second novel was warmly welcomed, although the *Athenaeum* noted that the characters 'speak too much like educated people' (15 June 1872; repr. in *CH*), which was to be a recurring theme of many reviews. *A Pair of Blue Eyes*, like several of Hardy's early works, was likened to George *Eliot's novels, and it was praised by the *Saturday Review* as being 'one of the most artistically constructed among recent novels' (2 August 1873; repr. in *CH*).

However, it was with his next novel, *Far from the Madding Crowd*, that Hardy's reputation was firmly established, the novel being widely reviewed, and often with enthusiasm. The curiously sophisticated language of the rustics was often thought to be unconvincing, but the beauty of the descriptive passages was praised, and even Henry *James, who declared in the New York *Nation* (24 December 1874; repr. in *CH*) that 'the only things we believe in are the sheep and the dogs', was obliged to acknowledge Hardy's success at creating a rural atmosphere.

The move away from rural life in Hardy's next novel, *The Hand of Ethelberta*, clearly disappointed reviewers, but more surprising is the decidedly mixed response to *The Return of the Native*, whose descriptive passages and dramatic scenes were praised but whose characters were widely deplored as unconvincing. Two years later, however, *The Trumpet-Major* was to become one of the most popular of Hardy's novels, with the *Athenaeum* beginning its review by observing that 'Mr Hardy seems to be in the way to do for rural life what Dickens did for that of the town' (20 November 1880; repr. in *CH*). The next two works, however, *A Laodicean* and *Two on a Tower*, were not at all well received: the *Saturday Review* neatly summarized the former as 'very queer people doing very queer things', while the latter was 'too full of minor incidents which really have nothing to do with its action' (18 November 1882; repr. in *CH*). Critics bemoaned the relative absence of rural life and rustic characters, a chorus which must have confirmed for Hardy the sources of his best work—sources to which he returned for most of his later novels.

The reception given to *The Mayor of Casterbridge* was not at all enthusiastic: as so often before, Hardy's descriptive powers were praised, but there was criticism of the rustics' conversation, the improbable plot, and the far-fetched and unpleasant similes. A new note of complaint, however, was struck by a leading critic, R. H. Hutton, in his review in the *Spectator*, which disliked the manner in which Hardy 'intersperses throughout his story hints of the fashionable pessimism, a philosophy which seems to us to have little appropriateness to the homely scenery and characters which he portrays' (5 June 1886; repr. in *CH*). *The Woodlanders* was much better received, and the *Athenaeum* shrewdly began its review by announcing that 'Mr Hardy seems to have fairly settled down into what his biographers will probably call his second manner. He is less vividly "sensational", less broadly comic' (26 March 1887; repr. in *CH*). The consensus of contemporary opinion was that *The Woodlanders* was a very powerful book, but also a very disagreeable one, and 'repulsive' is a term that appears in several discussions of the characters. Ominously, given Hardy's forthcoming troubles with his next two works, the *Athenaeum* ends its review by noting that 'the novel is distinctly not one for the "young person" of whom we have lately heard'.

Many reviews of *Tess of the d'Urbervilles* were highly enthusiastic and regarded the novel as Hardy's greatest to date, but there were four savage notices which greatly upset him. The first, in the *Saturday Review*, attacked the pessimism and spoke of 'the terrible dreariness of this tale, which, except during the few hours spent with cows, has not a gleam of sunshine anywhere' (16 January 1892: repr. in *CH*). At least Hardy had the satisfaction, however, of seeing that this review improved the novel's sales. The next attacks were by R. H. Hutton in the *Spectator*, scorning the idea of Tess as a 'pure woman' (23 January 1982; repr. in *CH*), and by Andrew Lang in the *New Review*, where he denounced the tale's theology: 'If there be a God, who can seriously think of Him as a malicious fiend?' (February 1892; repr. in *CH*). Finally, the *Quarterly Review* accused Hardy of lacking 'good taste' and 'intellectual cultivation', while 'poor Tess's sensual qualifications for the part of heroine are paraded over and over again with a persistence like that of a horse-dealer egging on some wavering customer to a deal' (April 1892; repr. in *CH*). The author of this last attack was Mowbray *Morris, who as editor of *Macmillan's Magazine* was one of those who had earlier declined to publish the novel.

It is no surprise to find Hardy writing in his diary at this time: '"Well, if this sort of thing continues no more novel-writing for me. A man must be a fool to deliberately stand up to be shot at"' (*LW* 259). The ferocious and sometimes crude attacks on *Jude* shocked Hardy, who, astonishingly, does not appear to have foreseen them, and he was unprepared for reviews titled 'Jude the Obscene' and 'Hardy the Degenerate' (this last a topical adjective in the year of Oscar Wilde's trial). The timing of *Jude*'s publication meant that it was wrongly understood to be a 'marriage question' novel, a subgenre for which there had recently been a vogue; but there were more predictable charges against the 'grimy' aspects of the novel, such as the pig-killing scene and the throwing of the pig's pizzle, while the principal characters were inevitably described as 'revolting' and 'coarsely indecent'. Of course, there were some sensible and highly appreciative reviews, and Hardy himself noted that it had been received with 'about equal voices for & against' (*L* i 103); but it is understandable that the sensational clamour should have made a more lasting impression on an acutely sensitive Hardy. He appreciated that sections of the press were insincere and commercially motivated in their outrage, and he acknowledged that he had upset those readers who had wanted 'something comfortable, resigned and conforming' (*L* vii 128); but he retained sufficient irony to observe that 'the only people who faint & blush over it are fast men at clubs' (*L* ii 100).

Hardy's first three volumes of poetry received an increasingly favourable reception, although the first of them, *Wessex Poems*, had left many reviewers puzzled by the turn to verse, as Hardy had foreseen: 'considering that the Britisher resents a change of utterance, instrument, even of note, I do not expect a particularly gracious reception of them' (*L* ii 208). The arrival of Hardy the poet had not been at all trumpeted in advance, and the bemusement was widespread among a reading public that Hardy saw as reluctant to have its lazy categorization of him challenged. There was even some open animosity towards the volume, such as the unsigned notice in the *Saturday Review*: 'it is impossible to understand why the bulk of this volume was published at all—why he did not himself burn the verse, lest it should fall into the hands of the indiscreet literary executor, and mar his fame when he was dead' (7 January 1899; repr. in *CH*). Other complaints echoed familiar ones from Hardy's earlier career, such as the unremitting grimness, the lack of humour, and the use of dialect. Three years later, *Poems of the Past and the Present* was generally well received. This was no doubt assisted by the topicality of the eleven War Poems near the start of the volume, most of which had been previously printed in journals and newspapers, helping to accustom readers to the notion of Hardy the poet.

However, as Hardy himself acknowledged, the best reviewed of all his volumes of verse was *Time's Laughingstocks* in 1909: 'the book has been received wonderfully well here—far better than I expected' (*L* iv 73). *Satires of Circumstance*, on the other hand, was seen as wholly pessimistic, and reviewers questioned whether Hardy could even be called a poet at all. Inevitably for one who had made his reputation in another medium, his verse was seen as 'prosaic', and even the appreciative Lytton Strachey felt obliged to defend the originality of Hardy's poetry by declaring that it 'bears everywhere upon it the impress of a master of prose fiction' (*New Statesman*, 19 December 1914; repr. in *CH*). Three years later, in 1917, *Moments of Vision* again attracted a mixture of puzzlement and repulsion. Hardy himself felt that this was possibly because he did not fit the romantic image of a poet, being neither young nor dead, and yet paradoxically he also found himself castigated as a poetic apprentice for daring to try something new in his old age. The *Athenaeum*, for instance, lamented that he showed 'something of the gracelessness of a youth learning to skate'. Among the mass of reviewers, it would appear that Hardy's collections of poetry were judged principally on their degree of sombreness, no matter how much Hardy himself might insist on the preponderance of reflection, love, and comedy in his verse.

The original reviewers of Hardy's fiction and poetry certainly helped to shape and predict the popular perception of his writing career which continues to this day. Hardy himself, writing to Edmund *Gosse in 1918, observed that 'I began writing novels, & made a sort of trade of it; but last night I found that I had spent more years in verse-writing than at prose-writing! (prose 25 yrs—verse 26 yrs) Yet my verses will always be considered a bye-product, I suppose, owing to this odd accident of the printing press' (*L* v 253). It was an accident that most of his reviewers served only to reinforce. (See also the discussions of this topic under the entries for individual volumes of fiction and verse.)

MR

R. G. Cox, Introduction to *Thomas Hardy: The Critical Heritage* (1970).

Laurence Lerner and John Holmstrom (eds.), *Thomas Hardy and His Readers* (1968).

Carl J. Weber, *Hardy in America: A Study of Thomas Hardy and his American Readers* (1946).

regionalism. In the 'General Preface to the Novels and Poems' attached to the first volume of the 1912 Wessex Edition of his works, Hardy enters a somewhat defensive plea for his opting to confine himself, in his fiction at least, to the geographical area 'bounded on the north by the Thames, on the south by the English Channel, on the east by a line running from Hayling Island to Windsor Forest, and on the west by the Cornish coast'. He rejects the view that novels restricted to 'a circumscribed scope' cannot be so 'inclusive' as those which cover 'large extents of country' and take in 'towns and cities', and even 'wander over the four quarters of the globe'. Without giving a precise refutation, he simply asserts that this is not true 'in respect of the elementary passions'. To the implied criticism that he limited himself to Wessex because that was the only region he knew well enough he replied more fully, claiming that it was a matter of deliberate choice, and defiantly offering a comparison with the drama of ancient Greece: 'I considered that our magnificent heritage from the Greeks in dramatic literature found sufficient room for a large proportion of the action in an extent of their country not much larger than the half-dozen counties here reunited under the old name of Wessex, that the domestic emotions have throbbed in Wessex nooks with as much intensity as in the palaces of Europe, and that, anyhow, there was quite enough human nature in Wessex for one man's literary purpose.' It is worth noting, however, that in both parts of his argument Hardy falls back, in the one instance on 'the elementary passions', and in the other on 'the domestic emotions'. The issue of 'inclusiveness' is slid over; and the last part of the quoted passage, with its slightly uneasy 'anyhow', almost concedes that a comprehensive treatment of human nature might well require venturing outside Wessex. (It is perhaps significant, too, that when he introduces the poems he claims that the 'limited stage' to which the novels are confined 'has not been adhered to here in the same proportion, the dramatic part especially [what follows makes it clear that this is a reference to *The Dynasts*] having a very broad theatre of action'.)

As Robin Gilmour suggests in his essay on 'Regional and Provincial in Victorian Literature' (*The Literature of Region and Nation*, ed. R. P. Draper (1989)), this defensiveness probably has to do with Hardy's contradictory feelings towards Matthew *Arnold's deprecating treatment of 'the provincial spirit' in his celebrated essay on 'The Literary Influence of Academies' (1864). Arnold compared what he regarded as the narrowness and zealotry of the provincial, its 'eruptive' and 'aggressive' manner, unfavourably with the urbanity and intellectual restraint of the cultural centre, which was for him located on the Oxford/London axis. Hardy himself deplored the abrasive Victorian self-confidence riding roughshod over delicate and sensitive issues which the liberal-minded consciousness found crudely inadequate. His most eloquent expression of this pro-Arnoldian sympathy is to be found in the poem 'In Tenebris II' (1895–6), where the brutal blitheness of typically Victorian 'stout upstanders', whose 'dust smokes around their career', is ironically poised against the speaker's own odd-man-out humility.

Yet Hardy could also contradict Arnold on the question of provincialism. In the *Life* he asserts that '"A certain provincialism of feeling is invaluable. It is of the essence of individuality, and is largely made up of that crude enthusiasm without which no great thoughts are thought, no great deeds done"' (*LW* 151). Hardy was, of course, provincial himself in that he was born in a rural hamlet just outside Dorchester, and lived most of his life in Dorset. But he was also very familiar with *London, where as a young man he had lodgings and did much of his work as a professional architect. The mature writer, both in style and in temperament, was a complex combination of the urban and the provincial—in Raymond Williams's phrases, both 'an educated observer' of his home background and 'a passionate participant' (*The Country and the City* (1975), 247). Unlike Arnold, he could appreciate the emotional commitment and the continuity embodied in customs and habits that went with a local affiliation, and see them as valuable corrections to the less rooted sophistication of the metropolitan centre. And though 'provincialism' is the word he uses, 'regionalism' better expresses the combined sense of community and place that his fictional Wessex represents. The derogatory implications of words such as 'provincial' and 'parochial' are themselves an indication of the extent to which Arnold has won the intellectual battle; but the counterbalancing virtues suggested by 'regionalism' are what give Wessex its powerful imaginative appeal.

Hardy belongs to the movement that came to consciousness in the late 18th century, in the work of writers like *Scott and *Wordsworth, as a reaction to industrialization, the growth of overcrowded cities, and the desiccating influence of utilitarianism. Regionalism is allied to *pastoralism, and like pastoralism has elements both of idealism and of criticism. In Hardy, however, the deep sense of identity with the people and places of which he writes coming from his own shared background, rarely blinds him to their limitations, and is accompanied by a realistic understanding of the forces of change that threaten the humane values he divines in the regional way of life. Even *Under the Greenwood Tree*, which is perhaps the closest among his novels to an idealized portrayal of Wessex, is written in a sophisticated style which tacitly acknowledges its appeal to a metropolitan readership, as well as presenting an old order which, no matter how charming it may be deemed, is recognized as inevitably yielding place to the new.

This is the theme, too, of *Far from the Madding Crowd* and *The Mayor of Caster-*

bridge, with increasing awareness not only of the strengths of region but of the developments undermining it. The Great Barn in *Far from the Madding Crowd* (22) stands as one of the most comprehensive symbols in all Hardy's fiction of the idea of regional wholeness and continuity. Originally forming (the narrator speculates) 'one of a group of conventual buildings', it has for four centuries been put to the secular purpose of the 'defence and salvation of the body by daily bread' which 'is still a study, a religion, and a desire'. It unites medievalism and modernity, and is the very focal point of the agricultural community of Weatherbury. Its scale is seemingly timeless: 'in comparison with cities, Weatherbury was immutable'. Ostensibly, the consciousness of London and Paris is introduced to heighten the permanence of Weatherbury, but ultimately the effect is to mesh it in with the 'great web' of change that demystifies and destabilizes all things in Hardy's Wessex.

The regional unity survives in *Far from the Madding Crowd*, but survives precariously. In *The Mayor of Casterbridge*, that unity is split, both from without and from within. Yet the theme of the regional is still more pronounced. Casterbridge itself is presented as almost the perfect union of city and surrounding countryside in the celebrated opening of Chapter 9, where 'Bees and butterflies in the cornfields at the top of the town who desired to get to the meads at the bottom, took no circuitous course, but flew straight down High Street without any apparent consciousness that they were traversing strange latitudes'.

The town is the regional centre by virtue of its integration with the region. But this includes decadent elements as well. Balancing Chapter 9 is the passage in Chapter 36 which describes Mixen Lane as 'the hiding-place of those who were in distress, and in debt, and trouble of every kind'. It is from there that the scurrilous skimmity-ride emerges. Casterbridge is a microcosm: different parts of the town are associated with different aspects of the social and psychological urban body—different houses and different inns belong to different degrees of prosperity and self-confidence, while the two bridges in Chapter 32 are the haunt of 'all the failures of the town'. Henchard at different stages of his career is linked with all of these; and even when he is self-exiled from Casterbridge, a magnetic pull keeps him wandering on the circumference of a circle the centre of which is Casterbridge and his once-supposed daughter, Elizabeth-Jane. That this joint sense of communal inclusiveness and topographical intimacy between town and country corresponded so well with the actual *Dorchester familiar to Hardy underlines the debt he owed to his native area, as well as reinforcing the metonymic bias of his imagination, which drove him to create depths of implication from the faithfully detailed reproduction of local material.

Yet Casterbridge is also the site of conflict between native and alien. Its Roman past, so much emphasized in the novel, is a reminder that it was once colonized by distant outsiders, and the title, *The Mayor of Casterbridge*, paradoxically both elides and foregrounds the fact that it is the story of not one but two mayors—Farfrae (with a name that speaks for itself) as well as Henchard. The Scotsman, Farfrae, is 19th-century man opportunistically on the make; in the contrast between his more up-to-date knowledge, greater social polish, and lack of serious local affiliation (though he sings sentimentally of Scotland, he loves it so well as never to return there) and the rugged inflexibility, but far more passionate commitment, of Henchard, there is another version of modern versus old-fashioned, provincial man. The virtues that make Henchard so much a part of his local world are also the vices that rob him of adaptability to change; the shallowness of Farfrae which makes him so much less impressive a figure also enables him to be freer and nimbler to adjust. In the end the latter ousts the former, and in so doing helps to bring Casterbridge more firmly into the 19th-century mainstream—but at the cost of that archaic unity which both the town and its older mayor embody.

The region as archaic is still more evidently the theme of *The Return of the Native*. Egdon Heath symbolizes the primitive, reinforced by such things as the superstition of Susan Nunsuch, the bonfire rituals of the Heath, the deliberately stilted form and language of the Mummers' Play, and the peculiarly Mephistophelean aspect given to Diggory Venn. Eustacia Vye also seems an emanation of this;

but in her own consciousness she chafes at the narrowness and awkwardness of the Heath. However, in projecting her longings to escape such restrictions, as she feels them to be, upon Clym Yeobright, glamorized for her by his connection with the quintessentially metropolitan Paris, she ironically chooses an earlier escapee who is now returning, disillusioned, to the very region of which he is a 'native'. Thus, the action, though confined to the narrow stage of Egdon, dramatizes conflicts that resonate with contradictory responses to the regional/metropolitan opposition.

Again, in *The Woodlanders*, a very restricted locality—hardly big enough to warrant the term 'region'—is made to take the impact of persons and ideas alien to its traditional inhabitants, whose lives, as suggested in the opening chapter, are characterized by 'concentrated passions and closely knit interdependence'. But in the two great novels that bring Hardy's fiction-writing career to a close, *Tess of the d'Urbervilles* and *Jude the Obscure*, there is a marked shift to peripatetic narrative and a widening of the regional geography to include the borderlands where region and metropolis confront each other. This is more notable in *Jude*, where major parts of the action take place in Melchester, Shaston, Aldbrickham, and Christminster (readily identifiable as fictional variants of, respectively, Salisbury, Shaftesbury, Reading, and Oxford). But in *Tess of the d'Urbervilles* also the action moves from Tess's home area, the Vale of Blakemore, 'an engirdled and secluded region', to the Valley of the Great Dairies, where 'the world was drawn to a larger pattern', and later encompasses Sandbourne (Bournemouth), Stonehenge, and Wintoncester (Winchester). The *railway, too, increasingly links these places. It is the means by which Dairyman Crick's milk is transported to London; and, strikingly, in *Jude*, in Sue Bridehead's jejune opinion the Melchester railway station displaces the cathedral as 'the centre of the town life now' (3.1), while Little Father Time's journey in the train to Aldbrickham, 'like Age masquerading as Juvenility' (5.3), offers a weirdly modern image of deracination.

With this widening-out of the region goes an increased sense of the subversion of region, accompanied by a dissolving of the categories that stratify society and, for better or worse, challenge the instinctive conservatism of region. In this respect *education, which had been an emerging theme in earlier novels, now attains a major status. It is there, at least marginally, in *Under the Greenwood Tree* with the schoolmistress values of Fancy Day, and more markedly in *The Return of the Native* with the earnest, didactic schemes of the would-be teacher, Clym. In *The Woodlanders* it is the education, limited though it may have been, ambitiously bought for Grace by her father, that makes her available to the outsider Fitzpiers—and less available to the essentially 'regional' Giles.

But education, and the development of a sceptical consciousness, become more damaging to the region in *Tess* and *Jude*. Tess herself is a girl with a modicum of board-school education—hardly enough to rank her as an educated woman, but enough to mark her off as in some way superior to her fellow-dairymaids (and certainly to Car Darch and her like), and enough to draw the attention of Alec and Angel. But it is the more fully developed education of the latter which is most damning to the regional. Angel's very enlightenment in looking to the regional for renewal of the jaded metropolitan within himself generates an abstract idealism, coupled with his immature, intellectualized (and, it must be said, insufficiently self-critical) moral standards, that is destructive of the fallible, living person of Tess.

This juxtaposition of Tess and Angel is something like an imaginative riposte to Arnold's exaltation of the values of the centre over those of the region—a riposte that is developed and expanded in *Jude the Obscure*. There Arnold's venerable city, Oxford, paradoxically 'home of lost causes' and yet speaking with the serenely unemphatic voice of the centre, is reflected sardonically in the walled-up arrogance of Christminster, which Jude envisions as the heavenly Jerusalem. The most 'modern' of Hardy's novels, this is correspondingly the least regional; and yet everywhere it reverberates with modern, progressive ideas which—though they challenge the hegemony of the centre, and to that extent should be enabling the regional to shake off its subordinate status—serve only to destabilize the regional. If Christminster is a curious perversion of these ideas, a fossilized medievalism masquerading as a superior culture rather than the true standard-bearer of 19th-century progress, the very un-Arnoldian Hellenism of Sue Bridehead (that is, before she commits her intellectual suicide) is too much ahead of its time, and yet, if anything, still more destructive of regional values. She might have survived in the Pre-Raphaelite Bohemianism of London, or the artistic colonies of Paris; but in Wessex she is inherently fragile, with a fragility that wrecks both herself and those around her. She has the perverse sophistication of the metropolis, matching the perverse equability of Christminster, but joining with it in an essentially anti-regional bias.

Regionalism is so pervasive in Hardy's work that a comprehensive survey would have to include virtually everything he wrote. However, some mention should be made of *The Dynasts* and the poems. *The Dynasts* would appear to be Hardy's most European, least regional, work. The comments of its supernatural Choruses, *sub specie aeternitatis*, and the 'bird's-eye prospects' of its elaborate stage-directions, suggest a distanced overview in which detail is subordinated to vast perspectives; but the author-director's camera (the pre-cinematic technique of *The Dynasts* has been noted by several critics) also zooms in to give vivid close-ups of the 'bang-up locals' of Wessex preparing for Napoleon's expected invasion, and the strangely defamiliarizing effect of the battlefield of Waterloo seen from the point of view of rabbits, moles, and snails (3.6.8). Here regionalism is opposed not to metropolitan values but to the Napoleonic grand design—the sentient, individual life to the dehumanizing abstraction of large-scale military-cum-political objectives.

The contribution of the poems, though more variable and piecemeal, runs parallel to this. Their dependence so often on the vividly particularized detail and the naming of places and people anchors them firmly to the felt reality of Wessex. Yet facile sentimentalizing of the regional is also avoided. If poems like 'In Front of the Landscape' and 'Wessex Heights' can be dubbed 'regional' by virtue of their topographical and nostalgic themes, they also cast a weirdly disenchanted light on Hardy's native region. The associations are both 'Dolorous and dear'; and, in 'Wessex Heights' especially, there is a sense of alienation that generates a disturbingly ambiguous attitude to region. These are not songs of regional Innocence, but of chilling Experience. They record a barrier between Hardy and Wessex that makes his 'breast beat out of tune', and, like *Jude the Obscure*, they imply a tragic/sardonic feel for region.

RPD

R. P. Draper (ed.), *The Literature of Region and Nation* (1989).

Shelagh Hunter, *Victorian Idyllic Fiction: Pastoral Strategies* (1984).

Dale Kramer (ed.), *Critical Approaches to the Fiction of Thomas Hardy* (1979).

John Lucas, *The Literature of Change: Studies in the Nineteenth-Century Provincial Novel* (1977).

relatives of Thomas Hardy. Both of Hardy's grandfathers died before he was born, but his grandmothers were known to him, his paternal grandmother particularly well. Born Mary Head in 1772, she had lost her parents very young and had spent a very unhappy childhood in the Berkshire village of Fawley—a place and name put to use in *Jude the Obscure*, where its actual name provides the hero's surname, while its fictional name of 'Marygreen' was surely suggested partly by Mary Head's name. At the other end of her life, in her seventies and eighties, she spent the whole of Hardy's early years, until her death in 1857, as a member of his parents' household. Known as 'Granny', she formed a close bond with the young Hardy and was a rich oral source of stories, traditions, and folklore, as well as of recollections of what Hardy came to perceive as the historical past: of the period when the threat of a French invasion seemed very real, and of even earlier times (she is said to have casually remarked on one hot day of his childhood, 'It was like this in the French Revolution, I remember'). Hardy's poem 'The Alarm' draws on such memories: as F. B. Pinion has noted (*A Commentary on the Poems of Thomas Hardy* (1976), 12), Hardy 'gave 1803 for the poem, since it was in the summer of that year that [his grandmother] ... was expecting her first-born'.

She thus made a significant and permanent contribution to the formation of his interests and outlook. His earliest surviving poem, 'Domicilium', perhaps prompted by her death, recalls her time as a young married woman in the Bockhampton cottage in the early years of the century, and she is the subject of a much later poem, 'One We Knew'. She has also been suggested as a model for Mrs Martin, the hero's grandmother in *Two on a Tower*.

Hardy's relationship with his maternal grandmother, Betty Hand (see HAND FAMILY), was inevitably less close, since she lived at some distance (in her later years she had moved from Melbury Osmond to Puddletown), and he was only 6 years old when she died. (On her husband George Hand, Hardy's maternal grandfather, see HAND FAMILY.)

Hardy's paternal grandfather, the first of three Thomas Hardys in successive generations, who married Mary Head in 1799, had been born in 1778 and took up his father's occupation as mason and bricklayer. He was a keen musician who had played the bass viol in Puddletown church before his marriage, and after his removal to the Bockhampton cottage that his father built for him upon his marriage (see HOMES) he took in hand, according to Hardy's account, the music-making in *Stinsford church, then in 'a deplorable condition'. Hardy notes with pride that his grandfather 'played in the gallery of Stinsford Church at two services every Sunday from 1801 or 1802 till his death in 1837' (*LW* 13).

Mary and Thomas Hardy had three sons and four daughters. Of the sons, Thomas Hardy, father of the writer, was the youngest. He and his brother James were taught the violin and in due course joined their father in the church choir until it was effectively disbanded in the early 1840s—a landmark in family history that is affectionately commemorated in *Under the Greenwood Tree*. Even after this time, they continued to play for weddings and other occasions, and made the traditional Christmas visits with the carol-singers to houses in the neighbourhood, as narrated in Hardy's story 'The Grave by the Handpost' and elsewhere. After the death of Thomas Hardy the First in 1837, his business was continued under his widow's name by their sons James and Thomas, the old lady playing an active part that included doing the accounts; the brothers' partnership seems, however, to have come to an end well before 1850, Thomas continuing it independently. (The third brother, John, had married and moved to Fordington, on the outskirts of Dorchester.) When he married at the end of 1839, Thomas brought his new bride, who was soon to become the writer's mother, to live with his own mother in the Bockhampton cottage, and, as noted above, this arrangement lasted until the old lady's death nearly twenty years later.

Hardy's account of his father in the early pages of his *autobiography is an attractive and affectionate one: 'handsome' in his prime, he was 'of good figure', with blue eyes, 'Vandyke-brown' hair and beard, and white and regular teeth (a much less common endowment then than now). 'The courtesy of his manners' made him popular, especially with women, and in his youth he seems (though Hardy does not quite say so) to have had the reputation of a womanizer. (Probably his marriage to Hardy's mother was largely motivated by the fact that he had made her pregnant.) He was 'a great walker', danced 'hornpipes and jigs, and other folk-dances', and, as noted above, inherited—and transmitted to his firstborn—a deep fondness for music (all quoted phrases in this paragraph are from *LW* 17–18). In his last years, sadly, he was an invalid.

Hardy's poem 'A Church Romance' presents an account of the beginning of his parents' relationship, significantly in a musical context. Jemima Hardy had known considerable hardship in her early years (see HAND FAMILY), and at the earliest possible moment had gone into service. Over the next few years, with characteristic energy and ambition, she had risen to be a cook, finding employment in households in London and Weymouth as well as at Kingston Maurward, the manor-house on whose estate the Hardy cottage stood.

In her marriage she was beyond question 'the dominant personality': if her husband was 'easy-going to the point of indolence', she was 'hard-driving' (Millgate 20, 19). Small in stature, she was vigorous and strong-minded, and Hardy draws a vivid composite portrait of her, with her 'chestnut hair and grey eyes', her 'Roman nose', and her walk 'buoyant' even in old age. 'She read omnivorously,' he adds, 'and sang songs of the date' (*LW* 19). By precept and example she must have exerted a profoundly formative influence on Hardy's life, and the phrasing of a notebook entry dated 30 October 1870 is revealing: 'Mother's notion, & also mine: That a figure stands in our van with arm uplifted, to knock us back from any pleasant prospect we indulge in as probable' (*PN* 6–7).

Some inkling of her passionate views on family loyalty and solidarity can be gained from the fact that she wished none of her children to marry, urging them to stick together, each brother living with a sister. In the event Hardy was the only one of the four to do so, and unsurprisingly Jemima's relationship with his wife Emma was not a cordial one. Perhaps partly for this reason she remained in the Bockhampton cottage until her death on Easter Sunday 1904, an event movingly commemorated in Hardy's poem 'After the Last Breath'. He arranged for a painting of her by her daughter Mary to be published, together with a report of her death, in some national newspapers (e.g. in the *Sphere* of 23 April 1904).

Robert Gittings has summed up some important aspects of Hardy's inheritance from his parents: 'His father's enjoyment of nature was matched by his mother's extraordinary store of local legend and story. Together they filled Hardy's world with landscape and human dealing, the special blend that was to mark his poems and novels...' (*Young Thomas Hardy*, 17).

Hardy was, as stated, the eldest of the four children of Jemima and Thomas Hardy. Closest to him in age and in other respects was his sister Mary (1841–1915), little more than eighteen months his junior and, as he told Sydney *Cockerell at the time of her death, 'almost my only companion in childhood' (*L* v 135). Their closeness in age conspired with a temperamental affinity to develop a much deeper relationship between the two of them than with either their younger sister or their brother. She trained as a teacher at the Church of England training college in Salisbury to which, much later, Hardy was to send (and from which he was to expel) Sue Bridehead in *Jude the Obscure*, and she followed the teaching profession in Dorchester and elsewhere.

Some of Hardy's earliest surviving letters were written to Mary, and the fact that she carefully kept them testifies to her own feelings. Within a few weeks of her death on 24 November 1915 (three years almost to the day after the death of Emma Hardy), he had written several poems prompted by memories of her ('In the Garden', 'Logs on the Hearth', 'Looking Across', 'The Sun's Last Look on the Country Girl'); another poem, 'Middle-Age Enthusiasms', is inscribed to Mary, and he also wrote an obituary of her for the *Dorset County Chronicle*. Among other poems referring to her are 'Molly Gone' and 'Conjecture'. He wrote that 'Her character was a somewhat unusual one, being remarkably unassertive, even when she was in the right...' (*LW* 402); the same passage praises, with evident pride, her skill as a portrait-painter, her work including a picture of their mother.

Hardy's relationship to his other sister, Katharine (1856–1940), usually known as Kate, was less intense, though they remained on good terms and continued to meet regularly until the end of his life. Like Mary, she trained as a teacher in Salisbury and followed that profession, the two sisters living together for much of their lives. Hardy was generous to his sisters, and when (for instance) they were both teaching at a National School in Dorchester, he bought them a small house in the town.

The youngest of the family was Hardy's brother Henry (1851–1928), and though the eleven-year age-gap meant that they had little in common in childhood, the two of them were on friendly terms in their adult years. In August 1891, for instance, they took a holiday together in Paris, and in August 1906 and again in April 1911 they toured English cathedrals. (On the latter trip they were accompanied by Florence Dugdale and her sister Constance, and Hardy seems to have ventured on matchmaking between Henry and Constance, though without producing any result.) More compelling evidence of the brothers' closeness, perhaps, is furnished by the fact that Henry accompanied Hardy on his painful visit to *Cornwall after Emma's death, and less than a year later Henry was one of the witnesses to his marriage to Florence Dugdale on 10 February 1914.

Henry had followed the family tradition by becoming a builder, and on occasion he and Hardy worked together. It was Henry who supervised the building of *Max Gate to his brother's designs, and in the 1890s Henry carried out extensive renovations to the church of St Peter's, West Knighton, Dorset, Hardy once more returning for the occasion to his former profession of architect. At about the same time Hardy also designed Talbothays Lodge, a house situated some two miles from Max Gate; built by Henry, it was at first occupied by tenants, but in 1911 he moved in, joined soon afterwards by his two sisters—belatedly and incompletely fulfilling Jemima Hardy's stubborn dream that the family square would remain solid and uninvaded by outsiders.

Though their elder brother, despite their mother's longings, had ventured on matrimony, he retained close bonds with his siblings to the end of his life, and as long as the Bockhampton cottage was occupied by Hardys he was in the habit of visiting it regularly every Sunday afternoon.

relativity. Albert Einstein (1879–1955), the German-born mathematical physicist, became world-famous with the publication of his special (1905) and general (1916) theories of relativity. Hardy took a keen interest in Einstein's ideas: Florence Hardy wrote that he 'ponders over Einstein's Theory of Relativity in the night' (letter of 21 June 1921, quoted in Gittings, *The Older Hardy*, 193). He owned copies of Einstein's *Relativity: The Special and the General Theory: A Popular Exposition* (3rd edn., 1920) and C. Nordmann's *Einstein and the Universe* (1922). His notebooks contain extracts from an article by A. S. Eddington, 'Einstein on Time and Space' (*Quarterly Review*, January 1920: see *LN* ii 228–9). His reaction to Einstein's ideas was to observe that 'the universe seems to be getting too comic for words' (letter to the philosopher J. E. McTaggart, 31 December 1919), and a similar spirit is expressed in the poem 'Drinking Song', which illustrates at some length how history proves the relative ephemerality of theories about the universe. Other poems touching on Einstein's ideas are 'The Absolute Explains' and 'So, Time'. The *Life* suggests that Hardy's philosophical ideas were not dissimilar to those implied in Einstein's work ('that neither chance nor purpose governs the universe, but necessity': *LW* 364).

In a broader, less specialized sense, man's insignificance in the scheme of things is a recurring theme in Hardy's work. As early as *Desperate Remedies* Manston associates the brief life of swarms of minute creatures with humanity's 'little day' (12.3). Egdon Heath remains 'as the very finger-touches of the last geological change' left it, and Clym Yeobright is of 'no more account in life than an insect' (*RN* 4.5); Clym's mother watches tiny creatures 'wallow with enjoyment', and her death occurs in an insect world 'busy in all the fulness of life' (*RN* 4.6). Blaming Eustacia for Mrs Yeobright's death, Clym walks home gazing at 'the imperturbable countenance of the heath, which having defied the cataclysmal onsets of centuries, reduced to insignificance . . . the wildest turmoil of a single man'. *Two on a Tower* sets the 'emotional history' of two 'infinitesimal lives against the stupendous background of the stellar universe', aiming (as the 1895 preface says) to suggest that of 'these contrasting magnitudes' the smaller would seem greater to readers. The early poem 'At a Lunar Eclipse' makes a similar point. In *The Dynasts* Christianity is no more than a transient local cult in comparison with 'the systems of the suns' that go 'sweeping on . . . | In mathematic roll unceasingly' (compare the poem 'Evening Shadows'), while great men like Napoleon are compared to 'meanest insects on obscurest leaves' in relation to 'the elemental ages'. FBP

religion. Hardy's life encompassed a period of exceptional religious vigour, debate, and uncertainty. Much early critical attention centred on the intellectual background to Hardy's doubt (see items by Rutland and Webster listed below); more recently, Hardy's ordination plans and his relationship with the Church have been more fully investigated (Hands, Jedrzejewski).

Biography

Hardy's religious biography and views possess a complexity and intensity which make them remarkable even in the context of this extraordinary period. Biography too commonly considers Hardy's religious faith without pausing to ask how fully he ever possessed it. His Christian baptism with the forename of Thomas the doubting apostle is perhaps a pale reflection of rustic traditions of chthonistic or fatalistic powers which extended deep into family history. Hardy's maternal grandfather, George Hand (see HAND FAMILY), was an unregenerate alcoholic who refused to have his children baptized.

The links of Hardy's family with Stinsford church were on the other hand strong ones, especially through his father's involvement with the Mellstock (i.e. Stinsford) choir (see MUSIC). Hardy himself was a regular attender, assisted in the instruction of the Sunday School, and contemplated entrance to the ministry (*LW* 30, 31). Though he suggested that religious practices at Stinsford were old-fashionedly 'High and Dry', the vicar, Arthur Shirley, was an early (and, in Dorset, isolated) product of the Tractarian movement: Hardy benefited from many of his reforms, such as the institution of the village school, even if he never warmed to Shirley personally (see Timothy Hands, 'Arthur Shirley (Vicar of Stinsford, 1837–91)', *THA* 2 (1984)).

In the late 1850s and early 1860s, Hardy developed interests, keen but probably transient, in the Baptists (chiefly through his friend Henry *Bastow) and in a remarkably strong Evangelical Revival (through which he perhaps developed his relationship with the *Moule family) which affected Dorchester from early 1860 onwards. These twin and strangely polarized interests in High and Low Church religion continued into the church-going of Hardy's London years. An erased marginal notation 'doubt', with the date 11 September 1864, marks, first, the end to any plans for the ministry; and, second, the onset of a decline in Hardy's regular church attendance, though the decline was never absolute, particularly at periods of emotional intensity such as the courtship with his stridently Evangelical first wife. The mid-1860s clearly mark the end of the retention of such unequivocal Christian beliefs as Hardy may ever have possessed. His subsequent biography is characterized by a (frequently simultaneous) interest in Christianity and rejection of it, though, in broad terms, the more outspoken and bitter criticism of Christianity detectable in the later novel-writing years (especially the 1890s) gradually modulates into a less strident recognition of the fundamental ethical values of Christianity and a more conservative approach to church attendance in the remarks and practice of Hardy's final decade.

Writings

Religious themes and events are central to Hardy's work. Shirley's Stinsford reforms provide the basis for *Under the Greenwood Tree* and the background to poems concerning the Mellstock choir, especially 'A Choirmaster's Burial'. Hardy's dispute with Bastow over infant baptism underlies the dispute on that topic in *A Laodicean*, in which the minister, Woodwell, is based on the character of the Dorchester Baptist Frederic Perkins. The Evangelical character of the Moule household, and the disputes between Horace and his father Henry, contributed greatly to *Tess*: Hardy admitted that Mr Clare was conceived as a partial portrait of Henry Moule, and intended the short story 'A Changed Man' as a compliment to him. Jude's religious views—the High Church interests, the considerations of the ministry, the doubts, and the anti-ecclesiastical outcries—partly reflect (as do so many other aspects of Jude's personality) Hardy's own experiences and concerns. Both in form and content, the poems are frequently and deeply concerned with or influenced by religious factors. Some of the most frequently anthologized poems have religious settings or themes (for example, 'A Church Romance', 'Afternoon Service at Mellstock', 'The Impercipient', 'The Oxen', and 'The Darkling Thrush'); and the stylistic influence of the *Bible, the *Book of Common Prayer, and hymnody (see HYMNS) is considerable.

Anti-Christian Tendencies

Hardy's opposition to Christianity caused much comment in his lifetime and has remained as a focus of critical attention since. 'What has Providence done to Mr Hardy,' Edmund *Gosse questioned in a review of *Jude the Obscure*, 'that he should rise up in the arable land of Wessex and shake his fist at his Creator?' Will Dyson's famous cartoon (reproduced in Millgate, facing p. 400) showed Hardy drawing from that same putative creator the excuse, 'But Mr Hardy, Mr Hardy, if you only knew all the circumstances.' For G. K. *Chesterton in *The Victorian Age in Literature* (1913), Hardy was 'the village atheist, brooding and blaspheming over the village idiot'.

Hardy saw himself as influenced by writers characterized by a reputation for an unorthodox approach to Christian belief: 'My pages show harmony of view with Darwin, Huxley, Spencer, Comte, Hume, Mill, and others', he told Ernest Brennecke in June 1924 (*L* vi 259). Hardy would perhaps on reflection have wished to add to the list Leslie *Stephen, in the words of the *Life* 'the man whose philosophy was to influence his own for many years, indeed, more than that of any other contemporary' (*LW* 102). Stephen had invited Hardy to witness his renunciation of Holy Orders on 23 March 1875, and his influential volumes *Essays on Free Thinking and Plain Speaking* (1873) and *An Agnostic's Apology* (1876) date from the period of Hardy's close association with him. 'Let us think freely and speak plainly,' the first of Stephen's *Essays* enjoins, 'and we shall have the highest satisfaction that man can enjoy' (*Essays* (1873), 362). For Hardy, the biblical narratives had no definitive status as truth. On 26 December 1927 he asked Florence to read him the seasonal gospel accounts of the nativity and the Massacre of the Innocents as well as articles in the *Encyclopaedia Biblica*: 'He remarked that there was not a grain of evidence that the gospel story was true in any detail' (*LW* 479). Poems such as 'Panthera' and 'The Wood Fire' court controversy by destabilizing the conventionally received view of scriptural veracity. Stephen's plain-speaking approach is much to the fore.

Hardy's descriptive eye and analytic method owe far more to the 19th-century geologist than to the 18th-century sermon-writer. This was in part temperamental rather than acquired. In the early 1840s Hardy's father had thrown a stone on a bitterly cold morning in the direction of a starving fieldfare and killed it: Hardy 'said he had never forgotten how the body of the fieldfare felt in his hand: the memory had always haunted him' (*LW* 479). Hardy had, however, been lent by Horace *Moule one of the seminal works of 19th-century geology, Gideon Algernon Mantell's *Wonders of Geology* (1838); and he somewhat self-aggrandizingly claimed to have been 'among the earliest acclaimers of *The Origin of Species*' (*LW* 158). He views time and existence, as regards both quality and quantity, with a Darwinian perspective. In poems such as 'In a Wood' and 'Winter Night in Woodland', life is regarded as a struggle for existence in which the fittest survive. In the later novels one species preys on another in what have almost become set-piece descriptions: the owls, rabbits, and stoats of *The Woodlanders* (4), the pheasants in *Tess* (41), the rooks and the pig in *Jude* (see also DARWINISM).

Hardy aims to show Christianity as one amongst many religions, viewing it with a detachment temporal and quizzical. In the words of *The Dynasts*, its status is that of a 'local cult'; in the set-piece description of Weatherbury barn it is a 'worn out religious-creed', quite unlike the barn itself, which embodies practices which have suffered no mutilations at the hands of time, and has proved itself not to be 'founded on a mistake' (*FFMC* 22). The landscape (for example, the cliff in *A Pair of Blue Eyes* and the heath in *The Return of the Native*) is full of reminders of prehistoric times, suggesting a timescale for creation extending back far beyond that of the conventional Christianity of Hardy's time (the 'Earth's long order' of 'At Castle Boterel'). Such reminders of the pre-Christian are frequently extended to the church buildings themselves ('A Tryst at an Ancient Earthwork', 'What the Shepherd Saw', and *The Well-Beloved*). The later novels, especially perhaps *The Woodlanders*, consistently suggest a peasant community largely unaffected by Christian doctrine: thus the countrywomen of *Tess* 'retain in their souls far more of the pagan fantasy of their remote forefathers than of the systematized religion taught their race at a later date' (16).

Hardy's native cynicism in this regard was encouraged by his early study of John Stuart *Mill's *On Liberty*. Hardy claimed to know the work almost by heart, and had marked in his copy of the text the passage '"Pagan self-assertion" is one of the elements of human worth, as well as "Christian self-denial"'. Later wide reading, particularly, in the 1870s (as documented in the 'Literary Notes'), of Matthew *Arnold and his notions of Hellenism and Hebraism, prepared for Hardy's broadened attention to this theme. The conflict of Hebrew and Hellene underpins ideologically many of the contrasts of viewpoint in the later fiction: Eustacia and Clym, Paula and Somerset, Angel and his father, Jude and Sue. '"It might have resulted far better for mankind if Greece had been the source of the religion of modern civilization, and not Palestine"', Angel tells his father (*TDU* 25). The bold counterpoint of the statuary scene in *Jude* (2.3) forms the prelude to Sue's tender exposition of Arnoldian theory to Jude in the curious auditorium of the Great Wessex Agricultural Show: '"I feel that we have returned to Greek joyousness, and have blinded ourselves to sickness and sorrow, and have forgotten what twenty-five centuries have taught the race since their time, as one of your Christminster luminaries says."'

The idea has a fundamental effect on Hardy's character-typology. He had had a fascination with the diabolical male figure keen on self-indulgence, which continued from his earliest fiction onwards: Manston, Troy, the Mountclere brothers, Wildeve, Dare, Louis Glanville, and Fitzpiers. There is a similar progression of contrasting women who combine generally orthodox religious views with a devotion to the concept of self-denial which is unhelpful or even unhealthy. These are Cytherea, Elfride, Ethelberta, Picotee, Charlotte, Viviette, and to a certain extent Grace. Other recognizable dynasties of viewpoint are agnostics with a specialized professional training and a breadth of philosophical and religious view (Knight, Somerset, Swithin, and Clym), and women who similarly have an unorthodoxy of ethical and social outlook (Bathsheba, Eustacia, Paula, Elizabeth-Jane). In the later novels, these conventional oppositions are rendered considerably more subtle and ironic: hence the sorts of religious conversion or behavioural volte-face made by Alec and Angel, Arabella and Sue, and the elevation of the fallen woman, Tess, for all her near-masochistic self-denial, into something of an ethical ideal. (The subject has lent itself to periodical articles, amongst which should be particularly mentioned John O. Bailey, 'Hardy's Mephistophelian Visitants', *PMLA* 61 (1946); John Paterson, '*The Return of the Native* as Antichristian Document', *Nineteenth-Century Fiction*, 14 (1959–60); and David J. De Laura, '"The Ache of Modernism" in Hardy's Later Novels', *Journal of English Literary History*, 34 (1967).)

Both novels and poems frequently set out to question divine creation and control, not least because the notion of Providence, of God's control of human affairs for the better, chimed ill with Hardy's notion of the history of his own times ('Channel Firing', 'Christmas: 1924') or his sense of what Christianity had accomplished for mankind ('In a Waiting Room', 'A Drizzling Easter Morning'). '"Well, it's the Lord's doing and marvellous in our eyes,"' remarks an observer of the death of Picton in *The Dynasts*. The idea, in the words of the short story 'To Please His Wife', that 'God would not forsake those who were faithful to him' forms the animus for many of the scenes in the novels. In *Desperate Remedies*, the Carriford church bells ring out the jubilant Old Hundred-and-Thirteenth psalm as fire devastates the life of the Springrove family. *Tess* reads, perhaps intentionally (as, for example, at the end of Phase the First), like a parody of a contemporary Evangelical tract: it documents not a young girl saved by Evangelicalism, but a heroine destroyed by exponents of it. *Jude*, as in its operatic concluding chapter, constantly counterposes conventional notions of divine love with contradictory evidence of insupportable human suffering. The overall impression derived from what W. H. *Auden famously referred to as Hardy's 'hawk's vision' of life is that, in the words of the *Life* (*LW* 378), human beings are, at best 'of no matter or appreciable value in this nonchalant universe'. Hardy's emendation in *Tess* (51) of the famous line from Browning's *Pippa Passes* was deliberate: 'God's not in his heaven: all's wrong with the world!'

These philosophical differences heightened Hardy's native tendency towards anticlericalism and hostility towards the established Church. The later novels, not least in their treatment of marriage, encountered (perhaps even courted) the disapproval of the Establishment. *Tess* sets out a natural law to contrast with that of the Establishment; the preface to *Jude* takes some pleasure at the novel having been burnt by a bishop. 'A Refusal' satirizes opposition to a memorial to *Byron in Westminster Abbey; Hardy himself was to be the subject of a similar debate, with a different outcome. The clergy generally come poorly out of Hardy's writings. Exceptions such as Raunham (*Desperate Remedies*), Torkingham (*Two on a Tower*), and Woodwell (*A Laodicean*) are starkly contrasted with the Bath clergy of *Far from the Madding Crowd* (33), the ineffective pastors of *The Return of the Native*, the snobbish Bishop Helmsdale of *Two on a Tower*, and, most of all, the blatantly hypocritical and socially repulsive Halborough brothers of 'A Tragedy of Two Ambitions'.

Consistently, Hardy shows little interest in the spiritual life of his clergy (for example, Parson Maybold in *Under the Greenwood Tree*), and a contrasting emphasis on their social and pastoral role. '"To tell the truth,"' Joshua Halborough remarks, '"the Church is a poor forlorn hope for people without influence, particularly when their enthusiasm begins to flag. A social regenerator has a better chance outside, where he is unhampered by dogma and tradition."' The poems (for example, 'The Collector Cleans His Picture', 'In the Days of Crinoline') tell no more flattering a tale.

Equivocality

Hardy's approach to religion was not, however, exclusively hostile. Michael Millgate notes, in Hardy's reluctance to adopt absolute or even firm positions, 'a willingness to see virtue in all sides of a question, an insistence upon the provisionality of his opinions and the need to register them rather as a series of tentative impressions than as the systematic formulations of a philosopher' (Millgate 220). Hardy's approach to religious issues is entirely consonant with this general analysis. He refused to be included in Joseph McCabe's *Biographical Dictionary of Modern Rationalists*, a decision which strained his friendship with the freethinker Edward *Clodd. Hardy's correspondence with Clodd, with its hopes for the abandonment of 'doctrines of the supernatural' (*L* iii 5), gave Clodd some justification for finding himself 'staggered' by 'so grave a blunder' (letter to Hardy, 9 February 1921). Hardy's attitude to the supernatural, a litmus test of religious orthodoxy for the Victorian mind, was predictably non-committal. 'I am most anxious', he told William *Archer, 'to believe in what, roughly speaking, we may call the supernatural—but I find no evidence for it' (Archer, *Real Conversations* (1904), 37). He claimed late in life to have seen a ghost, and peopled poem after poem with them (see GHOSTS). Well might Florence Hardy respond to McCabe that her husband 'says he thinks he is rather an irrationalist than a rationalist, on account of his inconsistencies' (*LW* 432).

Ecclesiastical Sympathies

Hardy's attitude to the church as a social institution is symptomatic of this ambiguity in his views. 'If there is no church in a country village, there is nothing', Hardy told a friend in 1922 (Edmund Blunden, *Thomas Hardy* (1967), 165). 'He could not forget', Robert *Graves recalled, 'that the church was in the old days the centre of all the musical, literary and artistic education in the country village' (Graves, *Good-bye to All That* (1929), 373). But Hardy's attachment to the church was more than a respect for its social function: sentiment had a more than equal influence. He confessed to being 'churchy; not in an intellectual sense, but in so far as instincts and emotions rule' (*LW* 376). Hardy enjoyed the ceremony in which he was installed as an honorary fellow at Magdalene College, Cambridge, because it 'recalled the old ecclesiastical times' (*LW* 391); and Florence Hardy could tell Sydney *Cockerell of a 'successful venture' when a reading and a hymn and chant at Stinsford in August 1920 reminded Hardy of his youth (*Friends of a Lifetime*, ed. V. Meynell (1940), 306). Passive campaigner though he was in the 1920s for a new liturgy that would allow church services to become 'representative of modern thinking minds' (*LW* 415; see also *LW* 358–9), he was capable of refusing to attend Stinsford church—an increasing habit in later years—if it involved 'new services and new prayers' (*Friends of a Lifetime*, 299).

Hardy did not, in short, ever see religion or church attendance as something which he had moved conclusively and improvedly beyond. Like his favoured characters, the Mellstock choir, Hardy had a congenital respect for religious tradition. Church music in *Under the Greenwood Tree* is less an expression of doctrinal faith than a gesture of solidarity with the traditions of one's ancestors. As a note of not earlier than 1907 expresses the matter, 'That the dogmatic superstitions read every Sunday are merely a commemorative recitation of old articles of faith held by our grandfathers, may not much matter... as long as this is well understood' (*LW* 333). Hardy could hypothesize in the *Life* about not attending church because of the hypocrisy of being thought to be a believer: 'This must not be; we must leave. And if we do, we reluctantly go to the door, and creep out as it creaks complainingly behind us' (*LW* 333). But the hypothesis did not correspond to his own practice.

Ethical Views

Hardy's early Bible-readings chronicle the strenuousness of his religious aspirations. 'Go ye into all the world, and preach the gospel to every creature' was among the texts which he marked on New Year's Day 1862. A sense of responsibility for moral influence and instruction remained with Hardy long after his plans for ordination had been discarded. 'What are my books but one plea against "man's inhumanity to man"?' he rhetorically demanded of William Archer, whilst also telling Maurice Hewlett of his determination to use his books to make apparent 'true morality, true religion, etcetera, quite freely to the end'. Hardy's correspondents, such as Frederic *Harrison, Edward Clodd, and Robert Lynd, testify to how fully this view of his writings was reciprocated by their audience.

His views of the responsibilities of the individual correspond to his views on the social desirability of the church. Both concepts have a Christian provenance. An 'ephemeral article' sketched out in the *Life* argues that '*Religions, religion*, is to be used in the article in its modern sense entirely, as being expressive of nobler feelings towards humanity and emotional goodness and greatness' (*LW* 358). Another passage suggests that Christianity 'now limits itself to the religion of emotional morality and altruism that was taught by Jesus Christ, or nearly so limits itself' (*LW* 358). Though the novels consistently criticize any excessive deference to the Christian concept of self-denial, a promulgation of a Christian ethic of charity is amongst the most strenuously and consistently communicated virtues in his writings. 'A Plaint to Man' (dated 1909–10) sees such charity (frequently termed 'loving-kindness' by Hardy) as man's logically inescapable and socially imperative response to the disappearance of orthodox religious belief:

> The truth should be told, and the fact be faced
> That had best been faced in earlier years:
>
> The fact of life with dependence placed
> On the human heart's resource alone,
> In brotherhood bonded close and graced
>
> With loving-kindness fully blown,
> And visioned help unsought, unknown.

Treatment of other parties, and sometimes in particular treatment of other animal parties, frequently forms an index of moral charitable worth: *The Mayor of Casterbridge* and the quasi-liturgical poem 'The Blinded Bird' testify as much to this habit of mind as do Emma Hardy's releasing of caged animals, or Hardy's own bequests to animal causes in his will (see also ANIMALS; ANIMALS, CRUELTY TO). Charity became Hardy's moral watchword and totem: Tess, for example, is 'Apostolic Charity', an allusion to Hardy's favourite Bible reading of 1 Cor-3, which also provides the basis for significant passages in *Two on a Tower* and *Jude* as well as poems such as 'Surview'. To a certain extent the development of this ethical code is Hardy's positive assertion against what 'The Impercipient' sees as the negativity of his loss of faith. The young Jude is repulsed by a Darwinist education—'Nature's logic was too horrid for him to care for' (*JO* 1.2)—whilst for Phillotson 'Cruelty is the law pervading all nature and society' (*JO* 5.8) (an observation omitted from the serial edition of the novel, perhaps because of its capacity to give offence).

Loving-kindness is Hardy's human and writerly response to these seemingly inescapable scientific imperatives. Hardy expands on this quasi-creed in the unusually lengthy 'Apology' prefixed to *Late Lyrics and Earlier*, where the philosophy of 'evolutionary meliorism' is developed. The belief that pain should be everywhere 'kept down to a minimum by loving-kindness, through scientific knowledge' depends on a reconciliation of religion and reason through 'the interfusing effect of poetry'. The influence here was partly that general belief in amelioration which characterized much Victorian thought: 'he entertains so many illusions, and hopes for the world, things which I, in my disillusioned middle-age, feel to be illusory', T. E. *Lawrence remarked of Hardy to Robert Graves in September 1923 (*Letters* (1964), 429).

A more particular influence was Auguste *Comte. Hardy had for a time a keen interest in Comte's quasi-religious system of Logical *Positivism, with its twin mottos of 'Order and Progress' and 'Live for Others', and corresponded with the English Positivist, Frederic Harrison. Hardy remarked that 'no person of serious thought in these times could be said to stand aloof from Positivist teaching and ideals' (*L* iii 53): a full study of Hardy's relationship with Positivism has yet to appear.

The higher qualified optimism of the 'Apology', albeit tentatively hedged around with provisionalities of ideas and oddities of expression, represents, however, only an Indian summer in that depression of spirits and ideas—so memorably expressed in the poem 'We Are Getting to the End'—which followed the events of the *First World War, and which led to an inevitable and widely shared despair at any concept of human progress. According to Florence Hardy, contemplation of the war led Hardy 'to despair of the world's history thenceforward' (*LW* 365–6). Hence partly the reflection in the *Life* on the occasion of Hardy's 80th birthday: 'Though my life, like the lives of my contemporaries, covers a period of more material advance in the world than any of the same length can have done in other centuries, I do not feel that real civilization has advanced equally. People are not more humane, so far as I can see, than they were in the year of my birth. Disinterested kindness is less' (*LW* 435).

'Hoping it might be so' ('The Oxen')

An overall impression is finally given of a regret, sometimes sentimental, sometimes wistful, for a religious belief which Hardy found constantly considerable, yet personally elusive and intellectually unacceptable. 'I have been looking for God 50 years,' he recorded in the *Life*, 'and think that if he had existed I should have discovered him' (*LW* 234). But as the same work subsequently speculates, 'We have to sing, "My soul doth magnify the Lord", when what we want to sing is, "O that my soul could find some Lord that it could magnify!"' (*LW* 358). In 'In a Whispering Gallery' the narrator experiences a momentary 'kindling vision': 'And for a moment I rejoice, | And believe in transcendent things | That would mould from this muddy earth | A spot for the splendid birth | Of everlasting lives, | Whereto no night arrives...'. Conversely, 'On Stinsford Hill at Midnight' presents with some irony a timbrel-playing woman from 'a body of religious enthusiasts' who 'had no heed of me'. The most celebrated of the religious or semi-religious anthology-pieces, 'The Oxen', 'The Darkling Thrush', and 'Afternoon Service at Mellstock', dramatize in an effortlessly communicating form the uncertainties of Hardy's religious life and thought: the tendency of his heart (as also his feet) frequently to move in a different direction from his head. They are entirely characteristic of one of his most impressive styles of articulation, and amongst the most-quoted expressions of contemporary religious dilemma.

Hardy's religious attitudes are *sui generis* and escape conventional labels and tidy categorization. He is neither believer, agnostic, nor atheist by an accepted or historical definition of these terms. His writings are characterized by many aspects of a religious search, but at the same time are dominated by many aspects of religious rejection. While there were few things that he could not contemplate believing, there were likewise few things that he could: the tensions between belief and unbelief are some of the most significant dynamics in his art. See also READING, HARDY'S. TRH

Timothy Hands, *Thomas Hardy: Distracted Preacher?* (1989).

Jan Jedrzejewski, *Thomas Hardy and the Church* (1996).

William Rutland, *Thomas Hardy: A Study of His Writings and Their Background* (1938).

Harvey Curtis Webster, *On a Darkling Plain: The Art and Thought of Thomas Hardy* (1947).

Return of the Native, The. The sixth of Hardy's published novels.

Composition

Most of *The Return of the Native* was written during what Hardy later called 'the Sturminster Newton idyll', the 'happiest time' of his first marriage (*LW* 122). The novel was probably begun in late 1876; by 5 February 1877 the manuscript had been sent 'as far as written' (*L* i 47) to Leslie *Stephen, who as editor of the *Cornhill Magazine* had accepted Hardy's previous two novels for serialization. A tentative rejection resulted in Hardy's sending the first fifteen chapters to *Blackwood's Magazine*, but John Blackwood also turned down the story, maintaining that the opening scenes lacked 'Novel interest' (24 April 1877, National Library of Scotland). Stephen was then approached again; according, however, to Hardy's later recollection, he 'feared that the relations between Eustacia, Wildeve, and Thomasin might develop into something "dangerous" for a family magazine, and he refused to have anything to do with it unless he could see the whole' (quoted in Frederic William Maitland, *The Life and Letters of Leslie Stephen* (1906), 276–7). Hardy, still attempting to establish himself financially, was not willing to wait; he offered the serial rights to the editor of *Temple Bar*—and perhaps to others—before finally coming to an arrangement on 28 June with Chatto and Windus, the publishers of *Belgravia*, who agreed to pay £20 per instalment without seeing any of the (as yet untitled) manuscript.

Hardy submitted the first two instalments (1.1–7) on 28 August and the next three (1.8–11 and 2.1–8) on 8 November. When he completed the novel is uncertain, though it was presumably early in 1878, either before or shortly after he and his wife moved to Upper Tooting on 22 March.

Deletions and false starts in the surviving manuscript (University College, Dublin; reproduced in facsimile by Garland Publishing, 1986) indicate that the novel was substantially revised before its submission to *Belgravia*, perhaps because Hardy's difficulty in placing the potentially 'dangerous' story had made him anxious not to risk a late rejection. Certainly some advance bowdlerization occurred: a passage deleted from the manuscript, for example, refers to Thomasin's spending a week away with her assumed husband before learning that they are not legally married. Another major revision, presumably intended to render the story potentially more interesting to a middle-class audience, raised the social status of the major characters—simultaneously eliminating the essential classlessness of the heath community by insisting upon Mrs Yeobright's gentility, transferring Clym's place of employment from Budmouth to Paris, and transforming 'Conjuror Toogood' the herbalist into Wildeve the engineer-innkeeper, and 'Mis'ess Avice' the reputed witch's daughter into 'Miss Eustacia' the naval gentleman's granddaughter. Other revisions sometimes clarified, sometimes obscured the characters' thoughts and motivations, an important example being the increase in ambiguity surrounding the intentionality or otherwise of Eustacia's death.

Serialization

The novel appeared in twelve monthly instalments (January–December 1878) in *Belgravia*, a not particularly prestigious magazine best known for its sensationalism and sentimentalism. The division was as follows: January, Book 1, Chapters 1–4; February, 1.5–7; March, 1.8–11; April, 2.1–5; May, 2.6–8; June, 3.1–4; July, 3.5–8; August, 4.1–4; September, 4.5–8; October, 5.1–4; November, 5.5–8; December, 5.9–6.4. (The 'books' were untitled.) Simultaneous American serialization occurred in *Harper's New Monthly Magazine* (February 1878–January 1879).

Illustrations

Each of the twelve *Belgravia* instalments was accompanied by a full-page woodblock illustration by Arthur Hopkins, a successful painter and illustrator, now remembered as the younger brother of Gerard Manley Hopkins. Only the first four illustrations appeared in *Harper's*, the difficulty of receiving the electrotype plates in time (the second and third illustrations appeared a month late) apparently having led to a decision to abandon them altogether.

Hardy took an active interest in the illustrations. His disappointment with the second (February) drawing, depicting a heavy-set, stiff, and somewhat 'masculine' Eustacia, led him to send Hopkins a sketch of Eustacia as he envisioned her and to suggest that she be 'represented as more youthful in face, supple in figure, &, in general, with a little more roundness & softness than have been given her' (*L* i 52). Hopkins achieved this in his August illustration, where Eustacia's elegant attire, curvaceous figure, and pouting attractiveness contrast markedly with the roughness of Clym and Humphrey. Hardy was delighted: 'I think Eustacia is charming—she is certainly just what I imagined her to be, & the rebelliousness of her nature is precisely caught in your drawing' (*L* i 59).

Hardy also praised Hopkins's opening illustration of the rural labourers gathered around the bonfire: an eminently 'safe' drawing lacking any suggestion of the mysteriousness or uncontrollability associated with the heath-dwellers in the written text. Clearly Hopkins preferred the conventional and unthreatening: he avoided the representation of Wildeve almost entirely, and only depicted Thomasin as the stereotypical 'womanly' heroine and Venn as the selfless hero, ignoring the more radical Thomasin and shadowy Venn. Hardy perhaps saw that the very conventionality of the illustrations might help to render publishable a text that pushed persistently against the limits of the then acceptable: as he wrote in response to Hopkins's decision not to depict Eustacia in mumming guise, 'Eustacia in boy's clothes, though pleasant enough to the imagination, would perhaps be unsafe as a picture' (*L* i 54).

Volume Publication

The three-volume edition was published by *Smith, Elder at 31*s.* 6*d.* (half-a-guinea per volume) on 4 November 1878. Included as a frontispiece to the first volume is a 'Sketch map of the scene of the story' drawn by Hardy himself and remarkable both for its geographical unspecificity (unlike the maps of 'Wessex' in the later collected editions, it posits no correspondence between the fictional and the actual), and for its unmistakable resemblance—at least for those familiar with Dorset—to the tract of heathland immediately adjacent to Hardy's childhood home. In revising the novel for volume publication, Hardy continued to enhance the major characters' social status, promoting Clym from jeweller's assistant to jeweller's manager and the youthful Venn from haulier to small dairy-farmer. He also rendered more complex—and acrimonious—the misunderstanding with respect to the undelivered guineas, replacing Mrs Yeobright's direct reference to Eustacia and Clym's not acknowledging receipt of the money with unintentionally ambiguous questions which suggest to Eustacia that her mother-in-law is accusing her of sexual misconduct.

Relatively few changes were made for the first one-volume edition, published by Charles Kegan *Paul in 1880, but the novel was extensively revised for its inclusion in the Wessex Novels collected edition (*Osgood, McIlvaine, 1895). Hardy eliminated at this point what Simon Gatrell has defined as the 'essential calculated vagueness' of the setting: Egdon Heath became limited in extent and fixed in location as Hardy, in keeping with his general 'Wessexization' of the fiction for this edition, introduced standard 'Wessex' place-names and altered distances and directions to conform more closely to geographical actuality. The 1895 text also made more explicit the sexual nature of Eustacia and Wildeve's original relationship, and of their future relationship should she agree to run away with him.

Most of Hardy's revisions for the Wessex Edition (Macmillan, 1912) continued the process of identifying fictional settings with recognizable geographical locations, though it was also in 1912 that he added to 6.3 his famous footnote to the effect that the marriage of Thomasin and Venn was dictated by 'certain circumstances of serial publication', and that in his original, more 'artistic' conception of the story Venn was to have 'retained his isolated and weird character to the last', disappearing mysteriously 'nobody knowing whither', while Thomasin remained a widow.

Reception

The Return of the Native was more widely and more positively noticed than has generally been assumed, though nearly all of the reviews were mixed, combining approbation and criticism in varying proportions. The *Evening Standard* (2 May 1878), for example, briefly noticing the novel in the midst of its serialization, praised both plot and expression while lamenting Hardy's 'tedious love of tiresome commonplace characters'.

More influential was the early and largely negative *Athenaeum* (23 November 1878) review of the first edition, which judged Hardy's new novel 'distinctly inferior to anything of his we have yet read', dismissed Eustacia and Wildeve as 'selfish and sensual', regretted that the 'keen observation of natural things' should be 'disfigured at times by forced allusions and images', and criticized as unrealistically cultivated the dialogue of both rustics and major characters (all of 'low social position'). Hardy responded to this last point in a letter to the *Athenaeum* (published 30 November), arguing that 'An author may be said to fairly convey the spirit of intelligent peasant talk if he retains the idiom, compass, and characteristic expressions, although he may not encumber the page with obsolete pronunciations of the purely English words, and with mispronunciations of those derived from Latin and Greek'. It was, however, precisely the characters' idiom and expressions (rather than their pronunciation) to which the *Athenaeum* reviewer had objected.

In the *London* review, also published on 23 November, admiration for Hardy's 'power of cumulative poetry' and 'observant imagination' was qualified by criticism of his 'needlessly cruel' plot, love of 'futile tragedy', and damaging penchant for 'the introduction of exaggerated circumstances, of an offensive personality, of an inopportune conceit'. Ranking Hardy, with the exception of Henry James, as perhaps the greatest of living English novelists, the reviewer none the less insisted that he could never attain the 'prime place' because he appealed to the intellect rather than to the emotions: 'He regards his world from above; his men and women are seen in bird's-eye view; and it is not as human beings but as studies that they interest you.'

The dozens of reviews that followed on both sides of the Atlantic mostly repeated in different combinations and with different emphases the points made by the *Athenaeum* and *London* reviewers. Hardy's powers of description, especially in the opening portraits of both Egdon and Eustacia and in the nocturnal dice-game scene, were nearly always singled out for commendation (sometimes with reservations), while criticism was directed chiefly at the eccentricities and affectations of his language—though the occasional dissenting voice was heard, including the *Graphic* (7 December 1878) review, which praised Hardy's increased clarity of style and freedom from mannerisms.

Opinion also differed with respect to the various characters. Responses to Eustacia ranged from the sympathetic—'a true woman, with all her faults', beside whom the 'good folks' seem 'insipid' (*Observer*, 5 January 1879)—to the vehemently condemnatory: 'never, perhaps, at least in fiction, has beauty lent a certain baleful charm to a more thoroughly selfish, cruel, unprincipled, and despicable woman' (New York *Eclectic*, March 1879). Clym attracted equally varied commentary: 'not a very interesting hero' (*John Bull*, 30 November 1878); 'a moonstruck dreamer' (*Saturday Review*, 4 January 1879); 'the first of Mr. Hardy's characters who is actuated by any large appreciation of human duty' (*New Quarterly Magazine*, October 1879). The other characters also had their detractors and admirers—even Christian Cantle, who was singled out from the rustics both as the least effective portrait (*London*) and as 'fresh, well drawn, and very amusing' (*Examiner*).

Plot (1878 version)

When the marriage between Damon Wildeve and Thomasin Yeobright fails to take place because of an invalid licence, Wildeve once again becomes fascinated by the beautiful, passionate, and imperious Eustacia Vye. Eustacia, however, does not hesitate to tell Wildeve that he is unworthy of her, while he, a less than adoring suitor, candidly acknowledges his feeling that he ought to marry the 'good little woman', Thomasin. Eventually he does ask Eustacia to run away to America with him, but before she has come to a decision she meets Thomasin's cousin Clym Yeobright, a native of Egdon Heath newly returned from Paris, whom she invests with all the glamour and romance of a knight in shining armour. Wildeve, offhandedly dismissed by Eustacia, hastily marries Thomasin, who is willing to accept him for the sake of her family's honour, even though she no longer has any illusions about his character.

Clym is an idealist, choosing, in the face of strong maternal opposition, to give up his position as a jeweller's manager and its possibilities of advancement in order to bring education and cultural enlightenment to the heathfolk. He marries Eustacia—again defying his mother—in spite of her lack of sympathy with either his beloved heath or his educational projects. Eustacia, for her part, refuses to acknowledge that Clym has no intention of returning to Paris. They remain on Egdon while he prepares himself to teach, but excessive studying severely damages his eyesight and he turns (quite contentedly) to furze-cutting. Eustacia, humiliated by his occupation and bitterly disappointed by the defeat of all her romantic dreams, attempts to shake off her depression by attending a gypsying, where she accidentally meets and then dances with Wildeve.

Wildeve's passion is rekindled and he eventually succeeds in seeing Eustacia again by calling openly at her home. While he is there, Mrs Yeobright unexpectedly arrives, having decided to attempt a reconciliation with her son and his wife; Eustacia, concerned that Wildeve's presence will be misconstrued, ignores her knocking, believing in any case that it has roused the sleeping Clym. But Clym is not awakened and Mrs Yeobright, having previously seen Eustacia's face at the window, assumes that she has been deliberately shut out. During her long, hot walk home across the heath Mrs Yeobright is bitten by an adder and dies. Clym is consumed with remorse and loss; he blames himself for his mother's death and then, when he learns more (but not all) of the circumstances, turns his fury on Eustacia. After a bitter confrontation during which she refuses to explain herself, Eustacia returns to her grandfather's house.

Wildeve now offers to help her leave Egdon, but she is reluctant (later texts make it clear that acceptance of his offer would mean a renewal of their sexual relationship). Desperate, she decides to go, journeying across the heath in the midst of a violent storm. The sound of her body falling into the weir stream leads both Wildeve and Clym to plunge in after her: she and Wildeve drown, but Clym survives.

Nearly two years later Thomasin marries Diggory Venn, the reddleman turned dairy-farmer, who loved her before she knew Wildeve and has consistently acted as her faithful friend and protector, first selflessly promoting her marriage to Wildeve and later attempting to thwart her husband's renewed pursuit of Eustacia. Clym, now bearing the guilt for the deaths of both his mother and Eustacia, withdraws from life, emerging only to deliver open-air sermons 'on morally unimpeachable subjects'.

Critical Approaches

As one of the most popular of Hardy's novels throughout the 20th century, *The Return of the Native* has attracted a great deal of critical attention, much of it centring on characterization, especially the representation of Eustacia. Writing to the novel's illustrator, Arthur Hopkins, Hardy himself defined Eustacia as the 'wayward & erring heroine', in contrast to the '*good* heroine', Thomasin (*L* i 53), and numerous critics have been happy to perpetuate this simplistic reading. More common, however, has been the recognition of Eustacia's complexity, which allows her to be categorized as classical divinity, mythic victim, biblical temptress, pagan witch, tragic heroine, Romantic hero, perceiving subject, exploited object, philosophic idealist, paranoid egotist—or any combination of the above. Indeed, she is often considered a divided figure, caught between mythologizing and irony, a 'Queen of Night' whose aspirations—to see the Paris boulevards, or even to walk again the Budmouth esplanades—seem so trivial. Recent critics have tended to view such contradictions as evidence not of authorial inconsistency but of conflicting ideological systems and expectations. Jennifer Gribble, for example, demonstrates that Eustacia's challenge to 'a traditionally masculine world of power and mobility' blends romantic notions of a girl's experience with 'forwardness of mind' (p. 248): even as Eustacia alternates between the roles of queen and victim, she is capable of acting as self-assertive (and self-destructive) sexual initiator in lighting the signal-fire or joining the mummers.

Marjorie Garson takes the concept of divided heroine a step further, arguing that the representation of Eustacia as physically fragmented, 'a catalogue of culturally coded parts'—lips, cheek, hair, and so forth—is perpetuated not only by the narrator and male characters but also by Eustacia herself, who endorses and promotes images absorbed from romantic literature: 'As a result, she can be seen as a victim not only of her husband's misreading but of all male readings of woman as Other (including the author's)' (p. 71). For Garson, Eustacia is ultimately a figure of pathos, but for many recent critics her victimization is invested with heroic status: she is scapegoat and ritual sacrifice, offering herself up 'as an act of tragic propitiation' (Brian Thomas, p. 115; see also Joseph Garver and Gribble), as well as romantic hero, 'in love with her tragic destiny' (Robert Langbaum, p. 109).

Hardy himself considered Eustacia of secondary importance to Clym (*L* i 53), and in his later years insisted that Clym was 'the nicest of all my heroes, and *not a bit* like me' (*LW* 520). Critics, however, have generally given Eustacia primacy of place, emphasized the resemblance between Hardy's life and his hero's (especially with respect to the intense mother–son relationship), and criticized Clym's ineffectualness and inconsistency. Even those most sympathetic to Clym remark upon the rapid collapse of his educational idealism, his persistent inability to comprehend Eustacia, and his wilful bondage to the past. Having determined to keep alive 'his mother's trust in him, his plan for becoming a teacher, and Eustacia's happiness' (3.4), he destroys all three. He is a failed tragic hero, lacking awareness both of self and of destiny's malignity (Dale Kramer, *Thomas Hardy: The Forms of Tragedy* (1975)); an ironic Christ-figure, preaching parodic sermons on the mount (Michael Millgate, *Thomas Hardy: His Career as a Novelist* (1971)); and an impotent St George, incapable of rescuing the maiden or restoring the community (Brian Thomas).

Psychoanalytic readings focus on Clym's relationship with his mother, pointing out the obvious Oedipus parallels, especially the Freudian connection between blindness and castration. Since separation from his mother ultimately results in Clym's (self-willed?) loss not only of his sight and virility but also of his wife and chosen vocation, he can in some ways be seen as a pathetic figure, a victim of his infantile sexuality, domineering mother, and passionate wife. But regardless of whether or not he is held personally responsible for his losses—regardless, indeed, of whether or not he is registered as a sympathetic character—nearly all critics respond to him with the kind of compassionate tolerance articulated in the novel's concluding words: 'everywhere he was kindly received, for the story of his life had become generally known'.

More critical controversy has arisen with respect to Diggory Venn, traditionally viewed either as a benign (if perhaps somewhat dull) agent of order, a second Gabriel Oak, loving with self-abnegating devotion and ultimately bringing about the communal happy ending, or as a weird, romantic figure, the luridly coloured reddleman who haunts the heath, alienating himself from society because of disappointed love. Both figure in Hardy's text, though their coexistence is somewhat uneasy, particularly in the later editions, where added references to the devil, Mephistopheles, and Ishmael serve together with the 1912 footnote (see above) to heighten the contrast between the other-worldly Venn and his more conventional *alter ego*. The sinister connotations of the devil imagery have been noted by some feminist critics, especially Rosemarie Morgan, for whom Venn is 'a power-mongering bully and degrader of voluptuous womankind' (*Women and Sexuality in the Novels of Thomas Hardy* (1988), 75), a malevolent spy taking pleasure in creating trouble and censoring female nonconformity. In a less polemical reading, Garson points out that because Venn's interventions lead to disaster—from the Thomasin–Wildeve and Eustacia–Clym marriages to the deaths of Mrs Yeobright, Eustacia, and Wildeve—the reader remains unclear as to whether they represent good intentions thwarted or, since the obstacles to Venn's courtship are successfully eliminated, 'canny bungling' (p. 59).

The other characters have received comparatively little critical attention, unless, echoing generations of readers, one considers Egdon Heath a character—or indeed *the* character. After all, as the 1879 *Observer* reviewer noted, Egdon's portrait in the form of a sketch-map does constitute the novel's frontispiece. Those 20th-century critics who see Egdon as the central character emphasize its omnipresence, its anthropomorphic representation, and especially its role in defining the characters and determining their fate. Eustacia, for example, is paradoxically defined both by her hatred for the heath ('Egdon was her Hades') and by her harmony with it, her sighs mingling with its winds and her hair combed by its furze, while her desire to escape from Egdon culminates in her death—if also in her permanent presence within its sombre confines. Critics seeking a more precise definition of Egdon have variously interpreted it as the tragic power of primitive, primal earth, the abyss of hell (Homeric, Dantean, or Miltonic), the subconscious hinterland of elemental myth, the nurturing female principle, the sublime, the unconscious, a Darwinian landscape, a parody of Eden, a (mere) backdrop, and a location in Dorset either realistically portrayed or nostalgically romanticized.

In his 1895 preface to *The Return of the Native* Hardy himself invoked the heath of Shakespeare's Lear in relation to Egdon, doubtless wishing to emphasize the novel's tragic elements. He had intentionally modelled the five-book structure, with its unity of place and approximate unity of time (a year and a day), on Greek and Elizabethan tragedy, and his dramatic technique and achievement were often the focus of early critical studies. His inclusion of the sixth 'Aftercourses' book has, however, always raised troubling questions in that it not only breaks the five-act pattern and disrupts the unity of time but also transforms tragedy into comedy, the marriage of Venn and Thomasin functioning in traditional fashion as the symbol of the community's renewal and restoration. This mixing of genres is highlighted by the insistence in Hardy's footnote that the comedic ending was a capitulation to the conventions of serial publication, and critics have long debated which ending would in fact have been artistically superior. Given that only one ending exists, the reader is not in any case presented with a genuine choice, and certainly in the text as published the current ending is anticipated by the opening scenes of Venn's solicitous care of Thomasin—though those who argue in favour of the unwritten ending find the domesticated dairy-farmer entirely out of keeping with the heath-haunting reddleman. Alternatively, as Sheila Berger has argued, one could read the happy ending with its 'neatly packaged new Diggory' as deliberately implausible and intrusive, Hardy's conscious exposure of the inadequacy of conventional concepts of closure (*Thomas Hardy and Visual Structures: Framing, Disruption, Process* (1990), 114).

The existing ending has also been interpreted as the triumph of Christianity over paganism. It is true that classical imagery dominates the first half of the novel and biblical imagery the second—and indeed that the Hellenistic Eustacia dies while the Hebraic Clym survives—but it is equally true that Clym's 'sermons' are humanistic and that the heathfolk are defined in relation to folk tradition, while church-going, in so far as it figures at all, is described as a marginalized social custom. Since ultimately it is only the heathfolk, and Egdon itself, who are neither destroyed nor forced to endure great suffering, it could perhaps be argued that the narrative in fact represents the triumph of the pagan. Some of the most persuasive readings of the novel focus precisely on its pagan and folk elements, demonstrating the metaphoric centrality both of the ancient conflict between light and darkness (Jean Brooks, in Bloom) and of fertility myths and rituals, from sun-hero to St George, bonfire to Maypole dance (see Garver, Thomas, and Gribble). If, as has frequently been observed, *The Return of the Native* enacts in Clym's story the impossibility of returning, of going home again, it perhaps also suggests the impossibility of not returning—the inescapability of the human compulsion to repeat (ironically or otherwise) time-worn patterns. PD

Harold Bloom (ed.), *Modern Critical Interpretations: Thomas Hardy's 'The Return of the Native' (1987).*

Marjorie Garson, *Hardy's Fables of Integrity: Woman, Body, Text* (1991).

Joseph Garver, *Thomas Hardy: The Return of the Native* (1988).

Simon Gatrell, 'Notes of Significant Revisions to the Text', in Thomas Hardy, *The Return of the Native*, Oxford World's Classics (1990).

Jennifer Gribble, 'The Quiet Women of Egdon Heath', *Essays in Criticism*, 43 (1996).

Robert Langbaum, *Thomas Hardy in Our Time* (1995).

Brian Thomas, *The Return of the Native: Saint George Defeated* (1995).

'Romantic Adventures of a Milkmaid, The', short story perhaps long enough to qualify as a novella. It originally appeared in the *Graphic* (Summer Number, 25 June 1883) and, in seven weekly instalments, in the New York publication *Harper's Weekly* (23 June–4 August 1883). After the appearance of the first of the seven instalments, in order 'to protect themselves from an immediate pirating of the story' (Purdy 48), Harper's issued it in a paper-covered edition, selling at 10 cents. It was nevertheless extensively pirated in America. Although he had not originally intended to collect it, Hardy included it, 30 years after its original appearance, in his final collection of stories, *A Changed Man*.

The deliberately jarring and mystifying conjunction in the title of 'romantic' and 'milkmaid' prepares the reader for a tale that will daringly cross generic frontiers. It opens at 'half-past four o'clock on a May morning in the eighteen forties', and this specificity, matched by a wealth of visual detail, seems to promise a traditional realistic narrative. Soon, however, it turns into a kind of fairy-tale, a version of the Cinderella story, with the milkmaid, Margery Tucker, straying into a world of glamour and mystery presided over by the Baron Xanten, imported into the English countryside from foreign parts. The simple girl is given a taste of high life that (a characteristically Hardyan motif) involves the crossing of normally impenetrable class barriers. Characteristic, too, is the dramatic use of a fascinating and aristocratic stranger (Fitzpiers in *The Woodlanders* was soon to follow in the Baron's footsteps) whose presence—and, more particularly, whose overt sexuality—disturbs the even tenor of rural life. To Margery this 'dark-mustachioed stranger' is at first sight 'quite a different being from any of the men to whom her eyes were accustomed. She had never seen mustachios before...'. Even at the end of the story, happily married to a man of her own class, she confesses that '"He was like a magician to me"', and that if he reappeared she '"should have no power to disobey"'. With its frank tribute to the power of the exotic and the erotic, this is something more complex than a conventional happy ending. As in 'The Fiddler of the Reels', considerable emphasis is placed earlier in the story on the erotic effects of music and dancing.

When Hardy collected this story in *A Changed Man* he made a few minor but interesting revisions to place-names, the effect of which is to shift its locale west from the neighbourhood of 'Casterbridge' (Dorchester) to that of 'Exonbury' (Exeter) in 'Lower Wessex'. If Purdy's conjecture (49) that he wished 'to remove the story from the scene of *Tess*' can be accepted, the implication may be that Margery is a modest prototype of the tragic heroine created a few years later.

Royal Academy. During Hardy's lifetime, the summer exhibition of the Royal Academy of Arts was the foremost venue for the sale of contemporary works of art. When Hardy arrived in London in 1862, these exhibitions were held in the *National Gallery, but in 1867 the Academy moved to its present home at Burlington House, Piccadilly. With increasing prosperity, Hardy became a regular frequenter of the Academy's fashionable private views, held at the beginning of May, and also at the soirées which took place in late July. These were always crowded occasions, and Hardy would meet his friends in the quieter gallery reserved for the display of architectural drawings, works in which he no doubt retained a professional interest. In 1911 Hardy was a guest at the annual dinner, where he enjoyed the company of John Singer Sargent, J. M. *Barrie, and Rudyard *Kipling, and he was there again in 1914 and 1919. In his later years, Hardy's attendance at Academy exhibitions became more erratic, although he still attended whenever possible, sometimes taking guests or, when he did not go himself, giving his invitation cards to his friends.

On his winter visits to London, Hardy usually saw the annual exhibitions of Old Masters and recently deceased Academicians which were inaugurated in 1870. These were loan exhibitions, drawing upon the riches of English private collections. In 1889, Hardy was particularly struck by the watercolours of J. M. W. Turner. He had expressed anxiety that the thick fog would prevent him from seeing the paintings in that year, but in the event his worst fears were not realized.

Hardy had a number of friends among the Associate and full Academicians, including the painter William Powell Frith and the sculptor Hamo *Thornycroft. In *The Well-Beloved*, the sculptor-hero, Jocelyn Pierston, becomes an Academician, as does his friend, the landscapist Alfred Somers. Like other successful Academicians of his day, including Frederic Leighton and Luke Fildes, Pierston builds himself a large house in Kensington, with a huge studio behind. LO

S

St Helier, Lady. See JEUNE, MARY.

Sampson Low, London publishing firm (in full, Sampson Low, Marston, Searle & Rivington). They agreed on 14 July 1882 to publish *Two on a Tower* in volume form; an edition in three volumes appeared in October of that year. Between 1881 and 1893 they published cheap editions of eight of Hardy's novels. His dealings were mainly with Edward Marston (1825–1914): see the latter's volume of memoirs, *After Work* (1904), 266–7.

Sassoon, Siegfried (1886–1967), poet and autobiographer. He was a nephew of Hardy's friend, the sculptor Hamo *Thornycroft. Sassoon met Hardy on 6 November 1918, five days before the Armistice and a few months after sending Hardy a copy of his *Counter-Attack and Other Poems* (1918). Even earlier he had corresponded with Hardy and had dedicated to him his collection of war poems *The Old Huntsman* (1917). A warm friendship developed, both Hardy and his wife being attracted to Sassoon, and he became a frequent visitor during Hardy's last years, and one of the group of younger writers in whom he took a strong personal interest during the postwar period: in July 1922, for instance, Sassoon went to Max Gate with Edmund *Blunden, and he was there again in August 1924, this time with T. E. *Lawrence. His poem 'At Max Gate' both commemorates such visits and claims a special intimacy with Hardy.

In 1919 Sassoon delivered to Hardy the 'Poets' Tribute', a collection of manuscript poems by 43 contemporary poets presented to Hardy to commemorate his 79th birthday. He was also one of the younger authors (the others including Robert *Graves, James Joyce, and Virginia *Woolf) who gave Hardy a first edition of Keats's 1820 *Poems* on his 81st birthday. Sassoon's visits to Max Gate continued to the end of Hardy's life, and after *Harper & Brothers had invited him to write an 'authorized biography' of Hardy he was let into the secret of the work later published under Florence Hardy's name. For his vivid impression of Hardy in extreme old age, quoted from an unpublished letter to Edmund *Gosse, see Millgate 564. Sassoon's published diaries, edited by Rupert Hart-Davis (1981, 1983), contain references to Hardy and his second wife. See also HARDY, POEMS ABOUT.

Satires of Circumstance. This was published on 17 November 1914. It was Hardy's fourth book of verse, contained 107 poems, and was his biggest collection so far. At the age of 74 he was getting into his stride as a poet. During the five years since the publication of *Time's Laughingstocks*, his wife, Emma, had died and he had married Florence Dugdale.

The first hint that *Satires of Circumstance* was on its way is to be found in a letter from Hardy to Maurice Macmillan dated 6 August 1913. Macmillan were clearly not in any hurry to publish the new book of verse, and it was not until 15 July 1914 that Hardy wrote again to tell Sir Frederick *Macmillan that he had accumulated enough verse in manuscript for another volume, and that it was ready whenever the firm wished to publish it. This letter may well have been precipitated by Hardy's awareness that the Great War was imminent and might slow down all publishing. The reply was favourable, and on 19 July Hardy told Sir Frederick that he was tidying up the manuscript, making 'the pages clear where confused', and that he hoped to send it to the publisher by the end of the month.

England declared war on Germany on 4 August, and on the 9th Hardy asked Macmillan whether they still wanted the manuscript. They did, and it was posted to them on the 10th, Hardy concluding his short covering letter with 'If you decide to print it, it could, of course, be published at any favourable time—say when people get tired of the war, if they do' (*L* v 41). That the publication of this volume was important to him is made clear in a letter he wrote to Sydney *Cockerell on 28 August, in which he said that what he cared about most at that time was that Macmillan should publish it. Hardy's special involvement with *Satires of Circumstance* is apparent here, and he did not have long to wait, as on 9 November Sir Frederick sent him an early copy of the book, telling him that it would be published on the 17th. 'I am afraid that we cannot look for a very large sale,' Macmillan warned, 'as the book business is terribly disorganised, but we must hope for the best.' Even with a war on, Macmillan took only three months to turn the manuscript into a book. The publishers' caution is perhaps shown, however, in the print-run, which was a mere 2,000 copies. A reprint was required early in 1915 and published in March after Hardy had sent 'some corrections' in February. His 'corrections' euphemistically included revisions. Thus, in line 4 of 'After a Journey', the first printing had 'the unseen waters' soliloquies', but the second printing 'the unseen waters' ejaculations'; the former was no printing error.

The manuscript, now in DCM, consists of 189 pages and is, perhaps somewhat surprisingly, made up of fair copies rather than transcriptions. Because of this the manuscript is of far more interest than Purdy (171) indicates. That these are the sheets used by the printer to set the first edition is shown by the presence of the typesetters' names on a number of pages throughout the volume. Also present are the indications made by the printer of where each signature is to begin.

Hardy's titles are carefully thought out, and *Satires of Circumstance* seems very much in the line of *Life's Little Ironies* and *Time's Laughingstocks* but was a strange choice for a volume containing some of his greatest love poetry. The title originates in a sequence of twelve poems Hardy wrote for the *Fortnightly Review* with the title 'Satires of Circumstance'. Published in April 1911, about eighteen months before Emma died, they are a return to the mood of *Jude the Obscure*: jaundiced and bitter, these short sketches portray the worst in humankind—deceit, conceit, greed, and lust. They are so misanthropic that one wonders what caused them. Hardy was aware of their strident nature because, in a letter to Florence *Henniker of 17 March 1911, he said that he would not be sending her a copy of the *Fortnightly*, 'as I *know* you won't like them, or some of them'. When she replied that she would like to see them, he asked her to remember that 'being *satires* they are rather brutal. I confess no feeling or opinion myself at all. They are from notes I made some twenty years ago, and then found were more fit for verse than prose' (*L* v 151). So many of them have as a subject unhappy marriages that it is difficult not to see them as a reflection of the state of Hardy's own marriage at that time, and these were certainly very difficult years in Hardy's life. Emma had become ever more critical of him and irresponsible in her conduct, he was beginning to feel his age, and Florence Dugdale, who was to become his second wife, was waiting off-stage. But Emma's death in 1912 had 'altered all'.

A complimentary copy of *Satires of Circumstance* was sent to Edmund *Gosse with Hardy's comment that this was 'the mixture as before, of unstable fancies, conjectures, and contradictions'. Shortly after, on 1 December 1914, Hardy wrote to Gosse as follows: 'Some—even many—of the pieces in the volume do not precisely express my attitude to certain matters nowadays—or rather they express what I would now prefer to leave unexpressed. They had, however, been printed in periodicals in past years, so I could hardly leave them out of the book though they seem to myself harsh beside the others. There is too, in me, a little of Pilate's feeling: "What I have written I have written"' (*L* v 66).

There is here a fascinating mixture of part apology, part justification which reveals how uncertain Hardy himself is about the 'Satires'. But he came down on the side of publishing everything, as he always did. In publishing this group of poems in the first edition he made a number of changes. He increased the number of poems in the series to fifteen by adding 'In the Study', 'At the Draper's', 'On the Death-Bed', and 'In the Moonlight' (dropping 'On the Doorstep', which was not published again until James Gibson's edition of the *Complete Poems* appeared in 1976). In his autobiography Hardy refers to the attention given to the 'Satires' when they were first published in the *Fortnightly*, and describes their reception as being 'curiously blundering' (*LW* 382). In these circumstances, it is surprising that he was so upset by their reception when they were published in book-form in 1914.

Once again in the autobiography he lambasts the critics:

> Through a lack of apprehension, or wilful guile in these judges, the pieces though they had been imitated all the world over were solemnly pronounced to be 'mistaken'... the critics apparently not perceiving that they were caustically humorous productions, and issued with a light heart before the war.... So much shadow domestic and public had passed over his head since he had written the Satires that he was in no mood now to publish humour or irony, and would readily have suppressed them if they had not already gained such currency from magazine publication that he could not do it. So, by their being put into the book, and by their receiving almost exclusive notice, they were made to give a false tone to the whole volume... (*LW* 396)

All this being so, one wonders why Hardy then took the title of these satirical poetical sketches for the title of the book.

Hardy's anxiety about the 'Satires' is further seen in his uncertainty about where to place them in the volume. He seldom does anything casually; there is a reason for everything. When he came to arrange the contents of the first edition of his new collection, he divided the poems he had assembled into four groups with the titles 'Lyrics and Reveries', 'Satires of Circumstance', 'Poems of 1912–13', and 'Miscellaneous Pieces'. Shortly before publication, he added as a 'Postscript' the poem 'Men Who March Away'.

This poem, as Hardy remarked, had 'won an enormous popularity', partly because he had very generously made it free of copyright when it appeared in *The Times* on 9 September 1914, only a few weeks after the outbreak of war. Edward Thomas thought that it was 'the only good one' of the poems written at that time, and if Hardy is the 'Friend with a musing eye' who observes the soldiers with 'doubt and dolorous sigh', as he said he was, then a muted patriotism is being expressed. Hardy himself had some worries about the overall tone of the piece, and he wrote to a friend on 12 September, 'I am glad to hear that you like the verses, though I fear that they were not free from some banalities which it is difficult to keep out of lines which are meant to appeal to the man in the street, and not to "a few friends" only' (*L* v 48).

Where was he, then, to place the 'Satires'? As they provided the title of the book, it might have been presumed that they would appear first, but Hardy was not keen to give them that much prominence. His solution—an unsatisfactory compromise—was to put them rather awkwardly in the middle of his first group, which he had decided should be 'Lyrics and Reveries'. They follow 'Ah, Are You Digging on My Grave?', which could be described as yet another 'satire of circumstance', and this group ends with another nine 'lyrics'. Hardy must soon have realized that this was unsatisfactory, and when the collection appeared in the Wessex Edition in 1919 the 'Satires' were placed at the end of the book, where they remained for all later editions. It was the appropriate place for them. 'Lyrics and Reveries' was followed by 'Poems of 1912–13', and the first edition ended with 'Miscellaneous Pieces' and the 'Postscript'.

Some of the poems in the first group, 'Lyrics and Reveries', could have been placed just as appropriately in the last group, 'Miscellaneous Pieces', and vice versa. But the former are generally more personal and subjective than the latter, which frequently have a narrative element and include a few more satires of circumstance. Hardy liked to finish his volumes of poetry with a strongly personal poem, so he ends the 'Miscellaneous Pieces' with 'A Poet'. He himself is, of course, the poet, and the poem ends:

> Some evening, at the first star-ray,
> Come to his graveside, pause and say:
>
> 'Whatever the message his to tell,
> Two thoughtful women loved him well'.
> Stand and say that amid the dim:
> It will be praise enough for him.

This tribute to his two wives—the poem is dated 'July, 1914', and he had married Florence in February of that year—is heartfelt but may also be an attempt to placate Florence to some extent for the fact that Emma features so largely in the book. There is significance in the way in which, in the 'Lyrics and Reveries', Hardy has arranged the poems about the different women in his life. Florence is put first, with the two poems that are known to be about her, 'After the Visit' and 'To Meet, or Otherwise', respectively fifth and sixth in the group. Ninth comes 'When I Set Out for Lyonnesse', which is about his first meeting with Emma in 1870. It seems possible that, ironically, Emma never saw this poem, which is so radiant with Hardy's love for her. In its lyrical energy it gives the impression of having been written at the time of their first meeting. This is not emotion recollected in tranquillity. But if it was written in the first flush of love in the 1870s, why did Hardy not publish it until 1914? Presumably because, when in 1898 he was looking through the poems he had available for *Wessex Poems*, it was yet another satire of circumstance.

Florence first, Emma second (and 'The Sun on the Bookcase', which was later dated by Hardy '1870', is also about her)—who was to come third? It had to be the Honourable Mrs Florence Henniker, with whom Hardy had fallen in love in the early 1890s; he had had his love rejected, and never quite got over it. F. B. Pinion sees 'A Thunderstorm in Town' as being about Hardy's brief flirtation with Mrs Henniker, and she is present again in one of Hardy's finest poems, 'Wessex Heights', together with Emma and his love of the 1860s, Tryphena *Sparks. Mrs Henniker is the 'one rare fair woman' of 'Wessex Heights', and 'In Death Divided' is also associated with her.

But Emma dominates this opening group of poems, and at least three others are about her: 'The Spell of the Rose', 'St Launce's Revisited', and 'Where the Picnic Was'. All three were taken out of 'Lyrics and Reveries' in 1919 and put at the end of 'Poems of 1912–13'. There is no obvious reason why they were not put there in the first edition, nor can one explain why 'Under the Waterfall', which is clearly another Emma poem, was left in 'Lyrics and Reveries', unless it was written before or after 1912–13 and Hardy was being meticulously honest. These changes meant that 'Poems of 1912–13', which comprised eighteen poems in 1914, had 21 in 1919 and all later editions. The 39 poems described as 'Miscellaneous' stayed unchanged, possibly indicating Hardy's lack of a deeply personal interest in most of them.

As Hardy had a habit of writing a poem and then sitting on it for years, it is at times very difficult to know just when a particular poem was written; or, if it is dated, one wonders why it was not published in the next book of verse. *Satires of Circumstance* is, however, an exception in that it seems to be almost entirely the work of the period 1910–14. 'When I Set Out for Lyonnesse' may, as already suggested, have been written in the 1870s, as may 'The Sun on the Bookcase'; 'A Thunderstorm in Town' has the subtitle '1893' added to later editions, as was '189–' to 'In Death Divided'. The 'Poems of 1912–13' date themselves, but it is unusual to be able to date with any accuracy such a large body of verse.

One indication of Hardy's growing fame as a poet was the increasing demand from journal and magazine editors for his work, and 35 of the poems collected in the first edition of this collection had been published previously. The special nature of the 'Poems of 1912–13' may be shown by the fact that not one of them had seen periodical publication. Among the well-known periodicals which published poems from this collection were the *Fortnightly Review* (15 poems), the *English Review* (4), *Harper's Monthly Magazine* (4), the *Saturday Review* (3), and the *New Weekly* (2). Publication of this kind meant that Hardy had yet another possibility of revision, and he made good use of this. He was now in a position where he found himself having to refuse invitations from editors to contribute. Thus we find him on 9 December 1914, shortly after the publication of *Satires of Circumstance*, declining a request from the editor of the *Saturday Review* because 'I raked together all the verses I could find to fill up my late volume—a heterogeneous lot' (*L* v 68).

After the success of *The Dynasts* it was not easy for the reviewers to be as unpleasant about Hardy's verse as they had been before. He was now the Grand Old Man of English Literature, to be attacked at one's peril. This resulted in some damning with faint praise, as when the *Boston Evening Transcript* (30 December 1914) accused Hardy of having been unsuccessful in transforming himself from a novelist into a poet, but concluded by describing the poems as powerful, original, and full of ideas. What Hardy had feared did occur. Because of the title of the book and the stridency of the 'Satires', reviewers concentrated on them and almost completely ignored the far more important 'Poems of 1912–13'. And, perhaps not unnaturally, they thoroughly disliked the 'Satires'.

Hardy 'places life upon the operating table, and with an uncannily skilful knife, lays it bare to the public gaze, a shuddering, trembling mass of anguished nerves, inexpressibly vile and appalling. His poems are a valuable, but not a welcome, contribution to English poetry', wrote a reviewer in the *Globe* (26 November 1914). *The Academy* (28 November 1914) thought that this new collection proved that Hardy would never get away from the seamy side of things: 'Some of the poems are really too horrible.' Most of the 'Satires', thought *The Times Literary Supplement* (19 November 1914), should have been in prose. As always, there was criticism of his 'technical faults' and his 'awkwardness of technique'. The *Daily Telegraph* (2 December 1914) asserted that his poems rarely had music, and dismissed him as not among the greatest poets. The *Sunday Times* (22 November 1914) mentioned Hardy's 'pedantic words', and its review, like so many of the others, concentrated on the 'Satires'.

Laurence Binyon in the *Bookman* (February 1915) did comment on the 'Poems of 1912–13', describing them as 'deeply personal' and 'intense with loss'. For him the 'Satires' have 'the effect of little, deeply-bitten etchings beside large, elaborate paintings'. However, Binyon was worried by Hardy's 'steady conviction of life's irony and pain', and he was grateful for the music of 'Men Who March Away'.

By far the most sympathetic and perceptive of the reviews is that of Lytton Strachey in the *New Statesman* (19 December 1914), but then Strachey was a master of satire himself. It was, he said, a 'baffling' book; it was 'full of poetry', and yet 'also full of ugly and cumbrous expressions, clumsy metres, and flat, prosaic turns of speech'. But these blemishes were 'in reality an essential ingredient in the very essence of his work'; Hardy 'has brought the realism and sobriety of prose into the service of poetry. The result is a product of a kind very difficult to parallel in our literature.... What gives Mr Hardy's poems their unique flavour is precisely their utter lack of romanticism, their common, undecorated presentment of things. They are, in fact, modern as no other poems are.'

The collection was subject to a considerable amount of revision by Hardy, and this may be another indication of his particularly personal relationship with many of its poems. Henry Gifford's article 'Hardy's Revisions' in the special Hardy number of *Agenda* (Spring–Summer 1972) discusses some of the most interesting of the revisions. They tell the reader a great deal about the movement of Hardy's mind as he pondered over the correctness of this or that word or phrase. In 'The Voice', for example, 'Woman much missed' is 'O woman weird' in the manuscript, and 'Even to the original hat and gown' becomes 'Even to the original air-blue gown'. 'Air-blue' conveys far more than the fact that Emma was wearing a blue gown: it suggests the happiness of summer and the open air in Cornwall, and we know that Emma did wear a blue gown, something that Hardy still remembered more than 40 years later.

Edmund Gosse thought that *Satires of Circumstance* was inferior to the early collections of verse, and he was not alone in doing so. The *Academy* reviewer was of the opinion that it was not as good a collection as *Time's Laughingstocks* or *Wessex Poems*, and others were of the same mind. This seems astonishing today, when most critics regard it and *Moments of Vision* as the pinnacle of a remarkable total achievement. To some extent this is the result of a growing appreciation of the 'Poems of 1912–13', a group almost entirely ignored by the 1914 reviewers. But there were some who recognized their greatness. Harold *Child, as early as 1916, described them in his book *Thomas Hardy* as 'Perhaps the pleasantest, the most musically and suggestively beautiful poems that Hardy ever wrote. They are intimate, they are personal, they are gentle' (p. 88). In November 1919 John Middleton *Murry in the *Athenaeum* described the 'Mr Hardy of the love poems of 1912–13' as 'not a man giving way to memory in poetry; he is a great poet uttering the cry of the universe'.

Slowly, as the years have passed, this volume of poems, so unappreciated in its early years, has become ever more highly regarded. One of those who recognized its greatness right from the beginning was Virginia *Woolf, who described it in a letter to Hardy dated 17 January 1915 as the most remarkable book of poetry published in her lifetime. By 1927 John Fletcher Gould in the *Saturday Review* (12 February) was able to say that Hardy's reputation would, apart from *The Dynasts*, stand on *Satires of Circumstance* and *Moments of Vision*. Trevor Johnson's interesting analysis of ten anthologies of Hardy's poems shows that eight out of the 24 most anthologized poems come from *Satires of Circumstance* (*Victorian Poetry*, Spring–Summer 1979).

In what, then, lies the greatness of this particular book of verse? Most important of all, it has at its centre the finest group of elegies written in our language. When Emma died in 1912 Hardy was at the peak of his poetic powers, and his grief, his remorse for the wasted years of their marriage, his nostalgia for the past, and his need to relive that past and eternalize the memories of Emma, all inspired his poetical creativity and resulted in these poems of 1912–13 with their passion and deeply felt emotion. But these feelings are powerfully controlled by poetic techniques which Hardy had brought to perfection. Here we have a superb group of variations on a theme, and the reader is moved by the way in which, to use Irving Howe's words, 'What begins with an obscure private hurt ends with the common wound of experience'. In a poem like 'Beeny Cliff' the sheer permanence and beauty of the opal and sapphire sea and the chasmal beauty of 'Old Beeny' add to the poignancy of human transience.

In all of Hardy's eight volumes of verse there are great poems, but they are particularly to be found in *Satires of Circumstance*—and not just in the 1912–13 sequence. Writing about Hardy's poetry, Michael Millgate comments on 'the trenchant simplicity of his assumption that poetry was an entirely natural medium of human expression and, as such, entirely appropriate to almost any human situation' (Millgate 474), and we see this again and again in this volume. The group of poems 'Lyrics and Reveries' contains not only the love poems already mentioned (and they range widely in mood and expression) but moving tributes to Leslie *Stephen ('The Schreckhorn') and to *Swinburne ('A Singer Asleep'). Another occasional poem which has a touch of greatness about it is 'The Convergence of the Twain' (see TITANIC DISASTER). Like Milton's in 'Lycidas', Hardy's lament moves from the particular to the universal. The tragedy of the sinking of the *Titanic* becomes for Hardy a contemplation of man's hubris. The poem contrasts the luxurious, 'unsinkable' liner and its wealthy passengers with their final resting-place so many fathoms below the ocean, amid cold currents, grotesque sea-worms, and 'dim moon-eyed fishes'.

Yet another fine poem is 'Channel Firing', which, written in April 1914, has a prophetic ring about it. Working in his study at Max Gate, Hardy would in those days have heard the British Fleet at gunnery practice. The twelve-inch guns could be heard many miles away, and out of his experience Hardy makes a poem that begins humorously with God rebuking the dead, who think it must be the Judgement Day and sit up in their tombs, and ends with a serious reflection on man's militaristic stupidity and a recollection of a past which was just as warlike. Will they never learn? he seems to be asking, just a few months before the most terrible of all wars was to begin.

What stands out in these 'Lyrics and Reveries' is Hardy's ability to make great poetry out of human situations, to see the divine in the ordinary, and to 'touch our hearts by showing his own'. He does it again in 'Beyond the Last Lamp', where he immortalizes a chance meeting, on a dark and rainy night, with a pair of lovers who walk up and down slowly and sadly because of some unknown trouble. We are not told what worries them, but that does not matter: what does matter is their unhappiness and Hardy's compassion for them. 'Wessex Heights' is another outstanding poem in this group. It is an intensely personal poem and one that fascinates with its enigmatic descriptions of people and incidents in Hardy's life. But it pulsates with strong feelings in such lines as 'Well, time cures hearts of tenderness, and now I can let her go', where, like Yeats with Maud Gonne, we can feel a subtext which tells us that he can never really do so. One other of the many memorable poems in this group which needs mention is 'Ah, Are You Digging on My Grave?'. Hardy loved animals and fought to protect them from unnecessary suffering, but he refused to become sentimental about them, and must have shocked many of his readers with his final stanza, where the dog reveals that he has completely forgotten his dead mistress and digs on her grave to bury a bone for future consumption. It may seem cynical, but it has a sadness and an honesty that make it one of his best poems.

The 'Miscellaneous Poems' are indeed miscellaneous and cover many different aspects of life. One or two of them are yet again about Emma, and may be about incidents that occurred during the Max Gate years, as in 'She Charged Me'. There are several poems about unhappy marriages, which once again suggests that they were written during the last distressing years of living with Emma. Two events of national interest are used: 'A King's Soliloquy on the Night of his Funeral' imagines a meditation by the spirit of the dead King Edward VII, and 'The Coronation' is a satire about the preparations for George V's coronation in 1911 in which the kings and queens lying in Westminster Abbey speak amusingly from their tombs (as so often happens in Hardy) and we are made aware of death the leveller. Most of these poems are technically competent and remarkable in their range of subject-matter, which even includes ballad-like narrative poems such as 'The Sacrilege' and a moving poetic dramatization of Peter's denial of his association with Christ, 'In the Servants' Quarters'. Here is, indeed, God's plenty. In his mid-seventies Hardy's poetic imagination and creative ability are at their height. JCG

Schopenhauer, Arthur (1788–1860), German philosopher. Hardy's *Literary Notebooks* suggest that he may first have approached Schopenhauer through secondary sources (*LN* i 141, 170, 182–3, 203) before he read *Studies in Pessimism* in May 1891 (*LN* ii 28–31). Hardy owned *The World as Will and Idea* as well as *On the Four-Fold Root of the Principle of Sufficient Reason* and *Two Essays* (see Walter F. Wright, *The Shaping of 'The Dynasts'* (1967), 39–40). Wright traces in the *Literary Notebooks* a development of Hardy's concept of the Will in Schopenhauer, from a focus on its relation to human tragedy towards an understanding of the Will as a cosmic unconscious force, reminiscent of the Immanent Will in *The Dynasts* (Wright, 40–6). Hardy himself, however, claimed in 1908 that the Will in *The Dynasts* is 'regarded as becoming conscious; & it teaches other evolutionary doctrines that have grown up since Schopenhauer's time' (*L* iii 351), a view that also makes him 'hope' in the following year that his own philosophy is 'much more modern than Schopenhauer' (*L* iv 37).

One explicit reference to Schopenhauer in Hardy's fiction is the basically negative characterization of old Clare's determinism, defined as amounting 'on its negative side, to a renunciative philosophy which had cousinship with that of Schopenhauer and Leopardi' (*TDU* 25). Other references to Schopenhauer are somewhat ambivalent. Hardy lists Schopenhauer among the philosophers 'who have my respect' (*Thomas Hardy's Personal Writings*, ed. H. Orel (1966), 58), and contrasts him favourably with *Nietzsche (*L* v 50–1) and Maeterlinck (*LW* 338). Yet in 1924 Hardy downgrades Schopenhauer's importance: 'my pages show harmony of view with Darwin, Huxley, Spencer, Comte, Hume, Mill, and others (all of whom, as a matter of fact, I used to read more than Sch[openhauer])' (*L* vi 259). LAB

'Science of Fiction, The.' This short essay was originally contributed by Hardy to a symposium published in the *New Review* in April 1891 to which the other contributors were the French novelist Paul Bourget and Hardy's friend Walter *Besant. The piece has been well described as 'a remarkably concise and coherent statement of the fundamental issues in the current debate over realism and naturalism' (Millgate 316); elsewhere the same critic describes it as Hardy's 'most incisive critical essay', and notes the significance of its appearance shortly before the publication in volume form of *Tess of the d'Urbervilles* (*Thomas Hardy: His Career as a Novelist* (1971), 263).

Its central argument is that, while any 'artistic performance in narrative' requires a 'comprehensive and accurate knowledge of realities', beyond this basis of raw materials there are strict limits to the extent to which fiction can be regarded as a 'science': 'directly the constructive stage is entered upon, Art—high or low—begins to exist'. He adds tellingly that 'The most devoted apostle of realism, the sheerest naturalist, cannot escape, any more than the withered old gossip over her fire, the exercise of Art in his labour or pleasure of telling a tale'. He takes issue with Zola's stated views on the subject, claiming them to be at variance with the same writer's practice as a novelist, and also questions the usefulness of 'realism' ('an unfortunate, an ambiguous word') as a term of critical discourse. More broadly, he finds a source for the attitude of the realist and naturalist schools towards 'creativeness in its full and ancient sense' in the scepticism of 'a world which no longer believes in the abnormal'. A writer, Hardy concludes, needs not only acute powers of observation of the external world but 'a sensitiveness to the intrinsic' and 'a sympathetic appreciativeness of life in all of its manifestations'. See also REALISM.

Scotland. Hardy appears to have paid four visits to Scotland. On 23 August 1881 he and his wife Emma set off from *Wimborne for a tour that took them by train to Edinburgh and thence to Roslin, Hawthornden, Stirling, Callander, the Trossachs, Loch Katrine, Inversnaid, Loch Lomond, and Glasgow. Almost exactly ten years later, in September 1891, they paid a visit to Hardy's friend Sir George *Douglas at his home, Springwood Park, near Kelso, and Hardy took the opportunity to visit numerous sites associated with Sir Walter *Scott. Thirdly, in 1905, Hardy received an honorary degree from the University of Aberdeen, and visited that city in early April for the ceremony. His later account of the occasion describes it as 'like a romantic dream' (*LW* 348), and the poem 'Aberdeen' is also a product of this visit. (By the time St Andrews University followed suit, in 1922, he was too old to visit Scotland for the ceremony.) Finally, in 1909, Edinburgh was included in a tour of various cathedrals. There is one major Scots character in Hardy's fiction, Donald Farfrae in *The Mayor of Casterbridge*, in connection with whom Hardy not only takes pains to present Scots speech, but introduces references to a number of traditional Scots songs.

Scott, Walter (1771–1832; created baronet 1818), novelist and poet. He exerted an early influence on Hardy, whose first published novel, *Desperate Remedies*, bears a quotation from Scott's *The Monastery* on the title-page and later, in Crickett's remarkable marriage service words (*DR* 8.3), alludes to *The Fortunes of Nigel*. Hardy was familiar with the poetry as well as the novels, as is evident from the fact that seven of the chapter-epigraphs in *A Pair of Blue Eyes* are taken from Scott's poems—from *Marmion* and *Rokeby* as well as shorter poems he would have encountered in Palgrave's *Golden Treasury*. Hardy reached the conclusion that Scott's verse was superior to his prose; 'never ceased to regret' that Scott had later 'declined on prose fiction'; and thought *Marmion* 'the most Homeric poem in the English language' (*LW* 51). He quotes from *Marmion* again in subsequent works of fiction (*FFMC* 55; *AL* 1.4; 'Alicia's Diary'). *The Mayor of Casterbridge* (9) contains an allusion to another famous Scott poem, *The Lay of the Last Minstrel*.

Yet the 'witching pen' of Scott the novelist (the phrase is used in the poem 'An Ancient to Ancients') never ceased to attract Hardy. He bought the illustrated edition of the Waverley Novels in 48 volumes (1877–9 edition), and thought *Kenilworth* superior to the Scottish novels; its heroine is referred to in *The Woodlanders* (31). The title of Hardy's poem 'My Cicely' assumes its full significance only when Scott's Cicely, 'the beauty of the bar' in *Kenilworth* (3), is recalled. Hardy had a high admiration for another tragic novel, *The Bride of Lammermoor*, which is referred to in his essay 'The Profitable Reading of Fiction': Ravenswood, muffled in deep mourning and reclined against a pillar in the sepulchral vault after Lucy's funeral service, probably suggested the belated return of the hero in *Desperate Remedies* after the wedding of his beloved is concluded. Again, Ravenswood's sudden death when swallowed by the quicksand is recalled in *The Mayor of Casterbridge*, while his delayed return and the heroine's attempt to murder her husband are paralleled in *Tess of the d'Urbervilles*.

No wonder Sir George *Douglas found Hardy bent in deep homage over Scott's death-mask on a visit to Abbotsford in 1891. Among the 'many Scott scenes' they visited together during Hardy's Scottish tour (see SCOTLAND), Hardy selects two for special mention: the grave of Edie Ochiltree, a memorable character in *The Antiquary*, buried in Roxburgh churchyard, and Smailholm Tower, the romantic setting of Scott's ballad 'The Eve of Saint John' (a favourite with Hardy). FBP

Selected Poems. In March 1916 Hardy's publishers, Macmillan, proposed that he produce a selection from his own poems, and Hardy did so willingly, in the hope that such a volume would gain a wider public for his verse. An edition of 2,000 copies, modestly priced at half-a-crown (2*s.* 6*d.*), was published on 3 October 1916. The volume contains 120 poems (for a complete listing, see Purdy 179–87), divided into the Wordsworthian categories of 'Poems chiefly lyrical', 'Poems narrative and reflective', and 'War poems, and lyrics from "The Dynasts"' (this last category a topical gesture). They are mainly drawn from the four volumes of verse that Hardy had published by that date and *The Dynasts*, but there are also nine poems that were to be included in his fifth collection, *Moments of Vision*, which was not to be published until more than a year later.

The book was quickly reprinted, and further impressions followed. More than a decade later, and very near the end of his life, Hardy prepared a revised and expanded edition that appeared posthumously in August 1929 under the title *Chosen Poems*. This selection was made in September 1927, and was thus one of his last literary undertakings. Of its 161 poems, 45 now included for the first time were taken from the volumes of verse published subsequent to *Selected Poems* and four were newly added from earlier volumes of verse; eight that had been included in the original selection were now dropped.

serialization. It was a fact of life for the writer of fiction in the second half of the 19th century, that if he intended to make a living by his writing, he had to publish in magazines; that was where the money was. It was the publisher of his first two novels, William *Tinsley, who gave Hardy his first break; in July 1872, desperately needing a story to begin in September for his relatively new *Tinsleys' Magazine*, he asked Hardy if he could do one for £200—to include all rights (which, considering that he had paid him only £30 for the copyright of *Under the Greenwood Tree* earlier in the year, must have seemed a not unreasonable sum). Hardy wrote back to offer Tinsley the serial and first edition rights only, which the publisher accepted, perhaps with a wry smile. The work in question was *A Pair of Blue Eyes*, and it introduced Hardy in a thorough way to the rigours of writing against a deadline; he had not very much, if any, of the novel in a finished state, and in the event he was sometimes only just able to provide copy by the last moment possible, a week or so before publication—which gives some idea of the speed with which Victorian compositors could work, and the efficiency of the postal system.

From the first, most of Hardy's serialized novels were illustrated (see also ILLUSTRATIONS). Readers of most magazines expected to be given some visual sense of the characters and their environment in this way, and though there were some excellent artists working in this field, there were also others decidedly second-rate. Hardy experienced both ends of this spectrum; Pasquier's drawings for *A Pair of Blue Eyes* are mostly awful, despite having sketches from Hardy for reference; but Hardy was much luckier with his next illustrator.

Ironically it was not this first serial, but the earlier *Under the Greenwood Tree* that provided the impetus for the subsequent development in Hardy's relationship with magazines. The strongest of the monthlies that published fiction was undoubtedly the *Cornhill*; its editor, Leslie *Stephen, had read and enjoyed the rural tale, and had found out the name of its author from a mutual friend. He wrote to ask whether Hardy would be willing to offer his magazine a serial for £400. Naturally Hardy jumped at the chance; it was more than twice as much as Tinsley had given him, since it did not include book-publication rights, and the *Cornhill* would offer his work prominence in London literary culture. It also suggested that he could count on a future as a writer, enabling him to give up architecture and to marry. The serial was *Far from the Madding Crowd*.

Tinsley, editing his own magazine, had made one or two mildly critical comments on *A Pair of Blue Eyes*, but from Leslie Stephen Hardy was to learn the first serious lesson in what eventually became an intolerable school, run by magazine editors for the instruction of authors in the topics and language unsuitable for their subscribers (see also CENSORSHIP). Stephen suggested, for example, that Hardy remove all evidence of Fanny Robin's illegitimate baby, and though Hardy could not agree to this, he went a very long way to minimize its presence. Stephen commented in this instance that Hardy could of course restore the omitted details when the novel was published in book form, and to some degree he did, thus establishing another lifelong pattern, by which the first edition of a novel represented more completely than the serial what he had wished to publish; but inevitably some of the changes made at the insistence of the magazine editor remained—and remain, unless a modern critical editor has decided to restore the original readings.

Far from the Madding Crowd was stunningly successful as a serial; it gave Hardy a wide audience, and provided the basis for his reputation. A small part of the success must have been due to the generally satisfactory nature of the accompanying illustrations and decorated initials. They were by Helen *Paterson, who became the wife of the Irish poet William Allingham while the novel was running in the *Cornhill.* Hardy was taken both by the images and their maker, whom he met at Stephen's house, but, as he was later to say, mischievous fate led them to other ends: Hardy married Emma Gifford in the same year. He corresponded with Paterson about details of the story, and sent sketches of one or two rural implements for her information, but, with the one exception of *The Return of the Native,* Hardy did not after this take much of a controlling hand in choosing the subject or the organization of the illustrations of any of his novels.

Stephen naturally asked Hardy for another story; he did not get quite what he had expected when Hardy sent in *The Hand of Ethelberta,* but he continued to give advice and gentle insistence when he sensed some indelicacy that might have offended some of his readers—most of which advice Hardy again took. The *Cornhill* proof-sheets survive for *Ethelberta;* they are dated, and show clearly how in this novel (and by implication in the two earlier novels), the primary process of creation was continually interrupted by the need to revise proof for earlier episodes. The first chapters of the novel were in print before he had more than sketched out the conclusion, leaving Hardy no possibility of revising them in the light of developments that occurred to him later: such revision would have to wait until preparation for the first edition. But the appearance of words in print fixes them to a degree, and the author has to overcome a strong inertia if he wishes to alter them; and since Hardy almost invariably used the serial text as copy for the book issue, radical rethinking of the early part of a novel in the light of the later part does not happen, as it might have done if the novel had remained in manuscript to the last—or if he had completed the novel in manuscript before submitting it to a magazine. It is not surprising that under these circumstances Hardy soon came to understand that the serial versions of most of his novels were still in a state of becoming, a temporary condition to be fixed by the relative permanence of three volumes.

Leslie Stephen also helped Hardy to understand that each monthly episode of his serial ought to have its own point of interest: that he should not think of the novel just as a single narrative, but should also take thought for the design of twelve smaller segments, each preferably with an incident of significance, a climax of its own—something Dickens was a master of. When Hardy wrote at this time that he was anxious to be thought of as a 'good hand at a serial', he was thinking of this kind of lesson that he hoped to absorb (as well as of his future livelihood).

A second potential source of serial income was from America, where the magazines paid well. Almost always Hardy sent copies of English proofs to America, sometimes in a somewhat different state of revision from the English proofs. Thus the American serial would often be doubly different from the English—as a result of Hardy's revision, and also as a result of the American editor and printer imposing their own standards and style. Hardy never read proof of an American serialization—not even of *Two on a Tower,* which was serialized exclusively in the *Atlantic Monthly* in 1881, occasioning some anxiety, with duplicate manuscripts being sent off across the Atlantic by different mailings.

In 1877 Hardy had some trouble in finding a purchaser for *The Return of the Native:* Leslie Stephen was disturbed by Hardy's outline, and wanted to see the whole thing before deciding; Blackwood, another leading editor, was fully committed. Eventually, needing money fairly promptly but with the writing unfinished, Hardy was obliged to come to terms with Chatto and Windus's *Belgravia,* and to return to the level of pay of *Far from the Madding Crowd*—still quite satisfactory. Also satisfying was the relationship he established with Arthur Hopkins, Gerard Manley's brother, who had been asked to draw the illustrations for *Belgravia*; Hardy's comments affected several of the pictures, the drawings of Eustacia Vye in particular. Hardy felt to the full the irony of his wildest fictional environment appearing in a magazine called *Belgravia*, and he must have enjoyed equally the experience of dealing with the Reverend Donald Macleod, a Presbyterian minister and editor of *Good Words*, in which *The Trumpet-Major* appeared. There was no real chance of offending him with this narrative, but Sunday-travelling was forbidden, as well as any hint of taking the Lord's name in vain. At this stage of his career Hardy was still able to accept the requirement for such revisions with wry amusement.

His next commission could have been his greatest opportunity. Hardy had established a good relationship with the American publishing firm of *Harper & Brothers, and when they decided to set up a European edition of *Harper's Monthly Magazine* in 1880 they asked Hardy to provide the lead serial. Unfortunately he became severely ill soon after starting *A Laodicean*, and had to dictate the remainder of the novel from his bed to his wife. Inevitably the result was disappointing, to Hardy and his audience.

When the *Graphic* asked Hardy for a serial in 1884, Hardy was faced with a different kind of problem, for the *Graphic* was published weekly rather than monthly, but the same fundamental criterion obtained: an incident to grasp the reader's attention in each episode. There was a further difference, in that the *Graphic* was essentially a magazine that depended for its reputation upon its illustrations, and required that the author of a serial submit the whole novel to the illustrator before publication began. So for once Hardy had finished writing before the first episodes began appearing in print: a new experience for him. (The illustrator was Robert Barnes, not a name to conjure with, but the majority of his drawings have grace and power, the large format of the *Graphic* permitting more dramatic effects for an artist who could use the space.)

These two conditions contributed substantially to the uniqueness of *The Mayor of Casterbridge* in Hardy's fictional output. It is perhaps the most deliberately considered of his novels, though others run it close, among them *The Return of the Native* and *Tess of the d'Urbervilles*; the pressure of deadlines was not a bad thing in itself, though Hardy usually regretted the compromises it necessitated, but it did not allow him second or third thoughts. And yet this is the novel he felt he had disfigured the most, artistically speaking, because of the multiplicity of incidents he had felt obliged to include; and though he removed a few for the first edition, he was unable to rework the novel as he thought it should be reworked. It is a characteristic aspect of Hardy's attitude to his texts that he was very anxious to refine what he had written, and at certain times anxious to reshape one or two significant narrative threads or character traits, but he was, with one exception, absolutely unwilling to do any major rewriting, even of a serial that he was clear was unrepresentative of his original intention.

Hardy had tried hard with *The Mayor of Casterbridge* to reconcile his art with a conscientious duty towards the magazine reader of the novel. The result had not pleased him, and his attitude to serialization hardened. It became a necessary source of income, but nothing more. If editors would buy his name and reputation, he was content; he would do anything they required. He tried, for instance, to get his next novel, *The Woodlanders*, published serially in America by offering to cut it as much as the editor required, seeing his novel in magazine form as merchandise rather than (instead of as well as) art.

With this novel, published without illustrations in *Macmillan's Magazine* in England, Hardy was forced to return to the old pattern of having to write from hand to mouth to keep ahead of the printer, and it might be thought that he would have been pleased to write for the *Graphic* again. But the disasters associated with *A Group of Noble Dames* and the initial difficulties surrounding the serial publication of *Tess of the d'Urbervilles* finally fixed his attitude to serialization. If the editors with whom he dealt did indeed represent accurately the desires and attitudes of their readership, then Hardy could no longer believe they cared in the slightest for the kind of truths that he was interested in embodying in his writing; consequently, the readers of *A Group of Noble Dames* and *Tess* in the *Graphic* were given mangled, vitiated stories, and Hardy did not care. When asked by the *Graphic* how *Tess* should be broken up episodically, since he had given no indication on the manuscript, Hardy replied that breaks could be made at any convenient place—implying that he had made no attempt to pay attention to the design of the novel as a serial. The novel was also unfortunate in its illustrations—normally a primary concern of the *Graphic*—for Sir Hubert Herkomer farmed out three-quarters of the work to members of his studio, and thus there are substantially different versions of the major characters from week to week (though it must be added that some of Herkomer's own designs are amongst the most powerfully memorable of any serial illustrations to Hardy's work).

It is a measure of Hardy's understanding of what would be forbidden him by most magazine editors, and the editor of the *Graphic* in particular, that before submitting the manuscript of *Tess* he abstracted from it the episodes of Tess's violation and the baptism of her child, and published them as separate short stories in more receptive journals—a process he called in his autobiography 'the dismemberment of a novel'. In place of the scene in the Chase, Hardy gave the readers of the *Graphic* Tess's cursory account of how Alec had taken her to be married before a fake registrar, a trick she had only discovered weeks afterwards. He also made dozens of other smaller bowdlerizations just for the *Graphic*.

For the most part the remoteness of the American market did not lead Hardy to give much thought to the potential differences between his two largest audiences, but by the 1890s he had come to recognize that they were considerable. When he was forced into gross bowdlerization of *A Group of Noble Dames* and *Tess*, Hardy felt, correctly, that his American audience would accept the original narratives (though in the case of *Tess* he could not restore the massively excised portions, since he was working with proofs of the English serial). And so, in New York and Boston, they were allowed to know that Tess had sexual relations with Alec although she knew they were not married, when in London and Edinburgh readers were not.

He must have hoped that when he agreed to write *Jude the Obscure* for *Harper's Monthly* he would have been able to meet American ideas of what was acceptable in serial fiction: indeed he told the editor at first 'that it would be a tale that could not offend the most fastidious maiden' (Purdy 89). But by the time he was well into writing the novel, he recognized that he was going in directions that would be unacceptable to any magazine, and asked to cancel the agreement; the publishers, however, objected, and Hardy was forced into more of the same kind of bowdlerization that he had made for *Tess*. On the other hand, Hatherell's illustrations were among Hardy's favourites, and he hung them on his study wall at Max Gate.

It is only possible to speculate, but it seems likely that Hardy had decided by 1897 that he could finally afford to do without the financial boost that serialization gave to a novel, if it meant that he would have to 'do despite to his best imaginative instincts by arranging a *dénouement* which he knows to be unreal and meretricious, but dear to the Grundyist and subscriber', as he wrote in an 1890 essay titled *'Candour in English Fiction'. In this essay Hardy explicitly blames 'the magazine in particular and the circulating library in general' for the *de facto* censorship which prevented the exploration in contemporary English literature of the 'subjects that have been made, by general approval of the best judges, the bases of the finest imaginative compositions since literature rose to the dignity of an art'. The consequence he describes angrily as 'the charlatanry pervading so much of English fiction'. Hardy gave up writing novels for a complex of reasons, including his relative affluence after the success of *Tess of the d'Urbervilles*, his perennial desire to write poetry rather than prose, and his awareness that the themes he was now interested in were hard to embody in the realist novel he had become accustomed to write; but not least among the reasons was his disgust at the treatment he was forced to give to the serializations of his finest fiction. SJG

Simon Gatrell, *Hardy the Creator* (1988).

sexuality. Hardy's exploration of sexuality is most obvious in his frequent portrayal of peripheral forms of sexuality. His first published novel, *Desperate Remedies* (1870), contains a suggestion of possible lesbianism. Miss Aldclyffe, who is interviewing the ladylike Cytherea Graye for the job of lady's maid, is described as largely masculine and is so smitten with Cytherea's looks that she hires her without writing for a reference. After Miss Aldclyffe's characteristic temper tantrum one evening, Cytherea threatens to leave the next morning. That night, however, Miss Aldclyffe whispers through the keyhole of Cytherea's bedroom, '"Let me come in, darling"', and once in bed kisses her warmly, asks to be kissed back as warmly, and sets herself up as a rival to Cytherea's suitor ('"Don't let any man stand between us"'). It is true that Miss Aldclyffe, having discovered that Cytherea, who shares her first name, is the daughter of the man she loved and abandoned, is offering to love her as a mother, but few mothers love so extravagantly: '"Put your hair round your mamma's neck, and give me one good long kiss."' 'This vehement imperious affection... was not of the kind that Cytherea's instincts desired', we are told. Nothing, however, follows from this spectacular scene, except perhaps Cytherea's promotion to 'companion' to keep her contented, and the later remark that she 'never cared to go to Miss Aldclyffe's room, though she was always welcome there'.

Another aspect of sexuality in this novel is Cytherea's frightening meeting with Aeneas Manston in a thunderstorm, and the touching of their clothes, which stimulates her sexually and causes him to fall in love with her. She, however, comes to fear him in earnest, without sexual titillation, and he turns out to be a murderer. Their initial meeting looks forward to the meeting of Bathsheba and Troy in *Far from the Madding Crowd*, when their clothes become entangled in the darkness of her garden. Cytherea's fear of Manston as they are about to be married looks forward to the emotions of later heroines toward their sadistic lovers—Grace Melbury's fear of Fitzpiers in *The Woodlanders*, and Tess's fear of Alec in *Tess of the d'Urbervilles*—except that the later heroines themselves also feel sexual emotions.

Homosexuality is suggested again in Henchard's sudden and excessive passion for Farfrae in *The Mayor of Casterbridge*, which is striking after Henchard's coolness toward women. (The homosexuality is on Henchard's side.) We read of Farfrae's slight stature compared to Henchard's masculine bulk, and of Henchard's prolonged 'holding [of] the young man's hand' as he tries to persuade Farfrae not to go to America, offering him residence with him and any business deal he wants (9). Henchard's turning against Farfrae when the latter challenges him for power might be interpreted either as leading away from the hypothesis of homosexuality or as showing Henchard's continuingly excessive preoccupation with Farfrae. Their wrestling combat begins erotically (Henchard 'gazed upon the lowered eyes of his fair antagonist'), but the details lead our thoughts away from eros toward power (38). Critical comment on the Henchard–Farfrae relationship ranges from Elaine Showalter's 'There is nothing homosexual in their intimacy' ('The Unmanning of The Mayor of Casterbridge', in *Critical Approaches to the Fiction of Thomas Hardy*, ed. Dale Kramer (1979), 107), to H. M. Daleski's acceptance of the homosexual dimension (*Thomas Hardy and the Paradoxes of Love* (1997), 123–4).

Most important is Hardy's understanding of sadomasochism, which to some extent came from *Swinburne, whose poetry he admired. Edmund *Gosse, Hardy's friend and Swinburne's biographer, wrote that Swinburne had 'prepared the way for an ultimate appreciation of Mr. Hardy' (quoted in Richard D. McGhee, '"Swinburne Planteth, Hardy Watereth": Victorian Views of Pain and Pleasure in Human Sexuality', in *Sexuality and Victorian Literature*, ed. D. R. Cox (1984), 84).

In his first major novel, *Far from the Madding Crowd* (1874), Hardy explores the sadomasochistic implications of the master–servant relationship in the way the masterful Bathsheba torments Gabriel Oak, her suitor-turned-employee, but also thrills sexually when brutally subdued by her servant's lover, Sergeant Troy. Sexual excitement passes between Gabriel and Bathsheba as she watches him shear a frightened ewe: '"She blushes at the insult", murmured Bathsheba, watching the pink flush' spread across the ewe (22). The invisible body-contact of her nocturnal meeting with Troy excites Bathsheba because of its outrageousness. This scene leads to the sealing of their union in the spectacular sword exercise scene, which, with its phallic and sadomasochistic symbolism, reveals to Bathsheba a stratum of sexual desire she knows nothing about. She stands still while Troy makes sword cuts within a hair's breadth of her body, making her feel penetrated: '"Have you run me through?"' The experience becomes psychologically an act of intercourse: 'She felt powerless to withstand or deny him' (27).

The relation between Tess and Alec also illustrates the sadomasochism implicit in the master–servant relationship. On their first meeting, when she is offered a job, he insists on feeding her strawberries in a sexually suggestive way: Tess ate 'in a half-pleased, half-reluctant state.... She obeyed like one in a dream' (*TDU* 5). This is the pattern of her later rape-seduction by Alec on the night when, despite her determined resistance to him, she suddenly leaps behind Alec on his horse, and allows herself to be carried into the dark wood, where she conveniently falls asleep. When Alec, near the end of the novel, insists that Tess return to him, she strikes him across the mouth with her heavy glove, drawing blood and crying, '"Now punish me!"' Alec in replying fulfils the role required of him: '"I was your master once! I will be your master again"' (47). Alec's blood points toward Tess's bloody murder of him: '"I feared long ago, when I struck him on the mouth with my glove, that I might do it some day"' (54).

Most of these novels turn on a contrast between the sexually ardent, sadistic lover, who initially attracts or wins the heroine, and the less ardent, more idealistic lover, who in most cases ultimately wins her. In *Tess* the less ardent lover is Angel Clare, who, because of his idealism, leaves Tess after she confesses on their wedding night to her affair with Alec. In *The Woodlanders*, the less ardent lover is the too spiritual Giles Winterborne, who willingly resigns to Fitzpiers his claim to Grace. The exception is Gabriel Oak in *Far from the Madding Crowd*, who is just as ardent as Troy but in a gentle, self-sacrificing way, offering Bathsheba support, as his phallic last name suggests, and spiritual enlightenment, as is suggested by his first name recalling the angel Gabriel. Gabriel is the best example in Hardy of a successfully normal sexuality; he is more convincingly rooted in the body than is Diggory Venn in *The Return of the Native*, another faithful, self-sacrificing lover. The marriage in the end of Bathsheba and Gabriel is offered as a model because the two are partners in both a working and a love relationship, a similarity of pursuits, 'romance growing up in the interstices of a mass of hard prosaic reality' (*FFMC* 56).

With the portrayal of Sue Bridehead in what is in effect his last novel, *Jude the Obscure* (1896), Hardy introduces a new problem in sexuality; for Sue does not desire, or desires little, a sexual relationship. She resists intercourse with her husband Phillotson; and after she has left him for Jude, she refuses to marry Jude, though she sleeps with him occasionally. After the deaths of their children, her return as a penance to Phillotson is initially a way of escaping sex altogether. Sue's fear of sex contradicts her commitment at the beginning to a neo-Pagan, anti-Christian ideal of free love.

The standard comments on Sue are represented by Edmund Gosse's 'She is a poor maimed "degenerate"... ready to... play at loving though she cannot love' (review in *Cosmopolis*, January 1896; repr. in *CH*), and D. H. *Lawrence's 'Sue is scarcely a woman at all' (*Study of Thomas Hardy*, in *Phoenix: The Posthumous Papers*, ed. E. D. McDonald (1936), 496). Recent feminist critics, however, argue that Sue is not deficient sexually, but is attempting to retain control of her body and sexuality. Her reserve, as Penny Boumelha puts it, is connected with the intellectual 'woman's sense of selfhood' (*Thomas Hardy and Women* (1982), 143). The sexual problems of Sue and Jude are part of Hardy's critique of idealism running through *Jude* and most of his other novels. Hardy explores sexuality as an aspect of his exploration of society with its problems of class and gender. See also WOMEN. RL

Margaret R. Higonnet (ed.), *The Sense of Sex: Feminist Perspectives on Hardy* (1993).

Rosemarie Morgan, *Women and Sexuality in the Novels of Thomas Hardy* (1988).

Shakespeare, William (1564–1616). It is evident from the numerous quotations from and allusions to Shakespeare's plays and poems throughout his work, from the 1860s

Notebook onwards, that Hardy was deeply immersed in Shakespeare. He bought the complete works in *Knight's Illustrated Edition* (1859), and as a young man in London frequented Samuel Phelps's productions at Drury Lane, following the performance in the text (*LW* 54). In 1916 he contributed the poem 'To Shakespeare after Three Hundred Years' to *A Book of Homage*, invoking Shakespeare's 'Bright baffling soul, least capturable of themes' (*LW* 368).

The comparison between Hardy and Shakespeare became commonplace among Victorian critics. Charles Whibley elected him 'the Shakespeare of his generation' (*CH* 420–1). Lord David Cecil, looking back from the 1940s, considered Hardy 'the last English writer to be built on the Shakespearean scale' (*Hardy the Novelist* (1943), 153). Cecil's view had been implicit in Virginia *Woolf's estimate of Hardy in her 1932 essay 'The Novels of Thomas Hardy' as 'the greatest tragic writer among English novelists'.

Among earlier critics, Edmund *Gosse's 'the Shakespearean richness of his humour' (*CH* 169) may stand for the reiterated praise of Hardy's rustics. Modern critics are divided on this point: Douglas Brown suggests that 'Hardy's sense of the facts of village life is far more important than his concealed memories of Shakespeare's rustics': Brown finds that in *Far from the Madding Crowd* 'the stylization is flawed, the whole manner over-insistent' (*Thomas Hardy* (1954), 49–50). Jean Brooks, however, considers the 'rustics' conversation full of pithy humour and a proverbial wisdom that is Shakespearean as well as Hardeian' (*Thomas Hardy: The Poetic Structure* (1971), 175). Neither Hardy's nor Shakespeare's rustics are strictly 'realistic'. Desmond Hawkins judges that 'the interplay of low comedy and high tragedy... is perhaps Hardy's greatest achievement—to find a parallel to it in English one really needs to look back to Shakespeare' ('Thomas Hardy and Radio', in *Thomas Hardy and the Modern World*, ed. F. B. Pinion (1974), 66).

Hardy's tragic protagonists have suggested Shakespearian parallels. Outstanding among them is Tess, whom W. P. Trent in 1892 thought 'fit to set in the gallery of Shakespeare's women' (*CH* 234)—and this despite Hardy's 'pessimism', which seemed a marked contrast with Shakespeare. Hardy's citation of 'As flies to wanton boys are we to the gods, | They kill us for their sport' (*King Lear*, IV i 36–7) in the preface to the fifth and later editions of *Tess of the d'Urbervilles* helps to underline this contrast, for the words are those of the despairing Gloucester, not his creator, who unlike Hardy never speaks authorially. In *Tess* (35) Hardy puts Lear's words into Angel Clare's mouth: '"You were more sinned against than sinning, that I admit"' (cf. *King Lear* III ii 60).

Another significant echo is in the final chapter of *The Mayor of Casterbridge*, of whose protagonist, Michael Henchard, the narrator comments, 'It was a part of his nature to extenuate nothing', close to Othello's dying admonition, 'Nothing extenuate...' (*Othello* v ii 342). Early on in writing *The Mayor*, Hardy had attended a strolling players' performance of *Othello*. Especially appropriate to this novel is A. J. Guerard's observation that 'Hardy recognized—as Shakespeare did three centuries before him—that the guilty not merely flagellate themselves but also thrust themselves in the way of bad luck; *create* what appear to be unlucky accidents' (*Thomas Hardy: The Novels and Stories* (1949), 146). R. A. Scott-James puts the matter perhaps more deeply, comparing Henchard to Lear as one embroiled in 'the tragedy of his own soul' (*Thomas Hardy* (1951), 26). In a less intense vein, Clym Yeobright in *The Return of the Native* was 'conceived, at least in the beginning, as a kind of Hamlet' (Leonard W. Dean, 'Heroism and Pathos in *The Return of the Native*', in *Hardy: The Tragic Novels*, ed. R. P. Draper (1975), 126), but the parallel is not sustained in this novel, the tragic-heroic interest transferring to Eustacia.

Overall, Hardy's approximately 150 allusions in his fiction to Shakespeare accord with his considering the playwright's 'distinction as a minister to the theatre... infinitesimal beside his distinction as a poet, man of letters, and seer of life', Hardy even prophesying that Shakespeare 'will some day cease altogether to be acted, and be simply studied' (*LW* 368). So Hardy actually opposed the foundation of a Memorial Theatre. F. B. Pinion reflects this attitude when he writes of Hardy that 'Incidental thoughts in Shakespeare impressed him, but it was the expression, or the poetry in Shakespeare, which fascinated Hardy more than anything else' ('"Chance, Choice, and Charity": Hardy and the Future of Civilization', in *Thomas Hardy and the Modern World* (1974), 71).

The clearest stylistic influences are in Hardy's earlier work. In his poetry of the 1860s, it appears in his use of the Shakespearian sonnet, exactly or with variations (see 'Hap' and the first and fourth poems in the sequence 'She, to Him'). William F. Buckler comments that 'Hardy put the Petrarchan sonnet to highly economical dramatic uses, concentrating into the conventions of the Shakespearean sonnet the meditative intensity of a Shakespearean soliloquy' (*The Poetry of Thomas Hardy* (1983), 201). By contrast, efforts to read the later *The Dynasts* as Shakespearian are not wholly convincing (see Harold Child in *CH* 366–71; Edmund Blunden, *Thomas Hardy* (1942), 232–4). In the fiction, there is the influence of *As You Like It* on the pastoral novel *Under the Greenwood Tree*, pervasive as *leitmotif* from the title onwards: according to Michael Millgate, '*As You Like It* was a lively presence in [Hardy's] imagination, prompting by its structural incorporation of music, song and dance his own adoption of comparable techniques, encouraging and sustaining him in his choice of a pastoral theme and treatment' (*Thomas Hardy: Three Pastoral Novels*, ed. R. P. Draper (1987), 99). Fittingly, in Hardy's 'Apology' prefaced to *Late Lyrics and Earlier*, the poet is described in Prospero's words as 'the shaper of such stuff as dreams are made on' (cf. *The Tempest* iv i 156). MT

Shelley, Percy Bysshe (1792–1832), poet. He may have influenced Hardy's thought more than any other writer. For Hardy, he was the 'Poet of Liberty' (*JO* 6.9), and the one whom he wished above all he could meet 'in the Elysian fields', because he was the champion of the oppressed (*L* ii 144). Hardy loved to remember that as a child he had stayed at the Cross-Keys, Clerkenwell, the inn where Shelley met Mary Godwin at weekends (*LW* 22); he visited in 1899 St Mildred's, Bread Street, London, the church where they were married (*LW* 327); and he never missed an opportunity of seeing places associated with 'that greatest of all our lyrists' (*L* vi 101). Of the illustrious group who had lived near Lake Geneva, Shelley in Mont Alegre cottage and Byron not far off in the Villa Diodati, Hardy had romantic memories in 1897: 'Ah, but *they* are gone now, and care for their chosen nooks no more!' (*LW* 313). In Italy, in the summer of 1887, he had visited Shelley's grave, an occasion commemorated in the poem 'Rome: At the Pyramid of Cestius'; had been prompted by the 'Ecstatic heights of thought and rhyme' in Shelley's 'To a Sky-Lark' to spend time near Leghorn (see the poem 'Shelley's Skylark'); and had been reminded of Shelley's 'Lines written among the Euganean Hills' as he passed them in the train. John Stuart *Mill's essay *On Liberty*, which Hardy had known 'almost by heart' in 1865, conspired with Shelley's revolutionary zeal to produce the multifarious satire of Hardy's first, unpublished, and lost novel *The Poor Man and the Lady*, 'the author's views... being those of a young man with a passion for reforming the world' (*LW* 58–64).

In *Queen Mab* Shelley stresses Nature's ruthlessness in terms of 'ceaseless frost', and frost becomes the symbol of grief and tyranny in his *The Revolt of Islam*. In Hardy's own writings, frost (or, more generally, winter) is a frequent symbol of endurance and suffering in deprivation and adversity, suggesting graphic scenes both early in *Desperate Remedies* and much later in *Tess of the d'Urbervilles*. The 'Frost's decree' ('The Caged Thrush Freed and Home Again') occurs frequently in his writings: see also 'Discouragement' (one of his earliest poems), 'Heiress and Architect', 'Before Knowledge', 'In Tenebris I', and 'Family Portraits', where 'fear fell upon me like frost' echoes a phrase used in *Two on a Tower* (28), 'fear sharp as a frost'. To Hardy frost always suggested that 'something is imminent of a tragic nature' (*L* ii 211), and its wintry overtones are implicit in the title of his last collection of poems, *Winter Words*.

One stanza of Shelley's lyric 'When the lamp is shattered' was much in Hardy's mind during his early years as a writer of fiction: he quotes from it in *Desperate Remedies* (6.2) as well as in the story *An Indiscretion in the Life of an Heiress* (which uses material from *The Poor Man and the Lady*), and its bird imagery, inimical sun, grey (frosted) leaves, and disillusionment with love combine to form the wintry scene of the fine early poem 'Neutral Tones'.

Queen Mab also refers to Nature as the 'world's mother', a concept incongruously expressed by the heroine of *Desperate Remedies* (13.1; see also *FFMC* 36), and made explicit in the poem 'The Mother Mourns'. Among the notes to Shelley's poem are some that affected Hardy's thinking. The statement that 'Love withers under constraints; its very essence is liberty' is a conviction held by Sue Bridehead in *Jude the Obscure*, while Hardy's own agreement with Shelley's claim that a couple should remain united only as long as they love each other is expressed both in that novel and in *The Woodlanders*. Again, Hardy's poem 'The Christening' reflects Shelley's statement that if a woman obeys 'the instinct of unerring nature', society, 'the pure and virtuous matron... casts her as an abortion from her undefiled bosom'. Among other poems by Shelley quoted in Hardy's fiction are the ode 'To the West Wind' (*TDU* 36), the 'Stanzas Written in Dejection near Naples' (*HE* 27), and 'The Witch of Atlas' (*W* 33). The most frequently alluded to are probably *The Revolt of Islam* (*MC* 44, 45; *WB* 2.1, 2.23; *W* 16; *JO* 5.4) and *Adonais* (*HE* 17; *W* 27; *D* 3.1.9). *The Revolt of Islam* also provides the epigraph on the title-page of *The Well-Beloved* as well as two further allusions in that novel (2.1, 2.23); the whole novel, indeed, is permeated by Shelley's version of Platonic idealism. Shelley's poem *Hellas*, and especially its image of hope's 'iris of delight', is recalled in two of Hardy's poems, 'To Outer Nature' and 'On a Fine Morning'.

Two other poems by Shelley that were especially significant to Hardy are *The Sensitive Plant* and *Epipsychidion*. Fitzpiers quotes from the latter as he rides towards the 'lodestar' of his desire (*W* 28), and Hardy had lines 75–82 of the same poem in mind in connection with his idealized feelings for Florence *Henniker (*L* ii 44)—as Jude likewise did in relation to Sue (*JO* 3.9). Shelley's supreme work in the cause of freedom is *Prometheus Bound*, and its greatest influence on Hardy is to be found in *The Dynasts*, where Shelley's lyrical choruses suggested Hardy's aerial spirits, his chorus of Pities, and other elements. FBP

Shirley, Arthur. See RELIGION.

short story. Though a prolific writer of short fiction, Hardy is not associated so readily with the genre as Edgar Allan Poe, Nathaniel Hawthorne, or Henry James—perhaps because the British literary marketplace of the 19th century, in contrast to the American, favoured three-volume novels over narratives of lesser length. In England the publication of stories was generally confined to the popular periodical press, while educated reviewers gave consideration chiefly to hardbound books. Hardy pointedly complained that 'in England' there was 'very little to be made commercially out of short tales', and that publishers were 'as a rule shy of them, except those that [were] written by people who cannot write long ones successfully—an odd exception!—and have established a speciality in that line' (*L* ii 37).

Hardy's position as a writer of short narratives was therefore anomalous: when he began publishing stories in noticeable numbers after 1874, he was already viewed as a specialist in long fiction, and he did not collect any of his short works in volume form until the appearance in 1888 of *Wessex Tales*. At that point in his career, Hardy could use his considerable reputation as a novelist to market the short fiction in a venue less ephemeral than the magazine, and could thus present the stories for the first time to British reviewers. Even so, he was defensive when recommending the stories to the publishing firm of Macmillan: 'Some well-known critics have often advised me to reprint them, informing me that they are as good as anything I have ever written (however good that may be)' (*L* i 174). Macmillan's response was to publish *Wessex Tales* in two volumes, a format that helped to foster the respectful and enthusiastic response the book received from readers and critics.

Not coincidentally, this collection also served indirectly to advertise the novels by emphasizing the interconnectedness of the entire fictional corpus. The first instance in any of Hardy's titles of the word 'Wessex', the volume contained traditional 'tales' which, like the novels up to that point, were set in south-western England during the earlier decades of the 19th century (it was grouped with the 'Novels of Character and Environment' in the 1912 Wessex Edition), and featured a narrative voice that mimicked the style of the ballad or the oral tale. The five stories in the original *Wessex Tales*—'The

Three Strangers', 'The Withered Arm', 'Fellow-Townsmen', 'Interlopers at the Knap', and 'The Distracted Preacher'—were thus an important part of Hardy's increasingly self-conscious strategy to identify his works with a particular regionalized past. In his 1896 preface to *Wessex Tales*, Hardy insisted on factual sources for even the most extraordinary events in these stories, and simultaneously on the status of these fictions as 'but dreams, and not records'. As with Casterbridge, which he was later to call both 'a dream-place' and 'a sort of essence of [Dorchester] as it used to be' (*LW* 378–9), the physical and historical settings in *Wessex Tales* establish it as a miniature version of the fictional universe inhabited by all of Hardy's narratives, short and long.

Such similarities between the stories and the novels, however, lie more in the content of the two kinds of narrative than in formal elements. For when the novels' typically sporadic moments of melodrama are framed by the form of the story, the effect is one of distillation: unmitigated by the longer rhythms of the novel, the unrealistic devices of Hardy's fiction—its contrivances, incongruities, and narrative intrusions—stand out in the stories in all their meta-fictional intensity. The very extremity of effect in the shorter narratives, in other words, gives them the potential to be radically experimental. Such an understanding of the stories sheds light on *A *Group of Noble Dames*, a collection of tales different in style and tone from anything else Hardy wrote. The volume is structured as a story cycle in which the speakers, members of the Wessex Field and Antiquarian Club, are forced indoors by inclement weather and tell their 'curious tales of fair dames' as substitutions for their accustomed 'regulation papers on deformed butterflies, fossil ox-horns, prehistoric dungmixens, and such like' ('The First Countess of Wessex'). These circumstances provide an ironizing context both for the extravagant content of the stories and for their sometimes complacent and prurient tone. These 18th-century women, whose histories date back much further than Hardy's standard 'Wessex' narratives, are not unlike the extinct, stuffed birds displayed in the museum where the amateur natural historians tell their stories: unknowable at multiple levels—alien in time, gender, and class from these middle-class men—the dames none the less are the focus for obsessive, myopic analysis. The information in the stories is loosely based on accounts of actual families in John *Hutchins's *History and Antiquities of the County of Dorset*, but the extent to which these narratives digress from and embellish the historical source draws attention to their status, clearly expressed in their categorization, for the Wessex Edition, as 'Romances and Fantasies'.

Even before its publication, *A Group of Noble Dames* was a controversial text. It was submitted to the *Graphic* in 1890 as a short novel in the form of six stories: 'Barbara of the House of Grebe', 'The Marchioness of Stonehenge', 'Lady Mottisfont', 'The Lady Icenway', 'Squire Petrick's Lady', and 'Anna, Lady Baxby'. The editor, however, was quick to demand changes, and the British periodical publication of the work (unlike the American) was heavily bowdlerized. For volume-publication in 1891, however, Hardy restored the stories to their earlier form and added four narratives that had previously appeared in periodicals. Of these, a significantly revised version of 'The First Countess of Wessex' was placed first in the volume, while three other stories were attached to the end: 'The Lady Penelope', 'The Duchess of Hamptonshire', and 'The Honourable Laura'.

Given the unconventional sexual careers of many of the dames, it is not surprising that the book received mixed reviews, both at the time of its publication and thereafter. In response to a particularly vitriolic assessment by the *Pall Mall Gazette*, Hardy emphasized the distancing device of the story framework: 'to guard against the infliction of "a hideous and hateful fantasy", as you call it, the action is thrown back into a second plane or middle distance, being described by a character to characters, and not point-blank by author to reader' (*Pall Mall Gazette*, 10 July 1891).

This kind of intra-diegetical narration was unusual for Hardy, however, and after *Noble Dames* he returned to the extra-diegetical perspective typical of his early stories, though now the focus was often placed on the contemporary scene rather than on the earlier decades of the 19th century. Thus startling reversals in plot were no longer mediated by the voice of oral tradition, but instead were presented directly as examples of late 19th-century domestic life; and Hardy's adaptation of structures from Greek drama, always an influence on his plots, was modified by his more recent contact with late Victorian drama, especially the works of *Ibsen, which were appearing in translation on London stages throughout the 1890s. The result was a series of narratives critiquing the social mores of Hardy's own time and presenting contemporary domestic life as tragic. He described this new notion of tragedy in *'Candour in English Fiction', an essay published in 1890, where he argued for a 'revived presentation' of classical 'high tragedy' characterized by an 'original treatment' that shows 'Nature's unconsciousness not of essential laws, but of those laws framed merely as social expedients by humanity'. This different understanding of tragedy as grounded in social rather than 'essential' laws also gave a satiric and even farcical dimension to Hardy's revision of the form.

This peculiar version of tragicomedy is suggested by the title of Hardy's 1894 volume of short stories, *Life's Little Ironies*, whose 'Tales', most of them contemporary, variously demonstrate the ways in which Victorian social codes could interfere with the achievement of individual happiness. This collection, published by *Osgood, McIlvaine, contained nine stories, all of which had been previously published in periodicals: 'The Son's Veto', 'For Conscience' Sake', 'A Tragedy of Two Ambitions', 'On the Western Circuit', 'To Please His Wife', 'The Melancholy Hussar of the German Legion', 'The Fiddler of the Reels', and 'A Tradition of Eighteen Hundred and Four'. For the 1912 Wessex Edition, which categorized *Life's Little Ironies*, along with *Wessex Tales*, among the 'Novels of Character and Environment', Hardy removed to *Wessex Tales* 'The Melancholy Hussar' and 'A Tradition of Eighteen Hundred and Four', both set in the early 19th century, and added at the beginning of the volume 'An Imaginative Woman', a narrative with a contemporary setting that had been collected in the 1896 reprint of *Wessex Tales* in the Osgood, McIlvaine Wessex Novels Edition.

Life's Little Ironies also included, as its subtitle announces, *Some Colloquial Sketches Entitled A Few Crusted Characters*, a work that had originally appeared as 'Wessex Folk' in *Harper's New Monthly Magazine* in 1891. This minor cycle, intermittently light and elegiac, features a group of villagers travelling in a carrier's van as John Lackland, whose family had emigrated to North America 35 years before, returns to his native Longpuddle. The 'Crusted Characters' swap stories about their shared past, many of them farcical, a few of them horrifically grim: 'Tony Kytes, the Arch-Deceiver', 'The History of the Hardcomes', 'The Superstitious Man's Story', 'Andrey Satchel and the Parson and Clerk', 'Old Andrey's Experience as a Musician', 'Absent-Mindedness in a Parish Choir', 'The Winters and the Palmleys', 'Incident in the Life of Mr George Crookhill', and 'Netty Sargent's Copyhold'. These sketches imitate in a slighter and looser form the subject-matter and technique of *Wessex Tales*, thus offering in nostalgic miniature a historical context for the more contemporary focus of *Life's Little Ironies.*

When Hardy published this volume in 1894, he was close to the end of his fiction-writing career, and he did not collect more stories until 1913, when, in conjunction with his work on the Wessex Edition, he decided to put together most of the remaining uncollected stories. *A Changed Man, The Waiting Supper, and Other Tales* does not have, therefore, a discernible organizing principle—the Wessex Edition gives it the separate category of 'Mixed Novels'—and it draws together twelve stories originally published over a nineteen-year period: 'A Changed Man', 'The Waiting Supper', 'Alicia's Diary', 'The Grave by the Handpost', 'Enter a Dragoon', 'A Tryst at an Ancient Earthwork', 'What the Shepherd Saw', 'A Committee-Man of "The Terror"', 'Master John Horseleigh, Knight', 'The Duke's Reappearance', 'A Mere Interlude', and 'The Romantic Adventures of a Milkmaid'. Only 'The Waiting Supper' and 'The Romantic Adventures of a Milkmaid' were significantly revised for this printing.

After 1913, seven extant stories remained unpublished in volume form: 'How I Built Myself a House', 'Destiny and a Blue Cloak', 'The Thieves Who Couldn't Help Sneezing', 'An Indiscretion in the Life of an Heiress', 'Our Exploits at West Poley', 'Old Mrs Chundle', and 'The Doctor's Legend'. Hardy also collaborated formally with Florence *Henniker in writing 'The Spectre of the Real', and informally with Florence Dugdale, who became his second wife, in the composition of 'Blue Jimmy: The Horse Stealer' and 'The Unconquerable'. These 'excluded and collaborative' stories have recently been edited by Pamela Dalziel (see also UNCOLLECTED STORIES).

With the notable exception of essays by Irving Howe, Alexander Fischler, A. F. Cassis, and Norman Page, the stories as a group did not receive much exclusive attention from modern critics until Kristin Brady's 1982 book-length analysis. Since then, T. R. Wright, Roger Ebbatson, and Norman D. Prentiss have offered poststructuralist interpretations, and in 1997 Martin Ray published a textual study of the stories.

Further discussion of individual stories will be found under the appropriate titles. KB

Kristin Brady, *The Short Stories of Thomas Hardy* (1982).
Pamela Dalziel (ed.), *Thomas Hardy: The Excluded and Collaborative Stories* (1992).
Martin Ray, *Thomas Hardy: A Textual Study of the Short Stories* (1997).

Shorter, Clement (1857–1926), journalist and editor. As editor of the *Illustrated London News* he published as a serial in 1892 *The Pursuit of the Well-Beloved*, the first version of *The Well-Beloved*. He was simultaneously editor of the *English Illustrated Magazine*, and subsequently founder and editor of the *Sketch* and the *Sphere* and editor of the *Tatler*. A number of Hardy's short stories and poems first appeared under Shorter's editorship; the two men corresponded frequently, and Shorter and his wife Dora Sigerson Shorter (1866–1918), the poet, visited Max Gate. When Hardy submitted his story 'Master John Horseleigh, Knight' on 28 March 1893, he invited Shorter to delete the word 'bastard' if he wished (*L* ii 6), but Shorter printed it in his magazine (Summer Number, 1893). 'A Tryst at an Ancient Earthwork' (December 1893) and 'A Committee-Man of "The Terror"' (Christmas Number, 1896) also first appeared in the *Illustrated London News*. 'A Changed Man' appeared in the *Sphere* (21 and 28 April 1900).

When Shorter launched the *Sphere* he invited Hardy to contribute a poem to the first number (27 January 1900): the result was 'At the War Office After a Bloody Battle', later retitled 'At the War Office, London'. Other poems first published in the *Sphere* included 'The Lost Pyx' (22 December 1900) and 'The Man He Killed' (22 November 1902). To commemorate the death of Hardy's mother, Shorter reproduced in the *Sphere* a painting of her by Mary Hardy (23 April 1904).

Hardy used his influence with Shorter to persuade him to publish stories by Florence *Henniker. Shorter also published in the *Sphere* a poem, 'Spring Song', submitted to him by Emma *Hardy (14 April 1900), with the transparently apologetic editorial comment that he was, 'as one of the most enthusiastic admirers of her husband's books', happy to print it. He and his wife were fellow-guests with Hardy and Florence Dugdale (later Florence Hardy) at the home of Edward *Clodd in April 1911. Later he published reviews of novels submitted by Florence *Hardy. For Shorter's slightly un-expected appearance in a Max Beerbohm parody, see HARDY, POEMS ABOUT.

Smith, Elder & Co., London publishers. The firm, which had offices at 65 Cornhill in Hardy's day, had been founded in 1816 by George Smith and Alexander Elder and had published novels by Thackeray, Charlotte Brontë, and others. Hardy's first contact with them was to send them in April 1869 the manuscript of his first (and never-to-be-published) novel *The Poor Man and the Lady*, which they promptly rejected. However, as proprietors of the highly prestigious *Cornhill Magazine*, which had been established in 1860 by the head of the firm, George Smith (1824–1901), a son of the co-founder, and was then under the editorship of Leslie *Stephen, they did publish the serial version (January–December 1874) of *Far from the Madding Crowd* as well as (23 November 1874) the first edition of that novel in volume form. Hardy's correspondence with the firm at this time includes advice on the illustrations.

In March 1876 Hardy had approached George Smith with the proposal that he should publish cheap editions of *A Pair of Blue Eyes* and *Far from the Madding Crowd* (*LW* 116–17; Millgate 180). Smith, Elder subsequently brought out *The Hand of Ethelberta* in both serial (July 1875–May 1876) and volume (3 April 1876) forms, though with less success than its predecessor, and also published *The Return of the Native* in book form (4 November 1878), though Hardy's wish to have this novel serialized in their magazine had not materialized; the edition of 1,000 copies brought Hardy a fee of £200. In July 1880 Hardy agreed with Smith, Elder on similar terms for the volume-publication of *The Trumpet-Major*, which appeared on 26 October of that year; they were also the publishers of the volume-edition of *The Mayor of Casterbridge*. Neither of these publications proved a commercial success, and we have Hardy's testimony that Smith, Elder did not have high hopes for *The Mayor*, their reader having reported to George Smith that (in Hardy's own later words) 'the lack of gentry among the characters made it uninteresting' (*LW* 186).

Hardy, who first met Smith in the spring of 1874, later described him as 'a man of wide experience, who had brought Charlotte Brontë before the reading public' (*LW* 104); a diary entry for 30 September 1878 notes that he called on Smith and 'agreed to his terms' for the publication of *The Return of the Native* (*LW* 125), and other meetings are recorded. Smith founded in 1865 the *Pall Mall Gazette*, a London evening newspaper which published a number of reviews of Hardy's work, and is also remembered as founder of the *Dictionary of National Biography*, of which Hardy's friend Leslie Stephen was editor.

Smith, Reginald Bosworth (1839–1908), schoolmaster and author. The second son of the rector of West Stafford, Dorset, he was educated at Marlborough and Oxford, where he became President of the Union and later Fellow and Tutor of Trinity College. He was a master, and later a housemaster, at Harrow for nearly 40 years from 1864, and Hardy and his wife spent a weekend with him there in June 1879. Hardy's autobiography contains an account of this visit and also of a later occasion (1892), when the Hardys dined at West Stafford with Smith and his father on an evening made memorable by their witnessing the fire that destroyed Stinsford House. Smith had a strong interest in the Middle East, and Hardy is known to have read his *Mohamedd and Mohameddanism* (1874).

smuggling: See ALCOHOL.

societies and journals. The Thomas Hardy Society (UK) was established in 1968 and has a current membership of about 1,250. It exists for the advancement of 'education in the works of Thomas Hardy by promoting in every part of the World appreciation and study of these works'. The Society holds a biennial conference (in even-numbered years), usually in Dorchester, organizes other events in Wessex and London, and since 1985 has published the *Thomas Hardy Journal* thrice yearly. (Earlier publications were the *Thomas Hardy Society Newsletter* and the *Thomas Hardy Society Review*.) Enquiries about the Society can be addressed to PO Box 1438, Dorchester, Dorset DT1 1YH. A Northern Branch is based in Sheffield.

The Thomas Hardy Society of Japan was founded in 1957 and has a membership of about 250. It holds an annual conference, and publishes an annual *Bulletin* (with articles in both Japanese and English) and a twice-yearly newsletter, as well as occasional publications, including *A Thomas Hardy Dictionary* (1984). Enquiries to Room 2957, Chuo University, Higashi-Nakano, Hachioji, Tokyo 192–0351, Japan.

The International Association for Thomas Hardy Studies (formerly The Thomas Hardy Society of North America) was established in 1996 and inaugurated a website (http:/www.yale.edu/hardysoc) under the sponsorship of Yale University in 1997. The website's LINKS page provides 'an exhaustive collection of reports on the one-hundred-odd Hardy-related websites across the globe'. Other pages are devoted to biography, novels, short stories, drama, poetry, and other topics. The President, Review Editor, and Resources Editor is Rosemarie Morgan (rm82@ pantheon.yale.edu).

The Thomas Hardy Year Book is published by the Toucan Press, The White Cottage, Rue de Carteret, Castel, Guernsey GY5 7YG, via Great Britain.

Society for the Protection of Ancient Buildings. The work of the Society, founded in 1877, can be seen as a reaction to the destruction wrought by Victorian 'restorers', and Hardy's own involvement with its activities over many years was among other things a form of atonement for his own part in, or at any rate connivance at, the damage done to medieval churches when he was a young architect (see his important essay 'MEMORIES OF CHURCH RESTORATION', which originated as a paper read to the Society in 1906). While living at Wimborne in 1882, he showed concern (humorously evident in the poem 'The Levelled Churchyard') at the ongoing restoration of the Minster; in 1890 he corresponded with the Society's Secretary concerning the planned demolition of the church at Stratton, near Dorchester; and in 1908 he drew the Society's attention to the drawbacks of a proposed restoration at St Mary's, South Perrott, and also gave advice on the restoration of St Catherine's Chapel, Abbotsbury. In 1910 he expressed great and repeated concern about plans to undertake the restoration of the church at Puddletown, a spot with significant personal and family associations. A few years earlier he had joined a committee charged with supervising extensive restorations to the church at Fordington St George, another place closely associated with his early years (see MOULE FAMILY), but resigned from the committee in protest at what he regarded as excessive and unnecessary changes to the original structure; in correspondence with the Society, for whom he inspected an ancient font at the church in 1903, he continued to deplore these radical alterations.

As these examples suggest, Hardy regarded himself as holding a kind of watching brief in his own neighbourhood on the Society's behalf, and was vigilant in spotting, and prompt in bringing to their attention, projects that seemed to threaten the county's architectural heritage. Some of the advice he gave was of a technical nature, as in the two reports submitted to the Society in 1898 concerning East Lulworth church and an old inn at Maiden Newton. Millgate notes, however, that when in 1893–4 Hardy took an active part in the renovations to St Peter's, West Knighton, elements in his design were 'quite contrary to the official doctrines' of the Society (345). See also ARCHITECTURE.

Claudius J. P. Beatty, *Thomas Hardy: Conservation Architect: His Work for the Society for the Protection of Ancient Buildings* (1995).

'Son's Veto, The', short story. It was published in the *Illustrated London News* (Christmas Number, 1891), and collected in *Life's Little Ironies.* The manuscript was given to the John Rylands Library, University of Manchester, by Hardy in 1911. He had completed this story early in 1891, at about the same time that he was correcting the proofs of *Tess of the d'Urbervilles,* and there are similarities between the situations of the two heroines. Like 'A Tragedy of Two Ambitions' in the same collection, the story explores the conflict between a young man's worldly ambitions and his feelings for a parent of humble origins: in both cases natural affection stands no chance against the drive for success.

The anti-hero's father, now dead, was a clergyman who married beneath him, choosing (like Angel Clare in *Tess*) a 'child of nature', a maiden from a Wessex village. The boy, an only son educated at Eton, corrects the grammatical errors in his mother's speech and is deeply ashamed of her. Lonely and unhappy in a London suburb, she has the opportunity to remarry, but the plan is vetoed by her snobbish son, who has become a priest. (As in 'A Tragedy of Two Ambitions', and in the presentation of Angel's brothers in *Tess,* Hardy's anti-clericalism is in evidence.) The story is a powerful study in monstrous egotism and unresisting suffering, and as in several other stories in the same volume the central concern is with the demands of society that work for the destruction of individual happiness. Subsidiary and related themes are the uprooted life, and the 'good' marriage that turns out to be a disaster: the strong implication is that the village girl would have been happier marrying a rustic than in accepting a man who transplanted her to another social class and an alien, urban environment, in neither of which she could feel at ease. The symbolism of her watching the loads of produce from the countryside passing through the suburban streets on their way to the London markets is felicitous and touching.

Sparks, Tryphena (1851–90), cousin of Thomas Hardy. She is the subject of his tender and touching poem 'Thoughts of Phena at News of Her Death', which bears the date March 1890 and was included in *Wessex Poems* (1898), where it is accompanied by a striking illustration. Its origins are described in an interesting diary entry quoted in Hardy's autobiography, where he states that the opening lines were written as a result of 'sympathetic telepathy' whilst Tryphena was dying, though Hardy knew nothing of the fact at the time, and the poem was apparently completed after learning of her death (*LW* 234). That event is also referred to more obliquely ('the death of a woman') in the 1895 preface to *Jude the Obscure*.

Tryphena was the youngest child of James and Maria Sparks, the latter being a sister of Hardy's mother (see RELATIVES OF THOMAS HARDY), and was born and brought up in Puddletown, Dorset. In his youth Hardy seems often to have visited the Sparks family, though Tryphena, eleven years younger than he, was only a small child at this time. After completing her own schooling, she was for a time a pupil-teacher in Puddletown and then did a two-year teacher-training course (1870–2) at Stockwell Normal College in South London, following which she took charge of a girls' elementary school in Plymouth. In 1877 she married Charles Gale, the proprietor of a public house at Topsham, near Exeter, by whom she had four children. As the poem poignantly makes clear, Hardy saw nothing of her in her later years, and the social gap between the successful author and the publican's wife might in any case have made a meeting awkward: there is, though, an unsubstantiated story that he visited her grave at Topsham.

Lois Deacon and Terry Coleman's *Providence and Mr Hardy* (1966) made sensational allegations about an affair between Hardy and his cousin (actually, the book suggested, his niece) and an illegitimate son; though these claims attracted wide attention in the period immediately following publication, they rest on no substantial evidence and are now generally rejected. What seems much more likely is that for about two years from the summer of 1867, when Hardy was living at Bockhampton and Tryphena a lively teenager, they saw a good deal of each other and one or both were perhaps romantically inclined. Tryphena's day-to-day experiences as a pupil-teacher in the Puddletown elementary school must have formed a subject of conversation, and memories of what she told him may have been drawn on when Hardy came to write *Jude the Obscure* a generation later. Millgate's persuasive conclusion is that 'there was certainly no child, probably no formal engagement, and perhaps not even a dramatic parting but simply a gradual erosion of intimacy, an eventual relapse into the friendly and cousinly terms of the past' (Millgate 106). The tone of wistful regret in the 1890 poem, one of a number expressing a sense of a lost opportunity, needs no further explanation in the context of Hardy's marital unhappiness at the time of its composition.

Of the other Puddletown cousins, Hardy seems at one stage to have been attracted to Martha, six years his senior, who became a lady's maid and in 1870 married and emigrated to Australia. He was also friendly with two of Tryphena's brothers, James and Nathaniel. See also POLE, CATHERINE.

Robert Gittings, *Young Thomas Hardy* (1975): Appendix on 'Hardy and Tryphena Sparks'.

'Spectre of the Real, The.' See UNCOLLECTED STORIES.

speeches. Hardy was a reluctant public speaker and occasionally failed to deliver a speech he had written. In May 1908 he was due to give the presidential address to the Society of Dorset Men in London, but anxiety about his health ('he was always a victim to influenza and throat trouble if he read or spoke in London': *LW* 367) led him—or perhaps gave him an excuse—to ask the Society's secretary to deliver it on his behalf. (The speech survives but was not read on that occasion.) Two years earlier he had composed his interesting 'Memories of Church Restoration' as a paper to be given to the Society for the Protection of Ancient Buildings, but it was read by another in his absence. He did, however, speak in public on several occasions, though one of them involved a very small audience indeed. On his 72nd birthday in 1912 the Royal Society of Literature awarded him its gold medal, and the presentation was made at his home, Max Gate, by Henry *Newbolt and W. B. Yeats, who were guests of the Hardys at the time. His speech of acceptance was reported in *The Times* on 4 June ('A Plea for Pure English'). A little earlier, on 16 November 1910, he had received the Freedom of the Borough of Dorchester, and the occasion had elicited from Hardy a speech of great charm, humour, and interest (for quotations from this speech, see DORCHESTER).

A generation earlier still, in 1884, he had spoken at a meeting in Dorchester of the Dorset Natural History and Antiquarian Field Club: the speech, published as 'Some Romano-British Relics Found at Max Gate, Dorchester' (see ARCHAEOLOGY), is of interest in relation to references to the Roman occupation in *The Mayor of Casterbridge*, which was in progress at the time. Even earlier, in May 1875, when his fame as a novelist was still in its early stages, he gave an after-dinner speech to an undergraduate club at Oxford (see OXFORD). And in the last months of his life, on 21 July 1927, he spoke in the open air, on a 'cold and windy' day, on the occasion of laying a commemoration stone for the new building of Dorchester Grammar School. It was his last public appearance. The speech is quoted at some length in the *Life* (*LW* 472–3).

Stephen, Leslie (1832–1904; knighted 1902), critic, essayist, biographer, and founding editor of the *Dictionary of National Biography*. He played a highly influential role in Hardy's early career by publishing *Far from the Madding Crowd* in 1874 and *The Hand of Ethelberta* in 1875–6 in the *Cornhill Magazine*, the day's foremost monthly, then under his editorship. Having read *Under the Greenwood Tree* (attributed on its title-page only to 'the author of "Desperate Remedies"') with 'very great pleasure', Stephen undertook to discover its writer's identity and approached Hardy, through Horace *Moule, in late November 1872 with an offer to publish his next novel in the *Cornhill*, should it prove to be of similar interest and quality.

The proposal marked a decided advance in Hardy's fortunes, for not only did the long-established *Cornhill* promise significantly more prestige than *Tinsleys' Magazine*, in which *A Pair of Blue Eyes* had recently begun to appear, but it offered a substantial increase in earnings. Although committed to *A Pair of Blue Eyes* for William *Tinsley, Hardy replied that he was contemplating a pastoral story about a woman-farmer, a shepherd, and a soldier.

In due course Hardy sent this story, *Far from the Madding Crowd*, to Stephen, who, unlike Tinsley, was a painstaking editor and himself a writer of standing, although not a novelist. Stephen's very first letter to Hardy of 30 November 1872, which comments on the lack of incident in *Under the Greenwood Tree* and suggests the nature of writing required for a serial, presages the tone of their later professional collaboration. When Hardy eventually submitted his work to Stephen, he received back detailed advice about recasting his materials and altering phrasing. Some of Stephen's suggestions were gingerly formulated, others outrightly apologetic about the necessity for changes. In *Far from the Madding Crowd*, for instance, Stephen advised Hardy to omit the shearing-supper scene because it was too long, and to suppress the presence of Fanny's illegitimate baby in her coffin. In *The Hand of Ethelberta*, he objected not only to a 'very close embrace' in a London churchyard, but also to the word 'amorous'. Hardy, who had the opportunity to restore deletions and wording when these novels were published in book form, obligingly revised, pruned, and rewrote to suit the *Cornhill*'s audience. But he may even have been influenced at the draft stage, composing with their preferences in mind once Stephen had made these clear. (Rosemarie Morgan's *Cancelled Words: Rediscovering Thomas Hardy* (1992) offers a detailed study of the revisions of *Far from the Madding Crowd*.)

Stephen exercised such *censorship partly with an eye to making Hardy's unconventional frankness about sexual matters conform to the high moral tone and propriety demanded by the *Cornhill*'s conservative, upper-middle-class readership, which, then in thrall to Mrs Grundy, fully expected to see its values reflected in a magazine destined for its drawing-rooms. But the extent to which, at moments, Stephen's strictures may have been motivated by his own desire to soften Hardy's handling of sexual matters has been the subject of some critical disagreement. When his association with Stephen began, Hardy appears not to have objected to altering his work to suit the *Cornhill*'s readership. This willingness to compromise his artistic aims may have been urged on by the blandishments of higher returns for his work and exposure to a well-heeled establishment audience. However, increased confidence about the integrity of his art and methods, and, possibly, the popular success of *Far from the Madding Crowd*, eventually emboldened him to refuse to make concessions. Thus when he offered Stephen *The Return of the Native* in 1877, Stephen's response caused Hardy to seek a less timid publisher and a more congenial, less conservative venue for his work. The outline of the story that Hardy sketched out had promised developments that Stephen considered 'dangerous for a family magazine', and he indicated that he wished to see the novel in its entirety before making an offer for publication. Apparently without animus, Hardy refused to bow to this request, and he never sent the novel to Stephen.

While his relationship with Stephen the editor came to an end, his fondness for Stephen the man weathered this difference. However, although they continued to maintain cordial relations, and Hardy regarded Stephen warmly, with the end of their professional connection the two men saw one another only infrequently. They were, however, strongly linked by shared free-thinking attitudes towards religious issues. Hardy praised Stephen's essay 'Are We Christians?' (published in the *Fortnightly Review* in March 1873), and in the spring of 1875, Stephen asked Hardy to act as a witness to his renunciation of Holy Orders.

For his part, Hardy paid homage to Stephen as a critic by alluding to his 1868 essay on Defoe in *The Hand of Ethelberta* (16). Hardy's recollections of Stephen, along with a sonnet to him, 'The Schreckhorn. With Thoughts of L.S.' (dated June 1897 and later included in *Satires of Circumstance*), were published in Frederick William Maitland's *The Life and Letters of Leslie Stephen* (1906). Stephen's letters to Hardy are housed in DCM. Some of these are printed in an appendix to Purdy and in *Selected Letters of Leslie Stephen*, ed. John W. Bicknell (1996). See also RELIGION; SERIALIZATION; WOOLF, VIRGINIA. JHS

Stevenson, Robert Louis (1850–94), novelist, essayist, and poet. He met Hardy in August 1885 when, after introducing himself as an admirer, he visited Max Gate with members of his family while travelling in south-west England. For the unflattering comments subsequently made by his wife Fanny on Hardy ('most painfully shy... a quite pathetic figure') and Emma ('*very* plain, quite underbred, and most tedious'), see Millgate 270. In the following year Stevenson wrote an enthusiastic letter to Hardy (quoted *LW* 186) concerning *The Mayor of Casterbridge*, with a request for permission to dramatize the novel; Hardy replied with similar enthusiasm (7 June 1886: *L* i 146), and shortly afterwards he and Stevenson met in London, but nothing came of the project. This appears to have been their last meeting. On Hardy's ironic references to his 'good-natured friends' Stevenson and James, see Henry *James. There is perhaps also a touch of malice in Hardy's suggestion (*LW* 126) that Stevenson's inclusion of a map in *Treasure Island* (1883) was 'adopted' from his own use of a map in *The Return of the Native*.

A short contribution by Hardy to Rosaline Masson's *I Can Remember Robert Louis Stevenson* adds little to the above record; it does, however, state that their first meeting was 'possibly' at the home of Sidney Colvin 'at the British Museum'.

Stinsford, about two miles east of Dorchester, is a Church of England parish in which are to be found the hamlets of Higher and Lower Bockhampton. There are two places of considerable importance in Hardy's life and writings in Stinsford: the cottage at *Higher Bockhampton in which he lived for most of the first 34 years of his life, and Stinsford church. In the cottage he was born, grew up, and wrote most of his first four novels, including *Desperate Remedies* (1871), which features Kingston Maurward House, the Stinsford home of the wealthy, upper-class Martin family (see MARTIN, JULIA AUGUSTA), and *Under the Greenwood Tree* (1872), in which he makes extensive use of his intimate topographical knowledge of Stinsford, to which he gave the fictitious name of Mellstock. Much of the action of this latter novel occurs in 1840, at about the time of Hardy's own birth, and the cottage and Stinsford church are clearly recognizable in the descriptions. Several of Hardy's poems feature the cottage, among the best-known being 'Domicilium' and 'The Self-Unseeing'.

Stinsford church had been associated with Hardy's family since 1801, when his grandfather Thomas Hardy had moved into the newly built cottage. His grandfather, father, and uncle had all played their musical instruments in the choir, and *Under the Greenwood Tree* is much concerned with the sad disbanding of the choir about 1841 and the replacement of the instrumentalists with a barrel-organ. Many of Hardy's close relatives were buried in the churchyard, and it is the scene of several of his poems, including 'Afternoon Service at Mellstock' and 'Voices from Things Growing in a Churchyard'. In building *Max Gate in 1883–5, Hardy chose a spot within easy walking distance of Stinsford church and the cottage in which his mother lived until her death in 1904. In his autobiography we read that 'Stinsford was a favourite haunt until the last few months of his life... and the churchyard, to him, the most hallowed spot on earth' (*LW* 477). Here he could mourn not just his father and mother and beloved sister Mary, but his 'late espoused saint', his first wife Emma. Hardy's heart was buried in Emma's grave in Stinsford churchyard on 16 January 1928.

JCG

Stopes, Dr Marie (1880–1958), pioneer of birth control and sex education. She began her scientific career as a botanist but later achieved fame (and often notoriety) through such best-selling works as *Married Love* (1918). In 1923 Hardy and his wife visited her at the converted lighthouse on Portland Bill where she often stayed; she later bought and restored the nearby house known as 'Avice's Cottage', associated with *The Well-Beloved.* In a letter written to Dr Stopes on 14 September 1923 (British Library), Florence Hardy comments on the possibility that she might conceive a child in the early years of their marriage. On 16 April 1926 Hardy declined Marie Stopes's request that he should make a public statement concerning her play *Vectia*, which had been refused a licence for public performance: Hardy's candid and interesting letter (*L* vii 16–17) questions the probability of the sexual situation presented therein. After Hardy's death his widow maintained her friendship and correspondence with Dr Stopes.

Sturminster Newton was a small but important market town when Hardy and his wife Emma moved there in July 1876. It is about fifteen miles north-east of Dorchester, on the eastern edge of the Blackmoor Vale, with the river Stour flowing around it. They had been married almost two years when they moved into 'Riverside Villa', the more northerly of a pair of houses standing on a small hill overlooking the river and its famous old mill. To furnish the house they went to Bristol, bought £100-worth of furniture, and settled down in what was to be their first real home. Later Hardy referred to this period as 'The Sturminster Newton Idyll'.

Hardy enjoyed walking along the river bank and rowing on the river. In his autobiography we read: '"Rowed on the Stour in the evening, the sun setting on the river. ...Rowed among the water-lilies to gather them. Their long ropey stems...Gathered meadow-sweet....A Cloud in the sky like a huge quill-pen"' (*LW* 115). A number of poems resulted from this period, of which 'Overlooking the River Stour' and 'On Sturminster Foot-Bridge' are among the best-known. His major work at Sturminster was the writing of *The Return of the Native.*

An incident which occurred in June 1877 may have had an influence on Hardy's later writing. Their servant Jane was discovered letting her lover into the house late at night, was sent to bed in disgrace, ran away in the early hours of the morning, and soon after had a baby which, after a private baptism, died within a day or two. Ironically, the following diary entry (quoted in *LW* 119) was made on 13 August: '"We hear that Jane, our late servant is soon to have a baby. Yet never a sign of one is there for us."'

The 'Idyll' came to an end when they moved to Tooting in South London on 18 March 1878. Emma had felt isolated at Sturminster, and Hardy decided that his profession as a novelist required him to live closer to London. It was a decision that took him away from Wessex and one that he must later have regretted. Hardy records two further visits to 'Riverside Villa'. The first was in June 1916, when he went there with his second wife Florence and his sister Kate to 'a house he had never entered for forty years' (*LW* 403). The second was on 9 June 1921, when he motored to Sturminster Newton to see the Hardy Players perform *The Mellstock Quire*, a dramatization of *Under the Greenwood Tree*, in the Castle ruins, and afterwards had tea in the house he had first entered 45 years before.

JCG

style, 'as far as the word is meant to express something more than literary finish, can only be treatment, and treatment depends upon the mental attitude of the novelist.... A writer who is not a mere imitator looks upon the world with his personal eyes, and in his peculiar moods; thence grows up his style, in the full sense of the term.' Thus wrote Hardy in his essay 'The Profitable Reading of Fiction' in 1888. A year earlier he had written in a letter: 'A writer's style is according to his temperament, & my impression is that if he has anything to say which is of value, & words to say it with, the style will come of itself' (*L* i 168–9).

When, several years earlier, Hardy had committed himself to writing novels, he gave serious consideration to prose style, as he recalled in the *Life* under the year 1875 in the following note: 'Read again Addison, Macaulay, Newman, Sterne, De Foe, Lamb, Gibbon, Burke, *Times* Leaders, &c. in a study of style. Am more and more confirmed in an idea I have long held, as a matter of commonsense, long before I thought of any old aphorism bearing on the subject: "Ars est celare artem". The whole secret of a living style... lies in not having too much style—being—in fact, a little careless, or rather seeming to be, here and there. It brings wonderful life into the writing.' Hardy then adds these lines from Robert Herrick's poem 'Delight in Disorder': 'A sweet disorder in the dress... | A careless shoe-string, in whose tie | I see a wild civility, | Do more bewitch me than when art | Is too precise in every part.' Hardy's 'note' ends with this observation: 'It is, of course, simply a carrying into prose the knowledge I have acquired in poetry—that inexact rhymes and rhythms now and then are far more pleasing than correct ones' (*LW* 108).

Hardy's temperament, his vision, his peculiar moods all contributed to producing a distinctive style, which ranges from lengthy, ponderous sentences to succinct statements in his prose and to what Margaret Drabble called 'Hardy's own characteristic wilting, delicate, hesitating cadences' in his verse. The laborious sentence of 92 words in the penultimate paragraph of *The Mayor of Casterbridge* is as much part of Hardy's style as are the terse statements in moments of dramatic tension: 'Presently the gurgoyle spat' (*FFMC* 46); 'Events mocked her on all sides' (*TT* 38); 'She had not told' (*TDU* 30); 'Only a wall—but what a wall!' (*JO* 2.2). Similarly in his verse. There is awkwardness in a line like 'I said, "Get out to her do I dare?"' ('Faintheart in a Railway Train'), but a striking economy of diction in 'The glebe cow drooled' ('Channel Firing') with its clerical as well as bovine connotations.

Hardy possessed a resourceful vocabulary. A single word, whether familiar or ancient, adopted from another language or invented, can contribute effectively to his writing. In 'a lone cave's stillicide' in 'Friends Beyond' he revives an evocative Renaissance word; when a cabinet minister in *The Dynasts* (1.1.5) prophesies that the allied armies will 'un-French Italy | From shore to shore', Hardy indulges his passion for coining new words; and when he speaks of 'an intoxicating *Weltlust*' (*MC* 38), or 'the *monstrari digito* of idle men' (*PBE* 1), or 'the idea of any such *arrière-pensée*' (*L* 3.2), he uses the foreign word which best expresses his thought.

Comic touches occur in Hardy's style in poems like 'The Ruined Maid' and especially in his earlier novels, like the 'cough, sneeze, or amen' in a church service (*UGT* 1.6), or that 'marvellously old man, whose skin seemed so much too large for his body that it would not stay in position' (*PBE* 26), or Ethelberta's stealthy exclamation 'like a parson's damn' (*HE* 26), or the large tray which 'arrived on the stomach of a footman' (*TT* 7). *The Trumpet-Major* is especially rich in comic writing; for example, Miller Loveday's ancestry (2), Oxwell Hall with its 'romantic excellencies and practical drawbacks' (6), and Festus Derriman's Falstaffian bombast (26). Even in *Jude the Obscure* there is a touch of comedy as Hardy itemizes the 'forlorn hope' that rallies to Phillotson's defence at Shaston, which includes 'two travelling broom-makers, who called themselves widows, a gingerbread-stall keeper, a swing-boat owner, and a "test-your-strength" man' (4.6).

In 1910 Hardy wrote to Lady Grove that 'A sentence may often be strictly correct in grammar, but wretched in style' (*L* iv 89), and his style is by no means free from occasional 'wretchedness', as critics have not been slow to remark with labels like 'stiff', 'angular', and 'bizarre'. The juxtaposition of a short, familiar word with a learned 'Latinate' one can be stylistically as inept as a long, convoluted sentence; for example, 'this father in early domiciliation' (*MC* 43), or 'a natural inappetency for evil things' in 'The Duchess of Hamptonshire' (*GND*), especially when the latter is contrasted with the powerful 'a good bomb-like oath' two pages earlier, with its echo of Shakespeare's 'a good mouth-filling oath' in *Henry IV, Part 1*.

Literary echoes like this, or allusions, or direct quotations, not least from the *Bible, so familiar to Victorian readers, are a recurrent feature of Hardy's style. His first published novel, *Desperate Remedies* (1871), with its rich harvest of biblical, classical, English, and contemporary writings, paved the way, and once it had taken root, the habit remained embedded in Hardy's subsequent fiction, 'according to his temperament', his inbred love of literature and learning. Both in his own voice as narrator and through the mouths of his fictional personae Hardy seasons his work with literary condiments. In *Under the Greenwood Tree* (5.1), grandfather William quotes the prophet Jeremiah; in *A Laodicean* de Stancy quotes from Keats's 'Ode to a Nightingale', and in the same chapter (2.7) Hardy's own enthusiasm for Paula Power's 'supple form' in the gymnasium longs for 'the poetic passion of some joyous Elizabethan lyrist like Lodge, Nash, or Greene' (the 1896 edition has 'Constable'). In *The Woodlanders* Fitzpiers rhapsodizes about Grace Melbury in the words of Shelley (16), early autumn evokes a quatrain from Chatterton (25), and the 'sad delight' of the meeting between Giles and Grace is illumined by a couplet from Swinburne (40), the poet whom Hardy commemorated in his poem 'A Singer Asleep'.

A writer's words may be incorporated in the text with or without the author's name: 'the flattering fancy that heaven lies about them' (*JO* 1.4) echoes *Wordsworth; 'She had, in Chaucer's phrase, "all the craft of fine loving" at her fingers' ends' occurs in 'The Marchioness of Stonehenge' (*GND*); and in the final paragraph of *Tess of the d'Urbervilles* the mention of Aeschylus recalls his *Agamemnon*, followed by the echo of Gloucester's words in *King Lear*—'As flies to wanton boys, are we to the gods, | They kill us for their sport.'

Endowed with remarkable visual and aural senses, Hardy noticed minute details of daily life, of his environment, of persons and animals, which constitute yet another distinctive feature of his style. We remember the timid heath-croppers 'looking on with erect heads' in the memorable glow-worm scene in *The Return of the Native* (3.8), or 'those marvellous sunset effects' colouring London on a mellow afternoon (*WB* 3.5), or the changing seasons in *The Woodlanders*, when in spring you could 'almost' hear 'the rush of sap in the veins of the trees' (19). Hardy did hear 'the baritone buzz of a holly tree' (*RN* 1.6), the 'singular symphonies' of the river at Casterbridge (*MC* 41), and the 'hiss' and 'patter' and 'paddling plash' of raindrops falling on different surfaces (*DR* 17.1). Sometimes Hardy mentions details not strictly germane to the narrative, like Angel Clare striking his toe against the edge of the door while sleep-walking (*TDU* 37), or the absence of pavements at Shaston (*JO* 4.3), but he noticed such things, just as he noticed the behaviour of animals before an approaching storm and a humble toad travelling across the path (*FFMC* 36), or 'the dew-fall hawk' and the furtive hedgehog in his poem 'Afterwards'.

Such observations also find expression in figurative language, metaphors and similes in prose and verse, which are often highly original, albeit sometimes far-fetched or incongruous. Thus Hardy writes that 'the red coals of the perishing fire greeted her like living eyes in the corpse of the day' (*RN* 1.6), and he sees Tess standing 'upon the hemmed expanse of verdant flatness, like a fly on a billiard table of indefinite length' (*TDU* 16). He sees the bodies of the dead in 'The Levelled Churchyard' 'mixed to human jam'. He notices how 'the sun rested his chin upon the meadows' (*TT* 38), how 'a pumpkin-like moon arose' (*TDU* 28), how crises were becoming as common 'as blackberries' (*HE* 27), and how Paula Power turns into 'a sort of optical poem' (*L* 2.7). Hardy writes of 'the milk-teeth of a suburb' (*HE* 41), and in his early poem 'She, to Him III' of being 'Numb as a vane that cankers on its point'. Hardy's imagery can be unobtrusive, arresting, even grotesque, according to his 'peculiar moods': 'He appeared on the dark ridge of heathland, like a fly on a negro' (*RN* 2.4), or (yet another fly!) 'This ancestor had a mole on his cheek, black and distinct as a fly in cream' (*L* 3.1).

Blackness is common in Hardy's writing, but it is offset by a profusion of colours, many in a variety of shades, to describe not only surface, but substance, character, mood, nature, landscapes, and seasons in all their changing manifestations. Tess's multicoloured eyes defy even Hardy's powers of description, while Elfride Swancourt's eyes inspired the title of *A Pair of Blue Eyes*. Emma Hardy had 'nut-coloured hair, | And gray eyes, and rose-flush coming and going' ('After a Journey'); 'The High-School Lawn' is filled with bright colours; mountains are clad in 'magnificent purples' in 'Alike and Unlike'; a day is 'yellow' in 'A Spellbound Palace'—in both verse and prose Hardy saw the world in all its colours, from the 'Neutral Tones' of a wintry pond in 1867 to 'finger-white' Iseult in *The Famous Tragedy of the Queen of Cornwall* in 1923.

Moreover, to describe colours, shades, contours, atmosphere, Hardy often turned to painters and specific paintings. The real-life Lady Camilla Gurdon is 'Raffaellesque' in the *Life* (July 1891), an epithet also associated with Paula Power (*L* 1.2) and Lucy Savile in 'Fellow-Townsmen' (*WT*). Turner is adduced to enhance the colouring of one of Gabriel Oak's dogs (*FFMC* 5) and gas-lit butchers' stalls in London (*PBE* 13), while skinny storks' legs remind Hardy of Carlo Crivelli's emaciated dead martyrs (*L* 5.1). Appropriately, a tree-lined road in 'The Romantic Adventures of a Milkmaid' recalls Hobbema's Dutch landscapes, but despite the dignified sorrow of the scene at the end of *Tess of the d'Urbervilles* not every reader will be happy with Hardy's appeal to a painting as Angel Clare and Liza-Lu move on hand in hand, 'the drooping of their heads being that of Giotto's "Two Apostles"'. (See also PAINTING AND SCULPTURE.)

Hardy's response to the plenitude and variety he saw in the world around him finds expression in his style in the frequent enumerations of things or attributes or features, from varieties of apples to such virtues as 'honesty, goodness, manliness, tenderness, devotion' (*W* 30). In the Christminster stone-cutter's yard it is Hardy the architect who notices 'the new traceries, mullions, transoms, shafts, pinnacles, and battlements standing on the bankers' (*JO* 2.2), and who details the many features seen from the roof of the great library (*JO* 2.6). It is Hardy the historian who ponders the men who had stood at the famous Fourways (*JO* 2.6), and it is Hardy the man of letters who delights in listing authors and books (*JO* 3.4, 4.3). Above all it is Hardy the countryman who not only records rustic speech and customs, but who observes and describes whatever feature of the natural world and the rustic community which nurtured him merits attention. Winter arrives with the help of snakes, ferns, pools, fogs, frost, fungi, and snow (*FFMC* 11); trees, bedding plants, flowers, and apples are lovingly listed in *The Woodlanders*; and, in a typically rustic touch, Hardy itemizes the 'singular presents' old Mrs Edlin brought as wedding gifts, complete with warming-pan and goose-feathers (*JO* 5.4).

A stylistic variant of such straightforward enumerations are the more elaborate sentences in which items are contrasted. Swithin St Cleeve is trying to explain to Lady Constantine the size of the universe in *Two on a Tower* (4): 'There is a size at which dignity begins . . . further on there is a size at which grandeur begins; further on there is a size at which solemnity begins; further on, a size at which awfulness begins; further on, a size at which ghastliness begins'—the word 'ghastliness' providing an unexpected climax. At its best, Hardy's style combines grammatical simplicity with profoundness of meaning. Such a sentence is this in *The Mayor of Casterbridge* (19): 'Henchard's wife was dissevered from him by death; his friend and helper Farfrae by estrangement; Elizabeth-Jane by ignorance.' The three clauses neatly juxtaposed comprise not only the major characters but the tragic essence of the novel in a few words, to which the more 'learned' word 'dissevered' adds a powerful note of finality. Such instances prove that, however idiosyncratic Hardy's style may be, 'it achieves its aim', in Virginia Woolf's words, 'so unmistakably'. RE

Margaret Drabble (ed.), *The Genius of Thomas Hardy* (1976).

Penelope Vigar, *The Novels of Thomas Hardy: Illusion and Reality* (1974).

Morton Dauwen Zabel, 'Hardy in Defense of His Art: The Aesthetic of Incongruity', in

Albert J. Guerard (ed.), *Hardy: A Collection of Critical Essays* (1963).

Swetman family. Hardy's mother Jemima was the fourth child of Elizabeth (Betty) Swetman (1778–1847) and George Hand (1773–1822), who were married at Melbury Osmond in north-west Dorset in 1804. Elizabeth's ancestors had leased and farmed land nearby since the 17th century. An indenture to the lease dated 27 May 1752 included John Swetman, father of Elizabeth and grandfather of Jemima. The house in Melbury Osmond leased to the Swetman family was called 'Townsend' and still stands. In his autobiography Hardy describes his Swetman grandmother as an omnivorous reader. After her mother's death she made an imprudent marriage to the often drunk and violent George Hand. Her father never forgave her, and after her husband died in 1822 she was left, according to Hardy, with several children to support. Because of this, Jemima 'saw during girlhood and young womanhood some very stressful experiences of which she could never speak in her maturer years without pain' (*LW* 12). Elizabeth was buried in *Puddletown, near her father- and mother-in-law, William and Betty Hand.

Hardy makes use of several oral traditions associated with the Swetman family which he had heard from his mother. In his autobiography he reports that the Swetmans 'seem to have been involved in the Monmouth rising', that one of them was 'brought before Judge Jeffreys, "for being absent from home att the time of the Rebellion"', and that after the Battle of Sedgemoor two of the Swetman daughters 'were beset in their house by some of the victorious soldiery, and only escaped violation by slipping from the upper room down the back stairs into the orchard' (*LW* 10–11). Hardy's short story 'The Duke's Reappearance' uses the Swetman tradition that a stranger, thought to be the Duke of Monmouth, called at the Swetman home after the battle. JCG

Swinburne, Algernon Charles (1837–1909), poet and critic. Although almost Hardy's contemporary, he was considerably more precocious as a writer, achieving early fame with his poetic drama *Atalanta in Calydon* (1865) and his *Poems and Ballads* (1866), the latter of which was savagely attacked for immorality. Hardy read these works with passionate enthusiasm as a young man in London; later he told Swinburne that he used to walk through the crowded streets regardless of the traffic and intently reading *Poems and Ballads.* Swinburne was one of the minority who praised *Jude the Obscure*, and Hardy's autobiography quotes his letter commending 'The beauty, the terror, and the truth' of the much-abused novel (*LW* 288–9).

Hardy developed a strong fellow-feeling with Swinburne, based on the shared experience of being attacked for outspokenness in their writings. When Hardy visited him at his Putney home in the summer of 1905, Swinburne told him of a critic who had remarked that 'Swinburne planteth, Hardy watereth, and Satan giveth the increase'; describing this visit in his autobiography, Hardy adds that they exchanged condolences on being 'the most abused of living writers' (*LW* 349–50). An earlier visit had taken place on 20 June 1899. On 23 March 1910, accompanied by Florence Dugdale (later Florence Hardy), Hardy visited Swinburne's grave at Bonchurch on the Isle of Wight; his poem 'A Singer Asleep', first published in the *English Review* (April 1910), commemorates the occasion. Swinburne's rejection by the guardians of public morality is referred to in another poem, the doggerel 'A Refusal' (see BYRON). Hardy's later novels contain a number of allusions to Swinburne's poems. He praised the biography of Swinburne (1917) by his friend Edmund *Gosse, as well as the same author's article on Swinburne in the *Dictionary of National Biography*, while Gosse's essay 'Mr Hardy's Lyrical Poetry' (*Edinburgh Review*, April 1918: repr. in *CH*) observes that Swinburne 'prepared the way for an ultimate appreciation of Mr Hardy'. See also GISSING, GEORGE.

Symons, Arthur (1865–1945), author. Although now remembered mainly for his association with the Decadents and his promotion in England of the French Symbolists, Symons was a prolific poet, prose writer, critic, and translator, as well as an influential editor. In 1900 Hardy sent him personal information for use in the *Encyclopaedia Britannica* article he was writing, and in the same year Hardy read Symons's *Images of Good and*

Evil (1899) and *The Symbolist Movement in Literature* (1899). In 1906 Symons published 'A Note on the Genius of Thomas Hardy' in the *Saturday Review*; the previous year he had dedicated to Hardy his collection of stories and sketches *Spiritual Adventures*, and Hardy had given high praise to one of the pieces in that volume, 'Seaward Lackland'. He also praised Symons's *Introduction to the Study of Browning* (enlarged edn., 1906) and his *Figures of Several Centuries* (1916). Later Symons published an article on Hardy in the *Dial* (1920) and a book-length *Study of Thomas Hardy* (1927). The two men met in London and Hardy invited Symons to Max Gate; their correspondence, mainly on literary topics, suggests sincere mutual admiration rather than intimacy.

T

Tauchnitz editions. Baron Christian Bernhard von Tauchnitz (1816–95) founded in 1837 in Leipzig a publishing house that in 1841 began to issue a series of English-language titles eventually known as the 'Collection of British and American Authors'. These small volumes, often in paper wrappers, though strictly speaking intended for sale only on the Continent, came to be sold worldwide over a period of more than a hundred years; by 1943, no fewer than 5,370 titles had appeared, and it has been estimated that sales totalled some 40 million.

Tauchnitz began in 1876 to purchase the rights to publish works by Hardy in this format: the first, *The Hand of Ethelberta* (for the Continental rights to which Tauchnitz paid the author £40), was followed by eight other novels and several collections of short stories, to a total of thirteen titles. Hardy's letters contain references to the negotiations involved, and his autobiography notes (*LW* 91) that he received from William *Tinsley, the publisher of *Under the Greenwood Tree*, the sum of £10 as a half-share of Tauchnitz's payment for the Continental copyright of that novel. The Tauchnitz editions are textually significant since Hardy sometimes took the opportunity to introduce corrections into his previously published texts: in 1882, for instance, he sent Tauchnitz a list of corrections for the edition of *Two on a Tower* published in the following year.

Tennyson, Alfred (1809–92), poet. The most widely admired poet of his time, he was Poet Laureate from 1850, and was elevated to the peerage in 1882. While admiring Tennyson's artistry, Hardy's own preference from the outset was for a less ornate style in which sense took precedence over euphony. He met Tennyson in London in March 1880; Tennyson told him on that occasion that his favourite among Hardy's novels was *A Pair of Blue Eyes*, a work that includes five quotations from *In Memoriam*. The same poem is quoted or referred to in several other works by Hardy (*TDU* 27; the 'Apology' to *Late Lyrics and Earlier*; *LW* 230, 275). Hardy's interest in Tennyson's work over a long period is illustrated by a wide range of allusions in his writings to Tennyson's poems: 'The Two Voices' provides an epigraph for *A Pair of Blue Eyes* (27); 'Oenone' is quoted in the same novel (11) as well as in *Two on a Tower* (37); *The Princess* is quoted (but misremembered) in *The Mayor of Casterbridge* (20), and also provides the title of *Time's Laughingstocks*; 'Morte d'Arthur' in *Tess of the d'Urbervilles* (52); 'Tithonus' in *The Well-Beloved* (chapter-title to 3.8); 'A Dream of Fair Women' in *Desperate Remedies* (9.3) and on the title-page of *The Dynasts*; and 'Locksley Hall' in the poem 'A Sign-Seeker'. 'The Lady of Shalott' may have exerted a more generalized influence on *Two on a Tower*. Whether by accident or design, the distant appearance of Camelot, the mists, wind, and rain, and the reference to wallowing swine in *The Idylls of the King* (representing 'the ideal . . . and the warring elements of the flesh'), have some resemblances to the 'deadly war waged between flesh and spirit' (1895 preface) and other elements in *Jude the Obscure*.

Hardy sympathized with the radical views expressed in *Maud*, which is also quoted from in the 'Apology' to *Late Lyrics and Earlier*, but he dismissed Tennyson as 'a mere Philistine of a thinker', thought his religious views outmoded (see the poem 'An Ancient to Ancients'), and could not accept the 'All is well' of *In Memoriam* (see 'The Impercipient' and 'In Tenebris II'). He attended Tennyson's funeral in Westminster Abbey, but found the service less impressive than 'a plain country interment' (*LW* 265), no doubt recalling that of his father a few months earlier. FBP

Tess of the d'Urbervilles. The twelfth of Hardy's fourteen published novels.

Composition

Hardy began writing *Tess* in the autumn of 1888 in response to a commission from the fiction syndicators W. F. Tillotson and Son of

Bolton, Lancashire. They had offered him 1,000 guineas for a serial that would be first issued in a range of English newspapers, and he had agreed on 29 June 1888 to provide the first four instalments a year later. In the event he did not get anything to Tillotson's until 9 September 1889, but he was regularly in touch with them through the summer, incidentally providing us with an early title (though not the first): 'The Body and Soul of Sue' (11 July 1889: *L* i 194). Sue is the third name given to the heroine in the extant manuscript of *Tess* (British Library), following 'Love' and 'Cis', and it appears as an original reading only on pages that run from her preparations to go to work at Trantridge to Dairyman Crick's story about William Dewy and the bull; the phrasing of the title suggests that Hardy had in mind his heroine's violation and the short life of her child. A little later he had changed his mind again, and called the novel 'Too late, Beloved' in a letter of 4 August (*L* i 196); when he sent Tillotson's about half of the novel on 9 September he called it 'Too Late Beloved' (*L* i 200)—thus offering for the student of Hardy's writing a vivid example of the difference a comma can make. By this time the heroine's name was Rose-Mary, and Hardy was chiefly struck by the bitter ironies involved in her relationship with Angel Clare.

The partial manuscript was sent by Tillotson's to the printers before they had read it; when they did look at what they had bought they were horrified—sex in the wood, an illegitimate baby, and an unauthorized baptism were not the kind of incidents they were used to considering in fiction, even in 1889. They asked for changes, but Hardy demurred; they agreed to pay, but would not publish, and Hardy suggested cancelling the agreement altogether—and this was done, on 25 September.

This bare record of exchanges conceals powerful emotions. For fifteen years Hardy had been aware that the truths of sexual relations and their consequences which he wished to embody in his fiction were not acceptable to the editors of serial-publishing magazines—and he had permitted himself to make such changes as they required. Now he absolutely refused to do this. Why? Perhaps in part because he was more intimately involved with the heroine he was creating than with the central figure of any of his earlier books, but also because his disgust at the moral hypocrisy of the class with which he had to deal had for once overflowed into resistance. He had to write for magazines in order to live, but for once he abandoned the largest payment he had ever been offered for a serial rather than mutilate on such grounds his growing work. His subsequent actions with regard to *Tess* can only be explained thus.

By the middle of November 1889 Hardy had offered the novel to two other magazine editors, both of whom he had every reason to think would reject it. Edward Arnold of *Murray's Magazine* told him, 'I know well enough that these tragedies are being played out every day in our midst, but I believe the less publicity they receive the better, and that it is quite possible and very desirable for women to grow up and pass through life without knowledge of them' (15 November; DCM). Mowbray *Morris of *Macmillan's Magazine*, who had requested bowdlerizing changes to the serialization of *The Woodlanders*, thought the story had too much 'succulence' and was too open about sexual matters (25 November; DCM). At the same time as these men were considering *Tess*, Hardy had offered to provide for Arthur *Locker of the *Graphic* an unnamed serial for July 1890, which could only have been *Tess*; terms were agreed by 21 November, and of course Locker saw none of the manuscript.

The key to these negotiations is the essay that Hardy was now writing for the *New Review's* January 1890 symposium entitled *'Candour in English Fiction', in which he at last released the frustration he felt at being compelled by the economic structure of publishing to lie in his fiction about the realities of human life if he wished to make a living. It is clear, from the phrases in the letters of Arnold and Morris that Hardy underlined, that this correspondence fuelled the fire under his essay, and he only offered the manuscript to them because he knew they would refuse it—he just wanted to see the terms in which they would refuse.

Serialization

In the end, though, Hardy had as much trouble with the *Graphic* as with any other journal. His story-sequence *A Group of Noble*

Dames was published in the magazine at Christmas 1890, but not before it had undergone the most humiliating bowdlerization. Hardy, thus forewarned, made special preparations for *Tess.* The violation scene and the baptism and burial of Tess's baby were removed from the manuscript when he sent it off in October 1890, and were published as separate short stories in more 'advanced' magazines, and a mock-marriage with Alec d'Urberville was substituted for the violation. (The account of Tess's seduction by Alec was published as 'Saturday Night in Arcady' in a Special Literary Supplement of the *National Observer* (Edinburgh) on 14 November 1891, and the description of the baptism and death of Tess's child appeared as 'The Midnight Baptism: A Study in Christianity' in the *Fortnightly Review* in May 1891. For these purposes 'new material was added to meet the demands of an independent sketch and indications of the real origin of the episode, particularly the name "Tess", removed' (Purdy 69).) Many other passages in the manuscript were deleted in blue pencil so that Hardy could restore them when the novel was published in volume form (not all of them, however, were thus restored). This process shows Hardy's growing contempt for the magazine readers who enforced such censorship, assuming that they would be satisfied that Angel could reject Tess for failing to distinguish between a real and a fake marriage ceremony. It is also highly probable that the second part of the novel is, in ways not now retrievable, different from Hardy's original intentions for it.

The diminished novel appeared in 26 instalments in the *Graphic* from 4 July to 26 December 1891, and also during the same period in various provincial newspapers in England (where the text was taken from the *Graphic* setting before Hardy revised proof), as well as in Indian and Australian newspapers. In America *Tess* appeared in *Harper's Bazar* from 18 July to 26 December. Each episode in the *Graphic* was accompanied by an illustration (on 10 October there were two). Six were drawn by Hubert von Herkomer, the rest by his pupils Wehrschmidt, Johnson, and Sydall, resulting in a rather wide variation in representation of the main characters (see also ILLUSTRATIONS). *Harper's Bazar* reproduced only eleven of these, and differed from the English serialization in other ways.

Hardy thought more highly of the intelligence of his American serial readers, and though he could not restore the excised chapters, he rewrote on the proofs a succinct account of Tess's violation and the birth and death of her child, and removed most of his *Graphic* bowdlerizations. On the other hand the editor of *Harper's Bazar* made her own changes, deleting passages that suggested the capacity for sexual excitement in the dairymaids, and anything that might be construed as irreligious.

For details of the division of the novel into instalments for serialization in the *Graphic*, see Purdy 68–9 (the matter is complicated by the fact that chapter-numbers in serial and later editions do not always correspond).

Volume Publication

When *Tess* was published in three volumes at the beginning of December 1891 (the price, as was usual for three volumes, was 31*s.* 6*d.*, or one-and-a-half guineas), Hardy brought together most of the scattered elements of his original manuscript, though the episode of the dance at Chaseborough, immediately antecedent to Tess's violation, was retrieved for the first time in the Wessex Edition of 1912. The final detail to be added to the first edition was the subtitle: 'A pure woman faithfully presented by Thomas Hardy', and this last-minute addition suggested what proved to be the case—that, for once, Hardy had not fundamentally finished with a novel once it reached book form. The revisions he made for the one-volume issue of 1892 were substantial, and it is with this edition that the text reached its first completion. In America the novel appeared in three different forms in three years, as Harper's scrambled (inadequately) to keep up with Hardy's revisions to the English editions.

Tess was the first volume to appear in the 1895–6 collected edition published by *Osgood, McIlvaine, but was only lightly revised for this purpose, and it was not until a paperbound edition of 1900 for Harper that Hardy made further important changes—to Alec d'Urberville's conversion. When the novel appeared as the first volume in the 1912 Wessex Edition it also contained a general preface to all Hardy's work, and Hardy made another series of revisions, some of which derive from the changes made in 1900. There are six other versions of the novel which Hardy revised to a lesser degree; no other of Hardy's novels has so complex a textual history.

Reception

The novel was an immediate success, both with the public and with most of the critics—much more of a success with the latter, indeed, than Hardy had expected. There were few dissentient voices, though some of the praise was mixed with criticism of his style and of the overt nature of his moral lesson. Perhaps the most hostile review was by Mowbray Morris for the *Quarterly*, only emphasizing what Hardy knew of Morris's views already; the *Saturday Review* was also outspoken against the novel. A number of the positive reviews suggested that here was Hardy's masterpiece, and the *Westminster* called it (quite correctly) one of the greatest novels of this century and the greatest since George Eliot died.

Plot

Tess Durbeyfield's family in Marlott is descended on the paternal side from the Norman family of d'Urberville, but has come down in the world. In order to repair the family fortunes she agrees to seek work on the estate of some rich d'Urbervilles near the village of Trantridge, unaware that the name has recently been bought by them along with the estate. The son, Alec Stoke-d'Urberville, a handsome, idle libertine, is attracted to Tess, and succeeds in getting her alone at night in woodland. Hardy avoids describing what follows. Tess remains at Trantridge for some weeks, apparently as Alec's mistress, and then leaves in self-disgust. She has a baby, who is sickly and likely to die. Since her father will not have the vicar in the house, she baptizes the baby herself; when it dies the vicar refuses it Christian burial.

Recovering her vitality, Tess goes south to work as a dairymaid at Talbothays farm in the valley of the Froom; there she again encounters Angel Clare, a young man whom she had once seen at a dance in Marlott. The son of a vicar, he has renounced his father's narrowly Pauline religion and is learning to be a farmer. The two fall in love, passionately and deeply, despite the class-difference between them, and he presses her to marry him. Tess believes her past history ought to prevent her marrying, and puts him off, but ultimately is overpersuaded. Before the ceremony she attempts an account of her past by sending a letter, which, as she discovers, he never receives; she cannot bring herself to tell him face to face, and the wedding goes ahead.

On the evening after their marriage Angel confesses an affair he has had in London, and this encourages her to tell him of her liaison with Alec d'Urberville and its consequence. She forgives him, but he cannot forgive her; it is the usual double-standard operating. For Angel she was one woman, is another: love is not enough in him to overcome the teaching of his class and his family's religion. He abandons her temporarily, and goes to Brazil to try to find a farm (and himself), giving her money and leaving more for her with his parents.

Tess meanwhile has had to support her parents, and by the winter the money has gone. She is working on a harsh arable farm at Flintcomb-Ash, with two of her dairymaid companions from Talbothays, Izz Huett and Marian, and resolves to go to Angel's parents to ask for help; but she is frightened away by overhearing Angel's awful brothers talk slightingly of her. On the way back to Flintcomb-Ash she comes across Alec d'Urberville again, who, in a fit of enthusiasm, has become an itinerant preacher; he tracks her down, renounces his conversion, and (after Tess's father dies and the family is made homeless) persuades her, by taking care of her mother and siblings, to live with him in a seedy seaside resort, Sandbourne.

This is the state of affairs when Angel returns to England, having come to realize that he should have valued Tess for what she intrinsically was, and not rejected her for what had been made to happen to her—a lesson, Hardy suggests, we would all do well to learn. Angel finds Tess in a boarding-house with Alec, and speaks with her. She thinks that she now belongs to Alec, and sends Angel away; as he disconsolately returns to the railway-station, Tess has a rapid revulsion of feeling, believing that if she kills Alec, who deceived her by making her believe that Angel would never return, she will kill the whole problem. She stabs him to the heart with a carving-knife, and rushes after Angel.

By happy chance they meet, and set out across country; eventually they find an empty manor-house to shelter in, which becomes a refuge in which their love is given a space of five days to flower. Eventually they are discovered by a caretaker, and they move on, pursued by the police, who catch up with them as Tess is sleeping at Stonehenge, on what Angel believes to be an altar. Tess is arrested, tried, and executed for Alec's murder; she is glad to die, because she has experienced perfect happiness with Angel at Bramshurst Court, and knows him well enough to recognize that at some time or another he would hold her past against her—and that she could not bear. The novel ends with Angel and Tess's younger sister Liza-Lu walking hand in hand from the scene of Tess's execution. Tess had hoped that Angel might marry Liza-Lu, 'a spiritualized image of Tess', and Hardy leaves open that possibility.

Critical Approaches

When Tess is hanged at Wintoncester, the light goes out of the world Hardy has created in the novel. Tess was capable of love in a way that is only matched by Michael Henchard (*MC*) in Hardy's fiction, and love, more deeply than anything else, is what Hardy writes about—mostly, though not always, failures of love. Of course he is concerned with a hundred other aspects of life, human and non-human, some of them of individual or cumulative significance; but love, for Hardy, was the most powerful passion known to us, and was most urgently to be accounted for by a novelist worth anything to read.

And yet much discussion of the novel has been concerned with other topics than love; the problem is that Tess loves a man most readers find hard to respect, let alone admire. He is not a hero, and if he is a villain to many, it is because he is weak where he should have been strong and vice versa, because he allows himself to be ruled by convention when it seemed he had got beyond it. And so Angel is dismissed, and Tess's love for him tacitly treated as some kind of aberration.

But, when the narrator asks bitterly why Tess should have encountered the wrong man rather than the right one when she met Alec, the inescapable implication is that she should have met Angel—that he was the missing half of the perfect whole who 'wandered independently about the earth waiting in crass obtuseness till the late time came'. Sadly, the narrator says, in 'the ill-judged execution of the well-judged plan of things' (5) such happy coincidences in love rarely happen. We are prepared, though, for 'the late time' to arrive.

Before it does, Tess experiences Alec, thanks to her d'Urberville ancestry and her father's inability to act as providence for his family (a role Tess is seduced into filling by her own morally sensitive nature, and after her father's death by Alec himself). She receives his imprint, takes on his sexual compulsion, bears the fruit of his sexual imperiousness, not just as the baby Sorrow, but (thanks to her Victorian socialization) as a bitter legacy in her consciousness, which she can only extirpate by killing its originator (and her own right to live in Victorian society). The inner conflict generated in her by the recognition of the 'missing half' when he appears is severe, and is intensified by his mutual recognition of her.

When Tess walks down to Talbothays for the first time, she praises the Lord, then says, '"But perhaps I don't quite know the Lord as yet."' It is one whom she accepts as her lord that she finds there, the lord of all her days. She recognizes him at once; beneath his milking-clothes 'was something educated, reserved, subtle, sad, differing'—the archetypal other to which she is irresistibly drawn.

But which other is it? The texts of the novel offer two quite different versions of Angel, one embedded in Hardy's manuscript, the other available in the first edition and all other book versions of the story. When the narrator tells us, at the beginning of Chapter 18, what Tess saw when she looked at him as he rose out of the past, it is, in versions read today, as 'an appreciative voice, a long regard of fixed, abstracted eyes, and a mobility of mouth, somewhat too small and delicately lined for a man's, though with an unexpectedly firm close of the lower lip now and then'. When Hardy first conceived Angel, though, the description went thus: 'a tender voice, an eloquent pair of eyes, and a small mobile mouth of somewhat too delicate a cut for a man, though with a sufficiently humorous turn now and then'.

The firm close of the lip and the fixed eyes belong to the man who embodies Victorian cultural rigidity, who abandons the other half of his perfect whole because the socio-religious law bred in the bone says he must, and because his internal logic sets love below the law: forgiveness does not enter the case. The tenderness, the eloquence, the humorous twist of the mouth belong to the lover who, idealizing the beloved, cannot bear that she has been invaded by another man. There is a paper-chase of revision through the next twenty chapters to the nature of Angel and of his love for Tess, all tending to move him from one who loves passionately with his body and his spirit to one who loves intensely with his mind and his spirit.

The crucial detail to keep in mind is that, when the novel was rejected by editors on the grounds of its inappropriate treatment of relations between the sexes, Hardy had only written half of it, and Angel and Tess were in love but not yet married. The editors' grotesquely revealing responses radically altered Hardy's understanding of what Tess's relationship with Angel and Alec should show his readers. He set the novel aside for a while, and when he came back to it, it was necessary for Angel to change.

Consider the force that lies behind the revision to one of the more notorious (and the first) of Angel's thoughts about Tess: 'What a fresh and virginal daughter of Nature that milkmaid is' (18). Hardy tried several adjectival versions in the manuscript: 'superb', 'true', 'real', 'superb' again; and, unhappy with all these, changed to 'genuine' for the serial. It was not until the battle over Tess's purity was well and truly waged after the publication of the first edition that he decided on 'fresh and virginal'. Angel, as he had then become, might well have thought this, but not the first Angel, whose love was not for Tess's purity but for her intrinsic closeness to Nature, her elemental quality.

Hardy is apparently clear that the environment and the girl were transforming Angel: 'Amid the oozing fatness and warm ferments of the Var Vale, at a season when the rush of juices could almost be heard below the hiss of fertilization, it was impossible that the most fanciful love should not grow passionate' (24). And he transmitted his passionate love: 'Every time she held the skimmer under the pump to cool it for the work, her hand trembled, the ardour of his affection being so palpable that she seemed to flinch under it like a plant in too burning a sun' (27). 'In this way Clare persistently wooed her in undertones like that of the purling milk—at the cow's side, at skimmings, at buttermakings, at cheesemakings, among broody poultry, and among farrowing pigs' (29); above all, 'It was for herself that he loved Tess; her soul, her heart, her substance'. But then, after all this, we are told 'he was in truth more spiritual than animal; he had himself well in hand, and was singularly free from grossness. Though not cold-natured he was rather bright than hot; less Byronic than Shelleyan. He could love desperately, but with a love more especially inclined to the imaginative and ethereal' (31). The description is an idea that does not fit what has been shown. Hardy realized that he needed to create a man whom Tess would love with all her heart, yet who would reject her if he knew her past. So the transformation of the man through experience at the dairy farm is not allowed to happen—or rather it is overwritten.

Tess was only two-parts a fully realized human before she loved Angel. She was animal and spirit (soul), but her intelligence was hardly awakened. Alec dulled her spirit, awoke her animal, for a short while. The passage in which Tess says she can feel her soul go out of her body (18) is important because it draws particular attention to the dissociability of the two in her; that when she needs to, she can live in her soul. She is drawn spiritually in this way to Angel by his cracked music—second-rate in itself, but enough to awaken her fascination. It is not that he teaches her, but that he shows her what her mind is and what it can be for; indeed she never thinks in his way, though she repeats some of his ideas by rote.

And Tess idealizes Angel also. She loses her faith in the end, and cannot hold out in love against Alec's temptations of security for her family. Hardy quite overtly considers Tess's love for Angel as a spiritual conviction, and Alec in the last part of the novel is explicitly a Satan figure—tempting not Eve, as Alec's *Paradise Lost* quotation suggests (50), but one like Christ in the wilderness, one who is already suffering like Christ on the cross ('why hast thou forsaken me?'). But the partial analogy only emphasizes the difference: Christ is superhuman, Tess is not. She succumbs again, in her flesh. But when Angel's return reunites her body and her spirit, she recognizes her own sin against love, and she slaughters the Satan who enticed and cajoled and bullied and blackmailed and lied her to it. She achieves momentary bodily redemption and transfiguration through union with the beloved, and permanent spiritual redemption and transfiguration through the self-sacrifice of her death. To this story Angel (as also Alec) is incidental yet essential: the perfect other flawed by social convention, who humbly confesses his own transgression of love, and is rewarded for his confession with loving absolution by Tess—and perhaps with Liza-Lu. See also LANDSCAPE. On the opera based on this novel, see *TESS OPERA*.

SJG

Simon Gatrell, *Thomas Hardy and the Proper Study of Mankind* (1993).
Dale Kramer, *Tess of the d'Urbervilles* (1991).
Peter Widdowson (ed.), *Tess of the d'Urbervilles*, New Casebooks series (1993).

***Tess* opera.** An opera based on *Tess of the d'Urbervilles* was first proposed to Hardy in 1900 by an American, Charlotte Pendleton, evidently inspired by the Fiskes' dramatic version in New York in 1897 (see DRAMATIZATIONS). Nothing came of this, however, and it was a more professional and determined approach in 1902 by Baron Frederic d'Erlanger which won Hardy's consent. D'Erlanger (1868–1943), a naturalized British subject of German-American extraction, was a distinguished composer who had already had one of his operas produced at Covent Garden. A friend and associate of Puccini, he engaged Puccini's librettist, Luigi Illica, to collaborate with him in a highly Italianate version of the novel.

The première of *Tess* in April 1906 in the San Carlo opera house in Naples was one of the most remarkable in operatic history, since Vesuvius honoured the occasion with a massive volcanic eruption: hot ash and fearsome rumblings filled the air, the expected audience dwindled, and next morning the authorities closed the theatre, fearing that it might collapse. Hardy's response to this sad news was philosophical: 'all of a piece with Tess's catastrophic career!' (28 April 1906: *L* iii 204). Puccini in Milan had received favourable reports of the work and sent a cheering message, 'Sempre avanti e con coraggio' ('Ever onward with courage').

It was in Milan that a fresh production was presented in 1908, after which d'Erlanger was able to tell Hardy that Tess was in Covent Garden's plans for the following year. Rehearsals for the London production began in July 1909 with the role of Tess played by Emmy Destinn, following up her spectacular success when she introduced Puccini's Butterfly to London. The opening night was an impressive occasion, with Queen Alexandra in the royal box and social London attending in force. The critics were generally favourable, though with doubts about the opera's connection with Hardy's novel, so great were the liberties taken. Hardy was quoted by the *Daily Chronicle*, however, as being 'quite satisfied' and adding that 'one must remember that opera is a convention'.

Further performances scheduled for the following season would have coincided happily with Hardy's award of the Order of Merit, but the death of King Edward VII cast a chill on theatrical London. In 1911 *Tess* was sung in German at Chemnitz and in Hungarian at Budapest, but a New York production at the Metropolitan Opera failed to materialize, and d'Erlanger was forced to recognize that his work was not going to win an enduring place in the international repertoire. A gracefully unassuming man, he apologized to Hardy in a letter for 'not having proved more worthy, or rather less unworthy, of such a partner as you'. He enclosed a cheque for the total of Hardy's royalties—£34. One further performance came as an unexpected bonus. On 2 March 1929 the BBC broadcast a full-scale studio production under the composer's supervision in an English translation with leading British soloists of the period.

DH

Desmond Hawkins, *The Tess Opera* (1984).
Marguerite Roberts, *Tess in the Theatre* (1950).
Discography: Angel's aria in Act I, sung by Amedeo Bassi (tenor), reissued as Rococo 5323 (*LP*, Cañada); the same, sung by Alessandro Bonci (tenor), reissued as Belcantodisc eb23 & Belcantodisc BC 214 (*LP*).

textual studies. Textual study of Hardy's work began, it is not frivolous to say, while he was still writing his novels. The comments of 'some good judges across the Atlantic' resulted in the restoration of a few pages from the ending of the serialized version of *The Mayor of Casterbridge* that had been omitted from the English first edition (see HARDY'S PREFACE TO THE NOVEL). Differences between the American and English versions of *Tess of the d'Urbervilles* were the cause of some journalistic debate, and resulted in three textually different American editions of the novel in the first three years of its publication. In more general terms, it was common knowledge, held almost scandalous in some quarters, that the texts of both *Tess* and *Jude the Obscure* were very different in serial and first edition.

However, the first scholarly attempt to analyse and understand the relationships between the different versions of any of Hardy's works was *Thomas Hardy from Serial to Novel* by Mary Ellen Chase, published in 1927. This is still a useful book, and contains some factual material as yet nowhere else in print. However, the work has a number of drawbacks: it deals with only three novels, it pays no attention to manuscript material, nor does it distinguish between English and American issues. It was a substantial pioneering work, but it had no successors for over 30 years.

The publication in 1954 of the first edition of Richard Little Purdy's remarkable bibliography (*Thomas Hardy: A Bibliographical Study*) raised by its very richness of detail many of the questions that needed to be answered by textual scholarship, and in the late 1950s scholars began to take up the question of Hardy's texts again. Foremost amongst them were John Paterson in America and Dieter Riesner in Germany, both of whom worked with *The Return of the Native*. Paterson's *The Making of 'The Return of the Native'* (1960) was the first book-length study of the way in which any of Hardy's major works developed from its first inscription to its final version. It was revolutionary in its day, and is still essential reading for anyone working on that novel; but because he worked from a reproduction of the manuscript rather than from the document itself, Paterson missed or misinterpreted crucial evidence, and thus some of his conclusions about the genesis of the novel are seriously flawed. Reisner, in an essay in German, 'Zur Textgeschichte von Hardys Romanen' ('On the Textual History of Hardy's Novels'), published in the journal *Archiv* in 1962, initiated debate over Paterson's book and other textual issues; and Simon Gatrell, in *Hardy the Creator* and elsewhere, has sought further to modify Paterson's conclusions. A little later (1964) Riesner also published a detailed account of the genesis of *The Mayor of Casterbridge*, again in German ('Kunstprosa in der Werkstatt: Hardys *The Mayor of Casterbridge*, 1884–1912', in *Festschrift fur Walter Hubner*) and, as far as I know, sadly still unpublished in an English translation.

There were from this time onward occasional essays published in journals which amplified and revised Chase's pioneering work, including Robert Schweik's 'The Early Development of Hardy's *Far from the Madding Crowd*' (*Texas Studies in Language and Literature*, 1967), and (a very substantial piece) Dale Kramer's two-part study of the texts of *The Woodlanders* in 1971 in the *Bulletin of the New York Public Library*, the result of his graduate work, and a preliminary to his scholarly edition of the novel. Christine Winfield published the heart of her doctoral research in 'The Manuscript of Hardy's *The Mayor of Casterbridge*' (*Publications of the Bibliographical Society of America*, 1973), and this was followed by J. T. Laird's monograph *The Making of 'Tess of the d'Urbervilles'* (1975), an excellent first attempt to understand the development of the most textually complex of Hardy's novels, and a book that should be read in conjunction with the introduction and apparatus of the Clarendon edition of the novel (1983) edited by Juliet Grindle and Simon Gatrell.

Patricia Ingham's study 'The Evolution of *Jude the Obscure*' was issued in two parts in the *Review of English Studies* (1976), while Simon Gatrell's 'Hardy the Creator: *Far from the Madding Crowd*' appeared in *Critical Approaches to the Fiction of Thomas Hardy*, ed. Dale Kramer (1979).

Kramer's own Clarendon edition of *The Woodlanders* appeared in 1981; this and the edition of *Tess* mentioned still represent the only full critical editions of Hardy's fiction to reach the general public. On the other hand, the texts issued in Oxford University Press's World's Classics Hardy series have all been critically edited, and most of the Oxford World's Classics editors have produced editions with full apparatus and textual annotation as doctoral dissertations. Much fascinating and necessary material is thus still only available on microfilm or through inter-library loan.

The first (and so far the only) attempt to synthesize much of the work being done with the texts of Hardy's fiction was Simon Gatrell's *Hardy the Creator: A Textual Biography* (1988). This makes generalizations both about the development of Hardy's work from manuscript, through various printed versions, to the final collected editions, and about his life as a man of books, his relations with editors and publishers and illustrators, and his financial dealings with the same. Primarily, it shows what all textual studies of Hardy show: that Hardy was an obsessive and mostly successful reviser.

Most recently there have been Rosemarie Morgan's controversial account of the manuscript of *Far from the Madding Crowd*, which takes issue with Gatrell's work on the novel, as well as with the critical edition by Suzanne Falck-Yi; and Martin Ray's *Thomas Hardy: A Textual Study of the Short Stories* (1997).

To turn to the edited texts themselves: it used to be thought that it was possible, through intense study and analysis of all the versions of a work and of the issues surrounding its production and publication, to produce the ideal text. This view is no longer tenable. Editors must still perform the same intense scrutiny, but they are now aware that there is a multiplicity of justifiable texts they might produce, so long as the process involved is fully explained and all the textual evidence presented. Much depends upon the editor's own theoretical orientation. The imminent advent of interactive electronic editions will render editorial establishment of any text unnecessary.

The primary issues in editing Hardy's fiction have been two. Since the publication of Gatrell's 'Hardy, House-Style, and the Aesthetics of Punctuation' (in Anne Smith (ed.), *The Novels of Thomas Hardy* (1979), 169–92) it has been accepted by most editors that Hardy's manuscript punctuation—in part ignored by the first compositors of all his novels—though occasionally deficient in marks that have no rhetorical significance, like closing inverted commas, has intrinsic value, and should be preserved where the manuscript has survived. Secondly, many editors have, in general terms, accepted the revisions that Hardy made at various times to his novels. The major revisions occurred during the primary process of writing from manuscript through serial to first edition; for the first one-volume edition some time shortly thereafter; and for the first and second *collected editions of his work in 1895–6 and 1912. However, some works have considerably complex histories of revision—for *Tess of the d'Urbervilles*, for example, there are seventeen substantively different versions revised by Hardy to some degree or other, some unpublished.

The very extent of Hardy's revision, particularly dense for the first collected edition of 1895–6, has raised in recent years another issue. It has been suggested that, as far as some early novels are concerned, the revisions made twenty or even forty years later change the reading experience of the work to such a degree that in certain respects it is no longer the same work, and that, at the very least, it is inaccurate to call the 1912 version of, say, *Far from the Madding Crowd* or *Under the Greenwood Tree* a novel of 1874 or 1872.

Readers who are interested to encounter the consequences of this concern should look at the Oxford World's Classics edition of *The Return of the Native*, in which the editor has chosen to exclude from his critically edited text the substantive revisions made after the first edition was published and the serial ended its run in *Belgravia* in 1878, and provides in the introduction the compelling reasons for so doing. The text differs in several marked ways from all others currently available; it is not better, it is just what Hardy intended at one time rather than at another—something worth knowing, especially since it makes clear that to call a work by a single title does not guarantee that it will in all its manifestations be anything like the same.

The situation with regard to the texts of Hardy's poetry and drama is much better, thanks to the editorial work of James Gibson and Samuel Hynes. Gibson's Variorum Edition of Hardy's poems (1978) is not in itself a critical edition; he appends to the standard *Collected Poems* text annotations of all variants to which he had access. Samuel Hynes's five-volume *Complete Poetical Works of Thomas Hardy* is a critical edition, and Hynes had the advantage of access to certain manuscript material from which Gibson was excluded. His annotation is thus somewhat more complete, but the complexities of the transmission of Hardy's poetry texts means that he is forced into making uncomfortable decisions.

The essential problem again is that Hardy revised so frequently, and in particular it is that there is one strand of revisions made for the Wessex Edition in 1912, and another made for the *Collected Poems* edition in 1919. Towards the end of his life Hardy tried to reconcile the differences between the two traditions, but he did not succeed, and Hynes decided that he should attempt to fulfil Hardy's expressed desire. This leads to some alterations to familiar poems, but, as in any good critical edition, the evidence upon which the decision was taken to make the change is present, and the reader who does not like the new version can return to the old, while enriched by a more vivid understanding of Hardy's creative process.

It is regrettable that Hardy critics in general pay little attention either to the processes by which Hardy's texts have become what they are, or to the quality and nature of the text from which they quote and which has formed their response to the work. This is particularly true of criticism of the fiction, since so many indifferently prepared paperback versions of the 1912 edition are readily available for the works most often discussed. Very many critics still take it on trust that what they are reading is what Hardy wrote, and many still believe (or act as if they believe) that the *Far from the Madding Crowd* they are reading is the novel Hardy published in 1874. At present it certainly requires some effort of will to locate all the materials required to take these aspects of Hardy's writing into account, especially if a study deals with many of his novels; but such effort is often very rewarding. SJG

theatre. Hardy's attitude to the theatre was a paradoxical blend of engagement and dismissiveness. While he was living in London during the mid-1860s, his theatre-going bordered on the obsessive. He attended every one of Samuel Phelps's Drury Lane Shakespeare productions, arriving 'among the first of the pit queue' and carrying 'a good edition of the play' (*LW* 54). At the Princess's Theatre he saw Charles and Ellen Kean, and at the Haymarket John Buckstone and Mrs Scott-Siddons, the latter sufficiently impressive in *As You Like It* to have inspired a poem ('To an Impersonator of Rosalind' [*TL*). He even appeared on stage at Covent Garden as a 'nondescript' in a 'Forty Thieves' pantomime. But the idea that he had formed in London of writing blank-verse plays soon evaporated: 'almost the first moment of his sight of stage realities disinclined him to push further in that direction' (*LW* 55).

Despite this disinclination, there is much evidence that Hardy maintained a broad interest in theatre throughout his life. He was an acquaintance of Henry Irving, and saw him perform in *Richard III* (1878), *Romeo and Juliet* (1882), *The Bells* (1890), *Becket* (1893), and *Coriolanus* (1901). One of his favourite actresses was Ada Rehan, whom he saw in *The Taming of the Shrew* (1888, 1893), *As You Like It* (1890), and *A Midsummer Night's Dream* (1895). He attended a number of *Ibsen's plays, including *Hedda Gabler* (1891, 1893), *Rosmersholm* (1893), and *The Master Builder* (1893). His theatre-going after the turn of the century included several products of the Anglo-Irish revival: Yeats's *Where There Is Nothing* (1904), Shaw's *John Bull's Other Island* and *Man and Superman* (1905), Wilde's *Salome* (1906), Synge's *The Playboy of the Western World* (1910), and Lord Dunsany's *The Glittering Gate* (1910).

But for Hardy theatre-going was clearly as much a social as an intellectual pleasure. It was associated with the London circles, which included minor aristocracy and major men of the theatre (such as James *Barrie and Henry Arthur Jones), in which his own increasing eminence in the 1880s and 1890s allowed him to move. His curiosity embraced popular comedies and music hall as well as serious drama. A diary entry from April 1892 reveals at once the catholicity of his theatrical tastes and the social range of his friendships: 'In the evening with Sir F[rancis] and Lady J[eune] to the Gaiety Theatre to hear Lottie Collins in her song "Ta-ra-ra."

A rather striking tune and performance, to foolish words' (*LW* 259).

His regular theatre attendance coexisted with forthright condemnations of the contemporary stage whenever he was called upon to advance an opinion. The most damning public judgement came in 'Why I Don't Write Plays' (1892), his contribution to a discussion in the *Pall Mall Gazette* (31 August 1892) of the relative merits of fiction and drama. He identifies in plays 'as nowadays conditioned' a plethora of inadequacies: 'parts have to be moulded to actors, not actors to parts... managers will not risk a truly original play... scenes have to be arranged in a constrained and arbitrary fashion to suit the exigencies of scene-building'. Many of the problems are ascribed to the contemporary taste for 'the presentation of mountains, cities, clothes, furniture, plate, jewels, and other real and sham-real appurtenances, to the neglect of the principle that the material stage should be a conventional or figurative arena'. He had earlier covered similar ground in a contribution to a discussion in the *Weekly Comedy* (30 November 1889) of the possible establishment of a British 'Théâtre Libre', advocating that 'the imagination should be appealed to rather than the bare eye-sight'.

His perennially jaundiced attitude to theatrical realities is encapsulated in his response to an invitation (1908) to join a committee to establish a Shakespeare Memorial Theatre at Stratford-upon-Avon. Doubting that Shakespeare 'appertains particularly to the theatrical world nowadays', and predicting that 'all poets of high rank whose works have taken a stage direction, will cease altogether to be acted some day, & be simply studied', Hardy saw no good in either a memorial theatre or 'any other material monument to him', and declined to assist (*L* iii 313). See also DRAMATIZATIONS. KW

Keith Wilson, *Thomas Hardy on Stage* (1995).

'Thieves Who Couldn't Help Sneezing, The.' See UNCOLLECTED STORIES.

Thornycroft, Hamo (1850–1925), sculptor and Royal Academician (1888); knighted in 1917. He met Hardy in 1884 and was, like Hardy himself, a close friend of Edmund *Gosse. As well as executing many public monuments, including the statue of King Alfred in Winchester, Thornycroft produced (1915) a marble bust of Hardy, now in the Dorset County Museum, and a bronze bust, exhibited at the Royal Academy in 1916 and later presented to the National Portrait Gallery by the sculptor's widow. Hardy, who admired Thornycroft's 'virile style of presentation' (Manning, *Marble and Bronze*, 169), gave his enthusiastic co-operation to these undertakings, sent the sculptor a careful drawing, with measurements of his head in profile as well as one of his old straw hats, and attended numerous sittings at Thornycroft's Kensington studio. In 1924 Hardy asked for the loan of one of his friend's chisels (and received two in response), in order to carve a gravestone for his cat Snowdove.

Thornycroft's wife Agatha (née Cox), whom he married in 1884, was a woman of striking beauty and was acknowledged by Hardy as a physical model for Tess. She and Hardy were dinner-companions at Gosse's home on 2 July 1889 and got on well; later Hardy told Gosse that he considered her the most beautiful woman in England. Less extravagantly, he judged her 'the most beautiful woman present' at a party at Lady *Jeune's home on 15 March 1890; his diary entry for this event, quoted in his autobiography (*LW* 235), also refers to 'Mrs T. and her great eyes'. The Thornycrofts met Hardy on many occasions and stayed at Max Gate in the summer of 1900; a letter of Hardy's (29 July: *L* ii 264–5) describes a bicycling expedition to Weymouth during this visit. When Thornycroft died, Hardy sent a laurel wreath to his funeral by the hand of Thornycroft's nephew, Siegfried *Sassoon, who happened to be staying at Max Gate at the time. See also PORTRAITS AND SCULPTURES OF THOMAS HARDY.

Elfrida Manning, *Marble and Bronze* (1982).
Helen Upton, *THJ* 13 (1997).
Donald J. Winslow, *THJ* 3 (1987).

'Three Strangers, The', short story. Originally published in *Longman's Magazine* (March 1883) and, in two instalments, in the American *Harper's Weekly* (3, 10 March 1883), it was collected in *Wessex Tales*. Set in the 1820s, its central situation is the confrontation between a jarringly jovial hangman on his way to Casterbridge to carry out an execution the next morning, and his intended but unrecognized victim, a poor man who has been condemned to death for sheep-stealing but has escaped captivity. A dramatically effective moment is created when the condemned man's brother (the third stranger) enters and sees executioner and victim drinking together. This black comedy, with its implications of a savagely repressive social and penal system, is ironically played out within a framework of celebration, song, and dance, and communal goodwill: the scene is a christening-party in a shepherd's isolated cottage, humble enough but an island of warmth and security in contrast to the wild night raging outside.

At the request of James *Barrie, Hardy later produced a one-act dramatic version titled *The Three Wayfarers*, successfully staged at Terry's Theatre, London, on 3 June 1893. In 1926 Hardy revised and expanded the play for an amateur performance at Keble College, Oxford. See also DRAMATIZATIONS.

Three Wayfarers, The. See DRAMATIZATIONS; 'THREE STRANGERS, THE'.

Tillotson & Son was a publishing firm based in Bolton, Lancashire, and owning a number of Lancashire weekly newspapers. In 1873 the head of the firm, W. F. Tillotson, established Tillotson's Newspaper Fiction Bureau, which became one of the leading syndicates supplying fiction to magazines and provincial newspapers in Britain and overseas, and conducting business with many of the leading novelists of the day. Beginning in 1881, they handled four of Hardy's short stories: 'Alicia's Diary', for instance, was sold to them and 'widely printed, especially in provincial papers' (Purdy 152).

Tillotson's are, however, chiefly remembered for commissioning, but failing to publish, *Tess of the d'Urbervilles.* In 1887 they had offered Hardy 1,000 guineas for a serial of similar length to *The Woodlanders*, and publication was planned to begin in late 1889. When, however, Hardy sent them on 9 September the manuscript of the first half of his novel, which included the seduction and baptism scenes, they were considerably alarmed, and requested deletions and revisions. Hardy refused, and although Tillotson's handsomely offered to pay his fee despite their unwillingness to proceed with publication, he expressed his agreement that the contract should be cancelled. (For a fuller account of this episode, see Purdy 71–2; Purdy also provides (340–1) a useful account of the firm.) This harmonious resolution of the situation led Hardy to sign an agreement with Tillotson's on 14 February 1890 for a much shorter and lighter novel: the result was *The Pursuit of the Well-Beloved*, later revised and retitled *The Well-Beloved.*

Time's Laughingstocks. Hardy's third collection of verse was published in an edition of 2,000 copies on 3 December 1909. It contains 94 poems. His first collection, *Wessex Poems*, had appeared in 1898 in an edition of only 500 copies, and had contained only 51 poems; it sold so slowly that it was not until 1903 that there was a small reprint. Of *Poems of the Past and the Present*, which followed in 1901, no more than 500 copies were again printed, but with 99 poems it was almost twice as large. The reception of these first two books was mixed, and the stridency of some of the reviews of *Wessex Poems* was such that Hardy devoted five pages of his autobiography (*LW* 319–24) to defending himself. Some of the attacks on Hardy at this time are reminiscent of the attacks on Wordsworth and Coleridge, who— exactly one hundred years before *Wessex Poems*—had published *Lyrical Ballads* in an attempt to bring poetry back into touch with everyday life. Most of Hardy's critics were unable to appreciate that there was a new voice in the land.

The reviews of *Poems of the Past and the Present* were not so dismissive. Although the *Spectator* concluded that Hardy was 'barely a poet' (5 April 1902), the *Saturday Review* was kinder—judging, it is true, that 'his verse often halts, or dances in hobnails', but also conceding that 'as far as it is possible to be a poet without having a singing voice, Mr Hardy is a poet, and a profoundly interesting one' (11 January 1902). The interest was such that, even if the book was hardly a best-seller, it did have a reprint of 500 copies in January 1902. What had happened in Hardy's professional life in the period of nearly eight years between *Poems of the Past and the Present* and *Time's Laughingstocks*, to lead to a first edition of 2,000 copies, a second impression early in the following year, and a more favourable reception by reviewers than he had previously known?

The answer, of course, is *The Dynasts*. In his introduction to the New Wessex edition (1978) of that work, Harold Orel states that 'At the time of its appearance, in the first decade of this century, it was immediately recognized as the greatest imaginative treatment by an English author of the Napoleonic Wars' (p. vii). This vast 'Epic-Drama' was published in three volumes in 1904, 1906, and 1908. The reviews of the first volume were generally unfavourable, but as the second and third followed the critics were won over by the remarkable epic qualities of the work. It was Hardy's 'Iliad of Europe', and the group of 106 young writers who presented him with a first edition of Keats in 1921 thanked him for all he had written, 'but most of all, perhaps, for *The Dynasts*'. It was almost certainly behind the award of the Order of Merit in 1910, and, as Dennis Taylor points out (*Hardy's Metres and Victorian Prosody* (1988), 169), it played an important part in Hardy's metrical development and in his use, in his later collections of verse, of longer stanza forms. It is interesting, too, that throughout *The Dynasts* there occur passages that are poems complete in themselves and provide evidence of Hardy's growing assurance as a poet. In his *Hardy: Novelist and Poet* (1976), Desmond Hawkins sums it up well:

> In fact, *Time's Laughingstocks* does not represent even a halfway point in Hardy's output of poems, for there were to be no fewer than five volumes to come after it. It can now be seen as the volume which signalled not his departure but his arrival. *Wessex Poems* was to some extent Hardy the novelist taking the temperature of the water. *Poems of the Past and the Present* did something to consolidate his new, second reputation, but it was *Time's Laughingstocks* which demonstrated incontrovertibly the stature he was to achieve as a poet. Of the 94 poems in the volume more than half can stand with his best work. (p. 185)

Several important events had taken place in Hardy's life between 1902 and 1909 and influenced poems in this collection. The death of his friend Henry Joseph Moule (see MOULE FAMILY) in March 1904 was soon followed by the death of his beloved mother in April of the same year, and with her death there came back a flood of memories from the past. 'She had been', he wrote, 'a woman with an extraordinary store of local memories, reaching back to the days when the ancient ballads were everywhere heard at country feasts, in weaving shops, and at spinning wheels . . .' (*LW* 345). In the non-human sphere, another of his cats, Snowdove, met death on the railway line adjacent to Max Gate. In April 1905 the University of Aberdeen conferred on him an honorary LL.D., the first of several such honours that he was to receive. About this time he met Florence Emily Dugdale, later to become his second wife, and the love that developed between them, but had to be concealed, obviously led to worry and frustration. Further deaths followed: in 1907 that of his friend the Reverend Thomas Perkins, writer, photographer, and active campaigner in humanitarian causes; in April 1909 the poet *Swinburne, whom Hardy had so much admired since reading *Poems and Ballads* when it was first published in 1866; and in May 1909 *George Meredith, whom Hardy had first met in 1869. With Hardy's own 70th birthday close at hand, it might have been expected that the new book of verse would be particularly retrospective and melancholy. Edmund Gosse thought that the verses seemed 'preponderantly sad', and Hardy defended himself in a letter of 12 December 1909: 'I fancied that, bulk for bulk, there would be as many of a cheerful or neutral pattern as of a deeper shade. But possibly gloom is more telling than brightness—in my effusions at least—so that a great deal of the latter is required to counteract a little of the former' (*L* iv 65).

The first reference in Hardy's autobiography to the publication of *Time's Laughingstocks* is as follows: 'In the meantime he had been putting together poems written between whiles, some of them already printed in periodicals—and in addition hunting up quite old ones dating from 1865, and overlooked in his earlier volumes, out of which he made a volume called *Time's Laughingstocks*, and sent off the MS. to his publishers the first week in September' (*LW* 374). In fact he sent the first eight pages to *Macmillan on 2 September and the remainder five days later. On 18 September he wrote a letter to Macmillan headed 'Private'; it enclosed the poem 'Panthera', which is based on an apocryphal story that Jesus was the offspring of an adulterous relationship between Mary and Panthera (or Pandera), an officer in the Roman army. Hardy said in his letter that he had asked several friends about this and had been given opinions for and against. As a result, he had 'rewritten the poem, and made the events a possibly erroneous fantasy of the narrator' (*L* iv 47). Macmillan could at that time have rejected the poem, but they decided to take the risk and publish it.

The title of this collection may be a Hardyan recollection of Shakespeare's *The Merry Wives of Windsor* (III i): 'Pray you, let us not be laughing-stocks', but it is more likely that he is remembering Tennyson's *The Princess* (IV.496), which has the phrase 'laughing-stocks of Time'. If he is using 'laughingstocks' in the usual sense of 'objects of laughter, baits for ridicule', it is not a comprehensive title for the collection. It was, however, the title Hardy had given to a poem that appeared in the *Fortnightly Review* on 1 August 1904 and which later, with the revised title of 'The Revisitation', became the first poem in the book.

In his preface to the volume, Hardy begins by thanking the editors and proprietors of the periodicals 'in which certain of [the poems] have appeared'. It is a sign of his growing recognition as a poet that as many as 29 had already appeared in periodicals of such distinction as the *English Review*, the *Pall Mall Magazine*, the *Cornhill Magazine*, and the *Graphic*. The preface continues by remarking on the 'lack of concord in pieces written at widely severed dates, and in contrasting moods and circumstances', and this draws attention to a difficulty Hardy faced in every one of his books of verse. Because of what Michael Millgate has called 'the trenchant simplicity of his assumption that poetry was an entirely natural medium of human expression and, as such, entirely appropriate to almost any human situation' (Millgate 474), his poetry was immensely wide-ranging in subject-matter, mood, and tone, and no matter how much Hardy, with his architect's mind, wanted to categorize his poems in each book under subtitles, he was never really successful in doing so.

Time's Laughingstocks begins with sixteen poems grouped under the heading 'Time's Laughingstocks', then has 26 poems headed 'More Love Lyrics', then seventeen headed 'A Set of Country Songs', and finally 35 under the catch-all title 'Pieces Occasional and Various'. He had used the heading 'Miscellaneous Poems' in *Poems of the Past and the Present*, and presumably wished to avoid it in his new collection, although he uses it again in both *Satires of Circumstance* and *Moments of Vision*. He must have known that his subtitles in *Time's Laughingstocks* were open to criticism because many of the poems could have been placed under other headings. One of the reviews of the volume observed that 'these subdivisions are quite arbitrary, since many of the lyrics are narrative, nearly all the narrative poems are in stanzas of lyrical quality, and love or the death of love is in all of them' (*Morning Post*, 9 December 1909). It is not surprising that such subtitles disappeared completely from his last three collections of verse. The preface significantly refers to the volume as a 'miscellany', and the manuscript of this collection, now in the Fitzwilliam Museum, Cambridge, shows that Hardy had considered using 'Miscellaneous Verses' and 'Miscellaneous Pieces' before deciding on 'Pieces Occasional and Various' as his heading for the final section of the book.

Hardy goes on in his preface to say that 'the sense of disconnection, particularly in respect of those lyrics penned in the first person, will be immaterial when it is borne in mind that they are to be regarded, in the main, as dramatic monologues by different characters'. Here it is worth recalling that Florence Hardy, obviously at the dictation of her husband, wrote a letter in which she asserted that 'Speaking generally, there is more autobiography in a hundred lines of Mr Hardy's poetry than in all the novels' (*LW* 425); and we are entitled to wonder whether Hardy is not protesting just a little too much. He had done the same in the prefaces to the first two collections of verse, describing the poems as 'in a large degree dramatic or personative' (*Wessex Poems*), and insisting that 'much is dramatic or impersonative even where not explicitly so' (*Poems of the Past and the Present*). Hardy obviously approved of Leslie *Stephen's dictum that 'The ultimate aim of the poet should be to touch our hearts by showing his own' (quoted in *LW* 131), but he found it difficult to reconcile this with his natural reticence. An interesting ambivalence is revealed here.

The preface ends with the information that 'some lines in the early-dated poems have been rewritten though they have been left substantially unchanged'. Once again Hardy has resurrected poems from the past, some written more than 40 years earlier. We know that while living in London in the 1860s he had written a great deal of poetry and failed to get it published. When he eventually published his first volume of verse in 1898, some of these early poems appeared in it. Where had they been during all the intervening years, during which Hardy had had some seven different homes, and why did he not publish all of them then? Whatever the reason, he did not do so, and these relics of past time kept on being disinterred and revised in volume after volume.

Two of them, dated respectively 1866 and 1868, are to be found as late as 1928 in *Winter Words*, and there is an obvious reason why they were not published earlier. Hardy's explanation in his 'Apology' prefaced to *Late Lyrics and Earlier* (1922) that such poems had been 'overlooked' takes some believing. *Time's Laughingstocks* contains seven poems written in London in the period 1865–7: 'Her Definition', 'From Her in the Country', 'Her Confession', 'To an Impersonator of Rosalind', 'To an Actress', '1967', and 'A Young Man's Epigram on Existence'. Two poems, 'At Waking' and 'The Dawn after the Dance', are ascribed to 'Weymouth 1869', when Hardy was in lodgings there, and others may belong to this *Weymouth period. 'Her Father' has the year 1869 on the manuscript and 'In the Vaulted Way' has 1870, while 'Four Footprints' refers to 'tracks upon the sand'. Perhaps Weymouth provided the time and the stimulus for a burst of poetic activity. One poem, 'The Minute before Meeting', is dated 1871, and this would suggest that it is about his wife-to-be, Emma Gifford, whom he visited in *Cornwall at that time. 'He Abjures Love' is dated 1883. With its 'I speak as one who plumbs | Life's dim profound', it would have been kinder of Hardy not to have published it during Emma's lifetime. Two poems come from the next decade, the 1890s: 'The Division' (dated 1893), and 'The Dead Quire' (dated 1897).

The retrospective Hardy becomes even more retrospective in this new collection of verse. The death of his mother in 1904 was the stimulus for 'A Church Romance', 'The Roman Road', and 'After the Last Breath', and other ancestors are remembered in 'Night in the Old Home', 'One We Knew', 'A Wet Night', and 'She Hears the Storm'. The choir that had played such a large part in the life of his family features in 'The Rash Bride', 'The Dead Quire', and 'The House of Hospitalities'. The seven poems that make up the sequence 'At Casterbridge Fair' are another delve into the past, with 'After the Fair', dated 1902, ending with a shift from the immediate past to a past in which the Romans 'loved, laughed, and fought, hailed their friends, drank their toasts, | At their meeting-times here, just as these'. Some of the poems, such as 'Geographical Knowledge', are reminiscences from the Wessex of Hardy's youth and earlier. The cottage in the last-named poem, in which 'Christiana C——' lived, can still be seen in Lower Bockhampton. The poem 'The Noble Lady's Tale' is about the 18th-century romance between Lady Susan, daughter of the first Earl of Ilchester, and an Irish actor (they married, and are buried in a vault constructed by Hardy's grandfather in Stinsford church). 'Autumn in King's Hintock Park' was, Hardy told Florence *Henniker, a memory of walking in the Ilchesters' park (Melbury Park) 'years ago, when the incident occurred on which the verses are based' (*L* iii 242). 'Yell'ham-Wood's Story' is yet another poem making use of the Wessex that Hardy knew so well, and, along with Wessex places, he continued to bring to life in these poems Wessex people such as 'Rose-Ann' and 'Julie-Jane', 'Carrey Clavel', 'John and Jane', and others who are not named. Wessex customs and events are used by him again and again. There was an election in Dorchester on 12 January 1906, and two weeks later a poem by Hardy titled 'The Ejected Member's Wife' was published in the *Spectator*; subsequently this was retitled 'The Rejected Member's Wife', and it is a remarkable example of his ability to endow a particular situation with a universal sense of sadness and sympathy. That Casterbridge moment lingers in the memory. Hardy is on his way to making his poetry a Wessex Epic.

Love in a variety of forms provides the subject-matter of at least half the poems, but the division of these poems into personal and impersonal is often made difficult by ambiguities and a lack of circumstantial evidence. What, for example, can one make of a poem like 'The Sigh', which might be based on a real-life experience of Hardy's, or might just as well have been imaginative? One clue to Hardy's personal involvement is that, as might be expected, the more he is involved personally, the better the poem. It is known that 'On the Departure Platform' is associated with Florence Dugdale—or so she told R. L. Purdy in the 1930s—and this is certainly one of the best poems in the volume. Two other poems that seem deeply personal are 'Shut Out That Moon' (1904) and 'The Dead Man Walking' (1896), and both were written out of the unhappiness of his relationship with Emma and before the beginning of his relationship with Florence. The other Florence in Hardy's life, Mrs Henniker, is almost certainly the 'Dear' referred to in 'The Division', which is dated 1893, the year in which he met her. Emma is not forgotten altogether, however. 'The Minute before Meeting', dated 1871, must have been written about a visit that year to Cornwall.

A guide to Hardy's estimate of his own verse is the selection he made which was published in 1916 with the title **Selected Poems.* It contained 120 poems drawn from *The Dynasts* and the four books of verse that he had published by that date, and this, of course, included *Time's Laughingstocks.* As his intention was to bring his poetry to the notice of a larger audience, it may not be that he chose the poems that meant most to him, but his own emotional involvement would have certainly played a part in the selection. Hardy chose 26 poems from *Time's Laughingstocks,* among which were 'I Say "I'll Seek Her"' (thought by some to be about his 'lost prize', Tryphena *Sparks), 'In a Cathedral City' (which may be about Mrs Henniker), 'Let Me Enjoy', 'The Division', 'The House of Hospitalities', 'Shut Out That Moon', 'Reminiscences of a Dancing Man', 'The Dead Man Walking', 'He Abjures Love', 'George Meredith', 'A Church Romance', 'The Roman Road', 'After the Last Breath', 'One We Knew', 'The Dead Quire', and 'The Man He Killed'. These are almost all poems close to Hardy's heart. Just before his death he was revising *Selected Poems* in order to include poems from the three books of verse that had been published since 1916. Four poems that had been in the 1916 selection were dropped, only one of them a major poem, 'One We Knew', the other three being 'News for Her Mother', 'The Dear', and 'The Pine Planters'. One of the best of his narrative poems, 'A Trampwoman's Tragedy', was added.

Yet another group of poems which stands out in this third collection is his narrative poems. Of these the two best are 'A Trampwoman's Tragedy' and 'A Sunday Morning Tragedy'. Hardy thought the first of these one of his most successful poems, but even so he had had difficulty in finding a journal that would publish it. The editor of the *Cornhill* declined it 'on the ground of it not being a poem he could possibly print in a family periodical' (*LW* 341). It is a ballad-like story of passionate love, jealousy, murder, and a hanging. With the aid of a clever rhyme-scheme and a refrain that repeats half the preceding line, it has become one of Hardy's most popular poems. 'A Sunday Morning Tragedy' uses the same kind of ballad treatment to tell a story of a girl who finds herself pregnant, is given by her mother a crude abortifacient of the kind used for sheep, and dies just as her lover, who has at first refused to marry her, comes to tell her that he will. Was Hardy, one wonders, the first poet to write about abortion?

Four other poems—'A Dream Question', 'Before Life and After', 'New Year's Eve', and 'God's Education'—make up a philosophical/religious group. In them Hardy asks the God in whom he claims not to believe questions about the nature of existence. In 'God's Education' he as good as accuses God of cruelty; in 'A Dream Question' God cares not a jot for what his 'creatures say'; and in 'New Year's Eve' God seems to be unaware of what he has done in creating humans who have developed a 'Consciousness'.

One of the reasons given by Hardy for abandoning the writing of fiction and returning to his first love, poetry, was that he could say things in verse that could not be said in prose: 'If Galileo had said in verse that the world moved, the Inquisition might have left him alone' (*LW* 302). The four poems mentioned above, together with 'Panthera', show how right Hardy was. If we add to these 'One Ralph Blossom Soliloquizes'—about a man now in Hell who thinks about the seven women to whom he made love, and regarding whom he has no regrets (and some of the women share his feelings)—we can see how outspoken and daring Hardy was for his time. And there are other poems in the collection that are almost as challenging to contemporary morality: see 'The Dark-Eyed Gentleman', a clever pastiche of a bawdy folk-song; the satirical mockery of 'The Conformers'; and 'The Christening', with its challenge to conventional marriage.

Hardy might be able to get away with these avant-garde ideas in his poetry, but the Establishment was still capable of showing its displeasure. When a new Poet Laureate was needed in 1913, Hardy was passed over in favour of Robert Bridges, a conventional minor poet. It was the same with the Nobel Prize, which during the years of Hardy's greatest fame was awarded to a number of writers now almost forgotten. In his *Thomas Hardy as Man, Writer and Philosopher* (1928), the Swedish author R. E. Zachrisson could find no good reason why his nomination of Hardy in 1921 was unsuccessful, but conjectured that it was the result of 'the adverse criticism which was bestowed on Hardy in the eighteen nineties, especially from clerical quarters, and which even now has a few spokesmen among English men of letters'; these latter 'had prevented the majority of the Academy, with its susceptibilities to traditional influences, from acknowledging Thomas Hardy's greatness'.

It is ironic that Hardy had a rare gift for writing 'occasional' verse and would have made an excellent Poet Laureate. A fine example of this in *Time's Laughingstocks* is 'George Meredith'. Hardy had known Meredith for almost exactly 40 years, and on 18 May 1909, 'walking along Dover Street on his way to the [Royal] Academy saw on a poster the announcement' of his death, whereupon 'He went on to the Athenaeum and wrote some memorial lines on his friend'. These appeared in *The Times* on 22 May and are an eloquent and moving tribute. No Poet Laureate could have done better. The poem 'Aberdeen', which resulted from his visit to that city to receive an honorary degree, is another very competent occasional poem. Hardy's greatness as a poet writing about war had been shown in the poems about the *Boer War included in *Poems of the Past and the Present*. One war poem written too late to get into that volume is 'The Man He Killed'. It is a dramatic monologue spoken by a bewildered ex-soldier, and a brilliant treatment of the stupidity and futility of war.

Time's Laughingstocks can now be seen as a stepping-stone on the way to *Satires of Circumstance*, which followed five years later and is regarded by many as the pinnacle of Hardy's poetic achievement. Although, as always, the earlier collection contains a few mediocre poems, there is an overall confidence and competence combined with a wide range of subject-matter and emotional involvement. In the words of the reviewer in the *Spectator* (29 January 1910), Hardy uses verse 'like a master'. JCG

Tinsley, William (1831–1902), publisher. In 1854 he had joined his younger brother Edward (d. 1866) in establishing the firm of Tinsley Brothers, with premises off the Strand. Until its failure in 1878, the firm issued works by leading novelists, including Anthony Trollope, Wilkie *Collins, Harrison *Ainsworth, Mary Elizabeth Braddon, and Mrs Henry Wood, and became 'the chief producer of novels and light literature in London' (*Dictionary of National Biography*). In 1869 Tinsley rejected Hardy's first novel, *The Poor Man and the Lady*, but later published its three successors: *Desperate Remedies* (at the author's expense), *Under the Greenwood Tree* (of which Hardy, to his later regret, sold Tinsley the copyright for £30), and *A Pair of Blue Eyes*. The last of these was serialized in *Tinsleys' Magazine* (founded in 1868) before its appearance in volume form, and the letter of 27 July 1872 (*L* i 17), in which Hardy discusses terms for this work, shows a marked increase in commercial *savoir-faire*. This proved to be the end of their association, and it is evident that Tinsley did not take it kindly when Hardy's next novel, *Far from the Madding Crowd*, was given to Leslie *Stephen for the *Cornhill Magazine*.

Hardy's autobiography gives a lively and engaging account of the inexperienced young author's dealings with the shrewd publisher, and a number of his somewhat laconic business letters to Tinsley survive. Tinsley's memoirs, *Random Recollections of an Old Publisher* (1900), contain references to Hardy.

***Titanic* disaster.** On 15 April 1912 the SS *Titanic* sank, with the loss of 1,513 lives, after colliding with an iceberg during her maiden voyage. Hardy was recruited as a member of a subcommittee that organized a 'Dramatic and Operatic Matinée in Aid of the "Titanic" Disaster Fund', and wrote the poem 'The Convergence of the Twain' for recitation as part of a programme given at Covent Garden on 24 May 1912. The poem represented a prompt reaction to news of the tragedy, having been completed on 24 April, little more than a week after the sinking of the ship. It first appeared in print in the souvenir programme, and soon afterwards received wider circulation by appearing, in a revised and expanded form, in the *Fortnightly Review* (June 1912). (It was later collected in *Satires of Circumstance.*)

All of this seems to place Hardy in the role of a kind of unofficial Poet Laureate—a post he failed to be offered when it fell vacant in the following year—and to raise expectations of an 'occasional' piece in the Tennysonian tradition; the poem itself, however, does not conform to such conventional expectations. Just as 'Drummer Hodge' (see BOER WAR) had defied orthodox assumptions concerning a poem about a dead soldier, 'The Convergence of the Twain' expresses a quirky response to a large-scale tragedy. The poem is dominated by the fanciful notion, somewhat reminiscent of Donne and the Metaphysicals, of ship and iceberg growing separately and far apart in relentless preparation for their fatal meeting at the behest of 'The Spinner of the Years'. The human loss and suffering involved earn scarcely a mention, and here Hardy's treatment of the theme must have been curiously out of line with the response of the majority. For him the sinking becomes a grim and ironic lesson in the vanity of human wishes: the phrase 'human vanity' occurs in the second line, and this theme dominates what follows. As for his vision of the luxury liner resting at the bottom of the Atlantic, the emphasis falls so strongly on the persistency and survival of the non-human world that the effect is almost that of a grim Darwinian joke: 'Over the mirrors meant | To glass the opulent | The sea-worm crawls—grotesque, slimed, dumb, indifferent.' A public subject has been treated from an entirely unpredictable and wholly personal angle: Hardy has appropriated the historical event and made it his own, the specificity and topicality shrinking in relation to the poem's philosophical framework. One can only wonder what the audience at Covent Garden made of it, but it remains one of his most striking and impressive poems on a public theme.

'To Please His Wife', short story. It was published in *Black and White* (27 June 1891) and collected in *Life's Little Ironies.* Hardy had sold the story to McClure's Syndicate in September 1890. Three themes—marriage, social differences, and education as an instrument of social mobility—one or more of which is explored in most of the other stories in this collection, are combined in this story. Joanna, who has cheated her friend Emily of her lover, is obsessed by social ambition, urging her husband to make money at any cost, and longing to send her sons to university to be turned into gentlemen. The outcome is tragic: like Henchard in *The Mayor of Casterbridge,* Joanna moves inexorably towards a doom that is largely of her own making. The story is set in 'Havenpool', based on Poole, Dorset, and takes place in an unspecified period in the past, in contrast to the markedly contemporary atmosphere of, for example, 'An Imaginative Woman' and 'On the Western Circuit' in the same volume.

Tolbort, T. W. Hooper (1841/2–83), an early friend of Hardy's. The stepson of a Dorchester ironmonger, he attended the school in South Street kept by William *Barnes, who encouraged his marked abilities. Tolbort became apprenticed to his uncle, a local chemist, and in about 1860 formed a friendship with Hardy. His intellectual brilliance and outstanding gift for languages attracted the attention of Horace *Moule, who encouraged him to take the Oxford Local Examinations in 1859 and in 1862 the competitive examination for entry into the Indian Civil Service introduced only nine years earlier, in both of which Tolbort was placed first in the entire country. Having risen by his late thirties to the rank of Deputy Commissioner in the Bengal Civil Service, he was invalided home as a result of consumption soon after 1880, and died in Dorchester in the summer of 1883. Hardy seems to have visited him on his deathbed, and his touching obituary of Tolbort appeared in the *Dorset County Chronicle* on 16 August 1883. Hardy's attempts to find a publisher for Tolbort's book *The Portuguese in India*, in accordance with his friend's dying request, were unsuccessful.

Tolbort is referred to in Hardy's autobiography as one of two 'literary friends' (*LW* 37) with whom he became acquainted while still working at John *Hicks's Dorchester office, the other being Moule. Tolbort's prodigious intellectual gifts overshadowed the young Hardy's less spectacular abilities, and Moule's eager encouragement to him to compete at the highest level was in contrast to his sober advice to Hardy to concentrate on architecture rather than Greek. In the early short story 'Destiny and a Blue Cloak' (see UNCOLLECTED STORIES), the character of Oswald Winwood owes something to Tolbort.

Tomson, Rosamund (1860–1911), author, journalist, and editor. Hardy met Rosamund Tomson, née Ball, in the late 1880s, while she was married to Arthur Tomson, a painter and illustrator, and was publishing under the pseudonym of 'Graham R. Tomson'. He was evidently attracted not only by her striking beauty and demonstrated poetic gifts, but also by the sexual promise of her beguiling freedom of manner and stylish participation (as poet, essayist, art critic, magazine editor, and fashion writer) in the contemporary Aesthetic movement. Sexual undercurrents are clearly detectable in his few surviving letters to her (all written between September 1889 and December 1891), but by July 1893 he was describing her as an ostensibly 'enfranchised woman' who was in fact interested only in parading him as one of her admirers (*L* ii 24).

Conceivably Hardy had ventured a sexual approach and suffered a rebuff, or even taken flight upon discovering the full extent of Mrs Tomson's enfranchisement: already divorced from her first husband, George Armytage, in 1887, she left Tomson for the Australian-born writer H. B. Marriott Watson in 1894, and was divorced by Tomson in 1896. Meanwhile, in November 1894, a two-part article about Hardy that she published in an American journal, the *Independent*, included a description of his personal appearance that he liked well enough to cut out and paste into his 'Personal' scrapbook (now in DCM).

The literary reputation of Rosamund Armytage/Tomson/Marriott Watson, already damaged by her changes of name, did not long survive her death, but she has in recent years effectively been reinstated as a significant poet of the 1890s. Hardy himself never forgot her: she was probably the 'original' of Mrs Pine-Avon in *The Well-Beloved*; his library contained several of her books, including the posthumously published *Poems of Rosamund Marriott Watson* (1912) and an inscribed copy of *The Bird-Bride* (1889); and his poem 'An Old Likeness (Recalling R.T.)', first published in 1922, speaks of kissing her picture in recollection of 'a far season | Of love and unreason'. MM

Linda K. Hughes, 'Rosamund Marriott Watson', *Dictionary of Literary Biography* (forthcoming). Millgate 297–8, etc.

'Tradition of Eighteen Hundred and Four, A', short story. First published in *Harper's Christmas* (December 1882), where it is titled 'A Legend of the Year Eighteen Hundred and Four', it was collected in *Life's Little Ironies* and transferred to *Wessex Tales* for the Wessex Edition of 1912 and subsequent editions. It briefly narrates an anecdote concerning a supposed clandestine and nocturnal visit by Napoleon to the Dorset coast in order to select a suitable site for an invasion. An unnamed opening narrator introduces the main narrative, recounted by an old man, Solomon Selby (now dead 'these ten years'), who was a small boy at the time and observed the scene while looking after his father's sheep. The name Selby occurs in Hardy's diary for 1877 (*LW* 119). For an interesting comment by Hardy, nearly 30 years after the story was written, on the treatment of his fiction as fact, see *LW* 424–5.

tragedy. Hardy did not have a single, consistent view of tragedy, nor does his practice conform with one overall idea. As so often with English writers, it would be more appropriate to speak of the tragic element in his work, rather than to use the term 'tragedy', if by that is meant conformity to a precise, classical formula such as Renaissance commentators derived (with exaggerated attempts at precision) from Aristotle's *Poetics.* The two works which might be considered exceptions to this statement are his somewhat uninspired verse-tragedy *The Famous Tragedy of the Queen of Cornwall* (1923) and *The Return of the Native.* The latter adheres more strictly than any other of Hardy's novels to the unities of time and place, and, as John Paterson demonstrates in the introduction to his 1966 edition of this novel, it shows signs of having been originally designed 'in terms of the five parts or "acts" of traditional tragedy'. But its more Gothic and primitive elements and the interweaving of the two plots (concerned, respectively, with Clym, Wildeve, and Eustacia, and with Diggory Venn and Thomasin) suggest the Shakespearian rather than the classical model.

Scattered comments in the autobiography also tend to point in different directions. A note dated April 1878, the year of publication of *The Return of the Native*, comments that 'A Plot, or Tragedy, should arise from the gradual closing in of a situation that comes of ordinary human passions, prejudices, and ambitions, by reason of the characters taking no trouble to ward off the disastrous events produced by the said passions, prejudices, and ambitions' (*LW* 123). This seems to fit the emphases of *The Return of the Native* reasonably well, and is especially appropriate to the disastrously contradictory emotions which drive Clym and Eustacia. In 1885, however, when Hardy's mind was still full of *The Mayor of Casterbridge*, his comments turn on the themes of the inexorability of fate ('a tragedy exhibits a state of things in the life of an individual which unavoidably causes some natural aim or desire of his to end in a catastrophe when carried out') and the tragic irony involved in human proneness to illusion ('the business of the poet and novelist is to show the sorriness underlying the grandest things; and the grandeur underlying the sorriest things'; 'Nature is an arch-dissembler. A child is deceived completely, the older members of society more or less according to their penetration: though even they seldom get to realize that *nothing* is as it appears').

The period from 1888 to 1895, encompassing *The Woodlanders, Tess of the d'Urbervilles*, and *Jude the Obscure*, reveals a shift towards blurring the distinction between tragedy and comedy ('If you look beneath the surface of any farce you see a tragedy; and, on the contrary, if you blind yourself to the deeper issues of a tragedy you see a farce': dated 15–21 October 1888), and an increased interest in natural versus social values—or, rather, what Hardy thinks is built into the instinctual, biological constitution of man, making him, so to speak, an extension of his natural environment, versus the arbitrary, and ultimately temporary, man-made conventions imposed by society.

Thus in 1889, after the publication of *The Woodlanders* in 1887 and two years before *Tess*, he comments: 'That which, socially, is a great tragedy may be in Nature no alarming circumstance', and in 1895, the year of *Jude*, he writes, in a notably combative spirit: 'Tragedy may be created by an opposing environment either of things inherent in the universe, or of human institutions. If the former be the means exhibited and deplored, the writer is regarded as impious; if the latter, as subversive and dangerous ...'.

Modern tragedy is predominantly social tragedy. To a number of critics this means that the tragic element in Hardy's work lacks the fundamental, mythic dimension, the sense of things inherent in the structure of the universe which informs classical Greek tragedy and the great Shakespearian tragedies. Most notably, for D. H. *Lawrence there is a failure of radical commitment in Hardy which undermines the tragic power of his work and leaves it in a halfway-house position. In his unfinished and posthumously published *Study of Thomas Hardy*, written in 1914, Lawrence argues that, although Hardy's protagonists often enough break through 'the shell of manner and convention', they succumb nevertheless to what must ultimately be recognized as no more than the arbitrary rules and customs of society. The natural environment against which they move, and of which they often seem to be potent emanations, allies them with the mythic tragedy of the Greeks and Shakespeare, but there is a point at which Hardy makes them hang back. With acute perceptiveness, Lawrence recognizes that novels such as *The Return of the Native*, *Tess*, and *Jude* succeed in juxtaposing the mythic with the social, that Hardy shares with the great tragedians 'this setting behind the small actions of his protagonists the terrific action of unfathomed nature'. But within the lives of those protagonists it is the conscious, human code rather than the deep, unconscious compulsion of their natures (where they share in the ineluctable laws of Nature) that brings about their destruction. What, Lawrence asks, was there in the position of Eustacia, Tess, or Sue—and, interestingly, he adds Tolstoy's Anna Karenina—that was 'necessarily tragic'? He concedes that it was painful: 'but they were not at war with God, only with Society'.

The comments by Hardy quoted above suggest that he was increasingly aware of the socially determined elements he was dealing with in his later novels. There seems, indeed, to have been some sort of progression from classical to modern in the conception of tragedy that underlies his novels. *The Return of the Native*, as already suggested, aims a little self-consciously at a classically tragic effect; and Henchard, the hero of *The Mayor of Casterbridge*, is Hardy's most Aristotelian tragic protagonist, clearly informed with a sense of *hamartia* and moving along a tragic path to ultimate *katharsis*. But there are also features in these novels which belong to purely social convention. If Eustacia is driven by her magnificently headstrong nature, the ironies and misunderstandings in her relations with Clym, and especially Clym's mother, which belong to a less deeply compulsive level, are also at least contributory factors in her undoing; and in *The Mayor of Casterbridge*, Lucetta's fear of society's ostracism, with the damaging effect upon her of the skimmity-ride, is likewise a complementary, if subordinate, part of the novel's overall tragic effect.

In *The Woodlanders*, *Tess*, and *Jude*, the damning power of social opinion becomes still more evident. It is Grace Melbury's fear of impropriety that brings about (or at least accelerates) Giles Winterborne's death; and Victorian moral values, ironically conditioning Angel Clare's judgement in spite of his nominally liberal outlook, that precipitate Tess's tragedy. With Jude and Sue, the contradictions inherent in Angel become grotesquely exaggerated. Sue's would-be rejection of the illiberal, lesser morality of the merely human consciousness is even more radically flawed, and the spurious enlightenment that Jude derives from her, though less brittle, is achieved only for him to find himself the victim of her psychological atavism. And in relation to the rest of society their status as free spirits merely exposes them to prejudices that exacerbate their insecure position, lacking as they do the cunning of an Arabella who knows how to cover her more radical amorality with acceptable masks of conformity.

In both *Tess* and *Jude*, the relevance of Hardy's 1888 comment on the interchangeability of tragedy and comedy also becomes more apparent. That Tess's father gets himself drunk, literally and metaphorically, on the news an antiquarian parson gives him of his noble ancestry is an unexpectedly fitting opening to *Tess*. It combines elements of heredity, farce, class distinction, and intellectual ignorance of the consequences of its own activities, in the kind of uneven mixture which characterizes much of the narrative that is to follow. Episodes that are deeply moving or searingly painful (whether in the Lawrentian sense 'necessarily' so or not) rub shoulders with others, like the painting in 'staring vermilion words' of 2 Peter 2: 3 (*TDU* 2. 12), that are almost caricature; and, as so frequently in all Hardy's novels, chance occurrences and coincidences like that of Tess's letter pushed under Angel's door, but left unread, operate almost equally as tragic ironies and bizarre sports of the immortals.

This process goes still further in Jude. Idealization that looks as much like ludicrous folly as noble enthusiasm is typical throughout of Jude's obsession with Christminster, and the tantalizing, often coquettish behaviour of Sue creates a generic ambiguity worthy of Polonius's 'tragical-comical-historical-pastoral'. Most comi-tragic/tragi-comic of all, the behaviour of Little Father Time and his killing of his siblings and himself ('*Done because we are too menny*') pose almost as great an interpretative problem with regard to genre, tone, and seriousness as a self-consciously postmodernist novel of the 1980s.

Hardy, arguably more than any other novelist who seeks to combine a full-length fiction with the more concentrated form of tragedy as practised in the theatre, varies his narrative to such a degree that all kinds of tragic, satiric, comic, and farcical effects can be found within the course of the same work. This is not incompetence but a result partly of the larger scale and more complex relationship between author and reader entailed in the novel as a literary form, and partly of the intellectual climate in which he as a late 19th-century writer was working. In common with other Victorian intellectuals, he was brought up in a Christian culture, with a strong emphasis in his particular rural background on the biblical and the 'churchy', but nevertheless found himself as an adult bound to accept a Darwinian science that undermined most of the accepted certainties of his childhood. A consequence was the opening up, or reopening, of the serious possibility of tragedy, since the fundamentally anti-tragic Christian belief in redemption and salvation no longer operated as an ultimate consolation for suffering and evil.

By the same token the kind of religious context which, in the tragedies of Aeschylus or Sophocles, made for a tragic subordination of merely human aspirations to the decrees of the gods was also undercut. Human rather than divine values became the measure of suffering, with the contradictory result that men and women appeared to suffer irremediable tragedies, which arose, however, from their own self-created mental tyrannies and were, to that extent, not irremediable. Attitudes in a Hardy tragedy therefore fluctuate. Tonal instability is endemic because the blame for human suffering shifts around in accordance with the uncertainty as to its fundamental cause, and with the shifting emotional attitudes of characters who now reject traditional ties felt as impeding their individual selves, for no inherent reason, and now feel the old-fashioned Christian sense of guilt and are ready in consequence to accept a supposedly deserved punishment for their crimes.

It is this process which reaches its culmination in *Jude*, making the novel at once the most and the least tragic of Hardy's novels and also the most elusive and kaleidoscopic in tone and style. Its tragedy, as Hardy suggests in his preface to the first edition (1895), is one of 'unfulfilled aims' rather than ineluctable destiny, and its form is not that of an organism, growing and decaying according to natural processes, but of a contrived 'shape and coherence' given to 'a series of seemings, or personal impressions'. To this Hardy adds, in a perhaps desperate attempt to ward off criticism based on traditional grounds of organic development, that the question of the 'consistency' of these impressions 'or their discordance, of their permanence or their transitoriness' is something to be regarded 'as not of the first moment'.

Most of the characters in Hardy's 'epic-drama' *The Dynasts* are, as John Wain suggests, too much like puppets 'to interest us as human beings' (Introduction to the Macmillan 1965 edition), and are therefore incapable of generating that sense of involvement essential to a tragic effect on the reader. However, this puppet status also belongs to an overall conception of an irresistible, impersonal Will, a bleak, latter-day version of the Greek immortals, which—though it catches up the characters, including Napoleon and his seemingly masterful grand designs, in the cogs of its universal mechanism—is the subject of commentary by a cast of 'Phantom Intelligences', including both 'Spirits Sinister and Ironic' and 'The Spirit of the Pities'. Their comments are unavailing as far as the action is concerned, but they articulate what are essentially human responses, sympathetic as well as malicious, to the destructive spectacle which unfolds beneath them.

And this, together with the particularized scenes which operate as a dramatic version of the 'series of seemings' of which *Jude* is composed, serves to project some sense of tragic perspective, if only in the form of a moving discrepancy between things as they immovably are and the pitiful wastefulness that the human consciousness feels in such an arrangement. For Hardy the tragic lies in the sense of the discrepancy, and here, as in the novels, it is his capacity to sharpen that sense in his readers that entitles him to be considered as a writer of tragedy. RPD

R. P. Draper (ed.), *Thomas Hardy: The Tragic Novels* (1991).

Jeannette King, *Tragedy in the Victorian Novel: Theory and Practice in the Novels of George Eliot, Thomas Hardy and Henry James* (1978).

Dale Kramer, *Thomas Hardy: The Forms of Tragedy* (1975).

Cedric Watts, *Jude the Obscure* (Penguin Guides) (1992).

'Tragedy of Two Ambitions, A', short story. First published in the *Universal Review* (December 1888), it was collected in *Life's Little Ironies*, but transferred to *Wessex Tales* for the Wessex Edition (1912). In late July 1888 Hardy offered the story, then only in outline, to Harry Quilter, editor of the above magazine; it was written quickly and sent to Quilter on 19 August. Like 'The Son's Veto' and 'To Please His Wife' (both also in *LLI* as finally ordered), it is deeply concerned with class barriers and social aspirations, while it looks forward to *Jude the Obscure* in its presentation of the difficulties of poor young men who wish to go to a university. Unlike Jude, however, Joshua is cannily conscious that education, the teaching profession, and a career in the Church are to be prized as rungs on the ladder of worldly advancement. In dealing with these themes, as also with the drunken father who proves a serious embarrassment to his ambitious sons, Hardy seems to be exploring personal anxieties and aspects of his own past. Like 'An Imaginative Woman' (also in *LLI*), the story has a richly ironic conclusion: Hardy's anti-clericalism is evident in the grimly comic scene in which Joshua, who has every reason to be grateful for his father's demise, conducts his burial service with exemplary propriety. The old man, however, has what amounts to the last word, since his walking-stick, stuck into a hedge, puts forth leaves—an unmistakably symbolic and felicitously poetic assertion of the naturalness and vitality of his far from 'respectable' life in contrast to the repression and sterility that are the price of his sons' success.

translations. Hardy's international reputation became well established during his lifetime both within and beyond the English-speaking world. Translations of a number of his novels began to appear soon after their original publication: a Dutch version of *Far from the Madding Crowd*, for instance, in 1876, and German (1897), Swedish (1900), and French (1901) versions of *Jude the Obscure*. A particular favourite among foreign translators was *Tess of the d'Urbervilles*, which within a decade of its appearance had become available in Russian (1893), Italian (1894), German (1895), Swedish (1900), and French (1901); later translations of this novel include versions in Danish, Norwegian, Spanish, Lettish, Czech, Bulgarian, Romanian, Hungarian, Chinese, Japanese, Korean, and Hindi. Other novels had to wait longer for attention: *Under the Greenwood Tree*, for instance, seems to have had no 19th-century translators, though versions in French (1910), Spanish (1921), Swedish (1937), and German (1949) were among those that appeared later. Of the other earlier novels *Far from the Madding Crowd* received more attention than most, with (apart from the Dutch version already noted) French, Swedish, and Spanish renderings appearing in Hardy's lifetime, and others in Polish, Russian, Italian, Hindi, and Serbo-Croat among those to appear later. *The Return of the Native* also received some attention, with translations during Hardy's lifetime into Hungarian (1898) and French (1923).

The 1920s—that is, the closing years of Hardy's life—appear to have been a particularly active period for translators, though some of the 'minor' or 'lesser' novels received little attention then or at other times. The short stories have not been neglected—examples range from a German version of *Life's Little Ironies* published as early as 1904, to 'Barbara dei Grebe', an Italian version of 'Barbara of the House of Grebe', which appeared in 1991—but for obvious reasons translators have shown themselves less eager to take on Hardy's verse (although see below for some notable exceptions to this generalization).

Outside Europe, Japan has been outstanding for having developed Hardy translation into a minor industry from the early years of the 20th century. Hardy's name had been introduced to the Japanese reading public by Shoyo Tsubouchi as early as 1890, and the first translation—a serial version of *Tess* by Seika Takase—began to appear in 1906 (discontinued 1909). Various short stories were also translated at this time: 'The Melancholy Hussar of the German Legion' by Shukotsu Togawa (1907), *Life's Little Ironies* by Meiyo Sato (1908), and 'A Tragedy of Two Ambitions' by Siyoshi Sato (1911). An unexpected item is an extract from *The Hand of Ethelberta*, translated by Tokuboku Hirata and published in 1912. The same year also saw the second attempt to translate *Tess*, this time by Koryo Yamada, though again the work was never completed. The first complete translation of this novel, by Hirata, was issued in two volumes in 1925–6. *Tess* has proved by far the most popular of Hardy's novels in Japan, and, among others, translations appeared in 1929 (by Shinzaburo Miyajima), 1930 (Kazuo Hirotsu), 1957 (Yoshio Yamanouchi), 1960 (Soji Inoue and Eiji Ishida), 1961 (Mamoru Osawa), 1969 (Tomoji Abe), 1980 (Hiroyuki Ide).

Several of these translators also tried their hand at other works by Hardy: Miyajima translated *Far from the Madding Crowd* (1933) and *The Mayor of Casterbridge* (1934), Abe *Under the Greenwood Tree* (1936), Osawa *The Return of the Native* (1952) and *Jude the Obscure* (1955). The last of these has proved the second most popular of Hardy's novels in Japan, and there are earlier translations by Seiichi Uchida (1925) and Yutaro Ito (1927) as well as a later one by Shizuko Kawamoto (1988). Meanwhile, Hardy's short stories continued to attract translators. Yoshisaburo Okakura translated 'A Tradition of Eighteen Hundred and Four' in 1915, Torajiro Sawamura 'Alicia's Diary' in 1924, and Junichiro Tanizaki 'Barbara of the House of Grebe' in 1927. In 1925 Tatsu Yaguchi published a selection of Hardy's stories in translation that included 'The Melancholy Hussar of the German Legion', 'What the Shepherd Saw', 'For Conscience' Sake', 'To Please His Wife', 'An Imaginative Woman', and 'The Three Strangers' (the last two in Shimpo Ishii's translation). Yutaka Morimura and Kentaro Omiya published a selection of nine stories in 1926, and Morimura later produced two further collections (1932, 1935).

Hardy's poems have by no means been neglected by Japanese translators. As early as 1930 Shigeo Yoshiwara translated 69 poems and Hirata published versions of 34 short lyrics; Osawa translated thirteen poems in 1955 and a further 25 (selected from *Wessex Poems*) in 1959. In 1967 Bunnsuke Yamamoto produced a collection of 121 Hardy poems in translation. But the outstanding work in this field has been done by Kensuke Morimatsu, whose two-volume translation of Hardy's complete poems was published in 1995. *The Dynasts* had been translated by Chuzo Uchidate in 1931. Polish translations of Hardy are comprehensively surveyed in an article by Jan Jedrzejewski (*THJ* 7, 1991). NP/YT

travels, Continental. Hardy made nine trips to various parts of the Continent of Europe between 1874 and 1897, all of which are recorded, in greater or lesser detail, in his autobiography. Other sources of information about the journeys are diaries kept by Emma Hardy, letters written while abroad, and notes made in guide-books still surviving from Hardy's library.

The nine visits are as follows:

(1) In September 1874 the Hardys went to Dieppe, Rouen, and Paris on their honeymoon (*LW* 104; Millgate 164–7; *L* i 31).

(2) In May and June 1876 they went to Holland (Rotterdam, The Hague, Scheveningen), the German Rhineland (Emmerich, Cologne, Bonn, Coblentz, Ehrenbreitstein, Mainz, Heidelberg, Carlsruhe, Baden, Strassburg, Metz), and Belgium (Brussels, Waterloo, Antwerp) (*LW* 113–14; Millgate 182–4).

(3) In July and August 1880 they went to Northern France (Boulogne, Amiens, Etretat, Le Havre, Trouville, Honfleur, Lisieux, Caen) (*LW* 142–3).

(4) In October and November 1882 they were in Paris (*LW* 160; Millgate 229).

(5) In March and April 1887 they went to France (Aix-les-Bains) and Italy (Turin, Genoa, Pisa, Florence, Rome, Venice, Milan) (*LW* 194–204; Millgate 280–3; *L* i 163).

(6) In May and June 1888 they were again in Paris (*LW* 217–18).

(7) In August 1890 Hardy went with his brother Henry to Paris (*LW* 240; Millgate 306).

(8) In September and October 1896 Hardy and Emma went to Belgium (Ostend, Bruges, Brussels, Namur, Dinant, Spa, Liège, Brussels, Waterloo) (*LW* 299–302; *L* ii 130, 134–5).

(9) In June and July 1897 they went to Switzerland (Neuchâtel, Berne, Interlaken, Grindlewald, Thun, Lausanne, Zermatt, Geneva) (*LW* 310–13; Millgate 386–7; *L* ii 166–9).

This might be a record of the Continental journeys of any middle-class English couple in the second half of the 19th century; however, it is striking that, in view of the growing emotional and intellectual estrangement between Hardy and his first wife, they should have continued taking elaborate and extensive foreign holidays together for so long. It seems that the habits of twenty years of living together were hard indeed to break.

It is natural that the novels in which Hardy drew most fully on his European experiences are primarily concerned with the lives of affluent people—*The Hand of Ethelberta* and *A Laodicean.* In the former Ethelberta visits Rouen, and there are some pretty descriptions of an inn and the view from the spire of the cathedral; in the latter novel, however, there is a more thoroughgoing use of Hardy's travels to date. When Hardy required some fluidity of movement to contrast with the massive stability of Stancy Castle, the architectural presence at the heart of the novel, he chose to send most of his personages to the Mediterranean, and then up the Rhine, reversing precisely the itinerary of his own 1876 trip. Subsequently the party moves, in leisurely fashion, through Holland and Belgium, and to Amiens, where the rambling tour concludes, as apparently does the equally rambling courtship by William de Stancy of Paula Power. It has been customary to dismiss this part of the novel as padding produced by the invalided Hardy, but there are some vivid and effective moments that catch, in a paragraph or two of description, a human significance: the image of the sand dunes of Scheveningen in the rain is one (5.9), enhanced by memories of the allusion to the same spot in the first chapter of *The Return of the Native.*

A Laodicean resolves itself in the pursuit to Normandy of the hero by the heroine, and Hardy's holiday of 1880 is pressed into use. A sharply described medieval street in Lisieux (6.1) provides a fresh stimulus to the medieval–modern contrast that is the central theme of the novel; the climax occurs on the beach at Etretat.

Hardy twice visited the field of the Battle of Waterloo, the climactic site of the Napoleonic drama that preoccupied him from time to time throughout his life—a preoccupation that issued in *The Dynasts.* The topographical details that help to make so vivid the last pages of that massive work are intimately shaped by his own explorations.

The journeys to Italy and Switzerland were perhaps the most fortunate in their transformation into Hardy's art, for they were made when he was turning in his mind to poetry, and, rather than forming the background colour for fragments of fiction, incidents that penetrated Hardy's imagination became poems, one or two amongst his most interesting. The majority were published in *Poems of the Past and the Present,* in the subsection he called 'Poems of Pilgrimage'.

In the Italian poems he is very conscious of the paradoxes the country presents in the relation of present to past: a Strauss waltz heard in the ruins of a Caesar's house 'blended pulsing life with lives long done, | Till time seemed fiction, Past and Present one'; a girl in the Roman theatre at Fiesole showed him a coin from Constantine's reign, and 'her act flashed home... the reach of perished Rome' as he recalled the same image on coins dug up in Dorchester; artisans in Rome build new in spite of the multitude of ruins about them that express clearly the futility of such enterprises. (A variant of this same favourite theme of Hardy's was stimulated later by the Matterhorn—first climbed by man in the 1860s, but, like Egdon Heath, utterly unchanged through all of man's paltry span of recorded history.) There are also poems on the historian Gibbon, on Shelley's Skylark, on the pyramid of Cestius (who was he? the poem asks—and answers, does it matter, when his memorial guides pilgrims to the graves of those matchless poets Keats and Shelley?), on Genoa and the Mediterranean. One final reminiscence of his Swiss travels is the memorial poem for Leslie *Stephen, 'The Schreckhorn', in which Stephen is merged with his 'spare and desolate' mountain, as *Swinburne is rocked by his white-frothed waves in 'A Singer Asleep', the companion elegy in *Satires of Circumstance.* SJG

Treves, Frederick (1853–1923). One of the leading surgeons of his day, he was the youngest son of a Dorchester upholsterer and traced his descent from generations of Dorset yeoman farmers. He had attended the school kept by William *Barnes in South Street, Dorchester, before going on to Merchant Taylors' School in the City of London and the London Hospital. Later he became a leading consultant, and was appointed Surgeon Extraordinary to Queen Victoria. In 1902 he became world-famous after operating on King Edward VII, who had developed appendicitis two days before his coronation; Treves was created a baronet in the same year.

As well as medical textbooks he published many works on travel and topography, including *Highways and Byways in Dorset* (1906), research for which had involved him in more than 2,000 miles of bicycling in order to visit every village and hamlet mentioned. Further evidence of his continuing interest in his native county is his becoming the first President of the Society of Dorset Men (1904–7), a position in which Hardy was his successor. Hardy attended, and chose the hymns for, Treves's funeral at Dorchester on 2 January 1924.

In the summer of 1907, which Treves and his Dorchester-born wife Anne spent in a rented house near Max Gate, he and Hardy met often and discussed among other topics 'the "poor whites" in Barbadoes' (*LW* 362). In 1915 the Hardys visited the Treves at their London home. Recording the death of Treves, Hardy notes that 'it was from the shop of Treves' father that as a boy he had purchased his first writing-desk' (*LW* 457). At least one guest was taken to Dorchester to see 'the shop that had been kept by the father of Sir Frederick Treves, the great surgeon' (Henry W. Nevinson, *Thomas Hardy* (1941), 17). Hardy's obituary tribute to Treves was published in *The Times* (text in Edmund Blunden, *Thomas Hardy* (1958)). Hardy's memorial verses to Treves are titled 'In the Evening' and also appeared originally in *The Times* (later revised and expanded); the last three lines of the original version appear on Treves's gravestone in Dorchester Cemetery. His fame has been revived in recent years by a film based on his association with Joseph Merrick, a patient known as 'the Elephant Man', recounted in his book *The Elephant Man and Other Reminiscences* (1923).

Fran Chalfont, *THJ* 6 (1990).

Trumpet-Major, The. The seventh of Hardy's fourteen published novels and the only one that can properly be described as a historical novel.

Composition

Hardy began his research for *The Trumpet-Major* in 1878 and probably began the actual writing in 1879. Set in 1804–8, during the *Napoleonic Wars, the book draws on several sources, including newspapers of the period, memoirs, regimental Standing Orders, and histories such as C. H. Gifford's *A History of the Wars Occasioned by the French Revolution* (1817). The Royal Library, Windsor Castle, holds the manuscript, which Hardy presented to King George V in 1911. Manuscript alterations suggest Hardy's shifting conceptions: he moved the Garlands' class slightly upwards, for instance (Anne's father was originally a schoolmaster, not a landscape-painter), and changed an earlier, possibly aristocratic character called 'Captain Delalynde' into Festus Derriman. He also enhanced the comic and dramatic possibilities of some episodes, as when he added Matilda Johnson to the press-gang rescue, replacing an earlier version in which Anne's helper is the servant Molly.

Serialization

The Trumpet-Major was serialized in the monthly magazine *Good Words* from January to December 1880, and in the United States in *Demorest's Monthly Magazine* from January 1880 to January 1881. Hardy had difficulty in placing *The Trumpet-Major* as a serial. He sounded out Leslie *Stephen, editor of the *Cornhill*, John Blackwood, publisher of *Blackwood's Magazine*, and *Macmillan's Magazine* before *Good Words* agreed to run the story. The *censorship enforced by the editor of *Good Words*, the Reverend Donald Macleod, was stringent even by the magazine standards of the day: Hardy was asked to excise swearing, Sunday travelling, and some sexually suggestive details. The excisions, apparently made in proof, did not affect the American serial; the *Demorest's* text also contains minor stylistic adjustments not made for *Good Words*, some of which were not transferred to later editions.

In the British serial version, the novel was divided as follows: January, Chapters 1–4; February, 5–7; March, 8–10; April, 11–14; May, 15–17; June, 18–21; July, 22–4; August, 25–7; September, 28–30; October, 31–4; November, 34 (contd.)–37; December, 38–41.

Illustrations

Hardy initially suggested the *Punch* artist Charles Keene (1823–91) as illustrator for *The Trumpet-Major* (*L* i 66). In the end, however, it was John Collier (1850–1934) who produced 32 illustrations for the *Good Words* run; perhaps the weakest done for Hardy's novels, these lacklustre productions scarcely distinguish the characters from each other, and add little to the novel.

Volume Publication

The Trumpet-Major was published in three volumes on 26 October 1880 by *Smith, Elder, at the standard price of 31*s.* 6*d.* (one-and-a-half guineas). For this edition Hardy restored some, though not all, of the bowdlerizations made for *Good Words*, made John Loveday's ultimate fate more explicit and Matilda's past more explicitly shady, removed some dates, and emphasized Festus's giant size for the first time. He also retitled some of the chapters, made stylistic revisions, and adjusted the amount of *dialect in characters' speech.

Of the later revisions to *The Trumpet-Major*, the most significant were done in 1895 for the *Osgood, McIlvaine Collected Edition. At that point Hardy moved the novel into his fictional 'Wessex', changing real place-names into their Wessex equivalents: Weymouth, for instance, became 'Budmouth' in 1895. He also adjusted style and dialect, and further eroded Matilda's character. Finally, a few more verbal changes were made for the Macmillan 1912 Wessex Edition of Hardy's works, and at the same time he added a little more detail to Matilda's sexual history.

Reception

Many reviewers contrasted *The Trumpet-Major*, usually favourably, with Hardy's earlier novels. Some noted with relief the departure from the sombre tone of its most recent predecessor, *The Return of the Native*, and welcomed what they saw as a return to Hardy's earlier manner. Others saw *The Trumpet-Major* as a novel which succeeds by restricting its aim: despite their generally positive tone, the reviews sometimes suggest that the novel is an achievement in miniature. Words such as 'charm' and 'quaintness' recur frequently, as does praise for the appealingly vivid 'picture' the book offers of a bygone age. John Loveday is a favourite character among Hardy's Victorian reviewers, for whom the hero's manliness is a key to a book's success. By contrast, Anne is usually chided for her bad taste in men, though in some reviews, such as Julian Hawthorne's in the *Spectator* (18 December 1880; repr. in *CH*), this 'perversity' becomes 'sweet' and lovable; heroines like Anne are all the more attractive 'for their tender naughtiness'.

Plot

In the midst of the Napoleonic Wars, John Loveday's regiment sets up camp near his father's mill at Overcombe. Both he and Festus Derriman fall in love with Anne Garland, whose widowed mother rents half of the elder Loveday's house. Mrs Garland would prefer Anne to choose the comparatively wealthy Festus, heir apparent to his uncle, old Squire Derriman. Hoping to help John win Anne, Miller Loveday proposes to Mrs Garland, whom he has long admired. She accepts, but Anne rejects John. Bob Loveday, the miller's sailor son and Anne's childhood sweetheart, returns home to help his father in the mill and to introduce his fiancée, Matilda Johnson. John recognizes Matilda as an actress with a shady past, and forces her to decamp. The miller and Mrs Garland marry, and John's regiment leaves the area.

Bob, initially disheartened by the collapse of his engagement, begins to cheer up and to court Anne, who remains angry with him for forgetting their early attachment, but shows signs of relenting. During a false invasion alarm, Festus traps Anne in a deserted house, proposes to her, becomes angry at her refusal, and seems about to rape her, but she escapes on his horse, which runs away with her. John, whose regiment has returned to the neighbourhood, rescues Anne and boxes Festus's ears, though Festus drunkenly mistakes him for Bob. Becoming aware that Bob and Anne are in love, John pretends that his heartsickness is for Matilda, who has found employment as an actress nearby. Matilda and Festus revenge themselves on the Lovedays by betraying Bob to a naval press-gang as an experienced seaman, but Matilda later repents and helps Anne rescue Bob. Once safe, however, Bob volunteers for the navy; life as a miller bores him, and he has discovered John's love for Anne. He tells John to take Anne for himself, but John altruistically ignores him.

Anne and the Lovedays hear about the great naval victory at Trafalgar, and some time later learn that Bob has survived and is courting a woman in Portsmouth. As Anne recovers from the shock, John writes to Bob to ask him whether he definitely intends to abandon her for good. Receiving no answer for months, John begins to approach Anne again, but just as she begins to respond, Bob writes to say that he will return to claim her. John retreats, but impresses Anne all the more by his self-sacrificing loyalty. She repulses Bob upon his return, despite his promotion to lieutenant. Later, however, Bob and Anne are reconciled, and Festus marries Matilda. Squire Derriman dies, making Anne his heir. John's regiment leaves for Spain, where he will die in battle.

Critical Approaches

Many of Hardy's novels are loosely 'historical' in the sense that they are set some decades before their date of publication and have elegiac overtones. Only in *The Trumpet-Major*, however, does he explicitly set out to explore interactions between characters and history by placing the action in a well-known and eventful historical period. From Walter *Scott on, and often with Scott's powerful example in their minds, most 19th-century novelists tried their hands at the historical novel at least once in their careers, but Hardy's use of the genre is so idiosyncratic that critics often refuse to call *The Trumpet-Major* historical fiction at all. Contemporary reviewers delighted in the 'picture' the book offers of a bygone age, but for most 20th-century critics the pictorialism produces an antiquarian rather than a historical vision, one that is far from the sort of engagement with history that historical novels characteristically involve. For many, the historical research the book's subject demanded is also too far from Hardy's conventional role as the self-educated creator of 'Wessex', whose most authentic material is assumed to come from tradition and memory rather than from research.

Hardy's sources were, however, diverse, and included many oral and anecdotal accounts remembered from childhood as well as documents and histories. The surviving notebook which records his research in the British Museum, 'Notes taken for "Trumpet-Major" & other books of time of Geo III. in (1878—1879—)' (reproduced in *PN*; see also NOTEBOOKS) sometimes shows him searching archival sources for references to a particular event already planned, such as the invasion scare of Chapters 26–8: 'N.B. The autumn of 1804 was one of alarm at the expected invasion, equally with 1803, though perhaps not to such an intense degree. So that the beacon-firing &c, may be in either year' (*PN* 142). The idea for 'the beacon-firing &c' most likely came not from printed records at all, but from local and familial traditions of wartime fears and invasion preparations; research merely helped Hardy to place the event chronologically.

Despite his fascination with the Napoleonic era, Hardy focuses less on recorded history than on characters who exist outside the record—on what H. A. T. Johnson, in the essay cited below, has called 'the ordinary, unremarkable, indeed often dull stuff of life' (p. 51). Indeed, the limitations of the historical perspective seem more interesting to Hardy than its fictional possibilities. George H. Thomson notes the paradoxical movement of time in several passages of *The Trumpet-Major*, where the past recedes from the narrator's grasp, moving backwards rather than forwards, and enforcing 'the contrast between the feeling that life is permanent and rich in future prospects and the fact that it is short and quickly lost in the vast reaches of unrecorded history' ('Trumpet-Major Chronicle', p. 54). The novel does in this sense part company with historical fiction of the kind Scott wrote, which tends rather to bring its characters into significant contact with recorded history, and to derive 'the individuality of characters from the historical peculiarity of their age' (Georg Lukács, *The English Historical Novel* (1937; trans. Hannah and Stanley Mitchell, 1962; repr. 1983), 19). With the exception of John Loveday's death, history in *The Trumpet-Major* has little significant impact, and nothing links that death firmly to 'the historical peculiarity' of the Napoleonic age: since death only dignifies his already bleak fate as the man Anne rejects, any war, or indeed any other form of early death, would remove him just as effectively. History to Hardy is anything but a sphere of significant action; it may even be an absurdity, as John Goode asserts in *Thomas Hardy: The Offensive Truth* ((1988), 66).

Ironically, the most resonant historical element in the novel may be the (absent) figure of Napoleon. Goode argues that 'the upstart who nearly ruled Europe' was a source of ambivalent fascination for Hardy, 'the *arriviste* who conquered by writing the culture which did not know him' (p. 65). Napoleon from this perspective is more important for the personal significance his name had for Hardy than for his directly historical role. Taking a similar class-oriented approach, George Wotton looks at *The Trumpet-Major* as a project of recovery, a deliberate turning away from written history, which is 'nothing more than the record of the private lives of the large owners of property, a record which conceals the *real* but unwritten history of the Lovedays and the class they represent' (*Thomas Hardy: Towards a Materialist Criticism* (1985), 47). Such a project is doomed to failure, however, because the past is itself unstable and marked by shifting economic and social exigencies: as Roger Ebbatson points out, there is no determinate 'past' to reclaim. Not only characters' class and economic circumstances but also the structures of buildings shift in Overcombe and Budmouth with marriages, deaths, inheritances, and military promotions (*Hardy: The Margin of the Unexpressed* (1993), 48).

It may be precisely its troubled and paradoxical involvement with history which has marked *The Trumpet-Major* out from the rest of Hardy's novels and made it difficult to place in many general accounts of Hardy's fiction, where it is often either overlooked or briefly praised as a limited achievement. Since Hardy himself classified it for the 1912 Macmillan edition of his works under 'Romances and Fantasies', a category which has tended to occupy a middle rank between the novels considered 'major' and those considered nearly unreadable, he could be said to have courted this critical reaction, although his 1895 preface certainly shows little self-deprecation as it asserts his faithfulness to his sources, especially to 'the recollections of old persons well known to the author in childhood, but now long dead'. Hardy had been accused of *plagiarism by some American readers, and the 1895 preface is in part intended to answer that charge, but the defence he mounts is spirited, positive, and by no means apologetic.

Shifting trends in Hardy criticism have had considerable impact on the status of *The Trumpet-Major.* Early 20th-century critics tend to see it as a charming but slight work. Towards the mid-century, the idea that Hardy's best vein was tragic gained considerable momentum, and accordingly *The Trumpet-Major*'s standing slipped; those few who did praise it began to focus on its 'darker' aspects. In 'Hardy the Novelist' (*Scrutiny* 3, 1934), for instance, Frank Chapman nods approvingly at its 'implicit conviction that things never come right' (p. 32), but few after Chapman read it this way. To Albert J. Guerard the novel is simply one of Hardy's 'worst books' (*Thomas Hardy: The Novels and Stories* (1949), 39), and for several decades after this brisk dismissal most critics saw it as irretrievably 'minor', often for precisely the same qualities that earlier critics had praised: its charm, and the absence of 'typically' Hardyan features such as sombreness of tone. Perhaps the most extreme example of this turn against *The Trumpet-Major* is John Bayley's assertion, in *An Essay on Hardy* (1978), that its form 'is too smooth, unified, and coherent', giving us none of the 'unbothered unevenness' which to Bayley is the characteristic source of pleasure in a Hardy text (p. 143).

Curiously, the idea of *The Trumpet-Major* as a weak link in the chain of Hardy's *œuvre* is often implicitly linked to Anne Garland, who at times seems almost to be blamed for the book's perceived failures. Guerard (p. 141) puts her with the *ingénues*, his own grouping of 'sweet, passive' (p. 143) Hardy women—mostly secondary characters, and in Guerard's view almost wholly uninteresting. Even feminist critics have tended to skip over Anne and *The Trumpet-Major*; no longer valued for the charm of her 'perversity', Anne seems to have become a blank to many modern critics, less interesting than Matilda, say (though beyond a few statements to that effect Matilda gets little of the critical limelight).

One notable exception is Richard H. Taylor, who finds Anne prim and 'colourless' (*The Neglected Hardy: Thomas Hardy's Lesser Novels* (1982), 90), but discovers perversity and disruption in her very primness, a combination that 'adds a new dimension of irony' (p. 91). For Taylor, as for Chapman, the novel's ending is dark, although less because things do not come right than because the 'rightness' they achieve has such a sour edge: Anne gets exactly what she deserves in Bob.

John Loveday's critical fortunes have declined in the 20th century; his love for Anne being as unalterable as her 'perverse' loyalty to Bob, nothing about him but his steadfastness (usually a source of irritation) and his death provokes much comment. Bob also receives scant attention, and his interestingly unstable gender has gone largely unnoticed. Although Guerard sees him as more 'masculine' than his brother (p. 118), Bob not only has the sailor's usual skill in household tasks, but also several physical traits which set him apart from most of the other men in the novel, such as a relatively small stature, a quiet step, and a marked resemblance to his mother.

Festus has attracted rather more critical notice than either of the Loveday brothers. Taylor suggests (p. 92) that his swaggering provides a parodic version of Napoleon; like Napoleon he embodies the tension in the novel between comedy and potential violence, and he excites both derision and fear as he tries to bully his uncle and Anne, the only 'enemies' he is not usually afraid of. For all his craven bluster, Festus/Napoleon suggests that 'history', absurd or not, can still erupt even in Overcombe, whether as invasion, sexual aggression, or the 'peaceful' incursion of several camping regiments.

Uncle Benjy's miserly fear of having soldiers billeted on him, comic though it is, nevertheless suggests the disruption war creates even outside combat zones. Roger Ebbatson analyses that disruption in a comment on the novel's opening scenes informed by the psychoanalytic theory of Jacques Lacan; he notes the implicit violence of Anne's rapid transformation from observing subject to observed object, 'a fetish which is stared at voyeuristically by the controlling male with his weaponry' (*Hardy: The Margin of the Unexpressed*, 55), and 'the covert alliance in bellicose masculinist ardour of Festus Derriman and the Loveday brothers with the invading emperor' (ibid. 57).

As this summary demonstrates, the focus of criticism on *The Trumpet-Major* has recently shifted towards elements which disturb and complicate the novel's apparent pictorial 'charm' and smooth surface. As it emerges from the work of such critics as Goode, Wotton, and Ebbatson, the novel is a more difficult and conflict-ridden text, but perhaps also a more interesting one. See also HISTORY. MPR

Avrom Fleishman, 'Hardy: The Avoidance of Historical Fiction', in *The English Historical Novel: Walter Scott to Virginia Woolf* (1971).

H. A. T. Johnson, 'In Defence of "The Trumpet-Major"', in F. B. Pinion (ed.), *Budmouth Essays on Thomas Hardy: Papers Presented at the 1975 Summer School* (1976).

George H. Thomson, 'The Trumpet-Major Chronicle', *Nineteenth-Century Fiction* (1962).

'Tryst at an Ancient Earthwork, A', short story. Originally published (as 'Ancient Earthworks and What Two Enthusiastic Scientists Found Therein') in the *Detroit Post* for 15 March 1885, and, in revised and expanded form (as 'Ancient Earthworks at Casterbridge'), in the *English Illustrated Magazine* for December 1893, it was collected in *A Changed Man and Other Tales*. A sketch rather than a story, its first-person narrative describes a nocturnal visit to Maiden Castle ('Mai-Dun'), near Dorchester, and a meeting with an archaeologist friend who, with surprising ease, proves his point that the site is Roman by uncovering a mosaic pavement and various objects, including a skeleton. Much of this short piece consists of scenic description graphically evoking the sensation of leaving the 'macadamized road', ascending 'this largest Ancient-British work in the kingdom', and entering a world of prehistory and ancient history. The 'original' of the archaeologist was Edward Cunnington, a local antiquary who had excavated at Maiden Castle and for whose methods Hardy seems to have had scant respect (see Millgate 244). The first edition of *A Changed Man* has a picture of 'The Castle of Mai-Dun' as a frontispiece.

Turner, J. M. W. See NATIONAL GALLERY; PAINTING AND SCULPTURE; ROYAL ACADEMY.

Two on a Tower. The ninth of Hardy's published novels. The title, decided on 'offhand', was one he 'afterwards disliked' (*LW* 155).

Composition

The work was prompted by an invitation from T. B. *Aldrich on 28 September 1881 to contribute a serial to the Boston magazine *Atlantic Monthly*. Before the end of the year Hardy, who was then living at *Wimborne, was researching the astronomical background of the novel; for his visit, under amusingly false pretences, to the Greenwich Observatory, see *LW* 155–6. The first nine chapters are known to have been in Aldrich's hands by March 1882. Composition continued after publication had begun in May, and the final portion had been dispatched to America by mid-September. The manuscript, retained by Aldrich, was in 1943 presented to Harvard University, an institution that makes a minor appearance in the novel.

Hardy's long-standing interest in astronomy, and his strong sense of the contrast between the vastness of the universe as revealed by the telescope and the minute scale of individual human lives, is demonstrated by such early poems as 'At a Lunar Eclipse' and 'In Vision I Roamed', both written in his twenties. Of specific sources, F. B. Pinion has plausibly suggested that Hardy may have taken a hint from a passage in George *Eliot's *The Mill on the Floss* (1860), where a character speculates whether all astronomers must hate women, and reflects that '"I suppose it's all astronomers: because, you know, because they live up in high towers, and if the women came there, they might talk and hinder them from looking at the stars"'.

Serial and Volume Publication

Two on a Tower appeared originally in eight monthly instalments from May to December 1882, copies of the magazine being sold simultaneously in America and England. There were no illustrations. The divisions of the story in the serial version were as follows: May, Chapters 1–4; June, 5–9; July, 10–15; August, 16–21; September, 22–7; October, 28–32; November, 33–7; December, 38–41.

The novel was published in book form in England by the firm of *Sampson Low, in the traditional three-volume format, at 31*s.* 6*d.* (half-a-guinea a volume), at the end of October 1882. American volume-publication followed in early December. A little later, in a letter to Edmund *Gosse (21 January 1883), Hardy bemoaned the fact that, while the story had been planned with care, the writing had been 'lamentably hurried' on account of the pressure of sending material across the Atlantic to meet the magazine's deadlines. He added that he had not been able to see proofs, and admitted that he had not carried out his original intention of rewriting the work for volume publication.

Hardy made a few minor revisions between the serial and publication in book form, and further revisions for a 'Second Edition' (actually a second impression) published early in 1883. Among the latter, Swithin's annuity from his uncle was increased from £400 to £600, and the incorrect form of Viviette's name after her marriage to the Bishop ('Lady Helmsdale') was corrected. More interestingly, he made revisions to show quite clearly that the child of Viviette and Swithin was conceived during their farewell meeting described in Chapter 36—that is, after they have learned that their marriage is legally invalid. Further revisions were made for the one-volume edition that appeared in April 1883, and the epigraph from Crashaw was added at this stage. The preface was written for the collected edition of the Wessex Novels in 1895 and slightly revised for the Wessex Edition in 1912. See also *Tauchnitz editions.

The 1912 edition had the benefit of Hardy's further careful revision 30 years after original publication. Among the changes introduced at this stage are the metrical psalm sung by the choir in Chapter 2 (with its thematically apposite reference to 'Heav'n's high tower') in place of the hymn 'Onward, Christian Soldiers!' in all earlier editions, and, near the end of the novel, the parson's innocently inaccurate reference to Viviette's son as 'a seven-months' baby'.

Reception

A Laodicean (1881) had not found favour with contemporary reviewers, and, as its immediate successor, *Two on a Tower* provoked little enthusiasm. Hardy told Edmund Gosse (10 December 1882) that he found the criticisms of the novel 'most extraordinary': while some 'eminent critics' praised its originality in private conversations, others (or possibly the same) attacked it in public for immorality. A similar grievance, evidently still rankling, is aired in the 1895 preface. Hardy even took the step of responding publicly to one of his critics. When the *St James's Gazette* (16 January 1883) published a review objecting that the portrayal of the Bishop might be viewed as holding up the Church of

England to ridicule, he promptly wrote a letter of self-defence, published in that newspaper on 19 January. In the original version of the 1895 preface, a phrase from the *St James's Gazette* review—'a studied and gratuitous insult'—was quoted, together with severe judgements (including 'repulsive' and 'little short of revolting') from two other reviews. The passage referring in detail to these contemporary reviews was deleted from the preface when Hardy revised it in 1902, but its appearance more than a dozen years after the reviews in question demonstrates how deeply these criticisms had been felt and resented.

It was an anonymous critic in the *Saturday Review* (18 November 1882: repr. in *CH*) who had described the story as having 'an extremely repulsive element'. What this reviewer had in mind is not quite clear, but it was presumably the sexual relationship between Viviette and Swithin as well as her deception of the Bishop. The review concludes by finding the work 'extremely disappointing'. A reviewer in the *Athenaeum* on the same day found a different cause for complaint, that the rustic dialogue was too idealized and literary, with an excessive debt to Shakespeare's clowns ('we must still take leave to doubt whether one Dorsetshire village ever produced quite so many Touchstones at one and the same time').

A particularly severe review was contributed by a well-known journalist, Harry Quilter, to the *Spectator* (3 February 1883: repr. in *CH*): it found the heroine unconvincing ('she is more of a shadow at the end of the book than she is in the first chapter'), and judged the novel as a whole 'unpleasant', 'improbable', 'melodramatic', 'unworthy of Mr Hardy's reputation', and 'the worst the author has written'. Evidently the critical establishment of the day was not ready for Hardy's defiance of convention in treating subjects normally excluded from fiction. However, a more positive note is sounded in a long and important survey of Hardy's work to date by the pioneering psychologist, sexologist, and man of letters Havelock Ellis, published in the prestigious *Westminster Review* (April 1883: repr. in *CH*). Ellis recognized *Two on a Tower* as 'the work of a writer who has a finer sense of his art than any living English novelist'.

Plot

Visiting for the first time a lonely tower on her absent husband's estate, Lady Constantine (Viviette) meets a beautiful youth, Swithin St Cleeve, who lives with his grandmother at a nearby cottage and is engaged in astronomical studies. At a later meeting she asks him to investigate a rumour that her husband, who has gone to Africa to hunt big game, has clandestinely returned to London; the rumour proves groundless. Lady Constantine encourages Swithin's studies, visits him frequently at the tower, and, despite the considerable difference in their ages, falls in love with him. Her resolve to avoid temptation by promoting his marriage to a village girl, Tabitha Lark, is abandoned when news arrives that her husband has died eighteen months earlier. Though his inexperience makes him slow to respond, Swithin eventually tells Viviette that he returns her love and proposes marriage; they agree that it should take place in private and remain secret until Swithin has achieved success in his career.

Viviette's brother Louis seeks to encourage a match between her and the pompous bachelor Bishop of Melchester, and during visits by these two men the secretly married couple have several narrow escapes from detection. The Bishop proposes marriage and soon afterwards Viviette learns that Sir Blount Constantine died much later than was originally supposed, with the result that her supposed marriage to Swithin is invalid.

Their intention of going through another form of marriage is frustrated, however, by Viviette's discovery that if he marries before the age of 25 Swithin will forfeit a legacy from his uncle, and she decides to postpone their marriage until he reaches that age, encouraging him in the meantime to pursue his researches in the southern hemisphere. Immediately after his departure, but too late to communicate with him, she learns that she is pregnant and in despair accepts the Bishop's renewed proposal, eventually bearing a son that she passes off as his. When Swithin returns to England after the Bishop's death several years later, he visits Viviette at the tower and is visibly shocked to discover how much she has aged. She relinquishes all claim on him and, when he tells her that despite this act of abnegation he wishes to marry her, she dies of joy. There is a strong implication that Swithin will marry Tabitha Lark and bring up his child.

Critical Approaches

The generally unfavourable contemporary reception of this novel, and Hardy's reactions to it, have been referred to above. Most modern readers are likely to be less distressed by the presentation of an Anglican Bishop as a figure of fun or by Hardy's initial failure to bestow on his heroine the correct aristocratic title; more importantly, they are also unlikely to raise objections to a story involving an older woman's love for a young man who is her social inferior, or even Viviette's ploy (born of desperation rather than calculation) in passing off her lover's child as that of the man she hastily marries. What now seems more problematic is the generic nature of the novel, the schematic quality of its characterization, its very circumscribed physical and social world, and a tone that seems, sometimes uneasily—or perhaps daringly and experimentally—to mingle seriousness and irony, tragedy and comedy.

Two on a Tower demands to be judged according to different criteria from those appropriate to, say, *The Mayor of Casterbridge*, the novel that followed it. Whereas the latter delineates in precise and circumstantial detail the topography, economy, and social order of a community at a specific stage of its historical development, the action of *Two on a Tower* takes place in a world that possesses the stark simplicity of allegory, fable, or fairy-tale: we are, metaphorically as well as literally, 'in a tower' rather than in a town. The story is almost entirely confined to three contrasting locations: Viviette's country house, the lonely tower, and Swithin's cottage. Though travels on a global scale are referred to, they all take place offstage, and the reader comes to share the heroine's sense of a confining, almost claustrophobic existence. The raven-haired lady living alone in the big house, the flaxen-haired youth (a prince in disguise in his grandmother's cottage), the wicked husband (heard of but never seen), the scheming brother, the foolish rival: all seem to belong to an earlier form of literature than the 19th-century realistic novel. The plot is full of contrivances and relies heavily on unexpected events occurring at the worst possible moment. And yet Viviette's infatuation and her entrapment by the inflexible conventions of her time and class have dramatic power.

At the outset, Swithin is a distinctly inept and even unconscious lover: believing that science will always come first in his life, he declares he will never marry. This naïve unawareness of the power of love produces a situation in which the woman takes the initiative, in feeling if not in action, and it was perhaps this defiance of orthodox Victorian ideology on the part of the heroine that (among other things) deeply offended so many early critics.

For almost 100 years after its first publication, *Two on a Tower* received little serious attention, and it seemed as though James *Barrie's glum prediction in the *Contemporary Review* in 1889 that 'the besom of oblivion will soon pass over it' was justified. During the striking upsurge of critical attention to Hardy during the 1970s, however, the novel became the subject of serious discussion. In a stimulating chapter in his *Thomas Hardy: His Career as a Novelist* (1971), Michael Millgate reminds us that Hardy consistently referred to the book as a 'romance' rather than a 'novel': it follows that the work needs to be located in a different tradition from the 'Novels of Character and Environment'. Millgate suggests, however, that it does not always explore very clearly or profoundly the moral implications of the situations it creates, with their marked 'patterns of contrast'.

Approaching the work from a different direction, Simon Gatrell has explored the physical world it depicts and has found it in this respect at odds with Hardy's normal practice of placing the action precisely on the map of Wessex and describing an environment that embodies a 'community of spirit, place and culture'.

The ending of the novel represents a problem for many critics and readers: what looks like a rapidly approaching happy ending suffers a reversal that may well be regarded as melodramatic or even preposterous, and the heroine's sudden death is followed by the portentous closing words 'The Bishop was avenged'. Unless these are taken as ironical, they are difficult to reconcile with what has gone before. For Richard H. Taylor (*The Neglected Hardy* (1982), 136) this is an example of 'the novel's failure in consistency in tone', which in turn derives from the difficulties

Hardy experiences in handling the genre of tragi-comedy: 'the conflicting demands of tragic irony and comic irony impose more strain on the narrative than it can comfortably withstand'.

Taylor also detects a failure of consistency in another area: the handling of the astronomical theme that is the novel's starting-point. Although the preface draws attention to the contrast between individual human destinies and the immensity of the 'stellar universe', this idea does not, according to Taylor, pervade the novel as it should; though prominent in the early chapters, it tends to be lost sight of, and the later complications of the love story derive from more mundane considerations. Taylor does concede, however, that the dominating presence of the tower, both location and symbol, is 'invested with a curiously poetic quality' (p. 129). J. Hillis Miller's influential study *Thomas Hardy: Distance and Desire* (1970) includes a discussion of the scientific and philosophical background of the novel and its relationship to 19th-century astronomy and ideas of 'the death of God'.

John Bayley, while sharing Taylor's view that the astronomical theme is not satisfactorily integrated with the love story, makes high claims for the novel, declaring that 'Nowhere else does [Hardy] give such an effective and in an involuntary sense such a complete picture of a love-relation'. For Rosemary Sumner, too, the novel demands to be taken seriously, since it 'contains some of Hardy's most original and adventurous experiments'. For Sumner, Hardy's portrayal of his heroine is wholly successful: 'She is, perhaps, Hardy's most heroic character.... Hardy has an almost Lawrentian delight in Viviette's sensuality' (pp. 78–9).

Taylor's reference to the 'poetic quality' of the tower draws attention to an important dimension of this story. Swithin is not just a scientist but a 'scientific Adonis', and this classical reference is part of a pattern of allusions that runs throughout the novel and embraces texts from the Bible to contemporary authors as well as classical mythology. Part research scientist, the young hero is also part figure of myth, legend, or fairy-tale, compared elsewhere to Apollo and Antinous. This dual role reflects the ambiguous nature of the story itself, part tale of contemporary life and modern science, part romantic and symbolic.

Similarly, Viviette herself is both a member of the Victorian ruling class and a figure from fairy-tale and from Romantic poetry, especially, perhaps, that of Keats and Tennyson. There are several fairly explicit references to both poets in this novel, including a direct quotation from Tennyson (37), but the most important Tennysonian allusion lies just beneath the surface. That is the parallel between Viviette and the Mariana (herself inspired by a phrase in Shakespeare's *Measure for Measure*) of Tennyson's poem of 1830, with further details supplied by the same poet's Lady of Shalott. Viviette, under a 'solemn oath' to live a solitary life during her husband's indefinite absence, resembles the woman of fairy-tale (that other tower-dweller, Rapunzel, for instance) living under a spell or curse and, more specifically, the isolated or deserted women of Tennyson's early poems. Like Mariana, she passes her days in an isolated house in the country, exchanging it only occasionally for the even more confined spaces of her carriage or the village church. As she tells Mr Torkingham, the parson, she lives '"like a cloistered nun"' and her '"life has become a burden"'. The epithet 'dreary', twice applied to her, may be a direct borrowing from Tennyson's 'Mariana', where it is a prominent rhyme-word. Viviette finds in her lonely tower first a new interest in life, then love and fulfilment, and later anxiety, despair, and death, and in most of these respects her story parallels that of the Lady of Shalott. Like Sir Lancelot, Swithin is hardly aware of how much devastation he has caused to the woman who loves him.

Viviette dominates the novel, and, as we have seen, she has sometimes polarized critical judgements. A pious Christian and a woman conscious of her social obligations, Viviette is, despite her infringements of the moral code, one for whom morality matters (in one of the earliest scenes she consults the parson about her conduct during her enforced quasi-widowhood). Her tragedy is to find herself racked by passion for a socially unacceptable lover whose own feelings are in any case of a different order. The theme of inequality (of many kinds) in loving is one of the most important in Hardy's fiction, and, despite the fairy-tale world she sometimes seems to inhabit, the heroine of *Two on a Tower* represents a powerful study in conflict in the individual conscience.

On the likely autobiographical basis of the central situation of this novel, see MARTIN, JULIA AUGUSTA.

John Bayley, 'The Love Story in *Two on a Tower*', *THA* 1 (1982).
Simon Gatrell, 'Middling Hardy', *THA* 4 (1986).
Rosemary Sumner, 'The Experimental and the Absurd in *Two on a Tower*', *THA* 1 (1982).

U

uncollected stories. Seven stories were excluded from the collective volumes published during Hardy's lifetime. The earliest of these, 'How I Built Myself a House' (*Chambers's Journal*, May 1865), is a short satirical sketch detailing a young man's house-building misadventures. Written to amuse the pupils in Arthur *Blomfield's architectural office, this 'humorous trifle'—as Hardy described it (*LW* 49)—is of interest primarily because of its status as Hardy's first published work, though it also heralds his later tendency to fictionalize his architectural experiences even as it provides a rare instance of his use of a fully dramatized and clearly non-authorial first-person narrator.

Nearly a decade later, during the successful *Cornhill* serialization of *Far from the Madding Crowd*, the *New York Times* solicited a story from Hardy; the result was 'Destiny and a Blue Cloak', published on 4 October 1874. Although somewhat crude in structure and language, 'Destiny' is recognizably Hardyan in its plot of mistaken identity, secret engagement, and thwarted love, culminating in a ruthlessly ironic mistiming. Substantial passages describing the heroine's courtship by an undesirable elderly suitor and her unsuccessful escape attempt were subsequently adapted for incorporation into *The Hand of Ethelberta*, and it was evidently Hardy's recognition of this reuse of material, combined with his own negative valuation of the over-plotted story, which prevented him from republishing it. 'Destiny' is, however, remarkable for its bleak representation—unsurpassed in Hardy's work—of the social marginalization of women: Agatha Pollin, regarded by both her uncle and Farmer Lovill as an object to be bargained with, and lacking any means of financially supporting herself, has no choice but to marry against her will.

Considerably lighter in tone and purpose is Hardy's first children's story, 'The Thieves Who Couldn't Help Sneezing' (*Father Christmas*, 1877), in which an adolescent boy uses wit and intelligence to triumph over a band of thieves. The moralizing is not overt, consisting only of a quiet emphasis on Hubert's courage and a minor but very Hardyan concern for the welfare of his stolen horse. No less Hardyan is the way in which the opening evocation of the world of fairy-tale is fulfilled solely in the archetypal romance movement towards recognition and reunion, the narrative events themselves—if hardly the stuff of everyday experience—remaining firmly grounded in the credible.

The following year (1878) saw both the completion of *The Return of the Native* and the publication of the most important and substantial of the uncollected stories, *An Indiscretion in the Life of an Heiress*, solicited by the *New Quarterly Magazine* in January and published in July. A somewhat different version, apparently set from unrevised proofs, was serialized in *Harper's Weekly* 29 June–27 July. When asked in 1913 why he had not included *Indiscretion* in his collective volume *A Changed Man*, Hardy replied that the story was 'a sort of patchwork of the remains of "The Poor Man & the Lady"', but since 'the point & force of the original story was abstracted from this pale shadow of it' he was considering reconstructing 'the original from the modification' (*L* iv 306). That reconstruction never materialized, however, and *Indiscretion* therefore remains of particular interest in its preservation of many of the elements—including much of the basic plot—of Hardy's lost first novel.

The poor man and the lady in *Indiscretion* are Egbert Mayne, the village schoolmaster, and Geraldine Allenville, daughter of the local squire. Realizing that they cannot marry unless he improves his social position, Egbert goes to London to make his name and fortune; after five years of separation and much effort, he is rewarded with a moderate literary success. He arranges to communicate with Geraldine at a concert and their youthful vows are renewed, only to fall victim to her sober second thoughts, dictated by societal convention and parental opposition. On the eve of her arranged marriage to Lord Bretton, she accidentally meets Egbert and confesses her unhappiness; early the following morning she runs away, marrying Egbert a few hours later. Within a week she is dead, the emotional stress of an attempt to be reconciled to her father having brought on a haemorrhage of the lungs.

While the plot insists on the ineradicability of social barriers and the narrative as a whole lacks the virulent satire criticized by the readers of *The Poor Man and the Lady*, social criticism none the less remains of central importance in *Indiscretion*. Both Egbert and Geraldine lament the class-driven prejudices which prohibit the union of two people who love each other, while Geraldine bitterly bewails the absence of options for an upper-class woman in a classist, patriarchal society. At the same time, conventional gender roles are questioned in the representation of the young lovers' relationship, since it is frequently Geraldine who (by virtue of her social status) assumes the dominant role.

More conventional in tone and subject-matter is 'Our Exploits at West Poley', a long children's story written by Hardy in 1883 at the invitation of the well-known American children's magazine, the *Youth's Companion*, but not published until nine years later. It was then serialized (apparently without his knowledge) from November 1892 to April 1893 in another Boston periodical, the *Household*, an obscure monthly 'Devoted to the Interests of the American Housewife'.

The story relates the adventures of two adolescent boys, Leonard (the retrospective narrator) and his 'somewhat masterful' elder cousin Steve, who in exploring local caves first inadvertently and then deliberately divert the source of their village's water supply. The unforeseen consequences of these actions ultimately lead to Steve's successful but dangerous destruction of access to the river head and call forth some explicit moralizing from the local authority-figure, the Man who had Failed: 'Quiet perseverance in clearly defined courses is, as a rule, better than the erratic exploits that may do much harm.' Frequently reprinted and twice filmed since its rediscovery by Richard Purdy in 1952, 'Exploits' has proved to be a modestly successful children's story, interpreted variously by its adult readers as a straightforward didactic tale, a self-conscious exploration of unreliable narration, and—drawing upon its cave and spring imagery—an allegory both of sexual initiation and repression, and of the processes of literary creation. (See also GEOLOGY.)

'Old Mrs Chundle' has attracted less critical attention. Alternately ironic, comic, and pathetic, it approximates moral fable more closely than is usual with Hardy. Its unnamed protagonist is a young curate whose inexperience leads him first to overzealous concern for the church attendance of the elderly Mrs Chundle and then, when her presence becomes an inconvenience, to conscious neglect, before her benevolent misinterpretation of his conduct brings him to the remorseful recognition of his own lack of Christian loving-kindness. The story, written *c.*1888–90, remained unpublished during Hardy's lifetime, presumably because it was based upon an actual event in the early career of the Reverend Henry Moule, the much-admired vicar of Fordington and father of seven sons, with all of whom Hardy was on friendly terms (see MOULE FAMILY); Hardy would not have wished to give offence by publishing a potentially identifiable and somewhat unsympathetic representation of Moule, for whom he in fact had considerable respect.

The use of potentially recognizable 'originals' in 'The Doctor's Legend' may also have led to that story's exclusion from Hardy's collective volumes—specifically from *A Group of Noble Dames*, for which its subject-matter and story-telling frame clearly mark it as intended. The doctor narrator tells the story of an unnamed squire whose terrorizing of a young girl transforms her into a living skull subsequently used by her distraught mother to frighten the squire's pregnant wife; years later the squire's son commits suicide, traumatized by the sight of a death's head he knows he has seen before.

Into this imaginary death's-head plot Hardy incorporated historical and legendary details of the lives of Joseph Damer, 1st Earl of Dorchester, and his son, most notably the former's death from a gruesome disease, popularly believed to be the result of a curse brought upon him by his desecration of ancient graves during the rebuilding and landscaping of Milton Abbey, Dorset. Given that some of Damer's descendants were his near neighbours, Hardy was evidently content to publish the story only in America, where it appeared in the Easter number of the New York *Independent* (26 March 1891). It is in keeping with Hardy's sense of irony that he should have insisted that 'The Doctor's Legend' was in harmony with the tone of this leading Congregationalist paper: certainly the moralizing is overt in its emphasis on the inevitable judgement of the wicked, but the story none the less remains a narrative of savage violence and revenge, disturbingly macabre and fundamentally directed towards the condemnation of social vanities and aristocratic tyrannies.

During his later years Hardy also contributed to the work of various women writers in whom he had a romantic interest, though he publicly acknowledged only one collaborative story, 'The Spectre of the Real', begun in July 1893 with Florence *Henniker and eventually published in *To-Day* (17 November 1894) and numerous American newspapers subscribing to Irving Bacheller's syndicate. Hardy's willingness both to embark upon and to acknowledge this collaborative project owed more to his emotional and sexual attraction to Henniker than to admiration for her literary abilities.

The somewhat strained collaborative process produced an equally strained story. Clearly Hardyan are the poor-man-and-the-lady plot, clandestine marriage, post-nuptial disillusionment, unexpected return of the spouse on the eve of a second marriage, convenient death by drowning, and inexorably ironic ending, as well as the centrality of sexual passion and articulation of advanced marital views. No less clearly Hennikerean are the banal prose style, sentimentalized set descriptions, and crudely judgemental narrator, whose conventional moral position reflects the stance Henniker was currently maintaining in her personal relationship with her collaborator. Henniker included a bowdlerized version of the story in her volume *In Scarlet and Grey* (1896), but Hardy evidently preferred not to authorize through collection this particular relic of his unfulfilled sexual passion. PD

Kristin Brady, *The Short Stories of Thomas Hardy* (1982).

Pamela Dalziel, Introduction to Thomas Hardy, *An Indiscretion in the Life of an Heiress and Other Stories* (1994).

—— (ed.), *Thomas Hardy: The Excluded and Collaborative Stories* (1992).

Roger Ebbatson, *Hardy: The Margin of the Unexpressed* (1993).

'Unconquerable, The.' See SHORT STORY.

Under the Greenwood Tree. The second of Hardy's fourteen published novels. Initially published anonymously, it is (like its predecessor, *Desperate Remedies*) exceptional among Hardy's novels in not having appeared initially in serial form.

Composition

A few pages at the beginning of *Under the Greenwood Tree* were originally written as incidents in Hardy's first rejected novel *The* *Poor Man and the Lady*. The scenes at the tranter's house at Christmas were thought strong and fresh by John Morley, who read the manuscript for *Macmillan, and this praise encouraged Hardy, while waiting in 1868 to hear from other publishers about *The Poor Man and the Lady*, to begin work on a novel exclusively of rural life. He set it aside when George *Meredith (who also read *The Poor Man*) advised a plot-centred piece, which emerged as *Desperate Remedies*. Reviews of the latter also remarked on the quality of the writing in the few passages of the novel given to the villagers and their life, and in the spring of 1871 Hardy took up the abandoned manuscript again, working on it both at *Higher Bockhampton and in *Weymouth, where he was making drawings for a local architect. Though William *Tinsley had published *Desperate Remedies*, and would have published *The Poor Man* if Hardy could then have afforded to share the risk with him, when *Under the Greenwood Tree* was ready (on 7 August 1871) Hardy sent the manuscript (now in DCM) again to Macmillan, who had turned down both his earlier pieces, but had also shown an unusually discriminating interest in the writing.

Publication

For a publisher the problem was the novel's length—too short to make the conventional three volumes which Mudie's and the other lending libraries preferred (their subscriptions were by the volume, and bulk-buying by Mudie alone could assure the publisher of a return on his investment). Thus Macmillan were hesitant, while not definitely refusing it. They did not wish to cramp Hardy by holding on to the manuscript, but hoped that, if he did not come to an agreement with anyone else, he would allow them to reconsider the novel in the spring. However, when Tinsley sent a cheque in settlement of the *Desperate Remedies* account on 19 March 1872, he also asked whether Hardy had anything else ready, and on 8 April Hardy sent *Under the Greenwood Tree*, somewhat revised as a consequence of John Morley's report for Macmillan (there were substantial deletions from the dialogue in the tranter's house at the beginning of the novel). Tinsley liked it enough to offer £30 for the copyright, which Hardy accepted on 22 April.

Under the Greenwood Tree was in proof in May, and published anonymously a month later, at 21*s.* (one guinea) for the two volumes. Though the reviews were good, it did not sell, and unbound sheets were remaindered after the success of *Far from the Madding Crowd* two years later. Despite this, Tinsley brought out a one-volume edition early in 1873, the printers repaging whatever type was still standing from the first edition, and resetting the rest of the text. The hybrid setting was issued in two formats that year—as number 40 in the yellowback 'Tinsley's Cheap Novels' series, and bound in cloth at half-a-crown (2*s.* 6*d.*)—and then as a Christmas book at the end of 1875 (dated 1876), with illustrations by R. Knight.

A year earlier Hardy had written to try to get the copyright back, but Tinsley asked £300 for the rights, plates, and stock, which was too much even for the author flush from the popularity of *Far from the Madding Crowd.* At the beginning of 1878 Tinsley took £100 from Chatto and Windus for the same material, but by then he was under considerable financial pressure; Hardy never regained the rights to the novel, it being unique among his work in this respect, and they reverted to his heirs only seven years after his death. This meant that when *Under the Greenwood Tree* was included in the two collected editions of 1896 and 1912, special arrangements had to be made with Chatto and Windus, and that until 1935 the text of Tinsley's one-volume edition of 187 was readily and cheaply available in many formats alongside the revised Macmillan versions.

Reception

The anonymous brief novel was hardly noticed amongst the mass of fiction published every month at this time, but those journals that did carry reviews were well-disposed, and Hardy's friend Horace *Moule was full of praise in the *Saturday Review* (28 September 1872; repr. in *CH*, which also prints the *Athenaeum* review of 15 June 1872).

Plot

Dick Dewy, the son of Reuben Dewy the village carrier, and one of the string-players and singers that comprise the Mellstock quire, falls in love with Fancy Day, the freshly appointed, London-trained schoolmistress of Mellstock, who is also daughter of the local head-gamekeeper. At the same time the young vicar Mr Maybold, also new to the parish, is attracted to Fancy, and a rich farmer in the neighbourhood, Mr Shiner, has Fancy's father's approval as her suitor. Fancy and Dick come to an understanding, but Mr Day disapproves. Nevertheless, after nearly starving herself to death as a protest at her father's attitude—gaining his acceptance thus—and then accepting and almost immediately rejecting an offer of marriage from the vicar, Fancy marries Dick at the end of the novel.

The novel is also concerned with the fate of the band of church musicians, composed primarily of village artisans. At first the band seems to be in a flourishing state, as they play and sing carols across the parish at Christmas; but soon the vicar, learning that Fancy can play, and prompted by Shiner, decides to replace the quire with a newfangled cabinet-organ. The players attempt in an interview with Maybold to postpone their demise until the following Christmas, but in the end settle for a compromise of about Michaelmas, accepting that the vicar has the right to order things as he wishes in his own shop. There is a poignant paragraph which marks the feelings of the musicians on the day that Fancy first plays the organ in church, and which concludes: 'the venerable body of musicians could not help thinking that the simpler notes they had been wont to bring forth were more in keeping with the simplicity of their old church than the crowded chords and interludes it was her pleasure to produce' (4.5).

The final scene of the novel is the wedding dance under the greenwood tree in which old and new customs and practices are reconciled—for the moment at least.

Critical Approaches

In Hardy's imagination in 1912, when he came to revise the novel for the last time, *Under the Greenwood Tree* was really two novels, the novel he had written in 1872 and the novel he would have written in the 1890s. The first of these was designed to sell: he had been told by readers whom he had reason to trust that one of the things he could do well was to depict the interaction between people such as those he had known all his life, his parents and relatives and their friends and acquaintances, and that descriptions of places he had known since childhood were fresh and interesting to the urban middle-class reading public. It was clear enough, as he considered the material he already had, that the story of the church-musicians would not be sufficient, and that to make the novel marketable he also had to have a romance of some sort: hence Dick and Fancy. At first in the manuscript there was a rather perfunctory courtship, but as the novel grew towards publication by Tinsley, this element became more and more prominent and complicated by more and more incident, until ultimately the novel became essentially their story. The context of their relationship remains the quire and the village community, but these latter are foregrounded no more.

The branch of the novel centred around the musicians had its source in one of the primary affections of Hardy's infancy, one that remained with him throughout his life: his love of music and dance. The writer's father, also Thomas, was an accomplished fiddler, who began to pass on his skill to his son as soon as the child could hold a violin. He had also been, before his son's birth, a member of the four-man band that played the music in Stinsford parish church; indeed Hardy's father, uncle, and grandfather all played, and though their connection with the church-music was severed before he could experience their playing for himself, they did carry on the tradition of carolling throughout the parish on Christmas Eve. Hardy was thus visiting in his imagination that most poignant of times, those years immediately before we were born that shaped our parents, of which we catch myriad echoes as we grow up, but which are always out of reach even to infantile memory. It is hard to know what it cost Hardy to prune this branch, as he did, to make room for the romance.

By the end of the novel it is possible to look back and see that the narrative has become in part a picture-gallery. At one point the narrator deliberately evokes the portrait of a shoemaker by 'some modern Moroni' (2.2)—Hardy must have seen Moroni's portrait of a tailor on one of his numerous visits to the *National Gallery—and it is as a collection of affectionate and heavily chiaroscuroed images that we experience Mellstock in the second half of the novel. Mrs Day, the innkeeper at Upway, the butcher in Casterbridge, Mrs Endorfield, trapper Enoch—we are given no time to understand such people otherwise than as the painter shows them, caught in one representative action, one fleeting revealing expression, whose individuality (even eccentricity) is striking. Each is a fragment of the richness of village life, part of 'A Rural Painting of the Dutch School', as the novel's subtitle calls it. Moreover, the same is true of the quire-members, keeper Day, Farmer Shiner, whose characteristic weaknesses, wrinkles, tricks of speech individualize them.

It is only Parson Maybold and the two lovers who seem less than distinctive, who are literary confections rather than life-studies. This difference does not diminish their success in the novel, rather it marks them as a different class of being, and leads to other cultural analogies. Fancy's nature has its origin, the manuscript makes clear, in Wordsworth's poem 'She Was a Phantom of Delight' (one of the group of 'Lucy' poems), and she embodies an idea of young womanhood given sufficient and satisfactory life; but she is not distinctive, she is any young woman, a puzzle to men. Dick too is an idea of a young man educated beyond his family but still dependent upon them, waiting to branch out, waiting to fall in love, but in a quite different way from his parents or their friends—a point Hardy makes clearly enough. Even though he is a member of the quire, during the novel Dick is much more noticeable by his absence from it.

When seen from this perspective, the novel is a romantic ballet, with Dick and Fancy as the handsome hero and beautiful heroine in standard tights and tutu; Shiner and Maybold, in more clumsy or subdued costume, represent the potential tragic fate overcome by love; the parents are comic figures, misunderstanding the younger generation; the other villagers are as character-dancers performing their version of a national or country dance, and melting back into the crowd that attends the merrymakings and weddings and fairs.

Indeed, a dance analogy is quite appropriate. It is in the two chapters devoted to the dance at the tranter's house (1.7–8) that Hardy lets us see the possibilities of intimacy between Fancy and Dick; indeed, it is hard to overestimate the importance of dancing in Hardy's novels, in particular as the only socially sanctioned and public intimate contact between young men and women. Hardy also shows the exaltation and intoxication, the suspension of usual inhibitions, the breaking down of barriers, that come in dance. Dick recognizes this: '"Look at this lovely Fancy—through the whole past evening touchable—squeezable—even kissable. For whole half-hours I held her so close to me that not a sheet of paper could have been slipped between us; and I could feel her heart only just outside my own, her life beating on so close to mine that I was aware of every breath in it. A flit is made upstairs—a hat and coat put on—and I no more dare to touch her than—"' (1.8). And it takes many months of anxious courtship before Dick gets into a position to kiss Fancy again.

The developing relationship between Dick and Fancy is in some ways a diminished version of the relationship between the poor man and his lady. In the end the success of their relationship depends upon competing ideas of whether Dick is good enough for Fancy; materially all concerned agree that he is not, and in her father's opposition there is (as in all comedy) the potential for various tragic outcomes, though the closest to this we get is Fancy going on hunger-strike in order to change his mind. Morally it is possible to argue that Fancy is not good enough for Dick, as she teases and toys with him, and accepts for a few hours the material temptations the vicar puts before her in his proposal of marriage. But, the narrator would claim, Fancy really loves Dick; she only acts as all young women act in such situations, and is not essentially culpable. When the narrator ends the novel with an allusion to Fancy's consciousness of the secret of the vicar's proposal and her determination never to tell it, he does not propose any sinister overtones, any suggestion of later narratives like *The Mayor of Casterbridge* or *Tess of the d'Urbervilles*—indeed the reverse, for it is the revelation of secrets that propels the tragic action in these novels.

This novel is also in contrast with almost all of Hardy's later work in that it is frankly a male novel that expresses most of the time the separateness of the sexes and the inability of the male part of the population to understand the female; and thus we understand that it is a characteristic of women that they like to have secrets. It was in the writing of *Far from the Madding Crowd* two years later that Hardy worked his way out of this essentialist position.

Hardy's narrator was designed with his potential audience in mind; intimately informed, affectionate towards his characters, with a sharp ear for the rhythms and varieties of speech and a sharp eye (and ear) for the distinctive details of his rural environment. However, he is distanced from the characters by education and breadth of experience, an interpreter of one world to the other, a mediator. Very occasionally this distance leads to an overt assumption of superiority and thus patronage; occasionally also his acute perception of the comic in life turns not upon intrinsic humour but the cheap farce to be found when the educated middle class observes the uneducated rural working class out of its element (the interview between the quire and the vicar (2.4–5) is an example of this).

This is the novel that Hardy wrote in 1871 and published in 1872. In 1912 he wrote in the preface to the Wessex edition of *Under the Greenwood Tree*: 'In rereading the narrative after a long interval there occurs the inevitable reflection that the realities out of which it was spun were material for another kind of study of this little group of church musicians than is found in the chapters here penned so lightly, even so farcically and flippantly at times. But circumstances would have rendered any aim at a deeper, more essential, more transcendent handling unadvisable at the date of writing . . .'. And undoubtedly he had such another kind of study in his imagination while writing this. What this other novel might have been it is of course impossible to suggest in detail, but there are some clues.

In 1871 Dorset village culture was only beginning to show the evidences of disintegration that the remainder of the decade would hurry on; and Hardy could not at that date anticipate what gradually became for him the full significance of the displacement of the traditional church-musicians by a product of modern industrial design and manufacture. What he was able then to view as an isolated incident of destruction of tradition and value by an insensitive modernizer (who after all was only following the fashion), the wound of which could be healed by time and communal goodwill, by 1890 would have seemed a part of the wholesale collapse of the world in which he grew up. This change in cultural and historical understanding is closely linked to the development in Hardy's imagination of the half-real, half-dream world of Wessex; but though Hardy would alter the environmental, and in a smaller way the cultural, context of *Under the Greenwood Tree* when he revised the novel in 1896 and 1912, he could not undertake the major rewriting that his later vision of the quire and its emblematic role in village society proposed.

In 1912 Hardy grouped *Under the Greenwood Tree* with the other novels conventionally thought of as his most satisfying, and called them 'Novels of Character and Environment'. This assignment has not often been thought to need any explanation, but the brevity of this novel, its minimal plot, and its predominantly optimistic view of the world do make the reading experience unique in Hardy's work; it seems in somewhat strange company with *The Mayor of Casterbridge* or *Jude the Obscure.* Though the environment is thoroughly harmonious with the other more celebrated novels, it is hard to suggest that there is a single character, or relationship between characters in this short novel which is developed in the way that readers of Hardy's later novels are accustomed to. The *Under the Greenwood Tree* that Hardy envisaged in 1912, however, might have been 'the' representative Wessex novel. The church musicians and their fate would become profoundly emblematic of the greater social and cultural upheaval, and their unease in church after the loss of their occupation would be the beginning of a narrative of displacement and confusion that could only end bleakly. SJG

Simon Gatrell (ed.), *Under the Greenwood Tree* (1985).

W

'Waiting Supper, The', short story. It was published in *Murray's Magazine* (January–February 1888) and in the American *Harper's Weekly* (31 December 1887, 7 January 1888), and collected in *A Changed Man and Other Tales.* Christine, the daughter of an impoverished squire, is in love with Nicholas, a young farmer, but their attempt to marry secretly is foiled by an obstructive clergyman (yet one more instance of the anti-clericalism endemic in Hardy's fiction). Christine then vacillates between Nicholas, who describes himself as '"A mere tiller of the soil"', and Bellston, a 'smart, new-lacquered man' who is the farmer's social superior. She marries Bellston, but he treats her badly, disappears, and is presumed dead (a situation used earlier in both *Far from the Madding Crowd* and *Two on a Tower*). Meanwhile Nicholas travels the world and after fifteen years returns, having made a fortune. Since Christine is now poor, their roles are now to some extent reversed. After long hesitation she agrees to marry him, only to receive, on the eve of their wedding, a message that her husband has returned. Bellston, however, fails to appear; years go by, and Christine is unwilling to renew the attempt to marry Nicholas in case her husband once again turns up, and the two of them grow old together, having spent years as friends and neighbours but never being united. At last Bellston's skeleton is discovered nearby: he has evidently drowned on the eve of the planned marriage, but even with the knowledge of his certain death they are unwilling to change their state.

Written in the autumn of 1887, soon after the completion of *The Woodlanders,* the story reproduces in Christine's situation some elements of Grace Melbury's in that novel: hesitating between a humble countryman and a middle-class sophisticate, both heroines choose the latter but live to regret it. More broadly, the story, like the novel, casts a critical eye on the institution of marriage and the societal pressures bearing down on loving relationships: the clergyman's jarring reference to '"The tragedy of marriage"' is sardonically justified ('"It is full of crises and catastrophes, and ends with the death of one of the actors"'), and when Nicholas reproaches Christine for being swayed by the dictates of society, she replies, '"Ah—you don't know what society is..."'.

*Browning is alluded to ('a sensible, new-risen poet') but not named, and his poem 'The Statue and the Bust' (included in *Men and Women,* 1855) is a source for the story. An interesting revision was made when the story was collected: in the original version Bellston actually turns up on the fateful evening, but the final version tellingly substitutes for his appearance in person that of a portmanteau bearing his initials.

war. See BOER WAR; FIRST WORLD WAR; LETTERS.

Ward, Mary (Mrs Humphry) (1851–1920), née Arnold. A prolific and successful novelist, she was also a member of a distinguished family, being the daughter of Thomas Arnold, the granddaughter of Dr Arnold of Rugby, and the niece of Matthew Arnold. She married (1872) Thomas Adolphus Ward, an Oxford don who later joined the staff of *The Times,* and was herself not only an energetic author but a tireless campaigner for social reform, especially among the London poor. She was also active in politics and worked to promote the higher education of women, but opposed female suffrage, founding in 1908 the Women's National Anti-Suffrage League.

Her depiction of a clergyman's religious doubts in *Robert Elsmere* (1888) made it one of the most widely read novels of its generation: Hardy read it with care and copied fifteen extracts from it into his notebooks. He also gave high praise to her later novel *The Coryston Family* (1913), which he considered her finest work (*L* iv 320). He had met the Wards in 1886 and became friendly with both of them. In 1916 he contributed a section on William *Barnes, consisting of a critical introduction and a selection of poems, to the fifth volume of T. H. Ward's *The English Poets*, published in 1918.

Mrs Ward's *A Writer's Recollections* (1918) expresses admiration for Hardy's novels and for *The Dynasts*, as well as paying tribute to his wide popularity, especially after the publication of *Tess of the d'Urbervilles*; she expresses the wish, however, that 'Mr Hardy had not written "Jude the Obscure"!'.

Weismann, August. See HEREDITY; 'IMAGINATIVE WOMAN, AN'.

Well-Beloved, The. The penultimate of Hardy's novels in respect of composition and first publication, but the last to appear—retitled and considerably revised—in volume form.

Composition

After the firm of *Tillotson had rejected the novel later titled *Tess of the d'Urbervilles*, they invited Hardy to write another serial for them and a contract was signed on 14 February 1890 by which Hardy undertook to supply 'something light' and relatively short (60,000 words). Most of 1890–1 was taken up with the composition and publication of *A Group of Noble Dames* and *Tess*, so that composition of the new novel was not begun until late in 1891: on 17 December Hardy told Tillotson's that he would make the work his first priority and expected to finish it by the following March.

The description of the proposed novel that Hardy sent to Tillotson's characterizes it as 'entirely modern in date and subject' and 'not a tragedy in the ordinary sense'. He emphasizes its social range and the alternation of scenes between fashionable London and an isolated region of the provinces. Most significantly, in view of the difficulties Hardy had for some time been experiencing from conventionally minded publishers, editors, and reviewers, the proposal contains the firm reassurance that 'There is not a word or scene in the tale which can offend the most fastidious taste; and it is equally suited for the reading of young people, and for that of persons of maturer years'. For the extensive rewriting of this first version undertaken by Hardy in 1896, see below.

Serial and Volume Publication

Serialization in the *Illustrated London News*, under the title *The Pursuit of the Well-Beloved*, began on 1 October, continued weekly, and was concluded on 17 December 1892. Each instalment included a headpiece and two illustrations by Walter Paget, and the serial appeared simultaneously in America in *Harper's Bazar*. The manuscript does not survive. Details of the division of the original novel into weekly instalments are given by Purdy (92–3). Volume publication did not follow until 1897, after the publication of *Jude the Obscure*, when it appeared on 16 March at the price of 6*s*. under the title *The Well-Beloved: A Sketch of a Temperament*. In the same month it was published in America. These editions include a preface, dated January 1897, slightly expanded for the Wessex Edition of 1912 and mainly devoted to a discussion of the locale of the novel. It describes the story itself, however, as 'differing from all or most others of the series in that the interest aimed at is of an ideal or subjective nature, and frankly imaginative, verisimilitude in the sequence of events has been subordinated to the said aim'. In Hardy's classification of his novels for the Wessex Edition, it is placed among the 'Romances and Fantasies'.

The volume edition of 1897 differs in important respects from the serial version, especially in its ending. Hardy had referred to the serial dismissively as an 'experimental issue' and to the work thus presented as 'short and slight, and written entirely with a view to serial publication', and he had reserved the right to revise it before its appearance in volume form. This right was extensively exercised towards the end of 1896, when he did much rewriting of the original version, adding or deleting many passages. A marked tendency of these revisions is in the direction of greater frankness and explicitness concerning the hero's infatuations. Two marriages in the earlier version, for instance (to Marcia near the beginning and to Avice the Third near the end), were now eliminated, and Pierston's account to Somers of the 'Well-Beloved' was added. The original opening chapter was discarded, and a powerfully ironic conclusion replaced a much cruder earlier version. For fuller information on the textual differences between the two versions, see the Appendix to the Oxford World's Classics edition (1986) by Tom Hetherington.

Reception

The novel's reception was generally favourable, though some reviewers were influenced by the hostile reception that *Jude* had received a year or so earlier, one remarking that 'Of all forms of sex-mania in fiction we have no hesitation in pronouncing the most unpleasant to be the Wessex-mania of Mr Thomas Hardy' (*World*, 24 March 1897). Hardy's skill in skating on thin ice without coming seriously to grief received some tributes: the *Academy* (27 March 1897) noted that 'never for one moment does the narrative verge on the ludicrous, comic though the scheme of it is in the abstract'. The *Athenaeum* (10 April 1897: repr. *CH*) included a similar tribute as well as praise for Hardy's skill in depicting the locale, perceptively summed up as 'a background which helps one not to be surprised at any of the action'.

Plot

Jocelyn Pierston, an aspiring young London sculptor, is highly susceptible towards women, though in a romantic rather than a carnal sense, and pursues the spirit of the 'Well-Beloved', a Platonic or Shelleyan ideal of the loved one, in its successive incarnations in various individual women over many years (this idea is expounded most fully in Chapter 7). At the beginning of the story, he returns after a long absence to his native place, the 'Isle of Slingers' (based on Portland, Dorset), where his father owns a quarry. There he sees again a childhood friend, Avice, to whom he becomes engaged. After meeting Marcia Bencomb, however, he is convinced that the spirit of 'the well-beloved' has migrated to Marcia from Avice. He and Marcia intend to marry, but after many delays they quarrel and separate.

Twenty years later, now successful in his profession, he hears that Avice, who has married soon after their parting, is dead. He revisits the Isle and meets her daughter, Ann Avice Caro, who bears such an uncanny resemblance to her mother that she seems like a reincarnation of her. Pierston becomes infatuated with the girl, thinks of marrying her, and engages her as a servant, but later learns that she is already married. After yet another twenty years, having lived mainly abroad in the meantime, Pierston, now 60, revisits Avice and meets *her* daughter, yet another Avice and seemingly a further incarnation of Avice the First. He wishes to marry the girl and receives encouragement from her mother, but the girl herself is shocked when she realizes how old he is and on her wedding day elopes with a young man, Leverre, who is Marcia's stepson. Avice the Second dies of shock, and at her funeral Pierston catches cold, becomes seriously ill, and is nursed by Marcia, now a widow. On recovering he finds that both his artistic gifts and his wish to pursue the Well-Beloved have alike deserted him. He and Marcia eventually marry and he becomes a pillar of the community on the Isle. Minor characters include Alfred Somers, an artist and confidant of Pierston, and Nichola Pine-Avon, a young widow who is attracted to Pierston but eventually marries Somers.

Critical Approaches

Hardy's classification of the novel among his 'Romances and Fantasies' is entirely intelligible: shorter and much more schematic than the 'Novels of Character and Environment', it presents a hero whose perception of and contacts with the external world are largely dominated by his imagination. Its three parts correspond to three stages of his life (at 20, 40, and 60), during which he falls in love successively with women belonging to three generations of the same family whose strong physical resemblance creates the illusion of reincarnation, renewal, and perpetual youth. Since Hardy, in his sixth decade at this time, seems to have been acutely conscious of the ageing process (see, for example, his poem 'I Look into My Glass', roughly contemporary with the novel), there are grounds for believing that the story may represent the working out of personal anxieties and fantasies.

As a sculptor specializing in ideal representations of the female figure, the hero's relationships with women involve less a sexual pursuit than a quest for ideal beauty, and there is in fact something curiously chaste about Pierston's contacts with women and about Hardy's presentation of desire and infatuation. Compared with the sensuousness and particularized physicality with which Tess and Arabella are depicted in Hardy's other two novels of the 1890s, the women in *The Well-Beloved* seem little more than shadows. To an unusual extent, indeed, the attention is focused on the central figure, and a pervasive concern is with the relationship between his romantic experiences and his art: though a source of personal distress, his restless and lifelong search for incarnations of ideal femininity seems to be one of the principal sources of his creative powers.

As Hardy had promised, the action alternates between Wessex and London, reflecting the two aspects of Pierston's life (as also of Hardy's own at this period): he is simultaneously a successful and affluent artist, at home in the drawing-rooms and at the dining-tables of fashionable London, and a 'native' impelled to return to his roots and hoping to find there the promise of satisfaction for his deepest emotional needs. The metropolitan figures such as the painter Somers and the society lady Nichola Pine-Avon offer him only superficial relationships. The Wessex scenes are placed on the 'Isle of Slingers' (Portland), a setting at least as much symbolic as realistic: itself a massive sculpture carved by nature, it is the home of an isolated and stubbornly independent community whose practice of intermarriage helps to render less implausible the uncanny resemblance between the successive generations of women.

The critical history of *The Well-Beloved* is one of long and unmerited neglect succeeded in recent years by serious attention. As late as 1949, A. J. Guerard could dismiss it in his otherwise perceptive study of Hardy as 'one of the most trivial' books ever published by a major writer. The past generation, however, has seen a notable increase in willingness to take the book seriously and to recognize that it needs to be judged *sui generis* rather than by canons more appropriate to, say, *Tess* or *Jude*. The impulse behind it is fanciful and poetic rather than sociological and realistic: its literary sources are in Plato and *Shelley, and its central concern is with the psychology of the artist-lover rather than with such public issues as marriage and education that are so important in Hardy's later fiction in general.

One of the earliest critics to grant sustained attention to this novel was J. Hillis Miller, who draws attention to its '"antirealistic" texture' (*Thomas Hardy: Distance and Desire*, 169) and significantly relates it to Hardy's poems, especially the elegies written after the death of his first wife, *'Poems of 1912–13'. (Among Hardy's poems is one titled 'The Well-Beloved'.) At about the same time Michael Millgate noted that Hardy himself described the work as 'half allegorical'. Millgate himself describes it as 'a kind of composite fable and romance', and suggests that the mythological allusions (notably to Aphrodite) may owe something to Hardy's recent reading of J. G. Frazer's *The Golden Bough*.

Michael Millgate was also one of the earliest critics to attempt to define the extent to which *The Well-Beloved* embodies a personal statement: 'It is not fictionalized autobiography but a carefully wrought fable which is both relevant to Hardy's experience and largely written out of that experience' (p. 307). Again the problem of genre is stressed, and it is true that much of the failure to appreciate the distinctive interest of this novel stems from inappropriate expectations.

Richard H. Taylor has explored further the relationship between character and creator, suggesting that 'there can be little doubt that it is as much about Hardy's artistic temperament as Jocelyn's' (p. 163). Taylor persuasively argues that Hardy, near the end of his career as a novelist, was casting a cold eye on the conditions to which, for a quarter of a century, that career had been subjected: the metropolitan public, especially at its more socially elevated levels; professional critics; fame and commercial success; and the compromises they enforce—all come under scrutiny. In contrast to all this is Pierston's consciousness of his own creative gifts and their relationship to his inner life.

Taylor also usefully stresses the comic and satiric elements in a novel that does not always demand to be read with solemnity. There are elements of social satire in the London scenes that are perhaps a throwback to Hardy's first, lost novel *The* *Poor Man and the Lady, but more interesting than these is his exploitation of the incongruity inherent in the older Pierston's infatuations. (A good instance of this occurs when the third Avice, some 40 years younger than her suitor, is amazed to learn that he has courted her grandmother and enquires innocently whether he perhaps also courted her great-grandmother.) Yet, as Taylor points out, the hero 'is saved from being ludicrous by Hardy's determination that his "inability to ossify", though wearing the aspect of comedy, is of the nature of tragedy'. (This tragic aspect can again be paralleled in 'I Look into My Glass'.) For Taylor, the story is 'a poetic tragi-comedy'.

An interesting attempt has been made by Michael Ryan (in *Critical Approaches to the Fiction of Thomas Hardy*, ed. Dale Kramer (1979)) to locate the novel in the context of the Aesthetic Movement of the 1890s and specifically the work of Wilde and Pater. For Ryan, Hardy's presentation of Pierston's refusal to grow old gracefully is 'ironic' and a conscious counterblast to Wilde's *The Picture of Dorian Gray* (1890).

As much of the above makes clear, the question of genre has loomed large in considerations of *The Well-Beloved*. Among other things it is a *Künstlerroman* (novel about an artist), and J. Hillis Miller has described it as 'one of the most important 19th-century novels about art'. In this respect it is closer to a work such as Thomas Mann's *Death in Venice* than to *Middlemarch* or to one of Hardy's own more realistic novels. A bald summary of the plot tends to draw attention to its improbability, but Miller has rightly insisted that as well as being an 'odd or even superficially absurd' novel it is also an 'important' one. Of its capacity to stimulate both enthusiasm and hostility there can be no doubt. D. H. *Lawrence described it as 'sheer rubbish', while John *Fowles, in the preface to his novel *The Magus*, has gone so far as to call it 'the most revealing of all modern novels about novelists'. Fowles's emphasis on its modernity is worth noting: at the end of his career as a writer of fiction (for some have argued that the final version of *The Well-Beloved* must be regarded as his last novel), Hardy seems to have been moving towards a new kind of fiction.

At the same time the work has affinities with some of the earlier novels that have traditionally been regarded as less central to his achievement. Marcel *Proust, another keen admirer of this novel, cites it in *A la recherche du temps perdu* as an example of the truth that 'great writers have never written more than a single work'—that is, they essentially write the same book over and over again—and specifically insists on its close relationship to the very early *A Pair of Blue Eyes*. *The Well-Beloved* is a work that has been not only greatly undervalued but seriously misunderstood—most notably in respect of its ending, in the final version (immeasurably superior at this point to the serial version) a masterpiece of controlled irony and precise symbolism. Its poetic qualities and its preoccupation with the power of the imagination ('fancy' and 'fantasy' are key-words throughout) make it a fitting prelude to the sustained period of self-dedication to poetry during the last 30 years of Hardy's life.

John Fowles, 'Hardy and the Hag', in Lance St John Butler (ed.), *Thomas Hardy after Fifty Years*.

J. Hillis Miller, *Thomas Hardy: Distance and Desire* (1970).

—— Preface to the New Wessex Edition of *The Well-Beloved* (1975).

Michael Ryan, '"One Name of Many Shapes": *The Well-Beloved*', in Dale Kramer (ed.), *Critical Approaches to the Fiction of Thomas Hardy* (1979).

Michael Millgate, *Thomas Hardy: His Career as a Novelist* (1971).

Richard H. Taylor, *The Neglected Hardy: Thomas Hardy's Lesser Novels* (1982).

Wells, H. G. (1866–1946), novelist. He met Hardy in 1907. In January 1919, Wells and his mistress, the novelist Rebecca West, were staying at Weymouth; when he wrote to Hardy proposing a visit, Hardy replied enthusiastically, though admitting that he had not read West's recent and successful novel *The Return of the Soldier*. The tea-time visit took place on 29 January, and afterwards Wells made some sketches with scraps of dialogue in West's copy of *Wessex Tales*. These, reproduced in Gordon N. Ray's *H. G. Wells and Rebecca West* (1974), pp. 94–5, constitute an amusing if not necessarily literal record of Hardy's 'boasts about the number of Roman skeletons and sepulchral urns that he found when digging the foundations of his house', which apparently prompted a lugubrious comment from Florence *Hardy. Perhaps hoping for more such gems, Wells and West paid another visit in August 1923. Wells sent presentation copies of some of his books to Hardy, who in a letter of 25 March 1923 (*L* vi 188) praised his productivity and freshness, and the excellence of his writing.

Wessex. Before 1874, the word 'Wessex' meant exclusively a Saxon kingdom which developed in the centre of southern England in the centuries between the Roman occupation and the Norman conquest, with King Alfred as its most celebrated monarch. Today the word is in popular use in much of southern England as the geographical element in the naming of many hundreds of institutions, societies, commercial undertakings, and assorted public bodies such as Wessex Water, Wessex Jewellers, and Wessex Golf Centre. The European Parliament even had a Member for Wessex until the constituency boundaries were reorganized.

This rejuvenation of a word which had lapsed into historical obscurity is the unique achievement of Hardy, who first restored the word to common usage in 1874, in *Far from the Madding Crowd*, as the fictitious name for the part of England in which this and the bulk of his novels, stories, and poems are set. His motive, as he explained in a subsequent preface, was to find a territorial definition larger than a single county to lend unity to the series of novels he was projecting, in which there would be a strong sense of place. Instead of inventing a name for this larger territory he chose to disinter the old one for his 'partly real, partly dream-country'. To his surprise Wessex became more and more popular as a provincial definition until, in his words, 'the dream-country has, by degrees, solidified into a utilitarian region which people can go to, take a house in, and write to the papers from'. In effect he reached out from his native county Dorset (which became South Wessex) to its neighbours—Devon (Lower Wessex), Somerset (Outer Wessex), Wiltshire (Mid-Wessex), and Hampshire (Upper Wessex). Later he added Berkshire (North Wessex) specifically for *Jude the Obscure*. Cornwall was a special problem, so unmistakably non-Saxon that Hardy tactfully named it Off-Wessex.

His development of Wessex was a gradual process with Dorset always remaining the strongest element, the outer reaches being drawn in by degrees as fresh opportunities offered. As a freelance writer with no private means and therefore dependent on his pen to earn a living, Hardy was not slow to recognize the commercial advantage of his Wessex concept, urging his publisher to employ the words 'Wessex novels' in advertisements of his books. This bestowed a degree of additional copyright, inhibiting other novelists from entering 'Wessex'. Dorchester might be common property. Casterbridge was not.

There were some inconsistencies at first. The years of his young manhood in London had helped him to see rural Dorset in a wider context and to understand the appeal to a national readership of those touches of 'quaintness' in rustic speech, dress, customs, and place-names associated with his native county. With a strong bent towards satire in his progress as a writer he turned an affectionate satire onto his own background, most noticeably in *Under the Greenwood Tree*, where he evidently enjoyed coining humorous names for people and places. Miss Vashti Sniff, Miss Mercy Onmey, and Farmer Kex ('kex' being a local word for the hollow dried-up stalk of a plant) are evidently introduced for our amusement; so too is the place-name of Tantrum Clangley (*UGT* 5. 2). More surprisingly, in view of its date, he included Puddle-sub-Mixen in *Two on a Tower* (23), published in 1882, eight years after the origination of Wessex.

Such momentary flippancies were quite out of place in the larger plan for a Wessex that Hardy increasingly recognized as the bordering frame of his life's work. It was in a more serious vein that he took advantage of each reprinting of his books to amend the proofs in ways which reinforced the overall Wessex character. In one instance he transferred the setting of a story, 'The *Romantic Adventures of a Milkmaid', from Dorset to Devon, a county which was not well represented in his Wessex. In other cases he made smaller revisions or additions to enhance the identification with a recognizable locality in Wessex.

It must be understood that his opportunities to get to know the whole of the territory at first hand were limited. He did not ride a horse or own a carriage, and he did not mount his first bicycle until the last of his novels had been written. His leisure was subject to the imperative of maintaining the momentum of his literary career. He made good use of the coastal shipping which linked the ports and little harbours of the English Channel, and no reader of his poetry can fail to recognize the important part that the railway played in Hardy's life. By one means or another the fictitious place-names multiplied on the map of Wessex, and its landscapes acquired fresh touches of animation, particularly in the rapidly growing body of his verse: such narrative poems as 'A Trampwoman's Tragedy' and 'The Sacrilege' were admirably adapted to enrich the Outer Wessex section which had received little attention in the novels. There was a separate problem, however, in the introduction of fresh Wessex elements into existing poems. The insertion or revision of a place-name in a sentence of prose was simple enough, but a line of verse made its own specific metrical and syllabic demands before it could accommodate alterations. Hardy was understandably less consistent in his use of Wessex pseudonyms in his poems and was sometimes ready enough to use whichever version came to hand, the real or the fictitious, even in the same line in one of the 'At Casterbridge Fair' group, 'The Market-Girl', where the village of Hermitage retains its proper name while Yeovil is 'wessexed' as Ivel.

With these reservations it can be seen that Hardy worked methodically to rules that he described in his preface to the Wessex Edition of 1912. The abiding landscape features of rivers, hill-tops, recognized landmarks, and well-defined antiquities retain their standard names, as do large towns and points which help to beat the bounds of Wessex. Those bounds, in Hardy's definition, were the Thames in the north, the English Channel on the south, on the west the Cornish coast and on the east a line running from Hayling Island to Windsor Forest. In effect, with some accretion at its eastern end, it is the south-west peninsula of England which thrusts out into the Atlantic, between the Severn Sea or Bristol Channel and the English Channel. It has few cities, many small market-towns, and a generally rural character.

The pseudonyms that Hardy scattered over his map of Wessex are usually transparent enough to allow the reader to glimpse the inner reality. In his earliest novels he had invented fictitious place-names in what was a generally accepted practice among novelists. It prevented odious comparisons, and provided a privacy for authors that might sometimes be essential: when Hardy wrote *A Pair of Blue Eyes* he certainly did not wish it to identify his visits to the home of his future wife. The anonymity imposed on Beeny Cliff as the Cliff without a Name emphasizes that. Occasionally he came up against an established pseudonym, notably in the case of Reading, which had been named Belford Regis by Mary Russell Mitford in her book of that title in 1835. In *Jude the Obscure* Hardy renamed Reading as Aldbrickham, a name which conjures up somewhere very different from the town where Miss Mitford's father practised as a doctor and was chairman of the magistrates.

When Hardy's Wessex was completed, and accompanied by a map drawn by his own hand, he had created an unofficial English province more closely and elaborately defined than any comparable example. It is in that sense one of the key developments in the 19th century's absorption in the subjects of regional identity, dialect speech, survivals of folklore and legend and anything that could be recognized as a local flavour in landscapes or people. Previously it had been the purpose of writers from the Restoration through the 18th century to establish national norms of language, of social behaviour, and of aesthetic taste, and eventually to entrench the genteel society of Georgian England—and more precisely of Georgian London and the Home Counties. Life outside that pale, apart from its outposts in manor-house and rectory, was ignored or represented only in jocular buffooneries. What disturbed this Augustan composure was a growing curiosity about the 'Gothick' past, which pointed the way to *Wordsworth and *Scott and the incoming tide of the Romantic Movement that was to dominate the 19th century with its emotional excesses, its cultivation of morbidity and horror, its antiquarian pursuits, and its intellectual radicalism. Under the pressure of new ideas the venerable deities of classical mythology had to yield space to accommodate Arthur and Guinevere, Tristan and Yseult and many another whose feet had never touched the soil of Greece or Rome.

At several levels the Victorians undertook what might be described as a national stock-taking, turning out neglected medieval cupboards and confronting familiar landscapes with a new set of questions. What the Age of Reason had been apt to dismiss was now seized upon by the Romantic imagination. Imperceptibly the living past and the picturesque present coalesced to create a spirit of place, a *genius loci*, which can now be recognized as a special attribute of 19th-century literature. There is no doubt in any literate mind as to where to look for the haunts of the Lake Poets, or the Brontë country, or the Lorna Doone country—or Hardy's Wessex.

There is a further change implicit in Wessex particularly. The events through which the plot of the traditional novel unfolded usually took place indoors for the most part and in a social setting. With Hardy, on the other hand, we are often confronted with a solitary figure in an unpeopled landscape. Tess, Fanny Robin, Henchard in his final hours, Clym cutting furze, Gabriel Oak on Norcombe Hill with his sheep—these are lonely figures walking in a Wessex countryside that gives an added dignity to them by the impassive timeless theatre it provides for the playing out of their destinies. Something elemental is added. The ambient atmosphere of Wessex reflects and reinforces the mood of the protagonist, and the human figure becomes almost an extension of the landscape.

In the make-up of his partly real, partly dream-country, Hardy drew extensively on the durable heritage of central southern England, its topography, its architecture, its history and its prehistory, its legends and its myths, its cultural and social distinctions. Time alters the surface reality as surely as it alters the features of a human face, but the inner character has its own slower momentum, just as each scenic vista has its own underlying geology. His ability to generate this sense of a long perspective is a feature of Hardy's writing: it gives a weightiness, a gravity to what might otherwise seem slight and transient. Wessex is rich in the kind of material that Hardy needed for this kind of writing. Its mixed geology of chalk downland, sandy heath, limestone, and blue lias give it variety in its basic qualities. It is exceptionally rich in its memorials of prehistory, in the Mendip caves, the many barrows on the Marlborough Downs and in Cranborne Chase, the national icons of Stonehenge, Avebury, Silbury Hill, and the Wansdyke (to choose at random from so many), and equally rich in the waveringly indistinct figures of early history—King Alfred holding out against the heathen invaders in his fastness at Athelney in the Somerset marshes, and the less substantial King Arthur believed to lie before the high altar of Glastonbury, between the ruined arches that still grope upwards like blinded giants.

It became almost second nature for Hardy to think in such terms. In April 1914, when he wrote the poem 'Channel Firing' after hearing naval gunfire practising in readiness for the imminent war, his closing verse invoked the symbols of Alfred's Tower at Stourton, of Arthur's Camelot, and of ancestral Stonehenge: 'Again the guns disturbed the hour, | Roaring their readiness to avenge, | As far inland as Stourton Tower, | And Camelot, and starlit Stonehenge.' And again, in his choice of the appropriate setting for Tess's final hours with Angel Clare, it is the so-called sacrificial stone at Stonehenge which seizes his imagination.

Combined with this visionary sense of the depth of Wessex history is a robust presentation of the here-and-now of the people among whom he lived. All attempts to convert dialect and the tonal shades of difference in vowel sounds into printed words are fraught with difficulty and seldom satisfy, but Hardy discarded phonetic devices and relied happily on his sensitivity to the phrasing, the rhythm, and the vocabulary of the speech that surrounded him in his formative years. It is these qualities which give such an endearing vividness to the murmuring vernacular background of Wessex speech that accompanies the major action of the novels and adds a convincing, down-to-earth authenticity to the most high-flown moments.

Nor is it only through speech that solidity and verisimilitude are given to Wessex. The scenes of daily life are so circumstantially graphic that they add an unsought but valuable documentary accuracy. Much that is now valued for its scenic qualities only was then a workplace, an economic necessity. The hazel coppices served to provide hurdles for the shepherd and spars for the thatcher. Peat and furze were the essential fuels for most of the population; in many villages coal was burnt only in the manor-house, the rectory, and the smithy. The springtime splendour of the blossoming orchards in *The Woodlanders* (19) leads at once to Mr Melbury's comment that '"All that apple-blooth means heavy autumn work"': he foresees a record yield of cider, the staple beverage of Wessex. As a young man Hardy himself liked to return home each autumn to help his father with the cider-making, and in *The Woodlanders* he gives a lovingly detailed picture of the itinerant cider-maker, who visited the smaller farms which had their own apples but lacked the necessary equipment. Hardy's liking for the genre paintings of the Dutch and Flemish artists seems to have encouraged him to create their equivalents in words. Another notable example (*W* 19) is the little cameo of Marty South in the canopy of a felled oak like a great bird, as she rips off the bark with the leg-bone of a horse as her ripping-tool. (The bark would go for tanning leather.)

It was the land itself that provided a livelihood in one form or another, the land and the surrounding sea. In Wessex the ratio of coastline to inland area is markedly high. To be a fisherman, a mariner, or a sailor was the main alternative to agricultural work on the land. In the moist and mainly benign climate of Wessex farming was predominantly livestock husbandry and dairying. Hardy's familiarity with what he called 'the life of the fields' is evident throughout his novels. Accompanying that familiarity was a realism that refused to sentimentalize the traditionally pastoral scene that increasingly faced radical changes. The steam-plough and the threshing-machine brought a new figure to the farming landscape, the engineer. 'Everything is mechanical or scientific', Richard Jefferies wrote in 1880 in *Hodge and His Masters*, sadly acknowledging that modernization had driven romance from the farmland. In his essay 'The *Dorsetshire Labourer' (1883) Hardy commented that 'progress and picturesqueness do not harmonize' and that the farm-folk could not be expected 'to remain stagnant and old-fashioned for the pleasure of romantic spectators'.

For modern readers Hardy's Wessex has a recurring elegiac tone, a lingering nostalgia which might have reduced him to the lesser stature of a purely regional writer, piously recording a fading legend. That this is not so is evident in the prevailing tension between his provincial background and the magnetic pull of London as his Mecca. In one of his *notebooks he wrote in 1922: 'I am convinced that it is better for a writer to know a little bit of the world remarkably well than to know a great part of the world remarkably little.'

Wessex gave him that, in full measure and at grass-roots level. When he went to London and his first taste of city life in the spring of 1862 he was indeed the complete provincial in social terms. His family background had no cultural, educational, or financial link with the gentry, no university sophistication or polish, no insight into the subtler codes of the Establishment. He had his innate talent, his own resolute pursuit of an education, and his recognition that for him what he called bohemian values were paramount. In Wessex he was secure: London was his challenge, and remained so for many years. He was of that first generation of ambitious young men to whom the railway offered an escape from rural obscurity to the stimulation, the wide intellectual horizon of the capital city.

In *Desperate Remedies* (1.3) Hardy wrote that 'provincial towns trying to be lively are the dullest of dull things'. The unspoken comparison was with London, whence he had recently returned to Wessex after five to six years there. He could now claim to know the streets of the city west of St Paul's like a born Londoner, and was proud to be mistaken for one. In 1866, in his London lodgings, he had written a poem, 'From Her in the Country', which contrasted the 'crass clanging town' with the peaceful tranquillity of rural Nature that should surpass 'all man's urban shows'. Such a wholesome attitude failed, alas, and the speaker 'mused again on city din and sin, | Longing to madness I might move therein!'

This was a recurring complexity in Hardy's thought. When *Far from the Madding Crowd* was published, with its first proclamation of Wessex, Hardy and his newly wedded wife were living on the dormitory fringe of London at Surbiton, not at Tantrum Clangley, Toller Porcorum, or any other Wessex village. Moreover, he was determined not to become typecast as a writer about sheepfarming; instead he developed what might be considered his most original and surprising plot in *The Hand of Ethelberta*. The central character in that novel is a trans-social woman, a butler's daughter transformed into an aristocrat, who advances the feminist cause by making every personal decision as a man would do and prospers accordingly, and who conceals her provincial background beneath a veneer of London sophistication. And for good measure he brings the servants' quarters into comparable prominence with the reception rooms.

The result is a display of somewhat revolutionary but unmatured ideas, which has not won much support from Hardy's critics and students but has a particular importance for the light it throws on Hardy's uncertainty at this time. He evidently wanted to keep alive his earlier interest in social satire, while developing his newly conceived plan to make Wessex the larger canvas for his novels. Ethelberta herself embodies the conflict between London mores and the provincial simplicities of her brothers and their sister Picotee. She is troubled by 'that old sense of disloyalty to her class and kin' (23). In a description of the well-bred style of laughter at a London dinner-party Hardy contrasts it with the boisterousness of 'contorted features, purple face, and stamping foot among the gentlemen in corduroy and fustian who adorn the remoter provinces' (7). In the same novel, Faith Julian argues that '"Mediocrity stamped 'London' fetches more than talent marked 'provincial'"' (11).

Hardy appears to have been caught in a state of tension at this time between the grass-roots background of Wessex and the first taste of the national success in London that could be within his grasp. There is even a hint of a doubt about the wisdom of adopting the profession of novelist as a full-time career in the anxious comment of Ethelberta's mother that '"A story-teller seems such an impossible castle-in-the-air sort of a trade for getting a living by"'.

After the completion of *Ethelberta* Hardy had decided to suspend writing for a longer time than usual. During the book's later stages he and Emma had lodged briefly in London, Swanage, and Yeovil, and it was from Yeovil that Hardy wrote to his publisher, George Smith, on 5 March 1876 (*L* i 43): 'I do not wish to attempt any more original writing of any length for a few months, until I can learn the best line to take for the future.' The choice to be resolved was evidently between the strong emotions and high tragedy that he could discern in the Wessex characters of *Far from the Madding Crowd* and the opportunities for satire and intellectual discussion that he had found in his most recent novel among 'that gentle order of society which has no worldly sorrow except when its jewellery gets stolen' (*HE* 11).

In the event he and Emma rented a house in Sturminster Newton, and lived there for two years while Hardy wrote *The Return of the Native*, which, in its evocation of Egdon Heath, pointed the way for his deeper poetic genius to accommodate itself to the task of writing serial fictions. Once more, however, he was drawn back to London and to novels of shallower draught in which the furze-cutters and heath-croppers of Egdon would have been horribly out of place. A serious illness ended this final London phase in a decision to build within a couple of miles of his birthplace the house, *Max Gate, that was to be his home and workplace for the rest of his life.

Workplace it certainly was in his estimation, for that is how he liked to describe it at first to his metropolitan friends: it was merely a little place that he used for writing in. To J. A. Symonds, who in 1889 was living in Switzerland, Hardy wrote that 'I, too, am in a sense exiled. I was obliged to leave Town after a severe illness some years ago' (*L* i 190). The compromise that Hardy established was to rent an apartment in Town for the London season each year, until Emma wearied of the housekeeping involved in their literary tea-parties. He enjoyed his membership of the Savile and the Athenaeum *clubs and the attentions of the hostesses of London society. When he returned to Wessex he might sometimes admit to longing for another reason to go away, but more often his study door closed and he was alone in that partly real, partly dream-country that was destined to be his abiding creation as we now know it in the great novels that came from Max Gate and the late flowering of the poet who succeeded the novelist. DH

William Cobbett, *Rural Rides* (1830).
Desmond Hawkins, *Hardy's Wessex* (1983).
Denys Kay-Robinson, *Hardy's Wessex Re-Appraised* (1972).
Peter Widdowson, 'Hardy, "Wessex", and the Making of a National Culture', *THA* 4 (1986).

Wessex Poems. The first of Hardy's eight collections of verse, it was published by *Harper & Brothers in December 1898 in an edition of only 500 copies. An American edition was issued in the following month. His last major work of fiction, the final version of *The Well-Beloved*, had appeared in volume form in March 1897, but plans for a volume of poems, and even its title, were in Hardy's mind before this date. On 4 February 1897 he had noted in his diary the tentative title *Wessex Poems: with Sketches of their Scenes by the Author*, and though the subtitle was dropped the sketches were carried out and included in the published volume (though, regrettably, not in all later editions).

Shortly before its appearance, Hardy told William *Archer that he had been 'going to publish it for years' (24 November 1898: *L* ii 206). The preface is dated September 1898, and by mid-October he was busy correcting the proofs. At the end of August he had told Florence *Henniker that he had recently been engaged in 'a mysterious occupation' (*L* ii 199), evidently the execution of the drawings, and by late September they were finished (*L* ii 201–2). He told Edward *Clodd (*L* ii 204) that he had enjoyed assembling the poems, but later expressed regret to Edmund *Gosse and Theodore Watts-Dunton—perhaps in response to criticisms from some reviewers—that he had not taken the opportunity to remove 'defects of form' (*L* ii 214, 216), a phrase that perhaps refers to diction as well as, or rather than, metrics.

The manuscript was given by Hardy to Birmingham City Museum and Art Gallery, through the agency of Sydney *Cockerell, in 1911. For the most part it is a fair copy intended for the printer rather than a working draft, Hardy's practice being to copy out poems and then to destroy the original manuscripts. Uniquely, it includes 31 pen and ink drawings, well worth careful attention; some of the most striking are referred to below.

Hardy's fame as a novelist led to the collection being widely reviewed but was also responsible for a certain puzzlement as to why he had turned from prose to verse, coupled with the suggestion that he lacked a distinctive lyrical gift. As R. G. Cox has said, 'reviewers were at first inclined to treat [the poems] as the usual sort of indulgence by a prose writer, not to be taken very seriously' (*CH* xxxvii). *The Academy* (14 January 1899; repr. in *CH*), however, while suggesting that 'Mr Hardy could scarcely have had time to master the mere *technique* of verse' and that 'his strong grim hand would be too heavy for poetry', acknowledged rather unexpectedly that the best of the volume was to be found in 'the lyrical and personal poems of the opening section'—some of these being in fact poems written more than twenty years earlier. This opinion was not shared by the influential *Saturday Review* (December 1898; repr. in *CH*), which found merit in individual poems but passed a severe overall judgement on 'this curious and wearisome volume, these many slovenly, slipshod, uncouth verses, stilted in sentiment, poorly conceived and worse wrought'.

With few exceptions, the other reviewers, while not always so harsh, were unenthusiastic: two particular areas of complaint that recur are the eccentricities of diction and the prevailing pessimism. A partial exception to the general lack of appreciation is the Shakespearian scholar E. K. Chambers: writing in the *Athenaeum* (14 January 1899; repr. in *CH*), he begins by censuring 'woodenness of rhythm and a needlessly inflated diction' but reaches the conclusion that, while Hardy's poetic range is 'very narrow', he achieves real power within his limitations ('strenuous, austere, forcible'). Chambers is perceptive, too, in noting that Hardy's 'vigorous and unworn provincialisms... should do something to renew and refresh a somewhat wilted vocabulary'.

Wessex Poems represented for Hardy the long-delayed fulfilment of his early and enduring ambition to become a poet, and one-third of the 51 poems in this volume date from the 1860s, before he turned to fiction. Like all his collections of verse, however, it includes work from different stages of his career to date, and some of the poems had been written quite recently. Thus, the second poem in the collection ('Amabel') has the date 1865 appended and is known to have been written when Hardy was living at 16 Westbourne Park Villas, Bayswater, London (see HOMES), while others were apparently written in 1869 ('Her Initials'), 1870 ('Ditty'), 1873 ('She'; later retitled 'She at His Funeral'), 1878 ('The Sergeant's Song'), 1890 ('Thoughts of Phena'), 1894 ('The Slow Nature'), and 1898 ('The Peasant's Confession'). This list is not complete, and many of the poems are undated and cannot be dated with any confidence, while some were taken up again after a long interval: 'Valenciennes', for example, was begun in 1878, but not completed until 1897. In sharp contrast to the writing to order, and often under pressure, that was demanded by his other career as a supplier of serialized fiction, Hardy could be infinitely patient and unhurried in giving his poems to the world.

The reader of 1898 who opened *Wessex Poems* and began to peruse its contents would have encountered poems that are often cast in traditional forms (there are, for instance, several sonnets), but that use language in ways that would have struck such a reader as unfamiliar and even disconcerting. In 1898 Tennyson had been dead for only six years, and the reaction against the prevailing late-Victorian style—fluid, musical, accessible, and remaining stubbornly within the boundaries of an established poetic diction—had not yet made itself seriously felt. Rudyard *Kipling's experiments in the vernacular could still be dismissed as exotic and eccentric, and though G. M. Hopkins was dead, his poems were to remain largely unpublished for another generation. Two other poets who published volumes in 1898 were the then-popular and highly conservative Henry *Newbolt and William Watson. The linguistic texture of Hardy's poems, gritty rather than fluid, and continually jarring rather than soothing, must have seemed bizarre, rebarbative, and affected, even perverse, and deprecatory or patronizing terms such as 'provincialisms' recur in contemporary criticism.

Among other features to strike the reader would have been Hardy's addiction to bleak and often ungainly negatives ('unchosen', 'unblooms'); to compounds that sometimes seem forced ('pleasure-caught', 'never-napping', 'omen-scouting'—though 'wind-wafts' has a Hopkinsian felicity); to unfamiliar archaisms, some so unusual that they may well have fallen under the suspicion of being neologisms ('showance', 'lippings', 'up-fingered', 'everywhen'); and to dialect words ('lewth', 'leazes'). Some of Hardy's locutions seem inspired by William *Barnes's campaign for a return to Saxon plainness and homeliness ('life-deed' rather than 'ambition', 'forthcome' rather than 'appear'), while at the same time there is a marked fondness for unfamiliar Latinisms ('prevision', 'intermissive'), many of which seem to subvert Barnes's principles ('ostent' for 'show', 'hodiernal' rather than 'daily').

What this adds up to is a remarkable eclecticism, a hospitality to all varieties of language, old and new, vernacular and learned, technical and everyday, familiar and strange, and an openness in startling contrast to the linguistic restrictions of most late-Victorian verse. Hardy's linguistic nonconformity makes him resistant to easy classification: though he uses dialect words, for instance, and even writes dialect poems ('The Bride-Night Fire'), he is not a dialect poet in the manner of Robert Burns, John Clare, or Barnes. Nor are his departures from linguistic decorum by any means uniform: while some poems, especially the earliest, are thickly studded with the kind of verbal experiments stigmatized by reviewers as uncouth, others are simpler, more lyrical, and closer to spontaneous everyday discourse. Some of the best poems in the volume achieve a happy blending of the two styles, 'Thoughts of Phena', for instance, moving forward with confident naturalness from a phrase almost banal in its simplicity ('Not a line of her writing have I . . .'), yet also accommodating such characteristic verbal oddities as 'unsight', 'Disennoble', and 'aureate nimb'. (This is the poem that Philip *Larkin specifically referred to in speaking of his own emergence, as a poet, from the influence of Yeats, and his falling, heavily and permanently, under the influence of Hardy.)

Hardy's arrangement of the contents of this volume is not consistently chronological, since although it opens with some very early poems, others of a similar date are found near the end. Broadly speaking the poems seem to fall into three groups: (1) early poems that combine a prevailingly gloomy mood with marked eccentricities of diction; (2) poems on historical themes, frequently employing ballad-forms, many of them connected with the *Napoleonic Wars or with local history; (3) poems for the most part written closer to the date of publication, and often expressing concern at the ageing process and the loss of loved ones. A group of poems on 'public' themes, in other words, is both preceded and followed by more intensely personal poems, many of which may be associated with particular individuals, whether or not these are readily identifiable.

In the first group, a notable preoccupation is the frustrations and disappointments of love, sometimes linked with a cosmic despair derived partly from the loss of belief in immortality and partly from an appalled sense of the vast indifferent universe revealed by Victorian science. Of several sonnets in this part of the collection, 'Hap' recognizes that in a godless universe the fate of human beings must be random and meaningless, while 'In Vision I Roamed' places individual emotions and relationships in the context of a universe that renders humanity insignificant. The latter, like 'At a Lunar Eclipse' (written at the same period, but published in Hardy's second collection, *Poems of the Past and the Present*), shows an interest in astronomy later exploited in his romance *Two on a Tower.*

Of the other sonnets, a form that Hardy was not much to practise in his later years, 'Revulsion' is Shakespearian in language and tone, though not strictly in form, and 'A Confession to a Friend in Trouble', associated with Horace *Moule, disturbing in its moral honesty and uncompromising self-awareness. The manuscript of the latter adds to the title the phrase '(a confession of selfishness)', later dropped.

If Hardy's dating is to be trusted, all these poems, and others, derive from the mid-1860s, when he was living in London: of the dated poems from this period, one belongs to 1865, two to 1867, one to 1869, and no fewer than thirteen to 1866—the year that saw the end of his romantic involvement with Eliza *Nicholls as well as his increasing recognition that he would be unlikely to obtain a university education. It was also the year that saw the publication, in April, of the first series of *Swinburne's *Poems and Ballads*, a volume that is known to have generated considerable excitement in Hardy.

Perhaps the most accomplished of these early poems is 'Neutral Tones', which, like the less successful 'A Meeting with Despair' later in the volume, exemplifies what was to become a characteristically Hardyan preoccupation, the exploration of parallels between the outer, visible world of nature and landscape and the hidden life of the emotions. The painterly title is a clue, if any is needed, to the poem's quest in external nature for a metaphor for unspoken feelings. Revealingly, 'Neutral Tones' is chaster and less affected in diction than many of the other poems in this group, its language and verse-movement coming much closer to suggesting natural speech. 'Her Dilemma' is a particularly striking example of a poem accompanied by an illustration that reinforces the verbal text.

In the middle section of the volume, 'Valenciennes', 'San Sebastian', and other poems attest to Hardy's lifelong interest in the Napoleonic Wars, developed at greater length in *The Trumpet-Major* and, above all, *The Dynasts.* (Part of 'The Sergeant's Song', later set to music by Gustav *Holst, had appeared in Chapter 5 of *The Trumpet-Major.*) 'The Dance at the Phoenix', a poem in which Hardy took great pride as an example of narrative art (see *L* ii 283), resembles a folksong or ballad in form, and was, according to Hardy, based on a local tradition; the ballad 'The Casterbridge Captains' links local figures with imperial history (two of the men referred to had died at the Khyber Pass in 1842); 'The Burghers' with its accompanying illustration also has a Dorchester setting. Nearer the end of the volume, the dialect poem 'The Bride-Night Fire' is another production of 1866 and was the first of Hardy's poems to appear in print: originally titled 'The Fire at Tranter Sweatley's', it appeared in the *Gentleman's Magazine* (November 1875) in a bowdlerized and somewhat shortened form.

Generally speaking, the poems in the closing part of the volume are later in date and more personal in nature. Several are associated with specified or unspecified individuals. One already mentioned, 'Thoughts of Phena At News of Her Death', is dated March 1890 and refers to Hardy's cousin Tryphena *Sparks (for his account of its curious origin, see *LW* 234); 'Middle-Age Enthusiasms' is inscribed 'To M.H.' (Mary Hardy, a beloved sister: see RELATIVES OF THOMAS HARDY); the '(E.L.G.)' in the subtitle of 'Ditty' is Emma Lavinia Gifford, later Emma *Hardy; 'Heiress and Architect', which is accompanied by a simple but striking illustration, is subtitled 'For A. W. Blomfield' and followed by the note '1867. 8 Adelphi Terrace', the time and place of Hardy's employment by the London architect *Blomfield; the woman in 'At an Inn', a poem said by Hardy to be associated with the George, Winchester, is unnamed but has been plausibly identified as Florence *Henniker.

In such poems as 'Middle-Age Enthusiasms', 'In a Eweleaze near Weatherbury', and the final item of the volume, 'I Look into My Glass', the standpoint is almost oppressively geriatric: the physical ravages of time, the loss of youth's joy, and the absence of hope for the future are intensely felt and communicated, while 'Friends Beyond', like 'Thoughts of Phena', is a poem of bereavement. In his fifties Hardy evidently felt like an old man, at least intermittently; he was in no position to know that he would live for almost thirty years after the publication of *Wessex Poems*, or that this would be a period of rich creativity, fame, and honour, as well as one of extensive activity and numerous friendships. The theme of ageing so dominant in these poems is also central to *The Well-Beloved*, the novel whose revision, completed at about the time he turned his attention to *Wessex Poems*, was his final major task as a writer of fiction.

Two other poems remind us that Hardy, an unbeliever, longed to believe: in 'A Sign-Seeker' his yearning for, and desperate quest for evidence of, personal immortality are frustrated, while 'The Impercipient (At a Cathedral Service)', titled in the manuscript 'The Agnostic (Evensong: —— Cathedral)', expresses a painful sense of reluctant self-exclusion from the community of believers. There is an ironic appropriateness in the metrical form of this poem, one familiar in Anglican hymnody, while the accompanying illustration suggests that Hardy had Salisbury Cathedral, one of his favourite ecclesiastical buildings, in mind. Like many other poems in this first collection, these touch on themes that recur in Hardy's work in prose and verse both before and after its publication.

Wessex Tales, Hardy's first collection of short stories, was proposed to *Macmillan on 29 February 1888, and in its earliest form was published in two volumes on 4 May 1888, priced 12*s.* and with the subtitle 'Strange, Lively, and Commonplace' (later dropped). An American edition was published by *Harper & Brothers in the same month. At this stage the collection comprised five stories: 'The Three Strangers', 'The Withered Arm', 'Fellow-Townsmen', 'Interlopers at the Knap', and 'The Distracted Preacher' (see separate entries for each of these stories). For an edition brought out by *Osgood, McIlvaine in 1896, Hardy added a preface and a sixth story, 'An Imaginative Woman', but in the Wessex Edition (1912) he moved this story to *Life's Little Ironies* and transferred two stories ('A Tradition of Eighteen Hundred and Four' and 'The Melancholy Hussar of the German Legion') from that volume to *Wessex Tales*, which henceforth contained seven stories. All seven had made their first appearance in magazines or newspapers. The preface was revised and expanded in 1912 and again for the Mellstock Edition of 1919. For a fuller account of the textual history of this collection, see the Oxford World's Classics edition by Kathryn R. King (1991).

All seven stories had been written during the period 1878–87, a period that opens with *The Return of the Native* and ends with *The Woodlanders*. In keeping with the 'Wessex' emphasis of the title, the stories are predominantly local and historical, drawing heavily on regional customs, traditions, and folk beliefs. 'A Tradition of Eighteen Hundred and Four' and 'The Melancholy Hussar of the German Legion' furnish evidence of Hardy's deep interest in the Napoleonic period, manifested a little earlier in *The Trumpet-Major* (1880); 'The Withered Arm' is based on a grisly superstition and set in the decade after Waterloo; 'The Three Strangers' is also set 'Fifty years ago', and 'The Distracted Preacher', a tale of smuggling on the Dorset coast based on oral tradition, at roughly the same time; 'Fellow-Townsmen' is set 'five-and-thirty years ago'; and while the action of 'Interlopers at the Knap' takes place 'Some few years ago', it appears to draw on a Hardy family tradition relating to a period before the writer's birth, and is firmly located in the area of 'Casterbridge'. The spirited, unconventional heroines of 'The Distracted Preacher' and 'Interlopers at the Knap' are in a line of descent traceable from some of Hardy's novels of the 1870s, including *Far from the Madding Crowd*, *The Hand of Ethelberta*, and *The Return of the Native*.

Weymouth. The influence of Weymouth ('Budmouth') on Hardy was, among Dorset towns, second only to that of *Dorchester. It was within easy distance of his birthplace. In his praise of cider in the poem 'Great Things', he speaks of 'spinning down to Weymouth town | By Ridgway thirstily'. In his boyhood, Weymouth with Melcombe Regis was the county's largest town with a population of 8,230 (1851 census). Its importance stemmed largely from the patronage of George III, who in his later years made it virtually the nation's summer capital. It appears in *The Dynasts* as 'King George's watering-place'. In the afterglow of this regal splendour Weymouth became to rural Dorset, and further afield to the railway workers of Swindon, what Blackpool was to the millworkers of Lancashire. Diggory Venn's description of it in *The Return of the Native* (1.10) eloquently expresses the glamour and excitement of the place where 'out of every ten folk you meet nine of 'em in love'. It seems no accident that Eustacia Vye in the same novel was born there. Weymouth is the antithesis of Egdon Heath: the acme of worldly pleasure, not of spiritual travail.

Chance brought Hardy in 1869 to live and work in Weymouth for a time. A Weymouth architect, G. R. *Crickmay, had bought the practice of Hardy's original employer, which included specialized church restoration work—notably in *Cornwall, at St Juliot—and he wanted to delegate this to Hardy. Taking lodgings at 3 Wooperton Street, Hardy could enjoy a morning swim in Weymouth Bay and an occasional row in a boat. He was also persuaded by a young colleague to join a quadrille class, which provided 'a gay gathering for dances and love-making by adepts of both sexes'. Here 'a good deal of flirtation went on' (*LW* 66). In this lively atmosphere Hardy turned again to verse which expresses more personal and intense emotions than hitherto, with an emphasis on the pains and pleasures of being in love. There are about a dozen such poems that Hardy identified as of this period in Weymouth. He was evidently ready for the great romance that awaited him when he set out from Weymouth to St Juliot. DH

Elizabeth Ham, *Elizabeth Ham by Herself*, ed. Eric Gillett (1945).

Desmond Hawkins, *Thomas Hardy, Novelist and Poet* (1976), 28–34.

'What the Shepherd Saw', short story written in the autumn of 1881, while the Hardys were living at *Wimborne, and first published in that year's Christmas Number of the *Illustrated London News*; collected in *A Changed Man and Other Tales*, where it is the earliest of the stories included. The setting is close to the ancient town of Marlborough in Wiltshire, and the country house of Shakeforest Towers is said to have been based on Clatford Hall in that neighbourhood, a prehistoric trilithon (used to dramatic effect in the story) standing nearby. A seasonal gesture towards the occasion of first publication is provided by rather perfunctory opening and closing references to Christmas; however, the situation of the shepherds, keeping lonely vigil over their flocks, seems intended to recall the Nativity story. Somewhat perfunctory, too, is the narrative frame, which has this tale of the distant past recounted by a 'genial Justice of the Peace'.

The main action is divided into four sections corresponding to 'four moonlight nights'. In the first three, a shepherd boy witnesses a drama involving an aristocratic lady who keeps a rendezvous with her cousin, Captain Fred Ogbourne, newly returned from Canada after a long absence; their meeting is observed and misinterpreted by her husband, who kills the young man and buries his body, then swears the boy to silence. As a reward for keeping the secret, the boy is removed from his home and educated, but his ascent to the middle class brings no happiness. In the final section, 'many years subsequent' to the events described, the former shepherd boy is now a steward in the Duke's employment, and the conclusion is reached after a confrontation, the revelation of a secret, a sleep-walking scene, and three deaths.

The story contains some vivid glimpses of the contrast between extreme poverty and quasi-feudal grandeur and power ('the Duke was Jove himself to the rural population, whom to offend was starvation, homelessness, and death, and whom to look at was to be mentally scathed and dumbfoundered'). It also makes generous use of Hardy's favourite motifs of spying and the watcher who is himself watched. The murdered man's surname is a place-name found in the Marlborough area.

Wimborne is a small but historically interesting town on the banks of the river Stour, about ten miles north-west of Bournemouth. It has a fine Norman Minster and in a poem entitled 'Copying Architecture in an Old Minster', published in 1914, Hardy remembered his experience of studying architecture there many years earlier. The first mention of Wimborne in his autobiography is an entry of 1875 in which Hardy writes: 'thence to Wimborne, where on arrival he entered the Minster at ten at night, having seen a light within, and sat in a stall listening to the organist practising, while the rays from the musician's solitary candle streamed across the arcades' (*LW* 110). He had been married for less than a year at that time and was looking for somewhere to live. However, it was not until June 1881 that he and his wife Emma moved into a rented house in the Avenue at Wimborne, where they were to live for two years. The house, 'Lanherne', had an attractive garden, and in the *Life* Hardy describes (with a quotation from his own diary) how in the sunny days of September he corrected the proofs of *A Laodicean* 'for the issue in volumes, sitting under a vine "which for want of training hangs in long arms over my head nearly to the ground. The sun tries to shine through the great leaves, making a green light on the paper, the tendrils twisting in every direction, in gymnastic endeavours to find something to lay hold of"' (*LW* 155).

The stay in Wimborne restored Hardy to health after the illness he had suffered in *London. It was a busy time both socially and professionally. He and Emma met a number of new friends, went to Shakespeare readings, made several visits to London, paid a visit to France and made a circular tour of Wiltshire, Devon, and Dorset, and were invited to a ball at Lady Wimborne's, an indication of his rise in the social world.

Professionally, his two years in Wimborne saw the publication of the first volume edition of *A Laodicean* and the writing and publication of *Two on a Tower*. In the latter, Wimborne is given the fictitious name of 'Warborne'. The tower that plays such an important part in the story is based largely on a tall tower located in Charborough Park which can be seen from the main road from Wimborne to Bere Regis. Charborough House is the model for 'Welland House' in the same novel, and was the home of the Drax family. Hardy drove by on 23 July 1881 and was told of a rich heiress of the family who had married a poorer man. Other of his work dating from the Wimborne period includes 'The Romantic Adventures of a Milkmaid' and his important sociological essay 'The *Dorsetshire Labourer'.

JCG

Winter Words. Hardy's eighth and final volume of verse was published by *Macmillan on 2 October 1928; in America it appeared a little later, on 28 November, and was chosen by the Book League of America as its December book. It had, as the 'Introductory Note' suggests with justified pride, originally been intended for publication on Hardy's 88th birthday (2 June 1928), but his death on 11 January meant that it was prepared for the press by his literary executors, Florence *Hardy and Sydney *Cockerell. No table of contents written by Hardy survives, and other details, including variants and titles, were left unresolved. However, the arrangement seems to be at least partially Hardy's, since Florence Hardy wrote to Macmillan on 11 February 1928 to tell them that 'the first few poems and the last few have been arranged, but I am not sure that the ones in the middle of the book are arranged'. There is some internal evidence for this 'arrangement': the volume opens, like Hardy's previous volume, with a poem on the poet's readiness to die, 'The New Dawn's Business', followed by a poem on birdsong, emblematic of nature's continuing; it ends with two powerful valedictory poems. Most of the 105 poems included in the collection were written after his previous collection, *Human Shows* (1925), had appeared, but a few are earlier in provenance, going back as far as his first decade of poetry in the 1860s. As elsewhere in Hardy's poetry, dating poems is often difficult given his tendency to rework earlier drafts: 'An Unkindly May', for example, is dated 1877 in the manuscript, though Hardy showed it to his wife as something he was working on a few months before he died; two poems have double dates attached to them to signal inception and revision.

The reception of *Winter Words* was affected by the volume's posthumous status: there had been an outpouring of writing on Hardy after his death, and the volume published several months later seemed something of an appendix to his career. Vita Sackville-West portrayed it in that way in the *Nation and Athenaeum* (13 October 1928), describing it as depicting a world in which 'carpenters are still making coffins; bastards are still born and furtively disposed of; lovers still fail to coincide; the old romance is still evoked and regretted'. The anonymous *Times Literary Supplement* reviewer ('Hardy's Last Poems', 4 October 1928) was more positive, seeing it as 'a piece with his other poems, with just that blend of similarity and contrast, of surprise and the familiar, which seems to mirror the world depicted in them', and raising the question, as many subsequent critics have done, of defining Hardy's 'exact poetic quality... that "middle flight" whose beat often looks laboured and yet follows instinct, and can be swift and true'—the problem, that is, of categorizing a poet who seems not to write 'major' poems but whose corpus is nevertheless important.

The most positive response to the volume was Richard Church's in the *Spectator* ('The Last Sheaf from Wessex', 6 October 1928). Arguing that 'Hardy's assumption of a settled attitude of mind is only a mask shielding his powerful and agonized sensibility', he praised the poet for a 'fine lyricism controlled by sixty years of technical practice' and for 'the dramatic genius which still burns in this last work, making many poems intense with such human aching that the heart is wounded as we read them'.

A notable later consideration of the volume is Harold Bloom's essay 'Poetic Origins and Final Phases', in *A Map of Misreading* (1975). Bloom declares hyperbolically that 'a few books of twentieth-century verse in English compare with *Winter Words* in greatness, but very few', adding that 'all through *Winter Words* the attentive reader will hear a chastened return of High Romantic Idealism, but muted into Hardy's tonality'. Hardy's final volume is an example of the last phase of a poetic career, in which a poet finally comes to terms with literary tradition (in Hardy's case, Bloom argues, predominantly with the influence of *Shelley).

Few other critics have singled out the volume as a whole for commentary, most placing it in a late phase that includes the previous two volumes of poetry. In *Hardy's Topographical Lexicon and the Canon of Intent* (1990), Margaret Faurot devotes a half-chapter to the text, arguing that it is the culmination of a drive towards silence and not-saying, and sees the poet's preoccupation with inscription and landscape as the ground of poetry undone. 'If there is a dialectic in *Winter Words*', she adds, 'it is one of tone shift, from resignation to recantation.' This comment reflects the general critical focus on the final two poems of the volume, and on a number of other poems in which Hardy seems to look back over his life and career. Critical treatment of the volume has, then, stressed its status as a late work, valedictory if not quite summational.

That said, the volume includes its share of the formal experimentation of Hardy's later verse-forms—the varied stanza-shapes even, according to Dennis Taylor, suggesting a shift towards modernist open-field compositions—and contains a variety of topics and styles. It ranges from impersonal songs and ballads (of which the best is probably 'Burning the Holly') to teasing reminiscences of women the poet has loved and outlived ('Concerning Agnes' remembers Agnes *Grove; 'To Louisa in the Lane' raises Louisa Harding's ghost (see LATE LYRICS AND EARLIER), to its 'spectral frail alarm'; from short lyrics to the bloody and dramatic extended fragment 'Aristodemus the Messenian', subtitled 'Dramatic Hendecasyllabics' and offering a fairly strict imitation of classical metres; from the lengthy interview with God in 'A Philosophical Fantasy' to the sardonic four-line epigram of 'Christmas: 1924':

> 'Peace upon earth!' was said. We sing it,
> And pay a million priests to bring it.
> After two thousand years of mass
> We've got as far as poison gas.

Like this poem, 'Unkept Good Fridays' (dated Good Friday, 1927) and 'Christmastide' are trenchant political and moral satire, the first remembering the 'nameless Christs' destroyed by the powerful and forgotten by history, and the second making a 'sodden tramp' heading for the workhouse the true bearer of the Christmas spirit. 'Whispered at the Church-Opening' offers a similar commentary on the ways of the world and the success of the corrupt, while poems like 'The Son's Portrait' and 'In the Marquee' reflect, like so many of Hardy's poems, on the plot of 'crossed fidelities' and the instabilities of love.

The volume also, as Hardy insists in the 'Introductory Note', includes a range of poems in a more positive mood, including the late pastoral manner exemplified by the pure observation and seasonal structure of 'Proud Songsters' and 'An Unkindly May'. 'I Watched a Blackbird' versifies an observation from a diary; 'We Field-Women' is a fragment of monologue relating to *Tess of the d'Urbervilles.* A number of short poems simply seek to record moments in the lives of others, with a minimal sense of an ironic twist to them. There is the woman who goes to the fair and is drenched and disappointed in 'Expectation and Experience'; the Mrs Masters of 'The Lodging-House Fuchsias', whose much-loved plants grow in profusion but have to be cut back to let her coffin pass; the starkly told episode of tree-felling in 'Throwing a Tree' (the latter a brilliant example of Hardy's use of mimetic verse forms, with its sawing rhythms and overbalancing last line); and the 'good death' described in 'Squire Hooper'.

Given the variety sketched above, it is difficult to characterize the volume as a whole. Perhaps the most single striking aspect of *Winter Words* (understandable in a man of Hardy's age) is its self-concentration. Fifteen or more poems describe the poet himself: watching and waiting for death ('The New Dawn's Business'; 'I am the One'; 'A Wish for Unconsciousness'; 'Lying Awake'); his various irreconcilable moods and aspects ('Concerning His Old Home'; 'So Various'); his inner nature, and particularly his minimal expectations of life (the moving 'Childhood among the Ferns'; 'A Self-Glamourer'; and less directly 'A Placid Man's Epitaph' and 'A Private Man on Public Men'). The latter mood is best represented by 'He Never Expected Much', with its unresolved alternative title 'A Consideration [A Reflection] on My Eighty-Sixth Birthday'. It stresses the compact since boyhood between poet and World. The 'neutral-tinted haps and such' which the World has always offered him are what Bloom describes as a final muting of *Wordsworth's 'visionary gleam', pessimism acting less as the 'sure game' (to borrow Hardy's phrase in the *Life*) than as a unique visionary mode, confirmed after a lifetime's experience.

Paradoxically, given this self-revelation, other poems insist that he remains a mystery: 'A Poet's Thought' and 'Not Known' both point towards the withdrawal of the final poem in the volume—here, as elsewhere in Hardy's poetry, the assertion that lyric represents an uncovering of the self coexists with the idea that it is also a self-cloaking, a point stressed once again in the insistence in the 'Introductory Note' that 'no harmonious philosophy is attempted in these pages'. 'A Wish for Unconsciousness' pursues an even more absolute path to silence and oblivion, implicitly seeking a state beyond Christian eschatology and recollection, in which 'I should hear no judgment-call, | Have no evil dreams or wakings, | No uncouth or grisly care; | In a word, no cross to bear'.

A number of major poems reflect Hardy's late accounting with his life, and require fuller commentary. 'Standing by the Mantelpiece (H.M.M., 1873)' is his last word on the mysterious suicide of his early friend and mentor Horace *Moule, ventriloquized cryptically in Moule's voice and addressed to an unidentified 'you' whom he loved (given the sensitive subject-matter, it is possible that Hardy wrote this poem earlier and held it over to his final volume). Hardy makes use of the folk-belief that a candle melting into a shroud-shape presages a death to have Moule—in a chilling final moment—accept his fate as part of an inevitable pattern:

And let the candle-wax thus mould a shape
Whose meaning now, if hid before, you know,
And how by touch one present claims its drape,
And that it's I who press my finger—so.

A more abstract accounting is provided by 'Family Portraits' (originally published as 'The Portraits', in a rather different form, in *Nash's Magazine* in 1924). This is one of the most phantasmagoric and gothic poems in Hardy's corpus, comparable only to 'The Pedigree' in its self-confrontational intensity; an astounding poem for a writer in his eighties, revealing that Hardy's sense of his life as enacting a pre-written text (whether conceived in terms of Darwin or the primal scene) could still produce a great crisis-poem. Hardy sees 'Three picture-drawn people' step from their frames and begin to enact an 'obscure' drama relating to 'the law-lacking passions of life'—a drama which is to shadow forth his own life. The fair and dark woman and the 'man of much gloom' represent a repeated pattern in Hardy's poetry—in 1924 he had only recently explored the same triangle in *The Famous Tragedy of the Queen of Cornwall*—and here they signal an 'ancestral mystery' which the narrator draws back from confronting, crying 'Let old ghosts be laid!', before living to regret his lack of courage to stay and 'see the play played', and thus to 'balk future pain'.

Other poems seem to represent less a personal accounting than a last word on a recurrent theme. Reflections on birds and birdsong are one such topic, ranging in Hardy's corpus from the descriptions of Tess as a caged bird to such poems as 'The Blinded Bird' (see BIRDS). In *Winter Words* 'The Boy's Dream' links the subject to a sense of maiming and identification: a lame and (literally) thin-skinned boy wishes to have 'a real green linnet' in a cage, a bird which might express his sorrow in song. 'Lying Awake' is a final example of inscription-poetry, as Hardy watches at dawn in the churchyard and sees 'The names creeping out everywhere' on the gravestones. 'Seeing the Moon Rise', the last dated poem Hardy wrote (August 1927), is a return to the moon-imagery of earlier volumes, reflecting on the fact that in old age he no longer climbs the hill to find her, but must gain his vision in snatched glances.

'Aristodemus the Messenian' is a grotesque final exploration of the topic of the aborted, bastard, unwanted, or displaced child—also explored in this volume in 'The Whaler's Wife' and 'Reluctant Confession'. 'Aristodemus' offers a literal investigation of the mysteries of paternity, climaxing in a father ripping open his daughter to reveal that there is in fact nothing there, that the child is a fiction. A group of poems provide a final version of Hardy's philosophical and religious scepticism. 'A Philosophical Fantasy' is a parodic dialogue with a rather bumbling and limited God. 'An Evening in Galilee' is the last of Hardy's poems exploring the life of Jesus: in a poem which perhaps incorporates memories of the realistic depiction of Mary in Holman Hunt's Pre-Raphaelite painting *The Shadow of Death*, we see a mother worried at her son's unconventional behaviour and cryptic utterances, uncertain of her relation to a history outside her understanding.

'Christmas in the Elgin Room' (subtitled 'British Museum: Early Last Century' and dated 1905 and 1926) was the last poem Hardy published in his lifetime. It reflects on the passing of gods, as the newly captured Greek deities in the British Museum shake at the Christmas bells which signal a new provenance. Since this was a subject Hardy knew well from poetic tradition—'The Gods of Greece' is marked in his copy of Heine's *Book of Songs*—and his treatment of it borrows its inflection from one of his early poems—'To Flowers from Italy in Winter', which has a similar sense of southern beauty exposed to northern cold—the reader cannot but read syncretically, and remember back to poems in earlier volumes like 'God's Funeral'. 'Drinking Song' is comparable in its treatment of belief, listing the extinction of superseded ideas in the hands of a range of thinkers from Copernicus to Darwin and Einstein (Hardy read the latter carefully in the early 1920s: see RELATIVITY). With its rollicking chorus 'Fill full your cups: feel no distress; | 'Tis only one great thought the less!', it suggests the fragility and contingency of all human knowledge.

The volume ends, like a number of previous volumes, with poems in the summational mode of the envoi, '"We Are Getting to the End"' and 'He Resolves to Say No More'. The first rejects reason and historical optimism in apocalyptic terms:

> We are getting to the end of visioning
> The impossible within this universe,
> Such as that better whiles may follow worse,
> And that our race may mend by reasoning.

Seeing the possibility of yet another cataclysmic war in which nations 'hack their pleasant plains in festering seams', impelled by 'some demonic force', Hardy declares an end to reason, progress, and the dream of a better world. In its intensity, it recalls the grotesque imagery of yet another Christmas poem in the volume, 'A Nightmare, and the Next

Thing', with its vision of 'a gray nightmare | Astride the day'.

'He Resolves to Say No More' is an example of the rhetorical figure known as *occupatio*, the refusal to speak (compare Hamlet's 'The rest is silence'). Clearly, Hardy felt that it would stand at the end of his corpus, and he took pains over the poem, extensively revising it in draft and using a rhyme-scheme he uses nowhere else. It takes its opening line from the Greek epigrammatist Agathias, and continues with the apocalyptic imagery of the previous poem:

> O my soul, keep the rest unknown!
> It is too like the sound of moan
> When the charnel-eyed
> Pale Horse has nighed:
> Yea, none shall gather what I hide!

In some ways the poem itself represents an impasse: each of the four stanzas simply restates in a different form the original determination not to speak, though the context shifts from the Pale Horse of the Book of Revelation to the 'By truth made free' of John 8: 32, as Hardy moves from voice to vision, beyond 'the blinkered sight of souls in bond', and implicitly into the freedom of death, beyond his readers. In a sense the poem is an anti-prophecy, reinforcing at the most abstract level the end of historical hope described in '"We Are Getting to the End"', as well as a farewell penned by the 'midnight quill' of the poet, seeking to allow him a freedom beyond his work.

If Hardy's career closes at that point, the two recent standard editions of his poems (edited, respectively, by James Gibson and Samuel Hynes) also offer a set of 'Uncollected Poems' which for various reasons he never included in the *Collected Poems*—choruses from plays, a translation ('Thoughts from Sophocles', written in the dark days of the mid-1890s), minor poems which he was persuaded not to publish. The 'Uncollected Poems' end with two 'Epitaphs' that Hardy dictated on his deathbed, violently attacking, respectively, G. K. *Chesterton and George *Moore, both of whom had hurt him in attacks on his novels. Like the posthumous *Life*, published under Florence Hardy's name but eventually revealed as very largely the poet's work, these fragments demonstrate that the closure offered by the final volume is always gestural, supplemented by other stories.

The manuscript of *Winter Words* is at Queen's College, Oxford, of which Hardy was an honorary fellow. TA

'Withered Arm, The', short story. Originally published in *Blackwood's Magazine* (Edinburgh) in January 1888, it was collected in *Wessex Tales*. Hardy had originally submitted it to *Longman's Magazine*, which rejected it on the grounds that its macabre theme was unsuitable for its readership. It is evident from Hardy's autobiography that at this time he was taking a close interest in Dorset traditions and superstitions, including some heard from his mother and grandmother (*LW* 211), and the plot turns upon a folk-remedy of a particularly sensational kind. Opening in a pastoral vein with a milking scene, the story quickly moves into the uncanny and the sinister, and reaches its climax in a tableau of *grand guignol* horror and tragedy.

Rhoda Brook, a dairymaid, has been seduced some years earlier by a prosperous local farmer and now lives with her young son in abject poverty. When the farmer brings home a young and pretty wife, Rhoda's obsession with the girl (Gertrude Lodge) leads to a nightmare in which the latter takes the form of an incubus which can only be shaken off by violence. Soon Gertrude befriends Rhoda and confides to her that she has developed inexplicable symptoms on her arm: a number of marks corresponding to the hand with which Rhoda has seized the arm of her ghostly visitant. It appears, too, that the symptoms have begun at precisely the moment of Rhoda's nightmare. Gertrude's condition deteriorates, her arm becomes partially paralysed, remedies are of no avail, and in time she loses her looks and her husband's love. From Conjuror Trendle, a local wise man and practitioner of white magic, she learns that a cure may be effected by laying the arm on the neck of one who has just been hanged, and in desperation she tries this remedy, with fatal results.

The sombre tale is powerfully narrated, with many details of local topography, including journeys across Egdon Heath, that provide a realistic frame for the central theme of the supernatural or paranormal.

Rhoda, who seems in the earlier part of the story to have some of the qualifications of a witch, is developed into a figure of genuine pathos, and an unexpected and touching intimacy develops between the two women. Conjuror Trendle has much in common with Mr Fall, the weather-prophet in *The Mayor of Casterbridge* a little earlier in the same decade. On Hardy's detailed account of the circumstances attending the hanging in Casterbridge, see EXECUTIONS, PUBLIC. A slight relief to the sombreness of the conclusion was given by 'a last-minute change in the manner of Farmer Lodge's death, from suicide to natural causes' (Millgate 288).

The 1896 Preface to *Wessex Tales* recalls that during Hardy's boyhood 'there was still living an old woman who, for the cure of some eating disease, had been taken in her youth to have her "blood turned" by a convict's corpse, in the manner described in "The Withered Arm"'.

women. The progression, over the past century, in critical attitudes to the women in Hardy's fiction has been marked by a noticeable shift from Victorian moral anxiety to, more recently, a disencumbered celebration of female sexuality. Havelock Ellis, in an important essay published in the *Savoy Magazine* in October 1896, regarded Hardy's resourceful, sensual, adventurous women as both 'very feminine' and very earthy, yet in no sense degenerate—in contrast to the prevailing cultural tendency to relegate the sexually active woman to what Ellis called 'the farmyard' (*CH* 306–10).

On the other hand, relegating Hardy himself to a kind of sexist backyard has become, for some latter-day feminist critics, an overt evaluation of a narrative stance ascribed not to the demands of publication politics but to authorial intention. The argument goes, in this instance, that in peppering the text with generalizations about the nature of women, Hardy betrays his own deeply rooted sexist assumptions. However, such generalizations partake of a stance of circumspection, a narratorial convention pure and simple. Behind this convention lay the stricture that the novel, a highly influential medium for the dissemination of cultural values, should provide edification for the Young British Person. Difficulties therefore abounded for Hardy in getting his unconventional women past the ever-vigilant Mrs Grundy. One solution was to employ an alternative narrator to perform the Grundyan task of interpolating a moralizing voice at carefully selected intervals in the text. This, in turn, ensured literary access to the Victorian middle-class drawing-room, which would otherwise be barred to all but the most decorous, conventional, and genteel of women. Proleptically skilled from the outset in adopting a wide variety of narratorial stances within the single text, some less intrusive than others, Hardy thus circumvented Mrs Grundy by means of subverting his own text—at various points of injudiciousness—with a proprietary narrator quick to point a moralizing finger whenever necessary.

One thing is clear: as soon as his reputation as a novelist was assured, Hardy started to dispense with this moralizing narrator—in later works such as *Tess*, *Jude*, and *The Well-Beloved* the proprietory voice of circumspection ceases to intrude. Moreover, if sexist assumptions were indeed deeply rooted in the Hardyan consciousness, the freer medium of poetry might reasonably be expected to express them. On the contrary, Hardy's verse, which adopts an even greater variety of voices than does his prose, invokes no such generalizations about women. Such a literary device is not called for in poetics.

Hardy bemoaned the fate of the novelist and the paralysing effect of censorship; in verse he found a far greater freedom, and, no doubt, an important aspect of this freedom lay in the fact that, therein, decorum and self-censorship was not an issue he needed to address. Then again, the kind of woman that attracted him, the type he portrays so compellingly in his fiction, is strong-minded, sensual, free-spirited, and sexually exciting to a degree not to be talked about in Victorian drawing-rooms. These women were an embarrassment to readers in polite circles. Sexuality apart, the female body remained not only unmentionable but also sufficiently restructured by the prevailing fashion as to be virtually invisible from the waist down. Hence Hardy's physically active women were disquieting: they remove their underwear to undertake cliff-top rescues, they ride horses bareback and with legs astride, they dress up, quite casually, as one of the 'young bucks', and they walk out at night unveiled, taking a forthright delight in the life of the senses, exhibiting their palpable exertions as they toil and labour, pulse and sweat, ache and strain.

The Victorian model of womanhood, to which all nice young ladies were expected to conform, either denied or concealed each and every one of these physical activities. A gentlewoman did not soil her hands but, instead, pampered them, whitened them; she did not allow herself to get heated by physical exertion, and if, by chance, she forgot herself in some momentary delight or other, she most certainly did not sweat, she simply perspired; nor did she laugh loudly with open mouth, nor did she raise her voice in anger; nor did she run—she glided; nor did she glow with health, but cultivated a pallid invalidism; and, most emphatically, she did not display any sign of sexual arousal or desire. Even Hardy's Sue Bridehead, perhaps one of his least sexually demonstrative heroines, roused disgust in one contemporary critic, Margaret *Oliphant, for no other reason than by 'keeping the physical facts' of life 'in constant prominence by denying them'.

The social usefulness of cultivating sexually anaesthetized models of womanhood has a deeply entrenched historical and political basis in patriarchy, involving strict controls relating to the position of women in society. Ruskin was to promote such models under the iconic 'Stainless Sceptre of Womanhood', Coventry *Patmore to do so under the imago of the 'Angel in the House'. Hardy, in characteristic iconoclastic vein, sought to demolish them all. Such rarefied models, he would attest, are not only tyrannical (since the 'Angelic', the 'Perfect', guarantees its own unattainability, therefore inculcating in women the guilt and shame of forever falling short of the ideal), but a self-image that remains unrealizable is also enslaving.

In line with John Stuart *Mill, Hardy would argue for a liberated world in which the sexual double standard is abolished (for no such idealized models were imposed upon men), and 'Each individual will prove his or her capacities in the only way in which capacities can be proved—by trial; and the world will have the benefit of the best faculties of all its inhabitants' (quoted by Gertrude Himmelfarb in *On Liberty and Liberalism* (1974), 173). Since women, like men, must fall short of perfection, the more worthy and desirable female model should, in all reasonableness, as Hardy saw it, embody less than perfect qualities. However, for removing the 'Stainless' paragon from her pedestal, for presenting readers with humanly imperfect, sexually challenging heroines, he was, to his hurt and indignation, charged not only with misogynism but also with misrepresenting womankind.

Here ideology conflicts with verisimilitude. For if, to Hardy, a fully realized, authentic female character is to come into being holistically, as an accessible figure endowed with a fair share of 'best faculties' which readers can identify with and care about, the culturally idealized model of womanhood has not only to be dismantled but radically opposed. There are attending risks to this. What, for example, would be the most desirable of representations? Which of the fresh active fictions bearing imaginative possibilities of challenge, renewal, and change, upon which women might wish to model themselves, are both realistic and engaging? If young Victorian males could dream of becoming warriors or conquerors, what kind of cultural icons could be offered to young Victorian females? Without educational opportunities and the freedom to move in the world, the only possible options seemed to be those figurations of dutiful wifehood and saintly motherhood—and these were not entirely lacking in power thresholds, especially for those willing to place an ideological investment in the 'separate spheres' doctrine advocated by the strongly influential Sarah Ellis and her colleagues (see, for example, Ellis's *The Wives of England* (1843); *The Daughters of England* (1845); *Education of the Heart: Woman's Best Work* (1869)).

These, then, were the limitations. Moreover, in an age that placed a high value on such 'feminine' attributes as delicacy of health, physical timidity, and intellectual meekness, would readers be alienated by such female characters as the robustly energetic Bathsheba, the rebelliously assertive Eustacia, the intellectually rigorous Sue Bridehead? The risk was real—but Hardy took it. And despite the hostility of some of his critics, for whom Bathsheba was a 'hussy',

Eustacia a 'Bovarian' voluptuary, and Sue thoroughly 'indecent', he continued, long beyond his novel-writing days, to stand by his earlier claim that 'In representations of the world, the passions ought to be proportioned as in the world itself, life being a physiological fact' (*'Candour in English Fiction'). Codes prescribing sexuality topically ineligible in popular works of fiction necessarily rendered a disproportioning of the world, in Hardy's view, and his first impulse, from the very outset of his novel-writing career, was to override these conventional codes. To some extent his first heroine, Cytherea Graye, in *Desperate Remedies* (1871), presents him with few problems of decorum, primarily because at surface level she is a thoroughly orthodox creation. Ironically, the only major point of critical contention, in this instance, was directed at a class issue. The complaint was that the author had dared 'to suppose it possible that an unmarried lady owning an estate could have an illegitimate child'. The irony here lies in the fact that the question of illegitimacy and class indecorum remains virtually elided by the narrator in *Desperate Remedies*—whereas the jealous, sensual passion borne by that same 'unmarried lady' for the young Cytherea, seeking her out in her bed at night and begging for caresses and kisses, would seem to constitute the far greater indiscretion—if only in terms of arousing, as opposed to edifying, the Young British Person. However, since female sexuality defined itself only in terms of man–woman contact, and did not, according to Victorian mores, exist beyond the compass of heterosexual encounters, this erotic intimacy between the two women did not, for the main part, register in the eyes of the wider critical public, as anything other than innocuously sisterly, or maternal.

Sensual intimacy between women, in Hardy's novels, features as normative homosocial female experience, but it is never once remarked upon by those selfsame critics who castigated Hardy for treating as normative those equivalent, heterosocial passions that take place between men and women. Where, in their night-time woodland meeting, Grace Melbury and Felice Charmond 'cling close', clasping each other in tight emotional embraces, 'each one's body, as she breathed, alternately heav[ing] against that of her companion' (*W* 33), there is clearly an erotic element nowhere to be found in Grace's physical contact with Edred Fitzpiers. Similarly, while Paula Power and her beloved Charlotte de Stancy express their homoemotional relationship so openly that the local innkeeper is driven to observe that the women ' "be more like lovers than maid and maid" ' (*AL* 1.6), there is no comparable physical passion in Paula's heterosexual relationship with Somerset.

But, if Hardy suffered no constraints in his representations of intimate relationships between women, he was still obliged to put all into reverse for the dénouement. Albeit reluctantly, Grace has to reunite with her husband, Fitzpiers; Paula, lukewarm in her affections, marries Somerset; Cytherea ends up with Edward Springrove, and in each case the novel has to conclude with 'the false colouring best expressed by the regulation finish that "they married and were happy ever after"... a *dénouement* ... indesc ribably unreal and meretricious, but dear to the Grundyist and subscriber' ('Candour in English Fiction').

With *A Pair of Blue Eyes* (1873), Hardy breaks this pattern and Elfride dies at the last, thus bringing her into line with the role of the tragic heroine for whom the commonplace middle-class solution of marriage-and-living-happily-ever-after would be glaringly 'unreal'. Elfride, who is no iconic maiden awaiting self-definition at the hands of man or marriage, shares with Cytherea Graye that capacity, so dear to Hardy's heart, of loving as an end in itself and not as a means to gaining a husband. Bringing together in the single characterization the qualities of intellectual strength, sexiness, and moral seriousness, Hardy flies in the face of current convention, code, and belief, and offers his reader, in his portrayal of Elfride, precisely that type of individual who has the potential to prove 'her capacities in the only way in which capacities can be proved—by trial'. 'Potential' is the keyword here. For, as Hardy shows, Elfride inhabits a world in which she can neither test her capacities nor escape the prejudices of those who put her on trial, so to speak. Subjected to proscriptive codes and prejudged attitudes, she is permitted to prove nothing. Yet as Hardy presents the case, she has the intellectual skills for writing her father's sermons, the physical courage and vigour for undertaking a cliff rescue (where, incidentally, Hardy reverses the chivalric story and has maiden-at-arms rescue the knight-in-distress), and the emotional fortitude to stand up to the perpetual bullying of her suitor, Henry Knight.

In the 'establishment' world that Knight inhabits, and which he brings into Elfride's domain, the Victorian conceptual bifurcation of woman into the paradigmatic types of 'madonna' and 'whore'—loosely speaking, the sexually inert and the sexually active female—carries sufficient influence within the society to generate its likeness in form. The form thus generated lies in the concept of two types of woman, one fit for wife, the other for sex. In Knight's eyes, Elfride's sexual experience with her two previous suitors (which has not, in fact, extended beyond the rites of courtship, exchanging kisses and declarations of love) ineluctably places her in the latter category and renders her unfit to be his wife. Inevitably, this destroys, in Elfride, all that she had held to be worthy, desirable, honourable, and accomplished in herself.

Possibly Elfride's demise saved *A Pair of Blue Eyes* from the kind of critical opprobrium Hardy next had to face with *Far from the Madding Crowd* (1874), in which a more overtly unconventional female character, Farmer Bathsheba Everdene, is also pursued by three lovers but does not, in the dénouement, die. Instead she marries: a nice, ordinary, middle-class marriage. Partly for this reason—and not being heroized by tragic death, or killed off by the author (the point of view depending on whether one is subscribing to the ideals of art or life, myth-making or author-intentionality)—she brings heavy opprobrium down upon her author's head.

Hardy had opted for the 'regulation finish', in *Far from the Madding Crowd*, for reasons of publication politics (reader-demand), although by no means without ambivalence. Henry *James, for one, was not convinced that Bathsheba had been tamed, subdued to wifely submission, sufficiently reformed, that is, to be married off to the 'worthy' Oak. James is outraged: Bathsheba, he remonstrates, 'is inconsequential, wilful and mettlesome, and we cannot say that we either understand or like her' (*Nation*, 24 December 1874; repr. in *CH*). The *Observer* liked her even less. So 'odious' is she that, 'if women in whatever rank of society are supposed to retain any trace of modesty and reserve... we confess we do not care one straw about her... and are only sorry that Gabriel Oak was not sufficiently manly to refuse to have anything more to say to such an incorrigible hussy' (quoted in *Thomas Hardy and His Readers*, ed. Laurence Lerner and John Holmstrom (1968), 30–1).

From the opening passages to her last tender enfolding of Troy's dying body, Bathsheba is self-commanding to the point of imperiousness. Supremely voluptuous, she stands her ground strongly in confrontations with men even in moments of crisis. Gabriel Oak takes her prideful manner and sexual self-delight to be 'feminine' vanity. But Hardy shows a more complicated, often contradictory, psychological make-up. Occasionally a fearful defensiveness, frequently a sense of self-endangerment, Bathsheba's impetuousness and risk-taking is at times far more alarming to herself than to those who spy upon and criticize her.

Victorians seriously debated the 'problem' of the strong woman: surely she would be unpleasantly manly, pitifully devoid of femininity? And in what sense would she be desirable if not softly shy, gently submissive, femininely passive, sweetly retiring—evoking strong manly feelings in the hearts of men? Confronted with a Bathsheba, who is manifestly none of these things but indisputably sexually exciting as well as rigorously strong-minded, many deeply rooted certitudes about the nature of women and sexual relationships were, undoubtedly, threatened. Her defiant nonconformity alone would upset the status quo: such an unwarranted intrusion of *difference* invariably acts as a wholly alienating element in any homogeneous community.

Hardy had set out upon his novel-writing career with the intention of unsettling not sexual but class attitudes. There was, to wit, the unpublished *The Poor Man and the Lady*, which portrayed satirical representations of the squirearchy in a class-ridden society. Then, subsequently, there was the melodramatic *Desperate Remedies*, which shares much in the way of scene and setting with *An Indiscretion in the Life of an Heiress* (adapted from *The Poor Man and the Lady*), and which takes manorial life as its backcloth to the story of mystery and murder. Indeed, issues of class conflict remained of deep concern to Hardy long beyond the publication of his last novel, *Jude the Obscure* (1896), but it was ultimately his treatment of women and marriage that brought the critical thunders down upon his head.

Bathsheba, as we have seen, was the first in the line of his unconventional heroines to rouse censure of this kind, and her attitude to marriage seems to have been at the crux of it—the marriage, that is, of a sexually progressive and rather combative young woman with decided views on *not* becoming some 'man's property'—and one, moreover, who can think in terms of marriage as a 'pollutant' of her person, and who perceives that for a woman to give herself to a man in wedlock out of conscience, atonement, or duty is an act of virtual prostitution. At the time of publication, in the early 1870s, a woman still lost her nominal identity and legal status upon marriage. And, as Bathsheba learns to her cost, whereas she had sole control of her earnings when single, as a married woman she loses this right: her husband is entitled to possession of both her property and her income. A husband could also lawfully lock up his wife, and could assert his conjugal rights by force if necessary. This, in an age when marriages were not only 'made in heaven' and therefore sacrosanct ('Holy'), but also vocational ('dutiful wifehood'), as well as robustly institutionalized, was nothing less than an outrage. If anyone at all might be permitted to criticize this enshrined domain, as did John Stuart Mill (endorsed by Hardy), it should not be Hardy's 'inconsequential, wilful and mettlesome' young heroine, who already has the unearned privilege of gaining in marriage the proverbial Good Man and True.

Bathsheba survived long enough in Hardy's imagination to undergo various permutations. There are aspects of her in Tess (though with, perhaps, additional touches of Fanny Robin), and much of her anti-marriage rationale recurs some twenty years later in Sue Bridehead's more radical diatribe against the institution of marriage.

Incensed by critical views suggesting that the author of *Far from the Madding Crowd* was writing in imitation of George *Eliot, Hardy next plunged into 'a new and untried direction' with *The Hand of Ethelberta* (1876). This meant abandoning Wessex for the city, quitting psychological drama for light comedy, discarding a microcosmic setting for sketchy scenes, and replacing imaginatively realized characters with restricted types. The kind of situation Hardy would customarily reserve for minor incident or anecdote is expanded, picaresque style, in *Ethelberta*, and derives, as do many of his short fictional pieces and verse topics, from a story handed down from his maternal grandmother. Forming the idea of being a club-house cook to help support her widowed mother and fatherless siblings, Hardy's mother, it is told, as a young unmarried woman, applied to the Earl of Ilchester for help; he sent her to his brother in London, where she settled as a cook, taking her six little brothers and sisters along with her. This is the autobiographical origin of Ethelberta's story: Hardy was deeply inspired by his grandmother's stories, and her voice comes down to us through a plethora of anecdotal sketches, poetic observations, and imaginative themes. Yet Ethelberta herself is possibly the least admirable, the most forgettable of Hardy heroines—perhaps, in creative terms, suggesting a classic case of memory blocking imagination, or reality blocking realism.

What *Ethelberta* lacks, or does not even aspire to, *The Return of the Native* (1878) achieves *par excellence*: an intense and vivid evocation of a woman's inner life, her emotional conflicts, the contradictoriness of her desires, her obsessive cravings, the psychological suffocation of the inertia of her life, her sexual restlessness, and her inability to stem the destructive force of her own passions in a world in which there is no place for a single one of them. In a world 'unfriendly to women', as the narrator describes it, Eustacia Vye longs for action, craves physical sensation, mental exertion, sexual passion, but unlike Eve Greensleeves in Hardy's poem 'Voices from Things Growing in a Churchyard', who exalts in being 'Kissed by men from many a clime', a comparable freedom of exploration is not available on Egdon Heath. On the contrary, in her 'Limbo' life on Egdon, Eustacia remains so confined, so emotionally arrested, and so starved of the life of the senses that, with the compulsive drive of one suffering severe mental conflict, she sets fires, sometimes needlessly, often extravagantly, occasionally to summon her lover whose instant response will frustrate her need for tension, her longed-for ache of anticipation—the smallest pain acting as an antidote to the suffocating boredom of her days. Alternatively, in constant want of sensation, she runs her hair, tearingly, through the prickly furze, or paces through the night across the heath, or treks miles to dance a whirling reel or two. Eustacia Vye hungers for what is denied to women of her background, time, and clime: the freedom of a challenging, active life as enjoyed by men.

Clearly, Hardy could not convey the fullness of Eustacia's intense erotic energy in any explicit way. As it was, the opening chapters, with their indications of impending sexual transgression, were too much for the family-minded Leslie *Stephen, editor of the *Cornhill*, and he declined publication. This is where Hardy's poetic sensibility comes fully into play, to embed within seemingly innocuous figures of speech a language of sexuality which is neither fastidious nor sanitized but, rather, earthy and physical and at all times embedded in figurations both synecdochic and eidetic.

For example, as Eustacia and her lover, Wildeve, wander off to make love in the twilight of the heath, so 'Their black figures sank and disappeared from against the sky. They were as two horns which the sluggish heath had put forth from its crown, like a mollusc, and had now again drawn in' (*RN* 9). Reinforcing the sense of mutuality and sexual equality which the hermaphrodite figure of the mollusc introduces, Hardy here invokes the metonym 'horns'—twinned erectile protuberances suggestive of sharpened sexual appetites and erotic arousal in woman and man alike.

Fundamentally, it is the character of Egdon Heath that enlarges the nature of individual consciousness in *The Return of the Native*. This manner of invoking an external correlative to give imaginative expression to inner experience (that is, Eustacia's inner life) goes some considerable way to alleviating public anxiety of the kind expressed by Leslie Stephen, who feared the novel might develop into something 'dangerous' for his readers. Nor does Eustacia's story end in conventional marriage (in line with her sexually questing forebear, Elfride Swancourt), to the good and deserving husband, the preacherly Clym. Instead, she dies. And *The Return of the Native* escapes the thunders.

Returning to his lifelong fascination with all things Napoleonic, Hardy produces, in *The Trumpet-Major* (1880), a heroine as colourless as Ethelberta (is this the fate of the plot-driven novel?), who vacillates tediously between the two brothers John and Bob Loveday, but with nothing of Eustacia Vye's passion or Bathsheba's flery intelligence. Sexual inconstancy necessarily invites a lightness of tone, and Anne Garland's perverse desire for the less worthy of the brothers does little to deepen the emotional level of the courtship theme in this novel. Possibly one of the book's more memorable moments occurred post-publication with Leslie Stephen's observation that he thought the woman married the wrong man, to which Hardy retorted that they usually do—to which Stephen snapped, 'Not in magazines' (quoted in F. B. Pinion, *A Hardy Companion* (1968), 35).

With *A Laodicean* (1881), despite dictating the greater part of this work to his wife while undergoing a long and serious illness, Hardy moves ingeniously into the age of telegraphy and railway engineering as background for a story in Gothic vein, while recurring boldly to the theme of sensual love between two women as originally broached in *Desperate Remedies*. As in the earlier novel, a heterosexual marriage concludes affairs in the dénouement. But in the case of Paula Power and Charlotte de Stancy, the erotic energy of restless desire, jealousy, quickening sensations, and physical satisfaction—sublimated by Paula in her gymnastic cult—rests with the women. The 'Laodicean' element of diffidence, of lukewarm feelings, has no place in this tale of scientific achievement, of accelerating mobility, of faster-moving communications, except at the level of marriage. With a chilling absence of love and passion at the last, in what would otherwise, in more conventional novels, feature as the closure-with-blissful-nuptials, the focus is upon atmospheric gloom, in which 'silence, chaos, and obscurity' provide the moody setting for the unhappy break between the two women. Simultaneously there is the destruction, by fire, of their home (Charlotte's ancestral home), as the bridal pair, Paula and Somerset, discuss an exchange of property and the 'provisional necessity' for what the former calls her 'lukewarmth' (*AL* 6.5). The only aspect of passionate love that rouses Paula to deep emotion in this scene originates with Charlotte de Stancy's farewell letter: 'my own very best friend, and more than sister, don't think that I mean to leave my love and friendship for you behind me. No, Paula, you will *always* be with me.... My heart is very full, dear—too full to write more...' (*AL* 6.5). Paula weeps. And her very last words, breathed with a 'repressed... sigh', frame only one desire and only one name as she turns to Somerset and says, '"I wish you were a de Stancy!"'

Hardy seems, in his 1880s writing period, to have been moving into a 'scientific' phase, topically speaking. In *Two on a Tower* (1882), in particular, he had wanted, he tells Edmund Gosse, 'to make science, not just the padding of a romance, but the actual vehicle of the romance' (Pinion, *A Hardy Companion*, 39). The technological devices of modernity, in so far as they inject a rhetoric of utilitarianism in *A Laodicean*'s lukewarm matrimonials, do feature in the slightly later novel as more than 'the padding of a romance', in contrast, say, to the pastoral rhythms of *Far from the Madding Crowd* or the indifferent universe of *The Return of the Native*, in which it is not 'science' but the vicissitudes of nature which shape the circumstances of struggling human lives. The 'scientific' backcloth of astronomy in *Two on a Tower* does, in turn, thematically set in opposition the tragic illusion of timeless love which, juxtaposed with the vastness of the stellar heavens, appears less than stupendous. In similar vein, just as the ravages of time take their toll upon the ageing Lady Viviette Constantine, so her appearance, in the eyes of her beloved Swithin, is subsumed to the magnitude of the astronomical world: 'the masses of hair that were once darkness visible had become touched here and there by a faint grey haze, like the Via Lactea in a midnight sky' (41).

Hardy has come a long way, from Cytherea Graye in *Desperate Remedies*, to the aristocratic Viviette, who also risks bearing an illegitimate child but does not bring the thunders down upon her author's head, despite the fact that she is forced to marry a bishop to make her child legitimate. Possibly, in the eyes of Victorian critics, for whom the novel should at all times be edifying, the psychological cruelty of this enforced marriage, like Eustacia's death by drowning, enacts, by transference, its own kind of comeuppance for the sexually active woman. This could also be said of Lucetta in *The Mayor of Casterbridge* (1885) and Felice Charmond in *The Woodlanders* (1887), both of whom, as unmarried women, act upon their sexual desires, and both of whom die an untimely death.

The agricultural 'science' of developing a disease-resistant grain against the background of the era of the Corn Laws influences the rise and fall of the two mayors of Casterbridge, but it is Michael Henchard's passionate desire to be loved as Elizabeth-Jane's biological father which renders him the vulnerable 'fallen' man at the centre of this novel. Ironically, just as Farfrae masters the grain-market as well as the mayoralty against Henchard's repeated attempts to domineer over him, so the father's attempts to subdue his daughter have a recoiling effect, and it is she, in the end, who gains mastery over him. Elizabeth-Jane is no 'Laodicean', neither is she one of Hardy's tempestuous rebels. Caught in a triangle of desire, in sensuous delight with Lucetta, in admiration with Farfrae, and in deep affection with Henchard, yet feeling herself to be peripheral to each one of their lives, Elizabeth-Jane's significant achievement lies in her capacity staunchly to hold her ground and to come through with sincerity and compassion at the last in each one of these relationships.

Elizabeth-Jane is noticeably the stronger for her continual experience of being displaced in the affections of those she loves. Hers is an education of the heart, and she is a rare instance in the Hardy canon of the exemplary Victorian heroine. Learning the 'lesson of renunciation', impelled to self-improvement, owning limited ambitions and an appreciation of Farfrae on account of his 'serious attitude to life' as well as his good looks, Elizabeth-Jane is as straitened a heroine as ever Hardy could have created for what he called, in reference to marketing

The Mayor of Casterbridge, 'mid-Victorian taste'.

Hardy's immediate turn to creating, in *The Woodlanders*, a daughter in rebellion against her father's strictures—that is, her resistance to his paternal efforts to upgrade her value on the marriage market—appears to be, in truth, a revival of a larger theme that was ultimately to preoccupy Hardy throughout his novel-writing career: the subjugation of women at the hands of the patriarchal male. In this instance, the fact that George Melbury scarcely knows what he is doing reinforces the sense of his total disregard for his daughter:

> She wished that she was not his worldly hope; the responsibility of such a position was too great.... Her father then insisted upon her looking over his cheque-book and reading the counterfoils. This also she obediently did, and at last came to two or three which had been drawn to defray some of the late expenses of her clothes, board and education.
>
> 'I, too, cost a good deal, like the horses and waggons and corn!' she said, looking up sorrily.
>
> 'I didn't want you to look at those; I merely meant to give you an idea of my investment transactions. But if you do cost as much as they, never mind. You'll yield a better return.'
>
> 'Don't think of me like that!' she begged. 'A mere chattel.'
>
> 'A what? Oh, a dictionary word...' (12)

Even in the light comic romance of *Under the Greenwood Tree* (1872), such patriarchal attitudes surface. Geoffrey Day may not embrace the ethics and ideological trappings of capitalism, as Melbury has done, but when it comes down to his daughter's marriage he most certainly regards her as marketable goods.

Later in the Wessex novels, the role of male-supremacist will, however, be divided between fathers and potential husbands. For Elfride, the assessor of her marriageable assets is Henry Knight; for Bathsheba it is Oak who, at one point in *Far from the Madding Crowd*, tells her she should marry Boldwood because she has emotionally cost him; and for Tess it will be Angel Clare, for whom the price of lost female virginity is high indeed—incalculably higher than his own.

The vexed question of Hardy's subtitle to *Tess of the d'Urbervilles* (1891), 'A Pure Woman', has dogged critics from Victorian days to the present. Attributing to Tess a spurious purity in order to morally cleanse her as a sexually active woman (who also happens to be an unmarried mother, a religious sceptic, and a murderer) was not at all what Hardy had in mind. To the preface of the fifth and later editions of the novel, he added the following words:

> The more austere of these [critics] maintain a conscientious difference of opinion concerning, among other things, subjects fit for art, and reveal an inability to associate the idea of the sub-title adjective with any but the artificial and derivative meaning which has resulted to it from the ordinances of civilisation. They ignore the meaning of the word in Nature, together with all aesthetic claims upon it, not to mention the spiritual interpretation afforded by the finest side of their own Christianity.

As the 'Nature' sequences in *Tess* reveal, the heroine's sexual vitality is at all times associated with pure physicality, pure naturalness. In the blissful Talbothays days when she falls in love with Angel Clare, the dawning of her sexual awakening and the natural world are as one: 'The sunrise drew forth the buds and stretched them into long stalks, lifted up sap in noiseless streams, opened petals, and sucked out scents in invisible jets and breathings.' There is no artifice, no empty flirtatiousness in her own nature, no pretence, no affectation of social mannerism, no guile—and, as the well-known 'Garden' scene poetically demonstrates, by analogical metaphor, her sexuality is as natural as the untamed wilderness itself: untended, unfettered, and wholly untainted by shame or guilt. Hardy purposefully situates Tess, in this autoerotic scene, *beyond* the confines of the proverbial Edenic garden, the implications being that she is at no point *within* that circumscribed arena of sin, temptation, and predestinate Fall. (See also Rosemarie Morgan, *Women and Sexuality in the Novels of Thomas Hardy*, 84–9.) Wandering to the outskirts of the 'garden' where there are earthy sensations of wetness, 'damp and rank' juicy grasses, bursting 'mists of pollen' at a touch, colours burning to the senses, hotly 'red and yellow', Virgilian 'purple', 'sticky', 'dazzling', 'staining... with thistle-milk', the erotic sensations that suffuse Tess's consciousness harmonize, in terms of pure physicality, with the organic world of nature almost in the same breath as they blissfully elevate her to a state of transcendence over time and space.

Devoting, in *Tess*, considerable narrative time and attention to the intimate life of female sensations, Hardy places a new emphasis—and to Victorians a shocking emphasis—upon the indivisible relationship between mind and body. Tess's capacity to 'love for its own sweet sake', as an end in itself and not a means to an end (marriage), remains fully a part of her emotional generosity, which itself remains integral to her sexual vitality—the healthy physical energy of the body elevating the moral strength of the mind to rise above what Christian mythology would designate her 'Fall'. That is to say (and this is a constituent part of her 'purity'), in her premarital days she transcends with sublime ease the shame and guilt attributed, by the Genesis story, to woman's concupiscence, to female moral turpitude, formulated, generated, and promulgated through generations and generations of patriarchy.

More often than not, natural instinct, for Hardy, is natural law. And this principle, lightheartedly touched into his next novel, later published in a revised version as *The Well-Beloved*, is subsumed to the Platonic Idea that all men are pursuing a shadow, the Unattainable; thus the women, as objects of beauty and desire, are treated by author and male principal alike as ciphers upon which to project a subjective notion of love. In *Jude the Obscure* (1896), however, this same principle becomes a major cause for Sue Bridehead. Jude himself shares her views, that instinctual love relationships should not need to be regulated by law. And this parity between them is important not only to the affinity Hardy wishes to emphasize as vital to their deep love-bond, but also to the notion that their partnership aspires to one of mutuality and sexual equality. Hence the male sex drive, in *Jude*, is as fragile, as vulnerable, as sensitive as Sue's. Hardy had this very much in mind at the time of writing this late novel: as he put it in his contribution to a symposium in the *New Review* of June 1894, 'it has never struck me that the spider is invariably male and the fly invariably female'.

Sue does, though, differ temperamentally from Jude in respect of her lower sexual energy, the tepidity of her sexual appetite. Apprehensive of his deeper needs, she feels far more strongly than he that a formal ratification of their union could exacerbate this imbalance: '"I think I should begin to be afraid of you... the moment you had contracted to cherish me under a Government stamp, and I was licensed to be loved on the premises by you"' (4.6). Polarized against Sue's coltish charms and intense intellectualism, Arabella Donn is earthily voluptuous and intuitively capable, manifesting to Jude all the contradictions of the attraction–repulsion aspects of sexuality. Arabella, who is at worst manipulative and crude, is largely redeemed by her emotional generosity and candour, which is matched by a rough-and-ready but insightful perceptiveness about human character. She 'sees' Sue where Jude is unseeing, and considerable narrative trust is placed in her observations. Sue, by contrast, is intense and mentally acute, 'a kindly star, an elevating power', yet all too often blind to Jude's needs.

Nevertheless, what this novel succeeds in evoking with extraordinary power is the fearful insecurity of the early liberationist's struggle to come into being, in personal autonomy, in social freedom, in an equitable sexual union—when having no female models to stand by. Battling with these conflicts, Sue flounders between the only cultural models she has available: on the one hand, the infantilized Daddy's-little-girl role, and on the other, the idealized Angel-in-the-House, to be enshrined, to be worshipped. Whether on or off the ideological 'pedestal', Sue is constantly testing Jude's responses, and is never fully assured of herself, her identity, her achievements, or her desirability, while he, in turn, remains equally uncertain and confused about himself, about her, and about the mutuality of their union.

Hardy's achievement in his portrayal of women lies indisputably in his profound understanding of their dilemma as strong, bright intelligences fully capable of proving their capacities in a world unwilling to grant them that right. Ironically, his endeavour to dismantle what he called 'The doll of English fiction', in his portraits of the less than perfect woman, struggling to define herself in a world that ill equips her to shape her own life, to explore her own needs, and to express her own desires, brought repeated accusations of misogyny. This is the more ironic for the fact that woman's struggle for self-definition, for recognition of her enterprise, for a way through to personal fulfilment, was precisely Hardy's own psychological struggle. His was not, of course, an issue of sexual oppression but of class. And, as with the women of the Wessex novels, the battle was bitter and lifelong. RM

Penny Boumelha, *Thomas Hardy and Women: Sexual Ideology and Narrative Form* (1982).
Rosemarie Morgan, *Women and Sexuality in the Novels of Thomas Hardy* (1988).

Woodlanders, The. The eleventh of Hardy's fourteen published novels.

Composition

The novel, written at *Max Gate, was first mentioned in July 1884, while Hardy was working on *The Mayor of Casterbridge*, and was planned as a serial in twelve monthly instalments for the firm of *Macmillan. Composition did not commence until the closing weeks of 1885 (*The Mayor* having been completed in April of that year), and the planning stage did not proceed smoothly: a diary entry of 17–19 November notes that Hardy is submerged in 'a fit of depression' but is hard at work planning the novel in detail (*LW* 182). The same entry records that he has 'gone back to my original plot' for the story. Writing continued throughout 1886 and was completed on 4 February 1887—at 8.20 p.m., as another diary entry scrupulously notes (*LW* 192)—nine months after serialization had begun. For much of the period of composition, therefore, Hardy had written under the pressure of strict deadlines. An alternative title, *Fitzpiers at Hintock*, had been wisely rejected by the publishers. The manuscript, now in DCM, reveals that among other revisions Hardy changed the names of the two principal male characters, Giles being originally 'Ambrose' and Edred Fitzpiers 'Edgar Fitz Rayne'.

Serialization

The Woodlanders appeared in twelve monthly instalments in *Macmillan's Magazine* from May 1886 to April 1887; there were no illustrations. The contents of the twelve numbers are as follows: May, Chapters 1–4; June, 5–8; July, 9–13; August, 14–18; September, 19–22; October, 23–5; November, 26–9; December, 30–3; January, 34–7; February, 38–40; March, 41–3; April, 44–8. In America it appeared roughly simultaneously as a weekly serial in *Harper's Bazar* from 15 May 1886 to 9 April 1887. On the Macmillan's editor's objections to Hardy's sexual frankness in treating the seduction of Suke Damson by Fitzpiers, see MORRIS, MOWBRAY; CENSORSHIP. These objections led to some minor but significant excisions in the serial version. In Chapter 20, for instance, the sentence 'Fitzpiers kissed her again, and pressed her close to him' was omitted, as was the slightly portentous sentence that closes the chapter ('It was daybreak before Fitzpiers and Suke Damson re-entered Little Hintock'). (On the persistence of some of these excisions in early volume editions, see below.)

Volume Publication

The first book edition, in three volumes, was published by Macmillan on 15 March 1887, thereby slightly anticipating, in accordance with common practice, the conclusion of the serial. This edition, mainly intended for libraries, was priced, again traditionally, at 31s. *6d.* (one-and-a-half guineas). A cheaper one-volume edition followed in September of the same year. The bowdlerization already noted in the British serial version (a foretaste of the more severe censorship soon to be imposed on *Tess* and *Jude*) to some degree persisted in the first and other early editions: Suke Damson's reference to obtaining the services of a doctor 'in a few months', with its clear implication of pregnancy, was still couched more vaguely as 'if I should require one' (44), while in Chapter 33 Grace's still startling cry of horror to Mrs Charmond ('"Oh, my great God!... He's had you! Can it be—can it be!"') was still toned down in the first edition, which reads '"Oh, my great heaven!... Can it be—can it be!"' (An interesting, if not wholly persuasive, discussion of this latter passage will be found in John Sutherland's *Can Jane Eyre Be Happy?* (1997).) On these and other textual points the critical edition of the novel by Dale Kramer (1981) may be consulted.

A preface, dated September 1895, was written for the collected edition of that year and a postscript added to the preface for the Wessex Edition of 1912, which also incorporated Hardy's final revisions to his text.

Reception

The novel was widely reviewed and, since Hardy had now been for some time an established novelist, some reviewers took the opportunity of relating it to his earlier work. The *Athenaeum* (26 March 1887: repr. in *CH*), for instance, suggested that it belonged to 'his second manner', 'less vividly "sensational", less broadly comic' than his earlier novels, but 'in a subdued key'. The same reviewer added that 'the general drift of the story is melancholy, and its ending unsatisfactory in any but an artistic point of view'. The well-known critic R. H. Hutton, writing in the *Spectator* on the same day (repr. in *CH*), took the high moral ground, declaring that 'This is a very powerful book, and as disagreeable as it is powerful', and complaining that Hardy seemed to exhibit 'an indifference to the moral effect' conveyed by his story. Like the *Athenaeum* reviewer's dissatisfaction with the ending, this complaint seems to originate in Hardy's failure to ensure that the good (notably Giles) receive their due reward whilst the immoral (notably Fitzpiers) are punished. Moreover, as Hutton observes, Hardy does not 'seem to paint his picture in any spirit of indignation that redeems the moral drift of the book'.

The poet Coventry *Patmore observed in the *St James's Gazette* (2 April 1887: repr. in *CH*) that, while Giles Winterborne, Marty South, and other rustic characters were finely drawn, Fitzpiers and Mrs Charmond 'are throughout repulsive' and Grace Melbury 'never takes hold of our sympathy very strongly'. On the same day, the *Saturday Review* (repr. in *CH*) perceptively praised Hardy's skill in the pervasive use of landscape, 'not as an outside adornment but as an essential part of the scheme of the story', but was less complimentary concerning the plot-devices, in particular the characteristic use of overheard conversations.

Plot

Marty South, a simple countrywoman, is in love with Giles Winterborne but finds that he loves Grace Melbury. The latter's father, a well-to-do timber merchant, has much earlier promised Giles that Grace will become his wife; he has, however, had Grace educated at a boarding-school and is now anxious for her to make a more socially advantageous match than the thoroughly decent but unassuming countryman Giles can offer. A series of social gaffes on Giles's part confirms Melbury's reluctance to view him as a suitable son-in-law, and eventually Giles, who has meanwhile lost much of his property (partly as a result of the death of John South, Marty's father), relinquishes his claim on Grace.

Edred Fitzpiers, a dissolute young doctor of good family who has settled in the district, is attracted by Grace and, overcoming his scruples about her humble social origins, marries her; soon after their marriage, though, Fitzpiers begins an affair with Mrs Charmond, a fine (and wealthy) lady of morally dubious background who has taken up residence in Little Hintock House, and this liaison becomes known to Grace, her father, and Giles. Fitzpiers and Mrs Charmond elope to the Continent. Grace hopes for a divorce that will enable her to marry Giles, but finds that this is not legally possible. Fitzpiers leaves Mrs Charmond, who is soon afterwards murdered by a former lover, and returns to Little Hintock, but Grace refuses to live with him. Instead she occupies Giles's hut whilst he removes himself to a rough shelter in which he falls ill; despite Grace's efforts and Fitzpiers's professional attention, he dies. After several months Grace and Fitzpiers are reconciled and resume their married life together. Suke Damson, a former lover of Fitzpiers, emigrates to Australia with her husband, Tim Tangs. Marty is left alone beside the grave of Giles.

Critical Approaches

The effect of social and economic status upon marriage-choices, which had been a favourite theme of Hardy's at least as early as *Under the Greenwood Tree* and *Far from the Madding Crowd*, persists in *The Woodlanders*, but in its consideration of marital disharmony, adultery, and divorce the novel looks forward to *Jude the Obscure* and the final phase of Hardy's work as a writer of fiction. It also shares common elements with the novel that immediately preceded it, *The Mayor of Casterbridge*: both explore the father–daughter relationship, and Mrs Charmond is to some extent a reworking of that earlier elegant lady and wealthy outsider, Lucetta. Whereas *The Mayor*, however, is set in a busy urban community (though admittedly one intimately dependent upon the surrounding countryside), the locale of its successor is an isolated and tiny rural community that recalls the scenes of Hardy's own early life.

At the heart of the novel is Grace Melbury's conflict over the choice of a husband—a choice that goes beyond personalities to involve questions of social class and education. The schooling, fashionable rather than profound, that her father's economic power has purchased for her has had the effect of uprooting her from her home and her past. (That metaphor is particularly appropriate in relation to a novel permeated by the contrasting ideas of natural and distorted growth, primarily in connection with vegetation but by extension also applicable to human life.) The narrator's sympathies, or prejudices, are made explicit: in embracing the bourgeois values of the boarding-school, Grace has 'fallen from the good old Hintock ways' (6). Yet the 'fall', with its Miltonic reverberations, is not absolute, since she continues to vacillate between the two worlds, those of childhood and maturity, roughly corresponding to country and town. Returning home from school, she 'sucked in this native air of hers like milk' (12), and when she meets Giles after her marriage, 'Her heart rose from its late sadness like a released bough; her senses revelled in the sudden lapse back to Nature unadorned' (28). But the pressures on her, both from within herself and from her father's ambitions on her behalf, are strong, and (unlike Fancy Day in the much earlier *Under the Greenwood Tree*) she makes the wrong marriage-choice—though to say so begs the question whether marriage to Giles would have brought perfect happiness to this refined and socially hypersensitive girl.

Giles himself is partly a realistic, partly an allegorical figure with mythological overtones. Both his mastery of rural skills such as tree-planting and cider-making and his unpretentious domestic life are presented with a fidelity, blending affection, respect, and humour, of which George *Eliot would not, and need not, have been ashamed. At times, however, Giles takes on a more impersonal significance. In a richly Keatsian passage (28), as 'Autumn's very brother', he resembles the representative figures in the 'Ode to Autumn'; later he seems to Grace, in terms that are reminiscent of Frazer's *The Golden Bough*, like 'the fruit-god and the wood-god in alternation' (38). (The first volume of Frazer's monumental work did not, though, appear until 1890.) In historical and evolutionary terms, Giles represents a vanishing world, and his death is perhaps symbolic as well as quixotic. Certainly his undemonstrative or passive nature equips him very inadequately as a rival to Edred Fitzpiers, with his aristocratic lineage, his education, his self-assurance, and his evident sexual prowess. Like Felice Charmond, Fitzpiers is an outsider whose intrusion into the 'sequestered' world of Little Hintock (this epithet perhaps borrowed from Gray's *Elegy*) portends nothing but harm. His Norman-French name anticipates the one adopted by the family of that slightly later seducer, Alec Stoke-d'Urberville. As with Alec, there are hints of diabolism that need not be taken very seriously; but, unlike Alec, Fitzpiers is an intellectual, or at least a pseudo-intellectual, with his dabblings in German metaphysics and his scientific research.

For these outsiders are the agents of change, accelerating, with dramatic results, a process already under way. Though Little Hintock lies 'outside the gates of the world' (1), it is not immune from the upheavals that the 19th century was inflicting on every corner and aspect of English life. It is characteristic of Hardy that such radical modifications of human life and consciousness should be mediated more often through some humble domestic object than by reference to major historical phenomena such as the railways or parliamentary reform: a pair of coffin-stools, long used for their traditional purpose, are now put to a different use after 'changes had led to the discontinuance of the custom' (2).

The novel opens, indeed, with a striking piece of symbolism marking the displacement of the familiar by what Hardy in *The Return of the Native* calls 'the irrepressible New': the sale of Marty South's hair to make a hair-piece for Mrs Charmond may be interpreted as representing (to employ terms used more often of the fate of Tess Durbeyfield) the rape of the peasantry by the *rentier* class. The symbolism is placed, moreover, in a precise socio-economic context: there are hints of eviction from her cottage if Marty refuses, and the loss of home (always a particularly poignant idea for Hardy) is a motif that recurs later in the novel. The connection between these scenes is made explicit when Giles confirms that the houses he possesses under the ancient 'lifehold' system will fall into Mrs Charmond's hands on the death of John South: as Marty ruefully reflects, '"They are going to keep company with my hair"' (5). Marty is referred to at one point as 'a heroic girl' (8) and it is striking that she is given the last word, after the more articulate and demonstrative characters have disappeared from the scene.

The final chapters of *The Woodlanders* have a curious ambivalence that raises questions concerning the novel's generic status. The temptation to regard it as a version of *pastoral ought to be resisted, as Irving Howe argued as long ago as 1967. While conceding that 'Some conventions of pastoral are present', Howe points out that while true pastoral involves 'a stylized bucolic setting drawn from a distance—a cosmopolitan willing of the natural', this novel offers 'a realistic picture of country life' and shows 'earth as a place, not as emblem'. The conclusion of the novel, he adds, is 'all too close to the gritty compromises of actuality'. Hardy had shown a willingness to express such concluding compromises as early as *Under the Greenwood Tree*, and there is perhaps a sense in which his intimate awareness, known and felt, of country life disqualified him for the role of pastoralist. For Douglas Brown, *The Woodlanders* is of all Hardy's novels the one that 'most comprehensively expresses Hardy's feeling towards agricultural life'.

There are also problems with regarding the novel as a *tragedy occupying a place in the series of late novels that runs from *The Mayor of Casterbridge* to *Jude the Obscure*. Hardy's reference very early in the text to the isolated locale of the action as hospitable to 'dramas of a grandeur and unity truly Sophoclean' (1) seems to point us firmly in the direction of Aristotelian theory and classical tragic practice, but what follows does not quite live up to this rather portentous promise. If Giles is the unobtrusive hero of the story (though that cannot be taken for granted), then his death may seem (as that of Mrs Charmond at about the same time assuredly does not) to justify the term 'tragic'—at least at a superficial glance, though as we shall see in a moment the precise circumstances of that death have led critics not only to question its tragic quality but even to detect in it an element of the comic or the absurd.

What, though, are we to make of the five chapters that follow Giles's unnecessary passing? Grace's renewal of her relationship with her husband, the melodrama of the man-trap set by Tim Tangs (and its anticlimactic outcome), and above all the search party that ends in the discovery that Grace and Fitzpiers have spent the night together comfortably in a hotel—all these represent a change, or several changes, of tone. The relaxed discussion of matrimony and womankind by the rustic chorus in the final chapter merely affirms the note of comedy and irony. Only Marty's final soliloquy reminds us of Giles, and the implication of that occasion is that he is now forgotten by all except this girl whose love for him has been unrequited. For Michael Millgate, the novel is 'a tragi-comedy of social and sexual mismatching', and the same critic suggests that 'tragedy' may be 'altogether too portentous a term to invoke' when we bear in mind that 'If Giles's fate is a sombre one, his final act of self-sacrifice has often been regarded as excessive, as almost comic in its strict observation of the proprieties, and certainly as undercut by Grace's eventual return to Fitzpiers' (pp. 257–8).

More recent critics have taken up more combative stances on the same generic issue. For Penny Boumelha, the novel 'draws on genres so widely disparate as to be at times incompatible', while for John Bayley, more positively, 'the ultimate ground of the novel' is 'social comedy'. Bayley sees Melbury, for instance, as 'more socially obsessed than any other Hardy character' and Giles as 'caught up in the unforgiving social process': the novel's message is that 'sex and class, and all that they bring in the way of obsession and possession, can be seen in the end as a comedy that is grim, certainly, but not so grim as all that'. Such readings interpret the novel as a more complex and elusive work than has often been supposed: Giles, for instance, can no longer be seen simply as a solidly innocent 'man of the woods' but as a more interesting figure, and one more distinctively of his (or Hardy's) time.

To recall Hardy's original title for this novel, *Fitzpiers at Hintock*, is to be compelled to consider the centrality of the character given primacy therein and the claims of other characters to a similar role. Dale Kramer has argued that, while Melbury may appear to perform 'the suffering and educative function of the tragic hero, the novel's central sufferers are his daughter and her woodland lover, Giles'. Some might also wish to make out a case for Marty South, but the truth may well be that we should not expect to find in this story a 'tragic hero' (or heroine) on the Shakespearian model: Hardy is more interested in the lines of force that connect characters than in rankings that separate them. Grace has received attention recently from feminist critics who have placed her, with Tess, Sue, and Arabella, in a line of women exhibiting 'spontaneous sexuality' (the phrase is Patricia Ingham's). Hardy brings out strikingly the conventional life-plan that Melbury has conceived for his daughter, with its limited and limiting notion of femininity and sexuality, as well as the very different reality of Grace's own feelings and impulses. It is instructive to contrast Grace's self-consciousness with the cheerful carnality of Suke Damson, a Tess without scruples and perhaps also a first sketch for the Arabella of *Jude*.

Like most of Hardy's novels, *The Woodlanders* has a rich impurity or many-sidedness: old-fashioned love story, psychological drama, sociological study of an archaic community threatened by historical change. What makes it distinctive is the importance of the setting, for this is a novel in which the 'background' is often part of the foreground and trees should be named in any truly comprehensive list of characters. At the beginning of *Under the Greenwood Tree* Hardy had written that 'To dwellers in a wood almost every species of tree has its voice as well as its feature', and, fifteen years later, *The Woodlanders* seems designed to elaborate that observation and to imitate its anthropomorphic language. For most of the 'dwellers in a wood' in the later novel, the woodlands are both lifelong home and place of work, the basis of their economic life and their social relationships. Grace's fate has set her apart from them without entirely severing the links; only Dr Fitzpiers and Mrs Charmond stand in emphatic isolation as figures entirely unconnected with their surroundings—except, that is, by legal and financial considerations, for she is prepared to use considerable power over those who belong to the spot as she does not, and he has his eye firmly fixed on the fortune Melbury has made as a timber-merchant. Though, almost inevitably, these two outsiders are involved in scenes in the woodlands to the extent of becoming temporary 'dwellers in a wood' (Fitzpiers rides home through the woods in his sleep, Mrs Charmond gets lost in the woods), the sense of belonging is totally absent and the hint of foreignness in both their names is not accidental.

Hardy's conception of the woodlands and the dwellers therein seems at first the Wordsworthian one of harmony between human lives and an environment regularly modified by seasonal change. It should be remembered, though, that what is in question is no virgin forest but plantations. Even so, an early passage points the contrast between the unnaturalness of Fitzpiers's light burning when working folk have gone to sleep and the immemorial pattern of existence in the woodlands: 'Almost every diurnal and nocturnal effect in that woodland place had hitherto been the direct result of the regular terrestrial roll which produced the season's changes; but here was something dissociated from these normal sequences, and foreign to local knowledge' (6). A few pages later, though, a remarkable paragraph depicts the woodlands as no tranquil refuge—as not essentially different, in fact, from the grimmest urban environment: 'Here, as everywhere, the Unfulfilled Intention, which makes life what it is, was as obvious as it could be among the depraved crowds of a city slum' (7). The rest of the novel proceeds to demonstrate that, for such as Giles and Marty, that Unfulfilled Intention operates no less disastrously on those who live and work among the trees.

In some respects this is also a very personal novel. *The Mayor of Casterbridge* had been the direct outcome of Hardy's return to the neighbourhood of Dorchester, but in a less obvious way *The Woodlanders* explores the insoluble predicament of the returned native. Like Grace, Hardy had left his home, had adopted middle-class values and attitudes, and had found that returning to one's roots was not just a matter of relocation.

John Bayley, 'A Social Comedy? On Re-Reading *The Woodlanders*', *THA* 5 (1987).
Penny Boumelha, *Thomas Hardy and Women: Sexual Ideology and Narrative Form* (1982).
Douglas Brown, *Thomas Hardy* (1954).
Irving Howe, *Thomas Hardy* (1967).
Patricia Ingham, *Thomas Hardy* (1989).
Dale Kramer, *Thomas Hardy: The Forms of Tragedy* (1975).
Michael Millgate, *Thomas Hardy: His Career as a Novelist* (1971).

Woolf, (Adeline) Virginia, née Stephen (1882–1941), novelist, short-story writer, and essayist. She was slightly acquainted with Hardy through her father Leslie *Stephen. On a visit to Max Gate in late July 1926 in the company of her husband Leonard, Woolf was regaled with Hardy's recollection of seeing her, or possibly her sister Vanessa, as an infant. The visit generated an especially vivid and sympathetic pen-portrait of Hardy in old age (see the entry for 25 July 1926 in *The Diary of Virginia Woolf*, ed. Anne Olivier Bell and Andrew McNeillie (1981), iii): her first impression of him on that occasion was of 'a little puffy-cheeked cheerful old man, with an atmosphere cheerful and business-like in addressing us, rather like an old doctor's or solicitor's....'. Woolf admired both Hardy's poetry and his fiction, and in May 1923, when her husband was appointed literary editor of the *Nation and Athenaeum*, she attempted to solicit a contribution from Hardy (*Letters of Virginia Woolf*, ed. Nigel Nicolson (1977), iii 37). (He eventually contributed the poem 'Coming Up Oxford Street—Evening', published in June 1925.)

Woolf's major commemorative essay, 'Thomas Hardy's Novels', was commissioned by *The Times Literary Supplement* as early as 1919 as an obituary appreciation. Written in December 1921 and January 1922, it duly appeared on 19 January 1928 (eight days after Hardy's death), and was subsequently collected under the title 'The Novels of Thomas Hardy' in *The Common Reader: Second Series* (1932). Acclaiming Hardy as 'the greatest tragic writer among English novelists', Woolf offers an enthusiastic assessment of his fiction. She praises highly *The Woodlanders, The Return of the Native, Far from the Madding Crowd*, and *The Mayor of Casterbridge* as novels in which the intensely tragic contradictions of individual experience and those of the human lot are captured movingly and convincingly. She none the less faults Hardy's tendency to allow argument to intrude upon the presentation of character in his late novels, and registers muted dissatisfaction with him as a stylist. The keywords of the essay, however, remain 'greatness' and 'genius'. Woolf also favourably reviewed F. E. Hardy's *The Early Life of Thomas Hardy* for the *Nation and Athenaeum* in November 1928. JHS

Wordsworth, William (1770–1850), poet. Writing in 1918, Hardy said that 'It bridges over the years to think that Gray might have seen Wordsworth in his cradle, and Wordsworth might have seen me in mine' (*LW* 417). Hardy was born in 1840, Wordsworth died ten years later, and by the time he was 18 Hardy knew Wordsworth's verse sufficiently well to write his earliest surviving poem, 'Domicilium', which he himself described as 'Some Wordsworthian lines' (*LW* 8–9). So competent is this as a pastiche that Hardy must already have acquired that admiration for Wordsworth the poet which is revealed by the many Wordsworthian allusions to be found in Hardy's writings (F. B. Pinion found more than 30, and thought that there were others). Hardy's favourite among Wordsworth's poems is the 'Ode on Intimations of Immortality', which is quoted at least nine times. Hardy made visits to Racedown and Grasmere, places with Wordsworthian associations, and in King's College, Cambridge, found that 'Wordsworth's ghost, too, seemed to haunt the place, lingering and wandering on somewhere alone in the fan-traceried vaulting' (*LW* 145). In 1869 Hardy notes that a cure for despair is to read Wordsworth's 'Resolution and Independence' (*LW* 59).

But if Hardy admired Wordsworth's poetry, he was critical of his philosophy. He knew enough about the nature that surrounded him in Dorset to realize that Wordsworth's 'Nature never did betray | The heart that loved her' was romantic nonsense, and in

Tess of the d'Urbervilles (3) we find: 'Some people would like to know whence the poet whose philosophy is in these days deemed as profound and trustworthy as his song is breezy, gets his authority for speaking of "Nature's holy plan"'. F. R. Leavis was near the mark when he suggested as an examination question, '"Hardy is Wordsworth one hundred years older and wiser." Discuss.'

JCG

work takes many forms in Hardy's fiction, which—unlike that of, say, Jane Austen or Evelyn Waugh—admits relatively few who are idle. Those not engaged in productive labour (Alec d'Urberville, for instance, and Lady Constantine's big-game-hunting husband in *Two on a Tower*) are often morally suspect: the work people do, or fail to do, serves to define not only social status but moral worth. The representation of work ranges from the humblest drudgery to the skilled practice of crafts, the professional activities of clergymen, doctors, and architects, and the creative lives of writers and artists.

The spectrum of labour presented by Hardy is very different from that offered by, say, Dickens, whose portrayal is almost exclusively based on urban life in an industrialized society. Hardy's characters include no factory-workers, London attorneys, crossing-sweepers, or proprietors of dust-heaps: although town and city scenes are not uncommon in his work, his world is for the most part a rural one, and in his best-known novels characteristic occupations include those of the farmer, the dealer in corn, the cider-maker, the reddleman, and the dairymaid.

Like city life, however, rural life embodies a definite hierarchy of pursuits, as of incomes, dwellings, education, and modes of speech and dress. As the son of a working man who was also an employer of labour, Hardy must have acquired very early a finely tuned sense of what were generally judged to be superior or inferior occupations. His early and intimate contact with the lady of the manor, Mrs Julia Augusta *Martin, introduced him to the landowning class, and the withdrawal of estate business from his father after Mrs Martin had taken offence at Jemima Hardy's plans for her son's education must have made him keenly aware of the power over their inferiors' work and livelihood that could be exerted by that class. Such ladies, without occupation but empowered, later made an appearance in his fiction (notably Miss Aldclyffe in *Desperate Remedies* and Lady Constantine in *Two on a Tower*). On the male side, the idle rich include such playboys as Alec d'Urberville and the passionate gentleman from South Carolina who murders Mrs Charmond (*The Woodlanders*). There are numerous representatives of the clergy, from a bishop (again in *Two on a Tower*) to village parsons, and Hardy's treatment of them is often critical or satirical: examples include the obnoxious brothers in 'A Tragedy of Two Ambitions', the even more obnoxious and undutiful son in 'The Son's Veto', the brothers of Angel Clare, and the clergyman consulted by Tess after she has 'baptized' her baby. The Christminster academics in *Jude the Obscure* have little more than walk-on or offstage parts (their most articulate moment is in the form of a letter from the head of a college), and when Hardy depicts intellectuals they are not necessarily university men: Swithin St Cleeve in *Two on a Tower* seems self-taught as an astronomer and hence something of an outsider in the scientific establishment. Knight in *A Pair of Blue Eyes* is a journalist of a superior kind (he writes for the London reviews that Hardy studied carefully), and Raye in 'On the Western Circuit' is a barrister.

These, however, are exceptions to the general rule that Hardy shows little interest in portraying intellectuals and members of the learned professions. Of special interest to Hardy is the role of the creative artist, and Pierston in *The Well-Beloved* is a full-length portrait of the artist (in this case a sculptor). Ethelberta, who writes and recites her own stories, is both artist and artiste. In the short story 'An Imaginative Woman' a poet plays a significant role though he takes no direct part in the action.

More prominent than any of these groups, however, is the gamut of those engaged in rural occupations, from the prosperous farmer (Boldwood in *Far from the Madding Crowd*, for instance) to the lowest unskilled labourer (the young Jude injudiciously hired to keep the birds from eating the crops). Between these extremes come skilled men and women such as Giles and Marty in

The Woodlanders. Within this and other occupational hierarchies (closely correlated, of course, with social and economic hierarchies), mobility is possible. In *Far from the Madding Crowd,* a novel that presents a rich variety of rural occupations, Gabriel Oak begins as a sheep-farmer but, after disaster strikes, is reduced to offering himself for hire as a bailiff, then (descending still further in the scale) a shepherd. In *The Mayor of Casterbridge* Henchard begins as a labourer with a specialized skill (hay-trussing), rises to become a well-to-do corn and hay merchant, then sinks again to his former position.

Middle-class characters sometimes opt for a change of occupation that has the effect of displacing them from one social class and social environment to another: in *The Return of the Native,* Damon Wildeve, a qualified engineer, becomes an innkeeper; Clym Yeobright abandons a promising career with a Paris jeweller to become a schoolmaster, and is further reduced to furze-cutting; Diggory Venn has declined to take on his father's business as dairyman and has become a reddleman. Another educated man, Angel Clare in *Tess,* throws in his lot with the struggling farm-workers who emigrate to Brazil. Mobility can also operate strikingly across generations: just as Hardy, a builder's son, became first an architect and then a writer, Pierston in *The Well-Beloved,* the son of a quarry-owner, becomes a fashionable sculptor. Another artist, Ethelberta, is the daughter of a servant, a class to which Hardy's mother had belonged.

Ethelberta is, however, one of the exceptions that prove the rule, since career choices and work opportunities were much more restricted for women. For Hardy, though, such exceptions were of special interest. As a teacher, Fancy Day in *Under the Greenwood Tree* can live independently in a way that would normally be impossible for a girl of her class—though on the other hand the social status of the teacher, male or female, at this time is a lowly one (a point of which the hero of *An Indiscretion in the Life of an Heiress* is painfully aware). When Jude first encounters Sue Bridehead, she is employed by a shop executing ecclesiastical artwork; she later begins (but does not complete) a course of teacher-training in one of the Church of England colleges of which a good number had been founded, especially in cathedral cities such as 'Melchester' (Salisbury), around the mid-century. (Hardy knew about such institutions through the experience of his sisters, who trained in Salisbury, and his cousin *Tryphena Sparks.) Through an unexpected inheritance, Bathsheba Everdene in *Far from the Madding Crowd* becomes the mistress of a farm and the employer of male and female workers. Elizabeth-Jane in *The Mayor of Casterbridge,* on the other hand, can only effect her escape from the parental (or quasi-parental) home by moving into another kind of servitude, as a lady's companion.

The above groupings leave out of account a number of other occupations depicted by Hardy, ranging from the itinerant quack (Physician Vilbert in *Jude*) to the pork butcher (the symbolically rich calling of Arabella's father in the same novel), and from the common hangman (in the stories 'The Three Strangers' and 'The Withered Arm') to the wealthy manufacturer of firearms ('An Imaginative Woman'). A final mention should be made of soldiers, always an object of fascination for Hardy—not only in *The Trumpet-Major* and *The Dynasts* but, colourfully, in Sergeant Troy (*FFMC*). Like the reddleman and the quack, these military figures follow a calling that grants them a physical mobility, and the ensuing opportunities for philandering, denied to most of their stay-at-home fellows. See also CLASS.

APPENDIX A: INDEX OF HARDY'S POEMS

This appendix lists all Hardy's poems by title (or, for untitled poems, by the first line). The abbreviation in parentheses after the title or first line indicates the volume in which the poem was first collected, thus:

(*WP*) *Wessex Poems* (1898)
(*PPP*) *Poems of the Past and the Present* (1901)
(*TL*) *Time's Laughingstocks* (1909)
(*SC*) *Satires of Circumstance* (1914)
(*MV*) *Moments of Vision* (1917)
(*LLE*) *Late Lyrics and Earlier* (1922)
(*HS*) *Human Shows* (1925)
(*WW*) *Winter Words* (1928)

Poems and fragments uncollected by Hardy and sometimes appearing in other works by him are designated '(uncoll.)'.

Next, the date of composition, if known, is given. In many cases this represents the date appended by Hardy (indicated here by 'dated'), and may signify the production of the final version of a poem begun earlier, often very much earlier. Sometimes Hardy has added both an earlier and a later date, and to some poems he has appended 'From an old copy' or some similarly vague but suggestive phrase. Finally, references to the poem in the present volume are listed.

Abbey Mason, The (*SC*) 187, 189
Aberdeen (*TL*) 389, 429
Absolute Explains, The (*HS*), dated 'New Year's Eve, 1922' 368
'According to the Mighty Working' (*LLE*), dated 1917 36
Aërolite, The (*HS*)
After a Journey (*SC*) 73, 212, 254, 280, 326, 383
After a Romantic Day (*LLE*) 125, 242, 353
After Reading Psalms XXXIX, XL, etc. (*LLE*), dated '187-' 29, 243
After Schiller (*PPP*)
After the Burial (*WW*)
After the Club-Dance (*TL*)
After the Death of a Friend (*WW*)
After the Fair (*TL*) 427
After the Last Breath (*TL*), dated 1904 427, 428
After the Visit (*SC*) 384
After the War (*LLE*) 242
Afternoon Service at Mellstock (*MV*) 16–17, 202, 283, 369, 374
Afterwards (*MV*) 19, 212, 409
Aged Newspaper Soliloquizes, The (*WW*)
Ageing House, The (*MV*) 285
Ἀγνωστωι θεωι [Agnostoi Theoi] (*PPP*) 331
A.H., 1855–1912 (uncoll.)
Ah, Are You Digging on My Grave? (*SC*) 150, 384, 387
Alarm, The (*WP*) 12, 190, 296
Alike and Unlike (*HS*)
Amabel (*WP*), dated 1865 (1866 in manuscript and *Selected Poems*) 279, 334, 465
Ancient to Ancients, An (*LLE*) 242, 243, 292, 339, 413
'And There Was a Great Calm' (*LLE*) 19, 29, 241, 338
Anniversary, An (*MV*)
Announcement, The (*MV*)
Any Little Old Song (*HS*) 212, 291
Apostrophe to an Old Psalm Tune (*MV*), dated 13 August 1916 286
Appeal to America on Behalf of the Belgian Destitute (*MV*), dated December 1914
Aquae Sulis (*SC*) 189
Architectural Masks (*PPP*)
Aristodemus the Messenian (*WW*) 471, 473
As 'Twere To-Night (*LLE*)
At a Bridal (*WP*), dated 1866
At a Country Fair (*MV*)
At a Fashionable Dinner (*HS*)
At a Hasty Wedding (*PPP*)

At a House in Hampstead (*LLE*), dated July 1920 224, 242, 338
At a Lunar Eclipse (*PPP*) 19, 318, 368, 467
At a Pause in a Country Dance (*HS*)
At a Rehearsal of One of J.M.B.'s Plays (uncoll.) 27
At a Seaside Town in 1869 (*MV*)
At a Watering-Place ('Satires of Circumstance' V) (*SC*)
At an Inn (*WP*) 184, 468
At Casterbridge Fair, sequence of poems in *TL* 104, 145, 427
At Castle Boterel (*SC*), dated March 1913 73, 149, 212, 318, 326, 337, 370
At Day-Close in November (*SC*) 37
At Lulworth Cove a Century Back (*LLE*), dated September 1920 224, 242
At Madame Tussaud's in Victorian Years (*MV*) 286
At Mayfair Lodgings (*MV*)
At Middle-Field Gate in February (*MV*) 285
At Moonrise and Onwards (*LLE*)
At Rushy-Pond (*HS*)
At Shag's Heath (*HS*)
At Tea ('Satires of Circumstance' I) (*SC*)
At the Altar-Rail ('Satires of Circumstance' IX) (*SC*)
At the Aquatic Sports (*HS*)
At the Dinner-Table (*LLE*) 241, 242
At the Draper's ('Satires of Circumstance' XII) (*SC*) 383
At the Entering of the New Year (*LLE*), dated '31 December. During the War' 241
At the Mill (*HS*)
At the Piano (*MV*)
At the Pyramid of Cestius near the Graves of Shelley and Keats: *see* Rome
At the Railway Station, Upway (*LLE*) 37, 242, 353
At the Royal Academy (*LLE*)
At the War Office, London (*PPP*), dated December 1899 35, 401
At the Wicket-Gate (*MV*) 16, 284
At the Word 'Farewell' (*MV*) 125
At Waking (*TL*) 211, 427
At Wynyard's Gap (*HS*)
August Midnight, An (*PPP*), dated 1899 212, 312, 331, 336
Autumn in King's Hintock Park (*TL*), dated 1901 427
Autumn Rain-Scene, An (*LLE*), dated October 1904

Background and the Figure, The (*MV*)
Backward Spring, A (*MV*), dated April 1917
Bad Example, The (*WW*) 66
Bags of Meat (*HS*)
Ballad of Love's Skeleton, The (*WW*)
Ballad-Singer, The (*TL*)
Ballet, The (*MV*)
Barthélémon at Vauxhall (*LLE*) 202
Beauty, The (*LLE*)
Beauty's Soliloquy during Her Honeymoon, A (*HS*), dated 1892
Bedridden Peasant, The (*PPP*)
Beeny Cliff (*SC*), subtitled '(March 1870–March 1913)' 73, 212, 326, 387
Before and after Summer (*SC*)
Before Knowledge (*MV*) 397
Before Life and After (*TL*) 37, 90, 138, 428
Before Marching and After (*MV*), dated September 1915 142
Before My Friend Arrived (*HS*) 288
Bereft (*TL*) 25, 311
Bereft, She Thinks She Dreams (*SC*)
Best She Could, The (*HS*) 195
Best Times (*LLE*) 241
Between Us Now (*PPP*)
Beyond the Last Lamp (*SC*) 193, 280, 387
Bird-Catcher's Boy, The (*HS*)
Bird-Scene at a Rural Dwelling, A (*HS*)
Birds at Winter Nightfall (*PPP*), dated December 1899 33
Blinded Bird, The (*MV*) 473
Blow, The (*MV*) 138
Boy's Dream, The (*WW*) 473
Boys Then and Now (*WW*)
Bride-Night Fire, The (*WP*), 1866 98, 199, 279, 466, 467
Bridge of Lodi, The (*PPP*) 230, 296
Broken Appointment, A (*PPP*) 184, 328, 331, 335
Brother, The (*WW*)
Budmouth Dears (uncoll.): extract from *The Dynasts*
Building a New Street in the Ancient Quarter: *see* Rome
Bullfinches, The (*PPP*) 33
Burghers, The (*WP*) 267, 467
Burning the Holly (*WW*) 471
By Henstridge Cross at the Year's End (*LLE*), dated 'During the War'
By Her Aunt's Grave ('Satires of Circumstance' III) (*SC*)
By the Barrows (*TL*) 12
By the Earth's Corpse (*PPP*) 149, 330
By the Runic Stone (*MV*)
Bygone Occasion, A (*LLE*)

Caged Goldfinch, The (*MV*) 33
Caged Thrush Freed and Home Again, The (*PPP*) 397
Calf, The (uncoll.)
Call to National Service, A (*MV*), dated March 1917
Cardinal Bembo's Epitaph on Raphael (*PPP*)
Caricature, The (*HS*)
Carrier, The (*HS*)
Casterbridge Captains, The (*WP*) 467
Casual Acquaintance, The (*LLE*)
Catching Ballet of the Wedding Clothes, The (*WW*), dated 1919
Cathedral Façade at Midnight, A (*HS*) 16
Catullus: XXXI (*PPP*), dated April 1887
Change, The (*MV*), dated January–February 1913 33, 125
Channel Firing (*SC*), dated April 1914 150, 212, 371, 387, 408
Chapel-Organist, The (*LLE*) 202, 242
Cheval-Glass, The (*SC*)
Child and the Sage, The (*LLE*), dated 21 December 1908
Childhood among the Ferns (*WW*) 107, 472
Children and Sir Nameless, The (*LLE*) 37, 242
Chimes, The (*MV*)
Chimes Play 'Life's a Bumper!', The (*LLE*), dated 1913
Choirmaster's Burial, The (*MV*) 37, 150, 291
Chorus of the Pities (uncoll.): extract from *The Dynasts*
Chosen, The (*LLE*)
Christening, The (*TL*), dated 1894 429
Christmas Ghost-Story, A (*PPP*), dated December 1899 35, 41, 150, 329
Christmas in the Elgin Room (*WW*), dated '1905 and 1926' 473
Christmas: 1924 (*WW*), dated 1924 41, 371, 471
Christmastide (*WW*) 41, 471
Church and the Wedding, The (*HS*)
Church Romance, A (*TL*) 16, 366, 369, 427, 428
Church-Builder, The (*PPP*)
Circular, A (*SC*) 327
Circus-Rider to Ringmaster (*HS*)
Clasped Skeletons, The (*WW*) 12
Clock of the Years, The (*MV*), dated 1916 232
Clock-Winder, The (*MV*) 16
Collector Cleans His Picture, The (*LLE*) 29, 372
Colonel's Soliloquy, The (*PPP*), dated October 1899 35, 189
Colour, The (*LLE*)
Come Not; Yet Come! (*HS*) 185
Comet at Yell'ham, The (*PPP*) 328, 331
Coming of the End, The (*MV*)
Coming Up Oxford Street: Evening (*HS*), dated 'As seen 4 July 1872' 253
Commonplace Day, A (*PPP*) 320, 330, 335
Compassion (*HS*), dated 22 January 1924
Concerning Agnes (*WW*) 155, 340, 471
Concerning His Old Home (*WW*) 472
Confession to a Friend in Trouble, A (*WP*), dated 1866 288, 467
Conformers, The (*TL*) 429
Conjecture (*MV*) 283, 284, 367
Contretemps, The (*LLE*)
Convergence of the Twain, The (*SC*), written April 1912 138, 387, 430
Conversation at Dawn, A (*SC*), dated 1910
Copying Architecture in an Old Minster (*MV*) 16, 338, 470
Coquette, and After, The (*PPP*)
Coronation, The (*SC*), dated 1911 388
Could I but Will (*LLE*)
Countenance, A (*WW*), dated 1884
Country Wedding, The (*LLE*) 144
Cross Currents (*LLE*)
Cry of the Homeless (*MV*), dated August 1915
Curate's Kindness, The (*TL*)
Curtains Now Are Drawn, The (*LLE*), dated 1913
Cynic's Epitaph (*HS*)

Dame of Athelhall, The (*PPP*) 331
Dance at the Phoenix, The (*WP*) 232, 279, 290, 334, 467
Dark-Eyed Gentleman, The (*TL*) 429
Darkling Thrush, The (*PPP*), dated 31 December 1900 (but first published 29 December) 33, 35, 233, 311, 319, 328, 331, 333, 336, 369, 374
Daughter Returns, A (*WW*), dated 17 December 1901
Dawn after the Dance, The (*TL*), dated 1869 279, 291, 427
Days to Recollect (*HS*)
Dead and the Living One, The (*MV*), dated 1915
Dead Bastard, The (*WW*)
Dead Man Walking, The (*TL*) 292, 428
Dead Quire, The (*TL*), dated 1897 144, 145, 292, 427, 428
Dead 'Wessex' the Dog to the Household (*WW*)
Dear, The (*TL*), dated 1901 428

Death of Regret, The (*SC*)
Death-Day Recalled, A (*SC*) 327
Departure (*PPP*), dated October 1899 35, 189
Destined Pair, The (*WW*)
Difference, The (*SC*)
Discouragement (*HS*), dated 1863–7 197, 198
Discovery, The (*SC*)
Dissemblers, The (*LLE*)
Ditty (*WP*), dated 1870 465, 467
Division, The (*TL*), dated 1893 184, 427, 428
Dolls, The (*MV*)
Domicilium (uncoll.), written not later than 1860; first printed 1916 187, 292, 311, 366, 489
Donaghadee (*HS*)
Doom and She (*PPP*) 138, 319, 330, 335
Drawing Details in an Old Church (*LLE*) 16
Dream Is—Which?, The (*LLE*)
Dream of the City Shopwoman (*LLE*), dated 1866
Dream or No, A (*SC*), dated February 1913 73, 327
Dream Question, A (*TL*) 428–9
Dream-Follower, The (*PPP*)
Drinking Song (*WW*) 90, 368, 473
Drizzling Easter Morning, A (*LLE*) 371
Drummer Hodge (*PPP*), dated 1899 9, 35, 126, 189, 212, 330, 331, 335
Duel, The (*MV*)
Duettist to her Pianoforte, A (*LLE*) 242, 292
During Wind and Rain (*MV*) 25, 212, 283, 338

East-End Curate, An (*HS*)
Echo-Elf Answers, The (*HS*)
Elopement, The (*SC*)
Embarcation (*PPP*), dated October 1899 35, 189, 329
End of the Episode, The (*TL*)
End of the Year 1912 (*LLE*) 241
Enemy's Portrait, The (*MV*) 286
England to Germany in 1914 (*MV*), dated Autumn 1914
Epeisodia (*LLE*) 33
Epigraph to 'The Woodlanders' (uncoll.)
Epilogue (uncoll.): 'Written for the production of "The Dynasts" at the Kingsway Theatre'
Epitaph (*LLE*)
Epitaph for George Moore (uncoll.) 287, 340, 474
Epitaph for G. K. Chesterton (uncoll.) 53, 474
Epitaph on a Pessimist (*HS*) 65–6
Eunice (uncoll.)
Eve of Waterloo, The (uncoll.): extract from *The Dynasts*
Evelyn G. of Christminster (*LLE*)
Evening in Galilee, An (*WW*) 29, 473
Evening Shadows (*WW*) 12
Every Artemisia (*HS*)
Everything Comes (*MV*)
Exeunt Omnes (*SC*), dated 2 June 1913
Expectation and Experience (*WW*) 472
Experience, An (*LLE*) 288
Expostulation, An (*HS*)

Face at the Casement, The (*SC*) 29
Faded Face, The (*MV*)
Fading Rose, The (*HS*)
Faintheart in a Railway Train (*LLE*) 230, 240, 353, 408
Faithful Swallow, The (*HS*)
Faithful Wilson (*WW*)
Fallow Deer at the Lonely House, The (*LLE*)
Family Portraits (*WW*) 186, 340, 397, 472
Farmer Dunman's Funeral (*HS*)
Farm-Woman's Winter, The (*TL*)
Felled Elm and She, The (*WW*)
Fetching Her (*LLE*)
Fiddler, The (*TL*)
Fight on Durnover Moor, The (*HS*)
Figure in the Scene, The (*MV*) 284, 286, 338
Fire at Tranter Sweatley's, The (*WP*): original title of 'The Bride-Night Fire'
First or Last (*LLE*)
First Sight of Her and After (*MV*) 283
Five Students, The (*MV*) 280, 283, 288
Flirt's Tragedy, The (*TL*)
Flower's Tragedy, The (*HS*)
For Life I Had Never Cared Greatly (*MV*)
Forbidden Banns, The (*HS*)
Forgotten Miniature, A (*WW*)
Former Beauties (*TL*) 212
Forsaking of the Nest, The (uncoll.)
Four Footprints (*TL*) 427
Four in the Morning (*HS*)
Fragment (*MV*) 138, 321
Freed the Fret of Thinking (*HS*)
Friends Beyond (*WP*) 143, 408, 468
From Her in the Country (*TL*), dated 1866 251, 427
From Victor Hugo (*PPP*)
Frozen Greenhouse, The (*HS*) 198

Gallant's Song (*WW*), dated November 1868
Gap in the White, The (*WW*)
Garden Seat, The (*LLE*) 241
Genitrix Laesa (*HS*) 196, 198

Genoa and the Mediterranean (*PPP*) 335
Gentleman's Epitaph on Himself and a Lady, A (*LLE*) 242
'Gentleman's Second-Hand Suit, A' (*WW*)
Geographical Knowledge (*TL*) 427
George Meredith (*TL*), dated May 1909 278, 428, 429
Ghost of the Past, The (*SC*)
Glimpse, The (*MV*)
God-Forgotten (*PPP*) 330
God's Education (*TL*) 138, 428
God's Funeral (*SC*), dated 1908–10 335
Going, The (*SC*), dated December 1912 73, 211
Going and Staying (*LLE*) 338–9
Going of the Battery, The (*PPP*), dated November 1899 35, 38, 329
Graveyard of Dead Creeds, The (*HS*)
Great Things (*MV*) 5, 311
Green Slates (*HS*) 149
Growth in May (*LLE*)

Had You Wept (*SC*)
Hap (*WP*), dated 1866 334, 397, 467
Harbour Bridge, The (*HS*)
Harvest-Supper, The (*HS*) 25, 145
Hatband, The (uncoll.)
Haunter, The (*SC*) 212, 327
Haunting Fingers (*LLE*) 242, 338
He Abjures Love (*TL*), dated 1883 427, 428
He Did Not Know Me (*WW*)
He Fears His Good Fortune (*MV*)
He Follows Himself (*LLE*) 339
He Inadvertently Cures His Love-Pains (*HS*)
He Never Expected Much (*WW*) 472
He Prefers Her Earthly (*MV*) 321
He Resolves to Say No More (*WW*) 66, 340, 473, 474
He Revisits His First School (*MV*)
He Wonders About Himself (*MV*), dated November 1893 184, 320
Head above the Fog, The (*MV*)
Heiress and Architect (*WP*), 1867 397, 467
Henley Regatta (*WW*)
Her Apotheosis (*LLE*)
Her Confession (*TL*), dated 1865–7 427
Her Death and After (*WP*) 12
Her Definition (*TL*), dated 'Summer: 1866' 427
Her Dilemma (*WP*), dated 1866 16
Her Father (*TL*) 427
Her Haunting-Ground (*HS*)
Her Immortality (*WP*) 321
Her Initials (*WP*), dated 1869 465
Her Late Husband (*PPP*) 267
Her Love-Birds (*MV*)
Her Reproach (*PPP*), dated 1867 328
Her Second Husband Hears Her Story (*WW*)
Her Secret (*SC*)
Her Song (*LLE*) 241
Her Temple (*LLE*)
Heredity (*MV*) 186, 283, 285
High-School Lawn, The (*HS*) 410
His Country (*MV*), dated 1913
His Heart (*MV*)
His Immortality (*PPP*), dated February 1899 321
His Visitor (*SC*), dated 1913
History of an Hour, The (*HS*)
Homecoming, The (*TL*), dated December 1901
Honeymoon Time at an Inn (*MV*)
Horses Abroad (*HS*) 9
House of Hospitalities, The (*TL*) 427, 428
House of Silence, The (*MV*)
House with a History, A (*LLE*)
How Great My Grief (*PPP*)
How She Went to Ireland (*WW*)
Hundred Years Since, A (uncoll.)
Hurried Meeting, A (*HS*)
Husband's View, The (*TL*)

I Am the One (*WW*) 472
I Found Her Out There (*SC*) 327
I Have Lived with Shades (*PPP*), dated 2 February 1899 230
I Knew a Lady (*LLE*)
I Look in Her Face (*LLE*)
I Look into My Glass (*WP*) 241, 468
I Looked Back (*WW*)
I Looked Up from My Writing (*MV*)
I Met a Man (*MV*), dated 1916 232
I Need Not Go (*PPP*)
I Rose and Went to Rou'tor Town (*MV*)
I Rose Up as My Custom Is (*SC*) 41, 144, 150
I Said and Sang Her Excellence (*MV*)
I Said to Love (*PPP*)
I Say, 'I'll Seek Her' (*TL*) 428
I Sometimes Think (*LLE*) 240
I Thought, My Heart (*MV*)
I Travel as a Phantom Now (*MV*), dated 1915 285
I Was Not He (*LLE*)
I Was the Midmost (*LLE*)
I Watched a Blackbird (*WW*) 472
I Worked No Wile to Meet You (*LLE*)
Ice on the Highway (*HS*) 281, 339
If It's Ever Spring Again (*LLE*) 37, 242

If You Had Known (*LLE*), dated 1920
Imaginings (*MV*)
Imitations, etc. (*PPP*): group of six short poems 335
Impercipient, The (*WP*) 16, 369, 373, 413, 468
In a Cathedral City (*TL*) 428
In a Eweleaze near Weatherbury (*WP*), dated 1890 468
In a Former Resort after Many Years (*HS*)
In a London Flat (*LLE*) 9
In a Museum (*MV*) 285
In a Waiting-Room (*MV*) 105, 371
In a Whispering Gallery (*MV*) 16, 374
In a Wood (*WP*), dated '1887; 1896' 311, 319, 370
In Childbed (*TL*)
In Church ('Satires of Circumstance' II) (*SC*) 16
In Death Divided (*SC*), dated '189-' 184, 385
In Front of the Landscape (*SC*)
In Her Precincts (*MV*) 283
In Sherborne Abbey (*HS*) 16
In St Paul's a While Ago (*HS*) 16
In Tenebris I (*PPP*) 29, 128, 230, 330, 331, 397
In Tenebris II (*PPP*), dated 1895–6 29, 128, 313, 339, 413
In Tenebris III (*PPP*), dated 1896 29, 128
In the British Museum (*SC*)
In the Cemetery ('Satires of Circumstance' VI) (*SC*)
In the Days of Crinoline (*SC*) 372
In the Evening (*HS*)
In the Garden (*MV*), dated 1915 144, 283, 367
In the Marquee (*WW*) 471
In the Mind's Eye (*TL*)
In the Moonlight ('Satires of Circumstance' XV) (*SC*) 383
In the Night She Came (*TL*)
In the Nuptial-Chamber ('Satires of Circumstance' X) (*SC*)
In the Old Theatre, Fiesole (*PPP*)
In the Restaurant ('Satires of Circumstance' XI) (*SC*)
In the Room of the Bride-Elect ('Satires of Circumstance' IV) (*SC*)
In the Servants' Quarters (*SC*) 29, 383
In the Seventies (*MV*) 29
In the Small Hours (*LLE*)
In the Street (*HS*)
In the Study ('Satires of Circumstance' VIII) (*SC*) 383
In the Vaulted Way (*TL*) 427
In Time of 'The Breaking of Nations' (*MV*), dated 1915 1, 29, 142, 286, 338
In Time of Wars and Tumults (*MV*), dated 1915
In Vision I Roamed (*WP*), dated 1866 19, 467
In Weatherbury Stocks (*WW*)
Inconsistent, The (*PPP*)
Inquiry, An (*HS*)
Inquiry, The (*TL*)
Inscription, The (*LLE*), dated 30 October 1907
Inscriptions for a Peal of Eight Bells (*HS*)
Interloper, The (*MV*)
Intra Sepulchrum (*LLE*)
It Never Looks Like Summer (*MV*), dated 8 March 1913
Ivy-Wife, The (*WP*)

January Night, A (*MV*) 285
Jezreel (*LLE*), dated 24 September 1918 242
Jingle on the Times, A (uncoll.), dated December 1914 195
Jog-Trot Pair, A (*LLE*)
John and Jane (*TL*) 427
Joys of Memory (*MV*)
Jubilate (*MV*) 150
Jubilee of a Magazine, The (*SC*)
Julie-Jane (*TL*) 427
June Leaves and Autumn (*WW*), dated 19 November 1898
Just the Same (*LLE*)

King's Experiment, The (*PPP*) 33
King's Soliloquy, A (*SC*), dated May 1910 388
Kiss, A (*MV*)
Known Had I (*HS*)

Lacking Sense, The (*PPP*) 319, 320, 330, 335
Lady in the Furs, The (*WW*), dated 1925
Lady of Forebodings, The (*HS*)
Lady Vi (*HS*)
Lament (*SC*) 327
Lament of the Looking-Glass, The (*LLE*)
Last Chorus (uncoll.): extract from *The Dynasts*
Last Chrysanthemum, The (*PPP*) 331
Last Journey, A (*HS*)
Last Leaf, The (*HS*)
Last Look Round St Martin's Fair (*HS*) 198
Last Love-Word (*HS*) 185
Last Performance, The (*MV*), dated 1912
Last Signal, The (*MV*), dated 11 October 1886 26, 283, 317
Last Time, The (*LLE*) 241
Last Week in October (*HS*)

Last Words to a Dumb Friend (*LLE*), dated 2 October 1904 242, 315
Later Autumn, The (*HS*)
Lausanne: In Gibbon's Old Garden: 11–12 p.m. (*PPP*), dated 1897 330
Leader of Fashion, A (*HS*)
Leaving, A (*HS*)
Leipzig (*WP*) 190, 296
Let Me Believe (*HS*)
Let Me Enjoy (*TL*) 428
Letter's Triumph, The (*WW*)
Levelled Churchyard, The (*PPP*), dated 1882 47, 409
Liddell and Scott (*WW*) 318
Life and Death at Sunrise (*HS*) 197
Life Laughs Onward (*MV*)
Light Snow-Fall after Frost, A (*HS*) 198
Lines Spoken by Miss Ada Rehan... (*WP*), dated 22 July 1890
Lines to a Movement in Mozart's E-Flat Symphony (*MV*), dated 'Begun November 1898' 286, 291
Little Old Table, The (*LLE*) 37, 241
Lizard, The (uncoll.)
Lodging-House Fuchsias, The (*WW*) 472
Logs on the Hearth (*MV*), dated December 1915 282–3, 338, 367
Lonely Days (*LLE*)
Long Plighted (*PPP*)
Looking Across (*MV*), dated December 1915 367
Looking at a Picture on an Anniversary (*MV*), dated Spring 1913 286
Looking Back (uncoll.)
Lorna the Second (*WW*)
Lost Love (*SC*)
Lost Pyx, The (*PPP*) 331, 401
Louie (*HS*), dated July 1913
Love the Monopolist (*MV*), dated 'Begun 1871: finished—'
Love Watches a Window (*WW*)
Love-Letters, The (*WW*)
Lover to Mistress (*HS*)
Lying Awake (*WW*) 339–40, 472, 473

Mad Judy (*PPP*)
Maid of Keinton Mandeville, The (*LLE*), dated '1915 or 1916' 241
Maiden's Pledge, A (*LLE*)
Man, A (*PPP*)
Man He Killed, The (*TL*), dated 1902 401, 428, 429
Man Was Drawing Near to Me, A (*LLE*) 241
Man Who Forgot, The (*MV*)
Man with a Past, The (*MV*)
Marble Tablet, The (*LLE*), dated 8 September 1916 240, 243
Marble-Streeted Town, The (*LLE*), dated '1914?' 241
Market-Girl, The (*TL*)
Masked Face, The (*MV*)
Master and the Leaves, The (*LLE*), dated 1917
Meditations on a Holiday (*LLE*), dated May 1921 292–3
Meeting with Despair, A (*WP*) 467
Memorial Brass: 186-, The (*MV*) 230
Memory and I (*PPP*)
Men Who March Away (*MV*), dated 5 September 1914 141, 384
Merrymaking in Question, A (*MV*) 338
Middle-Age Enthusiasms (*WP*) 367, 468
Midnight on Beechen, 187- (*HS*) 230
Midnight on the Great Western (*MV*) 37, 353
Milestone by the Rabbit-Burrow, The (*LLE*) 243
Military Appointment, A (*LLE*) 241, 242
Milkmaid, The (*PPP*)
Minute before Meeting, The (*TL*), dated 1871 427
Misconception (*TL*)
Mismet (*LLE*)
Missed Train, The (*HS*)
Mock Wife, The (*HS*) 25
Molly Gone (*MV*) 283, 367
Moments of Vision (*MV*)
Mongrel, The (*WW*)
Month's Calendar, The (*HS*) 185
Monument-Maker, The (*HS*), dated 1916 241, 281
Moon Looks In, The (*SC*)
More Love Lyrics, sequence of poems in *TL* 334
Mother Mourns, The (*PPP*) 33, 90, 319, 328, 335, 398
Moth-Signal, The (*SC*)
Mound, The (*WW*)
Murmurs in the Gloom (*LLE*), dated 22 September 1899 241
Music in a Snowy Street (*HS*)
Musical Box, The (*MV*)
Musical Incident, A (*WW*)
Musing Maiden, The (*WW*), dated 'October 1866 (recopied)'
Mute Opinion (*PPP*)
My Cicely (*WP*) 12, 230, 280, 389
My Love's Gone a-Fighting (uncoll.): extract from *The Dynasts*
My Spirit Will Not Haunt the Mound (*SC*)

Nature's Questioning (*WP*) 335
Near Lanivet, 1872 (*MV*) 25, 284
Necessitarian's Epitaph, A (*WW*)
Nettles, The (*MV*)
Neutral Tones (*WP*), dated 1867 279, 297, 311, 324, 334, 467
New Boots, The (*WW*) 200
New Dawn's Business, The (*WW*) 470, 472
New Toy, The (*HS*)
New Year's Eve (*TL*), dated 1906 90, 138, 428
New Year's Eve in War Time, A (*MV*), dated 1915–16 338
Newcomer's Wife, The (*SC*)
News for Her Mother (*TL*) 428
Night in November, A (*LLE*), dated '(?)1913'
Night in the Old Home (*TL*) 427
Night of Questionings, A (*HS*)
Night of the Dance, The (*TL*)
Night of Trafalgar, The (uncoll.): extract from *The Dynasts*
Nightmare, and the Next Thing, A (*WW*) 473–4
Night-Time in Mid-Fall (*HS*) 197
1967 (*TL*), dated 1867 427
No Bell-Ringing (*WW*)
No Buyers (*HS*) 9, 195
Noble Lady's Tale, The (*TL*) 427
Nobody Comes (*HS*), dated 9 October 1924 125, 195, 340
Not Known (*WW*) 472
Not Only I (*HS*)
Nothing Matters Much (*HS*)

O I Won't Lead a Homely Life (*LLE*) 293
Obliterate Tomb, The (*SC*)
Occultation, The (*MV*)
Often When Warring (*MV*), dated 1915
Old Excursions (*MV*), dated April 1913 284
Old Furniture (*MV*) 150, 186, 283
Old Gown, The (*LLE*)
Old Likeness, An (*LLE*) 240, 243, 431
Old Neighbour and the New, The (*LLE*) 241
Old Workman, The (*LLE*)
On a Discovered Curl of Hair (*LLE*), dated February 1913 241
On a Fine Morning (*PPP*), dated February 1899 398
On a Heath (*MV*)
On a Midsummer Eve (*MV*) 285
On an Invitation to the United States (*PPP*)
On Martock Moor (*HS*)
On One Who Lived and Died Where He Was Born (*LLE*)
On Stinsford Hill at Midnight (*LLE*) 241, 374
On Sturminster Foot-Bridge (*MV*) 407
On the Belgian Expatriation (*MV*), dated 18 October 1914 142, 286
On the Death-Bed ('Satires of Circumstance' XIII) (*SC*) 383
On the Departure Platform (*TL*) 428
On the Doorstep (*MV*), dated January 1914
On the Doorstep (uncoll.) 383
On the Esplanade (*HS*) 324
On the Palatine: *see* Rome
On the Portrait of a Woman about to be Hanged (*HS*), dated 6 January 1923
On the Tune Called the Old-Hundred-and-Fourth (*LLE*) 202–3, 242, 292
On the Way (*LLE*)
Once at Swanage (*HS*)
One Ralph Blossom Soliloquizes (*TL*) 47, 429
One We Knew (*TL*), dated 20 May 1902 25, 290, 366, 427, 428
One Who Married Above Him (*HS*)
Opportunity, The (*LLE*) 240, 312
Orphaned Old Maid, The (*TL*)
Our Old Friend Dualism (*WW*), dated 1920
Outside the Casement (*LLE*)
Outside the Window ('Satires of Circumstance' VII) (*SC*)
Over the Coffin ('Satires of Circumstance' XIV) (*SC*)
Overlooking the River Stour (*MV*) 192, 407
Oxen, The (*MV*), dated 1915 145, 283, 311, 338, 369, 374

Pair He Saw Pass, The (*HS*)
Panthera (*TL*) 29, 47, 233, 370, 426
Paphian Ball, The (*HS*) 150, 291
Paradox (*HS*) 321
Parting-Scene, A (*HS*)
Passer-By, The (*LLE*) 240
Pat of Butter, The (*HS*)
Paths of Former Time (*MV*), dated 1913 284
Paying Calls (*MV*)
Peace-Offering, The (*MV*)
Peace Peal, The (*HS*), dated 'At the end of the War'
Peasant's Confession, The (*WP*), dated 1898 25, 190, 296, 465
Pedestrian, The (*MV*)
Pedigree, The (*MV*), dated 1916 186, 338, 472
Penance (*LLE*)
Phantom Horsewoman, The (*SC*), dated 1913 280, 327, 337
Philosophical Fantasy, A (*WW*), dated '1920 and 1926' 471, 473

Photograph, The (*MV*) 285
Pieces Occasional and Various, group of poems in *TL*
Pine Planters, The (*TL*) 311, 428
Pine Frock, The (*MV*) 283
Pity of It, The (*MV*), dated April 1915 142, 286, 318
Place on the Map, The (*SC*)
Places (*SC*), dated March 1913 327
Placid Man's Epitaph, A (*WW*), dated 1925 472
Plaint to Man, A (*SC*), dated 1909–10 90, 373
Plena Timoris (*HS*)
Poems of 1912–13 (*SC*), sequence of 21 poems 127, 149, 164, 166, 212, 280, 284, 325–7, 337, 384, 387
Poems of Pilgrimage (*PPP*), sequence of eleven poems 330, 335, 437
Poems of War and Patriotism (*MV*), group of 17 poems 141, 286, 338
Poet, A (*SC*), dated July 1914 384
Poet's Thought, A (*WW*) 472
Poor Man and a Lady, A (*HS*) 16
Popular Personage at Home, A (*HS*), dated 1924
Portraits, The (uncoll.)
Postponement (*WP*), dated 1866 33, 279
Practical Woman, A (*WW*)
Premonitions (*HS*) 144
Private Man on Public Men, A (*WW*) 472
Problem, The (*PPP*)
Procession of Dead Days, A (*LLE*)
Prologue (uncoll.): *see* Epilogue
Prophetess, The (*WW*)
Prospect, The (*HS*) 339
Protean Maiden, The (*HS*)
Proud Songsters (*WW*) 37, 472
Puzzled Game-Birds, The (*PPP*) 33

Queen Caroline to Her Guests (*HS*)
Question of Marriage, A (*WW*)
Quid Hic Agis? (*MV*), dated '1916. During the War' 29, 36

Rain on a Grave (*SC*), dated 31 January 1913 327
Rake-Hell Muses (*LLE*), dated '189-' 232
Rambler, The (*TL*)
Rash Bride, The (*TL*) 145, 291, 427
Read by Moonlight (*LLE*)
Recalcitrants, The (*SC*)
Re-Enactment, The (*SC*) 150
Refusal, A (*HS*), dated August 1924 39, 371, 411
Regret Not Me (*SC*)
Rejected Member's Wife, The (*TL*) 427
Reluctant Confession (*WW*)
Reminder, The (*TL*)
Reminiscences of a Dancing Man (*TL*) 291, 428
Respectable Burgher, The (*PPP*) 47, 296
Retrospect (*PPP*): group of three poems at the end of that volume
Retty's Phases (*HS*), dated 'From an old draft of 1868' 197
Revisitation, The (*TL*) 12
Revulsion (*WP*), dated 1866 467
Riddle, The (*MV*)
Rift, The (*LLE*) 241
Rival, The (*MV*) 286
Robin, The (*MV*)
Roman Gravemounds, The (*SC*), dated November 1910
Roman Road, The (*TL*) 102, 427, 428
Rome: At the Pyramid of Cestius near the Graves of Shelley and Keats (*PPP*) 224, 397
Rome: Building a New Street in the Ancient Quarter (*PPP*) 229
Rome: On the Palatine (*PPP*)
Rome: The Vatican: Sala delle Muse (*PPP*) 305
Rose-Ann (*TL*) 427
Rover Comes Home, The (*HS*)
Royal Sponsors (*MV*)
Ruined Maid, The (*PPP*), dated 1866 47, 234, 281, 311, 331, 334, 408

'Sacred to the Memory' (*LLE*) 240, 243
Sacrilege, The (*SC*) 25, 388
Sailor's Mother, The (*LLE*)
San Sebastian (*WP*) 190, 296, 467
Sapphic Fragment (*PPP*)
Satin Shoes, The (*SC*)
Satires of Circumstance (*SC*), subtitled 'In Fifteen Glimpses' 336, 337, 384, 387
Saying Good-Bye (*LLE*)
Schreckhorn, The (*SC*), dated June 1897 387, 406, 437
Sea Fight, The (*HS*)
Seasons of Her Year, The (*PPP*) 33
Second Attempt, A (*HS*)
Second Night, The (*LLE*)
Second Visit, The (*WW*)
Seeing the Moon Rise (*WW*) 473
Seen by the Waits (*SC*) 145
Self-Glamourer, A (*WW*) 472
Selfsame Song, The (*LLE*) 224
Self-Unconscious (*SC*)

Self-Unseeing, The (*PPP*) 253, 290, 331
Sergeant's Song, The (*WP*), dated 1878, partly quoted in *The Trumpet-Major* (5) 296, 465, 467
Set of Country Songs, sequence of poems in *TL* 426
Seven Times, The (*LLE*)
Seventy-Four and Twenty (*SC*)
Sexton at Longpuddle, The (*HS*)
Shadow on the Stone, The (*MV*), dated 'Begun 1913: finished 1916'
She at His Funeral (*WP*), dated 1873 465
She Charged Me (*SC*) 388
She Did Not Turn (*LLE*)
She Hears the Storm (*TL*) 147, 427
She, I, and They (*MV*), dated 1916 283
She Opened the Door (*HS*), dated 1913
She Revisits Alone the Church of Her Marriage (*LLE*)
She Saw Him, She Said (*HS*)
She, to Him I (*WP*), dated 1866 297, 334, 397
She, to Him II (*WP*), dated 1866 297
She, to Him III (*WP*), dated 1866 409
She, to Him IV (*WP*), dated 1866 397
She Who Saw Not (*LLE*)
She Would Welcome Old Tribulations (uncoll.), dated 'About 1900'
Sheep-Boy, The (*HS*)
Sheep Fair, A (*HS*) 195, 197, 311
Shelley's Skylark (*PPP*) 330, 331, 335, 397
Shiver, The (*HS*)
Shortening Days at the Homestead (*HS*) 195
Shut Out That Moon (*TL*), dated 1904 19, 212, 428
Sick Battle-God, The (*PPP*) 35, 329
Side by Side (*LLE*)
Sigh, The (*TL*) 428
Sign-Seeker, A (*WP*) 212, 233, 321, 334, 468
Signs and Tokens (*MV*)
Silences (*WW*)
Sine Prole (*HS*) 186
Singer Asleep, A (*SC*), dated 1910 232, 387, 411, 437
Singing Lovers (*HS*)
Singing Woman, The (*LLE*)
Single Witness, The (*WW*)
Sitting on the Bridge (*MV*)
Six Boards, The (*HS*)
Sleep-Worker, The (*PPP*) 33, 319, 330, 335
Slow Nature, The (*WP*), dated 1894 465
Snow in the Suburbs (*HS*) 193, 195, 196, 339
So, Time (*HS*) 368
So Various (*WW*) 472
Something Tapped (*MV*), dated August 1913 284
Something that Saved Him, The (*MV*)
Song from Heine (*PPP*)
Song of Hope (*PPP*)
Song of the Soldiers' Wives and Sweethearts (*PPP*), dated 1899 36
Song to an Old Burden (*HS*)
Song to Aurore (*WW*)
Son's Portrait, The (*WW*) 472
Souls of the Slain, The (*PPP*), dated December 1899 35, 150, 212, 329, 331, 336
Sound in the Night, A (*LLE*)
Spectres that Grieve (*SC*)
Spell of the Rose, The (*SC*) 327, 385
Spellbound Palace, A (*HS*) 410
Spot, A (*PPP*)
Spring Call, The (*TL*)
Squire Hooper (*WW*) 472
St Launce's Revisited (*SC*) 327, 385
Standing by the Mantelpiece (*WW*) 288, 340, 472
Starlings on the Roof (*SC*)
Statue of Liberty, The (*MV*)
Strange House, The (*LLE*) 241
Stranger's Song, The (*WP*), incl. in 'The Three Strangers'
Subalterns, The (*PPP*)
Summer Schemes (*LLE*)
Sun on the Bookcase, The (*SC*), dated 1870 385
Sun on the Letter, The (*TL*)
Sunday Morning Tragedy, A (*TL*), dated January 1904 25, 47, 145, 428
Sundial on a Wet Day, The (*HS*)
Sun's Last Look on the Country Girl, The (*LLE*), dated December 1915 240, 367
Sunshade, The (*MV*) 212
Superseded, The (*PPP*)
Supplanter, The (*PPP*)
Surview (*LLE*) 29, 243
Suspense (*WW*)
Sweet Hussy, The (*SC*)

Tarrying Bridegroom, The (*WW*)
Telegram, The (*SC*)
Temporary the All, The (*WP*) 334
Ten Years Since (*HS*), dated November 1922
Tenant-for-Life, The (*PPP*)
Tess's Lament (*PPP*) 328, 331
That Kiss in the Dark (*WW*)
That Moment (*HS*)
Then and Now (*MV*), dated 1915 142, 286
There Seemed a Strangeness (*HS*)

They Are Great Trees (uncoll.)
They Would Not Come (*LLE*)
Thing Unplanned, The (*HS*)
Third Kissing-Gate, The (*WW*)
This Summer and Last (*HS*), dated '1913?' 195
Thought in Two Moods, A (*MV*)
Thoughts at Midnight (*WW*), carries note 'Part written 25 May 1906'
Thoughts from Sophocles (uncoll.) 474
Thoughts of Phena (*WP*), dated March 1890 173, 239, 281, 334, 403, 465, 466, 467
Three Tall Men, The (*WW*)
Throwing a Tree (*WW*) 472
Thunderstorm in Town, A (*SC*) 184, 385
Timing Her (*MV*) 292, 311
To a Bridegroom (uncoll.), dated '1866 (abridged)'
To a Lady Offended by a Book of the Writer's (*WP*)
To a Lady Playing and Singing in the Morning (*LLE*) 241
To a Motherless Child (*WP*)
To a Sea-Cliff (*HS*)
To a Tree in London (*WW*), dated '192-'
To a Well-Named Dwelling (*LLE*)
To an Actress (*TL*), dated 1867 427
To an Impersonator of Rosalind (*TL*), dated 21 April 1867 427
To an Unborn Pauper Child (*PPP*) 330, 332
To C.F.H. (*HS*)
To Carrey Clavel (*TL*)
To Flowers from Italy in Winter (*PPP*) 473
To Life (*PPP*)
To Lizbie Browne (*PPP*)
To Louisa in the Lane (*WW*) 240, 471
To Meet, or Otherwise (*SC*) 384
To My Father's Violin (*MV*), dated 1916 283, 338
To Outer Nature (*WP*) 397
To Shakespeare after Three Hundred Years (*MV*), dated 1916
To Sincerity (*TL*), dated February 1899
To the Moon (*MV*)
To-Be-Forgotten, The (*PPP*) 29, 321
Tolerance (*SC*)
Torn Letter, The (*SC*)
Tragedian to Tragedienne (*HS*)
Trampwoman's Tragedy, A (*TL*), dated April 1902 25, 428
Transformations (*MV*) 241, 285, 311
Tree, The (*PPP*)
Tree and the Lady, The (*MV*) 232
Tresses, The (*MV*)
Turnip-Hoer, The (*HS*)
Two Houses, The (*LLE*) 233
Two Lips (*HS*) 340
Two Men, The (*WP*), 1866
Two Rosalinds, The (*TL*)
Two Serenades (*LLE*)
Two Soldiers, The (*SC*)
Two Wives, The (*LLE*)
Two-Years' Idyll, A (*LLE*)

Unborn, The (*TL*)
Under High-Stoy Hill (*HS*)
Under the Waterfall (*SC*) 385
Unkept Good Fridays (*WW*), dated Good Friday, 1927 471
Unkindly May, An (*WW*) 470, 472
Unknowing (*WP*)
Unplanted Primrose, The (uncoll.), dated 1865–7
Unrealized (*TL*)
Upbraiding, An (*MV*) 284
Upper Birch Leaves, The (*MV*)

Vagg Hollow (*LLE*)
Vagrant's Song (*HS*)
Valenciennes (*WP*), dated '1878–1897' 280, 296, 466, 467
Vampirine Fair, The (*TL*)
Vatican, The: Sala delle Muse: *see* Rome
Victorian Rehearsal, A (uncoll.)
Voice, The (*SC*), dated December 1912 326, 337, 386
Voice of the Thorn, The (*TL*)
Voice of Things, The (*MV*) 41, 284, 286
Voices from Things Growing in a Churchyard (*LLE*) 91, 149–50, 241, 311, 339
V.R. 1819–1901 (*PPP*), dated 27 January 1901

Wagtail and Baby (*TL*) 37
Waiting Both (*HS*) 195, 197, 199
Walk, The (*SC*) 327, 337
Wanderer, The (*LLE*) 339
War Poems (*PPP*): sequence of eleven poems 328–9, 335–6
War-Wife of Catknoll, The (*WW*)
Wasted Illness, A (*PPP*)
Watcher's Regret, A (*HS*)
Watering-Place Lady Inventoried, A (*HS*)
We Are Getting to the End (*WW*) 374, 473
We Field-Women (*WW*) 472
We Sat at the Window (*MV*) 284
We Say We Shall Not Meet (*WW*)
Weary Walker, The (*HS*)
Weathers (*LLE*) 242, 311

Wedding Morning, The (*LLE*)
Week, A (*SC*)
Welcome Home (*LLE*)
Well-Beloved, The (*PPP*), written *c.*1897
Wessex Heights (*SC*) 147, 149, 185, 190, 226, 280, 385, 387
West-of-Wessex Girl, The (*LLE*), dated 'Begun...March 1913' 240
Wet August, A (*LLE*), dated 1920 241
Wet Night, A (*TL*)
Whaler's Wife, The (*WW*) 473
What Did It Mean? (*LLE*)
What's There to Tell? (*HS*), dated '190-' 198
When Dead (*HS*)
When I Set Out for Lyonnesse (*SC*) 71, 162, 211, 241, 284, 385
When Oats Were Reaped (*HS*), dated August 1913 195
When Warily We Shrink Away (uncoll.)
Where the Picnic Was (*SC*) 327, 385
Where They Lived (*MV*)
Where Three Roads Joined (*LLE*) 143
While Drawing in a Churchyard (*MV*) 16
Whipper-In, The (*LLE*) 242
Whispered at the Church-Opening (*WW*) 472
Whitewashed Wall, The (*LLE*)
Who's in the Next Room? (*MV*)
Why Be at Pains? (*MV*)
Why Did I Sketch (*MV*) 284, 286
Why Do I (*HS*) 199
Why She Moved House (*HS*)
Widow Betrothed, The (*PPP*)
Wife and Another, A (*TL*) 267
Wife Comes Back, A (*LLE*), dated 1867
Wife in London, A (*PPP*), dated December 1899 36, 329
Wife Waits, A (*TL*)
Wind Blew Words, The (*MV*)
Wind's Prophecy, The (*MV*) 33
Winsome Woman, A (*WW*)
Winter in Durnover Field (*PPP*) 33
Winter Night in Woodland (*HS*) 291, 370
Wish for Unconsciousness, A (*WW*) 472
Wistful Lady, The (*SC*)
Without Ceremony (*SC*) 327
Without, Not Within Her (*LLE*)
Wives in the Sere (*PPP*)
Woman Driving, A (*LLE*) 241
Woman I Met, The (*LLE*), dated 1918
Woman in the Rye, The (*SC*)
Woman Who Went East, The (*WW*)
Woman's Fancy, A (*LLE*)
Woman's Trust, A (*LLE*)
Wood Fire, The (*LLE*) 29, 370
Workbox, The (*SC*) 25
Wound, The (*MV*)

Xenophanes, the Monist of Colophon (*HS*), dated 1921

Year's Awakening, The (*SC*), dated February 1910 319
Yell'ham-Wood's Story (*TL*), dated 1902 427
Yellow-Hammer, The (uncoll.)
You on the Tower (*MV*)
You Were the Sort that Men Forget (*MV*)
Young Churchwarden, The (*MV*)
Young Glass-Stainer, The (*MV*), dated November 1893
Young Man's Epigram on Existence, A (*TL*), dated 1866 427
Young Man's Exhortation, A (*LLE*)
Your Last Drive (*SC*), dated December 1012 327
Youth Who Carried a Light, The (*MV*), dated 1915
Yuletide in a Younger World (*WW*)

Zermatt: To the Matterhorn (*PPP*)

APPENDIX B: CHARACTERS IN HARDY'S NOVELS

The following list indicates the novels in which Hardy's characters appear. Fuller information concerning the more important characters will be found in the entries for individual novels, especially in the section of each entry headed 'Plot'. A number of figures who are mentioned by name but play no part, or only a very insignificant part, in the action have not been included. The list has also been confined to human characters, though Hardy names a number of animals—for example, the Talbothays cows in *Tess of the d'Urbervilles* (Dumpling, Fancy, Lofty, Mist, Old Pretty, Tidy, Winker, and Young Pretty). One of the interests of a list such as the one that follows is its exemplification of the diversity of Hardy's practice in naming his characters, from the commonplace and realistic to the romantic, symbolic, and whimsical (see also NAMES).

Aldclyffe, Cytherea *DR*
Anny *JO*
Avice: *see* Caro

Baker, Farmer *DR*
Ball, Cain *FFMC*
Beaucock, Lawyer *W*
Bencomb, Marcia *WB*
Blowbody *MC*
Boldwood, William *FFMC*
Bollens, Adelaide: *see* Hinton
Bower o'Biss: *JO*
Bowman, Joseph *UGT*
Bradleigh, Cytherea: *see* Aldclyffe
Bridehead, Sue (Susanna Florence Mary) *JO*
Brooks, Mrs *TDU*
Brown, Abraham *DR*

Callcome, Nat *UGT*
Cannister, Martin *PBE*
Cantle, Christian *RN*
Cantle, Grandfer *RN*
Caro, Avice (the First) *WB*
Caro, Avice (the Second) *WB*
Caro, Avice (the Third) *WB*
Cartlett *JO*
Cawtree, Farmer *W*
Challow *JO*
Chant, Mercy *TDU*
Charl *MC*
Charley *RN*
Charmond, Felice *W*
Chickerel, Dan *HE*
Chickerel, Joey *HE*
Chickerel, Mr and Mrs *HE*
Chickerel, Picotee *HE*
Chickerel, Sol *HE*
Chimlen, Billy *UGT*
Clare, Angel *TDU*
Clare, Cuthbert, the Reverend *TDU*
Clare, Felix, the Reverend *TDU*
Clare, James, the Reverend *TDU*
Clare, Mrs *TDU*
Clark, Mark *FFMC*
Cleeve, Swithin St *TT*
Coggan, Jan *FFMC*
Coggan, Mrs *FFMC*
Coggan, Teddy *FFMC*
Constantine, Sir Blount *TT*
Constantine, Lady Viviette *TT*
Cornick, James *TM*
Creedle, Robert *W*
Crick, Christiana *TDU*
Crick, Richard ('Dairyman') *TDU*
Crickett, Richard ('Clerk') *DR*
Cripplestraw, Anthony *TM*
Crumpler, Mrs *UGT*
Crumpler, Simon *UGT*
Cunningham, Captain *TM*
Cuxsom, Mother *MC*

Damson, Suke *W*
Darch, Car ('Queen of Spades') *TDU*
Darch, Nancy ('Queen of Diamonds') *TDU*
Dare, Will(iam) *AL*
Day, Fancy *UGT*
Day, Geoffrey *UGT*
Day, Jane *UGT*
Day, John *DR*
de Stancy, Charlotte *AL*
de Stancy, Captain William *AL*
de Stancy, Sir William *AL*
Derriman, Benjamin ('Uncle Benjy') *TM*
Derriman, Festus *TM*

Dewy, Ann *UGT*
Dewy, Bessy *UGT*
Dewy, Charley *UGT*
Dewy, Dick *UGT*
Dewy, Jimmy *UGT*
Dewy, Reuben *UGT*
Dewy, Susan *UGT*
Dewy, William *UGT*
Dickson, Mr *DR*
Dollery, Mrs *W*
Dollop, Jack *TDU*
Doncastle, Mr and Mrs *HE*
Donn, Arabella *JO*
Dowden, Olly *RN*
Drew (later Vye), Captain *RN*
d'Urberville, Alec: *see* Stoke-d'Urberville
Durbeyfield, Abraham *TDU*
Durbeyfield, Hope *TDU*
Durbeyfield, Joan *TDU*
Durbeyfield, John (Jack) *TDU*
Durbeyfield, Liza-Lu (Eliza-Louisa) *TDU*
Durbeyfield, Modesty *TDU*
Durbeyfield, Tess (Teresa) *TDU*

Edlin, Mrs *JO*
Endorfield, Elizabeth *UGT*
Enoch (trapper) *UGT*
Everdene, Bathsheba *FFMC*
Everdene, James *FFMC*
Everdene, John *FFMC*

Fairway, Timothy *RN*
Fall, 'Conjuror' *MC*
Fawley, Drusilla *JO*
Fawley, Jude *JO*
Fitzpiers, Edred *W*
Flooks, Mr *DR*
Floy, Mr *DR*
Fontover, Miss *JO*
Fray, Henery *FFMC*
Fyander, Deborah *TDU*

Garland, Anne *TM*
Garland, Martha *TM*
Gillingham, George *JO*
Glanville, Louis *TT*
Goodman, Mrs *AL*
Gradfield, Mr *DR*
Graye, Ambrose *DR*
Graye, Cytherea *DR*
Graye, Owen *DR*
Grinham, Parson *UGT*
Groby, Farmer *TDU*
Grower, Benjamin *MC*

Hardy, Captain Thomas Masterman *TM*
Havill *AL*
Haylock (butcher) *UGT*
Henchard, Elizabeth-Jane *MC*
Henchard, Michael *MC*
Henchard, Susan *MC*
Hinton, Adelaide *DR*
Huett, Izz *TDU*
Humphrey *RN*
Huntway, Mr *DR*
Hurst, Mrs *FFMC*

James, Grandfather *UGT*
Jethway, Gertrude *PBE*
Joe (Joseph) *MC*
Johnson, Matilda *TM*
Jopp, Joshua *MC*
Julian, Christopher *HE*
Julian, Faith *HE*

Kail, Jonathan *TDU*
Kaytes, Grammer *UGT*
Kex, Farmer *UGT*
Knibbs, Beck *TDU*
Knight, Henry *PBE*

Ladywell, Eustace *HE*
Lark, Tabitha *TT*
Lawson, Sam *UGT*
Le Sueur, Lucetta (*see also* Templeman) *MC*
Leaf, Thomas *UGT*
Leat, Elizabeth *DR*
Ledlow, Farmer *UGT*
Lewell, Bill *TDU*
Lickpan, Robert *PBE*
Loveday, John *TM*
Loveday, Robert *TM*
Loveday, William ('Miller Loveday') *TM*
Luxellian, Lady Helen *PBE*
Luxellian, Kate *PBE*
Luxellian, Mary *PBE*
Luxellian, Spenser Hugo, Lord *PBE*

Mail, Michael *UGT*
Manston, Aeneas *DR*
Manston, Eunice *DR*
Marian (dairymaid) *TDU*
Maybold, Arthur, the Reverend *UGT*
Melbury, Grace *W*
Melbury, Mr *W*
Melbury, Mrs *W*
Melchester, Bishop of *TT*
Menlove (maid) *HE*

Miller, Soberness *FFMC*
Miller, Temperance *FFMC*
Mockridge, Nance *MC*
Money, Maryann *FFMC*
Moon, Matthew *FFMC*
Mountclere, Lord *HE*

Neigh, Alfred *HE*
Newson, Elizabeth-Jane *MC*
Newson, Richard *MC*
Noakes, Jacob *TM*
Nunsuch, Johnny *RN*
Nunsuch, Susan *RN*

Oak, Gabriel *FFMC*
Oliver, Grammer *W*
Onmey, Mercy *UGT*

Pearston: Pierston's name is spelt thus in serial version of *WB*
Penny, Mrs *UGT*
Penny, Robert *UGT*
Pennyways, Benjy *FFMC*
Percomb, Barber *W*
Petherwin, Ethelberta *HE*
Petherwin, Lady *HE*
Phillotson, Richard *JO*
Pierston, Jocelyn *WB*
Pine-Avon, Nichola *WB*
Poorgrass, Joseph *FFMC*
Power, Abner *AL*
Power, John *AL*
Power, Paula *AL*
Priddle, Retty *TDU*

Randle, Andrew *FFMC*
Raunham, Mr *DR*
Robin, Fanny *FFMC*
Rolliver, Mrs *TDU*

Sam *RN*
Samway, Sam *FFMC*
Seaway, Anne *DR*
Seedling, Amby *TDU*
Shiner, Frederic *UGT*
Smallbury, Jacob *FFMC*
Smallbury, Liddy *FFMC*
Smallbury, William *FFMC*
Smith, Jane (also called Maria) *PBE*
Smith, John *PBE*
Smith, Stephen *PBE*
Sniff, Vashti *UGT*
Somers, Alfred *WB*
South, John *W*
South, Marty *W*
Spinks, Elias *UGT*
Springrove, Edward *DR*
Stancy: *see* de Stancy
Stoke-d'Urberville, Alec *TDU*
Stoke-d'Urberville, Mrs *TDU*
Strickland, Captain *TM*
Stubb, Farmer *TM*
Swancourt, Christopher *PBE*
Swancourt, Elfride *PBE*

Tall, Laban *FFMC*
Tall, Susan *FFMC*
Tangs, Timothy (the older) *W*
Tangs, Timothy (the younger, who marries Suke Damson) *W*
Taylor, Tinker *JO*
Templeman: name adopted by Lucetta Le Sueur *MC*
Tetuphenay, T. *JO*
Thirdly, Parson *FFMC*
Time, Little Father *JO*
Torkingham, Mr *TT*
Traceley, Miss *JO*
Tringham, Parson *TDU*
Troutham, Farmer *JO*
Troy, Francis (Frank) *FFMC*
Troyton, Charlotte (later Charlotte Swancourt) *PBE*

Uncle Joe *JO*
Unity (later Unity Cannister) *PBE*
Upjohn, John *W*

Vilbert, 'Physician' *JO*
Viney, Dairyman *UGT*
Voss *UGT*
Vye, Captain: *see* Drew
Vye, Eustacia *RN*

Waywood, Ted *UGT*
Whittle, Abel *MC*
Wildeve, Damon *RN*
Wildway, John *UGT*
Winterborne, Giles *W*
Woodwell, the Reverend Mr *AL*
Worm, Barbara *PBE*
Worm, William *PBE*

Yeobright, Clym *RN*
Yeobright, Mrs *RN*
Yeobright, Thomasin *RN*

APPENDIX C: PLACE-NAMES IN HARDY'S WRITINGS

Topographical and touristic enthusiasm led Hardy's readers from an early stage to identify, sometimes excessively closely, the locations of his fiction and poetry with actual towns, villages, and landmarks. Hardy's reaction to this sincerest form of flattery could sometimes be ironic, and in the postscript added in 1912 to his preface to *The Woodlanders* he gently reproves, or at least discourages, such efforts: though he has often been asked where 'Little Hintock' is, he says, and has actually searched for it himself 'on a bicycle', he has failed to find it. The truth seems to be that, whereas there is a close correspondence between 'Wessex' and the world of the Ordnance Survey maps, Hardy wished to preserve his creative freedom; and though he often describes himself as a 'chronicler', he feels under no obligation to stick unswervingly to reality. He is, after all, a teller of tales, not the compiler of a guide-book. His readiness to take liberties with the observable world that is his starting-point is made explicit in the 1895 preface to *Two on a Tower*, where he writes: 'The scene of the action was suggested by two real spots in the part of the country specified, each of which has a column standing upon it. Certain surrounding peculiarities have been imported into the narrative from both sites, and from elsewhere.'

This is symbolized in his fictitious names, which often resemble real place-names but are slightly different from them: 'Abbots Cernel', mentioned in the opening chapter of *The Woodlanders*, may not be precisely the Dorset village of Cerne Abbas, but it clearly owes something to it. Even so, there is considerable variation in the closeness or otherwise of real to invented name: 'Emminster' is only a spoken consonant away from Beaminster, but a name like 'Alfredston' for Wantage (the Oxfordshire birthplace of King Alfred) is somewhat subtler.

For these reasons, the following list, in which the fictitious names precede the actual ones, gives not so much equivalents or aliases as approximations to the real places concerned. As Hardy warned, not all identifications can be made with complete confidence. Actual names used by Hardy, such as Bristol and Bath, are not listed here. Some locations cannot be identified with confidence, or at all, and may well be (in F. B. Pinion's phrase) 'composite or imaginary'. The map Hardy prepared for an edition of his works in 1895 includes both actual and fictitious names. For fuller information, see the works by Hermann Lea and Denys Kay-Robinson listed (under Topography) in the Bibliography. Useful information may also be found in the 'Dictionary of People and Places in Hardy's Works' included in F. B. Pinion's *A Hardy Companion* (1968).

Abbots Cernel: Cerne Abbas
Abbotsea: Abbotsbury
Aldbrickham: Reading
Alfredston: Wantage
Anglebury: Wareham

Blackmoor Vale: Blackmore Vale
Budmouth: Weymouth

Camelton: Camelford
Casterbridge: Dorchester
Castle Boterel: Boscastle
Castle Royal: Windsor
Chaldon: East Chaldon or Chaldon Herring
Chalk-Newton: Maiden Newton
Charmley: Charminster
Chase, The: Cranborne Chase
Chaseborough: Cranborne
Chene: Canford Magna
Christminster: Oxford
Cockdean: Cogdean
Corvsgate: Corfe
Cresscombe: Letcombe Bassett

Downstable: Barnstaple
Dundagel: Tintagel
Durnover: Fordington (Dorset)

East Egdon: Affpuddle
East Endelstow: Lesnewth (Cornwall)
East Quarriers: Easton (Portland)
Emminster: Beaminster

Endelstow: *see* East Endelstow, West Endelstow
Estminster: Yetminster
Evershead: Evershot
Exonbury: Exeter

Fensworth: Letcombe Regis
Flintcomb-Ash: ?Plush

Gaymead: Theale (Berkshire)
Great Forest: New Forest
Great Plain: Salisbury Plain
Greenhill: Woodbury Hill (near Bere Regis)

Haggardon: Eggardon Hill (near Bridport)
Havenpool: Poole
Hocbridge: unidentified (Banbury has been suggested)
Holmstoke: East Stoke (Dorset)

Idmouth: Sidmouth
Isle of Slingers: Portland

Kennetbridge: Newbury
Kingsbere: Bere Regis
Kingscreech: Kingston (Dorset)
Knollingwood: Wimborne St Giles
Knollsea: Swanage

Leddenton: Gillingham (Dorset)
Lewgate: Higher Bockhampton
Little Hintock: uncertain (?Minterne Magna or Melbury Osmond)
Longpuddle: Piddlehinton and Piddletrenthide
Lornton: Horton (Dorset)
Lower Mellstock: Lower Bockhampton
Lulwind Cove: Lulworth Cove
Lumsdon: Cumnor
Lyonesse [*sic*], Isles of: Scilly Isles
Lyonnesse: north Cornish coast, especially the area round Tintagel

Mai Dun: Maiden Castle
Markton: Dunster
Marlbury: Marlborough
Marlott: Marnhull
Marshwood: Middlemarsh
Marygreen: Fawley (Berkshire)
Melchester: Salisbury
Mellstock: Stinsford
Middleton Abbey: Milton Abbey
Mid-Wessex: Wiltshire
Millpond St Jude's: Milborne St Andrew
Monksbury: ?Abbotsbury (cf. 'Abbotsea')
Moreford: Moreton (Dorset)

Nether-Moynton: Owermoigne
Newland Buckton: Buckland Newton
North Wessex: Berkshire and Oxfordshire
Nuttlebury: Hazelbury Bryan

Oakbury Fitzpiers: Okeford Fitzpaine
Oozewood: Ringwood
Outer Wessex: Somerset
Overcombe: ?Sutton Poyntz
Oxwell: Poxwell

Pen-Zephyr: Penzance
Port-Bredy: Bridport

Quartershot: Aldershot

Ringsworth: Ringstead Bay

St Launce's: Launceston
Sandbourne: Bournemouth
Shaldon: Chaldon (Dorset)
Shaston: Shaftesbury
Sherton Abbas: Sherborne
Shottsford: Blandford Forum
Silverthorn: Silverton
Solentsea: Southsea
South Wessex: Dorset
Stickleford: Tincleton
Stoke-Barehills: Basingstoke
Stourcastle: Sturminster Newton
Stratleigh: Bude

Targan Bay: Pentargon Bay (Cornwall)
Tivworthy: Tiverton
Tolchurch: Tolpuddle
Toneborough: Taunton
Trantridge: Pentridge or Tarrant Hinton
Troy-Town: Troy Town
Trufal: Truro

Upper Wessex: Hampshire

Warborne: Wimborne Minster
Warm'll: Warmwell
Weatherbury: Puddletown
Wellbridge: Wool
West Endelstow: St Juliot
Weydon-Priors: Weyhill (Hampshire)
Wintoncester: Winchester

Yalbury: ?Yellowham (Dorset)

APPENDIX D: GLOSSARY OF DIALECT WORDS AND EXPRESSIONS

The following list includes not only terms that can properly be described as dialect but a number of colloquialisms, proverbial expressions, and slang terms, as well as non-standard spellings (representing regional or uneducated pronunciations) that might puzzle the reader.

a' all
'a I, he, she, it
afore before
afterclap setback
anigh, anighst near, almost
arrant errand
a-scram withered
athwart, ath'art across
avore before

back-brand log placed at the back of a fire
backy tobacco
ba'dy bawdy, wicked
bagnet bayonet
bain't is not, are not
ballet ballad, song
barton farmyard
bee bitch (euphemism)
beest are
benefit benefice
bide stay, remain
blackpot black pudding (sausage made from pig's blood)
blade young fellow
blooth bloom
bode remained, dwelt
bowse drink heavily
bruckle rough, unreliable
bruckle het (hit) mistake, failure
by-now a short time ago

cark worry, cause anxiety
carrel carol
'ch I
chainey china
chammer, chimmer chamber, room
chap o' wax promising young fellow
chaps cheeks
chaw chew, the action of chewing
chaw high be genteel, affect superior manners
chiel child
chimbley, chimley chimney
chimmer *see* chammer
chiney china
chit young person (term of disparagement)
chok' it all! mild oath (literally 'choke it all')
clammy cold and damp
clane clean, completely
clim climb
clink off disappear, go away
clitch crook of the arm or leg
coling embracing
coney rabbit
cow-barton cow-yard
crater creature
crowner coroner
culpet culprit
cussed, cust cursed

dand dandy
dang damn
danged damned
daze damn
dee damned
deedy earnest, serious
deppity deputy
dew-bit light meal taken early in the morning, before breakfast
diment diamond
doggery tricks, carryings-on
dree (1) three; (2) suffering
drong alley or narrow path between walls or hedges
droudge drudge, labour
drough through
drouth drought
dumbledores bumble-bees
dun-fly gadfly

'e, 'ee you
een eyes
ees yes
em them
emmet ant
empt empty
en him, it

er he
eweleaze meadow grazed by sheep

fay faith
fairy luck
fess proud, strong
fetch recover; an indrawn breath
feymel female
fidgets trifling matters
fleed fled, flew
fretted my gizzard green worried myself sick
full-buff face to face
furmity wheat boiled in spiced milk

gaberlunzie wandering beggar (Scots)
gaffer old man, master or employer
gallicrow scarecrow
gallied worried
gammer old woman, grandmother
gam'ster gambler
gawk-hammer fool, foolish (literally one 'gawking' or gaping)
gi'd, gi'ed gave, given
gie, gi'e give
glutch swallow, gulp
glutch-pipe gullet
goodman husband, householder
good-now I reckon, you may be sure
grandfer grandfather
gwine going

ha', hae have
hag-rid having had nightmares or a bad night's sleep
harlican urchin
harnet hornet
harum-skarum wild, reckless
hawk clear the throat
heft weight
hent hint
het (1) hot, heat; (2) swallow (verb)
hey has, have
ho long for, grieve
hob-and-nob talk intimately
hobble troublesome matter
holler (1) shout; (2) hollow
home-along in the direction of home
honeycombed emptied, robbed (like a honeycomb from which the honey has been eaten)
hontish proud, haughty
house-ridding moving house
husbird bastard

I wis truly, to be sure
idd is it . . . ?
idden, idn' is not
inching and pinching moving by slow degrees
inquiration inquiry

jackanapes foolish or pretentious person
jest just
jim-cracks machinery, apparatus
jine join
jineral general
jints joints
jown, be jowned mild oath (literally 'drown')
jumped-up conceited
jumps stays (woman's undergarment)
juvinals juveniles, young persons

keacorn windpipe, throat
ken know, knowledge
kex dried hollow stalk of cow-parsley
kip keep
knap hillock
knowed knew

lamiger, lammiger cripple
lammicken, lammocken awkward, clumsy, ungainly
lanch, lanchet, lynchet barren area left uncultivated in arable land
larry fuss, commotion, state of confusion
layers-out those who prepare a corpse for burial
leery tired and hungry
lew, lewth shelter
limberish weak, frail
linhay shed or other learn-to building
lirruping lazy, slovenly
lumpering walking heavily
lynchet *see* lanch
lynes loins

mampus crowd
mandy cheeky
mane mean
man-jack every one
maphrotight hermaphrodite
market-nitch full belly of liquor consumed on market-day
martel mortal, person
maul down take down
mawn-basket round wicker basket with two handles
med may, might

mee my
mid (1) with; (2) might (verb)
miff quarrel
milcher milking cow
mind recall, remember
mistchy mischief
mizzel, mizzle hurry off
mollyish soft, weak
mommet grotesque figure
mortal extremely
mossel morsel
mother-law stepmother
mumbudgeting creeping up quietly
mun must

'n him, it
nater nature
nation damnation
natomy body, skeleton
nesh delicate in health, weakly
night-rail nightdress
nipperkin small measure of alcohol
nitch bundle, load (*see also* market-nitch)
no'thern stupid (literally 'northern')
nunch nuncheon (snack taken between meals)
nunnywatch predicament

'od ('Od) God
'oman, 'ooman woman
on end, on-end ready
oneyer uncommon one, unusual person
onriddle unriddle, explain
orchet orchard
or'nary mediocre, inferior
o't of it
overlook bewitch, cast the evil eye on

pa'son parson
passiont passion
peckle pickle
picter picture
pinner pinafore, apron with bib
pins legs
pixy-led led astray
pizzle penis
plannard planet
plim swell
'pon upon
projick project; prodigy
pudden pudding
put-to troubled

quare queer
quat squat, stoop

raft rouse, upset, trouble
rale real
randy party, celebration
rantipole noisy, unruly
ratch reach
rathe early, soon
ray dress
rithe wildly
rozum quaint saying or person; bow (a violin) energetically

sappy simpleton
sarpless surplice
sartin certain
saur sir
says sayings
scallops stringy part of animal fat
scantling morsel
scrags scraps
scram small, trivial; puny, emaciated
scrammed, shrammed numbed
scrimp economize, be stingy
scrimped up screwed up
scroff, shroff scraps of wood or other material; rubbish
seed saw, seen
shadder shadow
shaddery shadowy, uncertain
shail shuffle, slouch
shet shut
shetters shutters
shoon shoes
shotten worthless
shrammed *see* scrammed
shroff *see* scroff
sich such
sight, a a great many
siller silver
skellington, skellinton, skillenton skeleton
skitty-boots heavy nailed boots
skiver fasten with a skewer
slack impudence
slat pounding, splintering
slent broken
slim-faced sly-faced
slittering restless
slummocky slovenly
smack-and-coddle kiss and cuddle
small weak and inferior beer
snacks shares; 'go snacks with' also means 'marry'

snap snack, light meal
snapper short period of bad weather
sniche stingy, greedy
sniff and snaff a friendly relationship
snipe mean person
snoach snore
snock knock
snoff snuff or charred wick of candle
sock sigh deeply
sodger soldier
sommit something
so's friends (rustic form of address; literally 'souls')
spak speak
sparrowgrass asparagus
sperrit spirit
spet spit
sprawl energy, activity
squail throw
squat strike, crush
squench quench
stap step
starving freezing cold
stitching getting married
stooded stationary
stoor disturbance (variant of 'stir')
stound astound
strappen strapping, well-built
strawmote single straw
strent slit or tear in a garment
strook struck, astonished
stud study, quandary (cf. 'studding', day-dreaming)
stunpoll stupid person (literally 'stonehead')
sumple supple
sware swore
swipes beer of poor quality

taters, taties potatoes
tay tea
teave toil, struggle
teuny weak, undersized
thik this
thirtingill perverse, wrong-headed
thirtover obstinate, bad-tempered
thrid thread
tidden, 'tidn it is not
tine shut
tisty-tosty round and plump, like the balls of cowslips made for a children's game
toil set a trap
tole draw, entice, persuade
topper topple, bring down in the world; a blow on the head
top-sawyer superior
totties the feet of small children
touse battering
tout hill
to-year this year
trangleys toys, odds and ends
trate treat
traypse walk (with the implication of weariness or aimlessness)
tuens tunes
turmit-head fool (literally 'turnip-head')
twanking grumbling, miserable

un'rayed undressed ('unarrayed')
unrind undress
up-sides equal to, good enough for

vallie value
varden farthing (coin of the lowest value)
varmint, varmit vermin; derogatory term for a person
'vation salvation
vell trace, sign
vinger finger
vitty fitting
vlankers sparks
vlee flee
vlock flock
volk folk
voot foot

wadden, wadn' was not
walm rise
wamble walk unsteadily
wanzing wasting away
warn warrant
werrit worry
whicker snigger
wi' with
widder widow
winder window
woak oak
wold, wuld old
woll, wool will
wo'th worth
wownd wound
wownded wounded, upset
wriggles sand-eels
wropper wrapper, overall
wuld *see* wold
wynd-pipes windpipes

yaller yellow
yer your

zeed, zid saw, seen
zell sell
zid *see* zeed
zilver silver
zixpence sixpence (small silver coin)
zot sat
zull plough
zummat something
zung sang
zwail sway

APPENDIX E: HARDY IN THE CINEMA AND ON RADIO AND TELEVISION

(For stage adaptations of Hardy's work, see DRAMATIZATIONS and OPERA.)

1913 An American adaptation of *Tess of the d'Urbervilles* marked the beginning of Hardy's appropriation by the silent cinema. The heroine was played by Minnie Maddern Fiske, who had played the same role in a New York stage adaptation in 1897. Hardy attended the British première on 21 October.

1916 *Far from the Madding Crowd* (GB), directed by Larry Trimble.

1921 *The Mayor of Casterbridge* (GB). In July Hardy witnessed scenes for this film being shot on location in Dorchester and at Maiden Castle.

1923 BBC broadcast of two short items performed by the Hardy Players from the local wireless station at Bournemouth, marking Hardy's entry into the medium of radio.

1924 Another American film version of *Tess*, directed by Marshall Neilan, with Blanche Sweet as the heroine. It is described by Desmond Hawkins as 'grotesque' and as showing 'a total disregard of place and period' (*Thomas Hardy: Novelist and Poet*, 231).

1926 The Hardy Players broadcast again from Bournemouth (see 1923 above), this time performing 'The Three Wayfarers', a dramatization of the short story 'The Three Strangers'.

1928 The BBC broadcasts an adaptation of *The Mayor of Casterbridge.*

1929 Film version of *Under the Greenwood Tree* (GB), directed by Harry Lachman.

1933 BBC radio version of *The Dynasts*, Part I (the first of six separate broadcasts devoted to *The Dynasts* between 1933 and 1967).

1937 BBC radio version of *Tess.*

1940 BBC radio version of *The Dynasts.*

1941 BBC radio version of 'A Tragedy of Two Ambitions'.

1942 BBC radio version of *Far from the Madding Crowd.*

1943 BBC radio versions of *Under the Greenwood Tree* and *The Dynasts.*

1945 BBC radio version of 'The Three Strangers'.

1948 BBC radio version of *Tess of the d'Urbervilles.*

1949 BBC radio versions of 'The Withered Arm', *Far from the Madding Crowd*, and *Under the Greenwood Tree.*

1951 BBC radio versions of *The Mayor of Casterbridge* and *The Dynasts.*

1952 BBC TV version of *Tess*, marking Hardy's entry into the television medium.

1953 Film version (titled *The Secret Cave*) of *Our Exploits at West Poley*, directed by John Durst (GB).

1955 BBC radio version of *The Woodlanders.*

1956 BBC radio version of *The Famous Tragedy of the Queen of Cornwall.*

1960 ITV television version of *Tess*. BBC radio versions of *The Dynasts* and *The Return of the Native.*

1967 Film version of *Far from the Madding Crowd*, directed by John Schlesinger. Film version (India) of *Tess of the d'Urbervilles* as *Dulhanek raat ki* (*Bride for a Single Night*), directed by Dharm Dev Kashyap. BBC radio version of *The Dynasts.*

1968 BBC radio version of *The Mayor of Casterbridge.*

1969 BBC radio versions of 'Fellow-Townsmen' and *Under the Greenwood Tree.* BBC TV version of 'The Distracted Preacher'.

1970 BBC TV version of *The Woodlanders.* BBC radio version of 'The Withered Arm' (revival of 1949 production).

1971 BBC radio version of *Tess of the d'Urbervilles.* BBC TV version of *Juda the Obscure.*

1973 BBC TV versions of six short stories ('The Withered Arm', 'Fellow-Townsmen', 'A Tragedy of Two Ambitions', 'An Imaginative Woman', 'The Melancholy Hussar', 'Barbara of the House of Grebe'), under the title 'Wessex Tales'.

1974 BBC radio version of *Far from the Madding Crowd.*

1975 BBC World Service radio version of 'On the Western Circuit', based on stage version (titled *The Day after the Fair*) produced in London in 1972 (see also 1986). BBC radio version of *Two on a Tower.*

1976 BBC radio version of *The Return of the Native.*

1977 BBC radio version of *The Trumpet-Major.*

1978 BBC radio version of *The Woodlanders.* BBC TV version of *The Mayor of Casterbridge.*

1979 Film version (*Tess*) of *Tess of the d'Urbervilles,* directed by Roman Polanski (GB/France).

1982 BBC radio version of *A Pair of Blue Eyes.*

1985 Film version of *Our Exploits at West Poley* (GB), directed by Diarmuid Lawrence, for Children's Film and Television Foundation.

1986 BBC radio version of *Jude the Obscure.* BBC TV version of 'On the Western Circuit' (as *The Day after the Fair*).

1988 BBC radio (Arabic Service) version of *The Mayor of Casterbridge* (in Arabic).

1995 Channel 4 TV version of *The Woodlanders.*

1996 Film version (*Jude*) of *Jude the Obscure* (GB), directed by Michael Winterbottom.

Radio and TV adaptations in recent years have been too numerous to list here. Further information on many of the above will be found in Appendix 2 of Desmond Hawkins's *Thomas Hardy: Novelist and Poet* (1988). For other references, see CINEMA.

BIBLIOGRAPHY

This select bibliography of writings by and about Hardy is arranged as follows:

A. Hardy's published writings
B. Bibliographies
C. Reference works
D. Textual studies
E. Biographies
F. Criticism: general
G. Criticism: specific texts
H. Criticism: special aspects

Inevitably, this bibliography includes only a small selection of the vast amount of secondary material that has been published, especially during the past 30 years. An attempt has been made to list the most significant and representative works that have appeared in volume form since 1894, together with a selection of articles dealing with specific texts and specialized aspects. Compilations of material that had previously appeared in print have not been included. Numerous other references are given at the end of entries in the body of this *Companion*, and discussion of many of the secondary works listed will be found in the entry on CRITICAL APPROACHES. For fuller information, the bibliographies listed in Section B may be consulted.

A. Hardy's published writings

Collected editions

The Wessex Novels, 16 vols. (1895–6).

The Wessex Edition, 24 vols. (1912–31). [The first 20 volumes appeared in 1912–13, and for the most part embody Hardy's final revisions of his novels.]

Collected Poems (1919). [Subsequent editions include later collections of verse; see also under 'Poems' below.]

The Mellstock Edition, 37 vols. (1919–20).

The Short Stories of Thomas Hardy (1928).

Novels

(Dates refer to first volume-publication; for details of serialization, see the entries on individual novels in the body of this work.)

Desperate Remedies (1871).

Under the Greenwood Tree (1872).

A Pair of Blue Eyes (1873).

Far from the Madding Crowd (1874).

The Hand of Ethelberta (1876).

The Return of the Native (1878).

The Trumpet-Major (1880).

A Laodicean (1881).

Two on a Tower (1882).

The Mayor of Casterbridge (1886).

The Woodlanders (1887).

Tess of the d'Urbervilles (1891).

Jude the Obscure (1895).

The Well-Beloved (1897).

Short stories

(For details of the contents of the first four volumes listed below, and of the original magazine publication of individual stories, see under the appropriate titles in the body of this work.)

Wessex Tales (1888).

A Group of Noble Dames (1891).

Life's Little Ironies (1894).

A Changed Man (1913).

Pamela Dalziel (ed.), *Thomas Hardy: The Excluded and Collaborative Stories* (1992).

Poems

(For details of the contents of the various volumes, see under the appropriate title in the body of this work.)

Wessex Poems (1898).

Poems of the Past and the Present (1901).

Time's Laughingstocks (1909).

Satires of Circumstance (1914).

Moments of Vision (1917).

Late Lyrics and Earlier (1922).

Human Shows (1925).
Winter Words (1928).
Of the numerous collected editions of Hardy's poems, the most convenient and widely useful is *The Complete Poems of Thomas Hardy*, ed. James Gibson (1976), which includes a section of 'Previously Uncollected Poems and Fragments'. For textual information, see James Gibson's *The Variorum Edition of the Complete Poems of Thomas Hardy* (1979), and Samuel Hynes's edition of *The Complete Poetical Works of Thomas Hardy*, 5 vols. (1982–95).

Drama

The Dynasts (originally published in three parts in 1904, 1906, 1908).
The Famous Tragedy of the Queen of Cornwall (1923).
The above are included in Samuel Hynes's edition of *The Complete Poetical Works of Thomas Hardy* (see above).

Miscellaneous prose

Thomas Hardy's Personal Writings, ed. Harold Orel (1966). (Includes prefaces, essays, etc.)

Letters, notebooks, autobiography

The Collected Letters of Thomas Hardy, ed. Richard Little Purdy and Michael Millgate, 7 vols. (1978–88).
One Rare Fair Woman: Thomas Hardy's Letters to Florence Henniker 1893–1922, ed. Evelyn Hardy and F. B. Pinion (1972).
Thomas Hardy, *Selected Letters*, ed. Michael Millgate (1990).
The Architectural Notebook of Thomas Hardy, ed. C. J. P. Beatty (1966).
The Personal Notebooks of Thomas Hardy, ed. Richard H. Taylor (1979).
The Literary Notebooks of Thomas Hardy, ed. Lennart Björk, 2 vols. (1985).
Thomas Hardy's 'Studies, Specimens &c.' Notebook, ed. Pamela Dalziel and Michael Millgate (1994).
Florence Emily Hardy, *The Life of Thomas Hardy 1840–1928* (1962) (originally published in two volumes: *The Early Life of Thomas Hardy* (1928) and *The Later Years of Thomas Hardy* (1930)). (Despite the attribution to Hardy's widow, this is very largely an autobiography.)
Thomas Hardy, *The Life and Work of Thomas Hardy*, ed. Michael Millgate (1984).

B. Bibliographies

W. Eugene Davis and Helmut Gerber, *Thomas Hardy: An Annotated Bibliography of Writings About Him, II, 1970–1978, and Supplement for 1871–1969* (1983).
Ronald P. Draper and Martin S. Ray, *An Annotated Critical Bibliography of Thomas Hardy* (1989).
George S. Fayen, Jr., 'Thomas Hardy', in Lionel Stevenson (ed.), *Victorian Fiction: A Guide to Research* (1964).
—— Hardy entry in *The New Cambridge Bibliography of English Literature*, 3 (1800–1900), ed. George Watson (1969).
Helmut E. Gerber and W. Eugene Davis, *Thomas Hardy: An Annotated Bibliography of Writings About Him* (1973) (covers the period 1871–1969).
Michael Millgate, 'Thomas Hardy', in George H. Ford (ed.), *Victorian Fiction: A Second Guide to Research* (1978).
Richard Little Purdy, *Thomas Hardy: A Bibliographical Study* (1954; rev. edn., 1968).
Lionel Stevenson, 'Thomas Hardy', in F. E. Faverty (ed.), *The Victorian Poets: A Guide to Research* (1956; rev. edn., 1968).
Richard H. Taylor, 'Thomas Hardy: A Reader's Guide', in Norman Page (ed.), *Thomas Hardy: The Writer and His Background* (1980).

C. Reference works

J. O. Bailey, *The Poetry of Thomas Hardy: A Handbook and Commentary* (1970).
Timothy Hands, *A Hardy Chronology* (1992).
Alan Hurst, *Thomas Hardy: An Illustrated Dictionary* (1980).
Glenda Leeming, *Who's Who in Thomas Hardy* (1975).
F. B. Pinion, *A Hardy Companion* (1968).
—— *A Commentary on the Poems of Thomas Hardy* (1976).
—— *A Thomas Hardy Dictionary* (1989).
F. O. Saxelby, *A Thomas Hardy Dictionary* (1911).

D. Textual studies

Joseph Warren Beach, 'Bowdlerized Versions of Hardy', *PMLA* 37 (1921).

Mary Ellen Chase, *Thomas Hardy from Serial to Novel* (1927).
Simon Gatrell, *Hardy the Creator: A Textual Biography* (1988).
J. T. Laird, *The Shaping of 'Tess of the d'Urbervilles'* (1975).
John Paterson, *The Making of 'The Return of the Native'* (1960).
Martin Ray, *Thomas Hardy: A Textual Study of the Short Stories* (1997).
Barbara Rosenbaum, *Index of English Literary Manuscripts, Volume 4, 1800–1900: Part 2, Hardy–Lamb* (1990).
Robert C. Schweik, 'Current Problems in Textual Scholarship on the Works of Thomas Hardy', *English Literature in Transition*, 14 (1971).
—— and M. Piret, 'Editing Hardy', *Browning Institute Studies*, 9 (1981).

E. Biographies (including memoirs, interviews, letters, and diaries)

William Archer, *Real Conversations* (1904).
Edmund Blunden, *Thomas Hardy* (1942).
Ernest Brennecke, *The Life of Thomas Hardy* (1925).
Vere H. Collins, *Talks with Thomas Hardy at Max Gate 1920–1922* (1928).
J. Stevens Cox (ed.), *Thomas Hardy: Materials for a Study of His Life, Times and Works*, Vols. I (1968) and II (1971) (originally published as a series of monographs).
Lois Deacon and Terry Coleman, *Providence and Mr Hardy* (1966).
Jo Draper, *Thomas Hardy: A Life in Pictures* (1989).
James Gibson, *Thomas Hardy: A Literary Life* (1996).
—— (ed.), Thomas Hardy: *Interviews and Recollections* (1999).
Robert Gittings, *Young Thomas Hardy* (1975).
—— *The Older Hardy* (1978).
—— and Jo Manton, *The Second Mrs Hardy* (1979).
F. E. Halliday, *Thomas Hardy: His Life and Work* (1972).
Emma Lavinia Hardy, *Diaries*, ed. Richard H. Taylor (1985).
—— *Some Recollections*, ed. Evelyn Hardy and Robert Gittings (1961; repr. with corrections, 1979).
Evelyn Hardy, *Thomas Hardy: A Critical Biography* (1954).
Florence Emily Hardy, *The Early Life of Thomas Hardy, 1840–1891* (1928).
—— *The Later Years of Thomas Hardy, 1892–1928* (1930).
—— *The Life of Thomas Hardy, 1840–1928* (1962) (single-volume edition of the preceding two items, which largely constitute Hardy's autobiography; see also second item under Millgate below).
Denys Kay-Robinson, *The First Mrs Thomas Hardy* (1979).
Michael Millgate, *Thomas Hardy: A Biography* (1982).
—— (ed.), *The Life and Work of Thomas Hardy by Thomas Hardy* (1984).
—— (ed.), *Letters of Emma and Florence Hardy* (1996).
Harold Orel, *The Final Years of Thomas Hardy* (1976).
—— *The Unknown Thomas Hardy* (1987).
Timothy O'Sullivan, *Thomas Hardy: An Illustrated Biography* (1975).
Kenneth Phelps, *The Wormwood Cup: Thomas Hardy in Cornwall* (1975).
F. B. Pinion, *Thomas Hardy: His Life and Friends* (1992).
Martin Seymour-Smith, *Hardy* (1994).
J. I. M. Stewart, *Thomas Hardy: A Critical Biography* (1971).
Carl J. Weber, *Hardy of Wessex: His Life and Literary Career* (1940; rev. edn., 1965).
—— *Hardy and the Lady from Madison Square* (1954).

F. Criticism: general

Lascelles Abercrombie, *Thomas Hardy: A Critical Study* (1912).
John Bayley, *An Essay on Hardy* (1978).
Joseph Warren Beach, *The Technique of Thomas Hardy* (1922).
Claudius J. P. Beatty, *Thomas Hardy: Conservation Architect. His Work for the Society for the Protection of Ancient Buildings* (1995).
Sheila Berger, *Thomas Hardy and Visual Structures* (1990).
Lina Wright Berle, *George Eliot and Thomas Hardy: A Contrast* (1969).
Lennart A. Björk, *Psychological Vision and Social Criticism in the Novels of Thomas Hardy* (1987).

Edmund Blunden, *Thomas Hardy* (1942).
Penny Boumelha, *Thomas Hardy and Women: Sexual Ideology and Narrative Form* (1982).
Ernest Brennecke, Jr., *Thomas Hardy's Universe: A Study of a Poet's Mind* (1924).
Jean Brooks, *Thomas Hardy: The Poetic Structure* (1971).
Douglas Brown, *Thomas Hardy* (1954).
Joanna Cullen Brown, *A Journey into Thomas Hardy's Poetry* (1990).
—— *Figures in a Wessex Landscape* (1987).
—— *Let Me Enjoy the Earth: Thomas Hardy and Nature* (1990).
William E. Buckler, *The Poetry of Thomas Hardy: A Study in Art and Ideas* (1983).
J. B. Bullen, *The Expressive Eye: Fiction and Perception in the Work of Thomas Hardy* (1986).
Lance St John Butler, *Thomas Hardy* (1976).
—— (ed.), *Thomas Hardy after Fifty Years* (1977).
—— (ed.), *Alternative Hardy* (1989).
Richard C. Carpenter, *Thomas Hardy* (1964).
Peter Casagrande, *Unity in Hardy's Novels: 'Repetitive Symmetries'* (1982).
—— *Hardy's Influence on the Modern Novel* (1987).
Lord David Cecil, *Hardy the Novelist* (1943).
Samuel C. Chew, *Thomas Hardy: Poet and Novelist* (1921; rev. edn., 1928).
Harold Child, *Thomas Hardy* (1916).
Patricia Clements and Juliet Grindle (eds.), *The Poetry of Thomas Hardy* (1980).
R. G. Cox (ed.), *Thomas Hardy: The Critical Heritage* (1970).
H. M. Daleski, *Thomas Hardy and the Paradoxes of Love* (1997).
Jagdish Chandra Dave, *The Human Predicament in Hardy's Novels* (1985).
Donald Davie, *Thomas Hardy and British Poetry* (1972).
—— (ed.), *Agenda: Thomas Hardy Special Issue* (1972).
Margaret Drabble (ed.), *The Genius of Thomas Hardy* (1976).
H. C. Duffi;n, *Thomas Hardy: A Study of the Wessex Novels* (1916).
Terry Eagleton, 'Thomas Hardy: Nature as Language', *Critical Quarterly*, 13 (1971).
Roger Ebbatson, *Hardy: The Margin of the Unexpressed* (1993).
Andrew Enstice, *Landscapes of the Mind* (1979).
Jo Fisher, *The Hidden Hardy* (1992).
Marjorie Garson, *Hardy's Fables of Integrity: Woman, Body, Text* (1991).
Simon Gatrell, *Thomas Hardy and the Proper Study of Mankind* (1993).
Frank R. Giordano, Jr., *'I'd Have My Life Unbe': Thomas Hardy's Self-Destructive Characters* (1984).
John Goode, *Thomas Hardy: The Offensive Truth* (1988).
Ian Gregor, *The Great Web: The Form of Hardy's Major Fiction* (1974).
H. B. Grimsditch, *Character and Environment in the Works of Thomas Hardy* (1925).
Joan Grundy, *Hardy and the Sister Arts* (1979).
Albert J. Guerard, *Thomas Hardy: The Novels and Stories* (1949; rev. edn., 1964).
Timothy Hands, *Thomas Hardy* (1995).
Evelyn Hardy, *The Countryman's Ear and Other Essays on Thomas Hardy* (1982).
Noorul Hasan, *Thomas Hardy: The Sociological Imagination* (1982).
Desmond Hawkins, *Hardy the Novelist* (1950).
—— *Hardy: Novelist and Poet* (1976; rev. edn., 1988).
E. C. Hickson, *The Versification of Thomas Hardy* (1931).
Margaret R. Higonnet (ed.), *The Sense of Sex: Feminist Perspectives on Hardy* (1993).
John Holloway, *The Victorian Sage* (1953).
Bert G. Hornback, *The Metaphor of Chance: Vision and Technique in the Works of Thomas Hardy* (1971).
Irving Howe, *Thomas Hardy* (1967).
Virginia R. Hyman, *Ethical Perspective in the Novels of Thomas Hardy* (1975).
Samuel Hynes, *The Pattern of Hardy's Poetry* (1961).
Patricia Ingham, *Thomas Hardy* (1989).
—— (ed.), *Thomas Hardy: Feminist Readings* (1989).
Arlene M. Jackson, *Illustration and the Novels of Thomas Hardy* (1981).
Pamela L. Jekel, *Thomas Hardy's Heroines: A Chorus of Priorities* (1986).
Bruce Johnson, *True Correspondence: A Phenomenology of Thomas Hardy's Novels* (1983).
Lionel Johnson, *The Art of Thomas Hardy* (1894; rev. edn., 1923).
Trevor Johnson, *Thomas Hardy* (1968).

—— *A Critical Introduction to the Poems of Thomas Hardy* (1991).

Arnold Kettle, *Hardy the Novelist* (1967).

Jeannette King, *Tragedy in the Victorian Novel: Theory and Practice in the Novels of George Eliot, Thomas Hardy and Henry James* (1978).

Dale Kramer, *Thomas Hardy: The Forms of Tragedy* (1975).

—— (ed.), *Critical Approaches to the Fiction of Thomas Hardy* (1979).

Robert Langbaum, *Thomas Hardy in Our Time* (1995).

D. H. Lawrence, 'A Study of Thomas Hardy', *Phoenix* (1936).

Laurence Lerner and John Holmstrom, *Thomas Hardy and his Readers* (1968).

Peter Levi, *John Clare and Thomas Hardy* (1975).

Charles Lock, *Thomas Hardy* (1992).

John Lucas, *The Literature of Change: Studies in the Nineteenth-Century Provincial Novel* (1977).

Arthur McDowall, *Thomas Hardy: A Critical Study* (1931).

Phillip V. Mallett and Ronald P. Draper (eds.), *A Spacious Vision: Essays on Hardy* (1994).

Kenneth Marsden, *The Poems of Thomas Hardy: A Critical Introduction* (1969).

Katherine Kearney Maynard, *Thomas Hardy's Tragic Poetry: The Lyrics and 'The Dynasts'* (1991).

Perry Meisel, *Thomas Hardy: The Return of the Repressed* (1972).

Anne Z. Mickelson, *Thomas Hardy's Women and Men: The Defeat of Nature* (1976).

Ruth Milberg-Kaye, *Thomas Hardy: Myths of Sexuality* (1983).

J. Hillis Miller, *Thomas Hardy: Distance and Desire* (1970).

Michael Millgate, *Thomas Hardy: His Career as a Novelist* (1971).

—— *Testamentary Acts: Browning, Tennyson, James, Hardy* (1992).

Kevin Z. Moore, *The Descent of the Imagination: Postromantic Culture in the Later Novels of Thomas Hardy* (1990).

Rosemarie Morgan, *Women and Sexuality in the Novels of Thomas Hardy* (1988).

—— *Cancelled Words: Rediscovering Thomas Hardy* (1992).

Roy Morrell, *Thomas Hardy: The Will and the Way* (1965).

Ross C. Murfin, *Swinburne, Lawrence, Hardy and the Burden of Belief* (1978).

Tess O'Toole, *Genealogy and Fiction in Hardy: Family Lineage and Narrative Line* (1997).

Norman Page, *Thomas Hardy* (1977).

—— (ed.), *Thomas Hardy: The Writer and his Background* (1980).

—— (ed.), *Thomas Hardy Annual*, 5 Vols. (1982–7).

Tom Paulin, *Thomas Hardy: The Poetry of Perception* (1975).

Charles P. C. Pettit (ed.), *New Perspectives on Thomas Hardy* (1994).

—— (ed.), *Celebrating Thomas Hardy: Insights and Appreciations* (1996).

—— (ed.), *Reading Thomas Hardy* (1998).

F. B. Pinion, *Thomas Hardy: Art and Thought* (1977).

—— (ed.), *Thomas Hardy and the Modern World* (1976).

—— (ed.), *Budmouth Essays on Thomas Hardy* (1974).

John Rabbetts, *From Hardy to Faulkner* (1989).

Martin Ray, *Thomas Hardy: A Textual Study of the Short Stories* (1997).

James Richardson, *Thomas Hardy: The Poetry of Necessity* (1977).

Beat Riesen, *Thomas Hardy's Minor Novels* (1990).

William R. Rutland, *Thomas Hardy: A Study of His Writings and Their Background* (1938).

C. H. Salter, *Good Little Thomas Hardy* (1981).

Benjamin Sankey, *The Major Novels of Thomas Hardy* (1965).

G. W. Sherman, *The Pessimism of Thomas Hardy* (1976).

Anne Smith (ed.), *The Novels of Thomas Hardy* (1979).

Southern Review, 6 (1940) (Hardy centennial issue, containing important essays by W. H. Auden, R. P. Blackmur, F. R. Leavis, etc.).

J. G. Southworth, *The Poetry of Thomas Hardy* (1947).

Ellen Lew Sprechman, *Seeing Women as Men: Role Reversal in the Novels of Thomas Hardy* (1995).

Marlene Springer, *Hardy's Use of Allusion* (1983).

Michael Squires, *The Pastoral Novel: Studies in George Eliot, Thomas Hardy and D. H. Lawrence* (1974).

J. I. M. Stewart, *Thomas Hardy: A Critical Biography* (1971).
—— *Eight Modern Writers* (1974).
Rosemary Sumner, *Thomas Hardy: Psychological Novelist* (1981).
Richard Swigg, *Lawrence, Hardy, and American Literature* (1972).
Arthur Symons, *A Study of Thomas Hardy* (1927).
Dennis Taylor, *Hardy's Poetry, 1860–1928* (1981; 2nd edn., 1989).
—— *Hardy's Literary Language and Victorian Philology* (1993).
Richard H. Taylor, *The Neglected Hardy: Thomas Hardy's Lesser Novels* (1982).
Geoffrey Thurley, *The Psychology of Hardy's Novels: The Nervous and the Statuesque* (1975).
Penelope Vigar, *The Novels of Thomas Hardy: Illusion and Reality* (1974).
John Powell Ward, *Thomas Hardy's Poetry* (1992).
Carl J. Weber, *Hardy in America: A Study of Thomas Hardy and His American Readers* (1946).
Harvey Curtis Webster, *On a Darkling Plain: The Art and Thought of Thomas Hardy* (1947).
R. J. White, *Thomas Hardy and History* (1974).
Peter Widdowson, *Hardy in History: A Study in Literary Sociology* (1989).
—— *Thomas Hardy* (1996).
Merryn Williams, *Thomas Hardy and Rural England* (1972).
—— *A Preface to Hardy* (1976).
—— *Women in the English Novel 1800–1900* (1984).
Keith Wilson, *Thomas Hardy on Stage* (1994).
George Wing, *Thomas Hardy* (1963).
George Wooton, *Thomas Hardy: Towards a Materialist Criticism* (1985).
T. R. Wright, *Hardy and the Erotic* (1989).
Paul Zietlow, *Moments of Vision: The Poetry of Thomas Hardy* (1974).

G. Criticism: specific texts (listed alphabetically)

(Further references are given at the end of entries for individual works.)

Desperate Remedies
Lawrence O. Jones, '*Desperate Remedies* and the Victorian Sensation Novel', *Nineteenth-Century Fiction*, 20 (1965).
Catherine Neale '*Desperate Remedics*: The Merits and Demerits of Popular Fiction', *Critical Survey*, 5 (1993).
Norman Page, 'Visual Techniques in Hardy's *Desperate Remedies*', *Ariel*, 4 (1973).

The Dynasts
Emma Clifford, 'The "Trumpet-Major Notebook" and *The Dynasts*', *Review of English Studies*, NS 8 (1957).
Susan Dean, *Hardy's Poetic Vision in 'The Dynasts'* (1977).
Harold Orel, *The Dynasts*, New Wessex Edition (1978).
—— *Thomas Hardy's Epic-Drama: A Study of 'The Dynasts'* (1963).
Keith Wilson, '"Flower of Man's Intelligence": World and Overworld in *The Dynasts*', *Victorian Poetry*, 17 (1979).
Walter F. Wright, *The Shaping of 'The Dynasts': A Study in Thomas Hardy* (1967).

Far from the Madding Crowd
John Bayley, Introduction to *Far from the Madding Crowd*, New Wessex Edition (1974).
Frank R. Giordano, Jr., 'Farmer Boldwood: Hardy's Portrait of a Suicide', *English Literature in Transition*, 21 (1978).
Lawrence Jones, 'George Eliot and Pastoral Tragi-Comedy in Hardy's *Far from the Madding Crowd*', *Studies in Philology*, 77 (1980).
—— '"A Good Hand at a Serial": Thomas Hardy and the Serialisation of *Far from the Madding Crowd*', *Journal of Narrative Technique*, 8 (1978).
Rosemarie Morgan, *Cancelled Words: Rediscovering Thomas Hardy* (1992).
Fred Reid, 'Art and Ideology in *Far from the Madding Crowd*', *THA* 4 (1986).

The Hand of Ethelberta
Sarah Davies, '*The Hand of Ethelberta*: De-Mythologising "Woman"', *Critical Survey*, 5 (1993).
T. Sasaki, Introduction to Everyman Edition (1998).
Clarice Short, 'In Defence of *Ethelberta*', *Nineteenth-Century Fiction*, 13 (1958).
Michael Slater, 'Hardy and the City', in Charles P. C. Pettit (ed.), *New Perspectives on Thomas Hardy* (1994).

Richard H. Taylor, *The Neglected Hardy: Thomas Hardy's Lesser Novels* (1982).

Paul Ward, '*The Hand of Ethelberta*', *THYB* (1971).

Peter Widdowson, *Hardy in History: A Study in Literary Sociology* (1989).

George Wing, '"Forbear, Hostler, Forbear!": Social Satire in *The Hand of Ethelberta*', *Studies in the Novel*, 15 (1972).

Jude the Obscure

Christine Brooke-Rose,. 'Ill Wit and Sick Tragedy: *Jude the Obscure*', in Lance St John Butler (ed.), *The Alternative Hardy* (1989).

A. R. Cunningham, 'The "New Woman" Fiction of the 1890's', *Victorian Studies*, 17 (1973).

R. P. Draper, 'Hardy's Comic Tragedy: *Jude the Obscure*', in Dale Kramer and Nancy Marck (eds.), *Critical Essays on Thomas Hardy: The Novels* (1990).

Lloyd Fernando, *'New Women' in the Late Victorian Novel* (1977).

John Sutherland, 'A Note on the Teasing Narrator in *Jude the Obscure*', *English Literature in Transition*, 17 (1974).

Dennis Taylor, 'The Chronology of *Jude the Obscure*', *THJ* 12 (1996).

Cedric Watts, *Thomas Hardy: 'Jude the Obscure'*, Penguin Critical Studies (1992).

Janet B. Wright, 'Hardy and his Contemporaries: The Literary Context of *Jude the Obscure*', *Inscape*, 14 (1980).

A Laodicean

Robert Y. Drake, Jr., '*A Laodicean*: A Note on a Minor Novel', *Philological Quarterly*, 40 (1961).

Barbara Hardy, Introduction to New Wessex Edition (1975).

Pearl R. Hochstadt, 'Hardy's Romantic Diptych: A Reading of *A Laodicean* and *Two on a Tower*', *English Literature in Transition*, 26 (1983).

J. H. Stape, Introduction to Everyman Edition (1997).

George Wing, 'Middle-Class Outcasts in Hardy's *A Laodicean*', *Humanities Association Review*, 27 (1976).

The Mayor of Casterbridge

Douglas Brown, *Thomas Hardy, 'The Mayor of Casterbridge'* (1962).

R. P. Draper, '*The Mayor of Casterbridge*', *Critical Quarterly*, 25 (1983).

Juliet M. Grindle, 'Compulsion and Choice in *The Mayor of Casterbridge*', in Anne Smith (ed.), *The Novels of Thomas Hardy* (1979).

Robert B. Heilman, 'Hardy's *Mayor* and the Problem of Intention', *Criticism*, 5 (1963).

—— 'Hardy's *Mayor*. Notes on Style', *Nineteenth-Century Fiction*, 18 (1964).

Frederick R. Karl, '*The Mayor of Casterbridge*: A New Fiction Defined', *Modern Fiction Studies*, 6 (1960).

Jeannette King, '*The Mayor of Casterbridge*: Talking about Character', *THJ* 8 (1992).

Craig Raine, 'Conscious Artistry in *The Mayor of Casterbridge*', in Charles P. C. Pettit (ed.), *New Perspectives on Thomas Hardy*, (1994).

Elaine Showalter, 'The Unmanning of the Mayor of Casterbridge', in Dale Kramer (ed.), *Critical Approaches to the Fiction of Thomas Hardy* (1979).

Christine Winfield, 'Factual Sources of Two Episodes in *The Mayor of Casterbridge*', *Nineteenth-Century Fiction*, 25 (1970).

A Pair of Blue Eyes

Arthur K. Amos, 'Accident and Fate: The Possibility for Action in *A Pair of Blue Eyes*', *English Literature in Transition*, 15 (1972).

Jo Devereux, 'Thomas Hardy's *A Pair of Blue Eyes*: The Heroine as Text', *Victorian Newsletter* (1992).

Mary Jacobus, 'Hardy's Magian Retrospect', *Essays in Criticism* (1982).

John Lucas, *The Literature of Change: Studies in the Nineteenth-Century Provincial Novel* (1977).

Judith Bryant Wittenberg, 'Early Hardy Novels and the Fictional Eye', *Novel* (1983).

The Return of the Native

Roger Loomis, *The Play of Saint George* (1928).

John Paterson, *The Making of 'The Return of the Native'* (1960).

R. W. Stallman, 'Hardy's Hour-Glass Novel', *Sewanee Review*, 55 (1947).

Brian Thomas, *'The Return of the Native': Saint George Defeated* (1995).

Carl J. Weber, 'Hardy's Chronology in *The Return of the Native*', *PMLA*, 53 (1938).

Tess of the d'Urbervilles

Kristin Brady, 'Tess and Alec: Rape or Seduction?', *THA* 4 (1986).

Jean R. Brooks, '*Tess of the d'Urbervilles*: The Move towards Existentialism', in F. B. Pinion (ed.), *Thomas Hardy and the Modern World* (1974).

David J. De Laura, '"The Ache of Modernism" in Hardy's Later Novels', *Journal of English Literary History*, 34 (1967).

Ian Gregor, 'The Novel as Moral Protest: *Tess of the d'Urbervilles*', in Ian Gregor and Brian Nicholas, *The Moral and the Story* (1962).

Mary Jacobus, 'Tess's Purity', *Essays in Criticism*, 26 (1976).

Arnold Kettle, 'Thomas Hardy: *Tess of the d'Urbervilles* (1891)', in *An Introduction to the English Novel*, Vol. 2 (1951).

J. T. Laird, *The Shaping of 'Tess of the d'Urbervilles'* (1975).

Vernon Lee, 'Hardy', in *The Handling of Words* (1923).

David Lodge, 'Tess, Nature, and the Voices of Hardy', in *Language of Fiction* (1966).

Tony Tanner, 'Colour and Movement in Hardy's *Tess of the d'Urbervilles*', *Critical Quarterly*, 10 (1968).

The Trumpet-Major

W. G. Bebington, *The Original Manuscript of 'The Trumpet-Major'* (1948).

Peter Collister, '"Past Things Retold"': A Study of Thomas Hardy's *Under the Greenwood Tree* and *The Trumpet-Major*', *Durham University Journal*, 36 (1974–5).

H. A. T. Johnson, 'In Defence of *The Trumpet-Major*', in F. B. Pinion (ed.), *Budmouth Essays on Thomas Hardy* (1976).

George H. Thomson, 'The *Trumpet-Major* Chronicle', *Nineteenth-Century Fiction*, 17 (1962).

Two on a Tower

John Bayley, 'The Love Story in *Two on a Tower*', *THA* 1 (1982).

Joan Grundy, '*Two on a Tower* and *The Duchess of Malfi*', *THJ* 5 (1989).

Pearl R. Hochstadt, 'Hardy's Romantic Diptych: A Reading of *A Laodicean* and *Two on a Tower*', *English Literature in Transition*, 26 (1983).

Glenn Irvin, 'High Passion and High Church in Hardy's *Two on a Tower*', *English Literature in Transition*, 28 (1985).

Rosemary Sumner, 'The Experimental and the Absurd in *Two on a Tower*', *THA* 1 (1982).

Richard H. Taylor, *The Neglected Hardy: Thomas Hardy's Lesser Novels* (1982).

Paul Ward, '*Two on a Tower*: A Critical Appreciation', *THYB* 8 (1978).

George Wing, 'Hardy's Star-Cross'd Lovers in *Two on a Tower*', *THYB* 14 (1987).

Under the Greenwood Tree

Peter Collister, '"Past Things Retold"': A Study of Thomas Hardy's *Under the Greenwood Tree* and *The Trumpet-Major*', *Durham University Journal*, 36 (1974–5).

John F. Danby, '*Under the Greenwood Tree*', *Critical Quarterly*, 1 (1959).

Robert A. Draffan, 'Hardy's *Under the Greenwood Tree*', *English*, 22 (1973).

Jeanne Howard, 'Thomas Hardy's "Mellstock" and the Registrar General's Stinsford', *Literature and History*, 6 (1977).

H. E. Tolliver, 'The Dance under the Greenwood Tree: Hardy's Bucolics', *Nineteenth-Century Fiction*, 17 (1962).

The Well-Beloved

John Fowles, 'Hardy and the Hag', in Lance St John Butler (ed.), *Thomas Hardy after Fifty Years* (1977).

Helmut E. Gerber, 'Hardy's *The Well-Beloved* as a Comment on the Well-Despised', *English Language Notes*, 1 (1963).

J. Hillis Miller, Introduction to New Wessex Edition (1975).

Alma Priestley, 'Hardy's *The Well-Beloved*: A Study in Failure', *Thomas Hardy Society Review*, 2 (1976).

Michael Ryan, '"One Name of Many Shapes": *The Well-Beloved*', in Dale Kramer (ed.), *Critical Approaches to the Fiction of Thomas Hardy* (1979).

The Woodlanders

John Bayley, 'A Social Comedy? On Re-Reading *The Woodlanders*', *THA* 5 (1987).

G. S. Fayen, 'Hardy's *The Woodlanders*: Inwardness and Memory', *Studies in English Literature*, 1 (1961).

Mary Jacobus, 'Tree and Machine: *The Woodlanders*', in Dale Kramer (ed.), *Critical Approaches to the Fiction of Thomas Hardy* (1979).

F. B. Pinion, 'The Country and Period of *The Woodlanders*', *THYB* 2 (1971).

Robert C. Schweik, 'The Ethical Structure of Hardy's *The Woodlanders*', *Archiv*, 211 (1974).

Michael Steig, 'Art versus Philosophy in Hardy's *The Woodlanders*', *Mosaic*, 4 (1971).

H. Criticism: special aspects

Language and style

Raymond Chapman, *The Language of Thomas Hardy* (1990).

Ralph W. V. Elliott, *Thomas Hardy's English* (1984).

Norman Page, 'Hardy and the English Language', in Norman Page (ed.), *Thomas Hardy: The Writer and His Background* (1980).

K. C. Philipps, *Language and Class in Victorian England* (1984).

J. B. Smith, 'Dialect in Hardy's Short Stories', *THA* 3 (1985).

Dennis Taylor, *Hardy's Literary Language and Victorian Philology* (1993).

Religion

Deborah L. Collins, *Thomas Hardy and His God: A Liturgy of Unbelief* (1990).

Timothy Hands, *Thomas Hardy: Distracted Preacher* (1989).

Jan Jedrzejewski, *Thomas Hardy and the Church* (1996).

Topography and folklore

David Daiches and John Flower, 'Thomas Hardy's Wessex', in *Literary Landscapes of the British Isles: A Narrative Atlas* (1979).

Ruth A. Firor, *Folkways in Thomas Hardy* (1931).

John Fowles and Jo Draper, *Thomas Hardy's England* (1984).

Denys Kay-Robinson, *Hardy's Wessex Reappraised* (1971).

—— *The Landscape of Thomas Hardy* (1984).

Hermann Lea, *Thomas Hardy's Wessex* (1913).

F. P. Pitfield, *Hardy's Wessex Locations* (1992).

Gayla R. Steel, *Sexual Tyranny in Wessex: Hardy's Witches and Demons of Folklore* (1993).

J. S. Udal, *Dorsetshire Folk-Lore* (1922).

Visual arts

J. B. Bullen, *The Expressive Eye: Fiction and Perception in the Work of Thomas Hardy* (1986).

Joan Grundy, *Hardy and the Sister Arts* (1979).

Lloyd Fernando, 'Thomas Hardy's Rhetoric of Painting', *A Review of English Literature*, 6 (1965).

Norman Page, 'Hardy's Pictorial Art in *The Mayor of Casterbridge*', *Études Anglaises*, 25 (1972).

Alastair Smart, 'Pictorial Imagery in the Novels of Thomas Hardy', *Review of English Studies*, 12 (1961).